The SAGE
Handbook of

Organizational
Behavior

Volume I

The SAGE
Handbook of

Organizational
Behavior

Volume I
Micro Approaches

Edited by
Julian Barling
and Cary L. Cooper

Los Angeles • London • New Delhi • Singapore

SAGE Publications Ltd
1 Oliver's Yard
55 City Road
London EC1Y 1SP

SAGE Publications Inc.
2455 Teller Road
Thousand Oaks, California 91320

SAGE Publications India Pvt Ltd
B 1/I 1 Mohan Cooperative Industrial Area
Mathura Road
New Delhi 110 044

SAGE Publications Asia-Pacific Pte Ltd
33 Pekin Street #02-01
Far East Square
Singapore 048763

Library of Congress Control Number: 2007936430

British Library Cataloguing in Publication data
A catalogue record for this book is available from the British Library

ISBN 978-1-4129-2385-9

Typeset by CEPHA Imaging Pvt. Ltd., Bangalore, India
Printed in Great Britain by The Cromwell Press, Trowbridge, Wiltshire
Printed on paper from sustainable resources

To my family, Janice, Seth and Monique at home, and Annette Lilly at work, all of whom nurture, support and ignore me when appropriate.

Julian Barling

I would like to thank Prof. Fred Massarik, formerly of UCLA and Prof. Peter Robinson, formerly of the University of Bristol, who both supported and mentored me in earlier stages of my career, and remain good friends and colleagues.

Cary Cooper

Contents

About the Editors

Julian Barling Fellow of the Royal Society of Canada and Queen's Research Chair, is Professor of Organizational Behavior and Psychology, and Associate Dean (PhD, MSc and Research) in the Queen's School of Business. Dr Barling is the author/editor of several books on topics such as work and family, unions, young workers, work safety, and co-editor of the *Handbook of Work Stress*, and the *Handbook of Workplace Violence*. He is the author/editor of well over 125 research articles and book chapters, and was editor of the American Psychological Association's *Journal of Occupational Health Psychology* (2000–2005). In 2001, Dr Barling received the National Post's 'Leaders in Business Education' award; in 2008, he was elected as a Fellow of the Society of Industrial and Organizational Psychology. His current research focuses on the nature of transformational leadership and unethical leadership, and on employees' psychological and physical well-being.

Cary L. Cooper is Distinguished Professor of Organizational Psychology and Health at Lancaster University Management School and Pro Vice Chancellor of Lancaster University. He is the Founding President of the British Academy of Management, Founding Editor of the *Journal of Organizational Behavior*, Chair of The Sunningdale Institute (a UK government think tank on management/organizational issues), President of the British Association of Counselling and Psychotherapy, and author of numerous scholarly articles and books. He has been awarded four honorary doctorates from various universities, and in 2006 was given an Honorary Fellowship of the Royal College of Physicians. In 2001, he was awarded the Commander of the Most Excellent Order of the British Empire by the Queen for his contribution to organizational health.

About the Contributors

Natalie J. Allen is a Professor in the Department of Psychology at the University of Western Ontario in London, Canada and Director of The TeamWork Lab at Western. Her research interests include the composition and processes within teams, methodological issues in team research, and the psychology of employee commitment. She is Associate Editor of the *Journal of Occupational and Organizational Psychology* and Past Chair of the Canadian Society of Industrial-Organizational Psychology. Dr Allen's work appears in numerous academic and practitioner journals and she is the co-author, with John Meyer, of *Commitment in the Workplace: Theory, Research and Application* (Sage, 1997).

Terry A. Beehr is a Professor in the PhD Program Industrial/Organizational (I/O) Psychology at Central Michigan University. He earned his PhD in Organizational Psychology from The University of Michigan in 1974 and previously was an Assistant Professor of psychology at Illinois State University. He has been on the editorial boards of several journals in I/O psychology and management and is currently an Associate Editor for the *Journal of Organizational Behavior*. He has published research on several topics, including retirement, occupational stress, leadership, and careers.

Misty M. Bennett is a Doctoral Candidate in the Industrial/Organizational (I/O) Psychology program at Central Michigan University. She has co-authored another book chapter in the area of retirement, and has additional research in progress in the areas of work-family conflict, occupational stress, and social support. She has been an instructor at CMU for the past three years and gives workshops on leadership and occupational stress for both managers as well as college students.

Jennifer L. Berdahl is an Associate Professor of Organizational Behavior at the University of Toronto. She received her PhD from the University of Illinois. Her research investigates the social psychology of power in work groups and organizations. She has studied the emergence of status hierarchies in groups, the role of harassment and undermining in maintaining social status hierarchies in organizations, and the effects of social power on individual cognition, emotion, and behavior in groups. Her work has appeared in such journals as *Academy of Management Review*, *Journal of Applied Psychology*, *Journal of Personality and Social Psychology*, and *Organizational Behavior and Human Decision Processes*.

Matt Bloom is an Associate Professor in the Management Department at the Mendoza College of Business, University of Notre Dame. His research interests center around understanding motivation in the workplace, employee engagement, and human well-being. Matt is especially interested in understanding the role that affect plays in intrinsic motivation and well-being at work. He teaches courses on innovation and high-performance organizations to undergraduates, MBAs, and executives. Matt received his PhD from Cornell University.

Wendy R. Boswell is an Associate Professor and Mays Research Fellow in the Mays Business School, Texas A&M University. She is also the Director of the Center for Human Resource Management. Her research focuses on employee attraction and retention, workplace conflict, and work stress. Dr Boswell's work has appeared in such journals as *Academy of Management Journal*, *Journal of Applied Psychology*, *Academy of Management Review*, *Personnel Psychology*, *Human Resource Management*, and *Journal of Management*. She serves on the editorial boards of *Journal of Applied Psychology and Personnel Psychology*, and is an Associate Editor for the *Journal of Management*.

Robyn L. Brouer is an Assistant Professor at Hofstra University. She received her PhD in Organizational Behavior and Human Resource Management from Florida State University. Brouer has research interests in leadership, the multi-dimensions of person-environment fit, social influence processes including impression management and politics, leader-member exchange, and work stress. Her work has been published in such journals as the *Journal of Management*, *Leadership Quarterly*, and *Human Resource Management Review*.

Adam Butler is Professor of Psychology and Director of the graduate program in Industrial-Organizational Psychology at the University of Northern Iowa. He conducts research on issues related to work-family balance, family-friendly employment practices, and college student employment. His research has appeared in *Journal of Applied Psychology*, *Journal of Vocational Behavior*, *Organizational Behavior* and *Human Decision Processes*, and *Journal of Occupational and Organizational Psychology*. He holds a PhD in Industrial-Organizational Psychology from the University of Nebraska-Lincoln.

Gerard A. Callanan is Professor in the Management Department at West Chester University. He received a PhD in Organizational Behavior from Drexel University. He was formerly a Vice President with the Federal Reserve Bank of Philadelphia. A member of the Academy of Management and the American Psychological Association, his research has appeared in a number of scholarly publications. In 2000, Dr Callanan co-authored (with J. H. Greenhaus & V. M. Godshalk) the third edition of the textbook *Career Management*, published by Thomson-Southwestern. He is co-editor (with Jeffrey H. Greenhaus) of the *Encyclopedia of Career Development*, published by Sage in 2006.

Anthony Carroll is a PhD Candidate at the Queen's School of Business at Queen's University in Kingston, Ontario. He conducts research on union commitment and participation, leadership and safety in the workplace. His research has appeared in the *Journal of Applied Psychology*, and *Journal of Business and Psychology*. His current interests include examining the structure and nature of safety behaviors within organizations and the predictors and consequences of such behaviors.

Jennifer Carson is completing her PhD in Organizational Behavior at the London Business School (www.london.edu). She received both her Bachelor of Commerce and MSc in Organizational Behavior from Queen's University, in Canada. She has also worked as an Associate for the international executive search firm, Heidrick & Struggles (www.heidrick.com). Jennifer's past research has included publications on groups, health and romantic relationships in the workplace.

Susan Cartwright is Professor of Organizational Psychology in the Manchester Business School at The University of Manchester, is a Chartered Psychologist and Fellow of the British Psychological Society. Susan is currently the President of the British Academy of Management and a Fellow of the British Academy of Management. She is a past Editor of the *Leadership and Organization Development Journal* and currently Associate Editor of the *British Journal of Management*. Susan has authored 13 books, over 40 scholarly articles and 30 book chapters. Her main research interests are occupational stress and well being, human aspects of mergers and acquisitions and emotional intelligence.

Amy Christie is an Assistant Professor in the School of Business and Economics at Wilfrid Laurier University in Waterloo, Ontario. Her research interests surround issues of status, power, and leadership in organizations. One stream of her research has centered on abuses of power and unethical leadership, while another has explored status structures and interpersonal processes in small groups.

Jason A. Colquitt is a Professor in the Management department at the University of Florida. He received his PhD from Michigan State University. His research interests include organizational justice, trust, and personality. He has published more than 20 articles on these and other topics in a number of journals. He is currently serving as an Associate Editor for *Academy of Management Journal* and is a recipient of the Society for Industrial and Organizational Psychology's Distinguished Early Career Contributions Award and the Cummings Scholar Award for early to mid-career achievement, sponsored by the Organizational Behavior division of the Academy of Management.

Catherine E. Connelly is an Assistant Professor of Organizational Behavior and Human Resource Management at the DeGroote School of Business at McMaster University in Hamilton, Canada. She earned her MSc and PhD degrees in Management at Queen's University in Kingston, Canada. Her research has appeared in several journals, including *Human Resource Management Review*, *Journal of Applied Psychology*, *Journal of Management*, *Journal of Management Information Systems*, and *Journal of Vocational Behavior*.

Lilia M. Cortina is Associate Professor of Psychology and Women's Studies at the University of Michigan. She received her PhD from the University of Illinois. Her research addresses sexual harassment, incivility, and gender in organizations, with a particular focus on how victimization undermines employee well-being. Her work has appeared in a variety of journals, including *Academy of Management Review*, *Journal of Applied Psychology*, *Journal of Personality and Social Psychology*, and *Journal of Abnormal Psychology*. She has served on the editorial boards of the *Journal of Applied Psychology*, *Journal of Occupational Health Psychology*, *Journal of Consulting and Clinical Psychology*, and *Psychology of Women Quarterly*.

Jacqueline A-M. Coyle-Shapiro is a Professor in Organizational Behavior in the Department of Management at the London School of Economics and Political Science (LSE), where she received her PhD in 1996. Her research interests include employment relationships, psychological contracts, perceived organizational support, organizational justice, organizational citizenship behavior, and communal relationships. She is Senior Editor at the *Journal of Organizational Behavior* and is on several editorial review boards. Her work has been published in outlets including the *Academy of Management Journal*, *Journal of Applied Psychology*, *Journal of Organizational Behavior*, *Journal of Vocational Behavior*, and *Journal of Management Studies*.

Marco S. DiRenzo is a PhD student in the Department of Management at Drexel University's LeBow College of Business. He is currently conducting research on job-level differences in work-family conflict, a boundaryless career perspective on organizational turnover, generational differences in conceptualizations of career success, and cognitive biases in entrepreneurial decision making and career orientations. His PhD dissertation will examine the role of a protean career orientation in employees' career management processes.

Jane E. Dutton is the Robert L. Kahn Distinguished University Professor of Business Administration and Psychology at the University of Michigan. She is a cofounder of the Center for Positive Organizational Scholarship (http://www.bus.umich.edu/Positive). Her current research focuses on positive identity processes, compassion and organizations, and high quality connections. She has edited a special issue in the *Journal of Positive Psychology* on positive organizing (forthcoming in 2008). Jane and Belle Ragins edited *Exploring Positive Relationships at Work*, published by Lawrence Erlbaum in 2007.

P. Christopher Earley is the Auran J. Fox Chair in Business and the Dean of the University of Connecticut School of Business and former Dean of National University of Singapore Business School. His interests include cross-cultural and international aspects of organizations, including the dynamics of multinational teams and motivation. Recent publications include *Cultural Intelligence: Individual Interactions Across Cultures* (with Ang Soon), *Multinational Work Teams: A New Perspective* (with Cristina Gibson), *The Transplanted Executive: Managing in Different Cultures* (with Miriam Erez), and 'Creating Hybrid Team Cultures: An Empirical Test of International Team Functioning' (with E. Mosakowski, in *Academy of Management Journal*).

Gerald R. Ferris is the Francis Eppes Professor of Management and Professor of Psychology at Florida State University. He received a PhD in Business Administration from the University of Illinois (Urbana-Champaign). He has research interests in social influence and effectiveness processes in organizations, and reputation in organizations, and has published articles in the *Journal of Applied Psychology*, *Organizational Behavior and Human Decision Processes*, *Organizational Dynamics*, *Personnel Psychology*, *Academy of Management Journal*, and *Academy of Management Review*. He served as Editor of the annual research series, *Research in Personnel and Human Resources Management* from its inception in 1983 until 2003.

Lori Francis received a PhD in Industrial/Organizational Psychology from the University of Guelph and is currently an Associate Professor in the Department of Psychology at Saint Mary's University in Halifax, Nova Scotia, Canada. Dr Francis has broad research interests in organizational psychology including occupational health and safety, industrial relations, and workplace fairness. She is a member of Saint Mary's University's CN Center for Occupational Health and Safety.

Michael R. Frone is a Senior Scientist at the Research Institute on Addictions, State University of New York at Buffalo. He has published extensively in the areas of organizational behavior and occupational health. He coedited *The Psychology of Workplace Safety* and the *Handbook of Work Stress*. He was an Associate Editor for the *Journal of Occupational Health Psychology* and has served on several editorial boards. His research has received federal funding totaling more than $7.5 million. He is currently the principal investigator on the National Survey of Workplace Health and Safety and the National Survey of Work Stress and Health.

Daniel G. Gallagher is the CSX Corporation Professor of Management at James Madison University, USA. He earned his MA and PhD degrees at the Institute of Labor and Industrial Relations at the University of Illinois with concentrations in the areas of industrial psychology and economics. He has also been a member of the faculty at the University of Iowa, and Queen's University, Canada. Professor Gallagher is currently an Associate Editor for *Human*

Relations (Tavistock Institute) and a member of the editorial board of *Industrial Relations* (Berkeley).

Heidi K. Gardner is an Assistant Professor of Organizational Behavior at Harvard Business School. One line of her research focuses on team-level issues such as status, expertise utilization, and multi-national perspectives; another stream of research focuses on knowledge-based innovation in professional service firms. She has published articles in the *Academy of Management Journal* and *Journal of Organizational Behavior*, as well as several book chapters. She has lived in the UK, South Africa, Germany, France and Japan. Formerly a management consultant, Heidi also worked with multinational clients in 16 nations on four continents. She holds a PhD from London Business School.

Mary Ann Glynn is a Professor of Organization Studies and, by courtesy, Professor of Sociology at Boston College. She is the Inaugural Fellow and Research Director for the Winston Center for Leadership and Ethics (http://www.bc.edu/schools/csom/leadership). Her current research focuses on organizational identity, institutionalization processes, and the positive dynamics of organizing and leadership.

Alicia A. Grandey is an Associate Professor and Chair of Industrial-Organizational Psychology at Penn State University. She earned her PhD at Colorado State University in 1999. Her research focuses on emotional labor, customer service and work-family, and is published in journals such as *Journal of Applied Psychology*, *Academy of Management Journal*, *Organizational Behavior and Human Decision Processes*, and *Journal of Occupational Health Psychology*. Her research has also been discussed in *Harvard Business Review*, *Ms. Magazine*, and *National Public Radio*.

Jeffrey H. Greenhaus is a Professor and William A. Mackie Chair in the Department of Management at Drexel University's LeBow College of Business. His research, which focuses on work-family relationships and career dynamics, has been published in many of the field's leading journals. In addition, Jeff is coauthor or coeditor of *Career Management*, now in its third edition, *Work and Family – Allies or Enemies*, *Integrating Work and Family: Challenges and Choices for a Changing World*, and the *Encyclopedia of Career Development*. He is currently studying decision-making and gender processes at the work-family interface and the meaning of work-family balance.

Mark Griffin is a Professor of Work Psychology in the Institute of Work Psychology at the University of Sheffield. He received his PhD in Industrial/Organizational psychology from The Pennsylvania State University and has published his research in journals such as *Academy of Management Journal*, *Journal of Applied Psychology*, *Journal of Management*, and *Personnel Psychology*. He has managed large-scale organizational studies in areas such as leadership, safety, work performance, organizational climate, and work stress. His research seeks to understand the multilevel relationship between performance and well-being for individuals, teams, and organizations.

Joseph G. Grzywacz is Associate Professor of Family and Community Medicine at Wake Forest University School of Medicine. He earned a PhD in Child and Family Studies from the University of Wisconsin and completed an National Institute of Mental Health Post-Doctoral Fellowship in the Social Ecology of Health from the University of California, Irvine. He has published extensively in the area of work, family, and health and has published his research in journals such as *Journal of Marriage and Family*, *Social Science and Medicine*, *Journal of Applied Psychology*, and the *Journal of Health and Social Behavior*. His research is supported by the National Institutes of Health and the Alfred P. Sloan foundation and is consistently recognized as among the 'best of the best' research in work and family.

Andrew T. Hinrichs is a doctoral student in human resources and organizational behavior at the Mays Business School, Texas A&M University. His research interests center around individual differences, workplace attitudes, work-family conflict, stress, and leadership. He has presented his research at both the Academy of Management and the Southwest Academy of Management. He obtained his MBA from University of New Mexico and his BA in business/economics from Wheaton College.

Ying Hong is a Doctoral Candidate in Human Resource Management in the School of Management and Labor Relations at Rutgers University, USA. Her research interests include macro perspectives such as strategic human resource management (HRM) and knowledge management; a combination of multi-level perspectives such as social capital and customer service linkage research; and micro perspectives such as leadership. Her dissertation examines the strategic capability of service organizations in differentiating HRM to enhance customer outcomes. She obtained her MS degree in Industrial/Organizational Psychology from Saint Mary's University, Canada, and BA degrees from Zhejiang University, China.

Colette Hoption is a Doctoral Candidate in Management at Queen's University in Kingston, Ontario, specializing in Organizational Behavior. Prior to her doctoral studies, she completed a Master of Science in Management, and undergraduate degrees in Psychology and French studies. Colette's primary research interests are in the area of leadership, and in particular examining leadership with a relational and dynamic lens. Her research has been presented at conferences such as Association for Psychological Science and the Society for Industrial and Organizational Psychology. Colette's work has also been published in the *Journal of Applied Psychology*.

Charlice Hurst is a PhD Student in the Department of Management at the University of Florida. She holds a BA from Harvard University with a dual concentration in social and biological anthropology and an International MBA from the University of South Carolina Moore School of Business. Charlice's current research interests are the influence of core self-evaluations and gender on interpersonal relationships at work, the role of interpersonal relationships in mood and well-being, and work-family issues among low-wage earners.

Remus Ilies received his Doctorate from the University of Florida and earned a Master in Business Administration degree from Iowa State University. He conducts research on topics such as employee satisfaction, affect, work-family balance, health and well-being, leadership and group processes, and motivation and self-regulation. His research has been published in scholarly journals such as *Academy of Management Journal*, *Journal of Applied Psychology* and *Journal of Organizational Behavior*, and has received multiple research awards. Dr Ilies currently serves on the editorial boards of *Journal of Applied Psychology*, *Journal of Organizational Behavior*, *Leadership Quarterly*, and *Psihologia Resurselor Umane*.

Roderick D. Iverson is a Professor of Human Resource Management in the Faculty of Business Administration, Simon Fraser University. He received his PhD in Industrial Sociology from the University of Iowa. His main research interests include high-performance work systems, workplace safety, voluntary and involuntary (downsizing) turnover, employee absenteeism, psychological contracts, organizational union and dual commitment, and union joining and leaving. He currently serves on the editorial boards of *Asia Pacific Journal of Human Resources*, *Human Relations*, *Human Resource Management Review*, *Journal of Occupational Health Psychology*, and the *International Journal of Selection and Assessment*.

Susan E. Jackson is a Professor of Human Resource Management in the School of Management and Labor Relations at Rutgers University, USA, and Research Fellow at GSBA-Zürich. Her research interests include knowledge-based competition, managing team effectiveness, and workforce diversity. She has published numerous articles and books on these and related topics, including *Managing Knowledge for Sustained Competitive Advantage: Designing Strategies for Effective Human Resource Management* (with Michael Hitt and Angelo DeNisi). She is a Fellow and active member of the Academy of Management, British Academy of Management, American Psychological Association and Society for Industrial and Organizational Psychology.

Timothy Jackson is a PhD Student in Industrial/Organizational Psychology at The University of Western Ontario. His research examines the link between leadership behavior and employee commitment. He has presented his work at meetings of the Society for Industrial and Organizational Psychology, the Gallup Leadership Institute, and the Canadian Psychological Association. He has also consulted with numerous organizations on leadership, selection, and assessment issues, including Lafarge Group, Sunopta Inc., Bayer Healthcare, Ontario Power Generation, Atomic Energy of Canada Ltd., Salus Global Corporation, and the City of York Region.

Karen A. Jehn is a Professor of Social and Organizational Psychology at Leiden University, The Netherlands. Her research examines intragroup conflict, group composition, and lying in organizations. Professor Jehn has authored numerous publications in these areas, including articles in the *Academy of Management Journal*, *Administrative Science Quarterly*, *Journal of Personality and Social Psychology*, and the *Journal of Business Ethics*. She has served as a Director of the Solomon Asch Center for the Study of Ethnopolitical Conflict and the Sloan Foundation's Diversity Research Network. Her most recent area of interest is in asymmetric perceptions within workgroups.

Steve M. Jex is currently an Associate Professor of Industrial/Organizational Psychology at Bowling Green State University. Dr Jex received his PhD in Industrial/Organizational Psychology from the University of South Florida and has spent most of his post-doctoral career conducting research on occupational stress. His also serves on three editorial boards, and was recently Associate Editor of *Journal of Occupational and Organizational Psychology*. In addition to his research and editorial activities, Dr Jex is the author of two books, *Stress and Job Performance: Theory, Research*, and *Implications for Managerial Practice and Organizational Psychology: A Scientist-Practitioner Approach*.

Gary Johns is a Professor of Management and the Concordia University Research Chair in Management in the John Molson School of Business, Concordia University, Montreal. He has research interests in absenteeism from work, presenteeism, personality, job design, self-serving behavior, research methodology, and the impact of context on organizational behavior. His scholarship has been published in *Journal of Applied Psychology*, *Academy of Management Journal*, *Academy of Management Review*, *Organizational Behavior and Human Decision Processes*, *Personnel Psychology*, *Journal of Management*, *Research in Organizational Behavior*, *Journal of Organizational Behavior*, *Human Relations*, and *Journal of Occupational and Organizational Psychology*.

Sophia Soyoung Jeong is a Management Doctoral Student in the Moore School of Business at the University of South Carolina. Her current research interests include ethical judgment and decision making, prosocial behavior, trust, and cross-cultural organizational behavior.

Timothy A. Judge is the Matherly-McKethan Eminent Scholar, Department of Management, Warrington College of Business, University of Florida. He received his PhD from the University of Illinois (Urbana-Champaign). Judge's previous academic appointments include Stanley Howe Professor of Leadership at the Tippie College of Business, University of Iowa, and associate and assistant professor at the School of Industrial and Labor Relations, Cornell University. Prior to graduate school, he was a manager with Kohl's Department Stores in Milwaukee, WI, Janesville, WI, and Rockford, IL. Judge's research interests include personality, leadership, job attitudes, and, most recently, moods and emotions.

E. Kevin Kelloway PhD is a Professor of Management and Psychology at Saint Mary's University and Senior Research Fellow/Director of the CN Center for Occupational Health and Safety. His research interests include occupational health psychology, leadership, and unionization.

M. Audrey Korsgaard received a PhD from New York University and is currently a Professor of Management and Organizational Behavior at the University of South Carolina. Her research addresses the topics of prosocial orientation, trust and organizational justice and their relationship to interpersonal and intragroup cooperation. She has studied these issues in a variety of work settings, including supervisor-subordinate relationships, investor-entrepreneur relations, work teams, and joint ventures.

Mary Dana Laird is an Assistant Professor at the University of Tulsa. She received a PhD in Management from Florida State University. Her research interests include organizational politics, political skill, and stress, but most of her current work focuses on personal reputation. Her research has been published in the *Human Resource Management Review*, the *Journal of Applied Social Psychology*, and the *Journal of Management*. In addition, she has contributed book chapters to the *Handbook of Organizational Behavior*, *Research in Personnel and Human Resources Management*, the *Handbook of Organizational Politics*, and *Stress and Quality of Working Life: Current Perspective in Occupational Health*.

Gary Latham is the Secretary of State Professor of Organizational Effectiveness in the Joseph L. Rotman School of Business, University of Toronto. He is a Fellow of the Association for Psychological Science, the American Psychological Association, the Society of Industrial-Organizational Psychology, the Canadian Psychological Association, the Academy of Management, and the Royal Society of Canada. He is the recipient of both the Distinguished Scientific and the Professional Contribution Awards from SIOP, the Scholar/Practitioner Award from the AOM, and the Career Achievement Awards from the HR and OB Divisions of the AOM. He is a Past President of CPA and the current President of SIOP.

Beth Livingston is a doctoral student at the University of Florida. Previously, she received her Master's in Business Administration from the University of Kentucky. Her research interests are in the areas of gender, work-family, and workplace moods and emotions. Her dissertation concerns the relationships among gender, gender roles, and negotiation of work-family roles.

Edwin A. Locke is Dean's Professor of Motivation and Leadership Emeritus at the R.H. Smith School of Business, University of Maryland. He is a Fellow of the Association for Psychological

Science, the American Psychological Association and the Academy of Management. He received the Distinguished Scientific Contribution Award (Society for I/O Psychology), the Career Achievement Award from the Academy of Management (OB Division), and the J. M. Cattell Award (APS). He, with Gary Latham, developed Goal Setting Theory, ranked No. 1 in importance among 73 management theories. He is internationally known for his research on motivation, job satisfaction, leadership, and other topics.

Sean Lux is a Visiting Instructor at the University of South Florida Center for Entrepreneurship. He received his PhD in Management from Florida State University. Sean's research examines how individual actors shape social structure over time. Sean has examined this phenomenon in the context of firms and political institutions and entrepreneurs and their social networks. His work has been published in the *Journal of Management* and *Academy of Management Conference Best Paper Proceedings*.

Elyse Maltin is a PhD Student in Industrial/Organizational Psychology at the University of Western Ontario. Elyse holds a Master's degree in I/O Psychology from Western and a BA in Psychology and English Literature from McGill University. Her research interests include workplace commitment, motivation, stress, and well-being. She has presented her work at national and international conferences, including the Canadian Psychological Association, the Administrative Sciences Association of Canada, and the Society for Industrial and Organizational Psychology.

Melissa M. McCrae is a PhD Student in Management and Organization Studies in the Faculty of Business Administration, Simon Fraser University. Her main research interests are high-performance work systems and work-life balance.

John Meyer is a Professor and Chair of the Graduate Program in I/O psychology at The University of Western Ontario. His research interests include employee commitment, work motivation, leadership, and organizational change. He has published in leading journals in the fields of I/O psychology and management, and co-authored two books: *Commitment in the Workplace* and *Best Practices: Employee Retention*. He is a fellow of the Canadian Psychological Association, the American Psychological Association, and the Society for Industrial and Organizational Psychology, and a member of the Academy of Management. He has consulted and served on editorial boards in Canada and abroad.

Stella M. Nkomo is the Bateman Professor of Business Leadership at the University of South Africa's Graduate School of Business Leadership, where she teaches courses in leadership, change management, and organizational behavior. A former Scholar-in-Residence at the Mary Ingraham Bunting Institute of Radcliffe College of Harvard University, her work on race and gender in organizations and managing diversity appears in numerous journals, edited volumes, and magazines. She is listed in *Who's Who* in the Management Sciences. Together with Ella L. J. Bell, she co-authored *Our Separate Ways: Black and White Women* and the *Struggle for Professional Identity* (Harvard Business School Press).

Sharon K. Parker is a Professor of Organizational Psychology and Director at the Institute of Work Psychology, University of Sheffield. Her research interests are focused on work design, proactive behavior, and employee perspective taking. She has published 5 books, over 30 internationally refereed journal articles (including publications in top tier journals such as the *Journal of Applied Psychology* and *Academy of Management Journal*), over 30 book chapters and encyclopedia entries, numerous articles in practitioner outlets, and more than 60 technical reports. Professor Parker is an Associate Editor for the *Journal of Applied Psychology*.

Marjo-Riitta Parzefall is an Assistant Professor in the Department of Management and Organization at the Swedish School of Economics and Business Administration (Hanken). She received her PhD from the London School of Economics and Political Science. Her research focuses on social exchange theory based concepts to study the employee-employer relationship, leadership and innovativeness in organizations. She has published her work in Finnish and international journals, including *International Journal of Human Resource Management*, *Personnel Review* and *Creativity & Innovation Management*.

Adrian H. Pitariu is a Lecturer in management at the University of Toronto. He received his PhD in Organizational Behavior from the Moore School of Business, University of South Carolina. His research interests include intra-team trust and conflict, as well as team processes and performance over time.

Tahira Probst is an Associate Professor of Industrial/Organizational Psychology at Washington State University, Vancouver. Her research focuses on occupational safety and health-related implications of organizational downsizing and employee job insecurity. In addition, she also conducts research related to issues of workplace diversity. She currently serves on the Editorial Boards of the *Journal of Occupational Health Psychology* and the *Journal of Business and Psychology*, and her research has appeared in outlets such as the *Journal of Applied Psychology*, *Group and Organization Management*, *Journal of Occupational and Organizational Psychology*, *Organizational Behavior and Human Decision Processes*, and *Teaching of Psychology*.

Alannah Rafferty is a Lecturer in the School of Psychology at The University of Queensland, Australia. Her research interests include organizational change and development, readiness for change, and transformational leadership. Alannah has extensive experience in the development, administration, and use of surveys to inform leadership development and strategic change and within a range of private and public sector organizations. Alannah has published in a number of international high quality peer-reviewed journals, including the *Journal of Applied Psychology*, *The Leadership Quarterly*, and the *Journal of Occupational and Organizational Psychology*.

Lily Run Ren is an Assistant Professor of Management at College of Business & Economics, Longwood University. She received her PhD from the Mays Business School, Texas A&M University. Her research interests include organizational justice, ethics, discrimination against people with disabilities, and cross-cultural studies. She has published in such journals as *Human Resource Management Review* and *Basic and Applied Social Psychology*.

Sonja Rispens is an Assistant Professor in Work and Organizational Psychology at Twente University, The Netherlands. She received her PhD in 2006 from Leiden University. Her research focuses on the effectiveness of groups in organizations, with special attention to intragroup conflict, perceptual differences regarding group processes, and deviant behavior.

Sandra L. Robinson is a Professor, and designated Distinguished University Scholar, in the Sauder School of Business at the University of British Columbia. Her past research has focused primarily on the dark side of organizational behavior, examining issues such as psychological contract breach, betrayal, workplace deviance, and aggression. She presently continues this theme by focusing on territorial infringement and ostracism at work. Sandra is a past recipient of the Western Academy Ascendant Scholar award, and the Cummings Scholar Award from the Organizational Behavior Division of the Academy of Management. Currently, she serves as program chair for the Organizational Behavior Division.

Sabine Sonnentag is a full Professor of Work and Organizational Psychology at the University of Konstanz, Germany and a visiting Professor at the Radboud University Nijmegen, the Netherlands. In her research she is mainly interested in how individuals can achieve sustained high performance at work and remain healthy at the same time. Sabine Sonnentag published in journals such as the *Journal of Applied Psychology*, *Journal of Occupational Health Psychology*, and *Personnel Psychology* and is currently the editor of *Applied Psychology: An International Review*. She is Fellow of the Society for Industrial and Organizational Psychology.

Matthias Spitzmuller is a PhD Student at the Eli Broad Graduate School of Management at Michigan State University with a major in Organizational Behavior. His major research interests focus on the antecedents and consequences of discretionary work behaviors and on team decision making. Before pursing a career in academia, Matthias worked as a consultant and as assistant to the CEO at Kienbaum/Hewitt Associates. He holds an MBA from the University of St. Gallen in Switzerland. He is a member of the Academy of Management and of the Society for Industrial/Organizational Psychologists.

Gretchen Spreitzer is a Professor of Management and Organizations at the Ross School of Business at the University of Michigan. Her research focuses on employee empowerment and leadership development, particularly within a context of organizational change and decline. Her most recent research examines how organizations can enable human thriving and help people become more of their best selves at work. She is a faculty member in the Center for Positive Organizational Scholarship (www.bus.umich.edu/positive) at the University of Michigan.

Anne Spychala is currently a Research Assistant and PhD Student at the Department of Work and Organizational Psychology at the University of Konstanz. In her research she is mainly interested in the interplay between job stressors and proactive work behavior of employees. Further research interests include relationships between personality characteristics as well as strategies of small business entrepreneurs and entrepreneurial success.

James K. Summers is a PhD Candidate in Management at Florida State University. He has research interests in the areas of leadership, coalition formation, attribution theory, and teams, including how structure, change, temporal issues, and processes affect team and individual effectiveness. He has published his research in the *International Journal of Organizational Theory and Behavior*, and he has presented his research at several professional conferences.

Nick Turner is an Associate Professor and the Head of Business Administration at the University of Manitoba's Asper School of Business. He joined the Manitoba faculty in 2006 after spending four years at Queen's School of Business. He obtained his PhD from the University of Sheffield. His research interests lie in the area of occupational health psychology, with a primary focus on the psychosocial predictors of psychological and physical well-being at work. His current projects include socio-moral dimensions of transformational leadership and the social construction of workplace safety. His research has appeared in *Journal of Applied Psychology* and *Journal of Business Ethics*.

Linn Van Dyne is a Professor in Michigan State University, has two major research programs: proactive employee behaviors and cultural intelligence. She received her PhD from the University of Minnesota. She has published in *Academy of Management Journal, Academy of Management Review, Journal of Applied Psychology, Organizational Behavior and Human Decision Processes, Research in Organizational Behavior*. She is Associate Editor of *Organizational Behavior* and *Human Decision Processes*, on numerous editorial boards (*Academy of Management Journal, Journal of Applied Psychology, Personnel Psychology, Journal of Organizational Behavior, Academy of Management Perspectives, Human Relations, Management and Organization Review*) and is a fellow in the Society of Organizational Behavior.

Judith Volmer is an Assistant Professor of Work, Organizational, and Social Psychology and lecturer at the University of Erlangen-Nuremberg, Germany. She obtained her PhD in 2006 from the Technical University of Braunschweig, Germany. Her current research interests include interpersonal effects of discrete emotions in negotiations, expertise in teams, and voluntary employee behavior (e.g., creativity, proactive behavior).

Heather C. Vough is a Doctoral Candidate in Organizational Behavior at the University of Illinois, Urbana-Champaign. Her research interests center on the relationship between individual identity and the workplace. She has done research investigating the dynamic nature of meaning of work, employee identification with multiple targets, and the role of self-esteem in organizational life.

Helen M. Williams is a Senior Lecturer in the School of Business and Economics at Swansea University in the UK. Her current research focuses on team working and has two themes. The first involves investigating the dynamics of work group composition and exploring the conceptual and methodological challenges of conducting group composition research. The second focuses on understanding how relational issues play out in teams, especially during the implementation of team working.

Erin R. Fluegge Woolf is a Professor in the Department of Management at Southeast Missouri State University. She holds a PhD in Business Administration from the University of Florida, and a Bachelor of General Studies and Master of Business Administration from Southeast Missouri State University. Prior to graduate school, Erin worked as a travel agent, specializing in both leisure and corporate travel. Her research interests include workplace fun, affect and emotions, job attitudes, and leadership.

Maya Yankelevich is a Doctoral Candidate at Bowling Green State University, working on her dissertation on user perceptions of error in selection devices. Ms Yankelevich's research interests center around manager decision making in the selection process, with a particular interest in why managers reject the use of decision aids. Ms Yankelevich is also involved in research on work stress and employer well-being. She received her MA in Psychology from BGSU and her BA in Psychology and Spanish from Stetson University in DeLand, Florida.

Anthony R. Yue is a PhD Candidate (Management) at Saint Mary's University. His interest is in how individuals navigate their experience of work. This broad interest has led to his research in a variety of areas which include disability and work, existentialism in organizational analysis, industrial relations, and entrepreneurship. He is currently pursuing a thesis regarding informal communication at work and is a member of Saint Mary's University's CN Center for Occupational Health and Safety.

Christopher D. Zatzick is an Assistant Professor of Management at the Faculty of Business Administration, Simon Fraser University. He received his PhD Assistant from the University of California, Irvine. He studies a variety of organizational issues including downsizing and layoffs, high-performance work systems, turnover, diversity, and organizational change. His research has been published in a number of top journals, including *Academy of Management Journal*, *Organization Science*, and *Industrial Relations*.

Introduction

Colette Hoption, Amy Christie
and Julian Barling

As we move into the 21st century, we are witnessing enormous changes in the workplace that deeply affect the people that work in them, such as changes in how, when, where, and with whom they work. In addition, workforce characteristics are changing in terms of how young employees start working and at what age employees then choose to stop working. Other seismic changes include the embedding of new information technologies into the fabric of our organizations (and, indeed, our lives), as well as often-intangible knowledge replacing observable units of production as the currency of work. These changes have occurred in public and private sector organizations, the organized and non-unionized sectors, non-profit businesses and family businesses. Structural changes too have deeply affected individuals in organizations, whether it be the push toward being 'leaner and meaner,' hence the downsizing and restructuring of many formerly large organizations, or toward growing into global behemoths through merging and acquiring other organizations. Furthermore, these massive changes in the nature of work pose considerable and new challenges to

work performance. Subsequently, we question whether the understanding of work, and people at work, generated over the past century, remains relevant to the workplace and workforce today.

This is a propitious moment to stop and gather our thoughts as to the origins, current status, and of equal importance, future directions of organizational behavior – and it is to these issues that this Handbook is directed.

This Handbook highlights the major topics in the field of micro-organizational behavior (OB). In many important respects, the intent underlying this Handbook differs somewhat from many other Handbooks. Traditionally, Handbooks focus mainly on integrating past and current knowledge. In contrast, the editors of this volume have specifically invited our contributors to be retrospective and prospective in their orientation. The authors explore leading research in their domain over the past several decades, and look toward future research that will lead us into the next decade.

Second, the chapters in most existing Handbooks are authored by leading academics and scholars who have left their footprint on the field. While respecting the value of accumulated wisdom in our choice of authors, we were also guided by the need for the field of OB to be able to generate new knowledge relevant to the changing environment. Therefore, emerging scholars who are already making substantial contributions to the field join long-standing experts in authoring this Handbook.

A third difference between this and other Handbooks is especially relevant from the perspective of this chapter. Many introductory chapters are authored by leading authorities who have earned the right to provide a retrospective account of the field. Consistent with the goal of looking both backward and forward in this Handbook, the authorship of this chapter is constituted differently. One academic already relatively long-in-the-tooth (Barling) joins with two new scholars (Hoption and Christie), and together they speculate about where micro-OB could or should be headed. The rest of this chapter, which considers conceptual and methodological issues, and their confluence, is the result of this collaborative effort.

ORGANIZATIONAL BEHAVIOR IN THE FUTURE

We open this discussion with a consideration of five different conceptual directions that hold considerable promise for pushing the limits of our understanding of micro-OB. We begin at the individual level of analysis, speculating about the potential benefits of incorporating a social neuroscience perspective into the study of behavior in organizations. Thereafter, we go beyond the individual and turn our focus to relational issues in the study of OB. We then discuss organizational and societal influences on individual behavior in organizations. Last, we underscore the need to extend our focus beyond the oft-asked questions of *what* effects can be expected to emerge from different organizational phenomenon and *why*, and raise the importance

of understanding and predicting *when* such effects might be expected.

Two consistent themes cut across these five different areas. First, individual behavior in organizations does not occur in isolation; instead, an individual's behavior in organizations is both influenced by, and exercises influence upon biological, relational, organizational and societal factors. Second, historically, theory and method were often viewed as separate, with one the 'means' and the other the 'end,' as is evident in the title of Signorelli's (1974) article 'Statistics: Tool or master of the psychologist?'. In contrast, as will be seen in the ensuing discussion, there is now a greater rapprochement between the two, and because of methodological and statistical advances, empirical answers to our questions about each of the five conceptual directions are possible.

OB MEETS SOCIAL NEUROSCIENCE

The 20th century saw many significant advances in our understanding of human behavior. Broadly speaking, most of these advances derived from research that focused broadly on either social *or* biological processes. Some of the most substantial advances in our understanding of individual behavior over the past two decades have come from the field now known as social neuroscience, which merges the social and the biological, using knowledge about how broadly-based biological processes activate social interactions and behaviors (Cacioppo et al., 2007). The breadth and depth of the lessons already learned make it imperative that the methods used in, and the knowledge derived from, social neuroscience no longer escape the purview of those wishing to expand our understanding of micro-OB. With only very few exceptions (for example, Arvey et al., 1989; Heaphy and Dutton, 2008; Nicholson, 1998), some of which are discussed in the following paragraphs, explanations of individual behavior in organizations rarely rely upon knowledge of biological processes. Yet three specific examples will be sufficient to demonstrate the enormous potential from merging OB with social neuroscience.

First, an intriguing question that continues to bedevil social and behavioral scientists is the extent to which particular behaviors are either learned, or inherited. Empirical research contrasting the roles of genetic and social factors in behavior was undoubtedly stimulated by the classic studies conducted by Bouchard and his colleagues on identical twins reared apart (see Bouchard et al., 1990). In a series of studies, they identified the extent to which genetic factors influence cognitive ability, personality, anti-social behavior and psychopathology (see Baker et al., 2007; Bouchard et al., 1990; McGue and Bouchard, 1998).

In an early application to OB of the methodology of studying identical twins reared apart, Arvey et al. (1989) demonstrated that approximately 30 per cent of the variance in job satisfaction was accounted for by genetic factors. While the implementation of this methodology is not without its problems (Cropanzano and James, 1990), it has also been extended to the study of leadership. Given recent findings within the burgeoning field of social neuroscience (see Cacioppo et al., 2007), the question of whether leaders are 'born or made' is often raised. Not surprisingly, several studies have identified the genetic and environmental contributions to leadership emergence (Arvey et al., 2006; Arvey et al., 2007). Despite these advances, genetic and biological effects on the development of leadership behaviors deserve attention and robust empirical examination. The need for this is accentuated when even recent calls for more integrative theory building on leadership make limited reference to the roles of genetic and biological factors (Avolio, 2007), and future calls for additional research on social neuroscience do not identify leadership development as a possible focus (Cacioppo et al., 2007).

Second, and related, a consistent finding from the broad field of social neuroscience might offer some additional ideas for our understanding of leadership, and in particular abusive leadership behaviors and entrepreneurship. The possible influence of biological factors on aggression (and related behaviors such as social dominance, social control, and risk propensity; Dabbs, 1992) has attracted considerable empirical attention and support. In brief, this research, conducted in the field and in experiments, shows that higher levels of testosterone predispose individuals to increased aggression and related behaviors. Consistent results are found in studies where naturally-occurring levels of testosterone are measured, as well as in studies where testosterone is manipulated directly (van Honk and Schutter, 2007). Furthermore, testosterone has also been linked to entrepreneurship. White et al., (2006) contrasted two groups in an intriguing study: one with a substantial history of experience in the creation of new business ventures (entrepreneurs), and the other with no such experience (non-entrepreneurs). They showed that entrepreneurs evidenced higher testosterone levels than their non-entrepreneur counterparts.

As with Arvey et al.'s (1989) research pointing to variance explained in job satisfaction by non-contextual factors, pursuing a social neuroscience approach might lead to an understanding of the genetic factors inherent in leadership behaviors, and an appreciation of just how much of a leader's behavior is under (or beyond) individual or organizational control. In addition, if biological and genetic factors explain meaningful variance in leadership emergence and behaviors, what other core organizational behaviors might be similarly influenced?

Third, an approach that honors the assumptions of social neuroscience would extend its search for the causes of organizational behaviors beyond the social realm, suggesting that some of the explanations for behavior in organizations might well emerge very early in an individual's life. One example of this phenomenon emerges from a recent study on the predictors of individuals' counterproductive behavior in organizations – a frequent topic of study, as evident from Robinson's chapter in this volume, and one which has primarily emphasized the role of situational factors and individual differences. Recently, Roberts et al. (2007) examined the extent to which counterproductive workplace behaviors might be predicted by factors outside of the workplace. Their longitudinal study carried out over 23 years showed that being diagnosed with a conduct disorder by the age of 11, but no later than 18 years of age, was a significant predictor of subsequent counterproductive behaviors within the organization (although having a criminal record was not a significant predictor). These results are intriguing; genetic factors have been implicated in the development of conduct disorders (Slutske et al., 1998), and early conduct disorders persist into adulthood (Campbell, 1995).

While each of the three examples presented are specific, the reason for drawing attention to them is more general: Our understanding of the causes of individuals' behaviors in organizations can be expanded in innovative ways and directions by embracing the methods and lessons from social neuroscience.

THINKING RELATIONALLY

To understand the way in which work is now suffused by relationships, and just how much this situation has changed, we need look no further than our own work: While single-authored publications were the norm several decades ago (and in many situations even a requirement for tenure), it is now rare in our field to find instances of single authorship and this handbook itself, our introduction and the majority of the chapters are no exception! Further evidence of the relational nature of work (if any is needed) is how, throughout our collaborations with others, our own unique ideas are shared freely and frequently, and on reading the end product, it often becomes difficult to tease apart original ownership of ideas. How do we know what was self- versus other-initiated? Mead (1934) earlier termed this phenomenon 'a conversation of gestures,' and its prevalence and importance provides the foundation for conducting relational research.

Mead's (1934) conversation of gestures illustrates the dilemma of understanding and predicting most organizational phenomena: What behaviors can we study and understand without accounting for 'the other'? Even demographic variables such as age and gender are studied relationally. As one example: it is not being female per se that is associated with negative work experiences, but rather, being female in a male-dominated work environment that is associated with such experiences (see Gutek and Morasch, 1982). Many additional variables in OB lend themselves equally to a relational lens, including workplace aggression, leadership, discrimination, emotions and power and politics, each of which is considered in separate chapters in this Handbook.[1]

Aquino and Lamertz's (2004) model of workplace victimization exemplifies the move toward relational models in OB. As they cogently argue, 'by proposing a relational approach, we are directly exploring the idea that such behavior must be understood as a function of a relationship that develops between a victim and perpetrator rather than solely by their individual attributes' (Aquino and Lamertz, 2004: 1024). While this statement might seem self-evident, most research on workplace aggression and violence (as but one example) proceeds by focusing separately on either the victim or the perpetrator. Aquino and Lamertz (2004) are moving beyond this towards an understanding of how factors associated with the victim, the perpetrator and the relationship between the two, give rise to victimization. Several other examples of existing relational research help to illustrate its potential value to an understanding of behavior in organizations.

First, with few exceptions, traditional attempts to understand the effects of leadership proceed as if the presence or absence of followers was largely irrelevant. Recognizing the active role of followers in what is still referred to as the leadership process invites a relational perspective. Meindl et al. (1988) initially begged this question when addressing the 'romance of leadership.' Later, Klein and House (1995) invoked a relational perspective in their conceptualization of charisma: the leader may be charismatic, but charisma can only surface and flourish if and when the follower is open to charisma. More recently, dyadic-based leader-follower studies have ensued (for example, Dvir et al., 2002; Dvir and Shamir, 2003). These dyadic studies enrich our understanding of the nature and effectiveness of leadership, because they draw attention to the leader's behavior *and* the follower's active participation in interpreting (and modifying) that behavior.

As documented in the relational model of victimization and the aforementioned leadership research, other workplace behaviors may also benefit from a relational perspective. For instance, the relational lens can be used when studying courageous acts in the workplace; heroic (or altruistic) behaviors are often conceptualized solely in terms of individual differences of the altruistic individual. Yet our understanding of such behaviors (which include phenomena such as empathy and compassion, bystander non-intervention and whistle blowing) may be further understood by understanding the relationship between the 'hero' and the 'rescued' rather than examining 'altruistic behavior' in isolation.

Some of the most captivating illustrations of Mead's (1934) conversation of gestures derive from instances where explicit intentions to influence or affect another individual are absent. Research findings from beyond the confines of OB have provided support both for positive and negative emotional contagion. For example, emotional contagion is evident when merely looking at others' happy faces induces more happiness in oneself (Wild et al., 2001), and when being around depressed individuals increases one's own depressive symptoms (Stevens and Prinstein, 2005). In a similar vein, recent research has demonstrated how indirect witnesses to displays of interpersonal injustice react negatively along with the victim (De Cremer and van Hiel, 2006). Extending the findings of emotional contagion and vicarious learning, might it be possible that other anxieties, fears or frustrations, can be understood relationally? Similarly, might optimism and hope be equally 'contagious'?

From the perspective of thinking relationally, perhaps the greatest insights stand to be gained from the study of marital and romantic relationship processes and interactions. Unfortunately, a common practice in the social sciences is to become specialized in one's own areas, at the expense of understanding and benefiting from conceptual and methodological advances in other areas. From a science that emphasized self-reports in the mid-twentieth century, marital research has gained substantial predictive power by incorporating interview, observational and self-report data, and sequential and time-series analyses (Gottman and Notarius, 2002). Like other areas within OB (for example, workplace aggression; Barling, 1996) where our understandings have been enhanced by lessons from marital research, our understanding of relational issues in organizations may benefit meaningfully from the techniques used in marital research, the study of which may be more likely given the thoughts shared by Gottman (2007) in a recent *Harvard Business Review* interview.

In conclusion, many phenomena long seen as core parts of OB derive special meaning from one's position relative to others. For example, holding more or less power in an organization (group or team), enjoying relatively more or less control (see Dupré and Barling, 2006), and being of higher or lower status (Aquino et al., 2001), necessitate relational approaches to theory and research. Embracing such a relational approach to the study of micro-OB would provide the opportunity to consolidate and extend our understanding of individuals' behaviors in organizations.

INDIVIDUALS ARE EMBEDDED IN ORGANIZATIONS

'Open systems' theory was widely-accepted as an organizing framework for understanding individuals and organizations from the middle of the 20th century. Within this framework, organizations were seen as being inseparable from the societies in which they existed, and the influence between organizations and the individuals within those organizations was reciprocal. Despite the conceptual promise offered by an open-system perspective, the practice of research was not necessarily affected; research in the latter part of the 20th century continued to study employee behavior in isolation.

Now, organizational scholars are again recognizing the complex interdependence of individuals, groups and organizations, both conceptually and methodologically. To this end, there has been a veritable surge in multilevel theory and methodology. It would be redundant for us to reiterate calls for multilevel research which are comprehensively described elsewhere (for example, Kozlowski and Klein, 2000); instead, we raise three issues for consideration in multilevel research that would plausibly expand our knowledge of individual behavior in organizations.

First, whether for the sake of conceptual simplicity or methodological feasibility, multilevel research has usually examined basic instances of individuals embedded within teams that exist within organizations. In sharp contrast, the reality is that many individuals hold multiple competing roles within organizations (Beehr and Glazer, 2005) and across different social systems (e.g., as reflected by work-family conflict; Bellavia and Frone, 2005; also see the chapter by Grzywacz and Butler in this volume). With the increasing number of individuals who hold different part-time jobs in different organizations (Barling and Gallagher, 1996; Gallagher, this volume), or who moonlight (Inness et al., 2005), the complexity of the interdependencies within and across levels requiring attention becomes apparent.

Our second question deals with the reciprocal influences within these multiple levels of analysis. Most often, research has investigated top-down processes, where upper-level phenomena are presumed to influence lower-level phenomena (Kozlowski and Klein, 2000), such as team efficacy influencing individual performance. As is often the case, the way in which we structure our research questions reflects philosophical assumptions, not all

of which are necessarily intended. In this case, top-down approaches ascribe a relatively passive role to employees. While recognizing obvious power imbalances in organizations, we suggest that it would be more appropriate to ascribe a greater agentic role to individuals in the many ways in which they actively structure their environments (Bandura, 2005). Consistent with Mead's (1934) conversation of gestures, we might even ask where this process begins and ends? Chen's (2005) model of newcomer adaptation to new team settings is instructive in this sense. Finding that individual performance was both a product of initial team performance, and a driver of future team performance, Chen suggests that 'the assumption underlying the hypothesized model is that newcomer adaptation is a longitudinal process that evolves within persons (newcomers) over time, and that newcomer adaptation both influences and is influenced by certain individual and team constructs' (p. 102). While exploring the intricacies of reciprocal effects across levels are no doubt challenging, doing so will produce knowledge that more accurately reflects the active role that individuals play in interacting with and creating their environments.

Third, we also encourage greater attention to the nature of higher-level variables, such as groups. Commonly, within-group agreement has been a requirement central to multilevel research; groups in which agreement is not reached are discarded from the research. However, the disagreement that exists within groups is equally interesting. We illustrate this with two examples. Roberson and Colquitt (2005) discussed how team-level justice can be characterized by shared or dissimilar perceptions of justice, the former being more closely related to team effectiveness. Likewise, Ng and Van Dyne (2005) showed that teams with greater variation in the level of helping behaviors were associated with worse team performance. However, this study goes further, showing that this effect emerged irrespective of the mean levels of helping behavior. Both of these studies point to the possibility that the differences in perceptions and behavior within groups may be just as informative as the within-group similarities.

Theoretical and methodological advances in multilevel modeling will no doubt increase in the future, and confronting the questions asked here have the potential to contribute to an ever-expanding body of knowledge about behavior in and of organizations.

ORGANIZATIONS ARE EMBEDDED IN SOCIETY

'Few people are capable of expressing with equanimity opinions which differ from the prejudices of their social environment. Most people are even incapable of forming such opinions.' Albert Einstein.

Ignoring Einstein's insights in general would surely be inadvisable; ignoring the implications of this particular observation for understanding the impact of the social context on the individual employee would result in a truncated appreciation of individuals' behavior in organizations. In this section, we focus on the influence of societal events and trends on employees, as well as the significance of social context on the individual employee. Specifically, we discuss corporate social responsibility, community and natural disasters, and sleep.

Organizations' attempts to recognize social issues are frequently captured under the umbrella of 'corporate social responsibility' (CSR), which 'reflect[s] the organization's status and activities with respect to its perceived societal obligations' (Dacin and Brown, 1997: 68). Most of the studies focusing on CSR have been conducted at the organization level (e.g., Bird et al., 2007); only rarely is empirical research on this topic investigated at the employee level. Employees remain the face of faceless organizations, and the success of any CSR initiative is dependent on the extent to which employees identify with the values expressed in the CSR initiative, and are willing to go beyond normal job expectations to make the initiative a success. Anecdotal evidence

of individual employee involvement in CSR initiatives exists. As one example, in the summer of 2007, employees at Lush, an organization specializing in handmade cosmetics, served customers naked to protest against the damaging effect of packaging on the environment (a frequent focus for CSR is environmental sustainability). Employees covered parts of their bodies with an apron that invited the question 'Ask me why I'm naked.' Ignoring the potential risks of sexual harassment and interpersonal injustices, Lush employees showed their identification with the company's values and ethics. Not only did Lush workers prompt questioning from the public, but they were willing to deal with any criticisms their behaviors raised.

Existing OB theories are already well-placed to provide an understanding of the employee identification with organizational values that would make CSR initiatives possible. Whether it be the 'collective sense of mission' and going 'beyond self-interest for the good of the group' (Bass and Riggio, 2006) inherent in transformational leadership, the sense of identification that is core to organizational commitment (Meyer and Allen, 1997), or the task significance and meaning that individuals seek in their work (Hackman and Oldman, 1980), these issues have been at the core of OB for several decades.

Moving beyond established organizational behavior theories will also invite new avenues for research. For example, Andersson et al. (2007) found that hope and gratitude were associated with pro-social behaviors in organizations, as well as stronger beliefs in social responsibility. Compassion might fulfil a similar predictive role in involvement in CSR. Confronting such possibilities might help involvement of CSR initiatives in the burgeoning move towards positive organizational scholarship (see the chapter by Dutton and Glynn in this volume).

Recognizing how societal forces influence the individual in other ways can also advance our understanding of OB. Organizations and their employees have long been subjected to the vicissitudes of natural and technological disasters (Baum et al., 1983). Consequently, it should not be surprising that research exists focusing on disasters, as well as on individual differences such as resilience (for example, Bonanno et al., 2006) and coping strategies (e.g., Tucker et al., 2002) to account for employee well-being. However, organizations and their employees have also suffered from acute violence perpetrated both by organizational insiders and outsiders (e.g., partners of employees exacting revenge at the worksite; disgruntled customers; Kelloway et al., 2006), as well as major terrorist attacks such as those of September 11, 2001 (Inness and Barling, 2005), all of which may include among their consequences some effects on the experience of work and individual well-being. As is evident (e.g., Beehr and Glazer, 2005; and Jex's chapter in this volume), a mountain of research exists on chronic work stressors. In contrast, acute societal traumas such as 9/11, critical moments that have lasting effects on organizations and their employees, have attracted much less conceptual and empirical attention (Pratt and Barling, 1988) despite indications that disasters such as 9/11 might be associated with subsequent employee absences (Byron and Peterson, 2002), and that levels of community violence influence levels of employee aggression at work (Dietz et al., 2003). Focusing on leadership during the tragedy of 9/11 has also led to an understanding of the role of compassion in times of existential crisis (Dutton et al., 2002).

Third, just how individual-level employee behaviors might be affected by societal events can be gleaned from a focus on sleep trends. According to the National Sleep Foundation, the amount of individuals who endure less than six hours of sleep per night has steadily increased based on data gathered from 1998 to 2005 (National Sleep Foundation, 2005). The perils of sleep deprivation have been well documented, including compromised safety (e.g., Muecke, 2005), physical health (e.g., Babkoff et al., 1989), and mental health (e.g., Morin et al., 2006). The phenomenon of *karoshi* referring in Japanese to death from overwork (Kanai, 2006) may be equally relevant in this regard (e.g., Uehata, 1991).

There is no reason to expect these trends will reverse themselves in the near future, and therefore, just how societal changes in sleep influences the nature and experience of work (e.g., shift work), as well as safeguards at work to protect against sleep deprivation, warrant future research.

In summary, given the continuing and increasing interdependence of organizations and societies, the attempts made by organizations to influence society, and the disturbances from the external environment on organizations and their members will likely continue. As a result, any explanation of individual-level employee behavior that ignores these external events will likely result in an narrow perspective of OB. Accordingly, an opportunity exists for research in this area to enhance our understanding of the interconnection between the environment in which organizations function and the individual employee.

TIME AND TIMING IN OB RESEARCH

The very idea that time is a core issue in OB research would come as no surprise to anyone who has completed a first-level course in the behavioral sciences, where the notion that temporal ordering is a necessary condition for causal inferences is likely introduced early and discussed often. The attention given to this issue in classic methodology texts (e.g., Shadish et al., 2002) would further reinforce this notion. Moreover, how many of us have not received feedback from reviewers on a manuscript submitted that did not in some way question whether longitudinal data were needed, whether the longitudinal data presented were sufficient, or whether the temporal periods between data points were adequate? Our raising of this issue is not simply an attempt to reinforce the methodological importance of considering these issues in research; this is appropriately and extensively dealt with elsewhere (Shadish et al., 2002). Instead, we introduce this section to refine and extend existing knowledge, and to invite new conceptual questions. In that sense, time will not only be used to disentangle cause-and-effect relationships, but become an issue worthy of scholarly attention itself.

Perhaps an appropriate way to begin this discussion is to point a finger at research that one of us was involved in more than two decades ago (Barling et al., 1987). In the study, the authors were presented with the opportunity to study the effects of a major explosion that took place in a dynamite factory just outside Johannesburg, South Africa which resulted in the deaths of 14 employees. The organization involved invited them to study the effects of the explosion on employee attitudes and mental health of survivors, helped them to construct two quasi-experimental control groups, and allowed them to collect data within two weeks of, and again two months following the disaster. Remarkably, no negative effects on employee attitudes or mental health were revealed, and these findings were explained in terms of the likelihood that employees believed that there was no longer any threat to their personal well-being, as a result of which the stressor was no longer present. With the benefits of hindsight, we might offer a different set of explanations. What if we had not only measured the outcome so soon after the disaster, but also one year later? Might it be possible that the results would then have suggested that the earlier pattern of relief for having survived the disaster was replaced by later post-traumatic stress disorder? Just when we collected the outcome data – which was dictated entirely by organizational realities rather than conceptual criteria – might have been critical in generating a potentially erroneous set of conclusions. We are by no means alone in this phenomenon. The appropriate timing of any measurement is an issue that continues to plague OB research, and it is frequently determined by opportunity rather than conceptual design.

Research on the mental-health benefits of respites from work further illustrates the importance of time. Westman and Eden (1997) demonstrated that job stress and burnout can be relieved through vacations, but the benefits of any respite from work dissipated over a short period of time. Specifically, burnout was reduced during and immediately following a vacation, but returned to its pre-vacation levels within three weeks of returning to work. Had Westman and Eden (1997) conducted their post-respite assessment at only one of these time periods, or perhaps at any other period, different conclusions might have been reached.

Such examples highlight how assumptions about time permeate and influence OB research. Other core areas of micro-OB are beset with similar issues. To illustrate, we provide an example based on transformational leadership research – today's most prominent theory of leadership (see Judge et al.'s chapter in this volume). Most of the research on transformational leadership uses either self- or other-reports based on various forms of the Multifactor Leadership Questionnaire (Bass and Avolio, 1995). Invariably, respondents are asked to report on how frequently their leaders display various leadership behaviors across time, often a period of six months. Averaged measures of leadership are then created based on these aggregated reports. Not only are such methods susceptible to memory biases and distortions, but they also make an assumption that merits attention. The inherent assumption is that leadership behaviors are highly stable across time, which rationalizes measures of leadership based on aggregated reports. Yet even individuals who indicated that they have charismatic or transformational leaders often report verbally that these leaders do not display these behaviors 'all the time,' but rather episodically. This is consistent with recent theoretical suggestions that leadership is reflected in critical moments (Tucker et al., 2006; Avolio and Luthans, 2005). To capture these critical 'moments' and take a different approach to studying leadership, researchers could pursue the methodological approach of daily studies which have been conducted in other areas of OB such as daily stress (e.g., Story and Repetti, 2006).

So far we have focused on methodological considerations of time; however, research can also benefit from explicit conceptualizations of temporal effects. While research in OB is frequently focused on asking whether effects emerge, ascertaining *when* any effects abate is of equal importance. Team-based research may show the greatest advancement in this respect. Gersick's (1988, 1989) punctuated equilibrium model shows that time is critical in shaping group development, which is marked by two phases, the first of which is characterized by little progress toward the group's goals, with the second yielding considerable effort toward task completion. These two phases are separated by a midpoint transition, occurring when approximately half of the group's allotted time has passed. At this point, group members' awareness and perceptions of time shift, and accordingly, they change their behaviors. The punctuated equilibrium model illustrates the importance of timing for groups, and suggests that researchers must be cautious of how relationships could differ during various stages of a team's shared tenure. For instance, Harrison et al. (1998) showed that the effects of demographic diversity on group outcomes weakened as groups spent a greater amount of time together as a team; however, the opposite was true for diversity based on deep-level attitudes that are revealed over time.

Our understanding of teams has benefited from a conceptual focus on time and timing in other ways as well. For example, creativity may only have positive team implications when it emerges *prior* to a team's transition point, at a time when individuals are willing to embrace it (Ford and Sullivan, 2004). Likewise, the benefits of shared team experience exist, but there is an optimal amount of shared experience, after which negative performance effects occur – a process referred to as knowledge ossification (Berman et al., 2002).

Not directly confronting the issue of time and timing presupposes that any effects that emerge do so immediately and permanently which is an unlikely situation. We have argued that asking conceptual questions of time and timing can protect against such presuppositions and enhance our theories of behavior in teams. Furthermore, we suspect that the scarcity of such questions in the current literature derives from the methodological challenges inherent in handling longitudinal data. Fortunately, newly-embraced statistical techniques available to micro-OB researchers now enable us to ensure that our understanding of individual behavior in organizations is not a function of the methodological tail wagging the conceptual dog.

Before concluding this section, we raise one final consideration about the conceptualization of time in existing OB research. The effects of time urgency, time management, and deadlines (e.g., Waller et al., 2001), as well as perceived control over scheduling, have all received considerable empirical scrutiny (e.g., Barton, 1994). Additionally, the effects of time away from work, whether in the form of breaks (Galinsky et al., 2000), vacations (e.g., Westman and Eden, 1997) or absenteeism (see Johns, this volume) have been extensively studied. We suggest, however, that what has been lacking from this research is a sufficient appreciation of cross-cultural differences in the understanding and influence of time. Research needs to account for the way in which time is conceptualized within OB research, wherein time as a linear, limited resource, is culturally bound (e.g., Adair and Brett, 2005). Consistent with recent research on national differences in the experience of work stress (e.g., Liu and Spector, 2005), and the general move toward organizational research that is more responsive to cross-national differences (see the chapter by Gardner and Early in this volume), greater understanding of OB will emerge from using a broader lens to conceptualize time.

In summary, individuals are inseparable from their personal and cultural histories, and future trajectories, making time an inherent property of individual behavior in organizations, and warranting a temporal lens to study OB (Ancona et al., 2001).

CONCLUSION

Each of the chapters in this Handbook takes a very specific approach in reflecting on the history, current status and future possibilities of the specific area under consideration. In this introduction we have raised several questions that cross all of the areas considered. Confronting these questions enhances our understanding of individual behavior in organizations, and in turn, reveal meaningful and new directions for OB research.

NOTE

1. See the chapters by Cortina and Berdahl, Judge et al., Nkomo, Grandey, and Lux et al. respectively.

REFERENCES

Adair, W.L. and Brett, J.M. (2005) 'The negotiation dance: Time, culture, and behavioral sequences in negotiation', *Organization Science*, 16 (1): 33–51.

Ancona, D.G., Okhuysen, G.A. and Perlow, L.A. (2001) 'Taking time to integrate temporal research', *Academy of Management Review*, 26 (4): 512–529.

Andersson, L.M., Giacalone, R.A. and Jurkiewicz, C.L. (2007) 'On the relationship of hope and gratitude to corporate social responsibility', *Journal of Business Ethics*, 70 (4): 401–409.

Arvey, R.D., Bouchard, T.J.Jr., Segal, N.L. and Abraham, L.M. (1989) 'Job satisfaction: Environmental and genetic components', *Journal of Applied Psychology*, 74 (2): 187–192.

Arvey, R.D., Rotundo, M., Johnson, W., Zhang, Z. and McGue, M. (2006) 'The determinants of leadership role occupancy: Genetic and personality factors', *Leadership Quarterly*, 17 (1): 1–20.

Arvey, R.D., Zhang, Z., Avolio, B.J. and Krueger, R.F. (2007) 'Developmental and genetic determinants of leadership role occupancy among women', *Journal of Applied Psychology*, 92 (3): 693–706.

Aquino, K. and Lamertz, K. (2004) 'A relational model of workplace victimization: Social roles and patterns of victimization in dyadic relationships', *Journal of Applied Psychology*, 89 (6): 1023–1034.

Aquino, K., Tripp, T.M. and Bies, R.J. (2001) 'How employees respond to personal offense: The effects of blame attribution, victim status, and offender status on revenge and reconciliation in the workplace', *Journal of Applied Psychology*, 86 (1): 52–59.

Avolio, B.J. (2007) 'Promoting more integrative strategies for leadership theory-building', *American Psychologist. Special Issue: Leadership*, 62 (1): 25–33.

Avolio, B.J. and Luthans, F. (2005) *The High Impact Leader*. New York: McGraw Hill.

Babkoff, H., Mikulincer, M., Caspy, T., Carasso, R.L. and Sing, H. C. (1989) 'The implications of sleep loss for circadian performance accuracy', *Work and Stress. Special Issue: Stress and Sustained Performance*, 3 (1): 3–14.

Baker, L.A., Jacobson, K.C., Raine, A., Lozano, D.I. and Bezdijan, S. (2007) 'Genetic and environmental bases of childhood antisocial behavior: A multi-informant twin study', *Journal of Abnormal Psychology*, 116 (2): 219–235.

Bandura, A. (2005) 'The evolution of social cognitive theory', in K.G. Smith and M.A. Hitt (eds) *Great Minds in Management: The Process of Theory Development*. New York: Oxford University Press, pp. 9–35.

Barling, J. (1996) 'The prediction, psychological experience and consequences of workplace violence', in G. VandenBos and E.G. Bulatao (eds) *Violence On the Job: Identifying Risks and Developing Solutions*. Washington, DC: American Psychological Association, pp. 29–49.

Barling, J., Bluen, S.D. and Fain, R. (1987) 'Psychological functioning following an acute disaster', *Journal of Applied Psychology*, 72 (4): 683–690.

Barling, J. and Gallagher, D.G. (1996) 'Part-time employment', in C.L. Cooper and I.T. Robertson (eds) *International Review of Industrial and Organizational Psychology* (Vol. II). London: Wiley and Sons, pp. 243–277.

Barton, J. (1994) 'Choosing to work at night: A moderating influence on individual tolerance to shift work', *Journal of Applied Psychology*, 79 (3): 449–454.

Bass, B.M. and Avolio, B.J. (1995) *Multifactor Leadership Questionnaire*. Palo Alto, CA: Mind Garden.

Bass, B.M. and Riggio, R.E. (2006) *Transformational Leadership* (2nd edn) Mahwah, NJ: Lawrence Erlbaum.

Baum, A., Fleming, R. and Davidson, L.M. (1983) 'Natural disaster and technological catastrophe', *Environment and Behavior*, 15 (3): 333–354.

Beehr, T.A. and Glazer, S. (2005) 'Occupational role stress', in J. Barling, E.K. Kelloway and M.R. Frone (eds) *Handbook of Work Stress*. Thousand Oaks, CA: Sage Publications, pp. 7–33.

Bellavia, G.M. and Frone, M.R. (2005) 'Work-family conflict', in J. Barling, E.K. Kelloway and M.R. Frone (eds) *Handbook of Work Stress*. Thousand Oaks, CA: Sage Publications, pp. 113–148.

Berman, S.L., Down, J. and Hill, C.W.L. (2002) 'Tacit knowledge as a source of competitive advantage in the National Basketball Association', *Academy of Management Journal*, 45 (1): 13–31.

Bird, R., Hall, A.D., Momentè, F. and Reggiani, F. (2007) 'What corporate social responsibility activities are valued by the market?' *Journal of Business Ethics*, 76 (2): 189–206.

Bonanno, G.A., Galea, S., Bucciarelli, A. and Vlahov, D. (2006) 'Psychological resilience after disaster: New York City in the aftermath of the September 11th terrorist attack', *Psychological Science*, 17 (3): 181–186.

Bouchard, T.J.Jr., Lykken, D.T., McGue, M., Segal, N.L. and Tellegen, A. (1990) 'Sources of human differences: The Minnesota Study of Twins Reared Apart', *Science*, 250 (4978): 223–228.

Byron, K. and Peterson, S. (2002) 'The impact of a large-scale traumatic event on individual and organizational outcomes: Exploring employee and company reactions to September 11, 2001', *Journal of Organizational Behavior*, 23 (8): 895–910.

Cacioppo, J.T. et al. (2007) 'Social neuroscience: Progress and implications for mental health', *Perspectives on Psychological Science*, 2(2): 99–123.

Campbell, S.B. (1995) 'Behavior problems in preschool children: A review of recent research', *Journal of Child Psychology and Psychiatry*, 36 (1): 113–149.

Chen, G. (2005) 'Newcomer adaptation in teams: Multilevel antecedents and outcomes', *Academy of Management Journal*, 48 (1): 101–116.

Cropanzano, R. and James, K. (1990) 'Some methodological considerations for the behavioral genetic analysis of work attitudes', *Journal of Applied Psychology*, 75 (4): 433–439.

Dabbs, J.M. Jr. (1992) 'Salivary testosterone measurements in behavioral studies', in D. Malamud and L.A. Tabak (eds), *Saliva as a Diagnostic Fluid*. New York: New York Academy of Sciences, pp. 177–183.

Dacin, P.A. and Brown, T.J. (1997) 'The company and the product: Corporate associations and consumer product responses', *Journal of Marketing*, 61 (1): 68–84.

De Cremer, D. and van Hiel, A. (2006) 'Effects of another person's fair treatment on one's own emotions and behaviors: The moderating role of how much the other cares for you', *Organizational Behavior and Human Decision Processes*, 100 (2): 231–249.

Dietz, J., Robinson, S.L., Folger, R., Baron, R.A. and Schulz, M. (2003) 'The impact of community violence and an organization's procedural justice climate on workplace aggression', *Academy of Management Journal*, 46 (3): 317–326.

Dupré, K.E., and Barling, J. (2006) 'Predicting and preventing supervisory workplace aggression', *Journal of Occupational Health Psychology*, 11 (1): 13–26.

Dutton, J.E, Frost, P.J, Worline, M.C, Lilius, J.M. and Kanov J.M. (2002) 'Leading in times of trauma', *Harvard Business Review*, 80 (1): 54–61.

Dvir, T. and Shamir, B. (2003) 'Follower developmental characteristics as predicting transformational leadership: A longitudinal field study', *Leadership Quarterly*, 14 (3): 327–344.

Dvir, T., Eden, D., Avolio, B.J. and Shamir, B. (2002) 'Impact of transformational leadership on follower development and performance: A field experiment', *Academy of Management Journal*, 45 (4): 735–744.

Ford, C. and Sullivan, D.M. (2004) 'A time for everything: How the timing of novel contributions influences project team outcomes', *Journal of Organizational Behavior*, 25 (2): 279–292.

Galinsky, T.L., Swanson, N.G., Sauter, S.L., Hurrell, J.J. and Schleifer, L.M. (2000) 'A field study of supplementary rest breaks for data-entry operators', *Ergonomics*, 43 (5): 622–638.

Gersick, C.J. (1988) 'Time and transition in work teams: Toward a new model of group development', *Academy of Management Journal*, 31 (1): 9–41.

Gersick, C.J. (1989) 'Marking time: Predictable transitions in task groups', *Academy of Management Journal*, 32 (2): 274–309.

Gottman, J.M. and Notarius, C.I. (2002) 'Marital research in the twentieth century and a research agenda for the 21st century', *Family Process*, 41 (2): 159–197.

Gottman, J.M. (2007) 'Making relationships work', *Harvard Business Review*, December, 45–50.

Gutek, B.A. and Morasch, B. (1982) 'Sex-ratios, sex-role spillover, and sexual harassment of women at work', *Journal of Social Issues*, 38 (4): 55–74.

Hackman, J.R. and Oldham, G.R. (1980) *Work Redesign*. Reading, MA: Addison-Wesley.

Harrison, D.A., Price, K.H. and Bell, M.P. (1998) 'Beyond relational demography: Time and the effects of surface- and deep-level diversity on work group cohesion', *Academy of Management Journal*, 41 (1): 96–107.

Heaphy, E.D. and Dutton, J.E. (2008) 'Positive social interactions and the human body at work: Linking organizations and physiology', *Academy of Management Review*, 33 (1): 137–162.

Inness, M. and Barling, J. (2005) 'Terrorism', in J. Barling, E.K. Kelloway and M.R. Frone (eds) *Handbook of Work Stress*. Thousand Oaks, CA: Sage Publications, pp. 375–397.

Inness, M., Barling, J. and Turner, N. (2005) 'Understanding supervisor-targeted aggression: A within-person between-jobs design', *Journal of Applied Psychology*, 90 (4): 731–739.

Kanai, A. (2006) 'Economic and employment conditions, *karoshi* (work to death) and the trend of studies on workaholism in Japan', in R.J. Burke (ed.) *Research Companion to Working Time and Work Addiction. New Horizons in Management.* Northampton, MA: Edward Elgar, pp. 158–172.

Kelloway, E.K., Barling, J. and Hurrell, J.J. (2006) *Handbook of Workplace Violence.* Thousand Oaks, CA: Sage Publications.

Klein, K.J. and House, R.J. (1995) 'On fire: Charismatic leadership and levels of analysis', *Leadership Quarterly*, 6 (2): 183–198.

Kozlowski, S.W.J. and Klein, K.J. (2000) 'A multilevel approach to theory and research in organizations: Contextual, temporal, and emergent processes', in K.J. Klein and S.W.J. Kozlowski (eds) *Multilevel Theory, Research, and Methods in Organizations: Foundations, Extensions, and New Directions.* San Francisco, CA: Jossey-Bass, pp. 3–90.

Liu, C. and Spector, P.E. (2005) 'International and cross-cultural issues', in J. Barling, E.K. Kelloway and M.R. Frone (eds) *Handbook of Work Stress.* Thousand Oaks, CA: Sage Publications, pp. 487–516.

McGue, M. and Bouchard, T.J.Jr. (1998) 'Genetic and environmental influences on human behavioral differences', *Annual Review of Neuroscience*, 21 (1): 1–24.

Mead, G.H. (1934) *Mind, Self and Society.* Chicago, IL: University of Chicago Press.

Meindl, J.R., Ehrlich, S.B. and Dukerich, J.M. (1985) 'The romance of leadership', *Administrative Science Quarterly*, 30 (4): 78–102.

Meyer, J.P. and Allen, N.J. (1997) *Commitment in the Workplace: Theory, Research, and Application.* Thousand Oaks, CA: Sage Publications.

Morin, C.M., Bélanger, L. and Fortier-Brochu, É. (2006) 'Sleep, insomnia, and psychopathology', *Canadian Psychology*, 47 (4): 245–262.

Muecke, S. (2005) 'Effects of rotating night shifts: Literature review', *Journal of Advanced Nursing*, 50 (5): 433–439.

National Sleep Foundation (2005) *2005 Sleep in America Poll.* Washington, DC: National Sleep Foundation.

Ng, K.Y. and Van Dyne, L. (2005) 'Antecedents and performance consequences of helping behavior in work groups: A multilevel analysis', *Group and Organization Management*, 30 (5): 514–540.

Nicholson, N. (1998) 'How hardwired is human behavior?' *Harvard Business Review*, 76 (4): 134–147.

Pratt, L. and Barling, J. (1988) 'Differentiating daily hassles, acute and chronic stressors: A framework and its implications', in J.R. Hurrell, L.R. Murphy, S.L. Sauter and C.L. Cooper (eds) *Occupational Stress: Issues and Developments in Research.* London, UK: Taylor and Francis, pp. 41–53.

Roberson, Q.M. and Colquitt, J.A. (2005) 'Shared and configural justice: A social network model of justice in teams', *Academy of Management Review*, 30 (3): 595–607.

Roberts, B.W., Harms, P.D., Caspi, A. and Moffitt, T.E. (2007) 'Predicting the counterproductive employee in a child-to-adult prospective study', *Journal of Applied Psychology*, 92 (5): 1427–1436.

Shadish, W.R. Cook, T.D. and Campbell, D.T. (2002) *Experimental and Quasi-experimental Designs for Generalized Causal Experiments.* New York: Houghton Mifflin.

Signorelli, A. (1974) 'Statistics: Tool or master of the psychologist?' *American Psychologist*, 29 (10): 774–777.

Slutske, W.S. et al. (1998) *Journal of Abnormal Psychology*, 106 (3): 266–279.

Stevens, E.A. and Prinstein, M.J. (2005) 'Peer contagion of depressogenic attributional styles among adolescents: A longitudinal study', *Journal of Abnormal Child Psychology*, 33 (1): 25–37.

Story, L.B. and Repetti, R. (2006) 'Daily occupational stressors and marital behavior', *Journal of Family Psychology*, 20 (4): 690–700.

Tucker, P., Pfefferbaum, B., Doughty, D.E., Jones, D.E., Jordan, F.B. and Nixon, S.J. (2002) 'Body handlers after terrorism in Oklahoma City: Predictors of posttraumatic stress and other symptoms', *American Journal of Orthopsychiatry*, 72 (4): 469–475.

Tucker, S., Turner, N., Barling, J., Reid, E. and Elving, C. (2006) 'Apologies and transformational leadership', *Journal of Business Ethics*, 63 (2): 195–207.

Uehata, T. (1991) 'Long working hours and occupation stress-related cardiovascular attacks among middle-aged workers in Japan', *Journal of Human Ergology*, 20 (2): 147–153.

van Honk, J., and Schutter, D.J.L.G. (2007) 'Testosterone reduces conscious detection of signals serving social correction: Implications for antisocial behavior', *Psychological Science*, 18 (8): 663–667.

Waller, M.J., Conte, J.M., Gibson, C.B. and Carpenter, M.A. (2001) 'The effect of individual perceptions of deadlines on team performance', *Academy of Management Review*, 26 (4): 586–600.

Westman, M. and Eden, D. (1997) 'Effects of a respite from work on burnout: Vacation relief and fade-out', *Journal of Applied Psychology*, 82 (4): 516–527.

White, R.E., Thornhill, S. and Hampson, E. (2006) 'Entrepreneurs and evolutionary biology: The relationship between testosterone and new venture creation', *Organizational Behavior and Human Decision Processes*, 100 (1): 21–34.

Wild, B., Erb, M., and Bartels, M. (2001) 'Are emotions contagious? Evoked emotions while viewing emotionally expressive faces: Quality, quantity, time course and gender differences', *Psychiatry Research*, 102 (2): 109–124.

PART ONE

Individual Attachment to, and Disengagements from, Work

Psychological Contracts

Jacqueline A-M. Coyle-Shapiro
and Marjo-Riitta Parzefall

The psychological contract has captured the attention of researchers as a framework for understanding the employment relationship. In terms of research, there has been an exponential growth in publications on the topic in the last 15 years (following the publication of Rousseau's 1989 article) giving the impression of a relatively new concept. Its introduction can however be traced to the 1960s. The concept developed in two main phases: its origins and early development covering the period 1958 to 1988, and from 1989 onwards. This chapter begins with a review of the initial phase in the development of the psychological contract highlighting the commonalities and differences amongst the early contributors. We then review Rousseau's (1989) reconceptualization of the psychological contract, as this has been very influential in guiding contemporary research. The two distinct phases in the development of the psychological contract have given rise to a number of key debates, which we discuss prior to outlining an agenda for future research.

HISTORICAL DEVELOPMENT OF THE PSYCHOLOGICAL CONTRACT

In tracing the development of the psychological contract, we focus on the seminal works of Argyris (1960), Levinson et al. (1962) and Schein (1965). We also review the work of Blau (1964) and Gouldner (1960) as these represent the foundational ideas of social exchange theory upon which subsequent theorizing on the psychological contract draws.

Classical early studies

Although Argyris (1960) was the first to coin the term 'psychological contract,' the idea of the employment relationship as an exchange can be traced to the writings of Barnard (1938) and March and Simon (1958). Barnard's (1938) theory of equilibrium posits that employees' continued participation depends upon adequate rewards from the organization. Here lies the idea of a reciprocal exchange underlying the employee-organization relationship. This was elaborated upon by March and Simon (1958) in their inducements-contributions model. They argued that employees are satisfied when there is a greater difference between the inducements offered by the organization and the contributions they need to give in return. From the organization's perspective, employee contributions need to be sufficient to generate inducements from the organization, which in turn need to be attractive enough to elicit employee contributions. The work of March and Simon (1958) is rarely acknowledged in the psychological contract literature (Conway and Briner, 2005) but the idea of a reciprocal exchange bears a remarkable resemblance to a core tenet of the psychological contract.

Argyris (1960) viewed the psychological contract as an implicit understanding between a group of employees and their foreman, and argued that the relationship could develop in such a way that employees would exchange higher productivity and lower grievances in return for acceptable wages and job security (Taylor and Tekleab, 2004). Argyris (1960) believed that employees would perform at a higher level if the organization did not interfere too much with the employee group's norms and in return employees would respect the right of the organization to evolve. The defining characteristics of this first explicit conceptualization of the psychological contract viewed it as an exchange of tangible, specific and primarily economic resources agreed by the two parties that permitted the fulfillment of each party's needs.

Subsequently, Levinson et al. (1962) introduced a more elaborate conceptualization of the psychological contract that was heavily influenced by the work of Menninger (1958). Menninger (1958) suggested that in addition to tangible resources, contractual relationships also involve the exchange of intangibles. Furthermore, the exchange between the two parties needs to provide mutual satisfaction in order for the relationship to continue (Roehling, 1996). Levinson et al. (1962) based their definition of the psychological contract on the data they gathered in interviewing

874 employees who spoke of expectations that seemed to have an obligatory quality. They defined the psychological contract as comprising mutual expectations between an employee and the employer. These expectations may arise from unconscious motives and thus each party may not be aware of their own expectations let alone the expectations of the other party.

The findings of Levinson et al.'s (1962) study highlighted the role of reciprocity and the effect of anticipated satisfaction of expectations. Specifically, the emphasis on the fulfillment of needs created a relationship in which employees would try and fulfill the needs of the organization *if* the organization fulfilled the needs of employees. Thus, the employee and organization held strong expectations of each other and it was the anticipation of meeting those expectations that motivated the two parties to continue in that relationship. Taylor and Tekleab (2004) note that the work of Levinson et al. (1962) contributed to the conceptualization of the psychological contract in the following ways: the two parties in the contract are the individual employee and the organization represented by individual managers; the psychological contract covers complex issues – some expectations are widely shared, others are more individualized and the specificity of expectations may range from highly specific to very general; the psychological contract is subject to change as the parties negotiate changes in expectations that may arise from changes in circumstances or a more complete understanding of the contributions of the other party.

Although Schein's (1965) definition shares some similarities with Levinson et al. (1962), he placed considerable emphasis on the matching of expectations between the employee and organization. The matching of expectations and their fulfillment is crucial to attaining positive outcomes such as job satisfaction, commitment and performance. Consistent with this, Schein (1965) by implication highlighted the importance of understanding both the employee's as well as the employer's perspective. Schein went further than previous researchers in discussing how organizations might express the organization's psychological contract through its culture.

Divergences amongst early contributors

The initial phase in the development of the psychological contract is marked by divergences between the early contributors. In particular, the work of Argyris (1960) stands apart in several ways. First, the psychological contract captures an implicit understanding of the exchange of tangible resources between employees and an organizational representative. As noted by Conway and Briner (2005), this view of the psychological contract was a simple although underdeveloped one. It is not clear, for example, how the implicit understanding developed and what it is based upon. Furthermore, Argyris (1960) presented the narrowest view of the psychological contract in terms of its focus on tangible resources. In contrast, Levinson et al. (1962) and Schein (1965) viewed the content of the exchange as including both tangible and intangible resources.

Second, although Schein (1965) and Levinson et al. (1962) conceptualized the psychological contract as encompassing expectations, Levinson et al. (1962) viewed these expectations as having an obligatory quality where the parties believe the other to be duty bound to fulfill those expectations. At the same time, however, Levinson et al. (1962) did not see these expectations as being based on promises but rather on needs (Conway and Briner, 2005). Schein's (1965) primary emphasis was on the matching of expectations between the employee and organization. The outcomes (positive or negative) of the psychological contract were contingent upon the degree to which the two parties were in agreement in terms of expectations and their fulfillment. In addition, Schein (1965) gave greater prominence to the organization's perspective and considered ways in which the organization could express the type of psychological contract it wished to develop. In fact, Schein's (1980: 99) subsequent position on the importance of considering both

perspectives is illustrated in the following: 'We cannot understand the psychological dynamics if we look only to the individual's motivations or only to the organizational conditions and practices. The two interact in a complex fashion that demands a systems approach, capable of handling interdependent phenomena.'

Thus, the early phase in the development of the psychological contract is marked by differing emphases and an absence of acknowledgment of how one conceptualization relates to prior work. This lack of cumulative work created ambiguities that come to the fore in terms of current debates in the field.

Social exchange as theoretical foundation of psychological contracts

Running parallel and independently to the early psychological contract work, the seminal works of Homans (1958), Blau (1964) and Gouldner (1960) characterized the beginnings of social exchange theory, and were themselves influenced by the earlier work of Mauss (1925) and Malinowski (1922). Homans (1958) provided a skeletal theory of exchange in the context of how individuals interacted within groups (Coyle-Shapiro and Conway, 2004) that was developed by Blau (1964). We focus on the work of Blau (1964) and Gouldner (1960) as, together, their work represents the foundational ideas of social exchange theory (for a more comprehensive review see Coyle-Shapiro and Conway, 2004; Cropanzano and Mitchell, 2005).

Blau (1964) differentiated social from economic exchange along a number of dimensions: specificity of obligations, time frame and the norm of reciprocity. In short, economic exchange is one in which the obligations of each party are specified typically in a formal contract, there is a mechanism in place to ensure fulfillment of those obligations and the exchange has a limited time frame. In contrast, social exchange involves unspecified obligations where one party needs to trust the other that the benefits received will be reciprocated. The reciprocation of benefits enhances trustworthiness which in turn facilitates the ongoing conferring of benefits and discharging of obligations over the long term. In short, social exchange theory examines how social exchange relationships develop in engendering 'feelings of personal obligations, gratitude and trust' (Blau, 1964: 94). The exchange of economic and socio-emotional resources and the adherence to the norm of reciprocity play a critical role – the actions of one party contingent upon the reactions of the other and it is this contingent interplay that characterizes how social exchange has been applied to the employment relationship.

The norm of reciprocity plays an important role in the development of social exchange relationships by perpetuating the ongoing fulfillment of obligations and strengthening indebtedness. Gouldner (1960) argued that the norm of reciprocity is universal and that individuals should return help received and not injure those who have previously helped them. He distinguished between two types of reciprocity: heteromorphic and homeomorphic reciprocity. The former captures an exchange where the resources exchanged are different but equal in perceived value; the latter captures exchanges where the content or the circumstances under which things are exchanged are identical. Regarding how the norm of reciprocity operates, Gouldner (1960) argues that the strength of an obligation to repay is contingent upon the value of the benefit received – highly valued benefits create a stronger obligation to reciprocate.

The work on social exchange theory shares some common elements with psychological contract theory. First and foremost, both view exchange relationships as comprising tangible and intangible resources governed by the norm of reciprocity. Second, each party brings to the relationship a set of expectations/obligations that they will provide in return for what they receive. However, the other party to the exchange (i.e. the organization) received more explicit consideration by psychological contract researchers while the norm of reciprocity was more prominent

and theoretically refined by social exchange theorists.

RECENT RESEARCH

Rousseau's (1989) seminal article on the psychological contract is credited with reinvigorating research on the topic. We start by reviewing her definition and how it departed from earlier work. Three stands of contemporary research are presented: formation, content and breach of the psychological contract.

Rousseau's reconceptualization of the psychological contract

Rousseau's reconceptualization of the psychological contract signals a transition from the early work to what is now considered contemporary research. She defined the psychological contract as an individual's beliefs concerning the mutual obligations that exist between the individual and the employer. These obligations arise out of the belief that a promise has been made either explicitly or implicitly and the fulfillment of promissory obligations by one party is contingent upon the fulfillment of obligations by the other. Therefore, the psychological contract comprises an individual's perception of the mutual obligations that exist in the exchange with their employer and these are sustained through the norm of reciprocity.

This conceptualization differs from the early definitions in a number of ways. As Conway and Briner (2005) highlight, while the early work emphasized expectations, Rousseau defined the psychological contract in terms of obligations. This appears to be similar to what Levinson et al. (1962) had in mind in their use of expectations that had an obligatory quality which created a sense of duty to be fulfilled. The focus on obligations brings Rousseau's definition of the psychological contract very close to Blau's (1964) social exchange theory. However, although these researchers are conceptually close in capturing the nature of the exchange, they diverge in terms of its development. Rousseau (1989) is perhaps the clearest in presenting obligations arising out of a perception that a promise has been made to commit to a future action. The idea of obligation based on promise is very different from Levinson et al.'s (1962) position that expectations arise from need. Blau (1964) remains more ambiguous in terms of how obligations arise except that they are based on benefits received. Whether these benefits are based on the donor's recognition of the recipient's needs or the donor's promises to provide benefits is unclear in Blau's (1964) work.

A second point of departure, in particular with the work of Schein (1965), who emphasized matching of expectations between the employee and organization, was Rousseau's (1989) emphasis on the psychological contract residing 'in the eye of the beholder.' The importance of the two parties having 'matched' expectations was downplayed by Rousseau (1989), who emphasized instead an individual's perception of agreement. Therefore, the psychological contract shifted from the contingent interplay between two parties' obligations in the exchange to an individual's perceptions of both parties' obligations in the exchange.

The emphasis on needs vs. promises has implications for the factors that shape the psychological contract. Given that Levinson et al. (1962) and Schein (1965) viewed expectations as arising from needs, the degree to which the other party can influence those needs is constrained and the critical element becomes the extent to which each party can fulfill those needs. In contrast, as Rousseau (1989) focuses on perceived promises, the organization's influence on an individual's psychological contract through explicit and implicit signals is much greater. However, the degree to which an organization can shape an individual's psychological contract is contingent to some extent on an individual's schema which serves to guide an individual's interpretations of obligations and allows an individual to operate in a loosely

pre-programmed unconscious manner until something out of the ordinary happens.

The distinguishing feature of Rousseau's (1989) reconceptualization of the psychological contract was locating it at the individual level. In doing so, it captured the psychological contract as a mental model of the exchange, which in turn influenced what an individual contributed to that relationship rather than as an agreed upon exchange between the employee and the organization. Consequently, Rousseau (1989) emphasized the 'psychological' in psychological contracts.

Contemporary research

Although a prominent strand of contemporary research has focused on the consequences of contract breach, two other strands of research merit attention: the formation of the psychological contract and its content.

Formation of the psychological contract

Rousseau (2001) proposed that psychological contracts are grounded in an individual's schema of the employment relationship. This schema develops early in life when individuals develop generalized values about reciprocity and hard work and these values are influenced by family, school, peer group and interactions with working individuals (Morrison and Robinson, 2004). Before an individual's first employment experience, they have developed assumptions about what they should give and receive in an employment relationship and it is this schema that influences how an individual interprets the cues and signals from the organization.

The socialization period seems to be particularly important in terms of organizational influence in shaping an individual's psychological contract. Once an individual's schema is fully formed, it becomes highly resistant to change; also during the early socialization period, newcomers are more inclined to search for additional information to 'complete' their psychological contract, thereby reducing uncertainty. Tekleab (2003) found that higher levels of socialization reduced employee perceptions of employer obligations during the first three months of employment. Thomas and Anderson (1998) found that new army recruits adjusted their psychological contract over an eight-week period and this change was influenced by social information processing that 'moved' their psychological contract closer to that of experienced soldiers. DeVos et al. (2003) found that newcomers changed their perception of employer obligations based on the inducements they had received and also their perceptions of what they had promised based on what they had contributed. Dulac et al. (2006) showed that newcomer proactivity and socialization tactics were important in influencing newcomer evaluation of their psychological contract during the first year of employment.

Additional organizational influences include human and structural contract makers (Rousseau, 1995). Human contract makers (recruiters, managers and mentors) play an important role in communicating reciprocal obligations to employees and in particular, the line manager (Guest and Conway, 2000). Structural contract makers (human resource management practices) have been positively linked to the number of promises made to employees as perceived by managers. Notwithstanding organizational influences, individual factors still shape how individuals construe their psychological contract and how they enact contractual behavior. Raja et al. (2004) found that personality predicted psychological contract type, while Coyle-Shapiro and Neuman (2004) found that exchange related dispositions influenced employee reciprocation. Robinson et al. (1994) argue that self-serving biases cause individuals to over-estimate their contributions and under estimate the costs of the inducements to organizations.

Pre-employment experiences, individual dispositions and organizational influences play an important role in shaping the psychological contract in its formation stage. In contrast, there is little empirical research that examines how psychological contracts are changed. Once formed, psychological contracts are quite stable and resistant to change (Coyle-Shapiro and Kessler, 2000; Rousseau, 2001), and we know little about the conditions under which psychological contracts are more amenable to change.

Content

In light of the subjective nature of the psychological contract, researchers have attempted to categorize psychological contract items (for example, job security, interesting work, career prospects, pay, training and developmental opportunities and autonomy in job) in terms of two underlying dimensions: transactional and relational. The distinction between the two draws upon the legal work of Macneil (1974, 1980) and also parallels Blau's (1964) distinction between economic and social exchange. Transactional and relational contracts can be differentiated based upon their focus, time frame, stability, scope and tangibility. Transactional contracts contain highly tangible exchanges that are economic in focus; the terms and conditions remain static over the finite period of the relationship and the scope of the contract is narrow. In contrast, relational contracts contain tangible and intangible exchanges; are open ended and the terms of the contract are dynamic; the scope may be broad in that there is spillover between an individual's work and their personal life.

The conceptual distinction between transactional and relational contracts is clear. Rousseau (1990) argues that they represent anchors on a continuum such that a psychological contract can become more relational and less transactional and vice versa. However, the empirical evidence is not so clear cut in terms of supporting the transactional-relational distinction. In interpreting the empirical findings, one should bear in mind that researchers have operationalized the psychological contract in terms of specific obligations and a features-based measurement approach may lend itself more easily to capturing the relational-transactional distinction. The key issue is the crossover of items (Taylor and Tekleab, 2004). For example, training may be a transactional or relational item (Arnold, 1996) and one study supports training as an independent dimension (Coyle-Shapiro and Kessler, 2000). Attempting to classify psychological contract items into relational-transactional factors has not yielded consistent results.

An alternative approach captures the features of the psychological contract. O'Leary-Kelly and Schenk (2000) operationalized relational and transactional contracts in terms of four dimensions: focus, time frame, inclusion and stability using a 15 item measure. Sels et al. (2004) extended the number of dimensions to six to include:

- tangibility – the degree to which the terms of the psychological contract are explicitly specified;
- scope – the extent to which the boundary between work and personal life is permeable;
- stability – the extent to which the psychological contract is subject to change without negotiation;
- time frame – the perceived duration of the relationship;
- exchange symmetry – the extent to which the relationship is unequal; and
- contract level – the extent to which the contract is regulated at the individual or collective level.

These two studies provide empirical support linking the features of the psychological contract to outcomes. O'Leary-Kelly and Schenk (2000) found that relational contracts were negatively associated with intentions to leave the organization. Sels et al. (2004) did not classify their dimensions into relational and transactional contracts but nonetheless found that the dimensions of long-term time frame, an unequal employment relationship and a collective contract level were positively associated with affective commitment.

So, in light of the empirical evidence, the question needs to be raised as to whether the transactional-relational distinction matters? Rousseau (1990) found that relational employer obligations were associated with employee relational obligations (e.g., job security in return for loyalty) and transactional employer obligations were associated with transactional employee obligations

(e.g., high pay for high performance). These findings would support Gouldner's (1960) homeomorphic reciprocity in that the resources exchanged are similar. Together with the empirical evidence of the features based approach, the emerging conclusion is that the type of psychological contract matters in terms of defining the potential resources to be exchanged and the nature of those resources. The difficulty for researchers is how to best capture the transactional-relational distinction.

Consequences of contract breach and violation

A dominant emphasis of current research has focused on the consequences of perceived contract breach on employees' feelings, attitudes and behavior. This topic has attracted considerable research attention and, consistent with Rousseau's (1989) definition, this has been investigated from the employee perspective – when employees perceive that the organization has failed to fulfill its obligations. Employees experience contract breach quite frequently (Conway and Briner, 2002; Lester et al., 2002; Robinson and Rousseau, 1994). Coupled with its role in explaining the consequences of the psychological contract, it is not surprising that it has received considerable attention (see Robinson and Brown, 2004 for a review).

Researchers used psychological contract breach and violation interchangeably until Morrison and Robinson (1997) distinguished between the two in terms of cognition and emotion. Contract breach captures a cognitive awareness that one or more obligations have not been fulfilled and contract violation captures the emotional experience that arises from the recognition that a breach has occurred (Morrison and Robinson, 1997). Contract violation would include emotional distress, feelings of betrayal, anger and wrongful harm that result from the individual's perception that although they have kept their promises to another party, the other party has broken their promises to the individual. Therefore, one can recognize a breach has occurred yet at the same time not experience feelings of viola-tion. In empirical research, the overwhelming emphasis has been directed to examining the consequences of perceived contract breach while the consequences of violation are under researched.

Empirical evidence suggests that contract breach leads to reduced psychological well-being (Conway and Briner, 2002), increased intentions to leave the organization (Tekleab and Taylor, 2003; Turnley and Feldman, 1999), reduced job satisfaction (Tekleab and Taylor, 2003), trust in the organization (Robinson, 1996), organizational commit-ment (Coyle-Shapiro and Kessler, 2000; Lester et al., 2002), lower employee obliga-tions to the organization (Coyle-Shapiro and Kessler, 2002; Robinson et al., 1994), and more cynical attitudes toward the organization (Johnson and O'Leary-Kelly, 2003). In terms of behavior, contract breach negatively affects in-role performance and extra-role behaviors (Lester et al., 2002; Robinson and Morrison, 1995). There have been a few studies that have examined moderators in the breach-outcome relationship. Conway and Briner (2002) found that the greater the importance of the promise, the stronger the negative reaction to breach, while Kickul et al. (2002) found that procedural and interactional justice moderated employee responses to breach. Even fewer studies have examined the relationship between breach and vio-lation. One study by Dulac et al. (2006) showed that violation fully mediated the effects of breach on employees' affective commitment and trust. Raja et al. (2004) found that equity sensitivity and external locus of control enhanced the relationship between breach and violation. The relation-ship between perceptions of breach and feel-ings of violation merits additional research. In addition, the relative effect of cognition and emotion on outcomes is another avenue for investigation.

Thus, the weight of the empirical evidence strongly supports the negative consequences of contract breach. Although the negative ramifications are clear, the potential expla-nations for this effect warrant empirical

examination (Robinson and Brown, 2004). The overwhelming emphasis of empirical studies have been on employee perceptions of employer contract breach, the consequences of employee contract breach are compara-tively neglected (an exception is Tekleab and Taylor, 2003). Future research could examine whether contract breach leads to a spiraling of tit for tat breaches between the employee and employer.

KEY DEBATES

There are a number of debates, challenges and unresolved issues in the domain of the psychological contract, and our aim here is to highlight some of the important debates.

Conceptualization of psychological contract

Although Rousseau's (1989) reconceptualiza-tion of the psychological contract remains the most prominent, there is some debate as to what the psychological contract is capturing. The use of varying terms such as expectations, obligations and promises has injected some controversy. As argued by Conway and Briner (2005), the differences between expectations, obligations and promises are important yet not widely discussed potentially, reflecting a limited concern with definitional clarity. Promises involve expectations, but expecta-tions may not necessarily involve a promis-sory element (Rousseau and McLean Parks, 1993). Expectations may arise based on past experience, probabilitistic beliefs about the future whereas promises are based on communication or behavior of another party that leads an individual to believe that a promise has been made. As Conway and Briner (2005) argue the key difference is that expectations represent a general stable belief of whether something will or should happen in the future (e.g., I will probably get a promotion at some point) whereas a promise is a specific belief that something will happen based on communication or behavior of an intention to do so (e.g., my line manager told me that

I would get promoted if I successfully reached a certain performance level).

Only obligations arising from explicit or implicit promises are part of the psychological contract (Morrison and Robinson, 1997). Therefore, obligations that arise from past employment relationships or moral values are not included in the psychological contract unless they were conveyed in a promissory manner to employees. Given that researchers use all three terms to capture the psychological contract, it suggests that a broken promise is given the same significance as an unmet expectation. If the psychological contract encompasses beliefs about promises, expectations and obligations, it then becomes a loosely defined construct with weakened analytical power (Conway and Briner, 2005). To what extent promises, obligations and expectations represent the essence of the psychological contract deserves greater scrutiny.

Exchange and reciprocity are central to the psychological contract as evidenced in the use of the terms 'reciprocal obligations' or 'reciprocal exchange agreement.' However, what remains unclear is whether this exchange occurs at a general level or whether a specific inducement is offered in return for a specific contribution. Consistent with social exchange theory, the emphasis of the empirical research has been on capturing the exchange at a general level. In other words, the organization offers a range of inducements (pay, promotion, training and interesting work) in exchange for a range of employee contributions (performance, effort and flexibility). Researchers have argued that the resources exchanged are underspecified (Conway and Briner, 2005). Here, the work of Foa and Foa (1975) might provide a useful starting point in specifying what is exchanged. Foa and Foa (1980) argued that resources sharing similar attributes in terms of particularism and concreteness are more likely to be exchanged with one another (homeomorphic reciprocity). The idea of a contingent exchange between employee and employer needs to address 'what is contingent upon what?' rather than 'everything is contingent upon everything.' Greater specification of resources would begin to unravel the degree of contingency that underlies exchange relationships.

The employer's perspective

The question of employer representation presents one of the major ambiguities in the psychological contract literature, and just who represents the employer is a subject of debate. As a consequence, the employer perspective on the contract has remained largely underdeveloped in psychological contract theory, although there seems to be an emerging consensus developing that the employer's perspective to the exchange with employees should be included in psychological contract research (Guest, 1998; Taylor and Tekleab, 2004).

A key issue when examining the employer perspective is that the employer side is most often represented by multiple agents (Shore et al., 2004). Organizations recruit, select, socialize and provide different inducements without specifying who personifies the organization in these activities (Liden et al., 2004). Consequently, who represents the organization has yielded a number of different positions. The first position examines the exchange relationship at the dyadic level between employees and their immediate managers (Lewis and Taylor, 2001; Tekleab and Taylor, 2003). Lewis and Taylor (2001) argue that immediate managers play three important roles in forming, maintaining and monitoring employees' psychological contracts. Employees usually have most contact with their immediate managers who often take the role of representing the organization's expectations to the employee and directly evaluate and respond to employee behavior at work. Guest and Conway (2000), however, challenge the view that immediate managers could be considered as organizational representatives. They argue that managers need to perceive themselves as representing the organization in order to be considered as 'legitimate' organizational representatives.

Guest and Conway (2000) also point out that employees may not perceive line managers as organizational representatives unless they occupy a high position in the organizational hierarchy.

The second position views the relationship at a global level between senior/middle level managers and employees (Coyle-Shapiro and Kessler, 2002; Porter et al., 1998). The argument presented is that decisions that affect the employment relationship are usually made by those higher up in the organizational hierarchy. For instance, Porter et al. (1998) examined the psychological contract perceptions of high-level executives, and argue that high-level executives are in the best position to know about employer inducements offered to employees. A similar argument was made by Guest and Conway (2002), who examined the role of organizational communication in influencing perceptions of psychological contract breach.

The roles of immediate and senior managers may be complementary in managing the employee-organization relationship. Coyle-Shapiro and Shore (2007) argue that one way of uniting these opposing views is to recognize that employees may develop multiple exchange relationships in their employment relationship – a distal relationship with senior managers and a proximal one with line managers. Therefore, while senior managers may be key decision-makers in defining the broad parameters of the exchange (e.g., the type of reward system, promotion system and job security), managers lower in the organizational hierarchy have to enact those policies. Furthermore, lower level managers may develop a psychological contract with employees over specific issues such as autonomy and flexibility, for example. Irrespective of managerial level, managers in that capacity have a role to play in managing the psychological contract with employees whether they feel they are representing the organization or not.

Although the debate on who acts as employer representatives continues, there is evidence suggesting that managers, as employer representatives, view the exchange with employees as one adhering to the norm of reciprocity (Coyle-Shapiro and Kessler, 2002; Tekleab and Taylor, 2003). Two studies have also captured the employer's perspective as a way of assessing mutuality in the relationship (Coyle-Shapiro and Kessler, 2000; Dabos and Rousseau, 2004). The employer's perspective is very much in its infancy but represents a rich avenue for additional work, allowing a focus on the *interaction* between the employee and the employer.

Reciprocity and iterative exchanges

The assumption that reciprocity explains the contingent interplay between employer and employee contractual behavior is rarely subject to explicit empirical investigation. Instead, the association between contract breach/fulfillment and outcomes is taken as evidence supporting the norm of reciprocity. It is surprising that the norm of reciprocity has not come under greater scrutiny given its prominence to the development, maintenance and termination of psychological contracts. Is reciprocity the explanation underlying exchange relationships? Conway and Briner (2005) argue that the psychological contract may provide goals (i.e. promises) which employees use to compare their behavior and regulate it to reduce the discrepancy between actual behaviors and goals akin to goal setting theory. Robinson and Brown (2004) emphasize that trust and injustice may be important explanations for the negative effects of contract breach beyond reciprocity. Future research needs to examine the extent to which reciprocity underlies the exchange relationship and also its relative effect vis à vis other potential mechanisms.

If reciprocity is the mechanism, what form does it take? Sahlins (1972) distinguished between generalized, balanced and negative reciprocity and this may shed light on how the exchange operates (see Cropanzano and Mitchell (2005) for a review). Further, Greenberg's (1980) theorizing on the motives underlying reciprocity may also be a useful starting point to unraveling the intricacies of the process of reciprocation. Greenberg (1980) highlighted the notion that reciprocity may be driven by three different motives:

(1) the desire to receive future benefits (utilitarian reciprocity);
(2) the recipient's increased attraction to the donor; and
(3) internal pressure to conform to the norm of reciprocity (normative reciprocity).

Not only do we not know whether reciprocity is the explanation but if it is, we know comparatively little about how it operates.

The iterative process of the exchange has not been adequately captured in empirical research which starts from the position that perceived employer contract fulfillment provides the stimulus for employee reciprocation. This assumes *a priori* that employees have fulfilled their side of the exchange as employer contract fulfillment is contingent upon the employee fulfilling their contract. What happens when employees fulfill their obligations? A study by Conway and Coyle-Shapiro (2006) attempts to address this by examining the relationship between employee performance – perceived employer contract fulfillment – employee performance – perceived employer contract fulfillment using longitudinal data. The study finds support for the norm of reciprocity irrespective of who makes the first 'move' and therefore highlights that the outputs of one exchange transaction provide the input to the next exchange transaction. However, the ongoing iterative and contingent exchange has not been empirically examined in sufficient detail and although it poses a methodological challenge, it is critical to capturing the 'ongoingness' in the exchange relationship.

EMERGING RESEARCH AGENDA

Recently, several researchers have noted that research into contract breach has reached its saturation point and led to an almost exclusive focus on the employee perspective, using static research designs that repeatedly examine the same set of outcome variables (Conway and Briner, 2005; Taylor and Tekleab, 2004). Furthermore, psychological contract theory has also been criticized for lacking scientific rigor and abandoning its theoretical origins in social exchange theory (Guest, 1998). Where social exchange has been applied to psychological contract research, it is often applied in an implicit and uncritical manner (Coyle-Shapiro and Conway, 2004). In addition, there have been calls for developing more comprehensive conceptual models of psychological contracts (Taylor and Tekleab, 2004). We attempt to direct attention to three embryonic research areas that, if developed, could help further develop how we research and understand psychological contracts.

Alternative methodological approaches to examining psychological contracts

Although the seminal works of Argyris (1960) and Levinson et al. (1960) used a qualitative approach (interviews) to collecting and analyzing data, the emphasis on qualitative research has been downplayed in contemporary studies of psychological contract in favor of quantitative cross sectional studies (a minority of studies have used a longitudinal study design). As stated by Taylor and Tekleab in their review of psychological contract research (2004: 279), 'our literature review […] has caused us to note, with more than little exasperation, that much psychological contract research seems to have fallen into a methodological rut.'

In a review of empirical studies on the psychological contract, Conway and Briner (2005) note that 10 per cent adopted a qualitative approach. These studies examined the content of the psychological contract (Herriot et al., 1997; Inkson et al., 2001), employee reactions to contract breach (Pate et al., 2003), the impact of organizational changes on the psychological contract (Saunders and Thornhill, 2005) and the processual nature of the psychological contract (Millward-Purvis and Cropley, 2003).

We illustrate the potential insights provided by three studies using alternative methodologies. First, Millward-Purvis and Cropley (2003) investigated contracting in the context of interviews conducted by parents looking for a live-in nanny to care for their children. These authors were interested in understanding how mutual expectations were addressed during the recruitment interview by the interviewing parents and their respective nannies among two different samples (first-time nanny-employer pairs and experienced nanny-employer pairs). Generally, relational expectations were referred to more implicitly whereas transactional expectations were discussed more explicitly. The study indicates the positive role of implicit means of conveying expectations in the process of psychological contracting. Implicit discussion was found to be more important to mutual understanding and trust than explicit discussion. This study demonstrated the complexities of contracting processes in arriving at a satisfactory formation of an exchange relationship – the intricacies could not have been captured through quantitative means.

The second study (Conway and Briner, 2002) adopted a daily diary approach to examining contract breach and exceeded promises over a 10-day period. The authors viewed the psychological contract as an ongoing chain of events whereby breach is both a cause of subsequent reactions (daily mood) and is the effect that stimulates a subsequent reaction. This study highlights the dynamic nature of the psychological contract and shows how it can be used to understand everyday fluctuations in emotions and daily mood. The authors conclude by stating that the exchange process captured by the psychological contract is an ongoing, unfolding and intra-individual level phenomenon that calls for more detailed in-depth study than the traditional survey approach. The benefits of this approach allow researchers to track employees' immediate perceptions of contract breach and their affective reactions as they evolve over time.

The third interview study examines employees' experience of perceived contract breach using a critical incident technique (Parzefall and Coyle-Shapiro, 2007). The study offers a more complex understanding of contract breach that is located in an individual's schema. In particular, employees ascribed different meanings to breach (a specific breach to a complex chain of events), and this was influenced by their mental model of the employment relationship. In coping with an incongruous event, employees search for meaning that fit their flow of experiences where their emotions and actions are part of their sense-making process which may extend and unfold over time.

The small body of published qualitative studies and the potential of qualitative research to capture the complex nature of the psychological contract has been recognized (Conway and Briner, 2005). The few studies adopting alternative methodological approaches highlight that exchange processes and psychological contracting within an organization are more complex than is captured by survey research. Therefore, as the pressure is mounting for psychological contract research to broaden its scope beyond the examination of contract breach (Conway and Briner, 2005; Taylor and Tekleab, 2004) and to truly capture the individualized employment experiences, the use of qualitative methods and study designs may extend our understanding of exchange relationships and concurrently recognize that relationships are complicated. Qualitative research methods may be particularly well suited to addressing the psychological contract as a process and also highlighting the role of context in exchange relationships.

Psychological contracts: Contribution to social exchange

Psychological contracts, Perceived Organizational Support (POS) and Leader-Member Exchange (LMX) all draw upon social exchange theory. As social exchange theory provides a common theoretical foundation, how the three constructs are related and whether the psychological contract adds something unique to our understanding of social exchange relationships is an issue that needs to be addressed.

POS was developed by Eisenberger and colleagues (1986) to capture an individual's perception concerning the degree to which an organization values their contributions and cares about his/her well being. Within organizational support theory, when employees perceive that the organization is supportive, they will reciprocate by helping the organization achieve its goals (Eisenberger et al., 2001). LMX captures the quality of the interpersonal relationship that evolves between the employee and their manager (Graen and Scandura, 1987) and the empirical research stems from the assumption that leaders form qualitatively different relationships with different subordinates (Sparrowe and Liden, 1997). LMX theory suggests that the relationships between leaders and employees can range from strictly contractual transactions to an exchange of unspecified benefits that extend beyond the formal job description (Liden and Graen, 1980).

POS, LMX and psychological contracts rely on the norm of reciprocity as the underlying explanatory mechanism for their effects on employee attitudes and behavior. Empirical evidence is supportive of the link between POS (LMX) and organizational commitment (Eisenberger et al., 1990; Scandura and Graen 1984; Shore and Wayne, 1993; Wayne et al., 2002), in-role performance (Eisenberger et al., 1986, 1990), organizational citizenship behavior (Settoon et al., 1996; Shore and Wayne, 1993; Wayne et al., 1997). All three constructs have been empirically linked to a similar set of outcomes.

There have been some attempts to distinguish between the constructs, and the research thus far seems to support their distinctiveness. Aselage and Eisenberger (2003) conceptually integrate POS and psychological contracts, while Coyle-Shapiro and Conway (2005) empirically demonstrate that POS acts as an antecedent and outcome to

the components that comprise psychological contract fulfillment. Wayne et al. (1997) empirically demonstrate that POS and LMX are different with a distinct pattern of antecedents and outcomes suggesting that two types of social exchange relationships exist in organizations. There is empirical evidence that suggests LMX may play an important role in affecting the degree to which employees and supervisors agree on each party's respective obligations (Tekleab and Taylor, 2003). Lewis and Taylor (2001) found that managerial responses to employee contract breach was dependent upon the quality of LMX.

Cropanzano and Mitchell (2005) review the foundational tenets of social exchange theory and argue that the seminal works contain conceptual ambiguity in terms of the relationship between 'exchanges' and 'relationship.' The authors argue that the exchanges may alter the nature of the relationship, and the relationship may alter the nature of the exchanges. It is the distinction between exchanges and relationships that may provide the basis to uniting these three social exchange constructs under the social exchange umbrella. Dulac et al. (2006) empirically examine the relationship amongst the three constructs. Adopting the position that psychological contract breach/fulfillment represents an event that may disrupt or enhance the quality of relationship – in this respect, psychological contract breach is viewed as a potential interruption in an ongoing relationship, the authors demonstrate that the quality of relationship an individual has (captured by POS and LMX) influences cognitions of breach and moderates how individuals respond to contract breach. In other words, the quality of the relationship influences how an individual interprets an event occurring in that relationship and also how he/she responds to that event. This idea seems to have merit both in terms of distinguishing between social exchange constructs and also in advancing our understanding of how exchange relationships work. Future research could distinguish between relationship quality and resources exchanged (or not exchanged) as a way of examining how relationships influence what is exchanged and the implications of what is exchanged (or not) on the subsequent quality of the relationship.

Complementary theories

We now briefly turn our attention to potential complementary theories that may enrich our understanding of psychological contracts. First, sense-making may shed light on the intricacies of how employees interpret and respond to contract breach. Current quantitative research gives the impression that the relationship between contract breach and employee reciprocation is a simple and linear one (Conway and Briner, 2005). A psychological contract is, however, a schema of the employee-employer relationship. It guides the individual's perception of incoming information, the retrieval of stored information and the inferences based on that information so that it is relevant to and preferably consistent with the existing schema (Fiske and Taylor, 1984).

Apart from Rousseau's (2001) theoretical work, there is relatively little knowledge about the psychological contract as a schema (Taylor and Tekleab, 2004) in terms of how it functions and changes (Morrison and Robinson, 1997). A perseverance effect is a major feature of a schema: schemas tend to persist stubbornly even in the face of contradictory evidence that could potentially prove them false (Fiske and Taylor, 1984). Consequently, individuals tend to ignore contradictory and inconclusive information and tend to make the incoming information fit the schema rather than vice versa. At times, schemas do however change and there are certain conditions that cause individuals to question their schema (Louis and Sutton, 1991). One such event is the perception of contract breach that may conflict with an individual's existing schema and hence trigger conscious sense-making. This offers researchers a unique opportunity to examine how an incongruous event is interpreted, how the individuals make sense of it and how it influences their schema and subsequent action (Parzefall and Coyle-Shapiro, 2007).

Further, existing studies on schema indicate that members of the same social system share cognitive structures that guide their interpretation and behavior (Louis and Sutton, 1991). Consequently, it would be interesting to examine the potential influence that group level schemas exert on individual psychological contracts or how individuals align their psychological contract schemas with those of their group.

Social influence may provide insight into how co-workers shape an individual's schema of the employment relationship. Current research has tended to treat an individual's psychological contract in a vacuum without considering the influence of co-workers, but some research now focuses on these interdependencies. Ho and Levesque (2005) provide empirical evidence that social influence plays an influence in how employees evaluate contract fulfillment. Therefore, although the psychological contract captures the exchange between the individual employee and the employer, its evaluation is subjected to the influence of third parties who remain outside the contract (e.g., co-workers). Future research could extend this line of investigation by examining the conditions under which the strength of social influence is stronger/weaker and this would give greater prominence to the group context in which psychological contracts operate.

The organizational context may also provide a rich avenue for future research integrating social capital theory with psychological contracts. Leana and Van Buren III (1999) suggest that social capital can be seen as a psychological contract between a group of employees and organizational representatives. Hence, social capital theorists refer to an 'organizational reciprocity norm,' which can be described as a force that makes the members of the organization behave and think in a certain way in their exchange relationships. Crucial to the creation of social capital is not only the stability and quality of a relationship between dyadic exchange partners, but the overarching organizational philosophy and corresponding norms with which different individuals enact that philosophy (Leana and

Van Buren III, 1999). Social capital theory, like theories on networks, could provide possibilities for psychological contract theorists to explore similarities and differences between psychological contract perceptions of groups of employees, and offer insights into the development and maintenance of employees' psychological contract in organizational contexts.

CONCLUSION

Our goal in this chapter was to review the literature on the psychological contract in terms of seminal studies, contemporary research, key debates and emerging research agenda. We highlighted that the psychological contract has become more 'psychological' as it developed while concurrently remaining consistent with the basic tenets of social exchange theory. We are at an interesting juncture in psychological contract research in terms of the continuing debate as to what the psychological contract is capturing, how the employer's perspective fits with an individual-level subjective phenomenon and how best to capture the iterative nature of the relationship. In outlining a future research agenda, we have highlighted the potential benefits to be realized from employing alternative research methodologies, the potential contribution of the distinction between 'exchanges' and 'relationships' as a way of integrating social exchange related constructs to provide a richer basis to examining exchange relationships and finally, complementary theories that may advance our understanding of the workings of the psychological contracts. We hope that the material covered serves as a guide to future work on the topic as there is much yet to be uncovered from studying such a fundamental aspect of organizational behavior.

REFERENCES

Argyris, C. (1960) *Understanding Organizational Behavior*. Homewood, IL: Dorsey Press.

Arnold, J. (1996) 'The psychological contract: A concept in need of closer scrutiny?', *European Journal of Work and Organizational Psychology*, 5 (4): 511–520.

Aselage, J. and Eisenberger, R. (2003) 'Perceived organizational support and psychological contracts: A theoretical integration', *Journal of Organizational Behavior*, 24 (5): 491–509.

Barnard, C.I. (1938) *The Functions of the Executive*. Cambridge, MA: Harvard.

Blau, P. (1964) *Exchange and Power in Social Life*. New York: Wiley.

Conway, N. and Briner, R.B. (2002) 'A daily diary study of affective responses to psychological contract breach and exceeded promises', *Journal of Organizational Behavior*, 23 (3): 287–302.

Conway, N. and Briner, R.B (2005) *Understanding Psychological Contracts at Work: A Critical Evaluation of Theory and Research*. Oxford: Oxford University Press.

Conway, N. and Coyle-Shapiro, J.A-M. (2006) *Reciprocity and Psychological Contracts: Employee Performance and Contract Fulfillment*. Paper presented at the Annual meeting of the Academy of Management, Atlanta.

Coyle-Shapiro, J.A-M. and Conway, N. (2004) 'The employment relationship through the lens of social exchange', in J.A-M Coyle-Shapiro, L.M. Shore, M.S. Taylor and L.E. Tetrick (eds) *The Employment Relationship: Examining Psychological and Contextual Perspectives*. Oxford: Oxford University Press, pp. 5–28.

Coyle-Shapiro, J.A-M. and Conway, N. (2005) 'Exchange relationships: An examination of psychological contracts and perceived organizational support', *Journal of Applied Psychology*, 90 (4): 774–781.

Coyle-Shapiro, J. and Kessler, I. (2000) 'Consequences of the psychological contract for the employment relationship: A large scale survey', *Journal of Management Studies*, 37 (7): 903–930.

Coyle-Shapiro, J. and Kessler, I. (2000) *Mutuality, Stability and Psychological Contract Breach: A Longitudinal Study*. Paper presented at the Annual Meeting of the Academy of Management, Toronto.

Coyle-Shapiro, J.A-M. and Kessler, I. (2002) 'Reciprocity through the lens of the psychological contract: Employee and Employer perspectives', *European Journal of Work and Organizational Psychology*, 11 (1): 1–18.

Coyle-Shapiro, J.A-M. and Neuman, J. (2004) 'Individual dispositions and the psychological contract: The moderating effects of exchange and creditor ideologies', *Journal of Vocational Behavior*, 64 (1): 150–164.

Coyle-Shapiro, J.A-M. and Shore, L. (2007) 'The employee-organization relationship: Where do we go from here?' *Human Resource Management Review*, 17 (2): 166–179.

Cropanzano, R. and Mitchell, M.S. (2005) 'Social exchange theory: An interdisciplinary review', *Journal of Management*, 31 (6): 874–900.

Dabos, G. and Rousseau, D.M. (2004) 'Mutuality and reciprocity: Psychological contracts in research teams', *Journal of Applied Psychology*, 89 (1): 52–72.

De Vos, A., Buyens, D. and Schalk, R. (2003) 'Psychological contract development during organizational socialization: Adaptation to reality and the role of reciprocity', *Journal of Organizational Behavior*, 24 (5): 537–559.

Dulac, T., Coyle-Shapiro, J.A-M. and Delobbe, N. (2006) *The Role of Socialization Tactics and Information Seeking Behavior in Newcomers' Psychological Contract Evaluation*. Paper presented at the Annual meeting of the Academy of Management, Atlanta.

Dulac, T., Coyle-Shapiro, J.A-M., Henderson, D. and Wayne, S. (2006) *The Development of Psychological Contract Breach and Violation: A Social Exchange Approach*. Paper presented at the Annual meeting of the Academy of Management, Atlanta.

Eisenberger, R., Huntington, R., Hutchison, S. and Sowa, D. (1986) 'Perceived organizational support', *Journal of Applied Psychology*, 71 (3): 500–507.

Eisenberger, R., Fasolo, P. and Davis-LaMastrro, V. (1990) 'Perceived organizational support and employee diligence, commitment, and innovation', *Journal of Applied Psychology*, 75 (1): 51–59.

Eisenberger, R., Armeli, S., Rexwinkel, B., Lynch, P.D. and Rhoades, L. (2001) 'Reciprocation of perceived organizational support', *Journal of Applied Psychology*, 86 (1): 42–51.

Fiske, S.T. and Taylor, S.E. (1984) *Social Cognition*. Reading, MA: Addison-Wesley.

Foa, U.G. and Foa, E.B. (1975) *Resource Theory of Social Exchange*. Morristown, NJ: General Learning Press.

Foa, U.G. and Foa, E.B. (1980) 'Resource theory: Interpersonal behavior as exchange', in K.J. Gergen, M.S. Greenberg and R.H. Willis (eds) *Social Exchange: Advances in Theory and Research*. New York: Plenum Press, pp. 77–94.

Gouldner, A.W. (1960) 'The norm of reciprocity', *American Sociological Review*, 25 (2): 161–178.

Graen, G., and Scandura, T.A. (1987) 'Toward a psychology of dyadic organizing', *Research on Organizational Behaviour*, 9: 175–208.

Greenberg, M.S (1980) 'A theory of indebtedness', in K.J. Gergen, M.S. Greenberg and R.H. Willis (eds) *Social Exchange: Advances in Theory and Research*. New York: Plenum Press, pp. 3–26.

Guest, D.E. (1998) 'Is the psychological contract worth taking seriously?' *Journal of Organizational Behaviour*, 19 (7): 649–664.

Guest, D. and Conway, R. (2000) *The Public Sector and the Psychological Contract*. IPD Research Report. London: IPD.

Guest, D. and Conway, R. (2002) 'Communicating the psychological contract: An employer perspective', *Human Resource Management Journal*, 12 (2): 22–38.

Herriot, P., Manning, W.E.G. and Kidd, J.M. (1997) 'The content of the psychological contract', *British Journal of Management*, 8 (2): 151–162.

Ho, V.T. and Levesque, L.L. (2005) 'With a little help from my friends (and substitutes): Social referents and influence in psychological contract fulfilment', *Organization Science*, 16 (3): 275–289.

Homans, G.C. (1958) 'Social behavior as exchange', *American Journal of Sociology*, 63 (6): 597–606.

Inkson, K., Heising, A. and Rousseau, D. (2001) 'The interim manager: Prototype of the 21st-century worker?', *Human Relations*, 54 (3): 259–284.

Johnson, J.L. and O'Leary Kelly, A.M. (2003) 'The effects of psychological contract breach and organizational cynicism: Not all social exchange violations are created equal', *Journal of Organizational Behavior*, 24 (5): 627–647.

Kickul, J., Lester, S.W. and Finkl, J. (2002) 'Promise breaking during radical organizational change: Do justice interventions make a difference?' *Journal of Organizational Behavior*, 23 (2): 469–488.

Leana, C.R. and Van Buren III, H. (1999) 'Organizational social capital and employment practices', *Academy of Management Review*, 24 (3): 538–555.

Lester, S.W., Turnley, W.H., Bloodgood, J.M. and Bolino, M.C. (2002) 'Not seeing eye to eye: Differences in supervisor and subordinate perceptions of and attributions for psychological contract breach', *Journal of Organizational Behavior*, 23 (1): 39–56.

Levinson, H., Price, C.R, Munden, K.J., Mandl, H.J. and Solley, C.M. (1962) *Men, Management and Mental Health*. Boston: Harvard University Press.

Lewis, K. and Taylor, M.S. (2001) *Reciprocity from the Organization's Side: Manager Reactions to Employee Psychological Contract Breach*. Paper presented at Society of Industrial/Organizational Psychology (SIOP) Meetings, May.

Liden, R.C., Bauer, T.N. and Erdogan, B. (2004) 'The role of leader-member exchange in the dynamic relationship between employer and employee: Implications for employee socialization, leaders, and organization', in J.A.-M. Coyle-Shapiro, L.M. Shore, M.S. Taylor and L.E. Tetrick (eds) *The Employment Relationship: Examining Psychological and*

Contextual Perspectives. Oxford: Oxford University Press, pp. 226–250.

Liden, R.C. and Graen, G.B. (1980) 'Generalizability of the vertical linkage dyad mode of leadership', *Academy of Management Journal*, 23 (3): 451–465.

Louis, M.R. and Sutton, R.I. (1991) 'Switching cognitive gears. From habits of mind to active thinking', *Human Relations*, 44 (1): 55–76.

Macneil, I.R. (1974) 'The many futures of contracts', *Southern California Law Review*, 47: 691–816.

Macneil, I.R. (1980) *The New Social Contract: An Inquiry into Modern Contractual Relations.* New Haven: Yale University Press.

March, J.G. and Simon, H.A. (1958) *Organizations.* New York.

Mauss, M. (1925) *The Gift.* Glencoe, IL: Free Press, 1954. (Republished, New York: Norton, 1967).

Malinowski, B. (1922) *Argonauts of the Western Pacific: An Account of Native Enterprise and Adventure in the Archipelagoes of Melanesian New Guinea.* London: Routledge (Republished, New York: Dutton, 1962).

Menninger, K. (1958) *Theory of Psychoanalytic Technique.* New York: Basic Books, Inc.

Millward-Purvis, L.J. and Cropley, M. (2003) 'Psychological contracting: Processes of contract formation during interviews between nannies and their employers', *Journal of Occupational and Organizational Psychology*, 76 (2): 213–241.

Morrison, E.W. and Robinson, S.L. (1997) 'When employees feel betrayed: A model of how psychological contract violation develops', *Academy of Management Review*, 22 (1): 226–256.

Morrison, E.W. and Robinson, S.L. (2004) 'The employment relationship from two sides: Incongruence in employees' and employers' perceptions of obligations', in J.A.-M. Coyle-Shapiro, L.M. Shore, M.S. Taylor and L.E. Tetrick (eds) *The Employment Relationship: Examining Psychological and Contextual Perspectives.* Oxford: Oxford University Press, pp. 161–180.

O'Leary-Kelly, A.M. and Schenk, J.E. (2000) *An Examination of the Development and Consequences of Psychological Contracts.* Paper presented at the Annual meeting of the Academy of Management.

Pate, J., Martin, G. and McGoldrick, J. (2003) 'The impact of psychological contract violation of employee attitudes and behaviour', *Employee Relations*, 25 (6): 557–573.

Parzefall, M.-R. and Coyle-Shapiro, J. (2007) *Psychological Contract Schema, Contract Breach and Sense-Making: A Qualitative Study.* Paper presented at The Annual Meeting of the Academy of Management, Philadelphia 3–8th August.

Porter, L.W., Pearce, J.L., Tripoli, A. and Lewis, K.M. (1998) 'Differential perceptions of employers' inducements: Implications for psychological contracts', *Journal of Organizational Behavior*, 19 (7): 769–782.

Raja, U., Johns, G. and Ntalianis, F. (2004) 'The impact of personality on psychological contracts', *Academy of Management Journal*, 47 (3): 350–367.

Robinson, S.L. (1996) 'Trust and breach of the psychological contract', *Administrative Science Quarterly*, 41 (4): 574–599.

Robinson, S.L. and Brown, G. (2004) 'Psychological contract breach and violation: A review', in Anne O'Leary-Kelly and Richard Griffin's (eds) *Darkside of Organizational Behavior.* Jossey-Bass, pp. 309–338.

Robinson, S.L., Kraatz, M. and Rousseau, D.M. (1994) 'Changing obligations and the psychological contract: A longitudinal study', *Academy of Management Journal*, 37 (1): 137–152.

Robinson, S.L. and Morrison, E.W. (1995) 'Psychological contracts and OCB: The effect of unfulfilled obligations on civic virtue behavior', *Journal of Organizational Behavior,* 16 (3): 289–298.

Roehling, M.V. (1996) *The Origins and Early Development of the Psychological Contract Construct.* Paper presented at the annual meeting of the Academy of Management, Cincinnati.

Rousseau, D.M. (1989) 'Psychological and implied contracts in organizations', *Employee Responsibilities and Rights Journal*, 2 (2): 121–139.

Rousseau, D.M. (1990) 'New hire perceptions of their own and their employer's obligations: A study of psychological contracts', *Journal of Organizational Behavior*, 11 (5): 389–400.

Rousseau, D.M. (1995) *Psychological Contracts in Organizations: Understanding Written and Unwritten Agreements.* Thousand Oaks, CA: Sage.

Rousseau, D.M. (2001) 'Schema, promise and mutuality: The building blocks of the psychological contracts', *Journal of Occupational and Organizational Psychology*, 74 (4): 511–541.

Rousseau, D.M. and McLean Parks, J. (1993) 'The contracts of individuals and organizations', in L.L. Cummings, and B.M. Staw (eds) *Research in Organizational Behavior.* Greenwich: JAI Press, pp. 1–43.

Sahlins, M. (1972) *Stone Age Economics.* New York: Aldine de Gruyter.

Saunders, M.N.K. and Thornhill, A. (2005) 'Forced employment contract change and the psychological contract', *Employee Relations*, 28 (5): 449–467.

Scandura, T. and Graen, G.B. (1984) 'Moderating effects of initial leader-member exchange status on the effects of a leadership', *Journal of Applied Psychology*, 69 (3): 428–437.

Schein, E.H. (1965) *Organizational Psychology*. Englewood Cliffs, NJ: Prentice Hall.

Schein, E.H. (1980) *Organizational Psychology*. 3rd edn. Englewood Cliffs, NJ: Prentice Hall.

Sels, L., Janssens, M. and Van den Brande, I. (2004) 'Assessing the nature of psychological contracts: a validation of six dimensions', *Journal of Organizational Behavior*, 25 (4): 461–488.

Settoon, R.P., Bennet, N. and Liden, R.C. (1996) 'Social exchange in organizations: The differential effects of perceived organizational support and leader member exchange', *Journal of Applied Psychology*, 16 (3): 289–298.

Shore, L.M., Porter, L.W. and Zahra, S.A. (2004) 'Employer-oriented strategic approaches to the employee-organization relationships', in J.A-M. Coyle-Shapiro, L.M. Shore, M.S. Taylor and L.E. Tetrick (eds) *The Employment Relationship: Examining Psychological and Contextual Perspectives*. Oxford: Oxford University Press, pp. 135–160.

Shore, L. and Wayne, S. (1993) 'Commitment and employee behavior: Comparison of affective commitment and continuance commitment with perceived organizational support', *Journal of Applied Psychology*, 78 (5): 774–780.

Sparrowe, R.T. and Liden, R.C. (1997) 'Process and structure in leader-member exchange', *Academy of Management Review*, 22 (2): 522–552.

Taylor, M.S. and Tekleab, A.G. (2004) 'Taking stock of psychological contract research: Assessing progress, addressing troublesome issues, and setting research priorities', in J.A-M. Coyle-Shapiro, L.M. Shore, M.S. Taylor and L.E. Tetrick, (eds) *The Employment Relationship: Examining Contextual and Psychological Perspectives*. Oxford: Oxford University Press, pp. 253–283.

Tekleab, A.G. (2003) *The Role of Realistic Job Previews and Organizational Socialization on Newcomers' Psychological Contract Development*. PhD Dissertation, University of Maryland.

Tekleab, A.G. and M.S. Taylor (2003) 'Aren't there two parties in an employment relationship? Antecedents and consequences of organization-employee agreement on contract obligations and violations', *Journal of Organizational Behavior*, 24 (5): 585–608.

Thomas, H.D. and Anderson, N. (1998) 'Changes in newcomers' psychological contracts during organizational socialization: A study of recruits entering the British Army', *Journal of Organizational Behavior*, 19 (7): 745–767.

Turnley, W.H. and Feldman, D.C. (1999) 'The impact of psychological contract violations on exit, voice, loyalty, and neglect', *Human Relations*, 52 (7): 895–922.

Wayne, S.J., Shore, L.M. and Liden, R.C. (1997) 'Perceived organizational support and leader-member exchange: A social exchange perspective', *Academy of Management Journal*, 40 (1): 87–111.

Wayne, S.J., Shore, L.M., Bommer, W.H. and Tetrick, L.E. (2002) 'The role of fair treatment and rewards in perceptions of organizational support and leader-member exchange', *Journal of Applied Psychology*, 87 (3): 590–598.

Commitment in the Workplace: Past, Present, and Future

John P. Meyer, Timothy A. Jackson
and Elyse R. Maltin

Theory and research pertaining to commitment in the workplace had its roots in the Human Relations movement in the mid-20th century, but arguably came to life in the 1970s due in large measure to a program of research conducted by Lyman Porter, Richard Mowday and Richard Steers. Their seminal book on commitment (Mowday et al., 1982) was a major impetus for subsequent theory development and research. Today, a literature search for publications pertaining to commitment in a work context yields close to 2000 entries.

Our objectives in this chapter are to provide a brief history of theory and research on workplace commitment and to illustrate the tremendous developments that have taken place, particularly those over the last three decades. We focus on three distinguishable 'eras,' beginning with the early years (pre-1980), followed by the expansionary period of the 1980s and 1990s, and finally the new age beginning at the turn of the millennium. Although it is impossible to do justice to all of the important contributions that were made in these three eras, we summarize major developments in theory, highlight some key research findings, and identify some of the more salient controversies. We close with a brief look ahead to what promises to be an exciting new agenda for commitment theory and research.

THE EARLY YEARS (PRE-1980)

Prior to 1980, the primary focus of commitment theory and research in the organizational behavior literature was on employees' commitment to organizations. In addition to its roots in the Human Relations movement, early theory and research on 'organizational commitment' (OC) was influenced by the work of sociologists (for example, Becker, 1960; Etzioni, 1961; Kanter, 1968), social psychologists (Kiesler, 1971), and management scientists (e.g., Hall et al., 1970; March and Simon, 1958). Interest in the topic received a major boost in the 1970s from the research of Porter and colleagues noted above, and from increasing concerns about the apparent decline in loyalty and increase in turnover in North American organizations (see Mowday et al., 1982).

Given the diversity of influences, one of the major challenges for early investigators was to reach some consensus on the meaning of commitment. Mowday et al. (1982) identified 10 'widely divergent definitions' of commitment as well as several typologies (Etzioni, 1961; Kanter, 1968; Salancik, 1977). Salancik's (1977) distinction between *attitudinal* and *behavioral* commitment was particularly noteworthy because it had implications not only for the meaning of commitment but also for how it should be studied. In the attitudinal tradition, commitment was viewed as a measurable psychological state and most research focused on identification of its 'antecedents' and 'consequences.' In the behavioral tradition, research focused on identifying conditions (e.g., volition and irrevocability) that bind individuals to a course of action and shape beliefs that sustain that action. Although Mowday et al. (1982) suggested that the two approaches are complementary, there was little systematic attempt at integration. Rather, the two approaches stimulated quite distinct lines of investigation. This review focuses on developments in the attitudinal tradition because of their wide-ranging implications for workplace behavior. The impact of early research in the behavioral tradition is arguably narrower, and is best reflected in subsequent theory and research pertaining to the escalation of commitment to failing courses of action (for a review, see Staw, 1997).

Within the attitudinal tradition, some of the more influential studies in the 1970s were conducted to demonstrate that commitment was a better predictor of turnover than was job satisfaction (e.g., Porter et al., 1974; Porter et al., 1976; Steers, 1977). Although there were studies linking commitment to other outcomes, particularly job performance (e.g., Mowday et al., 1974; Steers, 1977), later meta-analyses would reveal that these

relations were relatively weak (e.g., Mathieu and Zajac, 1990; Randall, 1990). This might be due in part to the emphasis on retention in the design of measures. For example, Farrell and Rusbult's (1981) measure of job commitment focuses almost exclusively on intention to remain. However, even the Organizational Commitment Questionnaire (OCQ) (Mowday, Steers and Porter, 1979), one of the earliest and most widely used measures of OC, includes several items pertaining to willingness to remain in the organization.

Another major focus of early research was the identification of the antecedents of OC (e.g., Buchanan, 1974; Steers, 1977). Steers suggested that the major influences on OC could be grouped into three general categories:

- personal characteristics – age, tenure, personality;
- job- or role-related characteristics – role ambiguity, role conflict; and
- work experiences – organizational dependability, importance to the organization.

Stevens et al. (1978) suggested a fourth category, organizational structure characteristics – size, centralization, span of control. Unfortunately, very little attention was given to understanding the underlying processes involved in the development of commitment, and most of the research was non-experimental. Consequently, implications for management were limited. Nevertheless, this early research was just a foreshadowing of what was to come.

THE EXPANSIONARY PERIOD (THE 1980S AND 1990S)

We refer to the 1980s and 1990s as the expansionary period for several reasons. First, there was tremendous growth in research examining the development and consequences of OC (see Mathieu and Zajac, 1990, and Meyer and Allen, 1997, for meta-analytic and narrative reviews, respectively). Second, the concept itself 'grew' as researchers began to elaborate on the meaning of commitment and identify its multiple 'dimensions' (e.g., Allen and Meyer, 1990; Jaros et al., 1993; O'Reilly and Chatman, 1986). In addition, attention shifted beyond OC to commitments to unions (e.g., Gordon et al., 1980), careers (e.g., Blau, 1985, 1989), and other foci within and outside the organization (e.g., Becker, 1992; Morrow, 1983; Reichers, 1985). Finally, research on commitment expanded beyond the boundaries of North America, most notably to the UK (e.g., Cook and Wall, 1980; Iles et al., 1990).

In this section we begin by reviewing research addressing the development and consequences of commitment, with emphasis on what is now commonly referred to as 'affective organizational commitment.' We then describe the development of multi-dimensional models of OC. Finally, we shift our focus away from OC to discuss commitments to other foci within and outside the organization.

Development of organizational commitment

Research on the development of commitment in the early 1980s was much like that in the preceding years. The ever-expanding list of potential antecedent variables was characterized by Reichers (1985) as a 'laundry list.' There was little theory beyond the simple principle of exchange (Blau, 1964; Gouldner, 1960) to guide the selection of variables or to explain their relations with commitment. By the late 1980s and early 1990s, things had changed somewhat. Although there was still relatively little attention paid to process, the research became more systematic and focused. Among the more widely studied antecedents were perceived organizational support (POS: e.g., Eisenberger et al., 1990), organizational justice (e.g., Sweeny and McFarlin, 1993), met expectations (e.g., Irving and Meyer, 1994) person/organization fit (e.g., Meglino et al., 1989), and leadership (e.g., Bycio et al., 1995). Researchers also began to examine links with human resource management (HRM) policies and practices (see Meyer and Allen,

1997, for a detailed review). In general, the findings of these studies suggested that organizations that 'invest' in their employees are rewarded with high levels of OC (see Tsui et al., 1997, for a particularly clear illustration).

Research methods also became more sophisticated with, among other things, more longitudinal studies and applications of causal modeling. For example, causal modeling analyses were applied to cross-sectional (e.g., Vandenberg and Lance, 1992), longitudinal (Farkas and Tetrick, 1989), and meta-analytically derived (Tett and Meyer, 1993) data to examine the direction of the relation between job satisfaction and commitment. The findings generally provided evidence for reciprocal relations. Similar studies were conducted to examine relations between employees' pre- and post-entry experiences and commitment (e.g., Meyer et al., 1991; Meyer et al., 1998). Not surprisingly, these studies revealed stronger relations within time, but also provided evidence for time-lagged relations. In general, on-the-job experiences accounted for more variance in commitment than did individual differences (e.g., values) or pre-entry (e.g., recruitment) experiences. There was also evidence that employees' commitment could influence subsequent perceptions of work experiences. Finally, polynomial regression and response surface methodology (Edwards, 1994) was used to test for the effects of met expectations (e.g., Irving and Meyer, 1994) and person-organization fit (e.g., Kalliath et al., 1999) on OC. The results of these studies challenged earlier findings and suggested that situational factors (e.g., work experiences and organizational values) were strongly related to commitment regardless of initial expectations or personal characteristics (e.g., values or preferences).

Consequences of organizational commitment

Studies examining the 'consequences' of OC were also largely cross-sectional – the major exception being studies involving actual turnover. The outcome variables of primary interest were turnover and/or turnover intention (e.g., Hackett et al., 1994), absenteeism (e.g., Somers, 1995), tardiness (e.g., Blau, 1995), performance (e.g., Meyer et al., 1989), and organizational citizenship behavior (OCB: e.g., Shore and Wayne, 1993). Findings were largely consistent with expectations but relations were generally weak (Mathieu and Zajac, 1990; Randall, 1990). The strongest relations were found for turnover intention and OCB – the former because of its strong conceptual relationship to commitment, and the latter because it is discretionary and generally more responsive to attitudinal influences than in-role performance (Organ, 1988).

With few exceptions (Ostroff, 1992; Ryan et al., 1996), most studies examining the consequences of commitment were conducted at an individual level. Ostroff (1992) argued that this might explain, in part, why the relations with job performance were generally weak. She found a stronger relation between teachers' commitment and performance at an organizational (school) level than is typically reported at the individual level. Similarly, Ryan et al. (1996) found a strong relation between employee satisfaction with the organization (a construct related to affective commitment) and performance when examined across units in a large finance company. One possible explanation for the stronger relations at higher levels of analysis is the increase in reliability resulting from aggregation. Another is that, when measured at a group or organizational level, performance reflects the sum of the individual-level outcomes (e.g., attendance, performance and OCB) as well as other synergistic outcomes that are only detectable at higher levels of analysis. These unit- and organization-level studies complemented studies demonstrating the financial benefits of 'commitment' (Arthur, 1994) and 'high-involvement' (Huselid, 1995) HRM systems, and suggested that employee commitment might indeed be an important mediating mechanism contributing to the effectiveness of these strategies.

Although the majority of 'consequence' research focused on outcomes relevant to the organization, there was an increase in the 1990s in attention to employee-relevant outcomes (e.g., health and well-being). For the most part, studies demonstrated a positive relation between employees' affective commitment to the organization and their own physical and psychological well being (e.g., Romzek, 1989; Wittig-Berman and Lang, 1990). Begley and Czajka (1993) and others (e.g., Hochwarter et al., 1999) demonstrated that affective commitment can also serve to buffer the potentially negative effects of workplace stressors, but this finding has not always been replicated (e.g., Leong et al., 1996). Thus, the evidence suggested that affective commitment can be a 'win-win' situation for employees and employers.

Multidimensional models of organizational commitment

The multidimensionality of commitment was acknowledged prior to 1980 (e.g., Etzioni, 1961; Kanter, 1968). However, organizational researchers rarely if ever conducted research, including more than one type of commitment in the same study. It was not until the 1980s that investigators began to develop multidimensional measures and look for differences in the antecedents and consequences of the different forms of commitment. Although several multidimensional frameworks were proposed (see Meyer and Herscovitch, 2001, for a summary and comparison), we focus here on the two that received the most attention in subsequent research: Meyer and Allen's (1991) three-component model and O'Reilly and Chatman's (1986) multiple bases model.

Meyer and Allen's three-component model

Meyer and Allen (1991) developed their three-component model based on the observation that there were both similarities and differences in existing uni-dimensional conceptualizations of OC (e.g., Becker, 1960; Mowday et al., 1979; Wiener, 1982). Common to all was the belief that commitment binds individuals to organizations thereby reducing the likelihood of turnover. The key differences were in the mindsets presumed to characterize the commitment. These mindsets reflected three distinguishable themes:

- affective attachment to the organization;
- perceived cost of leaving; and
- obligation to remain.

Meyer and Allen (1991) argued that commitment might be accompanied by one or more of these mindsets and therefore incorporated all three into their model. To distinguish among the different forms of commitments, they labeled them affective commitment, continuance commitment, and normative commitment, respectively.

Tests of the three-component model generally confirmed the multidimensionality of the construct (see Allen and Meyer, 1996, for a review). However, there was some disagreement about whether affective and normative commitment were distinguishable, and whether continuance commitment was a uni-dimensional construct. Although confirmatory factor analyses consistently demonstrated better fit when affective and normative commitment items were defined as separate factors (e.g., Hackett et al., 1994), correlations between affective and normative commitment were generally quite high. Results pertaining to the dimensionality of continuance commitment were mixed, with some studies (e.g., Dunham et al., 1994) reporting evidence for uni-dimensionality and others finding evidence for two factors: personal sacrifice and lack of alternatives (e.g., McGee and Ford, 1987). The three-component model has continued to stimulate research, some of which was intended to address these points of disagreement (see Meyer et al., 2002).

O'Reilly and Chatman's multiple bases model

Following Kelman's (1958) work on attitude and behavior change, O'Reilly and Chatman (1986) argued that attitudinal commitment could take three distinct forms, each reflecting a different motivation, or *basis*, for the acceptance of organizational influence. They labeled these:

- compliance – personal gain or cost avoidance;
- identification – establishment or maintenance of a satisfying relationship; and
- internalization – value-congruence.

They developed measures of each.

Although O'Reilly and Chatman (1986) provided support for the three-dimensional structure of their measures, subsequent investigators had difficulty in distinguishing identification and internalization (e.g., Caldwell et al., 1990; Vandenberg et al., 1994). These measures tended to correlate highly with one another and showed similar patterns of correlations with measures of other variables. Compliance was clearly distinguishable from identification and internalization, but it correlated *positively* rather than negatively with turnover. The latter finding raised some question about whether compliance should be considered a form of OC (see Meyer and Allen, 1997).

Although O'Reilly and Chatman's (1986) measures have not been used as extensively as the measures of affective, normative, and continuance commitment, the multiple bases model was a major impetus for Becker's (1992) multiple-foci model of workplace commitment. We discuss this model in more detail in a later section.

Other work-relevant commitments

As interest in commitment increased, it also expanded to include 'foci' other than the organization. In this section, we focus on developments in theory and research pertaining to union commitment and career (occupational) commitment. Both of these foci received considerable attention during the 1980s and 1990s. In the next section we discuss other foci of commitment within the context of multiple-foci models where the relative and combined effects of multiple commitments become the focus of attention.

Union commitment

One of the first attempts to extend theory and research on OC to other foci was Gordon et al.'s (1980) model of union commitment. Gordon et al. conceived of commitment as a multi-dimensional construct and developed a measure with four subscales: loyalty to the union, responsibility to the union, willingness to work for the union, and belief in unionism. The Gordon et al. model stimulated a great deal of research, with two major themes dominating researchers' attention. The first concerned the dimensionality of the construct and measures, and the second involved the identification of antecedents and consequences.

Although some support was obtained for the original four-dimensional conceptualization (e.g., Tetrick et al., 1989), the factors were highly related. Other researchers argued for more parsimonious two- (Friedman and Harvey, 1986) or three-factor models (Kelloway et al., 1992). Among the most contentious issues was whether belief in unionism should be considered a separate construct (Fullagar, 1986; Sverke and Kuruvilla, 1995).

Despite the lack of consensus on dimensionality, considerable research was conducted to examine the antecedents and consequences of union commitment (see Bamberger et al., 1999, and Snape et al., 2000, for reviews). In their meta-analysis, Bamberger et al. showed that two of the predominant predictors of union commitment were pro-union attitude and beliefs about union instrumentality. With regard to consequences, the primary focus was on participation in union activities. It was generally believed that union commitment provided the motivation necessary for involvement (Snape et al., 2000).

Career, professional and occupational commitment

Theory and research on career commitment was influenced by earlier work on career salience (Greenhaus, 1971; and see Greenhaus' chapter on careers in this volume) and career motivation (London, 1983). The concept was popularized by Blau (1985, 1989)

who developed measures and conducted a series of studies to examine its antecedents and consequences. Blau's approach was modeled after the OC literature but the focus of commitment shifted to the employee's 'line of work.' The term 'career commitment' was later replaced by 'occupational commitment' (Blau, 2003; Meyer et al., 1993) because the latter more accurately reflected the intended target of the commitment and encompassed related work on 'professional commitment' (e.g., Wallace, 1995).

In contrast to Blau's (1985) uni-dimensional conceptualization, two multi-dimensional models were subsequently introduced. Meyer et al. (1993) applied the three-component model to the study of occupational commitment, and Carson et al. (1995) proposed and tested a three-dimensional model of a related construct, career entrenchment. The three dimensions, career investments, emotional costs, and limited alternatives shared much in common with the Meyer et al. model, and Blau (2003) recently proposed an integrated four-dimensional framework.

Research through the 1980s and 1990s demonstrated that occupational commitment could be reliably measured and that it related to important outcomes such as continuation in a line of work and development of relevant knowledge and skills. Although clearly distinguishable from OC, occupational commitment was also found to account for unique variance in organization-relevant outcomes such as retention and performance (Lee et al., 2001).

Multiple foci models of commitment

Another major development was the recognition that employees form multiple work-relevant commitments that combine to influence behavior. This idea was introduced by Morrow (1983) and Reichers (1985) and was promoted by Becker (1992; Becker et al., 1996) and Cohen (1999), although many others also contributed to the popularization of the multi-foci approach (e.g., Hunt and Morgan, 1994; Randall and Cote, 1991).

Morrow (1983) initially identified five basic forms of employee commitment:

- organizational commitment;
- union commitment;
- career commitment;
- job involvement; and
- work ethic.

She later made a distinction between affective and continuance commitment to the organization and dropped union commitment from among the five universal forms of work commitment (Morrow, 1993). In addition, she offered a conceptual model to explain how these commitments might relate to one another.

Morrow's (1993) model located the five commitments in concentric circles with work ethic as the innermost circle, followed by career commitment, continuance organizational commitment, affective organizational commitment, and job involvement, respectively as one moves outward. Morrow considered the inner circles to reflect more dispositional and culturally-based forms of commitment, whereas the commitments in the outermost circles were more situationally determined. She further proposed that adjacent commitments would relate most strongly and that causal influence was stronger from inside out than from outside in.

Although it stimulated considerable interest in multiple commitments, Morrow's concentric circles model has not received much empirical support (see Cohen, 2003, and Lee et al., 2001, for reviews). For example, Cohen (1999) found little support for the model due primarily to misspecification of the role of job involvement. Cohen's findings were more consistent with a competing model developed by Randall and Cote (1991), in which job involvement plays a central role in linking the various commitments.

A potential limitation of both Morrow's (1993) and Randall and Cote's (1991) multiple-commitment models is the failure to specify exactly what makes something a commitment. Tests of their models clearly demonstrate that work ethic and job involvement are distinguishable from affective and continuance organizational commitment and career commitment, but are they really commitments? This is an issue that we will revisit later, but it serves here as a point of contrast with other multi-foci frameworks (e.g., Becker, 1992; Meyer et al., 1993) where a consistent conceptual definition was applied across foci. The latter frameworks stem from a seminal article by Reichers (1985).

Reichers (1985) argued that employees can develop commitments to multiple constituencies within and outside the organization and that commitment to these constituencies might have greater relevance for employees than does the organization itself. Reichers also developed a concentric circles model with the individual at the core and the surrounding circles reflecting constituencies with increasing psychological distance from self. For example, co-workers and managers were considered to be relatively proximal, with the union, profession, and customers being more distal. Those constituencies closer to the core were expected to exert the strongest influence on employees' personal identities and therefore their commitments.

Becker and his colleagues (e.g., Becker, 1992; Becker et al., 1996) combined Reicher's (1985) argument for multiple constituencies with O'Reilly and Chatman's (1986) proposition regarding multiple bases and proposed that employees can develop different forms of commitment to multiple foci (e.g., organization, top management, immediate supervisor and team). This research was guided by, and provided support for, the social-exchange notion that commitment to any particular constituency would have its greatest impact on behavior of direct relevance to that constituency. Looked at another way, any given behavior is influenced most by commitment to the constituency most likely to benefit from that behavior. Interestingly, Becker et al. (1996) found that job performance related more strongly to commitment to the supervisor than it did to OC, suggesting that employees may see their performance as more relevant to the immediate work group than to the organization. This might provide another explanation for the relatively weak relations observed between OC and job performance.

Other developments concerning multiple commitments include various attempts to understand how multiple foci and components of commitment relate to one another and combine to influence behavior. For example, Hunt and Morgan (1994) proposed three separate models:

- the key-mediating-model in which commitments to various internal foci exert their influence through their impact on OC;
- the one-of-many model in which all commitments, including OC, exert a direct influence on foci-relevant behaviors; and
- a hybrid model in which OC mediates the effects of some foci-specific commitments and behavior but not all.

Lawler (1992) and Mueller and Lawler (1999) suggested that commitments to internal foci can be considered to be 'nested' within one another and commitment to the global organization and that these commitments will have reciprocal influences. They also used the notion of 'cognitive distance' to generate testable hypotheses concerning the relative impact of the nested commitments on behavior. Finally, a few studies examined and found evidence for interactions among the different components of commitment in predicting behavior (e.g., Jaros, 1997; Somers, 1995). The impact of these developments has only been experienced recently, and will be discussed in more detail below.

Summary

The 1980s and 1990s saw a tremendous increase in research on commitment. Over the course of the two decades, research on the development and consequences became more systematic and theoretical, although most research continued to be cross-sectional and non-experimental, making it difficult to draw firm conclusions about causal direction. Arguably the two most significant developments were the recognition that commitment

(a) is multi-dimensional and (b) can be directed at numerous foci within and outside the organization. However, there were also points of disagreement, one concerning the nature of the dimensionality, and the other involving the relations among commitments to multiple foci. These were among the more salient issues to be addressed as we entered the new millennium. Although not mentioned above, another issue that became salient near the close of the millennium was the relevance of commitment in an era of change (Baruch, 1998). This too posed a challenge for researchers in the new age.

THE NEW AGE (2000 AND BEYOND)

Given the large body of work generated in the 1980s and 1990s, it is not surprising that we started the new millennium with numerous meta-analytic investigations intended to take stock of what we know about employee commitment. In some of these analyses (e.g., Cooper-Hakim and Viswesvaran, 2005; Lee et al., 2001; Meyer et al., 2002; Riketta, 2002; Riketta and Van Dick, 2004; Wright and Bonett, 2002) commitment was the primary variable of interest, whereas in others it was included as a potential antecedent or outcome of another focal variable (e.g., Colquitt et al., 2001; Kristof-Brown et al., 2005; LePine et al., 2002; Rhoades and Eisenberger, 2002; Thoresen et al., 2003). The latter analyses provide a particularly strong testament to the relevance that commitment theory and research have within the broader discipline of organizational behavior.

The findings of these meta-analyses are far more extensive and complex than can be captured here. Therefore, we focus on just a few major themes. First, although most primary studies examined relations involving affective commitment, it is clear from those including multiple forms (e.g., affective, normative and continuance) that the nature of the commitment does matter. The correlations with other variables differ in magnitude and, in some cases, direction (e.g., Cooper-Hakim and Viswesvaran, 2005; Meyer et al., 2002).

Second, although affective OC correlates positively with other work-relevant commitments (e.g., occupation) and work attitudes (e.g., job involvement, job satisfaction and organizational identification) they are distinguishable constructs (Cooper-Hakim and Viswesvaran, 2005; Lee et al., 2001; Riketta, 2005). Third, the findings reveal moderate to strong correlations between affective OC and several hypothesized antecedents including POS (Rhoades and Eisenberger, 2002), organizational justice (Colquitt et al., 2001), person-organization fit (Kristof-Brown et al., 2005), and transformational leadership (Meyer et al., 2002). Fourth, the findings confirm that OC relates negatively to intention to leave and, albeit less strongly, than actual turnover (Meyer et al., 2002). Moreover, they demonstrate positive relations with job performance (Riketta, 2002; Wright and Bonett, 2002) and OCB (LePine et al., 2002; Meyer et al., 2002). Finally, there is evidence that affective OC relates positively to various indices of employee well-being, including job satisfaction and positive affect and negatively to stress, work-family conflict, and negative affect (Meyer et al., 2002; Thoresen et al., 2003).

While providing useful summaries of bivariate relations, these meta-analyses do not address important questions concerning causal direction, additive and interactive effects, and mediation processes. Therefore, in the following section we describe some recent developments in theory, research, and methodology that have the potential to advance our understanding of workplace commitments.

New developments in theory, research, and research methodology

Because it is impossible to capture the full richness of recent and on-going developments, we focus here on four illustrative examples. These include

(a) advances in theory and research pertaining to the multidimensionality of commitment and, in particular, the analysis of commitment 'profiles';

(b) a continued shift away from the study of OC alone, toward the inclusion of commitment to other foci (e.g., teams, supervisors, customers);
(c) a steady increase in research conducted outside North America, and
(d) the application of new methods and data analytic strategies to investigate the development and consequences of commitment.

Profiles of commitment

Although not new, interest in the development and consequences of 'profiles' of commitment has increased in the last few years. We focus here on two complementary profile approaches, one focusing on multiple forms of commitment to a single target, and the other on commitments to multiple foci.

The idea that employees have profiles reflecting the relative strength of affective, normative, and continuance commitment was first suggested by Allen and Meyer (1990; Meyer and Allen, 1991). More recently, Meyer and Herscovitch (2001) provided a set of propositions concerning the behavioral implications of profile differences. Subsequent research has provided mixed support for these proposition, but has clearly demonstrated that behavior does vary across profile groups (e.g., Gellatly et al., 2006; Herscovitch and Meyer, 2002; Sinclair et al., 2005; Wasti, 2005). For example, Gellatly et al. (2006) found that stay intentions and OCB were greatest among employees with profiles reflecting the combination of strong affective and normative OC. Similarly, Herscovitch and Meyer (2002) found the highest levels of behavioral support for an organizational change among employees with profiles characterized by weak continuance commitment combined with strong affective and/or normative commitment to the change initiative.

Perhaps more importantly, examination of commitment profiles has led to some new and potentially interesting discoveries. For example, Gellatly et al. (2006) found that normative commitment related differently to stay intentions and OCB depending on whether it was paired with strong affective or strong continuance commitment. Gellatly et al. (2006) suggested that when combined with affective commitment (desire), normative commitment (obligation) reflects a 'moral imperative,' whereas when paired with continuance commitment (cost) it reflects an 'indebted obligation.' Employees with the former combination reported stronger intentions to stay and greater discretionary performance than did those with the latter. These findings shed new light on normative commitment and might address some of the current confusion concerning its relevance (see Bergman, 2006).

The second approach to profile research focuses on the relative strength of commitments to multiple foci and builds on earlier work in the 1990s. These studies typically involve the measurement of commitment to two or more foci and use cluster analyses to identify profile groups (e.g., Somers and Birnbaum, 2000; Swailes, 2004). For example, in a study with two accountant samples, Swailes (2004) identified four clusters reflecting varying degrees of commitment to the organization, top management, supervisor, and workgroup, and found meaningful differences in behavior (task achievement and innovation) across clusters. Although this appears to be a promising area for future investigation, research on profiles reflects only the tip of the iceberg in multiple foci research. Therefore, we turn now to a more general review.

Commitments to multiple foci

Interest in multiple foci of commitment has increased since 2000 due, in part, to recognition that employee-employer relationships are changing, and that organizations can neither expect nor rely on employee commitment the way they once did. This is not to say that commitment to organizations is irrelevant. Indeed, many organizations still rely on the commitment of core employees whose skills are in high demand. However, instability and unpredictability in the economic climate of the new millennium has reduced many organizations' ability to make long term commitments to their employees. While this might

mitigate expectations regarding employee commitment, it does not reduce performance requirements. Therefore, it is important to consider how commitments to other foci might combine with or substitute for OC. For present purposes, we focus on multiple-foci studies but acknowledge that researchers are also continuing to test and refine theories pertaining to specific foci, including commitment to occupations (Blau, 2003), unions (Bayazit et al., 2004; Fullagar et al., 2004), and goals (Klein et al., 2001).

Researchers have demonstrated that commitments to foci within (e.g., work group and supervisor) and outside (e.g., occupation and union) the organization are distinguishable from one another, and from OC (e.g., Bentein et al., 2002; Redman and Snape, 2005). However, commitments to the different foci are generally positively related, with the strongest correlations between foci with the greatest physical or psychological proximity (e.g., supervisor and work group; top management and organizations). The weight of the evidence seems to suggest that commitment to one focus (e.g., occupation or union) is not necessarily achieved at the expense of another (e.g., organization), but also that commitment to one focus (e.g., organization) is not a precondition for commitment to another (e.g., customer or work group). In a relatively unique and timely twist on this line of investigation, Coyle-Shapiro and Morrow (2006) demonstrated that 'contracted employees' can develop commitments to both the contractor and client organization, and that commitment to the contractor explained unique variance in commitment to the client organization beyond that explained by client characteristics (e.g., attractiveness and support).

Research concerning the consequences of commitment to multiple foci has provided evidence for both unique and additive predictive effects (Becker and Kernan, 2003; Redman and Snape, 2005; Siders et al., 2000). For example, Siders et al. examined relations between various objective indices of performance and commitment to the organization, supervisor, and customers. They found that OC was the best predictor of sales volume, and that commitment to the supervisor related most strongly to organization-rewarded outcomes (e.g., sales volume and growth rate) whereas commitment to customer related most strongly to customer-controlled outcomes (e.g., continued patronage). Similarly, Becker and Kernan (2003) found that commitment to the organization was a better predictor of organization-directed OCB, whereas commitment to the supervisor was a better predictor of team-directed OCB. These findings confirm earlier evidence that behavior might be best predicted by commitment to the target most likely to be affected. However, some behaviors will benefit multiple constituencies, so it is not surprising that other studies found evidence for additive effects in prediction (e.g., Siders et al., 2001; Somers and Birnbaum, 2000).

Researchers have also begun to make a more concerted effort to understand how and why multiple commitments relate to one another and combine to influence behavior. For example, Bentein et al. (2002) tested and found little support for Hunt and Morgan's (1994) complete mediation model described above (cf. Maertz et al., 2002). Instead, consistent with Lewin's (1943) field theory, they found that commitment to the most proximal (behavior-relevant) target tends to mediate the influence of related commitments, including OC. Thus, the bulk of the evidence continues to suggest that, relative to other commitments, the best predictor of a particular behavior is commitment to the target most affected by that behavior. However, it is still too early to draw any firm conclusions about whether and when the effects of other commitments will be direct, partially mediated, or fully mediated by the more proximal commitment.

Studies are also being conducted to determine whether commitments to multiple foci have unique or shared antecedents (e.g., Bishop and Scott, 2000; Clugston et al., 2000; Heffner and Rentsch, 2001; Stinglhamber and Vandenberghe, 2003). Bishop and Scott tested whether affective commitment to organizations and teams had unique antecedents and therefore might be influenced independently

(a situation they argue would be helpful if team commitment were to be used as a substitute for OC). They found that some situational variables related only to team commitment (e.g., satisfaction with co-workers) and others related only to commitment to the organization (e.g., satisfaction with supervisor). However, task interdependence related to both. Similarly, Heffner and Rentsch (2001) found that organization, department, and workgroup commitments related more strongly to foci-relevant social interactions, but that there were significant cross-over correlations as well. Stinglhamber and Vandenberghe (2003) found that POS related most strongly to OC, whereas perceived supervisor support related more strongly to commitment to supervisor. Moreover, the perceived support measures fully or partially mediated the effects of intrinsically- and extrinsically-satisfying conditions on the relevant commitment. These findings suggest that it might indeed be possible to develop strategies targeting commitment to foci of particular interest.

Although the majority of the multiple-foci research reviewed here treated commitment as a uni-dimensional construct (typically reflecting affective commitment), a few investigators attempted to integrate the multi-dimensional and multi-foci approaches. Perhaps the best example of this integration was the application of the three-component model of OC to examine commitments to multiple foci (e.g., Clugston et al., 2003; Herscovitch and Meyer, 2002; Stinglhamber et al., 2002). Clugston et al. and Stinglhamber et al. demonstrated that it was possible to develop distinguishable measures of affective, normative, and continuance commitment to multiple foci. Stinglhamber et al. (2002) also demonstrated that many of these measures contributed uniquely to the prediction of turnover intentions. Clugston et al. (2003) showed that internalized cultural values related in meaningful ways to various component/foci combinations. For example, they found that power distance related positively to normative commitment to all foci included in the study (organization, supervisor and workgroup), uncertainty avoidance related positively to continuance commitment to all foci, and collectivism related to all three components of commitment to the workgroup. Finally, Herscovitch and Meyer (2002) demonstrated that commitment to an organizational change combined with OC to predict employees' level of support for the change.

Cross-cultural applications

Given the increase in globalization (see the chapter by Sparrow in this volume), it is perhaps not surprising that research on commitment outside North America and the UK is occurring with increasing frequency. Indeed, most research conducted outside North America has been published since 2000. In a recent review of this research, Wasti and Önder (forthcoming) note that the majority of studies were conducted in a single country with the intent of testing the generalizability of North American models and measures. There have been relatively few true cross-cultural comparison studies (e.g., Glazer, Daniel and Short, 2004; Kwantes, 2003; Vandenberghe et al., 2001), and even these have limitations that preclude firm conclusions concerning the impact of culture on the nature, strength, development, or consequences of commitment (e.g., failure to establish equivalence of measurement and/or control for differences in sample characteristics or institutional context). Moreover, there have been relatively few attempts to develop theory or measures within cultures to identify uniqueness in the nature, development, and implications of commitment (Wasti, 2002). Consequently, important questions remain to be answered.

With all due caution to the limitations noted by Wasti and Önder (forthcoming), there is some evidence for the generalizability of commitment models and measures developed in North America. For example, the OCQ has been used successfully (e.g., Walumbwa and Lawler, 2003; Yousef, 2003), and findings supporting the three-component model (e.g., Cheng and Stockdale, 2003, Lee et al., 2001) and the multiple foci framework

(e.g., Chen et al., 2002; Snape et al., 2006) have been reported in non-Western cultures. Although this evidence for generalizability is encouraging, it should not overshadow important differences that have yet to be explained (e.g., the relative importance of normative commitment across cultures), or the fact that important insights might be gained by studies designed to address aspects of commitment that are unique to other cultures (Wasti, 2002).

Developments in methodology

As commitment theory evolves and as new issues arise, there is a corresponding need for advances in research methods. This was apparent, for example, in the foregoing discussions of commitment profiles and cross-cultural research. However, answering our 'older' questions about the nature, development, and consequences of commitment can also benefit from recent developments in methodology and analysis. To illustrate, we focus here on two such developments, one involving the investigation of change, and the other involving the study of cross-level effects. (For a more detailed discussion of these and other useful methodological developments as they pertain to commitment research, see Vandenberg and Stanley, forthcoming).

Commitment researchers have long been interested in understanding how changes in conditions at work relate to changes in commitment, or how changes in commitment relate to changes in behavior. Answering these questions using standard correlation- and regression-based procedures has been difficult. Fortunately, new procedures have been developed (e.g., latent growth modeling: LGM) and are now being applied to address these questions more directly. For example, Lance et al. (2000) used LGM analyses to demonstrate that newcomers' pre-entry perceptions (anticipatory met expectations and job-choice difficulty) were associated with post-entry changes in commitment. In a study of more established employees, Bentein et al. (2005) showed that rate of change in commitment was a better predictor of actual turnover than was level of commitment. Although it is still impossible to draw firm conclusions about causality, the use of LGM and related procedures allows researchers to get closer to addressing important questions about patterns of change in the development and outcomes of commitment than has been possible in the past.

A related issue has to do with the combined influence of variables at different 'levels' on the development of commitment. Although it has long been recognized that employee commitment is likely to be influenced by organization- , unit- , and individual-level characteristics, investigation of relations involving higher-level factors has generally been conducted by obtaining individual-level (perception) measures. Recent developments in multi-level analytic procedures such as hierarchical linear modeling (HLM) now allow researchers to measure variables at the appropriate level and to examine how these variables combine to account for variance in employee commitment. For example, Fedor et al. (2006) used HLM to show that employee commitment to the organization and to a change initiative could be best understood in terms of a 3-way interaction between the overall favorableness of the change for the work unit members, the extent of the change in the work unit, and the impact of the change on individuals' jobs. There is a need for more multi-level research – and the availability of HLM and related procedures will facilitate this endeavor. To uncover causal effects, more experimental or quasi-experimental studies are needed (see Barling et al., 1996, and Schweiger and DeNisi, 1991, for examples).

Summary

Despite concerns about the relevance of employee commitment in an era of change (e.g. Baruch, 1998), and perhaps in response to these concerns, commitment theory and research is alive and well in the new millennium. We continue to gain a better understanding of the nature of commitment,

its development, and how it relates to important employer- and employee-relevant outcomes. Researchers have responded to the changing work environment by examining commitments to different foci, including organizational change itself. They have also begun to function within a global context, and to take advantage of recent advances in research methodology and analysis. These are all positive developments and provide a solid foundation upon which to build in the future.

CONCLUSIONS AND A LOOK FORWARD

Considerable progress has been made over the last several decades in our understanding of commitment in the workplace. One of the future challenges, therefore, is to ensure that this knowledge gets translated into action in the form of organizational policy and practice. In the meantime, there are still many questions to be answered. In what follows, we identify areas of investigation that we believe should be priorities.

First, it is now well established that commitments can take different forms and be directed at different foci. In addition, recent research has begun to explore the additive and interactive effects of these different forms and foci of commitment on behavior. However, this line of investigation is still in its infancy and should be continued. For example, there is much yet to be learned about how profiles of commitment (across forms and foci) develop and relate to work behavior. We also need to know more about compatibilities and conflicts among commitments to different foci and whether, and when, commitment to one constituency might serve as a reasonable substitute for another.

Second, although there is strong evidence linking commitment to work behavior at the individual level, there is a need for more research at higher levels of analysis. Establishing links between unit or organizational commitment and objective indices of effectiveness will arguably provide stronger justification for investments in commitment-oriented HRM systems. There is also a need for more cross-level research designed to test the assumptions that (a) the demonstrated effects of 'commitment' or 'high involvement' HRM systems on organizational effectiveness are mediated by their effects on employee commitment, and (b) the behavioral consequences of employee commitment observed at the individual level combine to impact the organization's bottom line.

Third, there is a need for more research to examine the impact of culture on workplace commitments. This research should include more well-designed cross-cultural comparison studies, but should also go beyond attempts to evaluate the generalizability of North American models and include studies designed to identify culture-specific forms and foci of commitment. It would also be useful to know more about how commitments affect, and are affected by, interactions among employees in culturally-diverse organizations.

Fourth, as we noted earlier, organizations are coming under considerable pressure to adapt to changes in their environment and they are doing so in ways (e.g., downsizing, merging/acquiring, re-engineering and outsourcing) that are bound to have an impact on employer–employee relationships. Consequently, we need more research to determine how these changes affect commitment and how commitment influences the effectiveness of change.

Finally, as investigators pursue these and other potentially interesting lines of research, it would be beneficial to utilize recent advances in methodology and analysis. We mentioned latent growth modeling and hierarchical linear modeling as examples earlier, but there are others. Although admittedly more difficult to arrange and conduct, more experimental and quasi-experimental studies would also help to address the ubiquitous questions of causality.

Despite rumors to the contrary, employee commitment is alive and well in the modern workplace. Admittedly, it is more complex than in the past, with multiple forms and foci, but it is no less important. Gaining a fuller understanding of how theses commitments develop and can be managed most effectively for the mutual benefit of organizations and their employees remains a challenge for commitment scholars. There are indeed exciting times ahead!

NOTE

1 Preparation of this manuscript was supported by a research grant from the Social Sciences and Humanities Research Council of Canada.

REFERENCES

Allen, N.J. and Meyer, J.P. (1990) 'Organizational socialization tactics: A longitudinal analysis of links to newcomers' commitment and role orientation', *Academy of Management Journal*, 33 (4): 847–858.

Allen, N.J. and Meyer, J.P. (1996) 'Affective, continuance, and normative commitment to the organization: An examination of construct validity', *Journal of Vocational Behavior*, 49 (3): 252–276.

Arthur, J.B. (1994) 'Effects of human resource systems on manufacturing performance and turnover', *Academy of Management Journal*, 37 (3): 670–687.

Bamberger, P.A., Kluger, A.N. and Suchard, R. (1999) 'The antecedents and consequences of union commitment: A meta–analysis', *Academy of Management Journal*, 42 (3): 304–318.

Barling, J., Weber, T. and Kelloway, E.K. (1996) 'Effects of transformational leadership training on attitudinal and financial outcomes: A field experiment', *Journal of Applied Psychology*, 81 (6): 827–832.

Baruch, Y. (1998) 'The rise and fall of organizational commitment', *Human Systems Management*, 17 (4): 135–143.

Bayazit, M., Hammer, T.H. and Wazeter, D.L. (2004) 'Methodological challenges in union commitment studies', *Journal of Applied Psychology*, 89 (4): 738–747.

Becker, H.S. (1960) 'Notes on the concept of commitment', *American Journal of Sociology*, 66 (1): 32–42.

Becker, T.E. (1992) 'Foci and bases of commitment: Are they distinctions worth making?' *Academy of Management Journal*, 35 (1): 232–244.

Becker, T.E., Billings, R.S., Eveleth, D.M. and Gilbert, N.W. (1996) 'Foci and bases of commitment: Implications for performance', *Academy of Management Journal*, 39 (2): 464–482.

Becker, T.E. and Kernan, M. (2003) 'Matching commitment to supervisors and organizations to in–role and extra–role performance', *Human Performance*, 16 (4): 327–348.

Begley, T.M. and Czajka, J.M. (1993) 'Panel analysis of the moderating effects of commitment on job satisfaction, intent to quit, and health following organizational change', *Journal of Applied Psychology*, 78 (4): 552–556.

Bentein, K., Stinglhamber, F. and Vandenberghe, C. (2002) 'Organization-, supervisor-, and workgroup-directed commitments and citizenship behaviors: A comparison of models', *European Journal of Work and Organizational Psychology*, 11 (3): 341–362.

Bentein, K., Vandenberg, R.J., Vandenberghe, C. and Stinglhamber, F. (2005) 'The role of change in the relationship between commitment and turnover: A latent growth modeling approach', *Journal of Applied Psychology*, 90 (3): 468–482.

Bergman, M.E. (2006) 'The relationship between affective and normative commitment: Review and Research Agenda', *Journal of Organizational Behavior*, 27 (5): 645–663.

Bishop, J.W. and Scott, K.D. (2000) 'An examination of organizational and team commitment in a self–directed team environment', *Journal of Applied Psychology*, 85 (3): 439–450.

Blau, P.M. (1964) *Exchange and Powering is Social Life*. New York: Wiley.

Blau, G. (1985) 'The measurement and prediction of career commitment', *Journal of Occupational Psychology*, 58 (4): 277–288.

Blau, G. (1989) 'Testing the generalizability of a career commitment measure and its impact on employee turnover', *Journal of Vocational Behavior*, 35 (1): 88–103.

Blau, G. (1995) 'Influence of group lateness on individual lateness: A cross-level examination', *Academy of Management Journal*, 38 (5): 1483–1496.

Blau, G. (2003) 'Testing for a four–dimensional structure of occupational commitment', *Journal of Occupational and Organizational Psychology*, 76 (4): 469–488.

Buchanan, B. (1974) 'Building organizational commitment: The socialization of managers in work organizations', *Administrative Science Quarterly*, 19 (4): 533–546.

Bycio, P., Hackett, R.D. and Allen, J.S. (1995) 'Further assessments of Bass's (1985) conceptualization of transactional and transformational leadership', *Journal of Applied Psychology*, 80 (4): 468–478.

Caldwell, D.F., Chatman, J.A. and O'Reilly, C.A. (1990) 'Building organizational commitment: A multi–firm study', *Journal of Occupational Psychology*, 63 (3): 245–261.

Carson, K.D., Carson, P.P. and Bedeian, A.G. (1995) 'Development and construct validation of a career entrenchment measure', *Journal of Occupational and Organizational Psychology*, 68 (4): 301–320.

Chen, Z.X., Tsui, A.S. and Fahr, J.L. (2002) 'Loyalty to supervisor vs. organizational commitment: Relationships to job performance in China', *Journal of Occupational and Organizational Psychology*, 79 (3): 335–356.

Cheng, Y. and Stockdale, M.S. (2003) 'The validity of the three–component model of organizational commitment in a Chinese context', *Journal of Vocational Behavior*, 62 (3): 465–489.

Clugston, M., Howell, J.P. and Dorfman, P.W. (2000) 'Does cultural socialization predict multiple bases and foci of commitment?' *Journal of Management*, 26 (1): 5–30.

Cohen, A. (1999) 'Relationships among five forms of commitment: An empirical assessment', *Journal of Organizational Behavior*, 20 (3): 285–308.

Cohen, A. (2003) *Multiple Commitments at Work: An Integrative Approach*. Hillsdale, NJ: Lawrence Erlbaum.

Colquitt, J.A., Conlon, D.E., Wesson, M.J., Porter, C.O.L.H. and Ng, K.Y. (2001) 'Justice at the millennium: A meta–analytic review of 25 years of organizational justice research', *Journal of Applied Psychology*, 86 (3): 425–445.

Cook, J. and Wall, T. (1980) 'New attitudes measures of trust, organizational commitment and personal need fulfillment', *Journal of Occupational Psychology*, 53 (1): 39–52.

Cooper–Hakim, A. and Viswesvaran, C. (2005) 'The construct of work commitment: Testing an integrative framework', *Psychological Bulletin*, 131 (2): 241–259.

Coyle–Shapiro, J.A.M. and Morrow, P.C. (2006) 'Organizational and client commitment among contracted employees', *Journal of Vocational Behavior*, 68 (3): 416–431.

Dunham, R.B., Grube, J.A. and Castenada, M.B. (1994) 'Organizational commitment: The utility of an integrative definition', *Journal of Applied Psychology*, 79 (3): 370–380.

Edwards, J.R. (1994) 'The study of congruence in organizational behavior research: Critique and a proposed alternative', *Organizational Behavior and Human Decision Processes*, 58 (1): 51–100.

Eisenberger, R., Fasolo, P. and Davis–LaMastro, V. (1990) 'Perceived organizational support and employee diligence, commitment, and innovation', *Journal of Applied Psychology*, 75 (1): 51–59.

Etzioni, A. (1961) *A Comparative Analysis of Complex Organizations.* New York: Free Press.

Farkas, A.J. and Tetrick, L.E. (1989) 'A three–wave longitudinal analysis on the causal ordering of satisfaction and commitment on turnover decision', *Journal of Applied Psychology*, 74 (6): 855–868.

Farrell, D. and Rusbult, C.E. (1981) 'Exchange variables as predictors of job satisfaction, job commitment, and turnover: The impact of rewards, costs, alternatives, and investments', *Organizational Behavior and Human Performance*, 28 (1): 78–95.

Fedor, D.B., Caldwell, S. and Herold, D.M. (2006) 'The effects of organizational changes on employee commitment: A multilevel investigation', *Personnel Psychology*, 59 (1): 1–29.

Friedman, L. and Harvey, R.J. (1986) 'Factors of union commitment: The case for a lower dimensionality', *Journal of Applied Psychology*, 71 (3): 371–376.

Fullagar, C. (1986) 'A factor analytic study on the validity of a union commitment scale', *Journal of Applied Psychology*, 71 (1): 129–136.

Fullager, C.J., Gallagher, D.G., Clark, P.F. and Carroll, A.E. (2004) 'Union commitment and participation: A 10–year longitudinal study', *Journal of Applied Psychology*, 89 (4): 730–737.

Gellatly, I.R., Meyer, J.P. and Luchak, A.A. (2006) 'Combined effects of the three commitment components on focal and discretionary behaviors: A test of Meyer and Herscovitch's proposition', *Journal of Vocational Behavior*, 69 (2): 331–345.

Glazer, S., Daniel, S.C. and Short, K.M. (2004) 'A study of the relationship between organizational commitment and human values in four countries', *Human Relations*, 57 (3): 323–345.

Gordon, M.E., Philpot, J.W., Burt, R.E., Thompson, C.A. and Spiller, W.E. (1980) 'Commitment to the union: Development of a measure and an examination of its correlates', *Journal of Applied Psychology*, 65: 479–499.

Gouldner, A.W. (1960) 'The norm of reciprocity', *American Sociological Review*, 25: 165–167.

Greenhaus, H. (1971) 'An investigation of career salience in vocational behavior', *Journal of Vocational Behavior*, 1: 209–216.

Hackett, R.D., Bycio, P. and Hausdorf, P.A. (1994) 'Further assessments of Meyer and Allen's (1991) three–component model of organizational commitment', *Journal of Applied Psychology*, 79 (1): 15–23.

Hall, D.T., Schneider, B. and Nygren, H.J. (1970) 'Personal factors in organizational identification', *Administrative Science Quarterly*, 15 (2): 340–350.

Heffner, T.S. and Rentsch, J.R. (2001) 'Organizational commitment and social interaction: A multiple constituencies approach', *Journal of Vocational Behavior*, 59 (3): 471–490.

Herscovitch, L. and Meyer, J.P. (2002) 'Commitment to organizational change: Extension of a three–component model', *Journal of Applied Psychology*, 87 (3): 474–487.

Hochwarter, W.A., Perrewé, P.L., Ferris, G.R. and Guercio, R. (1999) 'Commitment as an antidote to the tension and turnover consequences of organizational politics', *Journal of Vocational Behavior*, 55 (3): 277–297.

Hunt, S.D. and Morgan, R.M. (1994) 'Organizational commitment: One of many commitments or key mediating construct?' *Academy of Management Journal*, 37 (6): 1568–1587.

Huselid, M.A. (1995) 'The impact of human resource management practices on turnover, productivity, and corporate financial performance', *Academy of Management Journal*, 38 (3): 635–672.

Iles, P., Mabey, C. and Robertson, I. (1990) 'HRM practices and employee commitment: Possibilities, pitfalls and paradoxes', *British Journal of Management*, 1: 147–157.

Irving, G.P. and Meyer, J.P. (1994) 'Reexamination of the met–expectations hypothesis: A longitudinal analysis', *Journal of Applied Psychology*, 79 (6): 937–949.

Jaros, S.J. (1997) 'An assessment of Meyer and Allen's (1991) three–component model of organizational commitment and turnover intentions', *Journal of Vocational Behavior*, 51 (3): 319–337.

Jaros, S.J., Jermier, J.M., Koehler, J.W. and Sincich, T. (1993) 'Effects of continuance, affective, and moral commitment on the withdrawal process: An evaluation of eight structural equation models', *Academy of Management Journal*, 36 (5): 951–995.

Kalliath, T.J., Bluedorn, A.C. and Strube, M.J. (1999) 'A test of value congruence effects', *Journal of Organizational Behavior*, 20 (7): 1175–1198.

Kanter, R.M. (1968) 'Commitment and social organization: A study of commitment mechanisms in utopian communities', *American Sociological Review*, 33 (4): 499–517.

Kelman, H.C. (1958) 'Compliance, identification, and internalization: Three processes of attitude change', *Journal of Conflict Resolution*, 2: 51–60.

Kelloway, E.K., Catano, V.M. and Southwell, R.R. (1992) 'The construct validity of union commitment: Development and dimensionality of a shorter scale', *Journal of Occupational and Organizational Psychology*, 65 (3): 197–211.

Kiesler, C.A. (1971) *The Psychology of Commitment: Experiments Linking Behaviour to Belief*. New York: Academic Press.

Klein, H.J., Wesson, M.J., Hollenbeck, J.R., Wright, P.M. and DeShon, R.P. (2001) 'The assessment of goal commitment: A measurement model meta–analysis', *Organizational Behavior and Human Decision Processes*, 85 (1): 32–55.

Kristof-Brown, A.L., Zimmerman, R.D., and Johnson, E.C. (2005) 'Consequences of individual's fit at work: A meta-analysis of person-job, person-organization, person-group, and person-supervisor fit', *Personnel Psychology*, 58 (2): 281–342.

Kwantes, C.T. (2003) 'Organizational citizenship and withdrawal behaviors in the USA and India: Does commitment make a difference?' *International Journal of Cross Cultural Management*, 3 (1): 5–26.

Lawler, E.J. (1992) 'Affective attachement to nested groups: A choice process theory', *American Sociological Review*, 57 (3): 327–339.

Lance, C.E., Vandenberg, R.J. and Self, R.M. (2000) 'Latent growth models of individual change: The case of newcomer adjustment', *Organizational Behavior and Human Decision Processes*, 83 (1): 107–140.

Lee, K., Allen, N.J., Meyer, J.P. and Rhee, K.Y. (2001) 'The three–component model of organisational commitment: An application to South Korea', *Applied Psychology: An International Review*, 50 (4): 596–614.

Lee, K., Carswell, J.J. and Allen, N.J. (2000) 'A meta–analytic review of occupational commitment: Relations with person- and work-related variables', *Journal of Applied Psychology*, 85 (5): 799–811.

Leong, C.S., Furnham, A. and Cooper, C.L. (1996) 'The moderating effect of organizational commitment on the occupational stress outcome relationship', *Human Relations*, 49 (10): 1345–1363.

LePine, J.A., Erez, A. and Johnson, D.E. (2002) 'The nature and dimensionality of organizational citizenship behavior: A critical review and meta-analysis', *Journal of Applied Psychology*, 87 (1): 52–65.

Lewin, K. (1943) 'Defining the "field at a given time"', *Psychological Review*, 50: 292–310.

London, M. (1983) 'Toward a theory of career motivation', *Academy of Management Review*, 8 (4): 620–630.

Maertz, C.P., Mosley, D.C. and Alford, B.L. (2002) 'Does organizational commitment fully mediate constituent commitment effects? A reassessment and clarification', *Journal of Applied Social Psychology*, 32 (6): 1300–1313.

March, J.G. and Simon, H.A. (1958) *Organizations*. New York: Wiley.

Mathieu, J.E. and Zajac, D.M. (1990) 'A review and meta–analysis of the antecedents, correlates, and consequences of organizational commitment', *Psychological Bulletin*, 108 (2): 171–194.

McGee, G.W. and Ford, R.C. (1987) 'Two (or more?) dimensions of organizational commitment: Reexamination of the affective and continuance commitment scales', *Journal of Applied Psychology*, 72 (4): 638–642.

Meglino, B.M., Ravlin, E.C. and Adkins, C.L. (1989) 'A work values approach to corporate culture: A field test of the value congruence process and its relationship to individual outcomes', *Journal of Applied Psychology*, 74 (3): 424–432.

Meyer, J.P. and Allen, N.J. (1991) 'A three–component conceptualization of organizational commitment', *Human Resource Management Review*, 1 (4): 61–89.

Meyer, J.P. and Allen, N.J. (1997) *Commitment in the Workplace: Theory, Research, and Application*. Newbury Park, CA: Sage.

Meyer, J.P., Allen, N.J. and Smith, C.A. (1993) 'Commitment to organizations and occupations: Extension and test of a three-component conceptualization', *Journal of Applied Psychology*, 78 (4): 538–551.

Meyer, J.P., Bobocel, D.R. and Allen, N.J. (1991) 'Development of organizational commitment during the first year of employment: A longitudinal study of pre- and post-entry influences', *Journal of Managment*, 17 (4): 717–733.

Meyer, J.P. and Herscovitch, L. (2001) 'Commitment in the workplace: Toward a general model', *Human Resource Management Review*, 11 (3): 299–326.

Meyer, J.P., Irving, P.G. and Allen, N.J. (1998) 'Examination of the combined effects of work values and early work experiences on organizational commitment', *Journal of Organizational Behavior*, 19 (1): 29–52

Meyer, J.P., Paunonen, S.V., Gellatly, I.H., Goffin, R.D. and Jackson, D.N. (1989) 'Organizational commitment and job performance: It's the nature of the commitment that counts', *Journal of Applied Psychology*, 74 (1): 152–156.

Meyer, J.P., Stanley, D.J., Herscovitch, L. and Topolnytsky, L. (2002) 'Affective, continuance and normative commitment to the organization: A meta–analysis of antecedents, correlates, and consequences', *Journal of Vocational Behavior*, 61 (1): 20–52.

Morrow, P.C. (1983) 'Concept redundancy in organizational research: The case of work commitment', *Academy of Management Review*, 8 (3): 486–500.

Morrow, P.C. (1993) *The Theory and Measurement of Work Commitment*. Greenwich, CT: JAI Press.

Mowday, R.T., Porter, L.W. and Dubin, R. (1974) 'Unit performance, situational factors, and employee attitudes in spatially separated work units', *Organizational Behavior and Human Performance*, 12 (2): 1974.

Mowday, R.T., Porter, L.W. and Steers, R.M. (1982) *Employee–Organization Linkages: The Psychology of Commitment, Absenteeism, and Turnover.* New York: Academic Press.

Mowday, R.T., Steers, R.M. and Porter, L.W. (1979) 'The measurement of organizational commitment', *Journal of Vocational Behavior*, 14: 224–247.

Mueller, C.W. and Lawler, E.J. (1999) 'Commitment to nested organizational units: Some basic principles and preliminary findings', *Social Psychology Quarterly*, 62 (4): 325–346.

O'Reilly, C.A. and Chatman, J. (1986) 'Organizational commitment and psychological attachment: The effects of compliance, identification, and internalization on prosocial behavior', *Journal of Applied Psychology*, 71 (3): 492–499.

Organ, D.W. (1988) *Organizational Citizenship Behavior: The Good Soldier Syndrome.* Lexington, MA: Lexington Books.

Ostroff, C. (1992) 'The relationship between satisfaction, attitudes, and performance: An organizational level analysis', *Journal of Applied Psychology*, 77 (6): 963–974.

Porter, L.W., Crampon, W.J. and Smith, F. (1976) 'Organizational commitment and managerial turnover: A longitudinal study', *Organizational Behavior and Human Performance*, 15 (1): 87–89.

Porter, L.W., Steers, R.M., Mowday, R.T. and Boulian, P.V. (1974) 'Organizational commitment, job satisfaction, and turnover among psychiatric technicians', *Journal of Applied Psychology*, 59 (5): 603–609.

Randall, D.M. (1990) 'The consequences of organizational commitment: Methodological investigation', *Journal of Organizational Behavior*, 11 (5): 361–378.

Randall, D.M. and Cote, J.A. (1991) 'Interrelationships of work commitment constructs', *Work and Occupations*, 18 (2): 194–211.

Redman, T. and Snape, E. (2005) 'Unpacking commitment: Multiple loyalties and employee behavior', *Journal of Management Studies*, 42 (2): 301–328.

Reichers, A.E. (1985) 'A review and reconceptualization of organizational commitment', *Academy of Management Review*, 10 (3): 465–476.

Rhoades, L. and Eisenberger, R. (2002) 'Perceived organizational support: A review of the literature', *Journal of Applied Psychology*, 87 (4): 698–714

Riketta, M. (2002) 'Attitudinal organizational commitment and job performance: A meta-analysis', *Journal of Organizational Behavior*, 23 (3): 257–266.

Riketta, M. and Van Dick, R. (2005) 'Foci of attachment in organizations: A meta–analytic comparison of the strength and correlates of workgroup versus organizational identification and commitment', *Journal of Vocational Behavior*, 67 (3): 490–510.

Romzek, B.S. (1989) 'Personal consequences of employee commitment', *Academy of Management Journal*, 32 (3): 649–661.

Ryan, A.M., Schmit, M.J. and Johnson, R. (1996) 'Attitudes and effectiveness: Examining relations at an organizational level', *Personnel Psychology*, 49 (4): 853–882.

Salancik, G.R. (1977) 'Commitment and the control of organizational behavior', in B.M. Staw and G.R. Salancik (eds), *New Directions in Organizational Behavior.* Chicago: St. Clair Press, pp. 1–54.

Schweiger, D.M. and DeNisi, A.S. (1991) 'Communication with employees following a merger: A longitudinal field experiment', *Academy of Management Journal*, 34 (1): 110–135.

Shore, L.M. and Wayne, S.J. (1993) 'Commitment and employee behavior: Comparison of affective and continuance commitment with perceived organizational support', *Journal of Applied Psychology*, 78 (5): 774–780.

Siders, M.A., George, G. and Dharwadkar, R. (2001) 'The relationship of internal and external commitment foci to objective job performance measures', *Academy of Management Journal*, 44 (3): 580–590.

Sinclair, R.R., Tucker, J.S., Cullen, J.C. and Wright, C. (2005) 'Performance differences among four organizational commitment profiles', *Journal of Applied Psychology*, 90 (6): 1280–1287.

Snape, E., Redman, T. and Chan, A.W. (2000) 'Commitment to the union: A survey of research and the implications for industrial relations and trade unions', *International Journal of Management Review*, 2 (3): 205–230.

Somers, M.J. (1995) 'Organizational commitment, turnover and absenteeism: An examination of direct and interaction effects', *Journal of Organizational Behavior*, 16 (1): 49–58.

Somers, M.J. and Birnbaum, D. (2000) 'Exploring the relationship between commitment and work attitudes, employee withdrawal, and job performance', *Public Personnel Management*, 29 (3): 353–365.

Staw, B. (1997) 'The escalation of commitment: an update and appraisal', in Z. Shapiro (ed.), *Organizational Decision Making.* Cambridge: Cambridge University Press, pp. 191–215.

Steers, R.M. (1977) 'Antecedents and outcomes of organizational commitment', *Administrative Science Quarterly*, 22 (1): 46–56.

Stevens, J.M., Beyer, J.M. and Trice, H.M. (1978) 'Assessing personal, role, and organizational predictors of managerial commitment', *Academy of Management Journal*, 6 (1): 380–396.

Stinglhamber, F., Bentein, K. and Vandenberghe, C. (2002) 'Extension of the three–component model of commitment to five foci: Development of measures and substantive test', *European Journal of Psychological Assessment*, 18 (2): 123–138.

Stinglhamber, F. and Vandenberghe, C. (2003) 'Organizations and supervisors as sources of support and targets of commitment: A longitudinal study', *Journal of Organizational Behavior*, 24 (3): 251–270.

Sverke, M. and Kuruvilla, S. (1995) 'A new conceptualization of union commitment: Development and test of an integrated theory', *Journal of Organizational Behavior*, 16 (Special Issue): 505–532.

Swailes, S. (2004) 'Commitment to change: Profiles of commitment and in-role performance', *Personnel Review*, 33 (2): 187–204.

Sweeney, P.D. and McFarlin, D.B. (1993) 'Workers' evaluations of the "ends" and the "means": An examination of four models of distributive and procedural justice', *Organizational Behavior and Human Decision Processes*, 55 (1): 23–40.

Tetrick, L.E., Thacker, J.W. and Fields, M.W. (1989) 'Evidence for the stability of the four dimensions of the Commitment to the Union Scale', *Journal of Applied Psychology*, 74 (5): 819–822.

Tett, R.P. and Meyer, J.P. (1993) 'Job satisfaction, organizational commitment, turnover intention and turnover: Path analyses based on meta-analytic findings', *Personnel Psychology*, 46 (2): 259–293.

Thoresen, C.J., Kaplan, S.A., Barsky, A.P., Warren, C.R. and de Chermont, K. (2003) 'The affective underpinnings of job perceptions and attitudes: A meta–analytic review and integration', *Psychological Bulletin*, 129 (6): 914–945.

Tsui, A.S., Pearce, J.L., Porter, L.W. and Tripoli, A.M. (1997) 'Alternative approaches to the employee-organization relationship: Does investment in employees pay off?', *Academy of Management Journal*, 40 (5): 1089–1121.

Vandenberg, R.J. and Lance, C.E. (1992) 'Examining the causal order of job satisfaction and organizational commitment', *Journal of Management*, 18 (1): 153–167.

Vandenberg, R.J. and Stanley, L.J. (forthcoming) 'What evils lurk in the shadows of commitment research?' in H.J. Klein, T.E. Becker and J.P. Meyer (eds), *Commitment in Organizations: Accumulated Wisdom and New Directions*. Florence, KY: Routledge/Taylor and Francis Group.

Vandenberg, R.J., Self, R.M. and Seo, J.H. (1994) 'A critical examination of the internalization, identification, and compliance commitment measures', *Journal of Management*, 20 (1): 123–140.

Vandenberghe, C., Stinglhamber, F., Bentein, K. and Delhaise, T. (2001) 'An examination of the cross-cultural validity of a multidimensional model of commitment in Europe', *Journal of Cross-Cultural Psychology*, 32 (3): 322–347.

Wallace, J.E. (1995) 'Organizational and professional commitment in professional and non–professional organizations', *Administrative Science Quarterly*, 40 (2): 228–255.

Walumbwa, F.O. and Lawler, J.J. (2003) 'Building effective organizations: Transformational leadership, collectivist orientation, work-related attitudes and withdrawal behaviors in three emerging economies', *International Journal of Human Resource Management*, 14 (7): 1083–1101.

Wasti, S.A. (2002) 'Affective and continuance commitment to the organization: Test of an integrated model in the Turkish context', *International Journal of Intercultural Relations*, 26 (5): 525–550.

Wasti, S.A. (2005) 'Commitment profiles: Combinations of organizational commitment forms and job outcomes', *Journal of Vocational Behavior*, 67 (2): 290–308.

Wasti, S.A. and Önder, Ç. (forthcoming) 'Commitment across cultures: Progress, pitfalls and propositions', in H.J. Klein, T.E. Becker and J.P. Meyer (eds), *Commitment in Organizations: Accumulated Wisdom and New Directions*. Florence, KY: Routledge/Taylor and Francis Group.

Wiener, Y. (1982) 'Commitment in organizations: A normative view', *Academy of Management Review*, 7 (3): 418–428.

Wittig–Berman, U. and Lang, D. (1990) 'Organizational commitment and its outcomes: Differing effects of value commitment and continuance commitment on stress reactions, alienation and organization-serving behaviors', *Work and Stress*, 4 (2): 167–177.

Wright, T.A. and Bonett, D.G. (2002) 'The moderating effects of employee tenure on the relation between organizational commitment and job performance: A meta-analysis', *Journal of Applied Psychology*, 87 (6): 1183–1190.

Yousef, D.A. (2003) 'Validating the dimensionality of Porter et al.'s measurement of organizational commitment in a non-western culture setting', *International Journal of Human Resource Management*, 14 (6): 1067–1079.

3

Taking Stock: A Review of More Than Twenty Years of Research on Empowerment at Work[1]

Gretchen Spreitzer

Today, more than 70 per cent of organizations have adopted some kind of empowerment initiative for at least part of their workforce (Lawler et al., 2001). To be successful in today's global business environment, companies need the knowledge, ideas, energy, and creativity of every employee, from front line workers to the top level managers in the executive suite. The best organizations accomplish this by empowering their employees to take initiative without prodding, to serve the collective interests of the company without being micro-managed, and to act like owners of the business (O'Toole and Lawler, 2006).

So what do we know about empowerment in work organizations? In this chapter, I will conduct an in-depth review of the literature on empowerment at work. I start by framing the two classic approaches to empowerment – social-structural and psychological – before outlining the current state of the literature. I then close the chapter by discussing key debates in the field and emergent directions for future research.

CLASSIC EMPOWERMENT APPROACHES

Over the last two decades, two complementary perspectives on empowerment at work have emerged in the literature (Liden and Arad, 1996). The first is more macro and focuses on the social-structural (or contextual) conditions that enable empowerment in the workplace. The second is more micro in orientation and focuses on the psychological experience of empowerment at work. The two perspectives can be distinguished by a focus on empowering structures, policies, and practices and a focus on perceptions of empowerment (which focuses on individual's reactions to the structures, policies, and practices they are embedded in; Eylon and Bamberger, 2000). Each perspective plays an important role in the development of a theory of empowerment and is described in the sections below.

Social-structural empowerment

The social-structural perspective on empowerment is rooted in theories of social exchange and social power. The classic study in the development of a social-structural theory of empowerment was Kanter's (1977) *Men and Women of the Corporation*, an award-winning ethnographic study of an industrial organization conducted at a time when more women were entering work organizations. Kanter showed how women were often 'tokens' as a function of their small numbers and as a result their successful advancement was impeded as they lacked access to 'power tools' – defined as opportunity, information, support, and resources. Kanter's original research has now served as the foundation of the large body of empowerment research from a social-structural perspective described below.

The social-structural perspective is embedded in the values and ideas of democracy – where power ideally resides within individuals at all levels of a system (Prasad, 2001; Prasad and Eylon, 2001). Employees at low levels of the organizational hierarchy can be empowered if they have access to opportunity, information, support and resources. Even the secretary, mail clerk, or janitor has potential in an organization with democratic principals. Of course, in contrast to a formal democracy, where each person has an equal vote in the system and the majority rules, most organizations stop short in behaving as a real democracy (Eylon, 1998). Yet, employees at all levels can still have a voice in a system even if they don't have a formal vote when they have access to opportunity, information, support and resources.

The essence of the social-structural perspective on empowerment is the idea of sharing power between superiors and subordinates with the goal of cascading relevant decision-making power to lower levels of the organizational hierarchy (Liden and Arad, 1996). Empowerment from the social-structural perspective is about sharing power (i.e., formal authority or control over organizational resources; Conger and Kanungo, 1988) through the delegation of responsibility throughout the organizational chain of command. By sharing decision-making power, upper management may thus have more free time to think strategically and innovatively about how to move the organization forward. In this perspective, power means having formal authority or control over organizational resources and the ability to make decisions relevant to a person's job or role (Lawler, 1986). Relevance is key – empowered employees have the power to make decisions that fit within the scope and domain of their work. For example, manufacturing employees might not be making decisions about firm strategy but instead make decisions about how and when to do their own work. Thus, social-structural empowerment is about employee participation through increased access to opportunity, information, support and resources throughout the organizational chain of command.

The social-structural perspective focuses on how organizational, institutional, social, economic, political, and cultural forces can root out the conditions that foster powerlessness in the workplace (Liden and Arad, 1996). Practically, organizations can change organizational policies, processes, practices, and structures away from top-down control systems toward high involvement practices where power, knowledge, information and rewards are shared with employees in the lower echelons of the organizational hierarchy (Bowen and Lawler, 1995). For example, management can change practices to allow employees to decide on their own how they will recover from a service problem and then surprise and delight customers by exceeding their expectations rather than waiting for approval from a supervisor.

Specific practices that indicate a high involvement or self-managing system include the following.

- Participative decision-making: Employees and/or teams may have input into and influence over decisions ranging from high-level strategic decisions to routine day-to-day decisions about how to do their own jobs (Lawler, 1986). Increasing self-managing teams are the mechanisms for building authority and accountability (Gibson et al., in 2007).
- Skill/knowledge-based pay: Employees share in the gains of the organization and are compensated for increases in their own skills and knowledge.
- Open flow of information: This includes the downward flow of information (about clear goals and responsibilities, strategic direction, competitive intelligence, and financial performance in terms of costs, productivity, and quality) and the upward flow of information (concerning employee attitudes and improvement ideas). The point is to create transparency so that employees have 'line of sight' about how their behavior affects firm performance (Gibson et al., 2007). Those with better information can work smarter and thus make better decisions.
- Flat organizational structures: Empowering organizations tend to be decentralized where the span of control (more subordinates per manager) is wide (Spreitzer, 1996). It becomes very difficult to micro-manage when managers have many people to manage (Quinn and Spreitzer, 1997).
- Training: Educative efforts enable employees to build knowledge, skills, and abilities – not only to do their own jobs better but also to learn about skills and the economics of the larger organization (Lawler, 1996).

Each of these practices contributes to employee empowerment by increasing access to opportunity, information, support, or resources.

Research has found that any one of these practices by itself will have only a marginal effect on empowerment. The real impact comes from the interaction and reinforcement among these practices (Lawler, 1996; MacDuffie, 1995).

In summary, then, the social-structural perspective on empowerment is embedded

in theories of social exchange and power. However, while this perspective has garnered much attention from practitioners because it links specific managerial practices to performance, it is limited because it provides an organizationally-centric perspective on empowerment. It does not address the nature of empowerment as experienced by employees. This is important because, in some situations, all of Kanter's empowerment tools – power, knowledge, information and rewards – have been provided to employees, yet they still feel disempowered. And in other situations, individuals lack all the objective features of an empowering work environment yet still feel and act in empowered ways. This limitation helped to spur the emergence of the psychological perspective on empowerment, which is described in the next section.

Psychological empowerment

Psychological empowerment refers to a set of psychological states that are necessary for individuals to feel a sense of control in relation to their work. Rather than focusing on managerial practices that share power with employees at all levels, the psychological perspective is focused on how employees experience their work. This perspective refers to empowerment as the personal beliefs that employees have about their role in relation to the organization.

The paper that motivated researchers to think differently about empowerment was a conceptual piece by Conger and Kanungo (1988). They argued that a social-structural perspective was incomplete because the empowering managerial practices discussed above would have little effect on employees if they lacked a sense of self-efficacy. To them, empowerment was a 'process of enhancing feelings of self-efficacy among organizational members through the identification [and removal] of conditions that foster powerlessness' (Conger and Kanungo, 1988: 484).

Thomas and Velthouse (1990) extended Conger and Kanugo's ideas with the development of a theoretical framework articulating empowerment as intrinsic task motivation manifest in four cognitions that reflect their orientation to work. Rather than a dispositional trait, Thomas and Velthouse defined empowerment as a set of cognitions or states influenced by the work environment that helps create an active-orientation to one's job.

To ensure that these four dimensions truly captured the essence of empowerment, Spreitzer (1997) distilled the interdisciplinary literature on empowerment, drawing on psychology, sociology, social work, and education. She found wide support for these four dimensions of empowerment across these disparate literatures. Based on these results, she further refined these four dimensions as follows.

- Meaning involves a fit between the needs of one's work role and one's beliefs, values and behaviors (Hackman and Oldham, 1980).
- Competence refers to self-efficacy specific to one's work, or a belief in one's capability to perform work activities with skill (Gist, 1987; Bandura, 1989).
- Self-determination is a sense of choice in initiating and regulating one's actions (Deci et al., 1989). It reflects a sense of autonomy or choice over the initiation and continuation of work behavior and processes (e.g., making decisions about work methods, pace, and effort; Bell and Staw, 1989).
- Impact is the degree to which one can influence strategic, administrative, or operating outcomes at work (Ashforth, 1989).

Together, these four cognitions reflect an active, rather than passive, orientation to one's work role. In other words, the experience of empowerment is manifest in all four dimensions – if any one dimension is missing, then the experience of empowerment will be limited (Spreitzer, 1995). For example, if people have discretion to make decisions (i.e., self-determination) but they don't care about the kinds of decisions they can make (i.e., they lack a sense of meaning), they will not feel empowered. Alternatively, if people believe they can make an impact but don't feel like they have the skills and abilities to do their job well (i.e., they lack a sense of competence), they will not feel empowered either. Thus, employees

feel psychologically empowered when they experience all four psychological states. In this way, empowerment is the 'gestalt' of the four dimensions.

As discussed above, while the social-structural perspective is limited because it is organizationally-centric, the psychological perspective is also limited because it is individually-centric. A complete understanding of empowerment at work requires the integration of both perspectives. We need to understand how social-structural empowerment can enable psychological empowerment – as well as understand how beliefs of psychological empowerment can enable the development of more social-structural empowerment through proactive behaviors aimed at changing the systems.

In the next two sections, we describe the key research findings on the two empowerment perspectives with an eye to research which might help us bring the two perspectives closer together.

RELEVANT RESEARCH ON EMPOWERMENT

Social-structural empowerment findings

Much of the research on social-structural empowerment has been conducted under the terms high involvement work practices and high performance work systems (see the chapter on high performance work systems in this volume) and has focused largely at the unit (e.g., MacDuffie, 1995) or firm level (e.g., Lawler, et al., 2001; Gibson, et al., 2007; Staw and Epstein, 2000). Programmatic research on high involvement work practices has been conducted by researchers in both industrial relations and human resource management. This research has shown that high involvement practices which involve sharing power, information, knowledge, and rewards with employees at all levels often have positive outcomes for organizations, particularly in terms of improvements to employee quality of work life, the quality of products and services, customer service, productivity, and reduced turnover (Lawler et al., 2001).

Broader research in the area of high performance work systems (these include employee involvement but also things like long-term job security, flexible scheduling, and multiskilling) shows similar findings (Guthrie, 2001; Huselid, 1995; MacDuffie, 1995; Wright et al., 2003). Research in this area also documents the higher labor costs that are incurred with these practices (Cappelli and Neumark, 2001) but that those costs are offset by the higher productivity these firms generate (Pfeffer, 1996). Yet, other studies have shown marginal or mixed effects (Huselid and Becker, 1996; Staw and Epstein, 2000). It may be that there are tradeoffs inherent in implementing the high involvement practices. For example, Gibson et al. (2007) found that different high involvement or empowering practices were related to distinctively different outcomes (information sharing → financial performance, boundary setting → customer service, and team enabling → quality). No single practice was related to more than one dimension of performance.

A significant body of research has focused on structures, systems, and processes for building empowered or self-managing teams. An alternative to traditional hierarchical management, these empowered teams can be cross-functional and often operate virtually (where team members are not co-located and may even be located across different time zones and continents; Cohen and Bailey, 1997). Empowered teams direct and control their own work, having the responsibility for scheduling work hours and vacations, placing orders, hiring and firing team members and determining wages (Lawler, 1986). Thus, managers of empowered teams need to play quite a different role from traditional managers in helping these teams be effective.

To this end, Arnold and colleagues (2000) conducted a qualitative study to determine the key roles for leaders of empowered teams. They found that empowering team leaders:

(1) coach;
(2) inform;

(3) lead by example;
(4) show concern; and
(5) encourage participative decision-making.

They then developed and validated a measure of empowering leadership, showing that it explains more than traditional leadership measures such as the Self-Management Leadership Questionnaire (Manz and Sims, 1987). Using this newly created measure with a sample of senior leadership teams of hotel properties, Srivastava et al. (2006) found that empowering team leadership is associated with more knowledge sharing and team efficacy, which in turn predicted unit performance. Burpitt and Bigoness (1997) found that empowering leader behavior was also related to team innovation among professional project teams as well as perceptions of fairness by team members (Keller and Dansereau, 1995). This is likely because those subordinates are involved in decision-making and thus have a say about what is fair.

Other researchers focus more on the relational aspects of empowerment (Fletcher, 1998). Derived from a woman's experience in relationships, this relational perspective on empowerment focuses on forming mutual and meaningful connections with others. It is through these connections that people are empowered and grow and develop as human beings (Walsh et al., 1998). This is a provocative addition to the social-structural perspective, but has received rather limited attention in the literature thus far.

In summary, many researchers have examined the empowering characteristics of systems and structures as well as the leaders who design them. In looking across this stream of research on social-structural empowerment, it appears that empowering systems and structures, while often more costly to implement, for the most part have positive outcomes for organizations in terms of firm, unit, and team performance. Interestingly, this stream of research pays less attention to their effects on individual employees. The second stream of empowerment research – on psychological empowerment – seeks to fill that void. In this way, it helps identify the mechanisms by which empowerment structures and practices impact organizational behavior and performance.

Psychological empowerment findings

Measuring psychological empowerment

Unlike the social-structural perspective, where there are many different instruments which have been used to measure empowerment, a single 12-item (3 items per dimension) measure of psychological empowerment developed by Spreitzer (1995) has been used predominately in empirical research. Using a 7-point Likert scale, the measure of psychological empowerment assumes that empowerment is continuous rather than dichotomous – employees may perceive different degrees of empowerment rather than feeling empowered or not. A second-order confirmatory factor analysis demonstrated that the four dimensions are distinct but do contribute to an overall sense of empowerment. Spreitzer (1995) also found that the measure was not susceptible to social-desirability bias. The measure was further validated at the individual level by Kraimer et al. (1999) and at the team level by Kirkman and Rosen (1999). Both convergent and discriminant validity of the four dimensions have been established, the structure of the measure has been shown to be invariant across gender (Boudarias et al., 2004), and the measure has been translated and validated in Chinese (Aryee, and Chen, 2006). It has also been used across cultures in Turkey (Ergeneli et al., 2007), the Philippines (Hechanova et al., 2006), Singapore (Avolio et al., 2004), the UK (Holdsworth and Cartwright, 2003), Australia (Carless, 2004), and Canada (Laschinger et al., 2004). The team version of the psychological empowerment instrument (Kirkman and Rosen, 1999) has been translated into Flemish and Finish as well as used in the Philippines (Kirkman and Shapiro, 2001).

This measure of psychological empowerment has been used and found to be valid in a variety of different contexts – a sampling includes big box retail (e.g., Chen et al., 2007); the insurance industry (e.g., Spreitzer, 1995), teams of engineers (Seibert et al., 2004), high tech project teams (Chen and Klimoski, 2003), sales and service teams (Kirkman et al., 2004), the hospitality industry (e.g., Corsun and Enz, 1999; Sparrowe, 1994), manufacturing (e.g., Spreitzer, 1996), health care (e.g., Koberg et al., 1999; Kraimer, et al., 1999), aerospace (e.g., Mishra et al., 1998), and education (Moye et al., 2004). It is interesting to see that findings about empowerment appear to generalize across so many different work contexts.

Having a well-validated, theoretically-driven measure has allowed this substantive stream of research to flourish because researchers can build on each others' work. This stands in contrast to the social-structural perspective where empowerment has been measured in many different ways (high involvement practices, participation, and empowering leadership to name but a few). As such, this variety of measures of social-structural empowerment has made it more difficult to build a cohesive body of empirical findings.

Psychological empowerment studies have focused on several different levels of analysis including individual (e.g., Spreitzer, 1996), team (e.g., Kirkman and Rosen, 1999; Kirkman et al., 2004; Srivastava, et al., 2006), and work unit level (e.g., Seibert et al., 2004). Both team and unit level studies have conceptualized team or unit empowerment as shared perceptions of experienced empowerment. For example, for team empowerment, all four dimensions are conceptualized as team level constructs (Kirkman and Rosen, 1999):

(1) team meaningfulness is defined as the team valuing its tasks as important and worthwhile;
(2) potency, or competence, is the collective belief the team can be effective;
(3) autonomy involves the team members experiencing substantial freedom and discretion in their work; and
(4) impact is about the team producing work that is significant and important for the organization.

Recent research has provided a multi-level design to examine the interaction between team and individual empowerment (Chen et al., 2007). This is important because of the need to determine whether it is the team as a whole or the individual team members who are empowered differentially. Moreover, we do not know whether a different set of practices empower individuals in contrast to those that empower teams. Their research found that team empowerment was strongly related to individual empowerment – and that team empowerment moderated the relationship between individual empowerment and performance.

In the next sections, we review recent research findings undergirding the nomological network of psychological empowerment at work.

Who is empowered?

Research indicates that certain types of people are likely to report stronger feelings of empowerment. Spreitzer (1995) found that those with stronger self-esteem scores reported more empowerment, while locus of control appeared to have no relationship to empowerment. In terms of demographics, employees with higher levels of education, more tenure, and greater rank report more feelings of empowerment (Spreitzer, 1995). At the team level, racial diversity on a team, and between the team leaders and their teams, was found to be negatively related to empowerment (Kirkman, et al., 2004). Yet other forms of demographic diversity, such as gender, tenure, and age diversity, had no bearing on empowerment. Drawing on social categorization theory, it may be that these other sources of diversity are less 'visible' than race and thus have less bearing on power sharing in the workplace

Antecedents of empowerment

Contexts   Are there certain kinds of work conditions where empowerment plays a particularly important role? Empowerment is especially important in virtual settings where team members do not have face-to-face interactions and must work independently

(Kirkman et al., 2004). Empowerment has also been shown to be particularly important to preserve the hope and attachment of survivors during times of organizational downsizing (Brockner et al., 2004; Mishra and Spreitzer, 1998). These findings indicate that empowerment helps employees adapt in weak situations – where they need to be more proactive in making sense of the situation and determining the appropriate course of action.

The role of leadership   Kark et al. (2003) found that transformational leadership was associated with more follower empowerment (defined narrowly as self- and collective-efficacy) among bank employees. Transformational leaders (who show consideration and inspire followers to become empowered at work) created more social identification with the group which in turn helped the bank employees feel more empowerment. The relationship between transformational leadership and follower empowerment was replicated by Avolio et al. (2004) and Fuller et al. (1999).

Employees who have developed better relationships with their leader (i.e., higher leader-member exchange (LMX) (Aryee and Chen, 2006; Chen et al., 2007; Chen and Klimoski, 2003; Liden et al., 2000; Wat and Shaffer, 2005), with their team members (i.e., higher team-member exchange (TMX) (Chen and Klimoski, 2003), and with customers (Corsun and Enz, 1999) report more empowerment. Wallach and Meuller (2006) found that supervisory and peer support were associated with stronger feelings of empowerment.

Trust in one's leader was also found to have an important relationship to experienced empowerment. Trust in one's manager was found to be particularly potent for empowerment – cognition-based trust predicts meaning and competence while affect-based trust predicts impact (Ergeneli, et al., 2007). Also, teachers who had higher interpersonal trust with their principals reported that they found their work more meaningful and had significant self-determination and impact (Moye, et al., 2004). Looking across these findings, it becomes evident that a supportive, trusting relationship with one's boss or leader (and to a lesser extent with team members and customers) is important for individuals to experience empowerment at work. Relationships matter for empowerment.

Job characteristics   Kraimer et al. (1999) linked Hackman and Oldham's job characteristics to the four dimensions of psychological empowerment. Where Hackman and Oldham's characteristics are considered to be objective features of the job, the dimensions of psychological empowerment are conceptualized as psychological states or cognitions which are shaped by one's relationship to work. Kraimer et al. (1999) found that job meaningfulness was related to the experience of meaning, job autonomy was related to the experience of self-determination, and task feedback was related to more feelings of competence and impact. Other job characteristics are also related to empowerment. Contrary to much of the popular literature which assumed that more organic or loose systems were empowering to employees, Spreitzer (1996) found that role ambiguity was related to lower levels of empowerment. Wallach and Meuller (2006) replicated the negative effect of role ambiguity and also found that role overload reduced feelings of empowerment in social service employees. Taken together, it appears that empowering jobs have an inherent tension in them (Spreitzer and Quinn, 2001). Empowering jobs provide autonomy but mitigate the ambiguity that can come from having less direction from others by also providing feedback about how one's work is going. These kinds of tensions are elements of a weak situation where employees need to be proactive to make sense of the situation and determine the appropriate course of action.

Outcomes of empowerment

Findings across a wide range of studies show that both employees and their organizations can benefit from empowerment. When people feel empowered at work, positive individual outcomes are likely to occur. The finding that empowered employees report high job satisfaction has been consistent across a large number of studies for both individuals (e.g., Aryee and Chen, 2006; Carless, 2004; Koberg et al., 1999; Liden et al., 2000; Seibert et al., 2004; Sparrowe, 1994) and teams (Kirkman and Rosen, 1999). Empowered employees also report higher levels of organizational commitment (Avolio, et al. 2004; Liden et al., 2000) and less propensity to turn over (Sparrowe, 1994; Koberg et al., 1999). Empowered employees also reported less job strain (Spreitzer et al., 1997).

Some research has investigated how each of the four dimensions of empowerment predicts these outcomes. The meaning and to a lesser extent competence dimensions inherent in empowerment appear to be driving the strong and consistent relationship with job satisfaction (Spreitzer, 1997). Kraimer et al. (1999) found that the meaning and competence dimensions predict career progression intentions while the self-determination and impact dimensions predict organizational commitment. The fact that different dimensions of empowerment are related to different outcomes supports the notion of a 'gestalt' of empowerment being necessary to achieve the range of outcomes. No single dimension of empowerment affords the range of outcomes that have been shown to link to overall construct of psychological empowerment.

But empowerment is not only related to positive work attitudes, it has also been found to be related to positive work performance – more specifically, managerial effectiveness (Spreitzer, 1995), employee effectiveness (Spreitzer et al., 1997), employee productivity (Koberg, et al., 1999), and newcomer role performance (Chen and Klimoski, 2003). Employees who feel more empowered are more motivated to perform effectively (Chen et al., 2007; Chen and Klimoski, 2003; Liden et al., 2000; Seibert et al., 2004). Do certain dimensions drive the link to performance? In a sample of managers, Spreitzer et al. (1997) found that the competence and impact dimensions were most strongly related to managerial effectiveness. It may be that competence is necessary for performance (competence indicates the skills and abilities necessary to do one's job well) and that impact comes from strong prior performance (employees have seen that their effort has made a difference in the past so they feel they can have impact moving forward as well). These results suggest that psychological empowerment likely enhances performance because people go above and beyond the call of duty and are more influential and innovative in their work.

Empowerment also enables proactive behaviors that may lead to more effectiveness at work. Spreitzer and Quinn (1996) found that when stimulated in a leadership development program, empowered middle managers engaged in more transformation change initiatives than less empowered middle managers who were more transactional in their change approach. Spreitzer et al. (1999a) found that supervisors who reported higher levels of empowerment were seen by their subordinates as more innovative, upward influencing, and inspirational. Empowerment is also associated with more innovation at work (Spreitzer, 1995) and with more organizational citizenship behaviors (OCBs; Wat and Shaffer, 2004). Wat and Shaffer (2004) found that different empowerment dimensions are related to different elements of OCBs:

(1) the meaning dimension relates strongly to courtesy;
(2) the competence dimension relates to both conscientiousness and sportsmanship;
(3) the self-determination dimension relates to altruism; and
(4) the impact dimension relates to conscientiousness.

Again, each dimension of empowerment contributes to different outcomes. No single dimension captures the gestalt of empowerment in terms of influencing OCBs.

Research on empowered teams also indicates positive outcomes. More empowered teams have better work-unit performance (Seibert, et al., 2004), productivity (Kirkman and Rosen, 1999), team process improvement (Spreitzer et al., 1999b), customer satisfaction (Mathieu et al., 2006) and team effectiveness (Chen et al., 2007; Kirkman et al., 2001). Empowered team members are also more proactive, satisfied with their jobs, and committed to the team and the organization (Kirkman and Rosen, 1999). For virtual teams, more empowerment facilitates more process improvement and higher customer satisfaction (Kirkman et al., 2004) – especially when they didn't have an opportunity to interact face-to-face at regular intervals.

FINDINGS LINKING THE SOCIAL-STRUCTURAL AND PSYCHOLOGICAL PERSPECTIVES ON EMPOWERMENT

In the last few years, it has been exciting to see more research examining the relationship between different elements of social-structural empowerment and the psychological experience of empowerment. A natural first step in this regard was to examine the extent to which Kanter's (1977) elements of social-structural empowerment are related to feelings of psychological empowerment. Spreitzer (1996) found that Kanter's power tools, including sociopolitical support, access to information, and access to resources was related to the psychological empowerment of middle managers. Other research has replicated a strong positive relationship between Kanter's power tools and psychological empowerment (Siu et al., 2005), even in longitudinal research (Laschinger, et al., 2004).

Moving beyond operationalizing social-structural empowerment as Kanter's power tools, Wallach and Meuller (2006) found that actual participation in decision making (both decisions that shape the direction of the organization and decisions pertinent to one's own work) were related to stronger feelings of psychological empowerment in human service agency employees. Similarly, Spreitzer (1996) found that employees in units with a more participative work climate, wider spans of control, and performance-based pay reported higher levels of psychological empowerment. While no study looks at the full set of social-structural empowerment elements, findings do suggest that social-structural empowerment is related to psychological empowerment at the individual level.

At the team level, leaders who

(1) encourage the team to set its own goals and self-manage its tasks (Kirkman and Rosen, 1999);
(2) coach, inform, and show concern for the team (Arnold et al., 2000); and
(3) create the structures, policies, and practices that support team empowerment (Seibert et al., 2004)

were found to be related to psychological empowerment of the team. In particular, team-based HR practices like cross-training, team-based pay, and participation in hiring, developing, evaluating, and firing team members have been found to be related to team-level psychological empowerment (Kirkman and Rosen, 1999), particularly in terms of the self-determination dimension of empowerment (Mathieu et al., 2006). These team-level findings also indicate that social-structural empowerment is related to team-level psychological empowerment.

A limitation of the research discussed thus far is that it has been conducted at either the individual or the team-level of analysis. More recently, two studies have taken a multi-level approach to understanding the relationship between social-structural empowerment and psychological empowerment. First, Seibert et al. (2004) conceptualized social-structural empowerment as unit empowerment climate. They then linked empowerment climate (measured as shared perceptions among members of the unit of information sharing, boundary setting, and team accountability) to work unit performance as well as to enhanced feelings of psychological empowerment at the individual

level of analysis. In turn, they hypothesized a link between psychological empowerment and increased individual performance and job satisfaction. They found strong support for the cross-level model of empowerment at work. This research provided an important contribution in showing how macro-level empowerment practices (i.e., empowerment climate) do influence micro-level feelings of empowerment (i.e., psychological empowerment) – both of which impact key organizational and individual outcomes (unit and individual performance as well as job satisfaction).

Second, Chen et al. (2007) examined how two empowering leadership practices, one at the team level (empowering leadership climate) and one at the individual level (LMX), affected both individual and team empowerment. They showed that team empowerment impacted team performance and that individual empowerment impacted individual performance – especially when team interdependence was high. Their research also makes an important contribution in developing an integrative multilevel model of leadership, empowerment, and performance.

Thus, there is clear evidence that core elements of social-structural empowerment are associated with psychological empowerment – and that both in turn are related to performance, whether at the individual, team, or unit level. Interestingly, in many of the studies, psychological empowerment is modeled as a mediator between social-structural empowerment and key individual or organizational outcomes (Morgeson and Campion, 2003). Psychological empowerment is conceptualized as a key mechanism that explains how social-structural empowerment contributes to improved satisfaction, performance and the range of other outcomes examined. What is perhaps most surprising is the consistency in findings across a wide variety of studies with very different operationalizations of social-structural empowerment – psychological empowerment has been found to be a significant mediator time and time again.

KEY DEBATES REGARDING EMPOWERMENT

As research on empowerment at work has blossomed, a number of debates, controversies and questions have emerged. These are indicative of the deep discourse in the field about what empowerment means and why it matters. Each is outlined below.

Where is the power in empowerment?

Critical and postmodern empowerment scholars often argue that empowerment is a ruse the managers use to get more out of their employees without increasing wages or real power. They argue that without formal power structures of direct worker ownership (like ESOPs) and representation (like labor councils and worker cooperatives in Europe), most empowerment interventions are, in fact, disempowering to employees because power remains centralized at the top echelons of the organization (Boje and Rosalie, 2001; Wendt, 2001). All too often, discussions of power are conspicuously absent in the discourse on empowerment (Hardy and Leiba-O'Sullivan, 1998; Jacques, 1996).

Critical theorists recognize how programs espousing empowerment often create more controls over employees through peer monitoring. For example, Barker (1993) found that an intervention focused on empowering employees through self-managing work teams, resulted in extensive peer pressure, which left employees feeling even more controlled and disempowered.

While empowerment may have had its roots in real power from its genesis in the civil and women's rights movements, Lincoln et al. (2002) argue that empowerment is a 'term with a radical left-wing lineage which has been transformed into right-wing management discourse' (pp. 272–273). Indeed, in a longitudinal analysis of empowerment across a variety of disciplines over the last 25 years, Bartunek and Spreitzer (2006) found that as the meaning of the term empowerment has evolved over time, it

has focused more attention on issues of fostering productivity and less on enabling human or societal welfare. Real empowerment, according to critical theorists, comes from real ownership and control of the firm (O'Connor, 2001) – something most organizations in the developed world are far from implementing.

Is the potency in empowerment in the gestalt or the individual dimensions?

Reviewing the literature, most of the research on psychological empowerment modeled empowerment as an overall construct composed of the four dimensions. The idea here is that empowerment is the gestalt of the four dimensions. The essence of empowerment is the interplay between the four dimensions rather than just the independent effects of each dimension.

Yet, some studies have modeled empowerment as four separate dimensions (e.g., Ergeneli, et al., 2007; Kraimer et al., 1999; Moye, et al., 2004; Spreitzer, et al., 1997). These studies help specify more of the mechanisms underlying the relationships of interest. They indicate how different dimensions of empowerment are predicted by different antecedents and predict different outcomes. In terms of antecedents, Ergeneli et al. (2007) found that cognition-based trust of immediate managers relates to the meaning and competence dimensions of empowerment while affect-based trust related to the impact dimension. In terms of outcomes, Spreitzer et al. (1997) found that while impact was related to work effectiveness, meaning and competence were related to increased satisfaction and reduced strain. Future research can help elucidate how the interaction of the four dimensions enables the gestalt of empowerment.

The dark side of empowerment

Empowerment represents a kind of moral hazard for managers (Pfeffer et al., 1998). Empowerment depends on the ability of the manager to reconcile the potential loss of control inherent in sharing power with the need to empower employees for higher levels of motivation and productivity that often come with empowerment (Mills and Ungson, 2003). To reduce the risk of the moral hazard, managers and organizations can:

(1) set clear limits and boundaries as to what level of empowerment is appropriate so employees know what is acceptable (Blanchard et al., 2001; Seibert et al., 2004);
(2) build trusting relationships in which employees are less likely to operate on self-interest (Mishra et al., 1997); and
(3) measure and reward key performance goals to ensure that individual and organizational goals are aligned (Spreitzer and Mishra, 1997).

Moreover, while most research has found positive outcomes of empowerment at work, other research has found some trade-offs regarding empowerment. For example, Spreitzer et al. (1997) found that those who reported more of the meaning dimension in their work also reported more strain. They speculated that those who felt a closer connection to their work took it more seriously and thus experienced more stress in their jobs.

It may also be that employees who are too empowered become disempowered over time because their bosses are threatened by their empowerment (Spreitzer and Quinn, 1996). Their bosses may worry about 'loose cannons' who are not aligned with the needs of the organization and take too many risks. Managers often act in risk-averse ways that work against more democratic work practices such as empowerment (O'Toole and Lawler, 2006).

EMERGING RESEARCH AGENDA

Directionality of empowerment relationships?

The findings discussed above focus on how social-structural empowerment enables psychological empowerment, which in turn is related to key outcomes. Yet, the directionality of the relationships between empowerment and performance may also go the other way. Understanding the possibility of reverse causality can be a fruitful area of research because it can help to uncover the deviation-amplifying and temporal dynamics of empowerment at work. For example, when they are performing well, employees may be given more autonomy, and even idiosyncrasy credits to take initiative beyond that accorded by their formal authority (e.g., Hollander, 1958). Idiosyncrasy credits are earned from one's boss by showing competence in helping to achieve the units' task goals and commitment to the units' norms. Those credits may then be drawn upon to take more innovative actions. Signs of competence and commitment enable initiative and nonconformity to be better tolerated. Thus, leaders of higher performing employees may give those employees more latitude and voice in how they do their work (i.e., create more social-structural empowerment) which enables more psychological empowerment. Said differently, better performance may lead to more social-structural empowerment which, in turn, contributes to more psychological empowerment.

In addition, until now most research has posited and found support for how social-structural empowerment enables psychological empowerment. However, employees who experience psychological empowerment may also enable more social-structural empowerment through their actions. Empowered employees may seek out and shape their work contexts to further enable their empowerment. To date, we don't know much about this relationship but the evidence that empowered employees behave in more transformational ways (Spreitzer and Quinn, 1996) suggests this may be a fertile direction for future research. Researchers might draw on recent research on job crafting (Wrzesniewski and Dutton, 2001) to show how self-determination can lead workers to define their work in new ways.

One recent study offers some insight into how individuals may enable their own empowerment. It focuses on the role of reflection in sustaining psychological empowerment, particularly during difficult times (Cyboran, 2005). Using an experimental design with a control group, this study had knowledge workers in a software company keep guided journals of their learning activities for three months. The findings suggest that reflection through guided journaling helped sustain employees' feelings of empowerment during difficult transitions in the company.

Dispositions at play?

With one exception, namely Spreitzer's (1995) study showing that high self-esteem individuals were more like to feel psychologically empowered, there has been very little research that has examined how dispositions influence empowerment. Dispositions may either predict or moderate empowerment. Proactive personality (Bateman and Crant, 1993) is the stable tendency to effect environmental change through one's actions. Because empowerment is defined as a more active orientation with respect to one's work, proactive personality may predict who feels more empowered in a given situation. A more proactive personality leads to more personal initiative (Frese and Fay, 2001) and proactivity (Grant and Ashford, in press). Empowerment may be an important mediator for how and why a proactive personality manifests in more personal initiative and proactivity.

Dispositions can also play the role of moderators in empowerment research. Growth-need-strength (Hackman and Oldham, 1980) is defined as the preference for stimulating and challenging work, which has some similarity to a promotion-regulatory focus. People with a promotion-regulatory focus are 'motivated by growth and development needs in which they attempt to bring their actual selves in alignment with their ideal selves' (Brockner and Higgins, 2001). It can be contrasted with a prevention focus where people are more security focused. Those with a higher promotion focus and with a higher growth-need-strength may be more likely to seek out opportunities for empowerment at work. Future research can also examine the Big 5 personality variables in relation to empowerment. For example, those who are conscientious may have a greater sense of the competence dimension because they bring order to situations with ambiguity. Those who are open to experience may see more of the impact of what they do because they find ways to learn from their experiences. Those who are neurotic may experience less empowerment because they are threatened by even ordinary situations. Neurotic individuals may miss opportunities to see the meaning in their work and may see themselves as more incompetent than competent. In summary, these Big 5 dimensions may be moderators describing who is likely to experience psychological empowerment amidst social-structural empowerment conditions.

Culture as a boundary condition?

While empowerment research has looked within different cultures (e.g., China, Israel and the Philippines) to demonstrate the validity of the four dimensions and pieces of the nomological network, only limited research has looked across cultural boundaries. One initial step would be to look in depth at the meaning of the four dimensions within a culture outside the US. A good model of this kind of research would be the qualitative work by Farh et al. (1997) who found that only three of the five dimensions of organizational citizenship were valid in a Chinese culture: courtesy and sportsmanship were two dimensions that had a very different meaning within this culture. It may be that a dimension like impact looks very different in a collectivist culture where groups are more important. In collectivistic cultures, the impact dimensions may have more of a group referent than an individual referent. Similarly, the self-determination dimension may look different in a culture with a high power-distance. In high power-distance cultures, it may be culturally inappropriate for employees at low levels of an organizational hierarchy to have a significant say in their work.

In addition, cultural values may also be a moderator on how people experience social-structural empowerment. For example, Seibert et al. (2004) suggest that individuals from a high power distance or uncertainty avoidance cultures may react to an empowering climate with feelings of stress and withdrawal. In this vein, Robert et al. (2000) found that empowering leadership was negatively related to job satisfaction in India (a high power distance culture) while empowering leadership was positively related to job satisfaction in the US (low power distance), Mexico (moderate power distance), and Poland (moderate power distance). And in a study of work teams in Belgium, Finland, the Philippines, and the US, Kirkman and Shapiro (2001) found that teams with higher collectivism and a more 'doing-orientation' reported more empowerment.

Culture may also moderate the effectiveness of employee empowerment (Eylon and Eu, 1999). It may be that employees with high levels of self-determination and impact are perceived as threatening to bosses in high-power distance cultures and thus not viewed as high performers. Clearly, future research on the cultural boundaries of empowerment can contribute to the body of knowledge on empowerment.

A broader range of outcomes associated with empowerment

Thus far, most research on the impact of empowerment has examined organizational performance and individual attitudes, behaviors, and performance. My hope is that future research will explore a broader range of impacts including societal and health outcomes.

Societal

Some recent research gives us some clues about the societal affects of empowerment. Feldman and Khademian (2003: 358) take a cross-level approach in examining how organizational empowerment can create 'dynamic potential in the relationship between the individual, organization and community.'

They show how more empowerment can create positive spirals that rejuvenate and enliven communities to action. Spreitzer (2007) also examines an interesting society outcome – peace. In a country-level analyses, she demonstrates how countries that embrace empowering organizational leadership have less social unrest and lower levels of corruption. She asserts when employees develop skills to have voice at work they are also likely to exercise that voice in civic and political domains, which in turn contributes to a more democratic and peaceful society.

Health

With health care costs escalating, organizations are increasingly interested in the health implications of work. To date, there is little direct research linking psychological empowerment and health. A substantial body of research has linked lack of control at work (e.g., job insecurity, low decision latitude) with health problems including exhaustion, depression, anxiety, and cardiovascular disease (Karasek, 1979; Kuper and Marmot, 2003). But what about the other dimensions of empowerment? Recent research with call center employees in the UK found that psychological empowerment (especially the meaning, self-determination, and impact dimensions) had a small direct effect on mental and physical health but an even bigger indirect effect through enhanced job satisfaction (Holdsworth and Cartwright, 2003).

Most of the research above has investigated how a lack of empowerment can impair health. Future research might focus more on the converse – that is, how can empowerment nurture and sustain positive health? There are emerging clues as to how psychological empowerment may enable positive health outcomes. For example, Turner et al. (2002) suggest that healthy work is enabled by work designs that engage employees. Keyes et al. (2001) suggest that positive health outcomes result from leadership that involves and respects employees. Future research can look at how empowerment may be related to indicators that capture notions of positive health, like flourishing and thriving (Spreitzer et al., 2005).

Empowerment may also enable individuals to be resilient in the face of difficulty or threat (Fredrickson et al., 2003). Empowerment may be a resource that buffers individuals and helps them to bounce back from extraordinary physical and financial devastation and loss of human life (Sutcliffe and Vogus, 2003). Through empowerment, individuals experience the purpose and efficacy to allow them to persevere. Empowerment can facilitate a sense of real hope that things will get better in the future (Spreitzer and Mishra, 2000). For these reasons we believe that the links between empowerment and resilience may also provide fertile ground for future research.

CONCLUSION

The last two decades have brought a substantial body of new research in understanding empowerment at work. The biggest contribution has been more integration of the social-structural and psychological perspectives on empowerment. That integration highlights that need to further develop a more comprehensive theory of empowerment at work. Thus far, we have many of the pieces of this theoretical puzzle but a theory would articulate how the pieces fit together into a whole. A theory would specify more than definitions, measures, and the antecedents and consequences of empowerment. It would identify the mechanisms and processes of empowerment, and specify the individual and organizational boundary conditions of when and under what conditions empowerment has potency. We have come a long way over the last two decades, but there is still work to be done in integrating the current knowledge base toward a more holistic theory of empowerment at work.

ACKNOWLEDGEMENTS

I would like to thank editor Julian Barling as well as Peter Bamberger, Jane Dutton, Dafna Eylon, Brad Kirkman and Ben Rosen for their insights on an earlier draft of this article.

NOTE

1 This review of empowerment builds on two earlier reviews: (1) Empowerment at work, forthcoming in the *Encyclopedia of Industrial/Organizational Psychology*, Sage Publications and (2) Musings on the Past and Future of Empowerment, Forthcoming, *Handbook of Organizational Development*, Sage Publications.

REFERENCES

Arnold, J.A., Arad, S., Rhoades, J.A., and Drasgow, F. (2000) 'The empowering leadership questionnaire: The construction and validation of new scale for measuring leader behaviors', *Journal of Organizational Behavior*, 21 (3): 249–269.

Aryee, S. and Chen, Z.X. (2006) 'Leader–member exchange in a Chinese context: Antecedents, the mediating role of psychological empowerment and outcomes', *Journal of Business Research*, 59 (7): 793–801.

Ashforth, B.E. (1989) 'The experience of powerlessness in organizations', *Organizational Behavior and Human Decision Processes*, 43 (2): 207–242.

Avolio, B.J., Zhu, W., Koh, W. and Bhatia, P. (2004) 'Transformational leadership and organizational commitment: Mediating role of psychological empowerment and moderating role of structural distance', *Journal of Organizational Behavior*, 25 (8): 951–968.

Bandura, A. (1989) 'Human agency in social cognitive theory', *American Psychologist*, September: 1175–84.

Barker, J.A. (1993) 'Tightening the iron cage: Concertive control in self–managing teams', *Administrative Science Quarterly*, 38 (3): 408–437.

Bartunek, J.M. and Spreitzer, G.M. (2006) 'The interdisciplinary career of a popular construct used in management: Empowerment in the late 20th century', *Journal of Management Inquiry*, 15 (3): 255–273.

Bateman, T.S. and Crant, J.M. (1993) 'The proactive component of organizational behavior', *Journal of Organizational Behavior*, 14 (2): 103–118.

Bell, N.E. and Staw, B.M. (1989) 'People as sculptors versus sculpture', in M.B. Arthur, D.T. Hall, and B.S. Lawrence (eds), *Handbook of Career Theory*. New York: Cambridge University Press.

Blanchard, K., Carlos, J. and Randolph, A. (2001) *Three Keys to Empowerment*. San Francisco: Berrett–Koehler.

Boje, D.M. and Rosalie, G.A. (2001) 'Where's the power in empowerment? Answers from Follett and Clegg', *Journal of Applied Behavioral Science*, 37 (1): 90–117.

Boudarias, J.S., Gaudreau, P. and Laschinger, H.K.S. (2004) 'Testing the structure of psychological empowerment: Does gender make a difference?', *Educational and Psychological Measurement*, 64 (5): 861–877.

Bowen, D.E. and Lawler, E.E. (1995) 'Empowering service employees', *Sloan Management Review*, 36 (4): 73–85.

Brockner, J., Spreitzer, G., Mishra, A., Pepper, L. and Hochwarter, W. (2004) 'Perceived Control as an Antidote to the Negative Effects of Layoffs on Survivors' Organizational Commitment and Job Performance', *Administrative Science Quarterly*, 49 (1): 76–100.

Brockner, J. and Higgins, E.T. (2001) 'Regulatory focus theory: Implications for the study of emotions at work', *Organization Behavior and Human Decision Processes*, 86 (1): 35–66.

Burpitt, W.J. and Bigoness, W.J. (1997) 'Leadership and innovation among teams: The impact of empowerment', *Small Group Research*, 28 (3): 414–423.

Cappelli, P. and Neumark, D. (2001) 'Do high–performance: Work practice improve establishment–level outcomes?', *Industrial and Labor Relations Review*, 54 (4): 737–752.

Carless, S.A. (2004) 'Does psychological empowerment mediate the relationship between psychological climate and job satisfaction', *Journal of Business and Psychology*, 18 (4): 405–425.

Chen, G. and Klimoski, R.J. (2003) 'The impact of expectations on newcomer performance in teams as mediated by work characteristics, social exchanges, and empowerment', *Academy of Management Journal*, 46 (5): 591–607.

Chen, G., Kirkman, B.L., Kanfer, R., Allen, D. and Rosen, B. (2007) 'A multilevel study of leadership, empowerment, and performance in teams', *Journal of Applied Psychology*, 92 (2): 331–346.

Cohen, S.G. and Bailey, D.E. (1997) 'What makes teams work: Group effectiveness research form the shop floor to the executive suite', *Journal of Management*: 23 (3): 239–290.

Conger, J.A. and Kanungo, R.N. (1988) 'The empowerment process: Integrating theory and practice', *Academy of Management Review*, 13 (3): 471–482.

Corsun, D.L. and Enz, C.A. (1999) 'Predicting psychological empowerment among service workers: The effect of support–based relationships', *Human Relations*, 52 (2): 205–225.

Cyboran, V.L. (2005) 'The influence of reflection on employee psychological empowerment: Report of an exploratory workplace field study', *Performance Improvement Quarterly*, 18 (4): 37–50.

Deci, E.L., Connell, J.P. and Ryan, R.M. (1989) 'Self–determination in a work organization', *Journal of Applied Psychology*, 74 (3): 580–590.

Ergeneli, A., Sag, G., Ari, I. and Metin, S. (2007) 'Psychological empowerment and its relationship to trust in immediate managers', *Journal of Business Research*, 60 (1): 41–56.

Eylon, D. (1998) 'Understanding empowerment and resolving its paradox: Lessons from Mary Parker Follett', *Journal of Management History*, 4 (1): 16–28.

Eylon, D. and Au, E.Y. (1999) 'Exploring empowerment cross–cultural differences along the power distance dimension', *International Journal of Intercultural Relations*, 23 (3): 373–385.

Eylon, D. and Bamberger, P. (2000) 'Empowerment cognitions and empowerment acts: Recognizing the importance of gender', *Group and Organization Management*, 25 (4): 354–372.

Fahr, J.L., Earley, P.C. and Lin, S.C. (1997) 'Impetus for action', *Administrative Science Quarterly*, 42 (3): 421–444.

Feldman, M. and Khademian, A. (2003) 'Empowerment and cascading vitality', in K. Cameron and J. Dutton and R.E. Quinn (eds), *Positive Organizational Scholarship*. San Francisco: Jossey–Bass, pp. 343–358.

Fletcher, J.K. (1998) 'Relational practice: A feminist reconstruction of work', *Journal of Management Inquiry*, 7 (2): 163–186.

Fredrickson, B.L., Tugade, M.M., Waugh, C.E. and Larkin, G.R. (2003) 'What good are positive emotions in crises? A prospective study of resilience and emotions following the terrorist attacks on the U.S. on September 11, 2001', *Journal of Personality and Social Psychology*, 84 (2): 365–376.

Frese, M. and Fay, D. (2001) 'Personal initiative: An active performance concept for work in the 21st century', in B.M. Staw and R.I. Sutton (eds), *Research in Organizational Behavior*. New York: Elsevier. Vol. 23, pp. 133–187.

Fuller, J.B., Morrison, R., Jones, L., Bridger, D. and Brown, V. (1999) 'The effects of psychological empowerment on transformational leadership and job satisfaction', *The Journal of Social Psychology*, 139 (3): 389–391.

Gibson, C., Porath, C.L., Benson, G. and Lawler III, E.E. (2007) 'What Results When firms Implement Practices: The Differential Relationship Between Specific Firm Practices, Firm Financial Performance, Customer Service, and Quality', *Journal of Applied Psychology*, 92 (6): 1467–1480.

Gist, M. (1987) 'Self–efficacy: Implications for organizational behavior and human resource management', *Academy of Management Review*, 12 (3): 472–485.

Grant, A. and Ashford, S. (in press) 'The Dynamics of Proactivity at Work', *Research in Organizational Behavior*.

Guthrie, J. (2001) 'High–involvement work practices, turnover, and productivity: Evidence from New Zealand', *Academy of Management Journal*, 44 (1): 180–192.

Hackman, J.R. and Oldham, G.R. (1980) *Work Redesign.* Reading, MA: Addison–Wesley.

Hardy, C. and Leiba–O'Sullivan, S. (1998) 'The power behind empowerment: Implications for research and practice', *Human Relations*, 51 (4): 451–483.

Hechanova, M., Alampay, R. and Franco, E. (2006) 'Psychological empowerment, job satisfaction, and performance among Filipino service workers', *Asian Journal of Social Psychology*, 9 (2): 92–78.

Holdsworth, L. and Cartwright, S. (2003) 'Empowerment, stress, and satisfaction: An exploratory study of a call centre', *Leadership and Organization Development Journal*, 24 (3): 131–140.

Hollander, E.P. (1958) 'Conformity, status, and idiosyncrasy credit', *Psychological Review*, 65 (2): 117–127

Huselid, M. (1995) 'The impact of human resource management practices on turnover, productivity, and corporate performance', *Academy of Management Journal*, 38 (3): 635–672.

Huselid, M. and Becker, B. (1996) 'Methodological issues in cross–sectional and panel estimates of the human resource–firm performance link', *Industrial Relations*, 35 (3): 400–422.

Jacques, R. (1996) *Manufacturing the Employee: Management Knowledge from the 9th to the 21st Centuries.* London: Sage.

Kanter, R.M. (1977) *Men and Women of the Corporation.* New York: Basic Books.

Karasek, R.A. (1979) 'Job demands, job decision latitude, and mental strain: Implications for job redesign', *Admin Science Quarterly*, 24 (2): 285–307.

Kark, R., Shamir, B. and Chen, G. (2003) 'The two faces of transformational leadership: Empowerment and dependency', *Journal of Applied Psychology*, 88 (2): 246–255.

Keller, T. and Dansereau, F. (1995) 'Leadership and empowerment: A social exchange perspective', *Human Relations*, 48 (2): 127–146.

Keyes, C.L.M., Hysom, S.J. and Lupo, K.L. (2001) 'The positive organization: Leadership legitimacy, employee well–being, and the bottom line', *The Psychologist-Manager Journal*, 4 (2): 143–153.

Kirkman, B. and Rosen, B. (1999) 'Beyond self–management: The antecedents and consequences of team empowerment', *Academy of Management Journal*, 42 (1): 58–71.

Kirkman, B.L. Rosen, B., Tesluk, P.E. and Gibson, C.B. (2004) 'The impact of team empowerment on virtual team performance: The moderating role of face-to-face interaction', *Academy of Management Journal*, 47 (2): 175–192.

Kirkman, B.L. and Shapiro, D.L. (2001) 'The impact of team members' cultural values on productivity, cooperation, and empowerment in self-managing work teams', *Journal of Cross-Cultural Psychology*, 32 (5): 597–617.

Kirkman, B.L., Tesluk, P.E. and Rosen, B. (2004) 'The impact of demographic heterogeneity and team leader–team member demographic fit on team empowerment and effectiveness', *Group and Organization Management*, 29 (3): 334–368.

Koberg, C.S., Boss, W., Senjem, J.C. and Goodman, E.A. (1999) 'Antecedents and outcomes of empowerment: Empirical evidence from the health care industry', *Group and Organization Management*, 34 (1): 71–91.

Kraimer, M.L., Seibert, S.E. and Liden, R.C. (1999) 'Psychological empowerment as a multidimensional construct: A test of construct validity', *Educational and Psychological Measurement*, 59 (4): 127–142.

Kuper, H. and Marmot, M. (2003) 'Job strain, job demands, decision latitude, and risk of coronary heart disease within the Whitehall II study', *Journal of Epidemiology and Community Health*, 57 (2), 147–153.

Laschinger, H.K.S., Finegan, J.E., Shamian, J. and Wilk, P. (2004) 'A longitudinal analysis of the impact of workplace empowerment on work satisfaction', *Journal of Organizational Behaviors*, 24 (1): 527–545.

Lawler, E.E. (1986) *High Involvement Management.* San Francisco: Jossey-Bass.

Lawler, E.E. (1996) *From the Ground Up: Six Principles for Building the New Logic Corporation.* San Francisco: Jossey-Bass.

Lawler, E.E., Mohrman, S.A. and Benson, G. (2001) *Organizing for High Performance: Employee Involvement, TQM, Reengineering, and Knowledge Management in the Fortune 1000.* San Francisco: Jossey-Bass.

Liden, R.C. and Arad, S. (1996) 'A power perspective of empowerment and work groups: Implication for HRM research', in G.R. Ferris (ed), *Research in Personnel and HRM.* Greenwich, CT: JAI Press. Vol. 14, pp. 205–252.

Liden, R.C., Wayne, S.J. and Sparrow, R.T. (2000) 'An examination of the mediating role of psychological empowerment on the relations between the job, interpersonal relationships, and work outcomes', *Journal of Applied Psychology*, 85 (3): 407–416.

Lincoln, N.D., Travers, C., Ackers, P. and Wilkinson, A. (2002) 'The meaning of empowerment: The interdisciplinary etymology of a new management concept', *International Journal of Management Reviews*, 4 (4): 471–290.

MacDuffie, J.P. (1995) 'Human resource bundles and manufacturing performance: Organizational logic and flexible production systems in the world auto industry', *Industrial and Labor Relations Review*, 48 (2): 197–221.

Manz, C.C. and Sims, H.P. (1987) 'Leading workers to lead themselves: The external leadership of self-managed work teams', *Administrative Science Quarterly*, 32 (1): 106–128.

Mathieu, J.E., Gilson, L.L. and Ruddy, T.M. (2006) 'Empowerment and team effectiveness: An empirical test of an integrated model', *Journal of Applied Psychology*, 91 (1): 97–108.

Mills, P.K. and Ungson, G.R. (2003) 'Reassessing the limits of structural empowerment: Organizational constitution and trust as controls', *Academy of Management Review*, 28 (1): 143–153.

Mishra, K., Mishra, A. and Spreitzer, G. (1998) 'Preserving employee morale during downsizing', *Sloan Management Review*, 39 (2): 83–95.

Mishra, A.K. and Spreitzer, G.M. (1998) 'Explaining how survivors respond to downsizing: The roles of trust, empowerment, justice, and work redesign', *Academy of Management Review*, 23 (3): 567–588.

Morgeson, F.P. and Campion, M.A. (2003) 'Work design', in W.C. Borman, D.R. Ilgen, and R.J. Klimoski (eds), *Handbook of Psychology: Industrial and Organizational Psychology*. Hoboken, NJ: John Wiley and Sons. Vol. 12, pp. 423–452.

Moye, M.J., Henkin, A.B. and Egley, R.J. (2004) 'Teacher–principal relationships: Exploring linkages between empowerment and interpersonal trust', *Journal of Educational Administration*, 43 (3): 260–277.

O'Connor, E. (2001) 'Back on the way to empowerment: The example of Ordway Tead and industrial democracy', *Journal of Applied Behavioral Science*, 37 (1): 15–32.

O'Toole, J. and Lawler, E.E. (2006) *The New American Workplace*. New York: Palgrave-Macmillan.

Pfeffer, J. (1996) *Competitive Advantage Through People*. Boston: Harvard University Press.

Pfeffer, J., Cialdini, R.B., Hanna, B. and Knopoff, K. (1998) 'Faith in supervision and the self–enhancement bias: Two psychological reasons why managers don't empower workers', *Basic and Applied Social Psychology*, 20 (4): 313–321.

Prasad, A. (2001) 'Understanding workplace empowerment as inclusion: A historical investigation of the discourse of difference in the United States', *Journal of Applied Behavioral Science*, 37 (1): 51–59.

Prasad, A. and Eylon, D. (2001) 'Narrative past traditions of participation and inclusion: Historic perspectives on workplace empowerment', *Journal of Applied Behavioral Science*, 37 (1): 5–14.

Quinn, R.E. and Spreitzer, G.M. (1997) 'The road to empowerment: Seven questions every leader should consider', *Organizational Dynamics*, Autumn, 26 (2): 37–51.

Robert, C., Probst, T.M., Martocchio, J.J., Drasgow, F. and Lawler, J.J. (2000) 'Empowerment and continuous improvement in the U.S., Mexico, Poland, and India: Predicting fit on the basis of the dimensions of power distance and individualism', *Journal of Applied Psychology*, 85 (5): 643–658.

Seibert, S.E., Silver, S.R. and Randolph, W.A. (2004) 'Taking empowerment to the next level: A multiple–level model of empowerment, performance and satisfaction', *Academy of Management Journal*, 47 (3): 332–349.

Siu, H.M., Laschinger, H.K.S. and Vingilis, E. (2005) 'The effect of problem-based learning on nursing students' perceptions of empowerment', *Journal of Nursing Education*, 44 (10): 459–470.

Sparrowe, R.T. (1994) 'Empowerment in the hospitality industry: An exploration of antecedents and outcomes', *Hospitality Research Journal*, 17 (3): 51–73.

Spreitzer, G.M. (2007) 'Participative Organizational Leadership, Empowerment, and Sustainable Peace', *Journal of Organizational Behavior*, 28 (8): 1077–1096.

Spreitzer, G.M. (2006) 'Empowerment', in S. Rogelberg (ed), *Encyclopedia of Industrial and Organizational Psychology*. Thousand Oaks, CA: Sage Publications.

Spreitzer, G.M. (1995) 'Psychological empowerment in the workplace: Dimensions, measurement, and validation', *Academy of Management Journal*, 38 (5): 1442–1465.

Spreitzer, G.M. (1996) 'Social structural characteristics of psychological empowerment', *Academy of Management Journal*, 39 (2): 483–504.

Spreitzer, G.M. (1997) 'Toward common ground in defining empowerment', in R.W. Woodman and W.A. Pasmore (eds), *Research in Organizational Change and Development*. Greenwich, CT: JAI Press.

Spreitzer, G.M., De Janesz, S., and Quinn, R.E. (1999a) 'Empowered to lead: The role of psychological empowerment in leadership', *Journal of Organizational Behavior*, 20 (4): 511–526.

Spreitzer, G.M., Noble, D.S., Mishra, A.K. and Cooke, W.N. (1999b) 'Predicting process improvement team performance in an automotive firm: Explicating the roles of trust and empowerment', in E. Mannix and M. Neale (eds), *Research on Managing Groups and Teams*. Greenwich, CT: JAI Press. Vol 2, pp. 71–92.

Spreitzer, G.M. and Mishra, A.K. (1997) 'Giving up control without losing control: Trust and its substitutes' effects on managers' involving employees in decision making', *Group and Organization Management*, 24 (2): 155–187.

Spreitzer, G.M. and Mishra, A. (2000) 'An empirical examination of a stress-based framework of survivor responses to downsizing', in R.J. Burke and C. Cooper (eds), *The Organization in Crisis: Downsizing, Restructuring, and Privatization*. Oxford: Blackwell Publishers, pp. 97–118.

Spreitzer, G.M., Kizilos, M.A. and Nason, S.W. (1997) 'A dimensional analysis of the relationship between psychological empowerment and effectiveness, satisfaction and strain', *Journal of Management*, 23 (5): 679–704.

Spreitzer, G.M. and Quinn, R.E. (2001) *A Company of Leaders: Five Disciplines for Unleashing the Power in your Workforce*. San Francisco, CA: Jossey-Bass.

Spreitzer, G. and Quinn, R.E. (1996) 'Empowering middle managers to be transformational leaders', *Journal of Applied Behavioral Science*, 32 (3): 237–261.

Spreitzer, G., Sutcliffe, K., Dutton, J., Sonenshein, S. and Grant, A. (2005) 'A socially embedded model of thriving at work', *Organization Science*, 16 (5): 537–549.

Srivastava, A., Bartol, K.M. and Locke, E.A. (2006) 'Empowering leadership in Management Teams: Effects on knowledge sharing, efficacy, and performance', *Academy of Management Journal*, 49 (6): 1239–1251.

Staw, B.M. and Epstein, L. (2000) 'What bandwagons bring: Effects of popular management techniques on corporate performance, reputation, and CEO pay', *Administrative Science Quarterly*, 45 (4): 523–559.

Sutcliffe, K. and Vogus, T. (2003) 'Organization Resilience', in K. Cameron and J. Dutton and R.E. Quinn (eds), *Positive Organizational Scholarship*. San Francisco: Berrett-Koehler.

Thomas, K.W. and Velthouse, B.A. (1990) 'Cognitive elements of empowerment', *Academy of Management Review*, 15 (4): 666–681.

Turner, N., Barling, J. and Zacharatos, A. (2002) 'Positive psychology at work', in C.R. Snyder and S.J. Lopez (eds), *Handbook of Positive Psychology*. New York: Oxford University Press, pp. 715–728.

Wallach, V.A., and Mueller, C.W. (2006) 'Job characteristics and organizational predictors of psychological empowerment among paraprofessionals within human service organizations: An exploratory study', *Administration in Social Work*, 30 (1): 95–115.

Walsh, K., Bartunek, J.M. and Lacey, C.A. (1998) 'A relational approach to empowerment', in C. Cooper and D. Rousseau (eds), *Trends in Organizational Behavior*. New York: Wiley.

Wat, D. and Shaffer, M.A. (2005) 'Equity and relationship quality influences on organizational citizenship behaviors: The mediating role of trust in the supervisor and empowerment', *Personnel Review*, 34 (4): 406–422.

Wendt, R.F. (2001) *The Paradox of Empowerment: Suspended Power and the Possibility of Resistance*. Westport, CT: Praeger

Wright, P.M., Gardner, T.M. and Moynihan, L.M. (2003) 'The impact of HR practices on the performance of business units', *Human Resource Management Journal*, 13 (1): 21–36.

Wrzesniewski, A. and Dutton, J. (2001) 'Crafting a job: Revisioning employees as active crafters of their work', *Academy of Management Review*, 26 (2): 179–201.

4

Two Decades of Organizational Justice: Findings, Controversies, and Future Directions

Jason A. Colquitt

Research on organizational justice focuses on how individuals gauge the fairness of their working lives and how those judgments impact their attitudes and behaviors. The modern inception of the 'organizational justice literature' can be traced to Greenberg's (1987) *Academy of Management Review* article that presented a taxonomy integrating previously distinct streams of research in the social psychology, industrial and organizational psychology, and organizational behavior literatures. Unlike terms like organizational commitment or organizational identification, 'organizational justice' is viewed more as an umbrella term than an actual construct, serving to unite a number of fairness relevant concepts. Moreover, 'organizational justice' is examined in the laboratory as often as the field – all that is required is a task-focused environment that can make fairness issues salient to individuals.

In the twenty years since Greenberg (1987) coined the term 'organizational justice,' research on justice has grown dramatically. As shown in Figure 1, four articles were published in the top ten organizational behavior journals in 1987 using 'justice' or 'fairness' as keywords. By 2001, that number had grown to 57, with the most recent year containing 52 such articles. This chapter provides an overview of the terrain carved out by the past two decades of research on organizational justice. A more extensive history of the justice domain can be found in Colquitt et al. (2005), who traced the literature back to Stouffer et al.'s (1949) research on relative deprivation. The present review will concentrate on three primary questions: (a) what constructs are included under the 'organizational justice' heading? (b) when are concerns about fairness particularly salient? and (c) how do judgments of fairness impact work attitudes and behaviors? The chapter will then close by focusing on key controversies and debates that characterize current and future research on organizational justice.

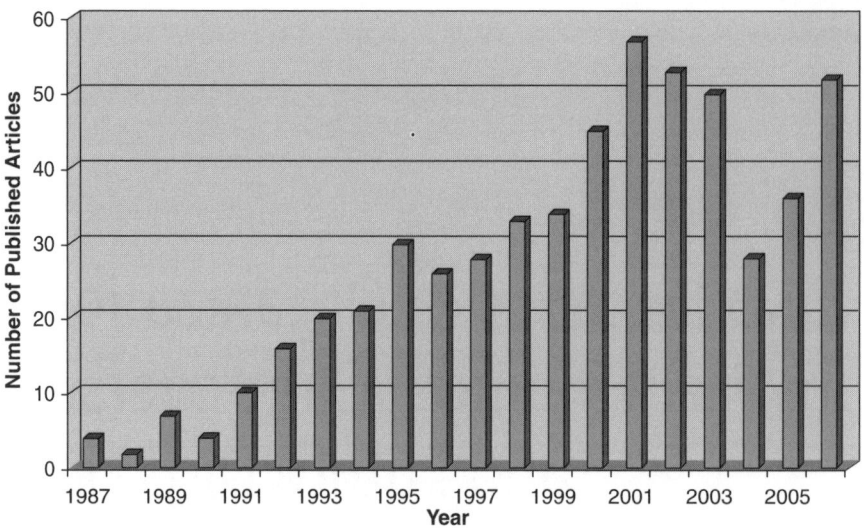

Figure 1   Number of published articles in the top ten organizational behavior journals with 'justice' or 'fairness' as keywords. The journal rankings were based on Podsakoff et al. (2005) and include *Administrative Science Quarterly, Academy of Management Review, Academy of Management Journal, Journal of Applied Psychology, Personnel Psychology, Organizational Behavior and Human Decision Processes, Journal of Vocational Behavior, Journal of Management, Journal of Occupational and Organizational Psychology,* and *Journal of Organizational Behavior.*

WHAT CONSTRUCTS ARE INCLUDED UNDER THE ORGANIZATIONAL JUSTICE HEADING?

The organizational justice umbrella includes a number of dimensions, many of which subsume more specific concepts. At a general level, however, all of the concepts can be viewed as capturing how an authority acts in a particular decision-making context. In some cases those actions refer to the decision itself, in some cases those actions reflect the process that led to that decision, and in other cases those actions capture interpersonal interactions between the authority and the recipient of the decision.

Distributive justice

At the point that Greenberg (1987) introduced his taxonomy of organizational justice, many scholars viewed justice solely in terms of outcome distributions. Distributive justice reflects the perceived fairness of outcome allocations, typically judged by comparing one's outcomes or rewards to one's inputs or investments (Adams, 1965; Homans, 1961; Leventhal, 1976). The dominant theory of distributive justice is equity theory, which argues that individuals compare their outcome/input ratio to that of some relevant comparison other (for a review, see Mowday and Colwell, 2003). Any imbalance in ratios creates a sense of distress that motivates a restoring of outcome/input balance. For example, a sense of under-reward may trigger a reduction in inputs, whereas a sense of over-reward may trigger a re-evaluation of one's inputs or a shift in the comparison other. Although equity remains the dominant conceptualization of distributive justice, it should be noted that other allocation norms may be relevant in some situations. For example, concerns about group harmony or individual welfare may increase the usefulness of allocations based on equality or need (Deutsch, 1975; Leventhal, 1976).

Procedural justice

Thibaut and Walker's (1975) work on dispute resolution procedures brought the first significant expansion to the justice landscape. In a comparison of the legal procedures used in the US and Europe, Thibaut and Walker (1975) argued that the primary determinant of procedural justice – the perceived fairness of decision-making processes – was the distribution of control. More specifically, dispute resolution procedures were judged to be most fair when the disputants had significant control over the evidentiary process. Presumably such process control would be valued because it can act as an indirect means of attaining decision control – actual influence over the result of the dispute. Although Thibaut and Walker (1975) eventually equated procedural justice with process control, Leventhal (1980) expanded the construct to include a number of rules relevant in resource allocation contexts. Those rules included consistency across persons and time, bias suppression, accuracy of information, correctability, representativeness, and ethicality. Taken together, Thibaut and Walker's (1975) and Leventhal's (1980) work carved out a profile for procedural justice that remains largely unchanged to this day.

Of course, it remained an empirical question whether process control, consistency, bias suppression, and so forth actually captured the fairness-related concerns of individuals in actual organizations. A study by Greenberg (1986) provided initial support for the notion that those justice rules truly were relevant to fairness in organizations. Greenberg asked a sample of managers to picture performance evaluations that were especially fair and unfair, and to identify the important factors that contributed to that judgment. Research across three different samples resulted in seven concepts that overlapped considerably with Thibaut and Walker's (1975) and Leventhal's (1980) ideas, most notably process control, consistency, accuracy, and correctability.

The next step for justice scholars was to begin differentiating 'the new construct on the block' (procedural justice) from its more venerable cousin (distributive justice). In other words, was procedural justice truly distinct from distributive justice or were both part of a single unitary fairness construct? Folger and Konovsky (1989) examined this issue in a study of manufacturing employees facing pay raise decisions. The authors constructed a measure of the procedural justice of the pay raise process using the rules validated by Greenberg (1986). Their study also included a measure of distributive justice, reflecting the perceived fairness of the pay raise, along with several other job attitudes (satisfaction with the raise, trust in supervisor and organizational commitment). Their results confirmed that procedural justice explained incremental variance in trust and commitment once distributive justice was controlled, with distributive justice explaining incremental variance in satisfaction with the raise once procedural justice was controlled. The conceptual rationale for these findings was that procedural justice was a key predictor of system-referenced attitudes, whereas distributive justice was more relevant to outcome-referenced attitudes.

Interactional justice

Although the justice literature had now expanded to cover both outcome and process, Bies and Moag (1986) called attention to one remaining omission. The authors reasoned that most dispute resolution or resource allocation contexts involve the implementation of a procedure, an interaction between the authority and the subjects of that procedure, and an eventual outcome. Bies and Moag (1986) argued that the authority's behaviors during the interaction phase could also be gauged in justice terms. They conceptualized interactional justice as the perceived fairness of interpersonal communication, noting that it depends on the fulfilment of four additional justice rules: respect, propriety, truthfulness, and justification. Those four interactional rules were based in Bies's research on job candidates' assessments of fairness during a recruitment process (Bies and Moag, 1986).

This new expansion to the justice landscape triggered a series of studies in the late 1980s and early 1990s, that provided initial tests of the interactional justice construct. Two studies by Bies and Shapiro supported the importance of providing justifications for decision events, particularly in the case of some perceived wrong by an authority (Bies and Shapiro, 1987, 1988). A subsequent study by Greenberg (1990) supported the importance of both the justification and respect rules in a study of manufacturing plants reacting to a pay reduction. Three plants were included in the study: a) a control plant that received no reduction; b) a plant that received a sincere, respectful, and comprehensive justification for the reduction; and c) a plant that received a terse and somewhat impersonal justification. The results of the study revealed that the combination of high justification and high respect significantly reduced employee theft (and turnover) during the course of the pay cut.

The tripartite structure for organizational justice was expanded once more when Greenberg (1993) suggested that interactional justice actually consisted of two distinct facets. Interpersonal justice reflects the sensitivity and politeness aspects of interactional justice, effectively subsuming Bies and Moag's (1986) respect and propriety rules. Informational justice reflects the explanations aspect of interactional justice, effectively subsuming Bies and Moag's (1986) justification and truthfulness rules. A study by Colquitt (2001) provided some support for Greenberg's (1993) four-factor conceptualization. Colquitt (2001) created a measure of organizational justice by operationalizing the justice rules described by Thibaut and Walker (1975), Leventhal (1976; 1980), and Bies and Moag (1986). Confirmatory factor analyses on data from undergraduates and automotive parts manufacturing employees revealed that a four-dimensional structure fit the data better than three-factor or two-factor structures. A subsequent analysis of 16 independent samples again supported a four-factor structure

for Colquitt's (2001) measure (Colquitt and Shaw, 2005).

Separate research has shed further insights into the structure of justice. Rupp and Cropanzano (2002) introduced a 'multifoci' perspective on justice by demonstrating that the various justice rules could be rooted in both supervisory and organizational sources. This perspective contrasted with the typical justice study that referenced procedural justice to organizational policies and interactional justice to supervisory actions. Blader and Tyler (2003) described a similar model, noting that procedural and interactional justice could be either formal (i.e., organization-originating) or informal (i.e., supervisor-originating). For example, organizational practices can build the provision of process control into key decision-making procedures or supervisors can grant employees voice by virtue of their own leadership styles. Similarly, organizational practices can build the provision of explanations into decision-making through websites, newsletters, and voice-mail updates or supervisors can offer such information in an informal, face-to-face manner. Taken together, these streams of research have brought further clarification to the constructs included under the organizational justice heading. Table 1 summarizes those concepts.

WHEN ARE CONCERNS ABOUT FAIRNESS PARTICULARLY SALIENT?

Having described the kinds of concepts individuals consider when judging fairness, it is time to consider when those concepts are made the focus of one's attention. What is it that causes individuals to attend to fairness issues in the first place? This question has garnered the attention of organizational scholars from the very beginning of the justice literature (Lind and Tyler, 1988). Although a number of potential answers have been provided, most of them can be viewed as a specific example of one of the more recent suggestions – that fairness is used as a means of dealing with uncertainty. Individuals face

Table 1　Constructs included under organizational justice heading

	Supervisor-originating	Organization-originating
Distributive justice		• Equity • Equality • Need
Procedural justice		• Process control • Decision control • Consistency • Bias suppression • Accuracy • Correctability • Representativeness • Ethicality
Interactional justice		*Interpersonal Justice* • Respect • Propriety *Informational justice* • Justification • Truthfulness

Note: Sources for justice rules include Adams (1965), Leventhal (1976, 1980), Thibaut and Walker (1975), Bies and Moag (1986), and Greenberg (1993).

a number of uncertainties in their working lives, including the kinds of outcomes they will receive in exchange for their work, how long they will be able to keep their job, and whether their relationship with their boss will continue to be functional. Van den Bos (2001) examined the effects of such uncertainty on procedural justice effects in a laboratory context. Specifically, he manipulated the process control afforded during a decision-making task, and also manipulated the uncertainty experienced by participants by having some participants picture how it felt to be uncertain or not in control. The results of the study revealed that process control had a stronger effect on participants' reactions when uncertainty was made salient (see also Van den Bos and Miedema, 2000).

Building on these results, Van den Bos and Lind introduced 'uncertainty management theory', which acknowledges that individuals face a number of uncertainties in their organizational lives surrounding their work outcomes, their relationship with their supervisor and co-workers, the health of the organization, and their future security

(Lind and Van den Bos, 2002; Van den Bos and Lind, 2002). The authors argued that fairness judgments can fulfil a particular psychological function, in that they can either remove or mitigate the negative effects of uncertainty. Fairness removes uncertainty when the fulfilment of justice rules speaks directly to the source of the uncertainty, as when employees wonder about the motives of their supervisor. In contrast, fairness only mitigates uncertainty when the fulfilment of justice rules has no direct connection to the source of the uncertainty, as when employees wonder about job insecurities resulting from a poor economy. In such cases, fairness is valued because it helps individuals maintain a positive state of mind and helps them feel secure about at least some aspects of working life. Although uncertainty management theory deals with uncertainty at a very general level, other justice scholars have dealt with more specific forms of uncertainty.

Uncertainty about outcomes

One of the earliest explanations for the importance of procedural justice centered on uncertainty about outcomes. The instrumental model suggests that justice is valued because it provides a sense of control over one's long-term economic interests (Lind and Tyler, 1988). The existence of a fair authority or a fair organization suggests that a 'level playing field' exists that will protect outcomes over the long run, even if one particular outcome allocation is unfavorable or disappointing. This instrumental view is consistent with Thibaut and Walker's (1975) original theorizing, in that process control was deemed valuable because it helped disputants exert some influence over the outcome of the dispute resolution context. Some support for the instrumental view can be seen in research on the interaction of procedural justice and outcome favorability, which shows that procedural justice has even more impact when outcome favorability is low than when it is high (Brockner, 2002; Brockner and Wiesenfeld, 1996).

Uncertainty about status

Although the instrumental model undoubtedly explains some of the appeal of organizational justice, research by Tyler and colleagues suggests that it paints an incomplete picture. For example, Tyler et al. (1985) showed that process control was associated with fairness perceptions even when it did not result in decision control. The authors summarized this finding by noting that process control has a 'value expressive' component, where individuals appreciate the opportunity to have their views considered for its own sake. In a subsequent study, Tyler (1987) showed that process control explained more variance than decision control in fairness perceptions, evaluations of authorities, and support for authorities. These results provided further evidence that the value of process control goes beyond its ability to reduce uncertainty about outcomes.

Tyler and Lind (1992) introduced the relational model to explain these findings (see also Lind and Tyler, 1988). The relational model emphasizes the collective character of working life, arguing that employees are motivated to join groups and to care about their standing in those groups. Importantly, the relational model suggests that the fulfilment of justice rules signals to employees that they are valued by the groups to which they belong. Those signals therefore reduce employees' concerns about status. In support of this model, studies have shown that the fulfilment of justice rules is associated with felt respect from one's group and pride in group membership (Tyler et al., 1996). These findings suggest that concerns about fairness are made more salient when one's status in a group is in doubt.

Uncertainty about authority trustworthiness

An offshoot of the relational model, fairness heuristic theory, devoted further attention to the cooperative context in which employees work (Lind, 2001; Van den Bos et al., 2001). Rather than emphasizing status in those

groups, however, this theory emphasized the potential for exploitation that existed in those groups. Lind (2001) described the 'fundamental social dilemma' wherein an incentive exists to cooperate in order to receive the kinds of outcomes that are not attainable through solitary activity – an incentive that is mirrored by the risk of being exploited by the other parties to the cooperative endeavor. The key question asked by employees when faced with the fundamental social dilemma is one of trustworthiness – is the authority in charge of the collective trustworthy? Unfortunately, it is often difficult to accurately gauge the trustworthiness of authorities, which depends on some combination of the authority's integrity, benevolence, and ability (Mayer et al., 1995).

Fairness heuristic theory argues that individuals draw on justice-relevant information to navigate that fundamental social dilemma, with the information used as a substitute for trustworthiness data (Lind, 2001; Van den Bos et al., 2001). When justice rules are fulfilled, individuals are more likely to assume that authorities are trustworthy and that cooperation can be risked. Two laboratory studies by Van den Bos et al. (1998) yielded empirical support for the key tenets of fairness heuristic theory. Both studies manipulated process control along with the availability of trustworthiness information. The results suggested that process control had a stronger effect on satisfaction and fairness ratings when trustworthiness information was unavailable. When trustworthiness information was available, process control did not matter to participants, regardless of whether that information depicted authorities as trustworthy or untrustworthy. Those results clearly show that concerns about fairness are made more salient when trustworthiness is uncertain.

Uncertainty about authority morality

Although concerns about outcomes, status, and trustworthiness provide three distinct reasons for caring about justice issues, all include some element of self-interest. In contrast, the last form of uncertainty described in this section is less self-interested. Folger's (1998; 2001) deontic model suggests that individuals care about fairness for its own sake, because adhering to justice rules is the moral and ethical thing to do. The model's label is based on the Greek word 'deon,' which refers to obligation or duty. The deontic model suggests that justice should be particularly salient whenever individuals feel a sense of uncertainty about an authority's morality. After all, working for an immoral authority threatens the meaning of one's working life (Cropanzano et al., 2001a). Some support for the deontic model can be seen in studies showing that decision-makers make self-sacrificial allocations in the interest of fairness, even when there are no short-term or long-term benefits for doing so (Turillo et al., 2002).

HOW DO JUSTICE JUDGMENTS IMPACT WORK ATTITUDES AND BEHAVIORS?

Assuming that individuals do consider the rules that comprise the organizational justice dimensions, perhaps out of concerns about outcomes, status, or the trustworthiness and morality of authorities, how do those justice judgments affect work outcomes? The early years of the organizational justice literature were marked by attempts to connect justice dimensions to the most visible outcomes in organizational behavior. Folger and Konovsky's (1989) study of pay raise decisions among manufacturing employees was indicative of a number of studies linking distributive and procedural justice to job satisfaction and organizational commitment (see also Alexander and Ruderman, 1987; Sweeney and McFarlin, 1993). In general, these studies showed that employees who perceived organizational authorities to be fair felt more satisfied with their jobs and felt a deeper sense of attachment to their organization. Such findings helped build a

momentum for the literature, as research began to expand beyond satisfaction and commitment by examining other potential consequences of justice (see Colquitt et al., 2001 for a meta-analytic review).

That expansion included an examination of the effects of justice on organizational citizenship behavior (OCB) – discretionary behaviors that go beyond one's formal job descriptions to benefit organizational functioning (Organ, 1990). The OCB construct had initially been cast as a version of job performance that would be more driven by job satisfaction than core task proficiency tends to be. Despite that origin, Organ (1990) speculated that fairness perceptions might actually represent a more powerful driver of OCB than job satisfaction. His conceptual rationale for that assertion was based in social exchange theory, which distinguishes between economic exchange relationships and social exchange relationships (Blau, 1964). The former are based in strict, *quid pro quo*, contractual relationships whereas the latter are based in more long-term, unspecified exchanges of tangible and intangible obligations. Organ (1990) conceptualized the justice-OCB relationship as indicative of an exchange of fair treatment on the part of authorities for discretionary behaviors on the part of employees.

A study of employees in the paint manufacturing industry by Moorman (1991) provided one of the more visible early tests of Organ's (1990) theorizing. Moorman's (1991) study examined the relationships among procedural, distributive, and interactional justice, job satisfaction, and five specific forms of OCB. The justice-OCB correlations were higher than the satisfaction-OCB correlations for four of the five forms of OCB. The positive results of such early tests had two distinct effects on the justice literature. First, OCB joined task performance as one of the most common behavioral outcomes associated with justice. Second, social exchange theory went on to become the dominant lens for explaining the effects of organizational justice on a variety of outcomes, even beyond OCB (for a review, see Cropanzano et al., 2001b).

That lens shaped the particular attitudes and behaviors that were examined most commonly in the late 1990s and into the next decade.

Attitudes supportive of reciprocation

Figure 2 depicts a social exchange relationship between an authority – either a formal organization or a particular supervisor – and an employee. The provision of benefits in the form of organizational justice is presumed to trigger an obligation to reciprocate on the part of the employee. This social exchange focus has prompted justice scholars to focus on a specific set of job attitudes – those that are somehow supportive of reciprocation. In cases where the justice benefits flow from the formal organization, the attitudes examined are referenced to that organization. In cases where the justice flows from a particular supervisor, the attitudes examined are referenced to that supervisor. Four specific attitudes have received the most attention in the literature: perceived support, trust, commitment, and exchange quality.

Perceived support reflects the degree to which the authority values the employee's contributions and cares about his or her well-being (Eisenberger et al., 1986). Perceived support has typically been referenced to the organization – abbreviated POS – but has also been referenced to the supervisor – abbreviated PSS (Eisenberger et al., 2002; Rhoades et al., 2001). The perceived support literature is built on a social exchange foundation (Eisenberger et al., 1986), making POS or PSS a natural construct to include in justice studies that utilize that same lens. For the most part, that inclusion has consisted of linking organization-originating procedural justice to POS (Masterson et al., 2000; Moorman et al., 1998; Wayne et al., 2002), though at least one study actually linked organization-originating informational justice to that support form (Rhoades et al., 2001). Despite this work, two concerns could be raised about pairing perceived support with justice in order to examine social exchange processes. First, perceived support seems to assess the provision of benefits portion of the exchange process, just as justice does, creating some ambiguity of causal direction.

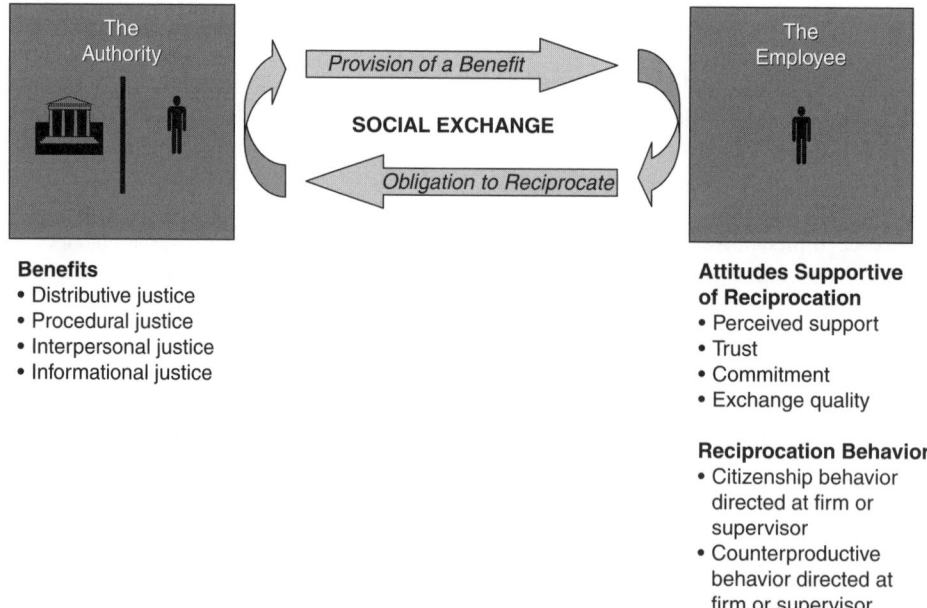

Benefits
• Distributive justice
• Procedural justice
• Interpersonal justice
• Informational justice

Attitudes Supportive of Reciprocation
• Perceived support
• Trust
• Commitment
• Exchange quality

Reciprocation Behaviors
• Citizenship behavior directed at firm or supervisor
• Counterproductive behavior directed at firm or supervisor

Figure 2   A social exchange explanation for organizational justice effects.

Second, measures of perceived support seem to share some of the same content as measures of interpersonal justice, potentially creating construct redundancy in cases where the referent for the measures is identical.

Trust reflects a willingness to be vulnerable to an authority based on positive expectations about the authority's character or competence (Mayer et al., 1995). Unlike perceived support, trust focuses less on the provision of benefits and more on the feasibility of developing and maintaining a social exchange relationship. After all, in the absence of trust, long-term unspecified exchanges of benefits and obligations would be impractical – one of the parties would demand an explicit repayment schedule (Blau, 1964). Past research has shown that justice is a significant predictor of trust. For example, Konovsky and Pugh (1994) connected supervisor-originating procedural justice to trust in the supervisor in a sample of hospital employees. Kernan and Hanges (2002) connected organization-originating procedural, interpersonal, and informational justice to trust in the organization among survivors of a restructuring effort.

Commitment can be generally defined as a willingness to persist in a course of action (Cooper-Hakim and Viswesvaran, 2005). Like trust, commitment impacts the feasibility of developing and maintaining a social exchange relationship. In the absence of commitment, one party cannot be sure that the other will remain long enough to repay favors over the long term. When referenced to an organization, commitment reflects a willingness to persist in employment. However, Meyer and Allen (1997) noted that the willingness to remain employed may actually be focused on a commitment to one's supervisor. Despite the possibility of a supervisory referent, the justice literature has focused exclusively on commitment referenced to the organization. Indeed, organizational commitment represents one of the most venerable outcomes in the literature, going all the way back to Folger and Konovsky's (1989) study. More recently, commitment has been included in articles utilizing a social exchange lens,

often falling 'downstream' from perceived support (Masterson et al., 2000; Wayne et al., 2002).

Exchange quality reflects the degree to which a working relationship is characterized by respect and mutual obligation (Gerstner and Day, 1997). Leader-member exchange (LMX) focuses on the quality of the supervisor-employee relationship whereas team-member exchange (TMX) focuses on the quality of the relationship between co-workers. Although one could conceive of an organization-referenced version of the construct, no one has examined such a version at this point in time. Of the four attitudes in Figure 2, exchange quality comes closest to directly assessing the social exchange dynamic by referencing the relationship itself. For the most part, justice scholars have linked supervisor-originating interactional forms of justice to LMX, often as a companion to a linkage between organization-originating procedural justice and POS (Masterson et al., 2000; Tekleab et al., 2005). However, it is important to note that any supervisor-originating justice form could be capable of increasing LMX levels.

Reciprocation behaviors

As shown in Figure 2, the social exchange explanation for justice effects implies that the support, trust, commitment, and exchange quality fostered by fairness will have behavioral ramifications. Those behaviors consist of reciprocation efforts aimed at repaying the original fairness benefit. As with the attitudes, those behaviors may be directed at either the overall organization or a particular supervisor. Some behaviors, such as task performance, lack an obvious referent, though some have speculated that task performance is more supervisor-directed given that supervisors ultimately rate the criterion (Masterson et al., 2000; Rupp and Cropanzano, 2002). Other behaviors, such as OCB, do possess an obvious referent, however. Helping co-workers or orienting new employees are clearly individual-benefiting, sometimes dubbed OCBI

(Williams and Anderson, 1991). Attending optional company functions or keeping up with organizational announcements are clearly organization-benefiting, sometimes dubbed OCBO (Williams and Anderson, 1991). Helping one's supervisor with optional work tasks or assisting the supervisor with heavy workloads are clearly supervisor-benefiting, sometimes dubbed OCBS (Malatesta, 1995). From a social exchange perspective, organization and supervisor-originating forms of justice should predict OCBO and OCBS, with effects on OCBI less explainable with that conceptual lens. Consistent with that assertion, organization and supervisor-originating forms of justice have been linked to OCBO and OCBS, with social exchange attitudes used as mediators (Aryee et al., 2002; Konovsky and Pugh, 1994; Masterson et al., 2000; Moorman et al., 1998; Rupp and Cropanzano, 2002; Wayne et al., 2002).

Counterproductive behaviors, which reflect intentional efforts to harm the firm or its employees (Sackett and Devore, 2001) also possess an obvious referent. Cursing at co-workers and publicly embarrassing co-workers are clearly individual-directed, sometimes referred to as interpersonal deviance (Bennett and Robinson, 2000). Theft, sabotage, and intentionally breaking organizational rules are clearly organization-directed, sometimes referred to as organizational deviance (Bennett and Robinson, 2000). Unlike research on OCB, scholars have given little attention to behaviors directed specifically at the supervisor. Nonetheless, social exchange arguments would suggest that organization and supervisor-originating forms of justice would be most directly linked to organization and supervisor-directed counterproductive behaviors, with effects on individual-directed actions less explainable. Although scholars have applied such arguments to the study of counterproductive behaviors (Greenberg and Scott, 1996), studies integrating justice, social exchange mediators, and counterproductive behaviors remain rare (see Kickul et al., 2002; Lim, 2002, for some exceptions).

CONTROVERSIES, DEBATES, AND FUTURE DIRECTIONS

The sections above have illustrated that scholars have learned a great deal about what justice is, when employees become concerned about it, and the attitudinal and behavioral consequences associated with those concerns. Even with those advances, however, the justice literature is marked by some emerging controversies and debates that promise to shape future research. Many of those debates center on the key issues covered in this review, including what organizational justice is and how justice affects attitudes and behaviors. Three such areas of debate are reviewed in this section.

Expansion of justice sources

Even as the literature expanded from distributive justice to procedural and interactional justice, a key boundary condition was maintained for justice constructs. Specifically, all of the constructs in Table 1 reflect how an authority acts in a particular decision-making context. Theorizing by Bies (2005) has recently relaxed the decision-making context portion of that boundary condition. Bies (2005) categorized the traditional view of organizational justice as an 'exchange perspective,' with justice concepts rooted in some sort of exchange between an authority and the subject of the decision event. However, Bies (2005) also pointed to the possibility of an 'encounter perspective,' where justice rules could be gauged in day-to-day encounters with a supervisor, regardless of whether something was really being decided. For example, a supervisor can be unbiased, ethical, respectful, or proper in or out of a decision-making context. Indeed, this encounter perspective brings a new element to the distinctions among justice dimensions, as interpersonal justice rules seem more encounter-relevant than informational justice rules, which require some decision event in order to make explanations necessary. The encounter perspective also highlights some of the differences within procedural justice, as some rules are more exchange-dependent than others.

Recent empirical research has relaxed the authority portion of the boundary condition for examining justice issues. For example, Simon and Sturmer (2003) examined whether an employee's fellow team members adhered to interpersonal justice rules, as opposed to examining whether a supervisor or more general organization acted fairly. In a laboratory study, individuals who received respectful treatment from their teammates were more likely to engage in OCB directed at those teammates. In a laboratory study simulating a call center help desk for a computer company, Rupp and Spencer (2006) examined whether customers adhered to interpersonal and informational justice rules when communicating with a service representative. Because there was no decision-making event per se, informational justice reflected whether the customers were honest and candid in their descriptions of their computer problem. The results of the study revealed that customers' violations of justice rules were associated with more emotional labor on the part of the customer service representatives.

These sorts of expansions raise critical questions that could impact future research in the literature. Are such studies really capturing 'justice' in the same sense as studies rooted in an authority's actions during a decision-making event? Are such studies better served by framing their predictions around constructs that might be labeled 'close cousins' of justice dimensions – constructs that have no explicit bounding in authority or decision-making contexts? Such constructs could include integrity (Mayer et al., 1995), ethical behavior (Schweitzer et al., 2004), courtesy (Podsakoff et al., 1990), incivility (Andersson and Pearson, 1999) and workplace dishonesty (Lewicki et al., 1997), to name a few.

Two suggestions seem warranted for studies that are looking to expand the justice construct by referencing rule adherence to sources that go beyond the supervisor or the organization. First, if a significant number of the rules in Table 1 cease to make sense with the new source, it may be that

another conceptual lens is warranted. Indeed, Simon and Sturmer (2003) utilized the term 'respectful treatment' rather than 'interpersonal justice' throughout their study. Second, if framing the manuscript as a justice study seems at all controversial, scholars should measure relevant 'close cousins' as controls, to ensure that the justice lens truly contributes to the outcome variables in question.

New directions in justice mediation

Although it remains unclear whether the expansion of justice sources will ultimately benefit the literature, it does seem clear that an expansion of mediators for justice effects would be useful. The social exchange lens depicted in Figure 2 has been invaluable to the literature on a number of levels, as it describes the types of attitudes and behaviors that justice should promote, as well as the specific targets to which those reactions will be directed. Still, there is a danger that justice scholars will view social exchange as *the* explanatory framework, eventually applying it to research questions and criteria that it is ill-suited to explain. The question then becomes, when individuals label a situation as 'fair,' what happens other than viewing the authority as supportive and trustworthy and the exchange relationship as high quality? Alternatively, when individuals label a situation as 'unfair' what happens other than doubting the strength of the social exchange relationship?

Affect represents a potentially powerful avenue for justice mediation that remains relatively untapped. Affect can be operationalized in a number of ways, including moods, emotions, and sentiments (Fridja, 1994). Moods represent relatively long lasting, low intensity affective states that are not connected to specific events or objects. Emotions are typically more intense and shorter in duration and are connected to specific events or objects. If those events or objects repeatedly trigger emotions over time, emotions evolve into sentiments – tendencies to respond affectively to a given stimulus. Of these affect forms, emotions and sentiments seem most relevant to organizational justice.

Cropanzano et al. (2001) noted that justice perceptions can be formed in relation to events (e.g., a performance appraisal, a dispute resolution) or entities (e.g., a supervisor, an organization). The fairness of events should have implications for emotions whereas the fairness of entities should have implications for sentiments.

Although emotions and sentiments come in many specific forms, Lazarus's (1991) core relational themes can provide a summarizing tool. A partial list of those themes is shown in Table 2, along with a justice theory that is relevant to the themes. The negative emotions and sentiments in Table 2 could arise when an authority fails to adhere to justice rules. For example, the deontic model and equity theory both suggest that anger should result from injustice (Adams, 1965; Folger, 1998; 2001), whereas uncertainty management theory emphasizes the anxiety and fear that could be amplified by injustice (Lind and Van den Bos, 2002; Van den Bos and Lind, 2002). The deontic model further implies that individuals will feel shame for being connected to an unjust authority (Folger, 1998; 2001), and equity theory describes a range of emotions – guilt, envy, and jealousy – that can result from outcome-input comparisons. In contrast, justice theories seem to have devoted less attention to positive emotions and sentiments, which could arise when an authority does adhere to justice rules. The relational model suggests that individuals will feel pride for being associated with an authority who acts fairly (Tyler and Lind, 1992). Fairness heuristic theory implies that justice will be associated with some sense of relief, as a trustworthy authority suggests that cooperation will not be met by exploitation (Lind, 2001; Van den Bos et al., 2001).

Empirical research has begun to support linkages between organizational justice and the kinds of emotions and sentiments shown in Table 2. In a laboratory study, Weiss et al. (1999) showed that, when outcomes were favorable, fair procedures produced happiness and pride and biased procedures produced guilt (see also Krehbiel and Cropanzano, 2000). A study by Barclay et al. (2005) went one step further by examining emotions as a mediator of the relationship between justice and counterproductive behaviors. For example, their study revealed that procedural and interactional justice reduced shame, guilt, and anger when outcomes were favorable, with anger mediating effects on counterproductive behaviors. That sort of emotion-based mediation is consistent with other models that have integrated justice constructs and counterproductive behavior (e.g., Fox et al., 2001), providing a valuable complement to social exchange-based theorizing.

Table 2   Core themes for emotions and sentiments

Emotions/sentiments	Relevant theories
Negative forms	
• Anger	• Deontic model, Equity theory
• Anxiety	• Uncertainty management theory
• Fear	• Uncertainty management theory
• Guilt	• Equity theory
• Shame	• Deontic model
• Sadness	• None
• Envy	• Equity theory
• Jealousy	• Equity theory
Positive forms	
• Happiness	• None
• Pride	• Relational model
• Relief	• Fairness heuristic theory
• Hope	• None

Note: Adapted from Lazarus, R.S. (1991) *Emotion and Adaptation.* New York: Oxford University.

CONCLUSION

In the two decades since Greenberg (1987) coined the organizational justice term, the literature has evolved from a niche topic to one of the more vibrant and visible areas in the organizational behavior literature. That expansion has helped scholars understand how employees think about justice, why they care about it, and how they react when it is found to be present or absent in the authorities for whom they work. If the past is any guide, the next decade will bring with it more opportunities to expand our understanding of justice and fairness.

REFERENCES

Adams, J.S. (1965) 'Inequity in social exchange', in L. Berkowitz (ed.), *Advances in Experimental Social Psychology*. New York: Academic Press. Vol. 2, pp. 267–299.

Alexander, S. and Ruderman, M. (1987) 'The role of procedural and distributive justice in organizational behavior', *Social Justice Research*, 1: 177–198.

Andersson, L.M. and Pearson, C.M. (1999) 'Tit for tat? The spiraling effect of incivility in the workplace', *Academy of Management Review*, 24: 452–471.

Aryee, S., Budhwar, P.S. and Chen, Z.X. (2002) 'Trust as a mediator of the relationship between organizational justice and work outcomes: Test of a social exchange model', *Journal of Organizational Behavior*, 23: 267–285.

Barclay, L.J., Skarlicki, D.P. and Pugh, S.D. (2005) 'Exploring the role of emotions in injustice perceptions and retaliation', *Journal of Applied Psychology*, 90: 629–643.

Bennett, R.J. and Robinson, S.L. (2000) 'Development of a measure of workplace deviance', *Journal of Applied Psychology*, 85: 349–360.

Bies, R.J. (2001) 'Interactional (in)justice: The sacred and the profane', in J. Greenberg and R. Cropanzano (eds), *Advances in Organizational Justice*. Stanford, CA: Stanford University Press, pp. 85–108.

Bies, R.J. (2005) 'Are procedural and interactional justice conceptually distinct?', in J. Greenberg and J.A. Colquitt (eds), *The Handbook of Organizational Justice*. Mahwah, NJ: Erlbaum, pp. 85–112.

Bies, R.J. and Moag, J.F. (1986) 'Interactional justice: Communication criteria of fairness', in R.J. Lewicki, B.H. Sheppard and M.H. Bazerman (eds), *Research on Negotiations in Organizations*. Greenwich, CT: JAI Press. Vol. 1, pp. 43–55.

Bies, R.J. and Shapiro, D.L. (1987) 'Interactional fairness judgments: The influence of causal accounts', *Social Justice Research*, 1: 199–218.

Bies, R.J. and Shapiro, D.L. (1988) 'Voice and justification: Their influence on procedural fairness judgments', *Academy of Management Journal*, 31: 676–685.

Blader, S.L. and Tyler, T.R. (2003) 'What constitutes fairness in work settings? A four-component model of procedural justice', *Human Resource Management Review*, 13: 107–126.

Blau, P. (1964) *Exchange and Power in Social Life*. New York: Wiley.

Brockner, J. (2002) 'Making sense of procedural fairness: How high procedural fairness can reduce or heighten the influence of outcome favorability', *Academy of Management Review*, 27: 58–76.

Brockner, J. and Wiesenfeld, B.M. (1996) 'An integrative framework for explaining reactions to decisions: Interactive effects of outcomes and procedures', *Psychological Bulletin*, 120: 189–208.

Colquitt, J.A. (2001) 'On the dimensionality of organizational justice: A construct validation of a measure', *Journal of Applied Psychology*, 86: 386–400.

Colquitt, J.A., Conlon, D.E., Wesson, M.J., Porter, C.O.L.H. and Ng, K.Y. (2001) 'Justice at the millennium: A meta-analytic review of 25 years of organizational justice research', *Journal of Applied Psychology*, 86: 425–445.

Colquitt, J.A., Greenberg, J. and Zapata-Phelan, C.P. (2005) 'What is organizational justice? A historical overview', in J. Greenberg and J.A. Colquitt (eds), *The Handbook of Organizational Justice*. Mahwah, NJ: Erlbaum, pp. 3–56.

Colquitt, J.A. and Shaw, J.C. (2005) 'How should organizational justice be measured?', in J. Greenberg and J.A. Colquitt (eds), *The Handbook of Organizational Justice*. Mahwah, NJ: Erlbaum, pp. 113–152.

Cooper-Hakim, A. and Viswesvaran, C. (2005) 'The construct of work commitment: Testing an integrative framework', *Psychological Bulletin*, 131: 241–259.

Cropanzano, R., Byrne, Z.S., Bobocel, D.R. and Rupp, D.E. (2001a) 'Moral virtues, fairness heuristics, social entities, and other denizens of organizational justice', *Journal of Vocational Behavior*, 58: 164–209.

Cropanzano, R., Rupp, D.E., Mohler, C.J. and Schminke, M. (2001b) 'Three roads to organizational justice', in G.R. Ferris (ed.), *Research in Personnel and Human Resource Management*. New York: Elsevier Science. Vol. 19, pp. 1–113.

Deutsch, M. (1975) 'Equity, equality, and need: What determines which value will be used as the basis for distributive justice?', *Journal of Social Issues*, 31: 137–149.

Eisenberger, R., Huntington, R., Hutchison, S. and Sowa, D. (1986) 'Perceived organizational support', *Journal of Applied Psychology*, 71: 500–507.

Eisenberger, R., Stinglhamber, F., Vandenberghe, C., Sucharski, I.L. and Rhoades, L. (2002) 'Perceived supervisor support: Contributions to perceived organizational support and employee retention', *Journal of Applied Psychology*, 87: 565–573.

Folger, R. (1998) 'Fairness as a moral virtue', in M. Schminke (ed.), *Managerial Ethics: Morally Managing People and Processes*. Mahwah, NJ: Erlbaum, pp. 13–34.

Folger, R. (2001) 'Fairness as deonance', in S.W. Gilliland, D.D. Steiner and D.P. Skarlicki (eds), *Theoretical and Cultural Perspectives on*

Organizational Justice. Greenwich, CT: Information Age Publishing, pp. 3–34.

Folger, R. and Konovsky, M.A. (1989) 'Effects of procedural and distributive justice on reactions to pay raise decisions', *Academy of Management Journal*, 32: 115–130.

Fox, S., Spector, P.E. and Miles, D. (2001) 'Counter-productive work behavior (CWB) in response to job stressors and organizational justice: Some mediator and moderator tests for autonomy and emotions', *Journal of Vocational Behavior*, 59: 291–309.

Frijda, N.H. (1994) 'Varieties of affect: Emotions and episodes, moods, and sentiments', in P. Ekman and R.J. Davidson (eds), *The Nature of Emotion*. New York: Oxford University Press, pp. 59–67.

Gerstner, C.R. and Day, D.V. (1997) 'Meta-analytic review of leader-member exchange theory: Correlates and construct issues', *Journal of Applied Psychology*, 82: 827–844.

Greenberg, J. (1986) 'Determinants of perceived fairness of performance evaluations', *Journal of Applied Psychology*, 71: 340–342.

Greenberg, J. (1987) 'A taxonomy of organizational justice theories', *Academy of Management Review*, 12: 9–22.

Greenberg, J. (1990) 'Employee theft as a reaction to underpayment inequity: The hidden cost of paycuts', *Journal of Applied Psychology*, 75: 561–568.

Greenberg, J. (1993) 'The social side of fairness: Interpersonal and informational classes of organizational justice', in R. Cropanzano (ed.), *Justice in the Workplace: Approaching Fairness in Human Resource Management*. Hillsdale, NJ: Erlbaum, pp. 79–103.

Greenberg, J. and Scott, K.S. (1996) 'Why do workers bite the hands that feed them? Employee theft as a social exchange process', in B.M. Staw and L.L. Cummings (eds.), *Research in Organizational Behavior*. Greenwich, CT: JAI Press. Vol. 18, pp. 111–156.

Homans, G.C. (1961) *Social Behaviour: Its Elementary Forms*. London: Routledge and Kegan Paul.

Kernan, M.C. and Hanges, P.J. (2002) 'Survivor reactions to reorganization: Antecedents and consequences of procedural, interpersonal, and informational justice', *Journal of Applied Psychology*, 87: 916–928.

Kickul, J.R., Neuman, G., Parker, C. and Finkl, J. (2002) 'Settling the score: The role of organizational justice in the relationship between psychological contract breach and anticitizenship behavior', *Employee Responsibilities and Rights Journal*, 13: 77–93.

Konovsky, M.A. and Pugh, S.D. (1994) 'Citizenship behavior and social exchange', *Academy of Management Journal*, 37: 656–669.

Krehbiel, P.J. and Cropanzano, R. (2000) 'Procedural justice, outcome favorability, and emotion', *Social Justice Research*, 13: 337–358.

Lazarus, R.S. (1991) *Emotion and Adaptation*. New York: Oxford University.

Leventhal, G.S. (1976) 'The distribution of rewards and resources in groups and organizations', in L. Berkowitz and W. Walster (eds), *Advances in Experimental Social Psychology*. New York: Academic Press. Vol. 9, pp. 91–131.

Leventhal, G.S. (1980) 'What should be done with equity theory? New approaches to the study of fairness in social relationships', in K. Gergen, M. Greenberg, and R. Willis (eds), *Social exchange: Advances in Theory and Research*. New York: Plenum Press, pp. 27–55.

Lewicki, R.J., Poland, T., Minton, J.W. and Sheppard, B.H. (1997) 'Dishonesty as deviance: A typology of workplace dishonesty and contributing factors', in R.J. Lewicki, R.H. Bies and B.H. Sheppard (eds), *Research on Negotiations in Organizations*. Greenwich, CT: JAI Press. Vol. 6, pp. 53–86.

Lim, V.K.G. (2002) 'The IT way of loafing on the job: Cyberloafing, neutralizing, and organizational justice', *Journal of Organizational Behavior*, 23: 675–694.

Lind, E.A. (2001) 'Fairness heuristic theory: Justice judgments as pivotal cognitions in organizational relations', in J. Greenberg and R. Cropanzano (eds), *Advances in Organizational Justice*. Stanford, CA: Stanford University Press, pp. 56–88.

Lind, E.A. and Tyler, T.R. (1988) *The Social Psychology of Procedural Justice*. New York: Plenum Press.

Lind, E.A. and Van den Bos, K. (2002) 'When fairness works: Toward a general theory of uncertainty management', in B.M. Staw and R.M. Kramer (eds), *Research in Organizational Behavior*. Boston, MA: Elsevier. Vol. 24, pp. 181–223.

Malatesta, R.M. (1995) Understanding the dynamics of organizational and supervisory commitment using a social exchange framework. Unpublished doctoral dissertation: Wayne State University, Michigan. Cited in Rupp and Cropanzano (2002).

Masterson, S.S., Lewis, K., Goldman, B.M. and Taylor, M.S. (2000) 'Integrating justice and social exchange: The differing effects of fair procedures and treatment on work relationships', *Academy of Management Journal*, 43: 738–748.

Mayer, R.C., Davis, J.H. and Schoorman, F.D. (1995) 'An integrative model of organizational trust', *Academy of Management Review*, 20: 709–734.

Meyer, J.P. and Allen, N.J. (1997) *Commitment in the Workplace: Theory, Research, and Application*. Thousand Oaks, CA: Sage.

Moorman, R.H. (1991) 'Relationship between organizational justice and organizational citizenship behaviors: Do fairness perceptions influence employee citizenship?' *Journal of Applied Psychology*, 76: 845–855.

Moorman, R.H., Blakely, G.L. and Niehoff, B.P. (1998) 'Does perceived organizational support mediate the relationship between procedural justice and organizational citizenship behavior?' *Academy of Management Journal*, 41: 351–357.

Mowday, R.T. and Colwell, K.A. (2003) 'Employee reactions to unfair outcomes in the workplace: The contributions of equity theory to understanding work motivation', in L.W. Porter, G.A. Bigley, and R.M. Steers (eds), *Motivation and Work Behavior*. Boston, MA: McGraw-Hill Irwin, pp. 65–113.

Organ, D.W. (1990) 'The motivational basis of organizational citizenship behavior', in L.L. Cummings and B.M. Staw (eds), *Research in Organizational Behavior*. Greenwich, CT: JAI Press. Vol. 12, pp. 43–72.

Podsakoff, P.M., MacKenzie, S.B., Bachrach, D.G. and Podsakoff, N.P. (2005) 'The influence of management journals in the 1980s and 1990s', *Strategic Management Journal*, 26: 473–488.

Podsakoff, P.M., MacKenzie, S., Moorman, R.H., and Fetter, R. (1990) 'Transformational leadership behaviors and their effects on followers' trust in leader, satisfaction, and organizational citizenship behaviors', *Leadership Quarterly*, 1: 107–142.

Rhoades, L., Eisenberger, R. and Armeli, S. (2001) 'Affective commitment to the organization: The contribution of perceived organizational support', *Journal of Applied Psychology*, 86: 825–836.

Rupp, D.E. and Cropanzano, R. (2002) 'The mediating effects of social exchange relationships in predicting workplace outcomes from multifoci organizational justice', *Organizational Behavior and Human Decision Processes*, 89: 925–946.

Rupp, D.E. and Spencer, S. (2006) 'When customers lash out: The effects of customer interactional injustice on emotional labor and the mediating role of discrete emotions', *Journal of Applied Psychology*, 91: 971–978.

Sackett, P.R. and Devore, C.J. (2001) 'Counterproductive behaviors at work', in N. Anderson, D.S. Ones, H.K., Sinangil and C. Viswesvaran (eds), *Handbook of Industrial, Work and Organizational Psychology*. London: Sage. Vol. 1, pp. 145–164.

Schweitzer, M.E., Ordonez, L. and Douma, B. (2004) 'Goal setting as a motivator of unethical behavior', *Academy of Management Journal*, 47: 422–432.

Simon, B. and Sturmer, S. (2003) 'Respect for group members: Intragroup determinants of collective identification and group-serving behavior', *Personality and Social Psychology Bulletin*, 29: 183–193.

Stouffer, S.A., Suchman, E.A., DeVinney, L.C., Star, S.A. and Williams, R.M., Jr. (1949) *The American Soldier: Adjustment During Army Life, Volume I*. Clinton, MA: Colonial Press.

Sweeney, P.D. and McFarlin, D.B. (1993) 'Workers' evaluations of the "ends" and the "means": An examination of four models of distributive and procedural justice', *Organizational Behavior and Human Decision Processes*, 55: 23–40.

Tekleab, A.G., Takeuchi, R. and Taylor, M.S. (2005) 'Extending the chain of relationships among organizational justice, social exchange, and employee reactions: The role of contract violations', *Academy of Management Journal*, 48, 146–157.

Thibaut, J. and Walker, L. (1975) *Procedural Justice: A Psychological Analysis*. Hillsdale, NJ: Erlbaum.

Turillo, C.J., Folger, R., Lavelle, J.J., Umphress, E.E. and Gee, J.O. (2002) 'Is virtue its own reward? Self-sacrificial decisions for the sake of fairness', *Organizational Behavior and Human Decision Processes*, 89: 839–865.

Tyler, T.R. (1987) 'Conditions leading to value-expressive effects in judgments of procedural justice: A test of four models', *Journal of Personality and Social Psychology*, 52: 333–344.

Tyler, T.R., Degoey, P. and Smith, H. (1996) 'Understanding why the justice of group procedures matters: A test of the psychological dynamics of the group-value model', *Journal of Personality and Social Psychology*, 70: 913–930.

Tyler, T.R. and Lind, E.A. (1992) 'A relational model of authority in groups', in M.P. Zanna (ed), *Advances in Experimental Social Psychology*. San Diego, CA: Academic Press. Vol. 25, pp. 115–191.

Tyler, T.R., Rasinski, K.A. and Spodick, N. (1985) 'Influence of voice on satisfaction with leaders: Exploring the meaning of process control', *Journal of Personality and Social Psychology*, 48: 72–81.

Van den Bos, K. (2001) 'Uncertainty management: The influence of uncertainty salience on reactions to perceived procedural fairness', *Journal of Personality and Social Psychology*, 80: 931–941.

Van den Bos, K. and Lind, E.A. (2002) 'Uncertainty management by means of fairness judgments', in M.P. Zanna (ed.), *Advances in Experimental Social Psychology*. Boston, MA: Elsevier. Vol. 34, pp. 1–60.

Van den Bos, K., Lind E.A. and Wilke, H.A.M. (2001) 'The psychology of procedural and distributive justice viewed from the perspective of fairness heuristic theory', in R. Cropanzano (ed.), *Justice in the Workplace*. Mahwah, NJ: Erlbaum. Vol. 2, pp. 49–66.

Van den Bos, K. and Miedema, J. (2000) 'Toward understanding why fairness matters: The influence of mortality salience of reactions to procedural fairness', *Interpersonal Relations and Group Processes*, 79: 355–366.

Van den Bos, K., Wilke, H.A.M. and Lind, E.A. (1998) 'When do we need procedural fairness? The role of trust in authority', *Journal of Personality and Social Psychology*, 75: 1449–1458.

Wayne, S.J., Shore, L.M., Bommer, W.H. and Tetrick, L.E. (2002) 'The role of fair treatment and rewards in perceptions of organizational support and leader-member exchange', *Journal of Applied Psychology*, 87: 590–598.

Weiss, H.M., Suckow, K. and Cropanzano, R. (1999) 'Effects of justice conditions on discrete emotions', *Journal of Applied Psychology*, 84: 786–794.

Williams, L.J. and Anderson, S.E. (1991) 'Job satisfaction and organizational commitment as predictors of organizational citizenship behaviors', *Journal of Management*, 17: 601–617.

5

Trust in Management: An Interpersonal Perspective

M. Audrey Korsgaard, Adrian H. Pitariu
and Sophia Soyoung Jeong

INTRODUCTION

The construct of trust has long been a central feature of theories of co-operation and collective action (Deutsch, 1962). In the organizational sciences, the relevance of trust to both theory and practice has arguably grown in recent decades as innovations in technology and organization have led to less formal and hierarchical modes of controlling and coordinating labor (Tyler, 2003). The volume of research generated in this field in recent years is illustrated in recent quantitative and narrative reviews of trust (Colquitt et al., 2007; Dirks and Ferrin, 2001, 2002; Lewicki et al., 2006). The findings summarized in these reviews represent a diverse and often disparate literature spanning discipline, levels of analysis, and methodologies. Despite this diversity, the importance of trust to collective action is a consistent finding.

Trust exists at organizational, group and individual levels of analysis and can target organizations, groups, or a particular individual. This chapter focuses on trust in the manager, an interpersonal phenomenon involving one individual's trust in a particular leader. Given the interpersonal context of leader-follower relationships, we approach interpersonal trust from a psychological perspective and mainly emphasize research and theory employing this perspective. Further, we focus primarily on recently published empirical evidence, so as to complement the aforementioned reviews of the field.

DEFINING TRUST

In the organizational sciences, interpersonal trust has been defined in various ways, but these definitions seem to converge on a few key elements (Lewicki et al., 2006). First, current definitions tend to reflect expectations about the consequences of trusting another party. Second, trust reflects a willingness to accept a risk involving the trustee. A third element of contemporary definitions of trust is that they differentiate interpersonal trust as a state from trust as a trait, such as propensity to trust (Rotter, 1967). Rousseau et al.'s (1998) definition is emblematic of this current and prevailing view of trust: '... a psychological state comprising the intention to accept vulnerability based upon positive expectations of the intentions or behavior of another.' (1998: 395).

As this definition reflects, interpersonal trust is thought to consist of three components: cognitive, affective and behavioral (Cummings and Bromiley, 1996). This structure is similar to the basic structure of attitudes described in expectancy-value models of attitudes (e.g., Ajzen, 2001). The cognitive component of an attitude is a belief regarding the object of the attitude. In the specific case of trust, the belief is an expectation about the actions of the other party. The affective component of an attitude reflects the individual values and preferences for the consequences associated with that belief. In the case of trust, the affective component is the value the trustor places on the consequences of his or her expectations being fulfilled or violated. The behavioral component of an attitude addresses the intentions associated with the belief. In the case of trust, the behavioral component is the willingness to make oneself vulnerable to the other party (Mayer et al., 1995). A noteworthy exception to this approach is the work of Currall and Judge (1995), who considered the expectancy-value components of trust (i.e., affective and cognitive components) as antecedents to trust and defined trust as behavioral intentions.

Other approaches to the dimensions of trust have distinguished between bases of trust. For example, McAllister (1995) distinguished between cognitive and affective trust. Similarly, Atkinson and Butcher (2003) distinguished between task-based trust and motive-based trust. Other scholars (Das and Teng, 2004; Dirks and Skarlicki, 2004) distinguish between character-based trust and relationship-based trust. These differing bases do not represent different definitions of trust but, rather, represent different reasons for trusting another. That is, at its core,

trust involves a willingness to make oneself vulnerable to another party; however, the nature and origins of the beliefs and values underlying trust may differ. As is discussed further below, the bases of trust relate to stage models of trust that depict distinct forms and causes of trust at different stages of a relationship.

THEORETICAL FRAMEWORKS

In this section, we review principal theoretical frameworks for understanding trust in the manager. Some of these frameworks are not exclusively pertinent to trust in the manager but are more broadly relevant to interpersonal trust. However, these approaches have been adapted or applied to the manager-subordinate context and are thus relevant to this review. Contemporary models of interpersonal trust in organizations have their roots in theories of social psychology (e.g., Deutsch, 1958), economics (Williamson, 1993), and sociology (e.g., Blau, 1964). Before addressing more contemporary approaches, we briefly review these underpinnings.

Theoretical underpinnings

The social psychological perspective on trust is represented by the work of Deutsch (1958; 1962). He developed a theory of co-operation and trust that delineated when trust is necessary and how it is related to co-operation. Deutsch argued that trust was relevant when:

(a) individuals' outcomes are interdependent;
(b) the actions of the other party are not controllable; and
(c) those actions may result in some harm or loss to the individual.

Trust is represented behaviorally in this theory as the choice to act in a way that makes the actor vulnerable to the other party. An individual's choice to trust is based on the stakes involved (i.e., the expected benefits must outweigh the potential losses) and the extent to which the actor possesses information about the other party's co-operative intent. Thus, according to this perspective, the interdependencies, the risk inherent in the situation and knowledge of and experience with the other party are the principal drivers of trust. The impact of these factors on trust reflects a largely rational process of weighing costs and benefits.

Microeconomic theories such as transaction cost economics (Williamson, 1993) and agency theory (Eisenhardt, 1989) provide a similar view of trust. Strictly speaking, these theories do not address trust but, rather, reduce the question of trust to one of risk taking. Indeed, Williamson (1993: 469) described the construct of trust as 'irrelevant to commercial exchange.' Risk taking is manifested in a party's choice to participate in an exchange relationship. These theories posit that the choice to take a risk is a function of the hazards associated with the exchange and the safeguards in place to protect against those hazards. For example, transaction cost economics suggests that when hazards are higher and safeguards are limited, a higher price is required for the transaction. Similarly, agency theory posits that when hazards are high, parties will require more safeguards to enter into or maintain the exchange relationship (e.g., formal contracts or monitoring). Simply put, trust is reflected in the extent to which parties will enter into more or less formal relationships and take measures to protect their vulnerability in those relationships.

Like Deutsch's definition of trust, the view of trust in the economic tradition is behavioral. The choice to trust is based on features of the context, such as the relative cost and benefits, and the ability to enforce reciprocation or punish violations. Also, in line with Deutsch's view, the underlying judgment process is assumed to be rational. This assumption was subsequently challenged, giving rise to the notion of less calculative bases of trust (Das and Teng, 2004; Kramer, 1999) that are characteristic of stage models of trust (Lewicki and Bunker, 1996; Shapiro et al., 1992) and presumptive trust (Meyerson et al., 1996), which are described later.

Social exchange theory (Blau, 1964) seeks to explain the dynamics of social, as opposed to economic, exchanges. Because the employment relationship involves both economic and social exchanges, this theory has been applied to the employment relationship and to the development of trust in organizations (Konovsky and Pugh, 1994; Robinson, 1996; Whitener et al., 1998). Like economic exchanges, social exchanges involve actions that are directed at another party and that are initiated with expectation of some returned benefit (Blau, 1964). However, unlike economic exchanges, the choices to initiate and reciprocate an exchange are voluntary. Moreover, the rate of exchange is not specified *a priori*. Thus, exchanges carry the risk of non-reciprocation or disproportionate reciprocation. Social exchanges also differ from economic exchanges in that social exchanges may involve extrinsic (e.g., job security) rewards as well as intrinsic rewards (e.g., respect).

In this framework, trust is both an antecedent of giving and a consequence of receiving benefits from the other party. Trust is strengthened through repeated exchanges that gradually expand in scope and value over time. Thus, direct experience is an important factor in determining trust. Additionally, Blau (1964) argued that the benefits that are exchanged in a social exchange relationship often carry symbolic meaning, such as respect, that communicates information about the giver's character and the value of the relationship to the giver. Thus, although not explicitly part of the theory, this perspective suggests that cognitive and affective processes involved in interpretation of exchanges are important factors in the evolution of trust.

CONTEMPORARY MODELS OF INTERPERSONAL TRUST

The decade of the 1990s was marked by a burst of theoretical and empirical work on trust in organizations (e.g., Kramer and Tyler, 1996; Rousseau et al., 1998) that continues through the current decade

(Bijlsma and Koopman, 2003; McEvily et al., 2003). Recent theoretical work has varied in its emphasis on direct experience, inference processes, the initial formation of trust, and on stage models of trust. We organize our review of the principal theoretical contributions around these areas of emphasis. First, we discuss models of trustworthiness that emphasize direct experience with the manager and its impact on perceptions of trustworthiness. Next, we review research and theory on attributions that underlie perceptions of trustworthiness and trust. Third, we review frameworks for explaining presumptive or swift trust in the initial stages of relationships. Finally, we review stage models that address the qualitative changes in trust over the life of the relationship.

Trustworthiness

Mayer et al. (1995) developed an integrated model of antecedents and consequences of trust. The focal consequence of trust in this model is risk taking in the relationship, which encompasses any act that exposes the trustor to risk based on the response of the other party. According to this model, trust must meet the level of risk inherent in the situation in order to produce risk taking behavior. The model also specifies that trust results from individual differences in trust propensity and perceptions of the manager's trustworthiness, which comprises three core perceptions: ability, benevolence and competence.

Although not explicitly incorporated into the model, the authors discuss the factors contributing to trustworthiness perceptions. They suggest that perceptions of ability, benevolence and integrity arise from interactions with the manager where the manager's behavior is interpreted as indicative of these traits. Building on this framework, Whitener et al. (1998) developed a typology of five broad categories of managerial trustworthy behavior:

- behavioral consistency (consistent treatment within and across employees);

- behavioral integrity (consistency between words and deeds);
- sharing and delegation of control;
- communication (e.g., accuracy, explanations, and openness); and
- demonstration of concern.

Somewhat in parallel, Bijlsma and van de Bunt (2003) identified six types of managerial behavior related to trust, including the following: support and guidance (similar to demonstrating concern), cooperation-related problem solving (similar to sharing control), listening, feedback giving, and communicating expectations (similar to two-way communication).

Mayer et al. (1995) also noted that context is apt to influence perceptions of trustworthiness and trust. Based on the requirements in the context, the authors speculated that a manager with certain attributes may be perceived as more or less trustworthy in a given situation. For example, depending on the task requirements, a manager with a certain skill set may be viewed as more or less competent. Context can also shape attributions of trustworthiness. If the organizational context (e.g., policy, structure) compels or constrains the manager's actions, an act is less likely to be attributed to the manager's character. Thus, for example, a manager who makes a decision that is beneficial to an employee may not be seen as particularly benevolent if the decision was mandated by company policy. Research and theory on the relationship between attributions and trust, discussed in the next section, delves further into this process.

Attributions of trust and trustworthiness

Perceptions of trustworthiness and trust can be viewed as a product of attributional processes (Atkinson and Bucher, 2003; Ferrin and Dirks, 2003). Attributions involve the process of inferring explanations for actions and events. Depending on the cues and processes employed, individuals may attribute an action or event to the actor, or to factors beyond the control of the actor. Attributions to an actor involve making inferences about the motives and ability of the actor. Thus, to the extent that an act or event has positive consequences and is attributed to the actor, the trustor will infer trustworthy attributes to the actor. Even when the event is not ascribed to the actor, it can influence trust in the actor. For example, Malhotra and Murnighan (2002) found that binding (i.e., enforceable) agreements inhibited trust because participants attributed the other party's trustworthy behavior to external factors (i.e., the presence of a binding agreement).

Trustworthy attributions are shaped by the manager's behavior as well as the context in which that behavior occurs. While attribution theory suggests that individuals are likely to attribute a negative event to the other party, the tendency to make internal attributions for negative events is offset by the manager's trustworthy behavior (Korsgaard et al., 2002). Existing levels of trust can also influence attributions about subsequent actions and events (Dirks and Ferrin, 2001). The potential for misattribution – and hence, misplaced trust or distrust – is considerable. For example, the fundamental attribution error would suggest that contextual factors, such as organizational policies, are likely to be attributed to the manager and influence trust in the manager (Dirks and Ferrin, 2002). Consistent with this view, Ferrin and Dirks (2003) found that a competitive reward system leads to negative perceptions of the trustee's motivations, which in turn leads to lower trust. Moreover, random contextual influences such as incidental mood, can lead to misattributions of trustworthiness (Dunn and Schweitzer, 2005).

The recent research and theory on attributions provides important insight into how direct experience with the manager is interpreted and how those inferences lead to trust. However, another theoretical stream on presumptive trust suggests that inferences of trust can occur rapidly based on minimal experience with the other party.

Presumptive trust

Theories of presumptive trust (McKnight et al., 1998; Meyerson et al., 1996; Williams, 2001) are based on the proposition that context can lead individuals to form trust rapidly in the initial stages of a relationship. There are three main reasons why trust may form presumptively. First, presumptive trust may result from a process of ascribing trustworthy attributes to the individual (Kramer, 1999). Unlike the deliberative attributional process described above, the process involved in presumptive trust is based on a relatively rapid cognitive process of categorization. That is, inferences regarding the individual are based on attributes associated with the category to which the individual belongs rather than on direct experience with the individual. Categorization may be based on shared group membership, roles or reputation (Kramer, 1999). Because categorization-based judgments are less effortful than calculated reasoning, factors that limit the motivation and ability to engage in more effortful processing, such as a lack of accountability and time pressure, should result in reliance on category-based processing (Kruglanski, 1989). For example, both Williams (2001) and Meyerson et al. (1996) argue that time pressure increases the propensity of individuals to adopt a presumptive trust stance.

Second, institutional or structural factors can lead to presumptive trust. Specifically, the existence of a structure of rules and regulations can impact interpersonal trust (McKnight et al., 1998; Zaheer et al., 1998). A similar concept is rule-based trust (Kramer, 1999), wherein individuals tend to trust others in the same organization to the extent that there is a shared understanding of the formal and informal rules for interacting. Theory and research also suggest that trust can be presumptively conferred based on third party ties. That is, trust may be 'transferred' from a trusted party to an unfamiliar party based on mere association or the sharing of information (Kramer, 1999; Stewart, 2003).

Finally, theory suggests that individual differences, such as the propensity to trust

(Rotter, 1967), may lead to presumptive trust. McKnight et al. (1998) argued that individual differences are likely to exert a relatively strong influence in the initial stages of a relationship and the impact of individual differences is likely to decline over time as direct experience overwhelms individual tendencies to trust. Theory on presumptive trust is clearly most pertinent to the initial stages of a relationship and the formation of trust. How trust changes as the relationship matures is not addressed in these models but rather is the focus of stage theories of interpersonal trust.

Stage theories

Stage models of trust focus on how trust evolves between parties over the life of the relationship. These models differ from other approaches to trust in that they depict trust as qualitatively different during different stages of the relationship; that is, the basis of trust changes over time (Lewicki et al., 2006). Shapiro et al. (1992) initially developed a three-stage model of trust consisting of deterrence-based trust, knowledge-based trust and identification-based trust. Lewicki and Bunker (1996) adapted this model, referring to deterrence-based trust as calculus-based trust and delving more deeply into the transitions between stages. Subsequently, Rousseau et al. (1998) presented a two stage model consisting of calculus-based trust and relational trust.

Deterrence- or calculus-based trust is an impersonal form of trust, based on the structure in place to enforce cooperation. This form is similar to institutional or rule-based trust (Kramer, 1999; McKnight, et al., 1998), and thus relates to the factors contributing to presumptive trust as well as the economic perspectives on trust (e.g., Williamson, 1993). Knowledge-based trust is derived from direct experience and interaction with the other party and it thus relates to exchange-based and behavioral views of trust (e.g., Mayer et al., 1995). Identification-based trust is based on the internalization of shared belief and values. This level of trust is similar to affect-based trust (McAllister, 1996) or relationship-based trust (Atkinson and Butcher, 2003) in that it is believed to develop through a strong interpersonal bond between individuals. Stage models presume that different factors influence trust at each stage. For example, structural controls such as binding agreements and exit costs (Eisenhardt, 1989) are likely to affect calculus-based trust but not knowledge-based or identification-based trust. Knowledge based trust is stimulated through regular interaction and communication, but, at least in the short term, this is insufficient for the formation of identification-based trust. Identification-based trust alone requires a shared identity and intensive, frequent interactions. Stage models also give attention to how relationships progress through these stages. For example, Lewicki et al. (2006) argued that progression from calculus-based to knowledge-based trust requires sufficient opportunity to exhibit voluntary trustworthiness. Further, interactions need to be frequent and complex enough to provide reliable and representative information about the trustee's intentions. As noted above, transition to identification requires more intensive interaction and a transformation of motivational orientation from an individualized perspective to a collective perspective (Lewicki et al., 2006).

ANTECEDENTS OF TRUST IN THE MANAGER

Although the aforementioned theories address disparate aspects of the development of trust, viewed together they suggest a finite set of influences on the development and maintenance of trust. The first broad class of factors is direct experience with the manager, which provides information about the character of the manager and builds a base of the exchange relationship. Second, contextual factors directly affect trust, particularly in early stages. Third, a consistent theme in theories of interpersonal trust is the role of individual differences among followers in the tendency to trust. Finally, theory suggests that individual differences and context influence trust by shaping perceptions and attributions of managerial behavior. Below, we review empirical evidence in each of these categories.

Direct experience

Trustworthy managerial behavior

Several studies have directly investigated Mayer et al.'s (1995) typology of trustworthiness (ability, benevolence, and integrity) by using a measure developed by Mayer and Davis (1999) that assesses behavior indicative of these three attributes. These studies, and others using similar measures, have consistently demonstrated that all three categories of behavior are uniquely predictive of trust in the manager (Davis et al., 2000; Ferrin and Dirks, 2003; Mayer and Davis, 1999; Mayer and Gavin, 2005; Shamir and Lapidot, 2003; Tan and Tan, 2000). In addition, Gill et al. (2005) manipulated perceived level of ability, benevolence, and integrity of a co-worker and found that higher level of these attributes led to increased trusting intentions. Furthermore, two studies (Bijlsma and van de Bunt, 2003; Korsgaard et al., 2002) investigated comprehensive typologies of managerial trustworthy behavior and found that the cluster of behaviors as a whole is significantly related to trust in the manager. Other studies have focused on a particular trustworthy behavior. The manager's communication style is one of the most frequently cited and reliable predictors of trust in the manager (Dirks and Ferrin, 2002). Communication is a multifaceted construct, involving two-way exchange, feedback giving, and listening, and its effects on trust may not be consistent across these facets. For example, Bijlsma and van de Bunt (2003) found that listening was significantly related to trust in the manager, but giving feedback was not. Other studies have focused on sharing and delegating control. This construct has been operationalized in a variety of ways such as participation in decision making (Gillespie and Mann, 2004), process control (Brashear et al., 2005), outcome control (Brashear et al., 2005), and delegation (Duffy and Ferrier, 2003) and, in its various manifestations, has been consistently related to trust in the manager (Dirks and

Ferrin, 2002). Additionally, studies show that dysfunctional leadership behaviors, such as a laissez-faire style (Gillespie and Mann, 2004), abusive behavior and excessive monitoring (Duffy and Ferrier, 2003) and opportunism (Brashear et al., 2003) are negatively related to trust.

In terms of a more global leadership style, the most frequently applied model is transformational leadership. Dirks and Ferrin's (2002) meta-analysis found significant relationships for both transformational leadership and transactional leadership to trust in the manager, ($\rho = 0.72$ and $\rho = 0.59$, respectively). As these findings and subsequent research suggest, transformational leadership tends to have a stronger relationship to trust in the manager than transactional leadership (Hoyt and Blascovich, 2003). Another approach to leadership style is to look at empowerment, which refers to the tactics that managers use to create a sense of intrinsic motivation (Spreitzer, 1995). For example, Moye and Henkin (2006) found that employees' feelings of empowerment were positively related to interpersonal trust in managers.

A final approach to modeling the interactions between leaders and followers is organizational justice theory. Organizational justice is not a theory of trust per se but some theoretical frameworks (e.g., Tyler and Lind, 1992) posit that justice perceptions are critical to the decision to trust persons in authority. There are four broad categories of justice (Colquitt, 2001):

- distributive (the fairness of the allocation of outcomes);
- procedural (the legitimacy of procedures to make allocation decisions);
- interactional (the quality of treatment when interacting with decision makers); and
- informational (the quality of communications during the process of decision making).

All four of these factors have shown a significant and positive relationship with trust (Dirks and Ferrin, 2002; Kernan and Hanges, 2002).

The elements of distributive, procedural, interactional, and informational justice correspond closely to the trustworthy behaviors reviewed above and inform on the integrity and benevolence of the manager. Interactional and informational justice are largely within the control of the manager, and thus capture the behavior of the manager. Distributive and procedural justice are less under the exclusive control of the manager. Thus, under some circumstances, these forms of justice represent contextual factors that shape the behavior of the manager.

Recent research suggests that employees differentiate between organization-based justice, and justice that is within the control of the manager, such that only supervisor-based justice tends to predict attitudes toward the manager, and organization-based justice predicts attitudes toward the organization. For example, Rupp and Cropanzano (2002) found that only supervisor justice predicted the quality of the exchange relationship with the supervisor. Similarly, several studies have found that distributive and/or procedural justice did not uniquely predict trust in the supervisor beyond the effect of interactional justice (Ambrose and Schminke, 2003; Aryee et al., 2002; Stinglhamber et al., 2006). These findings are consistent with theory on attributions of trust, for it suggests that justice is more apt to influence trust in the manager when it is more readily attributed to the manager.

In summary, although much of the research on managerial behavior and trust in the manager has been conducted in the context of other theories (e.g., leadership and organizational justice), the behaviors investigated correspond to the broad categories of ability, benevolence integrity. Consistent with this view, Colquitt et al.'s (2007) meta-analysis across these literatures found support for the unique effects of each of the components of trustworthiness on perceptions on trust.

Quality of the exchange relationship

Direct experience is also cumulatively represented in the quality of the exchange relationship. A variety of constructs capture the quality of the exchange relationship, such as leader-member exchange, perceived organizational support (POS), the extent that expectations in the psychological contract are met, all of which have been significantly related to trust (Dirks and Ferrin, 2002; Stinglhamber et al., 2005; Whitener, 2001). Not surprisingly, the mere duration of the relationship appears to be less important than the quality of the exchanges between manager and employee. Indeed, Dirks and Ferrin's (2002) meta-analysis indicated a non-significant effect of length of relationship ($r = -.01$, $k = 5$) on trust in the manager. However, a more recent study (Perry and Mankin, 2004) found a significant positive relationship between length of the relationship and trust in immediate supervisor.

There are two cautions about findings regarding the exchange quality and trust. First, most of the studies involving organization-level exchange variables (i.e., POS and psychological contract) focused on trust in organization-level management; thus, the link to trust in the manager at the interpersonal level is not clear. Second, it is not clear whether trust is conceptually distinct from some exchange constructs such as leader-member exchange (Dirks and Ferrin, 2002). Some scholars argue that trust is an aspect of the quality of the exchange (Ambrose and Schminke, 2003), and have incorporated trust into measures of exchange quality (Shore et al., 2006).

Context

As theories of presumptive trust suggest, context can predispose individuals to trust their managers. One reason is that contextual factors can minimize the risk of unprincipled behavior as well as compel, encourage or enable untrustworthy behavior. One such contextual factor that is likely to work in this fashion is HR policy. Some studies have examined HR policy systems, such as high performance work systems (e.g., Frenkel and Orlitzky, 2005; Whitener, 2001; Zacharatos et al., 2005) while others have focused on specific practices such as performance appraisal

(Mayer and Davis, 1999) or compensation (Coyle-Shapiro et al., 2002), all finding a positive relationship to trust. Most of these studies, however, have examined trust in organization's management as whole, rather than interpersonal trust in one's immediate manager.

While the link at the organizational level is consistently positive, the impact of HR policy on trust in the manager at an interpersonal level is less clear. Korsgaard et al. (2002) found that the general fairness of HR policy was positively related to both trustworthy behavior and trust in manager, but did not have a unique relationship to trust beyond the effect of trustworthy behavior. Similarly, Tzafrir et al. (2004) found that availability of training and development was positively associated with trust in the manager, and this relationship was mediated by perceptions of procedural justice. The findings of these studies suggest that HR policy does not have a direct effect on trust in the manager but rather affects trust indirectly by enabling or promoting trustworthy behavior. A similar argument might be made for the impact of organizational structure in that research suggests that structure influences justice perceptions (Schminke et al., 2002) and justice perceptions are related to trust in the manager. However, we know of no empirical work that directly examines this sort of mediated process. On the other hand, policy and structures that compel principled behavior may have the effect of inhibiting trust because such mechanisms serve as a replacement for trust (Husted and Folger, 2004; Sitkin and Roth, 1993).

Another factor determining presumptive trust is shared group membership or identity. In the context of supervisor-subordinate relations, shared identity has been investigated in terms of relational demography. That is, leaders and followers who are members of the same social category (e.g., gender) are expected, based on the shared social identity, to trust each other more than dyads composed of demographically dissimilar individuals. Consistent with this argument, Farh et al., (1998) found that subordinates trusted their supervisors more if they shared the same education level. Another manifestation of shared identity is Guanxi, a Chinese concept wherein individuals share a relational commonality (e.g., neighbors, alumni of the same school), which is also positively related to trust in the manager (Chen et al., 2004; Farh et al., 1998; Wong et al., 2003). Similarly, perceived value similarity is positively associated with interpersonal trust (Earle and Siegrist, 2006; Siegrist et al., 2000). Unlike social identity, which is apt to affect swift trust, this form of shared identity is likely to influence trust over time, as the perception of value similarity requires direct experience or information that indicates the trustee's value systems.

Trustee characteristics

Many models of trust posit that individual differences influence trust, and the most frequently cited characteristic is propensity to trust (e.g., Mayer et al., 1995). Two recent meta-analyses found significant relationships between propensity to trust and trust in the manager (Colquitt et al., 2007; Dirks and Ferrin, 2002). Demographic characteristics, namely gender, age, and ethnicity, have also been investigated as antecedents of trust. However, research has not demonstrated consistent relationships to trust in the manager (Moye and Henkin, 2006; Perry and Mankin, 2004).

Joint effects

An important implication of many of models of trust is that context and individual differences influence how direct experience with the leader is interpreted. That is, theory suggests a variety of ways in which direct experience interacts with context and individual differences. Consistent with this implication, Dirks and Ferrin (2002) reported substantial heterogeneity in effect sizes of the antecedents of trust, suggesting the existence of moderating variables. However, theory-driven moderated relationships have received limited empirical attention. Below, we highlight findings that inform on the joint effects of experience, individual differences and context. One of the implications of presumptive trust is that presumptive factors may alter the way individuals interpret their experiences with the leader. One such factor is social identity. Followers who share a social identity with their managers are likely to presume trust, and hence, engage in biased information processing that confirms this presumption. Thus, they may be less sensitive to leader behavior. In contrast, because they have little basis for trusting (or distrusting) their manager, individuals who do not share a group identity may be more vigilant and thus sensitive to leader behavior. Consistent with this implication, Duffy and Ferrier (2003) found that demographic similarity moderated the impact of leader behavior (delegation, procedural justice behavior, and excessive monitoring) on trust in the manager such that the relationship between leader behavior and trust was stronger for dissimilar dyads.

Another presumptive factor that is likely to interact with direct experience is the propensity to trust, although the pattern is likely to differ from that of group identity. Specifically, McKnight et al. (1998) argued that the propensity to trust is apt to more strongly affect trust early in relationships, because there is an absence of direct experience or information. Gill et al. (2005) provided evidence of this sort of relationship in a study comparing favorable, unfavorable, and ambiguous cues regarding trustworthiness. Specifically, they found that the relationship between the propensity to trust and trust was relatively strong when cues regarding the leader were ambiguous. In the presence of unambiguously favorable or unfavorable cues, the relationship between propensity to trust and trust was substantially smaller.

Stage models of trust suggest that, as the relationship progresses, trust grows more robust to violations (Lewicki et al., 2006), which suggests that the impact of a given experience on trust is weaker as the relationship matures. In contrast, trust in early-stage relationships is likely to be more fragile; thus leader behavior is apt to more strongly affect

trust. In line with this view, Lines et al. (2005) found that the effect of leader behavior, in the form of social accounts during organizational change, is weaker for employees with less tenure with the manager.

As noted earlier, Mayer et al. (1995) posited that context may affect perceptions of trust and trustworthiness by determining the relevance or significance of certain leader attributes. Ambrose and Schminke (2003) provided a test of this basic proposition in a study of the interaction of justice and mechanistic versus organic organizational structures. They reasoned that mechanistic organizations rely on formal rules and procedures and thus make procedural justice highly salient. In contrast, because organic organizations are based on interpersonal transactions, interactional justice is more salient. In support of these arguments, they found that structure significantly moderated the relationship of both procedural and interactional justice to trust. As expected, the relationship between procedural justice and trust was stronger in mechanistic organizations than organic organizations. As well, the relationship between interactional justice and trust was stronger in organic organizations than in mechanistic ones.

Further evidence of how context determines the relevance of leader behavior to trust was demonstrated in a study of culture and justice (Lee et al., 2000). These authors reasoned that the cultural value of power distance involves norms and expectations for egalitarian treatment. Individuals from cultures with a smaller power distance should therefore expect to be treated in an equal and consistent manner, regardless of their status. Hence, individuals from these cultures should be more sensitive to procedural and interactional justice. Their findings supported this contention for both forms of justice.

CONSEQUENCES OF TRUST IN THE MANAGER

Theories of trust broadly refer to risk taking behavior or co-operation under conditions of risk as the main consequences of trust (e.g., Deutsch, 1958; Meyer et al., 1995). Risk taking is manifested in employees in terms of organizational citizenship behavior (OCB) and in-role performance in that both of these behaviors are thought to be motivated by expectations of rewards or reciprocation from the manager. Additionally, risk taking is manifested in terms of particular choice behaviors such as the choice to share information openly. Manifestations of the non-cooperative behavior in employees, such as non-compliance with work rules, have also been investigated. Other studies have examined intentional or attitudinal indicators of cooperation. A final category of outcomes are indicators of the employees' willingness to remain in the relationship, such as loyalty, organizational commitment and intentions to leave.

Quantitative reviews of the literature indicate a significant relationship between trust in the manager and OCB both at the global level (Colquitt et al., 2007) and at the dimensional level of OCB (Dirks and Ferrin, 2002). Other studies have supported this relationship (e.g., Wat and Shaffer, 2005; Wong et al., 2003; Wong et al., 2005). However, research suggests that the relationship between trust and OCB may be more complex. Both Dirks and Ferrin (2002) and Colquitt et al. (2007) found indication of unmeasured moderators. Consistent with this view, Wong et al. (2005) found an interaction between trust and organizational form, such that the relationship between trust and OCB is stronger in state-owned enterprises as compared to joint ventures. However, this finding was obtained for trust in management at the organizational level, which Dirks and Ferrin found is not as strongly related to OCB as interpersonal trust in the manager. In many of these studies, trust functioned as an immediate antecedent of OCB, mediating the effects of more distal variables such as organizational justice or leader member exchange (e.g., Wat and Shaffer, 2005), but there is also evidence that the relationship between trust in the manager and OCB itself is mediated by attentional focus (Mayer and Gavin, 2005).

Trust in management is also significantly related to in-role performance (Colquitt et al., 2007; Dirks and Ferrin, 2002). As well, research suggests that trust in the manager is related to the performance of groups or units (Dirks and Ferrin, 2001). Both quantitative and narrative reviews (Colquitt et al., 2007; Dirks and Ferrin, 2001, 2002), indicate significant inconsistencies in these relationships, which suggest unmeasured moderators, with some studies finding no significant relationship (Mayer and Gavin, 2005). Consistent with these findings, Goris et al. (2003) found congruence between employees growth needs, and job scope moderated the relationship between trust and productivity, such that trust was related to productivity only under conditions of low congruence. Further, Wong et al. (2005) found that trust mitigated the relationship of job security to performance within state-owned enterprises and joint ventures. Colquitt et al. (2007) examined a broad category of specific risk-taking choices, including delegating important tasks, open sharing of information, and deferring to a trustee. They found that these choices are significantly related to trust in the manager, although the findings were based on a limited number of samples (6).

Non-cooperative behaviors on the part of the employee are indicated by a failure to comply with rules and meet minimum standards. These include a variety of counter-productive behaviors, such as disciplinary actions, disregard of work rules, tardiness and absenteeism, workplace deviance and aggression (Colquitt et al., 2007). As expected, the Colquitt et al. (2007) meta-analysis found a significant negative relationship between trust and these behaviors, and there were no indications of unmeasured moderators.

In terms of intentions and attitudes, research indicates that trust is positively related to job satisfaction and acceptance of decisions, and the credibility of information (Dirks and Ferrin, 2001, 2002). Finally, research indicates that trust in supervisors is related to various indicators of willingness to remain or exit the relationship, including organizational commitment, loyalty, and intentions to leave (Brashear et al., 2003; Dirks and Ferrin, 2002; Wong et al., 2002). As with many behavioral outcomes, some of these relationships may be more complex: Dirks and Ferrin (2002) found indications of unmeasured moderators of organizational commitment. Consistent with this finding, Watson and Papamarcos (2002) found that trust moderated the relationship between the reliability of communication and organizational commitment, such that the relationship was stronger when trust was higher. Further, Wong et al. (2003) reported evidence of an indirect effect of trust in managers in that the negative relationship between trust in managers and intentions to quit was fully mediated by trust in management.

UNRESOLVED ISSUES AND FUTURE DIRECTIONS

Construct and measurement

As noted earlier, there is growing consensus on the definition of trust as a multidimensional construct that comprises an affective, cognitive, and behavioral component (e.g., Clark and Payne, 1997; Cummings and Bromiley, 1996; Mayer et al., 1995; McAllister, 1995). However, as Lewicki et al. (2006) note, the measurement of trust lags behind theoretical developments due to insufficient effort directed at measuring the different facets of trust. In empirical research, trust is often measured with little regard to these distinctions, which is likely the cause of inconsistent and heterogeneous findings noted in narrative and quantitative reviews (Colquitt et al., 2007; Dirks and Ferrin, 2001, 2002). Furthermore, it appears that existing measures that attempt to differentiate between these facets sometimes fall short of this objective. For example, previous attempts to develop a comprehensive measure that taps into all three facets of trust have not been successful in distinguishing between cognitive and affective dimensions

(Clark and Payne, 1997; Cummings and Bromiley, 1996).

The behavioral facet of trust poses its own unique challenges. This facet generally refers to and has been operationalized as a trustor's intended risk taking behavior (Clark and Payne, 1997; Cummings and Bromiley, 1996; Currall and Judge, 1995). However, this approach risks confounding the construct of trust with it consequences (Das and Teng, 2004). Cummings and Bromiley (1996), for example, operationalize behavioral trust as the polar opposite of monitoring and control. However, while research to date found that monitoring is negatively related to trust, it is more appropriately considered a separate concept rather than a component or facet of trust (e.g., Langfred, 2004). In addition, Langfred (2004) raises the question of causality between monitoring and trust. A similar problem occurs in the treatment of control as an indicator of low trust. Das and Teng (2001) argue that trust and control are reciprocally related and may jointly affect outcomes.

Another challenge to the conceptual and operational definition of trust is its relation to distrust. Controversy persists over whether trust and distrust represent a single continuum or two separate dimensions (Lewicki et al., 2006). Most measures are based on the assumption of a single continuum. However, Lewicki et al. (1998) have argued that distrust is a distinct dimension with unique consequences. While there is some preliminary evidence of distinct dimensions (Lewicki et al., 2006), further work is needed on developing and documenting a two-dimensional measure. However this debate is resolved, greater attention should be directed toward distrust and the avoidance motivations associated with it.

Theory

One issue warranting greater theoretical and empirical consideration is the relationship between trust in the manager and follower behavior. Colquitt et al. (2007) examined four behavioral consequences in their meta-analysis:

- task performance;
- OCB;
- risk taking behavior; and
- counter-productive behavior.

While they found that all four consequences were significantly related to trust, all but counter-productive behavior exhibited significant heterogeneity to suggest the presence of moderators. In their narrative review, Dirks and Ferrin (2001) reached a similar conclusion that trust is more likely to function as a moderator of other predictors of behavior. However, theory and systematic empirical support regarding the complexities of the trust-behavior link is clearly lacking. Trust scholars should also give careful consideration to specifying and differentiating between behavioral consequences. Theories of trust typically specify a single, broad behavioral construct such as cooperation (Deutsch, 1962) or risk taking (Mayer et al., 1995). As Mayer and Gavin (2005) note, the findings for the impact of trust on some forms of employee behavior, such as OCB, are more consistent than for other forms of behavior such as in-role performance.

Moreover, greater attention should be given to the mechanisms underlying the effect of trust on behavior. For example, an oft-cited justification for the trust-OCB link is social exchange theory (Korsgaard et al., 2002). OCB is by definition a voluntary behavior that the employer is not contractually obligated to reward. Social exchange theory would suggest that employees engage in OCB when they trust their manager because they expect their manager reciprocate. This explanation does not fit as well with the relationship between trust and in-role performance which, unlike OCB, is typically specified, monitored and formally rewarded. Thus, the link between in-role performance and trust may be governed by other processes.

This chapter focused mainly on trust in the manager as an interpersonal phenomenon. Yet, most of the theory underlying the research

reviewed was not designed to specifically address trust in the leader. The hierarchical nature of the leader-follower relationship is unique (Atkinson and Butcher, 2003). Unlike peer relationships, the relationship between a manager and employee involves an asymmetric distribution of power; thus, all things being equal, the employee faces a greater degree of risk than does the manager. Further, the form of dependence between manager and employee differs in that each party expects a different set of rewards in the exchange relationship (Kramer, 1996). For example, the manager relies on the employee to perform certain tasks whereas the employee relies on the manager to provide support and resources to perform the task. Therefore, managers and employees face unique consequences of trusting the other party.

Addressing the unique aspects of trust in the context of leader-follower relationships does not necessitate developing a unique model of trust in the manager. Indeed, a proliferation of models specific to different forms of relationships is probably not warranted. Colquitt et al.'s (2007) meta-analysis found few instances where the type of relationship moderated the links between trustworthiness, trust and behavior. Only the relationship between integrity and trust differed, such that integrity was more strongly related to trust in the manager than trust in coworkers. Rather than directing efforts toward a specific model of trust in the manager, theory could incorporate the elements that differentiate forms of relationships in terms of the nature and degree of dependence (Sheppard and Sherman, 1998). To this end, more research is needed on trust in non-hierarchical relationships such as between co-workers and within work groups.

In addition to the hierarchical nature, trust in the manager is unique in that it is an interpersonal phenomenon. Thus, it is important to differentiate between effects of interpersonal trust in the manager and organizational trust in management (Dirks and Ferrin, 2002). As noted earlier, research on social exchange, organizational justice, and trust, all indicate that individuals are differentially affected by their experience with their immediate supervisor and with the organization as a whole. This differentiation necessitates a multi-level view of trust. Furthermore, cross-level effects should be considered in the formation of interpersonal trust itself. For example, as noted earlier, theory differentiates between what Atkinson and Butcher (2003) refer to as personal bases of trust, such as ability and integrity, and impersonal bases of trust, such as roles and regulation. Impersonally-based trust, wherein the manager is the agent or personification of the organization, represents a cross-level effect on the formation of trust. Moreover, Dirks and Skarlicki (2004) note that trust in the manager does not exist in isolation but influences and is influenced by trust in the subordinate. Trust in the manager can also impact the dynamics of the group and its aggregate performance (Dirks, 2000; Mayer and Gavin, 2005) which represents another cross-level effect. In sum, there is a clear need for cross-level theory and empirical research on the determinants and consequences of trust.

CONCLUSION

Trust in organizations has received considerable theoretical and empirical attention since the 1990s. This review sought to document the progress of research and theory on trust, as well as identify the remaining gaps. Among those gaps is the lack of an integrative theory (Kramer, 1999; Lewicki et al., 2006). The problem is not merely a lack of integration of theories within the field trust, but that scholarly interest in trust spans theories that focus on other phenomena (e.g., leadership). Indeed, it is interesting to note the sheer volume of empirical studies that involve measures of trust wherein the construct was the central component of the theory used to develop the hypotheses. Additionally, controversies over the definition of the construct persist, particularly regarding its dimensionality. Finally, empirical progress lags behind theoretical developments, which

demands more innovative and rigorous methods. These gaps also point to opportunities in the study of trust. Recent research in trust brought greater precision to the meaning and significance of interpersonal trust in organizations and in doing so, helped set the agenda for future research. This brings to attention a rich and promising area that calls for a theoretical integration and empirical contributions. We hope that this chapter not only provides an overview of the current standing of the literature, but also stimulates further inquiry regarding the role of interpersonal trust by providing suggestions and, more importantly, a useful framework for future researchers.

REFERENCES

Ajzen, I. (2001) 'Nature and operation of attitudes', *Annual Review of Psychology*, 52 (1): 27–58.

Ambrose, M.L. and Schminke, M. (2003) 'Organization structure as a moderator of the relationship between procedural justice, interactional justice, perceived organizational support, and supervisory trust', *Journal of Applied Psychology*, 88 (2): 295–305.

Aryee, S., Budhwar, P.S. and Chen, Z.X. (2002) 'Trust as a mediator of the relationship between organizational justice and work outcomes: Test of a social exchange model', *Journal of Organizational Behavior*, 23 (3): 267–286.

Atkinson, S. and Butcher, D. (2003) 'Trust in managerial relationships', *Journal of Managerial Psychology*, 18 (4): 282–304.

Bijlsma, K.M. and van de Bunt, G.G. (2003) 'Antecedents of trust in managers: A "bottom up" approach', *Personnel Review*, 32 (5): 638–664.

Bijlsma, K.M. and Koopman, P. (2003) 'Introduction: Trust within organisations', *Personnel Review*, 32 (5): 543–555.

Blau, P.M. (1964) *Exchange and Power in Social Life*. New York, NY: John Wiley and Sons.

Brashear, T.G., Boles, J.S., Bellenger, D.N. and Brooks, C.M. (2003) 'An empirical test of trust–building processes and outcomes in sales manager–salesperson relationships', *Journal of the Academy of Marketing Science*, 31 (2): 189–200.

Brashear, T.G., Manolis, C. and Brooks, C.M. (2005) 'The effects of control, trust, and justice on salesperson turnover', *Journal of Business Research*, 58 (3): 241–249.

Chen, C.C., Chen, Y. and Xin, K. (2004) 'Guanxi practices and trust in management: A procedural justice perspective', *Organization Science*, 15 (2): 200–209.

Clark, M.C. and Payne, R.L. (1997) 'The nature and structure of workers' trust in management', *Journal of Organisational Behaviour*, 18 (3): 205–224.

Colquitt, J.A. (2001) 'On the Dimensionality of Organizational Justice: A Construct Validation of a Measure', *Journal of Applied Psychology*, 86 (3): 386–400.

Colquitt, J.A., Brent, S.A. and LePine, J.A. (2007) 'Trust, trustworthiness, and trust propensity: A meta-analytic test of their unique relationships with risk taking and job performance', *Journal of Applied Psychology*, 92 (4): 909–927.

Coyle-Shapiro, J.A.M., Morrow, P., Richardson, R. and Dunn, S.R. (2002) 'Using profit sharing to enhance employee attitudes: A longitudinal examination of the effects on trust and commitment', *Human Resource Management*, 41 (4): 423–439.

Cummings, L.L. and Bromiley, P. (1996) 'The organizational trust inventory (OTI): Development and validation', in R.M. Kramer and T.R. Tyler (eds), *Trust in Organizations: Frontiers of Theory and Research*. Thousand Oaks, CA: Sage, pp. 302–330.

Currall, S.C. and Judge, T.A. (1995) 'Measuring trust between organizational boundary role persons', *Organizational Behavior and Human Decision Processes*, 64 (2): 151–170.

Das, T.K. and Teng, B.S. (2001) 'Trust, control, and risk in strategic alliances: An integrated framework', *Organization Studies*, 22 (2): 251–283.

Das, T.K. and Teng, B.S. (2004) 'The risk–based view of trust: A conceptual framework', *Journal of Business and Psychology*, 19 (1): 85–116.

Davis, J.H., Schoorman, F.D., Mayer, R.C. and Tan, H.H. (2000) 'The trusted general manager and business unit performance: Empirical evidence of a competitive advantage', *Strategic Management Journal*, 21 (5): 563–576.

Deutsch, M. (1958) 'Trust and suspicion', *Journal of Conflict Resolution*, 2 (4): 265–279.

Deutsch, M. (1962) 'Cooperation and trust: Some theoretical notes', in *Nebraska Symposium on Motivation*. Lincoln: Nebraska University Press, pp. 275–320.

Dirks, K.T. (2000) 'Trust in leadership and team performance: Evidence from NCAA Basketball', *Journal of Applied Psychology*, 85 (6): 1004–1012.

Dirks, K.T. and Ferrin, D.L. (2001) 'The role of trust in organizational settings', *Organization Science*, 12 (4): 450–467.

Dirks, K.T. and Ferrin, D.L. (2002) 'Trust in leadership: Meta–analytic findings and implications for research and practice', *Journal of Applied Psychology*, 87 (4): 611–628.

Dirks, K.T. and Skarlicki, D.P. (2004) 'Trust in leaders: Existing research and emerging issues', in R.M. Kramer, and K.S. Cook (eds), *Trust and Distrust in Organizations: Dilemmas and Approaches*. New York: Russell Sage Foundation, pp. 21–40.

Duffy, M.K. and Ferrier, W.J. (2003) 'Birds of a feather…? How supervisor-subordinate dissimilarity moderates the influence of supervisor behaviors on workplace attitudes', *Group and Organization Management*, 28 (2): 217–248.

Dunn, J.R. and Schweitzer, M.E. (2005) 'Feeling and believing: The influence of emotion on trust', *Journal of Personality and Social Psychology*, 88 (5): 736–748.

Earle, T.C. and Siegrist, M. (2006) 'Morality information, performance information, and the distinction between trust and confidence', *Journal of Applied Social Psychology*, 36 (2): 383–416.

Eisenhardt, K.M. (1989) 'Agency theory: An assessment and review', *Academy of Management Review*, 14 (1): 57–74.

Farh, J., Tsui, A.S., Xin, K. and Cheng (1998) 'The influence of relational demography and *guanxi*: The Chinese case', *Organization Science*, 9 (4): 471–488.

Ferrin, D.L. and Dirks, K.T. (2003) 'The use of rewards to increase and decrease trust: Mediating processes and differential effects', *Organization Science*, 14 (1): 18–31.

Frenkel, S. and Orlitzky, M. (2005) 'Organizational trustworthiness and workplace labor productivity: Testing a new theory', *Asia Pacific Journal of Human Resources*, 43 (1): 34–51.

Gill, H., Boies, K., Finegan, J.E. and McNally, J. (2005) 'Antecedents of trust: Establishing a boundary condition for the relation between propensity to trust and intention to trust', *Journal of Business and Psychology*, 19 (3): 287–302.

Gillespie, N.A. and Mann, L. (2004) 'Transformational leadership and shared values: The building blocks of trust', *Journal of Managerial Psychology*, 19 (6): 588–607.

Goris, J., Vaught, B.C. and Petit Jr., J.D. (2003) 'Effects of trust in superiors and influence of superiors on the association between individual-job congruence and job performance/satisfaction', *Journal of Business and Psychology*, 17 (3): 327–343.

Hoyt, C.L. and Blascovich, J. (2003) 'Transformational and transactional leadership in virtual and physical environments', *Small Group Research*, 34 (6): 678–715.

Husted, B.W. and Folger, R. (2004) 'Fairness and transaction costs: The contribution of organizational justice theory to an integrative model of economic organization', *Organization Science*, 15 (6): 719–729.

Kernan, M.C. and Hanges, P.J. (2002) 'Survivor reactions to reorganization: Antecedents and consequences of procedural, interpersonal, and informational justice', *Journal of Applied Psychology*, 87 (5): 916–928.

Konovsky, M.A. and Pugh, S.D. (1994) 'Citizenship behavior and social exchange', *Academy of Management Journal*, 37 (3): 656–669.

Korsgaard, M.A., Brodt, S.E. and Whitener, E.M. (2002) 'Trust in the face of conflict: The role of managerial trustworthy behavior and organizational context', *Journal of Applied Psychology*, 87 (2): 312–319.

Kramer R.M., and Tyler T.R. (eds) (1996) *Trust in Organizations*. Thousand Oaks, CA: Sage.

Kramer, R. (1996) 'Divergent realities and convergent disappointments in the hierarchic relation: Trust and the intuitive auditor at work', in R.M. Kramer, and T.R. Tyler (eds), *Trust in Organizations: Frontiers of Theory and Research*. Thousand Oaks, CA: Sage, pp. 216–45.

Kramer, R.M. (1999) 'Trust and distrust in organizations: Emerging perspectives, enduring questions', *Annual Review of Psychology*, 50 (1): 569–598.

Kramer, R.M., Brewer, H.B. and Hanna, B.A. (1996) 'Collective trust and collective action: The decision to trust as a social dilemma', in R.M. Kramer and T.R. Tyler (eds), *Trust in Organizations: Frontiers of Theory and Research*. Thousand Oaks, CA: Sage, pp. 357–389.

Kruglanski, A.W. (1989) *Lay Epistemics and Human Knowledge: Cognitive and Motivational Bases*. New York: Plenum Press.

Langfred, C.W. (2004) 'Too much of a good thing? Negative effects of high trust and individual autonomy in selfmanaging teams'. *Academy of Management Journal*, 47 (3): 385–399.

Lee, C., Pillutla, M. and Law, K.S. (2000) 'Power–distance, gender, and organizational justice', *Journal of Management*, 26 (4): 685–704.

Lewicki, R.J. and Bunker, B.B. (1996) 'Developing and maintaining trust in work relationships', in R.M. Kramer and T.R. Tyler (eds), *Trust in Organizations: Frontiers of Theory and Research*. Thousand Oaks, CA: Sage, pp. 114–139.

Lewicki, R.J., McAllister, D. and Bies, R. (1998) 'Trust and distrust: New relationships and realities', *Academy of Management Review*, 23 (3): 438–458.

Lewicki, R.J., Tomlinson, E.C. and Gillespie, N. (2006) 'Models of interpersonal trust development: Theoretical approaches, empirical evidence, and future directions', *Journal of Management*, 32 (6): 991–1022.

Lines, R., Selart, M., Espedal, B. and Johansen, S. (2005) 'The production of trust during organizational change', *Journal of Change Management*, 5 (2): 221–245.

Malhotra, D. and Murnighan, J.K. (2002) 'The effects of formal and informal contracts on interpersonal trust', *Administrative Science Quarterly*, 47 (3): 534–559.

Mayer, R.C. and Davis, J.H. (1999) 'The effect of the performance appraisal system on trust for management: A field quasi-experiment', *Journal of Applied Psychology*, 84 (1): 123–136.

Mayer, R.C. and Gavin, M.B. (2005) 'Trust in management and performance: Who minds the shop while the employees watch the boss?' *Academy of Management Journal*, 48 (5): 874–888.

Mayer, R.C., Davis, J.H. and Schoorman, F.D. (1995) 'An integrative model of organizational trust', *Academy of Management Review*, 20 (3): 709–734.

McAllister, D.J. (1995) 'Affect- and cognition-based trust as foundations for interpersonal cooperation in organizations', *Academy of Management Journal*, 38 (1): 24–59.

McEvily, B., Perrone, V. and Zaheer, A. (2003) 'Introduction to the special issue on trust in an organizational context', *Organization Science*, 14 (1): 1–4.

McKnight, D.H., Cummings, L.L. and Chervany, N.L. (1998) 'Initial trust formation in new organizational relationships', *Academy of Management Review*, 23 (3): 473–491.

Meyerson, D., Weick, K.E. and Kramer, R.M. (1996) 'Swift trust and temporary groups', in R.M. Kramer and T.R. Tyler (eds), *Trust in Organizations: Frontiers of Theory and Research*. Thousand Oaks, CA: Sage, pp. 166–195.

Moye, M.J. and Henkin, A.B. (2006) 'Exploring associations between employee empowerment and interpersonal trust in managers', *Journal of Management Development*, 25 (2): 101–117.

Perry, R.W. and Mankin, L.D. (2004) 'Understanding employee trust in management: Conceptual clarification and correlates', *Public Personnel Management*, 33 (3): 277–290.

Robinson, S.L. (1996) 'Trust and breach of the psychological contract', *Administrative Science Quarterly*, 41 (4): 574–599.

Rotter, J.B. (1967) 'A new scale for the measurement of interpersonal trust', *Journal of Personality*, 35 (4): 651–665.

Rousseau, D.M., Sitkin, S.B., Burt, R.S. and Camerer, C. (1998) 'Not so different after all: A cross–discipline view of trust', *Academy of Management Review*, 23 (3): 393–404.

Rupp, D.E. and Cropanzano, R. (2002) 'The mediating effects of social exchange relationships in predicting workplace outcomes from multifoci organizational justice', *Organizational Behavior and Human Decision Processes*, 89 (1): 925–946.

Schminke, M., Cropanzano, R. and Rupp, D.E. (2002) 'Organization structure and fairness perceptions: The moderating effects of organizational level', *Organizational Behavior and Human Decision Processes*, 89 (1): 881–905.

Shamir, B. and Lapidot Y. (2003) 'Trust in organizational superiors: Systemic and collective considerations', *Organization Studies*, 24 (3): 463–291.

Shapiro, D.L., Sheppard, B.H. and Cheraskin, L. (1992) 'Business on a handshake', *Negotiation Journal*, 8 (4): 365–377.

Sheppard, B.H. and Sherman, D.M. (1998) 'The grammars of trust: A model and general implications', *Academy of Management Review*, 23 (3): 422–438.

Shore, L.M., Tetrick, L.E., Lynch, P. and Barksdale, K. (2006) 'Social and economic exchange: Construct development and validation', *Journal of Applied Social Psychology*, 36 (4): 837–867.

Siegrist, M., Cvetkovich, G., and Roth, C. (2000) 'Salient value similarity, social trust, and risk/benefit perception', *Risk Analysis: An International Journal*, 20 (3): 353–362.

Sitkin, S.B. and Roth, N.L. (1993) 'Explaining the limited effectiveness of legalistic "remedies" for trust/distrust', *Organization Science*, 4 (3): 367–392.

Spreitzer, G.M. (1995) 'Individual empowerment in the workplace: Dimensions, measurement, and validation', *Academy of Management Journal*, 38 (5): 1442–1465.

Stewart, K.J. (2003) 'Trust transfer on the World Wide Web', *Organization Science*, 14 (1): 5–17.

Stinglhamber, F., De Cremer, D. and Mercken, L. (2006) 'Perceived support as a mediator of the relationship between justice and trust: A multiple foci approach', *Group and Organization Management*, 31 (4): 442–468.

Tan, H.H. and Tan, C.S.F. (2000) 'Toward the differentiation of trust in supervisor and trust in organization', *Genetic, Social and General Psychology Monographs*, 126 (2): 241–260.

Tyler, T.R. (2003) 'Trust within organisations', *Personnel Review*, 32 (5): 556–568.

Tyler, T.R. and Lind, E.A. (1992) 'A relational model of authority in groups', in M. Zanna (eds), *Advances in Experimental Social Psychology*. New York: Academic Press. Vol. 25, pp. 115–192.

Tzafrir, S.S., Harel, G.H., Baruch, Y. and Dolan, S.L. (2004) 'The consequences of emerging HRM practices for employees' trust in their managers', *Personnel Review*, 33 (6): 628–647.

Wat, D. and Shaffer, M.A. (2005) 'Equity and relationship quality influences on organizational citizenship behaviors: The mediating role of trust in the supervisor and empowerment', *Personnel Review*, 34 (4): 406–422.

Watson, G.W. and Papamarcos, S.D. (2002) 'Social capital and organizational commitment', *Journal of Business and Psychology*, 16 (4): 537–552.

Whitener, E.M. (2001) 'Do "high commitment" human resource practices affect employee commitment? A cross-level analysis using hierarchical linear modeling', *Journal of Management*, 27 (5): 515–535.

Whitener, E.M., Brodt, S.E., Korsgaard, M.A. and Werner, J.M. (1998) 'Managers as initiators of trust: An exchange relationship framework for understanding managerial trustworthy behavior', *Academy of Management Review*, 23 (3): 513–531.

Williams, M. (2001) 'In whom we trust: Group membership as an effective context for trust development', *Academy of Management Review*, 26 (3): 377–396.

Williams, O.E. (1993) 'Calculativeness, trust, and economic organization', *Journal of Law and Economics*, 36 (1): 453–485.

Wong, Y.T., Ngo, H.Y. and Wong, C.S. (2003) 'Antecedents and outcomes of employees' trust in Chinese joint ventures', *Asia Pacific Journal of Management*, 20 (4): 481–499.

Wong, Y.-T., Wong, C.-S. and Ngo, H.-Y. (2002) 'Loyalty to supervisor and trust in supervisor of workers in Chinese joint ventures: A test of two competing models', *International Journal of Human Resource Management*, 13 (6): 883–900.

Wong, Y.-T., Wong, C.-S., Ngo, H.-Y. and Lui, H.K. (2005) 'Different responses to job insecurity of Chinese workers in joint ventures and state-owned enterprises', *Human Relations*, 58 (11): 1391–1418.

Zacharatos, A., Barling, J. and Iverson, R.D. (2005) 'High–performance work systems and occupational safety', *Journal of Applied Psychology*, 90 (1): 77–93.

Zaheer, A., McEvily, B. and Perrone, V. (1998) 'Does trust matter? Exploring the effects of interorganizational and interpersonal trust on performance', *Organization Science*, 9 (2): 123–159.

6

Organizational Citizenship Behavior: A Review and Extension of its Nomological Network

Matthias Spitzmuller, Linn Van Dyne and
Remus Ilies

The purpose of this chapter is to provide an updated, conceptually-based overview of the nomological network of the organizational citizenship behavior construct, with an emphasis on implications for future research. In doing so, we will use the OCB categorization framework based on the target of the behaviors, differentiating between citizenship targeted at the organization and citizenship targeted at the individual (McNeely and Meglino, 1994; Williams and Anderson, 1991). Previous literature reviews have mostly focused on (1) attitudinal and dispositional factors as antecedents of citizenship and (2) individual and organizational performance as consequences of citizenship (LePine et al., 2002; Organ and Ryan, 1995; Podsakoff et al., 2000). We suggest that more recent research has widened the scope

of the nomological network of citizenship behavior, and thus, an updated literature review can help structure this emerging research on OCB. Accordingly, we discuss motivational and contextual antecedents of OCB, in addition to dispositional and attitudinal antecedents. In a similar fashion, we consider consequences of OCB for individual well-being in addition to consequences of OCB for individual, group, and organization performance.

There are at least four benefits of this broader perspective on citizenship behavior. First, with respect to the antecedents of OCB, we believe that a more dynamic understanding of the antecedents of citizenship behavior is needed to capture the complexities of the social environment in which OCB is embedded and to account for employee motivations to engage in OCB. Second, with respect to consequences of OCB, the managerial orientation of most prior research on citizenship (Organ, 1997) has ignored consequences of OCB which go beyond effectiveness and efficiency implications. Third, recent research in social and personality psychology demonstrates the positive implications which prosocial behavior can have for those who perform these behaviors. Incorporating this perspective into research on citizenship can help generate a more complete understanding of the consequences of OCB for individual well-being as well as factors that sustain high levels of citizenship over extended periods of time. Fourth, an updated literature review can help structure these emerging areas of OCB research and can add to the research agenda for citizenship behavior for the next decade.

RESEARCH ON ORGANIZATIONAL CITIZENSHIP BEHAVIOR – QUO VADIS?

It is almost thirty years now since Organ (1977) revisited the relationship between job satisfaction and job performance by differentiating quantitative measures of output from more subtle, qualitative aspects of work. Up to that point, a long tradition of research had failed to reach consensus on the nature of the relationship between job satisfaction and job performance (Brayfield and Crockett, 1955; Cherrington et al., 1971; Lawler and Porter, 1967; Vroom, 1964; see review by Judge et al., 2001), despite its practical appeal and its apparent face validity. By emphasizing more subtle, qualitative aspects of work, Organ widened the commonly accepted definition of job performance to include behaviors with positive effects on the psychological, social, and organizational context of work. Organ's idea set the stage for rapid growth in research on the nature, causes, and consequences of discretionary work behaviors, commonly referred to as organizational citizenship behavior (Organ, 1988) and contextual performance (Borman and Motowidlo, 1993).

Building on Organ's (1977) conceptualization, the first empirical studies on citizenship behavior were published in 1983. Bateman and Organ (1983) provided the first empirical support for the proposed relationship between job satisfaction and qualitative performance (later OCB); and Smith et al. (1983) developed the first measure of citizenship behavior which included subscales of helping and compliance. Further developing the concept, Organ defined OCB in 1988 as 'individual behavior that is discretionary, not directly or explicitly recognized by the formal reward system, and in the aggregate, promotes the efficient and effective functioning of the organization' (Organ, 1988: 4). Acknowledging the related research on contextual performance, Organ updated the definition to 'contributions to the maintenance and enhancement of the social and psychological context that support task performance' (Organ, 1997: 91) in response to challenges that OCB is not necessarily extra-role and discretionary. Most recently, Organ et al. (2006: 34) emphasized the discretionary nature of OCB by defining it as 'discretionary contributions that go beyond the strict description and that do not lay claim to contractual recompense from the formal reward system.'

Since the early work of Organ and colleagues, the domain of citizenship behavior has grown at an impressive rate (Podsakoff et al., 2000), with two primary effects. First, researchers have identified a large number of related constructs. Second, there is an impressive amount of substantive research on the antecedents and consequences of OCB and related constructs. For example, in their review of research on organizational citizenship behavior, Podsakoff and colleagues (2000) noted that close to 30 different forms of citizenship behaviors had been suggested since Smith, Organ, and Near coined the term 'organizational citizenship behavior' in 1983. These include altruism, courtesy, sportsmanship, conscientiousness, civic virtue (Organ, 1988), interpersonal facilitation, job dedication (Van Scotter and Motowidlo, 1996), helping co-workers (George and Brief, 1992), loyalty, obedience, participation (Van Dyne et al., 1994), loyal boosterism, personal industry, individual initiative (Moorman and Blakely, 1995), OCB-O and OCB-I (McNeely and Meglino, 1994; Williams and Anderson, 1991). The emergence of this large number of constructs demonstrates widespread interest in and relevance of organizational citizenship research. However, this proliferation of constructs has also been criticized.

First, some scholars have criticized the process used to introduce OCB-related constructs (LePine et al., 2002). For example, most research which proposed new types of OCB used factor analysis to identify and support different types of OCB. Unfortunately, however, very little research has investigated the potential conceptual overlap of the resulting constructs (see Van Dyne et al., 1995; and LePine et al., 2002, for two exceptions).

Second, because the convergent and discriminant validity of OCB constructs has not been examined conclusively, researchers could only speculate on the dimensionality of citizenship behavior. More recently, scholars have attempted to resolve this debate with meta-analytical techniques (LePine et al., 2002), multidimensional scaling, and cluster analysis (Coleman and Borman, 2000). However, conflicting results have prevented definitive resolution. For example, LePine and colleagues (2002) suggested that OCB should best be conceptualized as a latent construct, whereas Coleman and Borman (2000) suggested a three-factor structure of citizenship behavior. Moreover, other meta-analyses (Ilies et al., 2006a; Ilies et al., 2007) suggested that diverse facets of OCB differ in their relationships with common antecedents such as positive affect, agreeableness, conscientiousness, and leader-member-exchange. Thus, more recent findings support a multidimensional view of citizenship behavior.

Third, much of the construct work on citizenship behavior has been atheoretical. Based on Calder (1977), Van Dyne et al. (1995) criticized OCB research for developing first degree constructs derived from everyday explanations of socially constructed meaning, as opposed to using second degree constructs

supported by conceptual and empirical scientific evidence. Interestingly, even the first conceptualization of OCB proposed by Smith et al. (1983) has been criticized for being overloaded with socially constructed meaning. For example, Organ (1997) noted the managerial, status-quo bias of these behaviors that tend toward the mundane. Later research continued to introduce other first degree OCB constructs without clear theoretical rationale. There are, however, a small number of exceptions to this tendency. Van Dyne and colleagues (1994) developed a theoretically grounded approach to types of OCB based on political philosophy. Van Dyne and colleagues (1995) proposed a framework that differentiated affiliative versus challenging and promotive versus change-oriented behaviors. Finally, Moon et al. (2004) proposed a circumplex conceptualization of citizenship behavior as another example of a conceptually-based framework which can form the basis for cumulative research on OCB. Overall, however, we have to conclude that theoretically-based approaches to differentiating types of OCB are exceptions to the general tendency of researchers to list types of OCB.

Fourth, the lack of construct clarity becomes even more salient in light of the large body of substantive research that relates OCB to an increasingly complex network of antecedents and consequences. Schwab (1980) emphasized the critical importance of reaching consensus on construct definitions before moving on to substantive research, to avoid redundant and insufficiently distinct conceptualizations, construct contamination, and construct deficiency. Unfortunately, this has not been the case in OCB research. Instead, as noted by Van Dyne and colleagues (1995) and LePine and colleagues (2002), the large number of overlapping OCB constructs makes it increasingly difficult for the research domain to be cumulative, or to have a well-explicated nomological network (also see Moon et al., 2004; Organ et al., 2006; Organ, 1997; Podsakoff et al., 2000). In addition, although meta-analytic research has enhanced our understanding of the large body of OCB research (Harrison et al., 2006; Dalal, 2005;

Ilies et al., 2006a; Ilies et al., 2007; LePine et al., 2002; Organ and Ryan, 1995), these meta-analyses have also not resolved the debate over the nature and dimensionality of citizenship behavior.

Acknowledging these shortcomings of prior research, the remainder of this chapter is structured as follows. First, we argue that OCB research needs a conceptually-based framework which can help structure and summarize past research as well as guide future research. We then suggest that categorizing OCB based on the target of the behavior provides a parsimonious and conceptually meaningful framework which is supported by empirical research. Thereafter, we discuss the nomological network of citizenship behavior with a special focus on antecedents and consequences of citizenship which have received little or no attention in previous reviews. We conclude with a summary of past research that integrates these ideas and proposes an agenda for future citizenship research.

A SIMPLE CONCEPTUAL FRAMEWORK

Before reviewing antecedents and consequences of citizenship behavior, we discuss the organizing framework which we use in our review of the nomological network of citizenship behavior. To avoid proliferation of OCB constructs and to contribute to accumulation of OCB findings, we discuss the substantive literature on OCB in terms of the intended beneficiary of the behavior. Thus, we organize this review by differentiating between citizenship behavior targeted at the organization [OCB-O] and citizenship behavior targeted at individuals [OCB-I]. Our objective in adopting this simple conceptual framework is aimed at integration of the literature, rather than differentiation, so that big-picture general patterns in the relationships can emerge and serve as a foundation for guiding future research. We suggest that this simplified approach should highlight areas where future research is most likely to make important contributions. It also should help

to identify areas where research findings are clear and consistent, suggesting less need for additional studies of particular relationships.

Smith and colleagues' (1983) measure of OCB had two subdimensions – altruism and compliance – clearly differentiating citizenship targeted at the organization from citizenship targeted at individuals, with altruism representing interpersonal OCB-I and compliance representing impersonal OCB-O. The vast majority of subsequent OCB research can be subsumed into these two categories. For example, helping behavior (Van Dyne and LePine, 1998), task-focused interpersonal citizenship behavior, person-focused interpersonal citizenship behavior (Settoon and Mossholder, 2002), altruism (Organ, 1988), interpersonal facilitation (Van Scotter and Motowidlo, 1996), helping co-workers (George and Brief, 1992), and social participation (Van Dyne et al., 1994) reflect OCB targeted at individuals: OCB-I (Williams and Anderson, 1991). In contrast, loyal boosterism (Moorman and Blakely, 1995), loyalty, obedience, participation (Van Dyne et al., 1994), job dedication (Van Scotter and Motowidlo, 1996), conscientiousness, civic virtue (Organ, 1988), personal industry, and individual initiative (Moorman and Blakely, 1995) reflect OCB targeted at the organization: OCB-O (Williams and Anderson, 1991).

From a conceptual perspective, differentiating OCB-O and OCB-I is meaningful because OCB-I emphasizes interpersonal aspects of citizenship behaviors, whereas OCB-O focuses on impersonal citizenship. Based on this important conceptual distinction, there should be key differences in their respective nomological networks. Consistent with this, past theory and empirical research demonstrate that employees do not perform all types of OCB uniformly (Organ, 1997; Settoon and Mossholder, 2002; Van Dyne et al. 1995). In addition, research generally demonstrates that subdimensions of OCB differ in their relationships with antecedents and consequences only if they differentiate between citizenship behavior targeted at the organization, and citizenship behavior targeted at individuals. More specifically, past research has established differential relationships of OCB-O and OCB-I with attitudinal, dispositional, motivational, and contextual antecedents (Colquitt et al., 2001; Flynn et al., 2006; Kamdar and Van Dyne, 2007; Rioux and Penner, 2001; Van der Vegt et al., 2006; Van Dyne and Farmer, 2004). In sum, we use the OCB-O and OCB-I framework to organize our review of the nomological network of citizenship behaviors. This approach is parsimonious and consistent with the differential relationships of OCB-O and OCB-I with their antecedents and consequences. In addition, we suggest that the OCB-O and OCB-I framework is especially relevant for reviewing more recent research that has relied on this framework (i.e., Bowler and Brass, 2006; Ilies et al., 2006a; Ilies et al., 2007).

ANTECEDENTS OF ORGANIZATIONAL CITIZENSHIP BEHAVIOR

In this section, we review research on antecedents of citizenship behavior. Early OCB research focused primarily on dispositional and attitudinal predictors, whereas more recent research has broadened its perspective by considering social ties and networks as antecedents at the meso level as well as contextual and organizational antecedents at the macro level. Since earlier reviews provide excellent summaries of the literature (Organ, 1997; Organ and Ryan, 1995; Podsakoff et al., 2000), we emphasize more recent advancements in the literature.

The role of dispositions, attitudes, and motivations as antecedents of OCB

Dispositions
Since OCB is discretionary, it is more strongly influenced by personality and attitudinal factors than by ability, knowledge, or training (Podsakoff et al., 2000). Specifically, agreeableness and conscientiousness

are dispositional aspects of personality that predict performance of OCB in a wide variety of settings (Barrick et al., 1998; Organ and Ryan, 1995; Podsakoff et al., 2000). For example, LePine and Van Dyne (2001) demonstrated relationships for agreeableness and conscientiousness with helping and voice citizenship. More important, conscientiousness was more strongly related to voice than to helping – and agreeableness was positively related to helping, but negatively related to voice. Consistent with this, meta-analytic evidence shows that agreeableness is more strongly associated with OCB-I and conscientiousness is a more effective predictor of OCB-O (Ilies et al., 2006a; Organ and Ryan, 1995).

More recently, researchers have focused on traits that predict prosocial behavior in general (i.e., a prosocial personality). For example, Penner et al. (1995) and Penner et al. (2005) identified dispositional empathy and helpfulness, based on self-perceived potency and competence to help, as two dimensions which comprise prosocial personality. Kamdar et al. (2006) demonstrated that the dispositional trait of perspective taking was more predictive of OCB-I (interpersonal helping) than OCB-O (loyal boosterism). Finally, positive and negative affectivity have been identified as personality predictors of OCB, with positive affectivity as a significant (but weak) predictor of OCB-I and negative affectivity as a significant (but weak) predictor of OCB-O (Organ and Ryan, 1995; Podsakoff et al., 2000).

Research on dispositional antecedents of OCB has focused primarily on direct effect predictions. Unfortunately, research which examines the mediating (indirect) mechanisms through which personality impacts OCB is still in its nascent stages (Ilies et al., 2006a). Nevertheless, some studies consider moderated and/or mediated relationships. For example, some research suggests that personality influences citizenship behavior only to the extent that it influences thoughts and feelings about a job (Ilies et al, 2006; Organ and Ryan, 1995). This line of reasoning is congruent with trait activation theory

(Tett and Burnett, 2003), which suggests that attitudes and perceptions moderate the relationship between personality and work behavior (Kamdar and Van Dyne, 2007). In their recent meta-analysis on antecedents of OCB, Ilies and colleagues (2006) demonstrated that satisfaction mediated the effects of agreeableness and conscientiousness on organization-targeted behaviors. Moreover, both job satisfaction and positive affect mediated the effects of agreeableness and conscientiousness on individually-targeted behaviors. Another recent study investigated the interactive effects of personality traits and experienced states on intraindividual patterns of citizenship behavior (Ilies et al., 2006b). Results using experience-sampling methodology demonstrated that agreeableness moderated the intraindividual relationship between state positive affect and daily reports of citizenship behavior: highly agreeable employees exhibited more consistent patterns of citizenship behavior, such that their performance of OCB was less dependent on their state positive affect.

Building on the work of Campbell and colleagues (1993), Motowidlo et al. (1997) argued that personality would influence performance (comprised of contextual performance and task performance) through its influence on contextual knowledge or contextual work habits. Johnson (2003) noted, however, that this proposition has only received partial empirical support: Specifically, Schmit et al. (1996) reported that extraversion mediated the effect of contextual knowledge on contextual performance, but not for conscientiousness and agreeableness.

Finally, Organ and colleagues (2006) suggested that 'personality might influence manner or motive more than the substance of OCB' (p. 85). Specifically, they argued that dispositional traits may not explain differences in enacted levels of OCB, but they might explain why some individuals engage in citizenship. According to this line of reasoning, agreeable people are not predisposed to engage in citizenship behavior more frequently. Instead, their desire to mitigate the discomfort of coworkers or friends leads to higher levels of OCB. We discuss motivational antecedents of citizenship behavior in greater detail below.

Attitudes

Since the early work of Organ (1977) and Bateman and Organ (1983), attitudes have received a great deal of attention as predictors of citizenship behaviors. Job satisfaction has consistently been identified as one of the strongest predictors of OCB, irrespective of the intended beneficiary (Ilies et al., 2006; Podsakoff et al., 2000). Moreover, organizational commitment (Organ and Ryan, 1995; Podsakoff et al., 2000), justice and fairness perceptions (Colquitt et al., 2001; Organ and Ryan, 1995; Podsakoff et al., 2000), and state positive affect (Ilies et al., 2006) are other affective and cognitive constructs associated with OCB. Interestingly, and consistent with our emphasis on OCB-O and OCB-I, organizational commitment and procedural justice perceptions were more strongly associated with OCB-O (Colquitt et al., 2001; Organ and Ryan, 1995) and interpersonal justice was more strongly associated with OCB-I (Colquitt et al., 2001).

Motivations

Most motivational approaches to citizenship behavior differ from approaches which focus primarily on attitudinal antecedents. Research on attitudes and OCB is typically based on social exchange theory and assumes that individuals perform OCB as a reaction to positive treatment at work (Rioux and Penner, 2001). In contrast, research on individual motivations as antecedents to OCB positions discretionary behaviors as proactive efforts directed toward satisfying basic human needs (Penner et al., 1997; Rioux and Penner, 2001). For example, Krebs (1991) argued generically that helping behavior (i.e., OCB-I) is based on a combination of egoistic and altruistic motives. Helping others, thus, provides personal benefits that enhance the helper's welfare and well-being. Krebs and others (Hornstein, 1991; Kenrick, 1991), however, acknowledge the inherent difficulties of disentangling egoistic and altruistic motivational factors which trigger discretionary behaviors. Noting similarities between OCB and volunteering, Van Dyne and Farmer (2004) differentiated expressive functional motives and instrumental functional motives that lead to helping others (OCB-I). Expressive motives include helping for expression of role identity, ego protection, and self-enhancement. Instrumental motives, on the other hand, include economic and cost-benefit considerations.

To date, however, there is little empirical research on the motivational antecedents of citizenship. One notable exception is Rioux and Penner's (2001) measure of motives for engaging in OCB – the CMS or Citizenship Motivation Scale. This scale has a three-factor structure, consisting of:

- prosocial values (being motivated by helping others);
- organizational concern (being motivated by a sense of pride for being associated with the organization); and
- impression management (being motivated by looking good to obtain rewards).

Of these three motives, organizational concern and prosocial values predicted OCB. More importantly, organizational concern was more strongly associated with OCB directed at the organization and prosocial values were a stronger predictor of OCB directed at individuals. Although Bolino (1999) emphasized conceptual similarities between OCB and impression management, Rioux and Penner's (2001) self-report scale for impression management motives was not related to OCB. More recently, however, Bowler and Brass (2006) demonstrated that impression management can motivate citizenship behavior, especially when citizenship is targeted at employees with influential friends in the organization.

The role of task characteristics as antecedents of OCB

Podsakoff and Mackenzie (1997) suggested that task characteristics directly impact OCB,

and that they also moderate the effect of OCB on group performance. Consistent with this, Motowidlo et al. (1986) showed that high task demands reduced OCB-I. Podsakoff and colleagues' (2000) meta-analysis reported that task routinization reduced OCB-I. In contrast, job autonomy (Farh et al., 1990) and intrinsically satisfying tasks (Podsakoff et al., 2000) enhanced OCB. Recently, Bachrach et al. (2006) noted an increase in research on task characteristics and citizenship. Much of this research differentiates between OCB-I and OCB-O (Van der Vegt and Van de Vliert, 2005). For example, Bachrach and colleagues examined the moderating effect of task interdependence on the relationship between helping behavior (OCB-I) and group performance. Interestingly, they reported a non-monotic effect of helping on group performance in the low task interdependence condition such that both low and high levels of helping led to lower group performance. Anderson and Williams (1996) demonstrated that employees seek and receive more interpersonal help (OCB-I) in task environments characterized by high task interdependence. These results suggest the benefits of additional work on task characteristics and citizenship.

The role of social relationships as antecedents of OCB

Like research on task characteristics and OCB, we observe an increasing trend in research on social relationships and citizenship behavior. Bowler and Brass (2006) argued, for example, that our understanding of interpersonal citizenship behavior is incomplete without considering the social relationships in which work is embedded. Specifically, they proposed that attitudinal, dispositional, and motivational approaches to citizenship behavior fail to account for the social environment surrounding citizenship. Moreover, Dovidio et al. (2006) suggested that quality of interpersonal relationships is a powerful predictor of human behavior which should add to our understanding of discretionary work behavior. In line with this reasoning, we now review employee relationships with supervisors and co-workers as predictors of citizenship. Here, we focus primarily on OCB-I because interpersonal relationships have special relevance to OCB-I.

Relationships with supervisors as antecedents of OCB

Meta-analytic findings demonstrate that leadership and relationships of employees with their supervisors are powerful predictors of citizenship behavior. This includes leader supportiveness, transformational leadership, and contingent rewards (Podsakoff et al., 2000). Interestingly, dyadic relationships between leader and followers are more strongly related to OCB than universal leadership behaviors, such as transformational and transactional leadership (Organ and Ryan, 1995; Podsakoff et al., 2000). In fact, leader-member exchange (LMX) is one of the most powerful predictors of OCB. Based on their review of previous research on OCB, Podsakoff and colleagues (2000) find that LMX was not only the strongest predictor of OCB among leadership behaviors, but among all predictors considered in their analyses, including individual characteristics, task characteristics, organizational characteristics, and leadership behaviors. A recent meta-analysis by Ilies and colleagues (2007) shows particularly strong relationships between LMX and interpersonal citizenship. In addition, research demonstrates that employees reciprocate high-quality LMX relationships with OCB-I directed specifically at the leader (Kamdar and Van Dyne, 2007). Moreover, again consistent with trait activation theory (Tett and Burnett, 2003), the results of Kamdar and Van Dyne demonstrate that LMX weakens the effects of personality on OCB-I. Other research shows LMX mediates and moderates the effects of other predictors on OCB. For example, Wang et al. (2005) demonstrated that leader-member exchange fully mediated the effect of transformational leadership on citizenship. Also, Sparrowe et al. (2006) showed that LMX moderated the effect of leader influence tactics on employee helping behavior.

The majority of research on the relationship between leadership and citizenship behavior has focused on the positive effects of leadership behaviors on citizenship. Taking a different approach, Tepper et al. (2004) investigated potential negative consequences of abusive leadership on citizenship behavior. Results demonstrated that in the presence of abusive supervision, performance of OCB eventually led to lower levels of co-worker job satisfaction.

Relationships with co-workers as antecedents of OCB

Social relationships with peers also predict OCB (Bowler and Brass, 2006; Ng and Van Dyne, 2005; Van der Vegt et al., 2006). Consistent with social exchange theory (Blau, 1964), employees reciprocate quality relationships with co-workers by providing more interpersonal citizenship (Anderson and Williams, 1996; Kamdar and Van Dyne, 2007; Settoon and Mossholder, 2002). Likewise, interpersonal relationship quality (Anderson and Williams, 1996), intensity of friendship (Bowler and Brass, 2006), team member exchange (Kamdar and Van Dyne, 2007), group cohesiveness, and cooperative group norms (Ng and Van Dyne, 2005) are positively related to OCB-I. Research also suggests that relationships among co-workers (TMX) are strong proximal predictors of OCB-I that constrain expression of dispositional traits, thus reducing the effect of personality on citizenship (Kamdar and Van Dyne, 2007).

Research has started to investigate potential negative consequences of social relationships on citizenship behavior. For example, Ng and Van Dyne (2005) showed that group task conflict reduced OCB-I in work groups, and Twenge et al. (2007) demonstrated that social exclusion reduced prosocial behavior (i.e., OCB-I). Reflecting on this finding, Twenge and colleagues suggested that social exclusion temporarily interfered with emotional responses and thus impaired empathic reactions to co-workers, which in turn, reduced prosocial behavior. Finally, Van der Vegt and colleagues (2006) used a relational approach in their study of expertness diversity and interpersonal helping. Results demonstrated that team members who were not perceived as experts received less help, which lead to increased team member frustration, and reduced intragroup learning.

CONSEQUENCES OF ORGANIZATIONAL CITIZENSHIP BEHAVIOR

The consequences of organizational citizenship behavior have not been studied as extensively as antecedents of citizenship (Scott, 2007), perhaps because most empirical studies focus on OCB as a valuable outcome in and of itself. A few studies, however, consider OCB as the predictor of other outcomes. Most of these studies focus on OCB as a predictor of individual, group, and organizational performance. This tendency is not surprising due to the managerial bias of early work on OCB (Organ, 1997). Looking ahead, we view this as a major opportunity to expand our understanding of the nomological network of OCB. Specifically, we draw on research in social and personality psychology which provides strong evidence that helping behavior has important implications for those who do the helping.

We begin this section with a review of the literature on consequences of OCB for individual, group, and organizational performance. We then review the limited existing research on consequences of citizenship for those who perform OCB. We then make suggestions about future research on consequences of OCB for individuals, with special emphasis on individual well-being.

Consequences of OCB for individual and group performance, and organizational effectiveness

The conceptualization of job performance has been expanded to include citizenship behavior and contextual performance (Johnson, 2003; Motowidlo, 2003). Although this redefinition could be interpreted as reducing the need

for empirical research on OCB and job performance, and even though Podsakoff and Mackenzie (1997) summarized eight conceptual reasons to support the assumed relationship between citizenship behavior and performance, surprisingly few studies have examined this relationship empirically.

At the individual level of analysis, Mackenzie and Podsakoff demonstrated positive effects of citizenship for those who exhibit OCB as well as for those who are the targets of citizenship. For example, those who exhibit OCB are rated as higher performers by supervisors (MacKenzie and Podsakoff, 1999; MacKenzie et al., 1991, 1993). From a conceptual perspective, Podsakoff and MacKenzie (1997) argued that OCB helps new employees become productive more quickly, and helps to spread 'best practices' in organizations, thus enhancing the performance of those who learn these best practices.

Moving to higher levels of analysis, research has demonstrated relationships between OCB and unit performance in terms of customer service quality and sales performance, as well as performance quality and quantity. Several studies have demonstrated significant relationships between citizenship and unit sales (MacKenzie et al., 1998; Podsakoff et al., 1997; Podsakoff and MacKenzie, 1997). Walz and Niehoff (1996) showed citizenship was related to operating efficiency and customer service quality. Looking specifically at OCB-I and OCB-O, George and Bettenhausen (1990) demonstrated that group prosocial behaviors (OCB-I) were positively related to store sales. Explanations for these findings include enhanced coordination and reduced need for maintenance activities in units where employees regularly contribute OCB and enhanced coordination (Podsakoff and MacKenzie, 1997). Finally, at the macro level of analysis, Schnake and Hogan (1995) demonstrated that OCB was related to organizational flexibility and efficiency.

Together, these studies provide support for relationships between citizenship behavior and performance on the micro, meso, and macro levels. Unfortunately, studies which differentiate between OCB-I and OCB-O have produced inconsistent results. Podsakoff and MacKenzie (1997) commented that the relationship between helping (OCB-I) and performance may be stronger than the relationships for civic virtue and sportsmanship (OCB-O) with performance. Another study, however, reported a significant negative relationship (-0.49) between helping (OCB-I) and sales performance (Podsakoff and MacKenzie, 1994). In contrast, other research has reported positive relationships between helping (OCB-I) and group and organizational outcomes (e.g., sales performance, operating efficiency, customer satisfaction, and quantity/quality of performance: MacKenzie et al., 1996; Podsakoff et al., 1996; Walz and Niehoff, 1996). Finally, Ng and Van Dyne (2005) showed that the relationship between group helping (OCB-I operationalized with both average and minimum levels) and group performance failed to reach significance. Podsakoff and colleagues (1997) noted that differences might be due to the nature of the work being performed such that task interdependence influences whether OCB contributes to or detracts from performance. Consistent with this, Bachrach and colleagues' (2006) findings show that task interdependence influenced the effectiveness of helping. Perhaps other inconsistent findings are due to group norms and/or organizational culture. Clearly, more research is needed to address the inconsistent findings about relationships for OCB-I and OCB-O with performance.

The consequences of OCB for those who perform OCB

Organ's (1988) original conceptualization of OCB assumed that OCB was positively intended and in aggregate would have positive consequences for organizations. More recent research has continued this focus, including potential benefits for the well being of other individuals, groups, organizations, and society in general (e.g., Penner et al., 2005). Consequently, a considerable amount of research has investigated the effects of OCB on intended beneficiaries (individuals, groups, organizations).

Unfortunately, however, there is little research on the consequences of performing OCB for those who perform OCB. We are aware of only two studies that have considered satisfaction as an outcome of performing OCB (Bateman and Organ, 1983; Park and Van Dyne, 2006). Thus, we suggest that scholars have not fully recognized the positive implications of performing OCB for the actor – the person who performs OCB. In the next section, we develop specific ideas for ways that research in social psychology on prosocial behavior could inform research on the consequences of performing OCB for those who perform the behavior.

AGENDA FOR FUTURE RESEARCH ON CITIZENSHIP BEHAVIOR

We start by emphasizing the importance of establishing a conceptual rationale for the types of OCB considered in future research. Consistent with our earlier critique of the proliferation of OCB constructs, we propose that a simple conceptual framework that contrasts types of OCB based on intended beneficiary (OCB-I and OCB-O) would provide focus and help researchers integrate and consolidate research findings. Although we acknowledge the viability of more complex approaches to conceptualizing OCB such as 2×2 frameworks that contrast types of OCB based on two dimensions (Van Dyne et al., 1995) or circumplex frameworks that contrast OCB on bipolar continua (Moon et al., 2004), we suggest that the OCB literature would currently benefit most from more basic comparisons of OCB based on intended beneficiary of the behavior. This would enhance the focus of OCB research and, in turn, should clarify basic similarities and differences in the antecedents and consequences of basic forms of OCB. We note that this approach would be consistent with the observations of Podsakoff and colleagues (2000) who emphasized the importance of differentiating types of OCB only when there are differences in the nomological networks (antecedents and/or consequences) of these types of OCB. This approach is also consistent with the growing empirical consensus in the research community on the differences in OCB-I and OCB-O. We now consider specific areas for future research.

Consequences of OCB-I for those who perform it

Drawing on research from social and personality psychology on prosocial behavior (Brown et al., 2003; Kenrick et al., 1979; Penner et al., 2005; Thoits and Hewitt, 2001), we suggest that a new focus on implications of OCB for employees who engage in OCB offers a promising avenue for future research. Even though there is not a lot of social psychological research on the implications of prosocial behavior for individual well-being, existing research provides a rich source of information with the potential to enhance our understanding of the nomological network of organizational citizenship behavior. Not surprisingly, research in social and personality psychology on the consequences of prosocial behavior on individuals who enact them has focused almost exclusively on behavior directed at individuals, thereby ignoring the potential consequences of OCB-O on individuals. Because of that, this section will also focus primarily on prosocial behaviors directed at other individuals. Penner and colleagues' (2005) review chapter explicates positive consequences of performing prosocial behavior on individual well-being, psychological health, physical health, social behavior, and fitness. We review individual consequences for well-being, self-evaluation, physical and mental health, and personal development in the following section.

Individual well-being

Many studies have investigated the effects of prosocial behavior on individual well-being. In general, research demonstrates that prosocial behavior leads to higher positive affect (Piliavin et al., 1981). Furthermore, Cialdini

and Kenrick (1976) demonstrated that prosocial behavior can relieve/reduce bad moods. Kenrick and colleagues (1979) demonstrated that people learn to associate helping behavior with social rewards. Over time, people link helping others with positive outcomes, irrespective of social rewards provided in any particular instance. Restated, people internalize the rewards of prosocial behavior, such that helping can become intrinsically rewarding. This is one explanation for the mood-enhancing consequences of prosocial behavior.

Self-evaluation

Research also indicates that prosocial behavior leads to more favorable self-evaluations. Specifically, Van Willigen (1998) discussed the positive effect of prosocial behavior on life satisfaction, suggesting that prosocial behavior can convey a sense of personal control. Yogev and Ronen (1982) demonstrated positive effects of prosocial behavior on self-esteem. In a study of elderly volunteers and non-volunteers, Hunter and Linn (1981) showed that volunteers had a stronger will to live and more positive feelings of self-respect (compared to non-volunteers). Likewise, studies by Giles and Eyler (1994) and Yates and Youniss (1996) reported positive consequences of prosocial behavior for personal efficacy, self-esteem, and confidence.

Physical and mental health

Social psychological research has examined prosocial behavior effects on physical and mental health of those who engage in the behavior. This research provides strong support for the health-enhancing benefits of prosocial behavior. Based on a study of older married couples, Brown et al. (2003) demonstrated higher longevity for those who provided social support to spouses, friends, relatives, and neighbors. More importantly, results demonstrated lower mortality even when controlling for demographics, personality, health, mental health, and marital-relationship. Interestingly, Brown and colleagues reported a non-significant effect of receiving help on longevity and that providing help had more positive consequences for longevity than receiving help. In considering these findings, Brown and colleagues suggested that prosocial behavior may facilitate cardiovascular recovery from the after-effects of negative emotions, which in turn reduces mortality. Thoits and Hewitt (2001) demonstrated significant effects of volunteer work on physical health and decreased depression.

Penner and colleagues (2005) suggested three primary mechanisms as potential mediators of the relationships between prosocial behavior and physical and mental health: First, prosocial behavior can lead to more favorable self-assessments, which then translate into better mental and physical health. Second, helping others can provide distraction from personal troubles. Third, prosocial behavior includes a social component which facilitates social integration and interaction. Consistent with this, those who were isolated before engaging in prosocial behaviors benefited the most personally from engaging in prosocial behaviors (Musick and Wilson, 2003; Penner et al., 2005).

Personal development

Finally, research provides strong evidence that prosocial behavior has developmental consequences which facilitate individual development in subsequent life stages (Hansen et al., 2003; Johnson et al., 1998; Penner et al., 2005), Specifically, youth volunteers are less likely to smoke marihuana, abuse alcohol, perform poorly in school, or be arrested later in their lives (Barber et al., 2001; Eccles and Barber, 1999; Moore and Allen, 1996; Penner et al., 2005; Uggen and Janikula, 1999; Youniss et al., 1997).

To summarize, research in social and personality psychology demonstrates important positive consequences for those who engage in prosocial behavior. Prosocial behavior enhances psychological and physical health, individual well-being, and individual self-perceptions. It also has positive consequences for development in subsequent life stages. We note that the above social psychological research differs from that typically conducted in organizational settings. Specifically, it is important to consider whether results of research on older people, volunteers in not-for-profit organizations, and those in social settings outside of organizations can be applied to or generalized to those in work organizations. Thus, we argue that considering consequences of performing citizenship to the actor is an exciting area for future research because it provides a considerable opportunity to widen our perspective on consequences of citizenship behavior.

Additional recommendations for future research

Having considered implications of the social psychological research on prosocial behavior for future research on OCB, we now turn to other recommendations for future research, including consequences of performing OCB-O for positive mood at work, work-related attitudes, interpersonal and inter-group relationships, and organizational level outcomes. We also consider potential negative consequences of OCB for those who perform the behavior, work group peers, and organizational effectiveness. Finally, we recommend consideration of more complex models that consider causality, bidirectionality, and nonrecursive relationships.

Employee attitudes and moods

Since most social psychological research on prosocial behavior has occurred in non-work settings typically involving volunteers, adolescents, or older individuals, there is little evidence on the consequences of performing prosocial behavior for employee attitudes such as job satisfaction, organizational commitment, psychological ownership, and turnover intentions. We believe, however, that research on the consequences of OCB-O for affective, attitudinal and behavioral outcomes is a promising avenue for future research on citizenship behavior. Consistent with research on the mood-enhancing benefits of prosocial behavior, it seems reasonable that performing OCB-O should also have positive consequences (based on sense of personal control) for positive mood (see Parks and Van Dyne, 2006). Given that the intended beneficiary of OCB-O is the organization, these positive consequences should also include an enhanced sense of contributing to the organization and making a difference. This could include positive attitudes directed at the organization, such as enhanced job satisfaction, organizational commitment, organizational identification, and psychological ownership. In some cases, however, these consequences might be negative. For example, Bolino and Turnley (2005) demonstrated that individual initiative (OCB-O) was positively related to role overload and job stress.

Interpersonal and intergroup relationships

Another promising area for future research is investigating the consequences of prosocial behavior on interpersonal and intergroup relations. Penner and colleagues (2005), for instance, suggested that prosocial behavior could be related to forgiveness, reconciliation, and sustained cooperation between groups. This supports our recommendations for considering an expanded set of outcomes of OCB. It also suggests benefits of drawing on the social psychological literature on forbearance and forgiveness (McCullough et al., 2003). Although we would expect generally positive cross-level group effects, there also is the possibility of negative effects. For example, Van Dyne and Ellis (2004) developed a theoretical model of potential negative consequences of OCB based on reactance theory. This could occur if coworkers resent an employee who makes them look bad by performing exceptionally high levels of OCB. These sorts of contrast effects can lead to reactance, exclusion, and even sabotage in extreme cases. Moreover, Bolino and Turnley (2005) demonstrated a positive relationship between individual initiative (OCB-O) and work family conflict.

Negative organizational consequences

Another area for future research would be to consider potential negative consequences

of OCB on organizational outcomes. For example, some types of OCB-I can strengthen interpersonal relationships but run counter to overall business objectives. Although showing 'genuine concern and courtesy toward coworkers, even under the most trying business or personal situation' (Moorman and Blakely, 1995) or supporting others in confrontations 'by providing a united front' (Anderson and Williams, 1996) most likely have positive consequences for the target of the OCB, the behavior may not necessarily contribute to overall group or unit performance. In some cases, these acts of interpersonal helping might even detract from work performance, such as when employees are distracted from performing their in-role work responsibilities because they are helping others with personal problems. In some cases, providing personal support might have long term positive consequences for the group, but in other cases the long term costs might be more negative than positive. Van der Vegt and colleagues (2006), for example, demonstrated that the flow of helping behavior in teams characterized by high expertness diversity can be unidirectional, such that those with low expertness do not receive help. This could lead to group frustration and decreased performance. In sum, helping (OCB-I) can be viewed as 'double-edged sword' (Ilgen et al., 2005: 530) because consequences can be positive or negative. Closer investigation of positive and negative consequences of OCB-I over time, thus, becomes especially worthwhile.

More complex and causal models

Another implication for future research is the importance of considering causality and more complex models. For example, some potential consequences of citizenship behavior (i.e., the consequences of OCB-I on individual or group performance or organizational commitment as discussed above) have already been identified as antecedents of citizenship behavior. This suggests the benefits of studies of possible bidirectional and/or nonrecursive relationships between types of OCB and factors which might be both antecedents and consequences of OCB. Specifically, we recommend research on causal relationships between OCB and performance, positive affect, job satisfaction, and organizational commitment.

CONCLUSION

In this chapter, we have attempted to provide an updated overview of the nomological network of organizational citizenship. Using a conceptual framework based on the intended beneficiary of OCB, we have summarized previous research on dispositional, attitudinal, motivational, contextual, and social antecedents of OCB; consequences of OCB for individuals, groups, and organizations; as well as implications of OCB for individuals who perform these behaviors. We have argued that past research on consequences of OCB has been unduly narrow by focusing almost exclusively on performance implications of citizenship behavior. Drawing on social and personality psychology, we have outlined potential consequences of prosocial behavior (OCB-I) for individual well-being, physical and mental health, and social integration. Finally, we have developed a research agenda which we hope will stimulate future research on citizenship behavior.

REFERENCES

Anderson, S.E. and Williams, L.J. (1996) 'Interpersonal, job, and individual factors related to helping processes at work', *Journal of Applied Psychology*, 81 (3): 282–296.

Bachrach, D.G., Powell, B.C., Collins, B.J. and Richey, R.G. (2006) 'Effects of task interdependence on the relationship between helping behavior and group performance', *Journal of Applied Psychology*, 91 (6): 1396–1405.

Barber, B.L., Eccles, J.S. and Stone, M.R. (2001) 'Whatever happened to the jock, the brain, and the princess? Young adult pathways linked to adolescent activity involvement and social identity', *Journal of Adolescent Research*, 16 (5): 429–455.

Barrick, M.R., Stewart, G.L., Neubert, M.L. and Mount, M.K. (1998) 'Relating member ability and personality to work-team processes and team effectiveness', *Journal of Applied Psychology*, 83 (3): 377–391.

Bateman, T.S. and Organ, D.W. (1983) 'Job satisfaction and the good soldier: The relationship between affect and employee "citizenship"', *Academy of Management Journal*, 26 (4): 587–595.

Blau, P. (1964) *Exchange and Power in Social Life*. New York, Wiley.

Bolino, M.C. (1999) 'Citizenship and impression management: Good soldiers or good actors?' *Academy of Management Review*, 24 (1): 82–98.

Bolino, M.C. and Turnley, W.H. (2005) 'The personal costs of citizenship behavior: The relationship between individual initiative and role overload, job stress, and work-family conflict', *Journal of Applied Psychology*, 90 (4): 740–748.

Borman, W.C. and Motowidlo, S.J. (1993) 'Expanding the criterion domain to include elements of contextual performance', in N. Schmitt, W.C. Borman, and Associates (eds), *Personnel Selection in Organizations*. San Francisco: Jossey-Bass, pp. 71–98.

Brayfield, A.H. and Crockett, W.H. (1955) 'Employee attitudes and employee performance', *Psychological Bulletin*, 52 (2): 396–424.

Brown, S.L., Nesse, R.M., Vinokur, A.D. and Smith, D.M. (2003) 'Providing social support may be more beneficial than receiving it: Results from a prospective study of mortality', *Psychological Science*, 14 (4): 320–327.

Bowler, W.M. and Brass, D.J. (2006) 'Relational correlates of interpersonal citizenship behavior. A social network perspective', *Journal of Applied Psychology*, 91 (1): 70–82.

Calder, B.J. (1977) 'An attribution theory of leadership', in B.M. Staw and G.R. Salancik (eds), *New Directions in Organizational Behavior*. Chicago: St. Clair Press, pp. 179–204.

Campbell, J.P., McCloy, R.A., Oppler, S.H. and Sager, C.E. (1993) 'A theory of performance', in N. Schmitt and W.C. Borman (eds), *The Changing Nature of Performance: Implications for Staffing, Motivation, and Development*. San Francisco: Jossey-Bass, pp. 399–429.

Cherrington, D.L., Reitz, H.J. and Scott, W.E., Jr. (1971) 'Effects of reward and contingent reinforcement on satisfaction and task performance', *Journal of Applied Psychology*, 55 (6): 531–536.

Cialdini, R.B. and Kenrick, D.T. (1976) 'Altruism as hedonism: A social development perspective on the relationship of negative mood state and helping', *Journal of Personality and Social Psychology*, 34 (5): 907–914.

Coleman, V.I. and Borman, W.C. (2000) 'Investigating the underlying structure of the citizenship performance domain', *Human Resource Management Review*, 10 (1): 25–44.

Colquitt, J.A., Conlon, D.E., Wesson, M.J., Porter, C.O.L.H. and Ng, Y.K. (2001) 'Justice at the millennium: A meta-analytic review of 25 years of organizational justice research', *Journal of Applied Psychology*, 86 (3): 425–445.

Dalal, R.S. (2005) 'A meta-analysis of the relationship between organizational citizenship behavior and counterproductive work behavior', *Journal of Applied Psychology*, 90 (6): 1241–1255.

Dovidio, J.F., Piliavin, J.A., Schroeder, D.A. and Penner, L. (2006) *The Social Psychology of Prosocial Behavior*. Mahwah, NJ: Erlbaum.

Eccles, J.S. and Barber, B.L. (1999) 'Student council, volunteering, basketball, or marching band: What kind of extracurricular involvement matters?' *Journal of Adolescence Research*, 14 (1): 10–43.

Farh, J.L., Podsakoff, P.M. and Organ, D.W. (1990) 'Accounting for organizational citizenship behavior: Leader fairness and task scope versus satisfaction', *Journal of Management*, 16 (4): 705–721.

Flynn, F.J., Reagans, R.E., Amanatullah, E.T. and Ames, D.R. (2006) 'Helping one's way to the top: Self–monitors achieve status by helping others and knowing who helps whom', *Journal of Personality and Social Psychology*, 91 (6): 1123–1137.

George, J.M. and Bettenhausen, K. (1990) 'Understanding prosocial behavior, sales performance, and turnover: A group–level analysis in a service context', *Journal of Applied Psychology*, 75 (6): 698–709.

George, J.M. and Brief, A.P. (1992) 'Feeling good – doing good: A conceptual analysis of the mood at work – organizational spontaneity relationship', *Psychological Bulletin*, 112 (2): 310–329.

Giles, D.E. Jr. and Eyler, J. (1994) 'The impact of a college community service laboratory on students' personal, social, and cognitive outcomes', *Journal of Adolescence*, 17 (4): 327–339.

Hanson, D.M., Larson R.W. and Dworkin, J.B. (2003) 'What adolescents learn in organized youth activities: A survey of self–reported developmental experience', *Journal of Research on Adolescence*, 11 (1): 25–55.

Harrison, D.A., Newman, D.A. and Roth, Ph.L. (2006) 'How important are job attitudes? Meta-analytic comparisons of integrative behavioral outcomes and time sequences', *Academy of Management Journal*, 49 (2): 305–325.

Hornstein, H.A. (1991) 'Neither altruism nor egoism', *Psychological Inquiry*, 2 (2): 135.

Hunter, K.I. and Linn, M.W. (1981) 'Psychosocial differences between elderly volunteers and non-volunteers', *International Journal of Aging and Human Development*, 12 (1): 205–213.

Ilgen, D.R., Hollenbeck, J.R., Johnson, M. and Jundt, D. (2005) 'Teams in organizations: From input-process-output models to IMOI models', *Annual Review of Psychology*, 56: 517–543.

Ilies, R., Nahrgang, J. and Morgeson, F.P. (2007) 'Leader–member exchange and citizenship behaviors: A meta-analysis', *Journal of Applied Psychology*, 92 (1): 269–277.

Ilies, R., Fulmer, I.S., Spitzmuller, M. and Johnson, M. (2006) 'Personality and citizenship behavior: The role of affect and satisfaction'. Paper presented at the 66th Annual Meeting of the Academy of Management in Atlanta, Georgia.

Ilies, R., Scott, B.A. and Judge, T.A. (2006) 'The interactive effects of personal traits and experienced states on intraindividual patterns of citizenship behavior', *Academy of Management Journal*, 49 (3): 561–575.

Johnson, J.W. (2003) 'Toward a better understanding of the relationship between personality and individual job performance', in M.R. Barrick and A.M. Ryan (eds), *Personality and Work: Reconsidering the Role of Personality in Organizations*. San Francisco: Jossey Bass, pp. 83–120.

Johnson, M.K., Beebe, T., Mortimer, J.T. and Syner, M. (1998) 'Volunteerism in adolescence: A process perspective', *Journal of Research on Adolescence*, 8 (3): 309–332.

Judge, T.A., Thoresen, C.J., Bono, J.E. and Patton, J.K. (2001) 'The job satisfaction – job performance relationship – A qualitative and quantitative review', *Psychological Bulletin*, 127 (3): 376–407.

Kamdar, D., McAlister, D.J. and Turban, D.B. (2006) ' "All in a day's work": How follower individual differences and justice perceptions predict OCB role definitions and behavior', *Journal of Applied Psychology*, 91 (4): 841–855.

Kamdar, D. and Van Dyne, L. (2007) 'The joint effects of personality and workplace social exchange relationships in predicting task performance and citizenship performance', *Journal of Applied Psychology*, 92 (5): 1286–1298.

Kenrick, D.T., Baumann, D.J. and Cialdini, R.B. (1979) 'A step in the socialization of altruism as hedonism: Effects of negative mood on children's generosity under public and private conditions', *Journal of Personality and Social Psychology*, 37 (5): 747–755.

Kenrick, D.T. (1991) 'Proximate altruism and ultimate selfishness', *Psychological Inquiry*, 2 (2): 135–137.

Krebs, D.L. (1991) 'Altruism and egoism: A false dichotomy?' *Psychological Inquiry*, 2 (2): 137–138.

Lawler, E.E., III and Porter, L.W. (1967) 'Perceptions regarding management compensation', *Industrial Relations*, 3 (3): 41–49.

LePine, J.A., Erez, A. and Johnson, D.E. (2002) 'The nature and dimensionality of organizational citizenship behavior: A critical review and meta-analysis', *Journal of Applied Psychology*, 87 (1): 52–65.

LePine, J.A. and Van Dyne, L. (1998) 'Predicting voice behavior in work groups', *Journal of Applied Psychology*, 83 (6): 853–868.

LePine, J.A. and Van Dyne, L. (2001) 'Voice and cooperative behavior as contrasting forms of contextual performance: Evidence of differential relationships with Big Five personality characteristics and cognitive ability', *Journal of Applied Psychology*, 86 (2): 326–336.

MacKenzie, S.B. and Podsakoff, P.M. (1999) 'Do citizenship behaviors matter more for managers than for salespeople?' *Academy of Marketing Science*, 27 (4): 396–410.

MacKenzie, S.B., Podsakoff, P.M. and Fetter, R. (1991) 'Organizational citizenship behavior and objective productivity as determinants of managerial evaluations of salespersons' performance', *Organizational Behavior and Human Decision Processes*, 50 (1): 123–150.

MacKenzie, S.B., Podsakoff, P.M. and Fetter, R. (1993) 'The impact of organizational citizenship behavior on evaluations of salesperson performance', *Journal of Marketing*, 57 (1): 70–80.

MacKenzie, S.B., Podsakoff, P.M. and Ahearne, M. (1998) 'Some possible antecedents and consequences of in-role and extra-role salesperson performance', *Journal of Marketing*, 62 (3): 87–98.

McCullough, M.E., Fincham, F.D. and Tsang, J. (2003) 'Forgiveness, forbearance, and time: The temporal unfolding of transgression–related interpersonal motivations', *Journal of Personality and Social Psychology*, 84 (3): 540–557.

McNeely, B.L. and Meglino, B.M. (1994) 'The role of dispositional and situational antecedents in prosocial organizational behavior: An examination of the intended beneficiaries of prosocial behavior', *Journal of Applied Psychology*, 79 (6): 836–844.

Moon, H., Van Dyne, L. and Wrobel, K. (2004) 'The circumplex model and the future of organizational citizenship behavior research', in Turnipseed, D.L. (ed.), *Handbook of Organizational Citizenship Behavior*. New York: Nova Science, pp. 1–22.

Moore, C.W. and Allen, J.P. (1996) 'The effects of volunteering on the young volunteer', *Journal of Primary Prevention*, 17 (2): 231–258.

Moorman, R.H. and Blakely, G.L. (1995) 'Individualism–collectivism as an individual difference predictor of organizational citizenship behavior', *Journal of Organizational Behavior*, 16 (2): 127–142.

Motowidlo, S.J. (2003) 'Job performance', in W.C. Borman, D.R. Ilgen, and R.J. Klimoski (eds), *Handbook of Psychology: Industrial and Organizational Psychology*, New York: Wiley. Volume 12, pp. 39–53.

Motowidlo, S.J., Borman, W.C. and Schmit, M.J. (1997) 'A theory of individual differences in task and contextual performance', *Human Performance*, 10 (2): 71–83.

Motowidlo, S.J., Packard, J.S. and Manning, M.R. (1986) 'Occupational stress: Its causes and consequences for job performance', *Journal of Applied Psychology*, 71 (4): 618–629.

Musick, M.A. and Wilson, J. (2003) 'Volunteering and depression: The role of psychological and social resources in different age groups', *Social Science and Medicine*, 56 (2): 259–269.

Ng, K.Y. and Van Dyne, L. (2005) 'Antecedents and consequences of helping behavior in work groups', *Group and Organization Management*, 30 (5): 514–540.

Organ, D.W. (1977) 'A reappraisal and reinterpretation of the satisfaction–causes–performance hypothesis', *Academy of Management Review*, 2 (1): 46–53.

Organ, D.W. (1988) *Organizational Citizenship Behavior: The Good Soldier Syndrome*. Lexington, MA: Lexington Books.

Organ, D.W. and Ryan, K. (1995) 'A meta-analytic review of attitudinal and dispositional predictors of organizational citizenship behavior', *Personnel Psychology*, 48 (4): 755–802.

Organ, D.W. (1997) 'Organizational citizenship behavior: It's construct clean–up time', *Human Performance*, 10 (2): 85–97.

Organ, D.W., Podsakoff, Ph.M. and MacKenzie, S.B. (2006) *Organizational Citizenship Behavior: Its Nature, Antecedents and Consequences*. Thousand Oaks, CA: Sage Publications.

Park, G. and Van Dyne, L. (2006) 'Effects of motivational fit on satisfaction with organizational citizenship behaviors'. Paper presented at the Society for Industrial and Organizational Psychologists. Dallas. May.

Penner, L.A., Fritzsche, B.A., Craiger, J.P. and Freifeld, T.R. (1995) 'Measuring the prosocial personality', in J. Butcher and C.D. Spielberger, (eds), *Advances in Personality Assessment*. Hillsdale, NJ: LEA, pp. 147–163.

Penner, L.A., Midili, A.R. and Kegelmeyer, J. (1997) 'Beyond job attitudes: A personality and social psychology perspective on the causes of organizational citizenship behavior', *Human Performance*, 10 (2): 111–132.

Penner, L.A., Dovidio, J.F., Piliavin, J.A. and Schroeder, D.A. (2005) 'Prosocial behavior: Multilevel perspectives', *Annual Review of Psychology*, 56: 365–392.

Piliavin, J.A., Dovidio, J.F., Gaertner, S.L. and Clark, R.D. III (1981) *Emergency Intervention*. New York: Academic.

Podsakoff, P.M., Ahearne, M. and MacKenzie, S.B. (1997) 'Organizational citizenship behavior and the quantity and quality of work group performance', *Journal of Applied Psychology*, 82 (2): 262–270.

Podsakoff, P.M. and Mackenzie, S.B. (1994) 'Organizational citizenship and sales unit effectiveness', *Journal of Marketing Research*, 3 (3): 351–363.

Podsakoff, P.M. and MacKenzie, S.B. (1997) 'Impact of organizational citizenship behavior on organizational performance: A review and suggestions for future research', *Human Performance*, 10 (2): 133–151.

Podsakoff, P.M., MacKenzie, S.B. and Hui, C. (1993) 'Organizational citizenship behaviors and managerial evaluations of employee performance: A review and suggestions for future research', *Research in Personnel and Human Resources Management*, 11: 1–40.

Podsakoff, P.M., Mackenzie, S.B., Moorman, R.H. and Fetter, R. (1990) 'Transformational leader behaviors and their effects on followers' trust in leader, satisfaction, and organizational citizenship behaviors', *Leadership Quarterly*, 1 (1): 107–142.

Podsakoff, P.M., MacKenzie, S.B., Paine, J.B. and Bachrach, D.G. (2000) 'Organizational citizenship behavior: A critical review of the theoretical and empirical literature and suggestions for future research', *Journal of Management*, 26 (3): 513–563.

Rioux, S.M. and Penner, L.A. (2001) 'The causes of organizational citizenship behavior: A motivational analysis', *Journal of Applied Psychology*, 86 (6): 1306–1314.

Schmit, M.J., Motowidlo, S.J., Degrott, T., Cross, T. and Kiker, D.S. (1996) 'Explaining the relationship between personality and job performance'. Paper presented at the 11th Annual Conference of the Society for Industrial and Organizational Psychology, San Diego, CA.

Schnake, M. and Hogan, E. (1995) 'Organizational citizenship behavior and organizational effectiveness', in Southern Management Association Proceedings. Georgia: Southern Management Association, pp. 93–97.

Schwab, D.P. (1980) 'Construct validity in organizational behavior', *Research in Organizational Behavior*, 2: 3–43.

Scott, B.A. (2007) *Employee popularity: Measurement and identification of antecedents and consequences*. Unpublished dissertation.

Settoon, R.P. and Mossholder, K.W. (2002) 'Relational quality and relationship context as antecedents of person- and task-focused interpersonal citizenship behavior', *Journal of Applied Psychology*, 87 (2): 255–267.

Smith, C.A., Organ, D.W. and Near, J.P. (1983) 'Organizational citizenship behavior: Its nature and antecedents', *Journal of Applied Psychology*, 68 (4): 653–663.

Sparrowe, R.T., Soetjipto, B.W. and Kraimer, M.L. (2006) 'Do leaders' influence tactics relate to members' helping behavior? It depends on the quality of the relationship', *Academy of Management Journal*, 49 (6): 1194–1208.

Tepper, B.J., Duffy, M.K., Hobbler, J. and Ensley, M.D. (2004) 'Moderators of the relationships between coworkers' organizational citizenship behavior and fellow employees' attitudes', *Journal of Applied Psychology*, 89 (3): 455–465.

Tett, R.P. and Burnett, D.D. (2003) 'A personality trait–based interactionist model of job performance', *Journal of Applied Psychology*, 88 (3): 500–517.

Thoits, P.A. and Hewitt, L.N. (2001) 'Volunteer work and well-being', *Journal of Health and Social Behavior*, 42 (2): 115–131.

Twenge, J.M., Baumeister, R.F., DeWall, C.N., Ciarocco, N.J. and Bartels, J.M. (2007) 'Social exclusion decreases prosocial behavior', *Journal of Personality and Social Psychology*, 92 (1): 56–66.

Uggen, C. and Janikula, J. (1999) 'Volunteerism and arrest in the transition to adulthood', *Social Forces*, 78 (1): 331–362.

Van der Vegt, G.S., Bunderson, J.S. and Oosterhof, A. (2006) 'Expertness diversity and helping in teams: Why those who need the most help end up getting the least', *Academy of Management Journal*, 49 (5): 877–893.

Van der Vegt, G.S. and Van de Vliert, E. (2005) 'Effects of perceived skill dissimilarity and task interdependence on helping in work teams', *Journal of Management*, 29 (1): 729–751.

Van Dyne, L. and Ellis, J.B. (2004) 'Job creep: A reactance theory perspective on organizational citizenship behavior as over-fulfillment of obligations', in J.A.M. Coyle–Shapiro, L.M. Shore, M.S. Taylor and L.E. Tetrick (eds), *The Employment Relationship: Examining Psychological and Contextual Perspectives*. Oxford, UK: Oxford University Press, pp. 181–205.

Van Dyne, L. and Farmer, S.M. (2004) 'It's who I am: role identity and organizational citizenship behavior of volunteers', in Turnipseed, D.L. (ed.), *Handbook of Organizational Citizenship Behavior.* New York: Nova Science Publishers, pp. 181–207.

Van Dyne, L., Graham, J.W. and Dienesch, R.M. (1994) 'Organizational citizenship behavior: Construct redefinition, measurement, and validation', *Academy of Management Journal*, 47 (4): 765–802.

Van Dyne, L., Cummings, L.L. and McLean Parks, J. (1995) 'Extra–role behaviors: In pursuit of construct and definitional clarity (A bridge over muddied waters)', *Research in Organizational Behavior*, 17: 215–285.

Van Dyne, L. and LePine, J.A. (1998) 'Helping and voice extra–role behaviors: Evidence of construct and predictive validity', *Academy of Management Journal*, 37 (1): 765–802.

Van Scotter, J.R. and Motowidlo, S.J. (1996) 'Interpersonal facilitation and job dedication as separate facets of contextual performance', *Journal of Applied Psychology*, 81 (5): 525–531.

Vroom, V.H. (1964) *Work and Motivation.* New York: Wiley.

Van Willigen, M. (1998) *Doing Good, Feeling Better: The Effect of Voluntary Association Membership on Individual Well–Being.* Paper presented at the annual meeting of the American Sociological Association, August, San Francisco, CA.

Walz, S.M. and Niehoff, B.P. (1996) 'Organizational citizenship behaviors and their effect on organizational effectiveness in limited-menu restaurants', in J.B. Keys and L.N. Dosier (eds), *Academy of Management Best Papers Proceedings.* Briarcliff Manor, NY: Academy of Management, pp. 307–311.

Wang, H., Law, K.S., Hackett, R.D., Wang, D. and Chen, Z.X. (2005) 'Leader-member exchange as a mediator of the relationship between transformational leadership and followers' performance and organizational citizenship behavior', *Academy of Management Journal*, 48 (3): 420–432.

Williams, L.J. and Anderson, S.E. (1991) 'Job satisfaction and organizational commitment as predictors of organizational citizenship and in-role behaviors', *Journal of Management*, 17 (3): 601–617.

Yates, M. and Younnis, J. (1996) 'A developmental perspective on community service in adolescence', *Social Development*, 5 (1): 85–111.

Yogev, A. and Ronen, R. (1982) 'Cross–age tutoring: Effects on tutors' attributes', *Journal of Educational Research*, 75 (5): 261–268.

Younnis, J., Yates, M. and Su, Y. (1997) 'Social integration into peer and adult society: Community service and marijuana use in high school seniors', *Journal of Adolescence Research*, 12 (2): 245–262.

7

Teams at Work

Helen M. Williams and Natalie J. Allen

Over the past three decades, teams have become a major part of the organizational landscape. During the same period, there has been a dramatic, and welcome, increase in the body of theoretical and empirical research on team effectiveness. Our goal here is not to provide an exhaustive (or exhausting!) review of that literature but, rather, to highlight key research findings and emerging trends within the literature.

Consistent with other scholars (e.g., Guzzo, 1996), we use the terms groups, workgroups and teams interchangeably here. In doing so, however, we are confident that readers will recognize our interest is not in 'groups' such as those composed of people waiting together for a bus, but rather in those who interact in order to accomplish a common work-related goal. To that end, we find particularly useful and have adopted for use here, the definition provided by Sundstrom and colleagues who described work teams as 'interdependent collections of individuals who share responsibility for specific outcomes for their organizations' (Sundstrom et al., 1990: 120). Beyond this fairly generic definition, of course, teams vary considerably and, indeed, numerous typologies of teams appear in the literature. Some focus on the specific types of work/tasks that teams do. For example, Hackman (1990) distinguished between service and performing teams, while Sundstrom et al. (2000) distinguished between production, service, management, project, action and performing, and advisory, teams. Kozlowski et al. (1999) take a different approach, noting that teams vary along a continuum from simple through to complex, with five dimensions (task, goals, roles, process emphasis, and performance demands) distinguishing between teams at differing points on the continuum. Although we recognize the importance of these differences, we provide a broad overview of factors that have received most attention across various types of teams and, later in the chapter, address the contextual role that variation in team type can play.

ARE TEAMS EFFECTIVE?

The question of whether teams are effective is an intriguing, albeit complex question, that, obviously, requires one to grapple with the 'compared to what?' issue. Should we compare, for example, the effectiveness of interacting teams in organizations to that of similarly-sized 'nominal groups' of individuals working on a task, as is often done in laboratory-based studies (e.g., Mullen et al., 1991)? Or make pre-team, post-team comparisons (e.g., Wall and Clegg, 1981), or team/non-team comparisons (Wall et al., 1986), in field settings? Alternatively, should we hold out for more sophisticated designs that involve both team, and non-team, conditions to which individuals have been randomly assigned? In field settings, how should researchers deal with the fact that team implementation often comes bundled with other organizational and/or job interventions that may account for, amplify, or mute any true 'team effects'? Furthermore, what outcomes are appropriate indicators of 'effectiveness'?

Suffice it to say that studies in which team effectiveness is evaluated vary considerably in terms of research rigor/design, settings, and effectiveness measures. Although positive effects of interactive teams are reported in some laboratory studies, most report either null or negative effects (see reviews by Hill, 1982; Mullen et al., 1991). Moreover, careful examination of the body of empirical field research, and oft-cited reviews of such research (e.g., Beekun, 1989; Hackman, 1990; Macy and Izumi, 1993), does not reveal strong, consistent, evidence regarding the performance superiority of teams. Indeed, Allen and Hecht (2004a: 444), in their discussion of the 'romance of teams,' argued that 'overall, the evidence regarding the effectiveness of teams must be described as modest, at best' and noted the apparent mismatch between this evidence and the enthusiasm with which teams are greeted. Other scholars (e.g., Naquin and Tynan, 2003) have made a similar point (but see Allen and Hecht, 2004b and West et al., 2004 for differing views on the nature of the evidence).

Nonetheless, and critically, there is no doubt that organizations face numerous situations in which teams are the only possible way to get the work done. Further, as Allen and Hecht (2004a) have argued, there is good evidence suggesting that team-based activity has social-emotional benefits for members – itself a worthy outcome and, for some, an indicator in its own right of team effectiveness. Thus, for many organizations and tasks, the key question is not so much 'are teams effective?' but, rather, 'how can team effectiveness be enhanced?' As will be seen, researchers examine numerous indicators of effectiveness including productivity, creativity/innovation, adapting to change, team viability, and satisfaction of team members.

ENHANCING TEAM EFFECTIVENESS

As early as the Hawthorne studies in the 1920s, when groups were somewhat unexpectedly discovered to have a powerful effect on work behavior (see Mayo, 1933; Roethlisberger and Dickson, 1939) there has been research interest in group phenomena at work. Within this body of research, which peaked in the 1950s, many field studies still have an impact upon current thinking – especially with respect to the links between teams and the socio-technical, and organizational, systems in which they are embedded (e.g., Rice, 1953; Trist and Bamforth, 1951). The 1960s and 1970s saw a noticeable decline in such research and, in fact, team research can really be considered to have begun in earnest in the mid 1970s and throughout the 1980s. Classic contributions to the team literature during this time (e.g., Hackman, 1987; Hackman and Morris, 1975; McGrath, 1984; Steiner, 1972) conceptualized team effectiveness from a systems perspective and, thus, proposed that team inputs lead to team processes which, in turn, lead to outcomes. This general IPO (inputs-process-outcome) framework has several variations (e.g., Campion et al., 1993; Gladstein, 1984; Hackman, 1987) in which scholars emphasize different sets of variables within each of the IPO categories. The IPO framework is best considered an organizing heuristic used to examine team research, rather than a dynamic model of team behavior (Ilgen et al., 2005; Kozlowski and Ilgen, 2006), and it is within this spirit that we use it to structure the remainder of the chapter.

INPUT VARIABLES: TEAM DESIGN AND TEAM COMPOSITION

The most commonly examined team input variables involve characteristics of the team and its task (i.e., team design) and characteristics of the team's members (i.e., team composition).

Team design

Although interdependence is a defining feature of teams, teams vary considerably on this design dimension. Some research indicates a positive relation between interdependence and performance (e.g., Campion et al., 1993), while other research suggests a u-shaped relationship between the two (e.g., Stewart and Barrick, 2000), with high and low interdependence being best for performance. Taking a more contextualized approach, Wageman (1995) found that performance was higher when interdependence level and reward level were matched. Specifically, highly interdependent teams performed best when the reward system incorporated team rewards; those low in interdependence performed best in the absence of team rewards. This is consistent with the key idea that, in order to be effective, any form of job design (including teams) must be aligned with, and supported by, the organizational system in which it is embedded (e.g., Parker and Wall, 1998). Still other research suggests that interdependence moderates the relation between team-efficacy and performance (Gully et al., 2002).

Another key input factor is task design. Hackman and Oldham (1980) suggest that the job characteristic model (which asserts the importance of skill variety, task identity, task meaningfulness, autonomy and feedback from the job) can be meaningfully applied at the team-level. Given the prevalence of self-managed teams – and, more generally, the empowerment agenda in organizations – it is not surprising that team autonomy has received the most attention. In a recent meta-analysis, Stewart (2006) reported that it, as well as team task meaningfulness, has positive

effects on team outcomes, but that these effects vary across settings.

Although recommendations about team size abound within practitioner publications and textbooks, empirical evidence regarding its link with outcomes is quite mixed; some research shows no relation between size and performance (e.g., Martz et al., 1992), some a positive relation (Campion et al., 1993) and still other research, an inverted u-shaped relationship (Nieva et al., 1985). Not surprisingly, recent meta-analytic evidence suggests this relation depends upon type of team and its task (Stewart, 2006) and, indeed, of key importance here may be the fit between the task, its specific person requirements, and team size.

In sum, team design factors such as interdependence, task, and size appear to be important factors, though likely as moderators, or contextual variables, rather than direct antecedents of either team processes or outcomes.

Team composition

Although team composition research can involve any characteristic along which individuals differ, most research has focused on personality, cognitive ability, attitudinal, and demographic variables.

Team composition researchers are first challenged, of course, with how best to conceptualize (and operationalize) composition at the group level and, hence, how best to aggregate the scores of individual members to the group level.[1] Within the personality literature, the case has been made for four, quite different aggregation approaches: the team's mean, maximum member score, minimum member score, and variability (Barrick et al., 1998). These and other researchers reported that teams with higher mean levels of conscientiousness, agreeableness and emotional stability were more effective than those with lower mean levels (e.g., Barrick et al., 1998; Neuman and Wright, 1999; Neuman et al., 1999). Further, there is evidence that team performance is positively related to variability in extraversion and emotional stability (Newman et al., 1999) and negatively related to variability in conscientiousness (Barrick et al., 1998). Beyond the Big Five, recent evidence suggests that goal orientation, aggregated to the team level, influences the speed and effectiveness with which teams adapt to changing situations. Specifically, LePine (2003; 2005) reports that teams with a high mean level of learning orientation adapt well, while those with a high level of performance orientation adapt poorly. Finally with respect to personality, it is important to note that – just as at the individual level – relations between team-level personality and team performance are ideally considered in light of the task the team carries out (e.g., Allen and West, 2005; Barry and Stewart, 1997).

Team composition effects have also been found with respect to cognitive ability. In their meta-analysis, Devine and Philips (2001) reported that mean cognitive ability was a better predictor of performance than other operationalizations; the higher, the better. They noted, however, that this effect varied across studies, was stronger in laboratory-based studies than in field studies, and stronger in teams conducting ad-hoc tasks, or short-term groups engaged in complex tasks, than in ongoing teams engaged in standard, repetitive tasks. In some contrast, Stewart's (2006) meta-analysis showed mean cognitive ability was strongly related to performance with little variation across studies.

The evidence regarding 'surface-level' demographic variables (e.g., age, gender, racio-ethnic) – which have been primarily examined from a diversity (or variance) perspective – seems far less clear (e.g., Jackson et al., 2003; Mannix and Neale, 2005). Some studies find positive effects of demographic diversity on processes and outcomes, some find negative effects and still others report no effects at all. Nonetheless, research focused on the conditions under which effects are most likely to occur is bearing fruit. In particular, it appears that demographic diversity will exert more negative effects on teams that have not been together long (e.g., Chatman and Flynn, 2001;

Harrison et al., 1998; Harrison et al., 2002) and that such effects dissipate with experience/time together. Research also suggests the importance of examining how diversity, with respect to different variables, interacts with each other (Alexander et al., 1995), with informational diversity (Jehn et al., 1999) and with work style diversity (Williams et al., 2007). Attention has also been given to diversity with respect to 'deep-level' variables such as the attitudes and values of team members. Diversity with respect to job satisfaction is negatively related to team cohesion, especially for higher-tenure teams (Harrison et al., 1998). In addition Jehn et al. (1999) found that value diversity in teams increased conflict in teams and decreased team effectiveness and Williams et al. (2007) found that work style diversity was negatively related to within team perspective taking.

Finally, there is growing evidence that methodological differences across team diversity studies might partly account for the inconsistent pattern of effects within the literature. Critically, studies differ in the way that they conceptualize and operationalize the diversity construct (Harrison and Klein, 2007; Riordan, 2000; Williams and Meân, 2004) and, thus, comparison across studies is problematic. Further, recent evidence suggests that response rates (and, hence, missing data) vary considerably across the diversity literature and influence the accuracy of diversity measures and their relations with team outcomes (Allen et al., 2007; Newman and Sin, in press).

Overall, evidence suggests that team composition influences effectiveness, though much more research is needed in order to make strong statements regarding selection for teams (Allen and West, 2005) and for managing the 'people mix' within teams.

TEAM PROCESSES

The last decade has seen an increased focus on the 'P' in the IPO framework (Ilgen et al., 2005; Marks et al., 2001) and a distinction made between behavioral processes (team interaction) and emergent team states (both cognitive and affective).

Behavioral processes

Co-operation and helping among team members are key behavioral team processes. Unsurprisingly, most research has found a positive relationship between co-operation and team effectiveness (e.g., Wagner, 1995; Pinto and Pinto, 1990; Smith et al., 1994). In some contrast, within-team helping behavior appears to have both beneficial and negative effects on performance (e.g., Podsakoff et al., 1997; Podsakoff and MacKenzie, 1994). Key here might be whether or not the help enables an increase in the helped team member's performance that surpasses the productivity lost by the helpers taking time away from their own contributions to the team. Somewhat consistent with this, Bachrach et al. (2006) recently reported that, in their laboratory study, within-team helping behavior was positively related to team performance only in teams with high task interdependence.

Communication and information sharing is another core aspect of team behavioral processes. Unsurprisingly, both within-team communication (e.g., Barry and Stewart, 1997; Bunderson and Sutcliffe, 2002; Hyatt and Ruddy, 1997), and communication with those outside the team (e.g., Ancona and Caldwell, 1992) have been shown to be beneficial to team performance and related outcomes. A particularly interesting aspect of communication, in our view, is 'voice behavior,' communication defined as 'constructive challenge to the status quo with the intent of improving the situation rather than merely criticizing it' (LePine and Van Dyne, 1998: 358). LePine and Van Dyne examined voice behavior among work group members and found that team member characteristics (self-esteem and satisfaction with the group) and group characteristics of the group (autonomy and group size) interacted to influence the tendency to engage this type of communication; for example, while those with high self-esteem were unaffected by group size and group autonomy, those with

low self-esteem were less likely to engage in voice behavior if the group was small or autonomy was low. Other research has also found that functional diversity within teams can impact positively on information sharing in groups (e.g., Drach-Zahavy and Somech, 2001). Overall, it appears that communication and information sharing can be encouraged both through the design of the team and the composition of its members.

The final behavioral process considered here is group conflict. Within the team literature, a distinction is made between conflict regarding the task (task conflict) and more interpersonal difficulties between team members (relationship conflict). In a recent meta-analysis of the team conflict literature De Dreu and Weingart (2003) found that *both* types of conflict were detrimental for team performance and team member satisfaction. Given the inevitability of conflict – particularly task conflict – within teams, research focused on minimizing its effects on performance is particularly welcome. Lovelace et al. (2001), for example, found that collaborative communication, feeling a freedom to express doubts, and low levels of contentious communication eliminated the negative effects of task conflict on performance outcomes while Montoya-Weiss et al. (2001) found that performance outcomes were dependent upon the type of conflict management behavior that was adopted. Research such as this suggests that *how* conflict is managed within teams is critical in determining its effects on performance.

Affective states

Cohesion is one of the most studied aspects of teamwork (Sundstrom et al., 2000) and several meta-analytic reviews conclude that strong cohesion is beneficial to teams (Beal et al., 2003; Evans and Dion, 1991; Evans and Jarvis, 1980; Gully et al., 1995; Mullen and Copper, 1994). These meta-analyses also suggest moderators of the cohesion-performance relationship. In particular the positive relationship between cohesion and performance is higher when interdependence is high (Beal et al., 2003; Gully et al., 1995), when groups are small (Mullen and Copper, 1994); and when groups are real, as opposed to laboratory based (Mullen and Copper, 1994). Interestingly, Beal et al. (2003) also found that how performance is measured matters; specifically, they found that the positive effect of cohesion was strongest for performance behaviors (as opposed to performance outcomes) and for efficiency-based, rather than effectiveness-based, performance criteria.

Does the team's belief in itself matter? In this regard, researchers have examined both team efficacy, which focuses on the team's task-specific perception of their collective competency, and team potency, which represents the team's more general perception of their collective competency (e.g., Kozlowski and Ilgen, 2006). In their meta-analysis, Gully et al. (2002) found that both team efficacy and team potency were positively related to team performance. Moreover, Hecht et al. (2002) found that team potency predicted performance even after accounting for the collective ability of team members. Finally, although most research on efficacy and potency has focused on performance, there is also some evidence that potency is positively related to team member satisfaction (e.g., Campion et al., 1993).

Other affective states are trust and psychological safety. Despite considerable rhetoric regarding the importance of trust in teams, there are surprisingly few empirical studies that demonstrate the direct effects of team-level trust on performance and it has been suggested that the relations may be more complex (Langfred, 2004). In a laboratory based experiment, Dirks (1999) found that trust moderated the relationship between motivation and team processes and performance. Specifically, he found that in teams with low levels of trust, motivation led to individual effort, whereas in teams with high levels of trust, motivation led to joint efforts, and consequently higher team performance. Langfred (2004) cautions that trust can be 'too much of a good thing' and provides evidence that high-trust teams were associated

with superior performance only when the autonomy of individual team members was low and, hence, team members monitored each other; when autonomy was high (and little monitoring of others occurred), high-trust teams performed less well. *Psychological safety* is defined as 'a shared belief that the team is safe for interpersonal risk taking' (Edmondson, 1999: 354). This involves trust but it also incorporates issues relating to respect amongst team members, and feelings of comfort (or safety) in being themselves (Edmondson, 1999). Edmondson found that psychological safety and team performance were positively related and mediated by team learning behavior and, in another study, reported that creating a climate of psychological safety was related to successful implementation of new technology within cardiac teams (Edmondson et al., 2001).

In sum, research suggests that confident and cohesive teams with high levels of trust and psychological safety may be more effective under some conditions. However, relatively little is known about how to create these affective states and about the conditions under which they will produce optimal effects, suggesting these as important areas for future research.

Cognitive states

One aspect of team cognition that has received considerable attention of late is 'shared mental models' (SMM) which are defined as 'team members' shared, organized understanding and mental representation of knowledge about key elements of the team's relevant environment' (Mohammed and Dumville, 2001: 90). SMM theorists argue that teams whose members have highly shared mental models will outperform those whose mental models diverge, that the mental models of team members converge over time as they work together and, hence, that SMM-performance links will strengthen over time/practice (Mathieu et al., 2000). Further, it has been argued that the performance-enhancing effects of SMMs occur, in part, by preventing misunderstandings, allowing for rapid and accurate coordination, and by increasing time spent 'on task' rather than on conflict or misinterpretations. For all these reasons, SMMs are seen to have considerable human resource/managerial value – especially in settings/jobs such as policing, emergency response teams, some medical teams, and complex transportation teams – where co-ordination among team members is essential, but where time, distance, and/or other ambient conditions (e.g., noise, physical constraints) impede communication. To date, there have been only a few empirical studies examining SMM-performance links (all conducted using 2-person computerized simulator tasks). Evidence regarding this link appears promising, albeit quite mixed (e.g., Marks et al., 2000; Mathieu et al., 2000; Mathieu et al., 2005; Stout et al., 1999). The convergence-over-time hypothesis has fared somewhat less well but, admittedly, has received less attention (Mathieu et al., 2000). There is evidence that the impact of SMMs on performance may occur through team processes such as improved coordination (Marks et al., 2002) and that the impact of SMMs models on team performance is greater in novel, than routine, tasks, which supports the suggestion that SMMs may be particularly useful in teams that must respond to changing demands. Despite the fairly limited body of empirical evidence, reliance on laboratory studies, and measurement challenges (Mohammed et al., 2000; Ross and Allen, 2006), SMM work has emerged as a promising area of research that may well pay dividends.

Also promising, in our view, is work on another cognitive state: 'transactive memory' (TM). Originally proposed by Wegner and colleagues (Wegner, 1986; Wegner et al., 1985) in relation to intimate relationships, TM refers to a team-level system that describes team members' awareness of the distribution of knowledge within the team (i.e., knowledge among team members about 'who knows what?'). Thus far, numerous potential pitfalls relating to issues such as conflicts of expertise and diffusion of responsibility (Wegner,

1986), confusion (Kozlowski and Bell, 2003) and the possibility of important information being overlooked (Wegner, 1986) have been identified in the TM literature (Kozlowski and Ilgen, 2006). Nonetheless, theoretical work and some experimental work (e.g., Moreland, 1999; Moreland and Myaskovsky, 2000) supports the link between TM and effective teamwork. Presumably, a strong TM system can enable teams to pool expertise and reduce the redundancy of knowledge and skills across team members, thus enhancing cognitive efficiency (Hollingshead, 1998). Moreover, there is some recent research supporting the beneficial effects of TM within organizational teams. Austin (2003) found that two dimensions of task TM – transactive accuracy and knowledge specialization – were related to team performance. Transactive accuracy, defined as the degree to which 'individuals identified by others in the group as possessing particular knowledge actually posses that knowledge' (Austin, 2003: 867), predicted group performance in terms of goal attainment and both internal and external assessments. Knowledge specialization, focusing on the degree to which each team member has a specialist role within the team, was found to be positively associated with internal and external assessments, but not goal attainment. Further field evidence comes from a study by Lewis (2003) who, in testing the reliability and validity of a measure of perceived TM, demonstrated that the construct was positively related to team performance. Therefore, although research on TM in teams is in its infancy, the available evidence suggests that future research might profitably focus on its development and maintenance.

In conclusion, research suggests that team cognition plays an important role in shaping team effectiveness – particularly performance. Preliminary research in this area suggests that teams may be more effective when they think about the team and its task in similar ways (shared mental models) and when team members specialize in aspects of the teams overall knowledge base but have an accurate understanding of each others' knowledge (transactive memory).

MORE RECENT TEAM PERSPECTIVES

Over the past two decades, teams have been extensively studied, primarily within the overarching IPO framework. For several reasons, however, its dominant position in the team literature is beginning to be challenged. In particular, it is argued that the IPO perspective – and the research it has inspired – has not sufficiently captured the dynamic and temporal aspects of teams (e.g., Ilgen et al., 2005) nor given sufficient consideration to the importance of contextual factors in understanding team effects. It is to these two issues that we turn next.

The dynamic and temporal nature of teams

In line with the organizational literature (e.g., Zaheer et al., 1999), there is a growing recognition amongst team researchers that the role of time should be given explicit consideration. Although some seminal IPO models discussed temporal elements such as feedback loops (e.g., Tannenbaum and Yukl, 1992) and reciprocal linkages (e.g., Hackman, 1987), these were not incorporated into the general IPO framework and were given short shrift in most empirical research. To rectify this somewhat, Ilgen et al. (2005) suggest that the terminology should be changed from IPO to IMOI (inputs – mediators[2] – outputs – inputs) with the second 'I' invoking 'the notion of cyclical causal feedback' (p. 520). This IMOI framework is a move in the right direction. However, as with the early works identifying temporal elements of team working, the IMOI model simply recognizes a gap in our understanding, and highlights the need for future theory development and research to capture the complex dynamics of teams, it does not itself move our understanding forward. A notable exception is the recurring phase model of team processes

developed by Marks et al. (2001). This model suggests that rather than considering the IPO model as being relevant to the whole life cycle of the team, teams should be thought of as being engaged in multiple performance episodes or sub episodes at a time. Consequently it is suggested that a series of IPO episodes will occur within teams and these will vary in terms of both their onset and their duration. This seems a logical proposition, with potential for enhancing our understanding of teamwork; however, the model awaits empirical evaluation.

Other time-focused work has emphasized team development. Indeed, team development models could be considered an exception to the view that early team researchers ignored temporal aspects of teamwork. Half a century ago, several researchers attempted to identify the stages, or developmental phases, through which teams progressed (e.g., Bales and Strodbeck, 1951; Bion, 1961; Tuckman, 1965). Although more contemporary scholars (e.g., Kozlowski et al., 1999; Miller, 2003) note the similarity across these various models, it is likely that readers will be most familiar with the one outlined by Tuckman (1965). Tuckman proposed that groups progress through four hierarchical stages: forming, storming, norming and performing.

Forming is characterized by confusion and uncertainty with team members engaging in activities that involve assessing the situation, getting to know one another, and testing and establishing ground rules. Then, during storming, groups experience conflict, struggles for leadership, and tension. The norming stage, according to Tuckman, is when group identity is formed and consensus, trust and cohesion is developed; further, norms and standards for behavior and performance are established. Finally, during the performing stage, the team's effort is focused on goal attainment and the accomplishment of tasks. Although early stage/phase models considered teams from a temporal perspective, they have been criticized as being overly rigid and static in their approach. For example, the underlying assumption that all teams progress through the same stages in a linear sequence is considered unrealistic (e.g., Bettenhausen, 1991; Gersick, 1988; Sundstrom et al., 1990) and the process of team development is thought to be far more complex than these models suggest (Miller, 2003). Finally, it has been noted that there is very little evidence supporting the idea that teams that do progress through prescribed stages are more effective than those that do not (Ericksen and Dyer, 2004).

More recent theoretical contributions, perhaps, take better account of the complexities of team development. For example, McGrath's (1991) time-interaction-performance (TIP) model incorporates 'modes,' which are similar to the stages in hierarchical stage models; these include, inception and acceptance of a project (mode 1), solution of technical issues (mode 2), resolution of conflict (mode 3) and execution of performance requirements (mode 4).

In contrast to hierarchical stage theories, McGrath argues that teams may engage in more than one mode at a time (especially if they are engaged in multiple tasks or projects) and that the temporal progress of the team through the sets of activities, and the number and order of the modes the team goes through, is dependent upon the tasks and the context.

Particularly important, in our view, is Kozlowski et al.'s (1991) multi-level theory of compilation and performance across levels and time. Herein, it is proposed that teams progress through four phases that involve the transition in level of focus from individual, to dyadic, to team. In Phase 1, team formation, the focus is on the individual level with individual team members engaging in information seeking in order to understand that the team, its purpose, and their individual places within the team. Phase 2, task compilation, is also focused at the individual level and primarily involves team members' attempts to demonstrate their own task competency. In Phase 3, the level of focus shifts to the dyad as, having determined their individual roles, team members explore how that role links to others – at this point, this is framed as a series

of dyadic relationships. Finally, Phase 4, team compilation, involves a team focus with attention turning from dyadic relationships to the whole network of roles within the team. Although this theory conceptualizes teams in a more complex way, Kozlowski et al. (1991) acknowledge, that, as with many phase theories, it applies best to new teams and that, thus far, it awaits empirical testing.

Another approach to considering temporal aspects of team working, both theoretically and empirically, has been to focus on specific aspects of teamwork (e.g., communication, conflict) and explore their impact over time. For example, Maruping and Agarwal (2004) theorize that the communication needs of virtual teams differ depending upon the team's developmental stage and, thus, that a particular type of communication will be helpful at one point in the team's lifespan, but not at another. In a similar vein, Choi (2002) argues that, because there are temporal shifts in the external demands that teams encounter, external activities will only be beneficial to team effectiveness at certain times in the team's lifespan. As a final example, Berman et al. (2002) theorize, and in a study of basketball teams, find limited support for, what they call knowledge ossification. The idea is that shared team experience initially will have a positive relationship with team performance but that, as shared experience (and time together) grows, this positive effect will diminish, and eventually become negative.

The theories described above focus on specific aspects of team working and consider how there might be temporal fluctuations in their effects. There have also been a number of empirical attempts to incorporate time – in its various guises – into our understanding of teamwork. In such work, various research strategies have been adopted.

Some of this research involves laboratory experiments using ad-hoc teams. For example, in a study of face-to-face and virtual teams, Alge and colleagues (2003) investigated temporal scope – the degree to which teams have worked together in the past and expect to work together in the future. Results demonstrated that, when teams had no past experience of working together, trust and information exchange was higher in face-to-face than virtual teams. In teams that had worked together previously, however, there was no difference in the levels of trust and information exchange. In addition, Adelman et al. (2003) investigated teams' responses to increasing time pressure over time, finding that although initial time pressure was not detrimental to performance, depending upon the adaptation behaviors undertaken by the team, it can be in longer term. Moreover, once time pressure reached a certain level, adaptation behaviors were no longer successful at maintaining performance.

Other researchers have relied on student groups working on class projects or assignments. A good example of this is Jehn and Mannix's (2001) investigation of the dynamic nature of group conflict in which they found that although both high and low performing MBA student teams engaged in conflict they differed in the timing of that engagement. In other studies of student teams, Pescosolido (2001) found that the relation between self-efficacy and group efficacy was higher early, rather than later, in the semester, while Harrison et al. (2002) reported that the impact of surface-level diversity vs. deep-level diversity varies as a function of the time the team has been together.

The temporal nature of teamwork has also been examined in organizational teams. Perlow (1999), for example, conducted a nine-month qualitative investigation into how a software engineering team used its time, finding that changing the way that team members used their time increased team productivity. Also interesting is work by Maznevski and Chudoba (2000) who conducted an in-depth study of three virtual teams. They described temporal patterns within the teams, noting that effective virtual teams used periodic face-to face coordination meetings to define the structure of the team in a manner they likened to a heart beat, 'rhythmically pumping life into the team's processes' (p. 486).

These studies are excellent examples of in-depth qualitative work that seems to capture the dynamic nature of teams in ways that quantitative or laboratory based approaches often do not. They are, however, based on only a very few teams. Particularly impressive, therefore, is Ancona and Caldwell's (1992) comparatively larger scale study ($n = 45$) that relied on both qualitative and quantitative methods. The authors conducted semi-structured interviews with 38 team managers and examined detailed log data from two teams. In addition, questionnaire data were collected from members of 45 teams. On the basis of their qualitative and quantitative analyses, Ancona and Caldwell concluded that teams with long-term success 'enter positive cycles of external activities, internal processes and performance' (p. 634) and that although teams with differing strategies may both perform well in the early stages, over time they can be distinguished in terms of their levels of success. This study is a rare example of rigorous research that captures the dynamic nature of teams. Most research examines either a few teams in great depth, or many teams in less ecologically valid settings. The bulk of the evidence thus far suggests that 'time matters'; a more elaborate understanding of the temporal/dynamic nature of teams, however, awaits further research.

CONSIDERING CONTEXT

Over the past few years, increased emphasis has been placed on the role of context in understanding workplace phenomena in general (e.g., Johns, 2001, 2006) and teams in particular (Hackman, 1999). Johns (2006) describes contexts as 'situational opportunities and constraints that affect the occurrence and meaning of organizational behavior as well as functional relationships between variables' (p. 386) and notes that context can play numerous tricks – restricting range of variables within a sample, altering causal direction between variables, reversing the sign of relation, and so on.

Importantly, Johns notes that ignoring context is 'likely responsible for one of the most vexing problems in the [organizational behavior] field: study-to-study variation' (p. 389). As with non-team research, explicit considerations of context are still the exception, rather than the norm, in team research. Nonetheless, interest in context is growing, in tandem it seems, with the increasingly multi-level approaches to the study of teams (Klein and Kozlowski, 2000). Below we provide some examples, though by no means a comprehensive representation, of ways in which contextual factors have been considered by team researchers. Merely as a way of organizing these we have distinguished between the context in which the team is embedded and the team-as-context and, in keeping with the focus of the chapter, we emphasize studies that focus on team effectiveness.

The context in which the team (and its members) are embedded

As Hackman (1999: 238) has noted 'there are no truly freestanding groups' as each is embedded in several larger contexts – whether they be the organization, its environment (e.g., marketplace or industry), or the wider culture in which the team operates.

Internally, organizations communicate various – and sometimes mixed – messages about how 'teamy' they expect their teams to be, often as a function of human resource practices such as team selection strategies, compensation, and inter-team contact (Allen, 1996). Further, teams vary greatly in terms of how tightly connected their work is to the larger organization and in terms of the 'mix' of people both within and across the organization. Unquestionably, such organizational factors can serve to constrain – or expand – the range of various behaviors and attitudes among team members and the relations among variables. For example, in trying to better understand their empirical observation that, contrary to prediction, senior managerial support for teamwork contributed little to team empowerment within the

organization's teams, Mathieu et al. (2006) obtained contextual information suggesting that these managers were generally not 'on board' (p. 106) with the teamwork notion.

Contextual factors beyond the organization also shape team behavior. For example, even among teams within the same organization, those that must operate under strict regulatory controls (e.g., audit teams) are likely to develop a narrower tolerance for change – and potentially experience more difficulty adapting to change – than teams who work under fewer constraints. In a related vein, researchers are just beginning to examine the host of contextual factors created by the multi-team systems (e.g., Marks et al., 2005) in which various teams, from different organizations, and with different operating strategies, must work together.

Still other researchers have tried to account for the role that cultural context can play in shaping behavior within teams. For example, Kirkman and Shapiro (2000) report that employees in collectivist cultures are generally more accepting of team-based compensation for performance than those with more individualist orientations.

The team as a context

A key, and multi-faceted, contextual feature of any team is its task. Task complexity and task uncertainty seem particularly important. In the meta-analysis referred to earlier, De Dreu and Weingart (2003) observed that the negative relation between task conflict and performance was much stronger among groups doing uncertain/complex tasks than for those doing simple, routine tasks. Similarly, relationship conflict and performance were more strongly linked among decision-making teams than those engaged in more straightforward production. Overall, it appears that conflict may have more deleterious effects on performance as task complexity and uncertainty increases. It has also been argued that the degree to which a task is complex allows for, or renders unlikely, the development of meaningful team cognition variables such as transactive memory (Moreland and Myaskovsky, 2000) and alters their impact on performance if they do develop. Finally, Cordery et al. (1997) reported that waste management teams whose tasks involved high levels of operational uncertainty outperformed those faced with low uncertainty.

Another key contextual variable is the stability of the team's membership. Perhaps the most cogent examples of this come from research on airline cockpit crews (Helmreich and Foushee, 1993), in which it is suggested that crews whose members have worked together outperform those who have not, and from research on coal-mining crews (Goodman and Leyden, 1991) that suggests a link between crew familiarity and productivity. It may be that membership stability influences the development and impact of shared mental models and/or transactive memory systems. Difference in stability may also underlie development of norms and, hence, constrain or expand the range of 'acceptable' behaviors exhibited by team members – including those that drive various effectiveness indicators. Similar issues may help to explain differences in the behavior of teams that differ in terms of their 'virtuality' (Kirkman and Mathieu, 2005).

That context matters to teams, and their members, seems undeniable. Optimists would argue that fortunately, in describing context and in reflecting on its potential meaning for our understanding of team phenomena, team researchers are starting to do better. Pessimists, however, might suggest that this could not yet be called a trend.

CONCLUSION

Despite the prevalence of, and enthusiasm for, teams in the workplace, teams are not always effective. Consequently, we caution against an unquestioning use of teams within organizations. Nonetheless, given that teams persist – and are necessary for many tasks – it is important to gain an understanding of how team effectiveness can be enhanced. Most research investigating the antecedents of team effectiveness has been influenced by the IPO framework and, as we argue here, numerous key input and process variables appear to be related to team effectiveness. This research can help us understand how teams can be managed effectively, but more research is needed both in terms of more fully understanding the impact of some of these factors and in terms of discovering how these aspects of team functioning can be developed and maintained.

More recently, the dominant position of the IPO framework has been challenged – most notably because it does not capture the dynamic and temporal nature of teams and because it pays little attention to context. As we discuss above, despite the increased awareness of the need to capture the complex nature of teams, the empirical literature has done so with little consistency. Nonetheless, theoretical work is emerging and is beginning to receive much-needed empirical attention. In doing so, team researchers have become aware of the multi-level nature of teamwork (see Klein and Kozlowski, 2000) and are starting to make use of recent multi-level methodological and statistical advances. To be sure, much of this work resides in the laboratory or with 'student teams.' Although we see value in tightly focused laboratory studies, their limitations are well known. Consequently, we look forward to an increased coupling of new theoretical, multi-level perspectives within the context of in-depth and fine grained analyses of larger samples of organizational teams. We believe that if this challenge is met, future research will have the potential to greatly surpass existing research efforts.

ACKNOWLEDGEMENTS

Support for this work was provided to the authors from the Social Sciences and Humanities Council of Canada (Grant No. 410-03-1186).

NOTES

1 It is important to note that most researchers do not conceptualize these team-level composition variables as shared property variables (Klein and Kozlowski, 2000) and, hence, are not looking for evidence of within-group homogeneity.

2 The term mediator replaces process to reflect the importance of team cognitive and affective states in addition to behavioral processes.

REFERENCES

Adelman, L., Miller, S.L., Henderson, D. and Schoelles, M. (2003) 'Using Brunswikian theory and a longitudinal design to study how hierarchical teams adapt to increasing levels of time pressure', *Acta Psychologica*, 112 (2): 181–206.

Alexander, J., Nuchols, B., Bloom, J. and Lee, S.Y. (1995) 'Organizational demography and turnover: An examination of multiform and nonlinear heterogeneity', *Human Relations*, 48: 1455–1480.

Alge, B.J., Wiethoff, C. and Klein, H.J. (2003) 'When does the medium matter? Knowledge-building experiences and opportunities in decision-making teams', *Organizational Behavior and Human Decision Processes*, 91 (1): 26–37.

Allen, N.J. (1996) 'Affective reactions to the group and the organization', in M.A. West (ed.), *Handbook of Work Group Psychology*. Chichester: John Wiley & Sons Ltd, pp. 371–396.

Allen, N.J. and Hecht, T.D. (2004a) 'The "romance of teams": Toward an understanding of its psychological underpinnings and implications', *Journal of Occupational and Organizational Psychology*, 77 (4): 439–461.

Allen, N.J. and Hecht, T.D. (2004b) 'Further thoughts on the romance of teams: A reaction to the commentaries', *Journal of Occupational and Organizational Psychology*, 77 (4): 485–491.

Allen, N.J. and West, M.A. (2005) 'Selecting for teamwork', in A. Evers, N. Anderson, and O. Voskuijl (eds), *The Blackwell Handbook of Personnel Selection*. Oxford: Blackwell Press, pp. 476–494.

Allen, N.J., Stanley, D.J., Williams, H.M. and Ross, S.J. (2007) 'Assessing the impact of nonresponse on work group diversity effects', *Organizational Research Methods*, 10 (2): 262–286.

Ancona, D.G. and Caldwell, D.F. (1992) 'Bridging the boundary – External activity and performance in organizational teams', *Administrative Science Quarterly*, 37 (4): 634–665.

Austin, J.R. (2003) 'Transactive memory in organizational groups: The effects of content, consensus, specialization, and accuracy on group performance', *Journal of Applied Psychology*, 88 (5): 866–878.

Bachrach, D.G., Powell, B.C., Collins, B.J. and Richey, R.G. (2006) 'Effects of task interdependence on the relationship between helping behavior and group performance', *Journal of Applied Psychology*, 91 (6): 1396–1405.

Bales, R.R. and Strodbeck, F.L. (1951) 'Phases in group problem solving', *Journal of Abnormal and Social Psychology*, 46 (4): 485–495.

Barrick, M.R., Stewart, G.L., Neubert, M.J. and Mount, M.K. (1998) 'Relating member ability and personality to work-team processes and team effectiveness', *Journal of Applied Psychology*, 83 (3): 377–391.

Barry, B. and Stewart, G.L. (1997) 'Composition, process, and performance in self-managed groups: The Role of Personality', *Journal of Applied Psychology*, 82 (1): 62–78.

Beal, D.J., Cohen, R.R., Burke, M.J. and McLendon, C.L. (2003) 'Cohesion and performance in groups: A meta-analytic clarification of construct relations', *Journal of Applied Psychology*, 88 (6): 989–1004.

Beekun, R.I. (1989) 'Assessing the effectiveness of sociotechnical interventions: Antidote or fad?' *Human Relations*, 42: 877–897.

Berman, S.L., Down, J. and Hill, C.W.L. (2002) 'Tacit knowledge as a source of competitive advantage in the national basketball association', *Academy of Management Journal*, 45 (1): 13–31.

Bettenhausen, K.L. (1991) 'Five years of group research: What we have learned and what needs to be addressed', *Journal of Management*, 17 (2): 345–381.

Bion, W.R. (1961) *Experiences in Groups*. New York: Basic Books.

Bunderson, J.S. and Sutcliffe, K.M. (2002) 'Comparing alternative conceptualizations of functional diversity in management teams: Process and performance effects', *Academy of Management Journal*, 45 (5): 875–893.

Campion, M.A., Medsker, G.J. and Higgs, A.C. (1993) 'Relations between work group characteristics and effectiveness: Implications for designing effective work groups', *Personnel Psychology*, 46 (4): 823–850.

Chatman, J.A. and Flynn, F.J. (2001) 'The influence of demographic heterogeneity on the emergence and consequences of cooperative norms in work teams', *Academy of Management Journal*, 44 (5): 956–974.

Choi, J.N. (2002) 'External activities and team effectiveness – Review and theoretical development', *Small Group Research*, 33 (2): 181–208.

Cordery, J.I., Wright, B.M. and Wall, T.D. (1997) *Towards a more comprehensive and integrated approach to work design: Production uncertainty and self–managing team performance.* Paper presented at the annual meeting of the Society for Industrial and Organizational Psychology, St. Louis, MO.

De Dreu, C.K.W. and Weingart, L.R. (2003) 'Task versus relationship conflict, team performance, and team member satisfaction: A meta-analysis', *Journal of Applied Psychology*, 88 (4): 741–749.

Devine, D.J. and Philips, J.L. (2001) 'Do smarter teams do better. A meta-analysis of cognitive ability and team performance', *Small Group Research*, 32 (5): 507–532.

Dirks, K.T. (1999) 'The effects of interpersonal trust on work group performance', *Journal of Applied Psychology*, 84 (3): 445–455.

Drach-Zahavy, A. and Somech, A. (2001) 'Understanding team innovation: The role of team processes and structures', *Group Dynamics*, 5 (2): 111–123.

Edmondson, A. (1999) 'Psychological safety and learning behavior in work teams', *Administrative Science Quarterly*, 44 (2): 350–383.

Edmondson, A., Bohmer, R. and Pisano, G. (2001) 'Speeding up team learning', *Harvard Business Review*, 79 (9): 125–134.

Ericksen, J. and Dyer, L. (2004) 'Right from the start: Exploring the effects of early team events on subsequent project team development and performance', *Administrative Science Quarterly*, 49 (3): 438–471.

Evans, C.R. and Dion, K.L. (1991) 'Group cohesion and performance: A meta-analysis', *Small Group Research*, 22 (2): 175–186.

Evans, C.R. and Jarvis, P.A. (1980) 'Group cohesion: A review and re-evaluation', *Small Group Behavior*, 11: 359–370.

Gersick, C.J.G. (1988) 'Time and transition in work teams: Toward a new model of group development', *Academy of Management Journal*, 31 (1): 9–41.

Gladstein, D.L. (1984) 'Groups in context: A model of task group effectiveness', *Administrative Science Quarterly*, 29 (4): 499–517.

Goodman, P.S. and Leyden, D.P. (1991) 'Familiarity and group productivity', *Journal of Applied Psychology*, 76 (4): 578–586.

Gully, S.M., Devine, D.J. and Whitney, D.J. (1995) 'A meta-analysis of cohesion and performance: Effects of levels of analysis and task interdependence', *Small Group Research*, 26 (4): 487–520.

Gully, S.M., Incalcaterra, K.A., Joshi, A. and Beaubien, J.M. (2002) 'A meta-analysis of team-efficacy, potency, and performance: Interdependence and level of analysis as moderators of observed relationships', *Journal of Applied Psychology*, 87 (5): 819–832.

Guzzo, R.A. (1996) 'Fundamental considerations about work groups', in M.A. West (ed.), *Handbook of Work Group Psychology*. Chichester: John Wiley & Sons, pp. 3–21.

Hackman, J.R. (1987) 'The design of work teams', In J.W. Lorsch (ed.), *Handbook of Organizational Behavior*. Englewood Cliffs, NJ: Prentice-Hall, pp. 315–342.

Hackman, J.R. (1990) *Groups That Work (And Those That Don't): Creating Conditions For Effective Teamwork*. San Francisco: Jossey-Bass.

Hackman, J.R. (1999) 'Thinking differently about context', in R. Wageman, (ed.) *Research on Managing Groups and Teams: Groups in Context*. Stanford, CT.: JAI Press. Vol. 2, pp. 233–247.

Hackman, J.R. and Morris, C.G. (1975) 'Group tasks, group interaction process, and group performance: A review and proposed integration', in L. Berkowitz (ed.), *Advances in Experimental Social Psychology*. New York: Academic Press. Vol. 8, pp. 45–99.

Hackman, J.R. and Oldham, G.R. (1980) *Work Redesign*. Reading, MA: Addison-Wesley.

Harrison, D.A. and Klein, K.J. (2007) 'What's the difference? Diversity constructs as separation, variety, or disparity in organizations', *Academy of Management Review*, 32 (4): 1199–1228.

Harrison, D.A., Price, K.H. and Bell, M.P. (1998) 'Beyond relational demography: Time and the effects of surface- and deep-level diversity on work group cohesion', *Academy of Management Journal*, 41 (1): 96–107.

Harrison, D.A., Price, K.H., Gavin, J.H. and Florey, A.T. (2002) 'Time, teams, and task performance: Changing effects of surface- and deep-level diversity on group functioning', *Academy of Management Journal*, 45 (5): 1029–1045.

Hecht, T.D., Allen, N.J., Klammer, J.D. and Kelly, E.C. (2002) 'Group beliefs, ability, and performance: The potency of group potency', *Group Dynamics*, 6 (2): 143–152.

Helmreich, R.L. and Foushee, H.C. (1993) 'Why crew resource management? empirical and theoretical bases of human factors training in aviation', in E.L. Wiener, B.G. Kanki and R.L. Helmreich (eds), *Cockpit Resource Management*. San Diego: Academic Press, pp. 3–45.

Hill, G.W. (1982) 'Group versus individual performance: Are N+1 heads better than one?' *Psychological Bulletin*, 91 (3): 517–539.

Hollingshead, A.B. (1998) 'Group and individual training – The impact of practice on performance', *Small Group Research*, 29 (2): 254–280.

Hyatt, D.E. and Ruddy, T.M. (1997) 'An examination of the relationship between work group characteristics and performance: once more into the breech', *Personnel Psychology*, 50 (3): 553–585.

Ilgen, D.R., Hollenbeck, J.R., Johnson, M. and Jundt, D. (2005) 'Teams in organizations: From input-process-output models to IMOI models', *Annual Review of Psychology*, 56: 517–543.

Jackson, S.E., Joshi, A. and Erhardt, N.L. (2003) 'Recent research on team and organizational diversity: SWOT analysis and implications', *Journal of Management*, 29 (6): 801–830.

Jehn, K.A. and Mannix, E.A. (2001) 'The dynamic nature of conflict: A longitudinal study of intragroup conflict and group performance', *Academy of Management Journal*, 44 (2): 238–251.

Jehn, K.A., Northcraft, G.B. and Neale, M.A. (1999) 'Why differences make a difference: A field study of diversity, conflict, and performance in work-groups', *Administrative Science Quarterly*, 44 (4): 741–763.

Johns, G. (2001) 'In praise of context', *Journal of Organizational Behavior*, 22 (1): 31–42.

Johns, G. (2006) 'The essential impact of context on organizational behavior', *Academy of Management Review*, 31 (2): 386–408.

Kirkman, B.L. and Mathieu, J.E. (2005) 'The dimensions and antecedents of team virtuality', *Journal of Management*, 31 (5): 700–718.

Kirkman, B.L. and Shapiro, D.L. (2000) 'Understanding why team members won't share: An examination of factors related to employee receptivity to team-based rewards', *Small Group Research*, 31 (2): 175–209.

Klein, K.J. and Kozlowski, S.W.J. (eds) (2000) *Multi-level Theory, Research, and Methods in Organizations: Foundations, Extensions, and New Directions*. San Francisco: Jossey-Bass.

Kozlowski, S.W.J. and Bell, B.S. (2003) 'Work groups and teams in organizations', in W.C. Borman, D.R. Ilgen and R.J. Klimoski (eds), *Handbook of Psychology: Industrial and Organizational Psychology*. London: Wiley. Vol. 12, pp. 333–375.

Kozlowski, S.W.J. and Ilgen, D.R. (2006) 'Enhancing the effectiveness of work groups and teams', *Psychological Science in the Public Interest*, 7 (3): 77–124.

Kozlowski, S.W.J., Gully, S.M., Nason, E.R. and Smith, E.M. (1999) 'Developing adaptive teams. A theory of compilation and performance across levels and time', in D.R. Ilgen and E.D. Pulakos (eds), *The Changing Nature of Performance. Implications for Staffing, Motivation, and Development*. San Francisco: Jossey-Bass, pp. 240–292.

Langfred, C.W. (2004) 'Too much of a good thing? Negative effects of high trust and individual autonomy in self-managing teams', *Academy of Management Journal*, 47 (3): 385–399.

LePine, J.A. and Van Dyne, L. (1998) 'Predicting voice behavior in work groups', *Journal of Applied Psychology*, 83 (6): 853–868.

LePine, J.A. (2003) 'Team adaptation and post change performance: Effects of team composition in terms of members' cognitive ability and personality', *Journal of Applied Psychology*, 88 (1): 27–39.

LePine, J.A. (2005) 'Adaptation of teams in response to unforeseen change: Effects of goal orientation and team composition in terms of cognitive ability and goal orientation', *Journal of Applied Psychology*, 90 (6): 1153–1167.

Lewis, K. (2003) 'Measuring transactive memory systems in the field: Scale development and validation', *Journal of Applied Psychology*, 88 (4): 587–604.

Lovelace, K., Shapiro, D.L. and Weingart, L.R. (2001) 'Maximizing cross-functional new product teams' innovativeness and constraint adherence: A conflict communications perspective', *Academy of Management Journal*, 44 (4): 779–793.

Macy, B.A. and Izumi, H. (1993) 'Organizational change, design, and work innovation: A meta-analysis of 131 North American field studies – 1961–1991', *Research in Organizational Change and Development*, 7: 235–313.

Mannix, E. and Neale, M.A. (2005) 'What differences make a difference? The promise and reality of diverse teams in organizations', *Psychological Science in the Public Interest*, 6 (2): 31–55.

Marks, M.A., DeChurch, L.A., Mathieu, J.E., Panzer, F.J. and Alonso, A. (2005) 'Teamwork in multiteam systems', *Journal of Applied Psychology*, 90 (5): 964–971.

Marks, M.A., Mathieu, J.E. and Zaccaro, S.J. (2001) 'A temporally based framework and taxonomy of team processes', *Academy of Management Review*, 26 (3): 356–376.

Marks, M.A., Sabella, M.J., Burke, C.S. and Zaccaro, S.J. (2002) 'The impact of cross-training on team effectiveness', *Journal of Applied Psychology*, 87 (1): 3–13.

Marks, M.A., Zaccaro, S.J. and Mathieu, J.E. (2000) 'Performance implications of leader briefings and team-interaction training for team adaptation to novel environments', *Journal of Applied Psychology*, 85 (6): 971–986.

Martz, W.B., Vogel, R.R. and Nunamaker, J.F. (1992) 'Electronic meeting systems: Results from the field', *Decision Support Systems*, 8: 141–158.

Maruping, L.A. and Agarwal, R. (2004) 'Managing team interpersonal processes through technology: A task-technology fit perspective', *Journal of Applied Psychology*, 89 (6): 975–990.

Mathieu, J.E., Heffner, T.S., Goodwin, G.F., Cannon-Bowers, J.A. and Salas, E. (2005) 'Scaling the quality of teammates' mental models: Equity and normative comparisons', *Journal of Organizational Behavior*, 26 (1): 37–56.

Mathieu, J.E., Heffner, T.S., Goodwin, G.F., Salas, E. and Cannon–Bowers, J.A. (2000) 'The influence of shared mental models on team process and performance', *Journal of Applied Psychology*, 85 (2): 273–283.

Mathieu, J.E., Gilson, L.L. and Ruddy, T.M. (2006) 'Empowerment and team effectiveness: An empirical test of an integrated model', *Journal of Applied Psychology*, 91 (1): 97–108.

Mayo, E. (1933) *The Human Problems of an Industrial Civilization*. New York: Macmillan

Maznevski, M.L. and Chudoba, K.M. (2000) 'Bridging space over time: Global virtual team dynamics and effectiveness', *Organization Science*, 11 (5): 473–492.

McGrath, J.E. (1984) *Groups: Interaction and Performance*. Englewood Cliffs, NJ: Prentice Hall.

McGrath, J.E. (1991) 'Time, interaction, and performance (TIP) A theory of groups', *Small Group Research*, 22 (2): 147–174.

Miller, D.L. (2003) 'The stages of group development: A retrospective study of dynamic team processes', *Canadian Journal of Administrative Sciences*, 20 (2): 121–134.

Mohammed, S. and Dumville, B.C. (2001) 'Team mental models in a team knowledge framework: Expanding theory and measurement across disciplinary boundaries', *Journal of Organizational Behavior*, 22 (2): 89–106.

Mohammed, S., Klimoski, R.J. and Rentsch, J.R. (2000) 'The measurement of team mental models: We have no shared schema', *Organizational Research Methods*, 3 (2): 123–165.

Montoya-Weiss, M.M., Massey, A.P. and Song, M. (2001) 'Getting it together: Temporal coordination and conflict management in global virtual teams', *Academy of Management Journal*, 44 (6): 1251–1262.

Moreland, R.L. (1999) 'Transactive memory: Learning who knows what in work groups and organizations', in L.L. Thompson, J.M. Levine, and D.M. Messick (eds), *Shared Cognition in Organizations: The Management of Knowledge*. Mahwah, NJ: Erlbaum, pp. 3–31.

Moreland, R.L. and Myaskovsky, L. (2000) 'Exploring the performance benefits of group training:

Transactive memory or improved communication?' *Organizational Behavior and Human Decision Making Processes. Special Issue: The psychological foundations of knowledge transfer in organizations*, 82: 117–133.

Mullen, B. and Copper, C. (1994) 'The relation between group cohesiveness and performance: An integration', *Psychological Bulletin*, 115 (2): 210–227.

Mullen, B., Johnson, C. and Salas, E. (1991) 'Productivity loss in brainstorming groups: A meta-analytic investigation', *Basic and Applied Social Psychology*, 12 (1): 3–23.

Naquin, C.E. and Tynan, R.O. (2003) 'The team halo effect: Why teams are not blamed for their failures', *Journal of Applied Psychology*, 88 (2): 332–340.

Neuman, G.A. and Wright, J. (1999) 'Team effectiveness: Beyond skills and cognitive ability', *Journal of Applied Psychology*, 84 (3): 376–389.

Neuman, G.A., Wagner, S.H. and Christiansen, N.D. (1999) 'The relationship between work-team personality composition and the job performance of teams', *Group and Organization Management*, 24 (1): 28–45.

Newman, D.A. and Sin, H.P. (in press) 'How do missing data bias estimates of within-group agreement? Sensitivity of SD_{WG}, CV_{WG}, $r_{WG(J)}$, $r_{WG(J)*}$. and ICC to systematic nonresponse', *Organizational Research Methods*.

Nieva, V.F., Fleishman, E.A. and Reick, A. (1985) *Team Dimensions: Their Identity, Their Measurement and Their Relationships*. Washington, DC: ARRO.

Parker, S. and Wall, T.D. (1998) *Job and Work Design: Organizing Work to Promote Well–Being and Effectiveness*. London: Sage Publications.

Perlow, L.A. (1999) 'The time famine: Toward a sociology of work time', *Administrative Science Quarterly*, 44 (1): 57–81.

Pescosolido, A.T. (2001) 'Informal leaders and the development of group efficacy', *Small Group Research*, 32 (1): 74–93.

Pinto, M.B. and Pinto, J.K. (1990) 'Project team communication and cross-functional cooperation in new program development', *Journal of Product Innovation Management*, 7: 200–212.

Podsakoff, P.M. and MacKenzie, S.B. (1994) 'Organizational citizenship behavior and sales unit effectiveness', *Journal of Marketing Research*, 31 (3): 351–363.

Podsakoff, P.M., Ahearne, M. and MacKenzie, S.B. (1997) 'Organizational citizenship behavior and the quantity and quality of work group performance', *Journal of Applied Psychology*, 82 (2): 262–270.

Rice, A.K. (1953) 'Productivity and social organization in an Indian weaving shed: An examination of the socio-technical system of an experimental automatic loomshed', *Human Relations*, 6: 297–329.

Riordan, C.M. (2000) 'Relational demography within groups: Past developments, contradictions, and new directions', in G.R. Ferris (ed.), *Research in Personnel and Human Resource Management*. Oxford, UK: JAI Press/Elsevier Science. Vol. 19, pp. 131–173.

Roethlisberger, F.J. and Dickson, W.J., (1939) *Management and the Worker*. Cambridge, MA: Harvard University Press.

Ross, S.J. and Allen, N.J. (2006) 'Evaluating shared mental model assessment', Presented at the meeting of the Society for Industrial/Organizational Psychology, Dallas, TX, May, 2006.

Smith, K.G., Smith, K.A., Olian, J.D., Sims, H.P., Obannon, P. and Scully, J.A. (1994) 'Top management team demography and process – the role of social integration and communication', *Administrative Science Quarterly*, 39 (3): 412–438.

Steiner, I.D. (1972) *Group Process and Productivity*. New York: Academic Press.

Stewart, G.L. (2006) 'A meta-analytic review of relationships between team design features and team performance', *Journal of Management*, 32 (1): 29–55.

Stewart, G.L. and Barrick, M.R. (2000) 'Team structure and performance: Assessing the mediating role of intrateam process and the moderating role of task type', *Academy of Management Journal*, 43 (2): 135–148.

Stout, R.J., Cannon-Bowers, J.A., Salas, E. and Milanovich, D.M. (1999) 'Planning, shared mental models, and coordinated performance: An empirical link is established', *Human Factors*, 41 (1): 61–71.

Sundstrom, E., De Meuse, K.P. and Futrell, D. (1990) 'Work teams: Applications and effectiveness', *American Psychologist*, February: 120–133.

Sundstrom, E., McIntyre, M., Halfhill, T. and Richards, H. (2000) 'Work groups: From the Hawthorne studies to work teams of the 1990s and beyond', *Group Dynamics*, 4 (1): 44–67.

Tannenbaum, S.I. and Yukl, G. (1992) 'Training and Development in Work Organizations', *Annual Review of Psychology*, 43: 399–441.

Trist, E.L. and Bamforth, K.W. (1951) 'Some social and psychological consequences of the longwall method of coal getting', *Human Relations*, 4: 3–38.

Tuckman, B.W. (1965) 'Development sequence in small groups', *Psychological Bulletin*, 63 (6): 384–389.

Wageman, R. (1995) 'Interdependence and group effectiveness', *Administrative Science Quarterly*, 40 (1): 145–180.

Wagner, J.A. (1995) 'Studies of individualism-collectivism: Effects on cooperation in groups', *Academy of Management Journal*, 38 (1): 152–172.

Wall, T.D. and Clegg, C.W. (1981) 'A longitudinal field study of group work redesign', *Journal of Occupational Behavior*, 2 (1): 31–49.

Wall, T.D., Kemp, N.J., Jackson, P.R. and Clegg, C.W. (1986) 'An outcome evaluation of autonomous work groups: A long-term field experiment', *Academy of Management Journal*, 29 (2): 280–304.

Wegner, D.M. (1986) 'Transactive memory: A contemporary analysis of the group mind', in B. Mullen and G.R. Goethals (eds), *Theories of Group Behavior*. New York: Springer-Verlag, pp. 185–208.

Wegner, D.M., Giuliano, T. and Hertel, P. (1985) 'Cognitive interdependence in close relationships', in W.J. Ickes (ed.), *Compatible and Incompatible Relationships*. New York: Springer-Verlag, pp. 253–276.

West, M.A., Brodbeck, F.C. and Richter, A.W. (2004) 'Does the "romance of teams" exist? The effectiveness of teams in experimental and field settings', *Journal of Occupational and Organizational Psychology*, 77 (4): 467–473.

Williams, H.M. and Meân, L.J. (2004) 'Measuring gender composition in work groups: A comparison of existing methods', *Organizational Research Methods*, 7 (4): 456–474.

Williams, H.M., Parker, S.K. and Turner, N. (2007) 'Perceived dissimilarity and perspective taking within work teams', *Group and Organization Management*, 32 (5): 569–597.

Zaheer, S., Albert, S. and Zaheer, A. (1999) 'Time scales and organizational theory', *Academy of Management Review*, 24 (4): 725–741.

8

Dysfunctional Workplace Behavior

Sandra L. Robinson

INTRODUCTION

In the decade or so since researchers 'discovered' that employees sometimes behave in ways that cause harm to others and to their organizations, the field has witnessed an explosion in the number of studies and book chapters on the topic of dysfunctional behavior at work. Yet it is really more accurate to say that the field merely 'rediscovered' what classical organizational theorists (e.g., Cyert and March, 1964; Katz and Kahn, 1978), have said all along; namely, that from time to time employees are prone to act in ways that undermine efficiency, or conflict with the desires of the organization's dominant coalition (Cyert and March, 1964). This is the reasoning behind control systems, rules, and other methods for directing and monitoring employee behavior.

Despite all of the efforts made by organizations to channel employee behavior toward desired goals, dysfunctional behavior persists. If the growing body of evidence is to be believed, dysfunctional behavior is both prevalent and costly. For example, employee theft and fraud is the fastest growing crime in the US, with annual costs of $US50 billion (Coffin, 2003). Recent estimates suggest that as much as 90 per cent of the workforce has experienced bullying (Glendinning, 2001), and 5 per cent of workers are physically assaulted each year (see Schat et al., 2006). The costs of dysfunctional behavior range from increased insurance premiums, tarnished reputations, and costs associated with stress, to capital replacement costs, injury payouts, lawsuits, and lost productivity (Dunlop and Lee, 2004), to name a few. These statistics tell us why the study of the darker side of employee behavior is flourishing. Simply put: There is a lot of dysfunctional behavior in need of explanation.

Over the last decade, many researchers have heeded the call to study this important and costly problem (e.g., Giacalone and Greenberg, 1997; O'Leary-Kelly et al., 1996; Robinson and Bennett, 1995; Vardi and Weiner, 1996). At this stage, the topic has reached a period of maturity, and it is time to review what we have learned so far, where we currently stand, and where we need to go next. That is the goal of this chapter. In it, I selectively review the literature of the past decade, identify common streams and patterns, and highlight the limitations and unanswered questions that remain.

In doing so, I first provide a brief history of this domain of research. Next, I discuss some of the key studies and findings that have emerged in the last decade. Given the sheer volume of research in this area, this review is not meant to be exhaustive. From this review, I highlight some of the common patterns and themes that have emerged from this empirical work and, most importantly, identify the gaps that future research needs to explore next.

HISTORY

Various researchers have always shown some fascination with behaviors that are dysfunctional, although these behaviors might not have been referred to as such. For example, topics examined have included theft, social loafing, conflict, and withdrawal. Though these behaviors are clearly dysfunctional, the goal of these research efforts was to understand the particular behaviors themselves, not necessarily to understand or explain in a general sense why employees engage in dysfunctional behavior per se.

In the mid-1990s, several researchers independently began to focus on the phenomenon of dysfunctional or harmful workplace behavior in a more comprehensive fashion, attempting to conceptually integrate a range of dysfunctional behaviors into a meaningful whole. Robinson and Bennett (1995) developed a construct referred to as 'workplace deviance'; O'Leary-Kelly et al. (1996) theorized about 'organizationally-directed aggression;' and Vardi and Weiner (1996) developed a theory of 'organizational misbehavior.' As with most trends, it is difficult to know how and why this interest emerged simultaneously among different researchers. Perhaps it was due to the media's focus on what seemed to be an 'epidemic' of workplace violence and aggression in the middle of the last decade. Indeed, workplace

aggression peaked in 1994 (Schat et al., 2006). As is the case with many topics in our field, the public recognition of a workplace problem was probably what motivated some scholars in our field to try to make sense of these behaviors. When they attempted to do so, they discovered that the more traditional or popular topics in organizational behavior (e.g., leadership, motivation, commitment, satisfaction and organizational citizenship behavior) had disproportionately emphasized the positive aspects of organizations, and largely ignored dysfunctional behavior as a phenomenon unto itself. In other words, our field had little to offer in the way of either rigorous empirical research or sound theory on why people exhibit negative behaviors at work.

The first step toward building a body of knowledge on dysfunctional workplace behavior involved the introduction of constructs and definitional boundaries around this phenomenon. As a result many constructs, with somewhat different definitions, emerged: abusive workplace behavior (Keashly et al., 1994), bullying and harassment (Einarsen et al., 1994), workplace deviance (Robinson and Bennett, 1995), workplace retaliation and revenge (Bies and Tripp, 1996), organizational misbehavior (Vardi and Wiener, 1996), organizationally-motivated aggression (O'Leary-Kelly et al., 1996), and anti-social behavior (Giacalone and Greenberg, 1997). A few years later, additional conceptualizations emerged, such as organizational incivility (Andersson and Pearson, 1999), workplace victimization (Aquino et al., 1999), abusive supervision (Tepper, 2000), counterproductive work behavior (Sackett and DeVore, 2001), social undermining (Duffy et al., 2002), and identity threats (Aquino and Douglas, 2003).

Each of the conceptualizations listed above has a somewhat unique definition that sets it apart from the others (see Robinson and Greenberg, 1999 for a review of these differences). In some cases, those differences result in somewhat behaviors being included or excluded from consideration. Despite definitional differences, however, many labels have been used to capture the same broad set of dysfunctional behaviors in the workplace.

In the next section, I will separately review the empirical research that has been conducted on these various constructs, focusing on those that have come to dominate the field in the past decade.

REVIEW OF THE LITERATURE

Reviewing the literature on workplace dysfunction is challenging for several reasons. The body of literature is large, many constructs and operationalizations exist, and the lines are often blurred between one construct and the next. To make this task more manageable, I have created several arbitrary boundaries. First, I am focusing this review only on the last decade of empirical research appearing in peer-reviewed journals. Second, I am organizing this review around the constructs that dominated the literature in the past decade, grouping papers by how the authors chose to operationalize the construct. At the same time, it is important to note that these construct boundaries are somewhat artificial in the sense that, as I will explain later, studies focusing on supposedly different constructs often investigate the same construct; authors use different construct labels interchangeably; and different authors rely on somewhat different definitions for constructs – thus further blurring the distinctions between them.

During this time period, several distinct groupings of constructs around dysfunctional behavior have emerged. The first two are workplace deviance and counterproductivity, which most broadly capture potentially harmful behavior directed at either individuals or the organization itself. Related to these two conceptualizations are the constructs of organizational retaliation and revenge, which focus on the same behaviors, but only when they are motivated by retribution. Next is the conceptualization of aggression, which primarily focuses on behavior directed at others with the intent to cause harm. Finally, there is the loose grouping of

research focused on workplace bullying, emotional abuse, and abusive supervision, which captures the same interpersonally harmful behavior as aggression but tends to focus on prolonged episodes of behavior within a relationship, usually from the perspective of the target. I review each of these areas below.

Workplace deviance and counterproductive work behavior

A number of constructs have focused on the broad gamut of dysfunctional workplace behavior. Borrowing from the sociological tradition, Robinson and Bennett (1995) coined the term 'workplace deviance behavior'; the term 'counterproductive work behavior' emerged from the tradition of industrial/organizational psychology (Sackett and Devore, 2001). Similarly broad terms have also been developed, such as Vardi and Weiner's (1996) 'organizational misbehavior' and Greenberg and Giacoloni's (1997) 'anti-social behavior.' To date, the terms 'workplace deviance' and 'counterproductivity' seem to be the most common, with the phrases often being used interchangeably. They reflect potentially harmful workplace behavior, ranging from minor to more serious forms. Moreover, this harmful behavior can be directed either at individuals, as reflected in behavior such as harassment, back-stabbing, or physical aggression, or directed at the organization, as reflected in behavior such as theft, sabotage, or absenteeism. A distinguishing feature of these behaviors is that although they are intentional behaviors that are potentially harmful (as opposed to accidents or poor performance, which are not intentional but potentially harmful), they are not necessarily intended by the actor to be harmful or destructive.

The vast majority of empirical research to date on both workplace deviance and counterproductivity has focused on its predictors or antecedents. Identified antecedents include those at the individual level, group level, and organization level (Griffin et al., 1998). We will consider each of these in turn.

Individual predictors

In terms of individual factors, much of the focus has been on personality traits that correlate with counterproductive work behavior. Some of the most established predictive traits include a lack of conscientiousness (Collins and Schmidt, 1993; Salgado, 2002) and integrity (Sackett and Wanek, 1996). These studies suggest that dysfunctional behavior can be controlled by assessing and de-selecting employees on the basis of character qualities. Additional personality traits associated with workplace deviance and counterproductivity include trait anger (Chen and Spector, 1992; Fox and Spector, 1999; Lee and Allen, 2002), state hostility (Judge et al., 2006), agreeableness (Colbert et al., 2004), positive affect (Duffy, Ganster and Shaw, 1998), and locus of control (Fox and Spector, 1999), as well as trait anxiety (Fox and Spector, 1999), responsibility, and risk-taking (Ashton, 1998).

Other individual factors besides personality have been explored as predictors of workplace deviance and counterproductivity. For example, attitudes such as momentary hostility (Judge et al., 2006) and job satisfaction (Judge et al., 2006; Duffy et al., 1998) predict workplace deviance behavior. Henle et al. (2005) found workers high on idealism were less likely to engage in workplace deviance, although high relativism moderated this relationship. Relatedly, Bolin and Heatherly (2001) found that four attitude variables – theft approval, company contempt, intent to quit, and dissatisfaction – predicted various forms of workplace deviance. In a more complex model, Duffy et al. (1998) found that a lack of positive affectivity, job satisfaction, and tenure interact together to predict counterproductive work behavior. When multiple individual differences are considered simultaneously, considerable variance in workplace deviance is explained. As one outstanding example, Judge et al. (2006) accounted for over 50 per cent of variance in workplace deviance by examining individual differences.

Contextual predictors

Despite the significant role of individual differences in predicting workplace deviance and counterproductive work behavior, many researchers have focused on the role of contextual factors in explaining these behaviors, because situational factors such as job stressors (Fox et al., 2001) may serve as triggers or provocations for workplace deviance and counterproductive work behavior (Bennett and Robinson, 1997). Some researchers considered the roles of control and powerlessness, noting how work environments that undermine an individual's autonomy and sense of control may fuel counterproductivity and workplace deviance (Bennett, 1998; Lawrence and Robinson, 2007). Relatedly, contexts characterized by prolonged conflict lead to bullying and that more bullying, as a source of frustration and humiliation, fuels counterproductive behavior (Ayoko et al., 2003). Likewise, Penney and Spector (2005) found both incivility and interpersonal conflict to be positively related to counterproductive work behavior.

The impact of context on workplace deviance and counterproductivity might also be understood through affect events theory (Weiss and Cropanzano, 1996), which contends that the work environment and specific work events create affective reactions, which in turn influence attitudes and behaviors. One study using this perspective to predict workplace deviance (Judge et al., 2006) showed that perceptions of interpersonal injustice and state hostility lead to workplace deviance, although job satisfaction partially mediates this relationship.

Social exchange theory (Blau, 1964) coupled with the norm of reciprocity (Gouldner, 1960) offers another theoretical perspective on how context can produce deviant behavior. Specifically, employees reciprocate favorable work environments with productive behavior, and respond to unfavorable treatment at work with counterproductive behaviors. Consistent with this view, workplace deviance is negatively related to positive perceptions of one's work situation and perceived organizational support (Colbert et al., 2004). In contrast, perceptions of injustice predict workplace deviance (Aquino et al., 1999; Colquitt et al., 2001; Judge et al., 2006).

A distinct set of studies has focused on group-level antecedents of workplace deviance. Arguing from a social information process and social learning perspective, Robinson and O'Leary Kelly (1998), found that workplace deviance could be predicted by the degree of deviance engaged in by one's workgroup. In a more recent study, Liao et al. (2004), using social identification theory and exchange theory, show that dissimilarities between an individual and his/her group in terms of ethnicity, agreeableness and openness to experience, were significantly related to individual engaging in workplace deviance directed at the organization, and dissimilarity in terms of gender, conscientiousness, and extraversion predicted workplace deviance directed at the individual.

Interaction effects

More complex but interesting predictive models of workplace deviance and counterproductive work behavior emerge from examining the interaction between individual factors and contextual factors. In some cases, individuals' personality may act to constrain counterproductive behavior that would otherwise be triggered by contextual factors (Colbert et al., 2004). As Marcus and Schuler (2004) show, using Hirschi's theory of self control (1969), counterproductive behavior involves an interaction of triggers along with situational and individual constraints. Although negative perceptions of the work environment are related to workplace deviance (Colbert et al., 2004), conscientiousness, stability and agreeableness weaken this relationship.

From a cognitive appraisal perspective, it can be argued that individual differences will influence the interpretation of situational factors (Martinko and Zellars, 1998), and several studies found that injustice in the work environment interacts with individual traits to predict workplace deviance. Aquino et al. (1999) found interactional injustice, procedural injustice and distributive injustice

increase workplace deviance when negative affectivity is high. Relatedly, Henle et al. (2005) also found that interactional injustice predicted deviance, but only for employees low in socialization or high in impulsivity (in other words, individuals whose constraining personality traits are relatively weak). Similarly, Penney and Spector (2005) found that job stressors have a greater impact on counterproductive behavior when individuals are high in negative affectivity. Aquino and Douglas (2003) showed that being a frequent recipient of actions undermining one's sense of dignity or self-worth leads to higher workplace deviance, but this relationship is moderated by gender, age, and revenge attitudes, as well as situational factors such as aggressive modeling. These findings suggest that future studies would benefit from exploring the role of demographic variables in predicting workplace deviance and other dysfunctional behaviors.

Retaliation and revenge

Workplace deviant behavior and counterproductive work behavior capture a wide range of potentially harmful behaviors directed at the organization or individuals. Another set of constructs, also capturing a range of behaviors, focuses on those behaviors that serve as a means by which to seek revenge, retaliation or retribution. Revenge was initially established as a construct in organizational behavior by Bies and Tripp (1996, 1998a, 1998b), reflecting the desire to 'get even' with those who have mistreated you. Skarlicki and Folger (1997) subsequently coined the term 'organizational retaliatory behavior' to capture specific responses to perceived injustice in the workplace. Unlike researchers focused on workplace deviance and counterproductive work behavior, the focus of revenge and retaliation is most interested in a particular motivation for such behavior, and not necessarily the behavior itself. However, retaliation is operationalized such that it only captures whether a behavior or set of behaviors occurred, not whether the motivation for those behaviors includes retribution. In this sense, the measure for retaliation is almost identical to the measures for workplace deviance and counterproductive work behavior.

Given how retaliation is measured, the empirical research on retaliation overlaps fully with the many studies looking at the injustice antecedents of workplace deviance and counterproductive behavior. In the past decade, various forms of workplace injustice have been identified as antecedents of workplace deviance behavior. Likewise, Bies and Tripp (1996) found that employees who have engaged in revenge often identify unfair, arbitrary, or self-serving behavior on the part of others as the motivating force behind their actions. Skarlicki and Folger (1997) also found that distributive, procedural, and interactional injustice interact to predict retaliatory behavior. In a subsequent study (Skarlicki et al., 1999), they found that negative affectivity and agreeableness moderated the relationship between perceptions of injustice and retaliatory behavior.

More recently, Cortina and Magley (2003) provided an interesting twist on the retaliation construct. They examined the retaliation behavior perpetrated by those who have already committed abuse. They noted that victims of mistreatment manifest a variety of responses, and some of those responses – such as seeking social support, confronting the abuser, or whistle-blowing – can trigger retaliation by the original abuser against the victim. Whereas other perspectives of retaliation tend to focus on the retaliator as the original victim, in this particular conceptualization, the ultimate retaliator is the original bully or aggressor. As we will show later, this work extends and connects research on aggression, abuse, and retaliation, highlighting empirically how cycles or escalations of abuse can occur in organizations.

Workplace aggression and violence

Workplace aggression refers to purposeful behavior that is intended to be harmful or destructive to others with whom one works or has worked, or to the organization in which they are presently or were previously employed (Neuman and Baron, 1998; O'Leary-Kelly et al., 1996). Central to the definition of aggression and violence is the intent to cause harm, distinguishing it from workplace deviance or counterproductive work behavior, which are potentially harmful but not necessarily intended by the actor to be so. The terms 'workplace aggression' and 'workplace violence' are often used interchangeably, but aggression is generally understood to be the broader construct, reflecting behavior intended to cause harm to another, whereas violence more specifically reflects acts that are intended to cause physical harm (Barling et al., 1987). Neuman and Baron (1998) argue that aggression has three forms: overt, which reflects physical acts of aggression, obstructionism, which are actions designed to impede an individual's ability to perform their job and expressions of hostility, which include verbal or symbolic actions directed at others.

Workplace violence has been studied less frequently than the other forms of aggression (Barling et al., 2001, Budd et al., 1996), perhaps due to its relative infrequency and the difficulty in empirically assessing it in the workplace. Thus, the more frequently occurring construct of non-violent aggression has been the focus of most research (Greenberg and Barling, 1999; Harvey and Keashly, 2003). Although aggression can be directed at both the organization and individuals, and some studies have examined aggression directed at different targets (Herchovis et al., 2007), to date, most empirical research has either focused on aggression targeting individual or it has ignored the target altogether.

Individual antecedents

Several studies have examined individual predictors of workplace aggression. In that regard, aggression has been found to be related to negative affectivity (Hepworth and Towler, 2004), trait anger (Douglas and Martinko,

2001; Glomb and Liao, 2003; Herchovis et al., 2007), revenge attitudes (Douglas and Martinko, 2001), job dissatisfaction (Herchovis et al., 2007), hostile attributional styles (Hepworth and Towler, 2004), Type A personalities (Baron et al., 1999), low self-control (Hepworth and Towler, 2004) and low self-esteem (Einarsen, 2000, Harvey and Keashly, 2003, Inness et al., 2005). Moreover, aggression is exhibited more frequently by men (Herchovis et al., 2007) those who have consumed alcohol (Greenberg and Barling, 1999; Jockin et al., 2001), people who have a personal history of aggression (Greenberg and Barling, 1999; Inness et al., 2005) or have been exposed to aggressive cultures (Douglas and Martinko, 200). Taken together, it appears that individual differences play an important role in aggression in the workplace. For example, Douglas and Martinko (2001) were able to explain 62 per cent of variance in workplace aggression with personality traits alone.

Contextual antecedents

Researchers also have focused on how workplace aggression emanates from factors in the work environment (Greenberg and Barling, 1999). One stream of studies has examined aggression by organizational outsiders, identifying job and work environmental factors that put some employees at risk (Kraus, 1987). As a recent example, LeBlanc and Kelloway (2002) found numerous job risk factors, such as supervising others or collecting valuable items that were related to increased reports of violence and aggression at work. Relatedly, Harvey and Keashly (2003) found that such risk was enhanced by exposure; that is, to the extent one spent more time working in such environments, he or she was more likely to report incidents of violence and aggression at work.

Focused on aggression among co-workers, Greenberg and Barling (1999) found aggression to be more likely when workplace surveillance is low. Herchovis et al. (2007) found interpersonal conflict impacted aggression toward individuals, and situational constraints impacted aggression directed at the organization. In terms of social context, Glomb and Liao (2003) found that the level of aggression in a workgroup explained individual-level aggression above and beyond that explained by individual differences. This study parallels a similar social learning effect that Robinson and O'Leary-Kelly (1998) found for workplace deviance.

A prominent theme among those exploring antecedents of workplace aggression and violence is the influence of how one is treated at work. It appears that aggression leads to aggression! Using a social exchange perspective, Glomb and Liao (2003) found support for their argument that to the extent one is a target of aggression within a workgroup, that person is more likely to also engage in aggression. Relatedly, Jockin et al. (2001) found support for a relationship between feeling victimized and aggressive behavior. Mistreatment by the organization also matters. Workplace injustice, especially interactional injustice, is positively correlated with aggression (Baron et al., 1999; Dupre and Barling, 2006; Greenberg and Barling, 1999; Inness et al., 2005). Dietz et al. (2003) found climates of injustice to be positively related to both workplace aggression and violence. Similarly, abusive supervision has been identified multiple times as a potential antecedent of workplace aggression, possibly as a means by which to cope or respond to this form of interpersonal mistreatment (Folger and Baron, 1996; Inness et al., 2005; Tepper, 2000). In the opposite fashion, Hepworth and Towler (2004) demonstrated that the presence of charismatic leadership created a sense of empowerment through autonomy, fairness and control actually reduced aggression beyond reductions accounted for by individual differences.

Impact of aggression and violence at work

Unlike those studying workplace deviance and counterproductive work behavior, who focus almost exclusively on the causes of such behavior, researchers studying aggression have given considerable attention to both causes and consequences. Lapierre et al.'s (2005) meta-analysis showed that both sexual and non-sexual aggression reduced job satisfaction, with nonsexual aggression having the biggest impact. LeBlanc and Kelloway (2002) showed that exposure to violence and aggression by both organizational outsiders and by co-workers impacted emotional and psychosomatic well-being, affective commitment, and turnover intentions, albeit in different ways. Barling et al. (2001) found exposure to workplace aggression reduced commitment and perceptions of justice and increased cognitive difficulties and job neglect. They also found that negative mood and fear of future violence mediated the effects of aggression.

Interestingly, findings from this research stream reveal that one need not be the direct target of aggression for it to cause harm. Hall and Spector (1991) originally established that employees who only feel the threat of workplace violence – without having actually experienced that violence – show many of the same negative consequences as those who are direct victims. Indeed, Schat and Kelloway (2003) found vicarious violence in the workplace, such as witnessing or hearing about a violent act, has a similar impact to being directly targeted. Research has also shown that fear of workplace violence alone is strongly associated with mental and physical distress, turnover intentions, and reduced productivity (Budd et al., 1996). From the theoretical perspective of workplace stressors and strain (e.g., Barling, 1996; Pratt and Barling, 1988; Rogers and Kelloway, 1997) numerous other studies have demonstrated that fear of future violence mediates the relationship between exposure to aggression or violence and negative outcomes, such as psychological well-being, somatic symptoms, commitment and intent to leave (Barling, 1996; Rogers and Kelloway, 1997; Schat and Kelloway, 2003).

Several studies have explored potential buffers of the effects of aggression and violence. For example, gender makes a difference: Men tend to react less negatively to aggression than women (Barling et al., 1996; Breslau et al., 1999). Schat and Kelloway (2003) also find that organizational support weakens the relationship between aggression (including psychological aggression as well as direct and vicariously experienced violence) and negative outcomes (emotional well-being, somatic health, and job-related affect).

Workplace bullying and abusive treatment

The final category of dysfunctional behavior covered is workplace bullying and abuse. Research interest on workplace bullying emanated from earlier work examining bullying among children. Some of the first work actually appeared in the 1980s, under the term 'mobbing' (Leymann, 1990), language that is still used today, though the term 'workplace bullying' has largely dominated this arena with an explosion of research in Europe in the mid-1990s. While European research still dominates this arena, similar research in the North American sphere began in the late 1990s under the terms 'abusive behavior' (e.g., Keashley, 1998) and 'abusive supervision' (Tepper, 2000). One might also include in this domain 'petty tyranny' (Ashforth, 1997), 'workplace incivility' (Andersson and Pearson, 1999), and 'social undermining' (Duffy et al., 2002), as more specified kinds of interpersonal mistreatment at work.

Although debate continues regarding the definition of bullying (e.g., Einarsen, 2000; Rayner et al., 2002), a common definition is a repeat and prolonged pattern of exposure to negative acts by an individual or group (Einarsen and Skogstad, 1996; Vartia, 1996). This includes a range of behavior, such as verbal threats, criticism, withholding information, ostracization, ridicule, and deliberate overloading of work. Key characteristics of bullying, abuse, or mistreatment include:

(1) interpersonal in nature;
(2) verbal and emotional nature; and
(3) typically covert and relatively minor, rather than physical and more extreme. Although the specific behaviors composing bullying or abuse

might appear relatively trivial when examined in isolation, the target perceives this behavior as offensive, unfair, and demoralizing because of its persistent and ongoing nature.

The focus of research on this area is distinct from other kinds of dysfunctional work behavior. First, it addresses behaviors that occur as a pattern over time, rather than focusing on specific, episodic behaviors. Indeed, a specific behavior constituting one part of a pattern of bullying might itself go unnoticed, or be interpreted very differently in isolation. However, when a specific behavior is considered in light of other similar behaviors that have previously occurred, it is identified as part of a trend called bullying. This contrasts with research on workplace aggression, which is focused on potentially episodic behavior rather than behavior occurring in a pattern over time.

Second, this research focuses not so much on the behavior itself, or the intention of the actor behind the behavior, but instead on the experience of the 'victim.' Unlike the research on aggression, which focuses primarily on the harmful behavior, the work on bullying and abuse focuses on the victims' interpretation of the behavior. Third, this area of research focuses on behavior that resides not in an individual per se, but rather in a relationship. Fourth, unlike the study of aggression or retaliation, which are active behaviors perpetrated against a victim, the focus on bullying is both the active behaviors (e.g., criticism and belittlement), as well as the absence of behaviors (e.g., exclusion and withholding information), though relatively little work has addressed the latter.

Impact

The majority of research on bullying documents its impact on the target. Research has shown that exposure to bullying in the workplace can impact dissatisfaction (Einarsen and Raknes, 1997; Keashley et al., 1994; Keashley, 1998; Tepper, 2000); can reduce psychological well-being by increasing anxiety, stress, depression, anger, and helplessness; and create psychosomatic problems such as increased insomnia, stomach and back problems, and chronic fatigue (Einarsen et al., 1998; Keashley, 1998). Organizational costs include higher absenteeism and employee turnover, lower commitment, lower productivity, and less extra-role behavior (Hoel et al., 2003; Tepper, 2000; Zellars et al., 2002).

Individual antecedents

Additional research has addressed the specific correlates of workplace bullying. One set of potential antecedents of bullying are individual factors, though little empirical work has actually focused on the bullies (Rayner and Keashly, 2004). It has been argued that a number of factors encourage bullying, such as stress, lack of control over one's job, lack of clear goals, role conflict, and dissatisfaction with the social climate (Einarsen et al., 1994; Vartia, 1996; Zapf et al., 1996). Interestingly, one of the few empirical studies examining differences between bullies and non-bullies (Rayner and Cooper, 2003) found no differences between bullies and non-bullies in terms of self-reported mental health, stress levels, or personality.

Contextual antecedents

Others have identified deficiencies in the work environment as explanations for bullying behavior (Vartiai, 1996; Zapf et al., 1996). For example, bullying is more likely to occur in organizations characterized as large and bureaucratic (Einarsen and Skogstad, 1996), with high internal competition (O'Moore et al., 1998) and weak, frequently changing, or ineffective leadership (Hoel and Cooper, 2000; Leymann, 1996). One interesting empirical investigation by Tepper et al. (2006) found that supervisors' experiences of procedural injustice increased their subordinates' perceptions of being abused by the supervisors, and this relationship was fully mediated by the supervisor's depression. As with most predictive models of dysfunctional behavior, it is likely that bullying emanates from a variety of factors (Hoel and Cooper, 2001), and involves a combination or interaction of both the situation and the individuals involved (Aquino et al., 1999).

Numerous authors note the role of power imbalances between victim and bully, such that women, minorities, and people with disabilities experience more victimization (Aquino and Bradfield, 2000; Cortina et al., 2001; Hoel and Cooper, 2000) and supervisors are more typically the bully (Cortina et al., 2001; Hoel and Cooper, 2000, Knorz and Zapf, 1996). Some contend that bullying cannot occur between equals and thus such behavior is more appropriately considered as 'conflict' (Einarsen et al., 2003), yet this perspective seems to ignore the fact that even visible or hierarchical equals may not be interpersonal equals for any number of reasons. Thus, relationships between objectively defined peers may include bullying if one is able to exert social power or intimidation over the other.

Dynamics of bullying

Relatively few studies have addressed the process or dynamics of bullying or abuse. Although this is true for most areas of research on dysfunctional behavior, it is somewhat surprising that even the research on bullying has been largely static, given the fact that this type of behavior is, by definition, relational and dynamic in nature. There are a few exceptions in the theoretical realm. Andersson and Pearson (1999), in their theory of incivility, highlight the spiraling, self-reinforcing quality of mistreatment. Likewise, Salin (2003) has attempted to delineate the process of bullying, as did Lutgen-Sandvik (2003), who proposes emotional abuse to be a six-stage cyclical communicative process.

Coping with bullying

Some. research has focused on how people cope or respond to bullying. This is unique in that most studies in other domains have not addressed such responses. Tepper and colleagues (2001) note that employees subject to supervisor abuse were resistant to their supervisors' influence tactics. The relationship between abuse and dysfunctional resistance was stronger to the extent that

employees were low in conscientiousness, and the relationship between abuse and constructive resistance was stronger to the extent that employees were high in conscientiousness. Other research suggests that individuals change strategies as the experience of bullying continues, starting with more assertive or aggressive strategies and moving to more passive avoidance strategies over time as the prior strategies prove ineffective (Olafsson and Johannsdottir, 2004; Zapf and Gross, 2001).

COMMON PATTERNS ACROSS STUDIES ON DYSFUNCTIONAL BEHAVIOR

Considering the myriad of studies that have been conducted in these various areas, it is critical to identify commonalities across them. As such, in this section I take a broader perspective by identifying what we know about dysfunctional workplace behavior based on this collection of research considered together.

Although the empirical work covers different angles or subsets of many dysfunctional behaviors, the findings are quite similar. First, the findings point to the disruptive or harmful impact that these behaviors have upon individual organizational members, showing that being a target of dysfunctional behavior hurts psychological well-being (anxiety, depression and anger); physical well-being (increased absenteeism, insomnia and fatigue), and behavior (lowered productivity, reduced commitment and increased turnover). Although most of these negative effects have been documented for aggression and bullying, we can anticipate that similar effects would be found for other forms of interpersonal dysfunctional behavior. In addition, as research on aggression shows, individuals can be harmed by merely being exposed to, hearing about, or witnessing aggression. It is likely that being a vicarious target of bullying or other dysfunctional interpersonal behavior has a similarly negative impact on the individual.

Second, there is substantial commonality in the antecedents of the various forms of workplace dysfunction. These antecedents include individual-level factors (traits of conscientiousness, integrity, and anger, and state anxiety), and individual differences (dissatisfaction and perceived lack of situational control). Yet it also is important to note that while individual factors have accounted for many dysfunctional behaviors such as aggression and counterproductivity, relatively little empirical work has shown that bullying can be explained by such individual variables. Future research should further explore the potential individual predictors of bullying.

Many of these studies also demonstrate the impact of organizational factors in predicting dysfunctional workplace behavior. Ineffective leadership predicts various types of dysfunctional behavior. Weak or ineffective leadership increases the occurrence of bullying, abusive supervision increases aggression, and organizational support and charismatic leadership reduces workplace deviance and counterproductive work behavior. Relatedly, how individuals interpret their work environments and work experiences seems to stand out as a fundamental predictor of all types of dysfunctional behavior. Perceiving injustice or mistreatment in one's workplace seems to be a particularly important predictor. Procedural, distributive, and interactional injustice play separate and interactive roles in explaining all forms of workplace dysfunction. However, we still do not fully understand the mechanism underlying the injustice-dysfunction relationship. Several possibilities exist: Injustice may lead to dysfunctional behavior through affective events theory, whereby experiences of injustice cause negative affect (anger, frustration, depression), which in turn leads to dysfunctional behavior. Alternatively, exposure to injustice may lead to dysfunctional behavior because employees are following social cues or modeling the harmful behavior of those in higher organizational positions. Injustice may lead to dysfunctional work behavior through retribution – employees seek to remedy mistreatment by hurting those that hurt them. More generally, social

exchange and norms of reciprocity suggest employees will reciprocate 'negative' work experiences with counterproductive behavior. Though some studies have found support for one of these perspectives, future empirical research may be necessary to tease apart the potential role of these different mechanisms.

Considering how mistreatment and injustice lead to dysfunctional behavior raises the question of potential cycles or spirals of dysfunction. As already noted, dysfunctional interpersonal behavior begets more dysfunctional interpersonal behavior. Being the victim of bullying increases counterproductive behavior in the victim, and being the target of aggression increases one's own aggression. Likewise, being subject to actions that undermine one's sense of dignity or self-worth leads to workplace deviance. When supervisors experience unjust treatment, their subordinates end up feeling abused. Taken further, when victims of bullying strike out in retribution, the bullies in turn respond with more bullying. Andersson and Pearson (1999) articulated the 'tit-for-tat,' dynamic spirals of incivility in organizations, which perhaps might be extended to all forms of dysfunctional behavior in the workplace. Specifically, we need to develop and test a model involving the relational dynamics among a wide range of dysfunctional behaviors in the workplace, and examine how they feed and grow upon themselves.

Considering these various bodies of research together, some common patterns of knowledge emerge that can inform the field as a whole. However, knowledge gaps remain, and directions for future research on dysfunctional work behavior can be identified.

UNRESOLVED ISSUES AND FUTURE DIRECTIONS

In this section, I will discuss some important and unresolved issues remaining in the dysfunctional behavior research area. Identifying such issues will hopefully encourage future research to tackle them. The domain of research on dysfunctional workplace behavior could benefit from greater integration, more consideration given to motivations, more attention devoted to consequences, and the use of improved methodologies, each of which are now considered in turn.

More integration

Despite calls for integration in the study of dysfunctional workplace behavior as far back at the mid-1990s, greater integration is still needed. As Robinson and Bennett (1995) stated, the study of harmful workplace behavior to that point consisted largely of individual studies focusing only on one or two different behaviors, rather than considering multiple behaviors simultaneously. Since 1995, numerous conceptualizations of dysfunctional behavior have taken a broader perspective, integrating a disparate set of behaviors under one umbrella.

Yet the need for more integration remains. As this review shows, many terms and definitions exist for essentially the same behavior. These different labels have maintained a disconnection between very related streams of research. In some cases, this disconnect between constructs can be attributed to somewhat different fields or even different geography. For example, counterproductive work behavior is primarily the domain of industrial/organizational psychologists, while workplace deviance is the construct used primarily by organizational behaviorists; abusive supervision is a construct of interest primarily to American organizational researchers, whereas workplace bullying is primarily of interest to European psychologists.

Another explanation for the disconnect is the motivation by researchers to create new constructs. Rather than rely on existing constructs, many researchers have developed new approaches, with somewhat different names and definitions. Though precision is most often laudable, too often it seems the improvements or differences are too subtle to be justified (and not worth the loss of synergy that would be gained from using the same construct). Moreover, despite these subtle differences in definitions, the vast majority of these operationalizations for 'different' constructs are actually identical to each other. As such, all this activity has led to a disconnected, yet redundant, set of findings across these different constructs.

What this research area needs is convergence toward an agreed-upon construct label, definition, and operationalization. Barring that agreement, there are several things we as researchers in this area should be doing differently as we move forward. First, regardless of the construct or label used, we should at least incorporate and build upon all prior research that reflects similar behavior, even if it goes by a different name. Ignoring prior work just because a different label or definition was used will not advance our understanding. Second, new constructs should only be created when there are convincing reasons why a new construct is important. That is, when it is explained how this new construct will change the results of our prior research studies and improve our understanding of dysfunctional behavior in the workplace. Third, our constructs and operationalizations should be aligned, and operationalizations for a construct should be sufficiently different than operationalizations of other constructs.

Consider motivations

Many of the different conceptualizations of dysfunctional workplace behavior are distinguished on the basis of the motivation of the actor. For example, workplace deviance is defined as purposeful behavior, aggression is behavior intended to cause harm, and retaliation is behavior intended to get even with another who has mistreated you. Despite these different motivations, the operationalizations of these different constructs capture only the frequency of a set of behaviors, and seldom the intent of the actor engaging in them.

A greater focus on motivations – not just in defining behavior, but in operationalizing the construct – is critical for several reasons. First, we cannot distinguish between these different constructs if they do not capture motivation in their measures. To have valid constructs, we need our definitions and measures to be closely aligned. Without construct validity, we do not actually know what underlying motivation we are studying.

A greater focus on motivations will also build our understanding of why workplace dysfunction occurs and how we can more effectively manage it. Though a body of knowledge exists about the predictors of such behavior, we know little about individuals' actual or self-perceived intentions for engaging in these behaviors.

Consider consequences

The research on dysfunctional behavior would also benefit from more attention to the consequences of such behavior. Though considerable empirical work has shown the impact of dysfunctional behavior for the target of aggression or bullying, our understanding of consequences needs to be expanded in several directions.

First, more research is needed examining the impact of witnessing or being vicariously exposed to dysfunctional workplace behavior. Some empirical studies indicate that vicarious exposure to aggression has a similar impact as being a direct target. As such, perhaps witnessing bullying or other counterproductive or deviant behavior may also pose a threat to the individual. This would be an interest avenue for future empirical research.

Second, we need research that examines the impact of these behaviors on the actors themselves. Might 'dysfunctional behavior' be functional for the actor, meeting their goals or expectations? Or does exhibiting dysfunctional behavior hurt the actor, either through organizational consequences, or from internal feelings of guilt or shame?

Third, more research examining the consequences of dysfunctional behavior for the organizations in which it occurs would be informative. Although some studies have calculated the costs to organizations for specific behaviors (e.g., theft and absenteeism),

we do not yet know how organizations are hurt by the extent to which their employees engage in the range of various dysfunctional behaviors captured by aggression, bullying and workplace deviance. One exception is the study by Dunlop and Lee (2004) examining business-unit performance across 36 branches of a fast-food chain. They found that the degree of self-reported workplace deviance among employees in a unit was significantly related to supervisor's performance ratings and objective measures of performance of that unit. Interestingly self-reported ratings of organizational citizenship behavior were not predictive of business unit performance.

Finally, we should consider not only the potentially harmful effects of dysfunctional behavior but also ask whether there are any benefits. As Warren (2003) has argued, deviation from norms – which may appear to be potentially harmful – might have beneficial consequences to individuals, groups, and organizations. Relatedly, others have argued that workplace deviance (Bennett and Robinson, 2003), as well as revenge and retaliation, can also have positive implications (Bies and Tripp, 1998). Behavior that is deemed harmful from one perspective (e.g., short-term perspective of the organization), may be functional and constructive for the organization or others in the longer term. Thus, without condoning or justifying these behaviors, we can objectively note and investigate their potential benefits.

New methodological approaches

Finally, a methodological issue regarding the current study of dysfunctional workplace behavior: to date, most empirical research in this domain has relied primarily on self-report, retrospective accounts, typically taken at one point in time. Although this methodological approach is convenient and commonly used in our field, advances in our knowledge of dysfunctional workplace behaviors requires other methodological approaches be considered.

Beyond self-report

Following the lead of research on citizenship behavior which routinely uses reports from supervisors, future studies should seek reports of dysfunctional behavior from other sources, such as co-workers or supervisors. Although coworkers or supervisors might not be privy to harmful behavior engaged in by another, but it is likely that they can provide some unique data that self-report alone would not unearth. Moreover, examining the discrepancy between self-reports and other reports could itself present data that further informs this domain of inquiry. Looking for and utilizing data collected from organizational records also should be used to supplement or replace self-reports (e.g., Dietz et al. 2003).

A final alternative source of data that bears mentioning is qualitative data (e.g., naturalistic observations, content-analysis of interviews, open-ended survey questions, or journals). One exemplar paper of a more qualitative approach is Glomb (2002), who relied on a content analysis of structured interviews about specific experiences with aggression.

Longitudinal data

Data from multiple or ongoing periods of time should also be gathered. Social dynamics are inherent in many of our models, such as the increase in dysfunction over time, the transmission of counterproductive behavior from a group to the individual, or feedback loops of tit-for-tat mistreatment; yet most methods using a static approach cannot adequately account for such dynamics. In this respect, event or experience sampling methodology might be especially useful. A good example of such an approach is a study by Judge et al. (2006), who sent emails to respondents at the end of every work day for a three-week period, enabling them to capture daily moods, behaviors, and events and examine micro-processes over many intervals for each respondent.

Beyond the individual

As a final methodological prescription, I suggest that more research moves beyond the individual level of analysis. To date, most research has focused on individual-level predictors of individual-level dysfunctional behavior. However, the use of aggregated measures or hierarchical linear modeling presents a lot of future research opportunities to explore dysfunction at the group or organizational level, or between levels. Robinson and O'Leary- Kelly (1998); Glomb and Liao (2003); and Liao et al. (2004) provide interesting examples of group-level approaches. Some possible research questions might include how deviant individuals impact the group, the influence of group characteristics such as composition, longevity, and cohesion, on individual workplace deviance, whether groups learn dysfunctional behavior from another, and how do shared norms of deviance develop in a group or organizational context?

CONCLUSION

Employees have, and probably always will, engage in potentially harmful, dysfunctional behaviors in the workplace. Fortunately, many researchers, especially in the past decade, have been making a concerted effort to not only understand such behavior but possibly find ways to mitigate its occurrence and effects.

Thus far, we have learned a tremendous amount about dysfunctional workplace behavior. Yet as this review shows, we also have many more questions to answer in the years ahead. It is hoped that this review will guide current and future researchers in expanding our research horizons and knowledge base in the future.

REFERENCES

Andersson, L.M. and Pearson, C.M. (1999) 'Tit for Tat? The spiraling effect of incivility in the workplace', *Academy of Management Review*, 24: 452–471.

Aquino, K. and Bradfield, M. (2000) 'Perceived victimization in the workplace: The role of situational factors and victim characteristics', *Organizational Science*, 11: 525–537.

Aquino, K. and Douglas, S. (2003) 'Revenge attitudes and hierarchical status as moderators of the relation between identity threat and antisocial behavior in organizations', *Organizational Behavior and Human Decision Processes*, 90: 195–208

Aquino, K., Grover, S.L., Bradfield, M. and Allen, D.G. (1999) 'The effects of negative affectivity, hierarchical status, and self-determination on workplace victimization', *Academy of Management Journal*, 42: 260–272.

Aquino, K., Lewis, M.U. and Bradfield, M. (1999) 'Justice constructs, negative affectivity, and employee deviance: A proposed model and empirical test', *Journal of Organizational Behavior*, 20: 1073–1091.

Ashton, M.C. (1998) 'Personality and job performance: The importance of narrow traits', *Journal of Organizational Behavior*, 19: 289–303.

Ashforth, B. (1997) 'Petty tyranny in organizations: A preliminary examination of antecedents and consequences', *Canadian Journal of Administrative Sciences*, 14: 126–140.

Ayoko, O.B., Callan V.J. and Hartel, C.E. (2003) 'Workplace conflict, bullying and counterproductive behaviors', *International Journal of Organizational Analysis*, 11: 283–301.

Barling, J., O'Leary, K.D., Jouriles, E., Vivian, D. and MacEwen, K.E. (1987) 'Factor similarity of the Conflict Tactics Scales across samples, spouses and sites: Issues and implications', *Journal of Family Violence*, 2: 37–53.

Barling, J., Dekker, I., Loughlin C.A., Kelloway E.K., Fullagar C. and Johnson D. (1996) 'Prediction and replication of the organizational and personal consequences of workplace sexual harassment', *Journal of Managerial Psychology*, 11: 4–25.

Barling, J. (1996) 'The prediction, psychological experience, and consequences of workplace violence', in G. VandenBos and EG Bulatao (eds) *Violence on the Job: Identifying Risks and Developing Solutions*. Washington DC: APA, pp. 29–49.

Barling, J., Rogers, A.J. and Kelloway, E.K. (2001) 'Behind closed doors: Organizational and personal consequences of sexual harassment and workplace violence for in-home workers', *Journal of Occupational Health Psychology*, 6: 255–269.

Baron, R.A., Neuman, J.H. and Geddes, D. (1999) 'Social and personal determinants of workplace aggression: Evidence for the impact of perceived injustice and the Type A pattern', *Aggressive Behavior*, 25: 281–296.

Bennett, R.J. (1998) 'Perceived powerlessness as a cause of employee deviance', in S.B. Bacharach (ed) *Dysfunctional Behavior in Organizations: Violent and Deviant Behavior*. Stamford, CT: JAI Press, pp. 221–239.

Bennett, R.J. and Robinson, S.L. (1997) 'Workplace deviance: Its definition, its manifestations and its causes', in R. Lewicki, R. Bies, and B. Sheppard (eds) *Research on Negotiation in Organizations*. Stanford, CT: JAI Press. Volume 6, pp. 3–27.

Bennett, R.J. and Robinson, S.L. (2003) 'The Past, Present and Future of Workplace Deviance Research', in J. Greenberg, (ed.) *Organizational Behavior: The State of the Science*, 2nd edition. Mahwah, NJ: Lawrence Erlbaum.

Bies, R.J. and Tripp, T.M. (1996) 'Beyond distrust: Getting even and the need for revenge', in R.M. Kramer and T.R. Tyler (eds) *Trust in Organizations: Frontiers of Theory and Research*. Thousand Oaks, CA: Sage, pp. 246–260.

Bies, R.J. and Tripp, T.M. (1998a) 'Two Faces of the Powerless: Coping with Tyranny', in R.M. Kramer and M.A. Neale (eds) *Power and Influence in Organizations*. Thousand Oaks, CA: Sage, pp. 203–219.

Bies, R.J. and Tripp, T.M. (1998b) 'Revenge in organizations: The good, the bad and the ugly', in R.W. Griffin, A. O'Leary-Kelly and J. Collins, (eds) *Dysfunctional Behavior in Organizations: Vol. 1. Violent Behavior in Organizations*. Greenwich, CT: JAI Press, pp. 49–67.

Blau, P. (1964) *Exchange and Power in Social Life*. New York: Wiley.

Bolin, A. and Heatherly, L. (2001) 'Predictors of employee deviance: The relationship between bad attitudes and bad behavior', *Journal of Business and Psychology*, 15: 405–418.

Breslau N, Chilcoat H.D., Kessler R.C., Peterson E.L. and V.C. Lucia (1999) 'Vulnerability to assaultive violence: Further specification of the sex difference in posttraumatic stress disorder', *Psychological Medicine*, 29: 813–821.

Budd, J.W., Arvey, R.D. and Lawless, P. (1996) 'Correlates and consequences of workplace violence', *Journal of Occupational Health Psychology*, 1: 197–210.

Chen, P.Y. and Spector, P.E. (1992) 'Relationships of work stressors with aggression, withdrawal, theft and substance use: An exploratory study', *Journal of Occupational and Organizational Psychology*, 65: 177–184.

Coffin, B. (2003) 'Breaking the silence on white collar crime', *Risk Management*, 50: 8.

Colbert, A.E., Mount, M.K., Harter, J.K., Witt, L.A. and Barrick, M.R. (2004) 'Interactive effects of personality and perceptions of the work situation on workplace deviance', *Journal of Applied Psychology*, 89: 599–609.

Collins, J.M. and Schmidt, F.L. (1993) 'Personality, integrity, and white–collar crime: A construct validity study', *Personnel Psychology*, 46 : 295–311.

Colquitt, J.A., Conlon, D.E., Wesson, M.J., Porter, C. and Ng, K.Y. (2001) 'Justice at the Millennium: A meta–analytic review of 25 years of organizational justice research', *Journal of Applied Psychology*, 86: 425–445.

Cortina, L.M. and Magley, V.J. (2003) 'Raising voice, risking retaliation: Events following interpersonal mistreatment in the workplace', *Journal of Occupational Health Psychology*, 8: 247–266.

Cortina, L.M., Magley, V.J., Williams, J.H. and Langhout, R.D. (2001) 'Incivility in the workplace: Incidence and impact', *Journal of Occupational Health Psychology*, 6: 64–80.

Cyert, R.M. and March, J.G. (1964) 'A behavioral theory of the firm', *The American Economic Review*, 54: 144–148.

Dietz, J., Robinson, S.L., Folger, R., Baron, R.A. and Schulz, M. (2003) 'The impact of community violence and an organization's procedural justice climate on workplace aggression', *Academy of Management Journal*, 46: 317–326.

Douglas, S.C. and Martinko, M.J. (2001) 'Exploring the role of individual differences in the prediction of workplace aggression', *Journal of Applied Psychology*, 86: 547–559.

Duffy, M.K., Ganster, D.C. and Shaw, J.D. (1998) 'Positive affectivity and negative outcomes: The role of tenure and job satisfaction', *Journal of Applied Psychology*, 83: 950–959.

Duffy, M.K. Ganster, D. and Pagon, M. (2002) 'Social undermining and social support in the workplace', *Academy of Management Journal*, 45: 331–351.

Dunlop, P.D. and Lee, K. (2004) 'Workplace deviance, organizational citizenship behavior, and business unit performance: The bad apples do spoil the whole barrel', *Journal of Organizational Behavior*, 25: 67–80.

Dupré, K.E. and Barling, J. (2006) 'Predicting and preventing supervisory workplace aggression', *Journal of Occupational Health Psychology*, 11: 1–13.

Einarsen, S. and Raknes, B.I. (1997) 'Harassment at work and the vicimization of men', *Victims and Violence*, 12 (3): 247–263.

Einarsen, S. and Skogstad, A. (1996) 'Bullying at work: Epidemiological findings in public and private organizations', *European Journal of Work and Organizational Psychology*, 4: 185–202.

Einarsen, S., Raknes B.I. and Matthiesen, S.B.M. (1994) 'Bullying and harassment at work and their relationships to work environment quality: An exploratory study', *European Work and Organizational Psychologist*, 4: 116–137.

Einarsen, S. (2000) 'Harassment and bullying at work: A review of the Scandinavian approach', *Aggression and Violent Behavior*, 5: 379–401

Einarsen, S., Hoel, H., Zapf, D. and Cooper, C. (2003) 'Empirical findings on bullying', in S. Einarsen, H. Hoel, D. Zapf, and C.L. Cooper (eds), *Bullying and Emotional Abuse in the Workplace. International Perspectives in Research and Practice*. London: Taylor and Francis, pp. 3–30.

Einarsen, S., Matthiesen, S.B. and Skogstad, A. (1998) 'Bullying, burnout and well-being among assistant nurses', *Journal of Occupational Health and Safety*, 14: 563–568.

Folger, R. and Baron R.A. (1996) 'Violence and hostility at work: A model of reactions to perceived injustice', in G. VandeBos and E.Q. Bulatao (eds) *Violence on the Job: Identifying Risks and Developing Solutions*. Washington DC: APA, pp. 51–85.

Fox, S. and Spector, P.E. (1999) 'A model of work frustration-aggression', *Journal of Organizational Behavior*, 20: 915–931.

Fox, S., Spector, P.E. and Miles, D. (2001) 'Counterproductive work behavior in response to job stressors and organizational justice: Some mediator and moderator tests for autonomy and emotions', *Journal of Vocational Behavior*, 59: 291–309.

Glendinning, P.M. (2001) 'Workplace bullying: Curing the cancer of the American workplace', *Public Personnel Management*, 30: 269–286.

Glomb, T. (2002) 'Workplace anger and aggression: Informing conceptual models with data from specific encounters', *Journal of Occupational Health Psychology*, 7: 20–36.

Glomb, T.M. and Liao, H. (2003) 'Interpersonal aggression in work groups: Social influence, reciprocal, and individual effects', *Academy of Management Journal*, 46: 486–496.

Gouldner, Alvin W. (1960) 'The norm of reciprocity: A preliminary statement', *American Sociological Review*, 25: 161–178.

Greenberg, L. and Barling, J. (1999) 'Predicting employee aggression against coworkers, subordinates and supervisors: The roles of person behaviors and perceived workplace factors', *Journal of Organizational Behavior*, 20: 897–913.

Giacalone, R.A. and Greenberg, J. (1997) *Antisocial Behavior in Organizations*. Thousand Oaks, CA: Sage.

Griffin, R.W., O'Leary-Kelly, A. and Collins, J. (1998) *Dysfunctional Behavior in Organizations: Vol. 1. Violent Behavior in Organizations*. Greenwich, CT: JAI Press.

Hall, J.K. and Spector, P.E. (1991) 'Relationships of work stress measures for employees with the same job', *Work and Stress*, 5: 29–35.

Harvey, S. and Keashly, L. (2003) 'Predicting the risk for aggression in the workplace: Risk factors, self–esteem and time at work', *Social Behavior and Personality*, 31: 807–814.

Henle, C.A., Giacalone, R.A. and Jurkiewicz, C.L. (2005) 'The role of ethical ideology in workplace deviance', *Journal of Business Ethics*, 56: 219–230.

Hepworth, W. and Towler, A. (2004) 'The effects of individual differences and charismatic leadership on workplace aggression', *Journal of Occupational Health Psychology*, 9: 176–185.

Herschovis, M.S., Turner, N., Barling, J., Arnold, K.A., Dupre, K. E., Inness, M., LeBlanc, M.M. and Sivanathan, N. (2007) 'Predicting workplace aggression: A meta-analysis', *Journal of Applied Psychology*, 92 (1): 228–238.

Hirschi, T. (1969) *Causes of Delinquency*. Berkeley: University of California Press.

Hoel, H. and Cooper, C.L. (2000) 'Victims of workplace bullying', in H. Kemshall and J. Pritchard (eds) *Good Practice in Working with Victims of Violence*. London: Jessica Kingsley Publishers, pp. 101–118.

Hoel, H. and Cooper, C.L. (2001) 'Origins of bullying', in N. Tehrani (ed) *Building a Culture of Respect: Managing Bullying at Work*. London: Taylor and Francis, pp. 97–114.

Hoel, H., Einarsen, S. and Cooper, C. (2003) 'Organisational effects of bullying', in S. Einarsen, H. Hoel, D. Zapf and C. Cooper (eds) *Bullying and Emotional Abuse in the Workplace: International Perspectives in Research and Practice*. London: Taylor & Francis, pp. 145–162.

Inness, M., Barling, J. and Turner, N. (2005) 'Understanding supervisor-targeted aggression: A within-person between-jobs design', *Journal of Applied Psychology*, 90: 731–739.

Jockin, V., Arvey, R.D. and McGue, M. (2001) 'Perceived victimization moderates self-reports of workplace aggression and conflict', *Journal of Applied Psychology*, 86: 1262–1269.

Judge, T.A., Scott, B.A. and Ilies, R. (2006) 'Hostility, job attitudes, and workplace deviance: Test of a multilevel model', *Journal of Applied Psychology*, 91: 126–138

Katz, D. and Kahn, R.L. (1978) *The Social Psychology of Organizations*. New York: John Wiley & Sons.

Keashly, L. (1998) 'Emotional abuse in the workplace: Conceptual and empirical issues', *Journal of Emotional Abuse*, 1: 85–117.

Keashly, L., Trott, V. and MacLean, L.M. (1994) 'Abusive behavior in the workplace: A preliminary investigation', *Violence and Victims*, 9: 341–357.

Knorz, C. and Zapf, D. (1996) 'Mobbing–eine extreme Form sozialer Stressoren am Arbeitsplatz. [Mobbing–an extreme form of social stressors in the workplace]', *Zeitschrift für Arbeits- und Organisationspsychologie*, 40: 12–21.

Kraus J. (1987) 'Homicide while at work: Persons industries and occupations at high risk', *American Journal of Public Health*, 77: 1285–1289.

Lapierre, L.M., Spector, P.E. and Leck, J.D. (2005) 'Sexual versus nonsexual workplace aggression and victims' overall job satisfaction: A meta–analysis', *Journal of Occupational Health Psychology*, 10: 155–169.

Lawrence, T. and Robinson, S.L. (2007) 'Workplace deviance as organizational resistance', *Journal of Management*, 33: 378–394.

LeBlanc, M.M. and Kelloway, E.K. (2002) 'Predictors and outcomes of workplace violence and aggression', *Journal of Applied Psychology*, 87: 444–453.

Lee, K. and Allen, N. J (2002) 'Organizational citizenship behavior and workplace deviance: The role of affect and cognitions', *Journal of Applied Psychology*, 87: 131–142.

Leymann, H. (1990) 'Mobbing and psychological terror at workplaces', *Violence and Victims*, 5: 199–126.

Leymann, H. (1996) 'The content and development of mobbing at work', *Mobbing and Victimization at Work. A Special Issue of the European Journal of Work and Organizational Psychology*, 2: 165–184.

Liao, H., Joshi, A. and Chuang, A. (2004) 'Sticking out like a sore thumb: Employee dissimilarity and deviance at work', *Personnel Psychology*, 57: 969–1000.

Lutgen-Sandvik, P. (2003) 'The cycle of employee emotional abuse: Generation and regeneration of workplace mistreatment', *Management Communication Quarterly*, 16: 471–501.

Marcus, B. and Schuler, H. (2004) 'Antecedents of counterproductive behavior at work: A general perspective', *Journal of Applied Psychology*, 89: 647–660.

Martinko, M.J. and Zellars, K.L. (1998) 'Toward a theory of workplace violence: A cognitive appraisal perspective', in R.W. Griffin, A. O'Leary-Kelly, and J.M. Collins (eds) *Dysfunctional Behavior in Organizations: Violent and Deviant Behavior*. Stanford, CT: JAI Press, pp. 1–42.

Neuman, J.H. and Baron, R.A. (1998) 'Workplace violence and workplace aggression: Evidence concerning specific forms, potential causes, and preferred targets', *Journal of Management*, 24: 391–419.

O'Leary-Kelly, A.M., Griffin, R.W. and Glew, D.J. (1996) 'Organization-motivated aggression: A research framework', *Academy of Management Review*, 21: 225–253.

O'Moore, M., Seigne, E., McGuire, L. and Smith, M. (1998) 'Victims of bullying at work in Ireland', *Journal of Occupational Health and Safety: Australia and New Zealand*, 14 (6): 568–574.

Olafsson, R.F. and Johannsdottir, H.L. (2004) 'Coping with bullying in the workplace: The effect of gender, age and type of bullying', *British Journal of Guidance and Counselling*, 32: 319–333.

Penney, L.M. and Spector, P.E. (2005) 'Job stress, incivility, and counterproductive workplace behavior: The moderating role of negative affectivity', *Journal of Organizational Behavior*, 26: 777–796.

Pratt, L. and Barling, J. (1988) 'Differentiating daily hassles, acute and chronic stressors: A framework and its implications', in J.R. Hurrell, L.R. Murphy, S.L. Sauter and C.L. Cooper (eds), *Occupational Stress: Issues and Developments in Research*. London: Taylor and Francis, pp. 41–53.

Rayner, C. and Cooper, C.L. (2003) 'The black hole in "bullying at work" research', *International Journal of Management and Decision-Making*, 4 (1): 47–64.

Rayner, C., Hoel, H. and Cooper, C.L. (2002) *Workplace Bullying: What We Know, Who is to Blame and What Can We Do?* London: Taylor and Francis.

Rayner, C. and Keashly, L. (2004) 'Bullying at work: A perspective from Britain and North America', in S. Fox and P.E. Spector (eds) *Counterproductive Work Behavior*. Washington DC: American Psychological Association, pp. 271–296.

Robinson, S.L. and Bennett, R.J. (1995) 'A typology of deviant workplace behaviors: A multidimensional scaling study', *Academy of Management Journal*, 38: 555–572.

Robinson, S.L. and Greenberg, J. (1999) 'Employees behaving badly: Dimensions, determinants and dilemmas in the study of workplace deviance', in D.M. Rousseau and C. Cooper (eds) *Trends in Organizational Behavior*. New York: Wiley. Vol. 5, pp. 1–23.

Robinson S.L. and O'Leary-Kelly, A.M. (1998) 'Monkey see, monkey do: The influence of work groups on the antisocial behavior of employees', *Academy of Management Journal*, 41: 658–672.

Rogers, K. and Kelloway, K. (1997) 'Violence at work: Personal and organizational outcomes', *Journal of Occupational Health Psychology*, 2: 63–71.

Sackett, P.R. and Devore, C.J. (2001) 'Counterproductive behaviors at work', in N. Anderson, D. Ones, H. Sinangil and C. Viswesvaran (eds) *Handbook of Industrial, Work, and Organizational Psychology*. London: Sage, pp. 145–164.

Sackett, R.R. and Wanek, J.E. (1996) 'New developments in the use of measures of honesty, integrity, conscientiousness, dependability, trustworthiness and reliability for personnel selection', *Personnel Psychology*, 49: 787–830.

Salgado J.F. (2002) 'The big five personality dimensions and counterproductive behaviors', *International Journal of Selection and Assessment*, 10: 117–125.

Salin, D. (2003) 'Ways of explaining workplace bullying: A review of enabling, motivating and precipitating structures and processes in the work environment', *Human Relations*, 56: 1213–1232.

Schat, A.C., Frone, M.R. and Kelloway, E.K. (2006) 'Prevalence of aggression in the US workforce: Findings from a national study', in E.K. Kelloway, J. Barling and J.J. Hurrell, (eds) *Handbook of Workplace Violence*. Thousand Oaks, CA: Sage.

Schat, A.C.H. and Kelloway, E.K. (2000) 'Effects of perceived control on the outcomes of workplace aggression and violence', *Journal of Occupational Health Psychology*, 5: 386–402.

Skarlicki, D.P. and Folger, R. (1997) 'Retaliation in the workplace: The roles of distributive, procedural and interactional justice', *Journal of Applied Psychology*, 82: 434–443.

Skarlicki, D.P., Folger, R. and Tesluk, P. (1999) 'Personality as a moderator in the relationship between fairness and retaliation', *Academy of Management Journal*, 42: 100–108.

Tepper, B.J. (2000) 'Consequences of abusive supervision', *Academy of Management Journal*, 43: 178–190.

Tepper, B.J., Duffy, M.K., and Shaw, J.D. (2001) 'Personality moderators of the relationship between abusive supervision and subordinates' resistance', *Journal of Applied Psychology*, 86: 974–983.

Tepper, B.J., Duffy, M.K., Henle, C.A., Lambert, L.S. (2006) 'Procedural injustice, victim precipitation, and abusive supervision', *Personnel Psychology*, 59: 101–123.

Vardi, Y. and Wiener, Y. (1996) 'Misbehavior in organizations: A motivational framework', *Organizational Science*, 7: 151–165.

Vartia, M. (1996) 'The sources of bullying: Psychological work environment and organizational climate', *European Journal of Work and Organisational Psychology*, 5: 203–214.

Warren, D. (2003) 'Constructive and destructive deviance in organizations', *Academy of Management Review*, 28: 622–632.

Weiss, H.M. and Cropanzano, R. (1996) 'Affective events theory: A theoretical discussion of the structure, causes and consequences of affective experiences at work', in B.M. Staw and L.L. Cummings (eds) *Research in Organizational Behavior: An Annual Series of Analytical Essays and Critical Reviews.* Greenwich, CT: JAI Press, Inc. Vol. 18, pp. 1–74.

Zapf, D. and Gross, C. (2001) 'Conflict escalation and coping with workplace bullying: a replication and extension', *European Journal of Work and Organization Psychology*, 10 (4): 497–522.

Zapf, D., Knorz, C. and Kulla, M. (1996) 'On the relationship between mobbing factors, and job content, social work environment, and health outcomes', *European Journal of Work and Organizational Psychology*, 5: 215–238.

Zellars, K.L., Tepper, B.J. and Duffy, M.K. (2002) 'Abusive supervision and subordinates' organizational citizenship behavior', *Journal of Applied Psychology*, 87: 1068–1076.

9

Absenteeism and Presenteeism: Not at Work or Not Working Well

Gary Johns

Absenteeism is the failure to report for work as scheduled. Compared with many phenomena in the organizational sciences, absence has a venerable research history. For instance, as early as 1932, Kornhauser and Sharp examined the association between factory employee attitudes and absence. During World War II this usually innocuous work behavior was recast as menace to the war effort (Pattton and Johns, 2006; Tansey and Hyman, 1992), and research was conducted to better understand its causes (Fox and Scott, 1943; Schenet, 1945). With their influential 1953 study of absence in a steel mill, Hill and Trist gave particular traction to the idea that absenteeism represents temporary withdrawal from dissatisfying work. Less immediately influential was their cogent insight that an 'appropriate' level and patterning of absence behavior was learned by new employees as they observed the attendance behavior of veteran workers (Hill and Trist, 1955).

The withdrawal thesis, which was especially compatible with the tenets of the human relations movement, dominated the thinking of work psychologists and organizational behavior scholars for many years (Johns, 2001a). Basically, absence was treated as an individual level indicator of work ineffectiveness and suffered from the lack of theoretical development not uncommon for so-called criterion variables (Austin and Villanova, 1992). However, absence and attendance reflect something essential about the relationship between the worker and the organization. This recognition has been bolstered by an emergent multi-disciplinary interest in absence in which the behavior is variously viewed as a manifestation of worker deviance (sociology), a result of labor-leisure tradeoff, (economics), a product of labor strife (industrial relations), an indicator of stress (nursing), an implied contract violation (law), or a reaction to illness (medicine). It is these additional optics and the resulting fact that a behavior with a singular surface appearance can reflect such diverse causes that makes the study of absenteeism both interesting and challenging.

INDIVIDUAL-LEVEL CORRELATES OF ABSENTEEISM

As some illustration of the academic interest in absenteeism, over 25 meta-analyses of its various correlates have been published following McShane's initial effort in 1984. The summary properties of meta-analysis have been particularly helpful in the case of absence because its variable reliability, positively skewed distribution, and susceptibility to context effects constitute a recipe for uneven relationships with its correlates (Johns, 2003).

Table 1 summarizes the results of meta-analyses of the individual-level correlates of absenteeism, excluding those that have been superceded in terms of the number of studies or samples that have been assembled (k) (e.g., McShane, 1984) or various methodological refinements. (Table 2, which recounts the impact of interventions on absence, is constructed and presented in the same way.) In most cases the summary corrected $r(r_c)$ is adjusted for sampling error and for unreliability in absence and its reported correlate. Separate estimates for total time lost (TL) and frequency (F, number of instances irrespective of duration) are reported when they are of particular interest or the only data available. When absence type is undesignated, it generally indicates a mix of time lost and frequency. Results are reported selectively. For instance, data on the facets of job satisfaction (Hackett, 1989; Hackett and Guion, 1985; Williams, McDaniel and Nguyen, 2006) are omitted. Also, I have occasionally added or reversed a sign for clarity (e.g., if the original report omitted signs or reported correlations with attendance rather than absence).

Attitudes

As can be seen in Table 1, work attitudes are not particularly strong correlates of absenteeism, a point that Nicholson et al. (1976) recognized even before the advent of meta-analysis. In general, overall satisfaction evinces stronger associations than its facets, with the possible exception of satisfaction with the work itself, which is the best facet predictor (Hackett, 1989; Hackett and Guion, 1985). The generally weak performance for attitudes is all the more striking when it is acknowledged that these attitudes are generally highly correlated and that they are often considered proximal mediators of more distal influences on absence In fact, Goldberg and Waldman (2000) found little support for such implied mediation.

What accounts for these low relationships? One reason might be inattention to viable moderators. Unfortunately, little attention has been accorded to whom or when dissatisfaction might especially stimulate absence, although Hackett (1989) found that the association was stronger in samples with higher proportions of women. Another reason might be a lack of predictor-criterion commensurability. On one hand, the person who is dissatisfied with their supervisor has a variety of behavioral options in addition to going absent. On the other hand, a broad variable such as global satisfaction might not map well onto a specific job behavior such as absenteeism (Hanisch et al., 1998; Harrison et al., 2006). This will be explored more fully below.

Work experiences

As shown in Table 1, various work perceptions and experiences are not much more highly correlated with absenteeism than are job attitudes. In particular, the rather weak results for stress command attention in light of repeated references in the popular and business press as to how absence is a salient consequence of stress. However, Darr and Johns (in press) did find support for the contention that psychological and somatic

Table 1 Individual-level correlates of absenteeism: a meta-analytic summary

Variable	k	r_c	Source
Attitudes			
Overall job satisfaction (TL)	22	−.10	Hackett and Guion, 1985
Overall job satisfaction (TL)	8	−.23	Hackett, 1989
Overall job satisfaction (F)	33	−.13	Hackett and Guion, 1985
Overall job satisfaction (F)	17	−.15	Hackett, 1989
Organizational commitment	23	−.10	Mathieu and Zajac, 1990
Affective organizational commitment	10	−.15	Meyer et al., 2002
Job involvement (TL)	7	−.17	Farrell and Stamm, 1988
Job involvement (F)	4	−.43	"
Experiences			
Role ambiguity	5	.13	Jackson and Schuler, 1985
Role conflict	3	−.02	"
Stress (all)	56	.15	Darr and Johns, in press
Stress (TL)	40	.14	"
Stress (F)	14	.17	"
Perceived job autonomy	12	−.15	Humphrey et al., 2007
Distributive justice[a]	18	−.50	Colquitt et al., 2001
Procedural justice[a]	39	−.46	"
Behavior			
Lateness	25	.40	Koslowsky et al., 1997
Turnover	28	.20	Griffeth et al., 2000
Turnover (all)	33	.33	Mitra et al., 1992
Turnover (TL)	9	.32	"
Turnover (F)	22	.34	"
Performance (supervisory ratings)	49	−.29	Bycio, 1992
Performance (non-rating criteria)	23	−.24	"
Contextual performance	8	−.26	Harrison et al., 2006
Past absence (TL)	10	.71	Farrell and Stamm, 1988
Past absence (F)	15	.65	"
Self-reported absence	6	.64	Johns, 1994b
Demographic/disposition			
Age (TL)	37	−.07	Hackett, 1990
Age (F)	25	−.30	"
Tenure (TL)	33	−.05	"
Tenure (F)	28	−.27	"
Gender (all)[b]	29	.20	Côté and Haccoun, 1991
Gender (TL)[b]	13	.18	"
Gender (F)[b]	15	.22	"
Locus of control (external)	6	.13	Ng et al., 2006
Medical			
Psychological illness	128	.20	Darr and Johns, in press
Somatic illness	65	.22	"
Low back pain (all)	14	.18	Martocchio et al., 2000
Low back pain (TL)	10	.11	"
Low back pain (F)	4	.41	"

Notes: k = number of studies; r_c = corrected estimated population correlation; F = frequency of absence; TL = time lost absence.

[a] The criterion includes both absence and turnover.

[b] Women tend to exhibit more absence than men.

Table 2 Impact of organizational policies and practices on absenteeism: a meta-analytic summary

Policy/practice	k	r_c	Source
Telephone selection interview	7	−.19	Schmidt and Rader, 1999
Integrity tests (all)	28	−.20	Ones et al., 2003
Integrity tests (personality based)	18	−.36	"
Integrity tests (overt)	10	−.09	"
Control policies	12	−.46	Farrell and Stamm, 1988
Flextime	8	−.42	Baltes et al., 1999
Compressed workweek	5	.00	"
Low back pain interventions	31	−.10	Martocchio et al., 2000

Note: k = number of studies; r_c = corrected estimated population correlation.

illness mediates the connection between stress and absence, an often implied but seldom tested idea.

Humphrey et al. (2007) reported the associations between absenteeism and seven perceived job characteristics. As shown in Table 1, the largest of these was for autonomy ($r_c = 0.15$). However, meta-analytic regression employing all seven characteristics yielded an R of 0.26, accounting for 7 per cent of the variance in absence. This result corresponds to the finding that satisfaction with the work itself is the best facet predictor of absence. It also aligns with the ubiquitous finding that absence tends to decrease with increasing occupational status, both cross-sectionally and longitudinally (e.g., Akyeampong, 2005; Shirom and Rosenblatt, 2006).

Moderators may limit the observed bivariate connection between job characteristics and attendance behavior and indeed even reverse the typical sign, a not-uncommon result of strong contextual effects (Johns, 2006a). For instance, Fried et al. (2002) found an exception to the general rule that more complex jobs entail less absence. Women doing complex jobs in very noisy work environments were particularly prone to absence; men's attendance was not much affected by noise. Similarly, Hirschfeld et al. (2002) found that low paid clerical employees exhibited elevated absence when skill variety and task significance were reported to be high. In addition, for skill variety, the positive association was even higher when a low connection between rewards and performance was perceived, suggesting that justice motives were at play (Hirschfeld et al., 2002).

Although the justice-absence connection has not been the subject of a dedicated meta-analysis, Colquitt et al. (2001) reported associations with an absence-turnover composite. As shown in Table 1, both distributive and procedural justice were strong correlates of this withdrawal composite, although a uniqueness analysis showed that distributive justice was clearly dominant. Johns and Nicholson (1982) explained why equity in particular might be a salient predictor of attendance (absence constitutes an input reduction), and individual studies have repeatedly confirmed that distributive justice (and sometimes procedural) is negatively related to absence (Geurts et al., 1999; Lam et al., 2002; van Direndonck et al., 1998; Van Yperen et al., 1996). De Boer et al. (2002) also found an indirect effect for both types of justice via health complaints. Surely reflecting equity motives, Kristensen et al. (2006) found higher rates of absence frequency in bank branches in which higher proportions of employees had been placed under salary caps because they were deemed overpaid. In a related vein, recent research has also shown that psychological contract breach results in absence (Johnson and O'Leary-Kelly, 2003; Sturges et al., 2005), and Deery et al. (2006) revealed support for an indirect model in which breach lowered organizational trust, reduced cooperation, and resulted in absence.

In general, the research concerning justice and contract breach constitutes some of the best (albeit indirect) evidence for the strategic, proactive use of attendance as a means of managing one's relationship with the employer. It is also significant in light of the fact that the average corrected correlations of pay satisfaction with absence are trivial in size (i.e., between -0.08 and -0.05, Hackett, 1989; Williams et al., 2006). This suggests that the cognitive evaluation of work outcomes such as pay is less important for absence than the more affectively loaded perceptions of unfairness and breach (see Brief and Weiss, 2002).

Work behaviors

Two major themes concerning work behavior emerge from Table 1. The first is that past absenteeism is a particularly viable predictor of more recent absenteeism (Farrell and Stamm, 1988). In and of itself, this relative rank order stability could stem from disposition, chronic differences in health among respondents, or relatively unchanging work circumstances over time. However, several factors combine to suggest that the dispositional explanation is viable if not exclusive. First, Rentsch and Steel (1998) observed stability in absence over very long time frames, with Year 1 data correlating in the 0.50s with absence exhibited four to six years later. Next, such stability in attendance has been observed even in the face of intervening situational changes (Brenner, 1968; Ivancevich, 1985). Finally, Harrison and Price (2003) showed that people exhibited a fair degree of internal consistency ($\alpha = 0.62$) in self-reported absenteeism across 11 different social settings. Thus, people who were inclined to miss work were also inclined to miss social engagements, school, and church. In combination, these findings point to a dispositional explanation for absence stability, a point to be examined shortly.

A second theme occasioned by the behavioral data in Table 1, and an important one, is that the various behavioral correlations are among the higher correlations in the table. This is noteworthy because work behaviors are subject to more organizational constraints than privately held work attitudes (Johns, 1991). What accounts for these associations?

One idea is that there is an escalating continuum of withdrawal in response to the occurrence of negative work attitudes and experiences (Rosse and Miller, 1984). That is, more trivial withdrawal acts precede more consequential ones as a means of seeking adjustment to the unfavorable work setting. Although the continuum has been theorized to span everything from escapist drinking to early retirement (Hanisch et al., 1998), the best empirical evidence (reviewed in Johns, 2001a) supports a sequence in which lateness precedes absence and absence precedes turnover. More recently, Harrison et al. (2006) reaffirmed this progression using meta-analytic structural equation techniques and also provided some support for the idea that a reduction in contextual performance might indeed precede lateness. More broadly, despite progression, they also found support for the idea that the three withdrawal behaviors, in-role performance, and contextual performance comprise a higher order construct, contributions to the work role (cf. Hanisch et al., 1998). A combination of job satisfaction and organizational commitment correlated 0.59 with this construct. Contextual constraints (Johns, 1991, 2006a) probably dictate which behaviors are enacted, with rough progression being the default under lower constraint. For some caveats concerning such broadly defined constructs, the reader is directed to Blau (1998) and Johns (1998).

Disposition

As noted above, the relative stability of absence over both time and circumstance gives rise to the possibility that disposition might influence the behavior, giving credence to the idea of proneness to absence. Although there has been somewhat limited research in this area, extant work reveals a series of smallish relationships. Two of the more consistent dispositional correlates of absence appear to be conscientiousness and positive affectivity. Several studies reveal that Big Five measures of conscientiousness are negatively related to absenteeism (Conte and Jacobs, 2003;

Iverson and Deery, 2001; Judge et al., 1997). In addition (as revealed in Table 2), personality based measures of integrity, most of which draw heavily on this personality variable, are especially good predictors of absence (Ones et al., 2003). Given the well established connection between conscientiousness and job performance, the findings for absence make intuitive sense and lend nomological support for the broad contributions to the work role construct advocated by Harrison et al. (2006).

The connection between affect and absenteeism is confusing. Several studies reveal a negative association between positive affectivity and absence (George, 1989; Iverson et al., 1998; Iverson and Deery, 2001; Pelled and Xin, 1999). However, the results for negative affect and neuroticism are decidedly more spotty, a sure anomaly in light of the repeatedly demonstrated connection between depression and absence (Johns, 2002). These contradictions suggest the need to better address the mood-regulatory aspects of attendance, and this surely requires attention to its temporal dynamics (cf. Harrison and Martocchio, 1998) – a call also made by Grandey in her chapter on emotions elsewhere in this volume. Martocchio and Jimeno (2003) present an interesting model of personality, affect, and absence that positions absence as a particular 'affective event' for different personality types.

As shown in Table 1, Ng et al. (2006) reported a rather small positive association between external locus of control (LOC) and absence across six studies. The conventional interpretation of this would be that internals are better able to overcome obstacles to attendance or that externals are more likely to succumb to them. The small size of this association might reflect the fact that LOC is a somewhat narrow personality trait (cf. core self-evaluations, Judge and Bono, 2001). Conversely, it might reflect the rather diffuse nature of trait LOC, and more state-specific measures, such as health LOC (Johns, 1994c), might be more relevant to attendance behavior. Indeed, LeBreton, Binning, Adorno, and Melcher (2004) found that job-specific

affect was a better predictor of self-reported absence than the more general Big Five dimension emotional stability (neuroticism). Similarly, Conte and Jacobs (2003) found that polychronicity, a preference for simultaneous engagement in multiple tasks, was positively correlated with absence, and Addae (2003) found that high polychronics viewed absence as more legitimate than did the less polychronic. Again, the specificity of the trait to the task is notable, since work attendance is in essence a matter of time allocation.

To conclude, the role of disposition for absenteeism shows some promise, but more dedicated research is necessary. In particular, researchers need to think more about how particular dispositional characteristics might map onto the specific functions absence might serve (e.g., respite, protest, revenge, equity restoration, childcare) and when this might occur. For instance, Elovainio and colleagues (2003) found that, for men, hostility exacerbated the connection between procedural injustice and absence and that neuroticism did the same for interactional injustice. In these cases, absence probably reflected protest or revenge motives.

THE SOCIAL CONTROL OF ABSENTEEISM

The prominence of individual-level factors reflected in Table 1 is symptomatic of a bias that has positioned absence as a partial indicator of individual performance that follows from personal traits, attitudes, experiences, and illnesses. However, one of the signal findings of the past 25 years is the social nature of attendance dynamics and their susceptibility to social control. Two factors set the stage for social influence over absenteeism. First, the fact that it can have many causes, many of these stochastic or unobservable, makes it uncertain just how much absenteeism is reasonable and appropriate. Still, as Harrison and Martocchio (1998) remind us, absenteeism is the failure to report for scheduled work when other parties expect us to be there. Accordingly, absenteeism is widely viewed as mildly deviant behavior. The best evidence for this is the tendency for people to underreport their own absence and to portray their attendance record as superior to that of their colleagues (Harrison and Schaffer, 1994; Johns, 1994a,b; Johns and Xie, 1998).

Evidence for absence cultures

The research on the social determinants of absence has often been conducted in light of theoretical work positing the existence of absence cultures (Chadwick-Jones et al., 1982; Johns and Nicholson, 1982; Nicholson and Johns, 1985). Such cultures are assumed to be underpinned by norms dictating acceptable levels and patterns attendance and acceptable reasons for absence, and might apply conceptually to any level from work teams to nations. A number of reviews and commentaries concerning this research are available (Johns, 1997, 2001a, 2002, 2003; Kaiser, 1998a; Rentsch and Steel, 2003). Here, I will briefly summarize the essence of these works and then go on to integrate some of the newer research in this domain. Based on past reviews, the following findings, in ascending order of convincingness, point to the social control of absence and the existence of absence cultures:

- There are striking differences in absenteeism levels across social units such as work groups, departments, plants, industries, occupations, and nations. It was such differences that led Chadwick-Jones et al. (1982) to speculate about social causation.
- Variables meant to capture social processes are common and convincing correlates of absenteeism. These include perceptions of equity and group cohesiveness (which tends to be negatively correlated with absence, especially when properly expressed at the group level), and expectations about how others will react to absence. However, social norms concerning absenteeism comprise the most studied social correlates. For instance, Gellatly (1995) determined that perceived norms mediated the relationship between work group absence and an individual's absence exhibited

in the following year. Any particular measure of absence norms has its limitations, such as the projection of one's own predilection for absence onto one's group. However, absence norms have been operationalized in such a wide variety of ways (e.g., numeric estimates, verbal estimates, return-potential curves, subjective norms) that the strengths of one method offset the weaknesses of another (Johns, 2003). Norms are very important for understanding absence because they specify just how much deviant behavior is tolerated by others.

- The best evidence for absence cultures is cross-level research showing that work unit absence or opinion about attendance shapes the attendance of individual work unit members (Gellatly and Luchak, 1998; Johns, 1994c; Markham and McKee, 1995; Martocchio, 1994; Mathieu and Kohler, 1990; Schmidt, 2002; Xie and Johns, 2000).

Recent refinements concerning social influence

A number of more recent studies have refined our understanding of the social control of absence. Especially compelling is research showing that the absenteeism exhibited by branch bank managers was a viable predictor of the branch employees' absence rates (Kristensen et al., 2006). Although the direction of causality here cannot be ascertained, it is tempting to infer modeling on the part of the managers, since they would be unlikely to directly advocate absence by subordinates.

Harrison et al. (2000) speculated about how diversity of work group composition might affect absence taking, and empirical efforts have supported the value of examining this issue. Sanders (2004) determined that consensus in work ethic was positively related to team cohesiveness, which in turn was associated with lower short term absence. This provides at least one possible explanation for the mechanisms underlying the oft-seen but not well understood positive connection between cohesiveness and attendance. Iverson et al. (2003) examined how the union membership composition of work groups affected the permissiveness of their absence cultures. Greater similarity in union membership was associated with a culture that viewed absence as less legitimate (i.e., heterogeneity weakened attendance norms), and a better perceived industrial relations climate strengthened this relationship. Under conditions of high similarity and a good climate, the authors inferred a Nicholson and Johns (1985) Type II absence culture, one characterized by the salience of absence and trust between management and labor (cf. Gellatly and Luchak, 1998). Other studies relevant to diversity of attitudes and perceptions are described below.

In a study of German civil servants, Schmidt (2002) found that organizational tenure interacted with office-level absence to account for variance in individual time lost. Specifically, mirroring the classic observations of Hill and Trist (1955), he determined that those with higher tenure were more inclined to exhibit attendance in line with the office norm. However, the fact that norms affect group or team absence behavior does not rule out the possibility that they change over time. In a unique longitudinal multilevel study, Mason and Griffin (2003) examined the absence of an occupationally diverse set of work groups in an Australian state government agency over a period of 15 months, using quarterly time lost absence data. They discovered changes in absence levels over time, with the groups exhibiting a wide variety of trends. The positive affective tone in groups was associated with both absence differences between groups (similar to George, 1990) and changes in group absence over time, with more positive tone resulting in less absence. Within groups, an accelerating pattern of change was seen over time, again analogous to the 'shaping' of absenteeism implied by Hill and Trist (1955) and by Schmidt (2002).

One manifestation of social control is that workers sometimes put pressure on each other to attend, especially under highly interdependent team structures (Barker, 1993). However, the general expectation that self-managed teams should reduce absenteeism is not borne out, and increases have even been reported (see Harrison et al., 2000).

This might correspond to evidence that workers sometimes collude to 'manage' their attendance levels in an orderly way (Edwards and Scullion, 1982; Edwards and Whitston, 1993; Xie and Johns, 2000), a practice facilitated by team structures. Interestingly, Dineen et al. (2007) found that team members who were dissatisfied with their jobs or university courses were less likely to be absent from work or team meetings when their teammates shared their negative views. Thus, united opinion against an external source of dissatisfaction motivated attendance.

Despite the possibility of collusion, there is growing evidence that absenteeism is highest when social integration is low and social control has broken down. Contrasting the absence practices of garment workers and engineering workers, Edwards and Scullion (1982) attributed the higher absence among the former employees to a lack of social integration and cohesion. More recently, Xie and Johns (2000) found that Chinese work groups had the highest absence rates when group cohesiveness was low and absenteeism was not a salient referent for the group. Rather similarly, Sanders (2004) found that short-term absence was highest in teams that were low on cohesiveness and had a low work ethic. Colquitt et al. (2002) found that absenteeism was highest in teams where both the level and strength of the procedural justice climate were low. In other words, generally unfair procedures, coupled with diverse perceptions, resulted in the greatest absence. Very similarly, Dineen et al. (2007) found that absence peaked in teams in which mean job (or university course) satisfaction was low and dispersion around this mean was high. In a another study of student learning teams, Duffy et al. (2000) predicted and found a three way interaction showing that the combination of high task interdependence, relationship conflict, and low self-esteem was a recipe for high self-reported absence. Thus, a lack of social integration in the face of a need for it maximized absenteeism. In this otherwise diverse series of studies, it is tempting to infer that the common thread is depressed positive affective tone (Brief and Weiss, 2002; George, 1990; Mason and Griffin, 2003) due to poor social integration stemming from a lack of consensus concerning core group issues. If so, group affective tone joins culture and norms as a key element of the social control of absence.

Cross-cultural absence research

There has been very little research on organizational attachment and withdrawal across cultures. However, we might expect cross-cultural differences in views about absence and in actual absence behavior based on the same logic offered above for social control within cultures – vague standards about what constitutes a legitimate level of absence and the deviant connotations of the behavior. Although deviant connotations are not assured to be transcultural, they have been shown to operate in the West and in China (Johns and Xie, 1998). In addition, the accumulated empirical evidence for social control within cultures reviewed above is suggestive of the likelihood of cross-cultural differences. If nothing else, the well documented differences in time allocation and time management across cultures point to examining absenteeism.

Kuzmits (1995) found that Vietnamese and non-Vietnamese workers in a US food processing plant had similar levels of involuntary absence but that the Vietnamese exhibited less voluntary absence and fewer attendance discipline episodes. He explained this in terms of Confucian values. Rosenblatt and Shirom (2006) found that Arab-sector Israeli school teachers were considerably more prone to absence than their Jewish-sector counterparts. They attributed this difference to greater injustice in the Arab-sector educational administration and to greater collectivism among the Arab community.

Johns and Xie (1998) found that Canadian and Chinese workers were equally self-serving, underreporting their own absence and seeing themselves as superior in attendance to their co-workers. However, the Chinese still demonstrated collective solidarity by

viewing their peers' absence as much lower than the occupational norm, a viewpoint not held by the Canadians. Comparing Chinese and Americans, Lam et al. (2002) found that individual power distance, but not country, moderated the connection between distributive justice and absence frequency – the relationship was more strongly negative among those who endorsed low power distance.

Much cross-cultural research is grounded in general cultural values, and Kaiser (1998b) used the economic implications of such values to explain cross-national differences in absence patterns. However, Addae and Johns (2002) argue for a more targeted approach focusing on the perceived legitimacy of absence behavior (Edwards and Whitston, 1993; Harvey and Nicholson, 1999; Johns and Xie, 1998) across cultures. Dealing with particular work behaviors bypasses the generality of distal values for the specificity of more proximal norms. Thus, Johns and Xie (1998) found both similarities and differences in the extent to which Canadians and Chinese endorsed the legitimacy of various reasons for absence. Addae and Johns (2002) present a model of absence that might apply both within and between cultures but that is based on variables that have been shown to vary cross-culturally; these include work centrality, locus of control, time orientation, gender role differentiation, and available social support systems. Addae (2003) showed that these factors varied systematically across nine cultures and that they in turn were associated with perceptions of the legitimacy of absenteeism. Low work centrality, external control, polychronicity, the espousal of gender role differentiation, and low social support were associated with the view that absence was more legitimate.

NONWORK CONTEXT AND ABSENTEEISM

Both Table 1 and the previous discussion of social control highlight the fact that absenteeism is most commonly viewed from an organization-centric perspective. However, the discussion of the cross-cultural aspects of absenteeism suggests the importance of nonwork context on work attendance. Some research has addressed this issue, corresponding to more general calls for greater attention to the impact of context on organizational behavior (Johns, 1991, 2001b, 2006a; Rousseau and Fried, 2001). As will be seen, this research spans contextual stimuli, ranging from the most routine to the most dramatic, from chronic conditions to acute events.

At the more routine end of the scale, Coleman and Schaefer (1990) showed that lower ambient temperature, the occurrence of snowfall, and snow on the ground were associated with elevated absence. However, in a regression equation that accounted for 6 per cent of the variance in absence, it was colder days and fewer hours of sunlight that prevailed in predicting missed shifts. We might wonder if people would be differentially susceptible to such environmental conditions. Indeed, Smith (1977) found that job satisfaction predicted attendance on a single excessively snowy day in Chicago while it did not do so in snow-free New York. Evidently, bad weather removed constraints on acting in line with one's attitudes (cf. Johns, 1991).

Lee et al. (2004) reasoned that people who were more embedded in their local community would be less likely to exhibit voluntary absence so as not to threaten the continuity of their jobs. They supported this prediction and, importantly, illustrated that being embedded in the job was not predictive of absence, showing the relative power of nonwork context for absence. This finding is reminiscent of Morgan and Herman's (1976) earlier research showing that reported nonwork consequences were more predictive of absence than were work consequences. Childcare and eldercare obligations certainly imply potential nonwork consequences, and a small body of research does implicate their contribution to (mostly self-reported) absenteeism (Barling et al., 1994; Bekker et al., 2005; Erickson et al., 2000; Gignac et al., 1996; Hammer et al., 2003).

A longitudinal study of Finnish municipal workers in three towns further illustrates the impact of community influence on absenteeism (Virtanen et al., 2000; Virtanen et al., 2004). Although these workers performed the same work for the same compensation, their absence rates varied remarkably across towns, being highest in the town that was dominated by the working class and lowest in the town dominated by the middle class. Thus, the SES composition of the community overrode the occupational class of the employees, a variable that itself has been repeatedly shown to have a solid inverse relationship with absenteeism. This result is a reminder of the power that ambient social context can hold and a reminder that physical location can be a particularly potent omnibus contextual stimulus (Johns, 2006a). Thus, controlling for a large number of organizational variables, Kristensen et al. (2006) found that being located in Copenhagen was by far the most potent predictor of elevated absence rates among Danish branch banks. They speculated that rural versus urban family patterns or the sheer probability of contracting contagious illnesses might have been the reason. However, the availability of employment opportunities might also have been at play. For instance, Markham (1985) demonstrated that regional unemployment rates were negatively related to absenteeism rates.

Two studies illustrate how acute national events can affect attendance at work, both positing stress related mechanisms. Kushnir et al. (2001) examined absenteeism following the assassination of Israeli Prime Minister Rabin. Those who were more emotionally affected were more likely to go absent, particularly women and those who were pessimistic. Similarly, Byron and Peterson (2002) reported more absence following the 9/11 terrorist attacks among those who experienced more strain.

Gradually unfolding social events can also affect attendance dynamics and views about the behavior. During World War II, absenteeism in U.S. war plants took on the character of a national crisis, being the subject of 510 articles in the *New York Times* between

1941 and 1945. It also figured prominently over the years in the *Times* coverage of the Cold War and various national economic crises and social protest movements (Patton and Johns, under review).

THE ADVENT OF PRESENTEEISM

Although the term presenteeism has been used for a number of years, there has been only recent convergence on two complementary definitions (Johns, 2006b). One of these has to do with the act of going to work despite being ill or otherwise not fit for work (Aronsson et al., 2000; Aronsson and Gustafsson, 2005). The other portrays presenteeism as the individual productivity loss associated with this act (e.g., Burton et al., 2004).

Presenteeism is worth considering in the context of absenteeism for several reasons. First, there is the logical possibility that the act of presenteeism will occur when the option of absenteeism is not available or is perceived to be too costly. Next, it is feasible that presenteeism, most particularly as it represents a productivity decrement, is a precursor of absenteeism in the continuum of withdrawal described earlier. In other words, reducing one's work output is a less extreme step than going absent. Additionally, studying both absenteeism and presenteeism together holds promise for better understanding the process by which people go absent and return to work, fully ready to do so or not. This process is currently not well understood, and gaining insight into the transitions between full engagement and absenteeism would be invaluable. Finally, from an applied standpoint, there is extensive recent research purporting to show that productivity loss due to presenteeism much exceeds that due to absenteeism (e.g., Collins et al., 2005; Goetzel et al., 2004), even though it may have fewer surface manifestations than absence. Thus, researchers are obligated to consider the impact of this hidden sap on organizational effectiveness.

Why would employees attend work despite being unwell? In Swedish studies, personal financial insecurity, a lack of replacement personnel, and membership in care-giving occupations (with obligations to fragile clients) have been implicated (Aronsson et al., 2000; Aronsson and Gustafsson, 2005). A lack of paid sick leave (Lovell, 2004), draconian absence control systems, and team designs (Grinyer and Singleton, 2000) have also been identified. However, the most-speculated cause of presenteeism has been job insecurity stemming from downsizing and contingent, non-permanent (e.g., part time, contracted) work (e.g., Worrall et al., 2000). Unfortunately, almost all of the evidence bearing on this thesis consists of speculation concerning *absenteeism* patterns, and these patterns are not consistent or convincing. Briefly, as reviewed by Johns (2006b) most research on downsizing seems to point to an increase in absenteeism, which is usually attributed to stress mechanisms. Although this increase does not rule out a simultaneous increase in presenteeism, it does violate the most straightforward prediction that insecurity will decrease absenteeism and consequently increase presenteeism. Most research on non-permanent employment does show that non-permanent employees exhibit less absence, and some authors thus infer presenteeism. However, this research neither accounts for employment preferences (e.g., some people prefer part-time work) nor rules out the possibility that secure employment simply elevates absence for personal reasons. In the only studies in this domain that measured presenteeism directly, one detected no difference due to employment status (Aronsson and Gustafsson, 2005), and the other actually found that permanent employees reported engaging in *more* presenteeism (Aronsson et al., 2000). Clearly, more dedicated research on this topic is necessary, with the direct measurement of absenteeism, presenteeism, and employment security being priorities.

Finally, it is interesting to observe that presenteeism cultures have been described that resemble the absence cultures discussed earlier (Dew et al., 2005; Simpson, 1998).

For instance, Simpson described a culture of 'competitive presenteeism' in a firm that had suffered downsizing. Deserved absence was avoided to showcase one's organizational commitment to senior managers. Thus, social control can foster absence or attendance.

MANAGING ABSENTEEISM AND PRESENTEEISM

There has been virtually no research on the management of presenteeism other than clinical trials examining the efficacy of pharmaceutical interventions in reducing productivity loss. However, Johansson and Lundberg (2004) found only weak associations between self-reported adjustment latitude (the ability to alter work practices or output in the face of unwellness) and presenteeism. They note, though, that employees with such latitude might be less inclined to see themselves as unwell.

Table 2 summarizes the results of meta-analyses that estimate the effects of various organizational policies and practices on absenteeism. Perhaps the most noteworthy aspect of this table is the clear impact of various organizational controls on absence (Farrell and Stamm, 1988). These include practices such as limiting sick days, disciplining absence, and rewarding good attendance (e.g., Dalton and Mesch, 1991). These results show that absence behavior is malleable, and that organizations 'get what they ask for' when it comes to attendance. It does require mention that poorly designed control systems have occasionally been documented in the literature, however, and one suspects that many more exist. Common errors include draconian punishment for lateness, excessive concern with the number of absence incidents as opposed to total time lost (Grinyer and Singleton, 2000), and provisions requiring several day's absence for sick leave to take effect (Nicholson, 1976). Each of these policies can encourage elevated absenteeism. Some circumstantial proof of the tendency for potential lateness to get converted into absence is seen in the good performance of

flextime in reducing absenteeism. Although employees like compressed work weeks, they do nothing to stem absence, probably due to the fatigue factor associated with longer work days (Baltes et al., 1999). Lower back pain accounts for considerable absenteeism (and presenteeism), so the overall results for back pain interventions are disappointing. However, there is substantial variation across interventions, with exercise and reduced bed rest showing the best results ($r_c = -0.18$) (Martocchio et al., 2000).

The results shown in Table 2 are encouraging in that the use of one intervention does not rule out the use of others, and the mechanisms underlying them are unlikely to share much common variance. However, one gets the distinct impression that attendance management has not been much informed by the more recent absence research or by contemporary workplace themes. Conspicuously missing is the incorporation of the convincing evidence on the social control of absence. However, Gaudine and Saks (2001) did report on the effectiveness of a simple absence feedback mechanism (providing self and peer-average data) that capitalized on people's aforementioned tendency to underestimate their own absence and to hold an unrealistically positive view of their attendance compared to that of their work peers.

Harrison et al. (2000) submit that there are forces for improved attendance in contemporary organizations (the need for speed, quality, service, and teamwork) and countervailing forces that have shown a demonstrated connection with increased absence (downsizing, psychological contract breach, childcare, and eldercare). In consequence, they argue for the fostering of a culture of 'managed attendance' that recognizes that some absence is inevitable while fostering accountability for good attendance. Key elements include selecting employees prone to good attendance, providing them with repeated feedback about their attendance, and allowing more flexible, indigenous management of absence at the work unit level.

CONCLUSION

In comprehensive, independent reviews of the literature, both Harrison and Martocchio (1998) and Johns (1997) remarked on the vibrancy and cumulative progress of absenteeism research. A decade later, this chapter illustrates that this positive trend continues, particularly with the addition of presenteeism to the attendance research agenda. Multidisciplinary interest, an unusual variety of research methods, and welcome freedom from domination by a particular theory, paradigm, or research group have contributed to this progress (Johns, 1997, 2001, 2003). For instance, absence research (e.g., Mathieu and Kohler, 1990) pioneered the formal application of cross-level methods in organizational behavior.

For the continuity of this success, there are some avenues of research that show particular promise, and I highlight a few here.

- More attention needs to be devoted to the changing employment landscape, considering how restructuring, contingent employment, and emerging work design affect attendance dynamics. For instance, the apparent tendency for downsizing to stimulate absence and contingent employment to curtail it requires reconciliation with the prevalent idea that both conditions evoke employee insecurity. Harrison et al. (2000) have speculated about how factors such as telecommuting require a reconsideration of traditional conceptions of absenteeism. The changing nature of work is in part a function of nonwork matters, and more sophisticated research attention needs to be devoted as to how childcare and eldercare affect attendance.
- The aforementioned associations among absenteeism, lateness, turnover and performance (e.g., Harrison at al., 2006) need to be better understood. This is especially so if presenteeism is added to the mix. Viewing these behaviors as manifestations of some higher order construct does not obviate interest in their discrete connections. This applies especially to transitions between the behaviors and the conditions under which one behavior can substitute functionally for another.
- Absence research has not profited nearly enough from the recognition that behavior is a joint function of the person and the situation. Just who is likely to go absent, or be present while ill, and under what circumstances, is of great interest (e.g., Elovainio et al., 2003).
- There is a desperate need for organizational behavior scholars to take an interest in presenteeism and for better linkage between absenteeism and presenteeism research. Currently, almost all presenteeism research is conducted by scholars in medicine, epidemiology, and occupational health. Dedicated to showing the connection between various medical conditions and productivity reduction, this work is strikingly atheoretical and oblivious to the likely psychosocial contributors to both presenteeism and its biased self-report.

As can be seen from this short list of research avenues, there is plenty grist for the continued contribution of absence research to understanding organizational behavior.

ACKNOWLEDGEMENTS

Preparation of this chapter was supported by grants 410-2003-0630 and 410-2003-1014 from the Social Sciences and Humanities Research Council of Canada.

REFERENCES

Addae, H.M. (2003) *Dimensions, antecedents and consequences of absence legitimacy: From theory to empirical evidence in a nine–nation study.* Unpublished doctoral thesis, Concordia University, Montreal.

Addae, H.M. and Johns, G. (2002) 'National culture and perceptions of absence legitimacy', in M. Koslowsky and M. Krausz (eds), *Voluntary Employee Withdrawal and Inattendance: A Current Perspective.* New York: Kluwer/Plenum, pp. 21–51.

Akyeampong, E.B. (2005) 'Work absences', *Statistics Canada Perspectives*, 75–84.

Aronsson, G., Gustafsson, K. and Dallner, M. (2000) 'Sick but yet at work: An empirical study of sickness presenteeism', *Journal of Epidemiology and Community Health*, 54: 502–509.

Aronsson, G. and Gustafsson, K. (2005) 'Sickness presenteeism: Prevalence, attendance–pressure factors, and an outline of a model for research',

Journal of Occupational and Environmental Medicine, 47: 958–966.

Austin, J.T. and Villanova, P. (1992) 'The criterion problem: 1917–1992', *Journal of Applied Psychology*, 77: 836–874.

Baltes, B.B., Briggs, T.E., Huff, J.W., Wright, J.A. and Neuman, G.A. (1999) 'Flexible and compressed workweek schedules: A meta–analysis of their effects on work–related criteria', *Journal of Applied Psychology*, 84: 496–513.

Barker, J.R. (1993) 'Tightening the iron cage: Concertive control in self–managing teams', *Administrative Science Quarterly*, 38: 408–437.

Barling, J., MacEwen, K.E., Kelloway, E.K. and Higginbottom, S.F. (1994) 'Predictors and outcomes of elder–care–based interrole conflict', *Psychology and Aging*, 9: 391–397.

Bekker, M.H.J., Croon, M.A. and Bressers, B. (2005) 'Childcare involvement, job characteristics, gender and work attitudes as predictors of emotional exhaustion and sickness absence', *Work and Stress*, 19: 221–237.

Blau, G. (1998) 'On the aggregation of individual withdrawal behaviors into larger multi–item constructs', *Journal of Organizational Behavior*, 19: 437–451.

Brenner, M.H. (1968) 'Use of high school data to predict work performance', *Journal of Applied Psychology*, 52: 29–30.

Brief, A.P. and Weiss, H.M. (2002) 'Organizational behavior: Affect in the workplace', *Annual Review of Psychology*, 53: 279–307.

Burton, W.N., Pransky, G., Conti, D.J., Chen, C-Y. and Edington, D.W. (2004) 'The association of medical conditions and presenteeism', *Journal of Occupational and Environmental Medicine*, 46, 6 suppl: S38–S45.

Bycio, P. (1992) 'Job performance and absenteeism: A review and meta–analysis', *Human Relations*, 45: 193–220.

Byron, K. and Peterson, S. (2002) 'The impact of a large-scale traumatic event on individual and organizational outcomes: Exploring employee and company reactions to September 11, 2001', *Journal of Organizational Behavior*, 23: 895–910.

Chadwick-Jones, J.K., Nicholson, N. and Brown, C. (1982) *Social Psychology of Absenteeism*. New York: Prager.

Coleman, D.F. and Schaefer, N.V. (1990) 'Weather and absenteeism', *Canadian Journal of Administrative Sciences*, 7 (4): 35–42.

Collins, J.J., Baase, C.M., Sharda, C.E., Ozminkowski, R.J., Nicholson, S., Billotti, G.M., et al. (2005) 'The assessment of chronic health conditions on work performance, absence, and total economic impact for employers', *Journal of Occupational and Environmental Medicine*, 47: 547–557.

Colquitt, J.A., Conlon, D.E., Wesson, M.J., Porter, C.O.L.H. and Ng, K.Y. (2001) 'Justice at the millennium: A meta–analytic review of 25 years of justice research', *Journal of Applied Psychology*, 86: 425–445.

Colquitt, J.A., Noe, R.A. and Jackson, C.L. (2002) 'Justice in teams: Antecedents and consequences of procedural justice climate', *Personnel Psychology*, 55: 83–109.

Conte, J.M. and Jacobs, R.R. (2003) 'Validity evidence linking polychronicity and big five personality dimensions to lateness, absence, and supervisory performance ratings', *Human Performance*, 16: 107–129.

Côté, D. and Haccoun, R.R. (1991) 'L'absentéisme des femmes et des hommes: Une méta-analyse', *Canadian Journal of Administrative Sciences*, 8: 130–139.

Dalton, D.R. and Mesch, D.J. (1991) 'On the extent and reduction of avoidable absenteeism: An assessment of absence policy provisions', *Journal of Applied Psychology*, 76: 810–817.

Darr, W. and Johns, G. (in press) 'Work strain, health, and absenteeism from work: A meta–analysis', *Journal of Occupational Health Psychology*.

De Boer, E.M., Bakker, A.B., Syroit, J.E. and Schaufeli, W.B. (2002) 'Unfairness at work as a predictor of absenteeism', *Journal of Organizational Behavior*, 23: 181–197.

Deery, S.J., Iverson, R.D. and Walsh, J.T. (2006) 'Toward a better understanding of psychological contract breach: A study of customer service employees', *Journal of Applied Psychology*, 91: 166–175.

Dew, K., Keefe, V. and Small, K. (2005) ' "Choosing" to work when sick: Workplace presenteeism', *Social Science and Medicine*, 60: 2273–2282.

Dineen, B.R., Noe, R.A., Shaw, J.D., Duffy, M.K. and Wiethoff, C. (2007) 'Level and dispersion of satisfaction in teams: Using foci and social context to explain the satisfaction-absenteeism relationship', *Academy of Management Journal*, 50: 623–643.

Duffy, M.K., Shaw, J.D. and Stark, E.M. (2000) 'Performance and satisfaction in conflicted interdependent groups: When and how does self-esteem make a difference?' *Academy of Management Journal*, 43: 772–782.

Edwards, P. and Whitston, C. (1993) *Attending to Work: The Management of Attendance and Shopfloor Order*. Oxford: Blackwell.

Edwards, P.K. and Scullion, H. (1982) *The Social Organization of Industrial Conflict: Control and Resistance in the Workplace*. Oxford: Blackwell.

Elovainio, M., Kivimäki, M., Vahtera, J., Virtanen, M. and Keltikangas-Järvinen, L. (2003) 'Personality as a moderator in the relations between perceptions of organizational justice and sickness absence', *Journal of Vocational Behavior*, 63: 379–395.

Erickson, R.J., Nichols, L. and Ritter, C. (2000) 'Family influences on absenteeism: Testing an expanded process model', *Journal of Vocational Behavior*, 57: 246–272.

Farrell, D. and Stamm, C.L. (1988) 'Meta–analysis of the correlates of employee absence', *Human Relations*, 41: 211–227.

Fox, J.B. and Scott, J.F. (1943) *Absenteeism: Management's Problem*. Cambridge, MA: Harvard Business School.

Fried, Y., Melamed, S. and Ben–David, H.A. (2002) 'The joint effects of noise, job complexity, and gender on employee sickness absence: An exploratory study across 21 organizations—the CORDIS study', *Journal of Occupational and Organizational Psychology*, 75: 131–144.

Gaudine, A.P. and Saks, A.M. (2001) 'Effects of an absenteeism feedback intervention on employee absence behavior', *Journal of Organizational Behavior*, 22: 15–29.

Gellatly, I.R. (1995) 'Individual and group determinants of employee absenteeism: Test of a causal model', *Journal of Organizational Behavior*, 16: 469–485.

Gellatly, I.R. and Luchak, A.A. (1998) 'Personal and organizational determinants of perceived absence norms', *Human Relations*, 51: 1085–1102.

George, J.M. (1989) 'Mood and absence', *Journal of Applied Psychology*, 74: 317–324.

George, J.M. (1990) 'Personality, affect, and behavior in groups', *Journal of Applied Psychology*, 75: 107–116.

Geurts, S., Schaufeli, W.B. and Rutte, C.G. (1999) 'Absenteeism, turnover intention and inequity in the employment relationship', *Work and Stress*, 13: 253–267.

Gignac, M.A.M., Kelloway, E.K. and Gottlieb, B.H. (1996) 'The impact of caregiving on employment: A mediational model of work-family conflict', *Canadian Journal on Aging*, 15: 525–542.

Goetzel, R.Z., Long, S.R., Ozminkowski, R.J., Hawkins, K., Wang, S. and Lynch, W. (2004) 'Health, absence, disability, and presenteeism cost estimates of certain physical and mental health conditions affecting U.S. employees', *Journal of Occupational and Environmental Medicine*, 46, 398–412.

Goldberg, C.B. and Waldman, D.A. (2000) 'Modeling employee absenteeism: Testing alternative measures and mediated effects based on job satisfaction', *Journal of Organizational Behavior*, 21: 665–676.

Griffeth, R.W., Hom, P.W. and Gaertner, S. (2000) 'A meta-analysis of antecedents and correlates of employee turnover: Update, moderator tests, and research implications for the next millennium', *Journal of Management*, 26: 463–488.

Grinyer, A. and Singleton, V. (2000) 'Sickness absence as risk-taking behaviour: A study of organizational and cultural factors in the public sector', *Health, Risk and Society*, 2: 7–21.

Hackett, R.D. (1989) 'Work attitudes and employee absenteeism: A synthesis of the literature', *Journal of Occupational Psychology*, 62: 235–248.

Hackett, R.D. (1990) 'Age, tenure, and employee absenteeism', *Human Relations*, 43: 610–619.

Hackett, R.D. and Guion, R.M. (1985) 'A reevaluation of the absenteeism-job satisfaction relationship', *Organizational Behavior and Human Decision Processes*, 35: 340–381.

Hammer, L.B., Bauer, T.N. and Grandey, A.A. (2003) 'Work-family conflict and work-related withdrawal behaviors', *Journal of Business and Psychology*, 17: 419–436.

Hanisch, K.A., Hulin, C.L. and Roznowski, M. (1998) 'The importance of individuals' repertoires of behaviors: The scientific appropriateness of studying multiple behaviors and general attitudes', *Journal of Organizational Behavior*, 19: 463–480.

Harrison, D.A., Johns, G. and Martocchio, J.J. (2000) 'Changes in technology, teamwork, and diversity: New directions for a new century of absenteeism research', *Research in Personnel and Human Resources Management*, 18: 43–91.

Harrison, D.A. and Martocchio, J.J. (1998) 'A time for absenteeism: A 20-year review of origins, offshoots, and outcomes', *Journal of Management*, 24: 305–350.

Harrison, D.A., Newman, D.A. and Roth, P.L. (2006) 'How important are job attitudes? Meta-analytic comparisons of integrative behavioral outcomes and time sequences', *Academy of Management Journal*, 49: 305–325.

Harrison, D.A. and Price, K.H. (2003) 'Context and consistency in absenteeism: Studying social and dispositional influences across multiple settings', *Human Resource Management Review*, 13: 203–225.

Harrison, D.A. and Shaffer, M.A. (1994) 'Comparative examinations of self-reports and perceived absenteeism norms: Wading through Lake Wobegon', *Journal of Applied Psychology*, 79: 240–251.

Harvey, J. and Nicholson, N. (1999) 'Minor illness as a legitimate reason for absence', *Journal of Organizational Behavior*, 20: 979–993.

Hattrup, K., O'Connell, M.S. and Wingate, P.H. (1998) 'Prediction of multidimensional criteria: Distinguishing task and contextual performance', *Human Performance*, 11: 305–319.

Hill, J.M.M. and Trist, E.L. (1953) 'A consideration of industrial accidents as a means of withdrawal from the work situations', *Human Relations*, 6: 357–380.

Hill, J.M.M. and Trist, E.L. (1955) 'Changes in accidents and other absences with length of service', *Human Relations*, 8: 121–152.

Hirschfeld, R.P., Schmitt, L.P. and Bedeian, A.G. (2002) 'Job content perceptions, performance-reward expectancies, and absenteeism among low-wage public-sector clerical employees', *Journal of Business and Psychology*, 16: 553–564.

Humphrey, S.E., Nahrgang, J.D. and Morgeson, F.P. (2007) 'Integrating motivational, social, and contextual work design features: A meta-analytic summary and theoretical extension of the work design literature', *Journal of Applied Psychology*, 92: 1332–1356.

Ivancevich, J.M. (1985) 'Predicting absenteeism from prior absence and work attitudes', *Academy of Management Journal*, 28: 219–228.

Iverson, R.D., Buttigieg, D.M. and Maguire, C. (2003) 'Absence culture: The effects of union membership status and union-management climate', *Relations Industrielles*, 58: 483–514.

Iverson, R.D. and Deery, S.J. (2001) 'Understanding the "personological" basis of employee withdrawal: The influence of affective disposition on employee tardiness, early departure, and absenteeism', *Journal of Applied Psychology*, 86: 856–866.

Iverson, R.D., Olekalns, M. and Erwin, P.J. (1998) 'Affectivity, organizational stressors, and absenteeism: A causal model of burnout and its consequences', *Journal of Vocational Behavior*, 52: 1–23.

Jackson, S.E. and Schuler, R.S. (1985) 'A meta-analysis and conceptual critique of research on role ambiguity and role conflict in work settings', *Organizational Behavior and Human Decision Processes*, 36: 16–78.

Johansson, G. and Lundberg, I. (2004) 'Adjustment latitude and attendance requirements as determinants of sickness absence or attendance. Empirical tests of the illness flexibility model', *Social Science and Medicine*, 58: 1857–1868.

Johns, G. (1991) 'Substantive and methodological constraints on behavior and attitudes in organizational research', *Organizational Behavior and Human Decision Processes*, 49: 80–104.

Johns, G. (1994a) 'Absenteeism estimates by employees and managers: Divergent perspectives and self-serving perceptions', *Journal of Applied Psychology*, 79: 229–239.

Johns, G. (1994b) 'How often were you absent? A review of the use of self–reported absence data', *Journal of Applied Psychology*, 79: 574–591.

Johns, G. (1994c) 'Medical, ethical, and cultural constraints on work absence and attendance', Presentation at the International Congress of Applied Psychology, Madrid.

Johns, G. (1997) 'Contemporary research on absence from work: Correlates, causes and consequences', *International Review of Industrial and Organizational Psychology*, 12: 115–174.

Johns, G. (1998) 'Aggregation or aggravation? The relative merits of a broad withdrawal construct', *Journal of Organizational Behavior*, 19: 453–462.

Johns, G. (2001a) 'The psychology of lateness, absenteeism, and turnover', in N. Anderson, D.S. Ones, H.K. Sinangil, and C. Viswesvaran (eds), *Handbook of Industrial, Work and Organizational Psychology*. London: Sage. Vol 2, pp. 232–252.

Johns, G. (2001b) 'In praise of context', *Journal of Organizational Behavior*, 22: 31–42.

Johns, G. (2002) 'Absenteeism and mental health', in J.C. Thomas and M. Hersen (eds), *Handbook of Mental Health in the Workplace*. Thousand Oaks, CA: Sage, pp. 437–455.

Johns, G. (2003) 'How methodological diversity has improved our understanding of absenteeism from work', *Human Resource Management Review*, 13: 157–184.

Johns, G. (2006a) 'The essential impact of context on organizational behavior', *Academy of Management Review*, 31: 386–408.

Johns, G. (2006b) 'Presenteeism at work: An introduction for psychologists', Presentation at the annual convention of the Canadian Psychological Association, Calgary, Alberta.

Johns, G. and Nicholson, N. (1982) 'The meanings of absence: New strategies for theory and research', *Research in Organizational Behavior*, 4: 127–172.

Johns, G. and Xie, J.L. (1998) 'Perceptions of absence from work: People's Republic of China versus Canada', *Journal of Applied Psychology*, 83: 515–530.

Johnson, J.L. and O'Leary-Kelly, A.M. (2003) 'The effects of psychological contract breach on cynicism: Not all social exchange violations are created equal', *Journal of Organizational Behavior*, 24: 627–647.

Judge, T.A. and Bono, J.E. (2001) 'Relationship of core self-evaluation traits – self-esteem, generalized self-efficacy, locus of control, and emotional stability – with job satisfaction and job performance: A meta–analysis', *Journal of Applied Psychology*, 86: 80–92.

Judge, T.A., Martocchio, J.J. and Thoresen, C.J. (1997) 'Five–factor model of personality and employee absence', *Journal of Applied Psychology*, 82: 745–755.

Kaiser, C.P. (1998a) 'What do we know about employee absence behavior? An interdisciplinary interpretation', *Journal of Socio-Economics*, 27: 79–96.

Kaiser, C.P. (1998b) 'Dimensions of culture, distributive principles, and decommodification: Implications for employee absence behavior', *Journal of Socio-Economics*, 27: 551–564.

Kornhauser, A.W. and Sharp, A.A. (1932) 'Employee attitudes: Suggestions from a study in a factory', *Personnel Journal*, 10: 393–401.

Koslowsky, M., Sagie, A., Krausz, M. and Singer, A.D. (1997) 'Correlates of employee lateness: Some theoretical considerations', *Journal of Applied Psychology*, 82: 79–88.

Kristensen, K., Juhl, H.J., Eskildsen, J., Nielsen, J., Frederiksen, N. and Bisgaard, C. (2006) 'Determinants of absenteeism in a large Danish bank', *International Journal of Human Resource Management*, 17: 1645–1658.

Kushnir, T., Fried, Y. and Malkinson, R. (2001) 'Work absence as a function of a national traumatic event: The case of Prime Minister Rabin's assassination', *Work and Stress*, 15: 265–273.

Kuzmits, F.E. (1995) 'Differences in incidences of absenteeism and discipline between Vietnamese and non-Vietnamese employees', *The International Journal of Organizational Analysis*, 3: 303–313.

Lam, S.S.K., Schaubroeck, J. and Aryee, S. (2002) 'Relationship between organizational justice and employee work outcomes: A cross-national study', *Journal of Organizational Behavior*, 23: 1–18.

LeBreton, J.M., Binning, J.F., Adorno, A.J. and Melcher, K.M. (2004) 'Importance of personality and job-specific affect for predicting job attitudes and withdrawal behavior', *Organizational Research Methods*, 7: 300–325.

Lee, T.W., Mitchell, T.R., Sablynski, C.J., Burton, J.P. and Holtom, B.C. (2004) 'The effects of job embeddedness on organizational citizenship, job performance, volitional absences, and voluntary turnover', *Academy of Management Journal*, 47: 711–722.

Lovell, V. (2004) *No Time to be Sick: Why Everyone Suffers When Workers Don't Have Paid Sick Leave.* Washington, DC: Institute for Women's Policy Research.

Markham, S.E. (1985) 'An investigation of the relationship between unemployment and absenteeism: A multi–level approach', *Academy of Management Journal*, 28: 228–234.

Markham, S.E. and McKee, G.H. (1995) 'Group absence behavior and standards: A multilevel analysis', *Academy of Management Journal*, 38: 1174–1190.

Martocchio, J.J. (1994) 'The effects of absence culture on individual absence', *Human Relations*, 47: 243–262.

Martocchio, J.J., Harrison, D.A. and Berkson, H. (2000) 'Connections between lower back pain, interventions, and absence from work: A time-based meta-analysis', *Personnel Psychology*, 53: 595–624.

Martocchio, J.J., and Jimeno, D.I. (2003) 'Employee absenteeism as an affective event', *Human Resource Management Review*, 13: 227–241.

Mason, C.M. and Griffin, M.A. (2003) 'Group absenteeism and positive affective tone: A longitudinal study', *Journal of Organizational Behavior*, 24: 667–687.

Mathieu, J.E. and Kohler, S.S. (1990) 'A cross–level examination of group absence influences on individual absence', *Journal of Applied Psychology*, 75: 217–220.

Mathieu, J.E. and Zajac, D.M. (1990) 'A review and meta-analysis of the antecedents, correlates, and consequences of organizational commitment', *Psychological Bulletin*, 108: 171–194.

McShane, S.L. (1984) 'Job satisfaction and absenteeism: A meta-analytic re-examination', *Canadian Journal of Administrative Sciences*, 1 (1): 61–77.

Meyer, J.P., Stanley, D.J., Herscovitch, L. and Topolnytsky, L. (2002) 'Affective, normative, and continuance commitment: A meta–analysis of antecedents, correlates, and consequences', *Journal of Vocational Behavior*, 61: 20–52.

Mitra, A., Jenkins, G.D., Jr. and Gupta, N. (1992) 'A meta–analytic review of the relationship between absence and turnover', *Journal of Applied Psychology*, 77: 879–889.

Morgan, L.G. and Herman, J.B. (1976) 'Perceived consequences of absenteeism', *Journal of Applied Psychology*, 61: 738–742.

Nicholson, N. (1976) 'Management sanctions and absence control', *Human Relations*, 29: 139–151.

Nicholson, N., Brown, C.A. and Chadwick-Jones, J.K. (1976) 'Absence from work and job satisfaction', *Journal of Applied Psychology*, 61: 728–737.

Nicholson, N. and Johns, G. (1985) 'The absence culture and the psychological contract – Who's in control of absence?' *Academy of Management Review*, 10: 397–407.

Ng, T.W.H., Sorensen, K.L. and Eby, L.T. (2006) 'Locus of control at work: A meta-analysis', *Journal of Organizational Behavior*, 27: 1057–1087.

Ones, D.S., Viswesvaran, C. and Schmidt, F.L. (2003) 'Personality and absenteeism: A meta-analysis of integrity tests', *European Journal of Personality*, 17: S19–S38.

Patton, E. and Johns, G. (under review) 'Absenteeism in the news: Historical trends in absence from work in the 20th century'. Manuscript under review.

Pelled, L.H. and Xin, K.R. (1999) 'Down and out: An investigation of the relationship between mood and employee withdrawal behavior', *Journal of Management*, 25: 875–895.

Rentsch, J.R. and Steel, R.P. (1998) 'Testing the durability of job characteristics as predictors of absenteeism over a six-year period', *Personnel Psychology*, 51: 165–190.

Rentsch, J.R. and Steel, R.P. (2003) 'What does unit–level absence mean? Issues for future unit-level absence research', *Human Resource Management review*, 13: 185–202.

Rosenblatt, Z. and Shirom, A. (2006) 'School ethnicity and governance influences on work absence of teachers and school administrators', *Educational Administration Quarterly*, 42: 361–384.

Rosse, J.G. and Miller, H.E. (1984) 'Relationship between absenteeism and other employee behaviors', in P.S. Goodman and R.S. Atkin (eds), A*bsenteeism: New Approaches to Understanding, Measuring, and Managing Employee Absence*. San Francisco: Jossey-Bass, pp. 194–228.

Rousseau, D.M. and Fried, Y. (2001) 'Location, location, location: Contextualizing organizational research', *Journal of Organizational Behavior*, 22: 1–13.

Sanders, K. (2004) 'Playing truant within organisations: Informal relationships, work ethics and absenteeism', *Journal of Managerial Psychology*, 19: 136–155.

Schenet, N.G. (1945) 'An analysis of absenteeism in one war plant', *Journal of Applied Psychology*, 29: 27–29.

Schmidt, K-H. (2002) 'Organisationales und individu-elles abwesenheitsverhalten: Ein cross–level studie', *Zeitschrift für Arbeits–und Organisationpsychologie*, 46: 69–77.

Shirom, A. and Rosenblatt, Z. (2006) 'A panel study of the effects of school positions and promotions on absenteeism in the teaching profession', *Journal of Occupational and Organizational Psychology*, 79: 623–644.

Simpson, R. (1998) 'Presenteeism, power and organi-zational change: Long hours as a career barrier and the impact on the working lives of women managers', *British Journal of Management*, 9: S37–S50.

Smith, F.J. (1977) 'Work attitudes as predictors of attendance on a specific day', *Journal of Applied Psychology*, 62: 16–19.

Sturges, J., Conway, N., Guest, D. and Liefooghe, A. (2005) 'Managing the career deal: The psychological contract as a framework for understanding career management, organizational commitment, and work behavior', *Journal of Organizational Behavior*, 26: 821–838.

Tansey, R.R. and Hyman, M.R. (1992) 'Public relations, advocacy ads, and the campaign against absenteeism during World War II', *Business and Professional Ethics Journal*, 11: 129–164.

van Dierendonck, D., Schaufeli, W.B. and Buunk, B.P. (1998) 'The evaluation of an individual burnout intervention program: The role of inequity and social support', *Journal of Applied Psychology*, 83: 392–407.

Van Yperen, N.W., Hagedoorn, M. and Geurts, S.A.E. (1996) 'Intent to leave and absenteeism as reactions to perceived inequity: The role of psychological and social constraints', *Journal of Occupational and Organizational Psychology*, 69: 367–372.

Virtanen, P., Nakari, R., Ahonen, H., Vahtera, J. and Pentii, J. (2000) 'Locality and habitus: The origins of sickness absence practices', *Social Science & Medicine*, 50: 27–39.

Virtanen, P., Vahtera, J., Nakari, J., Pentti, J. and Kivimäki, M. (2004) 'Economy and job contract as contexts of sickness absence practices: Revisiting locality and habitus', *Social Science & Medicine*, 58: 1219–1229.

Williams, M.L., McDaniel, M.A. and Nguyen, N.T. (2006) 'A meta–analysis of the antecedents and consequences of pay level satisfaction', *Journal of Applied Psychology*, 91: 392–413.

Xie, J.L. and Johns, G. (2000) 'Interactive effects of absence culture salience and group cohesiveness: A multi-level and cross-level analysis of work absenteeism in the Chinese context', *Journal of Occupational and Organizational Psychology*, 73: 31–52.

10

Job Insecurity

Tahira M. Probst

INTRODUCTION

Commercial rivalries around the globe, government deregulation of industry, and the increasing pace of organizational technology change have led to widespread corporate layoffs, workplace restructuring, and the increasing use of a contingent workforce. These phenomena virtually ensure that the employees of the new millennium will experience a substantially different workplace environment than employees in decades past. Specifically, today's worker must contend with the reality of rising job insecurity.

According to the Society for Human Resource Management (2001), 43 percent of US organizations conducted employee layoffs in 2000 and 2001 (prior to the events of September 11), with corporate reductions averaging 10–13 percent of the workforce. Since then, annual layoffs within the US have hovered around 1 million permanent separations per year (Bureau of Labor Statistics, 2006). As a result, a large proportion of today's workforce is concerned about losing their job. Whereas only 11 percent of workers reported being fearful of involuntary job loss during the recession years of the early 1990s,

37 percent of workers were fearful of being laid off in the near future during the boom years of the late 1990s (Belton, 1999). Not surprisingly, the proportion of workers who reported being satisfied with their job security fell 10 percent from 1992 to 1996 with fewer than 50 percent of workers indicating they were satisfied with their job security (Organization for Economic Cooperation and Development [OECD], 1997).

These numbers are not unique to the US. Similar results exist in European nations where unemployment rates have been high for more than a decade. For example, between 1985 and 1995, an OECD study found a 12 percent decline in the proportion of surveyed European employees who felt their jobs were secure. Such trends have emerged in Asia. Of particular note, the Chinese economy has undergone significant reform during the past two decades, shifting away from the 'iron rice bowl' policy of lifetime employment to a market-oriented economy (Rust et al., 2003), which have had a significant impact on the employment security of Chinese workers who represent approximately 20 percent of the global workforce. Implementing plans to close or restructure all insolvent state industries, the Chinese government has laid off more than 17 million employees of state-owned enterprises, representing more than 20 percent of such employees (Rust et al., 2003).

Statistics alone, however, cannot fully capture the extent of job insecurity felt by today's employees. While the number of employee layoffs is relatively easy to track, it is much harder to quantify the extent to which employees are concerned that their job will be the next slated for 'right-sizing.' Nevertheless, based on the surveys described above, one can conclude that a significant portion of today's workforce is worried about their job security (OECD, 1997).

The purpose of this chapter is to provide an overview of research in the area of job insecurity. Although there are many topics closely related to job insecurity (e.g., under-employment, downsizing, unemployment and employment security), a broader discussion of economic stressors is beyond the scope of this chapter (see Probst, 2005 for a review). Therefore, we will begin by describing the results of seminal research in the area, and then discuss more recent research advances. Next, while interest in job insecurity as a research topic has grown, there are still many conceptual and theoretical debates that need to be resolved before the field can meaningfully progress. Finally, some of the emerging research trends among job insecurity researchers will be described and avenues for further research agendas will be proposed.

THE EARLY YEARS OF JOB INSECURITY RESEARCH

Without a doubt, the seminal article by Greenhalgh and Rosenblatt published in *Academy of Management Review* (1984) was the driving force behind the explosion of job insecurity research that was to follow in the next two decades. In that article, Greenhalgh and Rosenblatt proposed a theoretical model of the antecedents and consequences of job insecurity that would heavily influence the future research agenda in this area. In their model, they proposed that objective threats to the job security of individual employees (such as a planned reorganization, technological change, or impending layoffs) lead to intended organizational messages, unintended organizational clues, and the rise of rumors. Such messages result in a subjective threat experienced by employees, who could differ in the perceived severity of the threat and the level of powerlessness that employees feel they have to combat the threat. Higher levels of subjective job insecurity were then proposed to result in decreased work effort, higher turnover intentions, and an increased resistance to change – all of which would lead to an overall reduction in organizational effectiveness (e.g., productivity, adaptability). The extent to which workers perceive and react to a subjective threat was proposed to be moderated by a number of individual differences moderators, such as need for security, locus of control, and occupational mobility.

Shortly after the publication of this article, Ashford et al. (1989) reported the development of a multidimensional measure of job insecurity based on the Greenhalgh and Rosenblatt model, which defined job insecurity as the 'perceived powerlessness to maintain desired continuity in a threatened job situation' (p. 438). The 57-item measure (the Job Insecurity Scale; JIS) assessed job insecurity by measuring:

(1) the range of work situation features that could be in jeopardy;
(2) the valence of each such feature;
(3) the subjective probability of losing each feature; and
(4) the number of sources of threat.

Thus, job insecurity $= [(\Sigma$ importance of job feature $\times$ likelihood of losing job feature) $+ (\Sigma$ importance of job loss $\times$ likelihood of job loss)] $\times$ perceived powerlessness to resist threat (Ashford et al., 1989).

Using the JIS, Ashford et al. conducted one of the first comprehensive tests of the Greenhalgh and Rosenblatt model, finding that the purported antecedents (anticipated organizational change, role ambiguity, and locus of control) accounted for 34 percent of the variance in job insecurity perceptions, and that job insecurity explained on average 14 percent of the variability in outcomes such as turnover intentions, organizational commitment, and job satisfaction.

Other early job insecurity research continued in this vein, primarily focusing on individual correlates and outcomes of insecurity. Such research found that the effects of job insecurity were pervasive, overwhelmingly negative, and could be organized into three primary categories: attitudinal outcomes, behavioral outcomes, and physical and mental health outcomes.

Attitudinal and behavioral outcomes

Research has consistently shown that employees who perceive their jobs to be insecure report more negative job-related attitudes and lower levels of job satisfaction than secure employees (e.g., Büssing, 1986; Davy et al., 1998; Grunberg et al., 1998; Lim, 1996; Roskies and Louis-Guerin, 1990). In a study of a state government multi-agency reorganization, Probst (1998) also found that employees reported more negative affective reactions to the intended plans for organizational change when they were concerned about their job insecurity. Early research also consistently found that organizational commitment was adversely affected by employee perceptions of job insecurity (Armstrong-Stassen, 1998; Borg and Elizur, 1992; Davy et al., 1998; Probst, 1998). Researchers theorized that this was due to a breach of the traditional psychological contract of loyalty and hard work in exchange for a secure job (Hallier and Lyon, 1996). If a job was no longer perceived to be secure, then employees were no longer willing to maintain commitment to that organization. Not surprisingly, these negative attitudes mediated the effects of job insecurity on work-related behaviors and outcomes such as turnover intentions (Davy et al. (1998), work withdrawal behaviors (Probst, 1998),

and measures of performance (Abramis, 1994; Brockner et al., 1992).

Physical and mental health outcomes

In addition to adverse effects on employee attitudes and behaviors, data from as early as the 1970s suggested that job insecurity could also negatively effect employee health outcomes. Cobb (1974) found that the stress of possible job termination was associated with significant increases in norepinephrine excretion, serum creatinine, serum uric acid, and serum cholesterol. Research since then has replicated the finding that employees with low job security report a greater incidence of physical health problems (Cottington et al., 1986; Dooley et al., 1987; Kuhnert et al., 1989; Probst, 2000, 2002a, 2003b; Roskies and Louis-Guerin, 1990), have higher levels of blood pressure and cholesterol levels (Pollard, 2001), and an increased incidence of ischemic heart disease (Siegrist et al., 1990). Recent research suggests that one mechanism for these adverse physical effects may be body-mass-index (BMI) of insecure employees. Hannerz et al. (2004) found that job insecurity led to further weight gain among already obese employees, but was related to additional weight loss among low BMI employees. Thus, when exposed to the stress of job insecurity, employees who already overeat may do so even more, whereas underweight employees may begin to have diets that are nutritionally deficient.

In addition to physical consequences, job insecurity has also been associated with higher levels of general psychological distress (Dekker and Schaufeli, 1995; Probst, 2000, 2002a, 2003b) and increased medical consultations for psychological distress (Catalano et al., 1986). Job insecurity was related to overall increases in somatization, depression, anxiety and hostility (Kuhnert et al., 1989), lower levels of life satisfaction (Lim, 1996), and to an increase in anxiety, depression, and general distress among managers (Roskies and Louis-Guerin, 1990). Research also showed that not only does the loss of job security lead to worsened health and psychiatric outcomes, but that the removal of the threat to job security does not completely reverse these negative effects; further, these outcomes worsen as exposure to the stressor is more chronic (Ferrie et al., 2002).

Sverke et al. (2002) summarized the contributions of early job insecurity researchers in their meta-analysis and review of job insecurity's consequences. Aggregating from the results of 72 studies published between 1980 and 1999, they found that job insecurity was negatively correlated with job satisfaction (−.041), job involvement (−0.37), organizational commitment (−0.36), trust (−0.50), physical health (−0.16), mental health (−0.24) and job performance (−0.21). Job insecurity was positively related to turnover intentions (0.28). Thus, two decades of research overwhelmingly and clearly confirmed what most laypersons would suspect: job insecurity is a workplace stressor that results in significant adverse consequences.

RECENT RESEARCH ADVANCES

While early research in this area tended to focus on the individual-level attitudinal, behavioral, and health-related outcomes of job insecurity, there has been growing interest in delineating moderators of the effects of job insecurity on these outcomes. Additionally, recent research has begun to explore how this stressor might impact other important employee outcomes such as safety, creativity, and organizational citizenship behaviors. Finally, although difficult to conduct in the field, there have been some recent attempts to use experimental methods to explore issues of causality in the laboratory. Each of these recent advances will be discussed in turn below.

Moderators of job insecurity

Research into variables that might exacerbate or alleviate the relationship between job insecurity and its outcomes has largely focused on individual differences variables related

to the affected employees. Greenhalgh and Rosenblatt (1984) originally proposed that locus of control would moderate the effects of job insecurity such that individuals with an internal locus of control would be more troubled by the perception of powerlessness. However, subsequent research has found, in fact, that individuals with an external locus of control fare worse under conditions of job insecurity. Individuals with an external locus of control not only report higher levels of perceived insecurity (Hartley et al., 1991), but they also report more mental health complaints as a result of that insecurity than their internal locus of control counterparts (Näswall et al., 2005).

Research also suggests that positive and negative affectivity may not only influence the perception of job insecurity, but also moderate job insecurity's consequences. Negative affectivity (NA; Watson and Clark, 1984) is a personality disposition that is manifested by individuals (a) experiencing chronically high levels of distress and (b) accentuating the negative when appraising themselves, other people, and the world in general (Roskies, Louis-Guerin, and Fournier, 1993). Several studies have shown that NA may serve to inflate the relationship between work perceptions and affective symptoms (Parkes, 1990; Schaubroeck et al., 1992), although controlling for NA does not entirely eliminate the stressor-to-strain relationship. Positive affectivity, on the other hand, may serve to attenuate the relationship between job perceptions and affective symptoms. Individuals who cast a positive glow on situations will likely perceive less threat than is objectively present. As a result, they are also less likely to exhibit negative reactions to the threat. The results are mixed: Roskies et al. (1993) found that positive personality attributes exerted as strong an effect on mental health as negative ones, albeit in the opposite direction, in individuals experiencing job insecurity; other researchers (e.g., Näswall et al., 2005; Probst, 1998) have failed to find any significant interactive effects between job insecurity and either positive or negative affectivity.

Chan et al. (2004) found that a related construct, dispositional optimism (the generalized tendency to expect good things rather than negative events, Scheier and Carver, 1985), buffers the negative effects of job insecurity on psychological symptoms and life satisfaction; Specifically, optimists had more positive primary and secondary appraisals of job insecurity, and they were less likely to view a particular job situation as insecure and were less likely to interpret job insecurity as stressful.

A final personality variable that is now being examined in relation to job insecurity is emotional intelligence (Salovey and Mayer, 1990). Jordan et al. (2002) proposed that employees with low emotional intelligence are more likely to experience negative emotional reactions to job insecurity and adopt negative coping strategies than high emotional intelligence employees. However, other researchers (e.g., Becker, 2003) argue that the construct of emotional intelligence has not yet been adequately conceptualized or measured, and that it is therefore premature to speculate on its role as a moderator.

Three work-related attitudes and perceptions – job involvement, workplace control, and perceived powerlessness – have also been proposed as moderators to better understand the process by which job insecurity leads to negative outcomes. Greenhalgh and Rosenblatt (1984) theorized that increased job involvement would result in a stronger negative reaction to a perceived threat of job insecurity. By definition, individuals who are highly involved in their jobs derive much of their personal identity from the jobs with which they are associated and threatening that source of identity may have severe consequences. As Judge and Hulin (1993) noted, 'To do nothing may be to be nothing for many Americans (p. 413).' In support of this, Probst (2000) found that highly involved employees reported more negative job attitudes, more health problems, and a higher level of psychological distress than their less involved counterparts when they perceived their jobs to be threatened.

Perceived powerlessness and lack of workplace control have also been shown to moderate the effects of job insecurity on consequences such as satisfaction, irritation/strain, and psychosomatic complaints and other health outcomes (Barling and Kelloway, 1996; Büssing, 1999). Additionally, Reisel (2003) found that powerlessness was a significant moderator of the antecedents of job insecurity (e.g., environmental threats, role ambiguity, job alternatives) and the perception of job insecurity. Thus, as with other moderators, these variables may serve to influence both the primary and secondary appraisals of job insecurity.

Although individual differences moderators may explain who is most likely to negatively react to job insecurity, these variables are not always easily modified. Therefore, there is clearly a need for research into organizational-level moderators (i.e., interventions) that may be effectively utilized toward this end.

Moving beyond traditional outcomes of job insecurity

As Sverke et al.'s (2002) meta-analysis demonstrated, there should be little debate regarding the negative effects of job insecurity on variables such as job satisfaction, organizational commitment, physical and mental health and turnover intentions. Yet, recent research confirms that the effects of job insecurity are more pervasive than originally thought, and sometimes occur in unexpected directions. For example, while earlier research largely focused on physical and mental health consequences of insecurity, recent studies indicate that employee safety may be jeopardized as well.

In one of the first studies to address this, Landsbergis et al. (1999) reported detrimental effects on employee health and injury rates in a variety of industries that were implementing lean production cultures. Although job insecurity and lean production are unique constructs, it is accepted that one of the hallmarks of lean production is the implementation of organizational downsizing (American Management

Association, 1997; Landsbergis et al., 1999). Later research by Probst and Brubaker (2001) found that employees who perceive their jobs to be insecure report lower levels of safety knowledge, and reduced motivation to comply with safety policies. In turn, these variables were related to a decrease in safety compliance and an increase in job-related accidents and injuries. In a follow-up study, Probst (2002b) found that individuals threatened with layoffs subsequently violated more safety policies than their secure counterparts. A recent comprehensive review of more than 90 studies conducted in Europe, North and South America, Asia, and Africa (Quinlan, 2005) found evidence of consistent adverse associations between precarious employment, job insecurity, and occupational safety outcomes such as injury rates, safety knowledge, and safety compliance. Thus, there appears to be growing consensus that job insecurity can negatively affect both the health and safety of employees.

While organizations are rightly concerned with employee safety and health, it appears that organizational innovation may also be at risk when employees are insecure. While many organizations cite increased flexibility and enhanced innovation as 'benefits' of restructuring and downsizing, many researchers argue the exact opposite may occur. Pech (2001) reasons that while organizations may claim to encourage innovation and creative behavior organizational cost cutting and downsizing counters such behavior. Similarly, researchers have argued that innovation is likely to suffer as a result of downsizing due to an increase in risk-averse thinking (Cascio, 1993) and behavioral rigidity (Cameron et al., 1988). Another possibility is that this increased rigidity is not intentional, but rather reflects an underlying loss of cognitive flexibility (Carnevale and Probst, 1998).

In the first study to assess the effects of downsizing on creativity, Amabile and Conti (1999) found that the work environment for creativity significantly declined during organizational downsizing. In their study of 754 employees, respondents reported significantly less freedom, challenge, access to resources, supervisory encouragement, work group support, and organizational encouragement following the implementation of organizational downsizing. More recent research (Probst et al., 2007) demonstrated that individuals threatened with layoffs were less able to solve a subsequent creative problem solving task. Additionally, higher levels of job insecurity were related to lower scores on a series of tests measuring the ability to see relationships between ideas that are remote from each other. These latter findings support the contention that job insecurity may reduce creativity due to an underlying loss of cognitive flexibility (Carnevale and Probst, 1998), rather than (or in addition to) any intentional change on the part of the employees themselves (e.g., increased risk aversion).

While the effects of job insecurity on creativity are consistent, there are mixed results when it comes to determining how job insecurity might influence employees' likelihood to engage in organizational citizenship behaviors (OCBs). Rather than having a main effect on OCBs, job insecurity affects OCBs differently depending on the nature of the employment contract. In one of the first studies on this topic, Feather and Rauter (2004) found that OCBs and job insecurity were positively correlated among contract teachers, but were negatively correlated among permanent teachers. Thus, contract employees might increase their performance of OCBs as a means of securing their position, whereas permanent employees may withhold their engagement in OCBs as a means of expressing their dissatisfaction. Consistent with these results, Reisel et al. (under review) also found that job insecurity was related to fewer OCBs in a sample of MBAs who held permanent positions with their organization.

In addition to investigating novel and less-traditional consequences of job insecurity, researchers are also beginning to use novel and less-traditional methods of inquiry in their studies of insecurity. Most notably, the past few years have seen an increase in the number of studies that use experimental methods (e.g., Probst, 2002b; Probst and Brubaker, 2007; Probst et al., 2007). Given that most of the data on job insecurity stem from field-based survey research, the use of laboratory experiments as an alternative complementary research methodology has the potential to expand our knowledge of the processes involved beyond what correlational cross-sectional data has thus far provided us.

Despite concerns regarding ecological validity, a laboratory experiment is arguably the only way to definitively ascertain the true causal effects of job insecurity, as the threat of layoffs cannot be ethically or practically manipulated in a field setting. Nevertheless, laboratory experiments should be seen as a complementary research strategy rather than a replacement of field-based research. As Ilgen (1986) noted, laboratory research is a question of when, not if.

KEY DEBATES AMONG JOB INSECURITY RESEARCHERS

Despite the recent research advances noted above, there are many areas of debate among job insecurity researchers and much room for improvement in our field. In their seminal article, Greenhalgh and Rosenblatt (1984) noted that there were conceptual inadequacies involving the job insecurity construct, that the content domain needed to be better specified, and that many measures to assess job insecurity had undergone almost no psychometric development. In many ways, Greenhalgh and Rosenblatt's assessment of the state of research at that time remains valid. As Klandermans and Van Vuuren (1999) noted, the issues encompassing the key debates within the job insecurity field can be grouped into three categories:

(1) conceptual issues pertaining to the definition and dimensionality of the construct;
(2) theoretical questions related to the prediction of antecedents and consequences of job insecurity; and

(3) methodological challenges related to the measurement of job insecurity and the over-reliance on research designs that limit inferences of causality.

Conceptual issues regarding the job insecurity construct

Job security can be thought of as a subjective experience or an objective state. Objectively, the Bureau of Labor Statistics within the US Department of Labor (DOL) provides biennial estimates of the job outlook for hundreds of occupations (DOL, 2004–2005) based on whether employment opportunities within these occupations are growing, stable, or declining over the next decade. Organizations can also objectively identify positions within the company as being more or less likely to be outsourced, eliminated, retained, or expanded in the future. Often, this assessment can be made by upper-level management based on annual strategic planning and company economic forecasts. Some researchers (e.g., Büssing, 1999; Kozlowski et al., 1993) argued that more attention should be paid to this conceptualization of job insecurity. To a certain extent, one would expect to see some convergence between objective and subjective measures of insecurity. For example, Büssing (1986) found that employees in a downsizing steel plant reported significantly higher levels of subjective job insecurity compared to a similar sample of employees in a prospering steel plant. Likewise, Probst (2003b) found significant differences in the subjective perceptions of employees undergoing an organizational restructuring that corresponded to the extent to which their jobs had been objectively targeted for reorganization.

While job security can be described objectively, it is more commonly conceptualized and measured as a subjective perception on the part of the employee (e.g., Davy et al., 1997; Greenhalgh and Rosenblatt, 1984; Probst, 2002a; Sverke and Hellgren, 2002). From this perspective, a job can be defined as insecure if employees perceive their job to be unstable or at risk, regardless of any actual objective level of job security. Thus, it is possible to have a job which is objectively secure, but subjectively perceived to be insecure by the employee holding that position (e.g., Kinnunen et al., 1999). Thus, one can experience subjective insecurity in the face of objective security. The reverse situation may also occur, whereby individuals perceive their job to be secure, although the objective data indicate otherwise. Jacobson and Hartley (1991) argue that job insecurity should be viewed as the discrepancy between the level of security an employee experiences and the level preferred by that employee. Thus, regardless of objective security, it is the individual's subjective perception that is meaningful. The overarching implication is that individuals in the same environment may not only have different perceptions of job insecurity, but can also exhibit different reactions to that perception.

There are advantages and disadvantages to both approaches of conceptualizing and measuring job security (Probst, 2006). The objective approach removes individual perceptions from the equation and relies upon government or organizational forecasts of job security. This can be advantageous if one's purpose is to accurately categorize a position or occupation as having (or lacking) job security. On the other hand, the subjective approach explicitly relies upon individual perceptions of job security which can be colored by economic, social, organizational, and individual characteristics. However, many outcomes of job security are best predicted by such individual subjective perceptions rather than more objective assessments. Thus, if one's purpose is to predict individual outcomes, conceptualizing job security subjectively may be more informative.

There has also been much debate regarding the dimensionality of the job insecurity construct. Some researchers prefer a more global (i.e., unidimensional) definition of job insecurity that focuses primarily on the perceived probability of job loss (e.g., Klein Hesselink and Van Vuuren, 1999) or the amount of fear that one's job would be lost (e.g., Johnson et al., 1984). Many such studies

use one- or two-item indicators to measure job insecurity. Commonly, participants are asked to indicate 'the likelihood of losing their job in the next year,' or 'if they expected a change in their employment for the worse' (e.g., Büssing, 1986; Dooley et al., 1987). Others, however, use multi-item scales to capture the global or overall level of job insecurity perceived by employees (e.g., Probst, 2003a).

Most researchers, however, argue strongly for a multidimensional conceptualization of job insecurity. As noted earlier, Greenhalgh and Rosenblatt (1984) defined job insecurity as 'perceived powerlessness to maintain desired continuity in a threatened job situation' (p. 438). Based on this definition, Ashford et al. (1989) developed the JIS which measured job insecurity by assessing:

(1) the range of work situation features that could be in jeopardy;
(2) the valence of each such feature;
(3) the subjective probability of losing each feature; and
(4) the number of sources of threat.

Thus, powerlessness to maintain continuation of the job itself was equally important as the continuation of specific valued job features (Greenhalgh and Rosenblatt, 1984). Similarly, others have also argued for the inclusion of the perceived severity of loss in their definition of job insecurity (e.g., Klandermans et al., 1991) in addition to measuring the probability of loss. Yet others (Blau et al., 2004) have argued that job insecurity is comprised of three related but conceptually distinct constructs:

(1) job loss insecurity;
(2) human capital job feature insecurity (i.e., perceived threats against an individual's monetary or psychic income); and
(3) work condition job feature insecurity (i.e., perceived threats to job-specific situational characteristics, such as autonomy).

Clearly, there is little consensus regarding whether job insecurity should be more appropriately conceptualized as a unidimensional versus multidimensional construct; Sverke and Hellgren (2002), however, provide an excellent review of both global and multidimensional measures of job insecurity. Both approaches have their advantages and disadvantages. Proponents of the global approach often rely on single-item measures with unknown or poor psychometric properties. On the other hand, it is unclear how conceptually distinct various facets of the multidimensional measures truly are. For example, Roskies and Louis-Guerin (1990) concluded that the antecedents and consequences of threat of demotion and termination were sufficiently similar to be grouped together. Further, while Ashford et al. (1989) found that their multiplicative measure of job insecurity accounted for more variance than a global measure, others (Reisel and Banai, 2002) have found that global measures can account for more variance than the Ashford et al. measure. In that same study, Reisel and Banai (2002) showed that while the job threat items were significant predictors of outcomes, the threat to job features items were not, suggesting these additional items add little to our prediction of employee outcomes.

Some researchers (e.g., Hartley et al., 1991; Probst, 2003a) also argue that multidimensional measures may account for more variance because they include items that reflect the intended construct as well as other elements in that constructs nomological network. Therefore, when conceptualizing job security, it is important to clearly distinguish dimensions of the construct itself from those variables that moderate the relationships between the construct and outcome variables of interest. For example, although perceived powerlessness is clearly an important variable in the study of job insecurity, it may be a moderator of job insecurity, rather than an aspect of the construct itself. Similarly, the Greenhalgh and Rosenblatt definition implies that an individual experiences job insecurity only if the individual desires continuity in that work role. It would seem, however, that individuals experience job insecurity regardless of any desire for continuity, but

that desire for continuity would moderate the impact job insecurity has on outcome variables. Supporting this, research has shown that job importance moderates the relationship between perceived job security and several individual outcomes such as psychological distress, physical health, and job satisfaction (Orpen, 1993; Probst, 2000).

A final growing conceptual debate concerns the affective versus cognitive nature of the job insecurity construct, and some researchers (e.g., Borg and Elizur, 1992; Probst, 2003a) argue that both need to be measured in order to adequately capture the full domain. This distinction allows researchers to then explore the moderators of the relationship between an employee's perception of job insecurity and his or her evaluative and affective responses to that perception. Toward that end, Probst (2003a) and Borg and Elizur (1992) have developed measures to assess both cognitive perceptions and affective reactions. Borg and Elizur's (1992) measure of job insecurity contains cognitive items assessing belief that one's job is secure, whereas the affective items tap into concern or fear of losing one's job. Similarly, Probst (2003a) developed the Job Security Index (JSI) to assess individual's cognitive appraisal of the future of their job with respect to the perceived level of stability and continuance of that job. The second measure, the Job Security Satisfaction (JSS) scale, was designed to assess satisfaction with job security. Probst argued that two distinct measures are necessary because one's perceptions of job insecurity – although likely to be related to – are not the same as one's affective reaction to that job insecurity and each would have distinct antecedents and consequences.

According to Probst's (2002a) conceptual model, only if one is dissatisfied with one's level of job security should one experience stress as a result. And, in fact, employee stress levels were significantly predicted by job security satisfaction, but were not predicted by job security perceptions. Similarly, physical and mental health outcomes were predicted by satisfaction with job security, but not perceptions of security. On the other hand, individuals who reported more job changes as the result of an organizational restructuring reported lower levels of job security, but these job changes were unrelated to their satisfaction with their job security. In addition, individuals who had been with the organization for a greater period of time cognitively perceived their jobs to be more secure, but were not necessarily more satisfied with that security. Thus, there appears to be value in distinguishing between an employee's cognitive perceptions of job insecurity and their affective reactions or satisfaction with that perception.

Theoretical issues regarding the antecedents and consequences of job insecurity

There are several theoretical models that enhance our understanding and prediction of the antecedents and consequences of job insecurity, most notably Jahoda's (1982) model of 'latent deprivation' which theorizes that the possibility of unemployment threatens employee needs that are currently being satisfied by work (e.g., need for income, social contacts outside family, structuring of time). The potential disruption of those needs being met then account for the negative reactions to perceived insecurity. Similarly, Warr's (1987) *Vitamin Model* describes nine components of work that influence psychological well-being. Many of those are threatened under conditions of job insecurity (e.g., environmental clarity, environmental control). Other theoretical models may be applicable as well (see Winefield, 2002), such as the theory of learned helplessness (Seligman, 1975) where exposure to uncontrollable aversive situations can lead to negative cognitive, emotional, and motivational outcomes among individuals with an unhealthy attributional style, and relative deprivation theory (Feldman et al., 1997) which posits negative outcomes occur as a result of the perception of unjustified violated expectations.

While each of these models helps explain in general why job insecurity would lead to negative outcomes, more sophisticated models are needed to understand conflicting empirical data regarding the antecedents and consequences of: objective versus subjective insecurity, the threat of job loss versus job features, and probability versus severity of losses. For example, while Büssing (1999) found that both subjective and objective insecurity were related to lower levels of job satisfaction, only subjective perceptions of job insecurity were related to strain and psychosomatic complaints. Similarly, while researchers argue that both threat of job loss and threat to job features are important, others have found the threat of job loss to be a better predictor of outcomes (e.g, Reisel and Banai, 2002).

To provide a better explication of these disparate findings, Blau et al. (2004) proposed that three types of job insecurity: job loss insecurity, human capital job feature insecurity, and work conditions job feature insecurity form a continuum and that employees may progress from work condition insecurity to human capital insecurity and finally to job loss insecurity. Their data showed significantly different patterns of antecedents and subsequent withdrawal cognitions for each type of insecurity in the expected directions. For example, as employees moved along the continuum from work condition to human capital to job loss insecurity, the relationship with turnover intentions grew correspondingly strongly (0.16, 0.27, 0.39, respectively). While this model may be a step in the right direction, there is still a need to develop a better understanding of the intermediary mechanisms that account for the negative outcomes of job insecurity. For example, it appears that uncertainty is an important mediator of job insecurity and that control is important moderator, but further investigation is needed.

Recently, De Witte and Näswall (2003) proposed two competing hypotheses for the negative effects of job insecurity: the psychological contract violation hypothesis versus the intensification hypothesis. According to the psychological contract violation hypothesis, negative effects emerge because expectations of job security were violated. Thus, one should only see negative effects when job security could be reasonably expected. On the other hand, models such as proposed by Blau et al. (2004) would predict higher levels of job insecurity would result in more negative outcomes regardless of original expectations.

Results of these competing tests conducted comparing permanent and contingent workers favor the psychological contract violation hypothesis. For example, De Cuyper and De Witte (2006) found that job insecurity was related to lower job satisfaction and organizational commitment, but only among permanent employees; no effects were seen for temporary employees. Similarly, Mauno et al. (2005) found job insecurity had greater negative effects on permanent workers then fixed-term workers. These results suggest that job insecurity may only result in negative effects if job security was an expected part of the job (i.e., psychological contract violation), whereas adding job insecurity to an already insecure position (i.e. temporary workers) did not result in more negative effects disconfirming the intensification hypothesis. Thus, while many deplore the growth of flexible work arrangements (i.e. non-permanent employment contracts), and argue that most employees with fixed or temporary contracts would prefer a permanent one (Brewster et al., 1997), it appears that the added insecurity of such positions does not necessarily lead to more negative outcomes because security was not an expected benefit of the job in the first place.

Methodological challenges

The two primary methodological challenges facing the job insecurity field today are related to the measurement of job insecurity, and the over-reliance on research designs that limit our ability to draw inferences of causality.

For many years researchers in this field have invariably relied on single item scales to measure the construct of job insecurity. Commonly, participants are asked to simply indicate 'the likelihood of losing their job in the next year' or 'if they expected a change in their employment for the worse' (e.g., Büssing, 1986). Such measures possess either poor or unknown psychometric properties; and, rarely is any evidence provided to validate these measures. At the other extreme (Klandermans and van Vuuren, 1999) is the overly complex multiplicative formula proposed by Ashford et al. (1989). Many researchers would argue that collapsing all of the information gathered in such a scale into a single job insecurity score reduces our ability to disentangle mediators, moderators, and appropriate dimensions of job insecurity (see Kinnunen et al., 1999). However, until the conceptual debate is resolved, measurement challenges will remain.

Finally, research on job insecurity must move beyond the over-reliance on cross-sectional correlational research designs which limit our ability to draw inferences of causality. Unfortunately, that is often easier said than done. While organizational researchers often complain of the difficulty in gaining access to organizational sites for data collection, one could argue that researchers studying job insecurity face particular difficulties. When organizations face upcoming mergers, acquisitions, downsizings, and/or reorganizations, often the last thing an already overburdened HR department wants is outside researchers surveying their already frazzled employees. This is especially true with respect to longitudinal studies. Nevertheless, longitudinal research (e.g., Ferrie et al., 2002; Kinnunen, et al., 1999) is sorely needed to progress beyond the litany of individual and organizational correlates of job insecurity. An alternative strategy already described earlier in this chapter would be to increase the use of laboratory experiments. However, this can only be a complementary method of investigation and not a replacement for longitudinal field research.

EMERGING RESEARCH AGENDAS

As the economy becomes more global and technology continues its rate of change, organizations will continue to engage in practices that cause employees to be concerned about their job security. Given this, what questions need to be answered? Does employee job insecurity affect organizational outcomes such as innovation, performance, and customer service? What are the broader effects of job insecurity on the family and community? Are employees adapting to the new psychological contract; will job insecurity eventually become accepted by workers, and therefore, a moot line of inquiry?

While job insecurity clearly has pervasive negative effects for the affected individual, the effects are more widespread and affect organizations and society as well. Reisel et al. (2005) found that job insecurity was related to several negative organizational outcomes, ranging from reduced customer service, decreased adaptiveness, and less *esprit de corps* among co-workers. Schwebel (1997) and Neuman and Baron (1998) have argued that job insecurity may also be related to a rise in violence both within and outside of the workplace (see also Quinlan, 2005). Increasingly research suggests spouses, partners, and children may also be negatively affected, with research finding that the economic worries of one member of a couple crossover to predict the job security of the other partner (Mauno and Kinnunen, 2002). Similarly, Westman et al. (2001) found that job insecurity was related to burnout, and that the burnout experienced by one member of the couple influenced the burnout reported by the other member. More importantly, couples who were experiencing job insecurity exhibited higher levels of both given and received social undermining – behaviors that display negative affect and negative evaluation – toward one another.

Children of parents who are experiencing job insecurity at work are also not immune from its negative effects. Lim and Loo (2003) found that job insecurity is related to increased use of paternal authoritarian parenting behaviors and lower children's self-efficacy. Barling et al. (1998a) found that children's perceptions of work, work beliefs, and work attitudes are also influenced by their parents' job insecurity. Further, undergraduate student grades were negatively associated with children's perceptions of their parent's job insecurity (Barling and Mendelson, 1997). In an exploration of these findings, Barling et al. (1998b) report that this relationship is mediated by children's cognitive difficulties. This series of relationships is particularly alarming, as it suggests a potential negative cyclical relationship, whereby parental job insecurity is related to lower academic performance and potentially fewer and/or lower quality employment opportunities for their children.

Despite the negative effects of job insecurity, some researchers argue that the issue of job insecurity will one day be a moot point due to a changing psychological contract from one of life-time employment to one of life-time employability in exchange for hard work (Kanter, 1989; Kluytmans and Ott, 1999), raising a new series of questions: Do employees accept this new contract? Are employees more concerned with employability than employment? Preliminary data comparing so-called 'Generation X' employees to 'Baby Boomers' (Probst, 2007) found that job insecurity was unrelated to psychological distress for GenX employees (<29 years), but significantly so for Baby Boomer employees (45+ years). Health conditions were also unrelated to insecurity among the GenXers, but were modestly correlated among Boomers.

However, other research concluded that while younger workers do not expect job security, they still desire it (Smithson and Lewis, 2000). Many surveys repeatedly show that employees rank job insecurity as one of the major stressors facing them in the workplace (e.g., Ironson, 1992; De Witte, 1999). Additionally, the 1989 International Social Survey Programme asked workers from nine OECD countries (Austria, Hungary, Ireland, Italy, Netherlands, Norway, Germany, the UK, and US) to rate importance of nine different aspects of work, including job security, income, promotion opportunities, leisure time, independent work, being able to help others, being useful to society, and flexible work hours. Fully 59 percent said that job security was 'very important' and it was selected as the most important job feature in eight of the nine countries – Netherlands ranked it 2nd (OECD, 1997). Thus, while there may be some preliminary data to suggest that younger workers do not expect and therefore do not react negatively to the lack of job insecurity, job insecurity is far from becoming a moot issue.

Given that the job insecurity remains a primary concern of employees and employers, more research should be conducted to assess the effects of job insecurity over time. We need more information about how the process unfolds over time, and the implications, if any, for short-term job insecurity versus long-term insecurity. The results of early research have been mixed. Heaney et al. (1994) found that the effects of job insecurity become more potent as the time of exposure increases. Van Vuuren (1990) found that job insecurity reduced well-being in both short and long-term. On the other hand, Hellgren et al. (1999) found that effects of insecurity on outcomes became nonsignificant when controlling for baseline outcome levels, whereas Probst (2002a) found that earlier levels of job insecurity predicted outcomes at a six month follow-up date. Given the difficulty in conducting longitudinal research and the lack of theory to make time-related predictions regarding how the process unfolds, these mixed results are perhaps not surprising. Nevertheless, this remains an important area of inquiry.

The search for organizational-level moderators of the effects of job insecurity also remains a primary concern. There has been much research on individual differences moderators, yet as noted earlier, individual differences are difficult, if not impossible, to modify, thereby providing limited knowledge regarding preventive interventions. Preliminary research in this area is promising.

To assess whether enhanced organizational communication could dampen the dysfunctional effects of an organizational merger, Schweiger and DeNisi (1991) examined the effectiveness of a 'realistic merger preview' in reducing employee uncertainty. Analogous to a realistic job preview, a realistic merger preview provides detailed information regarding the timeline of the merger, how the merger will affect employees and other pertinent information. In a rare longitudinal field experiment in this context, Schweiger and DeNisi (1991) provided realistic merger previews to employees in one plant; in a control plant, the merger was managed more traditionally. Although both plants experienced initial negative effects as a result of the announced upcoming merger, the plant that was offered a realistic merger preview rebounded more quickly from the negative effects, whereas employees in the control plant continued to report negative job attitudes, a lack of trust toward the company, and lower levels of self-reported performance four months following the merger announcement. Thus, as the authors noted, 'a realistic merger preview seems to function at least as an inoculation that makes employees resistant to the negative effects of mergers and acquisitions, and its effects may go beyond that' (p. 129).

Increasing participative decision making opportunities has also been shown to reduce the negative effects of job insecurity. Whereas job insecurity is associated with a lack of control perceived by employees, participative decision making would be effective precisely because it allows employees to have a substantial voice in job-related decisions (Probst, 2005). Data on the job satisfaction and turnover intentions of 807 employees in six different companies confirmed this hypothesis (Probst, 2005). Employees with greater participative decision making opportunities reported fewer negative job-related consequences as a function of job insecurity compared to employees with fewer participative decision making opportunities.

Another organizational intervention that shows promise in attenuating some of the worst effects of job insecurity involves the organizational safety climate under which employees work. Research shows that job insecurity has a detrimental effect on employee safety attitudes, behaviors, and outcomes (Grunberg et al., 1996; Probst,

2002; Probst and Brubaker, 2001). However, the effects of job insecurity on safety are moderated by the extent to which the organization is seen as valuing and emphasizing safety. In a study of light manufacturing employees, Probst (2004) found that when employees perceived a weak organizational safety climate, job insecurity was related to lower levels of safety knowledge, less employee safety compliance, a greater number of employee accidents, more near miss incidents, a greater likelihood of workplace injury, and a greater incidence of repetitive motion injuries. However, when employees perceived that the organizational safety climate was strong, the slope of the relationships between job insecurity and these safety outcomes was consistently attenuated. Thus, particularly during times of organizational transition and employee economic stress, organizations would benefit by consistently sending strong messages regarding the importance of safety to their employees.

CONCLUSION

In conclusion, much remains to be learned about the consequences of job insecurity and their prevention. However, most of the cutting edge research on the topic of job insecurity has been conducted outside of the US, primarily in Europe and Canada, despite the fact that jobs are arguably more tenuous in the US where there are fewer government regulations protecting employees from layoffs. Thus, although a frequent topic in the popular press, the lack of attention given to job insecurity by researchers within the US is somewhat surprising. A brief keyword search of articles on job insecurity revealed 553 peer-reviewed journal articles since 1980, more than 80 percent of which were conducted by non-US researchers – in 27 years, only 97 articles (i.e., approximately 3–4 articles per year) were written by US-based researchers! Part of this stark difference in attention paid to the topic may be due to historically higher levels of unemployment within the European nations. But it may

also be due to fundamentally different approaches that these countries have with respect to labor market security. In a recent analysis (International Labor Organization, 2004), countries were categorized as 'pragmatists,' 'pacesetters,' 'conventionals,' or 'much-to-be-done countries.' Being labeled 'pragmatist' indicated a 'lack of policy commitment to labor market security,' whereas 'pacesetting' countries demonstrate a 'strong constitutional and policy commitment to social welfare' (p. 312). Canada and most Western European countries were categorized as pacesetters, whereas the US was found to be a pragmatist when it comes to employment security. Perhaps these governmental differences in attitudes (and presumably research funding) trickle down to the level of individual researchers and may account for the different levels of attention paid to the topic of job insecurity. Regardless of the reason, hopefully, the coming years will see greater attention devoted to this important organizational behavior topic.

REFERENCES

Abramis, D.J. (1994) 'Relationship of job stressors to job performance: Linear or an inverted-U?', *Psychological Reports*, 75: 547–58.

Amabile, T.M. and Conti, R. (1999) 'Changes in the work organization for creativity during downsizing', *Academy of Management Journal*, 42: 630–640.

American Management Association (1997) *Corporate Job Creation, Job Elimination and Downsizing*. New York: American Management Association.

Armstrong-Stassen, M. (1998) 'The effect of gender and organizational level on how survivors appraise and cope with organizational downsizing', *Journal of Applied Behavioral Science*, 34: 125–142.

Ashford, S., Lee, C. and Bobko, P. (1989) 'Content, causes, and consequences of job insecurity: A theory-based measure and substantive test', *Academy of Management Journal*, 32: 803–829.

Barling, J., Dupre, K.E. and Hepburn, C.G. (1998a) 'Effects of parents' job insecurity on children's work beliefs and attitudes', *Journal of Applied Psychology*, 83: 112–118.

Barling, J. and Kelloway, E.K. (1996) 'Job insecurity and health: The moderating role of workplace control', *Stress Medicine*, 12: 253–259.

Barling, J. and Mendelson, M.B. (1997) 'Parents' job insecurity affects children's grade performance through the indirect effects of beliefs in an unjust world and negative mood', *Journal of Occupational Health Psychology*, 4: 347–355.

Barling, J., Zacharatos, A. and Hepburn, C.G. (1998b) 'Parents' job insecurity affects children's academic performance through cognitive difficulties', *Journal of Applied Psychology*, 84: 437–444.

Becker, T. (2003) 'Is emotional intelligence a viable concept?', *Academy of Management Review*, 28: 192–195.

Belton, B. (1999, February 17) 'Fed chief: Tech advances raise job insecurity', *USA Today*, B2.

Blau, G., Tatum, D.S., McCoy, K., Dobria, L. and Ward-Cook, K. (2004) 'Job loss, human capital job feature, and work condition job feature as distinct job insecurity constructs', *Journal of Allied Health*, 33: 31–41.

Borg, I. and Elizur, D. (1992) 'Job insecurity: Correlates, moderators, and measurement', *International Journal of Manpower*, 13: 13–26.

Brewster, C., Mayne, L. and Tregaskis, O. (1997) 'Flexible working in Europe', *Journal of World Business*, 32: 133–151.

Brockner, J., Grover, S., Reed, T.F. and DeWitt, R.L. (1992) 'Layoffs, job insecurity, and survivors' work effort: Evidence of an inverted-U relationship', *Academy of Management Journal*, 35: 413–425.

Bureau of Labor Statistics (2006) *Archived news releases for extended mass layoffs*. Available: www.bls.gov/schedule/archives/mslo_nr.htm (accessed January 22, 2007).

Büssing, A. (1986) 'Worker responses to job insecurity: A quasi-experimental field investigation', in G. Debus and H.W. Schroiff (eds), *The Psychology of Work and Organization*. North Holland: Elsevier Science Publishers, pp. 137–144.

Büssing, A. (1999) 'Can control at work and social support moderate psychological consequences of job insecurity? Results from a quasi-experimental study in the steel industry', *European Journal of Work and Organizational Psychology*, 8: 219–242.

Cameron, K.S., Sutton, R.I. and Whetton, D.A. (1988) *Readings in Organizational Decline: Frameworks, Research and Prescriptions*. Cambridge, MA: Ballinger.

Carnevale, P.J. and Probst, T.M. (1998) 'Social values and social conflict in creative problem solving and categorization', *Journal of Personality and Social Psychology*, 74: 1300–1309.

Cascio, W. (1993) 'Downsizing: What do we know? What have we learned?', *Academy of Management Executive*, 7: 95–104.

Catalano, R., Rook, K. and Dooley, D. (1986) 'Labor markets and help-seeking: A test of the employment security hypothesis', *Journal of Health and Social Behavior*, 27: 277–287.

Chan, W., Kwok, K. and Yeung, S.A. (2004) 'Facing challenging circumstances: Optimism and job insecurity', *Journal of Psychology in Chinese Societies*, 5: 81–95.

Cobb, S. (1974) 'Physiologic changes in men whose jobs were abolished', *Journal of Psychosomatic Research*, 18: 245–258.

Cottington, E.M., Matthews, K.A., Talbot, E. and Kuller, L.H. (1986) 'Occupational stress, suppressed anger, and hypertension', *Psychosomatic Medicine*, 48: 249–260.

Davy, J., Kinicki, A. and Scheck, C. (1991) 'Developing and testing a model of survivor responses to layoffs', *Journal of Vocational Behavior*, 38: 302–317.

De Cuyper, N. and De Witte, H. (2006) 'The impact of job insecurity and contract type on attitudes, well-being and behavioral reports: A psychological contract perspective', *Journal of Occupational and Organizational Psychology*, 79: 395–409.

De Witte, H. (1999) 'Job insecurity and psychological well-being: Review of the literature and exploration of some unresolved issues', *European Journal of Work and Organizational Psychology*, 8: 155–178.

De Witte, H. and Näswall, K. (2003) '"Objective" vs. "subjective" job insecurity: Consequences of temporary work for job satisfaction and organizational commitment in four European countries', *Economic and Industrial Democracy*, 24: 149–188.

Dekker, S.W. and Schaufeli, W.B. (1995) 'The effects of job insecurity on psychological health and withdrawal: A longitudinal study', *Australian Psychologist*, 30: 57–63.

Dooley, D., Rook, K. and Catalano, R. (1987) 'Job and non-job stressors and their moderators', *Journal of Occupational Psychology*, 60: 115–132.

Feather, N.T. and Rauter, K.A. (2004) 'Organizational citizenship behaviours in relation to job status, job insecurity, organizational commitment and identification, job satisfaction and work values', *Journal of Occupational and Organizational Psychology*, 77: 81–94.

Feldman, D.C., Leana, C.R. and Turnley, W.H. (1997) 'A relative deprivation approach to understanding underemployment', in C.L. Cooper and D.M. Rousseau (eds), *Trends in Organizational Behavior*. London: Wiley, pp. 43–60.

Ferrie, J.E., Shipley, M.J., Stansfeld, S.A. and Marmot, M.G. (2002) 'Effects of chronic job insecurity and change in job security on self reported health, minor psychiatric morbidity, physiological measures, and health related behaviours in British civil servants: The Whitehall II study', *Journal of Epidemiology and Community Health*, 56: 450–454.

Greenhalgh, L. and Rosenblatt, Z. (1984) 'Job insecurity: Towards conceptual clarity', *Academy of Management Review*, 9: 438–448.

Grunberg, L., Moore, S. and Greenberg, E.S. (1998) 'Work stress and problem alcohol behavior: A test of the spillover model', *Journal of Organizational Behavior*, 19: 487–502.

Hallier, J. and Lyon, P. (1996) 'Job insecurity and employee commitment: managers' reactions to the threat and outcomes of redundancy selection', *British Journal of Management*, 7: 107–123.

Hannerz, H., Albertsen, K., Nielsen, M.L., Tüchsen, F. and Burr, H. (2004) 'Occupational factors and 5-year weight change among men in a Danish national cohort', *Health Psychology*, 23: 283–288.

Hartley, J., Jacobsson, D., Klandermans, B. and van Vuuren, T. (1991) *Job Insecurity*. London: Sage Publications.

Heaney, C.A., Israel, B.A. and House, J.S. (1994) 'Chronic job insecurity among automobile workers: Effects on job satisfaction and health', *Social Science and Medicine*, 38:1431–1437.

Hellgren, J., Sverke, M. and Isaksson, K. (1999) 'A two-dimensional approach to job insecurity: Consequences for employee attitudes and well-being', *European Journal of Work and Organizational Psychology*, 8: 179–196.

Ilgen, D.R. (1986) 'Laboratory research: A question of when, not if', in E.A. Locke (ed.), *Generalizing from Lab to Field Settings*. Lexington, MA: Heath, pp. 257–267.

International Labor Organization (2004) *Economic Security for a Better World*. Geneva, Switzerland: ILO.

Ironson, G.H. (1992) 'Job stress and health', in C.J. Cranny, P.C. Smith and E.F. Stone (eds), *Job Satisfaction: How People Feel About their Jobs and How it Affects their Performance*. New York: Lexington Books, pp. 219–239.

Jacobson, D. and Hartley, J. (1991) 'Mapping the context', in J. Hartley, D. Jacobson, B. Klandermans and T. van Vuuren (eds), *Job Insecurity: Coping with Jobs at Risk*. Sage: London, pp. 1–23.

Jahoda, M. (1982) 'Work, employment, and unemployment: Values, theories, and approaches in social research', *American Psychologist*, 36: 184–191.

Johnson, C.D., Messe, L.A. and Crano, W.D. (1984) 'Predicting job performance of low income workers: The Work Opinion Questionnaire', *Personnel Psychology*, 37: 291–299.

Jordan, P.J., Ashkanasy, N.M. and Hartel, C.E.J. (2002) 'Emotional intelligence as a moderator of emotional and behavioral reactions to job insecurity', *Academy of Management Review*, 27: 361–372.

Judge, T.A. and Hulin, C.L. (1993) 'Job satisfaction as a reflection of disposition: A multiple source causal analysis', *Organizational Behavior and Human Decision Processes*, 56: 388–421.

Kanter, R.M. (1989) 'Careers and the Wealth of Nations: A Macro-Perspective on the Structure and Implications of Career Forms', in M.B. Arthur, D.T. Hall and B.S. Lawrence (eds), *Handbook of Career Theory*. Cambridge: Cambridge University Press, pp. 506–522.

Kinnunen, U., Mauno, S., Natti, J. and Happonen, M. (1999) 'Perceived job insecurity: A longitudinal study among Finnish employees', *European Journal of Work and Organizational Psychology*, 8: 243–260.

Klandermans, B., Vuuren, T.V. and Jacobson, D. (1991) 'Employees and job insecurity', in J. Hartley, D. Jacobson, B. Klandermans and T. van Vuuren (eds), *Job Insecurity: Coping with Jobs at Risk*. Sage: London, pp. 40–65.

Klandermans, B. and van Vuuren, T. (1999) 'Job insecurity: Introduction', *European Journal of Work and Organizational Psychology*, 8: 145–153.

Klein Hesselink, D.J. and van Vuuren, T. (1999) 'Job flexibility and job insecurity: The Dutch case', *European Journal of Work and Organizational Psychology*, 8: 273–294.

Kluytmans, F. and Ott, M. (1999) 'Management of employability in the Netherlands', *European Journal of Work and Organizational Psychology*, 8: 261–272.

Kozlowski, S., Chao, G., Smith, E. and Hedlund, J. (1993) 'Organizational downsizing: Strategies, interventions, and research implications', *International Review of Industrial and Organizational Psychology*, 8: 263–332.

Kuhnert, K., Sims, R. and Lahey, M. (1989) 'The relationship between job security and employees health', *Group and Organization Studies*, 14: 399–410.

Landsbergis, P.A., Cahill, J. and Schnall, P. (1999) 'The impact of lean production and related new systems of work organization on worker health', *Journal of Occupational Health Psychology*, 4: 108–130.

Lim, V.K.G. (1996) 'Job insecurity and its outcomes: Moderating effects of work-based and nonwork-based social support', *Human Relations*, 2: 171–194.

Lim, V.K.G. and Loo, G.L. (2003) 'Effects of parental job insecurity and parenting behaviors on youth's self-efficacy and work attitudes', *Journal of Vocational Behavior*, 63 (1): 86–98.

Mauno, S. and Kinnunen, U. (2002) 'Perceived job insecurity among dual-earner couples: Do its antecedents vary according to gender, economic sector and the measure used?' *Journal of Occupational and Organizational Psychology*, 75: 295–314.

Mauno, S., Kinnunen, U., Mäkikangas, A. and Nätti, J. (2005) 'Psychological consequences of fixed-term employment and perceived job insecurity among health care staff', *European Journal of Work and Organizational Psychology*, 14: 209–237.

Näswell, K., Sverke, M. and Hellgren, J. (2005) 'The moderating role of personality characteristics on the relationship between job insecurity and strain', *Work and Stress*, 19: 37–49.

Neuman, J. and Baron, R. (1998) 'Workplace violence and workplace aggression: Evidence concerning specific forms, potential causes, and preferred targets', *Journal of Management*, 24: 391–419.

OECD (1997) 'Is job insecurity on the increase in OECD countries?', in OECD *1997 Employment Outlook*. Paris: OECD.

Orpen, C. (1993) 'Correlations between job insecurity and psychological well-being among White and Black employees in South Africa', *Perceptual and Motor Skills*, 76: 885–886.

Parkes, K.R. (1990) 'Coping, negative affectivity, and the work environment: Additive and interactive predictors of mental health', *Journal of Applied Psychology*, 75: 399–409.

Pech, R.J. (2001) 'Termites, group behaviour, and the loss of innovation: Conformity rules!', *Journal of Managerial Psychology*, 16: 559–574.

Pollard, T.M. (2001) 'Changes in mental well-being, blood pressure and total cholesterol levels during workplace reorganization: The impact of uncertainty', *Work and Stress*, 15: 14–28.

Probst, T.M. (1998) *Antecedents and consequences of job insecurity: Development and test of an integrated model*. Unpublished doctoral dissertation. University of Illinois at Urbana-Champaign.

Probst, T.M. (2000) 'Wedded to the job: Moderating effects of job involvement on the consequences of job insecurity', *Journal of Occupational Health Psychology*, 5: 63–73.

Probst, T.M. (2002a) 'The impact of job insecurity on employee work attitudes, job adaptation, and organizational withdrawal behaviors', in J.M. Brett and F. Drasgow (eds), *The Psychology of Work: Theoretically Based Empirical Research*. New Jersey: Lawrence Erlbaum Associates, pp. 141–168.

Probst, T.M. (2002b) 'Layoffs and tradeoffs: Production, quality, and safety demands under the threat of job loss', *Journal of Occupational Health Psychology*, 7 (3): 211–220.

Probst, T.M. (2003a) 'Development and validation of the Job Security Index and the Job Security Satisfaction Scale: A classical test theory and IRT approach', *Journal of Occupational and Organizational Psychology*, 76: 451–467.

Probst, T.M. (2003b) 'Exploring employee outcomes of organizational restructuring: A Solomon four-group study', *Group and Organization Management*, 28: 416–439.

Probst, T.M. (2004) 'Job insecurity: Exploring a new threat to employee safety', in J. Barling and M. Frone (eds), *Psychology of Workplace Safety*. Washington, DC: American Psychological Association, pp. 63–80.

Probst, T.M. (2005) 'Economic stressors', in J. Barling, K. Kelloway, and M. Frone (eds), *Handbook of Work Stress*. Thousand Oaks, CA: Sage Publication, Inc., pp. 267–297.

Probst, T.M. (2006) 'Job security', in J. Greenhaus and G. Callanan (eds), *Encyclopedia of Career Development*. Thousand Oaks, CA: Sage Publication, Inc.

Probst, T.M. (2007) *Baby Boomers and GenX: Generational Health and Safety Implications of Job Insecurity*. Unpublished manuscript. Washington State University Vancouver.

Probst, T.M. and Brubaker, T.L. (2001) 'The effects of job insecurity on employee safety outcomes: Cross–sectional and longitudinal explorations', *Journal of Occupational Health Psychology*, 6: 139–159.

Probst, T.M. and Brubaker, T.L. (2007) 'Organizational safety climate and supervisory layoff decisions: Preferences versus predictions', *Journal of Applied Social Psychology*, 37: 1630–1648.

Probst, T.M., Stewart, S., Gruys, M.L. and Tierney, B.W. (2007) 'Productivity, counterproductivity, and creativity: The ups and downs of job insecurity', *Journal of Occupational and Organizational Psychology*, 80: 479–497.

Quinlan, M. (2005) 'The hidden epidemic of injuries and illness associated with the global expansion of precarious employment', in C.L. Peterson and C. Mayhew (eds), *Occupational Health and Safety: International Influences and the New Epidemics*. Amityville, NY: Baywood Publishing, pp. 53–74.

Reisel, W.D. (2003) 'Predicting job insecurity via moderating influence of individual powerlessness', *Psychological Reports*, 92: 820–822.

Reisel, W.D. and Banai, M. (2002) 'Comparison of a multidimensional and a global measure of job insecurity: Predicting job attitudes and work behaviors', *Psychological Reports*, 90: 913–922.

Reisel, W.D., Chia, S.L. and Maloles, C.M. (2005) 'Job insecurity spillover to key account management: Negative effects of performance, effectiveness, adaptiveness, and esprit de corps', *Journal of Business and Psychology*, 19: 483–503.

Reisel, W.D., Probst, T.M., Chia, S., Maloles, C.M., Brown, J.W. and Hazen, J. (2007) 'An examination of the effects of job insecurity on job satisfaction, organizational citizenship behavior, deviant behavior, and negative emotions of employees'. Poster presented to the 2007 Conference of the Institute of Behavioral and Applied Management, Reno, NV.

Roskies, E. and Louis-Guerin, C. (1990) 'Job insecurity in managers: Antecedents and consequences', *Journal of Organizational Behavior*, 11: 345–359.

Roskies, E., Louis-Guerin, C. and Fournier, C. (1993) 'Coping with job insecurity: How does personality make a difference?' *Journal of Organizational Behavior*, 14: 617–630.

Rust, K.G., McKinley, W. and Zhao, J. (2003) '*Business ideologies and perceived breach of contract during downsizing: A China perspective.* Unpublished manuscript.

Salovey, P. and Mayer, J.D. (1990) 'Emotional intelligence', *Imagination, Cognition and Personality*, 9: 185–211.

Schaubroeck, J., Ganster, D.C. and Fox, M.L. (1992) 'Dispositional affect and work-related stress', *Journal of Applied Psychology*, 77: 322–325.

Scheier, M.F. and Carver, C.S. (1985) 'Optimism, coping, and health: Assessment and implications of generalized outcome expectancies', *Health Psychology*, 4: 219–247.

Schwebel, M. (1997) 'Job insecurity as structural violence: Implications for destructive intergroup conflict', *Peace and Conflict: Journal of Peace Psychology*, 3: 333–351.

Schweiger, D.M., and DeNisi, A.S. (1991) 'Communication with employees following a merger: A longitudinal field experiment', *Academy of Management Journal*, 34: 110–135.

Seligman, M.E.P. (1975) *Helplessness.* San Francisco: Freeman.

Siegrist, J., Peter, R., Junge, A., Cremer, P. and Seidel, D. (1990) 'Low status control, high effort at work and ischemic heart disease: Prospective evidence from blue-collar men', *Social Science Medicine*, 31: 1127–1134.

Smithson, J. and Lewis, S. (2000) 'Is job insecurity changing the psychological contract?' *Personnel Review*, 29: 680–702.

Society for Human Resource Management (2001) *Layoffs and Job Security Survey.* Alexandria, VA: Author.

Sverke, M. and Hellgren, J. (2002) 'The nature of job insecurity: Understanding employment uncertainty on the brink of a new millennium', *Applied Psychology: An International Review*, 51: 23–42.

Sverke, M., Hellgren, J. and Näswell, K. (2002) 'No security: A meta-analysis and review of job insecurity and its consequences', *Journal of Occupational Health Psychology*, 7: 242–264.

US Department of Labor (2004–2005) *Occupational Outlook Handbook* (Bulletin 2570). Washington, DC: Author.

van Vuuren, T. (1990) *Met Ontslag Bedreigd: Werknemers in Onzekerheid Over Hun Arbeidsplaats Bij Veranderingen in De Organisatie.* Amsterdam: VU Uitgeverij.

Warr, P.B. (1987) *Work, Unemployment and Mental Health.* Oxford: Clarendon Press.

Watson, D. and Clark, L. (1984) 'Negative affectivity: The disposition to experience aversive emotional states', *Psychological Bulletin*, 96: 465–490.

Westman, M., Etzion, D. and Danon, E. (2001) 'Job insecurity and crossover of burnout in married couples', *Journal of Organizational Behavior*, 22: 467–481.

Winefield, A.H. (2002) 'Unemployment, underemployment, occupational stress, and psychological well-being', *Australian Journal of Management*, 27: 137–148.

11

Voluntary Employee Turnover: Determinants, Processes, and Future Directions

Wendy R. Boswell, Lily Run Ren
and Andrew T. Hinrichs

Few would argue that the most valuable asset to an organization is its human capital. Retaining this asset is a critical task for supervisors, executives, and HR professionals. Indeed, employee retention is frequently cited as one of the most significant challenges facing employers (e.g., Byrne, 1999). At the time this chapter was written, organizations face a fairly tight labor market, struggling with acute labor and shortages, particularly within certain industries (e.g., accounting and energy) and professions/skill sets (e.g., nurses and geoscientists). Yet organizations are continuously confronted with challenges in retaining high-performing/high-impact talent even when the job market is tight. Understanding the processes and determinants of employees voluntarily leaving an organization is thus of theoretical interest and practical importance as employers struggle in the 'war for talent.'

Research is replete with conceptual models and empirical research examining employee retention, providing important insight into why employees leave (or stay with) an organization. The purpose of this chapter is to review early and recent research on employee turnover and suggest areas for future research. We first review the classic models and describe some of the corresponding empirical research. We then focus on the more recent turnover research, including issues such as different psychological paths that explain why people stay with vs. leave an organization, and the role of performance and dispositional factors in predicting employee turnover. Methodological and measurement issues are then examined. The chapter concludes with a discussion of potential future research areas on employee turnover, and the practical value of this research to organizations.

Our focus throughout is on *voluntary* employee turnover. This is to be contrasted with involuntary turnover (e.g., layoffs and dismissal) and retirements. More specifically, we follow prior research (e.g., Boswell et al., 2005; Bretz et al., 1994) that has conceptualized and operationalized voluntary employee turnover as being in a different position, in a new organization, and having left on one's own accord. That being said, studies have not always distinguished between voluntary vs. involuntary turnover. This is discussed in measurement issues, as research rely on turnover cognitions (e.g., quit intent) and/or seeking alternative employment rather than actual employee quits as outcome variables. We include such studies in our review, given the prevalence of the former constructs in empirical research as well as their importance in the turnover process.

CLASSIC TURNOVER THEORY AND EMPIRICAL RESEARCH

Early turnover models

Research on employee turnover dates back to March and Simon's (1958) pioneering work, which introduced the theory of organization equilibrium. They suggested that employees remain in their organization if the organization can provide sufficient inducement to motivate them to stay; and that the perceived desirability of movement and the perceived ease of movement are two primary factors that influence employee turnover. This model has evoked tremendous attention from researchers for decades. Inspired by March and Simon's (1958) 'explicit, formal, and systematic conceptual analysis of the withdrawal process' (Hom and Griffeth, 1995), turnover researchers endeavored to interpret the process through which employees voluntarily leave their organizations.

Other notable models of employee turnover followed from March and Simon's (1958) seminal work. Porter and Steers (1973) proposed that met expectations were the central determinant of employees' decision to leave the organization. Specifically, unmet expectations result in employees dissatisfied with their jobs and eventually the decision to leave. However, Locke (1976) noted that the relationship between job satisfaction and turnover is quite moderate, with job satisfaction rarely explaining more than 16 percent of the variance in turnover. In response, Mobley (1977) suggested that job satisfaction is not directly related to turnover. Mobley (1977) posited an intermediate linkage model of employee turnover, starting from the evaluation of the present job, which may lead to job dissatisfaction and thoughts of quitting, going through a process of searching for and evaluating alternatives, and resulting in an intention to quit before actual turnover behavior. Mobley et al. (1979) then proposed a more heuristic model within which quit intention and turnover are determined largely by job satisfaction, expected utility of the present work role, and expected utility of alternative work roles, which in turn, are influenced by a number of individual, organizational, and environmental factors. Steers and Mowday (1981) offered a dual sequence in their extension, suggesting that quit intentions directly lead to turnover or may trigger a search for and evaluation of alternative opportunities. Similarly, based on Mobley's (1977) model, Hom et al. (1984) proposed a revised intermediate-processes model. In addition to the original evaluation and search process, Hom et al. (1984) suggested another path, where some employees may expect to easily find an alternative job or do not consider finding an alternative and simply decide to quit the job.

At about the same time of Mobley's (1977) publication, Price (1977) developed a turnover model, in which the central thrust was that intent to quit and perceived alternative opportunities determine turnover, and job satisfaction influences turnover through its effect on intent to quit. Price and Mueller (1981, 1986) later incorporated various individual and structural determinants of job satisfaction. The most recent revision of the Price and Mueller model (Kim et al., 1996) consists of nearly 20 variables that are linked to turnover, including structural determinants, individual determinants, environmental determinants, and process variables.

The 1980s brought additional turnover models, including Muchinsky and Morrow's (1980) multidisciplinary model, Farrell and Rusbult's (1981) investment model, Sheridan and Abelson's (1983) cusp catastrophe model, and Hulin, Roznowski, and Hachiya's (1985) labor-economic model. Hom and Griffeth (1995) provide a thorough and insightful review of these models.

Early empirical research on employee turnover

Employee turnover is one of the most studied behaviors in management research (Griffeth et al., 2000). In this section, we briefly review the factors that were shown to predict turnover in early empirical research.

The role of work attitudes

Despite the numerous conceptual and somewhat diverse models, one common characteristic recognized in most early models is the role of work attitudes (e.g., job satisfaction, organizational commitment) in the turnover process. It has long been recognized that dissatisfied employees are more likely to quit their jobs (e.g., Hulin, 1966; March and Simon, 1958). Several meta-analyses demonstrate that job satisfaction moderately and negatively relates to turnover (e.g., Carsten and Spector, 1987; Hom and Griffeth, 1995; Steel and Ovalle, 1984), as do different facets of job satisfaction (e.g., satisfaction with the work, pay, or supervision; Cotton and Tuttle, 1986). A more recent meta-analysis by Griffeth et al. (2000) replicated these results.

Though a consistent and significant relationship exists, the correlation between job satisfaction and turnover is moderate (Griffeth et al., 2000; Locke, 1976), indicating that a great deal of variance in turnover is unexplained by job satisfaction. To address this, researchers have suggested different intermediate linkages between the two variables (e.g., Mobley, 1977; Porter and Steers, 1973; Price and Mueller, 1981), and studies support such mediators. For example, intent to quit appears to be a more proximal predictor of

employee turnover than job satisfaction (e.g., Michaels and Spector, 1982; Mobley et al., 1978).

The relationship between job satisfaction and turnover is also influenced by other factors, including the existence of alternative opportunities as well as general unemployment levels. Specifically, unemployment rates are likely to moderate the effect of job satisfaction on turnover such that under high unemployment, dissatisfied employees will be less able to quit (Carsten and Spector, 1987).

Beyond affective reactions to the job, affective responses to the organization (e.g., organizational commitment) also influence turnover (e.g., Cotton and Tuttle, 1986; Griffeth et al., 2000; Hom and Griffeth, 1995; Mathieu and Zajac, 1990; Mowday et al., 1982; and see the Chapter by Meyer et al. in this volume). Some research has examined which attitude – job satisfaction or organizational commitment – is the stronger and/or more proximal predictor of turnover (e.g., Currivan, 1999), and whether global measures are better predictors than specific ones (Porter et al., 1974; Wiener and Vardi, 1980). In support of this, early work generally found organizational commitment to be the strongest attitudinal determinant of voluntary turnover (e.g., Mowday et al., 1982; Porter et al., 1974). However, Tett and Meyer's (1993) test of competing models showed that the two work attitudes have reciprocal influence, as well as exerting direct and independent effects on intent to quit. They also found that intent to quit was predicted more strongly by job satisfaction than organizational commitment, and that intent to quit mediated the linkages between these attitudes and actual turnover.

Similarly, the role of organizational commitment on turnover appears to be moderated by other individual and contextual factors. Cohen and Hudecek (1993) showed that the negative relationship between organizational commitment and turnover was stronger for employees in higher-status occupations than those in lower-status occupations. Chang (1999) found that employees with higher levels of organizational commitment were less likely to leave the organization, and this relationship was stronger for those highly committed to their careers, arguably because of the fewer alternative opportunities limited by their career focus.

The role of turnover intentions

Turnover intention refers to a conscious and deliberate willingness to leave the organization (Tett and Meyer, 1993), and thus would precede (be more proximal to) actual turnover (e.g., Mobley's (1977) theory of intermediate linkages between job satisfaction and turnover). Hom and colleagues (e.g., Hom and Hulin, 1981; Hom et al., 1979) confirmed this, showing that intentions can explain as much as 49 percent of the variance in reenlistment decisions during a six-month period. Tett and Meyer's (1993) path analyses also showed that turnover intention/withdrawal cognitions mediate the attitudinal linkage with turnover (and see Griffeth et al. 2000; Steel and Ovalle, 1984). The important role of quit cognitions helps explain why attitudinal variables such as job satisfaction and organizational commitment (both distal predictors) account for only a small percentage of the variance in turnover. The role of turnover intentions have been acknowledged in most conceptual models (e.g., Farrell and Rusbult, 1981; Hulin et al., 1985; Steers and Mowday, 1981).

The role of alternative opportunities

Alternative opportunity is an important variable in most turnover models (e.g., Farrel and Rusbult, 1981; Mobley, 1977; Mobley et al., 1979; Price and Mueller, 1981, 1986; Steers and Mowday, 1981), and is directly linked to March and Simon's (1958) notion of ease of movement. Perceived alternatives refer to employees' perception of how easily they might find an alternative job, thus representing perceptions of their respective labor market. On the other hand, economic opportunities represent an objective condition of the labor market (e.g., employment rate). Both constructs have been shown to play an important role in the employee turnover process.

Alternative opportunities can directly impact turnover (e.g., Hom and Griffeth, 1991; Steers and Mowday, 1981). Gerhart (1990) found that both perceived alternatives and the unemployment rate significantly predicted turnover in young adults. Alternative opportunities can also influence turnover through the impact on variables such as job attitudes (Hulin et al., 1985).

Research shows that perceived alternative opportunities only modestly affect turnover (Griffeth et al., 2000; Hom and Griffeth, 1995; Steel and Griffeth, 1989); there is a stronger relationship between objective unemployment rate and turnover (e.g., Hulin et al., 1985; Kirschenbaum and Mano-Negrin, 1999). One explanation for this phenomenon is that unlike most studies examining perceived alternative opportunities with limited samples, labor economics use broader samples across industries and occupations (Hom and Griffeth, 1995). It is also possible that employees' perceptions are limited by the amount of information they have. In addition, Steel and Griffeth (1989) suggested that perceived opportunities were often operationalized by deficient and unreliable measures (e.g., single-item scale), thus accounting for its weak predictive validity.

Additional turnover correlates

The first meta-analysis by Cotton and Tuttle (1986), and other studies (see Hom and Griffeth, 1995) show that employees' personal characteristics (e.g., age, tenure, education, sex, and marital status) are modest predictors of turnover. Work-related factors (overall job satisfaction, satisfaction with job facets, organizational commitment, compensation level, job performance, and tenure) also consistently predict turnover.

Using a different categorization, research has discussed turnover antecedents as reflecting an individual's *motivation* to quit (e.g., salary and job satisfaction), thus providing 'push' vs. *human capital* traits (e.g., age and education) that influence an individual's attractiveness to the labor market, thus providing 'pull' (e.g., Blau, 1994; Boswell et al., 2006; Bretz et al., 1994). Despite finding significant relationships between such factors and turnover, the bivariate relationships are fairly moderate (correlations are generally below 0.40 in several meta-analyses). The remaining unexplained variance in turnover drives researchers to investigate other important determinants as well as potential moderators.

Summary of classic models

The classic models of turnover reviewed in this section result from researchers' attempts to understand the process and determinants of employees' voluntary turnover. Extensive research exists testing these models, though some relationships remain to be examined. For instance, Price and Mueller (1981) and Mobley et al. (1979) acknowledged that factors like professionalism could influence turnover, but it is rarely examined (see Cohen and Hudecek, 1993 for an exception). Many empirical studies have provided only partial tests of conceptual models (see Dalessio et al., 1986; Spector, 1991 for exceptions). Most early turnover studies were cross-sectional, focusing on single organizations or specific industries. In addition, the effect sizes for any single variable in predicting turnover are typically small to moderate and there remains a great deal of unexplained variance in turnover overall (Cotton and Tuttle, 1986; Hom and Griffeth, 1995; Griffeth et al., 2000). This suggests that additional factors need to be considered to understand employee turnover. This early work, both conceptual and empirical, provided important insight and a strong foundation for the more contemporary research on employee turnover.

RECENT DEVELOPMENTS IN EMPLOYEE TURNOVER THEORY AND RESEARCH

Unfolding model

Arguably the most notable contribution to the turnover literature in the past decade is Lee and colleagues' (Lee and Mitchell, 1994; Lee et al., 1996) 'unfolding model of voluntary turnover.' This model suggests that turnover and search processes may deviate from the traditional sequential model. Drawing on image theory (Beach, 1990), Lee and Mitchell (1994) argued that turnover is often triggered by a precipitating event such as an unsolicited job offer, the spouse's job transfer, or an extreme incident of mistreatment by one's boss. This event causes the person to 'pause and think about the meaning or implication of the event in relation to his or her job' (Lee and Mitchell, 1994: 60). The unfolding model presents four decision paths to employee voluntary turnover. The first path is characterized by the individual experiencing a 'shock to the system' which triggers a plan (or script) already in place. There is typically no accumulated job dissatisfaction or search for alternative employment, the employee simply experiences an incident that prompts a pre-determined plan to leave. The second path also involves a shock but, in this situation, there is no plan or script in place. The incident simply shocks an individual to leave unexpectedly without a search for alternative employment. The third path involves a shock that then prompts some level of job dissatisfaction, and a search for an alternative. Again, a specific event triggers the turnover, but in this case, the employee attempts to secure employment before leaving. The fourth path represents the more traditional view of turnover, in which there is a progression of job dissatisfaction, and ultimately the decision to leave with or without a search for alternative employment.

An important element to and contribution of the unfolding model is the notion of 'shock'-induced turnover. This notion of a single incident rather than a progression of withdrawal fostering employee exit has prompted a series of empirical studies and support for the different decision processes involved in staying vs. leaving a company (e.g., Donnelly and Quirin, 2006; Lee et al., 1999; Morrell et al., 2004). Interestingly, empirical research suggests that such 'shocks' cause more employee voluntary turnover than accumulated job dissatisfaction (Holtom et al., 2005).

Job embeddedness

In their 2001 work introducing job embed-dedness, Mitchell et al. pointed out that more research is needed to explain the significant, yet modest, relationships that attitudinal vari-ables, job search, and perceived alternatives have with turnover. The job embeddedness construct was introduced to understand fur-ther what influences employees' decisions to stay on a job. Embeddedness has been described as a web or net that encompasses the various aspects of a person's life (Mitchell et al., 2001). The more intricate or complex the web a person has, the more likely that this person has more responsibilities, active roles, and important relationships; those with more complex webs relative to their jobs are said to be more job-embedded.

The first dimension, links, involves the extent to which individuals have formal or informal connections to other people (work and non-work friends) and institutions. The number of links in both the community and organization contributes to the degree of embeddedness (Yao et al., 2004), given those links are salient to the individual. The second dimension, fit, reflects an employee's perceived compatibility or comfort with their organization or community, and research shows that fit is associated with retention (Chan, 1996), and that people consciously seek fit (Cable and Judge, 1996). The third dimension of embeddedness is sacrifice, the perceived cost of material or psychological benefits that would be forfeited by leaving the organization or community (Mitchell et al., 2001).

Each of these components can con-tribute to job embeddedness through on-the-job and off-the-job factors (Mitchell et al., 2001). Examples of on-the-job factors are relationships with co-workers, organi-zational fit between employee skills and demands, and organizational perks or spon-sored activities (e.g., in-house day care services, time-off for volunteer service). Off-the-job factors include family, community, religious, and personal commitments. These two domains give the embeddedness construct

six dimensions: links, fit, and sacrifice associ-ated with the organization or the community (Mitchell et al., 2001).

Mitchell et al. (2001) showed that those who are embedded in their jobs do not leave as freely as those who are less embedded in their current jobs. More importantly, job embed-dedness was shown to add to the prediction of turnover beyond which is attributable to desirability of movement (i.e., job satisfaction and organizational commitment) and ease of movement (i.e., perceived alternatives and job search; Mitchell et al. 2001).

A study by Allen (2006) focused on the mechanisms through which organizations can embed employees, and specifically, new employees into the company. This study revealed that socialization tactics such as collective (common learning experiences), fixed (informing of the timing associated with socialization steps), and investiture tactics (positive social support for organizational members) were positively related to on-the-job embeddedness, which in turn negatively predicted turnover. These findings indicate that organizations can use socialization tactics to actively embed new employees into their positions and reduce early voluntary turnover.

Lee et al. (2004) took a closer look at the on- and off-the-job dimensions of embeddedness. They found that off-the-job embeddedness predicted absence and turnover and that on-the-job embeddedness predicted organi-zational citizenship behavior and job perfor-mance. Interestingly, being embedded on the job moderated many relationships, such as the negative effect of organizational citizenship behavior on absence and the negative effect of job performance on turnover, and the positive effect of absence on turnover. These findings are consistent with the argument that on-the-job embeddedness is a key factor in decisions to stay with an organization (Lee et al., 2004).

The eight motivational forces

Maertz and Griffeth (2004) argued that 'there is no overarching framework available for researchers and practitioners hoping to comprehensively grasp the motivations for staying and leaving an organization' (p. 667) and that specifying the motivational mechanisms behind those predictors is crucial for better understanding turnover. To address this issue, they proposed eight motive categories, or 'forces,' which trigger engagement in the mental behavior of turnover deliberations, and the physical behavior of actually quitting (Maertz and Griffeth, 2004).

The forces have been categorized as follows:

(1) *Affective* (psychological comfort or discomfort with one's membership);
(2) *Calculative* (calculation of one's future value/goal attainment with the organization);
(3) *Contractual* (perceived obligations to stay);
(4) *Behavioral* (desire to avoid costs of quitting);
(5) *Alternative* (beliefs about obtaining an alternative job);
(6) *Normative* (perceived expectations to comply with others, i.e. family members);
(7) *Moral/ethical* (maintaining consistency between one's values and behaviors); and
(8) *Constituent* (attachment to coworkers or groups in their organization).

This approach is proposed to further turnover content-process (*how-why*) model integration by helping to identify psychological mechanisms behind the individual's reported reasons for quitting.

In an empirical study, Maertz and Campion (2004) examined how different motives systematically relate to different types of decision processes. Drawing from Lee and Mitchell and colleagues' work (Lee and Mitchell, 1994; Lee et al., 1996; Lee et al., 2004; Mitchell et al., 2001), Maertz and Campion (2004) discussed four generic decision paths (i.e., quitting as impulsive, comparative, preplanned, or conditional) as the 'how' regarding turnover. Then, integrating the eight motivational forces as the 'why' driving attachment vs. withdrawal, they proposed how the four decision paths would vary on the eight motives. Results generally confirmed the hypotheses regarding turnover motives systematically related to decision

process types. For example, comparison and conditional quitters had higher attraction to alternative jobs than preplanned or impulsive quitters, while impulsive quitters tended to be more affect-driven and impulsive in their decisions.

Though there is limited research in this area, this perspective provides an interesting opportunity for researchers to better integrate the *how* and *why* of quitting, ultimately providing 'more accurate and precise descriptions' (Maertz and Campion, 2004: 566) of turnover decision processes.

The performance-turnover link

Progress has also been made in understanding the complex relationship between job performance and employee turnover. Early work suggested a negative relationship between performance and turnover (e.g., Bycio et al., 1990; McEvoy and Cascio, 1987), while cautioning that simple linear relationships may not fully capture the complexity of the relationship nor the importance of the context. Consistent with this, research suggests that the performance-turnover relationship depends on reward contingencies (e.g., Allen and Griffeth, 2001; Williams and Livingstone, 1994). A study of sales representatives found that when commission accounted for 100 percent of pay, there was a stronger negative performance-turnover relationship (Harrison et al., 1996). Recognizing the dynamic nature of performance, this study also showed that voluntary employee turnover was better predicted (negatively) by current performance than by average performance level, and that the decline in performance over time increased the risk of turnover (and vice versa). Sturman and Trevor (2001) expanded on this research, showing that the performance slopes of 'leavers' were significantly less than those of employees that stayed, and that both short- and long-term trends in performance as well as current performance were important in predicting turnover.

Researchers continue to examine the possibility of a curvilinear (U-shaped) performance-turnover relationship (Jackofsky, 1984).

The rationale here is that low performers are likely to be 'pushed out' because of low rewards (intrinsic or extrinsic) as well as possible concern over termination, while high performers may perceive or experience being under-rewarded yet have high ease of movement. Though few studies test for the possibility of a curvilinear relationship, and some that explicitly test for it have failed (e.g., Birnbaum and Somers, 1993; Wright and Bonett, 1993), Williams and Livingstone (1994) found meta-analytic support for the U-shaped relationship. Trevor et al. (1997) replicated this phenomenon, and perhaps more importantly, found that the relationship was more pronounced when salary growth was low, reinforcing the importance of pay growth commensurate with performance to retaining talent. They also found evidence of a more pronounced curvilinear relationship when promotions are high, suggesting that promotions (particularly among low performers) facilitate ease of movement through visibility and signaling. Other recent research supports the curvilinear performance-turnover relationship, though the relationship appears to vary depending on sample characteristics such as gender (Hochwarter et al., 2001) or country/culture (Salamin and Hom, 2005).

Drawing on the notion that both low and high performers are generally more likely to leave, and that organizations can influence the 'performance distribution of leavers' (p. 998), Sturman et al. (2003) used a cost-benefit analysis to show the positive financial consequences to a firm for investing in performance-based pay. They showed how the benefits of a strong pay-for-performance link far outweigh the costs by prompting high-performing employees to stay and encouraging the turnover of low performers.

More distal determinants of employee turnover

Recent studies (including meta-analyses) have reconfirmed the earlier research findings and theoretical perspectives regarding the roles of work-related, personal, and external factors in relation to employee turnover. For example, Griffeth et al's (2000) meta-analysis confirmed work factors such as pay, supervisory and coworker relations, participative management, promotional opportunities, met expectations, job demands/stress, tenure, and both facets of and overall job satisfaction as correlates of employee turnover. The results also replicated earlier findings regarding a minimal role for personal characteristics (e.g., demographics, cognitive ability) and a moderate role for perceived alternative opportunities. New perspectives of the employment relationship and structures of work/HR practices have led researchers to incorporate such variables as perceived organization support (e.g., Rhoades and Eisenberger, 2002), relational variables (e.g., network centrality, Mossholder et al., 2005), organizational change (e.g., Baron et al., 2001), perceptions of the company's success (Bretz et al., 1994) as well as the role of stock options (e.g., Daily et al., 2002; Dunford et al., 2005) in predicting employee turnover.

The role of dispositional factors to employee turnover has received increasing attention (Barrick and Mount, 1991; Salgado, 2002). Zimmerman (2006) found that among the Big Five personality traits, emotional stability was the strongest (negative) predictor of intent to quit, while conscientiousness and agreeableness best predicted (negatively) actual turnover. Findings from this meta-analytic path model also revealed direct effects from the personality traits to turnover intent and turnover that are not captured through job satisfaction or performance, reflecting that individuals low on these traits may have adverse experiences in the work environment not related to the job itself and/or engage in unplanned/spontaneous turnover. Boudreau et al. (2001) found that executives higher in extroversion, neuroticism, openness to experience, and agreeableness (but not conscientiousness) as well as cognitive ability engaged in more job search activity, and that the effect emerged over-and-above situational variables such as job satisfaction, compensation, and tenure. Findings from this study differ somewhat from meta-analytic work on the personality-turnover link, particularly regarding the significant effect of extroversion but not conscientiousness. This is likely due to the specific turnover construct examined in Boudreau et al. (2001), namely job search activity rather than turnover.

Barrick and Zimmerman (2005) investigated how to identify employees with the propensity to quit during the selection process. Results showed that applicants' biodata, clear-purpose attitudes and intentions, and disguised-purpose dispositional retention variables predicted voluntary turnover six months after hiring. An interesting implication from this study is that while most turnover models view intent to quit as an immediate precursor to actual turnover, some individuals may be predisposed to quit 'even before starting the job' (Barrick and Zimmerman, 2005: 164). Krausz (2002) also discussed the issue of premeditated turnover (or 'time-bound commitment'). Drawing upon Mael and Ashforth's (1995) argument regarding individual differences in the propensity for organizational identification immediately upon joining the organization, Krausz (2002) took a more dire perspective that every employee may be 'a passive job seeker regardless of organizations' efforts to improve various aspects of work itself and the work environment' (p. 64).

In sum, recent research on employee turnover has continued to examine cognitive and affective bases for turnover decisions, drawing explicitly or implicitly on March and Simon's (1958) desirability and ease of movement framework. However, recent work also suggests that the turnover process is not fully captured by the traditional sequential model relating job dissatisfaction to turnover when alternatives are available. The unfolding model, job embeddedness, motivational forces, and the role of dispositions have contributed new insight to our understanding of employee turnover/retention.

METHODOLOGICAL ISSUES IN TURNOVER RESEARCH

In this section, we focus on an array of critical methodological issues in turnover research. In particular, we discuss issues surrounding the context of the sample examined, how turnover is measured, the role of time, and level of analysis and their implications. Though there are likely other important methodological issues relevant to this literature, we see these as particularly pertinent to understanding prior research findings as well as directing future research.

Understanding the context

One methodological-related issue particularly important to interpreting research findings and their practical applicability and generalizability is the nature of the employee sample examined. This is an important issue to examine because 'contextual' factors (an issue discussed further below) such as the labor market conditions and cultural and professional norms vary, and are likely to play an important role in an individual's turnover decision.

Many early studies of employee turnover focused on the nursing profession (see Hom et al., 1992). These studies offer important insight given the practical challenges healthcare organizations face in attracting and retaining qualified nurses in the face of nursing shortages (Health Resources and Services Administration, 2000), but the generalizability of the findings would remain an open question. More recently, other occupational groups have been the focus of empirical attention. Donnelly and Quirin (2006) examined the unfolding model among a sample of accountants – a profession also faced with employee retention challenges. This study explicitly recognized potential gender differences within the sample, finding for example, that women experienced more shocks than men presumably because of pregnancy and childbirth. Other studies have addressed the importance of understanding turnover at different levels of the organization (e.g., Boswell et al., 2005; Boudreau et al., 2001; Bretz et al., 1994) seeking for example to uncover the turnover determinants and processes of these particularly high-demand/high-impact individuals. In general, this research suggests that many of the key variables important in predicting turnover among lower-level employees are also important in understanding that of high-level employees, though some differences exist. In particular, compensation (including incentive pay) appears to be less important (though statistically significant) perhaps due to pay being less of a concern among this already highly-compensated group and/or that other elements such as stock options are more important. Related to this, a study of executives by Dunford et al. (2005) found that underwater stock options represent an important 'push' factor, particularly among those executives that feel they have more to lose if they stay.

Recent research has examined the generalizability to other settings of traditional predictors of employee turnover based on samples outside of the US. For example, Boswell et al. (2006) examined an array of personality (e.g., conscientiousness and extraversion), demographic (e.g., tenure and gender), and situational (e.g., job satisfaction and compensation level) variables as predictors of job search activity among a large sample of European executives, finding some differences from prior US-focused research. Contrary to Boudreau et al's (2001) study of US executives, compensation level and the personality traits of openness to experience and agreeableness did not predict job search activity for the executives in Europe.

Posthuma et al. (2005) compared retail grocery store employees in the US and Mexico, finding that job satisfaction and perceived ease of movement were stronger predictors of turnover intent in the US than in Mexico. Maertz et al.'s (2003) research on Mexican maquiladoras provides particularly important insight on the application of traditional employee turnover research and models to non-Anglo cultures. They found that beliefs that quitting is acceptable

behavior, negative or ambivalent attitudes toward the maquiladora, potential costs of quitting (i.e., sacrifice), fulfilment of work values (e.g., flexibility and development), and attachment to co-workers and the leader play a particularly important role in maquiladora workers' turnover decisions. As noted by the researchers, many of these constructs are consistent with Anglo-based findings, though there seems to be a greater role for perceiving job change as a 'hassle' (i.e., any small benefit is not likely worth it) as well as the role of family (i.e., family responsibilities, loyalty) among the Mexican sample.

Measuring turnover

Turnover proxies

A key issue in turnover research is whether turnover is even measured. Many studies that are focused on the general issue of employee turnover/retention assess turnover cognitions (e.g., quit intent) and/or related behaviors (e.g., job search) rather than actual turnover, though typically yield findings consistent with studies using actual turnover as the outcome variable.

As discussed above, intent to quit and related turnover cognitions (e.g., intent to search) are important intermediary variables linking personal and work factors to turnover (e.g., Mobley, 1977; Tett and Meyer, 1993). Turnover cognitions have also been examined as a proxy for employee turnover. The general argument is that as one of the strongest predictors of actual turnover (Hom and Griffeth, 1995), assessing quit intent as an outcome variable offers insight on employee exit from an organization.

Job search activity has also been examined as a proxy for employee turnover as well as an intermediary variable in the turnover process. In their study of high-level managers, Bretz et al. (1994) showed that variables such as job dissatisfaction motivate an individual to search for a new job and ultimately separate from the organization. Following up on this study, Boudreau et al. (2001) examined enduring individual characteristics (i.e., personality, cognitive ability) in relation to executive job search. A trend in the job search literature is to consider the nature of job search behaviors. In particular, Blau (1994) distinguished between preparatory (i.e., assessing whether desirable alternatives exist) and active (i.e., determining the availability of those alternatives to the individual) job search behaviors. Research has generally shown preparatory and active search as distinct dimensions, with different antecedents and outcomes (Blau, 1993). For example, preparatory job search tends to precede active job search, and active search is a stronger and more proximal predictor of turnover.

Nature of turnover

As previously noted, empirical research does not always distinguish between voluntary and involuntary turnover (see Campion, 1991). This was perhaps more common in early studies, although recent research, particularly at the unit- or firm-levels of analysis (e.g., Glebbeek and Bax, 2004; Kacmar et al., 2006; Koys, 2001; Simons and Roberson, 2003), does not always make this distinction. This is a concern given that the factors involved in quitting an organization and being involuntarily dismissed are quite distinct. From their organizational level analysis, Shaw et al. (1998) found that HRM practices that predicted voluntary turnover were quite different from those that predicted discharge. Specifically, pay and benefits and employer expectations were related to voluntary turnover, and staffing practices were related to discharge or involuntary turnover.

A related issue is distinguishing between avoidable and unavoidable turnover (Abelson, 1987; Dalton et al., 1981; Hom and Griffeth, 1995). Examining avoidable turnover is arguably of greater importance to an organization in understanding the employee withdraw process. Abelson (1987) found that employees who leave the organization for unavoidable reasons (e.g., spouse relocation, pregnancy) were similar to employees who stayed with the organization in terms of job attitudes and withdrawal cognitions. Making the avoidable-unavoidable turnover distinction is thus particularly important in studies seeking to understand the role of job attitudes, working conditions, and/or turnover cognitions to employee turnover. However, what researchers often label 'unavoidable' turnover (or unavoidable 'shocks') may not always be beyond the organization's control. For example, an organization may be able to accommodate an individual faced with a relocating spouse, childcare challenges, or return to school through telecommuting, a transfer to another division, or offering part-time work or flexible scheduling. Regardless, understanding the reasons for the turnover is likely to help researchers improve their understanding and prediction of turnover.

From a practical standpoint, data on the nature of turnover are not always available through organizational records. Even in organizations that distinguish among the nature of employees' turnover, the distinction made may not accurately reflect the situation. Failure to distinguish between and mis-categorization of the nature of turnover increases the error variance, thus arguably attenuating turnover relations and model viability (Tett and Meyer, 1993). Categorizing turnover through 'triangulation' whereby researchers utilize multiple sources (e.g., exit interviews with HR and input from direct supervisors, Barrick and Zimmerman, 2005) and/or verification by a neutral third-party (Hom and Griffeth, 1995) is likely to help enhance measurement validity (voluntary vs. involuntary) as well as the reasons (e.g., avoidable vs. unavoidable) for the turnover.

Also potentially relevant is the nature of the new job to which the individual 'turned over'. That is, where/what does the employee go to when they leave the current employer (i.e., job destination, Kirschenbaum and Weisberg, 2002)? Fields et al. (2005) investigated this issue, focusing on three 'destinations' – different job in the same company, same type of job in a different company, and different job in a different company. Findings revealed different predictors of the various destinations (e.g., less competent/concerned supervisor led to movement to a similar job in a different organization but not a different job in a different organization nor internally), and that failure to distinguish between the destinations of the job move may affect the effects of certain predictor variables. This later point may help explain equivocal findings across studies (e.g., role of pay level to turnover decisions, demographic differences) in that some studies may be comprised of different proportions of where employees leave to. That is, if the effect of a variable depends on the turnover destination, failure to assess the destination may obscure the findings. Such an approach thus recognizes the turnover process as involving an individual not only leaving an organization but also entering a new work situation. Understanding the nature of an employee's turnover is quite consistent with Lee et al.'s (1996) view of turnover as a decision process with multiple paths and decision steps.

Temporal nature of turnover research

The time-dependent nature of employee turnover is critical, not only because of methodological issues (e.g., when measuring job attitudes or the work environment simultaneously with quit intent), but because turnover is a process that develops over time. Indeed, multiple researchers have argued the importance of time in studying turnover to fully understand its process and determinants (e.g., Kammeyer-Mueller et al., 2005; Mobley, 1982; Steel, 2002). We thus see the temporal context as a particularly important issue in turnover research.

One critical issue involves the time lag between measuring antecedents (i.e., turnover predictors) and the outcome variable (e.g., turnover, intent to quit). The measurement window in prior studies varies between three (e.g., Peterson and Luthans, 2006) and nine months (e.g., Lee and Mowday, 1987), with a one-year period perhaps being most common (e.g., Blau, 1993; Boswell et al., 2005; Bretz et al., 1994; Mitchell et al., 2001; Trevor, 2001). Carsten and Spector's (1987) meta-analysis suggested that the negative

relationship between job satisfaction and turnover is stronger when the time span is relatively short (but this may be due to the military studies included in the analysis). Griffeth et al. (2000) suggested that while a longer time-period may help boost the base rate of turnover incidents, this may be counterproductive given that predictor values may change and thus become less relevant.

Peterson and Luthans (2006) examined unit-level outcomes including employee turnover at three different time intervals. Using a quasi-experimental design, this study showed that financial incentives had a greater impact than non-financial incentives (i.e., social recognition) in predicting turnover over time (at three, six, and nine months), though both types of incentives were significant negative predictors.

It seems that time period used in turnover studies is arbitrary, and chosen for practical convenience (see Peters and Sheridan, 1988), i.e., the turnover data were available within organizational records or existing archival data. Not surprisingly, measurement across multiple time periods is rare. Aside from practical difficulties, the challenge in collecting repeated measures of employee turnover is exacerbated as individuals move between multiple organizations. Boswell et al. (2004) took such an approach, examining the temporal interplay between job satisfaction and turnover of high-level managers as they left (or not) multiple firms. The researchers collected and analyzed individual turnover data over five years and across organizations. This study proposed and investigated the 'Honeymoon-Hangover Effect,' and showed the benefits of multiple measurement: They find that job satisfaction drops prior to a job change, increases significantly after the job change (honeymoon effect), and then tapers off (hangover effect), reinforcing the value of longitudinal data that enables researchers to better understand the temporal cycle in which individuals join and exit organizations.

Other research has modeled the time-dependent nature of employee turnover using survival (or event history) analysis. In the case of employee turnover, researchers examine survival time (i.e., tenure) rather than a simple dichotomous assessment of turnover to describe not only whether someone will quit but when (see Morita et al., 1989, 1993 for descriptions). For example, Trevor (2001) used survival analysis to show a stronger negative effect of job satisfaction on turnover when job availability and/or 'movement capital' (e.g., education, cognitive ability) is high. Trevor et al.'s (1997) study of the curvilinear relationship between voluntary turnover and job performance tracked the survival time of employees that entered the organization within a six-year window. Mossholder et al.'s (2005) study of relational variables as predictors of turnover used survival analysis and a five-year observation period. In an examination of Ghiselli's (1974) 'hobo syndrome' (i.e., the tendency to job-hop), Judge and Watanabe (1995) used event history analysis and a nine-year observation period to show that past turnover behavior significantly predicted present turnover behavior.

A recent study by Kammeyer-Mueller et al. (2005) used repeated measures (survey at organizational entry and every 4 months for 20 months) and survival analysis to examine both between- and within-persons changes in contextual variables (e.g., cost of turnover, perceived alternatives), work attitudes (e.g., organizational commitment, supervisor satisfaction), and behaviors (e.g., search). Findings from this analysis improved the prediction of turnover, and provided important insight on the progression of withdrawal from an organization. As noted by the researchers, there are important differences between 'leavers' and 'stayers' that occur over time (e.g., significant decreases in work satisfaction and increases in work withdrawal behaviors) that are not typically captured when predictor variables and behaviors are measured at only one point in time.

Macro-level studies

Voluntary turnover, particularly among high-performing employees, can be costly to an organization (Staw, 1980) because of its effects on efficiency, sales, and profits (e.g., Glebbeek and Bax, 2004; Kacmar et al., 2006; Koys, 2001). Accordingly, examining turnover at the macro- (firm or business unit) level of analysis is of increasing significance in understanding the 'strategic importance' of employee retention. Investing in high commitment or high involvement HRM systems is consistently associated with lower turnover (e.g., Arthur, 1994; Batt, 2002; Huselid, 1995; Shaw et al., 1998). Importantly this phenomenon extends beyond the US context. In his study of New Zealand business, Guthrie (2001) found a positive relationship between high-involvement work practices and employee retention, but also an interaction between employee retention and high-involvement work practices in affecting firm productivity. This latter finding reinforces the 'business case' for employee retention in that turnover is particularly costly when an organization has created a valuable and unique workforce.

High-involvement/commitment work practices arguably influence employee retention by fostering greater identification and commitment among employees. In support of this, a meta-analysis of the business-unit relationship between employee attitudes and business outcomes, including employee turnover rate, revealed that overall satisfaction and job engagement correlated (ρ) -0.36 and -0.30 with turnover rate respectively (Harter et al., 2002). It appears that aggregate employee attitudes play an important role in turnover rates consistent with the attitude-turnover link found at the individual level of analysis.

The industrial relations as well as the economics literatures have also contributed to our understanding of quit rates. For example, studies have used Exit-Voice-Loyalty theory (Hirschman, 1970) to examine the role of unions, employee involvement initiatives, teams, and alternative dispute resolution practices on employee exit from an organization. Union representation, higher wages, and use of problem-solving groups, self-directed teams, and internal promotion policies associated with lower quit rates, while use of contingent workers, electronic monitoring, and variable pay associated with higher quit rates (Batt et al., 2002). Economics research often examines wage and benefit levels (Campbell, 1995; Osterman, 1987), industry demand, and job vacancies (e.g., McCormick, 1988; Parsons, 1973) in explaining quit rates.

DIRECTIONS FOR FUTURE RESEARCH

In this section we highlight what we see as particularly fruitful areas for future research on employee turnover. Many of these suggestions involve methodological issues, though we also see opportunities for enriching turnover theory through more interdisciplinary work.

Understanding the context

Like many other topics in management research, the turnover literature would benefit from better understanding of the context in which studies are conducted. Many turnover studies are focused on specific professions such as nursing (e.g., Judge, 1993; Lee et al., 1996; Lee et al., 1999), high-level managers (e.g., Boswell et al., 2005; Bretz et al., 1994), or high-tech industries (e.g., Baron et al., 2001). Such approaches allow researchers to narrow in and provide insight on a specific and often unique context. Yet directly recognizing the implications of the context such as industry/professional norms and idiosyncrasies in the company's culture or environment would lead to more specific practical recommendations regarding how to manage the retention of different employee groups. Greater understanding of the context would also offer insight as to why cross-cultural differences exist.

Another important element of the context is the 'timing' of the study as macroeconomic conditions impose constraints on an individual's mobility options (Carsten and Spector, 1987). Though articles may provide information on when the data was collected, incorporating this element more directly into the theoretical model and the interpretation of the findings would be helpful. Most turnover models and empirical studies implicitly recognize the importance of the extant job market conditions to employee turnover by including perceived employment opportunities/alternatives as a predictor and/or moderator variable. Griffeth et al.'s (2005) development of a multidimensional measure of job market cognitions – the Employment Opportunity Index (EOI) – is helpful in capturing the richness of the alternative opportunities construct. They proposed and validated five factors involved in job market perceptions: ease of movement (i.e., accessibility and quantity of alternatives), desirability of movement (i.e., higher quality or better alternatives), networking (e.g., contacts, visibility), crystallized (concreteness of) alternatives, and mobility (e.g., family responsibilities). Though this provides a systematic measure of perceived employment alternatives, another interesting avenue would be to examine actual job market conditions (as well as actual human capital) in the turnover process and how/why accuracy of perceived alternatives may diverge from actual labor market conditions (Steel, 2002).

Longitudinal research: beyond single-time lag

The very issue of employee turnover is one that unfolds overtime. As discussed above, few studies take a longitudinal approach to studying the phenomenon beyond a single-time lag (i.e., Time 1-Time 2) despite the phases and decision stages involved in the process (Steel, 2002). Research designs involving repeated measures of multiple turnover antecedents and/or behaviors such as in Kammeyer-Mueller et al. (2005) and Trevor (2001) provide valuable insight on how the process of withdrawal plays out over time leading to turnover. Such approaches are likely to contribute practical information to organizations by assessing who is likely to stay vs. leave given changes in attitudes, cognitions, and behaviors, as well as intermediary (and causal) linkages in the withdrawal and turnover process.

Another fruitful area is examining the temporal cycle in which individuals exit one organization and join another. Boswell and colleagues' (2004) research on the honeymoon-hangover effect offers insight into this issue by examining the temporal interplay of work attitudes and job changes over time and across organizations. The notion that past experiences such as prior job changes play a role in future behaviors and experiences is not new, yet is seldom incorporated in empirical studies. This is of course due to the challenge of conducting longitudinal research more generally (e.g., time constraints); however, studying employee turnover adds complexity given that employees that leave are by definition no longer employed at the original research site. Longitudinal research spanning multiple years and potentially multiple job changes thus requires tracking individuals across organizations, necessitating research methodology that provides researchers access to individual contact information beyond their present employer. Given the evidence of stable and predictable attitude changes specifically related to the past and future job changes shown in Boswell et al. (2004), we would suggest research on how prior experiences affect an individual's future attitudes and behaviors upon re-employment is a particularly fruitful area for investigation.

Related to the issue of exit and re-employment is the nature of the employee's destination upon turnover (Fields et al., 2005). Further research distinguishing the individual's destination in terms of the nature of the organization (e.g., within-company move vs. new company/same industry vs. new industry) as well as the nature of the job (e.g., similar job/new company vs. promotion/new company vs. demotion/new company vs. career change) is another fruitful area for research. For instance, Staw and Ross (1985) found in their five-year longitudinal study that individuals showed significant stability of attitudes regardless if they changed employers and/or occupations. Such research would add valuable insight on what individuals are truly looking for in terms of future employment.

Specific issues that could be examined include factors leading to preventable (e.g., similar job in a new company) vs. less preventable (e.g., career changes) turnover, the cost/benefit of within-company movement, how jobs can be redefined to retain critical talent, factors leading to career changes, and the relative importance of job vs. organizational vs. career elements. We see the issue of internal movement particularly interesting given the changing nature of jobs within organizations (Krausz, 2002). For example, as organizations become more and more 'boundaryless' or 'jobless' (Ashkenas et al., 1995; Bridges, 1994), we have seen a paradigmatic shift from employees performing narrowly-defined job duties to an expectation that employees contribute as needed and in varying capacities (Lawler, 1994). This suggests organizations may have greater need as well as opportunities for individuals to move within the organization, assuming different responsibilities and developing skill sets. Examining 'internal turnover' would help us better understand the new employment relationship and evolution of job roles.

Bridging the micro-macro gulf

Research on workforce retention/turnover is consistent with understanding the 'strategic value' of human resources and HRM practices. Employee retention is an important organizational outcome, upon which HRM/work practices have a more direct and explainable influence relative to more distal and 'contaminated' outcomes such as firm profit or stock price. Continued research examining the role of employee retention as part of the 'black box' linking high-commitment/involvement work practices to organizational effectiveness would help us better explore the process through which HRM adds strategic value. Yet the detrimental impact of employee turnover on an organization is likely to depend on individual- (e.g., nature of the employee's work, cost to replace) and organizational-level (e.g., firm strategy, industry competition) factors. Accordingly, research examining *when* and *how* employee turnover affects business outcomes (e.g., sales, profits) is important in understanding the role of a firm's human capital to the bottom-line (Kacmar et al., 2006).

Macro-level research poses its own challenges (e.g., access to large samples), yet may provide an opportunity for expanding longitudinal research on how turnover rates vary over time and the consequences to organizational effectiveness. Examining industry and economic trends in workforce turnover would also offer greater context (as discussed above) to this issue. We also see studies at the establishment level (i.e., the individual workplace rather than firm) to be particularly helpful for understanding the factors (e.g., HRM practices, culture) that influence employee turnover. Within-industry (or within-firm) studies help control for extraneous factors and thus compare 'apples to apples,' while also accounting for possible variance in practices within a firm.

Interdisciplinary research and theory building

Employee turnover research crosses many disciplines. The topic is examined within fields such as OB/HRM, Industrial-Organizational psychology, sociology, economics, strategic management, and labor relations, each with a somewhat different perspective, approach, and even terminology. As examples, 'top management team turnover' is a significant area of research in the strategy literature (e.g., Boeker, 1997; Wiersema and Bantel, 1993), while economics and labor relations discuss 'quit rates' and 'employee exit' (e.g., Batt et al., 2002). Unfortunately, rarely do researchers in a specific field draw from other fields in developing their respective models or research approaches (e.g., measures) – our own review focused primarily on the OB/HRM literature. Interdisciplinary research and theory-building incorporating the collective role of psychological, organizational, economic, and societal factors would provide a clearer and more complete understanding of the complex issues involved in the employee turnover process.

CONCLUSION

Given the increasingly important role of human capital to an organization's success, we see the retention of that talent as one of the most critical issues facing organizations. Past research and theorizing on employee turnover has provided important insights into a complex process that varies with individual traits and is embedded within a complex set of life and work experiences. Prior work has added much to our understanding of why employees stay with vs. leave an organization. Yet there are many fruitful research questions to explore within this topic, several extending from our discussion of methodological and measurement issues in this chapter.

REFERENCES

Abelson, M.A. (1987) 'Examination of avoidable and unavoidable turnover', *Journal of Applied Psychology*, 72: 382–386.

Allen, D.G. (2006) 'Do organizational socialization tactics influence newcomer embeddedness and turnover?', *Journal of Management*, 32: 237–256.

Allen, D.G. and Griffeth, R.W. (2001) 'Test of a mediated performance-turnover relationship highlighting the moderating roles of visibility and reward contingency', *Journal of Applied Psychology*, 86: 1014–1021.

Arthur, J.B. (1994) 'Effects of human resource systems on manufacturing performance and turnover', *Academy of Management Journal*, 37: 670–687.

Ashkenas, R. Ulrich, D., Jick, T. and Kerr, S. (1995) *The Boundaryless Organization: Breaking the Chains of Organizational Structure.* San Francisco: Jossey-Bass.

Baron, J.N., Hannan, M.T. and Burton, M.D. (2001) 'Labor pains: Change in organizational models and employee turnover in young, high-tech firms', *American Journal of Sociology*, 106: 960–1012.

Barrick, M.R. and Mount, M.K. (1991) 'Five personality dimensions and job performance: A meta-analysis', *Personnel Psychology*, 44: 1–26.

Barrick, M.R. and Zimmerman, R.D. (2005) 'Reducing voluntary, avoidable turnover through selection', *Journal of Applied Psychology*, 90: 159–166.

Batt, R. (2002) 'Managing customer services: Human resource practices, quit rates, and sales growth', *Academy of Management Journal*, 45: 587–597.

Batt, R., Colvin, A.J. and Keefe, J. (2002) 'Employee voice, human resource practices, and quit rates: Evidence from the telecommunications industry', *Industrial and Labor Relations Review*, 55: 573–94.

Beach, L.R. (1990) *Image Theory: Decision Making in Personal and Organizational Contexts*. Chichester: Wiley.

Birnbaum, D. and Somers, M.J. (1993) 'Fitting job performance into turnover model: An examination of the form of the job performance-turnover relationship and a path model', *Journal of Management*, 19, 1–11.

Blau, G. (1993) 'Further exploring the relationship between job search and voluntary individual turnover', *Personnel Psychology*, 46: 313–330.

Blau, G. (1994) 'Testing a two–dimensional measure of job search behavior', *Organizational Behavior and Human Decision Processes*, 59: 288–312.

Boeker, W. (1997) 'Executive migration and strategic change: The effect of top manager movement on product-market entry', *Administrative Science Quarterly*, 42: 213–236.

Boswell, W.R., Boudreau, J.W. and Dunford, B.B. (2004) 'The outcomes and correlates of job search objectives: Searching to leave or searching for leverage?' *Journal of Applied Psychology*, 89: 1083–1091.

Boswell, W.R., Boudreau, J.W. and Tichy, J. (2005) 'The relationship between employee job change and job satisfaction: The honeymoon-hangover effect', *Journal of Applied Psychology*, 90: 882–892.

Boswell, W.R., Roehling, M.V. and Boudreau, J.W. (2006) 'The role of personality, situational, and demographic variables in predicting job search among European managers', *Personality and Individual Differences*, 40: 783–794.

Boudreau, J.W., Boswell, W.R., Judge, T.A. and Bretz, R.D. Jr. (2001) 'Personality and cognitive ability as predictors of job search among employed managers', *Personnel Psychology*, 54: 25–50.

Bretz, R.D., Boudreau, J.W. and Judge, T.A. (1994) 'Job search behavior of employed managers', *Personnel Psychology*, 47: 275–301.

Bridges, W. (1994) 'The end of the job', *Fortune*, (September 19): 62–72.

Bycio, P., Hackett, R.D. and Alvares, K.M. (1990) 'Job performance and turnover: A review and meta-analysis', *Applied Psychology: An International Review*, 39: 47–76.

Byrne, J. (1999, October 4) 'The search for the young and gifted', *Business Week*, 3649: 108–112.

Cable, D.M. and Judge, T.A. (1996) 'Person–organization fit, job choice decisions, and organizational entry', *Organizational Behavior and Human Decision Processes*, 67: 294–312.

Campbell, C.M. (1995) 'The relative impacts of the level and change in wages on quits', *International Journal of Manpower*, 16: 31–41.

Campion, M.A. (1991) 'Meaning and measurement of turnover: Comparison of alternative measures and recommendations for research', *Journal of Applied Psychology*, 76: 199–212.

Carsten, J.M. and Spector, P.E. (1987) 'Unemployment, job satisfaction, and employee turnover: A meta-analytic test of the Muchinsky model', *Journal of Applied Psychology*, 72: 374–381.

Chan, D. (1996) 'Cognitive misfit of problem–solving style at work: A facet of person-organization fit', *Organizational Behavior and Human Decision Processes*, 68: 194–207.

Chang, E. (1999) 'Career commitment as a complex moderator of organizational commitment and turnover intention', *Human Relations*, 52: 1257–1278.

Cohen, A. and Hudecek, N. (1993) 'Organizational commitment-relationship across occupational groups: A meta-analysis', *Group and Organization Management*, 18: 188–213.

Cotton, J.L. and Tuttle, J.M. (1986) 'Employee turnover: A meta-analysis and review with implications for research', *Academy of Management Review*, 11: 55–70.

Currivan, D.B. (1999) 'A causal order of job satisfaction and organizational commitment in models of employee turnover', *Human Resource Management Review*, 9: 495–524.

Daily, C.M., Certo, S.T. and Dalton, D.R. (2002) 'Executive stock option repricing: Retention and performance reconsidered', *California Management Review*, 44: 8–22.

Dalessio, A., Silverman, W.H. and Schuck, J.R. (1986) 'Paths to turnover: A re-analysis and review of existing data on the Mobley, Horner, and Hollingsworth turnover model', *Human Relations*, 39: 245–263.

Dalton, D.R., Krackhardt, D.M. and Porter, L.W. (1981) 'Functional turnover: An empirical assessment', *Journal of Applied Psychology*, 66: 716–721.

Donnelly, D.P. and Quirin, J.J. (2006) 'An extension of Lee and Mitchell's unfolding model of voluntary turnover', *Journal of Organizational Behavior*, 27: 59–77.

Dunford, B.B., Boudreau, J.W. and Boswell, W.R. (2005) 'Out-of-the-Money: The impact of underwater stock options on executive job search', *Personnel Psychology*, 58: 67–101.

Farrell, D. and Rusbult, C.E. (1981) 'Exchange variables as predictors of job satisfaction, job commitment, and turnover: The impact of rewards, costs, alternatives, and investments', *Organizational Behavior and Human Performance*, 28: 78–95.

Fields, D., Dingman, M.E., Roman, P.M. and Blum, T.C. (2005) 'Exploring predictors of alternative job changes', *Journal of Occupational and Organizational Psychology*, 78: 63–82.

Gerhart, B. (1990) 'Voluntary turnover and alternative job opportunities', *Journal of Applied Psychology*, 75: 467–476.

Ghiselli, E.E. (1974) 'Some perspectives for industrial psychology', *American Psychologist*, 29: 80–87.

Glebbeek, A.C. and Bax, E.H. (2004) 'Is high employee turnover really harmful? An empirical test using company records', *Academy of Management Journal*, 47: 277–286.

Griffeth, R.W., Hom, P.W. and Gaertner, S. (2000) 'A meta-analysis of antecedents and correlates of employee turnover: Update, moderator tests, and research implications for the next millennium', *Journal of Management*, 26: 463–488.

Griffeth, R.W, Steel, R P., Allen, D.G. and Bryan, N. (2005) 'The development of a multidimensional measure of job market cognitions: The employment opportunity index (EOI)', *Journal of Applied Psychology*, 90: 335–349.

Guthrie, J.P. (2001) 'High-involvement work practices, turnover, and productivity: Evidence from New Zealand', *Academy of Management Journal*, 44: 180–191.

Harrison, D.A., Virick, M. and William, S. (1996) 'Working without a net: Time, performance, and turnover under maximally contingent rewards', *Journal of Applied Psychology*, 81: 331–345.

Harter, J.K., Schmidt, F.L. and Hayes, T.L. (2002) 'Business-unit level relationship between employee satisfaction, employee engagement, and business outcomes: A meta-analysis', *Journal of Applied Psychology*, 87: 268–279.

Health Resources and Services Administration (HRSA) (2000) 'A National Agenda for Nursing Workforce: Racial/Ethnic Diversity' (National Advisory Council on Nurse Education and Practice: Report to the Secretary of Health and Human Services and Congress). September 2003.

Hirschman, A.O. (1970) *Exit, Voice, and Loyalty*. Cambridge, MA: Harvard University Press.

Hochwarter, W.A., Ferris, G.R., Canty, A.L., Frink, D.D., Perrewe, P.L. and Berkson, H.M. (2001) 'Reconsidering the job-performance-turnover relationship: The role of gender in form and magnitude', *Journal of Applied Social Psychology*, 31: 2357–2377.

Holtom, B.C., Mitchell, T.R., Lee, T.W. and Inderrieden, E.J. (2005) 'Shocks as causes of turnover: What they are and how organizations can manage them', *Human Resource Management*, 44: 337–352.

Hom, P.W., Caranikas-Walker, F., Prussia, G.E. and Griffeth, R.W. (1992) 'A meta-analytical structural equations analysis of a model of employee turnover', *Journal of Applied Psychology*, 77: 890–909.

Hom, P.W. and Griffeth, R.W. (1991) 'Structural equations modeling test of a turnover theory: Cross-sectional and longitudinal analyses', *Journal of Applied Psychology*, 76: 350–366.

Hom, P.W. and Griffeth, R.W. (1995) *Employee Turnover*. Cincinnati, OH: South–Western.

Hom, P.W., Griffeth, R.W. and Sellaro, C.L. (1984) 'The validity of Mobley's 1977 model of employee turnover', *Organizational Behavior and Human Performance*, 34: 141–174.

Hom, P.W. and Hulin, C.L. (1981) 'A competitive test of the prediction of reenlistment by several models', *Journal of Applied Psychology*, 66: 23–39.

Hom, P.W., Katerberg, R. and Hulin, C.L. (1979) 'Comparative examination of three approaches to the prediction of turnover', *Journal of Applied Psychology*, 64: 280–290.

Hulin, C.L. (1966) 'Job satisfaction and turnover in a female clerical population', *Journal of Applied Psychology*, 50: 280–285.

Hulin, C.L., Roznowski, M. and Hachiya, D. (1985) 'Alternative opportunities and withdrawal decisions: Empirical and theoretical discrepancies and an integration', *Psychological Bulletin*, 97: 233–250.

Huselid, M.A. (1995) 'The impact of human resource management practices on turnover, productivity, and corporate financial performance', *Academy of Management Journal*, 38: 635–672.

Jackofsky, E.F. (1984) 'Turnover and job performance: An integrated process model', *Academy of Management Review*, 9: 74–83.

Judge, T.A. (1993) 'Does affective disposition moderate the relationship between job satisfaction and voluntary turnover?', *Journal of Applied Psychology*, 78: 395–401.

Judge, T.A. and Watanabe, S. (1995) 'Is the past prologue? A test of Ghiselli's hobo syndrome', *Journal of Management*, 21: 211–229.

Kacmar, K.M., Andrews, M.C., Van Rooy, D.L., Steilberg, R.C. and Cerrone, S. (2006) 'Sure everyone can be replaced... but at what cost? Turnover as a predictor of unit-level performance', *Academy of Management Journal*, 49: 133–144.

Kammeyer-Mueller, J.D., Wanberg, C.R., Glomb, T.M. and Ahlburg, D. (2005) 'The role of temporal shifts in turnover processes: It's about time', *Journal of Applied Psychology*, 90: 644–658.

Kim, S., Price, J.L., Mueller, C.W. and Watson, T.W. (1996) 'The determinants of career intent among physicians at a U.S. air force hospital', *Human Relations*, 49: 947–975.

Kirschenbaum, A. and Mano–Negrin, R. (1999) 'Underlying labor market dimensions of "opportunities": The case of employee turnover', *Human Relations*, 52: 1233–1255.

Kirschenbaum, A. and Weisberg, J. (2002) 'Employee's turnover intentions and job destination choices', *Journal of Organizational Behavior*, 23: 109–125.

Koys, D.J. (2001) 'The effects of employee satisfaction, organizational citizenship behavior, and turnover on organizational effectiveness: A unit-level, longitudinal study', *Personnel Psychology*, 54: 101–114.

Krausz, M. (2002) 'The many faces of voluntary employee turnover: A multifacet and multilevel perspective', in M. Koslowsky and M. Krausz (eds), *Voluntary Employee Withdrawal and Inattendance: A Current Perspective*. New York: Kluwer Academic/Plenum Publishers, pp. 53–70.

Lawler, E.E. III (1994) 'From job–based to competency-based organizations', *Journal of Organizational Behavior*, 15: 3–15.

Lee, T.W. and Mitchell, T.R. (1994) 'An alternative approach: The unfolding model of voluntary employee turnover', *Academy of Management Review*, 19: 51–89.

Lee, T.W., Mitchell, T.R., Holtom, B.C., McDaniel, L.S. and Hill, J.W. (1999) 'The unfolding model of voluntary turnover: A replication and extension', *Academy of Management Journal*, 42: 450–462.

Lee, T.W., Mitchell, T.R., Wise, L. and Fireman, S. (1996) 'An unfolding model of voluntary employee turnover', *Academy of Management Journal*, 39: 5–36.

Lee, T.W., Mitchell, T.R., Sablynski, C.J., Burton, J.P. and Holtom, B.C. (2004) 'The effects of job embeddedness on organizational citizenship, job performance, volitional absences, and voluntary turnover', *Academy of Management Journal*, 47: 711–722.

Lee, T.W. and Mowday, R.T. (1987) 'Voluntarily leaving an organization: An empirical investigation of Steers and Mowday's model of turnover', *Academy of Management Journal*, 30: 721–743.

Locke, E.A. (1976) 'The nature and causes of job satisfaction', in M.D. Dunnette (ed), *Handbook of Industrial and Organizational Psychology*. Chicago: Rand McNally.

Mael, F.A. and Ashforth, B.E. (1995) 'Loyal from day one: Biodata, organizational identification, and turnover among newcomers', *Personnel Psychology*, 48: 309–334.

Maertz, C.P. and Campion, M.A. (2004) 'Profiles in quitting: Integrating process and content turnover theory', *Academy of Management Journal*, 47: 566–582.

Maertz, C.P. and Griffeth, R.W. (2004) 'Eight motivational forces and voluntary turnover: A theoretical synthesis with implications for research', *Journal of Management*, 30: 667–683.

Maertz, C.P., Stevens, M.J. and Campion, M.A. (2003) 'A turnover model for the Mexican maquiladoras', *Journal of Vocational Behavior*, 63: 111–135.

March, J.G. and Simon, H.A. (1958) *Organizations*. New York: Wiley.

Mathieu, J.E. and Zajac, D.M. (1990) 'A review and meta-analysis of the antecedents, correlates, and consequences of organizational commitment', *Psychological Bulletin*, 108: 171–194.

McCormick, B. (1988) 'Quit rates over time in a job rationed labour market: The British manufacturing sector, 1971–83', *Economica*, 55: 81–94.

McEvoy, G.M. and Cascio, W.F. (1987) 'Do good or poor performers leave? A meta-analysis of the relationship between performance and turnover', *Academy of Management Journal*, 30: 744–762.

Michaels, C.E. and Spector, P.E. (1982) 'Causes of employee turnover: A test of the Mobley, Griffeth, Hand, and Meglino model', *Journal of Applied Psychology*, 67: 53–59.

Mitchell, T.R., Holtom, B.C., Lee, T.W., Sablynski, C.J. and Erez, M. (2001) 'Why people stay: Using job embeddedness to predict voluntary turnover', *Academy of Management Journal*, 44: 1102–1121.

Mobley, W.H. (1977) 'Intermediate linkages in the relationship between job satisfaction and employee turnover', *Journal of Applied Psychology*, 62: 237–240.

Mobley, W.H. (1982) *Employee Turnover: Causes, Consequences, and Control*. Reading, MA: Addison-Wesley.

Mobley, W.H., Griffeth, R.W., Hand, H.H. and Meglino, B.M. (1979) 'Review and conceptual analysis of the employee turnover process', *Psychological Bulletin*, 86: 493–522.

Mobley, W.H., Horner, S.O. and Hollingsworth, A.T. (1978) 'An evaluation of precursors of hospital employee turnover', *Journal of Applied Psychology*, 63: 408–414.

Morita, J.G., Lee, T.W. and Mowday, R.T. (1989) 'Introducing survival analysis to organizational researchers: A selected application to turnover research', *Journal of Applied Psychology*, 74: 280–292.

Morita, J.G., Lee, T.W. and Mowday, R.T. (1993) 'The regression-analog to survival analysis: A selected application to turnover research', *Academy of Management Journal*, 36: 1430–1464.

Morrell, K., Loan-Clarke, J. and Wilkinson, A. (2004) 'The role of shocks in employee turnover', *British Journal of Management*, 15: 335–349.

Mossholder, K.W., Settoon, R.P. and Henagan, S.C. (2005) 'A relational perspective on turnover: Examining structural, attitudinal, and behavioral predictions', *Academy of Management Journal*, 48: 607–618.

Mowday, R.T., Porter, L.W. and Steers, R.M. (1982) *Employee–Organization Linkages*. New York: Academic Press.

Muchinsky, P.M. and Morrow, P.C. (1980) 'A multi-disciplinary model of voluntary employee turnover', *Journal of Vocational Behavior*, 17: 263–290.

Osterman, P. (1987) 'Turnover, employment security, and the performance of the firm', in M. Kleiner, M. Roomkin, and S.W. Salsburg (eds), *Human Resources and the Performance of the Firm*. IRRA Series. Madison, WI: Industrial Relations Research Association.

Parsons, D. (1973) 'Quit rates over time: A search and information approach', *The American Economic Review*, 63: 330–401.

Peters, L. and Sheridan, J. (1988) 'Turnover research methodology: A critique of traditional designs and a suggested survival model alternative', in K.M. Rowland (ed.), *Research in Personnel and Human Resource Management*. Greenwich, CT: JAI Press, pp. 231–262.

Peterson, S.J. and Luthans, F. (2006) 'The impact of financial and nonfinancial incentives on business-unit outcomes over time', *Journal of Applied Psychology*, 91: 156–165.

Porter, L.W., Steers, R.M., Mowday, R.T. and Boulian, P.V. (1974) 'Organizational commitment, job satisfaction, and turnover among psychiatric technicians', *Journal of Applied Psychology*, 59: 603–609.

Porter, L.W. and Steers, R.M. (1973) 'Organizational, work, and personal factors in employee turnover and absenteeism', *Psychological Bulletin*, 80: 151–176.

Posthuma, R.A., Joplin, J.R.W. and Maertz, C.P., Jr. (2005) 'Comparing the validity of turnover predictors in the United States and Mexico', *International Journal of Cross Cultural Management*, 5: 165–180.

Price, J.L. (1977) *The Study of Turnover*. Ames, IO: The Iowa State University Press.

Price, J.L. and Mueller, C.W. (1981) 'A causal model of turnover for nurses', *Academy of Management Journal*, 24: 543–565.

Price, J.L. and Mueller, C.W. (1986) *Absenteeism and turnover of hospital employees*. Greenwich, CT: JAI Press.

Rhoades, L. and Eisenberger, R. (2002) 'Perceived organizational support: A review of the literature', *Journal of Applied Psychology*, 87: 698–714.

Salamin, A. and Hom, P.W. (2005) 'In search of the elusive U-shaped performance-turnover relationship: Are high performing Swiss bankers more liable to quit?', *Journal of Applied Psychology*, 90: 1204–1216.

Salgado, J. (2002) 'The Big Five personality dimensions and counterproductive behaviors', *International Journal of Selection and Assessment*, 10: 117–125.

Shaw, J.D., Delery, J.E., Jenkins, G.D., Jr. and Gupta, N. (1998) 'An organization-level analysis of voluntary and involuntary turnover', *Academy of Management Journal*, 41: 511–525.

Sheridan, J.E. and Abelson, M.A. (1983) 'Cusp catastrophe model of employee turnover', *Academy of Management Journal*, 26: 418–436.

Simons, T. and Roberson, Q. (2003) 'Why managers should care about fairness: The effects of aggregate justice perceptions on organizational outcomes', *Journal of Applied Psychology*, 88: 432–443.

Spector, P.E. (1991) 'Confirmatory test of a turnover model utilizing multiple data sources', *Human Performance*, 4: 221–230.

Staw, B.M. (1980) 'The consequences of turnover', *Journal of Organizational Behavior*, 1: 253–273.

Staw, B.M. and Ross, J. (1985) 'Stability in the midst of change: A dispositional approach to job attitudes', *Journal of Applied Psychology*, 70: 469–480.

Steel, R.P. (2002) 'Turnover theory at the empirical interface: Problems of fit and function', *Academy of Management Review*, 27: 346–360.

Steel, R.P. and Griffeth, R.W. (1989) 'The elusive relationship between perceived employment opportunity and turnover behavior: A methodological or conceptual artifact?' *Journal of Applied Psychology*, 74: 846–854.

Steel, R.P. and Ovalle, N.K. II. (1984) 'A review and meta-analysis of research on the relationship between behavioral intentions and employee turnover', *Journal of Applied Psychology*, 69: 673–686.

Steers, R.M. and Mowday, R.T. (1981) 'Employee turnover and postdecision accommodation processes', in L. Cummings and B. Staw, *Research in Organizational Behavior*. Greenwich, CT: JAI Press, pp. 235–281.

Sturman, M.C. and Trevor, C.O. (2001) 'The implications of linking the dynamic performance and turnover literatures', *Journal of Applied Psychology*, 86: 684–696.

Sturman, M.C., Trevor, C.O., Boudreau, J.W. and Gerhart, B. (2003) 'Is it worth it to win the talent war? Evaluating the utility of performance-based pay', *Personnel Psychology*, 56: 997–1035.

Tett, R.P. and Meyer, J.P. (1993) 'Job satisfaction, organizational commitment, turnover intention, and turnover: Path analyses based on meta-analytic findings', *Personnel Psychology*, 46: 259–293.

Trevor, C.O. (2001) 'Interactions among actual ease-of-movement determinants and job satisfaction in the prediction of voluntary turnover', *Academy of Management Journal*, 44: 621–638.

Trevor, C.O., Gerhart, B. and Boudreau, J.W. (1997) 'Voluntary turnover and job performance: Curvilinearity and the moderating influences of salary growth and promotions', *Journal of Applied Psychology*, 82: 44–61.

Wiener, Y. and Vardi, Y. (1980) 'Relationships between job, organization, and career commitments and work outcomes: An integrative approach', *Organizational Behavior and Human Performance*, 26: 81–96.

Wiersema, M.F. and Bantel, K.A. (1993) 'Top management team turnover as an adaptation mechanism: The role of the environment', *Strategic Management Journal*, 14: 485–504.

Williams, C.R. and Livingstone, L.P. (1994) 'Another look at the relationship between performance and voluntary turnover', *Academy of Management Journal*, 37: 269–298.

Wright, T.A. and Bonett, D.G. (1993) 'Role of employee coping and performance in voluntary employee withdrawal: A research refinement and elaboration', *Journal of Management*, 19: 147–161.

Yao, X., Lee, T.W., Mitchell, T.R., Burton, J.P. and Sablynski, C.J. (2004) 'Job embeddedness: Current research and future directions', in R. Griffeth and P. Hom (eds), *Innovative Theory and Empirical Research on Employee Turnover*. Information Age: Greenwich, CT, pp. 153–188.

Zimmerman, R.D. (2006) *Understanding the Impact of Personality Traits on Individuals' Turnover Decisions*. Unpublished doctoral dissertation. University of Iowa.

12

Unemployment and Retirement

Terry A. Beehr and Misty M. Bennett

Most of the other chapters in this handbook examine people doing work for pay. Here, however, we focus on people who have been employees in the past but who are not presently in the employed workforce: unemployed people and retirees. Those people designated as unemployed can be of any age; furthermore, they desire and actively seek paid work. Retirees, on the other hand, are usually older, former workers who may or may not have any intention to work for pay again. As will be seen in a later section of this chapter, some retirees might even return to work and still be considered retired, a situation labeled bridge employment. Unemployment has always been a concern of government and society when the proportion of unemployed people becomes large. Retirement has become a concern to many countries in recent years – the ones experiencing the aging of the 'baby-boom' generation. Both unemployed and retired people tend to be supported tangibly (usually financially) in some ways by those who are still working. If their numbers become large, therefore, concerns are often raised. Some causes, effects, and correlates of these two phenomena are explored here.

UNEMPLOYMENT

Sometimes people have no paid employment even though they want to work, and a nation or region's official unemployment rate is an indicator of the extent of such unemployment. Overall unemployment rates, however, are only general indicators and do not reveal details such as the nature of the people who are unemployed (e.g., their work skills, personal qualities or the consequences to them of their unemployment) and the behavior of those people. Unemployment varies over time and across geographic locations, and across occupational sectors. It can appear to be cyclical and varies over time with the state of the economy (Vinokur et al., 2000). Unemployment can be due to a myriad of factors, some of which result in unemployment of masses of people at once rather than one person at a time. In some nations that have been economically developed for a long time, increased global competition can lead to lower profits and even financial losses to employers, who then 'lay off' 'redundant' workers in order to cut costs. In 2005 in the US, for example, there were 16,466 'mass' layoffs of at least 50 employees each (Mass Layoffs in 2005, 2006). The man-ufacturing sector of the economy accounted for about 30 per cent of those layoffs. Another, probably more unusual, example concerns the medical occupation. Again in 2005, Hurricane Katrina caused the offices of about 6,000 physicians along the US Gulf Coast to close (Industry Watch, 2005). Even though physicians might be in high demand for their skills, most of them presumably were at least temporarily unemployed.

Unemployment has some relation to turnover, but the research on these two topics usually differs in nature. Both unemployed and employed people might engage, for example, in efforts to find a new job, and so some of their behaviors are similar (Van Hooft et al., 2004b). From the employer's perspective, people who leave and find a new job 'look' similar to people who leave and do not find a new job; both were in the organization, and now they are gone. Beyond that, however, there are important differences. Research on and knowledge about the unemployed tends to focus on those people who are involuntarily unemployed. Research and knowledge about turnover more often (though not always) tends to focus on those who voluntarily leave the organization, often already with prospects for a new job. It is probable that unemployment rates are related to individuals' decisions that affect their own turnover behaviors and unemployment conditions. To avoid becoming unemployed themselves, people might tend to cling to the job they already have. That is, during times of high unemployment people are less likely to leave their jobs because there are fewer job alternatives. The relationship between unemployment rates and turnover is often very weak, however, nearly zero (Hom and Kinicki, 2001; Trevor, 2001). When people want to quit their jobs, because of low job satisfaction for example, they are probably less likely to do so during times of high unemployment because of few alternatives. This implies an interaction rather than in addition to a direct effect. That is, reasons for quitting (job dissatisfaction) interact with unemployment rates to determine employees'

turnover. A meta-analysis has reported data consistent with this assumption (Carsten and Spector, 1987).

When organizations decide to lay off employees, there are different ways in which they can make the decision and different ways in which they can notify and treat those being laid off. Those who are laid off can be chosen because of their low seniority as contracts sometimes officially specify, they can be targeted for layoffs because their jobs or func-tions are deemed less necessary than others, or they can be terminated because their own individual performance has been evaluated as poor. It seems likely that the people making the decisions, as well as those becoming unemployed, can make causal attributions about the layoff decisions. Research is needed, however, to determine the nature of such attributions, what might lead to the specific attributions, and what their consequences might be. When people are selectively chosen to have their employment terminated, this can take the form of being fired, being laid off, or retiring (Colarelli and Beehr, 1993). We discuss retirements elsewhere in this chapter, but for now we should note that retirements are often a (more or less) voluntary choice for older employees whose jobs are not in jeopardy. Firing, on the other hand, usually implies that the employee's work was not satisfactory. If an organization is forced to downsize because of economic difficulty, targeting specific people to be dismissed based on their performance might be called a layoff, but it seems psychologically similar to being fired. People who are laid off without the stigma of the decision being based specifically on their job performance behaviors might perceive, experience, and attribute causes of the event differently.

Job loss and becoming unemployed can be considered a process rather than a single, one-time event, i.e., it is a time of transition, as much a work life transition as obtaining one's first job, obtaining a promotion, or retiring. Compared to many other transitions, however, more unpleasant consequences are likely to result from unemployment (Viney and Tych, 1984–85). Over time the transition from employment to unemployment might include the experience of anticipation before the event, and shock, relief, new efforts at obtaining reemployment, self-doubt, anger, and resignation after the event of becoming unemployed (Colarelli and Beehr, 1993; Kaufman, 1982). The process through which the organization's representatives determine layoffs and other terminations should be related to perceptions of procedural justice. If those who are laid off perceive the procedures of the termination to be unjust, negative psychological reactions are likely to follow, including ill feelings and negative attitudes toward the organization (Colquitt et al., 2001).

People often think of employment vs. unemployment as a dichotomy. Instead of these being two discrete categories, however, we argue that these two terms are the ends of a continuum. That is, there are degrees of employment or unemployment. The present chapter considers anything between these endpoints to be varying degrees of underemployment. People on points of the continuum that are closer to the (full) employment end are considered to be less underemployed, and people closer to the unemployment end of the continuum are considered to be more underemployed. Governments often keep track of unemployment statistics, but they usually only include people who are unemployed and looking for work. Such statistics do not usually include those who are unemployed and gave up looking for a new job, even though they would like to have work. They also do not include people who are underemployed, but one could think of underemployment as partial unemployment. That is, the employed person could be and maybe would prefer to be employed more. This could mean a greater quantity of work, for example individuals working part-time would prefer full-time work but cannot find it. It could, however, also mean quality of work, such that the job being held does not use the individuals' skills as fully as they might prefer. It could also mean underemployment in terms of desired or needed income. There is not a unified, consistent agreement on

exactly what constitutes underemployment, or how it should be measured (Feldman, 1996), but these three types of underemployment have received some empirical scrutiny by researchers interested in unemployment and underemployment (e.g., Jensen and Slack, 2003; Johnson et al., 2002; Khan and Morrow, 1991; Sullivan and Hauser, 1978); in addition, some research (Clogg, 1979; Sullivan and Hauser, 1978) used a Labor Utilization Framework to disentangle the concepts of unemployment and underemployment into five different categories.

In order to understand the antecedents and consequences of unemployment, the related concept of underemployment probably needs to be considered (Dooley and Prause, 2004). While most of this discussion focuses on unemployment, it should be noted that underemployment can be related to potential outcomes such as lower job satisfaction and organizational commitment and to increased intentions to quit and stress-type reactions (e.g., depression, anxiety, frustration; Feldman and Turnley, 1995; Jones-Johnson and Johnson, 1992, Khan and Morrow, 1991). For a nation, keeping track of the unemployment rate but not the underemployment rate might provide an incomplete picture of its labor conditions.

Effects of unemployment

Unemployment theory

There are a few psychological theories of unemployment, focusing mostly on its negative effects on the individual. Perhaps the most dramatic theory derives from the counseling domain and labels unemployment 'the living death,' arguing that unemployed individuals go through Kubler-Ross' (1969) stages of death and dying (Winegardner et al., 1984). Of 300 unemployed people in the US (some of whom might have taken early retirement), over half reported experiencing four of the five Kubler-Ross stages a 'great deal.' These stages are:

- denial and isolation;
- anger;

- bargaining;
- depression; and
- acceptance.

The 'bargaining' stage was not experienced by most of the unemployed. Depression was by far the most frequently experienced stage, with 80 per cent of the respondents experiencing it a great deal. Given that one stage was not experienced 'a great deal' by a majority of unemployed people, and two others (denial and acceptance) were experienced a great deal by just over 50 per cent of the sample, this is not strong evidence that these stages are a pervasive reaction among most people who become unemployed. The very strong results for the depression stage, however, are important. As will be explained shortly, aversive emotional reactions such as depression are a common consequence across many studies of different types and in different locales over the years.

A second theoretical approach to understanding the effects of unemployment is the latent deprivation model of Jahoda (1982; Haworth, 1986). It is a functional approach, outlining the functions that employment serves for people, and by extension, functional losses that people might need to make up for if they become unemployed. Employment provides people with money so that they can live physically – an obvious manifest function of employment. The emphasis of the model, however, is on latent functions. The model proposes that there are five important, inter-related, social-psychological, latent functions that employment fulfils. Employment:

(1) structures the person's time, which it is argued should be the most important of the five functions;
(2) provides social contact;
(3) provides common goals for employed people;
(4) gives status; and
(5) provides activities for employed individuals.

Being unemployed potentially deprives the person of these, and therefore adverse effects on the person can ensue from deprivation. Among unemployed young adults in Queensland, Australia, all five latent functions were positively intercorrelated (median r = 0.35), with the strongest relationship between time structure and activity (r = 0.55) (Creed and Macintyre, 2001). Being able to fill one's time with meaningful activities might be the essence of structuring time (Haworth, 1986). The overall implication is that without these five latent functions being met by employment, individuals may suffer aversive psychological consequences. Among the unemployed in Queensland, the five functions were all negatively correlated with self-reported general health; status (r = −0.56) and time structure (r = −0.47) had the strongest relationships with health.

A third model of unemployment is a personal agency or agency restriction model (Creed and Macintyre, 2001; Haworth, 1986). It emphasizes the manifest effects (rather than the latent effects of the previous model). This primarily means negative economic effects or loss of income place people in danger of moving into poverty; a state in which they would no longer be able to act successfully upon their environment to satisfy their desires and needs. Even the ability to fulfil the latent functions through alternative or leisure activities might be more difficult without money. For example, it is harder to have desirable social contacts (a latent function of employment) by going with friends to events that charge admission, or that have some other costs attached.

Negative effects

The theories and models emphasize the negative effects of unemployment, and indeed, empirical research shows consistently that unemployment is associated with unpleasant and deleterious outcomes. The loss of both latent and manifest benefits of employment predicts lower overall well-being, poorer general health ratings, and poorer mental health (Creed and Macintyre, 2001; Frese and Mohr, 1987; McKee-Ryan et al., 2005; Viney and Tych, 1984–85). Furthermore, the length of unemployment is associated with more unfavorable outcomes (McKee-Ryan, et al., 2005), but becoming reemployed (or even retiring) minimizes some of these problems (Frese and Mohr, 1987; Hultman et al., 2006; Waters and Moore, 2002). Although there are occasional studies showing no effect of unemployment on health (e.g., Merriam, 1987), most theories, themes, and data are consistent with the idea that becoming unemployed is detrimental to well-being.

One of the most obvious problems with unemployment is the loss of income (e.g., Chan and Stevens, 1999; Hultman et al., 2006). Furthermore, consistent with agency theory and its emphasis on the manifest variable of finances, there is some evidence that the financial problems of unemployment are the key variable and might be one of the most important elements in the decrease in well-being among unemployed people (Creed and Macintyre, 2001; Frese, 1987; Frese and Mohr, 1987; Price et al., 2002; Winegardner et al., 1984). That is, financial loss and uncertainty might be a mediating variable between unemployment situations on the one hand, and general health and well-being reactions on the other (Frese and Mohr, 1987; Price, et al., 2002). Financial strain due to any cause can be a problem leading to poor health and well-being, as has been shown by research on many groups, including divorced rural mothers (Wickrama et al., 2006), urban African American women (Schulz et al., 2006), and the elderly (Kahn and Pearlin, 2006).

Our understanding of the effects of unemployment might well be enhanced by isolating the role of moderator variables. Based on the assumptions that many cultures expect men more than women to work for pay, unemployment might yield worse mental health effects for men; however, the results are mixed, with some research reporting no differences between males and females (e.g., Price, et al., 2002). Similarly, one might expect age differences, given that older workers have more difficulty gaining reemployment (e.g., Cockburn et al., 1972; Couch, 1998; Merriam, 1987); yet again no clear differences emerge in how younger and older workers respond psychologically to unemployment. One possibility is that

the oldest workers can sometimes retire, thereby adopting a new and socially legitimate role (Frese and Mohr, 1987), escaping the more stigmatized role of the unemployed. Regarding the health and well-being effects of unemployment, research has shown more consistently and convincingly the negative effects of unemployment on mental health than on physical health (Haworth, 1986), a phenomenon that probably remains true to this day. More examination of the physical effects, especially both self- and objective reports, is warranted. In general, though, it is abundantly clear that unemployment is bad for most people who experience it.

Gaining reemployment

In understanding unemployment and its effects, important questions to be answered include what are unemployed people doing to avoid or alleviate the aversive effects of unemployment? What are they doing to obtain employment, and how successful are they?

Job search

What characteristics or behaviors of unemployed people lead them to seek and obtain new jobs? As noted earlier, being unemployed leads to poor psychological and maybe poor physical well-being, and becoming reemployed alleviates some of these reactions (Frese and Mohr, 1987; Hultman et al., 2006; Waters and Moore, 2002). But different causal relationships among these variables might also be plausible, i.e., psychological distress (e.g., depression) might prevent unemployed people from becoming reemployed (e.g, Vinokur and Schul, 2002). Alternatively, distress might also lead to better job search success (Crossley and Stanton, 2004), perhaps because of a desperate need to obtain new employment.

Job search activity, effort, and/or intensity are sometimes used as surrogate criterion variables instead of actual attainment of a new job when studying unemployed people's attempts to find work. This approach is intuitively appealing, because the harder individuals search, the more likely they will find an acceptable job. Conceptually, the Theory of Planned Behavior is sometimes invoked as a reason why variables such as intention and effort should lead to finding a new job (e.g., van Hooft et al. 2004b; Wanberg et al., 2005). The relationship between searching and finding jobs is weak or maybe inconsistent, however (e.g., see van Hooft et al., 2004a; Wanberg et al., 2002; Wanberg, et al., 2005). This might be due to so many other factors that can influence finding another job (e.g., the labor market regarding one's specific skills in that particular time and place).

Expectancy theory variables (e.g., expectancy, valence, and instrumentality) are related to job search efforts (Prussia et al., 2001; van Hooft et al., 2004a; van Hooft et al., 2004b), as are subjective search norms among meaningful others (van Hooft, et al., 2004a; van Hooft, et al., 2004b; Wanberg et al., 2005), job search commitment (Wanberg et al., 1999), financial hardship (Wanberg et al., 1999), and self-related variables (Crossley and Stanton, 2005; Wanberg et al., 2005; Wanberg et al., 1999). However, some studies failed to find such relationships with job search (e.g., van Hooft, et al., 2004a, 2004b) and job search attitudes (Wanberg, et al., 2004), and overall, it should be noted that the effect sizes tend to be weak.

Evaluations of job search training programs

Because unemployment is harmful both to the unemployed individual and (en masse) to society, formal training programs aimed at helping people become reemployed have been developed. The workshops and training programs discussed here tend to follow the theory and research noted in the review above. That is, they focus on presumed mediating variables, i.e., elements resembling improvements in psychological well-being, confidence or self-efficacy, teaching job search skills and encouraging their use. Thus, they improve job search ability and give encouragement (e.g., frequent positive feedback and support) and direction to unemployed people to keep up their intentions, efforts, and beliefs in their ability to succeed in their job search.

The ultimate goal, of course, is for the unemployed trainees to obtain new jobs, preferably jobs as 'good' as the ones they lost.

In one study in the US, a randomized, two-year field experiment with over a thousand unemployed people showed that the training led to better psychological health and functioning, and to obtaining reemployment (Vinokur et al., 2000). The program had the largest positive effect on people with low pre-test levels of motivation to search for jobs, suggesting that those who might need help the most benefited more from the job-search training. Two similar studies were completed subsequently in Finland. One, a six-month randomized field experiment of over a thousand unemployed people, found no effect on overall reemployment, but the training may have had a small effect on the quality of jobs for those who did become reemployed (Vuori et al., 2002). In addition, the effects on mental health were small. A second Finnish study examined 278 unemployed people participating in groups in 30-hour workshops (Vuori et al., 2005). Trainers of the different groups varied in their skills and in some of the treatments they chose to administer. None of the training variations predicted reemployment six-months later, however. Younger males and people with fewer previous depressed symptoms were more likely to become reemployed, and trainers' skills predicted the quality of the jobs that people obtained. Overall, more interventions of this nature need to be implemented and evaluated rigorously, but at present it seems that the effects on the ultimate variable, reemployment, might be small.

Older workers

Older workers are increasingly becoming unemployed, and they are less likely to become reemployed as quickly as younger workers (Couch, 1998). At the other end of the age spectrum, a Swedish study found that being unemployed in one's early years predicted being unemployed seven years later (Franzen and Kassman, 2005), and it is possible that both temporal ends of the working career bring potential employment problems. For older workers in a US sample from the Health and Retirement Study, even among people over the age of 55 who were laid off, over 70 per cent had obtained employment within a 2-year period. Older workers, however, often obtain jobs that pay less than their original employment situation (Couch, 1998). Regarding the trainability of older workers, one study reported that age may not be related to the efforts of unemployed people to learn new, potentially job-related information and skills (Niessen, 2005). This is promising and suggests that older people can still find work involving newly acquired skills. In addition, among males, but not females, being laid off as an older worker was associated with an expectation of eventually working to an older age before retiring (Chan and Stevens 1999). As noted earlier, however, some older workers who become unemployed are in a position to choose to retire rather than to remain in the workforce but unemployed (Frese and Mohr, 1987).

RETIREMENT

Retirement is an important phenomenon that needs to be understood because it will affect nearly all workers at some point in their lives. As the baby boomers (those born between 1945 and 1960; Hatcher, 2003) approach retirement, organizations and society will have to adapt to changing demographics in the workforce and to the presence of a large older population in society. This creates an increased need for a thorough understanding of retirement and its associated issues, including driving forces that encourage people to retire, factors that keep people in the workforce, and the parties that are affected by retirement. Despite the fact that the life expectancy has increased in the US and people are generally healthier and live longer, the retirement age has slowly been decreasing. In the US, the traditional retirement age of 65 is not a uniform norm; in December 2006, 51.8 per cent of people aged 55–64 years were employed in the US, yet just 15.7 per cent

of people 65 years and over were employed. Information is needed to help understand not only why individuals are retiring, but also what effect this has on organizations and society.

There has been a surge of research activity regarding retirement in recent decades. A search in PsycINFO revealed that prior to 1980, only 230 articles had been written on retirement; between 1980 to the present, over 1100 articles were written on the topic! This surge in research on retirement reflects the importance of understanding retirement in society. Not surprisingly, therefore, there is simply too much information to review in one chapter. As a result, our approach is to focus on major themes that recur through the literature, with a special emphasis on more recent research (i.e., publications between January 2000 and January 2007), although some older, seminal articles on retirement and its related topics were also included.

Perhaps more so than other areas in organizational behavior, retirement has attracted attention from many different disciplines. In addition to organizational behavior, general management, and industrial and organizational psychology, fields such as sociology, gerontology, developmental and clinical psychology, and (more recently) economics have all investigated retirement through their own lenses. Although the main focus of this chapter is on retirement from the organizational behavior perspective, additional research perspectives are also included where appropriate.

Theoretical perspectives on retirement

A number of theories have been proposed that attempt to characterize retirement and its related processes. A common approach to investigating retirement is from a developmental or life-span perspective. Throughout their career life-span, employees are recruited, selected, trained, retained or fired and, at the end of their employment life cycles, the employees retire. Retirement itself may even be seen as a continuum or a process rather than a discrete event (Beehr, 1986).

That is, people tend to think about and plan for their retirement for some years prior to actual retirement, and they may even retire gradually by reducing the number of hours they work or by engaging in volunteer work (e.g., Erlinghagen and Hank, 2006) before retiring fully. Thus applying a developmental or life-span approach to understanding retirement is intuitively appealing.

Another useful theoretical perspective is role theory. Role theory considers the various roles one occupies, e.g., father, husband, and employee. Retirement marks the loss of one major role, which most people have occupied, often for 40 years or more, necessitating an adjustment in roles and a redefinition of one's self concept. Work, in fact, can serve an important purpose for older workers. Mor-Barak (1995) examined the meaning of work to older workers and found that work serves four basic needs:

- social contact;
- personal needs (e.g., feelings of self-worth and pride);
- financial needs; and
- generativity (the opportunity to pass knowledge and skills down to younger workers).

The loss of work may thus mark the loss of fulfilment of one or more of these needs.

A related concern for retirees may be the loss of one's identity after retirement. Research examining identities before and after retirement showed that pre-retirement identities influenced self-esteem two years after retirement (Reitzes and Mutran, 2006). Research investigating gender and identity after retirement found that identity shifts after retirement may affect men and women differently; Barnes and Parry (2004) posit that men may be more concerned with loss of status associated with no longer being the breadwinner in the family, whereas women may be more concerned with a decrease in sociability associated with the loss of colleagues.

Another useful way of understanding retirement is in terms of typologies or dichotomies. For instance, Beehr (1986)

categorized retirement along three dimensions: partial vs. complete (or full), early vs. on-time, and voluntary vs. involuntary (unemployment may be an involuntary form of retirement, if older workers decide to retire after losing one job and failing to find another). The traditional view is of retirement as complete, on-time, and voluntary. There are recent trends in retirement, however, away from these norms. For instance, people are now retiring earlier. Potential reasons for early withdrawal from the workforce include health, better employer retirement incentives or benefits, the availability of social security benefits, and the development of positive attitudes toward retirement in society (Quadagno and Hardy, 1995). Another trend in retirement is toward partial and away from full retirement. This is often referred to as bridge employment (e.g., Feldman, 1994). Bridge employment is usually defined as reentry (or continued inclusion) into the workforce following retirement, either on a full or part time basis, and either in a different or the same field. Many older workers retire from their main career job and then pursue another source of income by being self-employed. Bridge employment is especially popular in several countries, including the US, Canada, and Israel (Saba and Guerin, 2005; Leviatan, 1983), and it is a phenomenon that will likely increase in popularity in the coming decades.

There are numerous ways in which individuals can assume bridge employment, and such employment may be beneficial for many reasons. For example, people may experience a decline in physical abilities as they age, and this can affect their ability to perform their current jobs, forcing them to change careers; or they may simply wish to cut back on the number of hours that they work to spend more time with their families. Gradual transitions to retirement may be more beneficial to organizations as well. Employers may be able to hire new employees and allow them to job share with an older worker. The older worker can then train the new worker to perform the job, potentially saving the organization from spending money on training or from losing productivity during the transition from when the older worker leaves to when the new one is hired.

Retirement decision-making

One of the most fundamental questions regarding retirement is why do people retire? This is a basic question to ask, but the answer may not be very straightforward. In some forms of an ideal world, factors like health and economics would stay constant, and people would only retire when they want to, e.g., to spend more time with grandchildren or their spouse. Failing health may be one determinant that pushes people into retirement early, while low finances may be one that keeps people working when they otherwise might retire. Some studies have investigated such 'pushes' or factors that encourage workers to retire and 'pulls' or factors that keep workers in their current jobs (e.g., Feldman, 1994; Hanisch, 1994). A survey of 992 early retirees from the Health and Retirement Study found that push factors (poor health, inability to find work, dislike of work, health of a family member, employer's policy toward older workers, inability to get along with boss, and feelings that their work was not appreciated) were stronger differentiators of voluntary vs. involuntary retirement than pull factors (Shultz et al., 1998). Individuals may also be more likely to retire if their job skills are obsolete and their jobs have undesirable characteristics (Beehr, 1986).

Finances are one of the biggest concerns for older workers. There are a number of financial factors that influence the decision to retire (e.g., retirement savings, assets or wealth, expected contribution from social security, pensions, salary, eligibility for full retirement benefits, early retirement incentives, and other sources of income; Bahman, 2001; Wise, 1996). One of the difficulties facing older workers is the uncertainty of financial support from the organizations they work for and from the government. Many organizations are currently experiencing financial difficulties and may cut back on retirement benefits to save money. Because retirement benefits provided by organizations can be unstable, many individuals rely on their own financial contribution to retirement through private pension plans, e.g. 401(k)'s in the US. However, as Hansson et al. (1997) argue, pensions are not yet widely available to many, with just over half of workers between the ages of 45–64 having some form of pension coverage. Gender differences may also exist in this respect, as women tend to have poorer financial coverage than men and may have a greater need to rely on additional sources of income (Hansson et al., 1997).

Retirement outcomes

Another crucial area in which critical questions emerge concerns the consequences or effects of retirement. A concern for older people in general is the extent to which the aging process will affect their quality of life, and retirement is an important part of the aging process. Although retirement may be stressful for some, particularly if it is due to unexpected or unwanted factors such as poor health, most people find retirement an enjoyable experience. In fact, Hankin et al. (1999) found that only 30 per cent of retirees reported retirement to be a stressful event – in spite of it being a major life change that would seem to require a great deal of readjustment.

Life satisfaction after retirement is perhaps the most frequently studied outcome in research on retirement. A cross-cultural study of retirement in European countries ranked four major determinants of retirement satisfaction, and found that satisfaction with health and resources and anticipated satisfaction predicted retirement satisfaction better than satisfaction with marriage and family and regained freedom and control (Fouquereau et al. 2005). Satisfaction with retirement may be dependent upon other factors, however. One study of employed, unemployed, and retired men and women applied role theory to examine their life satisfaction and affective well-being (Warr et al., 2004). Retirees who expressed preference for their current roles, whose roles were clear, and who had an opportunity for control were more likely to have higher levels of well-being and life satisfaction. Control over the factors resulting in retirement is likely to exert important effects on the individual, as uncontrollable factors such as the unexpected disability of a spouse or loss of one's retirement benefits may well increase stress and have a negative effect on retirement outcomes. Additional factors that may moderate the link between retirement and subsequent well-being could include the amount and quality of planning for retirement, occupational goal attainment, and expectations about retirement (e.g., Beehr, 1986; Nuttman-Shwartz, 2004). One final consideration is whether retirement exerts lasting or only transient effects on satisfaction and well-being. Longitudinal data from the Normative Aging study exist on the life satisfaction and leisure activities of 293 male retirees, measured within the first three years of retirement at six monthly intervals (Ekerdt et al., 1985), and showed that optimism was greatest for recent retirees and that these positive effects dwindled over time, as some temporary dysphoria was experienced during the second year of retirement.

Organizational concerns

Older workers and job performance

A central concern for many organizations regarding older workers is the extent to which job performance is impaired as employees age. A typical concern from a utility perspective is whether older workers are costly to the organization, as they tend to earn higher salaries but may have reduced job performance. One study of 796 managers investigated managers' stereotypes about older workers' productivity, reliability, and adaptability (Henkens, 2005). Managers tend to hold stereotypes in all three categories, but older managers and managers who spent more time with their employees were more likely to hold positive opinions of older workers, rather than the negative stereotypes. The evidence clearly indicates, however, that managers hold some negative views regarding productivity of older workers, which has implications for job performance and performance appraisals.

Some researchers have examined how aging affects job performance, focusing especially on abilities or processes that typically decline with age. Researchers agree that several physical and mental abilities tend to decline with age, and performance dependent on those abilities is therefore likely to suffer. Examining the effects of aging from an occupationally-specific perspective, age may play a factor in dynamic jobs where the tasks required by the job change often or where new technologies are frequently introduced, and jobs that require physical ability. Jobs that require new tasks or additional training may be particularly problematic for older workers, as fluid intelligence tends to decrease with age (e.g., data from the German BASE study; Singer et al., 2003), and the brain is not able to create new circuits for new information as quickly.

There is some evidence that this deleterious effect of aging can be slowed down. Recent physiological evidence shows that exercise can combat the effects of aging by increasing neurogenesis (i.e., new neural growth) in the hippocampus in older adults, a brain region that plays a crucial role in learning and memory (vanPraag et al., 2005). Exercise may also help workers in jobs that require physical ability. Safety is especially crucial in some jobs and organizations, and a study using NIOSH data in the US showed that age accounted for 79.5 per cent of the variance in workplace fatalities (Agnew and Suruda, 1993). Regular exercise can help promote muscle growth and fight osteoporosis in older workers, which can help to prevent injuries on the job. Organizations may need to take additional precautions to ensure that the workplace is safe for older workers. Accommodations that the organization can make may range from simple adjustments to the physical structure of work to larger scale interventions.

Age discrimination and diversity in organizations

A major legal and ethical concern is the extent to which diversity affects the organization and group-level processes such as cohesion, conflict, and group performance. Although advocates of diversity argue that having a diverse work group leads to better group performance and lower levels of poor decision making processes such as groupthink, some critics maintain that diversity inhibits group cohesion and leads to conflict. A comprehensive review of the research surrounding diversity and demography in organizations revealed that diversity in tenure had particularly negative consequences on group cohesion and performance (Williams and O'Reilly, 1998); thus groups that were comprised of members who entered the organization at different times tended to experience more interpersonal difficulties working with each other than groups whose members entered at the same time. Although tenure is related to age (the median tenure for employees between the ages of 55 to 64 years was 9.3 years in 2006, which was three times as much for ages 25 to 34; BLS, 2006), age diversity was found to have only slightly negative consequences (Williams and O'Reilly, 1998), and therefore should be of little concern to organizations.

Organizations can mitigate any negative effects by ensuring that people of all ages feel welcome and accepted. Nonetheless, there is evidence that even if it is illegal, age discrimination still exists in the workplace. Older workers are less likely to receive training opportunities; a study found that older workers (55–64 years) were a third as likely to receive training opportunities as 35–44 year-old workers (Simon, 1996). This certainly does not aid in helping older workers adapt to new demands (physical or mental) in the workplace.

Special populations and considerations in retirement

A review of the research on social class and retirement from 1990 to 1996 in the US found that people of lower social class tend to retire earlier and for different reasons from those of higher social class (Brown et al., 1996). This might partly explain why women and African Americans are two groups in the US that retire earlier – they are often of lower social

and economic status. In particular, women tend to have inadequate retirement income and often need to rely on additional sources of income (e.g., social security or spouse's income). Interestingly, the lowest social class members among African-Americans were less likely to work after retirement than higher class members in that same group (Brown et al., 1996). Additional research suggests that African-Americans are more likely to retire early than Caucasians in the US (Elman, 1999); this may have significant implications for organizations that are concerned with maintaining diversity. Our understanding of why this difference exists is limited, and future research should seek to investigate this more fully.

Gender differences in retirement

Early research in retirement focused mainly on how retirement affected men, however as the demographics of the workforce have shifted, researchers are beginning to examine how retirement affects women as well. A study of Swedish early retirees aged 55–64 years found some of the factors that push one into retirement or pull one away from work differ for men and women; a difficult job pushed women into retirement and a socially-rewarding job tended to keep men in their current job (Soidre, 2005). Some evidence exists that a crucial component of retirement satisfaction is the extent of planning and building self-efficacy for retirement planning (e.g., Bidewell et al., 2006). Evidence exists that women spend less time planning for retirement, suggesting that women may need additional assistance preparing for retirement (Jacobs-Lawson et al., 2004). Organizations could provide such training (as could community programs) to help make sure that women are financially as well as psychologically prepared for retirement.

An additional difference between men and women from a role theory perspective is that women tend to take on additional non-work roles as older workers. They often play more involved roles in their families, and they often end up taking care of aging parents. Women may even find themselves unable to continue working, or need to transition to bridge jobs rather than continue full employment, to allow more time to care for loved ones. This undoubtedly adds substantial stress for women and may even contribute to role overload. However, being a caregiver for older parents has a negative impact on long term financial consequences as well (Orel et al., 2004). This is particularly concerning given that women already tend to be less financially prepared for retirement than men (Hansson et al., 1997). Again, organizations as well as society may help buffer these effects by providing financial training to women, but it may also help to provide counseling and support for those caring for aging parents.

Retirement and families

The decision to retire is more than an individual one; it affects one's spouse and family as well. Some research has examined the effect of retirement on marital quality (e.g., Szinovacz and Schaffer, 2000). A survey of couples comparing those where the wife retired vs. those where the husband retired found that wives' continued employment was related to increased marital conflict, reinforcing the notion that women serve an important role in maintaining healthy family functioning in the home (Davey and Szinovacz, 2004). The amount of involvement one has in a spouse's decision to retire must also be considered: A longitudinal study found that for both men and women, the more involvement one has in a spouse's decision to retire, the less satisfied the retiring spouse is with retirement (Szinovacz and Davey, 2005). The study also found that both male and female retirees were less likely to be satisfied if their spouse remained working, indicating that retirement may serve an important marital function, allowing couples to spend more time together. This research supports the assertion that retirement is not an individual decision, and that in fact, many parties are involved. This makes capturing the couple's decision to retire even more complex and multifaceted. Future research should examine the relative effect of different components of the retirement decision-making process.

Cross-cultural studies of retirement

Historically, there has been somewhat limited information comparing retirement across different countries. The situation is changing however, as is evident from the recent appearance of the *Journal of Cross-Cultural Gerontology*. Some of the available research suggests the important generalities in the retirement experiences. A study examining satisfaction with retirement in six European countries found that retirees in five of the countries (Belgium, Great Britain, Finland, France, and Spain) had similar levels of life satisfaction; Portuguese retirees, however, had significantly lower levels of satisfaction (Fouquereau et al., 2005). Countries have different laws and regulations governing retirement. In the US, forced retirement is illegal in most occupations, but in some countries retirement age is mandated by the government for some or all jobs (e.g., the Netherlands and India). For instance, in Israel, retirement is required at age 65 for men and 60 for women. A study of 56 Israeli men examined their retirement process and found that their psychological experience in response to retirement occurred in waves; the dominant perspective of retirement was viewing it as uncertainty and crisis prior to retirement, followed by a reduction in anxiety and improved well-being (Nuttman-Shwartz, 2004). For more thorough information comparing retirement in Western countries with non-Western cultures including Thai, Chinese, Fulani, and Lusi, among others, the interested reader should consult Leborsky and LeBlanc (2003).

Future directions for retirement research

As the literature on retirement increases, organizational behavior needs to address gaps that have been identified in the literature; in addition, the existing research needs to be synthesized to capture the major themes of our understanding of retirement. Related to the latter issue, upon reviewing the literature for this book chapter, we noted that there is a considerable inconsistency regarding basic concepts and definitions in retirement. For instance, even the definition of 'older worker' varies considerably – from beginning at 40 years- (Hansson et al., 1997) to 55 years-old (Noonan, 2005). In order to apply a useful framework to the variables involved in retirement, researchers need to find some consensus concerning such important issues.

There are additional areas of research that need further exploration. Although we have gained some ground in the study of gender differences in retirement and retirement across different cultures, more research is needed to understand how retirement differs for these groups and cultures. Research has also furthered our knowledge of how retirement affects individuals and other relevant parties, and we now have a better understanding of how to help prepare individuals for, or cope with, retirement (e.g., by providing training on financial planning, establishing exercise interventions). Research still needs to examine the effect of the interventions, or characteristics of interventions, that may be particularly helpful. Such research should examine how organizations and society can make the most effective interventions to help individuals adjust to and prepare for retirement.

CONCLUSION

Unemployment and retirement are both concerned with former workers who are no longer in the paid workforce. In both cases, the portion of society that is still working tends to support some or all of those who are not, regardless of the reason for people's absence from the workforce. This makes these two situations important for governments as well as for the people who experience these phenomena. Governments try to influence both unemployment and retirement through direct legislation (e.g., regarding retirement ages, public pensions,

unemployment benefits, obligations and taxes for employers aimed at supporting people in both situations). Trends for each can look cyclical, but they follow different cycles. For example, unemployment varies strongly with certain economic trends, and retirement strongly with demographic trends (e.g., aging of society). Furthermore, for some older employees facing unemployment, retirement is an option they might find more desirable. In this special case, unemployment and retirement can be either-or alternatives.

Thus unemployment and retirement differ in important ways. They carry different statuses in the eyes of societies, carry different expectations for the behavior of people (e.g., whether one *ought to* be seeking paid employment vs. taking it easy), usually are experienced by differently aged people, tend to be explained by different theories, and also tend to be studied by different sets of researchers. Furthermore, governments tend to pass separate laws regarding each of these states rather than considering their social and economic effects together. We have learned much about each of these forms of withdrawal or absence from the paid workforce, but as can be seen from the discussion in this chapter, much more remains to be learned.

REFERENCES

Agnew, J. and Suruda, A.J. (1993) 'Age and fatal work-related falls', *Human Factors*, 35 (4): 731–736.

Bahman, B. (2001) 'Factors affecting faculty retirement decisions', *Social Science Journal*, 38: 297–305.

Barnes, H. and Parry, J. (2004) 'Renegotiating identity and relationships: Men and women's adjustments to retirement', *Ageing and Society*, 24: 213–233.

Beehr, T.A. (1986) 'The process of retirement: A review and recommendations for future investigation', *Personnel Psychology*, 39: 31–55.

Bidewell, J., Griffin, B. and Hesketh, B. (2006) 'Timing of retirement: Including a delay discounting perspective in retirement models', *Journal of Vocational Behavior*, 68: 368–387.

Brown, M.T., Fukunaga, C., Umemoto, D. and Wicker, L. (1996) 'Annual review, 1990–1996: Social class, work, and retirement behavior', *Journal of Vocational Behavior*, 49: 159–189.

BLS, Bureau of Labor Statistics (2006) Median years of tenure with current employer for employed wage and salary workers 25 years and over by educational attainment, sex, and age, January 2006. Available: http://www.bls.gov/news.release/tenure.t04.htm.

Carsten, J. and Spector, P.E. (1987) 'Unemployment, job satisfaction, and employee turnover: A meta-analytic test of the Muchinsky Model', *Journal of Applied Psychology*, 72: 374–381.

Chan, S. and Stevens, A.H. (1999) 'Employment and retirement following a late-career job loss', *American Economic Review*, 89: 211–216.

Clogg, C.C. (1979) *Measuring Underemployment: Demographic Indicators for the United States.* New York: Academic Press.

Cockburn, C., Gilmour, D., Ginsberg, A., Kiefer, U.E., Kurzynowski, A., Omachi, C. and Sachs, B. (1972) 'Employment and retirement: Roles and Activities', *The Gerontologist*, 12: 29–55.

Colarelli, S.M. and Beehr, T.A. (1993) 'Selection Out: Firings, Layoffs, and Retirement', in N. Schmitt and W. Borman (eds), *Personnel Selection in Organizations.* San Francisco: Jossey-Bass Publishers, pp. 341–384.

Colquitt, J.A., Conlon, D.E., Wesson, M.J., Porter, C.O. and Ng. K.Y. (2001) 'Organizational justice at the millennium: A meta-analytic review of 25 years of organizational justice research', *Journal of Applied Psychology*, 86: 425–445.

Couch, K.A. (1998) 'Late life job displacement', *The Gerontologist*, 38: 7–17.

Creed, P.A. and Macintyre, S. R (2001) 'The relative effects of deprivation of the latent and manifest benefits of employment on the well-being of unemployed people', *Journal of Occupational Health Psychology*, 6: 324–331.

Crossley, C.D. and Stanton, J.M. (2004) 'Negative affect and job search: Further examination of the reverse causation hypothesis', *Journal of Vocational Behavior*, 66: 549–560.

Davey, A. and Szinovacz, M.E. (2004) 'Dimensions of marital quality and retirement', *Journal of Family Issues*, 25 (4): 431–464.

Dooley, D. and Prause, J. (2004) *The Social Costs of Underemployment: Inadequate Employment as Disguised Unemployment.* Cambridge: Cambridge University Press.

Ekerdt, D.J., Bosse, R. and Levkoff, S. (1985) 'An empirical test for phases of retirement: Findings from the Normative Aging study', *Journal of Gerontology*, 40 (1): 95–101.

Elman, C. (1999) 'Labor markets and opportunity structures', *Research on Aging*, 21 (2): 205–239.

Erlinghagen, M. and Hank, K. (2006) 'The participation of older Europeans in volunteer work', *Ageing and Society*, 26 (4): 567–584.

Feldman, D.C. (1996) 'Toward a new taxonomy for understanding the nature and consequences of contingent employment', *Career Development International*, 11: 28–47.

Feldman, D.C. (1994) 'The decision to retire early: A review and conceptualization', *Academy of Management Review*, 19: 285–311.

Feldman, D.C. and Turnley, W.H. (1995) 'Underemployment among recent business college graduates', *Journal of Organizational Behavior*, 16: 691–706.

Fouquereau, E., Fernandez, A., Fonseca, A.M., Paul, M.C. and Uotinen, V. (2005) 'Perceptions of and satisfaction with retirement: A comparison of six European union countries', *Psychology and Aging*, 20 (3): 524–528.

Franzen, E.M. and Kassman, A. (2005) 'Longer-term labour-market consequences of economic inactivity during young adulthood: A Swedish national cohort study', *Journal of Youth Studies*, 8: 403–424.

Frese, M. (1987) 'Alleviating depression in the unemployed: Adequate financial support, hope and early retirement', *Social Science and Medicine*, 25: 213–215.

Frese, M. and Mohr, G. (1987) 'Prolonged unemployment and depression in older workers: A longitudinal study of intervening variables', *Social Science and Medicine*, 25: 173–178.

Frone, M.R. and Yardley, J.K. (1996) 'Workplace family-supportive programmes: Predictors of employed parents' importance ratings', *Journal of Occupational and Organizational Psychology*, 69 (4): 351–366.

Hanisch, K.A. (1994) 'Reasons people retire and their relations to attitudinal and behavioral correlates in retirement', *Journal of Vocational Behavior*, 45 (1): 1–16.

Hankin, C.S., Bosse, R. and Spiro, A., III. (1999) 'Assessment and Treatment of Retirement Stress', in L. VandeCreek and T.L. Jackson (eds), *Innovations in Clinical Practice: A Source Book, 17.* Sarasota, FL: USource Press/Professional Resource Exchange, Inc., pp. 49–63.

Hansson, R.O., DeKoekkoek, P.D., Neece, W.M. and Patterson D.W. (1997) 'Successful aging at work: Annual review, 1992–1996: The older worker and transitions to retirement', *Journal of Vocational Behavior*, 51: 202–233.

Hatcher, C.B. (2003) 'The Economics of the Retirement Decision', in G.A. Adams and T.A. Beehr (eds), *Retirement: Reasons, Processes, and Results.* New York: Springer Publishing Company, pp. 136–158.

Haworth, J.T. (1986) 'Meaningful activity and psychological models of non-employment', *Leisure Studies*, 5: 281–297.

Henkens, K. (2005) 'Stereotyping older workers and retirement: The managers' point of view', *Canadian Journal on Aging*, 24 (4): 353–366.

Hom, P.W. and Kinicki, A. (2001) 'Toward a greater understanding of how dissatisfaction drives employee turnover', *Academy of Management Journal*, 44: 975–987.

Hultman, B., Hemlin, S. and Hornquist, J.O. (2006) 'Quality of life among unemployed and employed people in northern Sweden. Are there any differences?', *Work*, 26: 47–56.

Industry Watch (2005) *Healthcare Financial Management*, 59 (11): 28.

Jacobs-Lawson, J.M., Hershey, D.A. and Neukam, K.A. (2004) 'Gender differences in factors that influence time spent planning for retirement', *Journal of Women and Aging*, 16 (3/4): 55–69.

Jahoda, M. (1982) *Employment and Unemployment: A Social-Psychological Analysis*. New York: Cambridge University Press.

Jensen, L. and Slack, T. (2003) 'Underemployment in America: Measurement and evidence', *American Journal of Community Psychology*, 32: 21–31.

Johnson, W.R., Morrow, P.C. and Johnson, G.J. (2002) 'An evaluation of a perceived overqualification scale across work settings', *The Journal of Psychology*, 136 (4): 425–441.

Jones-Johnson, G. and Johnson, W.R. (1992) 'Subjective underemployment and psychosocial stress: The role of perceived social and supervisor support', *The Journal of Social Psychology*, 132 (1): 11–21.

Kahn, J.R. and Pearlin, L.I. (2006) 'Financial strain over the life course and health of older adults', *Journal of Health and Social Behavior*, 47: 17–31.

Khan, L.J. and Morrow, P.C. (1991) 'Objective and subjective underemployment relationships to job satisfaction', *Journal of Business Research*, 22: 211–218.

Kaufman, H.G. (1982) *Professionals in Search of Work: Coping with the Stress of Job Loss and Underemployment*. New York: John Wiley and Sons.

Kubler-Ross, E. (1969) *On Death and Dying*. New York: Macmillan.

Leborsky, M.R. and LeBlanc, I.M. (2003) 'Cross-cultural perspectives on the concept of retirement: An analytic redefinition', *Journal of Cross-Cultural Gerontology*, 18 (4): 251–271.

Leviatan, U. (1983) 'Work and aging in the kibbutz: Some relevancies for the larger society', *Aging and Work*, 6 (3): 215–226.

Mass layoffs in 2005 (2006) *Monthly Labor Review*, 129 (2): 2.

Merriam, S.B. (1987) 'The experience of job loss as perceived by young and middle-aged adults and those near retirement', *Journal of Employment Counseling*, 24: 107–114.

McKee-Ryan, F.M., Song, Z., Wanberg, C.R. and Kinicki, A.J. (2005) 'Psychological and physical well-being during unemployment: A meta-analytic study', *Journal of Applied Psychology*, 90: 53–76.

Mor-Barak, M.E. (1995) 'The meaning of work for older adults seeking employment: The generativity factor', *International Journal of Aging and Human Development*, 41 (4): 325–344.

Niessen, C. (2005) 'Age and learning during unemployment', *Journal of Organizational Behavior*, 27: 771–792.

Noonan, A.E. (2005) '"At this point now": Older workers' reflections on their current employment experiences', *International Journal of Aging and Human Development*, 61 (3): 211–241.

Nuttman-Shwartz, O. (2004) 'Like a high wave: Adjustment to retirement', *Gerontologist*, 44 (2): 229–236.

Orel, N.A., Ford, R.A. and Brock, C. (2004) 'Women's financial planning for retirement: The impact of disruptive life events', *Journal of Women and Aging*, 16 (3/4): 39–53.

Price, R.H., Choi, J., N. and Vinokur, A.D. (2002) 'Links in the chain of adversity following job loss: How financial strain and loss of personal control lead to depression, impaired functioning, and poor health', *Journal of Occupational Health Psychology*, 7: 302–312.

Prussia, G.E., Fugate, M. and Kinicki, A.J. (2001) 'Explication of the coping goal construct: Implications for coping and reemployment', *Journal of Applied Psychology*, 86: 1179–1190.

Quadagno, J. and Hardy, M. (1996) 'Work and Retirement', in R.H. Binstock and L.K. George (eds), *Handbook of Aging and the Social Sciences* (4th edn). San Diego: Academic Press, pp. 325–345.

Reitzes, D.C. and Mutran, E.J. (2006) 'Lingering identities in retirement', *The Sociology Quarterly*, 47: 333–359.

Saba, T. and Guerin, G. (2005) 'Extending employment beyond retirement age: The case of health care managers in Quebec', *Public Personnel Management*, 34 (2): 195–214.

Shultz, K.S., Morton, K.R. and Weckerle, J.R. (1998) 'The influence of push and pull factors on voluntary and involuntary early retirees' retirement decision and adjustment', *Journal of Vocational Behavior*, 53: 45–57.

Schulz, A.J., Israel, B.A., Zenk, S.N., Parker, E.A., Lichtenstein, R., Shellman-Weir, S. and Klem, A.B.L. (2006) 'Psychosocial stress and social support as mediators of relationships between income, length of residence, and depressive symptoms among African American Women on Detroit's eastside', *Social Science and Medicine*, 62: 510–522.

Singer, T., Verhaegen, P., Ghisletta, P., Lindberger, U. and Baltes, P.B. (2003) 'The fate of cognition in very old age: Six-year longitudinal findings in the Berlin Aging Study (BASE)', *Psychology and Aging*, 38: 318–331.

Simon, R. (1996) 'Too damn old', *Money*, 25 (7): 188–216.

Soidre, T. (2005) 'Retirement-age preferences of women and men aged 55–64 years in Sweden', *Ageing and Society*, 25: 943–963.

Sullivan, T.A. and Hauser, P.M. (1978) 'The labor Utilization Framework: Assumptions, Data, and Policy Implications'. Background paper No. 19. National Commission on Employment and Unemployment Statistics.

Szinovacz, M.E. and Davey, A. (2005) 'Predictors of perceptions of involuntary retirement', *Gerontologist*, 45 (1): 36–47.

Szinovacz, M.E. and Schaffer, A.M. (2000) 'Effects of retirement on marital conflict tactics', *Journal of Family Issues*, 21 (3): 367–389.

Trevor, C.O. (2001) 'Interactions among actual ease-of-movement determinants and job satisfaction in the prediction of voluntary turnover', *Academy of Management Journal*, 44: 621–638.

van Hooft, E.A.J., Born, M. Ph., Taris, T.W. and van der Flier, H. (2004a) 'Job search and the theory of planned behavior: Minority-majority group differences in The Netherlands', *Journal of Vocational Behavior*, 65: 366–390.

van Hooft, E.A.J., Born, M. Ph., Taris, T.W., van der Flier, H. and Blonk, R.W.B. (2004b) 'Predictors of job search behavior among employed and unemployed people', *Personnel Psychology*, 57: 25–59.

vanPraag, H., Shubert, T., Zhao, C. and Gage, F.H. (2005) 'Exercise enhances learning and hippocampal neurogenesis in aged mice', *The Journal of Neuroscience*, 25 (38): 8680–8685.

Viney, L.L. and Tych, A.M. (1984–1985) 'To work or not to work? An enquiry of men experiencing unemployment, promotion an retirement', *Psychology of Human Development*, 1: 57–66.

Vinokur, A.D. and Schul, Y. (2002) 'The web of coping resources and pathways to reemployment following a job loss', *Journal of Occupational Health Psychology*, 7: 68–83.

Vinokur, A.D., Schul, Y., Vuori, J. and Price, R.H. (2000) 'Two years after a job loss: Long-term impact of the JOBS program on reemployment and mental health', *Journal of Occupational Health Psychology*, 5: 32–47.

Vuori, J., Price, R.H., Mutanen, P. and Malmberg-Heimonen, I. (2005) 'Effective group training techniques in job-search training', *Journal of Occupational Health Psychology*, 10: 261–275.

Vuori, J., Silvonen, J., Vinokur, A.D. and Price, R.H. (2002) 'The Tyohon Job Search Program in Finland: Benefits for the unemployed with risk of depression or discouragement', *Journal of Occupational Health Psychology*, 7: 5–19.

Wanberg, C.R., Glomb, T.M., Song, Z. and Sorenson, S. (2005) 'Job-search persistence during employment: A 10-wave longitudinal study', *Journal of Applied Psychology*, 90: 411–430.

Wanberg, C.R., Hough, L.M. and Song, Z. (2002) 'Predictive validity of a multidisciplinary model of reemployment success', *Journal of Applied Psychology*, 87: 1100–1120.

Wanberg, C.R., Rotundo, M. and Kanfer, R. (1999) 'Unemployed individuals motives, job-search competencies, and job-search constraints as predictors of job seeking and reemployment', *Journal of Applied Psychology*, 84: 897–910.

Warr, P., Butcher, V., Robertson, I. and Callinan, M. (2004) 'Older people's well-being as a function of employment, retirement, environmental characteristics, and role preference', *British Journal of Psychology*, 95: 297–324.

Waters, L.E. and Moore, K.A. (2002) 'Self-esteem, appraisal and coping: A comparison of unemployed and re-employed people', *Journal of Organizational Behavior*, 23: 593–604.

Wickrama, K.A.S., Lorenz, F.O., Conger, R.D., Elder, G.H. Jr., Abraham, W.T., and Fang, S. (2006) 'Changes in family financial circumstances and the physical health of married and recently divorced mothers', *Social Science and Medicine*, 63: 123–136.

Williams, K.Y., and O'Reilly, C.A. (1998) 'Demography and diversity in organizations: A review of 40 years of research', *Research in Organizational Behavior*, 20: 77–140.

Winegardner, D., Simonetti, J.L. and Nykodym, N. (1984) 'Unemployment: The living death?', *Journal of Employment Counseling*, 21: 149–155.

Wise, D.A. (1996) 'Program report: The economics of aging', *NBER Reporter*, Summer 1996 (1).

PART TWO

Practices, Processes and Performance

13

Emotions at Work: A Review and Research Agenda

Alicia A. Grandey

'We should not have consented to write an article on work and emotion ... In order to do a review, one needs literature that can be reviewed' (Pekrun and Frese, 1992: 153).

Things looked bleak for the study of emotions at work 15 years ago. Though early OB research had gathered rich evidence about emotions in the workplace (see Weiss and Cropanzano, 1996), during the cognitive era of 1940–1970, OB research 'portrays organization members as cognitive stick figures whose behavior is unaffected by emotions' (Mowday and Sutton, 1993: 197). Job satisfaction, and survey data, was the way to study affect (Weiss and Brief, 2001). Starting in the 1980s, a cadre of researchers showed the value of studying moods in the workplace using a variety of methods (e.g., George, 1989; Isen and Baron, 1991; Isen et al., 1987; Staw et al., 1986), yet 'perhaps the most glaring example of the narrowness of organizational research is the overemphasis of the study of mood at the expense of discrete emotions' (Brief and Weiss, 2002: 297).

Then in the mid-1990s, theoretical articles gave emotions at work new life, providing arguments that rationality-emotionality were not dichotomies akin to good-bad for organizations (Ashforth and Humphrey, 1993; Putnam and Mumby, 1993) and new theoretical frameworks to guide future research. Weiss and Cropanzano's (1996) Affective Events Theory (AET) proposed that emotions were the key mechanism by which the situation and personality influenced work attitudes and behaviors and provided 'a different paradigm for studying affect at work' (Weiss and Beal, 2005: 1), specifically studying within-person experiences over time. In addition, sociologist Arlie Hochschild's (1983) book *The Managed Heart* 'seemed to kickstart more recent interest in emotion at work' (Briner and Kiefer, 2005: 282) by suggesting that some employees are required to manage emotions as part of their work role (i.e., emotional labor).

Today's reviewer of emotions find quite a different dilemma than did Pekrun and Frese in 1992. Now is the age of the 'affective revolution' in OB (Barsade et al., 2003); in the last five years the growth of the number of articles on affect in OB exceeds the growth in other mainstream topics (see Figure 1). An important part of this growth is attention to specific emotions, as encouraged by recent authors (Barsade et al., 2003; Brief and Weiss, 2002; Briner et al., 2005; Lazarus and Cohen-Charash, 2001) and the positive psychology movement (Fredrickson, 1998).

In addition to reviewing the mood research, this chapter highlights the emerging literature on discrete emotions[1] and provides an agenda for future emotion research. To provide a basis for understanding the literature, I first give an overview of emotion theory and methods. Then I review how emotion has been integrated with OB topics, and whether discrete emotion provides unique information beyond positive and negative affect. I close with a brief discussion of the challenges and suggestions for emotions research.

INTRODUCTION TO EMOTIONS IN OB

Below I define terms, discuss the structure of affect, differentiate discrete emotions, and review useful theoretical perspectives.

Defining affective terms

When researchers talk about 'affect' they might mean three different constructs.

- *Moods* refer to a state without a known cause that is weaker in intensity and potentially longer in duration than emotions (Frijda, 1993; Russell and Feldman Barrett, 1999). I may wake up in a particular mood (e.g., lethargic or pleasant) without knowing why I feel that way.
- *Affective dispositions*, typically studied as positive and negative affectivity (Staw et al., 1986; Weiss and Cropanzano, 1996), refer to relatively stable feeling states and response tendencies (Watson et al., 1988).
- *Emotion*, like mood, involves a transient feeling state, but is a response to an identified cause or target.

Emotion is dynamic and multifaceted, including feelings, expressive behavior, and neurological/physiological changes (Davidson et al., 2000; Frijda, 1993; Izard, 1991), or the 'emotional reaction triad' (Scherer, 2000: 156). In a prototypical emotional episode all of these components change together, but in reality, that is seldom the case (Russell et al., 1999). Research shows that using self-reported experienced feelings (e.g., felt irritation and annoyance), behavioral indicators (e.g., observed scowling or aggressive acts), and physiological indicators

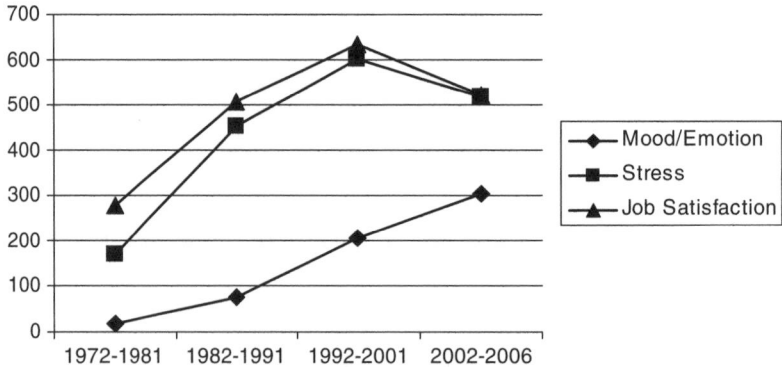

Figure 1   Number of articles in peer-reviewed management journals by topic during four time periods
Note: Search in ABI/Inform engine for the shown terms and 'workplace' or 'organization' in the citation or abstract. Note that the last time period is half the length of the first three.

of emotion (e.g., skin conductance and heart rate) can work independently and have different correlates (e.g., Gross and Levenson, 1993). Typically in OB, self-reported (feelings) or observational (expressions) methods are used to measure affect.

Structure of affect

The myriad of affective responses in self-reported studies can be reduced to two dimensions, depending on the rotation of axes in factor analyses (see Russell et al., 1999, for a review). A circumplex model of affect shows how affective terms group together by valence (also called hedonic tone or pleasantness) and arousal (also called activation) and can emerge as four different dimensions, or eight categories, see Figure 2 (Russell et al., 1999; Van Katwyk et al., 2000).

These dimensional approaches create a parsimonious way of studying affect, but important differences may be lost when aggregating across emotions. For example, both anger and fear are high activation–low

pleasantness, but they emerge from different situations and result in different behavioral tendencies (Lerner and Keltner, 2000). Emotion researchers tend to use indicators of specific prototypical emotions (e.g., anger, fear, happiness, see Larsen and Fredrickson, 1999; Weiss et al., 1996). Importantly, measuring specific emotions can later be aggregated into more parsimonious dimensions, while using measures like 'pleasantness–unpleasantness' cannot be formed into discrete emotions. Ultimately, the researcher needs to determine if specific emotions are likely to tell a different story than dimensions of pleasantness or activation.

Differentiating discrete emotions

If one decides to study specific emotions, which should be measured? There are multiple lists of 'basic' or core emotions (e.g., Izard, 1977; Plutchik, 1994) that vary depending on whether the list derives from variations in expressions, physiological responses, cognitive appraisals, action tendencies, or feeling labels (see Russell

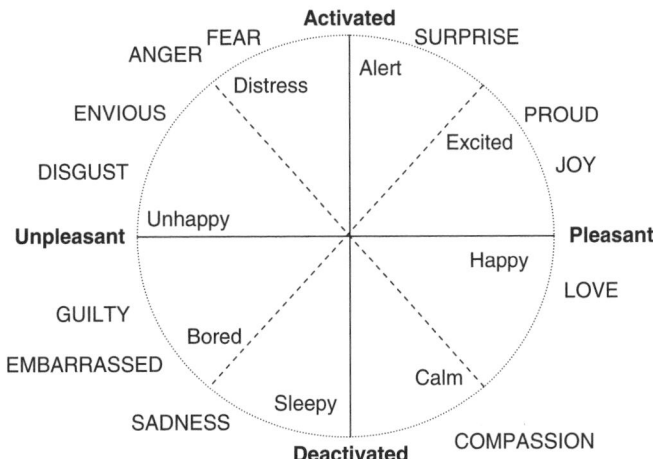

Figure 2 Conceptual structure of experienced affect (adapted from multiple sources: Larsen et al., 2002; Russell, 1980; Scherer, 2000)

Note: Terms that are more similar to each other are closer together around the circle. The words inside the circle represent mood states, while the words outside the circle represent prototypical emotions. The hedonic tone-activation two dimensional structure (Larsen and Diener) is shown with straight lines, the positive affect-negative affect two-dimensional structure (Watson and Tellegen) is shown with dashed lines.

and Barrett, 1999). Some common emotions across these lists are anger, fear, disgust, sadness, and joy/happy.[2] Other lists specify different categories of emotions, such as self-conscious (e.g., pride, embarrassment and shame) or social (e.g., love, hurt and contempt) emotions (Fredrickson, 1998; Leary, 2000; Lewis, 1993) (see Table 1 for categories).

When thinking about which emotions to study, consider the specific appraisals and action tendencies for each emotion.

Table 1 Appraisals and tendencies associated with discrete emotions

Discrete Emotion	Appraisal	Thought-Action Tendency
Goal Progress Emotions		
Happiness	Situation causes certain goal-consistent rewards; Making reasonable progress toward one's valued goals.	Urge to see connections, increase intimacy and openness, spontaneous play.
Pride*	Self-caused attribution for pleasant goal-consistent outcome; taking credit for valued object or achievement of self or group.	Urge to share achievements with others.
Anger	Blame other for goal-inconsistent outcome; a demeaning offense against me or what I care about.	Urge to attack, mobilize and sustain high levels of energy.
Sadness	Situation causes lack of obtaining reward with little controllability; experiencing irrevocable loss.	Urge to withdraw, reflect, to communicate need to others.
Personal Threat Emotions		
Fear	Uncertain causes of goal-inconsistency with little controllability; concrete and overwhelming danger.	Urge to escape, can mobilize or freeze resources to avoid threat.
Disgust	Situation unpleasant or threatening to self with little controllability.	Urge to expel, mobilize body to close off senses.
Social-Relational Emotions (how others feel about self)		
Guilt*	Self-caused goal-inconsistent situation with little power to correct situation; Having transgressed a moral imperative.	Urge to make amends with wronged others.
Shame/Embarrassment*	Self-caused goal-inconsistent situation with little means to correct situation; Failing to live up to an ego-ideal.	Urge to restore one's value in others' eyes (apology, excuse, seek forgiveness), or hide from others if cannot.
Envy/Jealousy	Feeling justified in wanting what another has/the person a third party has taken.	Urge to redress the situation by obtaining object/eliminating influence of the third party.
Social-Evaluative Emotions (how self feels about others)		
Liking/Love	Other-caused pleasant/goal-consistent; Desiring or participating in affection.	Urge to affiliate with specific other, for intimacy.
Compassion	Perception of another having unpleasant feelings; belief one has capability to help.	Urge to provide support to other to reduce discomfort.

*Also categorized as self-conscious emotions (Leary, 2000).
Note: Integrated from multiple sources (Fredrickson, 1998; Frijda et al., 1989; Lazarus and Cohen-Charash, 2001; Roseman, 1991).

Appraisals of the context are the meaning that the person ascribes to the situation, which impact the self-labeling of emotion (Frijda et al., 1989; Lazarus, 1991; Roseman, 1991).[3] The specific appraisal dimensions vary by researcher, but include assessments of goal progress, causal attributions, causal agents, or coping ability. For example, poor performance that hinders important goals induces guilt if appraised as self-caused, or anger if appraised as other-caused. Furthermore, emotions have the ability to interrupt ongoing thoughts and behaviors ('control precedence,' Frijda, 1993), such that emotions hijack a person and take their minds and bodies in a new direction. Guilt involves the tendency to make amends and improve work tasks, while the angry performer may lash out in counterproductive ways. Thus, action tendencies (Frijda et al., 1989) or thought-action tendencies (Fredrickson, 1998) impact motivation and behavior. Table 1 summarizes appraisals and action tendencies for a set of discrete emotions.

Theoretical perspectives

Below are summaries of several theoretical perspectives for understanding emotions in OB. They are organized into two broad categories: intrapersonal and interpersonal processes.

Intrapersonal theories of emotion

Many theories of emotion focus on how affect influences cognition or information processing. The *feelings-as-information model* (Schwarz and Clore, 1983, 1990) suggests that feelings without a clear cause (i.e., mood) are attributed to the situation. Negative moods suggest problems with the task such that systematic, analytical, and thorough processing is needed (Forgas, 1998b); positive moods suggest that the situation is safe and thus heuristic and flexible cognition is possible and there is more social awareness (Isen, 2001; Isen and Baron, 1991; Isen and Daubman, 1984). As an extension of these processes, the *Affect Infusion Model* (AIM) (Forgas, 1995) proposed that affect is most likely to infuse cognitions when the processing is automatic or ambiguous, and less so when processing is motivated or systematic.

Feelings influence motivated behavior as well. Ambiguous situations make it more likely that affect influences motivated behavior; according to the *mood-as-input* approach (Martin et al., 1993), positive moods inform the actor that they can stop working on the task and relax, while negative moods suggest further effort is needed. The *hedonic contingency model* states that people desire to remain in pleasant moods (Wegener and Petty, 1994), and will seek out ('approach') or withdraw from ('avoid') situations that do not meet that goal. The link between such tendencies and our emotional states is shown in neuroscientific evidence for two activation systems: the behavioral activation system (BAS – left prefrontal cortex, linked with joy, anger) and the behavioral inhibition system (BIS – right prefrontal cortex, linked with sadness) (Gray, 1971; Harmon-Jones and Allen, 1998).

Finally, how one regulates emotions also influences motivation and behavior. Higgins' (1987) *self-regulatory focus theory* argued that individual differences and situational factors (e.g., compensation systems) modify whether people direct behavior toward approaching or avoiding a goal, which is linked to emotions (Brockner and Higgins, 2001). According to the *ego depletion model* of self-regulation, regulating emotions per se depletes personal resources and requires recovery time to avoid failing at subsequent attempts at self-regulation (Baumeister et al., 1998; Muraven and Baumeister, 2000). In particular, this perspective suggests that regulating emotions reduces the future availability of any resource (e.g., physical strength, attention and willpower). This theoretical perspective provides rationale and empirical evidence for why emotion regulation may be effective in the short-term but have costs to the individual and task performance (Richards and Gross, 1999; Schmeichel et al., 2003).

Interpersonal perspectives of emotion

Felt emotion can also impact the motivation and behavior of others, which can be discussed as both passive and active processes. The most commonly used passive mechanism in OB is *emotional contagion* (Hatfield et al., 1994) where the 'sender' expresses his or her emotional state, the receiver automatically mimics this expression resulting in 'facial feedback' processes (Zajonc, 1985) and the imitated vocal or facial expression induces a congruent emotional state in the receiver (Stepper and Strack, 1993). Thus, in order for contagion to occur affect needs to be expressed and observed, though contagion need not be a conscious goal of either party (Neumann and Strack, 2000).

As a more active process, emotion is highly intertwined with power and influence (Gibson and Schroeder, 2002; Keltner et al., 2003; Kemper, 1978). Having power is associated with feeling more positively and having freedom to express emotions toward others as a form of influence, while lower-power persons experience more negative emotions but are expected to hide them or express positive emotions (Côté and Morgan, 2002; Hecht and LaFrance, 1998; Levine and Feldman, 1997; Ridgeway and Johnson, 1990). Moreover, expressing dominant emotion (e.g., anger versus sadness) increases the power one is seen as holding (Tiedens and Fragale, 2002), creating a reinforcing cycle of power and expressed emotion (Tiedens, 2000). The role of power in emotional contagion is unclear; contagion may be stronger from the more powerful to the less powerful, or power differences may encourage complementary (e.g., dominant-submissive) emotions (Anderson et al., 2003; Hsee, et al., 1990; Tiedens and Fragale, 2002).

EMOTIONS AS PART OF INTRAPERSONAL OB EXPERIENCES

Below I review theory and research on felt emotions as part of employee work motivation, contextual performance, and organizational justice.

Emotion and work motivation

Emotional mechanisms are beginning to be explicitly included in understanding work motivation, goals, and job performance (e.g., Seo et al., 2004).

Job characteristic approaches

Affective events theory (Weiss and Cropanzano, 1996) proposed that certain job characteristics increased the likelihood of affective events and reactions (see Figure 3). Brief and Weiss (2002) proposed five main categories of work characteristics that create affective reactions:

(1) stressful/aversive events;
(2) leaders;
(3) interpersonal/group characteristics;
(4) physical settings; and
(5) organizational rewards and punishments.

Research has provided some evidence in each category (e.g., Avolio et al., 1999; Humphrey, 1985; Oldham et al., 1995; Spector and Jex, 1991).

More comprehensively, Saavedra and Kwun (2000) demonstrated that the dimensions of the job characteristics theory (JCT, Hackman and Oldham, 1976) had differential relationships with affect. Some task dimensions improved enthusiasm at work (i.e., task significance, task feedback, and autonomy), others impacted the likelihood of nervousness (i.e., task identity reduced it, while skill variety increased it). Those with strong desire for growth (growth need strength; GNS) had stronger emotional reactions to these characteristics than those with weaker GNS (Saavedra et al., 2000). Future work is needed to compare how job design influences employee motivation; such as how the characteristics exacerbate or buffer each other over time and impact specific emotions with withdraw or approach action tendencies.

Goals

Most attention in this area has been with a two-dimensional approach to affect as predictors of goal choice (distal motivation)

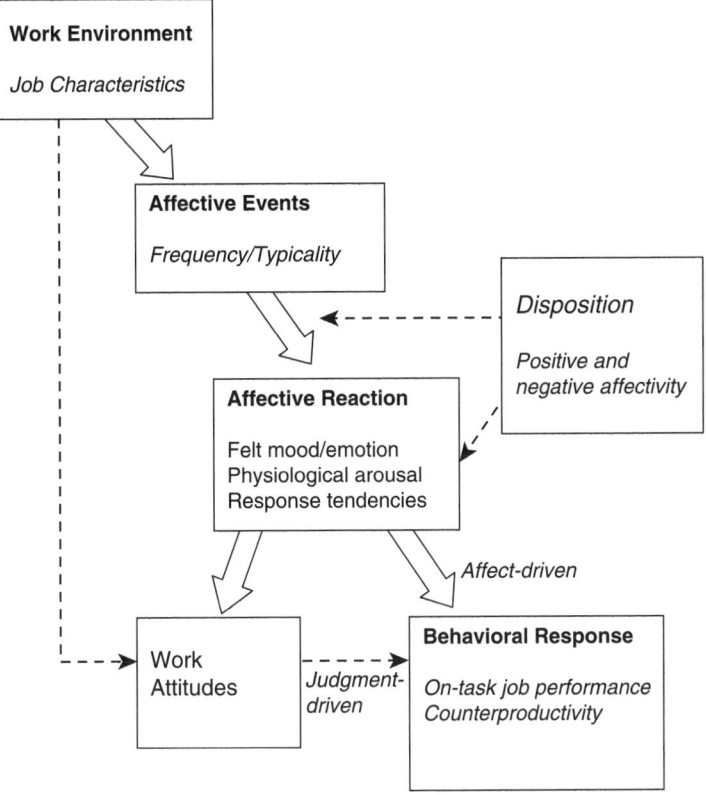

Figure 3   Conceptual model of affective events theory (adapted from Weiss and Cropanzano, 1996)

Note: The thick arrows represent the dynamic within-person associations that are unique to the AET, while the dashed arrows are the more stable aspects of the person and environment that might affect the dynamic relationships. Terms in the boxes are examples of the categories shown.

and reactions to goal progress/achievement (proximal motivation) (George and Brief, 1996; Kanfer, 1991; Seo et al., 2004).

Positive mood elevates beliefs about self-efficacy and the value of outcomes, increasing subsequent goal difficulty, goal quantity, and commitment. For example, feeling positive affect in response to feedback resulted in upward goal adjustment while negative affect led to adjusting goals downward (Ilies and Judge, 2005). This may depend on whether the negative affect is interpreted as motivational information: Negative emotions in response to feedback were less likely to result in goal reductions for employees with a strong orientation to improve skills than those with a weaker learning goal orientation (Cron et al., 2005). Specific negative emotions can increase goals too: Hong Kong bank tellers who experienced envy from observing a colleague receive a promotion increased their performance compared to those with a weaker envy response (Schaubroeck and Lam, 2004).

In turn, goal progress influences emotions. According to control theory and consistent with mood-as-input, positive discrepancies (i.e., making better than expected progress toward goals) lead to positive affect and a decrease in effort expended, whereas negative discrepancies (i.e., making worse progress than desired) result in negative affect and an increase in effort to diminish that discrepancy (Carver and Scheier, 1990). Discrete emotions may be predicted from the velocity of discrepancy reduction (i.e., the rate of progress) depending on the type of goal (Brockner et al., 2001). If moving toward an approach goal quickly, enthusiasm should occur; if too slowly, depression; anxiety is expected if moving toward an avoidance goal quickly, while goal contentment is the result if moving away from an avoidance goal (Carver et al., 2002). Empirical tests of this view are not altogether supportive but still emerging (Holman et al., 2005). These relationships may depend on the ability of the employee to respond effectively to these discrepancies: when hospital employees had a higher workload rather than a more manageable workload there was a stronger association between goal-disrupting events and negative emotion, while goal-enhancing events were more weakly related to positive emotions (Zohar et al., 2003). Such attention to the work context is an important direction for future research.

Goals may also be held for one's emotional displays (Diefendorff and Gosserand, 2003). When there is a discrepancy between organizationally-specified display rules and natural emotional expressions, emotion regulation is needed to re-align expressions with the display rules. Recent research has demonstrated that commitment to these goals about displays moderates the extent of self-regulation to meet the display goals (Gosserand and Diefendorff, 2005). Thus, goal theory seems directly applicable to emotional performance as well.

Emotions and job performance

The long-standing 'happy-productive' worker thesis suggests a link between emotions and performance, presumably because the happy worker will be more on-task and energized. Early longitudinal work by Hersey in the 1930s suggested that an unhappy railroad worker was less productive than one who felt more positively (see Weiss and Cropanzano, 1996) and more recent tests on within-person mood fluctuations show better prediction of ongoing performance than between-person differences in affect (Fisher, 2003; Fisher and Noble, 2004). However, it is difficult to tease apart the direction of causality – performing

better is also likely to make people feel better.

The influence of emotion regulation beyond the felt emotions is a current direction in this area. Building on the AET (Weiss et al., 1996) and ego depletion theories (Muraven et al., 2000), a recent model proposed that emotions and emotion regulation within a performance 'episode' impact ongoing on- and off-task performance due to resource allocation, depletion and recovery processes (Beal et al., 2005; Weiss et al., 2004). Recent experimental evidence showed that increasing the emotion regulation requirements decreased on-task performance in a call center simulation (Goldberg and Grandey, 2007), consistent with this new theoretical view.

The ambiguity and complexity of two specific types of job performance, creativity and decision-making, makes it likely that affect infuses their processes (Forgas, 1995). Positive mood increases flexible thinking (Isen et al., 1984; Isen et al., 1987) but negative mood increases effort expended in ambiguous tasks (Martin et al., 1993). So which leads to better creativity and decision making outcomes? George (2002) demonstrated that more creative manufacturing designs occurred with negative moods than positive moods, at least when employees had explicit rewards for creativity and were aware of their own feelings. Experiencing both strong positive and negative emotions (i.e., emotional ambivalence) may provide the best of both worlds (Fong, 2006). However, a comparison of these perspectives found that daily positive mood, and not negative or ambivalent moods, was positively related to other-rated daily creative thoughts and monthly creativity (Amabile et al., 2005), leading to a cyclical and integrative model of affect and creativity. Discrete emotions have not typically been part of creativity research, although case studies on depression and bipolar mood disorders suggest that strong emotions may aid the creative process.

With decision-making, managerial candidates who had moderate or high positive affectivity (a composite of self and other ratings) had more accurate decisions than those with low positive affectivity (Staw and Barsade, 1993). But positive mood does not always equal 'good' decision-making due to unrealistic optimism and an over-reliance on heuristics (Forgas, 1999). In fact, negative affect decreased the escalation of commitment to a poor decision when one was personally accountable (Wong et al., 2006). Discrete emotions research suggests some interesting directions. Emotions that imply certainty (e.g., anger, disgust or joy) result in more automatic processing, whereas feeling emotions that imply uncertainty (e.g., hope, fear or surprise) result in more systematic processing and less risky decisions (DeSteno et al., 2000; Lerner and Keltner, 2000; Lerner and Keltner, 2001; Tiedens and Linton, 2001). Thus moving beyond the two-dimensional approach to affect seems useful to understand effective decision-making in future research.

Emotion and voluntary work behaviors

Voluntary productive and counterproductive contextual behaviors may be more 'affect-driven behavior' (AET, see Figure 3) than in-role job behaviors (George and Brief, 1992; Spector and Fox, 2002).

Extra-role/helping behaviors

In social psychology research, both positive and negative moods have been associated with spontaneous helping behavior as a form of mood maintenance or repair (Carlson, 1988; Carlson and Miller, 1987; George and Brief, 1992). In field survey research, employees with higher positive moods at work are more likely to help supervisors, co-workers and customers, and the effect of mood is stronger than dispositional affectivity or fairness cognitions (George, 1991; see Lee and Allen, 2002 for an exception; Podsakoff et al., 2000).

The effect of positive mood on helping is short-lived (less than 20 minutes) (Isen et al., 1976), and thus survey measurement may not be the best approach. Experience sampling

methods (ESM) that capture momentary moods and behaviors have shown mixed results: positive mood predicted citizenship behavior (Ilies et al., 2006), negative mood predicted an increase in helping (Glomb et al., 2006), and in a third, there was no relationship (Miner et al., 2005). Employee disposition (i.e., agreeableness, Ilies et al., 2006) and motives (i.e., voluntary helping, Glomb et al., 2006) seem to help explain the mood-helping relationship. Discrete emotions may also be needed in this research rather than moods. Emotions that motivate affiliation tendencies (compassion or joy) may move people to engage in interpersonal helping, while emotions that are self-focused (pride) may not (Fredrickson, 1998).

Counterproductive behaviors

Consistent with the AET, negative mood has been shown to explain why certain events (e.g., conflicts, injustice and negative feedback) predict counterproductive work behaviors (CWB) (e.g., Fox et al., 2001). More specifically, anger has the action tendency of 'approach' and act compared with other negative emotions such as sadness (Harmon-Jones and Allen, 1998), and is often used to understand aggression within CWB research (Fitness, 2000; Glomb, 2002). In a daily diary and a survey study, felt hostility at work was associated with counterproductive behaviors, beyond work attitudes and negative dispositions (Judge et al., 2006; Lee et al., 2002).

However, the assumption that anger leads to counterproductive behavior needs to be examined more closely. In one study, only 24 per cent of employees who engaged in counterproductive behaviors felt angry, and anger emotions were related to interpersonal abuse and sabotage of equipment, but not theft or withdrawal (Spector et al., 2006; Tunstall et al., 2006). Anger can also lead to corrective actions. Anger in response to sex discrimination or layoffs was associated with action to rectify wrongs (Gill and Matheson, 2006; Goldman, 2003), and employees acknowledge that relationships were improved by the expression of anger

(Averill, 1983; Glomb, 2002). How and when this is the case is an interesting way of examining discrete emotions and the work context.

The hedonic contingency model and 'approach-avoid' associations with emotions suggest an association of affect with withdrawal. Limited research has examined the link between affect and actual absences or turnover (see Johns in this volume), and the existing research is contradictory. Though survey research typically finds that positive moods are negatively related to absences, they were positively related to withdrawing from job tasks in one ESM study (Miner et al., 2005) and there was no association in another (Glomb et al., 2006). Furthermore, negative moods sometimes have positive and sometimes negative associations with absences (George, 1989; George and Bettenhausen, 1990; Hardy et al., 2003; Iverson and Deery, 2001; Pelled and Xin, 1999; Spector and Jex, 1991). The link between felt moods and withdrawal seems to depend on general job attitudes; those who are dissatisfied with the job are more likely to let their moods drive their withdrawal decisions (Iverson and Deery, 2001; Pelled and Xin, 1999). The relationship may also depend on the specific negative emotion (e.g., hopelessness or anger), its target (e.g., tasks, supervisor and customers), and its typicality or duration. For example, being the target of aggression predicts fear at work (Barling et al., 2001); when managers used intimidation tactics (e.g., threats and yelling) or degradation (e.g., shaming publicly and gossip) over time such experiences resulted in pervasive fear and complete emotional breakdowns, and yet an irrational inability to leave the organization (Harlos and Pinder, 2000).

Emotions and organizational justice

Specific emotions have long been part of justice research. Early theories about fairness proposed that inequitable outcomes in the form of over-reward or under-reward created guilt and anger, respectively (Homans, 1961), and more recent experimental research

showed that procedural fairness (e.g., cheating by a team member) and outcome favorability (e.g., team winning) interacted to predict anger (favorable outcome–unfair procedure) and guilt (favorable outcome–unfair procedure) (Weiss et al., 1999a). In fact, the authors stated, 'the justice paradigm can be understood as a special instance of the more general appraisal models of emotion and ... the typical justice situation can be seen as an affective event' (Weiss et al., 1999a). Interestingly, fair procedures do not necessarily lead to positive emotions if unfavorable outcomes then must be attributed to oneself (Van den Bos et al., 1999). In a field study, unfairness perceptions of layoff decisions were likely to predict anger and retaliation, especially when there were unfair procedures, but fair procedures were likely to create self-conscious negative emotions (shame, guilt) due to self-blame (Barclay et al., 2005).

Finally, interpersonal injustice (e.g., violating norms of courtesy and respect for others) generally results in 'moral outrage' (Bies, 1987) and retaliation (Andersson and Pearson, 1999; Skarlicki and Folger, 2005), though overt retaliation is less likely toward those higher in power such as supervisors and customers (Grandey et al., 2002; Rafaeli et al., in press; Rupp and Spencer, 2006). Observing injustice toward others also evokes guilt and anger (Spencer and Rupp, under review), suggesting justice-emotion links are not only from self-interests. This may depend on the relationship with the unfairly treated other such that a stronger emotional response is likely when one is more similar or connected to the victim (De Cremer and van Hiel, 2006). At the same time, the deontic model of fairness suggests humans are driven by an underlying fairness motive, such that there is an emotional response to observed unfairness that goes beyond self interests (Cropanzano et al., 2003; Skarlicki and Folger, 2005).

Though most research in this area is on how (in)justice creates emotion, it should be recognized that emotions influence the formation of, and can be the target of, justice perceptions. Consistent with AIM (Forgas, 1995), manipulated moods influenced subsequent distributive justice perceptions of reward allocation when social comparison information was unknown, and did not influence the perceptions when the distribution was clearly inequitable or equitable (van den Bos, 2003). Furthermore, employees hold fairness perceptions about emotional displays as a job requirement (Grandey and Fisk, 2005), though more work is needed to see if this construct is useful to the fairness and emotions literature (see Rupp et al., in press).

EMOTIONS AS PART OF INTERPERSONAL OB EXPERIENCES

I now turn to research focusing on emotions as part of interactions between negotiators, leader-followers, and employee-customers.

Negotiator-opponent interactions

Positive mood has been argued to influence the entire negotiation process, from the decision to negotiate to the outcomes (Barry and Oliver, 1996; Pillutla and Murnighan, 1996). Positive mood decreases competitive or antagonistic bargaining strategies (Allred et al., 1997; Carnevale and Isen, 1986) and improves outcomes (Anderson and Thompson, 2004; Forgas, 1998a).

The strategic use of emotional expressions during negotiations suggests more complex associations. Positive expressions may improve negotiation outcomes compared to negative or neutral displays (Kopelman et al., 2006); however, negative expressions may also improve outcomes by communicating a toughness or inflexibility. In a computer-mediated negotiation, when a simulated partner communicated anger he received more concessions from the participant than when the opponent stated feeling happy or neutral (van Kleef et al., 2004a). Benefits of anger expressions are most likely when the opponent is motivated to process the information that anger communicates, such as due to a lack of negotiating options or high time pressure (Sinaceur and Tiedens, 2006; van Kleef et al., 2004a; Van Kleef et al.,

2004b). Expressing self-conscious emotions (e.g., guilt and shame), which communicate a desire to 'appease' the other, resulted in higher demands from the opponent, compared with expressing disappointment or worry (Van Kleef et al., 2006a).

Much of the existing research relies on laboratory experiments with manipulated written expressions of emotions from one opponent. Written emotions ('I feel angry') diminishes possible differences in the accuracy of emotion communication and perception, though such differences are a key aspect of negotiations (Elfenbein et al., in press; Morris and Keltner, 2000). Future research must attempt to understand the reciprocal (and probably cyclical) effects of emotions between negotiation dyads in real settings (see Butt et al., 2005), and compare facial and verbal communication of emotion.

Leader-follower interactions

Leaders create affective events (Brief and Weiss, 2002); for example, they can increase excitement and pride through recognizing employees (Basch and Fisher, 2000; Dasborough, 2006; Grandey et al., 2002), or strong negative emotions when mishandling employee discipline (Ball et al., 1992). Leader emotions are studied as a critical aspect of transformational leadership style, and as a contingency approach to effective leadership.

Positive emotions and transformational leadership

High-energy positive expressions are associated with charismatic and transformational leader ratings, which explained why such leaders were perceived as more effective (Bono and Ilies, 2006; Damen, van Knippenberg, and van Knippenberg, 2006). Contagion of these expressed emotions is thought to energize followers. The transfer of leader's emotions – positive and negative – to followers has been well-demonstrated (Bono and Ilies, 2006; Cherulnik et al., 2001; Lewis, 2000; Sy et al., 2005). For example, in an ESM study of health care workers, interacting with supervisors resulted in less positive moods than when interacting with peers (consistent with the power-emotion literature), but when those leaders were transformational this effect reversed (Bono et al., in press).

However, there is mixed evidence whether emotional contagion of leader expressions impacts follower performance. In one study, sales representatives with transformational leaders had higher sales, which were fully explained by the representatives' felt optimism and frustration (McColl-Kennedy and Anderson, 2002). In contrast, the link of leaders' emotion on performance was not explained by follower affect in laboratory and field studies using group, store, and individual level performance (Bono and Ilies, 2006; George, 1995; George and Bettenhausen, 1990; Sy et al., 2005). Instead, charismatic and transformational leaders may increase performance and moods through effective use of humor, though humor hurt performance for those with a contingent-reward style (Avolio et al., 1999).

Contingencies for effectiveness of leaders' negative emotions

In general, leaders' negative expressions decrease liking and evaluations compared to positive expressions (Gaddis et al., 2004; Glomb and Hulin, 1997; Lewis, 2000); however, the impact on follower motivation and performance depends on characteristics of both the leader and followers (see van Knippenberg et al., in press). Consistent with gender norms, expressed anger resulted in higher ratings for male than female CEOs, while expressed sadness resulted in higher ratings for women than men (Lewis, 2000). In contrast, angry feedback resulted in lower ratings of leader effectiveness than neutral expressions for both men and women (Glomb and Hulin, 1997). These were both experimental studies using video stimuli, while field research has shown little difference by gender (Damen et al., in press). Emotional ambivalence – strong positive and negative emotions – has been shown to be more likely with women in high than

low power roles (Fong and Tiedens, 2002); attention to mixed feelings may provide some insight into the role of gender and leader emotions.

Characteristics of the leader, followers, and tasks also moderate the impact of leader emotion. The emotional ability of leaders, such as empathy, emotional intelligence, and emotional recognition (Elfenbein and Ambady, 2002; Kellett et al., 2006; Rubin et al., 2005; Thomas et al., 2006), may impact how to effectively use negative emotions due to awareness of when and which emotions to show. Negative leader mood increased group effort and performance more than positive leader mood when the affect provides needed information about task progress (Sy et al., 2005), the group's motivational goals are to prevent problems (prevention-focused regulation) (Brockner and Higgins, 2001; Gaddis et al., 2004; Higgins et al., 1994), or the followers desire to fully understand and master the task (Van Kleef et al., 2006b). The congruence of leaders' expressions with their message and the followers' affect is also an important contingency; if they are incongruent the expressions may seem manipulative (Newcombe and Ashkanasy, 2002). Finally, the affective match of the leader's expressions and the followers' trait affectivity predicted performance and OCBs (Damen et al., in press).

Most of this research is short-term experimental designs, but examining the quality of the long-term relationship is likely to make a difference; for example, the stage of the leader-member exchange (LMX) relationship (Dasborough and Ashkanasy, 2002). Would expressed anger be more or less motivating for those in a high LMX relationship? A nonlinear relationship of expressed anger with follower motivation outcomes is also possible, as followers 'habituate' to the emotion and it no longer communicates useful information (Tiedens, 2001). Finally, initial research on specific emotions besides anger suggests interesting directions; when leaders expressed shame while giving negative feedback they received lower effectiveness ratings than when expressing disappointment to the group due to the impact on followers' self-esteem (van Knippenberg et al., 2005).

Employee–customer interactions

The importance of employees' emotions with customers, often studied as 'emotional labor' (Hochschild, 1983) has long been part of OB research. This research can be organized as focusing on emotion display rules, emotion regulation strategies, and observed expressions/performance (see Bono and Vey, 2005; Grandey, 2000; Zapf, 2002, for reviews).

Display rules

Display rules in customer service refer to emotional requirements communicated by the organization (Ashforth and Humphrey, 1993; Rafaeli and Sutton, 1987). 'Service with a smile' is perceived as an in-role job requirement for those with frequent interpersonal contact (Diefendorff et al., 2006), and is related to expressive performance with customers (Diefendorff and Richard, 2003). Though this may be an additional job demand creating strain (Goldberg and Grandey, 2007; Schaubroeck and Jones, 2000), studies also find that positive display rules are associated with job satisfaction and personal accomplishment (Brotheridge and Grandey, 2002; Brotheridge and Lee, 2002; Côté and Morgan, 2002; Diefendorff and Richard 2003). More attention is needed to explain when display rules are beneficial to the employee, such as high job experience (automaticity) or high task meaningfulness. Cultural differences surrounding the effect of shame expressions were found in sales interactions (Bagozzi et al., 2003), while display rules about suppressing anger with customers were consistent across cultures (Rafaeli et al., 2006). Research on the organizational policies (e.g,. monitoring and rewards) surrounding display rules, rather than relying on perceptions of display rules, is needed.

Emotion regulation

When employees tend to suppress negative emotions ('surface acting'), it may improve expressive performance with customers (Beal et al., 2006; Brown et al., 2005), though such regulation is also associated with poor service ratings and employee health in other studies (Brotheridge and Lee, 2002; Grandey, 2003; Totterdell and Holman, 2003). The detrimental effects of surface acting exists beyond negative affectivity, seems to be moderated by job autonomy, and is not found for other types of regulation such as 'deep acting' (Brotheridge and Grandey, 2002; Grandey et al., 2005b). New measures exist to assess how specific emotions are regulated in different ways (Glomb and Tews, 2004), and can guide future research. For example, regulating by amplifying/faking happiness is proposed to have beneficial results compared to suppressing negative emotions (Côté, 2005).

Observed expressions

Observed positive displays from employees (i.e., smiling or eye contact) result in better customer service ratings (Barger and Grandey, 2006; Pugh, 2001; Tsai, 2001; Tsai and Huang, 2002). Though emotional contagion effects explained the effect of employee displays on customer satisfaction for bank tellers and shoe salespersons (Pugh, 2001; Tsai, 2001), customer mood did not mediate this relationship for food service encounters or a video rental simulation (Barger and Grandey, 2006; Hennig-Thurau et al., 2006). Moderators of the effect of displays on customer reactions include the busyness of the store (Rafaeli and Sutton, 1990; Sutton and Rafaeli, 1988) and the authenticity of expressions (Grandey et al., 2005a; Hennig-Thurau et al., 2006). Less attention has been paid to negative displays to customers (see Mattila et al., 2003; Sutton, 1991, for exceptions), and still less to the specific emotion (e.g., irritation, sadness or boredom) which may be critical to customer attributions. Customers' affective tendencies can also influence employees' moods (Tan et al., 2004); might there be a spiral of incivility (Andersson and Pearson, 1999) that spreads from one customer, to employee, to the next customer, for example? How can employees resist contagion effects from hostile customers?

Group member interactions

Affects has been shown to develop and exist at the group level (Barsade, 2002; George, 1990). Below I describe the inputs, process, and outputs of group affect.

Group inputs

A work group may experience mood convergence due to common external factors and experiences such as leaders, resources, hassles and organizational procedures (Kelly and Barsade, 2001). Beyond these experiences, groups may share affect because of emotional contagion among members, as shown by the influence of three factors on group mood. First, frequent interactions increase the chance to observe and 'catch' emotions, it is not enough to simply work in the same environment (Totterdell, 2000; Totterdell et al., 1998; Totterdell et al., 2004). Moreover, mood of group members was more convergent the longer the group members worked together and had more interdependent tasks (Bartel and Saavedra, 2000).[4]

Second, individual and group characteristics of members impact the strength of convergence. Ethnic and cultural familiarity with group members (e.g., Elfenbein and Ambady, 2003) and higher group level susceptibility to contagion (Totterdell, 2000) increase convergence, though may be most likely when high arousal emotions are expressed (Bartel and Saavedra, 2000). Greater power/status of group members, such as the highly committed and older members (Totterdell, 2000; Totterdell et al., 1998), may set the affective tone for others' moods to converge toward (Anderson et al., 2003).

Finally, emotion norms regulate the extent that emotions are expressed and thus can be 'caught' (Ashforth and Humphrey, 1995). These group norms arise from socialization processes, or 'emotion managers' who enforce or model appropriate expressions (Pescosolido, 2002; Rafaeli and Sutton, 1987;

Wilk and Moynihan, 2005) and influence the extent that the group can share and benefit from conflict (Barsade et al., 2005; Yang and Mossholder, 2004).

Group process/outputs

Groups with higher mean levels of positive affect (PA) have more cooperation, less conflict, and better group performance in studies of front-line employees, upper-level managers, and sports teams (Barsade, 2002; Barsade et al., 2000; George, 1990; George and Bettenhausen, 1990; Totterdell, 2000). Moreover, this was most true when that affect was more 'shared'; more affective diversity in managerial teams (heterogeneity of trait PA of members) reduced the association of the group mean-level PA with cooperation and conflict, and meant lower team satisfaction and financial returns (Barsade et al., 2000). In contrast, diversity of affect may be valuable if it encourages more systematic processing than convergent PA. Affective diversity increased the thoroughness of information seeking and accuracy in experiments on decision-making, compared to groups with shared positive or negative mood (Tuncel and Doucet, 2006).

There is little work on strong emotions in groups (Kelly and Barsade, 2001), probably due to the combined practical difficulties of studying both groups and fleeting emotions. Higher mean levels of envy in student groups increased social loafing and reduced group performance (Duffy and Shaw, 2000); would strong levels of any emotion be effective or would they hijack task behaviors? The role of power and status and how that influences group emotional convergence still needs attention (Hsee et al., 1990). Identifying when and for what tasks it is best to have affective diversity versus convergence is an interesting direction with practical implications.

CHALLENGES FOR FUTURE OB EMOTION RESEARCHERS

Theoretical, empirical and practical challenges need to be overcome to advance the current state of knowledge on emotions in OB.

Theoretical challenges

Familiarity with extensive literature

Emotion has been studied since the beginning of psychology with William James' 1884 classic text. Moreover, emotion is a multi-disciplinary topic, including biology, genetics, personality, neuroscience, health, anthropology, sociology and psychology (Rosenberg and Fredrickson, 1998). To best approach a question of emotions in OB, one must be familiar with a wide literature. Several good chapters provide a review of the topics, questions and issues that are the focus of emotion researchers in the social sciences (see Ekman and Davidson, 1994; Gross, 1998; Scherer, 2000).

Considering the context

It is then up to the OB researcher to identify predictions that may be unique to the work context. Studies of relationships that could be predicted in any setting (e.g., injustice-anger) 'are not especially novel in the sense of failing to contradict what we think we already know...if the study of moods and emotions are to become woven into the fabric of organizational behavior it must be seen widely in the discipline as interesting' (Brief, 2001: 136). To uniquely study emotions in OB, we must consider the role of context more directly in our theory and research (see Johns, 2006; Waldron, 2000). Exacerbating or boundary conditions of emotion theory in OB include:

- formal power roles/hierarchical structure;
- multiple shareholders to please (e.g., self, supervisor, coworkers, subordinates, clients);
- balancing affiliation and achievement goals;
- interdependent work relationships and social networks;
- financial rewards and scarce desired resources;
- sense of choice or autonomy over behavior;
- variability in skill/ability at both emotion and work tasks.

Tomorrow's theories should not simply apply basic emotion theory to the workplace, but should argue why and how the workplace is a context that needs unique theoretical attention.

Methodological challenges

Until now, emotion researchers have focused more on *what* should be studied than *how* (Briner and Kiefer, 2005). Conceptual advances will be more likely if we follow psychologists' advice regarding methodology (Russell and Feldman Barrett, 1999).

Measuring multiple facets of emotion

Though the self-reported measure of emotion may be the best approach available in OB, it is not sufficient for several reasons. First, how one reports feeling may be different from what the body, brain, or expressions suggest due to ambivalence (i.e., mixed feelings), a lack of self-awareness, or display rules (i.e., social norms about emotional expressions) (Ekman and Friesen, 1971). Second, simply asking about emotional states may change their impact (Berkowitz et al., 2000; Schwarz and Clore, 1983). In fact, unconscious processing of emotions and how it impacts performance is beginning to be examined in OB (Moon and Lord, 2006). Third, using self-reports for emotion and other variables increases the likelihood that common method variance can explain found relationships. In short, triangulation across multiple approaches is necessary to interpret effects. If relationships are found for physiological measures but not self-reported, it suggests different conclusions.

Tools to measure emotions in OB include self-reported ratings of mood (e.g., Fisher, 2000; Van Katwyk et al., 2000), emotions (Wallbott and Scherer, 1989), and emotion regulation (Glomb and Tews, 2004; Grandey et al., 2004); coder ratings of emotions or expressions (see Bartel and Saavedra, 2000; Pugh, 2001); and physiological measures (e.g., cortisol levels, ambulatory physiological monitors) (Davidson et al., 2000; Harenstam et al., 2000). There are strengths and limitations of each approach, but combined they provide a more complete picture of emotion (see Larsen and Fredrickson, 1999).

Matching the time frame to the research question

Relatively few empirical studies on emotions in work settings measured emotions when they were 'experienced' (Briner and Kiefer, 2005); however, the longer the time lag between the event and the assessment of emotion, the more likely we are tapping beliefs about emotion or dispositional affectivity than emotional experience (Robinson and Clore, 2002). More critically, the effect of mood on behavior and cognitions is short-lived (Isen et al., 1976) and may even reverse itself over time (Forgas and Ciarrochi, 2001). The approach that seems most able to capture *in vivo* moods is experience sampling methodology (ESM), and involves the use of diaries or palm pilots to obtaining repeated momentary assessments (e.g., Beal and Weiss, 2003). This approach is not a panacea – it still relies on how well people understand and are willing to report their own feelings, may still change the nature of the experience by asking about those emotions, and is more likely to capture mood than emotion. Longitudinal survey or qualitative research during a change (e.g., layoffs) may help to capture the dynamic and short-term nature of emotion.

Obtaining real emotional episodes

Laboratory studies can capture emotional responses to manipulated events, though are less likely to reflect the strong prototypical emotional response than a real-life situation (Russell and Feldman Barrett, 1999). This is where OB researchers, with their connections to field settings, could make a contribution to the general emotion theory and research. We can identify situations where there are real relationships and emotional issues, resulting in higher likelihood of capturing prototypical emotional episodes. Naturalistic observational methods and surveys have been used to study emotions in organizational groups (Bartel and Saavedra, 2000), customer service (Pugh, 2001; Rafaeli and Sutton, 1990), and leadership (Staw and Barsade,

1993). Capturing emotional responses to real organizational events (e.g., Barclay et al., 2005) involves both fostering organizational connections and being in the right place at the right time.

Practical challenges and suggestions

Given relationships between emotions and work outcomes, is it then practically ethical to use this information in applications to the workplace? Or should our research be primarily 'basic' and descriptive in nature? It seems reasonable to suggest that management should enhance employees' positive affect, which has been shown to relate to some critical OB outcomes (Isen and Baron, 1991). At the same time, enhancing positive affect in the workplace is not always effective for businesses (Fineman, 2006), and negative emotions and expressions may also be effective for certain types of performance. The contingencies that would make certain feelings and expressions effective suggest a complexity that cannot easily be translated into a training and development tool. For other topics the practical applications to selection or training seem to outrun the scientific evidence, creating strong reactions in our field (e.g., Fineman, 2004; Locke, 2005). Perhaps the selling point of emotions research is its ability to help managers and employees better understand their day to day work situations. OB emotions research can do more to communicate this value to organizational audiences, thus increasing the likelihood of access to field data as well as helping the intra- and inter-personal functioning of organizations.

CONCLUSION

The workplace is an emotional place. This is commonsense to anyone who has ever dealt with annoying colleagues, a disrespectful boss, or frustrating tasks. It has even been argued that the workplace is a particularly emotional place, and 'arguably the best place to study feeling' (Lively and

Powell, 2006; Sandelands and Boudens, 2000: 47). The growth of research on emotions in organizational behavior since Pekrun and Frese's (1992) review has been truly impressive. In some ways, however, emotions will have truly arrived when future handbooks no longer have an emotions chapter but emotions are integrated into every chapter, just as they are interwoven into every aspect of organizational behavior.

ACKNOWLEDGEMENTS

I greatly appreciate suggestions on specific sections from Sigal Barsade, Jim Diefendorff, Theresa Glomb, Doug Pugh, and Deborah Rupp. Special thanks to Aiwa Shirako and Hillary Elfenbein for sharing their references, and to my research group – April Jones, Jennifer Diamond, Allison Gabriel, and Jane Shumski – for their assistance with the emerging literature.

NOTES

1 I have had to omit certain topics due to space; including emotional intelligence (Mayer et al., 2000) and the more specific abilities to perceive or recognize emotion (Elfenbein and Ambady, 2003); the reader interested in these topics is directed toward another review chapter (Elfenbein, in press). I also omitted stress research (Lazarus, 2000), job attitudes (Fisher, 2000; Weiss et al., 1999b), and macro topics such as diversity and culture, assuming they will get attention elsewhere in this book.

2 The higher differentiation of negative emotions is consistent with the positive-negative asymmetry effect and evolutionary view of emotion – we tend to be more attentive and reactive to negative stimuli than positive (Taylor, 1991; Willemsen and Keren, 2002).

3 The necessary role of brain centers or cognitive appraisals to emotion has been the subject of debate (Lazarus, 1982; Zajonc, 1980). There is now recognition that both direct automatic processing through physiological reactions and indirect processing through the cortex occur (Gross, 1998).

4 Some field research suggests that negative moods are more likely to be 'caught' (Bartel and Saavedra, 2000; Totterdell et al., 2004) while other work suggests positive moods are (Totterdell, 2000).

REFERENCES

Allred, K.G., Mallozzi, J.S., Matsui, F. and Raia, C.P. (1997) 'The influence of anger and compassion on negotiation performance', *Organizational Behavior and Human Decision Processes*, 70 (3): 175–187.

Amabile, T.M., Barsade, S.G., Mueller, J.S. and Staw, B.M. (2005) 'Affect and creativity at work', *Administrative Science Quarterly*, 50 (3): 367–403.

Anderson, C., Keltner, D. and John, O. (2003) 'Emotional convergence between people over time', *Journal of Personality and Social Psychology*, 85 (5): 1054–1068.

Anderson, C. and Thompson, L. (2004) 'Affect from the top down: How powerful individuals' positive affect shapes negotiations', *Organizational Behavior and Human Decision Processes*, 95 (2): 125–139.

Andersson, L.M. and Pearson, C.M. (1999) 'Tit for tat? The spiraling effect of incivility in the workplace', *Academy of Management Review*, 24: 452–471.

Ashforth, B. and Humphrey, R.H. (1995) 'Emotion in the workplace – A reappraisal', *Human Relations*, 48 (2): 97–125.

Ashforth, B.E. and Humphrey, R.H. (1993) 'Emotional labor in service roles – The influence of identity', *Academy of Management Review*, 18 (1): 88–115.

Averill, J.R. (1983) 'Studies on anger and aggression: Implications for a theory of emotion', *American Psychologist*, 38: 1145–1160.

Avolio, B.J., Howell, J.M. and Sosik, J.J. (1999) 'A funny thing happened on the way to the bottom line: Humor as a moderator of leadership style effects', *Academy of Management Journal*, 42 (2): 219–227.

Bagozzi, R., Verbeke, W. and Gavino, J. (2003) 'Culture moderates the self-regulation of shame and its effects on performance: The case of salespersons in the Netherlands and the Philippines', *Journal of Applied Psychology*, 88 (2): 219–233.

Ball, G.A., Trevino, L.K. and Sims, H.P., Jr. (1992) 'Understanding subordinate reactions to punishment incidents: Perspectives from justice and social affect', *Leadership Quarterly*, 3 (4): 307–333.

Barclay, L.J., Skarlicki, D.P. and Pugh, S.D. (2005) 'Exploring the role of emotions in injustice perceptions and retaliation', *Journal of Applied Psychology*, 90 (4): 629–643.

Barger, P. and Grandey, A. (2006) ' "Service with a smile" and encounter satisfaction: Emotional contagion and appraisal mechanisms', *Academy of Management Journal*, 49 (6): 1229–1238.

Barling, J., Rogers, A.G. and Kelloway, E.K. (2001) 'Behind closed doors: In-home workers' experience of sexual harassment and workplace violence',

Journal of Occupational Health Psychology, 6 (3): 255–269.

Barry, B. and Oliver, R. (1996) 'Affect in dyadic negotiation: A model and propositions', *Organizational Behavior and Human Decision Processes*, 67 (2): 127–143.

Barsade, S. (2002) 'The ripple effect: Emotional contagion and its influence on group behavior', *Administrative Science Quarterly*, 47 (4): 644–675.

Barsade, S.G., Brief, A.P. and Spataro, S.E. (2003) 'The affective revolution in organizational behavior: The emergence of a paradigm', in J. Greenberg (ed.), *Organizational Behavior: The State of the Science*, 2nd edn. Mahwah, NJ: Lawrence Erlbaum Associates, pp. 3–52.

Barsade, S.G., Gibson, D.E. and Putzel, R. (2005) *Expressing Anger in Groups: Catharsis or Catastrophe?* Paper presented at the The Role of Emotions in Organizational Life: An Interdisciplinary Approach, Toronto, Ontario.

Barsade, S., Ward, A., Turner, J. and Sonnenfeld, J. (2000) 'To your heart's content: A model of affective diversity in top management teams', *Administrative Science Quarterly*, 45 (4): 802–836.

Bartel, C. and Saavedra, R. (2000) 'The collective construction of work group moods', *Administrative Science Quarterly*, 45 (2): 197–231.

Basch, J. and Fisher, C.D. (2000) 'Affective events-emotions matrix: A classification of work events and associated emotions', in N. Ashkanasy, C. Hartel and W. Zerbe (eds), *Emotions in the Workplace: Research, Theory, and Practice*. Westport, CT: Quorum, pp. 36–48.

Baumeister, R., Bratslavsky, E., Muraven, M. and Tice, D. (1998) 'Ego depletion: Is the active self a limited resource?', *Journal of Personality and Social Psychology*, 74 (5): 1252–1265.

Beal, D., Trougakos, J., Weiss, H. and Green, S. (2006) 'Episodic processes in emotional labor: Perceptions of affective delivery and regulation strategies', *Journal of Applied Psychology*, 91 (5): 1053–1065.

Beal, D.J. and Weiss, H. (2003) 'Methods of ecological momentary assessment in organizational research', *Organizational Research Methods*, 6: 440–464.

Beal, D.J., Weiss, H.M., Barros, E. and MacDermid, S.M. (2005) 'An episodic process model of affective influences on performance', *Journal of Applied Psychology*, 90 (6): 1054–1068.

Berkowitz, L., Jaffee, S., Jo, F. and Troccoli, B.T. (2000) 'On the correction of feeling-induced judgmental biases', in J.P. Forgas (ed.), *Feeling and Thinking: The Role of Affect in Social Cognition*. New York: Cambridge University Press, pp. 131–152.

Bies, R.J. (1987) 'The predicament of injustice: The management of moral outrage', *Research in Organizational Behavior*, Vol. 9: 289–319. JAI Press.

Bono, J. and Ilies, R. (2006) 'Charisma, positive emotions, and mood contagion', *Leadership Quarterly*, 17 (4): 317–334.

Bono, J., Foldes, H.J., Vinson, G. and Muros, J.P. (in press) 'Workplace emotions: The role of supervision and leadership', *Journal of Applied Psychology*.

Bono, J. and Vey, M. (2005) 'Toward understanding emotional management at work: A quantitative review of emotional labor research', in C.E. Härtel and W.J. Zerbe (eds), *Emotions in Organizational Behavior*. Mahwah, NJ: Lawrence Erlbaum Associates, pp. 213–233.

Brief, A. (2001) 'Organizational behavior and the study of affect: Keep your eyes on the organization', *Organizational Behavior and Human Decision Processes*, 86 (1): 131–139.

Brief, A. and Weiss, H. (2002) 'Organizational behavior: Affect in the workplace', *Annual Review of Psychology*, 53: 279–307.

Briner, R.B. and Kiefer, T. (2005) 'Psychological research into the experience of emotion at work: Definitely older, but are we any wiser?', in N.M. Ashkanasy, W.J. Zerbe and C.E.J. Hartel (eds), *The Effect of Affect in Organizational Settings*. Boston: Elsevier. Vol. 1: 281–307.

Brockner, J. and Higgins, E.T. (2001) 'Regulatory focus theory: Implications for the study of emotions at work', *Organizational Behavior and Human Decision Processes*, 86 (1): 35–66.

Brotheridge, C. and Grandey, A. (2002) 'Emotional labor and burnout: Comparing two perspectives of "people work"', *Journal of Vocational Behavior*, 60: 17–39.

Brotheridge, C. and Lee, R.T. (2002) 'Testing a conservation of resources model of the dynamics of emotional labor', *Journal of Occupational Health Psychology*, 7 (1): 57–67.

Brown, S.P., Westbrook, R.A. and Challagalla, G. (2005) 'Good cope, bad cope: Adaptive and maladaptive coping strategies following a critical negative work event', *Journal of Applied Psychology*, 90 (4): 792–798.

Butt, A.N., Choi, J.N. and Jaeger, A.M. (2005) 'The effects of self-emotion, counterpart emotion, and counterpart behavior on negotiator behavior: a comparison of individual-level and dyad-level dynamics', *Journal of Organizational Behavior*, 26 (6): 681–704.

Carlson, M. (1988) 'Positive mood and helping behavior: A test of six hypotheses', *Journal of personality and social psychology*, 55 (2): 211–229.

Carlson, M. and Miller, N. (1987) 'Explanation of the relation between negative mood and helping', *Psychological Bulletin*, 102 (1): 91–108.

Carnevale, P.J.D. and Isen, A.M. (1986) 'The influence of positive affect and visual access on the discovery of integrative solutions in bilateral negotiation', *Organizational Behavior and Human Decision Processes*, 37 (1): 1–13.

Carver, C.S., Lawrence, J.W. and Scheier, M.F. (2002) 'Self-discrepancies and affect: Incorporating the role of feared selves', *Journal of Personality and Social Psychology*, 25: 783–792.

Carver, C.S. and Scheier, M.F. (1990) 'Origins and functions of positive and negative affect: A control-process view', *Psychological Review*, 97 (1): 19–35.

Cherulnik, P.D., Donley, K.A., Wiewel, T.S.R. and Miller, S.R. (2001) 'Charisma is contagious: The effect of leaders' charisma on observers' affect', *Journal of Applied Social Psychology*, 31: 2149–2159.

Côté, S. (2005) 'A social interaction model of the effects of emotion regulation on work strain', *Academy of Management Review*, 30 (3): 509–530.

Côté, S. and Morgan, L. (2002) 'A longitudinal analysis of the association between emotion regulation, job satisfaction, and intentions to quit', *Journal of Organizational Behavior*, 23 (8): 947–962.

Cron, W.L., Slocum, J.W., Vandewalle, D. and Fu, Q. (2005) 'The role of goal orientation on negative emotions and goal setting when initial performance falls short of one's performance goal', *Human Performance*, 18 (1): 55–80.

Cropanzano, R., Goldman, B. and Folger, R. (2003) 'Deontic justice: The role of moral principles in workplace fairness', *Journal of Organizational Behavior*, 24: 1019–1024.

Damen, F., van Knippenberg, B. and van Knippenberg, D. (2006) 'The role of follower arousal in determining the effectiveness of leader emotional displays', *Annual Meeting of the Academy of Management*. Atlanta, GA.

Damen, F., van Knippenberg, B. and van Knippenberg, D. (in press) 'Affective match: Leader emotional displays, follower positive affect, and follower performance', *Journal of Applied Social Psychology*.

Dasborough, M.T. (2006) 'Cognitive asymmetry in employee emotional reactions to leadership behaviors', *Leadership Quarterly*, 17 (2): 163–178.

Dasborough, M.T. and Ashkanasy, N.M. (2002) 'Emotion and attribution of intentionality in leader-member relationships', *Leadership Quarterly*, 13 (5): 615–634.

Davidson, R.J., Jackson, D.C. and Kalin, N.H. (2000) 'Emotion, plasticity, context, and regulation: Perspectives from affective neuroscience', *Psychological Bulletin*, 126 (6): 890–909.

De Cremer, D. and van Hiel, A. (2006) 'Effects of another person's fair treatment on one's own emotions and behaviors: The moderating role of how much the other cares for you', *Organizational Behavior and Human Decision Processes*, 100 (2): 231–249.

DeSteno, D., Petty, R., Wegener, D.T. and Rucker, D.D. (2000) 'Beyond valence in the perception of likelihood: The role of emotion specificity', *Journal of Personality and Social Psychology*, 78: 397–416.

Diefendorff, J.M. and Gosserand, R.H. (2003) 'Understanding the emotional labor process: A control theory perspective', *Journal of Organizational Behavior*, 24 (8): 945–959.

Diefendorff, J.M. and Richard, E. (2003) 'Antecedents and consequences of emotional display rule perceptions', *Journal of Applied Psychology*, 88 (2): 284–294.

Diefendorff, J.M., Richard, E.M. and Croyle, M.H. (2006) 'Are emotional display rules formal job requirements? Examination of employee and supervisor perceptions', *Journal of Occupational and Organizational Psychology*, 79 (2): 273–298.

Duffy, M.K. and Shaw, J.D. (2000) 'The Salieri Syndrome: Consequences of envy in groups', *Small Group Research*, 31: 3–23.

Ekman, P. and Davidson, R.J. (1994) *The Nature of Emotion: Fundamental Questions*. New York: Oxford University Press.

Ekman, P. and Friesen, W. (1971) 'Constants across cultures in face and emotion', *Journal of Personality and Social Psychology*, 17 (2): 124–129.

Elfenbein, H.A. (in press) 'Emotion in organizations: A review in stages', in A. Brief and J. Walsh (eds), *Academy of Management Annals* (Vol. 1.) Amsterdam: Elsevier.

Elfenbein, H.A. and Ambady, N. (2002) 'Predicting workplace outcomes from the ability to eavesdrop on feelings', *Journal of Applied Psychology*, 87 (5): 963–971.

Elfenbein, H.A. and Ambady, N. (2003) 'When familiarity breeds accuracy: Cultural exposure and facial emotion recognition', *Journal of Personality and Social Psychology*, 85 (2): 276–290.

Elfenbein, H.A., Foo, M.D., White, J., Tan, H.H. and Aik, V.C. (in press) 'Reading your counterpart: The benefit of emotion recognition accuracy for effectiveness in negotiation', *Journal of Nonverbal Behavior*.

Fineman, S. (2004) 'Getting the measure of emotion – and the cautionary tale of emotional intelligence', *Human Relations*, 57 (6): 719–740.

Fineman, S. (2006) 'On being positive: Concerns and counterpoints', *Academy of Management Review*, 31 (2): 270–291.

Fisher, C.D. (2000) 'Mood and emotions while working: Missing pieces of job satisfaction?', *Journal of Organizational Behavior*, 21: 185–202.

Fisher, C.D. (2003) 'Why do lay people believe that satisfaction and performance are correlated? Possible sources of a commonsense theory', *Journal of Organizational Behavior*, 24: 753–777.

Fisher, C.D. and Noble, C.S. (2004) 'A within-person examination of correlates of performance and emotions while working', *Human Performance*, 17 (2): 145–168.

Fitness, J. (2000) 'Anger in the workplace: An emotion script approach to anger episodes between workers and their superiors, co-workers and subordinates', *Journal of Organizational Behavior*, 21: 147–162.

Fong, C.T. (2006) 'The effects of emotional ambivalence on creativity', *Academy of Management Journal*, 49 (5): 1016–1030.

Fong, C. and Tiedens, L. (2002) 'Dueling experiences and dual ambivalences: Emotional and motivational ambivalence of women in high status positions', *Motivation and Emotion*, 26 (1): 105–121.

Forgas, J. (1995) 'Mood and judgment – The affect infusion model (AIM)', *Psychological Bulletin*, 117 (1): 39–66.

Forgas, J. (1998a) 'On feeling good and getting your way: Mood effects on negotiator cognition and bargaining strategies', *Journal of Personality and Social Psychology*, 74 (3): 565–577.

Forgas, J. (1998b) 'On being happy and mistaken: Mood effects on the fundamental attribution error', *Journal of Personality and Social Psychology*, 75 (2): 318–331.

Forgas, J.P. (1999) 'On feeling good and being rude: Affective influences on language use and request formulations', *Journal of Personality and Social Psychology*, 76: 928–939.

Forgas, J.P. and Ciarrochi, J. (2001) 'On being happy and possessive: The role of mood and personality on the evaluation of personal possessions', *Psychology and Marketing*, 18: 239–260.

Fox, S., Spector, P.E. and Miles, D. (2001) 'Counter-productive Work Behavior (CWB) in response to job stressors and organizational justice: Some mediator and moderator tests for autonomy and emotions', *Journal of Vocational Behavior*, 59: 291–309.

Fredrickson, B.L. (1998) 'What good are positive emotions?' *Review of General Psychology*, 2: 300–319.

Frijda, N.H. (1993) 'Moods, emotion episodes, and emotions', in M. Lewis and J.M. Haviland (eds), *Handbook of Emotions*. New York: Guilford, pp. 381–403.

Frijda, N.H., Kuipers, P. and Terschure, E. (1989) 'Relations among emotion, appraisal, and emotional action readiness', *Journal of Personality and Social Psychology*, 57 (2): 212–228.

Gaddis, B., Connelly, S. and Mumford, M.D. (2004) 'Failure feedback as an affective event: Influences of leader affect on subordinate attitudes and performance', *Leadership Quarterly*, 15 (5): 663–686.

George, J.M. (1989) 'Mood and absence', *Journal of Applied Psychology*, 74 (2): 317–324.

George, J.M. (1990) 'Personality, affect, and behavior in groups', *Journal of Applied Psychology*, 75 (2): 107–116.

George, J.M. (1991) 'State or trait – Effects of positive mood on prosocial behaviors at work', *Journal of Applied Psychology*, 76 (2): 299–307.

George, J.M. (1995) 'Leader positive mood and group performance: The case of customer service', *Journal of Applied Social Psychology*, 25: 778–794.

George, J.M. and Bettenhausen, K. (1990) 'Understanding prosocial behavior, sales performance, and turnover – a group-level analysis in a service context', *Journal of Applied Psychology*, 75 (6): 698–709.

George, J.M. and Brief, A.P. (1992) 'Feeling good doing good – a conceptual analysis of the mood at work organizational spontaneity relationship', *Psychological Bulletin*, 112 (2): 310–329.

George, J.M. and Brief, A.P. (1996) 'Motivational agendas in the workplace: The effects of feelings on focus of attention and work motivation', in B.M. Staw and L.L. Cummings (eds), *Research in Organizational Behavior: An Annual Series of Analytical Essays and Critical Reviews*. Greenwich, CT: Elsevier Science/JAI Press. Vol. 18: 75–109.

Gibson, D.E. and Schroeder, S.J. (2002) 'Grinning, frowning, and emotionless: Agent perceptions of power and their effect on felt and displayed emotions in influence attempts', in N.M. Ashkanasy, W.J. Zerbe and C.E.J. Hartel (eds), *Managing Emotions in the Workplace*. Armonk, NY: M.E. Sharpe, pp. 184–211.

Gill, R. and Matheson, K. (2006) 'Responses to discrimination: The role of emotion and expectations for emotional regulation', *Personality and Social Psychology Bulletin*, 32 (2): 149–161.

Glomb, T.M. (2002) 'Workplace anger and aggression: Informing conceptual models with data from specific encounters', *Journal of Occupational Health Psychology*, 7 (1): 20–36.

Glomb, T.M., Bhave, D., Miner, A.G. and Wall, M. (2006) In Search of the Pause that Refreshes?: Examining the Role of Work Withdrawal and Organizational Citizenship Behavior in Changing Mood. Paper presented at the meeting of the Academy of Management. Atlanta, GA.

Glomb, T. and Hulin, C. (1997) 'Anger and gender effects in observed supervisor-subordinate dyadic interactions', *Organizational Behavior and Human Decision Processes*, 72 (3): 281–307.

Glomb, T.M. and Tews, M.J. (2004) 'Emotional labor: A conceptualization and scale development', *Journal of Vocational Behavior*, 64 (1): 1–23.

Goldberg, L. and Grandey, A. (2007) 'Display rules versus display autonomy: Emotion regulation, emotional exhaustion, and task performance in a call center simulation', *Journal of Occupational Health Psychology*, 12 (1): 63–79.

Goldman, B. (2003) 'The application of referent cognitions theory to legal-claiming by terminated workers: The role of organizational justice and anger', *Journal of Management*, 29: 705–728.

Gosserand, R.H. and Diefendorff, J.M. (2005) 'Emotional display rules and emotional labor: The moderating role of commitment', *Journal of Applied Psychology*, 90 (6): 1256–1264.

Grandey, A. (2000) 'Emotion regulation in the workplace: A new way to conceptualize emotional labor', *Journal of Occupational Health Psychology*, 5 (1): 95–110.

Grandey, A. (2003) 'When "the show must go on": Surface and deep acting as predictors of emotional exhaustion and service delivery', *Academy of Management Journal*, 46 (1): 86–96.

Grandey, A., Dickter, D. and Sin, H. (2004) 'The customer is not always right: customer aggression and emotion regulation of service employees', *Journal of Organizational Behavior*, 25 (3): 397–418.

Grandey, A. and Fisk, G. (2005) 'Display rules in service jobs: What's fairness got to do with it?', in P. Perrewe and D. Ganster (eds), *Research in Occupational Stress and Well Being*. San Diego, CA: Elsevier Ltd. Vol. 4: 269–297.

Grandey, A., Fisk, G., Mattila, A., Jansen, K.J. and Sideman, L. (2005a) 'Is service with a smile enough? Authenticity of positive displays during service encounters', *Organizational Behavior and Human Decision Processes*, 96 (1): 38–55.

Grandey, A., Fisk, G.M. and Steiner, D.D. (2005b) 'Must "service with a smile" be stressful? The moderating role of personal control for American and French employees', *Journal of Applied Psychology*, 90 (5): 893–904.

Grandey, A., Tam, A. and Brauburger, A. (2002) 'Affective states and traits in the workplace: Diary and survey data from young workers', *Motivation and Emotion*, 26 (1): 31–55.

Gray, J. (1971) 'The psychophysiological basis of introversion/extraversion', *Behavior research and therapy*, 8: 249–266.

Gross, J. (1998) 'The emerging field of emotion regulation: An integrative review', *Review of General Psychology*, 2 (3): 271–299.

Gross, J. and Levenson, R. (1993) 'Emotional suppression: Physiology, self-report, and expressive behavior', *Journal of Personality and Social Psychology*, 64: 970–986.

Hackman, J.R. and Oldham, G.R. (1976) 'Motivation through the design of work: Test of a theory', *Organizational Behavior and Human Performance*, 16: 250–279.

Hardy, G.E., Woods, D. and Wall, T.D. (2003) 'The impact of psychological distress on absence from work', *Journal of Applied Psychology*, 88: 306–314.

Harenstam, A., Theorell, T. and Lennart, K. (2000) 'Coping with anger-provoking situations, psychosocial working conditions, and ECG-detected signs of coronary heart disease', *Journal of Occupational Health Psychology*, 5: 191–203.

Harlos, K.P. and Pinder, C.C. (2000) 'Emotion and injustice in the workplace', in S. Fineman (ed.), *Emotion in Organizations*, 2nd edn. Thousand Oaks, CA: Sage, pp. 255–279.

Harmon-Jones, E. and Allen, J.J.B. (1998) 'Anger and frontal brain activity: EEG asymmetry consistent with approach motivation despite negative affective valence', *Journal of Personality and Social Psychology*, 74: 1310–1316.

Hatfield, E., Cacioppo, J. and Rapson, R.L. (1994) *Emotional Contagion*. New York: Cambridge University Press.

Hecht, M.A. and LaFrance, M. (1998) 'License or obligation to smile: The effects of power and gender on amount and type of smiling', *Personality and Social Psychology Bulletin*, 24: 1332–1342.

Hennig-Thurau, T., Groth, M., Paul, M. and Gremler, D.D. (2006) 'Are all smiles created equal? How emotional contagion and emotional labor affect service relationships', *The Journal of Marketing*, 70 (3): 58.

Higgins, E.T. (1987) 'Self-discrepancy: A theory relating self and affect', *Psychological Review*, 94 (3): 319–340.

Higgins, E.T., Roney, C.J.R., Crowe, E. and Hymes, C. (1994) 'Ideal versus ought predilections for approach and avoidance distinct self-regulatory systems', *Journal of Personality and Social Psychology*, 66 (2): 276–286.

Hochschild, A.R. (1983) *The Managed Heart: Commercialization of Human Feeling*. Berkeley, CA: University of California Press.

Holman, D.J., Totterdell, P. and Rogelberg, S.G. (2005) 'A daily diary study of goal striving: The relationship between goal distance, goal velocity, affect, expectancies and effort', in N.M. Ashkanasy, W.J. Zerbe and C.E.J. Hartel (eds), *The Effect of Affect in Organizational Settings*. San Diego, CA: Elsevier. Vol. 1: 95–121.

Homans, G.C. (1961) *Social Behavior: Its Elementary Forms*. London: Routledge & Kegan Paul.

Hsee, C.K., Hatfield, E., Carlson, J.G. and Chemtob, C. (1990) 'The effect of power on susceptibility to emotional contagion', *Cognition and Emotion*, 4 (4): 327–340.

Humphrey, R.H. (1985) 'How work roles influence perception: Structural-cognitive processes and organizational behavior', *American Sociological Review*, 50: 242–252.

Ilies, R. and Judge, T.A. (2005) 'Goal regulation across time: The effects of feedback and affect', *Journal of Applied Psychology*, 90 (3): 453–467.

Ilies, R., Scott, B. and Judge, T.A. (2006) 'The interactive effects of personal traits and experienced states on intraindividual patterns of citizenship behavior', *Academy of Management Journal*, 49 (3): 561–575.

Isen, A. (2001) 'An influence of positive affect on decision making in complex situations: Theoretical issues with practical implications', *Journal of Consumer Psychology*, 11 (2): 75–85.

Isen, A.M., Clark, M. and Schwartz, M.F. (1976) 'Duration of the effects of good mood on helping: "Footprints on the sands of time"', *Journal of Personality and Social Psychology*, 34: 385–393.

Isen, A.M. and Daubman, K.A. (1984) 'The influence of affect on categorization', *Journal of Personality and Social Psychology*, 47: 1206–1217.

Isen, A.M., Daubman, K.A. and Nowicki, G.P. (1987) 'Positive affect facilitates creative problem solving', *Journal of Personality and Social Psychology*, 47: 1122–1131.

Isen, A.M. and Baron, R.A. (1991) 'Positive Affect as a Factor in Organizational Behavior', in L. Cummings and B. Staw (eds), *Research in Organizational Behavior*. Greenwich, CT: JAI. Vol. 13: 1–52.

Iverson, R.D. and Deery, S.J. (2001) 'Understanding the "personological" basis of employee withdrawal: the influence of affective disposition on employee tardiness, early departure, and absenteeism', *Journal of Applied Psychology*, 86: 856–866.

Izard, C.E. (1977) *Human Emotion*. New York: Plenum Press.

Izard, C.E. (1991) *The Psychology of Emotion*. New York: Plenum Press.

James, W. (1884) 'What is an emotion?', *Mind*, 9: 188–205.

Johns, G.G. (2006) 'The essential impact of context on organizational behavior', *The Academy of Management review*, 31 (2): 386–408.

Judge, T.A., Scott, B.A. and Ilies, R. (2006) 'Hostility, job attitudes, and workplace deviance: Test of a multilevel model', *Journal of Applied Psychology*, 91 (1): 126–138.

Kanfer, R. (1991) 'Motivation theory and industrial and organizational psychology', in M.D. Dunnette and L.M. Hough (eds), *Handbook of Industrial and Organizational Psychology*. Palo Alto, CA: Consulting Psychologists Press. Vol. 1: 76–170

Kellett, J.B., Humphrey, R.H. and Sleeth, R.G. (2006) 'Empathy and the emergence of task and relations leaders', *Leadership Quarterly*, 17 (2): 146–162.

Kelly, J.R. and Barsade, S.G. (2001) 'Mood and Emotions in Small Groups and Work Teams', *Organizational Behavior and Human Decision Processes*, 86 (1): 99–130.

Keltner, D., Gruenfeld, D.H. and Anderson, C. (2003) 'Power, approach, and inhibition', *Psychological Review*, 110 (2): 265–284.

Kemper, T.D. (1978) *A Social Interactional Theory of Emotions*. New York: Wiley and Sons.

Kopelman, S., Rosette, A.S. and Thompson, L. (2006) 'The three faces of Eve: Strategic displays of positive, negative, and neutral emotions in negotiations', *Organizational Behavior and Human Decision Processes*, 99 (1): 81–101.

Larsen, R.J., Diener, E. and Lucas, R.E. (2002) 'Emotion: Models, measures, and individual differences', in R. Lord, R. Klimoski and R. Kanfer (eds), *Emotions in the Workplace: Understanding the Structure and Role of Emotions in Organizational Behavior*. San Francisco, CA: Jossey-Bass, pp. 64–106.

Larsen, R. and Fredrickson, B.L. (1999) 'Measurement issues in emotion research', in E. Diener and D. Kahneman (eds), *Well-being: The Foundations of Hedonic Psychology*. New York: Russell Sage Foundation, pp. 40–60.

Lazarus, R.S. (1982) 'Thoughts on the relations between emotion and cognition', *American Psychologist*, 37 (9): 1019–1024.

Lazarus, R.S. (1991) 'Progress on a cognitive-motivational-relational theory of emotion', *American Psychologist*, 46: 819–834.

Lazarus, R.S. (2000) *Stress and Emotion*. New York, NY: Springer.

Lazarus, R.S. and Cohen-Charash, Y. (2001) 'Discrete emotions in organizational life', in R.L. Payne and C.L. Cooper (eds), *Emotions at Work*. New York, NY: John Wiley and Sons, pp. 45–84

Leary, M.R. (2000) 'Affect, cognition, and the social emotions', in J.P. Forgas (ed.), *Feeling and Thinking: The Role of Affect in Social Cognition*. New York: Cambridge University Press, pp. 351–356.

Lee, K. and Allen, N.J. (2002) 'Organizational citizenship behavior and workplace deviance: The role of affect and cognitions', *Journal of Applied Psychology*, 87 (1): 131–142.

Lerner, J. and Keltner, D. (2000) 'Beyond valence: Toward a model of emotion-specific influences on judgement and choice', *Cognition and Emotion*, 14 (4): 473–493.

Lerner, J. and Keltner, D. (2001) 'Fear, anger, and risk', *Journal of Personality and Social Psychology*, 81 (1): 146–159.

Levine, S.P. and Feldman, R.S. (1997) 'Self-presentational goals, self-monitoring, and nonverbal behavior', *Basic and Applied Social Psychology*, 19 (4): 505–518.

Lewis, K.M. (2000) 'When leaders display emotion: How followers respond to negative emotional expression of male and female leaders', *Journal of Organizational Behavior*, 21: 221–234.

Lewis, M. (1993) 'Self-conscious emotions: Embarrassment, pride, shame, and guilt', in M. Lewis and J.M. Haviland (eds), *Handbook of Emotions*. New York, NY: Guilford Press, pp. 563–573.

Lively, K.J. and Powell, B. (2006) 'Emotional expression at work and at home: Domain, status or individual characteristics?' *Social Psychology Quarterly*, 69 (1): 17–38.

Locke, E.A. (2005) 'Why emotional intelligence is an invalid concept', *Journal of Organizational Behavior*, 26 (4): 425–431.

Martin, L.L., Ward, D.W., Achee, J.W. and Wyer, R.S., Jr. (1993) 'Mood as input: People have to interpret the motivational implications of their moods', *Journal of Personality and Social Psychology*, 64: 317–326.

Mattila, A., Grandey, A. and Fisk, G. (2003) 'The interplay of gender and affective tone in service encounter satisfaction', *Journal of Service Research*, 6 (2): 136–143.

Mayer, J.D., Caruso, D. and Salovey, P. (2000) 'Emotional intelligence meets traditional standards for an intelligence', *Intelligence*, 27: 267–298.

McColl-Kennedy, J.R. and Anderson, R.D. (2002) 'Impact of leadership style and emotions on subordinate performance', *Leadership Quarterly*, 13 (5): 545–559.

Miner, A.G., Glomb, T.M. and Hulin, C. (2005) 'Experience sampling mood and its correlates at work', *Journal of Occupational and Organizational Psychology*, 78: 171–193.

Moon, S.M. and Lord, R.G. (2006) 'Individual differences in automatic and controlled regulation of emotion and task performance', *Human Performance*, 19 (4): 327–356.

Morris, M. and Keltner, D. (2000) 'How emotions work: The social functions of emotional expression in negotiations', *Research in Organizational Behavior*, 22: 1–50.

Mowday, R.T. and Sutton, R.I. (1993) 'Organizational behavior: Linking individuals and groups to organizational context', *Annual Review of Psychology*, 44: 195–229.

Muraven, M. and Baumeister, R.F. (2000) 'Self-regulation and depletion of limited resources: Does self-control resemble a muscle?', *Psychological Bulletin*, 126 (2): 247–259.

Neumann, R. and Strack, F. (2000) ' "Mood contagion": The automatic transfer of mood between persons', *Journal of Personality and Social Psychology*, 79: 211–223.

Newcombe, M. and Ashkanasy, N. (2002) 'The role of affect and affective congruence in perceptions of leaders: an experimental study', *Leadership Quarterly*, 13 (5): 601–614.

Oldham, G.R., Cummings, A., Mischel, L.J., Schmidtke, J.M. and Zhou, J. (1995) 'Listen while you work – Quasi-experimental relations between personal-stereo headset use and employee work responses', *Journal of Applied Psychology*, 80 (5): 547–564.

Pekrun, R. and Frese, M. (1992) 'Emotions in work and achievement', in C.L. Cooper and I.T. Robertson (eds), *International Review of Industrial and Organizational Psychology*. New York: John Wiley & Sons, Ltd., pp. 154–200.

Pelled, L. and Xin, K. (1999) 'Down and out: An investigation of the relationship between mood and employee withdrawal behavior', *Journal of Management*, 25 (6): 875–895.

Pescosolido, A.T. (2002) 'Emergent leaders as managers of group emotion', *Leadership Quarterly*, 13 (5): 583–599.

Pillutla, M.M. and Murnighan, J.K. (1996) 'Unfairness, anger, and spite: Emotional rejections of ultimatum offers', *Organizational Behavior and Human Decision Processes*, 68 (3): 208–224.

Plutchik, R. (1994) *The Psychology and Biology of Emotion*. New York: Harper Collins.

Podsakoff, P.M., MacKenzie, S.B., Paine, J.B. and Bachrach, D.G. (2000) 'Organizational Citizenship Behaviors: A critical review of the theoretical and empirical literature and suggestions for future research', *Journal of Management*, 26 (3): 513–563.

Pugh, S. (2001) 'Service with a smile: Emotional contagion in the service encounter', *Academy of Management Journal*, 44 (5): 1018–1027.

Putnam, L.L. and Mumby, D.K. (1993) 'Organizations, emotion and the myth of rationality', in S. Fineman (ed.), *Emotion in Organizations*: London: Sage, pp. 36–57.

Rafaeli, A. and Sutton, R.I. (1987) 'Expression of emotion as part of the work role', *Academy of Management Review*, 12 (1): 23–37.

Rafaeli, A. and Sutton, R.I. (1990) 'Busy stores and demanding customers: How do they affect the display of positive emotion?', *Academy of Management Journal*, 33 (3): 623–637.

Rafaeli, A., Grandey, A., Ravid, S., Wirtz, J. and Steiner, D. (2006) *Culture, Display Rules and Organization: The Effects of Globalization*. Paper presented at the Annual Meeting of the Academy of Management, Atlanta.

Rafaeli, A., Rozilio, R., Ravid, S. and Derfler, R. (in press) 'The costs of encountering others' anger: Emotional exhaustion, cognitive resources, and work performance', *Academy of Management Journal*.

Richards, J.M. and Gross, J.J. (1999) 'Composure at any cost? The cognitive consequences of emotion suppression', *Personality and Social Psychology Bulletin*, 25 (8): 1033–1044.

Ridgeway, C. and Johnson, C. (1990) 'What is the relationship between socioemotional behavior and status in task groups?', *American Journal of Sociology*, 95: 1189–1212.

Robinson, M.D. and Clore, G.L. (2002) 'Belief and feeling: Evidence for an accessibility model of emotional self-report', *Psychological Bulletin*, 128 (6): 934–960.

Roseman, I.J. (1991) 'Appraisal determinants of discrete emotions', *Cognition and Emotion*, 5 (3): 161–200.

Rosenberg, E.L. and Fredrickson, B.L. (1998) 'Understanding emotions means crossing boundaries within psychology', *Review of General Psychology*, 2 (3): 243–246.

Rubin, R.S., Munz, D.C. and Bommer, W.H. (2005) 'Leading from within: The effects of emotion recognition and personality on transformational leadership behavior', *Academy of Management Journal*, 48 (5): 845–858.

Rupp, D., Holub, S. and Grandey, A. (in press) 'A cognitive-emotional theory of customer injustice and emotional labor: Implications for customer service, fairness theory, and the multifoci perspective', in D. DeCremer (ed.), *Advances in the Psychology of Justice and Affect*.

Rupp, D.E. and Spencer, S. (2006) 'When customers lash out: The effects of customer interactional injustice on emotional labor and the mediating role of discrete emotions', *Journal of Applied Psychology*, 91 (4): 971–978.

Russell, J.A. (1980) 'A circumplex model of affect', *Journal of Personality and Social Psychology*, 39: 1161–1178.

Russell, J.A. and Feldman Barrett, L. (1999) 'Core affect, prototypical emotional epsiodes, and other things called "emotion": Dissecting the elephant', *Journal of Personality and Social Psychology*, 76 (5): 805–819.

Saavedra, R. and Kwun, S.K. (2000) 'Affective states in job characteristics theory', *Journal of Organizational Behavior*, 21: 131–146.

Sandelands, L.E. and Boudens, C.J. (2000) 'Feeling at work', in S. Fineman (ed), *Emotion in Organizations*, 2nd edn. Thousand Oaks, CA: Sage, pp. 46–63.

Schaubroeck, J. and Jones, J.R. (2000) 'Antecedents of workplace emotional labor dimensions and moderators of their effects on physical symptoms', *Journal of Organizational Behavior*, 21: 163–183.

Schaubroeck, J. and Lam, S. (2004) 'Comparing lots before and after: Promotion rejectees' invidious reactions to promotees', *Organizational Behavior and Human Decision Processes*, 94 (1): 33–47.

Scherer, K.R. (2000) 'Emotion', in M. Hewstone and W. Stroebe (eds), *Introduction to Social Psychology: A European Perspective*, 3rd edn. Oxford: Blackwell, pp. 151–191.

Schmeichel, B.J., Vohs, K.D. and Baumeister, R.F. (2003) 'Intellectual performance and ego depletion: Role of the self in logical reasoning and other information processing', *Journal of Personality and Social Psychology*, 85: 33–46.

Schwarz, N. and Clore, G.L. (1983) 'Mood, misattribution, and judgments of well-being – Informative and directive functions of affective states', *Journal of Personality and Social Psychology*, 45 (3): 513–523.

Schwarz, N. and Clore, G.L. (1990) 'Feelings as information: Informational and motivational functions of affective states', in E.T. Higgins and R.M. Sorrentino (eds), *Handbook of Motivation and Cognition*. New York: Guilford. Vol. 2: 527–561.

Seo, M.G., Barrett, L.F. and Bartunek, J.M. (2004) 'The role of affective experience in work motivation', *Academy of Management Review*, 29 (3): 423–439.

Sinaceur, M. and Tiedens, L.Z. (2006) 'Get mad and get more than even: When and why anger expression is effective in negotiations', *Journal of Experimental Social Psychology*, 42 (3): 314–322.

Skarlicki, D.P. and Folger, R. (2005) 'Beyond counterproductive work behavior: Moral emotions and deontic retaliation versus reconciliation', in S. Fox and P.E. Spector (eds), *Counterproductive Work Behavior: Investigations of Actors and Targets*. Washington, D.C.: APA, pp. 83–105.

Spector, P.E. and Fox, S. (2002) 'An emotion-centered model of voluntary work behavior: Some parallels between counterprodutive work behavior (CWB) and organizational citizenship behavior (OCB)', *Human Resources Management Review*, 12: 269–292.

Spector, P.E. and Jex, S.M. (1991) 'Relations of job characteristics from multiple data sources with employee affect, absence, turnover intentions, and health', *Journal of Applied Psychology*, 76 (1): 46–55.

Spector, P.E., Fox, S., Penney, L.M., Bruursema, K., Goh, A. and Kessler, S. (2006) 'The dimensionality of counterproductivity: Are all counterproductive behaviors created equal?', *Journal of Vocational Behavior*, 68 (3): 446.

Spencer, S. and Rupp, D. (under review) 'Angry, guilty and conflicted: Injustice toward coworkers heightens emotional labor through cognitive and emotional mechanisms'.

Staw, B.M. and Barsade, S.G. (1993) 'Affect and managerial performance: A test of the sadder-but-wiser vs. happier-and smarter hypotheses', *Administrative Science Quarterly*, 38 (2): 304–331.

Staw, B.M., Bell, N.E. and Clausen, J.A. (1986) 'The dispositional approach to job attitudes: A lifetime longitudinal test', *Administrative Science Quarterly*, 31 (1): 56–77.

Stepper, S. and Strack, F. (1993) 'Proprioceptive determinants of emotional and nonemotional feelings', *Journal of Personality and Social Psychology*, 64: 211–220.

Sutton, R.I. (1991) 'Maintaining norms about expressed emotions – The case of bill collectors', *Administrative Science Quarterly*, 36 (2): 245–268.

Sutton, R.I. and Rafaeli, A. (1988) 'Untangling the relationships between displayed emotions and organizational sales: The case convenience stores', *Academy of Management Journal*, 31 (3): 461.

Sy, T., Côté, S. and Saavedra, R. (2005) 'The contagious leader: Impact of the leader's mood on the mood of group members, group affective tone, and group processes', *Journal of Applied Psychology*, 90 (2): 295–305.

Tan, H.H., Foo, M.D. and Kwek, M.H. (2004) 'The effects of customer personality traits on the display of positive emotions', *Academy of Management Journal*, 47 (2): 287–296.

Taylor, S.E. (1991) 'The assymetrical impact of positive and negative events: The mobilization-minimization hypothesis', *Psychological Bulletin*, 110: 67–85.

Thomas, S., Susanna, T. and O'Hara, L.A. (2006) 'Relation of employee and manager emotional intelligence to job satisfaction and performance', *Journal of Vocational Behavior*, 68 (3): 461.

Tiedens, L.Z. (2000) 'Powerful emotions: The vicious cycle of social status positions and emotions', in N.M. Ashkanasy, C.E.J. Hartel and W.J. Zerbe (eds), *Emotions in the Workplace: Research, Theory and Practice.* Westport, CT: Quorum, pp. 71–81.

Tiedens, L.Z. (2001) 'Anger and Advancement Versus Sadness and Subjugation: The Effect of Negative Emotion Expressions on Social Status Conferral', *Journal of Personality & Social Psychology*, 80 (1): 86.

Tiedens, L. and Fragale, A. (2002) 'Power moves: Complementarity in dominant and submissive nonverbal behavior', *Journal of Personality and Social Psychology*, 84: 558–568.

Tiedens, L.Z. and Linton, S. (2001) 'Judgment under emotional certainty and uncertainty: The effects of specific emotions on information processing', *Journal of Personality and Social Psychology*, 81 (6): 973–988.

Totterdell, P. (2000) 'Catching moods and hitting runs: Mood linkage and subjective performance in professional sport teams', *Journal of Applied Psychology*, 85 (6): 848–859.

Totterdell, P. and Holman, D. (2003) 'Emotion regulation in customer service roles: Testing a model of emotional labor', *Journal of Occupational Health Psychology*, 8 (1): 55–73.

Totterdell, P., Kellett, S., Teuchmann, K. and Briner, R. (1998) 'Evidence of mood linkage in work groups', *Journal of Personality and Social Psychology*, 74 (6): 1504–1515.

Totterdell, P., Wall, T., Holman, D., Diamond, H. and Epitropaki, O. (2004) 'Affect networks: A structural analysis of the relationship between work ties and job-related affect', *Journal of Applied Psychology*, 89 (5): 854–867.

Tsai, W.-C. and Huang, Y.-M. (2002) 'Mechanisms linking employee affective delivery and customer behavioral intentions', *Journal of Applied Psychology*, 87 (5): 1001–1008.

Tsai, W.C. (2001) 'Determinants and consequences of employee displayed positive emotions', *Journal of Management*, 27 (4): 497–512.

Tuncel, E. and Doucet, L.(2006) *Working paper.* Mixed feelings: Impact of mood diversity on confirmation bias and decision accuracy in groups.

Tunstall, M.M., Penney, L.M., Hunter, E.M. and Weinberger, E. (2006) 'A closer look at CWB: Emotions, targets, and outcomes', *Meeting of the Society of Industrial and Organizational Psychologists.* Atlanta, GA.

van den Bos, K. (2003) 'On the subjective quality of social justice: The role of affect as information in the psychology of justice judgments', *Journal of Personality and Social Psychology*, 85 (3): 482–498.

van den Bos, K., Bruins, J., Wilke, H.A.M. and Dronkert, E. (1999) 'Sometimes unfair procedures have nice aspects: On the psychology of the fair process effect', *Journal of Personality and Social Psychology*, 77 (2): 324–336.

Van Katwyk, P.T., Fox, S., Spector, P.E. and Kelloway, E.K. (2000) 'Using the job-related affective well-being scale (JAWS) to investigate affective responses to work stressors', *Journal of Occupational Health Psychology*, 5 (2): 219–230.

van Kleef, G.A., De Dreu, C.K.W. and Manstead, A.S.R. (2004a) 'The interpersonal effects of anger and happiness in negotiations', *Journal of Personality and Social Psychology*, 86 (1): 57–76.

Van Kleef, G.A., De Dreu, C.K.W., and Manstead, A.S.R. (2004b) 'The interpersonal effects of emotions in negotiations: A motivated information processing approach', *Journal of Personality and Social Psychology*, 87 (4): 510–528.

Van Kleef, G.A., De Dreu, C.K.W. and Manstead, A.S.R. (2006a) 'Supplication and appeasement in conflict and negotiation: The interpersonal effects of disappointment, worry, guilt, and regret', *Journal of Personality and Social Psychology*, 91: 124–142.

Van Kleef, G.A., Homan, A.C., Beersma, B., van Knippenberg, D., van Knippenberg, B., and Damen, F. (2006b) *Understanding the Effects of Leader Emotions on Team Performance. The Effectiveness of Angry Versus Happy Leaders Depends on Followers' Cognitive Style.* Paper presented at the Annual Meeting of the Academy of Management. Atlanta, GA.

van Knippenberg, D., van Knippenberg, B., Damen, F. and Van Kleef, G.A. (2005) 'Leader self-relevant emotions, follower self-esteem, and leadership effectiveness', *Annual meeting of Society of Industrial-Organizational Psychologists.* Los Angeles, CA.

van Knippenberg, D., van Knippenberg, B., Van Kleef, G.A. and Damen, F. (in press) 'Leadership, affect, and emotions', in N. Ashkanasy and C.D. Cooper (eds), *Research Companion to Emotions in Organizations.* Edgar Eldar.

Waldron, V.R. (2000) 'Relational experiences and emotion at work', in S. Fineman (ed.), *Emotion in Organizations*, 2nd edn. Thousand Oaks, CA: Sage, pp. 64–82.

Wallbott, H.G. and Scherer, K.R. (1989) 'Assessing emotion by questionnaire', in R. Plutchik and H. Kellerman (eds), *Emotion Theory, Research, and Experience: The Measurement of Emotions.* San Diego: Academic Press, Inc., pp. 55–82.

Watson, D., Clark, L. and Tellegen, A. (1988) 'Development and validation of brief measures of positive and negative affect – the PANAS scales', *Journal of Personality and Social Psychology*, 54 (6): 1063–1070.

Wegener, D.T. and Petty, R.E. (1994) 'Mood management across affective states: The hedonic contingency hypothesis', *Journal of Personality and Social Psychology*, 66: 1034–1048.

Weiss, H. and Cropanzano, R. (1996) 'Affective events theory: A theoretical discussion of the structure, causes and consequences of affective experiences at work', *Research in Organizational Behavior*, 18: 1–74.

Weiss, H., Suckow, K. and Cropanzano, R. (1999a) 'Effects of justice conditions on discrete emotions', *Journal of Applied Psychology*, 84 (5): 786–794.

Weiss, H., Ashkanasy, N.M. and Beal, D. (2004) 'Attentional and regulatory mechanisms of momentary work motivation and performance', in J.P. Forgas, K.D. Williams and W.V. Hippel (eds), *Social Motivation: Conscious and Unconscious Processes.* New York, NY: Plenum Press, pp. 314–331.

Weiss, H. and Beal, D. (2005) 'Reflections on affective events theory', in N.M. Ashkanasy, W.J. Zerbe and C.E.J. Hartel (eds), *Research on Emotions in Organizations: The Effect of Affect in Organizational Settings.* Oxford, UK: Elsevier. Vol 1: 1–21.

Weiss, H.M., Nicholas, J.P. and Daus, C.S. (1999b) 'An examination of the joint effects of affective experiences and job beliefs on job satisfaction and variations in affective experiences over time', *Organizational Behavior and Human Decision Processes*, 78 (1): 1–24.

Weiss, H.M. and Brief, A.P. (2001) 'Affect at work: An historical perspective', in R.L. Payne and C.L. Cooper (eds), *Emotions at Work: Theory, Research, and Application in Management.* Chichester: Wiley, 133–171.

Wilk, S.L. and Moynihan, L.M. (2005) 'Display rule "regulators": The relationship between supervisors and worker emotional exhaustion', *Journal of Applied Psychology*, 90 (5): 917–927.

Willemsen, M.C. and Keren, G. (2002) 'Negative-based prominence: the role of negative features in matching and choice', *Organizational Behavior and Human Decision Processes*, 88: 643–667.

Wong, K.F.E., Yik, M. and Kwong, J.Y.Y. (2006) 'Understanding the emotional aspects of escalation of commitment: The role of negative affect', *Journal of Applied Psychology*, 91 (2): 282–297.

Yang, J. and Mossholder, K. (2004) 'Decoupling task and relationship conflict: the role of intragroup emotional processing', *Journal of Organizational Behavior*, 25 (5): 589–605.

Zajonc, R.B. (1980) 'Feeling and thinking – Preferences need no inferences', *American Psychologist*, 35 (2): 151–175.

Zajonc, R.B. (1985) 'Emotion and facial efference: An ignored theory reclaimed', *Science*, 5 (April): 15–21.

Zapf, D. (2002) 'Emotion work and psychological well-being: A review of the literature and some conceptual considerations', *Human Resource Management Review*, 12 (2): 237–268.

Zohar, D., Tzischinski, O. and Epstein, R. (2003) 'Effects of energy availability on immediate and delayed emotional reactions to work events', *Journal of Applied Psychology*, 88 (6): 1082–1093.

14

Conflict in Workgroups

Karen A. Jehn and Sonja Rispens

Conflict in general is defined as perceived incompatibilities (Boulding, 1963) by the parties involved, and is an inherent aspect of organizational life. Conflict has been studied in diverse contexts ranging from the effects of conflict between married couples (e.g., Gottman and Krokoff, 1989) to managing conflict between nations (e.g., Hopmann, 1996). In organizations, conflicts can occur between co-workers (e.g., Amason, 1996; Jehn, 1995; Pelled, 1996), between an employee and supervisor (e.g., Rahim et al., 2001), or between groups or departments (e.g., Nauta et al., 2002). Interorganizational relationships can also be marked by conflicts (e.g., Pondy, 1969; Putnam and Poole, 1987). Our focus in this chapter is on workgroups, defined as groups with three or more members who perceive themselves as a group, whom others perceive as a group, and who are interdependent for completing a common task goal (Rispens, 2006).

Our aim in this chapter is to briefly review the past work on conflict in organizations. We then focus on three frameworks that attempt to explain the effectiveness (group performance and viability) of organizational workgroups engaged in conflict. Workgroup

effectiveness has been the focus of much past conflict research, with the main emphasis on group performance (De Dreu and Weingart, 2003; Jehn and Bendersky, 2003). However, it is also critical to examine the attitudes of members within the group, and their intent to remain, when considering conflict as an antecedent of group outcomes. Recent research on group effectiveness has focused on the performance of the group as well as team viability, or the ability of the team to retain its members through members' willingness to remain part of the team (Balkundi and Harrison, 2006; Barrick et al., 1998; Hackman, 1987; Hackman and Wageman, 2005). This construct incorporates aspects of member satisfaction as well as members' behavioral intentions to continue working together. According to Balkundi and Harrison (2006), these two constructs (group performance and team viability) are essential for team functioning, as they reflect not only the current group performance but also the success and continuation of a workgroup.

After discussing the past research on conflict, we present three frameworks to integrate the views of workgroup conflict as a positive or negative force. The first framework addresses the constructive debate perspective, which proposes that certain types of conflict (i.e., task-related conflict) can be effective under certain group conditions. The second framework speaks to cognitive processing, which assumes that all conflict is negative in groups because it interferes with effective processing of information. The third framework we introduce is that of asymmetrical conflict. This reflects a relatively new view of conflict that challenges past group research, which assumes that all members within the group perceive the same level of conflict. However, we now turn first to the review of the classic literature on workgroup conflict, which we divide into two sections: conflict as a negative process and conflict as a positive process. At this point we do not make any assumptions that conflict is good or bad, or that the authors referred to below take a certain stand; rather, we choose this categorization as a way to identify the main reasons that research has found that conflict can be both positive and negative in organizational workgroups.

CONFLICT IN WORKGROUPS: PAST RESEARCH

Conflict as a negative process

In the past, organizational researchers were convinced that conflict could only have negative effects. The general view regarding conflict was mainly negative. For example, Rapoport (1960) defined conflict as non-rational fights fueled by aggressive feelings among individuals, even further underscoring this negative view of conflict. March and Simon (1958) viewed conflict as a malfunction of standard working procedures. A similar perception was that organizational conflict causes imbalance in the cooperative system (Pondy, 1967). In related areas, such as negotiation and decision-making research, this negative view of conflict also prevailed. In the organizational decision-making literature, for example, researchers argued that conflicts

constrained the search for information (e.g., Argyris, 1976).

Literature on negotiations also presumes that conflict between negotiating parties is mainly negative and needs to be resolved, or at least an agreement among parties should be reached. In this line of research, the basic assumption is that negotiators behave rationally; that is, they always decide on a course of action that optimizes their own outcome, which often results in a poorer outcome for the other party. Researchers in this tradition have often investigated the effect of incomplete information in decision-making. For example, Heckathorn (1980) suggests that incomplete information leads to conflict between negotiators, and in order to reach a mutual decision, individuals need to bargain and tactically exchange information. Mandel (1979) suggests that conflict between negotiators (between dyads and in groups) leads to suboptimal outcomes. People may behave irrationally in conflict situations because of the way in which controversies are framed and interpreted (Bazerman, 2002). The original perspective of conflict within this negotiation literature certainly viewed conflict as an unwanted state that needs to be resolved quickly.

A totally different line of past research investigated conflict within the domestic setting. Conflict between married couples (Arellano and Markman, 1995; Christiansen and Shenk, 1991), between parent and child, or between siblings (Katz et al., 1992) have all been studied. Much of the past research in this area regards conflict as negative and troublesome for the people involved in the relationships. Within the literature of family therapy, several models for conflict resolution can be found. Rollin and Dowd (1979) for example, describe a dynamic model consisting of the following steps: (1) own your own position, (2) attend to the conflicting party, and (3) resolve the conflict.

Another model, for example, includes four steps but has strong similarities to the Rollin and Dowd (1979) model: (1) the conflict, (2) blaming, (3) shame, feeling guilty, or being in denial, and (4) repairing, reconciling, or retaliating the conflict (Zuk and Zuk, 1989; Zuk, 1988).

Even in the hands of past therapeutic models of conflict management, conflict is rarely viewed as a constructive force. This perspective may well be changing: more recently, some authors within the established area of marital and family conflict have suggested that conflict is not only 'normal,' but may even contribute constructively to the family system (Bernstein et al., 1997) or the marital relationship (Gottman and Krokoff, 1989).

Conflict style, that is, how people react or respond to conflict, is also a topic of interest in past communication research (Cloven and Roloff, 1993; Johnson and Roloff, 2000). Much of this research has investigated the influence of an aggressive or dominating style of conflict management (e.g., Jones and Remland, 1993), or what the preferred strategy is for managing conflict (Rahim and Magner, 1995) within organizational settings (De Dreu et al., 2001). Again, conflict in this research stream is considered as negative – it causes psychological distress, stress, and reduced well-being (De Dreu et al., 2001). The assumption, again, is that conflict therefore should be resolved as quickly as possible to reduce the stress it has on the communicating parties.

This earlier negative view of conflict was supported by empirical research. Conflict has been shown to interfere with the cognitive processing of group members (e.g., Carnevale and Probst, 1998). When involved in conflicts, group members also waste energy on non-task fighting, avoiding, or attempting to resolve rather than focusing on the actual work of the group. Research on intragroup relationships in organizations has found that conflict harms effective group processes (e.g., Amason, 1996; Evan, 1965; Jehn, 1995), group performance (e.g., De Dreu and Weingart, 2003; Jehn, 1995; Li and Hambrick, 2005; Nibler and Harris, 2003; Pelled, 1997; Rau, 2005; Tjosvold, 1991), as well as innovation (e.g., Matsuo, 2006). Conflict also leads to distrust (Deutsch,

1973, 1990; Pruitt and Rubin, 1986), and decreased satisfaction with the job and the workgroup (e.g., Amason, 1996; Jehn, 1995; Tjosvold, 1991). The frustration associated with conflict is a normal reaction of most people that leads to dissatisfaction and the intent of members to leave the group (Ross, 1989). Despite the overwhelming amount of evidence and logical theoretical reasoning about the negative effects of conflict, there is still a groundswell of support that challenges this absolutist view of conflict as negative, and proposes that there are circumstances when conflict can be a positive force in organizational workgroups. We now present some of the past theorizing underlying the positive perspective.

Conflict as a positive process

In contrast to the negative view of conflict listed above, conflict may be constructive under certain conditions (Jehn and Bendersky, 2003). Indeed, some 50 years ago, Coser (1956) suggested that conflict may serve a useful purpose by establishing and maintaining the identity and boundaries of the parties involved. Conflict (with out-groups) increases in-group cohesion, establishes and maintains power-balances, and creates allies and coalitions. According to Deutsch (1973), creativity is also a potentially positive result of conflict. The more recent study by De Dreu (2006) suggested that a moderate level of conflict is positively related to innovation in teams. With respect to decision making, Amason's (1996) empirical results show that conflict can increase the quality of decisions made by a top management team. A survey among scientists by Pelz and Andrews (1966) indicated that high performing scientists had conflicts with colleagues about how to approach their task.

Intragroup conflict research has shown that conflict can be beneficial for the performance of student groups (Jehn, 1994) as well as organizational groups (Jehn, 1995; Pelled, 1996), if the conflict is task-focused. In fact, one of the ideas that had the greatest influence in moving the research on organizational conflict forward, and allowing researchers to empirically examine whether conflict is negative or positive in workgroups, was the distinction between task-related and personal or relationship-focused conflict (Amason, 1996; Jehn, 1995, 1997; Pelled, 1996). More recently, research on organizational conflict has focused primarily on three types of conflict: relationship, task, and process (e.g., Amason, 1996; Jehn et al., 1999; Pelled, 1996) and four conflict dimensions (emotions, importance, resolution efficacy, and norms; Jehn et al., 2008b). Relationship conflicts reflect disagreements and incompatibilities among group members about personal issues that are not task related, such as social events, gossip, and world news. Task conflicts comprise disagreements among group members regarding ideas and opinions about the task being performed, such as disagreements regarding an organization's current strategic position or determining the correct data to include in a report. Process conflicts encompass disagreements about logistical and distribution issues such as how task accomplishment should proceed in the work unit, appropriate assignment of responsibilities and task delegation.

Past research (Amason, 1996; Jehn, 1995; Pelled, 1996) and recent reviews of intragroup conflict (Jehn and Bendersky, 2003) suggest that task conflict, or conflict among group members regarding issues of the specific job they are working on, can be beneficial to group performance. Research has demonstrated that task conflicts can improve workgroup performance through the increased consideration of different alternatives during group problem-solving (Amason, 1996; Greer et al., 2006; Jehn, 1997; Jehn and Bendersky, 2003; Matsuo, 2006; Pelled et al., 1999). Despite their conclusion from their meta-analysis that task conflict is basically detrimental, De Dreu and Weingart (2003) agree that under certain conditions task conflicts may still be constructive in workgroups. Specifically, they suggest that task conflict provides an open, trusting, and psychologically safe environment in workgroups focusing on non-routine tasks may result in improved group performance. Additionally, some research has proposed that process conflict (i.e., conflicts about appropriate assignment of tasks within the group), can enhance performance through an improved fit between an individual group member's ability and preferences and the groups' specific tasks that need to be delegated (e.g., Jehn et al., 1999).

CONFLICT IN WORKGROUPS: PRESENT RESEARCH AND PERSPECTIVES

The debate over whether any kind of conflict can be beneficial is still ongoing. In fact, a recent meta-analysis by De Dreu and Weingart (2003) indicates that, on average, task conflict (as well as relationship conflict) among group members is detrimental to performance. To reconcile these past results and reviews, we present three different frameworks of intragroup conflict:

- constructive debate;
- cognitive processing; and
- asymmetry.

We use these perspectives as an avenue to summarize the various perspectives we uncovered when reviewing the past research, and to provide information for researchers considering the directions for future research on workgroup conflict.

The past research on conflict often assumes that all group members perceive the same amount and types of conflict, neglecting the fact that members may have different perceptions about the level or type of conflict that exists in their group. To address this, we develop a model of asymmetrical perceptions of conflict in workgroups. This work builds on Jehn and Chatman's (2000) concept of perceptual conflict composition, which they define as 'the degree to which each individual in a group perceives levels of conflict differently compared to other member perceptions in the group' (p. 61). Their research showed that this asymmetry in perceptions of conflict is not beneficial to group functioning. In fact, in some circumstances the asymmetry was more detrimental than all members perceiving high levels of conflict (Jehn and Chatman, 2000). This asymmetry is considered a meta-conflict construct (conflict about conflict), which can influence outcomes such as commitment, cohesiveness, satisfaction, and individual and group performance (Jehn and Chatman, 2000). We contrast the past approaches, which we label the constructive debate and cognitive processing approaches to intragroup conflict, with this more recent approach to conflict regarding the asymmetry of group member perceptions.

Recent work by Jehn and Barreto (2005) and Bijleveld et al. (2005) suggests three general hypotheses about conflict in workgroups and the relationships to group processes and performance: the constructive debate hypothesis, the cognitive processing hypothesis, and the asymmetry hypothesis. Each is based on past theory, and predicts different relationships of conflict to group processes and performance. In this review of conflict in organizational workgroups, we examine the contributions of each of the three theories to our understanding of conflict in organizational groups. We briefly describe the first two theories, constructive debate and cognitive processing, as they are the most commonly used to date and are based in the past research we already reviewed in the sections on conflict as a negative and positive process in workgroups. We then elaborate on the asymmetry hypothesis, a relatively new addition to conflict theory, to predict the effects of intragroup conflict in organizational workgroups.

Constructive debate

The constructive debate framework of conflict suggests that, in general, while relationship and process conflict are detrimental to effectiveness, task conflict can enhance performance through discussions and debates that improve decision-making and the quality of the outcomes. Regarding relationship conflict, a recent review of the conflict literature (Jehn and Bendersky, 2003), as well as a meta-analysis (De Dreu and Weingart, 2003), suggest that relationship conflict is associated with negative outcomes such as dissatisfaction and decreased performance, due to the interference with constructive group processes. The research on process conflict has yielded mixed results. Jehn et al. (1999) proposed that process conflict would enhance performance due to discussions that would increase efficiency, such as a better fit between individual ability and task requirements; however, they found that high levels of process conflict deterred constructive discussions and actually delayed implementation. Jehn (1997) noted that process conflicts often include insults about members' preferences and abilities, and thus detract from performance. Jehn and Mannix (2001) also found that high performing groups had low to moderate amounts of process conflict. Therefore, past research supports this aspect of the constructive debate hypothesis – relationship and process conflict will decrease, not enhance performance in groups.

Task conflict, however, has been shown to improve decision quality and strategic planning of groups and organizations (Eisenhardt and Bourgeois, 1988; Mitroff et al., 1977). Bourgeois' (1985) study of top management teams indicates that too little task debate can interfere with successful strategic decisions, and studies of top management teams has shown that decision-quality is positively linked to the management teams' constructive conflict (Amason, 1996; Eisenhardt and Schoonhoven, 1990). Schweiger et al. (1989) found that groups of middle and upper-level managers in an experimental setting made higher quality decisions when challenging and conflicting views were presented. Nemeth (1986, 1995, 2001) has also demonstrated that minority dissent stimulates divergent thought processes, which leads people to consider a problem from multiple perspectives, generate more original ideas, and arrive at superior decisions and performance outcomes. These lines of research suggest that task-related team conflict improves performance through enhanced understanding of various viewpoints stimulated by debate. Task-related conflict improves strategic decisions and creative performance in groups, as well as inhibits groupthink (Amason and Schweiger, 1994; Jehn, 1995; Schweiger et al., 1989).

In sum, within this theoretical framework of constructive debate, the distinction in type of conflict is of critical importance. Task conflict is theorized to enhance group performance, constructive group processes such as, for example, cooperation. Both relationship and process conflict are considered to be detrimental for group performance and viability. Fights over personal issues or work strategies do not trigger any constructive debates, and as such cannot be of any positive value for workgroups.

Cognitive processing

The recent meta-analysis by De Dreu and Weingart (2003) suggests support for an alternative view of conflict, specifically, task conflict. Their results suggest that both relationship and task conflict are detrimental for performance. The perspective that all conflict is detrimental to performance is what we label the cognitive processing perspective, because all conflict is proposed to increase the cognitive load, which in turn interferes with complex thinking and processing of information. Both organizational and laboratory studies have shown that the threat and anxiety associated with conflict can inhibit employees' cognitive functioning in their processing of complex information (Roseman et al., 1994; Staw et al., 1981) and thus inhibit individual performance. According to this perspective, the distraction associated with all types of conflict has a negative effect (De Dreu and Weingart, 2003) as a negative conflict schema, or mental set (Carnevale and Probst, 1998), narrows the range of attention and impairs integrative problem solving in workgroups. Carnevale and Probst (1998) also argue that the conflict mental set triggers negative memory material which, in addition to interfering with performance,

also negatively influences commitment, cohesiveness, and satisfaction. Recent theorizing on the effects of conflict also suggests that conflict is detrimental for the well-being and health of individual organizational members (De Dreu et al., 2004).

In sum, the amount of processing needed to deal with conflict detracts from the cognitive capacity available for other aspects, such as performing a task and solving problems. Given this and the past research on conflict as a negative process, this perspective suggests that all conflicts (task, relationship, and process) decrease both performance effectiveness and viability (satisfaction and intent of the members to remain in the groups).

Conflict asymmetry

One of the major shortcomings of the past research on intragroup conflict from both of the above perspectives is that it assumes that all parties involved in the conflict perceive the same types and levels of conflict (Jehn and Chatman, 2000), thus largely ignoring asymmetrical conflicts (Pruitt, 1995). We describe conflict asymmetry based on the concept of perceptual conflict composition developed by Jehn and Chatman (2000). Perceptual conflict composition is the degree to which one person perceives that a conflict is present compared to the other group members involved in the conflict. Jehn and Chatman (2000) compare this to the concept of relational demography in diversity research. Relational demography (Riordan and Shore, 1997; Tsui et al., 1992; Tsui and O'Reilly, 1989) reflects the degree to which an individual is different from other members of a group (or dyad) on demographic variables. We extend this idea to conflict perceptions among group members. The concept of asymmetry thus examines the differences in perceptions of conflict among the group members involved in the conflict, where one person may perceive that a serious conflict exists, while the other group members may perceive that there is no, or a very low level of, conflict present. Thus, our definition of asymmetry of conflict is that in an asymmetrical conflict, group member A

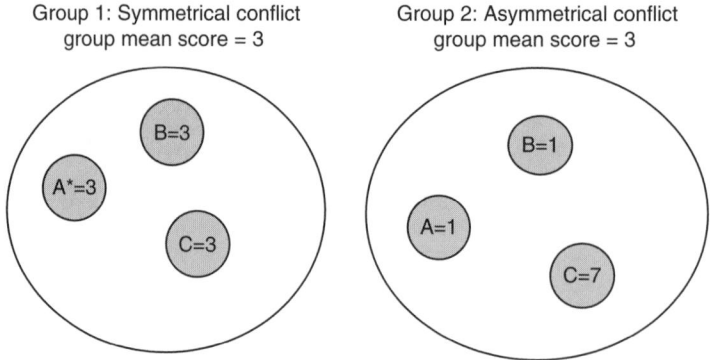

Example survey item: 'How much conflict is there in your workgroup?' (Scale 1–7)

Figure 1   Examples of conflict asymmetry in workgroups
*The gray circles indicate members in the group; thus, each group has member A, B, and C.

perceives more (or less) conflict than the other group members (see Figure 1 for a pictorial representation of conflict asymmetry). Note that while both groups A and B have the same average level of conflict (both group mean scores on the conflict survey item are 3), in group A all members agree on the level of conflict and in group B there is disagreement, or asymmetry, over the level of conflict perceived.

Drawing on procedural justice literature, we argue that when one party believes there is conflict and the other does not, discomfort and inequity will exist between the parties (Lind and Tyler, 1988; Tyler, 1986). This will cause the parties involved in the conflict to be less satisfied than when symmetrical views of the conflict experience exists. In addition, if party A believes that his/her view of the situation is not validated by the other party, or party B, he/she may question his/her own view of the situation. According to self-verification theory, this may decrease motivation, effort, satisfaction, and performance (Swann, 1999). According to self and identity theorists, individuals strive for confirmation of their own perceptions, often comparing their views with others', and the responses of others to their own views (Burke and Stets, 1999; Swann, 1990; Swann et al., 1994). Individuals search for coherence in their interactions and social environment (Swann et al., 2002), and those inconsistencies can negatively affect the

processes and outcomes of the group members involved.

Research on asymmetrical conflict structures also suggests similar processes. An asymmetrical conflict structure exists when one party wants to change the status quo, and the other party wants to keep the status quo as is (Kluwer and Mikula, 2002). This work, often based in a research setting of gender-related inequality in the division of family work, suggests that cognitions of injustice cause more problems than actual injustice (Major, 1987; Thompson, 1991). This distributive justice framework states that feelings of injustice are the result of a comparison process. The unfairness that individuals feel can cause decreased motivation, depression, and dissatisfaction with the relationship (see Kluwer and Mikula, 2002 for a review of the research in the marital setting). Based on the above perspective, asymmetrical conflict, we propose that asymmetry of conflict (task, relationship, and process) decreases effectiveness.

EMERGING ISSUES

Directional conflict asymmetry: individuals in workgroups

Some research has begun to examine the asymmetrical perspective of conflict in groups

(Bijleveld, 2005; Jehn and Chatman, 2000; Jehn et al., 2008a) and find that workgroup asymmetry decreases group performance and viability (e.g., decreased satisfaction, increased absenteeism, decreased commitment, decreased cohesiveness). These studies, however, focused on the magnitude of the asymmetry rather than the direction; that is, they examined only the degree to which members perceived differences in the amount of conflict but they did not take into account the difference or effects on those members who feel *more* conflict than the rest of the group (see Figure 1; Group 2, member C) vs. those who perceive *less* conflict than the rest of the group members (Group 2, member A). We introduce the concept of directional asymmetry – that is, the direction in which the individual's perceptions relate to the general group perceptions as an important aspect of the conflict asymmetry perspective.

We propose that group members who experience less conflict than the others in the group will be more trusting, more satisfied, and perform better (or perceive that they perform better) than the rest of the group. They will not be distracted by the conflict that the rest of the group experiences, thus their cognitive processes will not be as taxed as the other group members, allowing them to perform at a higher level (Carnevale and Probst, 1998). They will not be affected by the negative emotions and affect associated with conflict (Jehn and Bendersky, 2003; Pinkley, 1990; Thomas, 1992) and therefore their perception of group processes is likely to be positive and they will be quite satisfied with their group, especially in contrast to members who perceive that there is a high level of conflict within the group.

In contrast, members who perceive a higher level of conflict than the rest of the group will not be verified in their views (Burke and Stets, 1999; Swann, 1999), and may feel diminished and disrespected because they are not listened to (Tyler, 1999). When members feel different from others and perceive a high level of conflict, they are less receptive to the ideas of other group members, thus often interfering with constructive group processes

and individual performance (Pelled, 1996). In addition, such members will tend to spend the time and energy that should be devoted to working on the task to discussing, resolving, or ignoring conflicts that may not even be perceived by the other group members. This misspent effort used to resolve non-existent conflicts (at least non-existent according to the other group members), will detract from the energy this individual puts into performance-relevant tasks, but also will cause huge levels of frustration. These members' inability to communicate their views with the rest of the group regarding the reality of the group problems can cause frustration and withdrawal (Swann, 1999), thus decreasing satisfaction and task effort. These negative emotions can lead to irrational decisions and behaviors, because emotions such as frustration and anger overwhelm and oversimplify rational and instrumental reasoning (Brief and Weiss, 2002; Thomas, 1992). Pelled (1996) also found that high levels of perceived conflict were associated with the member also perceiving a low level of productivity in the group, which she suggests can reduce effort and thus individual performance due to a self-fulfilling prophecy effect. Therefore, a directional asymmetry perspective would suggest that team members who perceive more conflict than the other group members will be less effective or viable as members of the team (lower performance level, less satisfaction, and lower intent to remain with the group) than those who perceive less conflict compared to the rest of the group.

In a recent study, we tested the asymmetry hypothesis on 49 pre-existing organizational workgroups participating in executive education courses (Jehn et al., 2008a). The members from existing workgroups participated in an information exchange exercise based on the hidden profile task (Stasser and Stewart, 1992) in their intact groups (all group members were present). Individuals were given a number of clues, in the form of pieces of information, and were informed that none of the other participants had exactly the same clues and that group discussion was required to find the best solution. There was no manipulation of amount or content of information across groups or members; that is, amount and content of information was held constant. The exchange was restricted to a verbal exchange of information; showing the other group members your written information was prohibited. Performance was determined by the number of correct answers the individual provided. After this task, group members filled in questionnaires and reported on the level and type of conflict in their group, and group processes such as cooperation and commitment. The results showed that members who perceive more relationship or process conflict exhibit lower levels of effectiveness than other group members, above and beyond the main effect of the general level of conflict within the group. Those members who perceived more conflict than other group members also perceive lower levels of cooperation, commitment, communication, trust, and respect.

Asymmetry of type of conflict and proportional conflict

Jehn et al. (2008c) propose three other interesting areas for future research on conflict asymmetry and perceptions in workgroups. First, they suggest that there may also be an asymmetry of conflict *type*; that is, it is not just that one person perceived a high level of relationship conflict and the other group member a low level, but what one person perceives as a conflict about non-task personal issues the other may perceive as actually task-related, or task conflict. In this case, a meta-conflict exists concerning the nature of type of conflict. One group member perceives the conflict to be task related, and maybe even constructive, while the other person perceives it as a personal, non-task related attack. This can lead to its own interesting dynamics that should be further investigated in future research.

Second, Jehn et al. (2008c) refer to Jehn and Chatman's (2000) concept of proportional conflict as a future direction for conflict researchers to disentangle the positive and negative effects of conflict. In this framework, all conflict types are considered simultaneously. Jehn and Chatman (2000) criticize past research on group conflict for examining only one type of conflict at a time, rather than the interplay or connectedness of the conflict types. In past research, two groups with high levels of task conflict but differing levels of relationship conflict would be hypothesized to have the same task conflict effects (see Figure 2). But it is possible that, when the proportional amount of task conflict is considered (task conflict divided by the overall level of conflict; see Figure 2), that the group with high task conflict and *no*, or very little, relationship conflict (Group 2) will perform better and fit the constructive debate perspective predictions. On the other hand, performance of the group with high levels of both task and relationship conflict may follow the cognitive processing perspective predictions, thereby exhibiting problems processing any constructive debate that may come from the task conflict due to the presence of the high amount of relationship conflict (Figure 2; Group 1). If researchers only take into account one type of conflict without examining the overall conflict profile, they will ignore other aspects of the group functioning that may explain the full effect of the workgroup conflict on performance and viability.

The third direction for future research suggested by Jehn et al. (2008c) is considered below: the possibility that even relationship conflict can have positive consequences.

Functional relationship conflict

According to Davis (1971) in his classic article, research can be especially interesting when researchers theorize about a phenomenon and predict that it can behave differently than is generally accepted. While the debate continues regarding task conflict, research has consistently determined that relationship conflict is a negative process in workgroups. Fights over personal issues or personality clashes are associated with feelings of dissatisfaction, turnover intentions,

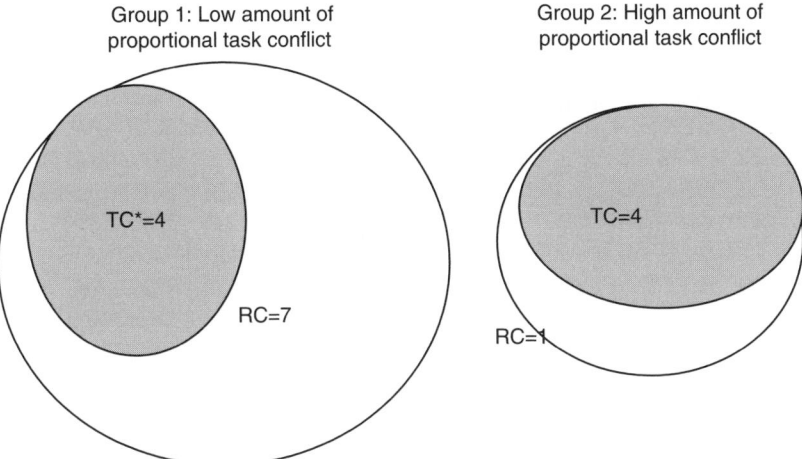

Group 1: Low amount of
proportional task conflict

Group 2: High amount of
proportional task conflict

TC*=4

RC=7

TC=4

RC=1

Figure 2   Examples of proportional conflict in workgroups
*The gray circle indicates the amount of task conflict within the group; the white area is the relationship
conflict; and the large overall circle indicates the overall amount of conflict within the group.

and decreased effectiveness of workgroups
(e.g., Amason, 1996; De Dreu and Weingart,
2003; Jehn, 1995). However, the negative
effects of relationship conflict are sometimes
not empirically supported. In the meta-
analysis by De Dreu and Weingart (2003), for
example, several unpublished working papers
were listed in which the negative effect of
relationship conflict did not emerge. In one
of those papers, the results even showed a
positive association between relationship conflict and an objective performance measure
(Nijdam, 1998).

We suggest that an interesting path for
future research is to examine under which
conditions relationship conflict may not
be as detrimental, or even positive, for
workgroups. What are the conditions and
the mediating processes that underlie the
possible positive effect of relationship conflict
on group processes and outcomes? It may
be that under certain conditions, in certain
group tasks, non-work related fights serve a
constructive purpose, such as an emotional
release of frustration (Coser, 1956; Jehn,
1997) that does not interfere with group
performance. Indeed, recent studies show a
positive effect of relationship conflict (Greer
and Jehn, 2005; Rispens et al., 2005a). In a

study of conflict occurring within political
organizing groups, Greer and Jehn (2005)
found that conflict management tactics and
communication styles allowed relationship
conflict to have both positive performance
and viability effects. In addition, the negative
effect of relationship conflict is buffered when
group members like each other (Rispens
et al., 2006) and when they are actively
involved in the group such that it enables
group members to know who knows what
and to share that knowledge within the group
(Rispens et al., 2006). The explanation for
these effects derives from the established
literature suggesting that conflict may help to
create and maintain boundaries (Coser, 1956).
Relationship conflicts may allow members of
a relationship to air their frustrations with
each other and discuss them, which can allow
for eventual improvement of the relationship
through an increased understanding of the
issues and others' perspectives on them
(Bernstein et al., 1997). Indeed, the improvement of the relationship may not be possible
in the absence of relationship conflict. Future
research is needed to determine if it is
possible that relationship conflict may also
have functional effects in workgroups and
under what conditions this can be achieved.

FUTURE RESEARCH AND THEORIZING

In this chapter we have reviewed the past research on workgroup conflict and two current summarizing theoretical approaches, which we labeled the constructive debate and cognitive processing approaches to workgroup conflict. We have also presented a more recent approach to conflict regarding the asymmetry of group member perceptions. We review results from past research and also provide some current findings regarding the asymmetry perspective. In support of the constructive debate hypothesis, findings suggest that task conflict may be constructive in non-routine task groups that require information exchange and constructive debate to perform well (Amason, 1996; Jehn, 1995; Jehn et al., 2005). Relationship, process, and task conflict in general decrease constructive group processes and satisfaction which supports the cognitive processing hypothesis (Carnevale and Probst, 1998; De Dreu and Weingart, 2003). The threat and anxiety associated with all types of conflict (task, relationship, and process) may interfere with cognitive and social processing of group members, which in turn may decrease constructive group processes and satisfaction. We thus suggest one way to reconcile the competing view of task conflict from the constructive debate and the cognitive processing perspectives. We suggest that task conflict may increase performance (constructive debate) but decrease group processes and satisfaction, therefore inhibiting *social* processes more so than cognitive processes.

This review also provides information to add to the literature on differences of conflict perceptions within groups. In general, asymmetrical perceptions of conflict in workgroups has been shown to decrease group performance and viability (e.g., decreased satisfaction, increased absenteeism, decreased commitment, decreased cohesiveness; Bijleveld, 2005; Jehn and Chatman, 2000; Jehn et al., 2006). In some recent studies, however, asymmetry of task and process conflict shows a positive effect on the amount of the debate within the group

(Bijleveld, 2005; Jehn et al., 2008a) which may lead to increased performance of the group (Rispens et al., 2005b). This finding seems to indicate that the more task (or process) conflict asymmetry a group member perceives, the greater the likelihood of that member expressing meta-conflict (conflict about conflict) to other group members. Meta-conflict may result in constructive debates about the task or process conflict among group members. In accordance with past research on task conflict, those debates may improve performance (e.g., Amason and Schweiger, 1994; Jehn, 1995; Schweiger et al., 1989).

We also provide new directions for conflict research by presenting the directional asymmetry and proportional conflict ideas. Directional asymmetry suggests that team members who perceive more conflict than other group members is less likely to perform well. We propose that this may be due to the member being less receptive to the ideas and opinions of other group members. Resolving nonexistent conflicts (at least non-existent according to the other group members), may lead to high levels of frustration and withdrawal consistent with self-verification predications (Swann, 1999), hence decreasing satisfaction and effort. The concept of proportional conflict takes into account the level of each type of conflict in consideration of the overall amount of conflict (see Figure 2), something lacking in past workgroup conflict research.

Another interesting direction for future conflict research is the investigation of positive effects of relationship conflict. In an increasing number of studies (De Dreu and Weingart, 2003; Greer and Jehn, 2005; Rispens et al., 2006), relationship conflict is being shown to have the potential to increase the performance of group members. This finding contradicts the literature which has stated that relationship conflict is detrimental for group performance. However, research on family conflicts (e.g., Bernstein et al., 1997; Jehn and Bendersky, 2003) suggest that interpersonal, relationship conflicts are necessary and even helpful to maintain a secure family group. This literature, as well as

De Dreu and Weingart's (2003) observation from their meta-analysis that six working papers all found relationship conflict to have positive effects on performance, suggests that the effect of relationship conflict on performance in groups be re-evaluated. It may be that in some circumstances, in certain group tasks, the non-work related fights serve a purpose, such as an emotional release of frustration (Jehn, 1997), that does not interfere with, and actually assists in task performance.

SUMMARY

The original research on conflict in organizations suggested that conflict was a negative force, but some of the early theorizing also suggested some positive effects (e.g., idea generation, constructive criticism, creativity). A resurgence of research on workgroup conflict in the past 15 years indicates that conflict can be beneficial for workgroups under certain conditions, but the debate is ongoing. We propose that the emerging new perspectives on conflict (e.g., conflict asymmetry, proportional conflict; functional relational conflict aspects) will enable future research to provide a clearer picture of the benefits and detriments of workgroup conflict.

REFERENCES

Amason, A.C. and Schweiger, D.M. (1994) 'Resolving the paradox of conflict, strategic decision making, and organizational performance', *International Journal of Conflict Management*, 5: 239–253.

Amason, A. (1996) 'Distinguishing the effects of functional and dysfunctional conflict on strategic decision making: Resolving a paradox for the top management teams', *Academy of Management Journal*, 39: 123–148.

Arellano, C. and Markman, H. (1995) 'The managing affect and differences scale (MADS): A self report measure assessing conflict management in couples', *Journal of Family Psychology*, 9: 319–334.

Argyris, C. (1976) 'Single loop and double loop models in research on decision making', *Administartive Science Quarterly*, 21: 363–375.

Balkundi, P. and Harrison, D.A. (2006) 'Ties, leaders, and time in teams: Strong inference about network structure's effects on team viability and performance', *Academy of Management Journal*, 49: 49–68.

Barrick, M., Stewart, G., Neubert, M.J. and Mount, M. (1998) 'Relating member ability and personality to work–team processes and team effectiveness', *Journal of Applied Psychology*, 83: 377–391.

Bazerman, M. (2002) *Judgement in Managerial Decision Making* (5th edn). New York: Wiley.

Bernstein, D.A., Clarke–Stewart, A. Roy E.J., and Wickens C.D. (1997) *Psychology* (4th edn). New York: Houghton Mifflin.

Bijleveld, E., Jehn, K.A. and Barreto, M. (2005) 'Asymmetries of perception in organizational conflict', *Working Paper*, Leiden University, The Netherlands.

Boulding, K. (1963) *Conflict and Defense*. New York: Harper and Row.

Bourgeois, L.J. (1985) 'Strategic goals, perceived uncertainty, and economic performance in volatile environments', *Academy of Management Journal*, 28: 548–573.

Brief, A.P. and Weiss, H.M. (2002) 'Organizational behavior: Affect in the workplace', *Annual Review of Psychology*, 53: 279–307.

Burke, P.J. and Stets, J.E. (1999) 'Trust and commitment through self-verification', *Social Psychology Quarterly*, 62: 347–360.

Carnevale, P.J. and Probst, T.M. (1998) 'Social values and social conflict in creative problem solving and categorization', *Journal of Personality and Social Psychology*, 74: 1300–1309.

Christiansen, A. and Shenk, J. (1991) 'Communications, conflict, and psychological distance in nondistressed, clinic, and divorcing couples', *Journal of Consulting and Clinical Psychology*, 59: 458–463.

Cloven, D. and Roloff, M. (1993) 'The chilling effect of aggressive potential on the expression of complaints in intimate relationships', *Communication Monographs*, 60: 199–219.

Coser, L. (1956) *The Functions of Social Conflict*. Glencoe, IL: Free Press.

Davis, M.S. (1971) 'That's interesting! Toward a phenomenology of sociology and a sociology of phenomenology', *Philosphy of the Social Sciences*, 1: 309–344.

De Dreu, C.K.W. and Weingart, L.R. (2003) 'Task versus relationship conflict, team performance, and team member satisfaction: A meta-analysis', *Journal of Applied Psychology*, 88: 741–749.

De Dreu, C.K.W. (2006) 'When too much and too little hurts: Evidence for a curvilinear relationship between task conflict and innovation in teams', *Journal of Management*, 32: 83–107.

De Dreu, C.K.W., Evers, A., Beersma, B., Kluwer, E.S. and Nauta A. (2001) 'A theory based measure of conflict management strategies in the workplace', *Journal of Organizational Behavior*, 22: 645–668.

De Dreu, C.W.K., Van Dierendock, D. and Dijkstra, M.T. (2004) 'Looking back, looking ahead: Conflict at work and individual health and well-being', *International Journal of Conflict Management*, 15 (1): 6–26.

Deutsch, M. (1973) *The Resolution of Conflict*. New Haven: Yale University Press.

Eisenhardt, K.M. and Bourgeois, L.J. (1988) 'Politics of strategic decision making: Toward a mid-range theory', *Academy of Management Journal*, 31: 737–770.

Eisenhardt, K.M. and Schoonhoven, C.B. (1990) 'Organizational growth: Linking founding team, strategy, environment and growth among U.S. semiconductor ventures', *Administrative Science Quarterly*, 35: 504–529.

Evan, W. (1965) 'Conflict and performance in R&D organizations', *Industrial Management Review*, 7: 37–46.

Gottman, J.M. and Krokoff, L.J. (1989) 'Marital interaction and satisfaction – A longitudinal view', *Journal of Consulting and Clinical Psychology*, 57: 47–52.

Greer, L.L. and Jehn, K.A. (2005) 'Relationship and task conflict in e-mail: Performance effects moderated by influence tactic usage', International Association of Conflict Management Conference, Seville, Spain.

Greer, L.L., Jehn, K.A. and Thatcher, S.M.B. (2006) 'Demographic faultline token splits, Effects on conflict and performance', *Academy of Management*, Atlanta, GA.

Hackman, J.R. (1987) 'The design of work teams', in J.W. Lorsch (ed.), *Handbook of Organizational Behavior*. Englewood Cliffs, NJ: Prentice–Hall, pp. 315–342.

Hackman, J.R. and Wageman, R. (2005) 'A theory of team coaching', *Academy of Management Review*, 30: 269–287.

Hekathorn, D. (1980) 'A unified model for bargaining and conflict', *Behavioral Science*, 25: 261–284.

Hopmann, P.T. (1996) *Negotiation Process and the Resolution of International Conflicts*. Columbia: University of South Carolina Press.

Jehn, K.A. (1994) 'Enhancing effectiveness: An investigation of advantages and disadvantages of value-based intragroup conflict', *International Journal of Conflict Management*, 5 (3): 223–238.

Jehn, K.A. (1995) 'A multimethod examination of the benefits and detriments of intragroup conflict', *Administrative Science Quarterly*, 40: 256–282.

Jehn, K.A. (1997) 'A qualitative analysis of conflict types and dimensions in organizational groups', *Administrative Science Quarterly*, 42: 530–557.

Jehn, K.A. and Barreto, M. (2005) 'The effects of conflict asymmetry on workgroup outcomes', *European Association of Experimental Social Psychology Conference*, Wurzburg, Germany.

Jehn, K.A., De Wit, F., Barreto, M. and Rink, F. (2008a) 'Conflict asymmetries: Effects on motivation, attitudes, and performance', *International Association for Conflict Management*.

Jehn, K.A. and Bendersky, C. (2003) 'Intragroup conflict in organizations: A contingency perspective on the conflict-outcome relationship', *Research in Organizational Behavior*, 25: 187–242.

Jehn, K.A. and Chatman, J.A. (2000) 'The influence of proportional and perceptual conflict composition on team performance', *The International Journal of Conflict Management*, 11: 56–73.

Jehn, K., Greer, L., Levine, S. and Szulanski, G. (2008b) 'The effects of conflict types, dimensions, and emergent states on group outcomes', *Group Decision and Negotiation*, forthcoming.

Jehn, K.A. and Mannix, E. (2001) 'The dynamic nature of conflict: A longitudinal study of intragroup conflict and group performance', *Academy of Management Journal*, 44: 238–251.

Jehn, K.A., Northcraft, G. and Neale, M. (1999) 'Why differences make a difference: A field study of diversity, conflict, and performance in workgroups', *Administrative Science Quarterly*, 44: 741–763.

Jehn, K.A., Rispens, S. and Thatcher, S.M.B. (2008c) 'Do you hear what I hear?: The effects of conflict asymmetry on workgroup and individual outcomes mediated by emergent states and social', *Academy of Management*.

Jehn, K.A., Rupert, J. and Nauta, A. (2006) 'The effects of conflict asymmetry on mediation outcomes: Satisfaction, work motivation and absenteeism', *International Journal of Conflict Management*, 17 (2): 96–109.

Johnson, K.L. and Roloff, M.E. (2000) 'Correlates of the perceived resolvability and relational consequences of serial arguing on dating relationships: Argumentative features and the use of coping strategies', *Journal of Social and Personal Relationships* 17 (4–5): 676–686.

Jones, T. and Remland, M. (1993) 'Nonverbal communication and conflict escalation: An attribution-based model', *The International Journal of Conflict Management*, 4: 119–137.

Katz, L.F., Kramer, L. and Gottman, J. (1992) 'Conflict and emotions in marital, sibling, and peer relationships', in C.U. Shantz and W.W. Hartup (eds), *Conflict in Child and Adolescent Development*. New York: Cambridge University Press, pp. 122–149.

Kluwer, E.S. and Mikula, G. (2002) 'Gender related inequalities in the division of family work in close relationships: a social psychological perspective', *European Review of Social Psychology*, 13: 185–216.

Li, J. and Hambrick, D.C. (2005) 'Factional groups: A new vantage on demographic faultlines, conflict, and disintegration in work teams', *Academy of Management Journal*, 48: 794–813.

Lind, E. and Tyler, T. (1988) *The Social Psychology of Procedural Justice*. New York: Plenum.

Major, B. (1987) 'Gender, justice, and the psychology of entitlement', in P. Shaver and C. Hendrick (eds), *Review of Personality and Social Psychology*. Beverly Hills, CA: Sage Publications Inc., pp. 124–148.

Mandel, R. (1979) *Perception, Decision Making and Conflict*. Washington, DC: University Press of America.

March, J. and Simon, H. (1958) *Organizations*. New York: Wiley.

Matsuo, M. (2006) 'Customer orientation, conflict, and innovativeness in Japanese sales departments', *Journal of Business Research*, 59: 242–250.

Mitroff, I., Barabba, V. and Kilmann, R. (1977) 'The application of behavioral and philosophical technologies to strategic planning: A case-study of a large federal agency', *Management Science*, 24: 44–58.

Nauta, A., De Dreu C.K.W. and Van der Vaart T. (2002) 'Social value orientation, organizational goal concerns and interdepartemental problem solving behavior', *Journal of Organizational Behavior*, 23: 199–213.

Nemeth, C.J. (1986) 'Differential contributions of majority and minority influence', *Psychological Review*, 93: 23–32.

Nemeth, C.J. (1995) 'Dissent as driving cognition, attitudes, and judgments', *Social Cognition*, 13: 279–291.

Nemeth, C.J. (2001) 'The art of mentoring: It's personal', in F. Buschini and E. Lage (eds), *Penser la Vie, le Social, la Nature: Mélanges en l'honneur de Serge Moscovici*. Paris: Editions de la Maison des Sciences de l'Homme.

Nibler, R. and Harris, K.L. (2003) 'The effects of culture and cohesiveness on intragroup conflict and effectiveness', *The Journal of Social Psychology*, 12 (1): 613–631.

Nijdam, N.E. (1998) *The Functioning of Work Teams*. Unpublished master's thesis, University of Amsterdam, The Netherlands.

Pelled, L.H. (1996) 'Relational demography and perceptions of group conflict and performance: A field investigation', *The International Journal of Conflict Management*, 7: 230–246.

Pelled, L.H. (1997) 'Relational demography and perceptions of group conflict and performance, A field investigation', *International Journal of Conflict Resolution*, 22 (1): 54–67.

Pelled, L.H., Eisenhardt, K.M. and Xin, K.R. (1999) 'Exploring the black box. An analysis of work group diversity, conflict, and performance', *Administrative Science Quarterly*, 44 (1): 1–28.

Pelz, D.C. and Andrews, W.P. (1966) *Scientists in Organizations: Productive Climates for Research and Development*. New York: Wiley.

Pinkley, R. (1990) 'Dimensions of the conflict frame: Disputant interpretations of conflict', *Journal of Applied Psychology*, 75: 117–128.

Pondy, L.R. (1967) 'Organizational conflict: Concepts and models', *Administrative Science Quarterly*, 12: 297–320.

Pondy, L.R. (1969) 'Varieties of organizational conflict', *Administrative Science Quarterly*, 14: 499–506.

Putnam, L.L. and Poole, M.S. (1987) 'Conflict and negotiation', in F.M. Jablin, L.L. Putnam, K.H. Roberts and L.W. Porter (eds), *Handbook of Organizational Communication: An Interdisciplinary Perspective*. Beverly Hills, CA: Sage, pp. 549–599.

Pruitt, D.G. (1995) 'Process and outcome in community mediation', *Negotiation Journal on the Process of Dispute Settlement*, 11: 365–377.

Pruitt, D. and J. Rubin. (1986) *Social Conflict: Escalation, Stalemate and Settlement*. New York: Random House.

Rahim M.A., Antonioni D. and Psenicka, C. (2001) 'A structural equations model of leader power, subordinates' style of handling conflict and job performance', *International Journal of Conflict Mangement*, 12: 191–211.

Rahim, M.A. and Magner, N. (1995) 'Confirmatory factor-analysis of the styles of handling interpersonal conflict – First-order factor model and its invariance across groups', *Journal of Applied Psychology*, 80 (1): 122–132.

Rapoport, A. (1960) *Fights, Games, and Debates*. Ann Arbor, University of Michigan Press.

Rau, D. (2005) 'The influence of relationship conflict and trust on the transactive memory', *Small Group Research*, 36 (6): 746–771.

Riordan, C.M. and Shore, L.M. (1997) 'Demographic diversity and employee attitudes: An empirical examination of relational demography within work units', *Journal of Applied Psychology*, 82: 342–358.

Rispens, S. (2006) *Multiple Interdependencies and Workgroup Effectiveness.* Doctoral dissertation, Ridderkerk: Ridderprint B.V.

Rispens, S. Greer, L.L. and Jehn, K.A. (2006) 'Can relationship conflict be positive? Exploring the moderating role of interdependence on the link between relationship conflict and workgroup performance', *International Association for Conflict Management.*

Rispens, S., Jehn, K.A. and Thatcher, S.M.B. (2005a) 'Creating constructive task conflict: reward structures and group process training', *International Association for Conflict Management*, Seville, Spain.

Rispens, S., Jehn, K.A. and Thatcher, S (2005b) 'Asymmetric conflict in workgroups: Effects on group processes and performance', *Work and Organizational Psychology Conference*, Rotterdam, The Netherlands.

Rollin, S. and Dowd, T. (1979) 'Conflict resolution: A model for effective marital and family relations', *American Journal of Family Therapy*, 7: 61–67.

Roseman, I.J., Wiest, C. and Swartz, T.S. (1994) 'Phenomenology, behaviors, and goals differentiate discrete emotions', *Journal of Personality and Social Psychology*, 67: 206–221.

Ross, R. (1989) 'Conflict', in R. Ross and J. Ross (eds), *Small Groups in Organizational Settings.* Englewood Cliffs, NJ: Prentice-Hall, pp. 139–178.

Schweiger, D., Sandberg, W. and Rechner, P. (1989) 'Experiential effects of dialectical inquiry, devil's advocacy, and consensus approaches to strategic decision making', *Academy of Management Journal*, 32: 745–772.

Stasser, G. and Stewart, D.D. (1992) 'The discovery of hidden profiles by decision making groups: Solving a problem versus making a judgment', *Journal of Personality and Social Psychology*, 63: 426–434.

Staw, B.M., Sandelands, L.E. and Dutton, J.E. (1981) 'Threat–rigidity effects in organizational behavior: A multilevel analysis', *Administrative Science Quarterly*, 26: 501–524.

Swann, W.B. (1990) 'To be adored or to be known? The interplay of self–enhancement and self-verification',

in E.T. Higgins and R. M. Sorrentino (eds), *Handbook of Motivation and Cognition.* New York, NY: Guilford, pp. 408–450.

Swann, W.B. (1999) *Resilient Identities: Self, Relationships, and the Construction of Social Reality.* New York: Basic Books.

Swann, W.B., de la Ronde, C. and Hixon, J.G. (1994) 'Authenticity and positivity strivings in marriage and courtship', *Journal of Personality and Social Psychology*, 66: 857–869.

Swann, W.B., Jr., Rentfrow, P.J. and Guinn, J. (2002) 'Self-verification: The search for coherence', in M. Leary and J. Tagney (eds), *Handbook of Self and Identity.* Guilford, New York.

Thomas, K.W. (1992) 'Conflict and negotiations in organizations', in M. Dunnette and L. Hough (eds), *Handbook of Industrial and Organizational Psychology.* Palo Alto, CA: Consulting Psychologists Press, pp. 651–718.

Thompson, L. (1991) 'Family work: Women's sense of fairness', *Journal of Family Issues*, 12: 181–196.

Tjosvold, D. (1991) 'Rights and responsibilities of dissent: Cooperative conflict', *Employee Responsibilities and Rights Journal*, 4: 13–23.

Tsui, A.S. and O'Reilly, C.A. (1989) 'Beyond simple demographic effects: The importance of relational demography in superior-subordinate dyads', *Academy of Management Journal*, 32: 402–423.

Tsui, A.S., Egan, T.D. and O'Reilly, C.A. (1992) 'Being different: Relational demography and organizational attachment', *Administrative Science Quarterly*, 37: 549–577.

Tyler, T.R. (1986) 'Procedural justice in organizations', in R.J. Lewicki, B.H. Sheppard and M.H. Hazerman (eds), *Research on Negotiation in Organizations.* Greenwich, CT: JAI Press, pp. 7–23.

Tyler, T.R. (1999) 'Why people cooperate with organizations: An identity based perspective', *Research in Organizational Behavior*, 21: 201–246.

Zuk, G.H. (1988) 'The confict cycle in families and therapy', *Contemporary Family Therapy*, 10 (3): 45–153.

Zuk, C. and Zuk, G. (1989) 'The conflict cycle in the case of an adolescent in crisis', *Contemporary Family Therapy*, 11: 259–266.

15

A Boundaryless Perspective on Careers

Jeffrey H. Greenhaus, Gerard A. Callanan
and Marco DiRenzo

One of the most significant themes emerging in the literature over the past several decades has been the decline of traditional, organizational careers characterized by upward mobility in a single employment setting (Arthur and Rousseau, 1996). A turbulent economic environment has forced organizations to become more flexible to remain competitive. As a result of ever-increasing market pressures, organizations have become leaner, psychological contracts increasingly transactional, and long-term linear careers within a single organization have been replaced by boundaryless careers.

Obituaries for the 'job,' the 'career,' and 'career jobs' have appeared in the professional (Cappelli, 1999; Hall and Associates, 1996) and popular (Bridges, 1994) literatures. Although some skepticism about the presumed demise of the traditional, organizational career remains (Dany, 2003; Guest and Mackenzie Davey, 1996), there is no doubt that novel career forms are unfolding in the context of these new economic realities.

Scholars at the forefront of this movement have noted that careers are increasingly boundaryless, disconnected from a single employment setting and untethered from traditional organizational career arrangements (Arthur and Rousseau, 1996). Boundaryless careers characterized by frequent interorganizational mobility have been observed in countries other than the US, such as New Zealand (Arthur et al., 1999), the UK (Jackson, 1996), and Japan (Yamashita and Uenoyama, 2006), and the boundaryless career concept has been applied to individuals pursuing global careers (Cappellen and Janssens, 2005; Carr et al., 2005) as 'international itinerants' (Banai and Harry, 2004).

Another trend that predated the concept of the boundaryless career was the assertion that careers are increasingly protean in nature. In his book *Careers in Organizations*, Hall (1976) described the emerging protean career as managed by the individual, rather than the organization, and guided by the search for self-fulfilment. Named after the mythological Proteus, the Greek God who could change his shape at will, the protean career has been characterized as self-directed, flexible, adaptable, versatile, and initiated by the individual to achieve psychological success. In recent years, Hall and his colleagues have elaborated on the protean career (Briscoe and Hall, 2006b), developed scales to assess protean career attitudes (Briscoe et al., 2006), and explored the implications of protean careers for individuals and organizations (Hall and Mirvis, 1995; Hall and Moss, 1998).

Despite the timeliness and popularity of these emerging concepts, several ambiguities remain. First, there is little consensus regarding the meaning and measurement of a boundaryless career. In addition, the similarities and differences between a boundaryless career and a protean career raise important questions about the meaning of each concept. Moreover, despite claims regarding the widespread nature of boundaryless and protean careers, it is not clear whether they have replaced (or will replace) more traditional organizational careers.

In this chapter, we critically examine boundaryless and protean careers and explore the implications of each for research on careers.[1] First, we discuss how economic and organizational changes are thought to be responsible for the emergence of boundaryless and protean careers. We next review the meaning of boundaryless and protean careers, noting the ambiguities in the literature, and similarities and differences between the two concepts. We then propose a 'boundaryless perspective' that integrates the themes in the emerging literature, and review theory and research that bear on the boundaryless perspective. We conclude with an agenda for future research to examine the elements of a boundaryless perspective and to incorporate this perspective into traditional research streams within the careers literature.

THE BOUNDARYLESS CAREER

Impact of the economy

Discussions of the boundaryless career often begin with an analysis of the economic

conditions that have spurred this career pattern. Economic environments that are increasingly technologically-driven, global, highly competitive, and turbulent have changed the way organizations conduct business and manage human resources. Cappelli (1999) argued that the 1981–1982 recession triggered fundamental changes in organizational structures and processes. Pressures to increase shareholder value encouraged organizations to shed poorly-performing or unrelated businesses, and acquire new businesses to enhance profitability. The need for increased flexibility and focus led organizations to outsource less central functions and partner with other organizations to acquire capabilities that no longer had to be developed internally (Cappelli, 1999).

Moreover, because of rapid changes in technology, market demands, and opportunities, organizations became reluctant to establish long-term relationships with employees whose skill sets might quickly become irrelevant, and turned increasingly to the external labor market to acquire new capabilities. The increasing use of temporary or contract employees and other forms of peripheral employees (see the chapter by Gallagher in this volume) also assured that a firm's human resources could be terminated when their skills were no longer consistent with the organization's business strategy (Handy, 1989). Increasing rates of job loss were also due to organizational restructuring activities that flattened organizational hierarchies by reducing the number of managerial layers through empowerment, the use of teams, and advanced technology (Callanan and Greenhaus, 1999; Cappelli, 1999).

All of these changes were driven by market conditions (Cappelli, 1999) that changed organizational career systems and individuals' career opportunities within the organization in a number of ways. The de-layering of organizations provided employees with fewer opportunities for continuous hierarchical advancement within their current organization, a hallmark of a successful organizational career (Arthur and Rousseau, 1996). Moreover, career paths within organizations became more unstructured and unpredictable because of the increasing likelihood that jobs would be eliminated, outsourced, or substantially changed to ensure that organizations could move in different strategic directions if necessary.

The need for flexibility in the deployment of human resources produced changes in organizations' psychological contracts with their employees, reducing their emphasis on a long-term relational focus in favor of a short-term transactional emphasis (Greenhaus, 2002; Rousseau, 1995). As a result of the loss of internal advancement opportunities and the uncertainty of an organization's future human resource needs, employees' feelings of long-term job security diminished (Cappelli, 1999). In organizations that adopted dominant transactional orientations, providing employees with the traditional form of job security was replaced with presenting them with opportunities to remain 'employable' (Fugate, 2006; Waterman et al., 1994), although not necessarily in their current organization, by developing new, more portable skills for continued professional development.

Variations in the definition of a boundaryless career

Despite apparent agreement on the economic conditions triggering boundarylessness, it is challenging to arrive at a single unambiguous definition of a boundaryless career. Table 1 presents a sample of definitions and descriptions of a boundaryless career provided in the literature.

Several points are worth noting. First, the seminal definition provided by Arthur and Rousseau (1996) positioned a boundaryless career as the opposite of an organizational career, and this is also reflected in Bird's (1994) definition and in comparisons of a boundaryless career vs. an organizational or traditional career (Sullivan, 1999). Boundaryless careers are different from organizational careers in that they represent 'independence from, rather than dependence on, traditional organizational career arrangements' (Arthur and Rousseau, 1996: 6). Traditional organizational career arrangements or traditional employment assumptions include upward hierarchical

Table 1 Sampling of definitions and descriptions of a boundaryless career

Author(s)	Definition or description of a boundaryless career
Arthur and Rousseau (1996: 5)	'Put simply, boundaryless careers are the opposite of "organizational careers" – careers conceived to unfold in a single employment setting.'
Arthur and Rousseau (1996: 3)	'A boundaryless career is not a single career form but a range of possible forms that "defies traditional employment assumptions." The orderly employment arrangements they refer to are "vertical coordination in mainly large, stable firms."'
Baker and Aldridge (1996: 135)	'Employees who are able to build work lives characterized by high interemployer mobility, high cumulation of competencies, and high identity' fall into the cell that they characterize as pursuing a boundaryless career.
Bird (1994: 335)	Boundaryless careers are a 'response to a more common view of careers as being bounded: bounded in organizations, bounded in well-defined roles, positions, or jobs.'
Briscoe (2006: 650)	'… the primary association with it (boundaryless career) is that the career plays out across multiple *organizational* boundaries' (italics in original).
DeFillippi and Arthur (1996: 116)	'… career paths may involve sequences of job opportunities that go beyond the boundaries of single employment settings. Such career paths are defined here as boundaryless careers.'
Eby (2001: 344)	'Boundaryless careers transcend specific organizational memberships and refer to sequences of experiences across organizations and jobs.'
Robinson and Miner (1996: 78)	'… career that unfolds unconstrained by clear boundaries around job activities, by fixed sequence of such activities, or by attachment to one organization.'
Van Buren (2003)	'… a career that unfolds over time in multiple employment settings.'
Weick (1996: 40)	'… boundaryless career, which I view as improvised work experiences that rise prospectively into fragments and fall retrospectively into patterns – a mixture of continuity and discontinuity.'

mobility in large, stable organizations with well-defined roles and positions connected to each other in fixed, predictable sequences (Arthur and Rousseau, 1996; Bird, 1994; Miner and Robinson, 1996). Not surprisingly, therefore, many scholars view boundaryless careers as crossing organizational boundaries (Briscoe, 2006; Briscoe and Hall, 2006b; DeFillippi and Arthur, 1994; Eby, 2001; Van Buren, 2003). Indeed, the literature often equates a boundaryless career with extensive inter-organizational mobility (Colakoglu, 2006).

Despite the emphasis on inter-organizational mobility as the hallmark of a boundaryless career, Arthur and Rousseau (1996) cautioned that boundaryless careers do not represent a single career pattern but can take many different forms or 'emphases' that deviate from traditional employment assumptions, the most prominent six of which are careers that:

(1) move across the boundaries of separate employers;
(2) draw validation and marketability outside the present employer;
(3) are sustained by external networks or information;
(4) depart from mobility across traditional organizational career boundaries, such as hierarchical advancement;
(5) involve the rejection of career opportunities for personal or family reasons;
(6) are perceived by employees as boundaryless regardless of constraints on physical mobility.

Only the first of these refers to inter-organizational mobility; the rest depart from other, interrelated traditional organizational assumptions, for example, that employees derive their identity and their perceived mobility opportunities from within the organization, rely on intra-organizational social capital, pursue hierarchical advancement within their organization, base career decisions solely on work-related criteria, and perceive their future as tied to their current organization.

Other scholars have recognized that the boundarylessness of a career is not defined exclusively by extensive inter-organizational mobility. Thus, in addition to inter-employer mobility, Baker and Aldridge's (1996) view of a boundaryless career includes an accumulation of competencies and a personal identity that affects and is affected by employees' work histories. Robinson and Miner (1996) believe that boundaryless careers are not only unconstrained by an attachment to a single organization but are also unconstrained by organizational environments with clear boundaries and sequences around job activities.

The notion of career competencies is closely connected to Arthur and Rousseau's (1996) conception of a boundaryless career. Drawing an analogy to a firm's core competencies, Arthur and colleagues (Arthur et al., 1999; DeFillippi and Arthur, 1994) identified three career competencies – knowing-why, knowing-how, and knowing-whom – that are forms of career capital that individuals can accumulate during their careers. Knowing-why competencies have to do with self-awareness and personal identity (often with one's profession rather than organization) and provide motivation and direction to a career. Knowing-how competencies are the skills and knowledge that individuals accumulate and generally include portable skills and know-how that can be transferred to new employment settings. Knowing-whom competencies refer to networks of relationships (especially extra-organizational networks) and one's reputation within those networks that can provide information, guidance, and social contacts. The career competencies directly relate to Arthur and Rousseau's (1996) second and third meanings of a boundaryless career, deriving validation, marketability, and networks or information from outside the present employer.

If nonlinear, inter-organizational mobility is often an objective marker of a boundaryless career, the process of enactment powers the boundaryless career. Borrowing from Weick (1996; Weick and Berlinger, 1989) and Marshall (1989), Arthur et al. (1999: 41) view enactment as 'the imposition of individual will in situations where choice is possible.' Weick's (1996) description of a boundaryless career as improvised work experiences (Table 1) is based on the assertion that the ambiguity and fluidity of boundaryless organizations provide employees with 'weak situations' (Mischel, 1977) with few explicit guides for action. In large, stable, hierarchical organizations that represent strong situations, there is a sense of clarity regarding desirable outcomes (climbing the organizational ladder) and behaviors (performing well in positions that constitute well-established career paths) necessary to attain the outcomes. Flat organizations with few advancement opportunities, unpredictable career paths, and a willingness to substantially change, eliminate, or outsource jobs no longer provide clear guides for effective behavior. The absence of explicit organizationally-provided guidelines for action in weak situations requires employees to develop internal guides, which provide greater latitude for their personal dispositions to determine their behavior.

In enacting careers, individuals improvise, exerting their will spontaneously in response to changing situations and the prospect of new opportunities. This adaptability enables career actors to learn and accumulate knowledge that permits ongoing growth and development. Moreover, individuals come to understand their careers and their evolving identity only after the fact through post-decisional sense making (Arthur et al., 1999). Enactment also displays the qualities of agency and communion. Whereas agency involves assertive independence and control over the environment, communion represents openness to (and acceptance of) change, living in the present, and an interdependence with other people (Arthur et al, 1999; Marshall, 1989). Weick (1996) argues that the enactment of boundaryless careers requires both agency and communion.

Ambiguities in the meaning of a boundaryless career

In sum, boundaryless careers are seen as a counterpoint to traditional organizational careers that assume continuous, linear mobility within a single employment setting in which an employee's identity, social capital, and future career possibilities are anchored to the current organization. Despite the apparent straightforwardness of this conception, the literature contains a number of ambiguities regarding the meaning of a boundaryless career.

First, because Arthur and Rousseau (1996) provided six meanings or emphases of a boundaryless career, one might ask whether any one of these emphases in and of itself constitutes a boundaryless career or whether clusters of emphases are necessary to consider a career to be boundaryless. For example, individuals might reject a promotion because of the demands of a partner's career even though they have been pursuing hierarchical advancement in a single organization for many years. Is the career boundaryless (rejection of career opportunities for family reasons) or organizational (hierarchical advancement within a single employment setting)? The specification of multiple criteria of a boundaryless career, such as inter-organizational mobility, the accumulation of competencies and personal identity (Baker and Aldridge, 1996) or unclear boundaries and sequences around job activities (Robinson and Miner, 1996) implies that one 'emphasis' may not be sufficient to consider a career boundaryless. Although it is possible that the interconnections among the emphases make it unusual for an individual to pursue a career with only one emphasis, the intercorrelations among the emphases or meanings of a boundaryless career have not been established empirically.

Relatedly, it is unclear whether career boundarylessness is a categorical or a continuous variable. Although much of the literature implies the former, Briscoe and Hall (2006a) suggest that career boundarylessness is a matter of degree and Sullivan and Arthur (2006) propose a continuum in which boundarylessness is highest when physical mobility and psychological mobility (the perception of the capacity to make transitions) are extensive, lowest when physical and psychological mobility are restricted, and intermediate when one form of mobility is high and the other is low. However, the limited empirical research conducted on boundaryless careers has not assessed boundarylessness as a continuous variable. One notable exception is Colakoglu's (2006) assessment of boundarylessness as the extent to which inter-organizational moves are accompanied by other transitions (e.g., change in occupation, move from full-time to part-time work) that depart from traditional organizational career arrangements.

A related unresolved issue is whether inter-organizational mobility is a necessary condition for the pursuit of a boundaryless career. Colakoglu (2006) included only inter-organizational moves in her measure of boundarylessness. This decision is understandable in light of the number of definitions in Table 1, indicating that boundaryless careers move across organizational boundaries. Although researchers have cautioned against viewing inter-organizational mobility as the defining characteristic of boundaryless careers (Briscoe and Hall, 2006b; Sullivan and Arthur, 2006), the literature generally equates boundarylessness with movement between firms.

The persistent tendency to equate boundarylessness with inter-organizational mobility raises a broader question of whether *any* mobility is required to consider a career to be boundaryless. Sullivan and Arthur (2006) argue that psychological mobility is as important a component of a boundaryless career as actual physical mobility, a view that is consistent with Arthur and Rousseau's sixth meaning of a boundaryless career, a perception of boundarylessness even in the absence of actual mobility. So we are left to wonder whether individuals who feel boundaryless are truly boundaryless in their career. Moreover, it is not clear whether Sullivan and Arthur's concept of psychological mobility refers only to the perceived capacity to cross physical boundaries or whether it refers more broadly to the perceived capacity to cross psychological boundaries such as incorporating a family situation into a career decision.

These ambiguities in the meaning of boundarylessness do not threaten to invalidate the notion of a boundaryless career. However, they do require answers to achieve agreement on an empirical assessment of boundarylessness that can be used in research on boundaryless careers.

THE PROTEAN CAREER

As noted earlier, Hall (1976) introduced the concept of the protean career more than 30 years ago. He originally defined a protean career as

> ...a process which the person, not the organization, is managing. It consists of all the person's varied experiences in education, training, work in several organizations, changes in occupational field, etc. The protean career is *not* what happens to the person in any one organization (Hall, 1976: 201, italics in original).

There are thought to be two dimensions or elements of a protean career (Briscoe and Hall, 2006b). First, a protean career is proactively *self-directed*. Individuals pursuing a protean career feel responsible for managing their career and take the initiative in exploring career options and making career decisions. Second, it is *values-driven* in that individuals make career decisions to meet their personally meaningful values and goals, resulting in feelings of psychological success, in contrast to striving to achieve values and goals imposed upon them by organizations and society. Moreover, the personal values and goals that protean careerists attempt to achieve are relevant to the 'whole life space' (Briscoe and Hall, 2006b) or 'life's work' (Mirvis and Hall, 1996) rather than focused solely on employment. The results of Briscoe et al.'s (2006) factor analysis of their 'Protean Attitude Scale' are consistent with these two dimensions, and Briscoe and Hall (2006b) further combine levels of the dimensions to create four career categories from a protean perspective, ranging from dependent (low on values-driven and self-directedness) to protean (high on values-driven and self-directedness).

Although the self-directed dimension is straightforward, the values-driven dimension has been interpreted in different ways. The essence of a protean career is that the individual determines the values and goals that are personally meaningful. Nevertheless, it is sometimes assumed that individuals pursuing a protean career hold different values or goals (freedom, growth, life balance) than individuals pursuing an organizational career (Hall, 1976; Mirvis and Hall, 1996). We believe that it is the individual determination of meaningful values and goals rather than the content of the values and goals that best captures the notion of the values-driven dimension of a protean career. Consistent with this notion, Briscoe (2006: 650) has observed that '... strictly speaking, a person could independently (in a protean fashion) select traditional career contexts and value some of the symbols of success they portend, including income and advancement.'

In addition to these two dimensions, adaptability and flexibility have long been associated with a protean career (Hall, 1976; 1996) reflecting its namesake, Proteus, who could change shape at will. In fact, Briscoe and Hall (2006b) incorporate adaptability regarding performance and learning demands into their conception of self-directed. Because adaptability and flexibility seem central to the pursuit of a protean career, it makes sense to consider them an enabler and also, as Inkson (2006) suggests, a by-product of a protean career rather than as a characteristic of a protean career. Individuals need to be (or they become) adaptable in managing their careers proactively to attain personally meaningful values and goals, especially in times of personal or organizational change.

A COMPARISON OF THE BOUNDARYLESS CAREER AND THE PROTEAN CAREER

Although boundaryless and protean careers are occasionally linked together (Dowd and Kaplan, 2005; Hall et al., 1997), it is more likely that they are 'overlapping but distinct' concepts (Briscoe and Hall, 2006b; Inkson, 2006). Nevertheless, the distinctions between

the two concepts are somewhat elusive and depend upon how widely one defines a boundaryless career. Symptomatic of the confusion is that both the boundaryless career (Arthur and Rousseau, 1996) and the protean career (Hall, 2002; Hall and Mirvis, 1995; Hall and Moss, 1998) have been contrasted to a traditional organizational career. If both of these career forms are thought to be the opposite of the organizational career, how are they different from one another?

Briscoe and Hall (2006b) suggested that a protean career is best viewed as an orientation, attitude, or approach to a career rather than an actual structure of a career. Several studies show that protean career attitudes are *not* strongly related to extensive inter-organizational mobility preferences and behaviors (Briscoe and DeMuth, 2003; Briscoe et al., 2006). Consistent with this, Briscoe and Hall (2006b) have proposed a categorization of career types based upon different levels of protean (self-directed and values-driven) and boundaryless (physical and psychological mobility) characteristics.

In a similar vein, Inkson (2006) observed that a protean career reflects a psychological career orientation that produces specific career behaviors, whereas a boundaryless career generally involves boundary-crossing behaviors that are produced by an 'internal' focus on the world. The distinction between attitude or orientation and behavior makes sense as long as boundaryless careers are defined primarily in terms of physical boundary-crossing. However, the distinction seems hazier when boundaryless careers are viewed as encompassing psychological mobility (Sullivan and Arthur, 2006) or *all* career phenomena that defy traditional organizational career arrangements (Arthur and Rousseau, 1996).

HOW PREVALENT ARE BOUNDARYLESS AND PROTEAN CAREERS?

The multiple meanings of a boundaryless career make it difficult to determine its prevalence. Understandably, the evidence regarding the emergence of boundaryless careers comes primarily from an examination of career mobility patterns. For example, 63 of the 75 participants in Arthur et al.'s (1999) study either changed employers at least once or became self-employed over a 10-year period, prompting Arthur and colleagues to conclude that 84 per cent of their sample engaged in a boundaryless career.

Although a one-time change of employer in 10 years seems to be a rather lenient threshold for a boundaryless career, Arthur et al. (1999) also observed that their respondents worked for an average of nearly three employers during the 10-year period. Moreover, more than 62 per cent of the inter-organizational moves and 20 per cent of the intra-organizational moves did not involve mobility to a higher-level position, the objective signal of traditional career advancement. In addition, moves between companies were often accompanied by changes in industry (35 per cent) or occupation (34 per cent). At the very least, these findings suggest that many careers do not follow a trajectory of continuous upward mobility in a single organization over time.

Whether the mobility reported by Arthur et al. (1999) signals the death of a traditional organizational career is a matter of debate. Reitman and Schneer (2003) found that one-third of the American MBAs in their sample followed what they called the 'promised path' of continuous full-time employment in one organization over a 13-year period. In addition, scholars in France (Dany, 2003) and Nigeria (Ituma and Simpson, 2006) conclude that organizational careers are still alive in these countries, and Pringle and Mallon (2003) have questioned the generalizability of the individual-oriented boundaryless career perspective beyond industrialized western cultures.

What does seem clear is that long-tenure associations with employers have declined, even for managers who have traditionally been most strongly protected from job loss. The massive downsizings and job loss over the past 25 years have been extensively documented. In his thorough and compelling analysis of the fate of career jobs, Cappelli (1999) examined changes over time in employee tenure as well as employers' human resource policies, and concluded that job security is not only declining but is also not a product of a poor economy. Instead, diminished job security is a function of a market-based employment relationship in which employers increasingly rely on the external labor market to cope with the need to remain competitive in times of rapid change. This produces a churning of jobs (Cappelli, 2006) – hiring new employees with needed skills and letting go current employees who do not possess these skills – that inevitably increases inter-organizational mobility.

Although these mobility patterns are consistent with the emergence of boundaryless careers, boundaryless and protean careers are often thought to represent far more than physical mobility (Briscoe and Hall, 2006b; Sullivan and Arthur, 2006). Do contemporary employees draw their identity primarily from their profession rather than their employer? Do they regularly extend their network of relationships outside the boundary of their employer? Are they self-directed and values-driven toward the pursuit of psychological success? And do they eschew planning for a more improvisational enactment of their careers? Extensive data are not available to determine the prevalence of these facets of boundaryless and protean careers.

Although we are not willing to pronounce the death of the organizational career or its universal replacement by the boundaryless or protean career, it is likely that a continuous, upwardly mobile linear career within a single employer is not a dominant career pattern. Employees now pursue an increasingly wide range of career patterns, many of which have boundaryless or protean elements. Therefore, it is important to understand how these elements have been – and could be – incorporated into research on careers. To help in this task, we turn to a discussion of a boundaryless perspective.

A BOUNDARYLESS PERSPECTIVE

Because of the ambiguities and unresolved issues in the literature, it is difficult to derive a consensual definition of a boundaryless career and to determine where boundarylessness ends and protean begins. Instead, we propose a boundaryless perspective (Figure 1) that encompasses the major themes that run through the protean career and boundaryless career literatures. In this section, we discuss the boundaryless perspective and examine the literature that bears on each component of this perspective.

Figure 1 shows three components of a boundaryless perspective (represented by variables enclosed in boxes with thick borders). We view the variables enclosed in boxes with dashed borders as antecedents or outcomes of the variables captured by a boundaryless perspective. One component of a boundaryless perspective includes mobility patterns that depart from traditional organizational career arrangements. Most of the mobility patterns reflect the first and fourth meanings of a boundaryless career specified by Arthur and Rousseau (1996). Collectively, they represent intra-organizational and inter-organizational mobility that diverges from a continuous, linear career pattern. Much of the literature on boundaryless careers speaks to these 'nontraditional' forms of boundary crossing, especially inter-organizational mobility.

One specific form of boundary crossing that is not generally discussed in the context of career mobility or a boundaryless career is job crafting, 'the actions employees take to shape, mold, and redefine their jobs' (Wrzesniewski and Dutton, 2001: 180). Job crafting involves modifying (1) the task boundaries of a job, either physically by changing the nature or number of job activities or cognitively by changing the way one perceives the job and/or modifying (2) the relational boundaries, thereby determining the people with whom one interacts on the job.

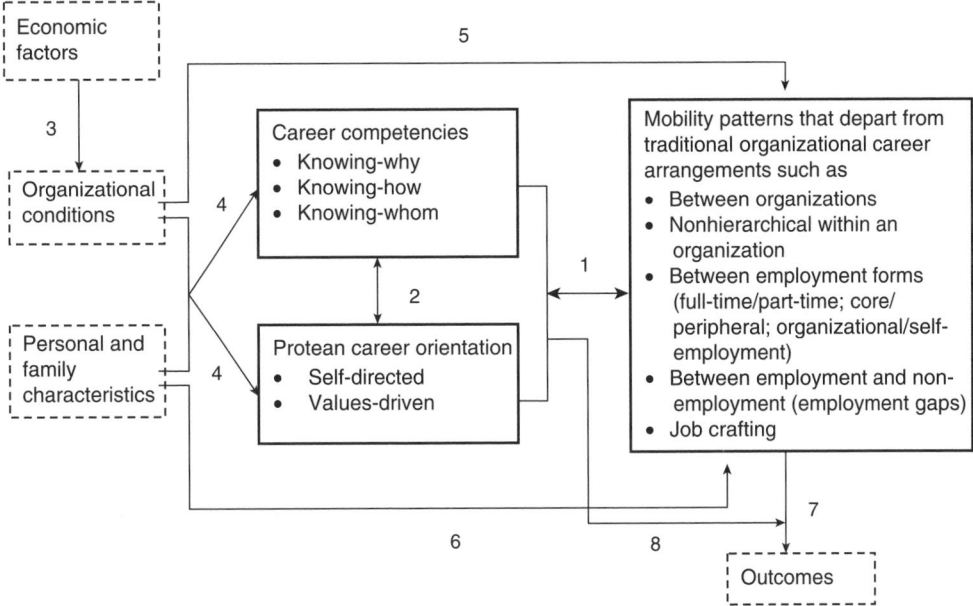

Figure 1   A boundaryless perspective on careers.
Note: The variables enclosed in boxes with thick borders are the three elements of a boundaryless perspective, and the variables enclosed in boxes with dashed borders are antecedents or outcomes of the variables captured by a boundaryless perspective.

Although the 'mobility' inherent in job crafting is within- rather than between-jobs or organizations, it is a strategy that seems increasingly relevant in situations where intra-organizational or inter-organizational mobility opportunities are not present or not desired. Moreover, job crafting is highly consistent with both dimensions of a protean career orientation; self-direction because of the proactive nature of job crafting and values-driven because job crafting can enable an individual to fashion a job to be more consistent with personally meaningful values and goals. For these reasons, we incorporate job crafting as another type of nontraditional boundary crossing.

The second component of a boundaryless perspective includes the three career competencies proposed by Arthur and colleagues (Arthur and Rousseau, 1996; Arthur et al., 1999; DeFillippi and Arthur, 1994). The career competencies necessitate boundary crossing in that they require looking *outside the organization* for identity (knowing-why), marketability (knowing-how), and the establishment of networks of information and influence (knowing-whom). This boundary crossing can be psychological (e.g., identifying primarily with a profession rather than an organization) or physical (e.g., establishing networks of relationships outside the organization) but does not represent mobility per se. The third component of a boundaryless perspective contains the two dimensions of a protean career orientation identified by Hall and colleagues (Briscoe and Hall, 2006b; Briscoe et al., 2006).

Figure 1 indicates several interconnections among the three components of a boundaryless perspective. Path 1 proposes that the career competencies and a protean career orientation influence – and are influenced by – nontraditional mobility patterns. DeFillippi and Arthur (1994) suggested that the acquisition of the career competencies permits an individual to realize or pursue a boundaryless career, presumably because the competencies enable individuals to identify and take advantage of boundary crossing opportunities. Moreover, because career competencies

are believed to accumulate throughout an individual's career (DeFillippi and Arthur, 1994), the bidirectional nature of path 1 signifies that extensive boundary crossing mobility experiences can further enhance one's career competencies. To our knowledge only Arthur et al. (1999) have explored connections between career competencies and nontraditional mobility patterns in their qualitative study.

The relationship between a protean career orientation and nontraditional mobility patterns has not been extensively studied or supported. Briscoe et al. (2006) found no substantial relationships between either element of a protean career orientation and preferences for inter-organizational mobility or actual mobility. Of course there are other forms of nontraditional boundary crossing besides changing employers. Briscoe et al.'s (2006) finding that self-directed and values-driven individuals are comfortable interacting with others outside of their department or organization reflects a preference for a different type of boundary crossing. Nevertheless, more research is needed to determine whether and under what conditions a protean career orientation is associated with a variety of nontraditional career mobility patterns.

Path 2 represents bidirectional interdependencies between the career competencies and a protean career orientation. For example, a strong values-driven approach to careers should encourage an individual to engage in knowing-why activities (career exploration) which in turn should help the individual clarify the priorities of different life values. Similarly, self-directed individuals are likely to initiate exploratory and strategic activities that enable them to acquire the career competencies. However, we are not aware of any research that has examined the relationships between these two concepts.

We should also comment on the other variables and linkages represented in Figure 1. As mentioned earlier, the literature generally attributes the emergence of boundaryless careers to changes in the economy (highly competitive, global, advanced technology) that have produced significant alterations in organizational practices, such as acquisitions, reorganizations, reductions in force, and the use of temporary employees all within the context of an increasingly transactional psychological contract with employees (path 3).

These organizational conditions can contribute to the development of the three career competencies and the adoption of a protean career orientation (path 4). That is, faced with diminishing and/or unpredictable career opportunities within their organization, employees see the virtue of looking outside the organization for identity, marketability, and social capital, and appreciate the importance of meeting their significant life values in a self-directed manner. We are not aware of studies examining the relationships of organizational conditions with career competencies or a protean career orientation.

Path 4 in Figure 1 also proposes that personal and family characteristics can trigger the acquisition of career competencies and the adoption of a protean orientation. Two personality characteristics – proactivity and openness to experience – have been positively related to the self-directed and values-driven elements of a protean career orientation (Briscoe et al., 2006) and perceived external marketability (Eby et al., 2003). Moreover, other personal characteristics (age, career authenticity, and a mastery learning orientation) are positively related to both dimensions of a protean career orientation (Briscoe et al., 2006). In light of the growing representation of dual-earner couples and single parents in the workforce, it is also plausible that attitudes toward family role participation, gender role attitudes, parental responsibilities, stage of family development, and spouses' commitment to their careers can affect protean career orientations and individuals' motivation to acquire the three career competencies.

Figure 1 indicates that organizational conditions and personal/family characteristics can have effects on nontraditional mobility patterns that do not operate through the career competencies or a protean career orientation (paths 5 and 6). Carr et al. (2005) and

Cappellen and Janssens (2005) proposed models to predict the pursuit of a boundaryless global career. Although not identical, both models included individual (e.g., career competencies) and environmental (political, cultural, organizational) predictors of the decision to pursue a global career path.

Mallon (1998) studied nontraditional mobility of another type: movement from a management position in the UK public sector to a 'portfolio' career of self-employment. She concluded that shifts toward a more boundaryless career involving self-employment were due to a combination of push factors (dislike of current employer, termination) and pull factors (opportunity to be more creative, to achieve balance, to attain financial security) suggesting that specific circumstances rather than general predispositions produced migration from an organizational career to a portfolio career. One important push factor is a low level of organizational commitment, especially affective and continuance commitment (Kondratuk et al., 2004).

Path 7 in Figure 1 shows a connection between nontraditional mobility patterns and outcomes. Although boundaryless and protean careers generally have positive implications, many scholars acknowledge the potential negative consequences of pursuing these nontraditional career patterns (Eby, 2001; Hall, 1996; Hall and Mirvis, 1995; Hirsch and Shanley, 1996; Mirvis and Hall, 1996; Pringle and Mallon, 2003; Van Buren, 2003). Colakoglu (2006) invoked two perspectives – enactment and stress – to explain the positive and negative consequences respectively.

An enactment perspective (Weick, 1996; Weick and Berlinger, 1989) emphasizes the positive consequences of boundaryless careers. As noted earlier, weak situations found in many contemporary organizations provide opportunities for individuals to exercise individual choice relatively unfettered by the restrictions found in highly structured and predictable organizations. Through improvisation, facilitated by a combination of agency and communion, boundaryless careers can provide opportunities for learning and growth, although not without conflicts and challenges (Weick, 1996). Similarly, a self-directed, values-driven protean career orientation enables individuals to pursue a 'path with a heart' (Hall, 1996) to achieve feelings of psychological success.

A stress perspective acknowledges the potential risks of pursuing a boundaryless or protean career (Colakoglu, 2006). Economic turbulence and transactional employment relationships produce uncertainty and ambiguity with subsequent feelings of insecurity. Moreover, independence from traditional, organizational career arrangements requires individuals to manage their own careers, change employers, periodically upgrade or broaden skills, adjust expectations regarding hierarchical mobility, shift identities away from a single employer, and manage increasingly fluid boundaries between work and home (Mirvis and Hall, 1996), all of which can produce extensive stress.

Do nontraditional career mobility patterns enhance or diminish well-being? Extensive inter-organizational mobility has been found to result in lower earnings (Mao, 2004; Valcour and Tolbert, 2003), although one can argue that salary attainment is not the most suitable indicator of success or well-being in a boundaryless career. The finding that mobility across employers is unrelated to subjective career success (Valcour and Tolbert, 2003) is more damaging to the notion that boundaryless careers inevitably promote individual well-being. Because crossing organizational boundaries does not fully capture a boundaryless career, Colakoglu (2006) explored the impact of different facets of boundarylessness on well-being. Her findings reflect the complexity of the consequences of boundary crossing on individual outcomes. For example, whereas perceived career autonomy was enhanced by frequent inter-organizational moves and by a shift to self-employment, it was diminished by changes in occupation as well as by lateral and downward mobility across organizations. Moreover, career insecurity decreased with changes in geographical location, self-employment, and long career interruptions, but increased with changes in occupation and large numbers of career interruptions.

It is probably more appropriate to ask when – rather than whether – a boundaryless career promotes individual well-being (path 8 in Figure 1). Most of the factors thought to facilitate the successful pursuit of a boundaryless career are personal characteristics, orientations, and behaviors that enable individuals to cope with the ambiguities and changes inherent in such careers. Baker and Aldridge (1996) suggest that individuals who experience boundarylessness early in their career, who are in a relationship where both partners have well-paying jobs, and whose identity is rooted in work rather than other life roles will benefit most from a boundaryless career. Hall and colleagues (Briscoe, 2006; Hall and Mirvis, 1995; Mirvis and Hall, 1996) suggest that identity, adaptability, and a protean orientation equip individuals to succeed in a boundaryless career, and Lichtenstein and Mendenhall (2002) emphasize the importance of 'response-ability,' that is responsiveness to changing circumstances, in managing nonlinear careers. Scholars have also identified social capital (Forret and Sullivan, 2002; Jackson, 1996; Raider and Burt, 1996), continuous learning (Hall and Mirvis, 1995; Hall and Moss, 1998), experimentation and failure (Saxenian, 1996), and perseverance and resilience (Jackson, 1996) as important ingredients of a successful boundaryless career.

In one of the few studies of boundaryless variables, Eby et al. (2003) found that all three career competencies were positively related to perceived internal and external marketability and subjective career success. External marketability was most strongly associated with the knowing-how competency, whereas subjective career success and internal marketability were most strongly related to the knowing-why competency. However, because Eby et al. (2003) did not assess the boundarylessness of individual careers, it cannot be determined whether the usefulness of the career competencies is limited to boundaryless situations. Similarly, Colakoglu (2006) found that individuals' career competencies and protean career orientations were generally associated with positive outcomes (e.g., career autonomy, subjective career success) *regardless* of the boundarylessness of their careers.

AN AGENDA FOR FUTURE RESEARCH

Whether or not boundaryless and protean careers become the norm, they are likely to represent increasingly significant career patterns and orientations in contemporary society. Therefore, understanding their nature is essential for the advancement of career theory and for the well-being of individuals and organizations. We believe that two types of research can contribute to our understanding of boundaryless and protean careers.

First, because the literature regarding the variables in Figure 1 has been primarily conceptual, the need for more empirical research on the components of the boundaryless perspective, including their antecedents and outcomes, is apparent. Second, because of the increasing salience of boundaryless and protean careers, research on traditional career-related topics should benefit from incorporating a boundaryless perspective into their goals and methodologies. We next propose future research on a boundaryless perspective and then discuss the incorporation of this perspective into research on mentoring, a career-related topic that has been extensively researched for the past 25 years.

Research on a boundaryless perspective

The meaning of boundarylessness
The most immediate need is to clarify the meaning and measurement of boundarylessness. Researchers need to address and agree on whether boundarylessness is a dichotomous or continuous variable, inter-organizational mobility is an essential ingredient, and the specific types of nontraditional mobility patterns that should comprise the concept and measure of boundarylessness.

Like Briscoe and Hall (2006b) and Sullivan and Arthur (2006), we believe that boundarylessness is a continuous variable. However, we prefer to view boundarylessness in terms of physical mobility patterns like those shown in Figure 1. Although psychological mobility – the perceived capacity to make changes (Sullivan and Arthur, 2006) – is central to a boundaryless perspective, we believe that it is captured best by personal characteristics (e.g., proactivity) and a protean career orientation (self-directedness) that produce boundary crossing behavior rather than as boundarylessness per se. Moreover, despite the widespread characterization of boundaryless careers as involving extensive inter-organizational mobility, we believe that *any* form of mobility that departs from traditional career assumptions (Arthur and Rousseau, 1996) can represent boundaryless or boundary crossing (Inkson, 2006) behavior.

Therefore, one of the first tasks is to identify various forms of nontraditional career mobility, recognizing that the examples given in Figure 1 are probably not exhaustive. The development of a measure of boundarylessness requires the assessment of the frequency of each type of nontraditional mobility as revealed through respondents' job histories (Colakoglu, 2006). This would enable researchers to examine the impact of boundarylessness as an accumulation of different types of nontraditional mobility as well as the effects of different forms of non-traditional mobility (e.g., inter-organizational mobility versus nonhierarchical intra-organizational mobility). There are currently rich and valuable streams of research on specific nontraditional mobility patterns such as employment gaps (Schneer and Reitman, 1990, 1997), reduced work loads (MacDermid et al., 2001), and contingent employment (Smith and Neuwirth, 2006) that should continue. Nevertheless, it would also be useful to assess the presence of these different mobility patterns in the same study so that their comparative effects on outcomes can be assessed.

The specification of outcomes

It is also essential to understand the potential consequences of boundaryless mobility patterns. Perhaps the most relevant outcome is career success, a prominent variable in the careers and organizational behavior literatures. We agree with Arthur et al.'s (2005: 179) definition of career success as 'the accomplishment of desirable work-related outcomes at any point in a person's work experiences over time.' The literature frequently distinguishes objective and subjective career success (Seibert, 2006). Objective career success is typically reflected by the accomplishment of objectively-observable outcomes such as organizational level, promotion rates, and compensation. Objective career success is represented by achievements that reflect 'shared social understanding' (Arthur et al., 2005) within organizations or in society. Subjective career success is derived from a 'distinctive individual understanding' (Arthur et al., 2005) of those things that matter to a particular person. Subjective career success is an individual's perception or evaluation of his or her achievement of personally-desirable work outcomes.

We believe that the ultimate criterion for the success of a boundaryless career (or any career for that matter) is subjective career success: To gauge the success of a boundaryless career through achievements in salary or rank is inconsistent with the emphasis on the subjective career that runs through the boundaryless and protean career literature. Moreover, society may no longer hold a shared understanding that advancement or money are reflections of career success, as other manifestations of success (e.g., balance, happiness) emerge in social consciousness.

This is not to suggest that money, advancement, and power are unimportant. However, because accomplishments on these dimensions will undoubtedly be incorporated into a subjective assessment of success by those individuals who value these outcomes, we question the place of traditional objective indicators in research programs designed to understand the meaning of a career from an individual's perspective. A detailed criticism of existing measures of subjective career success or career satisfaction (Arthur et al., 2005) is beyond the scope of this chapter. Nevertheless, measures of subjective career success should be constructed in a way that enables respondents to invoke idiosyncratic attributes (interesting work, challenge, life balance) in judging success, rather than relying on researcher-provided attributes that may not capture criteria that are most important to the individual (Greenhaus, 2002).

Moreover, a more complete understanding of the consequences of boundaryless careers requires the specification of factors that mediate the effect of boundarylessness on career success. Colakoglu (2006) proposed that boundarylessness has proximal effects on career autonomy and career insecurity which in turn affect feelings of subjective career success. Other factors that might explain the effect of boundarylessness on career success include perceived marketability (Eby et al., 2003), life balance (Colakoglu, 2006), and learning and growth (Weick, 1996).

Future research should also examine whether a protean career orientation and the acquisition of career competencies not only promote nontraditional career mobility patterns but also are affected by nontraditional mobility, as suggested by the bidirectional path 1 in Figure 1. This research would require a longitudinal design, a prospective or retrospective qualitative approach (Arthur et al., 1999), or a critical incident methodology (Powell and Greenhaus, 2006) in which respondents report on the consequences of a particular nontraditional career move.

A contingency approach

We noted earlier that the impact of nontraditional career mobility on career success and other outcomes is probably dependent on a variety of factors. The most theoretically-grounded variables for examination are a protean career orientation and the acquisition of the three career competencies. Colakoglu (2006) made a strong case for why a protean orientation and the career competencies should strengthen the positive effect of boundarylessness on feelings of career autonomy and weaken the negative effect of bound-arylessness on feelings of career insecurity, although her findings did not provide strong support for her predictions. It is possible that a range of personal, organizational, and cultural factors determine the consequences of boundarylessness, either directly or indirectly through their impact on a protean orientation or the career competencies.

Because boundarylessness takes different forms, it may be fruitless to expect a simple relationship between boundaryless-ness and career outcomes. Extensive inter-organizational mobility is likely to have different consequences than nonhierarchical intra-organizational mobility, an employment gap, job crafting, a reduced workload, or a contingent work arrangement. Moreover, the relationships between different forms of nontraditional mobility and outcomes may be moderated by different variables; the factors that determine the success of temporary contract employees may not be the same as the factors that determine the success of employees who make extensive lateral or downward moves as a permanent employee in an organization. Therefore, we encourage researchers to test theoretically-grounded pre-dictions regarding the facilitators of different types of nontraditional career mobility.

Because a protean career orientation and career competencies are likely to influ-ence boundarylessness and its consequences, future research should examine the factors that promote these orientations and skills. Hall (2004) questioned whether a protean orientation is a trait or a state and suggested that predispositions and experiences are both important. It is plausible that nontraditional mobility experiences can enhance or rein-force a protean orientation, just as Arthur et al. (1999) have argued that the career competencies constitute career capital that is accumulated as a result of prior career experiences. Nevertheless, it is likely that individual predispositions also play a role as suggested by the positive relationships of proactive personality, openness to experience, and a mastery learning goal orientation with the self-directed and values-driven

components of a protean orientation (Briscoe et al., 2006). Future research should explore a variety of personal characteristics, family-related variables, and organizational factors as antecedents to the development of a protean career orientation and the acquisition of the career competencies.

Gender and boundarylessness

It has been suggested that women are more likely than men to prefer self-directed and self-designed careers (Sullivan et al.,1998) and have rejected linear careers in favor of self-crafted careers for decades (Mainiero and Sullivan, 2005). However, research findings have been inconsistent. Briscoe et al. (2006) found nonsignificant relationships between gender and self-directed and values-driven elements of a protean career orientation; Reitman and Schneer (2003) found that women were *less* likely than men to pursue a protean path (full-time employment across multiple employers). On the other hand, Valcour and Tolbert (2003) found that women experience more inter-organizational mobility than men.

Several studies may explain the com-plex relationship between gender and career boundarylessness. First, it is possible that gender moderates the factors that drive the pursuit of nontraditional mobility patterns. Valcour and Tolbert (2003) found that number of children was positively related to inter-organizational mobility for women but not for men. Moreover, Reitman and Schneer (2003) observed that whereas women on a protean career path were as likely as men on a protean path to be married and have children, women on an organizational path were less likely than men on an organizational path to be married and have children. Together these findings suggest that women – but not men – may pursue inter-organizational mobility because it enables them to balance work and family responsibilities more effectively. Consistent with this, Mainiero and Sullivan (2005) found that women were more likely than men to make career transitions for family reasons and to achieve a more satisfying balance between work and family. Like Reitman and Schneer (2003), they also observed that women were more likely than men to experience employment breaks or interruptions.

These studies also suggest that the relationship between gender and boundarylessness depends on the type of nontraditional mobility examined. As already noted, movement between organizations does not fully capture the range of boundaryless mobility patterns, and women may be more likely than men to pursue some patterns and not others. Future research might also examine Sullivan and Arthur's (2006) proposition that opportunities for physical mobility are more prevalent for men and opportunities for psychological mobility are more prevalent for women.

Research should also examine whether women benefit more from a boundaryless career than men because women possess relational or communal qualities thought to be important in boundaryless careers (Sullivan, 1999). Reitman and Schneer (2003) examined the income and advancement of men and women on protean paths and organizational paths. They showed that although women do not benefit more than men from a protean path, they do benefit more from a protean path than an organizational path. Clearly, more research is needed to understand whether – and under what conditions – men and women experience different outcomes from pursuing nontraditional career patterns.

The impact of the individual on the environment

A basic premise of the boundaryless career movement is that individuals accumulating career capital as they move across organizations have a substantial impact on employers, industries, and society (Arthur, 1994; Arthur et al., 1999). The literature suggests that extensive inter-organizational mobility among employees can affect an organization's skills and knowledge (Saxenian, 1996), decision making (Becker and Haunschild, 2003), choice of strategy (Gunz and Jalland, 1996), and delivery of human resource practices (Dany et al., 2003; Yamashita and Uenoyama (2006). Moreover, Carr et al. (2005) illustrate how migrant global careers can affect talent

flows across countries that have implications for national human resource policies. More research is required to understand the full impact of individual careers on the larger social environment.

The role of enactment in boundaryless careers

As discussed earlier, the improvised enactment of choice and will in weak situations is central to the original concept of a boundaryless career (Arthur et al., 1999; Weick, 1996). Spontaneous improvisation to changing circumstances with understanding resulting from post-decisional sensemaking contrasts sharply with future-oriented career planning, whose advantages Arthur et al. (1999: 47) consider 'overstated.' We consider the concept of enactment to be the most fascinating and yet the most under-researched element of boundaryless careers.

Arthur et al. (1999) suggest that future-oriented career goal setting is neither characteristic of boundaryless careers nor particularly useful for individuals pursuing these careers. However, much of the empirical research regarding nontraditional mobility patterns, psychological attitudes (such as the protean career orientation), or career competencies neither assumes nor tests the fundamental role of enactment in boundaryless careers. Future research should devote more attention to the *process* by which boundaryless careers evolve to understand the roles of strong versus weak situations, improvisation, sensemaking, goal setting, agency, and communion in these careers.

Incorporating a boundaryless perspective into careers research: the case of mentoring

The purpose of this section is to examine the extent to which a boundaryless perspective has been incorporated into a mainstream career-related topic, and to suggest ways in which this perspective can guide future research. To provide depth to our discussion, we chose to illustrate the implications of a boundaryless perspective for only one career-oriented research area, and we selected mentoring for several reasons.

First, mentoring, a popular research topic in the careers literature, has positive effects on protégés' work outcomes (Allen et al., 2004; Noe et al., 2002; Wanberg et al., 2003). Second, research on the mentoring process has usually assumed the dominance of a linear organizational career, reflected by the traditional view that a mentor is located in the same organization as the protégé and by the selection of salary and advancement (intra-organizational indicators) as central dependent variables. Third, the mentoring literature now recognizes the impact of increasingly boundaryless careers on the mentoring process (de Janasz et al., 2003; Higgins and Kram, 2001; Higgins and Thomas, 2001; Whiting and de Janasz, 2004).

Therefore, it is instructive to examine how a boundaryless career perspective has been incorporated and can be further incorporated into mentoring research. The emerging mentoring literature is increasingly compatible with a boundaryless perspective in three respects:

(1) the recognition that a mentor can reside outside a protégé's organization;
(2) the incorporation of a wide array of outcomes of the mentoring process; and
(3) the adoption of a relational perspective that emphasizes growth, learning, and flourishing in mentor-protégé relationships.

Extra-organizational mentoring

The mentoring literature has revitalized Kram's (1985) early assertion that protégés can benefit from establishing a constellation of developmental relationships rather than a single mentoring relationship (Baugh and Fagenson-Eland, 2005; Eby, 1997; Higgins and Kram, 2001; Higgins and Thomas, 2001; de Janasz et al., 2003; Ragins and Verbos, 2007). Consistent with this is the discussion of the advantages and limitations of establishing a relationship with a mentor who resides outside a protégé's organization.

Individuals may seek an extra-organizational or external mentor for several reasons. First, organizational downsizings have reduced the pool of available middle- and upper-level managers (de Janasz et al., 2003). Second, advanced technology makes it feasible to establish online mentoring relationships (Ensher et al., 2003) that cross organizational boundaries. Third, employees pursuing nontraditional career mobility patterns may benefit from the knowledge and influence provided by mentors in different organizations, industries, and occupations (Baugh and Fagenson-Eland, 2005). On the other hand, external mentors' limited information and power in a protégé's current organization can restrict their ability to provide career support (Chao, 1998; Higgins and Thomas, 2001), and limited opportunities for face-to-face interaction may make it difficult to achieve the trust and intimacy necessary for external mentors to provide substantial psychosocial support (Baugh and Fagenson-Eland, 2005).

Empirical research on the relative advantages of extra- versus intra-organizational mentors is limited and inconsistent. External mentors provide less career support than internal mentors (Baugh and Fagenson-Eland, 2005; Higgins and Thomas, 2001) and either more (Higgins and Thomas, 2001) or less (Baugh and Fagenson-Eland, 2005) psychosocial support than internal mentors. Moreover, whether attorneys' primary developmental relationship was outside or inside the organization was unrelated to their work satisfaction, likelihood of staying in the organization, or likelihood of being promoted to partner (Higgins and Thomas, 2001).

Clearly, more research is required to understand effects of extra-organizational mentoring on protégés' careers. Higgins and Thomas (2001) have suggested distinguishing different characteristics of external mentors, such as whether the mentor is part of the protégé's occupational community. In fact, external mentors can be distinguished in several respects; they may be a member of the protégé's family or community, in the same or different industry as the protégé, and of equal or unequal status and work experience as the protégé. Moreover, the examination of extra-organizational mentoring relationships raises broader issues about the meaning and measurement of mentoring functions. It is not mentoring per se that affects a protégé's career but rather the functions that a mentor provides, which have traditionally included career support (sponsorship, protection, coaching, challenging assignments, and exposure/visibility), psychosocial support (counseling, acceptance, and friendship), and role modeling.

Career support has generally been conceptualized and measured from an intra-organizational perspective (e.g., providing sponsorship, exposure/visibility, and protection has a clear organizational focus in which protégés receive advocacy, key assignments providing contact with senior managers, and buffering from potentially damaging exchanges with senior managers respectively). Therefore, it would be useful to expand the meaning of several of the career mentoring functions to incorporate support regarding a wider range of career options, mobility patterns, and settings. For example, protégés can receive sponsorship for positions in a different organization, exposure to members of the community with extensive career contacts, and coaching on how to move from one industry to another or how to start a new business. These forms of career support can be provided by an internal or an external mentor. Scales designed to assess these functions should be revised either by broadening the scope of the items or by including additional items with an extra-organizational focus, similar to Eby's (1997) distinction between mentoring to provide job related skills (largely internal to the organization) and career related skills (internal and external). The other two career functions – providing challenging assignments and protection – may have an inherent intra-organizational focus that needs to be retained.

The preceding discussion has focused on the meaning and measurement of the career functions, not on who provides the support. Research that adopts a boundaryless

perspective should also describe the meaning of a mentor broadly enough so that respondents can specify – and assess the functions provided by – extra-organizational mentors (Baugh and Fagenson-Eland, 2005). Similarly, research that examines multiple developmental relationships should enable respondents to identify intra-organizational and extra-organizational sources of support and assess the functions and relationships with each source of developmental support (Higgins and Thomas, 2001).

Mentoring outcomes

Although the effect of a mentoring relationship on the mentor has been the subject of recent research (Allen, 2007), most of the research has examined the impact of mentoring on the protégé. At the very least, research regarding the effect of mentoring on protégés' career success should assess subjectively-defined success. Moreover, because proximal outcomes of mentoring contributing to career success are rarely included in mentoring studies (Wanberg et al., 2003), research should test mediated models of mentoring relevant to protégés who pursue a wide variety of career patterns. Such outcomes could include motivational variables, self-efficacy, learning outcomes, and the establishment of social networks (Day and Allen, 2004; Lankau and Scandura, 2002; Wanberg et al., 2003). It would also be useful to determine whether mentoring enhances a protégé's career competencies, identity, adaptability, and protean career orientation, all of which might contribute to success in a boundaryless career.

Just as a protégé's hierarchical mobility can mediate the effect of mentoring on the subjective success of protégés who pursue an organizational career, nontraditional career mobility patterns (e.g., lateral or downward mobility, part-time employment, career change) should be examined as mediators of the effect of mentoring on the success of protégés who pursue careers that are not tied to traditional organizational career arrangements. The effect of these mobility patterns on career success is contingent on the values and preferences of the protégé and the quality of the mobility experiences. Because mentoring is intended to help protégés become successful, it is important to understand the conditions under which the mentoring process enables protégés to undertake a wide variety of mobility experiences that ultimately contribute to a successful career.

Relational mentoring

Ragins and Verbos (2007) suggest that the mentoring process has historically been viewed too narrowly as an exchange-oriented relationship intended to benefit protégés on a restricted range of economic, instrumental outcomes. In its place, Ragins and Verbos (2007) proposed a relational perspective (characterized by mutual empathy, disclosure, sensitivity, empowerment, and learning) that views mentoring as an interdependent generative relationship based on communal norms responsive to the needs of the other person in the relationship. Ragins and Verbos (2007) distinguish relational mentoring not only from traditional mentoring, with its exchange-based assumptions, but also from dysfunctional mentoring based on exploitative norms that produce negative outcomes.

Relational mentoring may be particularly useful for protégés pursuing nontraditional career mobility patterns. Because mentors whose actions are guided by a relational mentoring schema (Ragins and Verbos, 2007) are sensitive to the needs of the protégé, they should be less constrained by stereotypes about the type of career a protégé should pursue and more responsive to the idiosyncratic circumstances and aspirations of a particular protégé. If relational mentoring enhances a protégé's authenticity, self-confidence, optimism, and resilience (Ragins and Verbos, 2007), it should provide the protégé with the self-knowledge and self-assurance to pursue a self-crafted career that is driven by the achievement of personally-meaningful values.

The integration of a boundaryless perspective into a relational mentoring framework provides a fertile area for future research. Greenhaus and Singh (2007) suggest that some mentors view their relationships through a work-family lens, a facet of a relational mentoring schema that makes them sensitive to, and supportive of, their protégés' attempts to achieve work-family balance. In the same vein, some mentors might approach their relationships through a boundaryless lens that enables them to appreciate the variety of career patterns inside or outside a particular organization that can potentially meet a protégé's needs and values.

Future research can examine the consequences of relational mentoring for protégés pursuing different career patterns. For example, it would be useful to study whether mentors who enact a relational schema are also likely to adopt a boundaryless lens in their mentoring relationships. Research can then determine whether protégés of mentors who adopt a relational and boundaryless approach perceive their mentors as responsive to their career and psychological needs, experience extensive learning and self-awareness, and are capable of exploring, assessing, and ultimately choosing satisfying career options that meet their needs.

CONCLUSION

The recent literature on boundaryless and protean careers has provided a framework in which to align research on careers with contemporary work. The introduction of these two concepts has provoked excitement and creativity that promise to strengthen scholarship on career dynamics. Further attention should be directed to enhancing the clarity of the concepts and the validity of the measures, testing theoretically-grounded hypotheses, identifying the boundary conditions that undoubtedly place limits on theoretical frameworks, and applying a boundaryless perspective to additional well-established career-related research streams.

In proposing a boundaryless perspective linking career competencies, a protean career orientation, and nontraditional boundary crossing, we avoided providing our definition of a boundaryless career. Although departure from traditional organizational career arrangements has been a useful unifying theme to tie together the different meanings or emphases of a boundaryless career (Arthur and Rousseau, 1996), it may be time to separate the different forms of nontraditional boundary crossing rather than trying to unite them under the umbrella of a boundaryless career.

Even a differentiated approach to nontraditional boundary crossing is not entirely satisfying, because a career mobility pattern that is nontraditional today may become commonplace tomorrow. Perhaps our boundaryless perspective should be renamed a boundary crossing perspective, the notion of departure from traditional organizational career arrangements should be omitted as a qualifier for the mobility patterns identified in Figure 1, and crossing hierarchical boundaries within a single organization should be included as an additional career mobility pattern. This more inclusive approach has several potential virtues.

First, it enables a more comprehensive examination of the effects of different career patterns as illustrated by Reitman and Schneer's (2003) comparison of a promised path and a protean path. Second, it encourages examination of a protean career orientation in the context of *all* careers, not only careers that are nontraditional at a given point in time; it is likely that self-directedness in pursuit of personally meaningful values can facilitate success in linear and nonlinear careers. Third, because of the value of self-awareness, skill development, and social capital, it is possible that the three career competencies, despite their extra-organizational orientation, can promote successful linear and nonlinear careers.

In conclusion, scholars who study career-related issues owe a debt of gratitude to the pioneers who have pushed the envelope by focusing attention on emerging career patterns. We can repay the debt by expanding the incorporation of these new frameworks into careers research, testing their viability in different organizational and cultural contexts, and improving theory along the way in order to further our understanding of individual careers that unfold in the 21st century.

NOTE

1 We agree with Inkson's (2006: 54) observation that although boundaries have become more permeable they have not disappeared, as well as his suggestion that '... strictly speaking we should not talk about the boundary-less career but about the boundary-crossing career.' Nevertheless, we use the term boundaryless to be consistent with the terminology in the literature.

REFERENCES

Allen, T.D. (2007) 'Mentoring Relationships from the Perspective of the Mentor', in B.R. Ragins and K.E. Kram (eds), *Handbook of Mentoring at Work*. Thousand Oaks, CA: Sage, pp. 123–147.

Allen, T.D., Eby, L.T., Poteet, M.L., Lentz, E. and Lima, L. (2004) 'Career benefits associated with mentoring for protégés: A meta-analytic review', *Journal of Applied Psychology*, 89: 127–136.

Arthur, M.B., Inkson, K. and Pringle, J.K. (1999) *The New Careers: Individual Action and Economic Change*. London: Sage.

Arthur, M.B., Khapova, S.N. and Wilderom, C.P.M. (2005) 'Career success in a boundaryless career world', *Journal of Organizational Behavior*, 26: 177–202.

Arthur, M.B. and Rousseau, D.M. (1996) 'Introduction: The Boundaryless Career as a New Employment Principle', in M.B. Arthur and D.M. Rousseau (eds), *The Boundaryless Career*. New York: Oxford University Press, pp. 3–20.

Baker, T. and Aldridge, H.E. (1996) 'Prometheus Stretches: Building Identity and Cumulative Knowledge in Multiemployer Careers', in M.B. Arthur and D.M. Rousseau (eds), *The Boundaryless Career*. New York: Oxford University Press, pp. 132–149.

Banai, M. and Harry, W. (2004) 'Boundaryless global careers', *International Studies of Management and Organization*, 34 (3): 96–120.

Baugh, S.G. and Fagenson-Eland, E.A. (2005) 'Boundaryless mentoring: An exploratory study of the functions provided by internal versus external organizational mentors', *Journal of Applied Social Psychology*, 35: 939–955.

Becker, K.H. and Haunschild, A. (2003) 'The impact of boundaryless careers on organizational decision making: An analysis from the perspective of Luhmann's theory of social systems', *International Journal of Human Resource Management*, 14: 713–727.

Bird, A. (1994) 'Careers as repositories of knowledge: A new perspective on boundaryless careers', *Journal of Organizational Behavior*, 15: 325–344.

Bridges, W. (1994, September 19) 'The end of the job', *Fortune*, 62–74.

Briscoe, J.P. (2006) 'Protean career', in J.H. Greenhaus and G.A. Callanan (eds), *Encyclopedia of Career Development*. Thousand Oaks, CA: Sage. Vol. 2: pp. 649–652.

Briscoe, J.P. and DeMuth, R.F. (2003, April) *The impact of the protean career on executive development practice: Evidence from 30 North American companies*. Paper presented at the annual meeting of the Society for Industrial and Organizational Psychology, Orlando, FL.

Briscoe, J.P. and Hall, D.T. (2006a) 'Special section on boundaryless and protean careers: Next steps in conceptualizing and measuring boundaryless and protean careers', *Journal of Vocational Behavior*, 69: 1–3.

Briscoe, J.P. and Hall, D.T. (2006b) 'The interplay of boundaryless and protean careers: Combinations and implications', *Journal of Vocational Behavior*, 69: 4–18.

Briscoe, J.P., Hall, D.T. and DeMuth, R.L.F. (2006) 'Protean and boundaryless careers: An empirical exploration', *Journal of Vocational Behavior*, 69: 30–47.

Callanan, G.A. and Greenhaus, J.H. (1999) 'Personal and Career Development: The Best and Worst of Times', in A.I. Kraut and A.K. Korman (eds), *Evolving Practices in Human Resource Management: Responses to a Changing World of Work*. San Francisco: Jossey-Bass, pp. 146–171.

Cappellen, T. and Janssens, M. (2005) 'Career paths of global managers: Towards future research', *Journal of World Business*, 40: 348–360.

Cappelli, P. (1999) 'Career jobs are dead', *California Management Review*, 42 (1): 146–167.

Cappelli, P. (2006) 'Churning of jobs', in J.H. Greenhaus and G.A. Callanan (eds), *Encyclopedia of Career Development*. Thousand Oaks, CA: Sage. Vol. 1: pp. 165–167.

Carr, S.C., Inkson, K. and Thorn, K. (2005) 'From global careers to talent flow: Reinterpreting "brain drain"', *Journal of World Business*, 40: 386–398.

Chao, G.T. (1998) 'Invited reaction: Challenging research in mentoring', *Human Resource Development Quarterly*, 9: 333–338.

Colakoglu, S.N. (2006) *The relationship between career boundarylessness and individual well-being: A contingency approach*. Unpublished doctoral dissertation, Drexel University.

Dany, F. (2003) '"Free actors" and organizations: critical remarks about the new career literature, based on French insights', *International Journal of Human Resource Management*, 14: 821–838.

Dany, F., Mallon, M. and Arthur, M.B. (2003) 'The odyssey of career and the opportunity for international comparison', *International Journal of Human Resource Management*, 14: 705–712.

Day, R. and Allen, T.D. (2004) 'The relationship between career motivation and self-efficacy with protégé career success', *Journal of Vocational Behavior*, 64: 72–91.

DeFillippi, R.J. and Arthur, M.B. (1994) 'The boundaryless career: A competency-based perspective', *Journal of Organizational Behavior*, 15: 307–324.

de Janasz, S.C., Sullivan, S.E. and Whiting, V.R. (2003) 'Mentor networks and career success: Lessons for turbulent times', *Academy of Management Executive*, 17 (4): 78–91.

Dowd, K.O. and Kaplan, D.M. (2005) 'The career life of academics: Boundaried or boundaryless?', *Human Relations*, 58: 699–721.

Eby, L.T. (1997) 'Alternative forms of mentoring in changing organizational environments: A conceptual extension of the mentoring literature', *Journal of Vocational Behavior*, 51: 125–144.

Eby, L.T. (2001) 'The boundaryless career experiences of mobile spouses in dual-earner marriages', *Group and Organization Management*, 26: 343–368.

Eby, L.T., Butts, M. and Lockwood, A. (2003) 'Predictors of success in the era of the boundaryless career', *Journal of Organizational Behavior*, 24: 689–708.

Ensher, E.A., Heun, C. and Blanchard, A. (2003) 'Online mentoring and computer-mediated communication: New directions in research', *Journal of Vocational Behavior*, 63: 264–288.

Forret, M.L. and Sullivan, S.E. (2002) 'A balanced scorecard approach to networking: A guide to successfully navigating career changes', *Organizational Dynamics*, 31 (3): 245–258.

Fugate, M. (2006) 'Employability', in J.H. Greenhaus and G.A. Callanan (eds), *Encyclopedia of Career Development*. Thousand Oaks, CA: Sage. Vol. 1: pp. 267–271.

Greenhaus, J.H. (2002) 'Career dynamics', in W.C. Borman, D.R. Ilgen, and R.J. Klimoski (eds), *Comprehensive Handbook of Psychology, Volume 12: Industrial and Organizational Psychology*. New York: Wiley, pp. 519–540.

Greenhaus, J.H. and Singh, R. (2007) 'Mentoring and the work-family interface', in B.R. Ragins and

K.E. Kram (eds), *Handbook of Mentoring at Work*. Thousand Oaks, CA: Sage, pp. 519–544.

Guest, D. and Mackenzie Davy, K. (1996) 'Don't write off the traditional career', *People Management*, 2 (4): 22–25.

Gunz, H.P. and Jalland, R.M. (1996) 'Managerial careers and business strategies', *Academy of Management Review*, 21: 718–756.

Hall, D.T. (1976) *Careers in Organizations*. Glenview, IL: Scott Foresman.

Hall, D.T. (1996) 'Protean careers of the 21st century', *Academy of Management Executive*, 10 (4): 8–16.

Hall, D.T. (2002) *Careers In* and *Out of Organizations*. Thousand Oaks, CA: Sage

Hall, D.T. (2004) 'The protean career: A quarter-century journey', *Journal of Vocational Behavior*, 65: 1–13.

Hall, D.T. and Associates (1996) *The Career is Dead – Long Live the Career: A Relational Approach to Careers*. San Francisco, CA: Jossey-Bass.

Hall, D.T., Briscoe, J.P. and Kram, K.E. (1997) 'Identity, Values and Learning in the Protean Career', in C.L. Cooper and S.E. Jackson (eds), *Creating Tomorrow's Organizations*. London: John Wiley and Sons, pp. 321–335.

Hall, D.T. and Mirvis, P.H. (1995) 'The new career contract: Developing the whole person at midlife and beyond', *Journal of Vocational Behavior*, 47: 269–289.

Hall, D.T. and Moss, J.E. (1998) 'The new protean career contract: Helping organizations and employees adapt', *Organizational Dynamics*, 26 (3): 22–37.

Handy, C. (1989) *The Age of Unreason*. Boston, MA: Harvard Business School Press.

Higgins, M.C. and Kram, K.E. (2001) 'Reconceptualizing mentoring at work: A developmental network perspective', *Academy of Management Review*, 26: 264–268.

Higgins, M.C. and Thomas, D.A. (2001) 'Constellations and careers: Toward understanding the effects of multiple developmental relationships', *Journal of Organizational Behavior*, 22: 223–247.

Hirsch, P.M. and Shanley, M. (1996) 'The rhetoric of boundarylessness – or, how the newly empowered managerial class bought into its own marginalization', in M.B. Arthur and D.M. Rousseau (eds), *The Boundaryless Career*. New York: Oxford University Press, pp. 218–234.

Inkson, K. (2006) 'Protean and boundaryless careers as metaphors', *Journal of Vocational Behavior*, 69: 48–63.

Ituma, A. and Simpson, R. (2006) 'The chameleon career: An exploratory study of the work biography of information technology workers in Nigeria', *Career Development International*, 11: 48–65.

Jackson, C. (1996) 'Managing and developing a boundaryless career: Lessons from dance and drama', *European Journal of Work and Organizational Psychology*, 5: 617–628.

Kondratuk, T.B., Hausdorf, P.A., Korabik, K. and Rosin, H.M. (2004) 'Linking career mobility with corporate loyalty: How does job change relate to organizational commitment?', *Journal of Vocational Behavior*, 65: 332–349.

Kram, K.E. (1985) *Mentoring at Work*. Glenview, IL: Scott, Foresman, and Company.

Lankau, M.J. and Scandura, T.A. (2002) 'An investigation of personal learning in mentoring relationships: Content, antecedents, and consequences', *Academy of Management Journal*, 45: 779–790.

Lichtenstein, B.M.B. and Mendenhall, M. (2002) 'Nonlinearity and response-ability: Emergent order in 21st-century careers', *Human Relations*, 55: 5–32.

MacDermid, S.M., Lee, M.D., Buck, M. and Williams, M.L. (2001) 'Alternative work arrangements among professionals and managers', *Journal of Management Development*, 20: 305–317.

Mainiero, L.A. and Sullivan, S.E. (2005) 'Kaleidoscope careers: An alternate explanation for the "opt-out" revolution', *Academy of Management Executive*, 19 (1): 106–123.

Mallon, M. (1998) 'The portfolio career: pushed or pulled to it?', *Personnel Review*, 27: 361–377.

Mao, H.-Y. (2004) 'Voluntary employer changes and salary attainment of managers', *International Journal of Human Resource Management*, 15: 180–195.

Marshall, J. (1989) 'Re-visioning Career Concepts: A Feminist Invitation', in M.B. Arthur, T. Hall and B.S. Lawrence (eds), *Handbook of Career Theory*. New York: Cambridge University Press, pp. 275–291.

Miner, A.S. and Robinson, D.F. (1994) 'Organizational and population level learning as engines for career transitions', *Journal of Organizational Behavior*, 15: 345–364.

Mirvis, P.H. and Hall, D.T. (1996) 'Psychological Success and the Boundaryless Career', in M.B. Arthur and D.M. Rousseau (eds), *The Boundaryless Career*. New York: Oxford University Press, pp. 237–255.

Mischel, W. (1977) 'The Interaction of Person and Situation', in D. Magnuson and N.S. Endler (eds), *Personality at the Crossroads*. Hillsdale, NJ: Erlbaum, pp. 252–283.

Noe, R.A., Greenberger, D.B. and Wang, S. (2002) 'Mentoring: What we know and where we might go', *Research in Personnel and Human Resources Management*, 21, 129–173.

Powell, G.N. and Greenhaus, J.H. (2006) 'Managing incidents of work-family conflict: A decision-making perspective', *Human Relations*, 59: 1179–1212.

Pringle, J.K. and Mallon, M. (2003) 'Challenges for the boundaryless career odyssey', *International Journal of Human Resource Management*, 14: 839–853.

Ragins, B.R. and Verbos, A.K. (2007) 'Positive Relationships in Action: Relational Mentoring and Mentoring Schemas in the Workplace', in J.E. Dutton and B.R. Ragins (eds), *Exploring Positive Relationships at Work: Building a Theoretical and Research Foundation*. Mahwah, NJ: Lawrence Erlbaum and Associates, pp. 91–116.

Raider, H.J. and Burt, R.S. (1996) 'Boundaryless careers and social capital', in M.B. Arthur and D.M. Rousseau (eds), *The Boundaryless Career*. New York: Oxford University Press, pp. 187–200.

Reitman, F. and Schneer, J.A. (2003) 'The promised path: A longitudinal study of managerial careers', *Journal of Managerial Psychology*, 18: 60–75.

Rousseau, D.M. (1995) *Psychological Contracts in Organizations: Understanding Written and Unwritten Agreements*. Newbury Park, CA: Sage.

Saxenian, A. (1996) 'Beyond boundaries: Open Labor Markets and Learning in Silicon Valley', in M.B. Arthur and D.M. Rousseau (eds), *The Boundaryless Career*. New York: Oxford University Press, pp. 23–39.

Schneer, J.A. and Reitman, F. (1990) 'Effects of employment gaps on the careers of M.B.A.s: More damaging for men than for women?', *Academy of Management Journal*, 33: 391–406.

Schneer, J.A. and Reitman, F. (1997) 'The interrupted managerial career path: A longitudinal study of MBAs', *Journal of Vocational Behavior*, 51: 411–434.

Seibert, S.E. (2006) 'Career success', in J.H. Greenhaus and G.A. Callanan (eds), *Encyclopedia of Career Development*. Thousand Oaks, CA: Sage. Vol. 1: pp. 148–154.

Smith, V. and Neuwirth, E.B. (2006) 'Contingent Employment', in J.H. Greenhaus and G.A. Callanan (eds), *Encyclopedia of Career Development*. Thousand Oaks, CA: Sage. Vol. 1: pp. 193–197.

Sullivan, S.E. (1999) 'The changing nature of careers: A review and research agenda', *Journal of Management*, 25: 457–484.

Sullivan, S.E. and Arthur, M.B. (2006) 'The evolution of the boundaryless career concept: Examining physical and psychological mobility', *Journal of Vocational Behavior*, 69: 19–29.

Sullivan, S.E., Carden, W.A. and Martin, D.F. (1998) 'Careers in the next millennium: Directions for future research', *Human Resource Management Review*, 8: 165–185.

Valcour, P.M. and Tolbert, P.S. (2003) 'Gender, family and career in the era of boundarylessness: Determinants and effects of intra- and inter-organizational mobility', *International Journal of Human Resource Management*, 14: 768–787.

Van Buren, H.J. (2003) 'Boundaryless careers and employability obligations', *Business Ethics Quarterly*, 13: 131–149.

Wanberg, C.R., Welsh, E.T. and Hezlett, S.A. (2003) 'Mentoring research: A review and dynamic process model', *Research in Personnel and Human Resources Management*, 22: 39–124.

Waterman, R.H., Waterman, J.A. and Collard, B.A. (1994) 'Toward a career resilient workforce', *Harvard Business Review*, 72 (4): 87–95.

Weick, K.E. (1996) 'Enactment and the Boundaryless Career: Organizing as We Work', in M.A. Arthur and D.M. Rousseau (eds), *The Boundaryless Career*. New York: Oxford University Press, pp. 40–57.

Weick, K.E., and Berlinger, L. (1989) 'Career Improvisation in Self-designing Organizations', in M.B. Arthur, Dr.T. Hall, and B.S. Lawrence (eds), *Handbook of Career Theory*. New York: Cambridge University Press, pp. 313–328.

Whiting, V.R. and de Janasz, S.C. (2004) 'Mentoring in the 21st century: Using the internet to build skills and networks', *Journal of Management Education*, 28: 275–293.

Wrzesniewski, A. and Dutton, J.E. (2001) 'Crafting a job: Revisioning employees as active crafters of their work', *Academy of Management Review*, 26: 179–201.

Yamashita, M. and Uenoyama, T. (2006) 'Boundaryless career and adaptive HR practices in Japan's hotel industry', *Career Development International*, 11: 230–242.

16

A Century of Compensation Research

Matt Bloom

H. L. Mencken famously quipped that the happy man makes $100 more than his wife's sister's husband. There is a great deal of insight in Mencken's quip about the challenges and complexities of understanding employee compensation. He points out, for example, that compensation has influences beyond its economic utility and also that pay can influence our happiness. For over 100 years scholars have been seeking a better understanding of how and why pay systems work. At first blush it seems clear that compensation matters in work organizations, after all, how many of us work for free? Indeed, both researchers and practitioners have asserted that compensation is a fundamental part, perhaps *the* fundamental part, of the value and meaning that employees, employers, and other stakeholders ascribe to the employment relationship (Gerhart and Milkovich, 1992; Opsahl and Dunnette, 1966; Rynes et al., 2005). But closer inspection has revealed that compensation is a subject fraught with complexity and nuance. George Milkovich, one of the leading compensation scholars, has mused that decisions about the design of

compensation systems can sometimes seem like a series of approximate solutions to unsolvable problems. Indeed, compensation practitioners often lament the difficulty in finding a compensation system that works, especially one that is effective over the long term (Milkovich and Newman, 2005).

In 1892, Schloss published what was perhaps the first research text book on compensation systems. He not only provided evidence about the effectiveness of different forms of compensation for motivating employee performance, but also explored the broader impact of compensation systems. Reviewing the piece rate and profit-sharing systems in use at that time, Schloss (1892) noted that they not only had rather dismal track records for motivating workers, but he also worried that these systems created a 'sweating system' wherein workers were co-opted into unduly hard work for unfairly risky pay. He also recognized that organizations develop their own cultures, which he suggested must be reflected in the compensation systems which they use. In 1923, Bloomfield published a textbook on compensation systems in which five of the chapters focused on how bonus systems can be used to increase performance. He suggested that bonuses must be designed, among other things, 'to promote confidence and understanding between employer and employees' (quoted in Milkovich and Stevens, 1999). As both scholars illustrate, micro-organizational issues have been important parts of research on compensation systems since the earliest published studies.

In their seminal review of the compensation literature, Opsahl and Dunnette (1966: 94) characterized the state of compensation research at that time by stating that:

> We know amazingly little about how money either interacts with other factors or how it acts individually to affect job behavior . . . . Speculation, accompanied by compensation fads and fashions, abounds; research studies designed to answer fundamental questions about the role of money in human motivation are all too rare.

Since that time many well-designed studies about compensation have been conducted and much has been learned. Nonetheless, important questions linger about how and when compensation influences employees' cognitions, behaviors, and affect. Many boundary conditions that interact with compensation to enhance or limit its effectiveness remain relatively unexplored. We know little about the relative importance of compensation vis-à-vis other potential work place motivators like challenging jobs, trust, and meaningful work which are heralded by some as the most important work place motivators (Colvin, 2006). We also know very little about how compensation affects human well-being.

There is good news in this for micro-organizational scholars. Most compensation research conducted over the past 20 years has relied on economic or macro-organizational theory, and leading scholars have emphasized that research using micro-organizational theory is needed to advance the state of knowledge on the causes and consequences of organizational reward systems (Barkema and Gomez-Mejia, 1998; Gerhart and Milkovich, 1992; Opsahl and Dunnette, 1966; Rynes et al., 2005) However, there are also important

reminders for OB scholars to recognize the gaps in our current understanding and to avoid overstepping what we know about compensation.

One of the challenges researchers interested in compensation face is that the compensation literature is so vast. It includes work by scholars from many fields, including management, psychology, sociology, finance, accounting, and economics, and so their interests often overlap with ours. Micro-organizational scholars need to be aware of this research and take account of it in their own work, but this can seem like a daunting challenge. Fortunately, several seminal reviews of the research literature exist. Three of these are, I believe, particularly important: Opsahl and Dunnette (1966); Gerhart and Milkovich (1992), and Rynes, et al., (2005). I have organized a brief historical review of the field around these three seminal pieces. I provide a short overview of the focus of each review, and then highlight some of the important research questions they raise that remain relevant for micro-organizational researchers today. Within this structure I review select studies that have addressed these open questions and then suggest some possible ways to continue advancing our knowledge in each area. Debates have developed around several of these research questions. I review these debates and offer some possible ideas about how scholars might proceed toward resolving them. Because these reviews provide such a complete and comprehensive review of the literature, I focus more of my attention on what I regard as the major gaps in our understanding of compensation systems. I end by suggesting some new ideas for compensation research.

CLASSICS OF COMPENSATION RESEARCH

Opsahl and Dunnette (1966)

Opsahl and Dunnette (1966) published the earliest review of compensation research in the management literature and much of their wisdom remains important, although often overlooked, today. Their focus was 'to identify and summarize research studies designed to show how opportunities to get money affect the way people actually do their work' (p. 94) and they omit the very few studies of compensation and employee attraction and retention. They provide a concise overview of major compensation theories, a thorough review and critique of published empirical studies, and an insightful and still relevant research agenda. Two over-arching themes play a central role in their review. They emphasize that 'money functions in many ways, depending upon the setting, the antecedent conditions, and the particular person involved' (Opsahl and Dunnette, 1966: 97) and stress the need to consider how contextual factors influence the effects that compensation systems have on employees. They also suggest that compensation may interact with other work place 'motives' (rewards) and that 'we must know more about the motives of employees – which motives are dominant, and how employees differ from one another in the configuration of their motives. We must also determine which of these motives can be linked to money as an incentive' (p. 114). Four topics that received special attention from Opsahl and Dunnette (1966) remain important subjects for research today: the secrecy of pay systems, how time figures into employee conceptions of compensation, the valence of compensation, and the outcomes of incentive pay.

Secrecy of pay systems

Opsahl and Dunnette (1966) note that, at the time of their review, most pay systems were governed by policies that mandate pay secrecy; and this remains true of many organizations today. Pay secrecy refers to the amount of formal information employees are given about the pay of other employees at the same organization. Although research on pay secrecy was in its early stages, the available empirical evidence suggested that secret pay systems may be problematic,

resulting in lower pay satisfaction, lower employee performance, and reductions in the efficacy of compensation as a signal of good performance (e.g., Lawler, 1965). In the years that followed, several published studies yielded results consistent with Opsahl and Dunnette's conclusions. For example, Lawler (1967) found that pay secrecy led to inaccurate employee perceptions of others' pay, and subsequently reduced the motivational effects of pay. Lawler (1971) noted that, while pay secrecy does not keep employees from making pay comparisons, it does increase the likelihood that employees will base their comparisons on inaccurate, and often inflated, estimates of others' pay. Other studies offered a contrasting view. Milkovich and Anderson (1972) found that pay secrecy was not related to pay satisfaction and Leventhal et al. (1972) found that laboratory subjects were less likely to inflate the pay of poor performers when they knew pay levels would be kept secret. Since the publication of these studies, there has been almost no research on pay secrecy, yet the debate about its efficacy continues. While most organizations continue to mandate pay secrecy, some, like Whole Foods Markets, have claimed that making information about individuals' pay packages open to all employees increases employee trust and commitment.

Recently, Colella et al. (2007) have developed a comprehensive conceptual model of pay secrecy in hopes of re-igniting research on the topic. They begin with a thorough discussion of the costs (e.g., the potential negative impact on employees' justice perceptions) and benefits (e.g., the potential to prevent employees from making detrimental pay comparisons) of pay secrecy. They then discuss several contextual factors that mitigate both the use and outcomes of pay secrecy. They suggest, for example, that information about internal pay levels is more useful and important to employees with firm-specific human capital since they are less mobile. They also explore how organizational choices about pay secrecy might influence employees' attitudes, such as their organizational justice perceptions, and the potential implications of pay secrecy for employee motivation. For example, Colella et al. (2007) suggest that pay secrecy might reduce or destroy pay-performance linkages, thereby diminishing instrumentality perceptions or causing employees to perceive negative pay inequities. Milkovich and Newman (2005) suggest that pay can serve as a signal of organizational values and objectives, and Colella et al. (2007) build on this notion by developing a conceptual model for how and what pay secrecy might signal to employees. They end by suggesting the broader, societal implications of pay secrecy, exploring, for example, what effects pay secrecy might have on income inequalities in communities and how national cultures might influence the way employees respond to pay secrecy.

Opsahl and Dunnette (1966) note that other pay administration policies also need research attention. For example, employee participation in the design of a pay plan and the type and amount of communication that accompanies compensation systems have been suggested as potentially important administrative polices. Like pay secrecy, all are in need of empirical research (Milkovich and Newman, 2005).

Pay curves

Pay curves represent an employee's pay over their entire tenure at a particular organization and reflect changes in the amount, type and variability of pay over time. The notion of a pay curve suggests that employees think about their pay over time and that such considerations influence employee outcomes. This idea has not been well-researched, yet several important forms of compensation are premised on the idea that employees do think about pay over time. For example, most uses of stock options are grounded in the idea that employees think and care about their future compensation and that such considerations influence current employee attitudes and behaviors. Other forms of compensation (e.g., retirement benefits) share the assumption that employees are concerned about their future income. Do employees

think about their future pay? If so, how far into the future do they project pay? What, if any, affects do these considerations have on current attitudes and behaviors? What role do individual differences play in these considerations? These and other important questions remain largely unstudied.

Pay preferences and the valence of compensation

Do people value money as a return from their work? Do they prefer money over other potential returns and rewards from work? Do people have preferences for how they are compensated and, if so, what affects do these preferences have on employee reactions to pay? Questions like these are of perennial interest to compensation researchers. Theory suggests that monetary compensation should be an important motivator because it is instrumental for obtaining so many other valued outcomes. At the time of their review, several empirical studies on the motivational value of pay had been done, but Opsahl and Dunnette (1966) note there was considerable discrepancy in findings across those studies. Some indicated that people place low value on money, while others suggested that it is the most important workplace motivator. Opsahl and Dunnette (1966) suggested that this disparity in results is due largely to the atheoretical nature of the studies, and urged researchers to develop theory about the role and meaning of money as a work place motivator. Since that time, some theory development work has occurred (e.g., Mitchell and Mickel, 1999) but the few more recent published studies tend to suffer from either significant theoretical or methodological shortcomings. Even so, debate continues over the importance of money as a workplace motivator (e.g., Pfeffer, 1998; Rynes et al., 2005). While some (e.g., Pfeffer, 1998) assert that it is a 'myth' that employees work for pay, others (e.g., Locke et al., 1980) assert that pay is the most important motivator in the work place. Despite disagreements about employee preferences, scholars uniformly seem to hold one assumption in common: that pay preferences matter. To this assumption,

Opsahl and Dunnette issue an important caveat:

> the implicit, but unwarranted, assumption ... is that if a person has a pay plan he likes, this plan will motivate behavior more than one that he does not like. Although this is an appealing assumption, future studies, in addition to determining employees' payplan preferences, should seek to map the relation between such preferences and the incentive value of different plans. (p. 108)

In addition to studies on the value of pay, we need more research on whether preferences for different forms of pay, such as fixed vs. incentive pay, matter for employee attraction, retention, and motivation. Cable and Judge's (1994) study was among the first to explore these relationships. They found that job applicant's preferences (e.g., for fixed vs. incentive pay or job- vs. skill-based pay) influence how attractive they found different organizations. Some additional research on these effects has been conducted (see Chapman et al., 2005 for a review), but much more research is needed for a comprehensive understanding of how pay preferences influence employee attitudes and behaviors.

Incentive pay

Of the many important compensation topics Opsahl and Dunnette (1966) reviewed none has received more research attention than incentive pay. They summarized the state-of-the-science noting that, 'very little is known about the behavioral laws regulating the effectiveness of incentives. We continue to dole out large sums of money under the guise of "incentive pay" without really knowing much about its incentive character' (p. 115). Since this review, there has been extensive research on incentive pay, and two meta-analyses of this research have also been conducted (Locke, et al., 1980; Jenkins et al., 1998). These meta-analytic studies suggest that a fairly strong relationship exists between pay and performance. Locke et al., (1980) conclude that incentive pay is the most important workplace motivator, better even than goal setting and Jenkins et al. (1998) reported an estimated population correlation between incentive pay and overall

performance of 0.30. Unfortunately, there are some limitations to these studies. Locke et al. (1980) highlight many methodological concerns with the studies covered in their review, including that many fail to use advanced experimental designs. In addition, they were not able use standard statistical meta-analytic techniques. The vast majority of the studies included in Jenkins et al.'s (1998) meta-analysis were laboratory studies, and the dependent variables in virtually all of the studies were simple, highly-prescribed tasks such as sorting index cards, solving puzzles, or assembling toy models. So, while the existing research indicates a positive relationship between incentive pay and performance, much more research is needed to establish whether this relationship generalizes across performance contexts and also what factors enhance or diminish these incentive effects.

There is a significant body of incentive pay research on managerial samples (see Gerhart and Milkovich, 1992), yet the results from this research may be even more equivocal. Summarizing this research, Barkema and Gomez-Mejia (1998: 135) concluded that:

> Researchers using different data sets, measurements of variables, statistical techniques, and model specifications have often found weak or even statistically insignificant relationships between pay and performance .... In short, after at least six decades of research, the failure to identify a robust relationship between top management compensation and firm performance has led scholars into a blind alley.

Unfortunately, significant gaps remain in our understanding of the motivational effects of incentives, especially when work is complex, difficult to prescribe, and dynamic, such as is often the case with professionals, knowledge and creative workers, and the like.

There has been less research on group-based incentive plans such as profit and gain sharing, but some critics of individual-incentive plans have advocated their potential advantages (e.g., Pfeffer, 1998) and organizational use of such plans is increasing (Milkovich and Newman, 2005). Although, historically, there has been very little theory explaining how and why such plans work, recent contributions seek to fill those gaps. Pfeffer (1998) suggests that group-based pay may enhance positive team processes such as fostering cooperative effort directed towards team performance and strengthening the bonds among team members. Gomez-Mejia et al. (2000) propose that the risk-sharing properties of group-based incentives might influence their effectiveness and Hollensbe and Guthrie (2000) propose a model of how group-based pay may foster goal setting activities on teams. None of these theories has received much empirical attention. Milkovich and Newman's (2005) idea that group-based plans may help foster organizational learning is one proposition that has been studied. Arthur and Aiman-Smith (2001) found that implementation of a gain sharing plan increased the innovativeness of employee suggestions.

Even given the limited or equivocal evidence, it is hard to imagine that incentive compensation simply does not work. Rather, as Opsahl and Dunnette (1966) emphasize, the key to understanding incentive pay probably lies in discovering what contextual factors mediate and moderate its affects. (This is also a central theme in Gerhart and Milkovich (1992), which I review below.) Longitudinal studies are also particularly important here. We need to know not only whether there are positive incentive effects, but also how long those effects last, and whether they change over time. Field studies of how pay packages influence employee attraction and retention would also be of significant value in advancing a broader understanding of the effects of incentive pay (Cable and Judge, 1994). In each of these areas, micro-organizational researchers have much to contribute. Theories such as organizational justice theory (Brockner 2002; Colquitt, Chapter 4, this volume); perceived organizational support (Rhoades and Eisenberger, 2002); person-organization fit (Kristof, 1996); psychological contracts (Coyle-Shapiro and Parzetall, Chapter 1, this volume; Rousseau and Ho, 2000); and social exchange theory (Cropanzano et al., 2001), provide important perspectives for

understanding how context, time, and pay system design influence employees. Since very little research has been done using these powerful theoretical lenses, opportunities abound.

Gerhart and Milkovich (1992)

Gerhart and Milkovich's (1992) masterful review and synthesis of compensation research has become another seminal piece in the literature. In addition to their review of a broad range of compensation studies, they provide important insights and guidance for enhancing knowledge and understanding of compensation systems. Their review takes the organization's perspective, seeking to understand factors which influence the choices organizations make about their pay systems and also the outcomes those choices produce. Like Opsahl and Dunnette (1966), they highlight the importance of contextual or contingency factors for understanding the design and outcomes of compensation systems. They emphasize (p. 545) that 'pay decisions are made in a complex world where many other influences are at work. The more recognition of this fact given by research, the more valuable its contribution is likely to be.' Gerhart and Milkovich (1992) discuss four broad classes of contingency factors:

- organizational (e.g., business strategy, HRM strategy, organization of work);
- job (e.g., complexity, programmability);
- individual (e.g., personality, values, skills); and
- external (e.g., competitive environment, economic conditions).

Throughout their review, they highlight how specific contingency factors might influence both the design and outcomes of compensation systems. In most cases, they point to the need for more research on what contingency factors matter and why they matter.

Another important contribution of Gerhart and Milkovich's (1992) review is that they develop and apply a 'return on investment' (ROI) perspective. They note that any organizational decisions about how to attract, retain, and motivate employees with compensation involve the investment of scarce resources. Like most resource allocation decisions, organizations should expect a positive return that exceeds the costs of those allocations. Gerhart and Milkovich (1992) emphasize that researchers need to include ROI considerations in their studies, especially when drawing conclusions about the superiority of compensation choices. They remind us – and this is a very important reminder – that it is the 'bang for the buck' that matters to organizations. Very little research on the ROI of various compensation systems exists, with virtually no studies comparing the ROI of different compensation systems.

Pay structures

One of the most important topics that Gerhart and Milkovich (1992) discuss is pay structures, 'the array of rates paid for different work within a single organization' (Milkovich and Newman, 2005: 611). Organizations almost never pay all jobs and all employees the same and these differences are usually designed to influence employee behaviors. Although Gerhart and Milkovich (1992) emphasize that, at the time of their review, little was known about the impact of pay structures on employee and organization, their review helped stimulate empirical research on the subject (e.g., Becker and Huselid, 1992; Bloom, 1999; Pfeffer and Langton, 1993).

There is currently an active debate over whether more or less dispersed structures are advantageous (Bloom, 1999). More dispersed pay structures create larger differences in pay between job levels, people, etc., like the prizes in a golf tournament. Some researchers have argued that more dispersed pay structures will lead to higher performance because they create a meritocracy and encourage lower performers to work harder (Lazear, 1995). Others have argued that more dispersed structures will lead to lower performance because they produce feelings of inequity, promote dissatisfaction, and create disincentives for cooperation (Pfeffer, 1998). Research is mixed, with some studies indicating more dispersed pay structures are positively related

to performance (e.g., Becker and Huselid, 1992) and others indicating the relationship is negative (e.g., Bloom, 1999; Pfeffer and Langton, 1993). Rynes and Gerhart (2005) argue that the results from the latter studies are overly pessimistic. For example, they argue that the negative effects of pay dispersion found in Bloom (1999)[1] obtain because he controlled for team talent and team pay in his analyses which, they argue (p. 588), 'parcels out the positive effects of pay dispersion, i.e., the attraction and retention of star players who are paid a great deal, thus resulting in better team performance, higher team pay, and greater dispersion.' Of course, empirical investigations of their ideas need to be conducted, but Rynes and Gerhart's (2005) propositions also beg important theoretical questions as to how and why pay dispersion might lead to the outcomes they propose. For example, how and why might pay dispersion influence the attraction and retention of employees? Are there differences for stars and non-stars and, if so, why? How and why does pay dispersion influence the talent composition (e.g., average talent level, dispersion of talent) of a group? Does pay dispersion effect the attitudes and performance of stars and non-stars differently, and if so, why? The objective of research on pay dispersion should be to increase our understanding of how and why pay dispersion leads to different individual and organizational outcomes.

For example, greater dispersion might cause employees to focus on specific performance outcomes (i.e., those that will help them move up the pay hierarchy) to the exclusion of others. Or, pay dispersion might affect employees' justice perceptions. When employees view distribution as unfair they might respond by withholding effort, reducing their cooperation, or even sabotaging the performance of other employees. Most of the concerns expressed about pay dispersion have centered on the potential detrimental effects that it might have on employees' sense of fairness, but with few exceptions (e.g., Miceli et al., 1991), little research exists investigating justice issues. Most of the existing studies, including Bloom (1999), measure outcome distributions and do not directly measure employees' justice perceptions. One excellent exception is the study by Trevor and Wazeter (2006) exploring how different dimensions of compensation – pay dispersion, external competitiveness, pay ranges – influence the pay equity perceptions of public school teachers. They found that employees' pay equity perceptions were dependent upon comparisons with multiple referents, both inside and outside the organization. They suggest that pay dispersion might be a proxy for other kinds of justice comparisons that employees make. As Trevor and Wazeter (2006) emphasize, much more research needs to be conducted to determine what employees are actually responding too when evaluating the justice of pay systems. Tekleab et al. (2005) also investigated multiple components of pay systems and multiple justice perceptions. They showed that distributive justice perceptions meditated the relationship between pay level and pay satisfaction, but that procedural justice perceptions matter for relationships between pay raise and pay satisfaction. They also found that only pay raise satisfaction influenced turnover decisions. Studies like these suggest, among other things, the value of organizational justice theory for studying compensation, and the importance of including more than one component of a pay system in research studies.

In their concluding statements on pay structures, Gerhart and Milkovich (1992) reiterate the need to study multiple pay decisions simultaneously. For example, in their study of pay dispersion in top management teams, Bloom and Michel (2002) found that paying above market salaries to managers seemed to mitigate some of the negative effects of pay dispersion on their tenure and turnover. Other dimensions of the compensation system, such as the use of incentives or the types and amounts of benefits and perquisites offered, might also influence the effects of pay dispersion. Employees might, for example, respond more favorably to dispersion in incentive pay because of its potentially closer link to individual performance. Again,

scholars have just begun to explore this important area of research. Researchers also need to examine the ROI of pay structures and pay dispersion. Even assuming that greater pay dispersion leads to better team performance, still unresolved is whether the cost of this difference is justified. As Gerhart and Milkovich (1992) emphasize, even pay systems that lead to better outcomes may not be worth their cost.

Benefits

A second important topic to which Gerhart and Milkovich (1992) give considerable attention is benefits. They note that despite the fact that employee benefits have become an important inducement in the employment relationship, benefits have attracted relatively little research attention. Most of the research has focused on satisfaction with traditional benefits (e.g., various forms of insurance, time off from work, retirement benefits; Dreher et al., 1988; Williams et al., 2002) and very little research has addressed whether and how benefits are related to employee attraction, retention, and motivation. Despite this, somewhat extravagant claims are made about the potential impact benefits can have on employees (Milkovich and Newman, 2005). Recently some researchers have begun to explore benefits, especially family-friendly work policies (Edwards and Rothbard, 2000; Lambert, 2000; Grzywacz and Butler, Chapter 24, this volume; Rothbard and Edwards, 2003). Edwards and Rothbard (2000) provide some much-needed theory for understanding work-family relationships. One of the several notable strengths of their theory is that they seek to explain first how work life and family life are related, and then use this theory to explain how the effects of one domain might spillover into the other. Lambert (2000) examined whether family-friendly work policies create high quality social exchanges that encourage employees to engage in OCBs. Rothbard and Edwards (2003) found that there are complex relationships in how people balance their investments of time between work and family. Their research indicates that role theory might offer important insights into how people make these trade-offs.

One of the challenges of doing research on benefits is that there is little theory to guide explorations (see Barringer and Milkovich, 1998, for an exception). For example, do employees value health care insurance only for financial reasons, or is health care insurance worth more to them somehow because it allows them to care for their dependents? How does life insurance, which by definition pays only upon employees' death, motivate employees? Do retirement plans, which provide for employees' future income, create a safety net that influences the way employees respond to current incentive programs? Do different kinds of retirement plans have different kinds of effects on employee attraction, retention, and motivation? These questions, and many more like them, remain unanswered and are in need of research. Following the lead of scholars like Edwards, Lambert, and Rothbard, researchers also need to explore a wider set of benefits to incorporate the array of choices organizations are adopting today. Finally, researchers need to address the potential interplay between benefits and the various forms of cash compensation, especially salaries and incentive pay.

Rynes, Gerhart and Parks (2005)

Rynes et al.'s (2005) review offers two important perspectives. First, they focus on psychological research and offer a number of important insights and suggestions to encourage greater use of psychological theories in compensation research. Second, they integrate theory and research on two important constructs, pay-for-performance (PFP) and performance evaluation, to develop a deeper understanding of both areas. Although relationships between these constructs seem intuitive, Rynes et al. (2005) note that little research has assessed this possible connection. The review should be explored in concert with two recent books by the lead authors (Gerhart and Rynes, 2003; Rynes and Gerhart, 2000) which also provide excellent reviews of compensation research.

Rynes et al. (2005) summarize the existing research by noting that (p. 581):

> our reading of the evidence on PFP is generally positive. To be sure, there are some very important caveats: pay is not the only important motivator in organizations, and PFP programs can yield serious, unintended negative results. Nevertheless, it can also deliver powerful improvements in performance. This combination of upside potential and downside risks is part of what makes PFP so interesting.

They remind us that PFP can operate in two ways, through incentive effects on employee performance, and through 'sorting effects' on workforce composition (i.e., influence employee attraction and selection). This is a very important conceptual issue, especially because important interactions between these effects are likely to exist, although they remain largely unexplored. They then provide a concise overview of select topics in performance evaluation research and discuss the implications of this research for future PFP studies. For example, Rynes et al. (2005) discuss how differences between subjective and objective performance measures might influence the effectiveness of incentive pay. They also discuss the potentially important mediating role that psychological variables, such as employee attitudes, beliefs, and behaviors, might play between PFP and performance evaluation.

One intervening variable that has received almost no research is employees' affect – moods and emotions – at work. Research on affect has been growing rapidly in recent years and yet it is under-represented in the compensation literature. This body of research indicates that affect plays an important, indeed critical, role in people's cognitions and behaviors (Brief and Weiss, 2002; Grandy, this volume; Isen, 2000, 2004). For example, Isen's (2000, 2004) work indicates that mood states are powerful determinants of performance in diverse contexts, yet very little is known about whether and how PFP and employees' affect may interact. Given the strong reactions that PFP appears to elicit in people (Milkovich and Newman, 2005), theory and research on affect may be a unique and useful way to advance our understanding of how and why PFP influences employees.

EMERGING ISSUES IN COMPENSATION RESEARCH

These excellent reviews indicate that significant contributions have been made to our knowledge of compensation systems, but they also suggest that more research is needed, especially research that extends beyond the topics that have historically dominated compensation research. Where can we go from here? Three topics stand out to me as important for enhancing our understanding of compensation and rewards systems: total returns, intrinsic motivation, and happiness.

Total returns

Many companies have adopted a 'total returns' perspective where compensation is viewed as just one part of the 'bundle of valued returns' that are important for attracting, retaining, and motivating employees (Milkovich and Newman, 2005; Rousseau and Ho, 2000). For example, non-cash returns like a sense of purpose, trust, and recognition are featured very prominently among the companies that make *Fortune* magazine's annual '100 Best Places to Work' (Colvin, 2006). Scholars, including Herbert Simon (1991: 334), have asserted that non-cash returns are vitally important work place motivators:

> Although economic rewards play an important part in securing adherence to organizational goals and management authority, they are limited in their effectiveness. Organizations would be far less effect systems than they actually are if such rewards were the only means, or even the principle means, of motivation available. In fact, observation of behavior in organizations reveals other powerful motivations that induce employees to accept organizational goals and authority as bases for their actions.

The idea of total returns goes back at least as far as Chester Barnard (1938), in his inducement-contribution model of the employment relationship. He maintained that the types of inducements offered by an organization are critically important determinants of the contributions employees provide to the organization and he placed particular emphasis on non-economic inducements, asserting that without them, 'most business would be a lifeless failure' (quoted in Mahoney, 2002: 167). The total returns perspective draws attention not only to a wider array of returns, but also to the potential for important relationships among the elements of a total returns package. Consider a simple example: an organization offers its employees rich retirement, life insurance, health care, and disability benefits along with cash compensation that heavily emphasizes incentive pay. Given that the organization has provided strong income protection for employees' future and that of their dependants would this provision influence the way employees respond to risky incentive pay? Does this combination of benefits and incentive pay influence employee behaviors and attitudes? Does it influence the way employees view their employment relationship? When we consider more complex bundles of returns, our knowledge is very limited. For example, *Fortune*'s writers assert that trust, recognition, and challenging work are the most important work place motivators (Colvin, 2006), more important than compensation, but we have almost no empirical evidence about whether these assertions are correct.

The limited empirical research on total returns does support the notion that non-cash returns, such as social recognition and performance feedback, are important determinants of individual and group performance (Peterson and Luthans, 2006; Stajkovic and Luthans, 2001). However, research has not examined relationships among these returns, and it is these synergies that may be most important for understanding how the bundle of valued returns affects employees. To advance knowledge on total returns, conceptual models that guide our research must first be developed. The micro-organizational literature contains a number of theories that may be useful for studying total returns, including perceived organizational support (Rhoades and Eisenberger, 2002), person-organization fit (Kristof, 1996), and psychological contracts (Rousseau and Ho, 2000). I briefly discuss three theories that provide unique perspectives for total returns research, but which have not, to my knowledge, been used in compensation studies. These theories are also advantageous in that they could be used together to provide a more comprehensive model of total returns.

Social exchange theory (SET; Cropanzano et al., 2001) suggests that the types of 'resources' exchanged by two or more parties determines the nature and quality of their on-going relationship and the outcomes of that relationship. SET assumes exchanges exist essentially in two forms. In economic exchanges, all of the resources can be easily monetizable so these relationships a short-term, quid-pro-quo exchanges. Social or reciprocal exchanges may involve economic resources, but they also involve intangible and symbolic resources, such as recognition, esteem, and trust. As a consequence, they are more durable and flexible, and, because the parties to the exchange can rely on the goodwill and discretion of the other, social exchanges comprise a wider variety of contributions by both parties. Foa and Foa's (1974) model of interpersonal resources has been used to distinguish the kinds of resources that create economic and social exchanges (Rousseau and Ho, 2000). This model suggests that more intangible and relationship-specific resources (e.g., recognition, autonomy and discretion) foster social exchanges, whereas more concrete and socially generic resources (e.g., money, goods and information) foster economic exchanges. One straightforward application is to compare the employee perceptions, attitudes, and behaviors created by total return bundles that offer only economic returns against those that include recognition, autonomy, and discretion. For example, some researchers suggest that the trust and personal obligation that are possible under a social exchange cannot be created under economic exchanges (e.g., Molm et al., 2000;

Pfeffer, 1998). Total returns bundles that foster social exchanges might foster higher levels of innovation and greater willingness among employees to accept changes in their work assignments. While seemingly simple, examples such of these, which have not been empirically studied, indicate the kinds of research questions that SET suggests.

Cropanzano et al. (2001) emphasize the importance of distinguishing between the nature of the relationship and the type of resources that are exchanged. For example, an economic exchange is different from economic resources that might be exchanged. Traditionally, SET has maintained that the nature of the resources exchanged influences the nature of the relationship, but this model suggests that the nature of the relationship might also influence the meaning people ascribe to and the way they respond to the resources being exchanged. For example, an economic resource like pay can be allocated using more economic or more relationship-based rules. Cropanzano et al. (2001) offer as an example an office manager who is willing to forego a year-end bonus to help save the job of a long-time, well-liked staff member. This suggests that the nature of the relationship might have important affects on how employees perceive the returns they receive, and also on how those returns affect employees' subsequent attitudes and behaviors.

Transformational leadership model (TLM, Bass, 1985; Judge et al., Chapter 18, this volume) also distinguishes among different kinds of work place relationships, but TLM focuses on how leaders shape whether employees identify with the organization and act to advance the collective good or whether they focus and act on their own self-interest. TLM distinguishes between transformational leaders, who use inspirational visions, challenging work, displays of personal convictions, and individualized considerations to elevate and broaden followers' goals and inspire them to high performance, and transactional leaders, who use conventional rewards and management practices to harness their follower's self-interest and thereby gain follower's compliance. Straightforward propositions, such as whether there are interactions between leadership style and incentive pay on employee outcomes, or whether transformational leadership enhances the effects of benefits on employee outcomes, could be investigated. For example, the sense of shared values and goals that transformational leaders create might enhance the effects of group-based incentives and egalitarian pay structures, but clash with the effects of individual incentives and more dispersed pay structures. The individualized consideration that transformational leadership provide to their employees might enhance the effects of benefits that protect employees and their dependants, which might then foster greater employee loyalty. Digging further, researchers might investigate whether leadership style influences the meaning employees ascribe to the compensation, benefits, or relational returns they receive.

An example of how this might work comes from private conversations with a VP of HR for a company in the pharmaceutical industry. The VP lamented that he has installed on-site day care centers at two organizations with the hopes that doing so would positively affect employee attitudes and performance. Employees at one organization responded with suspicion – 'This organization doesn't give us anything without expecting something in return' – and at the other, employees responded with a sense of entitlement – 'You're finally giving us what we deserve.' Neither installation produced positive responses. However, employees at other organizations, for example SAS, seem to view this same benefit as a signal of how much managers care about them (Florida and Goodnight, 2005). Did the leadership style of the managers at these three organizations influence the way employees responded to the same return? Are employees more likely to view their pay as fair when they work for a transformational leader? TLM provides a rich conceptual basis for exploring questions not only about how returns shape the relationship, but also about how the relationship might influence the way different bundles influence employees and also the way employees view their bundle of returns.

Self-concept theory (Sedikides and Brewer, 2001) proposes that there are three important levels to people's sense of self. The individual level focuses on oneself as a distinct, unique person and matters of self-interest are basic motivations in this context. The interpersonal level focuses on dyadic relationships with significant others. Protecting and enhancing the significant other and the relationship itself are basic motivations here. The collective level focuses on inclusion in a larger group. Basic motivations at this level are the welfare of the collective and placing a premium on the common fate and shared norms of the group. Much of the compensation research has assumed that only the individual level matters, but self-concept theory suggests that all three levels are important, although in differing degrees depending upon the person and situation. For example, in work situations where individuals identify very strongly with their work group, the collective self may dominate their self-concept. In such cases, group-based pay and egalitarian pay structures might be more effective. In other work situations, work is oriented toward the individual. Many sales jobs are illustrative, where individuals work largely on their own. Here, the individual level might dominate a person's self-concept at work and so commissions based upon individual performance might have more effect.

Integrating self-concept theory with SET and TLM might provide even more theoretical power. Transformational leaders will probably enhance the importance of the relational and collective selves and, perhaps, diminish the importance of the individual self. There are certainly other important theories in the micro-organizational literature, and my review of these three is meant as much to illustrate the importance of applying micro-organizational theories as it is to advance work using these three.

Compensation and intrinsic motivation

Another interesting and lively debate that has surfaced in the micro-organizational research focuses on the relationships between extrinsic motivation (EM) and intrinsic motivation (IM). EM occurs when employees work for rewards like compensation; the use of incentive pay is a classic example. IM has been defined as 'a cognitive state reflecting the extent to which the worker attributes the force of his or her task behaviors to outcomes derived from the task per se; that is, from outcomes which are not mediated by a source external to the task-person situation' (Brief and Aldag, 1977: 497),' or more simply, when 'there is no apparent reward except the activity itself' (Deci, 1971: 105). Because IM can be a powerful motivator, and because it has self-generating and self-perpetuating properties, it represents a potentially important motivation construct for investigation (Hackman and Oldham, 1980; Ryan and Deci, 2000; Sprietzer, 1996).

The debate centers around the question of whether EM has detrimental effects on IM (Deci et al., 1999; Eisenberger and Cameron, 1998; Eisenberger et al., 1999; Ryan and Deci, 2000). Ryan and Deci (2000; Deci, et al., 1999) maintain that EM undermines an individual sense of self-determination which, they argue, is the most important determinant of IM. Eisenberger and Cameron (1998; Eisenberger, et al., 1999) counter by proposing that properly-designed EM can overcome any potentially detrimental effects. They also discuss learned industriousness theory which proposes that when individuals put forth significant effort towards a challenging task, 'the sensation of high effort acquires secondary reward properties' (p. 1161) which can be enhanced with properly designed extrinsic rewards. Eisenberger et al. (1999) offer meta-analytic data to support their position, but neither side has offered definitive data, and because there is very little research on IM in field settings, the debate remains unresolved.

One of the challenges of research in this area is that there are several cognitive theories of IM including Hackman and Oldham's (1980) job characteristics theory, Ryan and Deci's (2000) self-determination theory, and Thomas and Velthouse's (1990) psychological empowerment theory. Although empirical research supports all of these theories, they each suggest different causal factors are important, and no definitive conclusion has emerged from the research. In hopes of advancing research in this area, Bloom and Colbert (2007) have developed an integrated cognitive model of IM that combines these three cognitive theories. They also integrate affect into their model to help explain, among other things, what causes lower or higher levels of IM, what kinds of returns may enhance or diminish IM, and when IM may reach a tipping point where its effects can become detrimental.

Compensation and well-being

Read through the compensation research that has been published over the past 20 years and look for trends in the dependent variables. With strikingly few exceptions, a clear pattern emerges: the importance of compensation is judged primarily by its impact on economic outcomes. This assumption resonates well with the traditional 'business' perspective which emphasizes financial outcomes for organizations and economic outcomes for employees. A hallmark of micro-organizational research, however, has been its endorsement of other outcomes, including the well-being of the individuals who populate and patronize business organizations (see Carson and Barling, Chapter 35, this volume). While economics and finance rightly emphasize economic outcomes for organizations and individuals, one of the important roles that micro-organizational scholars can fulfil is to advance the importance of the well-being of people as being of at least equal importance to the well-being of organizations. In many ways, micro-organizational scholars are the guardians of the individual in organizational life and it is important for compensation scholars to reclaim this perspective in their research.

The large and rapidly increasing research in positive psychology (see Dutton and Glynn, Chapter 36, this volume) has recently given special attention to individual well-being, and several important theoretical and empirical perspectives have emerged from this line of inquiry that hold promise for advancing our understanding of compensation systems (Diener, 2000; Lyubomirsky et al., 2005a; Seligman, 2002). Despite the surging activity in this field, there is strong consensus on what the broad concept of human well-being or happiness comprises. Minimally, happiness refers to the state in which a person experiences a preponderance of positive, as opposed to negative, affect (Lyubomirsky, et al., 2005a) but many scholars suggest that true happiness also includes a sense that one's life has meaning and purpose and that one is living life well (Ryan and Deci, 2001; Seligman et al., 2005).

Researchers have made extensive progress in determining the causes and outcomes of happiness (for a meta-analysis see Lyubomirsky, et al., 2005a; see also Isen, 2000, 2004; Lyubomirsky et al., 2005b; Seligman, 2002; Snyder and Lopez, 2001). Happier people appear to be more productive, more creative, better problem solvers, producers of higher quality work, and earners of higher incomes (Isen, 2000, 2004; Lyubomirsky et al., 2005a, 2005b; Seligman, 2002). They also seem to have higher self-esteem, be more likeable and cooperative, have more high-quality social relationships, perform better in negotiation and conflict resolution situations, be mentally and physically healthier, and be more resilient to both physical and psychological threats (Isen, 2000, 2004; Lyubomirsky et al., 2005a). All of these outcomes have direct parallels in organizations, and given their variety and importance, happiness seems like a construct worthy of consideration by micro-organizational scholars.

One set of research findings that is particularly germane to the study of compensation is studies on money and happiness. Researchers from both psychology and economics have found, across studies, samples, and nations, that once people rise above the poverty level for their nation, there is, *at best*, a very weak positive relationship between income (or wealth) and happiness (Csikszentmihalyi, 1999, Diener, 2000; Kahneman et al., 2006; Layard, 2005; Myers, 2000). Even positive changes in income have a negligible relationship

with happiness. While increases in income may produce short-term increases, these happiness-increasing effects tend to dissipate quickly. People seem to adapt quickly to their income and, consequently, they require successively larger increases in income to achieve the same short-term change in happiness. In spite of this adaptation effect, many people still seem to invest considerable personal resources in the pursuit of happiness through money (Csikszentmihalyi, 1999; Layard, 2005; Myers, 2000). This creates a hedonic treadmill: as peoples' economic desires and expectation rise with their income, the happiness they seek remains just out of reach *and* they have to work harder just to stay in place (Csikszentmihalyi, 1999; Layard, 2005; Myers, 2000). The hedonic treadmill hypothesis might provide an excellent conceptual lens for studying why compensation systems seem to have limited durability, why incentives might become ineffective, and how people respond to internal and external equity.

Another interesting explanation for the paradoxical relationship between money and happiness centers on the role of social comparisons. Although absolute income is important to people, they seem to care even more about their relative income and these comparisons also have important implications for their happiness (Csikszentmihalyi, 1999; Diener, 2000; Frank and Cook, 1995). In a study of eight industrialized nations, including the US, Hagerty (2000) found that the distribution of incomes within communities and nations affects the happiness of citizens. He also found that happiness was negatively related to both the dispersion of incomes and to the number of rich people in a community. Research on ultimatum games indicates that people are willing to forego significant sums of money if it means that they can maintain a superior financial position to others (Guth and Tietz, 1990; Pillutla and Murnighan, 1996). Frank and Cook (1995) propose that relative income is one very important signal of status. They note that because income and other signals of status change over time, people are prone to getting stuck on comparative treadmills and so keeping up with the Joneses is a never-ending, ever-losing game. Among other topics, this research seems particularly apropos for studying pay structures and pay dispersion. It suggests, for example, that more dispersed pay structures may have negative implications for people's happiness and that this diminution of happiness may build over time as hedonic and comparative treadmill effects accumulate.

A final stream of happiness research that has implications for the study of compensation systems focuses on materialism and the value people place on money. Early research by Kasser and Ryan (1993, 1996) indicated that people who attach high importance to money and financial goals have significantly lower subjective well-being. Srivastava et al. (2001) pursued this research further and suggest that it is not money per se, but the reasons people pursue money that matter. People who attached greater importance to money had lower well-being when their motives were externally-oriented: money as means for making social comparisons, to seek power, to show off, or to overcome self doubt. However, the importance of money was unrelated to well-being when people's motives were internally-oriented: money as a means to create financial security, support their family, or create more leisure time. Similarly, Crawford Solberg et al. (2002) found that the more unrealistic a person's desire for income and material goods, the less satisfied they were with their income. Vansteenkiste et al. (2006) found that students who were more materialistically oriented displayed lower psychological well-being, showed more signs of psychological distress, and engaged in more substance abuse than other students. Further research by Sheldon et al. (2004: 484) indicates that 'its both what you pursue *and* why you pursue it,' that matters for happiness.

This research on happiness and money raises some potentially provocative questions. We do not know, for example, whether compensation affects well-being, although the research on pay satisfaction suggests that it does (Williams et al., 2006). How are different forms of pay – base pay, incentives, benefits, relational returns – related to happiness? Is happiness an important mediator or moderator of the affects or compensation?

Are we intensely motivated at work by things that will, at best, have little positive effect on our long-term happiness? Are we prone to keeping up with co-workers and other peers even though doing so reduces our well-being? Do incentive pay and more dispersed pay structures create higher performance, but at the expense of employees' well-being? These are just a very few of the important questions that can be addressed by integrating research from positive psychology into the study of compensation systems.

CONCLUSION

In 1966 Opsahl and Dunnette lamented that not much was known about pay systems. Because of the devotion, ingenuity and perseverance of many researchers, significant advances in our knowledge of the causes and consequences of compensation systems in organizations have been achieved. Even so, many important research questions remain unanswered. By bringing their unique theories and viewpoints into the study of compensation, micro-organizational scholars can make important contributions toward discovering those answers. These perspectives bring new insights that advance our understanding of not only cash compensation, but also the other important returns and motivators in the modern work place.

ACKNOWLEDGEMENT

Herbert Simon quote (page 309) reprinted with permission. Professor Herbert Simon is the original author of this quote.

NOTE

1 In unpublished results, Bloom (1999) did drop these variables. The coefficient for pay dispersion remained negative and significant.

REFERENCES

Arthur, J.B. and Airman-Smith, L. (2001) 'Gainsharing and organizational learning: An analysis of employee suggestions over time', *Academy of Management Journal*, 44: 737–754.

Barkema, H.G. and Gomez-Mejia, L.R. (1998) 'Managerial Compensation and Firm Performance: a General Research Framework', *Academy of Management Journal*, 41: 135–145.

Barnard, C.I. (1938) *The Functions of the Executive*. Cambridge, MA: Harvard University Press.

Barringer, M.W. and Milkovich, G.T. (1998) 'A theoretical exploration of the adoption and design of flexible benefit plans: A case of human resource innovation', *The Academy of Management Review*, 23: 305–324.

Bass, B.M. (1985) *Leadership and Performance Beyond Expectations*. New York: Free Press.

Becker, B.E. and Huselid, M.A. (1992) 'The incentive effects of tournament compensation systems', *Administrative Science Quarterly*, 37: 336–351.

Bloom, M. (1999) 'The Performance Effects of Pay Dispersion on Individuals and Organizations', *Academy of Management Journal*, 42: 25–40.

Bloom, M. and Colbert, A. (2007) *Towards An Enhanced Model Of Intrinsic Motivation*. Working paper, Mendoza College of Business, University of Notre Dame.

Bloom, M. and Michel, J.G. (2002) 'The relationships among organizational context, pay dispersion, and among managerial turnover', *Academy of Management Journal*, 45: 33–42.

Bloomfield, D. (1923) *Financial Incentives for Employees and Executives*. New York: The H.W. Wilson Co.

Brief, A.P. and Aldag, R.J. (1977) 'The intrinsic-extrinsic dichotomy: Toward conceptual clarity', *Academy of Management Review*, 2: 496–500.

Brief, A.P. and Weiss, H.M. (2002) 'Organizational behavior: Affect in the workplace', *Annual Review of Psychology*, 53: 279–307.

Brockner, J. (2002) 'Making Sense of Procedural Fairness: how High Procedural Fairness can Reduce or Heighten the Influence of Outcome Favorability', *Academy of Management Review*, 27: 58–76.

Cable, D.M. and Judge, T.A. (1994) 'Pay preferences and job search decisions: A person-organization fit perspective', *Personnel Psychology*, 47: 317–348.

Chapman, D.S., Uggerslev, K.L., Carroll, S.A., Piasentin, K.A. and Jones, D.A. (2005) 'Applicant attraction to organizations and job choice: A meta-analytic review of the correlates of recruiting outcomes', *Journal of Applied Psychology*, 90: 928–944.

Colella, A, Paetzold, R.l., Zardkoohi, A. and Wesson, M. (2007) 'Exposing pay secrecy', *Academy of Management Review*, 32: 55–71.

Colquitt, J.A. (2001) 'On the dimensionality of organizational justice: A construct validation of a measure', *Journal of Applied Psychology*, 86: 386–400.

Colvin, G. (2006) 'The 100 Best Companies to Work For', *Fortune*, 153: 71–74.

Crawford Solberg, E., Diener, E., Wirtz, D., Lucas, R.E. and Oishi, S. (2002) 'Wanting, having, and satisfaction: Examining the role of desire discrepancies in satisfaction with income', *Journal of Personality and Social Psychology*, 83: 725–734.

Cropanzano, R., Rupp, D.E., Mohler, C.J. and Schminke, M. (2001) 'Three Roads to Organizational Justice', in J. Ferris (ed), *Research in Personnel and Human Resources Management*. Greenwich, CT: JAI Press. Vol. 20: pp. 1–113.

Csikszentmihalyi, M. (1999) 'If we are so rich, why aren't we happy?', *American Psychologist*, 54: 821–827.

Deci, E.L. (1971) 'Effects of externally mediated rewards on intrinsic motivation', *Journal of Personality and Social Psychology*, 18: 105–115.

Deci, E.L., Koestner, R. and Ryan, R.M. (1999) 'A meta-analytic review of experiments examining the effects of extrinsic rewards on intrinsic', *Psychological Bulletin*, 125: 627–668.

Diener, E., Suh, E.M., Lucas, R.E. and Smith, H.E. (1999) 'Subjective well-being: Three decades of progress', *Psychological Bulletin*, 125: 276–302.

Diener, E. (2000) 'Subjective well-being: The science of happiness and a proposal for a national index', *American Psychologist*, 55: 34–43.

Dreher, G.F., Ash, R.A. and Bretz, R.D. (1988) 'Benefit coverage and employee cost: Critical factors in explaining compensation satisfaction', *Personnel Psychology*, 41: 237–254.

Edwards, J.R. and Rothbard, N.P. (2000) 'Mechanisms linking work and family: Clarifying the relationship between work and family constructs', *Academy of Management Review*, 25: 178–199.

Eisenberger, R. and Cameron, J. (1998) 'Reward, intrinsic interest, and creativity: New findings', *American Psychologist*, 53: 676–679.

Eisenberger, R., Rhoades, L. and Cameron, J. (1999) 'Does pay for performance increase or decrease perceived self-determination and intrinsic motivation?', *Journal of Personality and Social Psychology*, 77: 1026–1040.

Florida, R. and Goodnight, J. (2005) 'Managing for Creativity', *Harvard Business Review*, 8: 124–131.

Foa, U.G. and Foa.B. (1974) *Societal Structures of the Mind*, Springfield, IL: Charles C. Thomas.

Frank, R.H. and Cook, P.J. (1995) *The Winner-Take-All Society*. New York: Penguin Books.

Gerhart, B. and Milkovich, G . T. (1992) 'Employee compensation: Research and practice', in M.D. Dunnette and L.M. Hough (eds), *Handbook of Industrial and Organizational Psychology* (2nd edn). Palo Alto, CA: Consulting Psychologists Press. Vol. 3: pp. 481–570.

Gerhart B. and Rynes S.L. (2003) *Compensation: Theory, Evidence, and Strategic Implications*. Thousand Oaks, CA: Sage.

Gomez-Mejia, L.R., Welbourne, T.M. and Wiseman, R.M. (2000) 'The role of risk sharing and risk taking under gainsharing', *Academy of Management Review*, 25: 492–507.

Grandy, A. (2008) 'Emotions at work', in C.L. Cooper and J. Barling (eds), *The SAGE Handbook of Organizational Behavior*.

Guth, W. and Tietz, R. (1990) 'Ultimatum bargaining behavior: A survey and comparison of experimental results', *Journal of Economic Psychology*, 11: 417–449.

Hackman, J.R. and Oldham, G.R. (1980) *Work Redesign*. Reading, MA: Addison-Wesley.

Hagerty, M.R. (2000) 'Social comparisons of income in one's community: Evidence from national surveys of income and happiness', *Journal of Personality and Social Psychology*, 78: 764–771.

Hollensbe, E.C. and Guthrie, J.P. (2000) 'Group pay-for-performance plans: The role of spontaneous goal setting', *Academy of Management Review*, 25: 864–872.

Isen, A.M. (2000) 'Some perspectives on positive affect and self-regulation', *Psychological Inquiry*, 11: 184–187.

Isen, A.M. (2004) 'Some Perspectives on Positive Feelings and Emotions: Positive Affect Facilitates Thinking and Problem Solving', in A.S.R. Manstead, N. Frijda, and A. Fischer (eds), *Feelings and Emotions: The Amsterdam Symposium*. New York: Cambridge University Press, pp. 263–281.

Jenkins, G.D. Jr., Mitra, A., Gupta, N. and Shaw, J. (1998) 'Are financial incentives related to performance? A meta-analytic review of empirical research', *Journal of Applied Psychology*, 83: 777–787.

Judge, T. (2008) 'Leadership', in C.L. Cooper and J. Barling (eds), *The SAGE Handbook of Organizational Behavior*.

Kahneman, D., Krueger, A.B., Schkade, D., Schwarz, N. and Stone, A.A. (2006) 'Would you be happier if you were richer? A focusing illusion', *Science*, 312: 1908–1910.

Kasser, T. and Ryan, R.M. (1993) 'A dark side of the American dream: Correlates of financial success as a central life aspiration', *Journal of Personality and Social Psychology*, 65: 410–422.

Kasser, T. and Ryan, R.M. (1996) 'Further examining the American dream: Differential correlates of intrinsic and extrinsic goals', *Personality and Social Psychology Bulletin*, 22: 280–287.

Kristof, A.L. (1996) 'Person-organization fit: An integrative review of its conceptualizations, measurement, and implications', *Personnel Psychology*, 49: 1–49.

Lambert, S.J. (2000) 'Added benefits: The link between work-life benefits and organizational citizenship behavior', *Academy of Management Journal*, 43: 801–815.

Lawler III, E.E. (1965) 'Managers' perceptions of their subordinates' pay and of their superiors' pay', *Personnel Psychology*, 18: 413–430.

Lawler III, E.E. (1967) 'Secrecy about management compensation: Are there hidden costs?', *Organizational Behavior and Human Performance*, 2: 182–189.

Lawler III, E.E. (1971) *Pay and Organizational Effectiveness*. Boston: McGraw-Hill.

Layard, R.M. (2005) *Happiness: Lessons From a New Science*. New York: Penguin Press.

Lazear, E.P. (1995) *Personnel Economics*. Cambridge, MA: MIT Press.

Leventhal, G.S., Michaels, J.W. and Sanford, C. (1972) 'Inequity and interpersonal conflict: Reward allocation and secrecy about reward as methods of preventing conflict', *Journal of Personality and Social Psychology*, 23: 88–102.

Locke E.A., Feren D.B., McCaleb V.M., Shaw, K.N. and Denny, A.T. (1980) 'The Relative Effectiveness of Four Ways of Motivating Employee Performance', in K.D. Duncan, M.M. Gruenberg, and D. Wallis (eds), *Changes in Working Life*. New York: Wiley, pp. 363–388.

Lyubomirsky, S., King, L. and Diener, E. (2005a) 'The benefits of frequent positive affect: Does happiness lead to success?', *Psychological Bulletin*, 131: 803–855.

Lyubomirsky, S., Sheldon, K.M. and Schkade, D. (2005b) 'Pursuing happiness: The architecture of sustainable change', *Review of General Psychology*, 9: 111–131.

Mahoney, J.T. (2002) 'The relevance of Chester I. Barnard's teachings to contemporary management education: Communicating the aesthetics of management', *International Journal of Organizational Theory and Behavior*, 5: 159–172.

Miceli, M.P., Jung, I., Near, J.P. and Greenberger, D.B. (1991) 'Predictors and Outcomes of Reactions to Pay-for-Performance', *Journal of Applied Psychology*, 76: 508–521.

Milkovich, G.T. and Anderson, P.H. (1972) 'Management Compensation and Secrecy Policies', *Personnel Psychology*, 25: 293–302.

Milkovich, G.T. and Newman, J.M. (2005) *Compensation*, 8th edn. Boston: McGraw-Hill Irwin.

Milkovich, G.T. and Stevens, J. (1999) '*Back to the Future: A Century of Compensation*'. Working Paper # 99–08. Ithaca, NY: Center for Advanced Human Resource Studies.

Mitchell, T.R. and Mickel, A.E. (1999) 'The meaning of money: An individual-difference perspective', *Academy of Management Review*, 24: 568–578.

Molm, L.D., Takahashi, N. and Peterson, G. (2000) 'Risk and trust in social exchange: An experimental test of a classical proposition', *American Journal of Sociology*, 105: 1396–1427.

Myers, D. (2000) 'The funds, friends, and faith of happy people', *American Psychologist*, 55: 56–67.

Opsahl, R.L. and Dunnette, M.D. (1966) 'Role of financial compensation in industrial motivation', *Psychological Bulletin*, 66: 94–118.

Peterson, S.J. and Luthans, F. (2006) 'The impact of financial and nonfinancial incentives on business-unit outcomes over time', *Journal of Applied Psychology*, 91: 156–165.

Pfeffer, J. (1998) 'Six dangerous myths about pay', *Harvard Business Review*, 76: 109–119.

Pfeffer, J. and Langton, N. (1993) 'The effect of wage dispersion on satisfaction, productivity, and working collaboratively: Evidence from college and university faculty', *Administrative Science Quarterly*, 38: 382–407.

Pillutla, M.M. and Murnighan, J.K. (1996) 'Unfairness, anger, and spite: Emotional rejections of ultimatum offers', *Organizational Behavior and Human Decision Processes*, 68: 208–224.

Rhoades, L. and Eisenberger, R. (2002) 'Perceived organizational support: A review of the literature', *Journal of Applied Psychology*, 87: 698–714.

Rothbard, N.P. and Edwards, J.R. (2003) 'Investment in work and family roles: A test of identity and utilitarian motives', *Personnel Psychology*, 56: 699–729.

Rousseau, D.M. and Ho, V.T. (2000) 'Psychological contract issues in compensation', in S.L. Rynes and B.A. Gerhart (eds), *Compensation in Organizations: Current Research and Practice*. San Francisco: Jossey-Bass, pp. 273–310.

Ryan, R.M. and Deci, E.L. (2000) 'Self-determination theory and the facilitation of intrinsic motivation, social development, and well-being', *American Psychologist*, 55: 68–78.

Ryan, R.M. and Deci, E.L. (2001) 'On happiness and human potentials: A review of research on hedonic and eudaimonic well-being', *Annual Review of Psychology*, 52: 141–166.

Rynes S.L. and Gerhart B.A. (eds) (2005) *Compensation in Organizations: Current Research and Practice*. San Francisco: Jossey-Bass.

Rynes, S.L., Gerhart, B. and Parks, L. (2005) 'Personnel Psychology: Performance Evaluation and Pay for Performance', *Annual Review of Psychology*, 56: 571–600.

Schloss, D.F. (1892) *Methods of Industrial Remuneration*. London: Williams and Norgate.

Sedikides, C. and Brewer, M.B. (2001) *Individual Self, Relational Self, Collective Self*. Philadelphia, PA: Psychology Press.

Seligman, M.E. P. (2002) *Authentic Happiness: Using the New Positive Psychology to Realize Your Potential for Lasting Fulfillment*, New York: Free Press.

Seligman, M.E. P., Steen, T.A., Park, N. and Peterson, C. (2005) 'Positive Psychology Progress', *American Psychologist*, 60: 410–421.

Sheldon, K.M., Ryan, R.M., Deci, E.L. and Kasser, T. (2004) 'The independent effects of goal contents and motives on well-being: It's both what you pursue and why you pursue it', *Personality and Social Psychology Bulletin*, 30: 475–486.

Simon, H.A. (1991) 'Organizations and markets', *Journal of Economic Perspectives*, 5: 25–44.

Snyder, C.R. and Lopez, S.J. (2001) *Handbook of Positive Psychology*, New York: Oxford University Press.

Sprietzer, G.M. (1996) 'Social structural characteristics of psychological empowerment', *Academy of Management Journal*, 3: 483–504.

Srivastava, A., Locke, E.A. and Bartol, K.M. (2001) 'Money and subjective well-being: It's not the money, it's the motives', *Journal of Personality and Social Psychology*, 80: 959–971.

Stajkovic, A.D. and Luthans, F. (2001) 'Differential effects of incentive motivators on work performance', *Academy of Management Journal*, 44: 580–590.

Tekleab, A.G., Bartol, K.M. and Liu, W. (2005) 'Is it pay levels or pay raises that matter to fairness and turnover?', *Journal of Organizational Behavior*, 26: 899–921.

Thomas, K.W. and Velthouse, B.A. (1990) 'Cognitive elements of empowerment: An "interpretive" model of intrinsic task motivation', *Academy of Management Review*, 15: 666–681.

Trevor, C.O. and Wazeter, D.L. (2006) 'A contingent view of reactions to objective pay conditions: Interdependence among pay structure characteristics and pay relative to internal and external referents', *Journal of Applied Psychology*, 91: 1260–1275.

Vansteenkiste, M., Duriez, B., Simons, J. and Soenens, B. (2006) 'Materialistic values and well-being among business students: Further evidence of their detrimental effect', *Journal of Applied Social Psychology*, 36: 2892–2908.

Williams, M.L., Malos, S.B. and Palmer, D.K. (2002) 'Benefit system and benefit level satisfaction: An expanded model of antecedents and consequences', *Journal of Management*, 28: 195–215.

Williams, M.L., McDaniel, M.A. and Nguyen, N.T. (2006) 'A meta-analysis of the antecedents and consequences of pay level satisfaction', *Journal of Applied Psychology*, 91: 392–413.

17

Employee Motivation

Gary P. Latham[1] and Edwin A. Locke

We discover the concept of motivation through our own experiences of desire and aversion. A motive is a physiological or psychological based desire that incites a person to action. Motivation affects choice, effort and persistence (Latham, 2007). Employees make choices as to what they will aim for, the amount of effort they will exert, and how long they will persist in pursuing what it is that they want to attain. A taxonomy for predicting, understanding, and influencing motivation in organizational settings includes needs, traits, values, cognition, affect, and the environment/context (Latham and Pinder, 2005; Locke and Henne, 1986). This chapter examines theories and empirical research that underlie this taxonomy. The value of these theories is that they provide frameworks for selecting employees and developing interventions for ensuring that an organization has a motivated work force.

NEEDS

The conditions required for life as well as an employee's well being are called needs.

When a need is not met, discomfort in the form of anxiety or pain is experienced. In extreme cases, need deprivation leads to death. Hence individuals are incited to take action to fulfill their needs.

Maslow (1943, 1954) developed a need hierarchy theory. This theory posits five needs ranging from physiological to psychological. Specifically, these needs are hierarchically ordered from lower to higher: physiological, safety, affiliation, esteem and self-actualization. A core assumption underlying this theory is that lower order needs must be satisfied before action is taken to satisfy higher order needs. However, all needs are cyclical; thus no need is ever permanently satisfied. The theory implies that needs lower in the hierarchy must be routinely satisfied before one can move up to needs higher in the hierarchy.

Although Ronen (2001) found empirical support for Maslow's taxonomy of needs, Maslow (1965) himself expressed skepticism of a universal hierarchy. Suffice it to say that, ordering aside, needs can be readily dichotomized as physiological (e.g., need for food) or psychological (e.g., need for self-esteem). Most importantly, people can prioritize their needs in different ways. For example, an employee may quit a much needed job to protest a perceived slight to self-esteem.

Needs provide an explanation for the choice, effort and persistence to seek and retain a paying job. People choose to work in order to fulfil their needs. In fact, working in an organization can help, in different ways, to fulfill all five needs posited in Maslow's theory. For example, to the extent that an employee's on-going choices, effort, and persistence increase knowledge, skills and abilities that foster the attainment of personally valued goals, the need for self-actualization, (that is, maximizing one's potential) may be met. This latter need, although not precisely defined by Maslow, typically incites a long range pursuit for challenging assignments of interest to an employee.

PERSONALITY TRAITS

Among the fastest growing bodies of literature on organization behavior is research on personality (Mitchell and Daniels, 2003). This is in stark contrast to the first 80 odd years of the 20th century. The reasons for this, as Barrick et al. (2001) pointed out, are at least two-fold. First, there was lack of clarity regarding the traits that were assessed. Consequently, researchers often used different names for traits with the same meaning or the converse, they ascribed different meanings for the same trait. Second, the hypothesized trait-performance linkage lacked a theoretical basis. There was not even an accepted classification system for reducing the myriad traits to a manageable number.

In the mid-1980s, two influential studies by Staw and his colleagues (Staw and Ross, 1985; Staw et al., 1986) suggested that there is a dispositional source of job satisfaction. This peaked the interest of the research community. This interest was soon followed by progress on the above two issues.

The Five Factor Model

The lack of an accepted taxonomy changed in the 1990s as a result of the development of the Five Factor Model or FFM (Wiggins, 1996). The FFM assesses extroversion, conscientiousness, neuroticism, openness to experience, and agreeableness. Bouchard (1997) found genetic influences on measures of these five personality traits, with heritability estimates ranging from 0.39 for agreeableness to 0.49 for extroversion. These five traits have also been shown to be relatively stable across a person's life-span (Barrick et al., 2001).

In an analysis of previous meta-analyses, Barrick et al. (2001) found that conscientiousness was the best and most consistent predictor of job performance, followed by emotional stability. This was the only other Big Five factor for which the mean validity fell within a positive 90 per cent credibility range. As Barrick et al. (2001) observed, it is difficult to think of a job where it is beneficial to be irresponsible rather than conscientious. The authors (p. 22) concluded that: 'Both the validity of conscientiousness and emotional stability generalize across all occupations and criterion types.' Emotional stability and agreeableness correlate with effective teamwork. Extroversion and openness to experience correlate with training performance.

Several subsequent meta-analyses have revealed that conscientiousness and emotional stability correlate positively with job performance in virtually all jobs (Anderson and Viswesvaran, 1998; Barrick and Mount, 1991). Salgado (1997) reached a similar conclusion based on studies conducted in Europe.

Despite these consistent findings, little is known about the mechanisms through which these distal traits affect job performance. One can argue that the 'Big Five' are simply cluster scores of behaviors, in which case they are predictive but not explanatory. Or one might argue, given the wording of some of the trait items measured in the Big Five, that they reflect a person's underlying values. But traits may reflect temperament which is heritable.

More conceptual work is clearly required here.

Additional knowledge is also needed on how traits lead to action if they are, in fact, causal. There is evidence that self-efficacy and goals mediate trait effects (Locke, 2000). In the domain of academic achievement, there is evidence suggesting that self-efficacy almost fully mediates the relationship between the FFM and performance (Caprara et al., 2004).

Core self evaluations

Judge et al. (1997) proposed a higher order concept related to internal psychological states which they labeled core self-evaluations (CSEs). They defined these evaluations as a broad trait that subsumes four specific traits, namely, self esteem, generalized self-efficacy, locus of control and emotional stability (the converse of neuroticism) that are sufficiently inter-related to be grouped together as a single measure. A subsequent study showed that CSEs are related to employee motivation (Judge et al., 1998). A meta-analytic review revealed that each of these four traits is related positively to job performance in addition to job satisfaction (Judge and Bono, 2001).

Goal orientation

Dweck's (1999) goal orientation theory predicts and explains a person's behavior in terms of an approach-avoidance disposition. People with a learning goal orientation are predisposed to acquiring knowledge and increasing their skill set. Hence, they typically seek tasks that are challenging for them. They view errors as inherent in the learning process, and as valuable to the extent they can learn from each mistake. The theory states that people with a performance goal orientation are predisposed to avoiding tasks that might lead others to question their competence. Consequently, they strive to choose tasks where they can easily excel (Vandewalle et al., 2001).

Research shows that a learning goal orientation correlates positively with performance.

The mediators are goal setting, planning and effort (Vandewalle, 1999; Brett and Vandewalle, 1999). A criticism of this theory is that these two goal orientations are as much a state as they are a disposition. The positive effects of a learning goal orientation are easily induced (Seijts et al., 2004).

Self-determination theory

Self determination theory, developed by Deci and Ryan (Deci, 1975; Deci and Ryan, 1990; Ryan and Deci, 2000), states that motivation, typically measured as the amount of time one persists at a task during one's free time, increases to the extent that the source of motivation is inferred by the person to be intrinsic rather than extrinsic. The theory further asserts that three relatively stable personality traits explain how people initially regulate themselves when striving to attain their goals.

An autonomy orientation leads people to attend to cues in the environment that suggest 'free choice.' Scores for autonomy correlate positively with assessments of a person's self-esteem; they correlate negatively with boredom at work. People with this orientation are said to have an intrinsic motivation to work hard at their job.

People with a control orientation have an extrinsic motivation for work. They see their behavior as constrained/controlled by others. Those with an impersonal orientation are sensitized to signals that suggest their incompetence. Scores suggesting a control orientation correlate negatively with self esteem. People who score high on this trait do not see themselves as being able to control external events. These three personality dispositions, autonomy, control, and impersonal affect performance via the mediating processes of a person's goal orientation as well as the difficulty level of the goal that is set (Ryan and Deci, 2000).

A core assumption of this prediction is the 'over-justification effect,' namely, that there is a negative reciprocal relationship between intrinsic and extrinsic rewards. Thus, the greater the extrinsic reward (e.g., money), the lower one's subsequent intrinsic motivation and satisfaction. The theory asserts that people are motivated to the extent that they feel that their actions are chosen by them freely. The administration of a monetary reward for doing what an individual might have done anyway, because of a task's intrinsic appeal, causes the person to make an attributional shift regarding the cause of behavior from self to others. This causal mechanism, however, has yet to be validated.

This theory has been criticized for its naïveté regarding the workplace. Bandura (1977) attacked its logic. Decreases in performance typically reflect a response to how extrinsic incentives are presented rather than to the incentives themselves. It is unlikely, Bandura noted, that concert pianists lose interest in the keyboard just because they are offered high recital fees. If a monetary reward is given for high performance, it does not undermine motivation (Miner, 2002). The feeling of competency appears to negate any feeling of loss of control. Eisenberger and Cameron (1996) attacked the theory for failing to specify the mechanism which explains why dissatisfaction emanating from a decline in perceived self determination decreases a person's intrinsic value for performing a task, rather than anger toward the person who is the source of the external incentive. Fay and Frese (2000) questioned the very relevance of this theory to organizational behavior. Work assignments, they said, are just that – assignments. In organizational settings, one can rarely describe work as being performed 'freely.' Moreover, people expect to be paid by the organization that employs them. It is unlikely that self-determination is the wellspring of employee motivation if it is so fragile that its effects are negated by the most common of life's exigencies (Locke and Latham, 1990). Finally, it is extremely difficult to differentiate situations that are characterized solely by intrinsic vs. extrinsic incentives. A so-called intrinsic setting, for testing the validity of self-determination theory, would have to be completely free of any and all external inducements (e.g., situational, physical and social structures, the materials

they contain, as well as expectations of and recognition from others). Yet, paradoxically, from a competency viewpoint, these factors could enhance an employee's motivation.

VALUES

Values are similar to needs in their ability to affect a person's choices, effort, and persistence. Values, however, as opposed to inborn needs, are an individual's conceptions of the 'good' or 'desirable' which are acquired through learning and experience. As is the case with needs, the satisfaction of values leads to pleasure, and lack of fulfilment is a source of displeasure (Allport, 1951). When the job requires people to behave in ways that are counter to their personality traits, they experience negative affect (Moskowitz and Cote, 1995). The same is likely true for values. Values are the proximal basis for the goals that people choose, though all motivation, as previously stated, begins with needs. Values can be defined as trans-situational goals in that they are relatively enduring, and they serve as guiding principles throughout an adult's life-span (Schwartz and Sagie, 2000). Because values transcend situations, they are able to influence choice, effort and persistence beyond the attainment of an individual's immediate goals to more ultimate goals (Chatman, 1991). Goals, discussed in the subsequent section, are the mechanisms by which values incite action.

Relevant to self determination theory, Malka and Chatman (2003) found that values act as a moderator of one's job satisfaction with respect to the money a person receives. Business school graduates who scored high on a measure of external work orientation valued money far more than those who had an orientation toward the intrinsic aspects of their work. Srivastava et al. (2001) assessed the motives underlying entrepreneurs' value for money. They found that positive motives for valuing money (e.g., enhancing their family's security, gaining a sense of justice) had a neutral effect on a person's self evaluation of one's overall life. However, there was a negative relationship between the value people attached to money and their self evaluation when their motive for money was negative (e.g., a way to feel superior to others; a way to gain power).

COGNITION

Knowledge is required to identify and satisfy an individual's needs and to choose and attain values/goals. In the absence of knowledge, an employee cannot determine ways to satisfy a need or to behave in ways consistent with, or leading to, the attainment of a value. Hence motivation in the absence of knowledge is useless. The reverse is also true. At least four motivational theories emphasize the important role of cognition in motivation.

Vroom's (1964) expectancy theory states that an employee's choice to exert effort is a multiplicative product of the person's expectancy that:

(1) effort will lead to performance (E);
(2) performance will be instrumental to the attainment of one or more outcomes (I); and
(3) the valence or value of the outcome(s) for that employee (V).

Hence, the theory is often referred to as valence-instrumentality-expectancy or VIE theory. The practical significance of this theory is that it provides a language and framework for formulating questions about the role of an employee's beliefs and values on that person's performance.

The mathematical operations are at best heuristics, as Vroom acknowledged (Latham, 2007: 47–48). People do not actually make these calculations before making a decision. As discussed in a subsequent section, many decisions are based on the subconscious. A further limitation of this theory is that a core assumption is that employees are hedonistic, that is, they consistently choose to act in ways that maximize valued outcomes. This is not always the case (Locke, 1975). Further, the theory says nothing about goals. It is silent on what arouses an employee to take action.

Even if an employee has the cognitive ability to derive complex mental representations of the environment, having no goal or a low one mitigates a person taking action.

GOAL SETTING

Goals are a task and situationally specific outgrowth of an individual's values. Consequently, they are both an end state to attain and a standard by which performance is evaluated. To the extent an employee values education, for example, that employee is likely to go back to school and master the chosen subject matter. Pursuing and attaining a goal that an employee values provides job satisfaction. Given that a person has sufficient knowledge/skill, a primary determinant of job satisfaction, as noted earlier, is cognitive challenge regarding work assignments an employee values (Judge et al., 2000). A specific high performance goal incites effort, and in addition cues an individual to draw upon knowledge that will likely lead to its attainment.

These conclusions are captured in Locke and Latham's (1990, 2002) goal setting theory. This theory, unlike need hierarchy and expectancy theory, was developed inductively rather than deductively from more than 400 laboratory and field experiments. The number of experiments currently exceeds 1000 (Mitchell and Daniels, 2003) In particular, the theory states that

(1) a specific high goal leads to higher performance than no goal setting or even an abstract goal such as 'to do your best';
(2) given goal commitment, the higher the goal the higher an employee's performance;
(3) Variables such as participation in decision making, performance feedback, incentives, and competition increase performance to the extent that they lead to the setting of and commitment to a specific high goal.

Boundary or conditional variables that can limit the effectiveness of goal setting include an employee's lack of ability or task knowledge, little or no goal commitment, no knowledge of results on goal progress, and situational constraints. If a task is complex for an employee, that is, if an employee has yet to acquire the requisite knowledge or ability to attain a performance goal, a specific high learning rather than a performance goal should be set (Latham and Seijts, 2006; Winters and Latham, 1996). This is because a performance goal, unlike a learning goal, may focus an employee's attention on the desired outcome to the exclusion of the attention required for the discovery of solutions to an impasse, the implementation of one or more appropriate discoveries, and the monitoring of their effectiveness (Latham, 2007; Seijts and Latham, 2001).

Goal setting is a key variable that ties studies of motivation to those of leadership. This is because leadership is a tripod consisting of leader(s), followers, and the common goal they want to attain (Bennis, 2007).

SOCIAL COGNITIVE THEORY

In addition to goal setting, Bandura's (1977, 1986, 1997) social cognitive theory specifies a core set of determinants, the mechanism through which they work, and the optimal ways of translating this knowledge into effective practices. The core determinants include knowledge of risks and benefits of different practices, outcome expectations of the expected costs and benefits for different practices, perceived self-efficacy that one can exercise control over one's performance outcomes, and the perceived facilitators and social structural impediments to the changes they seek. Outcome expectancy stresses the importance of seeing the relationship between what one is doing and the outcome that one can expect from doing it. For example, employees in a forest products company chose to expend a great deal of effort stealing from the company, and persisted in doing so when the outcome they expected from theft was a sense of thrill and excitement. When this expected outcome was removed, the theft stopped (Latham, 2001).

Self-efficacy is the extent to which employees believe that they can perform a specific task effectively. Employees with high self-efficacy not only set high goals, they persist until they attain them despite the obstacles that they encounter. Those with low self-efficacy give up readily when confronted by the same impediments to goal attainment.

Self-efficacy in organizational settings can be increased most readily in one of the following ways.

(1) Enactive mastery whereby tasks are sequenced in such a way as to increase the probability of skill acquisition, and hence an early win; early wins instill/restore confidence.
(2) Modeling the behaviors with whom the individual identifies, who has either mastered the task or is in the process of doing so. 'If that person can, so can I.'
(3) By persuasion from an individual with high credibility. 'If that person believes I can do so, it must be true.'

Persuasion can also involve giving the person task strategy information. Further, persuasion can include an individual's self talk. Displaced managers were re-employed (Millman and Latham, 2001), Native North Americans excelled in a selection interview and obtained employment (Latham and Budworth, 2006), and MBA students increased their team playing skills as a result of training in verbal self guidance (Brown and Latham, 2006). Related to self talk is positive mental imagery, which like self talk, increases self-efficacy. Morin and Latham (2000) found that as a result of this training, supervisors increased their effectiveness in their interactions with union officers. This finding is consistent with Action Theory, discussed next.

In short, self-efficacy is based on the conclusions employees draw regarding their capabilities to attain performance outcomes, including overcoming obstacles to goal attainment. Outcomes expectancies (e.g., rewards) will not affect performance if performance self-efficacy is low. Conversely, self efficacy will not affect performance if a person's outcome expectancies are not perceived as positive. Napier and Latham (1986) found that managers in a newspaper facility had high self-efficacy that they could conduct fair and objective performance appraisals of their subordinates. Nevertheless, they chose not to conduct appraisals, because the outcome they expected for doing so was 'nothing.' They anticipated that those who received a positive appraisal would be treated no differently by upper management than those who received a negative appraisal. The extent to which people mobilize their effort is determined by the outcomes they expect from the goals that are set, and their self-efficacy that the goal is attainable.

ACTION THEORY

Action theory, developed in Germany by Frese (2005), is consistent with goal setting and social cognitive theories. A goal, this theory asserts, can be an employee's wish or it can be derived from an organizational task. What differentiates a momentary wish from a true goal is whether a person has formulated a plan for attaining it. A core premise of this theory in that a goal is motivating to the extent that an individual can visualize its attainment. Goal importance, opportunity to take action, and knowledge of ways to effectively pursue the goal are moderator variables affecting goal attainment.

The above three theories presuppose the existence of goal commitment. In the absence of goal commitment, goal setting has no effect on behavior. Ways of gaining goal commitment were reviewed by Locke et al. (1988) and subsequently by Locke and Latham (1990). They include external influences (leadership, peer influence, and external rewards), interactive influences (participation) and internal factors (self efficacy, self regulation, goal importance).

When leaders assign a goal, they are implicitly communicating their belief that an employee is capable of attaining it (Salancik, 1977). To the extent that a leader is supportive, people set high goals (Latham and Saari, 1979), and to the extent that a leader is trusted,

the extent to which employees work hard increases (Earley, 1986; Oldham, 1976).

The effect of peer influence on performance is a well-known phenomenon (Kozlowski and Ilgen, 2006). Peers serve as models for one another. If employees commit to a goal, the likelihood increases that an individual, new to the group, will do likewise.

Monetary incentives for attaining goals may increase goal commitment as compared to hourly pay plus goals. Much depends, however, on whether the goals are viewed by an individual as attainable. Monetary incentives may reduce commitment (which may be reflected in lower self-set goals and self-efficacy) compared to hourly pay with goals when the goals with bonuses are viewed as impossible to attain (see Lee et al., 1997, Table 2).

If a goal is assigned curtly, it is unlikely to engender commitment. If a goal assignment includes a rationale, however, it is as effective as one that is set participatively (Latham et al., 1988). Communicating the goals to subordinates in a clear and compelling way is a hallmark of an effective leader who is able to gain the commitment of subordinates (Locke, 2000).

The benefits of participative decision-making, are primarily cognitive rather than motivational. Participative decision making on tasks that are complex for people is effective to the extent that it promotes the sharing of knowledge (Latham et al., 1994; Locke et al., 1997; Quigley et al., 2007). Participation in decision making can sometimes lead to the setting of higher goals than those that are assigned (Latham et al., 1978). The higher the goal, the higher the performance.

With regard to internal factors, a person's self-efficacy, as noted earlier, leads to the setting of, as well as effort for attaining a high goal (Bandura and Cervone, 1983). Studies of self management involving unionized state government employees revealed that self set goals that were accompanied by self generated feedback and self administered rewards brought about an increase in self-efficacy and goal commitment as well as increased job attendance (Frayne and Latham, 1987). Contrary to self-determination theory, there is no evidence in the organizational behavior literature that a self-set goal leads to better performance than one that is assigned or set participatively.

CONTROL THEORY

Carver and Scheier (1981) developed control theory on the basis of cybernetic engineering principles. This theory too champions the importance of goals on a person's behavior. Nevertheless, this theory differs from the preceding theories in its emphasis on a negative feedback loop. The loop is said to be a primary source of motivation in that a person, similar metaphorically to a thermostat, is incited to take action that will reduce, if not eliminate, goal-performance discrepancies. This assertion is in stark contrast to both goal setting and social cognitive theories which assert that goal setting also leads to a discrepancy production process. Once a goal is attained, an employee who has high self efficacy sets an even higher goal rather than becoming complacent. Control theorists try to get around this by claiming there are higher order goals but this only pushes the problem back a step further. Why do people have higher order goals? The answer lies in biological rather than in engineering principles. Life is a process of goal-directed action; thus human life requires a continual process of setting and pursuing hierarchically related goals. Task-specific goals (e.g., achieve X on my job) are tied (in a means-ends relationship) to higher order goals (e.g., keep my job and get promoted) which are tied to yet higher order goals (e.g., earn a 'good living').

Vancouver (2005), a control theorist, has been critical of self efficacy. The notion of self efficacy is discordant with the sole belief in a negative feedback loop. Hence, Vancouver has argued that high self efficacy leads to lower effort, thereby decreasing motivation over time within individuals. This may be true if the person becomes over-confident.

But, as noted earlier, people with high task-specific self efficacy routinely set their goals higher following goal attainment. This is a problem with control theory as originally conceived. The theory stresses that it does not model what goes on inside an organism psychologically, that is, consciously. This makes it impossible for the theory to explain action without resorting to unconscious or mechanistic processes. Thus, the cybernetic system is posited to respond mindlessly to its own performance. This is conceptual incoherence.

AFFECT

Emotion is the form in which one experiences subconscious value judgments (Locke, 1976). In the absence of emotion, a value would be experienced as a 'dry' abstraction (e.g., 'another pay raise; so what?'). Inherent in emotion are action tendencies to approach or avoid that which one appraises as beneficial or harmful (e.g., a safety hazard on the job). Emotion reflects cognition as well as values. To fear a safety hazard on the job, an employee must have knowledge of the plant site as well as the required job duties. Thus the causal sequence is: object –> cognitive appraisal –> value appraisal –> emotion. With repetitious experience, the appraisal becomes automatic, namely, object –> emotion.

Two cognitive/affect theories that focus specifically on emotion are Adams' equity theory and Folger and Greenberg's conceptualizations of organizational justice.

Equity theory

Few issues are more important to employees that being treated justly. For example, most employees become angry if they believe that someone is getting paid more than they for performing the same or comparable work. Adams' (1963) equity theory captures this emotional phenomenon. Specifically, the theory states that employees make cognitive appraisals of their inputs (e.g., education level, years of experience, amount of effort) relative to the outputs they receive (e.g., pay, promotion). They then compare the input/output ratio with that of comparison others, which is a form of value judgment. This process determines the extent to which they experience tension or anger from feelings of over-equity or inequity, and the likelihood they will be incited to take action to reduce that tension. If they feel over-paid, the theory predicts, and the research shows, that they are likely to increase the quantity and/or quality of their work (Mowday, 1991). If they learn that their comparison other is receiving more money than they are for exerting no more effort, and producing no more work, the resulting emotion is likely to be feelings of inequity (i.e., outrage).

Equity theory has been criticized for its lack of precision. For example, Pritchard (1969) pointed out that the theory does not explain how a person decides what constitutes relevant inputs and outputs. Nor does the theory suggest the basis by which an employee chooses a comparison other or when or how an employee will seek to change the situation.

Organizational justice

Folger, whose mentor was Adams, and Folger's colleague, Greenberg, built on equity theory to develop conceptualizations of organizational justice, that is, factors that affect perceptions/feelings of fairness. Whereas the focus of equity theory is on perceptions of distributive justice, that is, what is distributed to whom, Folger (Folger and Cropanzano, 1998) and Greenberg (1987) added the concept of procedural justice. This latter concept emphasizes the importance of developing procedures, processes or systems for determining 'what should be distributed to whom'. The crux of distributive justice is treating people on the basis of merit. Because this frequently requires judgment on the part of a person's manager (e.g., performance appraisal, amount of pay increase, or the lack of a promotion), an employee may feel that an outcome is unfair. When this occurs, the necessity for having the principles of procedural justice in place becomes

paramount (Brockner and Wiesenfeld, 1986). The crux of procedural justice is having a priori, agreed upon, understood procedures in place for determining 'who receives what,' and applying these procedures consistently.

A meta-analysis revealed that the application of distributive and procedural justice increases both job performance and satisfaction (Colquitt et al., 2001). This same meta-analysis also showed that both distributive and procedural justice are unique though inter-related concepts. Justice researchers have suggested a third dimension, namely, interactional justice. This concept refers to the relationship between a manager and an employee, particularly in regard to the extent to which the latter perceives the former as considerate and ethical. Locke (2003), however, has criticized the legitimacy of this term as consideration is arguably, the ethics part aside, no more than an already thoroughly studied variable in the early literature on leadership (Fleishman, 1957). Consideration is not a means to give 'just desserts,' rather it is an appropriate way of treating all employees. A meta-analysis by Judge et al. (2004) found that leader consideration toward employees has a positive effect on group performance.

Regardless of whether interactional justice is a new concept, Inness et al. (2005) found that a failure on a supervisor's part to be considerate can be the source of the most deeply felt types of resentment experienced by an employee. And not surprisingly, it can lead to retaliation by the aggrieved employee.

Affective events theory

Affective events theory (AET), developed by Weiss and Cropanzano (1996), states that environmental events affect a person emotionally, and that emotional consequences influence an employee's job performance. This influence is relatively immediate. Using AET as a framework, Ilies and Judge (2005) showed that goal regulation explains the links among emotions, a person's action tendencies and intentional behavior. For example, the performance feedback that is given to an employee is typically experienced as an affective event, because it involves a value appraisal of the employee's actions and achievements. This influences the emotions the person experiences, and through the goals this person subsequently sets, job performance.

ENVIRONMENT/CONTEXT

The importance of the environment on an employee's behavior has long been recognized. A person who is motivated in one setting may be demotivated in another. Personality traits typically predict an employee's behavior in 'weak' rather than in 'strong' situations (Mischel, 1977). This is because the job context allows or restricts the extent to which an employee is able to express whatever traits or potentials that person possesses. The job context for an assembly line worker is so highly structured (i.e., strong) that personality differences among employees have little chance to be expressed. The job context for high level managers is much less structured (i.e., weak); hence, their job context allows them much more leeway and therefore does not overwhelm differences in traits.

Behaviorism

The importance of the environment is espoused in the philosophy of behaviorism (Watson, 1913; Skinner, 1953). The underlying thesis is that the environment alone shapes behavior. This is said to occur through operant conditioning. That is, an employee's response, operating on the job environment, is rewarded, ignored or punished. The frequency of desired responses of an employee can be increased by management changing the schedule on which an external incentive is administered. For this reason, the behaviorists argue that an employee's behavior is solely a function of its consequences. Employees learn contingent relationships between what they do and the concomitant result (incentive, punishment, or neither). Behavior that is followed by a valued incentive 'reinforces' or strengthens the behavior, hence the likelihood that it will be repeated. Behavior for which there is no consequence, or which is followed by punishment, extinguishes. The causes of behavior are said to reside in the structural features of one's environment rather than in needs, traits, values, or goals. The attributes of a person are considered irrelevant. Cognition is said to be an explanatory fiction.

Kaufman et al. (1966) showed that when people are reinforced or rewarded on the same schedule, yet are led to believe (cognition) that they are being rewarded on a fixed interval, a variable ratio, or a variable interval schedule, they behave consistent with their belief. In short, environmental events affect behavior as a function of a person's beliefs, rather than the actual schedule with which an incentive/'reinforcer' is administered. What employees think affects how they act which in turn affects their environment. How the environment affects a person depends upon how it is interpreted (Bandura, 1997).

The philosophy of behaviorism has been discredited (Locke, 1977, 1978). Nevertheless, this does not negate the effectiveness of its techniques. Administering valued rewards on a continuous schedule typically improves the performance of new employees. Changing the schedule from continuous to variable ratio typically increases the performance of their experienced colleagues (e.g., Latham and Dossett, 1978; Komaki, 2003; Saari and Latham, 1982).

Organizational and societal culture

Context affects the extent to which an employee's needs are met and values are fulfilled (Latham, 2007). Context can have a direct effect, or it can interact with traits to affect a person's behavior (Johns, 2006). As a result of the increasing number of organizations who are conducting business globally, Hofstede (1984; 2001) conducted a landmark study regarding the analysis of responses to 32 value questions from approximately 116,000 employees in 50 countries. His results led to the discovery of four basic values, namely, low vs. high power distance (extent to which a society views inequality, regardless of merit, as acceptable/unacceptable), individualism vs. collectivism (value a society places on enlightened self interest vs. subserving self interest for the overall enhancement of the group), masculinity vs. feminity (value a society holds for assertiveness and competitiveness vs. nurturing and cooperation) and uncertainty vs. certainty (extent to which society is or is not structured, clear and predictable in its use of strict codes of conduct and beliefs in absolute truths).

Voluminous studies have shown that these values influence behavior. Motivational techniques used by superiors have a greater effect on employees in high power distance cultures (such as India) than they do in low power distance cultures (such as Canada; Leung, 2001). For example, Sue-Chan and Ong (2002) found that power distance moderated the effect of assigned versus participative goal setting on goal commitment and performance. Commitment and performance were higher for assigned goals in high as opposed to low power distance cultures. Employees in individualistic cultures (e.g., the US) are more motivated when they work alone than when they are members of a team (Aguinis and Henle, 2003). This is because in the West, the self is viewed/valued as a relatively independent, autonomous entity, whereas in the East, self is valued to the extent the person is seen as fitting into a shared network of social relationships (Bagozzi et al., 2003).

The practical significance of these findings regarding the effect of context on values is that they show the importance of adapting a behavioral science intervention to the values of society where it will be implemented.

The context in which one is working also moderates the effectiveness of goal setting. To the extent that a work environment is dynamic, proximal or sub-goals should be set rather than one distal goal. Inherent in proximal goals is additional feedback that enables people to discern whether they are pursuing an effective strategy for distal goal attainment (Latham and Seijts, 1999). Moreover, the attainment of proximal goals

maintains commitment to attaining the distal goal (Bandura, 1997).

When the group's goal is in conflict with an individual's goal, group performance suffers. A social dilemma is a boundary condition for the typical positive effects of goal setting (Seijts and Latham, 2000).

Even the context within which a goal is framed by one's supervisor may moderate its effect on performance. Performance is lower when the goal is framed in terms of avoiding a negative outcome rather than attaining a positive one (Drach-Zahavy and Erez, 2002).

NEW DIRECTIONS

Intriguing findings in social psychology suggest that research in organizational behavior will soon be exploring the subconscious side of an employee's motivation. The subconscious is a storehouse of knowledge and values beyond that which is found in a person's awareness at any given point in time (Locke and Latham, 2002). Because one can only hold about seven disparate items in focal awareness at the same time (Miller 1956), subconscious storage is essential for allowing people to free their attentional resources to focus on new facts and make new integrations

Gollwitzer (1999) and his colleagues (e.g., Brandstatter et al., 2001) found that on tasks that are complex for people, implementation intentions facilitate goal attainment. Implementation intentions are mental links that are created with regard to a specific future situation (context), and an internal goal directed response. An implementation intention specifies when, where and how one's actions are likely to lead to the attainment of one's goal. In short, the implementation intention commits a person to take goal-directed action once the person is in an appropriate situation to do so. Through this formation of implementation intentions, people are able to switch from conscious effortful control of their goal-directed behavior to becoming automatically influenced by their pre-selected contextual cues. This occurs as a result of the mental act of pairing their desired goal-directed behavior with a pre-determined situation. Subsequently, the environment activates goal directed behavior, without the person being aware of it, as a result of a pre-conscious analysis of what constitutes an appropriate setting for facilitating goal attainment. Gollwitzer (1999) found that implementation intentions affect a person's behavior even after considerable time has elapsed following the formation of them.

Consistent with Gollwitzer, Shah (2005) has obtained similar results through what he called instrumental priming, that is, by surrounding a person with various means to attain a specific goal. This causes a person, without awareness, to move that goal to the center of attention, thus increasing the individual's commitment to pursue it.

Shah (2003) also found that by presenting a person's significant other's name on a screen subliminally, goal pursuit increases or decreases dependent upon that individual's perceived support of goal attainment. Shah labeled this procedure interpersonal priming.

Bargh and his colleagues have studied the effects of semantic priming on perfor-mance (Bargh and Ferguson, 2000). People are randomly assigned to (1) a condition where they find words in a matrix or unscramble sentences that are achievement oriented or to (2) a condition where the words they seek/create are neutral. Those in the achievement condition perform better than those in the neutral condition on a subsequent unrelated task. Stajkovic et al. (2006) conducted the first study to compare the effect of subconsciously primed goals with those of consciously assigned goals as derived from goal setting theory (Locke and Latham, 1990). They found that both types of goals significantly affect performance on a brainstorming task, though the conscious goal had a stronger effect on performance. Further, they found that there is an interaction between the two types of goals. The effects of assigned do best and specific difficult goals, but not easy ones, were enhanced significantly by subconscious priming. These findings

regarding the priming of the subconscious beg for replication and extension in organizational settings. To date, it is not known how long priming effects, in the context of a dynamic work environment, last or how priming effects are influenced by conflicting demands.

CONCLUSION

Whereas theory and practice in the 20th century focused on conscious choices, effort, and persistence by employees, research in the 21st century will likely expand our knowledge to the role played by the subconscious in motivating individuals in tomorrow's workforce. There is now a taxonomy of motivation to facilitate this discovery. The taxonomy includes an employee's needs, personality traits, values, cognition, affect and the environment or context in which these variables occur.

NOTE

1 Preparation of this chapter was funded in part by a grant to the first author from the Social Sciences and Humanities Research Council of Canada.

REFERENCES

Adams, J. S. (1963) 'Toward an understanding of inequity', *Journal of Abnormal and Social Psychology*, 67: 422–436.

Allport, G. W. (1951) 'Basic principles in improving human relations', in K. W. Bigelow (ed.), *Cultural Groups and Human Relations*. Oxford: Bureau of Publications, pp. 8–28.

Aguinis, H. and Henle, C. A. (2003) 'The search for universals in cross-cultural organizational behavior', in J. Greenberg (ed.), *Organizational Behavior: The State of Science*. Mahwah, NJ: Erlbaum, pp. 373–419.

Anderson G. D. and Viswesvaran C. (1998) 'An update of the validity of personality scales in personnel selection: A meta-analysis of studies published between 1992–1997'. Presented at Annual Meeting of the Society of Industrial and Organizational Psychologists, Dallas.

Bagozzi, R. P., Verbeke, W. and Gavino, J. C. (2003) 'Culture moderates the self-regulation of shame and its effects on performance: The case of salespersons in the Netherlands and the Philippines', *Journal of Applied Psychology*, 88: 219–233.

Bandura, A. (1977) *Social Learning Theory*. Englewood Cliffs, NJ: Prentice-Hall.

Bandura, A. (1986) *Social Foundations of Thought and Action: A Social-Cognitive Theory*. Englewood Cliffs, NJ: Prentice Hall.

Bandura, A. (1997) *Self-Efficacy: The Exercise of Control*. Stanford: W. H. Freeman and Co.

Bandura, A. and Cervone, D. (1983) 'Self-evaluative and self-efficacy mechanisms governing the motivational effects of goal systems', *Journal of Personality and Social Psychology*, 45: 1017–1028.

Bargh, J. and Ferguson, M. J. (2000) 'Beyond behaviorism: On the automaticity of higher mental processes', *Psychological Bulletin*, 126: 925–945.

Barrick, M. R. and Mount, M. K. (1991) 'The Big Five personality dimensions and job performance: A meta-analysis', *Personnel Psychology*, 44: 1–26.

Barrick, M. R., Mount, M. K. and Judge, T. A. (2001) 'Personality and performance at the beginning of the new millennium: What do we know and where do we go next?', *International Journal of Selection and Assessment*, 9: 9–30.

Bennis, W. (2007) 'The challenges of leadership in the modern world: Introduction to the special issue', *American Psychologist*, 62: 2–5.

Bouchard, T. J. Jr. (1997) 'The genetics of personality', in K. Blum, E. P. Noble, R. S. Sparkes, T. H. J. Chen and Cull, J. G. (eds), *Handbook of Psychiatric Genetics*. Boca Raton, FL, US: CRC Press, pp. 273–296.

Brandstätter, V., Lengfelder, A. and Gollwitzer, P. M. (2001) 'Implementation intentions and efficient action initiation', *Journal of Personality and Social Psychology*, 81: 946–960.

Brett, J. F. and VandeWalle, D. M. (1999) 'Goal orientation and goal content as predictors of performance in a training program', *Journal of Applied Psychology*, 84: 863–873.

Brockner, J. and Wiesenfeld, B. M. (1986) 'An integrative framework for explaining reactions to decisions: Interactive effects of outcomes and procedures', *Psychological Bulletin*, 120: 189–208.

Brown, T. C. and Latham, G. P. (2006) 'The effect of training in verbal self-guidance on performance effectiveness in a MBA program', *Canadian Journal of Behavioural Science*, 38: 1–11.

Caprara, G. V., Barbaranelli, C., Pastorelli, C. and Cervone, D. (2004) 'The contribution of self-efficacy beliefs to psychosocial outcomes in adolescence: Predicting beyond past behavior and global dispositional tendencies', *Personality and Individual Differences*, 37: 751–763.

Carver, C. S. and Scheier, M. F. (1981) *Attention and Self-regulation: A Control-theory Approach to Human Behavior*. New York: Springer-Verlag.

Chartrand, T. L., and Bargh, J. A. (2002) 'Nonconscious motivations: Their activation, operation and consciousness', in A. Tesser, D. A. Stapel and J. V. Woods (eds), *Self and Motivation: Emerging Psychological Perspectives*. Washington, DC: American Psychological Association, pp. 13–41.

Chatman, J. A. (1991) 'Matching people and organizations: Selection and socialization in public accounting firms', *Administrative Science Quarterly*, 36: 459–484.

Colquitt, J. A., Conlon, D. E.,Wesson, M. J., Porter, C. O. and Ng, K. Y. (2001) 'Justice at the millennium: A meta-analysis of 25 years of organizational justice research', *Journal of Applied Psychology*, 86: 425–445.

Deci, E. L. (1975) *Intrinsic Motivation*. New York: Plenam.

Deci, E. L. and Ryan, R. M. (1990) 'A motivational approach to self: Integration in personality', in R. Dienstbier (ed.), *Nebraska Symposium on Motivation* (Vol. 38). Lincoln: University of Nebraska Press, pp. 237–288.

Drach-Zahavy, A. and Erez, M. (2002) 'Challenge versus threat effects on the goal-performance relationship', *Organizational Behavior and Human Performance*, 88: 667–682.

Dweck, C. S. (1999) 'Self-theories: Their Role in Motivation, Personality, and Development', in C. S. Dweck (ed.), *Essays in Social Psychology*. Philadelphia, PA: Psychology Press, p. xiii.

Earley, P. C. (1986) 'Trust, perceived importance of praise and criticism, and work performance: An examination of feedback in the United States and England', *Journal of Management*, 12, 457–473.

Eisenberger, R. and Cameron, J. (1996) 'Detrimental effects of reward: Reality or myth', *American Psychologist*, 51: 1153–1166.

Fay, D. and Frese, M. (2000) 'Self-starting behavior at work: Toward a theory of personal initiative', in J. Heckhausen (ed.), *Motivational Psychology of Human Development*. Amsterdam: Elsevier, pp. 307–324.

Fleishman, E. (1957) 'A leader behavior description for industry', in R. M. Stogdill and A. E. Coons (eds), *Leader Behavior: Its Description and Measurement*. Columbus, OH: Ohio State University, pp. 103–119.

Folger, R. and Cropanzano, R. (1998) *Organizational Justice and Human Resource Management*. Thousand Oaks, CA: Sage.

Frayne, C. A. and Latham, G. P. (1987) 'The application of social learning theory to employee self management of attendance', *Journal of Applied Psychology*, 72: 387–392.

Frese, M. (2005) 'Grand theories and midrange theories. Cultural effects on theorizing and the attempt to understand active approaches to work', in K. G. Smith and M. Hitt (eds), *The Oxford Handbook of Management Theory: The Process of Theory Development*. New York: Oxford University Press, pp. 84–108.

Gollwitzer, P. M. (1999) 'Implementation intentions and effective goal pursuit: Strong effects of simple plans', *American Psychologist*, 54: 493–503.

Greenberg, J. (1987) 'A taxonomy of organizational justice theories', *Academy of Management Review*, 12: 9–22.

Hofstede, G. (1984) 'The cultural relativity of the quality of life concept', *Academy of Management Review*, 9: 389–398.

Hofstede, G. (2001) *Culture's Consequences*. Thousand Oaks, CA: Sage.

Ilies, R. and Judge, T. A. (2005) 'Goal regulation across time: The effects of feedback and affect', *Journal of Applied Psychology*, 90: 453–467.

Inness, M., Barling, J. and Turner, N. (2005) 'Understanding supervisor-targeted aggression: A within-person, between-jobs design', *Journal of Applied Psychology*, 90: 731–739.

Johns, G. (2006) 'The essential impact of context on organizational behavior', *Academy of Management Review*, 31: 386–408.

Judge, T. A. and Bono, J. E. (2001) 'Relationship of core self-evaluations traits-self-esteem, generalized self-efficacy, locus of control, and emotional stability-with job satisfaction and job performance: A meta-analysis', *Journal of Applied Psychology*, 86: 80–92.

Judge, T. A., Bono, J. E. and Locke, E. A. (2000) 'Personality and job satisfaction: The mediating role of job characteristics', *Journal of Applied Psychology*, 85: 237–249.

Judge, T. A., Erez, A. and Bono J. E. (1998) 'The power of being positive: The relationship between positive self-concept and job performance', *Human Performance*, 11: 167–187.

Judge, T. A., Locke, E. A. and Durham, C. C. (1997) 'The dispositional causes of job satisfaction: A core self-evaluation approach', *Research in Organizational Behavior*, 19: 151–188.

Judge, T. A., Piccolo, R. F. and Ilies, R. (2004) 'The forgotten ones? The validity of consideration and initiating structure in leadership research', *Journal of Applied Psychology*, 89: 36–51.

Kaufman, A., Baron, A. and Kopp, R. E. (1966) 'Some effects of instructions on human operant behavior', *Psychonomic Monograph Supplements*, 1: 243–250.

Komaki, J. L. (2003) 'Reinforcement Theory at Work: Enhancing and Explaining What Employees Do', in L. W. Porter, G. A. Bigley and R. M. Steers (eds), *Motivation and Work Behavior*, 7th edn. Burr Ridge, IL: Irwin/McGraw Hill, pp. 95–113.

Kozlowski, S. W. J. and Ilgen, D. R. (2006) 'Enhancing the effectiveness of work groups and teams', *Psychological Science in the Public Interest*, 7: 77–124.

Latham, G. P. (2001) 'The importance of understanding and changing employee outcome expectancies for gaining commitment to an organizational goal', *Personnel Psychology*, 54: 707–716.

Latham, G. P. (2007) *Work Motivation*. Thousand Oaks, CA: Sage.

Latham, G. P. and Budworth, M. (2006) 'The effect of training in verbal self-guidance on the self-efficacy and performance of Native North Americans in the selection interview', *Journal of Vocational Behavior*, 68: 516–523.

Latham, G. P. and Dossett, D. L. (1978) 'Designing incentive plans for unionized employees: A comparison of continuous and variable ratio reinforcement schedules', *Personnel Psychology*, 31: 47–61.

Latham, G. P., Erez, M. and Locke, E. A. (1988) 'Resolving scientific disputes by the joint design of crucial experiments by the antagonists: Application of the Erez-Latham dispute regarding participation in goal setting', *Journal of Applied Psychology Monograph*, 73: 753–772.

Latham, G. P. and Pinder, C. C. (2005) 'Work motivation theory and research at the dawn of the twenty-first century', *Annual Review of Psychology*, 56: 485–516.

Latham, G. P., Mitchell, T. R. and Dossett, D. L. (1978) 'The importance of participative goal setting and anticipated rewards on goal difficulty and job performance', *Journal of Applied Psychology*, 63: 163–171.

Latham, G. P. and Saari, L. M. (1979) 'The importance of supportive relationships in goal setting', *Journal of Applied Psychology*, 64: 151–156.

Latham, G. P. and Seijts, G. H. (1999) 'The effects of proximal and distal goals on performance on a moderately complex task', *Journal of Organizational Behavior*, 20: 421–429.

Latham G. P. and Seijts, G. H. (2006) 'The effects of learning goal difficulty and cognitive ability on strategy development and performance'. Paper presented at the Annual Meeting at the Academy of Management.

Latham, G. P., Winters, D. C. and Locke, E. A. (1994) 'Cognitive and motivational effects of participation: A mediator study', *Journal of Organizational Behavior*, 15: 49–63.

Lee, T. W., Locke, E. A. and Phan, S. H. (1997) 'Explaining the assigned goal-incentive interaction: The role of self-efficacy and personal goals', *Journal of Management*, 23: 541–559.

Leung, K. (2001) 'Different Carrots for Different Rabbits: Effects of Individualism-Collectivism and Power Distance on Work Motivation', in M. Erez and U. Kleinbeck (eds), *Work Motivation in the Context of a Globalizing Economy*. Mahwah, NJ: Lawrence Erlbaum, pp. 329–339.

Locke, E. A. (1975) 'Personnel attitudes and motivation', *Annual Review of Psychology*, 26: 457–480.

Locke, E. A. (1976) 'The nature and causes of job satisfaction', in M. Dunnette (ed.) *Handbook of Industrial and Organizational Psychology*. Chicago: Rand McNally, pp. 1297–1349.

Locke, E. A. (1977) 'The myths of behavior mod in organizations', *Academy of Management Review*, 2: 543–553.

Locke, E. A. (1978) 'The ubiquity of the technique of goal setting in theories of and approaches to employee motivation', *Academy of Management Review*, 3: 594–601.

Locke, E. A. (2000) 'Motivation, cognition, and action: An analysis of studies of task goals and knowledge', *Applied Psychology: An International Review*, 49: 408–429.

Locke, E. A. (2003) 'Foundations for a Theory of Leadership', in S. E. Murphy and R. E. Riggio (eds), *The Future of Leadership Development*. Mahwah, NJ: Lawrence Erlbaum, pp. 29–46.

Locke, E. A. (2007) 'Control theory vs. cognitive theory: Which is the proper model for understanding human motivation?', under review.

Locke, E. A., Alavi, M. and Wagner, J. (1997) 'Participation in Decision Making: An Information Exchange Perspective', in G. Ferris (ed.), *Research in Personnel and Human Resources Management*. Greenwich, CT: JAI Press. Vol. 15: pp. 293–331.

Locke, E. A. and Henne, D. (1986) 'Work Motivation Theories', in C. L. Cooper and I. Robertson (eds), *International Review of Industrial and Organizational Psychology*. New York: Wiley, pp. 1–36.

Locke, E. A. and Latham, G. P. (1990) *A Theory of Goal Setting and Task Performance*. Englewood Cliffs, NJ: Prentice-Hall.

Locke, E. A. and Latham, G. P. (2002) 'Building a Practically Useful Theory of Goal Setting and Task Motivation: A 35-year Odyssey', *American Psychologist*, 57: 705–717.

Locke, E. A., Latham, G. P. and Erez, M. (1988) 'The determinants of goal commitment', *Academy of Management Review*, 13: 23–39.

Malka, A. and Chatman, J. A. (2003) 'Intrinsic and extrinsic orientations as moderators of the effect of annual income on subjective well-being: A longitudinal study', *Personality and Social Psychology Bulletin*, 29: 737–746.

Maslow, A. H. (1943) 'A theory of human motivation', *Psychological Review*, 50: 370–396.

Maslow, A. H. (1954) *Motivation and Personality*. New York: Harper.

Maslow, A. H. (1965) *Eupsychian Management: A Journal*. Illinois: Irwin, Homewood.

Miller, G. A. (1956) 'The magical number seven, plus or minus two: Some limits on the capacity for processing information', *Psychological Review*, 63: 81–97.

Millman, Z. and Latham, G. P. (2001) 'Increasing re-employment through training in verbal self guidance', in M. Erez, U. Kleinbeck and H. K. Thierry (eds), *Work Motivation in the Context of a Globalizing Economy*. Hillsdale, NJ: Lawrence Erlbaum, pp. 87–98.

Miner, J. S. (2002) *Organizational Behavior: Foundations, Theories and Analysis*. New York: Oxford.

Mischel, W. (1977) 'The interaction of person and situation', in D. Magnusson and N. S. Endler (eds), *Personality at the Crossroads: Current Issues in Interactional Psychology*. Hillsdale, NJ: Lawrence Erlbaum, pp. 333–354.

Mitchell, T. R. and Daniels, D. (2003) 'Motivation', in W. C. Borman, D. R. Ilgen, and R. J. Klimoski (eds), *Comprehensive Handbook of Psychology: Industrial Organizational Psychology*. New York: Wiley and Sons. Vol. 12: pp. 225–254.

Morin, L. and Latham, G. P. (2000) 'Effect of mental practice and goal setting as a transfer of training intervention on supervisors' self-efficacy and communication skills: An exploratory study', *Applied Psychology: An International Review*, 49: 566–578.

Moskowitz, D. S. and Cote, S. (1995) 'Do interpersonal traits predict affect? A comparison of three models', *Journal of Personality and Social Psychology*, 69: 915–924.

Mowday, R. T. (1991) 'Equity theory predictions of behavior in organizations', in R. M. Steers and L. W. Porter, (eds), *Motivation and Work Behavior*, 5th edn. New York: McGraw-Hill, pp. 111–130.

Napier, N. K. and Latham, G. P. (1986) 'Outcome expectancies of people who conduct performance appraisals', *Personnel Psychology*, 39: 827–837.

Oldham, G. R. (1976) 'Job characteristics and internal motivation: The moderating effect of interpersonal and individual variables', *Human Relations*, 29: 559–569.

Pritchard, R. D. (1969) 'Equity theory: A review and critique', *Organizational Behavior and Human Performance*, 4: 176–211.

Quigley, N., Tesluk, P. E., Locke, E. A. and Bartol, K. M. (2007) 'The effects of incentives and individual differences on knowledge sharing and performance effectiveness', *Organization Science*, 18: 71–88.

Ronen, S. (2001) 'Self-actualization Versus Collectualization: Implications for Motivation Theories', in M. Erez, U. Klenbeck and H. K. Thierry (eds), *Work Motivation in the Context of a Globalizing Economy*. Hillsdale, NJ: Lawrence Erlbaum, pp. 341–368.

Ryan, R. M. and Deci, E. L. (2000) 'Self-determination theory and the facilitation of intrinsic motivation, social development, and well-being', *American Psychologist*, 55: 68–78.

Saari, L. M. and Latham, G. P. (1982) 'Employee reactions to continuous and variable ratio reinforcement schedules involving a monetary incentive', *Journal of Applied Psychology*, 67: 506–508.

Salancik, G. R. (1977) 'Commitment and the Control of Organizational Behavior and Belief', in B. M. Staw and G. R. Salancik (eds), *New Directions in Organizational Behavior*. Chicago, IL: St. Claire Press, pp. 1–54.

Salgado, J. (1997) 'The five factor model of personality and job performance in the European community', *Journal of Applied Psychology*, 82: 30–43.

Schwartz, S. H. and Sagie, G. (2000) 'Value consensus and importance: A cross-national study', *Journal of Cross Cultural Psychology*, 31: 465–497.

Seijts, G. H. and Latham, G. P. (2000) 'The effects of goal setting and group size on performance in a social dilemma', *Canadian Journal of Behavioural Science*, 32: 104–116.

Seijts, G. H. and Latham, G. P. (2001) 'The effect of learning, outcome, and proximal goals on a moderately complex task', *Journal of Organizational Behavior*, 22: 291–307.

Seijts, G. H., Latham, G. P., Tasa, K. and Latham, B. W. (2004) 'Goal setting and goal orientation: An integration of two different yet related literatures', *Academy of Management Journal*, 47: 227–239.

Shah, J. (2003) 'Automatic for the people: How representations of significant others implicitly affect goal pursuit', *Journal of Personality and Social Psychology*, 84: 661–681.

Shah, J. Y. (2005) 'The automatic pursuit and management of goals', *Current Directions in Psychological Science*, 14: 10–13.

Skinner, B. F. (1953) *Science and Human Behavior*. New York: Macmillan.

Srivastava, A., Locke, E. A. and Bartol, K. M. (2001) 'Money and subjective well-being: It's not the money, it's the motives', *Journal of Personality and Social Psychology*, 80: 959–971.

Stajkovic, A. D., Locke, E. A. B. and Blair E. S. (2006) 'A first examination of the relationship between primed subconscious goals, assigned conscious goals, and task performance', *Journal of Applied Psychology*, 91: 1172–1180.

Staw, B. M., Bell, N. E. and Clausen, J. A. (1986) 'The dispositional approach to job attitudes: A lifetime longitudinal test', *Administrative Science Quarterly*, 31: 56–77.

Staw, B. M. and Ross, J. (1985) 'Stability in the midst of change: A dispositional approach to job attitudes', *Journal of Applied Psychology*, 70: 469–480.

Sue-Chan, C. and Ong, M. (2002) 'Goal assignment and performance: Assessing the mediating role of goal commitment and self-efficacy and the moderating role of power distance', *Organizational Behavior and Human Decision Processes*, 89: 1140–1161.

Vancouver, J. B. (2005) 'The depth of history and explanation as benefit and bane for psychological control theories', *Journal of Applied Psychology*, 90: 38–52.

VandeWalle, D. M. (1999) 'Goal orientation comes of age for adults: A literature review'. Paper presented at the annual meeting of the Academy of Management, Chicago, IL.

VandeWalle, D. M., Cron, W. L. and Slocum, J. W. (2001) 'The role of goal orientation following performance feedback', *Journal of Applied Psychology*, 86: 629–640.

Vroom, V. H. (1964) *Work Motivation*. New York: Wiley and Sons.

Watson, J. B. (1913) 'Psychology as the behaviorist views it', *Psychological Review*, 20: 158–177.

Weiss, H. M. and Cropanzano, R. (1996) 'Affective events theory: A theoretical discussion of the structure, causes, and consequences of affective experiences at work', in B. M. Staw and L. L. Cummings (eds), *Research in Organizational Behavior*. Greenwich, CT: JAI Press. Vol. 18: pp. 1–74.

Wiggins, J. S. (ed.) (1996) *The Five Factor Model of Personality*. New York: Guilford.

Winters, D. and Latham, G. P. (1996) 'The effect of learning versus outcome goals on a simple versus a complex task', *Group and Organization Management*, 21: 236–250.

18

Leadership

Timothy A. Judge, Erin Fluegge Woolf,
Charlice Hurst and Beth Livingston

It is hardly a bold statement to argue that leadership is one of the more foundational topics in organizational behavior. Every organizational behavior text has at least one, and often two, chapters on leadership, and leadership concerns are regularly at the forefront of business organizations and social policy debates. In all societies – human and nonhuman alike – individuals organize themselves into groups, and leaders emerge. Leaders are, by definition, at the pinnacle of these groups and organizations, and their actions, while not occurring in a vacuum, often change the course of the groups and organizations they lead and, in some cases, entire societies. Although the stakes are high, and the importance of their decisions are fundamental, effective leadership is all too often in the eye of the beholder. For instance, in a recent three-day period, one prominent Princeton historian proclaimed George W. Bush the worst US President in history (Wilentz, April 21, 2006), whereas a former deputy prime minister of Israel and survivor of the Soviet Gulag argued that Bush is a modern dissident whose doctrine is likely to forever change the international political landscape (Sharansky, April 24, 2006). It sometimes seems, to paraphrase Shakespeare, 'There is no good or bad leader but thinking makes it so.'

It might be argued that two of the greatest difficulties that undermine rational discourse are naïve realism and hindsight biases. Both have special significance to leadership research. If one defines naïve realism as the assumption that things are as they seem (Russell, 1940), we often find that it is generalized, so that we assume that others see things as they appear to us. Ichheiser (1949) notes:

> We tend to resolve our perplexity arising out of the experience that other people see the world differently than we see it ourselves by declaring that these others, in consequence of some basic intellectual and moral defect, are unable to see things 'as they really are' and to react to them 'in a normal way.' We thus imply, of course, that things are in fact as we see them, and that our ways are the normal ways. (p. 39)

One can quickly see how naïve realism poses special problems for leadership research. We tend to fall into the solipsism of arguing that an effective leader is one who is seen as effective. Like all solipsisms, at a practical level, this is an intellectual dead-end – impossible to refute, and impossible to validate. However, the problem is even greater than that. Because people tend to rationalize their naïve realism, they tend to assume that their subjective appraisal is the 'right' appraisal – that no reasonable person could see it any other way.

With respect to the other psychological-philosophical difficulty that we raised – hindsight bias – we often succumb to the tautology of judging effective leadership by the results. If one admits that many outcomes are beyond a leader's control, then one must wonder how history might have judged a leader quite differently if fate had twisted a different way. It seems that the perception of leadership is not merely immersed in our own values, but in the perceived outcomes under a leader's watch, irrespective of the leader behaviors that may or may not have produced the outcome. Moreover, we also tend to confuse leadership emergence with leadership effectiveness. According to Fortune magazine's poll of businesspeople, the world's five most-admired corporations are: General Electric, Toyota Motor, Procter and Gamble, FedEx, and Johnson and Johnson. How would we measure the effectiveness of the leaders of these organizations? Most of us seem to measure effectiveness by either ascendance (the leader of General Electric must be a good leader or he wouldn't have become a leader), or by the results (any leader who doesn't produce results is a poor leader).

Thus, the leadership scholar's task is a difficult one. We study an important concept. In theory, most of us would agree that Carlyle was telling the truth when he wrote of the importance of great leaders to societies. However, in applying that concept, we should not lose sight of conceptual and empirical difficulties in the study of leadership. Not every scholar agrees on what is effective leadership, or the behaviors that produce this effectiveness. Moreover, the situation can become even more muddied when one seeks to apply the concepts empirically. Our point is not to suggest that effective leadership is impossible to define or measure. Rather, our point is that unless we discipline ourselves to recognize these conceptual traps, we run the risk of doing more harm than good. This is the path taken by most of the business process: Carly Fiorina is a hero and great leader one minute and, once she is deposed at Hewlett-Packard, she is a poor leader or, worse, a corporate villain.

Keeping these difficulties ever in mind, there are and have been, we believe, important insights to be gleaned from the study of leadership. In this review, we focus our attention on a concept of leadership – charismatic or transformational leadership – which has been the dominant focus of contemporary leadership research. One may well question the wisdom of confining our analysis to only one theory of leadership when indeed there are scores of studies on many different theories of leadership. We do for several reasons. First, there is the simple issue of length. Given the (understandable) desire of the editors to keep each review relatively brief, there is simply not sufficient space to give anything but a superficial review of other leadership theories. Forced to choose between complete omission and superficial treatment, we chose the former sin over the latter. Second, charismatic/transformational leadership is the dominant conceptualization of leadership in organizational behavior. It has been for the past several decades, and promises to be so even when this review is outdated.

Accordingly, in this article we review the charismatic/transformational leadership literatures. In so doing, we discuss measurement, validity, moderating factors, and finally return to some of the issues above in offering an agenda for future research. Although we do not explicitly consider other theories of leadership, we will in several places make reference to either classic or what we see as emerging leadership concepts.

REVIEW OF CHARISMATIC AND TRANSFORMATIONAL LEADERSHIP RESEARCH

Charismatic leadership

Although the term has ancient origins ('kharisma' appeared in Ancient Greek, meaning 'divine favor'), the first scholar to discuss charismatic leadership was Max Weber. Weber argued that in organizational systems, there are three types of authority to which people will submit: traditional, legal/rational, and charismatic. Weber (1922/1947: 358–359) defined charisma as being 'set apart from ordinary people and treated as endowed with supernatural, superhuman, or at least specifically exceptional powers or qualities ... regarded as of divine origin or as exemplary, and on the basis of them the individual concerned is treated as a leader.' Despite Weber's importance as a sociologist and political economist, his work on charisma lay mostly dormant until the mid 1970s.

House (1977) further developed Weber's concept in articulating a theory of charismatic leadership that, at its core, argued that followers are motivated by leaders based on the attributions they make about them (which in turn are based on certain leader behaviors). House focused specifically on behaviors that followers attribute as extraordinary or heroic. Based on House's theory, researchers then began to uncover and identify key characteristics of charismatic leadership. Conger and Kanungo (1998), for example, argued that charismatic leadership is typified by four behaviors:

- possessing and articulating a vision;
- willingness to take risks to achieve the vision;
- exhibiting sensitivity to follower needs; and
- demonstrating novel behavior.

Three interesting conceptual issues are worthy of discussion here. First, much of the work on charismatic leadership has eschewed the Weberian perspective that charismatic leaders are rare or extraordinary. Conger (1989: 161),

for example, opined that charisma 'is not some magical ability limited to a handful.' As Trice and Beyer (1986) and Beyer (1999) argue, such approaches 'tame' charismatic leadership in that they assume that charisma is a property possessed by all individuals (to a greater or lesser degree). On the one hand, if we are to empirically study charismatic leadership, we cannot do so based on the assumption that it is a quality held by a handful of individuals (there are not enough such leaders to study). Moreover, most human characteristics seem to follow a normal distribution, or some semblance of one. Why should charisma be any different? On the other hand, if charisma is seen as relatively commonplace, have we damaged the concept? Clearly, the charismatic qualities of political leaders from Lincoln to Hitler, religious leaders from Martin Luther to Pope Jean Paul II, and business leaders from Estée Lauder to Jack Welch, do not seem to be a general commodity.

Second, some researchers would distinguish charisma as a trait or personal quality from the charismatic leadership process. House, for example, argues in favor of the latter. Locke and colleagues, conversely, clearly distinguish a charismatic communication style from other leadership qualities. These approaches are not necessarily in conflict – charismatic leadership may be a particular type of influence process, but that does not necessarily mean that some individuals are more predisposed to use this form of influence, or use it effectively, more than others. This is a topic to which we return later.

Finally, though Conger (1990) has written extensively about the dark side of charismatic leadership, judging from the research literature, he seems like a lone voice. As the aforementioned examples of charismatic leaders suggest, however, charismatic leadership seemingly can be used for either good or bad ends, depending on one's perspective and the hindsight of history. It seems obvious that charismatic leadership is neither inherently good nor evil, but the implicit assumption in the literature has been that it is a positive force in organizations. Our own view is that if we are to resist tautological thinking, we must distinguish charismatic behavior from its outcomes. In so doing, we recognize that if charisma is a form of influence, it can be used for good or ill. Moreover, we are not talking about lawful relations here – one can find many examples or ineffective charismatic leaders, and effective non-charismatic leaders.

Transformational leadership

At nearly the same time that House (1977) was developing his theory of charismatic leadership, Bass (1985) – drawing from Burns' (1978) book on political leadership – was developing his theory of transformational leadership. Subsequently, Bass and Avolio joined forces, and developed a revised model of transformational and transactional leadership. The Full Range Leadership Model,

developed by Bass and Avolio (see Avolio and Bass, 1991), contains both transactional and transformational leadership (see Figure 1). Components of transactional and transformational leadership are arranged in two-dimensional space, where the vertical axis is leadership effectiveness (rising from ineffective to effective), and the horizontal axis is involvement (moving from passive to active). Transactional leadership styles tend to fall in the ineffective and passive quadrant, while transformational leadership styles largely fall in the effective and active quadrant of the model. Although this seems to indicate that transformational leadership is superior to transactional leadership, transformational leadership researchers argue that the two may actually complement each other.

The four dimensions of transactional leadership are contingent reward, management by exception (active), management by exception

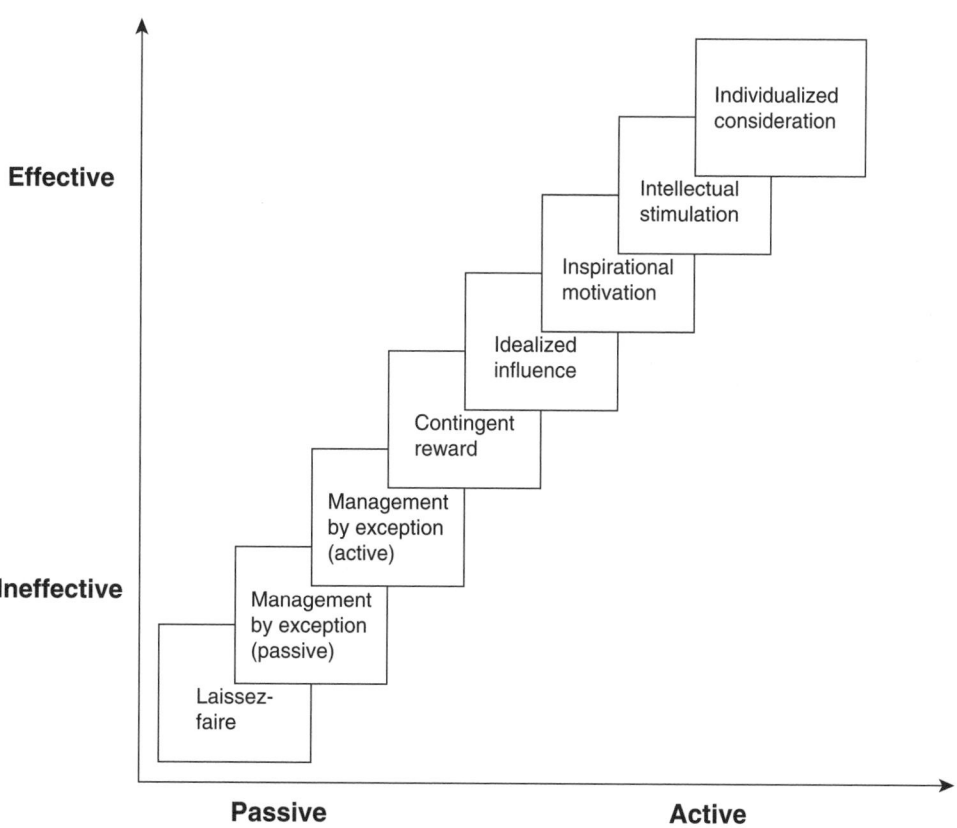

Figure 1 The full range leadership model (adapted from Avolio and Bass, 1991)

(passive), and laissez-faire. In contingent reward leadership, leaders provide resources in exchange for follower support (Bass and Riggio, 2006). Management by exception has two aspects – active and passive. In the active case, leaders monitor followers' performance and take corrective action when needed. In the passive case, known as management by exception-passive, leaders do little monitoring and only intervene when the problem becomes serious. In laissez-faire leadership, leaders simply avoid leadership responsibilities. These transactional leadership behaviors become decreasingly effective as leader participation declines. Thus, contingent reward is thought to be the most effective form of transactional leadership whereas laissez-faire is considered the most ineffective, the latter so much so that some argue is it not even transactional leadership (see Judge and Piccolo, 2004).

Transformational leadership supplements the characteristics of transactional leadership, and followers are inspirationally influenced. Bass (1985) explained that transformational leadership is accomplished through the four I's:

- idealized influence;
- inspirational motivation;
- intellectual stimulation; and
- individualized consideration (Bass, 1985).

Idealized influence is demonstrated when the transformational leader serves as a charismatic role model to followers. By articulating an inspiring vision to their followers, transformational leaders are said to foster inspirational motivation. Intellectual stimulation is generated when transformational leaders stimulate followers' creativity by questioning and challenging them. Finally, attending to individual needs of followers allows transformational leaders to promote individualized consideration. It is argued that the effects of transformational leadership actually augment the effects of transactional leadership, which suggests that the best leaders tend to be both transactional and transformational (Bass, 1985).

Charismatic and transformational leadership

Some debate exists regarding the synonymy or interchangeability of charismatic and transformational leadership. House has argued that the two are more similar than different, with the differences being relatively small. House and Podsakoff (1994), for example, characterized the disagreements among authors of these theories as 'modest' and 'minor' (pp. 71–72). Conger and Kanungo (1998) appear to agree, noting, 'There is little real difference' between charismatic and transformational leadership (p. 15). On the other hand, the main developers and proponents of transformational leadership, Bass and Avolio (1994), argue that charismatic leadership is a lower-level component of transformational leadership, so that transformational leadership is a broader concept than is charisma. Bass (1985), while arguing that charisma is part of transformational leadership, also argues that it, in and of itself, is insufficient to 'account for the transformational process' (p. 31). While scholars may still disagree on the specifics of these two types of leadership, scores on the measures are very highly correlated, meaning that in the vast majority of the cases, a leader who scores high on one measure type is very likely to score high on the other, and vice-versa. We now turn to a discussion of such measures.

Measurement

Bass and Avolio's (1990) Multifactor Leadership Questionnaire (MLQ) is the most extensively validated and commonly used measure of transformational and transactional leadership, so much so that one is hard-pressed to point out a viable alternative. Several different versions of the MLQ exist, such as the MLQ-Form 5R and the MLQ-Form 10. The former addresses both leadership behaviors and effects and has been therefore criticized (see Hunt, 1991). The latter, however, only examines leadership behaviors. For these reasons, the MLQ-Form 5X has been established in order to replace the MLQ-Form 5R and resolve several inadequacies.

There are several important, unresolved issues in measuring transformational leadership. First, there is some debate about whether the MLQ dimensions are distinct. Some writers argue that the evidence supports the distinctiveness of the dimensions (e.g., Avolio et al., 1999). However, the dimensions are highly correlated (the correlations among the dimensions are nearly always greater than 0.70, and often in the 0.90 range), and many researchers combine the dimensions into a single factor (see Judge and Piccolo, 2004). Yukl (1999: 288) concluded, 'The partially overlapping content and the high inter-correlation found among the transformational behaviors raise doubts about their construct validity.'

A second and perhaps an even more disturbing problem is the distinctiveness of the transformational and transactional leadership dimensions. Judge and Piccolo (2004) found, in a meta-analysis of 87 correlations, that transformational and contingent reward leadership correlated 0.80 (the 80 per cent credibility interval was 0.65 to 0.95, meaning that 80 per cent of the individually corrected correlations were between 0.65 and 0.95). Since this correlation is roughly the same as the correlation among the transformational leadership dimensions, this calls into question the distinctiveness of the measures of transformational and contingent reward leadership. Third, although charismatic and transformational leadership may be conceptually distinct, we are not aware of distinct measures of charismatic leadership. Conger et al. (1997) did develop a measure of charismatic leadership. However, their measure appears quite similar to measures of transformational leadership such as the MLQ, and it has not achieved widespread adoption. More work comparing and contrasting measures of charismatic, transformational, and transactional leadership is needed.

Finally, perhaps explaining the aforementioned result, there are the continuing measurement problems endemic to all such rating instruments. Specifically, there is little doubt that, to a moderate or even strong degree, such instruments suffer from halo effects. If a rater has a positive attitude toward one aspect of a leader, or toward the leader overall, it is likely that this attitude spills over and contaminates the ratings of other specific dimensions. There may be a general factor in leadership, independent of halo effects, as has been found in the job performance literature (Viswesvaran et al., 2005). However, this does not mean that halo is not a serious problem in the leadership literature. Positive halo occurs when raters' general impression affects their ratings of specific behaviors. As Palmer et al. (2003) noted with respect to performance ratings, 'Positive halo means a reduction in the specificity of performance ratings, making assessment of individual strengths and weaknesses, and thus performance feedback, difficult' (p. 83). We see no reason why this problem is any less significant in the leadership literature.

Second, the attributional biases we noted at the beginning of this review loom large. Some evidence suggests that once individuals form an impression of leadership effectiveness, they then attribute characteristics or behaviors to those leaders based on their implicit theories (which may be culturally conditioned) of leadership (Lord and Hall, 1992). As noted by Brown and Lord (1999), because experimental research designs can obviate or even eliminate this problem, more experimental leadership studies need to be conducted. Unfortunately, as has often been noted in organizational psychology (Locke, 1986), many have biases against experimental research, despite its many advantages, including its ability to address the attributional bias.

OUTCOMES: VALIDITY OF CHARISMATIC AND TRANSFORMATIONAL LEADERSHIP

Examinations of the validities of charismatic and transformational leadership reveal that both have important effects on criteria of interest to organizational behavior researchers.

In a meta-analysis of the relationship between transformational leadership, as measured by the MLQ, and leader effectiveness, Lowe et al. (1996) found validities of 0.71 for charisma, 0.62 for individualized consideration, and 0.60 for intellectual stimulation. In contrast, contingent reward and management-by-exception exhibited validities of 0.41 and 0.05, respectively. Corrected correlations were significantly higher for follower ratings of effectiveness ($\rho = 0.81$) than organizational measures ($\rho = 0.35$). Two other meta-analyses provide equivalent results, albeit with minor variations (DeGroot et al., 2000; Fuller et al., 1996).

The most recent meta-analysis of transformational leadership is by Judge and Piccolo (2004). This study differed from the previous meta-analyses in several ways. First, it included a larger number of studies than the others. Second, it tested the hypothesis that charismatic and transformational leadership have similar validities, seeking to add clarity to the long-running debate about the difference between them. Third, consistent with Bass' (1985) augmentation hypothesis, Judge and Piccolo sought to establish whether transactional leadership behaviors offer unique contributions to outcomes or recede entirely in significance when transformational leadership is controlled.

The validities Judge and Piccolo (2004) found are displayed in Table 1. All confidence intervals for transformational leadership excluded zero, as did all credibility intervals except the one for longitudinal designs. This means that the average validities can be distinguished from zero, and that the vast majority of the individual correlations in each study were nonzero. Supporting the view that measures of charismatic and transformational leadership are functionally equivalent, there was no significant difference in the overall validities of charismatic versus transformational leadership. Judge and Piccolo also found that measures of transformational leadership were substantially correlated with several dimensions of transactional leadership, most notably with contingent-reward (0.80) and laissez-faire

Table 1   Transformational leadership validities

	$\bar{r}$	ρ
Overall		
• Average across all conditions	.38	.44
By Criteria		
• Follower Job Satisfaction	.49	.58
• Satisfaction with Leader	.64	.71
• Follower Motivation	.46	.53
• Leader Job Performance	.23	.27
• Group/Organization Performance	.21	.26
• Leader Effectiveness	.56	.64
By Data Collection		
• Cross-Sectional	.44	.50
• Longitudinal	.23	.27
By Source of Data		
• Same-Source	.48	.55
• Multi-Source	.24	.28
By Study Design		
• Laboratory	.35	.40
• Field	.39	.45
By Leader Level		
• Lower- or supervisory-level	.41	.47
• Mid-level	.33	.37
• Upper-level or CEO	.48	.56

Notes: $\bar{r}$ = uncorrected average correlation.
ρ = correlation corrected for measurement error.

leadership (–0.65). Notably, the differences in validities between transformational leadership and contingent-reward leadership were fairly small. Contingent-reward even displayed somewhat higher validities in studies of business (as opposed to military or educational) organizations, and with follower job satisfaction, follower motivation, and leader job performance. However, the validities of transformational leadership were stronger under better research designs and were more consistent across study settings. Finally, with the exception of leader job performance, transformational leadership positively predicted all criteria in regressions that entered all of the leadership types, though the validities were quite a bit lower than the zero-order relationships. Contingent reward also positively predicted the criteria, though the magnitudes of these relationships were considerably lower than those of transformational leadership.

Beyond these meta-analyses, recent research has sought to link charismatic and transformational leadership to other criteria. These criteria can be broadly grouped into:

(a) follower attitudes and psychological states;
(b) follower behaviors and specific performance dimensions; and
(c) group processes.

In the first category, transformational leadership has been consistently positively associated with commitment (Meyer et al., 2002); self-efficacy (e.g., Dvir et al., 2002); psychological empowerment (Avolio et al., 2004; Hepworth and Towler, 2004); organizational identification (Epitropaki and Martin, 2005); and safety consciousness (Barling et al., 2002). It has also been negatively associated with employee cynicism about organizational change (Bommer et al., 2005).

With regard to specific performance dimensions and behaviors, transformational leadership positively predicts organizational citizenship (e.g., Podsakoff et al., 1996). Little work has been done on the influence of transformational leadership on counterproductive behavior, though one study (Hepworth and Towler, 2004) found a negative relationship with workplace aggression while another (Walumbwa and Lawler, 2003) found that followers of transformational leaders were less likely to exhibit job and work withdrawal. Several experimental studies have also examined the effect of transformational leadership on creativity and creative performance. Most have found that, relative to transactional leadership, transformational leadership has a significantly more positive impact on creative performance (e.g., Hoyt and Blascovich, 2003; Jung, 2001), although one found the reverse (Kahai et al., 2003).

There have also been numerous experimental inquiries into the impact of transformational leadership on group processes, providing substantial evidence that charismatic leaders enhance group cohesiveness (e.g., Bass et al., 2003; Hoyt and Blascovich, 2003); group potency (Bass et al., 2003; Lester et al., 2002); and collective efficacy (Kark et al., 2003). One study, furthermore, found that social loafing was less likely in groups led by transformational leaders (Kahai et al., 2003).

Falling somewhat outside of these three categories, another study (Bono and Anderson, 2005) examined the influence of transformational leaders on informal network positions of leaders and followers. They found that managers scoring higher on transformational leadership were more central in advice and influence networks. Moreover, their direct and indirect reports were more central in advice networks, while their direct reports were also more central in influence networks. These findings are interesting because they illuminate a previously unconsidered mechanism by which transformational leaders may exert influence on their own and their followers' outcomes.

There is sufficient laboratory and field evidence to convince us that transformational leadership has important effects on criteria of interest to organizational behavior researchers. There is still much to be learned, however, about the process by which transformational leadership exerts influence, its relative validity, and its generalizability across cultures. We examine these issues in the following sections, beginning with what influences charismatic and transformational leadership and moving to variables that may moderate their effectiveness.

INFLUENCES ON CHARISMATIC AND TRANSFORMATIONAL LEADERSHIP

Over the past decade, a number of influences on transformational and charismatic leadership have been identified. The antecedents studied are separated into individual and contextual variables for the purpose of this review. Transformational leadership has recently been the subject of two large-scale meta-analyses examining dispositional and demographic antecedents: one summarizing its relationship with gender, and the other with personality. According to Eagly et al. (2003), women are more likely to exhibit transformational leadership behaviors than men, though the average difference is quite small ($\bar{d} = -0.10$, meaning that women, on average, score one-tenth of a standard deviation higher on transformational leadership than do men). In terms of personality, Bono and Judge (2004) reported that extraversion is the strongest predictor of transformational leadership behaviors ($\rho = 0.24$), although all of the Big Five, except for conscientiousness, exhibit significant relationships with transformational leadership (neuroticism: $\rho = -0.17$; openness: $\rho = 0.15$; and agreeableness: $\rho = 0.14$).

Other individual differences variables that have been found to positively influence charismatic and transformational leadership are proactive personality (Crant and Bateman, 2000); traditional, self-transcendent (altruistic) and self-enhancement (egotistic) values (Sosik, 2005); and, somewhat ominously, narcissism (Judge et al., 2006) and Machiavellianism (e.g., Deluga, 1997, 2001). Also, Bommer et al. (2004) found that leaders who are cynical about organizational change are less likely to be judged as transformational.

Several contextual antecedents of charismatic and transformational leadership have also been the subject of research. The presence of peer leadership behaviors increases the likelihood of a leader exhibiting transformational leadership (Bommer et al., 2004). In a 'meso' level examination of charismatic leadership, Pillai and Meindl (1998) report a positive relationship between organic structure (as opposed to mechanistic) and charismatic leadership and between collectivistic cultural orientation (as opposed to individualistic) and charismatic leadership. These, in concert with Sosik's (2005) findings that charismatic leadership is positively predicted by collectivistic work characteristics, support additional examination of contextual factors related to charismatic leadership.

MODERATORS OF CHARISMATIC AND TRANSFORMATIONAL LEADERSHIP

In addition to influences on transformational and charismatic leadership, recent research has begun to identify moderators of the relationship of charismatic and transformational leadership with various outcomes. The five leader-or follower-level outcomes most investigated are:

(a) effectiveness (e.g., Fuller et al., 1996; Spreitzer et al., 2005; Wofford et al., 2001);
(b) performance (Fuller et al., 1996; Whittington et al., 2004);
(c) motivation (Felfe and Schyns, 2002);
(d) satisfaction (Fuller et al., 1996); and
(e) commitment (Meyer et al., 2002).

Individual differences variables that have been found to be moderators of transformational leadership are goal setting, growth need strength, need for autonomy, and values. These variables reflect characteristics of the rater or the follower that influence the effects found for transformational leadership. One study, for example, found that goal-setting moderated the effects of transformational leadership on both affective commitment and performance, such that, for both, goal-setting enhanced the strength of the relationship (Whittington et al., 2004).

Growth need strength and need for autonomy also appear to enhance the effects of transformational leadership. Wofford et al. (2001) found that, when need for autonomy and growth need strength of the employee are high, transformational leadership leads to greater group effectiveness. They also found that growth need strength enhanced the effects of transformational leadership on satisfaction with the leader.

Other research has investigated individual differences that suppress the effects of transformational leadership. Spreitzer et al. (2005) found that valuing traditionality (emphasizing respect for hierarchy) moderated the relationship between transformational leadership and ratings of effectiveness by superiors, such that transformational leaders are perceived to be less effective when the superior is a traditionalist in both the US and Taiwan.

Contextual variables also may moderate the relationship of transformational leadership with various outcomes. The effects of transformational leadership have been found, in particular, to vary by organizational sector. Lowe et al.'s (1996) meta-analysis revealed that relationships between transformational leadership behaviors and effectiveness were significantly higher in public than private organizations. Fuller et al. (1996) found that validities for performance were significantly higher in student and military samples than in civilian samples, while the validity for perceived effectiveness was higher in military than in civilian samples. Likewise, Judge and Piccolo (2004) found that transformational leadership was more valid in military settings.

Meta-analytic evidence also suggests that leader level moderates the effects of charismatic and transformational leadership. Fuller et al. (1996) found that the relationship between charismatic leadership and performance is somewhat stronger for upper-level leaders, and Judge and Piccolo (2004) showed that transformational leadership has a stronger impact on performance for leaders at the supervisory level ($\rho = 0.48$) than for those in middle- or upper-management ($\rho = 0.37$). Further supporting the moderating effects of leader level, Avolio et al. (2004) found that the relationship between transformational leadership and organizational commitment is more strongly positive when the supervision is indirect (i.e., leader-follower structural distance is high).

Job characteristics also moderate the relationship between transformational leadership and organizational commitment. Whittington et al. (2004) found that job enrichment substitutes for the effect of transformational leadership on organizational commitment, and the relationship is more positive when the supervision is indirect (structural distance is higher). Additional evidence that job characteristics act as moderators of transformational leadership effects was offered by Felfe and Schyns (2002). They found that high task demands neutralize the relationship between transformational leadership and self-efficacy, such that the relationship is zero when task demands are high and negative when they are low (Felfe and Schyns, 2002).

Finally, the internal and external organizational contexts influence the effects of transformational leadership. Felfe and Schyns (2002) found that climate moderates the relationship between transformational leadership and self-efficacy, such that the relationship is positive when climate is good and negative when it is bad. With regard to external context, another study found that high levels of environmental uncertainty strengthen the positive relationship between CEOs' charismatic leadership and subordinates' perception of their performance (de Hoogh et al., 2004). Furthermore, the relationship between charismatic leadership and firm profitability was stronger when the CEO was a firm owner rather than a managing director.

There is a potpourri of evidence that individual differences and contextual factors moderate the effects of charismatic and transformational leadership. Yet, systematic study and integration are still needed. Shamir and Howell (1999) advanced a model of organizational and contextual influences on the transformational leadership process, which suggested that factors like situational strength, organizational governance, and linkage of organizational goals to dominant society values should influence whether transformational leaders emerge and their likely effects. Their framework may be useful in guiding future research on contextual moderators as well as inspiring further specification of a model of individual differences moderators and the relationships between the two.

CROSS-CULTURAL EVIDENCE

Bass (1997) has posited that the effects of transformational leadership are universal, generalizing across cultures. This is a strong assertion given that cultural values vary as, presumably, do implicit assumptions about leadership. While some research supports the universality of charismatic and transformational leadership (e.g., Walumba et al., 2005), other studies challenge the role charismatic leaders may play in different cultures (e.g., Zagorsek et al., 2004).

The GLOBE studies – a study of leadership, organizational culture, and national culture in three industries across 62 nations – are particularly noteworthy with regard to the cross-cultural relevance of transformational leadership (e.g., Dorfman et al., 2004; Den Hartog et al., 1999). Although there is some variation in the findings across countries, in general, the results support the importance of charismatic or transformational leadership across cultures. Den Hartog et al. (1999: 250) conclude, 'The combined results of the major GLOBE study and the follow-up study demonstrate that several attributes reflecting charismatic/transformational leadership are universally endorsed as contributing to outstanding leadership.'

Broad and convincing support exists for the relevance of transformational and charismatic leadership in various cultural settings, yet there are some characteristics of national cultures that can influence the emergence, perceptions, and effects of these leadership styles. For example, Stajkovic et al. (2005) examined data from senior managers in the US (an individualistic culture) and China (a collective culture). Results suggested that culture moderated the positive relationship between charismatic leadership and social network extensiveness. In similar fashion, Walumbwa and Lawler (2003) found that collectivism moderated the relationship between transformational leadership and several job outcomes such as job satisfaction, withdrawal behavior, and organizational commitment in a sample of Chinese, Indian, and Kenyan workers; the form of the interaction was such that the relationships were stronger for collectivists. Finally, Javidan and Carl (2004) compared Iranian and Canadian managers and found the former to be significantly lower-rated, suggesting a difference in either manifestations of leadership behaviors or in the ways in which such behaviors are interpreted.

In addition to culture at the nation-state level, culture may also be considered at the organization level, wherein organizational cultures may vary in their charismatic or transformational styles. For example, although Carly Fiorina was hailed as the first 'rock star' CEO when she became head of Hewlett-Packard in 1999, when she was ousted in 2005, people argued that she may have been too flashy for HP's conservative culture (though HP's 50 per cent drop in stock price during her tenure certainly precipitated her fall; Cowley and Rohde, 2005). A theoretically-relevant cultural attribute may thus be analyzed at the national or organizational level.

Kotter and Heskett (1992) offered a perspective of adaptive and non-adaptive cultures. Adaptive cultures are more prone to emphasizing innovation, integrity, enthusiasm, teamwork, frank communication, and risk taking. On the contrary, non-adaptive cultures do not promote risk taking, innovation, or change and are instead focused on efficiency and order. Based on these characteristics, adaptive cultures may be more amenable to the emergence and effects of charismatic leadership compared to non-adaptive cultures.

DIRECTIONS FOR FUTURE RESEARCH

As is true of any literature that has reached a certain stage of maturation, the low hanging fruit has been picked, which leads to the paradox that the most important topics to be researched are also the least tractable.

Causal inference

Although there have been some studies of charismatic leadership that would satisfy the reader skeptical of causal inference, the literature is dominated by cross-sectional correlational designs, where causal inferences are highly suspect. Alternatively, some studies that would support causal inference are often conducted in the laboratory, which often constitutes a 'weak' situation in leadership research (Judge et al., 2002). To be sure, some field studies do support causal inferences to varying degrees. However, we think the problem is a greater one than that often recognized in the literature. The reason for our concern is a research stream showing that individuals have implicit stereotypes of charismatic or transformational leaders, meaning that, if a leader is deemed to be effective, attributional labels comporting with stereotypes of charismatic, transformational, or visionary leadership often will be invoked (Epitropaki and Martin, 2004). Although we realize it is much easier to call for rigorous designs than it is to design and execute rigorous studies, we do not think the ease of the call renders it invalid. To repeat an earlier refrain, we think laboratory studies have much to offer here.

Distinction between charismatic and transformational leadership

As noted by Hunt and Conger (1999), the vast majority of leadership research uses the terms charisma and transformational leadership interchangeably. However, we tend to agree with Hunt and Conger (1999: 340): 'We conclude that there needs to be more differentiation than there has typically been in the use of the two terms.' Although we agree with Conger (1999) that various models of charismatic and transformational leadership (e.g., House's model, the Bass-Avolio model, Conger and Kanungo's model, Shamir and associates' model) share more similarities than differences and that the models appear to be converging, we are not altogether certain this is a positive development.

We think there is a clear distinction to be made – at least in concept – between vision (a desired end-state) and charisma (a personal quality that is manifested in a dynamic, expressive communication style). A vision may transcend an individual, and be passed on from leader to leader (Collins and Porras, 1991). Charisma, conversely, is necessarily a personal quality. This is not to say that individuals who are charismatic might not be more likely to also have a vision. We suspect, measurement problems aside, that charismatic

leaders are probably more likely to develop and communicate visions. But we think these concepts have not been measured in a way that reflects their actual distinctiveness. If one examines the MLQ and other popular measures, the items often confound the two: 'Talks *enthusiastically* about what needs to be accomplished' (emphasis added).

The best work here has been done by Locke and colleagues. Baum et al. (1998) found that entrepreneurial visions that possessed certain attributes (e.g., brief, clear, future-oriented), were well-communicated, and focused on growth were associated with higher levels of business venture growth. They also found that the communication of a vision also mattered, though they did not measure charismatic communication style per se. Using trained actors as leaders, Kirkpatrick and Locke (1996) found that vision quality and cues for vision implementation each affected satisfaction and performance, whereas a charismatic communication style was unrelated to these outcomes. However, with the exception of Locke, Kirkpatrick and colleagues, no research has distinguished visionary leadership from a charismatic communication style.

Ignoring transactional leadership

In the largest meta-analytic review to date, Judge and Piccolo (2004) found that transactional leadership was as or more important than transformational leadership for many criteria. Collapsed across all criteria, the overall validity of transformational leadership was only slightly greater than contingent reward leadership ($\rho = 0.44$ vs. $\rho = 0.39$, respectively). Judge and Piccolo (2004) also found that the negative effects of laissez-faire leadership were far from trivial. Thus, current thinking about transformational leadership needs to take into account that, in many cases, transactional leadership may be at least as important. What are the situations in which transactional leadership may be particularly important, even more important than transformational leadership? Are there situations, as Avolio and Bass (1994) argue, that both are needed, or are there situations when high levels of one can substitute for low levels of the other?

Mediating mechanisms

In 1999, Bass concluded, 'Much more explanation is needed about the workings of transformational leadership' (p. 24). Since that time, there have been a large number of efforts to explore mediators of charismatic and transformational leadership (e.g., Avolio et al., 2004; Bono and Anderson, 2005; Bono and Judge, 2003; Jung and Avolio, 2000; Jung et al., 2003; Kark, et al., 2003; McCann et al., 2006; Purvanova et al., 2006; Shin and Zhou, 2003; Walumbwa et al., 2005; Wang et al., 2005). However, this focus on mediators has occurred in such a rush that it is difficult to integrate and make sense of the efforts. Indeed, it is scarcely the case that any of the same mediators have been investigated across studies. It is beyond the scope of this review to provide an integration of these mediators. We call for relatively more focus on integrative efforts and relatively less focus on the continued generation of individual mediator variables. Studies that make use of meta-analytic path analyses, as has been advocated in general (Viswesvaran and Ones, 1995), and carried out in other areas (e.g., Colquitt et al., 2000), would be particularly valuable here.

Are leaders made: development of charismatic/transformational leadership

We have already noted that there is clear evidence that good leaders are born. But this does not necessarily mean that good leaders cannot be made, anymore than a genetic component to intelligence means that individuals cannot learn. There is evidence that individuals can be trained to exhibit transformational leadership behaviors (Barling et al., 1996; Dvir et al., 2002; Frese et al., 2003). Although these studies are noteworthy for their use of control groups, there are three ways in which future research is needed to

fully validate the developmental nature of charismatic or transformational leadership. First, the longevity of training effects needs to be studied. The studies above were of relatively short duration (several months). What happens as more time passes? Is there a permanency to what is learned, or do the learning and learned behaviors decay? Second, we need to determine whether and when there are specific aspects of transformational leadership training that are meaningful. Is it possible that most *any* leadership training program would have an effect? Only through a comparison of transformational leadership training with other leadership models can this question be answered. Finally, if one is to separate a charismatic communication style from visionary leadership (Kirkpatrick and Locke, 1996), then can the former be developed? Although Kirkpatrick and Locke (1996) successfully trained professional actors to display a charismatic communication style (a powerful, confident, and dynamic presence through both verbal and nonverbal behaviors), it is not clear whether the average person would similarly benefit from charisma training, nor how long such development might last.

Moral leadership

One troubling aspect of transformational leadership theory is the presumption that transformational leadership is inherently positive. Bass (1985: 21) originally argued that 'transformational leadership is not necessarily beneficial leadership.' However, he later appeared to modify that position, arguing, 'Transformational leaders move followers to transcend their own self-interests for the good of the group, organization, or country' (Bass, 1997: 133). Research on transformational leadership has overwhelmingly been based on the assumption that transformational leadership is universally positive. There is no reason to believe that all change is good, nor is there any reason to believe that persuasive leadership is always directed toward positive ends. Indeed, we would submit that in the realm of the most salient leaders in human history, there are as many leaders deemed evil as benevolent. For every Churchill, there is a Hitler. Moreover, to most acts of transformational leadership, there is a moral ambiguity. Jack Welch may be viewed a great business leader by many, but what about the employees he was responsible for firing? Even his critics would have to acknowledge that Franklin Roosevelt was a transformational US President, but he also tried to usurp the power and independence of the judicial branch of government when they threatened his power. Our point is that we see the presumption that transformational leadership is a force for good to be heavy ontological baggage for the theory to carry.

Although not necessarily resolving this implicit contradiction, Avolio and colleagues have recently focused on a concept they term authentic leadership. According to Avolio and Gardner (2005: 321), authentic leaders are

> those who are deeply aware of how they think and behave and are perceived by others as being aware of their own and others' values/moral perspectives, knowledge, and strengths; aware of the context in which they operate; and who are confident, hopeful, optimistic, resilient, and of high moral character.

Although the lines of demarcation between this model of leadership and transformational leadership are yet to be clearly drawn, it does open up the intriguing possibility of transformational leaders who project an image of good leadership, but act in the service of their interests at the expense of their followers. Avolio and Gardner (2005) further distinguish authentic from transformational leadership. In the former, 'the leader may not actively set out to transform the follower into a leader, but may do so simply by being role model for followers,' thus viewing authentic leadership 'as being much more relational, where both follower and leader are shaped in their respective development' (p. 327).

Authentic leadership may or may not be the *deus ex machina* that resolves the issue of whether transformational leadership is necessarily benevolent. After all, as can be

clearly seen in the case of Osama bin Laden, whether a leader is judged as moral or evil very much depends on the perspective of the perceiver. Moreover, it is not entirely clear whether transformational leadership is a necessary condition for authentic leadership, or authentic leadership a necessary condition for transformational, or neither. Despite these difficulties, we think this is a pivotal issue for future research.

Integration with behavioral school

Yukl (1989) noted, '… most researchers deal only with a narrow aspect of leadership and ignore the other aspects' (p. 254). Only a few studies examine the relative influence of different leadership conceptualizations (Bycio et al., 1995; Howell and Avolio, 1993; Howell and Hall-Merenda, 1999; Judge and Piccolo, 2004; Jung, 2001; Seltzer and Bass, 1990), or the extent to which theories of leadership overlap. This is particularly a concern given conceptual overlap in the theories. One of the four transformational leadership dimensions – individualized consideration – appears to directly overlap with the Ohio State dimension of consideration. In transformational leadership theory, individualized consideration is the degree to which the leader attends to each follower's needs, acts as a mentor or coach to the follower, and listens to followers' concerns and needs (Bass, 1985). The Ohio State dimension of consideration refers to the degree to which a leader shows concern and respect for followers, looks out for their welfare, and expresses appreciation and support. Bass (1999) argued that these two ideas are conceptually distinct, but such a distinction is a fine one. Thus, there is a need for future research to compare and contrast transformational and transactional leadership with the Ohio State leadership dimensions.

CONCLUSION

'One of the most universal cravings of our time is a hunger for compelling and creative leadership,' wrote Burns in his 1978 Pulitzer Prize-winning book on leadership (p. 1). Accordingly, scholars and researchers have long been fascinated with leadership concepts and continue to study effects and antecedents of the phenomenon decades after its original inception in the literature. In this review, we sought to provide an overview of current knowledge about charismatic and transformational leadership and to suggest an agenda for future research. Sufficient laboratory and field evidence convinces us of the validity of charismatic and transformational leadership across many different settings. However, there is still a need for scholars to elucidate upon some of the puzzles that remain in this literature. Carrying out some of our recommendations for future research may require more rigorous research designs and the challenging of some generally-accepted pieces of wisdom in the field. Yet, we believe that more thorough investigation of transformational leadership along these lines is critical to our gaining a thorough understanding of leadership in general.

NOTE

Some portions of this review appear in: Judge, T. A., Woolf, E. F., Hurst, C., and Livingston, B. (2006). Charismatic and transformational leadership: A review and an agenda for future research. *Zeitschrift für Arbeits- und Organistionspsychologie*, 50: 203–214.

REFERENCES

Avolio, B. J. and Bass, B. M. (1991) *The Full Range of Leadership Development: Basic and Advanced Manuals*. Binghamton, NY: Bass, Avolio, and Associates.

Avolio, B. J., Bass, B. M. and Jung, D. I. (1999) 'Re–examining the components of transformational and transactional leadership using the Multifactor Leadership Questionnaire', *Journal of Occupational and Organizational Psychology*, 72: 441–462.

Avolio, B. J. and Gardner, W. L. (2005) 'Authentic leadership development: Getting to the root of positive forms of leadership', *Leadership Quarterly*, 16: 315–338.

Avolio, B. J., Zhu, W., Koh, W. and Bhatia, P. (2004) 'Transformational leadership and organizational commitment: Mediating role of psychological empowerment and moderating role of structural distance', *Journal of Organizational Behavior*, 25: 951–968.

Barling, J., Loughlin, C. and Kelloway, E. K. (2002) 'Development and test of a model linking safety-specific transformational leadership and occupational safety', *Journal of Applied Psychology*, 87: 488–496.

Barling, J., Weber, T. and Kelloway, E. K. (1996) 'Effects of transformational leadership training on attitudinal and financial outcomes: A field experiment', *Journal of Applied Psychology*, 81: 827–832.

Bass, B. M. (1985) *Leadership and Performance Beyond Expectations*. New York: Free Press.

Bass, B. M. (1997) 'Does the transactional/ transformational leadership transcend organizational and national boundaries?', *American Psychologist*, 52: 130–139.

Bass, B. M. (1999) 'Two decades of research and development in transformational leadership', *European Journal of Work and Organizational Psychology*, 8: 9–32.

Bass, B. M. and Avolio, B. J. (1990) *Manual for the Multifactor Leadership Questionnaire*. Palo Alto, CA: Consulting Psychologists Press.

Bass, B. M. and Avolio, B. J. (1994) 'Transformational leadership and organizational culture', *International Journal of Public Administration*, 17: 541–555.

Bass, B. M., Avolio, B. J., Jung, D. I. and Berson, Y. (2003) 'Predicting unit performance by assessing transformational and transactional leadership', *Journal of Applied Psychology*, 88: 207–218.

Bass, B. M. and Riggio, R. E. (2006) *Transformational Leadership* (2nd edn). Mahwah, NJ: Erlbaum.

Baum, J. R., Locke, E. and Kirkpatrick, S. (1998) 'A longitudinal study of the relation of vision and vision communication to venture growth in entrepreneurial firms', *Journal of Applied Psychology*, 83: 43–54.

Beyer, J. M. (1999) 'Taming and promoting charisma to change organizations', *Leadership Quarterly*, 10: 307–330.

Bommer, W. H., Rich, G. A. and Rubin, R. S. (2005) 'Changing attitudes about change: Longitudinal effects of transformational leader behavior on employee cynicism about organizational change', *Journal of Organizational Behavior*, 26: 733–753.

Bommer, W. H., Rubin, R. S. and Baldwin, T. T. (2004) 'Setting the stage for effective leadership: Antecedents of transformational leadership behavior', *Leadership Quarterly*, 15: 195–210.

Bono, J. E. and Anderson, M. H. (2005) 'The advice and influence networks of transformational leaders', *Journal of Applied Psychology*, 90: 1306–1314.

Bono, J. E. and Judge, T. A. (2003) 'Self-concordance at work: Toward understanding the motivational effects of transformational leaders', *Academy of Management Journal*, 46: 554–571.

Bono, J. E. and Judge, T. A. (2004) 'Personality and transformational and transactional leadership: A meta-analysis', *Journal of Applied Psychology*, 89: 901–910.

Brown, D. J. and Lord, R. G. (1999) 'The utility of experimental research in the study of transformational/charismatic leadership', *Leadership Quarterly*, 10: 531–539.

Burns. J. (1978) *Leadership*. New York : Harper & Row, Publishers, Inc.

Bycio, P., Hackett, R. D. and Allen, J. S. (1995) 'Further assessments of Bass's (1985) conceptualization of transactional and transformational leadership', *Journal of Applied Psychology*, 80: 468–478.

Collins, J. C. and Porras, J. (1991) 'Organizational vision and visionary organizations', *California Management Review*, 34: 30–52.

Colquitt, J. A., LePine, J. A. and Noe, R. A. (2000) 'Toward an integrative theory of training motivation: A meta-analytic path analysis of 20 years of research', *Journal of Applied Psychology*, 85: 678–707.

Conger, J. (1990) 'The dark side of leadership', *Organizational Dynamics*, 19: 44–55.

Conger, J. A. (1989) *The Charismatic Leader: Beyond the Mystique of Exceptional Leadership*. San Francisco: Jossey-Bass.

Conger, J. A. (1999) 'Charismatic and transformational leadership in organizations: An insider's perspective on these developing streams of research', *Leadership Quarterly*, 10: 145–179.

Conger, J. A. and Kanungo, R. (1998) *Charismatic Leadership in Organizations*. San Francisco: Jossey-Bass.

Conger, J. A., Kanungo, R. N., Menon, S. T. and Mathur, P. (1997) 'Measuring charisma: Dimensionality and validity of the Conger-Kanungo scale of charismatic leadership', *Revue Canadienne des Sciences de l'Administration*, 14 : 290–302.

Cowley, S. and Rohde, L. (February 9, 2005) Update: HP board ousts Fiorina. *Computerworld* , Available at http://www.computerworld.com/hardwaretopics/hardware/story/0,10801,99622,00.html

Crant, J. M. and Bateman, T. S. (2000) 'Charismatic leadership viewed from above: the impact of proactive personality', *Journal of Organizational Behavior*, 21: 63–75.

DeGroot, T., Kiker, D. S. and Cross, T. C. (2000) 'A meta-analysis to review organizational outcomes related to charismatic leadership', *Canadian Journal of Administrative Sciences*, 17: 356–371.

De Hoogh, A. H. B., den Hartog, D. N., Koopman, P. L., Thierry, H., van den Berg, P. T., van der Weide, J. G. and Wilderom, C. P. M. (2004) 'Charismatic leadership, environmental dynamism, and performance', *European Journal of Work and Organizational Psychology*, 13: 447–471.

Deluga, R. J. (1997) 'Relationship among American presidential charismatic leadership, narcissism, and rated performance', *Leadership Quarterly*, 8: 49–65.

Deluga, R. J. (2001) 'American presidential Machiavellianism: Implications for charismatic leadership and rated performance', *Leadership Quarterly*, 12: 339–363.

Den Hartog, D. N., House, R.J., Hanges, P. J., Ruiz–Quintanilla, S. A. and Dorfman, P. W. (1999) 'Culture specific and cross–culturally generalizable implicit leadership theories: Are attributes of charismatic/transformational leadership universally endorsed?', *Leadership Quarterly*, 10: 219–256.

Dorfman, P. W., Hanges, P. J. and Brodbeck, F. C. (2004) 'Leadership and Cultural Variation: The Identification of Culturally Endorsed Leadership Profiles', in R. J. House, P. J. Hanges, M. Javidan, P. W. Dorfman, and V. Gupta (eds), *Culture, Leadership, and Organizations: The GLOBE Study of 62 Societies*. Thousand Oaks, CA: Sage, pp. 669–719.

Dvir, T., Eden, D., Avolio, B. J. and Shamir, B. (2002) 'Impact of transformational leadership on follower development and performance: A field experiment', *Academy of Management Journal*, 45: 735–744.

Eagly, A. H., Johannesen-Schmidt, M. C. and van Engen, M. L. (2003) 'Transformational, transactional, and laissez-faire leadership styles: A meta-analysis comparing women and men', *Psychological Bulletin*, 129: 569–591.

Epitropaki, O. and Martin, R. (2004) 'Implicit leadership theories in applied settings: Factor structure, generalizability, and stability over time', *Journal of Applied Psychology*, 89: 293–310.

Felfe, J. and Schyns, B. (2002) 'The relationship between employees' occupational self-efficacy and perceived transformational leadership: Replication and extension of recent results', *Current Research in Social Psychology*, 7: 137–162.

Frese, M., Beimel, S. and Schoenborn, S. (2003) 'Action training for charismatic leadership: Two evaluations of studies of a commercial training module on inspirational communication of a vision', *Personnel Psychology*, 56: 671–697.

Fuller, J. B., Patterson, C. E. P., Hester, K. and Stringer, D. Y. (1996) 'A quantitative review of research on charismatic leadership', *Psychological Reports*, 78: 271–287.

Hepworth, W. and Towler, A. (2004) 'The effects of individual differences and charismatic leadership on workplace aggression', *Journal of Occupational Health Pyschology*, 9: 176–185.

House, R. J. (1977) 'A 1976 theory of charismatic leadership', in J.G. Hunt and L.L. Larsen (eds), *Leadership: The Cutting Edge*. Carbondale, IL: Southern Illinois University Press.

House, R. J. and Podsakoff, P. M. (1994) 'Leadership effectiveness: Past perspectives and future directions for research', in J. Greenberg (ed.), *Organizational Behavior: The State of the Science*. Hillsdale, NJ: Erlbaum, pp. 45–82.

Howell, J. M. and Avolio, B. J. (1993) 'Transformational leadership, transactional leadership, locus of control, and support for innovation: Key predictors of consolidated-business-unit performance', *Journal of Applied Psychology*, 78: 891–902.

Howell, J. M. and Hall–Merenda, K. E. (1999) 'The ties that bind: The impact of leader-member exchange, transformational and transactional leadership, and distance on predicting follower performance', *Journal of Applied Psychology*, 84: 680–694.

Hoyt, C. L. and Blascovich, J. (2003) 'Transformational and transactional leadership in virtual and physical environments', *Small Group Research*, 34: 678–715.

Hunt, J. G. (1991) *Leadership: A New Synthesis*. Newbury Park, CA: Sage.

Hunt, J. G. and Conger, J. A. (1999) 'From where we sit: An assessment of transformational and charismatic leadership research', *Leadership Quarterly*, 10: 335–343.

Ichheiser, G. (1949) *Misunderstandings in Human Relations: A Study in False Social Perception*. Chicago: University of Chicago Press.

Javidan, M. and Carl, D. E. (2004) 'East meets west: A cross-cultural comparison of charismatic leadership among Canadian and Iranian executives', *Journal of Management Studies*, 41: 665–691.

Judge, T. A., LePine, J. A. and Rich, B. L. (2006) 'The narcissistic personality: Relationship with inflated self-ratings of leadership and with task and contextual performance', *Journal of Applied Psychology*, 91: 762–776.

Judge, T. A. and Piccolo, R. F. (2004) 'Transformational and transactional leadership: A meta-analytic test of their relative validity', *Journal of Applied Psychology*, 89: 755–768.

Jung, D. I. (2001) 'Transformational and transactional leadership and their effects on creativity in groups', *Creativity Research Journal*, 13: 185–195.

Jung, D. I. and Avolio, B. J. (2000) 'Opening the black box: An experimental investigation of the mediating effects of trust and value congruence on transformational and transactional leadership', *Journal of Organizational Behavior*, 21: 949–964.

Jung, D. I., Chow, C. and Wu, A. (2003) 'The role of transformational leadership in enhancing organizational innovation: Hypotheses and some preliminary findings', *Leadership Quarterly*, 14: 525–544.

Kahai, S. S., Sosik, J. J. and Avolio, B. J. (2003) 'Effects of leadership style, anonymity, and rewards on creativity-relevant processes and outcomes in an electronic meeting system context', *Leadership Quarterly*, 14: 499–524.

Kark, R., Shamir, B. and Chen, G. (2003) 'The two faces of transformational leadership: Empowerment and dependency', *Journal of Applied Psychology*, 88: 246–255.

Kirkpatrick, S. A. and Locke, E. A. (1996) 'Direct and indirect effects of three core charismatic leadership components on performance and attitudes', *Journal of Applied Psychology*, 81: 36–51.

Kotter, J. P. and Heskett, J. L. (1992) *Corporate Culture and Performance*. New York: The Free Press.

Lester, S. W., Meglino, B. M. and Korsgaard, M. A. (2002) 'The antecedents and consequences of group potency: A longitudinal investigation of newly formed work groups', *Academy of Management Journal*, 45: 352–368.

Locke, E. A. (1986) 'Generalizing from Laboratory to Field: Ecological Validity or Abstraction of Essential Elements?', in E. A. Locke (ed.), *Generalizing from Laboratory to Field Settings*. Lexington, MA: Lexington Books, pp. 1–9.

Lord, R. G. and Hall, R. J. (1992) 'Contemporary views of leadership and individual differences', *Leadership Quarterly*, 3: 137–157

Lowe, K. B., Kroeck. K. G. and Sivasubramaniam, N. (1996) 'Effectiveness correlates of transformational and transactional leadership: A meta-analytic review of the MLQ literature', *Leadership Quarterly*, 7: 385–425.

McCann, J. A. J., Langford, P. H. and Rawlings, R. M. (2006) 'Testing Behling and McFillen's syncretical model of charismatic transformational leadership', *Group and Organization Management*, 31: 237–263.

Meyer, J. P., Stanley, D. J., Herscovitch, L. and Topolnytsky, L. (2002) 'Affective, continuance, and normative commitment to the organization: A meta-analysis of antecedents, correlates and consequences', *Journal of Vocational Behavior*, 61: 20–52.

Palmer, J., Thomas, A. and Maurer, T. (2003) 'Moderating effects of context on the relationship between behavioral diaries and performance rating halo and accuracy', *North American Journal of Psychology*, 5: 81–90.

Pillai, R. and Meindl, J. R. (1998) 'Context and charisma: A "meso" level examination of the relationship of organic structure, collectivism, and crises to charismatic leadership', *Journal of Management*, 24: 643–671.

Podsakoff, P. M., MacKenzie, S. B. and Bommer, W. H. (1996) 'Meta-analysis of the relationships between Kerr and Jermier's substitutes for leadership and employee job attitudes, role perceptions, and performance', *Journal of Applied Psychology*, 81: 380–399.

Purvanova, R. K., Bono, J. E. and Dzieweczynski, J. (2006) 'Transformational leadership, job characteristics, and organizational citizenship performance', *Human Performance*, 19: 1–22.

Russell, B. (1940) *An Inquiry into Meaning and Truth*. New York: W. W. Norton & Company.

Seltzer, J. and Bass, B. M. (1990) 'Transformational leadership: Beyond initiation and consideration', *Journal of Management*, 16: 693–703.

Shamir, B. and Howell, J.M. (1999) 'Organizational and contextual influences on the emergence and effectiveness of charismatic leadership', *Leadership Quarterly*, 10: 257–283.

Sharansky, N. (April 24, 2006) 'Dissident President: George W. Bush has the courage to speak out for freedom', *Wall Street Journal*. Available at http://www.opinionjournal.com/editorial/feature. html?id=110008281

Shin, S. J. and Zhou, J. (2003) 'Transformational leadership, conservation, and creativity: Evidence from Korea', *Academy of Management Journal*, 46: 703–714.

Sosik, J. J. (2005) 'The role of personal values in the charismatic leadership of corporate managers: A model and preliminary field study', *Leadership Quarterly*, 16: 221–244.

Spreitzer, G. M., Perttula, K. H. and Xin, K. (2005) 'Traditionality matters: An examination of the effectiveness of transformational leadership in the United States and Taiwan', *Journal of Organizational Behavior*, 26: 205–227.

Stajkovic, A. D., Carpenter, M. A. and Graffin, S. D. (2005) 'Relationships among charismatic leadership, social network extensiveness, and self–set career goals: A cross–cultural examination in the United States and China', *Academy of Management Proceedings*, G1–G6.

Trice, H. M. and Beyer, J. M. (1986) 'Charisma and its routinization in two social movement groups', *Research in Organizational Behavior*, 8: 113–164.

Viswesvaran, C. and Ones, D. S. (1995) 'Theory testing: Combining psychometric meta-analysis and structural equations modeling', *Personnel Psychology*, 48: 865–885.

Viswesvaran, C., Schmidt, F. L. and Ones, D. S. (2005) 'Is there a general factor in ratings of job performance? A meta-analytic framework for disentangling substantive and error influences', *Journal of Applied Psychology*, 90: 108–131.

Walumbwa, F. O. and Lawler, J. J. (2003) 'Building effective organizations: Transformational leadership, collectivist orientation, work-related attitudes and withdrawal behaviors in three emerging economies', *International Journal of Human Resource Management*, 14: 1083–1101.

Walumbwa, F. O., Orwa, B., Wang, P. and Lawler, J. J. (2005) 'Transformational leadership, organizational commitment, and job satisfaction: A comparative study of Kenyan and U.S. financial firms', *Human Resource Development Quarterly*, 16: 235–256.

• Wang, H., Law, K. S. and Hackett, R. D. (2005) 'Leader-member exchange as a mediator of the relationship between transformational leadership and followers' performance and organizational citizenship behavior', *Academy of Management Journal*, 48: 420–432.

Weber, M. (1947) *Max Weber: The Theory of Social and Economic Organization*. A.M. Henderson and T. Parsons (trans). New York: Free Press.

Whittington, J. L., Goodwin, V. L. and Murray, B. (2004) 'Transformational leadership, goal difficulty, and job design: Independent and interactive effects on employee outcomes', *Leadership Quarterly*, 15: 593–606.

Wilentz, S. (April 21, 2006) The worst president in history? One of America's leading historians assesses George W. Bush. *Rolling Stone*. Available at http://www.rollingstone.com/news/profile/story/ 9961300/the_worst_president_in_history?andrnd= 1146141676435andhas-player=true

Wofford, J. C., Whittington, J. L. and Goodwin, V. L. (2001) 'Follower motive patterns as situational moderators for transformational leadership effectiveness', *Journal of Managerial Issues*, 13: 196–211.

Yukl, G. (1989) 'Managerial leadership: A review of theory and research', *Journal of Management*, 15: 251–289.

Yukl, G. (1999) 'An evaluation of conceptual weaknesses in transformational and charismatic leadership theories', *Leadership Quarterly*, 10: 285–305.

Zagorsek, H., Jaklic, M. and Stough, S. J. (2004) 'Comparing leadership practices between the United States, Nigeria, and Slovenia: Does culture matter?', *Cross Cultural Management*, 11: 16–34.

19

A Multi-Level Conceptualization of Organizational Politics

Sean Lux, Gerald R. Ferris, Robyn L. Brouer,
Mary Dana Laird and James Summers

Organizational politics is predominately viewed as the exercise of power amongst individuals and groups within an organization (Leary, 1995; Pfeffer, 1992, 1997). The basic assumption behind this perspective is that individuals are rationally bounded, self-interested actors who pursue power and detract from others' power for their own gain (Emerson, 1962; Pfeffer and Salancik, 1978). Previous organizational politics scholarship largely has focused on social influence or effective political tactics (Ferris et al., 2002b) and the effects of perceived political behavior on organizational members (Ferris et al., 2002a). However, aspects of these largely sociology-based assumptions are at odds with economic and psychology-based assumptions of decision making and behavior.

Proponents of the economic organizational perspective (Barney and Ouchi, 1986; Coase, 1937; Williamson, 1975) have asserted that economic rewards, rather than the accumulation of power, influence individual decisions and behavior. Although the relationship between the successful use of power and economic rewards is implicit in political scholarship, economic competition in open markets ensures that ineffective organizations are short lived. Thus, power obtained through political behavior that is detrimental to economic performance is viewed as temporal at best.

Focusing on power over economic factors has other drawbacks in developing a comprehensive approach to organizational politics. First, the effect of politics on individual and organization economic performance cannot be directly examined. This relationship is mediated by accumulation and subsequent use of power in the power-based perspective. Considering economic factors as a motivator behind political behavior enables us to examine how politics both positively and adversely affects firm economic outcomes, thus delivering valuable insights to managers.

Second, we believe the lack of an overall organizational politics perspective or theory is due largely to differences in how scholars have viewed politics. Organization-level scholars often have suggested that politics are essential in coalition building and organization survival, and largely have viewed politics in more neutral, or even positive ways (e.g., Bacharach and Lawler, 1980; Cyert and March, 1963; Pfeffer, 1981; Mintzberg, 1983). Scholars at the individual or 'micro' level of analysis have tended to characterize politics as largely self-interested, manipulative, and potentially destructive behavior, which ultimately could be harmful to both individuals and organizations (e.g., Hall et al., 2004). However, these perspectives place subjective limits on our understanding of organizational politics, and create difficulties in integrating scholarship across levels of analysis. Considering economic factors enables us to examine how politics, both positively and negatively, affect economic performance, thus providing a more objective approach to organizational politics scholarship.

Factors other than rational evaluation of power and economic rewards affect decision-making and subsequent behavior. Whereas economic factors enable us to expand our understanding of why political behavior occurs and how it affects economic performance outcomes, intrinsic factors outside rational choice provide a great deal of insight into organizational politics. Attitudes, social norms, and perceived control over an action all affect the decision to engage in a behavior (Ajzen, 1991).

Considering both economic and psychological factors together enables us to build a more comprehensive understanding of organizational politics across levels of analysis. The purpose of this chapter is to develop a multi-level organizational politics framework that integrates theory and research across the individual and organization levels of analysis. The chapter proceeds as follows. We review the organizational economics literature with emphasis on the role of informal governance,

and then introduce our organizing model. We then integrate previous scholarship into the proposed model, discuss future research directions, ending the chapter with final conclusions.

ORGANIZATIONAL ECONOMICS

Firms exist in the economic organizational perspective because they reduce the level of uncertainty between economic exchange participants (Barney and Ouchi, 1986; Coase, 1937; Williamson, 1975). Firms are governance mechanisms that exist for two primary reasons. First, there are costs in any economic exchange associated with contracting (e.g., search, negotiation, enforcement, opportunistic behavior), and these costs increase as uncertainty surrounding the transaction increases (Coase, 1937). Effective governance moderates the relationship between exchange uncertainties and contracting costs, however, governance itself is not without cost. Williamson's (1975) basic theoretical proposition is that exchange parties will choose to organize economic exchanges through firms rather than contracts when the cost of firm governance is less than the costs associated with repeated contracting.

Second, firms exist because they are simply better at coordinating activities and information than markets (Alchian and Demsetz, 1973; Connor and Prahlahad, 1996; Grant, 1996). Uncertainty due to complexity rather than opportunism creates the need for organization in this perspective. Because firms enable individuals to share information and coordinate activities more effectively than market forms of organization, firms can create new knowledge and unique value unlikely to be developed by individuals in markets (Barney, 1991; Grant, 1996). Although these two perspectives of economics have advanced largely independently, scholars generally agree that firms likely exist to both reduce opportunism and create unique value through information and activity coordination (Madhok, 2002; Williamson, 1999).

Firms reduce uncertainty through formal and informal governance. Formal governance examples include employment contracts, hierarchical reporting relationships, and organizational policies, whereas trust and social norms are the predominant informal governance forms. While formal governance means are viable in market exchanges, few organizational members other than firm leadership can utilize formal governance means to coordinate intra-organizational economic and social exchanges. Most organizational members must rely on informal governance means to coordinate these intra-organizational exchanges.

Informal governance has two primary advantages over formal governance. First, informal governance is much more cost effective than formal governance. Social norms developed and reinforced through interpersonal relationships have an opportunity cost (Blau, 1964), but are far less costly than developing and maintaining formal governance mechanisms. Second, although formal governance seeks to reduce opportunistic behavior, it may actually encourage opportunism through negatively influencing individual attitudes towards the organization (Ghoshal and Moran, 1996). Increased monitoring of organizational members suggests that ownership does not trust them. This engenders mistrust as an organizational norm, and creates or enhances negative attitudes towards ownership and the organization.

Effective informal governance is based on trust. Self-interested, rational actors are most likely to trust each other when cooperation, rather than competition, results in optimal outcomes. Cooperation is likely only when three conditions are met: there are a limited number of exchange participants; future, repeated exchange is likely; and all participants have complete information about each other (North, 1990). Firms provide an environment where, to varying degrees, the first two conditions for cooperation are met. However, the level of uncertainty among firms varies greatly depending on a number of external and internal factors. The greater the uncertainty, the more information

asymmetries are likely to exist among firm members, and the less likely cooperation will exist.

Social norms reduce uncertainty by establishing acceptable behavior within the organization. Norms prescribe behavior not specified by formal governance forms. How individuals make decisions, communicate with superiors, and treat peers are all largely determined by organizational norms. Social norms also prescribe the level of sanction an individual faces for violating behavioral norms. Thus, norms enhance trust and cooperation through mitigating the range of behaviors individuals may engage in to a set of known and acceptable behaviors.

Social norms typically evolve over time through repeated interaction and behavior (Blau, 1964). As individuals engage in rounds of subsequent interaction and exchange, social norms develop that establish acceptable behavior and set the consequences for acting outside of behavioral norms. Individuals influence the development of social norms through their own behavior and their reactions to other's behavior. The extent to which social norms exist and are enforced in an organization is thus largely based on individual motivation and ability. Just as firms influence the institutional environment to their favor (Boddewyn, 1993; North, 1990), individuals will seek to influence organizational informal governance to their favor (Fligstein, 2001).

SHAPING FIRM INFORMAL GOVERNANCE

In this chapter, we define organizational politics as influence actions intended to shape firm informal governance. Unlike previous organizational politics definitions derived from the power and behavior literatures, this definition focuses on how politics affects economic organization, and thus economic outcomes. The interaction between organizational uncertainty and informal governance (mutual trust/cooperation) creates or limits opportunities for opportunistic behavior, and determines the level of effective information

A Multi-Level Conceptualization of Organizational Politics

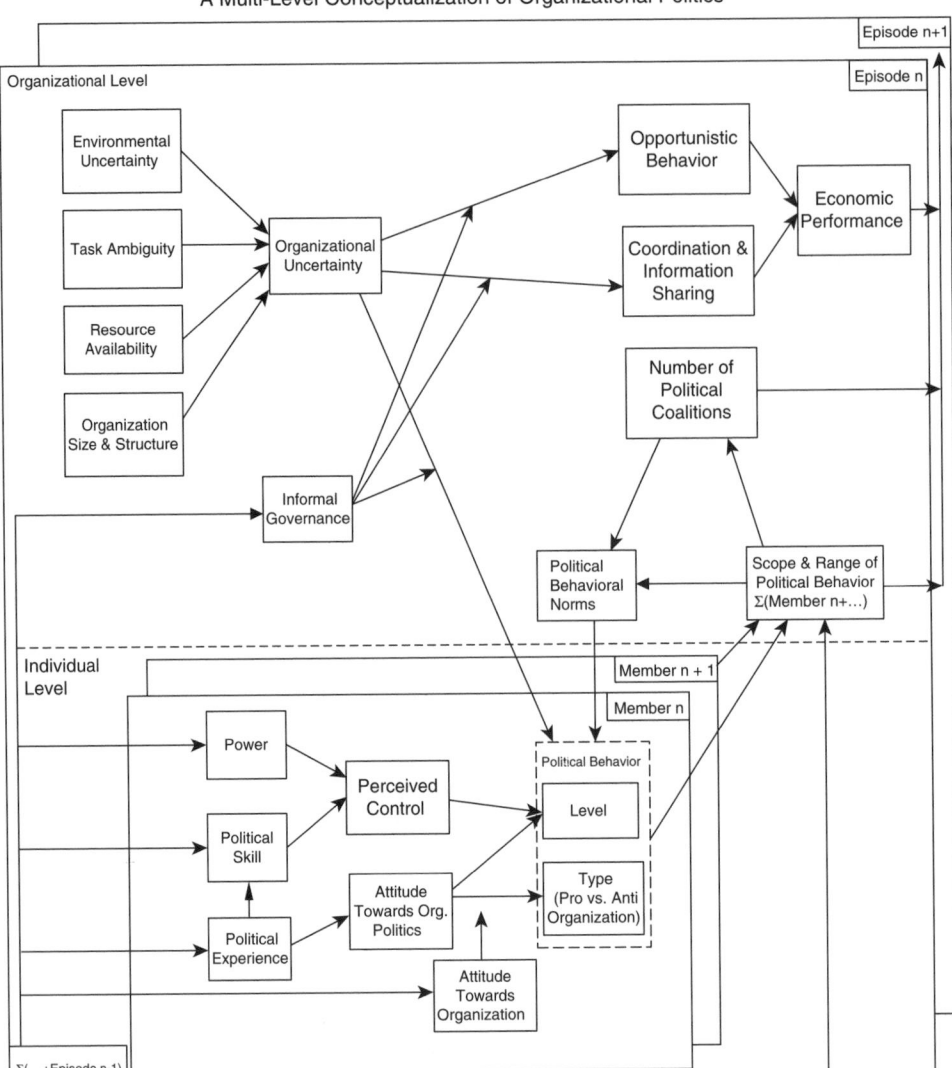

Figure 1   A multi-level conceptualization of organizational politics.

sharing and coordination, as illustrated in Figure 1.

Informal governance is a powerful double-edged sword in relation to firm performance. Effective informal governance enhances firm value creation through information sharing and coordination, and reduces the occurrence of opportunism. However, ineffective governance simultaneously increases opportunities for opportunistic behavior, while reducing the level of information sharing.

The level of organizational uncertainty and informal governance effectiveness also creates and limits the opportunity for political behavior. High levels of uncertainty and ambiguity create the conditions for political behavior to flourish (Ferris et al., 1989). When informal governance is ineffective or nonexistent, individuals are not restricted by social norms, and are able to engage in a greater variation of behaviors and actions without facing social sanction. Individuals have the most

Table 1 Organizational political opportunities

		Organizational Uncertainty	
		Low	High
Informal Governance	Effective	Low	Medium
	Ineffective	Medium	High

influence in shaping informal governance under these conditions. Table 1 illustrates that when organizational uncertainty is high and informal governance is ineffective or nonexistent, political opportunities are most prevalent. Subsequently, when organizational uncertainty is low and informal governance is effective, political opportunities are less available and so individuals are less likely to be able to shape informal governance.

An interaction based model of political behavior

The extent that political opportunities lead to political behavior is determined by both organizational and individual factors. Although organizational uncertainty and ineffective informal governance create conditions conducive to political behavior, individuals also engage in such behavior due to intrinsic factors. We use Ajzen's (1991) Theory of Planned Behavior to provide insight beyond rational choice as to why individuals engage, or fail to engage in political behavior. Ajzen (1991) asserted that an individual's decision to engage in a planned behavior is a function of the individual's attitude towards the behavior, the individual's perceived control over the behavior, and social norms regarding such behavior. Political behavior requires an individual to consider a multitude of factors before engaging in politics, and is fundamentally a planned behavior.

The decision to engage in political behavior is affected by perceived political opportunity, attitude towards politics, perceived ability to

engage in politics, and social norms regarding political behavior. Figure 1 illustrates how these factors affect the level and nature of political behavior. Engaging in a behavior positively affects an individual's attitude towards engaging in that behavior (Ajzen and Fishbein, 1977). As individuals engage in political activities, they become increasingly predisposed towards engaging in politics in the future. Power (resources) and political skill (ability) are the primary factors in determining an individual's perceived control over political behavior. Group norms of political behavior also affect the decision to engage in political behavior, and the range, or number of different political behavior level and types.

The individual's attitude towards the organization (pro or anti-organizational) determines the type of political behavior. Opportunistic individuals will seek to degrade firm informal governance through politics in order to increase opportunities for opportunistic behavior. Pro-organizational individuals will utilize political behavior to enhance informal governance. This is illustrated in Figure 1 through the use of multiple episodes. Organizational and individual factors influence the level and type of political behavior, and this behavior subsequently shapes informal governance in future episodes.

A few examples are useful in illustrating the interaction amongst these primary causal factors. Anti-political norms will likely lead to sanction of political behaviors. As an individual is sanctioned by others, they are less likely to develop attitudes towards engaging in political behavior. The initial negative effect on political behavior through sanction is amplified when the individual fails to acquire power and political skills through repeated political activities. However, an individual with strong attitudes towards engaging in politics (developed from experience in another organization with high political behavior norms) may continue to engage in politics despite negative sanction, while developing an increasing negative attitude towards the organization. This individual is likely to either modify their range and types of political behaviors or exit from the organization.

Political coalitions

Organizations are populated by coalitions to varying degrees (Cyert and March, 1963). Coalition or group norms affect the individual's decision to engage in political behavior. Groups develop around similar political agendas and activity levels. The divergence in the type and level of organizational politics among organization members determines the numbers of different coalition's agendas, and activity determines the level of cooperation and competition among groups. Pro-organizational politics leads to decreased uncertainty and more effective informal governance. Anti-organization politics leads to increased uncertainty and decreased informal governance effectiveness, which increases in political opportunities, enabling opportunistic individuals/groups to further themselves at some cost to the organization.

The number of episodes is perhaps the most important factor in influencing the number of coalitions in an organization. As organization members engage in successive rounds of political behavior, dominant coalitions form around certain levels and types of political behavior. Powerful and politically skilled individuals within the organization are likely to be at the center of these coalitions. The number of coalitions is inversely related to the strength of political behavior norms. Multiple coalitions enable individuals to engage in a wider range of behaviors, whereas a few or a single dominant coalition can restrict politics to a set of acceptable behaviors.

ANTECEDENTS OF ORGANIZATIONAL UNCERTAINTY

Some organizations are more conducive than others to high levels of uncertainty. Formal governance is highly effective in reducing organizational uncertainty, but this requires that intra-organizational exchange and behavior follow specific routines. The context and operations of some organizations requires the use of informal rather than formal governance means. Because informal governance evolves over time through repeated interaction and behavior, organizations face periods when formal governance is not applicable and informal governance has not evolved. This is when the opportunity to shape informal governance through political behavior is at its highest.

Perhaps the greatest source of uncertainty is the organization's task environment (Thompson, 1967). Environmental changes often radically alter the organization and even threaten its survival (Hannar and Freeman, 1977). Both the frequency (dynamism) and level of change contribute to organizational uncertainty (Dess and Beard, 1984), as well as organizational access to resources (Pfeffer and Salancik, 1978).

The level of uncertainty in an organization is not only affected by external factors. Task ambiguity makes planning and coordination more difficult (Thompson, 1967). The learning benefits obtained through repeating a task are diminished and may even negatively affect the organization's ability to solve new problems. New tasks require new behaviors and subsequently create the conditions for more political activities.

The availability of key resources is another source of organization uncertainty and subsequent political opportunity. Pfeffer and Salancik's (1978) basic assertion was that individuals and organizations must obtain essential resources to survive, and thus actions to obtain these resources to a large extent become the focus and the purpose of the organization. Resource scarcity is perhaps the greatest organization-level factor affecting political opportunity. Not only is organizational uncertainty high, but also individuals and groups that are successful in obtaining resources often wield a high degree of influence and power (Pfeffer, 1981; Pfeffer and Salancik, 1978). Resource scarcity thus provides the opportunity to engage in politics and the opportunity to enhance one's ability to engage in politics.

Organization structure also affects the level of uncertainty in an organization.

Hierarchical organization structures create information asymmetries both horizontally and vertically within an organization. These information asymmetries provide opportunities for politically savvy individuals. Although network structure is more effective in transferring information among organizational members, social norms (i.e. informal governance) can enhance or limit the extent and speed that information is shared. Thus, politically astute individuals are likely to see opportunity in shaping informal governance to their favor, even in these forms of organization.

Future political antecedent research directions

Organizational politics scholarship typically focuses on the consequences rather than the antecedents of politics within organizations. Perceptions of politics (POPS) has been utilized to assess the subjectively experienced level of political behavior in the organization, and its subsequent outcomes. We propose two primary lines of future research inquiry into this area of organizational politics.

First, we propose theoretical development and empirical research examining which factors have the greatest influence on political activity within an organization. As previously suggested, resource scarcity may have the greatest influence on political behavior because it creates both political opportunity and the means to acquire the power needed to exploit those opportunities.

Second, we propose examining which types of organizations are likely to be more conducive to organizational politics. Neo-institutional scholars (e.g., Meyer and Rowan, 1977) have suggested that organizations can survive even without achieving viable outcomes if their task ambiguity becomes great enough. The Federal Government bureaucracy in the US is an excellent example. The government bureaucracy lacks an agreed upon purpose or mission. Because there is a high degree of task ambiguity, the size of the organization is able to grow substantially. Future scholarship should examine whether political behavior is more prevalent in organizations with greater task ambiguity than in smaller, more task-centric organizations.

INDIVIDUAL LEVEL

Individuals' perceptions of control and attitudes toward organizational politics affect their demonstration of political behavior. However, it is important to understand what influences individual perceptions of control and political attitudes. In the following section, we explain how political experiences can enhance individuals' political skill and attitudes. This section proposes that power, much like political skill, produces increased perceptions of control. Ultimately, perceptions of control and political attitudes will affect the level of political behavior, whereas the interaction of political attitudes and organizational attitudes will determine the type (i.e., pro- or anti-organization) of political behavior.

Political experience and political skill

In order to explain how political experience might improve an individual's political skill, it is important to provide an overview of the political skill construct. Initially, political skill was defined as an individual characteristic that engenders effectiveness in political arenas (Mintzberg, 1983). However, more recent definitions suggest that political skill is 'the ability to effectively understand others at work, and to use such knowledge to influence others to act in ways that enhance one's personal and/or organizational goals' (Ferris et al., 2005b: 127).

Political skill is similar, yet divergent from other social effectiveness concepts (Ferris et al., 2005b). Some overlap exists between political skill and other personality and social effectiveness concepts such as political savvy, self-monitoring, conscientiousness, and emotional intelligence. However, these other concepts measure specific dimensions of social effectiveness. For example, emotional intelligence is an individual's ability to comprehend emotions, and political savvy is the ability to perceive and adopt to the nuances of organizations. However, no other social effectiveness concept examines all of the skills required to successfully engage in social interaction and influence (Ferris et al., 2005b).

Political skill consists of four dimensions: social astuteness, interpersonal influence, networking ability, and apparent sincerity. These dimensions enable individuals to influence others in ways that appear to be sincere, thus inspiring support and trust (Ferris et al., 2005b). Specifically, social astuteness provides individuals with the ability to read social situations and to understand their own and others' actions in these situations. Interpersonal influence allows individuals to select the most appropriate influence tactics, and to use these tactics easily and effectively (Ferris et al., 2005b). Networking ability helps politically skilled individuals develop diverse networks, alliances, coalitions, and social capital (Ferris et al., 2005b; Perrewé, et al., 2000), thus providing information access and a better understanding of the work environment (Baron and Markman, 2000). Lastly, politically skilled individuals are able to use influence tactics with sincerity and genuineness.

Although political skill has dispositional antecedents, it can be shaped, developed, and improved (Ferris et al., 2000). Specifically, when individuals utilize their political skill (i.e., participate in political experiences), they gain tacit knowledge, thus becoming more politically skilled (Perrewé et al., 2005). For example, individuals just entering the workplace may not be as adept at networking as those who have been with the same company for many years. However, organizationally tenured individuals know who is important in the company, how to position themselves within the company's network, from whom they can gain the most information, and from whom they can most benefit. In preliminary support of this theory, mentoring increases individuals' political

understanding, thus increasing networking ability (Blass et al., 2006).

Political skill and perceived control

Regardless of how one gains political skill, this ability should provide an individual with increased perceptions of control. Politically skilled individuals are adept at the 'development and leveraging of social capital' (Perrewé et al., 2000: 117). Not only does this social capital provide an enhanced social support system, but also it affords greater control in the work environment (Perrewé et al., 2004).

Politically skilled individuals are privy to increased information from their networks, and are able to use their influence to garner important resources and the support of key individuals. Thus, such individuals are able, through their political skill, to enhance their control (Ferris et al., 2005b). Perrewé and colleagues (2004) found political skill to moderate the relationship between role conflict and strain reactions, such that individuals with low political skill report greater increases in psychological and somatic complaints than individuals with high political skill when role conflict is increased (Perrewé et al., 2004).

Power and perceived control

Much like political skill, power should provide an individual with an increased sense of control as well. According to Hollander and Offermann (1990), power in organizations has three identifiable forms:

(1) *power over*, which is explicit or implicit dominance;
(2) *power to*, which gives individuals the opportunity to act more freely within organizational operations; and
(3) *power from*, which is the ability to resist the power of others by fending off their unwanted demands.

Furthermore, high status provides the potential for all of these forms, whereas low status only offers one or two of the latter forms.

Regardless of the form, power can have a profound psychological impact on the 'powerholder.' For example, Kipnis' (1976) work on the 'metamorphoses of power' indicated that power can cause individuals to experience feelings of exalted self-worth, isolation, and devaluation of less powerful others. Due to the fact that high status (i.e., powerful) individuals are seen as more likely to be influential and less likely to be influenced than low status individuals (Berger et al., 1980), it is likely that these perceptions will have a profound effect on a powerful individual's self-assessment, thus producing or instilling a strong sense of control.

Political experience and political attitudes

Just as political experience can enhance political skill, it also can exhibit a positive effect on an individual's attitude towards organizational politics. According to Cooper (Scher and Cooper, 1989; Cooper, 1992), dissonance is aroused whenever individuals feel responsible for aversive outcomes, regardless of whether the behavior that caused those outcomes is consistent with their attitudes. For example, when students were asked to write an essay strongly opposing an increase in tuition, but were then lead to believe that their essay inadvertently made their target group more in favor of tuition increases, they reported being more in favor of tuition increases themselves (Scher and Cooper, 1989). This attempt at dissonance reduction following pro-attitudinal behavior suggests that aversive consequences play an important role in motivating attitude change (Olson and Zanna, 1993).

Based on this reasoning, it is likely that individuals who engage in political behavior will develop positive attitudes about organizational politics. Regardless of an individual's attitude towards organizational politics, engaging in political behavior can be an effective way to get ahead or remedy perceived injustices (Dulebohn and Ferris, 1999). However, individuals who engage in organizational politics must also deal with the fact that perceptions of organizational politics can have deleterious consequences (e.g., job anxiety, job dissatisfaction, organizational withdrawal, etc.) for others. Therefore, in an attempt to reduce the dissonance that is caused by these aversive consequences, individuals with political experiences are likely to develop positive attitudes about organizational politics.

Furthermore, individuals who are successful at politics are likely to view it in a positive fashion. In preliminary support of this, Vigoda and Cohen (2002) found that when political behavior leads to desired outcomes, individuals feel that their organization is fair. However, when political behavior does not result in desired outcomes, individuals feel that the entire work setting is unjust and unfair. Thus, individuals receiving the benefits of political behavior are likely to hold a positive attitude toward organizational politics. On the other hand, individuals not benefiting from organizational politics are likely to have a more negative attitude toward politics.

Perceived control, political attitude, and level of political behavior

In the past three decades, the literature has primarily classified political behavior by action (Ferris et al., 2002b). However, in an attempt to explain how political behavior can affect informal governance, which, in turn, can affect organizational performance, we classify political behavior by level and motivation. Level of organizational politics is defined as the degree to which an individual is actively engaged in shaping his or her organization's informal governance. Furthermore, political behavior is either pro- (i.e., building trust, cooperation, and consensus) or anti- (i.e., competition, opportunism, etc.) organizational in nature.

According to expectancy theory (Vroom, 1964), motivation is a multiplicative function of valence (i.e., how valuable is the outcome?), instrumentality (i.e., if I do the behavior, will I be able to perform?), and expectations (i.e., if I perform the behavior, will I get the reward?). Based on this reasoning, it is likely that individuals with weak perceptions of control would have little instrumentality with regard to their ability to influence informal governance through political behavior.

Therefore, it is reasonable to believe that individuals with weak perceptions of control would either avoid political behavior altogether or participate in commonplace political activities (e.g., rationality, exchange of benefits). Conversely, individuals with strong perceptions of control would be more likely to use more proactive political activities (e.g., assertiveness, sanctions, blocking, coalitions.) to influence the firm's informal governance for their own benefit.

Much like perceptions of control, it is likely that an individual's attitude towards organizational politics would also affect his or her political behavior. As previously stated, organizational politics often is viewed in a negative light, thus causing negative outcomes (Ferris et al., 2002a and b). Therefore, it is likely that an individual who views organizational politics negatively would avoid engaging in political behavior in the hopes of eluding its negative repercussions. However, some individuals recognize that the ability to play the political game, or influence informal procedures, actually mitigates negative outcomes such as stress reactions (Zaleznik et al., 1977). It is reasonable to believe that these individuals would participate in a high degree of politics.

Political attitude, organizational attitude, and type of political behavior

We propose that the interaction between individuals' attitudes towards their organization in particular and their attitude towards organizational politics in general will determine the type of political behavior that they conduct. Research has found that individuals who are high in negative affectivity often view their environments with disdain (Watson and Clark, 1984), whereas individuals who are high in positive affectivity often are pleasantly engaged with their inhabited setting (George and Brief, 1992).

Based on this research, Ferris and colleagues (2002b) proposed that high-NA individuals would be more likely to use aggressive influence tactics whereas high-PA individuals would be more apt to use more palatable influence tactics. Drawing on this line of reasoning, it is plausible that individuals with negative and positive attitudes toward their organizations would participate in anti-organizational and pro-organizational politics, respectively. Further, if individuals feel negatively about their organization, it is likely that they will participate in political behavior regardless of the ultimate consequence to the organization. As a result, these individuals likely will engage in more anti-organizational political actions. Conversely, individuals with positive attitudes towards their organization will most likely consider the organizational consequences of their political actions, thus resulting in more pro-organizational political behaviors.

Political behaviors

Four predominant types of political behavior emerge based on individual attitudes towards politics and the organization, as noted in Table 2. Individuals with anti-organizational and pro-political attitudes are perhaps one of the greatest threats to organizational performance. Often described as Machiavellians, these individuals actively

Table 2   Effects of attitudes on political behavior types

		Organizational Attitude	
		Negative	Positive
Political Attitudes	Positive	Active, Self-Interested	Active, Stewardship
	Negative	Passive, Self-Interested	Passive, Stewardship

seek to create mistrust and weaken social norms encouraging pro-organizational behaviors. By doing so, these individuals create and increase information asymmetries among organizational members creating the conditions for opportunistic behavior. Individuals with both anti-organization and political attitudes are likely to act opportunistically when informal governance is ineffective, but their disdain for political activity suggests that they are unlikely to actively undermine firm informal governance.

Individuals with pro-organizational and anti-political attitudes are likely to engage in pro-organizational, or stewardship behaviors, and are unlikely to engage in actively shaping informal governance. Job satisfaction and performance are likely highest for such individuals when effective informal governance and anti-political behavioral norms exist. Individuals with both pro-organization and political attitudes are likely to actively seek to strengthen firm informal governance. These individuals are essential in developing effective informal governance when social norms and trust are low.

Moreover, individuals may not see all types of political behavior in the same manner. Certain political behaviors might be accepted, such as ingratiation, while others are seen as negative, such as intimidation. That is to say, individuals might participate actively in some political behaviors while shunning others. This acceptance of some political behaviors and rejection of others would lead individuals to engage in a variety of political behaviors.

In an extension, individuals also might feel that certain anti-organizational political behaviors are acceptable whereas others are not. For instance, individuals might think that leaving work early to pick up their supervisors' dry cleaning (i.e., favor doing) is acceptable, even though this may hurt the company (e.g., lower production because of leaving early). However, these same individuals may not approve of using intimidation in the workplace, which could potentially increase turnover and decrease morale. Therefore, individuals might be engaging in both pro- and anti-organizational political behavior simultaneously.

DIRECTIONS FOR FUTURE MICRO-LEVEL RESEARCH

An obvious direction for future research would be to test the proposed model (see Figure 1). Although it has been argued that political skill should enhance perceptions of control (e.g., Perrewé et al., 2004, 2005; Ferris et al., 2005), this has never been directly tested. Also, it is necessary to gain an understanding of how political skill increases perceived control. Is perceived control enhanced via the procurement of important resources, or is it drawn solely from politically skilled individuals' abilities to influence others?

Another area for future research would be to examine the impact of individuals' past political experiences on their political skill and attitudes toward organizational politics. Although this could be accomplished through survey research, it might be interesting to shadow employees or have these individuals write daily logs in order to pinpoint their political experiences and monitor their increases in political skill and changing attitudes toward organizational politics. Only by conducting this type of longitudinal research could we ascertain causation in these important relationships.

This style of data collection also would be interesting in monitoring individuals' level of political behavior, and the type of behaviors in which they engage (pro- vs. anti-organizational political behaviors). Another area for investigation would be an examination into the effects of NA and PA on the types of political behaviors in which individuals engage.

Examining the effects of power on perceived control and ultimately on the level of political behavior is appropriate. Do individuals in formal positions of power have increased perceptions of control, and does this further their level of political behaviors? Do individuals with the ability to resist others' power feel more in control of their work environment? And ultimately, does this lead to more or less political behavior?

Lastly, future research needs to examine political behaviors in the terms of pro- and anti-organizational. Most research on political behavior has examined specific tactics, such as ingratiation or upward appeal (Kipnis and Schmidt, 1988; Bolino and Turnley, 1999). Researchers also have examined the combinations of tactics, such as self-focused, other-focused, and job focused (Wayne and Ferris, 1990). However, whether a political behavior is pro-organizational versus anti-organizational has received far less attention.

Farrell and Peterson (1982) classified political behaviors as being either legitimate (i.e., allowed by the organization) or illegitimate (i.e., not allowed by the organization). At first, it might seem as if these authors have addressed the pro- vs. anti-organizational issue of political behaviors, but that is not necessarily true. Individuals can engage in political behaviors that their organization may not sanction, but that help the organization, none the less. For instance, organizations may not approve of favor-doing (i.e., a type of political behavior), but employees may engage in this behavior because it helps them accomplish the tasks and duties of their jobs.

Therefore, future researchers are encouraged to focus on not only which types of political behaviors are being performed, but also the intention behind their performance. To understand whether individuals are engaging in political behavior in order to achieve organizational goals, it is necessary to understand why they are engaging in such behavior. In order to study this, it most likely will be necessary to develop a measure of political behavior intentionality. This type of study may first be conducted through exploratory qualitative research, including interviews and case studies.

ORGANIZATIONAL POLITICS

Group or coalition formation, competition, and survival are essential to our understanding of politics as organizational and individual factors. In this chapter, we do not delve into great detail as to how political coalitions form and act. Instead, we examine how individual political behaviors lead to coalition development, and how this subsequently affects individual and organizational factors. We assume that coalitions form around similar political behaviors, and that the aggregate of individual political behavior types and levels is useful in explaining how coalitions develop. We adopt this perspective because group-level political scholarship is limited, which we discuss in further detail as an area of future research.

Political coalitions

Although group-level political research is limited, a rich foundation has been developed describing the impact that coalitions (e.g., Bacharach and Lawler, 1980; Cyert and March, 1963) and subunits (e.g., Pfeffer and Salancik, 1974) have on decision-making, resource allocation, uncertainty avoidance, and organizational learning. This foundation is a departure from the conventional view of groups within the firm as based on the assumption that they operate to maximize the interests of the organization (Cyert and March, 1963). However, this position is one in which coalitions and subunits are 'essential to the firm's continuing existence' (Cyert and March, 1963: 240) rather than considered as dysfunctional to organizational operations. In addition to reviewing this literature, more recent research regarding politics of organizational groups and teams also is reviewed.

Coalitions form as individuals within organizations coalesce around some broad goal (e.g., to secure scarce resources), although specific goals usually differ (Cyert and March, 1963). Just as uncertainty and ambiguity are catalysts for individual political behaviors (Ferris et al., 1989), partnerships form in organizations in order to control and/or acquire more resources, and establish and reinforce behavioral norms, for example. Coalitions form as organizational goals do not align with that of individuals, and internal conflicts result, which provide for the opportunity for coalition formation (Cyert and March, 1963).

Baldridge (1971) described that when conflict arises among participants, the decision outcomes are based more on which coalition has the power to influence the outcomes rather than what is optimal for achieving some organizational objective. In fact, Stagner (1969) found that executives believed that influential divisions within the organization probably get their way regardless of the impact on the entire firm. Whereas Perrow (1970) examined perceptions of power in industrial firms and found that the marketing department was nearly always perceived to be the most influential, Hickson et al. (1971) developed a theory attempting to account for variations in subunit power in organizations based on the idea that power is accumulated to those subunits which could best deal with critical organizational uncertainty (Thompson, 1967).

Bacharach and Lawler (1980) advanced the notion of politics as necessary for everyday survival in an organization, which are also 'the result of the conscious political decisions of particular actors and interest groups' (p. 2). Their primary agenda was to identify the conditions under which interest groups would form coalitions, and how coalitions relate to each other politically. By describing how factors such as subjective utility, boundary spanning, the environment, conflict of interest, communication, and retaliatory capacity affect group political activity, Bacharach and Lawler (1980) specified some of the principal conditions that affect a group's decision whether or not to form a coalition.

Perhaps the most well-known study on political decision making is Pfeffer and Salancik's (1974) examination of the budget allocation process at the University of Illinois. Due to the fact that resources are generally scarce, organizational subunits vie for a share of these resources, which, they contend, is an inherently political process. They found that the use of subunit power in organizational decision making ultimately affected the allocation of resources to those subunits that were found to have the highest levels of power across various measures, including interviews and departmental representation on thirteen major committees.

More recently, Lawrence et al. (2005) proposed an integrative framework describing the impact of politics on organizational learning. They addressed the role that groups play in this process by explaining the function that integrating, or 'the process of developing a shared understanding among individuals and of taking coordinated action through mutual adjustment' (Crossan et al., 1999: 525) has on this process. They argued that the process of integrating involves episodes of power on the part of involved players. Furthermore, for learning to occur at the group level, innovations must be championed at opportune moments and affirmed during moments of doubt. Additionally, for these same innovations to move to the organization level, they must be conveyed to upper management by appropriate individuals and/or groups at suitable times and, in many circumstances, revisited on several occasions. This implies that integrating new ideas is based largely on episodic forms of power (Lawrence et al., 2005), and the ability (e.g., political skill) to convince various constituents of the need adopt these new ideas.

In addition to research on coalitions and subunits, others have moved toward explaining team politics perceptions and behaviors. More specifically, Witt et al. (2001) examined the impact of team member perceptions of team-level politics on executive and member ratings of effectiveness, and to member expressions of satisfaction with and commitment to the team. As predicted, an inverse relationship between organizational politics and organizational commitment, job satisfaction, and organization-level effectiveness was found. Additionally, they discovered a moderating effect of member-team goal congruence that implies that attempts to improve member-team congruence on goal priorities may lessen the effect of politics perceived at the team level.

Coalition competition and outcomes

In this chapter, we assume that political coalitions form around similar political agendas and activity levels. The number of different political behaviors, or range, and the level of deviation among different types of political activity, or scope, increases the number of different coalitions. It should be noted that political norms are an aspect of overall informal governance that affects the level and type of political behavior by limiting the range of acceptable political behaviors. The two have been separated here to illustrate how political behavior influences overall informal governance, while political behavioral norms largely determine the range of acceptable behaviors.

Individuals come together due to similar interests, and groups form that participate to varying degrees within the organization (Bacharach and Lawler, 1980). Individuals often will form groups around the level (low to high political activity) and type (pro- vs. anti-organizational) of political behavior that, then, shapes group political norms in organizations over time. The extent to which individuals identify with the type of political behavior and the extent to which political behaviors are manifested, the greater the likelihood that groups coalesce around a shared set of norms.

The range of political behaviors is positively related to the number of different coalitions. When numerous different coalitions exist within an organization, consensus is difficult to reach and political norms and informal governance will subsequently be weaker. The scope or the degree of difference in political behaviors in an organization is perhaps best illustrated in Figure 2. Scope is highest when significant differences exist among political coalitions (i.e., high anti-organizational political activity and high pro-organizational political activity). Competition among coalitions is at its greatest, which further reduces cooperation and the development of strong political norms and effective informal governance. In Figure 2, the dashed line represents high scope of coalitions and only moderate range. This results in two predominant types of coalitions that exist within the organization: (1) one both pro-organization

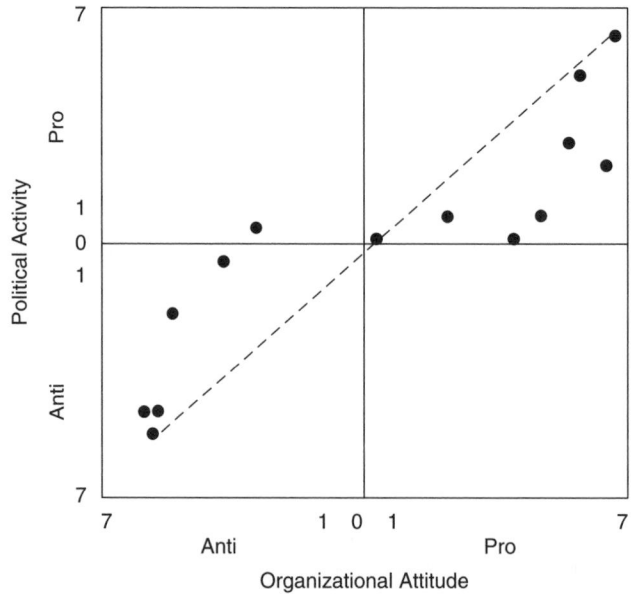

Figure 2   Scope and range of organizational political behaviors.

and pro-political; and (2) one pro-political and anti-organizational.

When organizations have high range and scope, the likely outcome is the development of multiple coalitions. This can be expected to lead to weak political behavior norms within the organization because no single core ideology becomes present. As a result, no dominant political behavior or coalition forms. However, this should increase the political opportunity within the organization as well, because individuals have greater behavioral range within to act. Because individuals are not constrained by dominant coalitions or specific types of political behavior, they have the opportunity to develop any type of coalition.

Dominant coalitions

Organizations divided by multiple coalitions with competing agendas are likely to become ineffective and noncompetitive in the marketplace. These organizations will either fail to survive, or a few dominant coalitions will emerge that institute informal governance to varying degrees of effectiveness. Economic performance, or the lack thereof, thus creates the impetuous for organizations to either increase cooperation, or develop more effective forms of formal governance (i.e., which can create its own set of issues and problems; Ghoshal and Moran, 1996). Two factors play into the reduction in political behavior type and level, and the subsequent reduction in the number of competing coalitions.

First, some coalitions will be more successful simply due to the individuals that comprise the coalition. Coalitions succeed over time as they create more influential power bases (Cyert and March, 1963) by acquiring more resources (Pfeffer and Salancik, 1978), and/or because of politically skilled members (Ferris et al., 2000). As a result of being more influential or dominant, the political norms of the coalition become stronger, which impacts organizational membership. Following Schneider's (1987) Attraction-Selection-Attrition framework, individuals adopting these political norms are more apt

to stay in the organization and participate in the coalition. Existing members not wanting to embrace the current political norms likely leave the organization. Furthermore, with a dominant coalition present in the organization, new members selected into the organization are also more prone to accept the dominant political norms of the coalition. Thus, the number of previous episodes is negatively related to political behavior range and scope.

Time is the second factor that reduces the variation of political behaviors. Over time, both pro- and anti-organizational group norms manifest into much larger organizational political norms. If pro-organizational group norms are established, over time, the opportunities for anti-organizational political behaviors become virtually nonexistent. However, as groups form for their own personal agendas, anti-organizational group political norms develop into larger organizational political norms that can create a very opportunistic political environment. In either case, this takes constant reinforcement of current norms, and, as time elapses, a strong sense of shared norms develops. The cohesiveness that ensues as a result of the norms developed reinforces group political behavior, regardless of the type.

FUTURE RESEARCH

Because the prior section is without direct empirical examination, a first step for future research would be to empirically investigate the theoretical framework that was just explicated. Although some past research has addressed the issues of group-level political phenomenon, much work is left to be both theoretically expounded and empirically investigated. Prior research has barely scratched the surface of group and team-level research regarding politics in organizations.

Second, cross-functional work teams are an interesting medium for the study of organizational politics. The idea of individuals coming from multiple areas of an organization, or as Bacharach and Lawler (1980) called it, 'segmentation,' implies that actors may come together with their own personal goals and agendas. Consequently, cross-functional work teams inherently develop an environment that, at least at first, permits political activity to arise.

Third, the utilization of technology in organizations also has created some interesting questions in the area of politics. With the advent of virtual organizations, the opportunity for political activity, such as coalitions, to form as a result of uncertainty and ambiguity could be excessive. The idea that individuals could form coalitions without ever meeting face-to-face is a fascinating one that should be examined. Also, investigating how these coalitions vie for resources that span international boundaries is another question that would shed light on the political landscape.

A fourth area of inquiry encompasses how political behavior can lead to both highly effective or potentially corrupt coalitions, and thus organizations over time. Identifying the processes and factors that lead to such a potentially high variance in the type of coalitions formed is an important endeavor that could shed light on the 'black box.' Also, it has ethical and moral implications because understanding how dominant corrupt coalitions form may perhaps allow researchers and practitioners to possibly prevent unethical behaviors that destroyed organizations like Enron. Likewise, knowing how to develop highly effective coalitions would greatly benefit organizations.

CONCLUSION

The organizing framework presented in this chapter incorporates psychological, economic, and power factors that influence organizational politics. Two primary contributions are made to the organizational behavior field. First, explaining how political behavior shapes governance and subsequent performance provides a great deal of insight into the 'black box' of the firm. This type of scholarship provides an example for how the organizational behavior field can impact and inform the broader and more established field of economics.

Second, the organizing model also is illustrative of how multiple levels of analysis can be integrated utilizing organizational science concepts and theory. Staw (1991) asserted that micro-level theory could inform macro-level theory. Here, we illustrate how integrating theories at different levels of analysis can provide a more informed understanding of the nature of organizational politics, and a more complete picture of organization and economic performance.

REFERENCES

Alchian, A.A., and Demsetz, H. (1972) 'Production, information costs, and economic organization', *American Economic Review*, 62: 777–795.

Ajzen, I. (1991) 'The theory of planned behavior', *Organizational Behavior and Human Decision Processes*, 50: 179–211.

Ajzen, I. and Fishbein, M. (1977) 'Attitude-behavior relations: A theoretical analysis and review of empirical research', *Psychological Bulletin*, 84: 888–918.

Ammeter, A.P., Douglas, C., Gardner, W.L., Hochwarter, W.A. and Ferris, G.R. (2002) 'Toward a political theory of leadership', *The Leadership Quarterly*, 13: 751–796.

Bacharach, S.B. and Lawler, E.J. (1980) *Power and Politics in Organizations.* San Francisco: Jossey-Bass.

Baldridge, J.V. (1971) *Power and Conflict in the University.* New York: Wiley.

Barney, J.B. (1991) 'Firm resources and sustained competitive advantage', *Journal of Management*, 17: 99–120.

Barney, J.B. and Ouchi, W.G. (1986) *Organizational Economics.* San Francisco: Jossey-Bass Publishers.

Baron, R.A. and Markman, G.D. (2000) 'Beyond social capital: How social skills can enhance entrepreneurs' success', *Academy of Management Executive*, 14: 106–116.

Berger, J., Rosenholtz, S.J. and Zelditch, M., Jr. (1980) 'Status organizing processes', *Annual Review of Sociology*, 6, 479–5

Blass, F.R., Brouer, R.L. and Ferris, G.R. (2006) *Socialization Tactics, Content, and Career Effectiveness: The Role of Political Skill in Contextual Adjustment and Effectiveness.* Paper presented at the Southern Management Association, Clearwater, Florida.

Blau, P.M. (1964) *Exchange and Power in Social Life.* New York: John Wiley & Sons, Inc.

Boddewyn, J.J. (1993) 'Political resources and markets in international business: Beyond Porter's generic strategies', in A. Rugman and A. Verbeke (eds), *Research in Global Strategic Management.* Greenwich, CT: JAI Press. Vol. 4: pp. 162–184.

Bolino, M. and Turnley, T. (1999) 'Measuring impression management in organizations: A scale development based on the Jones and Pittman taxonomy', *Orgazational Research Methods,* 2 (2): 187–206.

Coase, R. (1937) 'The nature of the firm', *Economica,* 4: 386–405.

Connor, K.R. and Prahalad, C.K. (1996) 'A resource-based theory of the firm: Konwledge versus opportunism', *Organization Science,* 7: 477–501.

Cooper, J. (1992) 'Dissonance and the return of the self-concept', *Psychological Inquiry,* 3: 320–323.

Crossan, M., Lane, H. and White, R. (1999) 'An organizational learning framework: From intuition to institution', *Academy of Management Review,* 24: 522–537.

Cyert, R.M. and March, J.G. (1963) *A Behavioral Theory of the Firm.* Englewood Cliffs, NJ: Prentice-Hall.

Dess, G.G. and Beard, D.W. (1984) 'Dimensions of organizational task environments', *Administrative Science Quarterly,* 29: 52–73.

Dulebohn, J.H. and Ferris, G.R. (1999) 'The role of influence tactics in perceptions of performance evaluations' fairness', *Academy of Management Journal,* 42: 288–303.

Emerson, R. (1962) 'Power-dependence relationships', *American Sociological Review,* 27: 31–41.

Farrell, D. and Petersen, J.C. (1982) 'Patterns of political behavior in organizations', *Academy of Management Review,* 7 (3): 403–412.

Ferris, G.R., Russ, G.S. and Fandt, P.M. (1989) 'Politics in organizations', in R.A. Giacalone and P. Rosenfeld (eds), *Impression Management in the Organization.* Hillsdale, NJ: Lawrence Erlbaum, pp. 143–170.

Ferris, G.R., Perrewé, P.L., Anthony, W.P. and Gilmore, D.C. (2000) 'Political skill at work', *Organizational Dynamics,* 28(4): 25–37.

Ferris, G.R., Adams, G., Kolodinsky, R.W., Hochwarter, W.A. and Ammeter, A.P. (2002a) 'Perceptions of organizational politics: Theory and research directions', in F.J. Yammarino and F. Dansereau (eds), *Research in Multi-level Issues, Volume 1: The Many Faces of Multi-level Issues.* Oxford, UK: JAI Press/Elsevier Science, pp. 179–254.

Ferris, G.R., Hochwarter, W.A., Douglas, C., Blass, R., Kolodinsky, R.W. and Treadway, D.C. (2002b) 'Social influence processes in organizations and human resources systems', in G.R. Ferris and J.J. Martocchio (eds), *Research in Personnel and Human Resources Management.* Oxford: JAI Press/Elsevier Science. Vol. 21: pp. 65–127.

Ferris, G.R., Davidson, S.L. and Perrewé, P.L. (2005a) *Political Skill at Work: Impact on Work Effectiveness.* Palo Alto, CA: Davies-Black Publishing.

Ferris, G.R., Treadway, D.C., Kolodinsky, R.W., Hochwarter, W.A., Kacmar, C.J., Douglas, C. and Frink, D.D. (2005b) 'Development and validation of the political skill inventory', *Journal of Management,* 31: 126–152.

Fligstein, N. (2001) 'Social skill and the theory of fields', *Sociological Theory,* 19, 105–125.

George, J. and Brief, A.P. (1992) 'Feeling good-doing good: A conceptual analysis of the mood at work-organizational spontaneity relationship', *Psychological Bulletin,* 112: 310–329.

Ghoshal, S. and Moran, P. (1996) 'Bad for practice: A critique of transaction cost theory', *Academy of Management Review,* 21: 13–47.

Grant, R.M. (1996) 'Toward a knowledge-based theory of the firm', *Strategic Management Journal,* 17 (Winter Special Issue): 109–122.

Hall, A.T., Hochwarter, W.A., Ferris, G.R. and Bowen, M.G. (2004) 'The dark side of politics in organizations', in R.W. Griffin and A.M. O'Leary-Kelly (eds), *The Dark Side of Organizational Behavior.* San Francisco: Jossey-Bass, pp. 237–261.

Hannan, M.T. and Freeman, J. (1977) 'The population ecology of organizations', *American Journal of Sociology,* 82: 929–984.

Hickson, D.J., Hinings, C.R., Lee, C.A., Schneck, R.E. and Pennings, J.M. (1971) 'A strategic contingencies' theory of intraorganizational power', *Administrative Science Quarterly,* 16: 216–229.

Hollander, E.P. and Offermann, L.R. (1990) 'Power and leadership in organizations: Relationships in transition', *American Psychologist,* 45: 179–189.

Kipnis, D. (1976) *The Powerholders.* Chicago: University of Chicago Press.

Kipnis, D. and Schmidt, S.M. (1988) 'Upward influence styles: relationship with performance evaluations, salary, and stress', *Administrative Science Quarterly,* 33: 528–542.

Lawrence, T.B., Mauws, M.K., Dyck, B. and Kleysen, R.F. (2005) 'The politics of organizational learning: Integrating power into the 4I framework', *Academy of Management Review,* 30: 180–191.

Leary, M.R. (1995) *Self Presentation: Impression Management and Interpersonal Behavior.* Boulder, CO: Westview Press.

Madhok, A. (2002) 'Reassessing the fundamentals and beyond: Ronald Coase, the transaction cost and resource-based theories of the firm and the institutional structure of production', *Strategic Management Journal*, 23: 535–550.

Mintzberg, H. (1983) *Power In and Around Organizations*. Englewood Cliffs, NJ: Prentice-Hall.

Meyer, J. and Rowan, B. (1977) 'Institutional organizations: Formal structures as myth and ceremony', *American Journal of Sociology*, 83: 340–363.

North, D.C. (1990) *Institutions, Institutional Change, and Economic Performance*. Oxford: Cambridge University Press.

Olson, J.M. and Zanna, M.P. (1993) 'Attitudes and attitude change', *Annual Review of Psychology*, 44: 117–154.

Perrewé, P.L., Ferris, G.R., Frink, D.D. and Anthony, W.P. (2000) 'Political skill: An antidote for workplace stressors', *Academy of Management Executive*, 14: 115–123.

Perrewé, P.L., Zellars, K.L., Ferris, G.R., Rossi, A.M., Kacmar, C.J. and Ralston, D.A. (2004) 'Neutralizing job stressors: Political skill as an antidote to the dysfunctional consequences of role conflict stressors', *Academy of Management Journal*, 47: 141–152.

Perrewé, P.L., Zellars, K.L., Rossi, A.M., Ferris, G.R., Kacmar, C.J., Liu, Y., Zinko, R. and Hochwarter, W.A. (2005) 'Political skill: An antidote in the role overload-strain relationship', *Journal of Occupational Health Psychology*, 10 (3): 239–250.

Perrow, C. (1970) 'Departmental power and perspective in industrial firms', in M.N. Zald (ed.), *Power in Organizations*. Nashville: Vanderbilt University Press, pp. 59–89.

Pfeffer, J. (1981) *Power in Organizations*. Boston: Pitman.

Pfeffer, J. (1992) *Managing with Power: Politics and Influence in Organizations*. Boston: Harvard Business School Press.

Pfeffer, J. (1997) *New Directions for Organization Theory: Problems and Prospects*. New York: Oxford University Press.

Pfeffer, J. and Salancik, G.R. (1974) 'Organizational decision making as a political process: The case of a university budget', *Administrative Science Quarterly*, 19: 135–151.

Pfeffer, J. and Salancik, G.R. (1978) *The External Control of Organizations*. New York: Harper & Row.

Scher, S.J. and Cooper, J. (1989) 'Motivational basis of dissonance: The singular role of behavioral consequences', *Journal of Personality and Behavioral Consequences*, 56: 899–906.

Schneider, B. (1987) 'The people make the place', *Personnel Psychology*, 40: 437–453.

Sederberg, P.C. (1984) *The Politics of Meaning: Power and Explanation in the Construction of Social Reality*. Tucson: University of Arizona Press.

Stagner, R. (1969) 'Corporate decision making: An empirical study', *Journal of Applied Psychology*, 53: 1–13.

Staw, B.M. (1991) 'Dressing up like an organization: When psychological theories can explain organizational action', *Journal of Management*, 17: 805–819.

Stepanski, K., Kershaw, T.S. and Arkakelian, A. (2000). *Perceptions of work politics: Meta-analytic investigation of individual differences and outcome variables*. Paper presented at the Fifteenth Annual Conference of the Society for Industrial and Organizational Psychology, New Orleans.

Thompson, J.D. (1967) *Organizations in Action*. New York: McGraw-Hill.

Vigoda, E., and Cohen, A. (2002) 'Influence tactics and perceptions of organizational politics: A longitudinal study', *Journal of Business Research*, 55: 311–324.

Vroom, V. (1964) *Work and Motivation*. New York: Wiley.

Watson, D. and Clark, L.A. (1984) 'Negative affectivity: the disposition to experience aversive emotional states', *Psychological Bulletin*, 96: 465–490.

Wayne, S.J. and Ferris, G.R. (1990) 'Influence tactics, affect, and exchange quality in supervisor-subordinate interactions: A laboratory experiment and field study', *Journal of Applied Psychology*, 75: 487–499.

Williamson, O.E. (1975) *Markets and Hierarchies: Analysis and Antitrust Implications*. New York: Free Press.

Williamson, O.E. (1999) 'Strategy research: Governance and competence perspectives', *Strategic Management Journal*, 20: 1087–1108.

Witt, L.A., Hilton, T.F. and Hochwarter, W.A. (2001) 'Addressing politics in matrix teams', *Group and Organization Management*, 26: 230–246.

Zaleznik, A., Kets de Vries, M. and Howard, J. (1977) 'Stress reactions in organizations: Syndromes, causes, and consequences', *Behavioral Science*, 22: 151–162.

20

Knowledge Work

Susan E. Jackson and Ying Hong

Characterized by global competition and rapid technological change, the 21st century competitive market landscape creates numerous opportunities and challenges for organizations (Matusik and Hill, 1998; Miles, 1989). Organizations increasingly compete on the basis of cost reduction, as well as continuous innovation, quality improvement, and customer service. Among the many factors that contribute to organizational survival and success, knowledge is a resource that can serve as the foundation for an organization's sustained competitive advantage (Barney, 1991). The ability to create and successfully manage knowledge resources stands out as one of the key capabilities of successful organizations (Grant, 1996). Indeed, a search of the keyword 'knowledge management' in the Business Source Premier data base generated 8,289 articles, of which 5,805 were published between 2001 and 2006; only 89 were published before 1980.

As the value of knowledge resources has become evident, many companies have invested in electronic knowledge management systems. The expectation was that electronic systems would increase the ability to store, sort, distribute, and (perhaps) analyze the vast array of knowledge residing within the organization. Experienced users of electronic knowledge management systems now realize that electronic systems can be effective only when they are integrated into a total management system that supports the complex array of activities referred to as knowledge work. Besides electronic knowledge systems, work designed around multidisciplinary teams and communities of practice with decentralized decision-making are perhaps the most prevalent features of knowledge-intensive organizations.

As electronic systems for managing knowledge have evolved in recent years, managers have found that employee behavior is less malleable than information hardware and software. Often subtle social barriers that are difficult to see and control interfere with the effectiveness of electronic knowledge management systems. Increasingly, it is being recognized that effectively managing knowledge-intensive organizations requires an understanding of how social dynamics influence the speedy and efficient creation and transfer of knowledge (Kogut and Zander, 1996: 503). Of particular interest is the configuration of organizational facilities, routines, principles, practices and capabilities that contribute to the performance of knowledge-intensive firms (Jackson et al., 2006). In this chapter, we examine the social dynamics of two aspects of knowledge work, namely knowledge creation and knowledge sharing, We recognize that a much larger constellation of knowledge work activities contributes to the success of firms engaged in knowledge-based competition, but a full discussion of those is beyond the scope of this chapter.

Knowledge creation and knowledge sharing are closely related to two strategies adopted by firms in knowledge-intensive industries: knowledge exploitation and knowledge exploration. Knowledge exploitation refers to the refining and deepening of existing knowledge, and knowledge exploration refers to the pursuit of new knowledge that does not exist within a firm (Kang et al., 2006; Taylor and Greve, 2007). Presumably, knowledge work serves as a source of sustainable competitive advantage when the type of knowledge work employees engage in matches the strategic imperatives of the organization (Taylor and Greve, 2007). Using knowledge sharing and knowledge creation as examples of the types of knowledge work found in organizations, we present a multi-level overview of recent research and offer some suggestions for future research.

A GENERAL FRAMEWORK FOR UNDERSTANDING KNOWLEDGE WORK

Previous research has documented the criticality of knowledge in sustaining organizational success, but scant effort has been devoted to organizing the empirical endeavors into a general framework. Building on previous work, we offer a multi-level framework for organizing research on knowledge work conducted at three levels of analysis: the individual, the team or unit, and the organization.[1]

Knowledge

We use the term knowledge to refer to subjectively construed information. Following Davenport and Prusak (1998), we view knowledge as 'a fluid mix of framed experience, values, contextual information, and expert insight that provides a framework for evaluating and incorporating new experiences and information' (p. 5). That is, knowledge accrues as a result of learning through action, and reflects the justified beliefs and commitments of its holder (see Nonaka et al., 2003).

Unlike many other organizational resources, knowledge is renewable and regenerative. Knowledge that is context specific (to an organization, for example) is also relatively difficult for competitors to imitate effectively. The inimitability of knowledge is an especially important attribute that differentiates it from other types of resources that contribute to sustainable competitive advantage (Barney, 1991).

Explicit and tacit knowledge

Two types of knowledge resources are relevant to understanding knowledge work: explicit knowledge and tacit knowledge (Polyani, 1967). Explicit knowledge is easily codified and recorded. It can be formulated into sentences and equations, which are easily and reliably shared through written documents and oral presentations. Due to these characteristics, explicit knowledge can usually be obtained by competing firms and thus it is not a likely basis for sustainable competitive advantage (Jackson et al., 2003).

In contrast to explicit knowledge, tacit knowledge is more complex and ambiguous, making it difficult to codify and transmit. People accumulate tacit knowledge through observation, imitation, and repeated interactions, which produce actionable skills or 'know how.' Tacit knowledge is also 'sticky' and cannot be transferred easily from one person to another or from one organization to another (see Von Hippel, 1994; Szulanski, 1996). Tacit knowledge is often shared during casual interactions (Lubit, 2001) that unfold within a trusting relationship. The stickiness of tacit knowledge makes it potentially more valuable than explicit knowledge as a source of competitive advantage (Lado and Wilson, 1994).

Knowledge stocks and flows

Another typology of knowledge resources that has implications for understanding knowledge work differentiates between knowledge stocks and knowledge flows. Knowledge stocks are more tangible and accessible (Amit and Schoemaker, 1993); included here are the specific knowledge and expertise of employees as well as resources that are at least partially controlled and sometimes owned by the organization, such as patented technologies and production processes.

To assure adequate knowledge stocks, firms must effectively manage knowledge flows. Dierickx and Cool (1989) likened knowledge flows to the movement of water into and out of a bath tub. In a bathtub, the water level (knowledge stock) is equal to the amount of water that has flowed in minus the amount that has flowed out. By analogy, a firm's knowledge stock is equal to the amount of knowledge it accumulates – through means such as knowledge creation and knowledge sharing – minus the amount it loses.

Likening knowledge to water emphasizes the power of knowledge aggregation and knowledge in motion. A single molecule of standing water has far less power to transform a landscape than does a river of moving water (cf. Fiol, 2003; Hass and Hansen, 2005). Knowledge that flows only between individuals is not likely to create competitive advantage for a large firm with global operations. Sustained competitive advantage is gained by firms that understand how to manage knowledge flows between teams, throughout and among business units, through ill-defined social networks, and beyond organizational boundaries. In other words, the concept of knowledge flows includes both horizontal knowledge transfers and cross-level dynamics.

Knowledge work

Knowledge work occurs when one or more individuals endeavor to move and transform knowledge.[2] It is through knowledge work that an organization can transform the knowledge held by an individual into something of value to the organization as a whole. The specific behaviors and activities that comprise knowledge work include knowledge acquisition, knowledge sharing, knowledge combination, knowledge creation, knowledge application, and knowledge revision (Jackson et al., 2006). Activities such as these are central to the work of scientists and engineers engaged in new product development, experts from various backgrounds who work together to serve customer-focused accounts, multi-functional sales teams, managers charged with planning and implementing a merger, and so on.

Knowledge work is not a category of work. Instead, it refers to a type of activity that may occur relatively frequently or infrequently, and that may be of more or less importance for a particular individual, team or organization. What differentiates knowledge work from other types of organizational behavior is the extent to which knowledge-centered activities dominate the interactions. For some employees, knowledge work may be their only responsibility, requiring all their time and effort. For others, knowledge work may be central to only one of their several responsibilities.

Unlike many other resources, an organization's knowledge is difficult to separate from the people and human relationships within which it exists. As noted by Subramaniam and Youndt (2005: 459), 'unless individual knowledge is networked, shared, and channeled through relationships; it provides little benefit to organizations in terms of innovative capabilities.' Likewise, Nahapiet and Ghoshal (1998) argued that 'knowledge and meaning are always embedded in a social context – both created and sustained through ongoing relationships in such collectivities' (p. 253).

Furthermore, knowledge work is inherently a multi-level construct – it can involve interactions between individuals, between an individual and a team, between teams, between organizations, and/or among a combination of individuals, teams and other social groupings of participants who are linked together in a network of collaboration. In this chapter, we use the term knowledge work broadly to refer to all of the knowledge-related behaviors and activities that employees can engage in, as individuals or collectively.

Knowledge sharing

While knowledge itself may be possessed independently by individuals, knowledge sharing occurs through interactions involving at least two individuals. Knowledge is shared when it is transferred from one person or group to another person or group. It is a critical intermediate process that aligns the acquisition and application of knowledge (Jackson et al., 2003; Snell et al., 1996). Knowledge sharing is the most frequently used method for individual employees and managers to obtain new knowledge (Cross et al., 2001); it is also essential to an organization's ability to secure and leverage the knowledge held by individual members of an organization (Starbuck, 1992). In addition, knowledge sharing can stimulate new knowledge creation (Nahapiet and Ghoshal, 1998).

Deriving competitive advantage from internal knowledge transfers while preventing knowledge from leaking to competitors is a key challenge for organizations in knowledge-intensive industries (Argote and Ingram, 2000). Transferability of knowledge can threaten competitiveness, for the issue of knowledge inimitability lies at the heart of competitive advantage and its sustainability (Spender and Grant, 1996). Indeed, one approach to gaining a competitive advantage may be to maximize knowledge acquisition, while minimizing knowledge sharing with external entities. In international joint ventures, for example, a firm's ability to keep an appropriate balance between its own knowledge acquisition (e.g., an improved understanding of the market) and knowledge transfers to partners (e.g., technological and management know-how) can be a major determinant of success (Tsang, 2002).

The importance of appropriate knowledge-sharing has been emphasized in many discussions of knowledge-based competition and innovation (e.g., Hargadon and Sutton, 2000). One objective of effective knowledge sharing is efficiency. No individual knows everything, and no individual can keep up with all of the relevant new knowledge continually being created. Knowledge sharing among employees conserves resources, and frees up time for people to use the knowledge they have. Moreover, knowledge sharing promotes knowledge application. As employees attempt to share knowledge, they are forced to articulate what they know; this makes it possible to evaluate the knowledge and apply it to solve problems or create new products (Von Krogh et al., 2000). Thus, the successful management of knowledge sharing should promote organizational effectiveness (Cross et al., 2001; Davenport and Prusak, 1998).

Given the presence of knowledge, knowledge sharing is not an automatic process, however. Sharing knowledge often incurs costs, such as the time and effort required to communicate (Reagans and McEvily, 2003). Other potential barriers to knowledge sharing include lack of awareness about the existence or location of relevant knowledge, loss of power associated with being the sole source of knowledge, and difficulties in articulating or absorbing available knowledge. Therefore, deliberate efforts may be needed to encourage, support and sustain knowledge sharing within an organization.

Knowledge creation

Whereas knowledge sharing is mostly concerned with the mobilization of existing knowledge, knowledge creation is a process through which novel knowledge is generated and added to the existing knowledge stock. New knowledge is defined as 'discoveries about phenomena that were not known previously' (McFadyen et al., 2004); it can take the form of ideas, processes, or solutions (Perry-Smith and Shalley, 2003). Knowledge creation is useful when it contributes to an organization's growth or effectiveness (Amabile et al., 1996). Generally, knowledge creation requires the acquisition and combination of existing knowledge (Kogut and Zander, 1992).

The creation of new knowledge often begins with an idea generated by an individual or perhaps a small group of individuals. The process is enabled by exposure to diverse ideas through network positions and dynamics (Burt, 2004; Perry-Smith and Shalley, 2003). As the initial idea is explored and developed, a wider circle of people typically become involved in discussions and other interactions that go beyond solitary individual activities such as reading, writing, and experimenting (McFadyen et al., 2004). Eventually, novel ideas contribute to an organization's success when they are made available to others in the organization (Oldham, 2003). By ensuring they have exclusive access to such knowledge and using it effectively, firms can gain a competitive advantage (Barney, 1986). At the same time, when the organization gives legitimacy to the creative ideas of individuals, it reinforces their centrality in the organizational network, which further enables them to gather more information and further contribute to the innovation process (Perry-Smith and Shalley, 2003).

Thus, both knowledge sharing and knowledge creation have substantial implications for the success of knowledge-intensive organizations. Next we examine these activities at three levels of analysis: individuals, teams and other collectives, and organizations.

DYNAMICS OF INDIVIDUAL-LEVEL KNOWLEDGE WORK

Several studies shed light on the dynamics of individual-level knowledge work. This work serves as a basis for understanding the social dynamics that unfold at higher levels of analysis.

Individual knowledge sharing

Knowledge sharing at the individual level refers to the transfer of knowledge from one individual to another. Relevant studies conducted at this level of analysis include those that treat individuals as the recipients and disseminators of knowledge (Nebus, 2006). The dynamics of knowledge reception are addressed in studies that investigate the motivation or ability of individuals to obtain knowledge from others. The dynamics of knowledge dissemination are addressed in studies that investigate the conditions that encourage or discourage the social interactions required for knowledge sharing to occur.

Recipients of knowledge

Research on social networks is central to an understanding of the conditions that increase focal actors' receipt of knowledge. The strength and redundancy of an individual's social ties have been proposed as two predictors of the knowledge a person is likely to receive from others.

According to one argument, people with strong social ties are more likely to be knowledge recipients. One rationale for this prediction is that frequent (i.e., strong) contacts are associated with positive affective relationships, which often are friendly in nature and supportive of 'reciprocal favors' (Nelson, 1989: 380), including the sharing of knowledge.

An alternative and more common perspective argues that more advantages accrue to individuals with more diverse 'weak ties.' Ideally, these weak ties create bridges across structural holes as well, giving the recipient access to sources of non-redundant information (Burt, 1992). In addition, diverse ties provide exposure to different perspectives, which also are a form of nonredundant knowledge (Perry-Smith and Shalley, 2003). Evidence to support these arguments was provided by Seibert et al. (2001), who found that people with more weak ties to contacts at higher levels and in other functions had access to more information. Similarly, individuals acting as brokers across structural holes were shown to have greater access to diverse and often contradictory and innovative ideas (Burt, 2004).

The competing views of the value of weak versus strong ties seems to pose a dilemma – should organizations that wish to maximize knowledge sharing at the individual level create conditions that support the development of a smaller network of strong ties or a larger network of more diverse weak ties? The answer to this question may depend on what types of knowledge sharing are most valuable to the organization. Weak ties with a wide range of contacts that provide access to non-redundant information are likely to be more valuable when the organization or work team values efficient knowledge transfer (Reagans and McEvily, 2003; Seibert et al., 2001). In contrast, when organizations wish to reinforce norms of reciprocity and create common perspectives and language for effective knowledge sharing, developing strong ties may be more valuable (Levin et al., 2006; Reagans and McEvily, 2003). In other words, the superiority of one form of network ties over the other may depend on the relative importance of efficiently accessing knowledge versus enabling effective knowledge transfers.

The type of knowledge to be shared may also be an important consideration when choosing between managerial practices that promote the development of weak and strong ties. As explained previously, explicit knowledge is easily codified and can be transferred without direct face-to-face communication, but tacit knowledge is learned through experience and is more difficult to articulate and communicate. When the knowledge to be transferred is explicit and codified, individuals who are connected to a diverse set of colleagues by weak ties can easily access and retrieve that knowledge (see Reagans and McEvily, 2003). Regarding tacit knowledge, however, merely knowing who knows what is not sufficient; transferring tacit knowledge requires more frequent and direct socialization and the development of a shared cognitive map. Individuals tend to trust others

with whom they have strong ties and are more likely to share the perspectives and language base that facilitates tacit knowledge transfer (Reagans and McEvily, 2003). Therefore, the nature of knowledge also dictates whether access to or transfer of knowledge is more valuable, and thus whether strong or weak ties are more desirable.

Disseminators of knowledge

When knowledge sharing is considered from the perspective of disseminators, a large literature on training and development make it clear that issues of individual motivation, opportunity and ability are all relevant to understanding what knowledge individuals are likely to disseminate (e.g., Goldstein and Ford, 2002). Recent research on knowledge sharing reinforces an appreciation for the role of informal social ties as conduits of learning (Nebus, 2006). Discussions of knowledge sharing have also brought more attention to the importance of understanding knowledge dissemination processes. Whereas traditional approaches have often assumed that knowledge disseminators shared knowledge freely in the process of enacting their formal roles (e.g., as supervisors or trainers), studies of knowledge-intensive organizations recognize that effective knowledge dissemination may require that managers find ways to motivate employees whose roles are not formally construed to include training and development activities.

An individual's motivation to disseminate knowledge is likely to reflect his or her view of whether his or her knowledge is a private good (individual social capital) or a public good (communal social capital) (Ibarra et al., 2005). If knowledge is viewed as a private good, individuals may be less likely to share it freely with others, because doing so diminishes their own worth. When knowledge is viewed as a private good, its dissemination is likely to follow the predictions of social exchange theory (Blau, 1964) – that is, individuals are likely to share knowledge with the expectation that others will reciprocate immediately or in the near future. Knowledge dissemination, therefore, is preceded by a weighing of its potential costs and benefits to the individual (Bock et al., 2002, 2005). As Ibarra et al. (2005) noted, organizations suffer from a 'tragedy of the commons' when their members take advantage of collective knowledge but do not freely contribute their own knowledge.

In contrast, individuals who view their knowledge as a public good may be more likely to share it without expecting something in return. This happens when individuals are committed to the organization, feel that their own personal interests are aligned with the organization's interests, perceive the organization climate as supporting affiliation and believe that organizational relationships are governed by a strong norm of reciprocity (Bock et al., 2002, 2005; Connelly and Kelloway, 2003). A state of 'network congruence' exists when individual's knowledge sharing behaviors satisfy the interests of both individuals and the organization (Ibarra et al., 2005).

The success of knowledge sharing behaviors also depends on others' interests in learning from the disseminator. Burt (2004) shows that managers who are situated at the gap of network structural holes are more likely to discuss their ideas with others, and more importantly, are more likely to have their ideas attended to by senior management and evaluated as valuable. The ideas of people who are peripheral in the network get less attention, which reduces their motivation to engage in further knowledge sharing. Thus, the contours of social networks have substantial implications for knowledge sharing amongst individuals.

Individual knowledge creation

The dynamics of individual knowledge creation are illuminated by studies of individual creativity and innovation. Individual creativity has traditionally been treated as an outcome that can be explained largely by individual attributes and capabilities, including domain expertise, creative thinking skills, and task motivation (Amabile, 1998; Taggar, 2002). More recently, however, scholars

have drawn attention to the potentially important role of unit and organization factors (e.g., Oldham, 2003). Thus, for example, individuals who are surrounded by creative coworkers tend to be more creative themselves (Zhou, 2003). Another study found that the innovation performance of managers was greater when managers had close and trusting relationships with others (Moran, 2005). Mehra et al. (2001) found that social network position and self-monitoring personality both had unique and additive influences on individual creativity performance. Broader organizational contextual factors, such as a sense of reciprocity, learning goal orientation, and team learning may also influence individual creativity (Da Silva et al., 1999).

Leaders influence an individual's creativity, too. A leader's role expectations, problem solving style, and the leader-member exchange relationship all influence perceptions of innovation support and innovation behavior (Scott and Bruce, 1994). Zhou (2003) found that individuals display more creativity when their supervisors provide developmental feedback, and when their supervisors display less monitoring behavior.

Finally, we note that the value of an individual's creative ideas will not be fully realized unless others recognize the potential of those ideas (Burt, 2004). Creativity is not only a business of 'genius' but also a business of 'import-export' communication and centrality (Burt, 2004; Perry-Smith and Shalley, 2003). The same ideas that are considered useless and dismissed in one environment may be perceived as highly innovative and valuable by others in a different context; the same ideas that are discounted as not credible when they come from someone who is peripheral in a network may be accepted and acted up when offered by someone more centrally located. Indeed, Burt (2004) showed that to some extent the value of 'an idea resides in a situation, in the transaction through which an idea is delivered to an audience; not in the source of the idea, nor the idea itself' (p. 388). Network position therefore comes into play in facilitating and realizing individual creativity.

Interplay between knowledge sharing and knowledge creation

Scholars who study individual knowledge sharing and knowledge creation typically focus on one or the other type of behavior. In practice, these two components of knowledge work are not so easily separated. Indeed, they may be completely intertwined. Knowledge sharing often stimulates new knowledge creation (Taylor and Greve, 2007). In a study of research scientists, for example, McFadyen et al. (2004) found that both the number and strength of contacts that researchers had were positively related to the knowledge they created. Presumably, these scientists benefited from a wide network of weak ties, which brought them into contact with a more diverse range of ideas, and a (perhaps) smaller network of strong ties that they were able to effectively leverage for creative productivity. Conversely, it is also the case that organizations can benefit from individual knowledge creation when it is accompanied by knowledge sharing. To date, however, the question of whether individuals who are more creative are also more likely to be effective knowledge disseminators (vs. recipients) remains largely unexplored.

Looking ahead, we believe knowledge-intensive organizations could benefit from individual-level research that improves our understanding of the interplay between knowledge sharing and knowledge creation. Also needed is research that examines more closely the dynamics of sharing and creating tacit knowledge versus explicit knowledge. Perhaps these knowledge activities are mutually reinforcing. If so, organizations need not choose which to maximize. More likely, individual employees make choices among these various activities, either intentionally or unintentionally. Knowledge-intensive organizations need to understand the individual knowledge activities that are likely to contribute to their effectiveness, as well as the conditions that are likely to maximize the most valuable activities.

DYNAMICS OF UNIT-LEVEL KNOWLEDGE WORK

We now consider research that examines knowledge work within or between teams and other organizational units, such as departments or divisions. The outcome of interest at this level is the knowledge work of a unit as a collective. We begin by focusing separately on the within-unit and between-unit social dynamics of knowledge work, and then consider the implications of jointly accounting for both types of dynamics.

Within-unit knowledge sharing

Within-unit knowledge sharing refers to the transfer of knowledge among unit members. To understand within-unit knowledge work, researchers have examined three social components of collectivities: the cognitive, relational, and structural (Nahapiet and Ghoshal, 1998).

Cognitive component of within-unit knowledge sharing
The cognitive dimension of within-unit dynamics corresponds to the ability of the unit to avoid misunderstandings (Nahapiet and Ghoshal, 1998). When members share a common language, narrative, and cognitive map or mental model, they communicate more effectively; knowledge can be shared more easily and with higher fidelity (for a review of the literature on team mental models, see Langan-Fox, 2003). In addition, corresponding to the public good perspective, common goals and interests mean that team members are more likely to expect positive outcomes from knowledge sharing (Tsai and Ghoshal, 1998).

Relational component of within-unit knowledge sharing
The relational dynamics among members of a team or unit can nurture or impede

many aspects of the collective's knowledge work. Trust, trustworthiness, active empathy, lenience in judgment, courage and access to help, norms, sanctions, expectations, and obligations all facilitate the achievement of collective outcomes (Zarraga and Bonache, 2005), and in this case, knowledge sharing.

Trust is necessary in situations characterized by vulnerability and risk (Mayer and Davis, 1995). Trust refers to 'the belief that an exchange partner would not act in self-interest at another's expense and … a predilection to assume the best when interpreting another's motives and actions' (Uzzi, 1997: 43). Trustworthiness, on the other hand, reflects how much one is trusted by others (Tsai and Ghoshal, 1998). With mutually favorable beliefs, actors are less concerned that their sharing behavior will be taken advantage of and are more likely to effectively cooperate and engage in knowledge sharing behavior (Nahapiet and Ghoshal, 1998).

Kang et al. (2006) further differentiated between generalized trust towards members of a group, and dyadic resilient trust towards direct contacts; these have differential implications for knowledge work. It is generalized trust towards a group of individuals (e.g., members of a work team or unit) that is likely to facilitate knowledge sharing. Norms favoring cooperation and openness should encourage broad knowledge sharing among individuals of the collective (Starbuck, 1992). Identification with the collectivity, in turn, instils individuals with the motivation to share knowledge that might contribute to collective outcomes (Nahapiet and Ghoshal, 1998). Leaders who encourage active involvement and empower employees to participate in decision making and social events also facilitate knowledge sharing within teams (Zarraga and Bonache, 2005).

Structural component of within-unit knowledge sharing

The structural component of knowledge work refers to social relationships that bind together members of the collective. The social structures (hierarchical vs. horizontal, mechanistic vs. organic) of a collective entity,

physical proximity at work, and personal ties established at work are all relevant to the development of conditions that support knowledge sharing.

The structural component of social networks creates and frames opportunities for knowledge work. Dense social networks appear to facilitate complex knowledge sharing (Reagans et al., 2004). Because actors in such a network interact with each other frequently, they have more opportunities to share fine-grained and in-depth knowledge; such interactions also increase the ability of the collective to effectively exploit their shared knowledge (Reagans and Zuckerman, 2001). Sparse networks, on the other hand, may present actors with more non-redundant information and stimulate the entrepreneurial behaviors associated with knowledge creation (Kang et al., 2006). Therefore, the optional structural configuration for unit knowledge sharing also depends on the knowledge in focus.

Between-unit knowledge sharing

Analogous to knowledge sharing among individuals, knowledge sharing among units involves searching for and identifying new knowledge, as well as transferring and incorporating existing knowledge. In this case, however, the focal actors are units taken as a collective. Cognitive, relational and structural factors may again serve as determinants of knowledge sharing at this higher level of analysis.

Cognitive and relational influences

When units within an organization share common interests or goals, they may be more likely to establish a cooperative relationship; knowledge sharing and joint learning can then create a win-win situation that has benefits to everyone involved. When units compete with each other for internal resources, however, knowledge sharing may be less likely (Tsai, 2002; Ingram and Simons, 2002). As to the relational component, when multi-national corporation (MNC) subsidiaries trust and identify with headquarters' management, it is more likely that organizational practices will be transferred to subsidiaries (Kostova and Roth, 2002).

Relational influences

While cognitive and relational factors are undoubtedly important to understanding inter-unit knowledge sharing, studies of knowledge work at this level of analysis have typically focused on the structural component. Units that are interconnected in a rich network seem to benefit from greater knowledge flow, which provides greater information access and timeliness (Burt, 1992). For example, research shows that when project teams have short inter-team network paths (structural social capital) with other teams, they are able to obtain more knowledge from other teams and complete their projects sooner (Hansen, 2002). Within a single network, some units may also reap more gains due to their position and ties. For example, those units that are most central in the network and those with the largest number of weak ties are more likely to engage in knowledge exchange and combination with other units (Tsai and Ghoshal, 1998). While weak ties to external entities provide greater access to nonredundant knowledge, a denser network of stronger ties seems to be more conducive to the sharing of complex and tacit knowledge among units (Hansen, 1999; Nahapiet and Ghoshal, 1998).

Hierarchical relationships among units may also influence knowledge flows. When units have a vertical relationship with one another and the locus of decision making lies at the upper level, the lower-level units may be reluctant to voluntarily share knowledge unless directed by the authority to do so (Tsai, 2002). Thus, the structural position of a unit may influence its ability, motivation, and opportunity to share knowledge.

Within-unit knowledge creation

An extensive literature informs our understanding of unit-level knowledge creation. Indeed, the prevalence of team-based work reflects the commonly held belief that teamwork enhances knowledge creation. As individuals with different knowledge stocks collaborate, the continual (re)combination of their knowledge serves as the basis for incremental change (Noe et al., 2003), and occasionally leads to radical changes such as significant new ideas, products, or procedures. Reviews of past work clearly illustrate the importance of cognitive and relational factors as determinants of knowledge creation within teams and other organizational units (e.g., see West and Hirst, 2003).

Cognitive influences

The increasing prevalence of team-based organizations reflects a belief in the ability of teams to create new and valuable knowledge. When creativity is the objective, work teams are typically designed to include people who bring a variety of differing perspectives to the problems at hand. While substantial evidence supports the assumption that new knowledge creation is more likely to occur in teams and work units that are more cognitively diverse, the evidence is sufficiently mixed to suggest that cognitive diversity alone is not a sufficient condition for new knowledge creation. For a unit to effectively use its stock of cognitive diversity, it must also have a social fabric that supports effective knowledge flows (Reagans et al., 2004; Reagans and Zuckerman, 2001).

Relational influences

The presence of diverse knowledge within teams may provide opportunities for knowledge creation, but those opportunities are more likely to be realized when the social relations among team members are positive (Reagans and Zuckerman, 2001). Those with minority viewpoints must feel free to express them, and the majority must be willing to actively engage in a consideration of the minority's ideas. A team climate characterized by active empathy and lenience in judgment, courage, and mutual trust and support is conducive to the creation of knowledge in teams (Zarraga and Bonache, 2005).

Unless knowledge sharing occurs among team members with diverse knowledge stocks, there is no basis for the analysis and problem solving activities that lead to new insights and ideas. The use of team building and other practices designed to develop strong interpersonal relationships reflect an understanding of this point among managers, and there is some empirical evidence to support this view (Schulze and Hoegl, 2006). In addition, research on creative organizational climates has identified organizational support, supervisory encouragement, work group support, sufficient resources, challenging work, and flexibility as elements of creative organizations. Conversely, creativity is impeded by internal political problems, harsh criticism of ideas, destructive internal competition, risk avoidance, and protecting the status quo. Too much emphasis on productivity and excessive workloads also appear to reduce creativity (Amabile et al., 1996).

Between-unit knowledge creation

The between-unit collaboration required for new knowledge creation is fraught with difficulties. One source of difficulty is that knowledge is not easily transferred between units due to its 'sticky' nature. Other barriers to inter-unit collaboration include conflicting goals and incentives as well as lack of motivation or opportunity (Dyer and Hatch, 2006).

To encourage the types of inter-unit collaborations that are likely to lead to the creation of new knowledge, managers may need to intentionally adopt management practices that both reduce knowledge stickiness and promote the use of knowledge from one part of the organization for solving problems in other parts of the organization. Attending to the organizational culture seems to be an obvious imperative for promoting inter-unit collaboration.

Just as within-unit trust facilitates knowledge sharing among members of a unit, a culture of cooperation and solidarity creates a relational atmosphere conducive to joint problem solving and knowledge creation between units. Commitment-based human resource management practices that foster trust and cooperation among employees include collective-based incentives, internal promotion, team-based work design, and training. Human resource practices such as cross-training, company-wide social events, and internal promotions may also help cultivate a shared cognitive schema among employees, which should also facilitate cooperation (Collins and Smith, 2006). The ongoing and continuous nature of knowledge creation suggests that actively managing turnover rates and patterns may also prove useful at the organizational level (Inkpen and Tsang, 2005; Nahapiet and Ghoshal, 1998).

Interplay between individual-level and unit-level knowledge work

Studies of knowledge work at the individual and unit or team-level share much in common. Many of the same theoretical explanations are used as the foundations of research at these two levels of analysis. The use of network theory and its related analytic techniques may prove to be especially useful for identifying general principles that hold across both levels of analysis. For example, the differential usefulness of weak vs. strong ties seems to transcend levels of analysis. Despite some similarities in the arguments applied to individuals and teams or units, however, it would be overly simplistic to view knowledge sharing and knowledge creation processes as directly parallel across these levels of analysis.

Given that teams are comprised of individuals, it is reasonable to expect that creativity at the individual level may aggregate to team-level innovation. But team innovation is not a simple aggregation of individual creativity. A more useful model views team innovation (i.e., team knowledge creation) as a two-stage process (West, 2002). The first stage resembles the simple aggregation of individual creativity, but this alone can lead to at most the sum of the individuals' ideas (Zarraga and Bonache, 2005). To ensure a team produces more value than the sum of its parts, contextual factors must also be considered. Thus, for example, Taggar

(2002) proposed a multi-level model in which individual creativity combines with 'team creativity-relevant processes' to produce new knowledge creation. West and Hirst (2003) argue that team and organizational processes combine with individual inputs to determine the number of innovations produced by teams. Such processes include developing shared objectives, reflexivity, leadership, and participation (Anderson and West, 1998). Such team-level factors support the aggregation of individual knowledge and also make it possible to realize an exponential gain that would not be achieved by individuals acting alone.

DYNAMICS OF ORGANIZATION-LEVEL KNOWLEDGE WORK

Whereas teams and work units can bring together diverse knowledge located within the organization, inter-organizational arrangements can bring together knowledge distributed among several organizations. Strategic alliances and network forms of organization support knowledge sharing and knowledge creation by encouraging knowledge flows between companies.

The US biotechnology industry is characterized by strategic alliances and networked relationships between new biotechnology firms and established firms. Strategic alliances allow older, established firms to gain access to the new discoveries of scientists employed by universities and small start-ups. Dedicated to research and new product development, small biotechnology firms often excel in the creation of new technical knowledge. In return for sharing their technical knowledge with larger firms, such as pharmaceutical companies, the smaller firms gain access to their partners' resources for product testing, marketing, and distribution (Liebeskind et al., 1996).

The concept of a 'network organization' has prevailed as an intermediate form of organization that complements markets and bureaucracies to facilitate organizational success (Borgatti and Foster, 2003). Central to network organizations are knowledge sharing routines that engage other organizations in the transfer, recombination, and/or creation of specialized knowledge (Dyer and Singh, 1998). Multinational corporations often take the form of a network of semi-autonomous business units. Indeed, some scholars (Gupta and Govindarajan, 2000) have argued that 'the primary reason why MNCs exist is because of their ability to transfer and exploit knowledge more effectively and efficiently in the intracorporate context than through external market mechanisms' (p. 473).

As organizational boundaries become more permeable, managers must weigh the value of the knowledge that might be gained against the associated costs. Thus, research on strategic management is actively focused on improving our understanding of the dynamics of inter-organizational knowledge sharing and knowledge creation. For example, researchers are asking how competing organizations that rely on the same suppliers can manage to share knowledge with suppliers while preventing them from using the knowledge to serve other competitors (Dyer and Hatch, 2006). Although reviewing that literature is beyond the scope of this chapter, we discuss it briefly here to encourage research that incorporates this higher level of analysis.

Inter-organization knowledge sharing

Increasingly, organizations need to absorb knowledge from outsiders to compete effectively, as no organization can possibly possess all required knowledge to deal with change (Anand, et al., 2002; Powell et al., 1996). Firms gain access to knowledge and learning opportunities through the network of relationships they have with other firms (Powell et al., 1996). Thus, one key role of top management teams is building social networks with, for example, suppliers, customers, competitors, and government agencies, thereby obtaining access to first-hand and valuable information that can be used to enhance organizational performance (Collins and Clark, 2003).

Actively sharing knowledge with others also can be beneficial. A study of the automotive industry found that by sharing knowledge with its suppliers, Toyota enabled them to learn more quickly and provide better products to Toyota, which helped Toyota outperform its American competitors (Dyer and Hatch, 2006). Strategic alliances, joint ventures, joint technical committees, and industrial districts are all examples of inter-organizational arrangements that can support knowledge sharing (Rosenkopf et al., 2001). Another approach used to obtain knowledge is hiring contingent workers and consultants who possess specialized knowledge that is not held by the firm's regular or core employees (Davis-Blake and Hui, 2003).

Aside from the structural connection with networking organizations, it is equally important for firms in knowledge-intensive industries to cultivate relational and cognitive social capital (Maurer and Ebers, 2006). When the knowledge to be shared between organizations is explicit, it is relatively easy to transmit and record (Zollo and Singh, 2004). The use of email, telephones, and face-to-face meetings facilitate the sharing of explicit knowledge among organizations.

When sharing tacit knowledge, organizations face the same challenges as individuals and teams – they must establish relationships that support knowledge sharing. Uzzi (1997) found that inter-organizational relationships characterized by trust were more conducive to fine-grained knowledge transfer compared to arms-length transactional relationships. Likewise, partners in a strategic alliance gain most from freely flowing knowledge when they establish noncompetitive relationships guided by common goals (Inkpen and Tsang, 2005). Activities such as visiting the facilities of other companies, attending industry consortia, and benchmarking against other firms are useful knowledge sharing mechanisms (Appleyard, 2006). Thus, just as social capital promotes knowledge sharing between individuals and between teams, it also promotes knowledge sharing between an organization and various external partners or stakeholders. Lessons learned about the dynamics of knowledge sharing at lower levels of analysis (individual and team) provide opportunities to develop new insights into organization-level phenomena, and vice versa.

Inter-organizational knowledge creation

When organizations are the unit of study, the notion of knowledge creation is often referred to as organizational innovation. Analogous to team-level research, work conducted at the organization level generally assumes that knowledge sharing contributes to knowledge creation (Huber, 2006). Thus, just as positive and cooperative relationships between organizations facilitate knowledge sharing, they are assumed to promote the creation of new organizational knowledge, both by accident as well as by design (Nahapiet and Ghoshal, 1998). Consistent with this assumption, studies have found that organizational innovation is facilitated by external ties with other organizations (Subramaniam and Youndt, 2005; Uzzi, 1997).

Multiple forms of network organizations that support knowledge sharing also are conducive to knowledge creation. Inter-organizational embeddednesss, including relationships with suppliers and clients, promotes joint problem solving (Uzzi, 1997). When top management teams of high tech firms have strong and wide ranging social ties with external entities, the firms experience greater sales growth and stock returns (Collins and Clark, 2003). External venturing, in which companies invest in start-up ventures outside the firm, enables investing firms to quickly access newly created knowledge even when they are not directly involved in the process of knowledge creation (Wadhwa and Kotha, 2007).

In some cases, the diverse knowledge obtained from external sources complements internal knowledge, which in turn can facilitate knowledge creation that stimulates incremental innovation. For example, Matusik and Hill (1998) showed that contingent workers bring in fresh and valuable public knowledge that helps stimulate the creation of new private knowledge within firms. Likewise, Yli-Renko et al. (2001) reported that the knowledge of customers facilitates product innovation. In their study of technology firms, customer network ties and strong relationships with customers were associated with both new product development and technology renovation. Thus, organizational social capital appears to promote both incremental innovation and radical innovation (Subramaniam and Youndt, 2005).

While networking organizations are likely to benefit from social capital, they are also subject to the constraints brought by their structural, relational, and cognitive social capital. For example, frequent interaction with contacts in a dense network, strong obligations for reciprocity with contacts, and homogeneous cognitive schema with contacts may cause relational and cognitive 'lock-in,' which prevents organizations from innovating and changing (Maurer and Ebers, 2006).

Interplay between team and organization knowledge work

Studies that jointly investigate team- and organization-level knowledge sharing and knowledge creation are needed to develop a better understanding of how the dynamics of knowledge work are influenced by the types of boundaries that must be spanned. Conceptually, the arguments used to explain the dynamics and potential outcomes of inter-organization knowledge work are quite similar to those used to explain inter-unit (within-organization) knowledge work. However, more research is needed to fully understand the similarities and differences in knowledge work at these levels of analysis.

Management scholars generally assume that inter-organization knowledge sharing carries with it more risks than inter-team knowledge sharing. Nevertheless, not all firms are likely to face the same risks. For example, companies in the semiconductor industry are less likely to share private knowledge with other companies than those in the steel industry, because the rapidly changing nature

of the semiconductor industry places more threats to competitive advantage if companies share knowledge with others (Appleyard, 1996).

Meanwhile, scholars who conduct research at the level of teams generally assume that knowledge sharing and knowledge creation within organizations are essentially risk-free. For example, one study included as impediments to the transfer of best practices within companies social distant, lack of ability, and ambiguity, but not potential risks associated with transferring best practices to other units (Szulanski, 1996). The consequences of differing levels of risk for the behavior of the individuals and teams involved in knowledge work are not yet well understood.

FUTURE DIRECTIONS

In reviewing the research on knowledge work conducted at the individual, team and organization levels of analysis, we found many similarities, some differences and several gaps. Strong ties and network embeddedness appear to facilitate knowledge sharing; when actors trust one another, they are perhaps less likely to view knowledge sharing as risky (Reagans and McEvily, 2003). Strong and cohesive networks characterized by frequent interaction allow the development of a common language and perspective, which enables the sharing of tacit knowledge. Yet weak ties are also desirable because they are more likely to provide access to non-redundant information, which is conducive to new knowledge creation. In addition, when actors are connected by weak ties to multiple diverse entities, they are more likely to develop the ability to communicate complex ideas to dissimilar recipients, which contributes to knowledge sharing (Hansen, 1999). What is not yet understood, however, are the management practices that nurture the development of networks with the appropriate structures and characteristics. Therefore, research on social networks and knowledge work provides scant guidance to practicing managers. To conclude, we discuss a few directions for future research that may yield additional insights to practicing managers.

Managing competencies and capabilities

For organizations that rely on knowledge work, both the competencies of individuals and the capabilities of collectives (e.g., teams, units, networks) are likely to influence knowledge sharing and knowledge creation. The dynamic nature of knowledge work and the importance of tacit (vs. explicit) knowledge pose two special challenges to building and maintaining the needed competencies and capabilities. In addition, managing the ability component of knowledge work involves bridging across multiple units of analysis. Thus, one objective for future research should be improving our understanding of the linkages and disconnects between individual-level competencies and the capabilities of collectives.

Individual competencies

At the level of individual employees, competencies associated with creative and innovative behavior include cognitive skills, some personality characteristics and deep task knowledge (Taggar, 2002). Staffing an organization with people who have these competencies should facilitate effective knowledge work (Pulakos et al., 2003), so standard selection and training practices may be of some use in maintaining the needed individual competencies. However, as Jackson et al. (2006) noted, traditional top-down training may be inadequate because it underestimates the dynamic, problem-driven nature of knowledge work. Rather than 'spoon feeding' employees *what* they need to know, knowledge-intensive organizations may find it is more effective to teach employees *how* to use social dynamics to access knowledge when they need it and recognize potentially useful or outdated knowledge when they encounter it.

Employees with technological know how – conducting effective internet searches, using electronic bulletin boards to communicate with experts, and participating in webcasts – can quickly acquire up-to-date information on almost any topic. If collaborators know how to use intranets, groupware, and myriad other information technologies, it makes it easier to perform their work despite their being geographically distributed. But knowledge work also requires interpersonal skills to navigate and leverage the tacit knowledge that is available in organizations; useful interpersonal skills include conflict resolution, collaborative problem-solving and communication (Stevens and Campion, 1999). In their analysis of talent contracting situations, Davis-Blake and Hui (2003) reported that contracting relationships typically require managers who are adept at managing the interface between contract employees and regular employees. Such managers should build mutual trust and engender feelings of identification with the contracting firm to encourage the flow of knowledge between contract and regular employees. Additional empirical work is needed to determine the degree to which improving the interpersonal competencies of managers results in the development of effective social networks.

Collective capabilities

At the individual level, knowledge work competencies constitute knowledge stocks. The knowledge work of teams, networks organizations and other social units draws upon such knowledge stocks. Capabilities of a collective are not isometric with the competencies of individual members, however. Group-level knowledge can increase even when not all individuals in the group gain knowledge. Conversely, individual knowledge can increase without a concurrent change in the knowledge of the collective, which is likely to bring little advantage to the organization (Turner and Makhija, 2006)

Research on team performance provides insights into the capabilities needed by collectives engaged in knowledge work. For example, effective teams are skilled at constructive controversy (Jehn, 1995). When creativity is needed, useful team capabilities include non-evaluative brainstorming, goal setting, the appropriate use of breaks, and scheduling of iterative team and individual idea sessions (Paulus et al., 2001). In rapidly changing environments, adaptation skills are likely to be important to success also (LePine et al., 2000). Adaptation occurs when members of the collective recognize changes in task demands and respond by re-evaluating and perhaps reformulating their approach.

Developing the capabilities of collectives may be more difficult than simply ensuring that individuals have the needed competencies for knowledge work. Rather than focusing on the development of individual competencies as most organizations do, it may be preferable to focus on developing the knowledge work capabilities of intact collectives. Currently, there is little empirical work to guide the design of learning approaches for developing the capabilities of collectives. Research that improves our understanding of how social collectives can develop the capabilities that facilitate knowledge work is clearly needed.

Tacit competencies and capabilities

In addition to extending what we know about developing individual competencies to include the development of collective capabilities, more research is needed to improve our understanding of how tacit competencies and capabilities can be developed. Like tacit knowledge, tacit competencies and capabilities are embedded in experience, and are not easily articulated and codified. For individual knowledge workers, creativity and political savvy may be useful tacit competencies. For collectives engaged in knowledge work, useful tacit capabilities may include building consensus, managing changes in membership, and maintaining network ties. Research that improves our understanding of the tacit competencies and capabilities that are needed for effective knowledge work should be given high priority. Subsequently, research can investigate how to develop such tacit competencies and capabilities. For example, when dealing with the ambiguities of tacit process-related and outcome-related knowledge, it may be appropriate for organizations

to rely on informal socialization and 'clan control' (Turner and Makhija, 2006).

Managing motivation

Developing individual competencies and collective capabilities may help ensure that individuals and collectives can engage in knowledge work, but motivation must also be present. Next we consider the motivational question of whether employees *will* engage in knowledge work.

Participation in knowledge work

Descriptions of knowledge-based competition often highlight the ability of knowledge workers to exercise their free will when deciding which organizations to join, which projects to work on, whether to participate in various informal communities of practice, and whether to share their ideas (see Kelloway and Barling, 2000). Thus, employers need to understand how employees decide to exert the effort needed for effective knowledge work, e.g., joining a particular project team, accepting informal leadership and advocacy roles, participating as an instructor or mentor, developing relationships that have no immediate utility in anticipation of the future, and so on. Such decisions to participate may reflect purely rational choices, but it is more likely that they also reflect political considerations (Arthur and Kim, 2005). Establishing trust between employees and managers may be the fundamental challenge that must be met to ensure that knowledge workers choose to participate and stay actively engaged.

Rewards and recognition

Scholars disagree about the effects of rewards as motivators of knowledge work. Lawler (2003) argued that contingent rewards should be effective motivators if they direct employees' attention to the most important aspects of their work. His view is consistent with research showing that organizations are more likely to achieve their goals when they reward employees for results that reflect those goals (Montemayor, 1996; Shaw et al., 2002). The design of contingent rewards that support knowledge work is fraught with difficulties, however. For example, it seems likely that rewarding the development of individual knowledge stocks may inadvertently dilute employees' motivation to share their knowledge.

An alternative perspective suggests that tying rewards to the achievement of creative outcomes may *reduce* creative output (Oldham, 2003). To address the organization's desire for accountability while providing room for individuals to take the risks associated with creating new knowledge, Oldham (2003) recommended offering only small rewards, and giving them after considerable time had elapsed. In addition, rewards that focus attention on quality over quantity may be more consistent with knowledge-centered activities (Zenger and Marshall, 2000).

Some field studies have reported that monetary rewards are not the main motivators of collaborative behavior (Swart and Kinnie, 2003), but research also shows that people tend to underestimate the importance of pay due to social desirability considerations and lack of self-insight (Rynes et al., 2002). Research that yields practical suggestions for how to develop effective reward and recognition systems for employees engaged in knowledge work (as individuals as well as participants in teams, networks, communities-of-practice) is needed to resolve this ongoing debate.

Motivation to learn

Research on individual learning has found that emotions and goals are two factors that influence learning outcomes. However, the implication of this work for managing knowledge-intensive organizations has yet to be closely examined.

Learning is inherent in knowledge work, but often the emotional cost of learning is more salient than the need for learning. The costs associated with learning are perhaps most salient when learning is construed as a remedy for knowledge deficiencies – i.e., as a remedial fix that corrects inaccurate or obsolete knowledge. Admitting that a remedial fix is needed may threaten an individual's

self-esteem or a group's sense of efficacy. Determining how to best motivate employees to critically evaluate and perhaps revise existing knowledge may require an improved understanding of the emotions associated with knowledge work. Research that examines the role of positive and negative emotions in knowledge-intensive organizations may provide new insights into how organizations can promote learning without reprisals (and see Grandey in this volume).

Additional research on the use of goal setting for knowledge work may prove useful, also. The motivational effectiveness of specific and difficult goals is well-established for tasks that are simple and routine (Locke and Latham, 1990). Studies of innovation processes indicate that specific and difficult goals enhance the performance of R&D teams (Zirger and Maidique, 1990). Contrary evidence indicates that individual creativity is impeded by productivity goals and excessive workloads (Amabile et al., 1996), perhaps because specific performance goals interfere with experimentation and learning (Dweck and Leggett, 1988). The tacit nature of knowledge may also reduce the usefulness and feasibility of setting specific goals. For example, Turner and Makhija (2006) argued that outcome control is viable only when outcome-related knowledge is explicit and complete, thus setting goals for developing tacit knowledge may not be appropriate.

When innovation is the objective, motivation seems to be enhanced by challenging work and autonomy, which suggests that 'do your best' goals may be most appropriate for complex knowledge work (Kanfer and Ackerman, 1989). Nonetheless, the practical value of vague goals is questionable. The size and complexity of knowledge-intensive projects may make it difficult to identify with the project as a whole, and see one's impact on the final outcome. Specific team goals may prove useful for establishing a definite 'line of site.' In other words, a mixed goal model might prove most effective, with teams having specific difficult goals while individual members work under more general 'do your best' goals. Research that examines the combined use of individual and collective goals is needed to resolve this issue.

Managing opportunities for knowledge work

If an organization's workforce has both the motivation and competencies/capabilities required for effective knowledge work, is it possible that knowledge work will fail to flourish? The answer is yes, unless opportunities for knowledge work are also present. Considerable research documents the value of contacts among people who have dissimilar information, perspectives and experiences. A variety of management policies and practices may be useful tools for increasing knowledge work opportunities.

An organization's culture – i.e., it's norms and rituals – can create opportunities for people to cross or span boundaries that might otherwise be barriers to knowledge flow (Bouty, 2000). In knowledge-intensive organizations, such opportunities should pervade organizational life. In addition to the structure of work itself, events such as meetings, celebrations, training programs, conferences, and myriad other occasions for social contact can be designed to encourage contact and learning among employees with different perspectives (Turner and Makhija, 2006).

Management practices and the organizational culture can also create opportunities for employees to engage in knowledge work outside the organization. Practices that create such opportunities include short-term leaves for community service work and other non-employment activities, paying the costs associated with professional memberships and conference travel, staffing practices that draw in a *broad* pool of external applicants, maintaining positive relationships with 'alumni' and supporting alumni-centered events that encourage current employees to mingle and learn from former employees, and supporting mentoring relationships that cross organizational boundaries (e.g., seasoned employees serving as mentors for college students).

The extant literature paints a clear picture of the importance of developing social connections among members of the organization and beyond. Less clear are the specific management practices that can be used to create and sustain such connections, which practices are especially harmful to them, and how to maximize benefits and avoid harms of building network connections.

CONCLUSION

To successfully compete on the basis of knowledge, organizations must learn to effectively manage knowledge work at multiple levels of analysis, including individuals, teams, departments, business units, and boundary-crossing networks. The management literature offers many insights into the dynamics of knowledge work at each of these levels of analysis. It offers fewer insights into the challenge of sustaining knowledge work at all of these levels of analysis simultaneously. We hope this chapter illuminates some of the many opportunities for conducting multi-level research that advances our understanding of how organizations can effectively manage the knowledge work of individuals as well as the knowledge work of the collectives in which they are embedded.

NOTES

1 A more complete framework would also include research conducted at higher levels of analysis, such as studies at the level of strategic groups, industries, and organizational networks; the development of such a framework is a project for the future.

2 For a discussion of other perspectives on how to define knowledge work, see Kelloway and Barling, 2000.

REFERENCES

Amabile, T. M. (1998) 'How to kill creativity', *Harvard Business Review* (September–October): 77–87.

Amabile, T. M., Conti, R., Coon, H., Lazenby, J. and Herron, M. (1996) 'Assessing the work environment for creativity', *Academy of Management Journal*, 39: 1154–1184.

Amit, R. and Schoemaker, P. J. H. (1993) 'Strategic assets and organizational rent', *Strategic Management Journal*, 14 (1): 33–46.

Anand, V., Glick, W. H. and Manz, C. C. (2002) 'Thriving on the knowledge of outsiders: Tapping organizational social capital', *Academy of Management Executive*, 16 (1): 87–101.

Anderson, N. R. and West, M. A. (1998) 'Measuring climate for work group innovation: Development and validation of the team climate inventory', *Journal of Organizational Behavior*, 19 (3): 235–258.

Appleyard, M. M. (1996) 'How does knowledge flow? Interfirm patterns in the semiconductor industry', *Strategic Management Journal*, 17: 137–154.

Argote, L. and Ingram, P. (2000) 'Knowledge transfer A basis for competitive advantage in firms', *Organizational Behavior and Human Decision Processes*, 82 (1): 150–169.

Arthur, J. B. and Kim, D.-O. (2005) 'Gainsharing and knowledge sharing: The effects of labour management co-operation', *International Journal of Human Resource Management*, 16 (9): 1564–1582.

Barney, J. (1991) 'Firm resources and sustainable competitive advantage', *Journal of Management*, 17: 99–129.

Barney, J. B. (1996) 'The resource-based theory of the firm', *Organization Science*, 7 (5): 469–469.

Blau, P. (1964) *Exchange and Power in Social Life*. New York: Wiley.

Bock, G.-W., Zmud, R. W., Kim, Y.-G. and Lee, J.-N. (2002) 'Breaking the myths of rewards: An exploratory study of attitudes about knowledge sharing', *Information Resources Management Journal*, 15 (2): 14–21.

Bock, G.-W., Zmud, R. W., Kim, Y.-G. and Lee, J.-N. (2005) 'Behavioral intention formation in knowledge sharing: Examining the roles of extrinsic motivators, social–psychological forces, and organizational climate', *MIS Quarterly*, 29 (1): 87–111.

Borgatti, S. P. and Foster, P. C. (2003) 'The network paradigm in organizational research: A review and typology', *Journal of Management*, 29 (6): 991–1013.

Bouty, I. (2000) 'Interpersonal and interaction influences on informal resource exchanges between R&D researchers across organizational boundaries', *Academy of Management Journal*, 43: 50–65.

Burt, R. S. (1992) *Structural Holes*. Cambridge, MA: Harvard University Press.

Burt, R. S. (2004) 'Structural holes and good ideas', *American Journal of Sociology*, 110 (2): 349–399.

Collins, C. J. and Clark, K. D. (2003) 'Strategic human resource practices, top management team social networks, and firm performance: The role of human resource practices in creating organizational competitive advantage', *Academy of Management Journal*, 48 (6): 740–751.

Collins, C. J. and Smith, K. G. (2006) 'Knowledge exchange and combination: The role of human resource practices in the performance of high-technology firms', *Academy of Management Journal*, 49 (3): 544–560.

Connelly, C. E. and Kelloway, E. K. (2003) 'Predictors of employee's perceptions of knowledge sharing cultures', *Leadership and Organization Development Journal*, 24 (5): 294–301.

Cross, R., Parker, A., Prusak, L. and Borgatti, S. P. (2001) 'Knowing what we know: Supporting knowledge creation and sharing in social networks', *Organizational Dynamics*, 30 (2): 100–120.

Da Silva, N., Tetrick, L. E., Jones, A. P., Slack, K., Kantambu, L. J. and Back, M. H. (1999) *Development of an organizational learning assessment instrument: An examination of its dimensionality and correlates*. Paper presented at the Society of Industrial and Organizational Psychology.

Davenport, T. H. and Prusak, L. (1998) *Working Knowledge*. Boston, MA: Harvard Business School Press.

Davis-Blake, A. and Hui, P. P. (2003) 'Contracting Talent for Knowledge–Based Competition', in S. E. Jackson, M. A. Hitt and A. S. Denisi (eds), *Managing Knowledge for Sustained Competitive Advantage*. San Francisco, CA: Jossey-Bass, pp. 178–206.

Dierickx, I. and Cool, K. (1989) 'Asset stock accumulation and sustainability of competitive advantage', *Management Science*, 35 (12): 1504–1511.

Dweck, C. S. and Leggett, E. L. (1988) 'A social-cognitive approach to motivation and personality', *Psychological Review*, 95: 256–273.

Dyer, J. H. and Hatch, N. W. (2006) 'Relation-specific capabilities and barriers to knowledge transfers: Creating advantage through network relationships', *Strategic Management Journal*, 27: 701–719.

Dyer, J. H. and Singh, H. (1998) 'The relational view: Cooperative strategy and sources of interorganizational competitive advantage', *Academy of Management Review*, 23 (4): 660–679.

Fiol, C. M. (2003) 'Organizing for Knowledge-Based Competitiveness: About Pipelines and Rivers', in S. E. Jackson, M. A. Hitt and A. S. Denisi (eds), *Managing Knowledge for Sustained Competitive Advantage*. San Francisco, CA: Jossey-Bass, pp. 64–93.

Goldstein, I. L. and Ford, J. K. (2002) *Training in Organizations*, 4th edition. Belmont, CA: Wadsworth.

Grant, R. M. (1996) 'Toward a knowledge–based theory of the firm', *Strategic Management Journal*, 17 (Winter Special Issue): 109–122.

Gupta, A. K. and Govindarajan, V. (2000) 'Knowledge flows within multinational corporations', *Strategic Management Journal*, 21: 473–496.

Hansen, M. T. (1999) 'The search–transfer problem: The role of weak ties in sharing knowledge across organization subunits', *Administrative Science Quarterly*, 44: 82–111.

Hansen, M. T. (2002) 'Knowledge networks: Explaining effective knowledge sharing in multiunit companies', *Organization Science*, 13 (3): 232–248.

Hargadon, A. and Sutton, R. I. (2000) 'Building an Innovation Factory', *Harvard Business Review*, 78 (3): 157–166.

Hass, M. R. and Hansen, M. T. (2005) 'When using knowledge can hurt performance: The value of organizational capabilities in a management consulting company', *Strategic Management Journal*, 26: 1–24.

Huber, G. P. (2006) 'Designing Firms for Knowledge Acquisition and Absorptive Capacity', in R. M. Burton, B. Eriksen, D. D. Hakonsson, and C. C. Snow (eds), *Organization Design: The Evolving State-of-the-Art*. New York: Springer.

Ibarra, H., Kilduff, M. and Tsai, W. (2005) 'Zooming in and out: Connecting individuals and collectivities at the frontiers of organizational network research', *Organization Science*, 16: 359–371.

Ingram, P. and Simons, T. (2002) 'The transfer of experience in groups of organizations: Implications for performance and competition', *Management Science*, 48 (12): 1517–1533.

Inkpen, A. C. and Tsang, E. W. K. (2005) 'Social capital, networks, and knowledge transfer', *Academy of Management Review*, 30 (1): 146–165.

Jackson, S. E., Chuang, C.-H., Harden, E. E. and Jiang, Y. (2006) 'Toward developing human resource management systems for knowledge-intensive teamwork', in J. Martocchio (ed.), *Research in Personnel and Human Resources Management*. The Netherlands: Elsevier, pp. 27–70.

Jackson, S. E., Hitt, M. A. and DeNisi, A. S. (2003) 'Managing Human Resources for Knowledge-Based Competition: New Research Direction', in S. E. Jackson, M. A. Hitt, and A. S. Denisi (eds), *Managing Knowledge for Sustained Competitive Advantage*. San Francisco: Jossey-Bass, pp. 399–428.

Jehn, K. A. (1995) 'A multimethod examination of the benefits and detriments of intragroup conflict', *Administrative Science Quarterly*, 40: 256–282.

Kanfer, R. and Ackerman, P. L. (1989) 'Motivation and cognitive abilities: An integrative/aptitude–treatment interaction approach to skill acquisition', *Journal of Applied Psychology*, 74: 657–690.

Kang, S.-C., Morris, S. S. and Snell, S. A. (2006) 'Relational archetypes, organizational learning, and value creation: Extending the human resource architecture', *Academy of Management Review*, 32 (1): 236–256.

Kelloway, E. K. and Barling, J. (2000) 'Knowledge work as organizational behavior', *International Journal of Management Reviews*, 2 (3): 287–304.

Kogut, B. and Zander, U. (1992) 'Knowledge and the firm, combinative capabilities, and the replication of technology', *Organization Science*, 3 (3): 383–397.

Kogut, B. and Zander, U. (1996) 'What do firms do? Coordination, identity and learning', *Organization Science*, 7 (5): 502–518.

Kostova, T. and Roth, K. (2002) 'Adoption of an organizational practice by subsidiaries of multinational corporations: Institutional and relational effects', *Academy of Management Journal*, 45: 215–233.

Lado, A. A. and Wilson, M. C. (1994) 'Human resource systems and sustained competitive advantage: A competency-based perspective', *Academy of Management Review*, 19 (4): 699–727.

Langan-Fox, J. (2003) 'Skill Acquisition and the Development of a Team Mental Model', in M. A. West, D. Tjosvold, and K. G. Smith (eds), *International Handbook of Teamwork and Cooperative Working*. Chichester, UK: Wiley, pp. 322–360.

Lawler, E. E. (2003) 'Reward Practices and Performance Management System Effectiveness', *Organizational Dynamics*, 32 (4): 396–406.

LePine, J. A., Colquitt, J. A. and Erez, A. (2000) 'Adaptability to changing task concerns: Effects of general cognitive ability, conscientiousness and openness to experience', *Personnel Psychology*, 53: 563–594.

Levin, D. Z., Whitener, E. M. and Cross, R. (2006) 'Perceived trustworthiness of knowledge sources: The moderating impact of relationship length', *Journal of Applied Psychology*, 91 (5): 1163–1171.

Liebeskind, J. P., Oliver, A. L., Zucker, L. and Brewer, M. (1996) 'Social networks, learning, and flexibility: Sourcing scientific knowledge in new biotechnology firms', *Organization Science*, 7: 428–443.

Locke, E. A. and Latham, G. P. (1990) *A Theory of Goal Setting and Task Performance*. Englewood Cliffs, NJ: Prentice Hall.

Lubit, R. (2001) 'Tacit knowledge and knowledge management: The keys to sustainable competitive advantage', *Organizational Dynamics*, 29 (3): 164–178.

Matusik, S. F. and Hill, C. W. L. (1998) 'The utilization of contingent work, knowledge creation, and competitive advantage', *Academy of Management Review*, 23 (4): 680–697.

Maurer, I. and Ebers, M. (2006) 'Dynamics of social capital and their performance implications: Lessons from biotechnology start-ups', *Administrative Science Quarterly*, 51: 263–292.

Mayer, R. C. and Davis, J. H. (1995) 'An integrative model of organizational trust', *Academy of Management Review*, 20 (3): 709–734.

McFadyen, M. A., Cannella, J. and Albert, A. (2004) 'Social capital and knowledge creation: Diminishing returns to the number and strength of exchange relationships', *Academy of Management Journal*, 47 (5): 735–746.

Mehra, A., Kilduff, M. and Brass, D. J. (2001) 'The social networks of high and low self-monitors: Implications for workplace performance', *Administrative Science Quarterly*, 46: 121–146.

Miles, R. E. (1989) 'Adapting to technology and competition: A new industrial relations system for the 21st century', *California Management Review*, 31 (2): 9–28.

Montemayor, E. F. (1996) 'Congruence between pay policy and competitive strategy in high-performance firms', *Journal of Management*, 22: 889–908.

Moran, P. (2005) 'Structural vs. relational embeddedness: Social capital and managerial performance', *Strategic Management Journal*, 26: 1129–1151.

Nahapiet, J. and Ghoshal, S. (1998) 'Social capital, intellectual capital, and the organizational advantage', *Academy Of Management Review*, 23 (2): 242–266.

Nebus, J. (2006) 'Building collegial information networks: A theory of advice network generation', *Academy of Management Review*, 31 (3): 615–637.

Nelson, R. E. (1989) 'The strength of strong ties: Social networks and intergroup conflict in organizations', *Academy of Management Journal*, 32 (2): 377–401.

Noe, R. A., Colquitt, J. A., Simmering, M. J. and Alvarez, S. A. (2003) 'Knowledge management: Developing intellectual and social capital', in S. E. Jackson, M. A. Hitt and A. S. Denisi (eds), *Managing Knowledge for Sustained Competitive Advantage*. San Francisco: Jossey-Bass, pp. 209–242.

Nonaka, I., Toyama, R. and Byosière, P. (2003) 'A theory of organizational knowledge creation: Understanding the dynamics of creating knowledge', in M. Dierkes, A. B. Antal, J. Child and I. Nonaka (eds), *Handbook of Organizational Learning and Knowledge*. Oxford: Oxford University Press, pp. 491–517.

Oldham, G. R. (2003) 'Stimulating and supporting creativity in organizations', in S. E. Jackson, M. A. Hitt and A. S. Denisi (eds), *Managing Knowledge for Sustained Competitive Advantage*. San Francisco: Jossey-Bass, pp. 243–273.

Paulus, P. N., Larey, T. S. and Dzindolet, M. T. (2001) 'Creativity in groups and teams', in M. E. Turner (ed.), *Groups at Work: Theory and Research*. Hillsdale, NJ: Erlbaum, pp. 319–338.

Perry-Smith, J. E. and Shalley, C. E. (2003) 'The social side of creativity: A static and dynamic social network perspective', *Academy of Management Review*, 28 (1): 89–106.

Polanyi, M. (1967) *The Tacit Dimension*. London: Routledge.

Powell, W. W., Koput, K. W. and Smith–Doerr, L. (1996) 'Interorganizational collaboration and the locus of innovation: Networks of learning in biotechnology', *Administrative Science Quarterly*, 41: 116–145.

Pulakos, E. D., Dorsey, W. D. and Borman, W. C. (2003) 'Hiring for knowledge-based competition', in S. E. Jackson, M. A. Hitt and A. S. DeNisi (eds), *Managing Knowledge for Sustained Competitive Advantage: Designing Strategies for Effective Human Resource Management*. San Francisco: Jossey-Bass, pp. 155–177.

Reagans, R. and McEvily, B. (2003) 'Network structure and knowledge transfer: The effects of cohesion and range', *Administrative Science Quarterly*, 48 (2): 240–267.

Reagans, R., Zuckerman, E. and McEvily, B. (2004) 'How to make the team: Social networks vs. demography as criteria for designing effective teams', *Administrative Science Quarterly*, 49 (1): 101–133.

Reagans, R. and Zuckerman, E. W. (2001) 'Networks, diversity, and productivity: The social capital of corporate R&D teams', *Organization Science*, 12: 502–517.

Rosenkopf, L., Metiu, A. and George, V. P. (2001) 'From the bottom up? Technical committee activity and alliance formation', *Administrative Science Quarterly*, 46 (4): 748–772.

Rynes, S. L., Brown, K. G. and Colbert, A. E. (2002) 'Seven common misconceptions about human resource practices: Research findings versus practitioner beliefs', *Academy of Management Executive*, 16: 92–103.

Schulze, A. and Hoegl, M. (2006) 'Knowledge creation in new product development projects', *Journal of Management*, 32 (2): 210–236.

Scott, S. G. and Bruce, R. A. (1994) 'Determinants of innovative behavior: A path model of individual innovation in the workplace', *Academy of Management Journal*, 37 (3): 580–607.

Seibert, S. E., Kraimer, M. L. and Liden, R. C. (2001) 'A social capital theory of career success', *Academy of Management Journal*, 44 (2): 219–237.

Shaw, J. D., Gupta, N. and Delery, J. E. (2002) 'Pay dispersion and workforce performance: Moderating effects of incentives and interdependence', *Strategic Management Journal*, 23: 491–512.

Snell, S. A., Youndt, M. A. and Wright, P. M. (1996) 'Establishing a framework for research in strategic human resource management: Merging resource theory and organizational learning', in G. R. Ferris (ed.), *Research in Personnel and Human Resources Management*. Greenwich, CT: JAI Press, pp. 61–90.

Spender, J. C. and Grant, R. M. (1996) 'Knowledge and the firm: Overview', *Strategic Management Journal*, 17: 5–9.

Starbuck, W. H. (1992) 'Learning by knowledge intensive firms', *Journal of Management Studies*, 29 (6): 713–740.

Stevens, M. J. and Campion, M. A. (1999) 'Staffing work teams: Development and validation of a selection test for teamwork settings', *Journal of Management*, 25: 207–228.

Subramaniam, M. and Youndt, M. A. (2005) 'The influence of intellectual capital on the types of innovative capabilities', *Academy of Management Journal*, 48 (3): 450–463.

Swart, J. and Kinnie, N. (2003) 'Sharing knowledge in knowledge-intensive firms', *Human Resource Management Journal*, 13: 60–75.

Szulanski, G. (1996) 'Exploring internal stickiness: Impediments to the transfer of best practice within the firm', *Strategic Management Journal*, 17: 27–43.

Taggar, S. (2002) 'Individual creativity and group ability to utilize individual creative resources: A multilevel model', *Academy of Management Journal*, 45 (3): 315–330.

Taylor, A. and Greve, H. R. (2007) 'Superman or the fantastic four? Knowledge combination and experience in innovative teams', *Academy of Management Journal*, 49 (4): 723–740.

Tsai, W. (2002) 'Social structure of "competition" within a multiunit organization: Coordination, competition, and intra-organizational knowledge sharing', *Organizational Science*, 13: 179–190.

Tsai, W. and Ghoshal, S. (1998) 'Social capital and value creation: The role of intrafirm networks', *Academy of Management Journal*, 41 (4): 464–476.

Tsang, E. W. K. (2002) 'Acquiring knowledge by foreign partners from international joint ventures in a transition economy: learning-by-doing and learning myopia', *Strategic Management Journal*, 23 (9): 835–854.

Turner, K. L. and Makhija, M. V. (2006) 'The role of organizational controls in managing knowledge', *Academy of Management Review*, 31 (1): 197–217.

Uzzi, B. (1997) 'Social structure and competition in interfirm networks: The paradox of embeddedness', *Administrative Science Quarterly*, 42: 35–67.

Von Krogh, G., Ichijo, K. and Nonaka, I. (2000) *Enabling Knowledge Creation*. New York: Oxford University Press.

Von Hippel, E. (1994) ' "Sticky Information" and the locus of problem solving: Implications for innovation', *Management Science*, 40 (4): 429–439.

Wadhwa, A. and Kotha, S. (2007) 'Knowledge creation through external venturing: Evidence from the telecommunications equipment manufacturing industry', *Academy of Management Journal*, 49 (4): 819–835.

West, M. A. (2002) 'Ideas are ten a penny: It's team implementation not idea generation that counts', *Applied Psychology: An International Review*, 51 (3): 411–424.

West, M.A. and Hirst, G. (2003) 'Cooperation and teamwork for innovation', in M.A. West, D. Tjosvold and K.G. Smith (eds), *International Handbook of Organizational Teamwork and Cooperative Working*. Chichester: John Wiley, pp. 297–319.

Yli-Renko, H., Autio, E. and Sapienza, H. J. (2001) 'Social capital, knowledge acquisitions, and knowledge exploitation in young technology-based firms', *Strategic Management Journal*, 22 (6/7): 587–613.

Zarraga, C. and Bonache, J. (2005) 'The impact of team atmosphere on knowledge outcomes in self-managed teams', *Organization Science*, 26 (5): 661–681.

Zenger, T. R. and Marshall, C. R. (2000) 'Determinants of incentive intensity in group-based rewards', *Academy of Management Journal*, 43: 149–163.

Zhou, J. (2003) 'When the presence of creative coworkers is related to creativity: Role of supervisor close monitoring, developmental feedback, and creative personality', *Journal of Applied Psychology*, 88 (3): 413–422.

Zirger, B. J. and Maidique, M. (1990) 'A model of new product development: An empirical test', *Management Science*, 36 (7): 867–883.

Zollo, M. and Singh, H. (2004) 'Deliberate learning in corporate acquisitions: Post-acquisition strategies and integration capability in U.S. bank mergers', *Strategic Management Journal*, 25: 1233–1256.

21

High-Performance Work Systems

Roderick D. Iverson, Christopher D. Zatzick
and Melissa M. McCrae

INTRODUCTION

Over the past decade, researchers have examined the use of high-performance work systems (HPWS) and the potential of HPWS for generating increased productivity and performance for organizations (Becker and Huselid, 2006; Wood and Wall, 2002). Although there is some debate about what constitutes a high-performance work system, at the broadest level it involves a strategic approach to the management of human resources such that employees at all levels have an impact on their jobs as well as the organization as a whole. HPWS are synergistic and mutually reinforcing bundles of human resources (HR) practices that are intended to improve employee performance by an increase in the knowledge, skills, and abilities (KSA) of employees, the motivation to use those KSA, and the empowerment to act. HPWS, when supported by an organization's overall human resource management (HRM) strategy, positively impact quality and productivity and generates a sustainable competitive advantage for an organization.

The broader field encompassing HPWS is Strategic Human Resources Management (SHRM). SHRM emphasizes the ability of HRM to move beyond a merely functional role to one that is essential to the development and implementation of organizational strategy. In particular, SHRM focuses on the bundles of HR practices that align an HPWS with the organization's strategy. Various terms have been used to reflect this perspective including innovative (Ichniowski et al., 1997), high-commitment (Wood and de Menezes, 1998), and high-involvement work practices (Guthrie, 2001; Lawler, 1992; Zatzick and Iverson, 2006). Throughout this chapter we will use the term HPWS to cover them all.

Our chapter begins with a review of the origins of HPWS followed by a summary of the key assumptions and classic studies that have shaped the field. Next, we examine the recent research that utilized international samples, moderators of the HPWS-performance relationship, and non-performance outcomes.

We then examine the key debates in the field including some of the major theoretical and methodological issues. Finally we discuss several emerging research areas in the field.

ORIGINS OF HPWS

The emergence of HPWS occurred in response to several major changes in the work environment. First, the transformation of Japanese manufacturing plants played an influential role in the development of HPWS. A number of researchers and practitioners have highlighted the value creation potential through the implementation of Japanese management practices (Ouchi, 1981; Pascale and Athos, 1981; Peters and Waterman, 1982). In the face of the growing threat from overseas, the US manufacturing industry adopted many of the practices fuelling the success of Japanese manufacturers. These practices included job rotation, teamwork, training, total-quality management (TQM), quality circles, and employment security (Cappelli and Neumark, 2001). Deming's original work in the 1950s in Japan also influenced many organizations to adopt these practices (see Deming, 1986). As these practices began to diffuse into US manufacturing plants, researchers examined the potential benefits (i.e., increased quality and productivity) from implementing them (Katz et al., 1983; Katz et al., 1985; Womack et al., 1990). Thus, the emergence of HPWS was in part a response to competitive forces in the increasingly global environment.

Second, as traditional sources of competitive advantage, such as price, product quality, and technology, became easier to imitate, the importance of HR systems increased. To respond to quickly changing environments, organizations needed to be faster and more flexible in shifting internal resources and processes. Becker and Huselid (1998) noted that placing the responsibility for the development and maintenance of the HR system solely within the traditional HRM department would be a strong impediment to the development of a strategic HR system that

was aligned to the needs of the firm. Thus, an increasing emphasis on the strategic role of HRM was evident in the development of HPWS.

Finally, Guest (1987) noted that during this time period there was a push for HR to be distinctive from other paradigms (e.g., personnel management and industrial relations). This entailed managing employees for competitive advantage and moving beyond the Tayloristic approach where employees and their skills were not valued or developed. Likewise, the command and control management styles were non-responsive to changing work environments. Thus, rather than keeping employees under tight control with little or no discretion, HR began to advocate the devolution of responsibility. As such, HR could increase its value to the organization by moving from a guardian of employees to a value generating strategic partner within the organization (Barney and Wright, 1998).

KEY ASSUMPTIONS

Several key assumptions underpin HPWS. These comprise the resource-based view of the firm, the synergy of practices, and the fit and configuration between HR practices and organizational strategy. We address each of these below.

Resources-based view of the firm

A primary theoretical foundation of HPWS derives from the resource-based view (RBV) of the firm (Barney, 1991). The underlying assumption of the RBV is that firms are heterogeneous with respect to the strategic resources that they possess, and these strategic resources are not perfectly mobile across firms, so are therefore a potential source of competitive advantage. If managed properly, the internal resources within a firm can provide excess returns to an organization. Researchers use the RBV to provide a theoretical foundation for the argument that investments in employee capabilities can contribute to a sustainable competitive advantage

(Barney and Wright, 1998; Huselid, 1995; Wright et al., 2001). The RBV argues that a competitive advantage is created when a firm's human resource management system is valuable, rare, difficult to imitate, and non-substitutable (Barney, 1991). Value creation comes from the development of HPWS that facilitates the implementation of firm strategy. However, the advantage can only be sustained over time when such a system is rare and has low imitability, and is non-substitutable. The issue of inimitability requires more discussion.

The two main features of HPWS that make them difficult to imitate are path dependency and causal ambiguity (Collis and Montgomery, 1995). Path dependency suggests that resources and systems are developed over time, and the experiences and learning that accompany that process are difficult to quickly attain. Therefore, a competitor would need to follow a similar path to the development of a new HR system, and the competitive advantage would remain intact for a longer period of time. In addition, causal ambiguity makes it difficult to imitate resources when competitors cannot fully understand the underlying cause of a particular advantage, and therefore cannot reproduce the advantage in their firm. Because HR systems result in complex social phenomena, they are difficult for other firms to interpret and replicate, helping maintain a sustainable competitive advantage (Barney, 1991, 1995). Finally, as we will discuss later, HPWS comprise one part of an organization's HR architecture (Lepak and Snell, 1999), increasing the difficulty for competitors to imitate.

Synergies of practices

A second major assumption is that HPWS are a system of interconnected HR practices. The systemic and interrelated nature of HPWS provides a competitive advantage that cannot be obtained from implementing individual HR practices. Barney (1995) contends that individual practices 'have limited ability to generate competitive advantage in isolation' (p. 56). Some argue that HR practices have an additive effect, where more practices present within a system result in higher performance returns (MacDuffie, 1995). Others propose that a combination of practices can be of greater benefit than the sum of the impact of each individual practice (Delery and Doty, 1996; Huselid, 1995). Hence, the additive effects of practices are difficult to imitate. For these reasons, many researchers study the effects of systems or bundles of practices on performance, rather than individual HR practices in isolation.

HPWS consist of a diverse set of practices that encompass both work design and the support systems used to develop, attract, motivate, and retain high-quality employees in the organization. MacDuffie (1995) referred to these two bundles as Work Systems and HRM policies indices. Work design practices such as team-based work structures, TQM, job rotation, and quality circles are designed to engage employees in their work by offering increased autonomy, decision-making, and information sharing. In addition, these practices are designed to increase flexibility and efficiencies in the product and service delivery process. Employees' roles are expanded through multi-skilling and job variety, which enables team members to do each other's jobs and rotate roles as needed. Further, employees can be part of problem-solving groups or consultative committees that discuss issues such as quality management or performance, and make important decisions related to products, services, finances, and HR management.

General or supportive HR practices are essential to supporting work reorganization initiatives by aligning hiring, training, and compensation practices with the new work designs. These practices typically include comprehensive recruitment and selection procedures, extensive training, performance-based compensation, information sharing, and flexible working arrangements (Jones and Wright, 1992). Sophisticated recruitment and selection mechanisms are necessary to hire employees who fit the organization's culture, work design, and strategic needs. Additionally, training and development is needed to increase employees' knowledge, skills and abilities, and better enable them to take on additional roles and responsibilities and participate in increased team-oriented work. HPWS also have increased upward and downward communication, such as sharing information on financial performance or staffing plans, and attaining employee feedback through surveys and opportunities to voice questions and comments. Pay in HPWS generally consists of a higher degree of contingent pay than traditional organizations. This includes profit-sharing, gain-sharing, share purchase plans, and performance-based pay, including pay tied to group performance. Finally, HPWS often include family friendly practices, such as child care, elder care, sick leave, male and female parental leave, and flexible working arrangements, which better enable employees to balance the demands of home and work. Flexible working arrangements often give employees greater control over how they do their job and the pace at which they work.

In their book *Manufacturing Advantage,* Appelbaum et al. (2000) argue that HR practices need to be supported by an overall strategic orientation reflected in practices throughout the organization. Specifically, the degree of autonomy that workers enjoy on the job needs to be complemented by greater access to information, the use of self-directed teams on the production floor, as well as off-line problem-solving and quality improvement teams. The authors identify some of the practices supporting HPWS within a manufacturing plant, including extensive selection mechanisms, investments in training, employment security, and gainsharing programs. Furthermore, the authors conclude that it is necessary to adopt practices related to all aspects in order for HPWS to be effectively in place. It is important to note that these types of practices are not exclusively the domain of manufacturing and can be implemented in other industries. Therefore,

although there is substantial variety as to the specific practices that encompass HPWS, there is general agreement that the practices cover a variety of work designs and HR systems throughout the organization.

Fit and configuration

Another key assumption of HPWS is the alignment among the HR practices and strategy (Huselid, 1995; Jackson and Schuler, 1995; Schuler, 1992; Wright and McMahan, 1992). At issue here is whether the universal, contingency, or configurational approach provides the best description of how systems of connected practices influence performance. In terms of the universal approach, there are certain 'best-practice' HR practices that organizations should adopt regardless of the organizational strategy pursued. That is, these practices when internally or horizontally consistent lead to greater organizational performance. Internal, or horizontal, consistency refers to the synergy between the practices that enables these to support each other and create a mutually reinforcing system (Barney, 1995). Hence, best-practice HR practices with good internal fit lead to optimal outcomes for all types of organizations.

The contingency approach focuses on external or vertical consistency. External consistency refers to alignment of an HR system with the firm's corporate strategy (Schuler and Jackson, 1987; Youndt et al., 1996) and emphasizes external fit. Thus, the effect that HPWS have on an organization's performance is contingent on their fit with the organization's strategy.

The third approach, configurational, extends the contingency approach by highlighting the need for both external consistency between HR practices and organizational strategy and internal consistency among HR practices. The two types of consistency are required to achieve organizational effectiveness (Delery and Doty, 1996). Basically, this perspective also allows for the formulation of an ideal bundle for an organization.

As noted by Becker and Huselid (2006) the debate among the universal, contingency, and configurational approaches in explaining the HPWS-performance relationship has been empirically rather than theoretically driven. We concur with Bowen and Ostroff (2004) that in order to build a strong HR system, it must be high on consistency (internal and external) and visibility, whereby HPWS are salient and observable to employees. These send an unequivocal message to employees about their value to the organization and how they fit with the strategy of the organization. At the end of this chapter, we discuss some opportunities for future research on the contingency and configurational approaches.

CLASSIC STUDIES

Several studies provide the empirical foundation for studying the link between HPWS and firm performance. We provide a brief summary of each article, including an emphasis on the treatment of HPWS (or the equivalent term) and firm performance.

In the early and mid-1990s, Arthur (1992) took the first steps towards operationalizing HPWS in a study of American steel minimills. Using two questionnaires sent to both HR managers and mill managers, Arthur analyzed the use of HR systems and business strategies at 30 mills. Overall, he concluded that HPWS fit best for firms with a differentiation strategy rather than a cost reduction strategy. He reasoned that firms with a differentiation strategy need their employees to be committed, flexible, and multi-skilled to allow for greater adaptability and performance, whereas firms with a cost reduction strategy can easily replace their employees, making employee involvement and contentment less important.

Subsequently, Arthur (1994) examined the effects of control vs. commitment HR systems on productivity. He found that high-commitment systems were associated with higher levels of productivity (measured in labor hours), and lower scrap rates and turnover than more traditional control HR systems. Although he had proposed that the contingency perspective was appropriate in his previous study, his follow-up study led him to conclude that the commitment approach was a better system for improving firm performance (i.e., universal perspective). In addition, he posited that the adoption of HPWS would result in less union conflicts and would be better for the successful implementation of new technologies.

In 1995, two highly influential studies with dramatically different methodologies were published. MacDuffie (1995) examined the independent and interactive effects of the bundles of HRM policies and Work Systems on labor productivity. Using a survey of 62 automotive assembly plants, he found that these bundles of HR practices contributed to productivity and quality improvements to the highest extent when they were implemented within a flexible production system versus a traditional mass production plant. These results confirm the interconnected nature of practices throughout HPWS, as well as provide evidence that fits with the operational strategy is important (i.e., contingency).

In an attempt to address a number of methodological limitations with previous HPWS studies, Huselid (1995) undertook a study to assess the impact of HPWS on organizational performance. Huselid argued that a number of methodological issues were limiting the value of previous studies. Often, previous research was cross-sectional, making it difficult to infer causation. Further, most of the recent research before his study used questionnaires for all data collection. Huselid dealt with these problems by using productivity and turnover as intermediate performance measures, as well as comprehensive financial information from 10-K reports for financial outcomes. Using a sample of 968 firms from a variety of industries, Huselid (1995) showed that HPWS have economically and statistically significant impacts on organizational performance. Specifically, HPWS affected the intermediate employee outcomes of turnover and productivity, and both short- and long-term corporate financial performance. His study found limited support for the contingency perspective; the HPWS and performance relationship was evident across industries and strategies.

Delery and Doty (1996) provided an empirical test of the universalistic, contingency, and configurational perspectives. Using Miles and Snow's typology (1978), they developed a theoretical rationale for why certain HR practices (internal career opportunities, formal training systems, appraisal measures, profit sharing, employment security, voice mechanisms, and job definition) were more appropriate for a defender strategy, analyzer strategy, and prospector strategy, as well as for internal and market-based employment systems. Delery and Doty predicted that organizations that align their practices with their strategy will have greater performance. Using a sample of 114 firms from the banking industry, they collected HR practice information from HR managers and strategy information from bank presidents. Performance information was taken from an external database. They found strong support for the universal perspective in that some HR practices resulted in increased performance regardless of firm strategy. They also reported some support for the contingency and configurational perspectives, where firm strategy moderated the relationship between several HR practices and performance. Importantly, they focused on individual HR practices rather than bundles of practices. The authors concluded that the study of HR practices will likely continue to increase in complexity with a greater focus on the contingency and configurational perspectives.

Similar to Delery and Doty (1996), Youndt et al. (1996) attempted to determine whether the universal or contingency perspectives were better at predicting the HPWS–performance relationship. Using a longitudinal study of 97 manufacturing plants, they measured productivity relative to other firms in terms of product quality, employee morale, on-time delivery, inventory management, employee productivity, machine efficiency, production lead time, and scrap minimization. They surveyed general and functional managers initially and then again after one and a half years. Controlling for organization size and industry, they found that HR systems that were focused on human capital enhancement were related to operational performance when the organization's manufacturing strategy focused on quality. Therefore, Youndt et al. found support for the contingency perspective, rather than the universal perspective for HR system effectiveness.

Finally, Ichniowski et al. (1997) investigated the effects of innovative employment practices on the productivity of steel finishing lines. They used 2190 monthly observations on productivity at 36 homogeneous steel production lines owned by seventeen companies. Their data collection was quite extensive: they conducted standardized interviews with HR, labor relations, and operations managers, superintendents, line workers, and union representatives, and reviewed other primary source documents, such as personnel files and manuals, collective bargaining agreements. Ichniowski et al. compared the productivity of lines that used innovative work practices, including incentive pay, teams, flexible job assignments, employment security, and training, to lines with a more traditional approach, including narrow job definitions, strict work rules, and hourly pay with close supervision. From their analysis, they found that HPWS were positively related to firm productivity. In addition, they compared the productivity effects of the HR systems and individual HR practices, and found that the individual practices had no additional impact on productivity.

Taken together, the results of the classic studies provide support for a positive relationship between various systems, indices, and bundles of HR practices and firm productivity and performance.

RECENT RELEVANT STUDIES

International samples

The majority of samples in the classic studies discussed above consisted of companies located in the US. This raises an important question of whether or not the link between HPWS and firm performance translates to companies outside of the US. We do not discuss all studies in detail, but do focus more attention on some non-western studies.[1] The evidence on the HPWS-performance link is accumulating and we find support across the UK (e.g., Hoque, 1999; Wood and de Menezes, 1998); Canada (e.g., Zatzick and Iverson, 2006); New Zealand (e.g., Guthrie, 2001); and Spain (e.g., de Saa-Perez and Garcia-Falcon, 2002; Kintana et al., 2006). Interestingly, one might expect countries that differ from the US in terms of cultural dimensions (e.g., individualism-collectivism; see the Chapter by Gardner and Earley in this volume) would have varying HPWS-performance relationships. Several studies of Taiwan-based organizations found support for a positive relationship between HPWS and performance (Chen et al., 2005; Shih et al., 2006; Tsai, 2006). In addition, researchers have reported positive effects of HPWS on firm performance in samples from other countries in the East and Southeast Asian regions (Bae et al., 2003; Bae and Lawler, 2000; Rowley and Benson, 2002). These findings provide affirmation of Katz and Darbishire's (2001) work, who in their global study concluded that there tends to be a convergence of HR practices across seven countries (e.g., US, Australia, Japan, UK, Sweden, Germany, and Italy) within the automotive and telecommunications industries. Hence, although there appears to be a globalization of HPWS, future theorizing and research is required to examine the potential for cross-cultural effects.

Meta-analysis results

As the research on HPWS continued to mount, the need to undertake a meta-analysis was warranted. In their meta-analysis, Combs et al. (2006) examined 92 studies and concluded that the use of HPWS was positively related to firm performance, with an overall correlation of 0.20. Moreover, in investigating the effects of HPWS against individual HR practices they found that the positive relationship between HPWS and organizational performance was significantly larger (0.28) than the relationship between individual HR practices and performance (0.14). Further, they proposed that because of extraneous factors and the time delay between HPWS implementation, operational measures and overall financial performance, the operational measures (productivity and retention) would display a stronger relationship with HPWS than financial measures (accounting returns, growth, and market returns). They did not find support for this hypothesis, and therefore conclude that researchers can use either operational or financial measures of organizational performance when studying the effect of HPWS.

Moderators

The robustness of the relationship between HPWS and performance has been well-established with a variety of samples and measures. Yet, a number of recent studies have examined factors that moderate the relationship between HPWS and performance. Three key moderators in the literature include employee turnover, organizational downsizing, and industry characteristics.

Employee turnover

Given the importance of employees in the implementation of HPWS, it is likely that changes in workforce composition will influence the relationship between HPWS and performance. Employee turnover will be costly as the departure of high performers includes the loss of valuable firm-specific skills. Likewise organizational learning may be lost when key employees leave the organization (Sung-Choon et al., 2007). Initially, Huselid (1995) showed a main effect of HPWS on employee turnover. Subsequently, Guthrie (2001), in an analysis of New Zealand organizations, observed that employee turnover was associated with decreased productivity when the level of HPWS was high and with increased productivity when the level of HPWS was low.

Organizational downsizing

There are also data to suggest that downsizing plays a moderating role. Zatzick and Iverson (2006), in a study of around 3,000 Canadian workplaces, reported that workplaces with higher layoff rates have a negative relationship between HPWS and productivity. Yet workplaces that continue to invest in HPWS during the layoff period were able to avoid productivity losses, as compared to workplaces that discontinue investments in HPWS. A number of other studies have also found a positive relationship between HPWS and the use of downsizing or layoffs (Cappelli and Neumark, 2004; Helper et al., 2002; Osterman, 2000).

Industry characteristics

Industry differences were also supported in the meta-analysis conducted by Combs et al. (2006). They found that the effect of HPWS on performance was greater for manufacturing than service organizations. They posited that this is likely because manufacturing organizations depend more on the ability of their workers and HR systems to adapt to changes in physical and technical infrastructure, which is a characteristic of HPWS. Datta and colleagues in their 2005 study examined the moderating effect of industry characteristics (capital intensity, growth, and differentiation) on the relationship between HPWS and productivity. Using survey data from a sample of 132 publicly traded firms from the manufacturing sector, they measured the percent of employees that were covered by 18 HR practices in exempt and non-exempt groups. Their performance measure was labor productivity, measured as total output divided by labor inputs. Overall, they found that industry capital intensity moderated the positive relationship between HPWS and labor productivity, where industries with lower capital intensity exhibited a stronger relationship. Further, they discovered that industry growth also moderated the relationship between HPWS and labor productivity, where more high-growth industries displayed a stronger relationship. Finally, they found that industry product differentiation moderated the relationship between HPWS and labor productivity, where industries with higher product differentiation exhibited a stronger relationship. Therefore, in addition to finding a positive relationship between HPWS and labor productivity, they also found that the industry context can affect the HPWS-productivity relationship.

We posit that the importance of moderators will continue to grow as researchers attempt to disentangle the HPWS-performance relationship.

Non-performance outcomes

A growing body of research has examined the implications of HPWS for employees. One such implication, wage outcomes for employees in HPWS, has received considerable attention from researchers. Handel and Levine (2004) provide a comprehensive review of over 20 studies that have examined the effects of HPWS on both individual (e.g., hourly or weekly earnings) and organizational (e.g., labor costs) wage outcomes. Small wage gains were found in some of the industry- and firm-specific studies, while few significant effects were found in studies using nationally representative samples. The authors conclude that employee involvement programs 'probably have no effect, but the average effect appears to be a few percentage points increase' (p. 39). Nevertheless, more research is required on this topic, as a recent study by Osterman (2006) reported wages gains for employees using a nationally representative sample (i.e., the 1997 National Establishment Survey).

In addition, a number of studies have examined individual reactions to the implementation of HPWS. Boselie et al. (2005) characterize these as HR outcomes (e.g., attitudinal and behavioral impacts such as job satisfaction, organizational commitment, and intention to leave). Indeed, studies have confirmed that employees working in HPWS have greater satisfaction (Appelbaum et al., 2000; Hunter et al., 2002) and organizational commitment (Agarwala, 2003). Recently, Batt (2004) found that satisfaction increased for employees working in self-managed work teams, but decreased for the supervisors of those employees. Other non-performance outcomes linked to HPWS include reduced work-family conflict (Batt and Valcour, 2003), fewer workplace injuries (Barling et al., 2003; Zacharatos et al., 2005), and lower grievance rates (Colvin, 2004).

THEORETICAL DEBATES

There are several major theoretical perspectives that have been advanced to explain the process by which HPWS impact on organizational performance. These approaches essentially focus on consensus or conflict between management and employees and comprise social exchange, psychological contract, organizational trust, labor process and numerical flexibility theory. As discussed below, all approaches have been drawn on in the literature, with social exchange being the most prominent.

Social exchange
In understanding the influence of HPWS on employees' attitudes and behaviors, some scholars apply a social exchange and norm of reciprocity framework (see Coyle-Shapiro and Conway, 2005 for a comprehensive discussion). Tsui et al. (1997) used the term 'employee-organization-relationship strategy' to characterize an organization's approach to the employment relationship, including balanced and unbalanced relationships. Whitener (2001) drawing on the work of Blau (1964) and Homans (1961), proposes that HPWS involve using HR practices to encourage employees to align to the goals of the organization and exert discretionary effort to achieve them. HPWS are designed to promote employee development, improve work and employee quality, and protect employee interests. Other researchers such as Farrell and Rusbult (1981) proposed an investment model, where employees consider HR practices as rewards, which are then reciprocated back to the organization in terms of their attitudes (e.g., commitment

and involvement) and behavior (e.g., performance) (Zacharatos et al., 2005). Essentially, HPWS involves using HR practices to build an environment of positive exchange and reciprocity between an organization and it's employees.

HPWS can also be viewed through the lens of psychological contract (see Chapter by Coyle-Shapiro in the Handbook). Argyris (1960), Levinson (1962), and Schein (1965) originally used the concept of psychological contract to describe an implicit agreement, or overlap of expectations, between the parties to an employment relationship. Rousseau (1989) utilized the concept to explain the exchange relationship, where employees provide their contributions in exchange for inducements from their employers. Hannah and Iverson (2004) note that inducements may include such HR practices as pay, benefits, and job security; contributions can include exerting effort and loyalty. Each inducement and contribution, that is, each component of an employment relationship, can be classified as either 'hard' or 'soft.' Hard or transactional components comprise the economic part of the employment relationship and are measurable, tangible, and monetizable (e.g., pay for performance; being punctual). Soft or relational components are those that are non-monetizable, less tangible, and hard-to-measure (e.g., devolution of responsibility; loyalty). Within the HPWS paradigm, the exchange of hard and soft inducements with their associated expectations, leads to employee engagement and higher organizational performance.

Organizational trust
Also implicit within the HPWS framework is the notion of organizational trust. Deery et al. (2006) argue that the degree to which an organization has fulfilled its contractual obligations in the employment relationship will affect the level of trust. Kramer (1999) defines trusts as a '... state of perceived vulnerability or risk that is derived from individuals' uncertainty regarding the motives, intentions, and prospective actions of others on whom they depend (p. 571). Although

few studies have empirically examined the HPWS-trust relationship, Zacharatos et al. (2005) observed HPWS to be positively related to trust in management. Hence, when organizations fulfil their obligations via HPWS, employees trust in management increases.

Labor process theory

An alternative approach to explain the HPWS-performance link is labor process theory. Orlitzky and Frenkel (2005) note that in an era of flexible specialization or post-Fordism, employees are coerced to work harder by management providing them with greater job discretion and additional job responsibilities. That is, HPWS leads to work intensification for employees. HPWS promote employees working harder with less job security. HR practices such as incentive pay have found to be linked to higher effort levels (Green and McIntosh, 1998). However, the evidence supporting the labor process theory is mixed. Appelbaum et al. (2000), for example, found no relationship between HPWS and role overload or increased stress, while Godard (2001) found a U-shaped relationship between HR practices and stress. Although Ramsay et al. (2000) found some evidence for the labor process, they concluded from their results that we should not accept the assumption that 'gains to management always come at the expense for labor of degradation of work' (p. 521).

Numerical flexibility theory

Another conflict approach is numerical flexibility theory, which assumes that labor is a cost to be minimized. That is, the use of various HR practices such as contingent (i.e., part-time, temporary, contract) employment helps to contain costs. Associated with the cost containment approach are reduced job security, reduced hours, intense supervision and a lack of attention to training and development. Employees are seen to be disposable and easy to replace. This precarious situation motivates employees to perform. In testing this model, Orlitzky and Frenkel (2005) found some support, although the effects varied across industries. Part-time employees were associated with numerical flexibility, which in turn impacted on labor productivity (relative to competitors). This was substantially higher in manufacturing than service workplaces.

At present there appears to be more support for the consensus rather than conflict approaches in understanding the HPWS-performance relationship. Nevertheless, given the lack of standardization in measures and study designs (to be discussed below), we need to be somewhat circumspect about this conclusion.

METHODOLOGICAL DEBATES

Similar to the theoretical debates, there are major issues surrounding the methodology employed in HPWS research. These debates focus on research design, configurations of HR practices, and the measurement of HPWS and outcomes.

Research design

Reviewing 68 empirical studies on HPWS and performance, Wright et al. (2005) concluded that causation tends to be inferred rather than empirically supported. They observed few studies (less than 15 per cent) use a 'predictive' design, where HR practices effect performance. Moreover, when researchers control for past performance, the correlation between HR practices and subsequent performance significantly decreases (Guest et al., 2003; Wright et al., 2005). Interestingly, the vast majority of studies (over 70 per cent) use a 'post-predictive' design where HR practices are measured after performance. A third type of design is 'retrospective,' whereby HR managers are asked to recall the practices that existed prior to the performance data. Other researchers collect data on HPWS and performance contemporaneously. Finally, few studies examine reverse causation, whereby firm performance predicts HR practices. In sum, most studies apply a cross-sectional rather than a longitudinal design, which limits the claims of causation.

Configurations of HR practices

Reviewing the literature, it becomes apparent that there is little consensus over the nature and number of practices in HPWS. As discussed previously, a recent meta-analysis by Combs et al. (2006) highlights that HPWS have a significantly better impact on firm performance than individual practices. Early studies tended to focus on a set of general core HR practices (e.g. internal career opportunities, formal training systems, appraisal measures, profit sharing, employment security, voice mechanisms, and job definition (Delery and Doty, 1996). However, there was little standardization across studies (e.g., Huselid, 1995; MacDuffie, 1995). In terms of bundles there is also little agreement. For example, Datta et al. (2005) combined 18 diverse HR practices to form a single HPWS bundle, while Zatzick and Iverson (2006) used six HR practices focused on employee involvement. Multiple bundles have also been popular in the research, such as MacDuffie's (1995) work systems and HRM policies and Huselid's (1995) skills and structures and motivation.

Measures of HPWS have advanced from an initial focus on the presence or absence of a HR practice (MacDuffie, 1995) to a focus on the degree of coverage of practices within an organization (Datta et al., 2005; Guthrie, 2001). Future studies should assess the effectiveness of HR practices, rather than simply who does or does not receive the practices (Boselie et al., 2005). In other words, workplaces offering flextime may only do so superficially, rather than actually having an efficacious flextime policy where employees are encouraged to arrange their work and personal schedules according to their needs. With respect to the question of which HR practices fit in HPWS, researchers need to justify the inclusion or exclusion of practices based on the theoretical processes with which the practices are expected to influence performance. For example, the industry differences (between manufacturing and service industries) identified by Combs et al. (2006) reflect the need to contextualize the practices grouped together. While HPWS in manufacturing operations require work reorganization practices, HPWS in service industries require HR practices increasing employee involvement (Combs et al., 2006).

Measurement error bias

When one respondent is the key informant (e.g., HR manager), there is potential for measurement error bias. If that person provides self-report data on HR practices and business performance, conflation may also occur. That is, the HPWS-performance relationship is artificially increased (Wood and Wall, 2002). While some researchers call for multiple informants (at multiple levels) to address these types of issues (Gerhart et al., 2000; Wall et al., 2004), other researchers have questioned the feasibility of such a research design. Typically, these studies have low response rates, a small sample of firms with multiple respondents, and inter-rater reliability being estimated on these samples (Becker and Huselid, 2006). Podsakoff et al. (2003) recommend that to mitigate common method bias, researchers need to collect objective (e.g., hours of training and performance data) and longitudinal data.

Performance measurement

Two contentious issues surround performance measurement. The first is self-report (i.e., perceptual) versus objective data. Boselie et al. (2005) note that there is a temptation for HR managers to portray their organizations in a positive light (i.e., social desirability bias). Wall et al. (2004) comparing subjective (relative to other establishments in same industry) and objective performance measures note that 'across the studies they (correlations) were typically in the order of 0.40 to 0.60, which leaves considerable independent variation in each' (p.113). Moreover, the issue of 'nonequivalence' between subjective and objective performance measures needs to be addressed. Second, there is great debate regarding what performance actually means. Guest (1997) recommended using 'outcomes' in preference to performance as it better captures the broad array of variables, while others have bifurcated variables into operational and financial performance (Combs et al., 2006; Huselid, 1995). Wall and Wood (2005) argue that greater attention to industry-specific indicators is required. For example, in non-profit organizations such as foodbanks, the number of food baskets distributed per staff member could be calculated. We suggest that it is prudent to consider performance as multi-dimensional, which is comprised of operational (i.e., productivity, quality, safety and retention) and financial (i.e., accounting returns, growth, and market returns) dimensions.

EMERGING RESEARCH AREAS

Disentangling the complex relationship between HPWS and organizational performance remains at the forefront of the research agenda. Clearly, more research is required to resolve the key debates discussed above, particularly related to the issues of measurement and causality. Improved research design is essential to increasing the validity and generalizability of HPWS. The existing evidence suggests that measuring a system of practices rather than individual practices alone is preferable, both theoretically (Barney, 1995) and empirically (Combs et al., 2006). Further, using multiple sources at multiple levels of analysis (i.e., CEO, HR managers, and front-line employees) provides greater information about the processes through which HPWS has an effect on performance. However, this may not always be practical. Any methodological advances must be considered concurrently with expanded theoretical models to better understand the processes of HPWS on performance.

A rather simplistic theoretical assumption in the literature is that one set of HR practices is used throughout an entire workplace or organization. Lepak and Snell's (1999) HR architecture offers a theoretical framework for understanding how different employment modes within a firm are needed for value creation. The four employment modes identified by Lepak and Snell (1999) are knowledge work, job-based employment, contract work, and alliance/partnerships. Each employment mode must be managed by different HR configurations, whereby a workplace can generate value through both numerical flexibility and employee involvement. In other words, employers treat employees differently. For example, organizations can hire and invest in core workers, while simultaneously using contingent or temporary employees for non-core or periphery work (Tsui et al., 1997).

This framework may explain why a number of studies have found a positive relationship between HPWS and downsizing (Cappelli and Neumark, 2004; Helper et al., 2002; Osterman, 2000; Zatzick and Iverson, 2006). It is common for workplaces to downsize one group of employees while continuing to hire and invest another group of employees. It may also explain why HPWS would downsize in an employee-friendly manner by using natural attrition and voluntary layoffs rather than the harsher downsizing practice of compulsory layoffs (Iverson and Zatzick, 2007). By taking care of employees when downsizing, organizations are able to maintain morale for employees throughout the organization. Therefore, the seemingly contradictory practices of HPWS and downsizing can coexist within a differentiated HR architecture.

Becker and Huselid (2006) argue that the strategic element of SHRM has been missing in the literature. Although early research found limited support for the contingency perspective, Becker and Huselid contend that strategic fit and implementation will mediate the relationship between HPWS and performance. In accordance with Lepak and Snell's HR architecture, they suggest that linking strategic direction with the various employment modes will provide the best approach for understanding the relationship between HPWS and performance. They posit that the 'black box' between HPWS and performance requires greater specification of how HPWS facilitates strategy implementation of core business processes. In other words, a contingency perspective at the level of business processes will provide the most direct link to value creation. A number of studies have focused on core employees (e.g., Delery and Doty, 1996; Osterman, 2006) or specific value chains (Collins and Smith, 2004) in an effort to increase the theoretical and empirical precision of their studies.

One such attempt to utilize strategic management theories is the incorporation of dynamic capabilities theory (Teece et al., 1997) into SHRM models. Within the resource-based view, the dynamic capabilities approach suggests firms will need 'processes to integrate, reconfigure, gain, and release resources to match and even create market change' (Wright et al., 2001: 713). In other words, dynamic capabilities theory suggests that high-performance workplaces need to make internal adjustments to structure and processes to renew organizational capabilities and sustain a competitive advantage. This theory informs the types of processes required for strategy implementation of core business processes (Becker and Huselid, 2006). Thus, future research would benefit from examining how organizations renew their HPWS.

The renewal of HPWS over time may be extremely difficult for organizations. The intractability of organizational systems and routines (Hannah and Freeman, 1984) suggest that HPWS will suffer from the same inertial forces that make it difficult for workplaces to change (Snell and Dean, 1994). HR practices are linked via an overall system making the removal or addition of an HR practice a potential shock to the system. For example, when an organization cuts back on HR as part of a larger restructuring plan, it can have negative consequences on employee productivity. We found that firms conducting downsizing suffer productivity losses, particularly when they cut back on HR practices at the same time (Zatzick and Iverson, 2006). Thus, future research needs

to investigate how workplaces adjust HPWS in response to environmental and competitive pressures. This will provide greater insights into the causal relationship between HPWS and productivity.

Other theoretical approaches in the strategic management literature could provide greater specification in strategy implementation. For example, the Value, Price, and Cost (VPC) framework posits that competitive advantage derives from an organization's ability to leverage its existing resources to create greater value and/or lower costs in the production process (V-C) (Hoopes et al., 2003). The VPC model allows a more precise test of strategic orientation as a factor influencing the successful implementation of core business processes. This theory can help explain how HPWS operate within an organization. One prediction would be that organizations seeking primarily a cost-based competitive advantage will experience greater performance outcomes from HR practices and work redesign that emphasize efficiencies (Zatzick et al., 2007). In contrast, workplaces emphasizing a competitive advantage through value creation will need HR practices that encourage innovation and employee discretionary effort. The VPC framework is more specific than the generic Miles and Snow (1978) typology used in prior research to test the consistency and configurational perspectives. It also recognizes the potential for firms with a cost reduction strategy to create value through HPWS. Therefore, additional research is needed to understand both the differentiated employment modes within an organization's HR architecture, as well as the various strategic orientations associated with the multiple employment modes.

CONCLUSION

During the past two decades, HPWS has emerged at the forefront of research on HRM. We believe that improved theoretical and methodological development will reconcile many of the conflicting findings in the literature. Researchers need to be attentive to potential mediators and moderators and explicate the conditions under which these operate. Clearly, there is a halo effect surrounding HPWS, with all stakeholders purporting to benefit. Although, this view is too simplistic and neglects the complexity of employment relationships, we are heartened by the most recent meta-analysis by Combs et al. (2006: 524) who conclude that 'organizations can increase their performance by .20 of a standard unit for each unit increase in [HPWS]…'

NOTE

1 We focus on HPWS at the organizational or workplace level and acknowledge that there is growing evidence at the individual level (e.g., Browning's 2006 study in South Africa).

REFERENCES

Agarwala, T. (2003) 'Innovative human resource practices and organizational commitment: an empirical investigation', *International Journal of Human Resource Management*, 14 (2): 175–197.

Appelbaum, E., Bailey, T., Berg, P. and Kalleberg, A.L. (2000) *Manufacturing Advantage: Why High Performance Work Systems Pay Off*. Ithaca, NY: Cornell University Press.

Argyris, C. (1960) *Understanding Organizational Behavior*. Homewood, IL: The Dorsey Press, Inc.

Arthur, J.B. (1992) 'The link between business strategy and industrial relations systems in American steel minimills', *Industrial and Labor Relations Review*, 45 (3): 488–506.

Arthur, J.B. (1994) 'Effects of human resource systems on manufacturing performance and turnover', *Academy of Management Journal*, 37 (3): 670–687.

Bae, J., Chen, S., Wan, D., Lawler, J.J. and Walumbwa, F. (2003) 'Human resource strategy and firm performance in Pacific Rim countries', *International Journal of Human Resource Management*, 14 (8): 1308–1332.

Bae, J. and Lawler, J.J. (2000) 'Organizational and HRM strategies in Korea: impact on firm performance in an emerging economy', *Academy of Management Journal*, 43 (3): 502–517.

Barling, J., Kelloway, E.K. and Iverson, R.D. (2003) 'High quality work, job satisfaction and occupational injuries', *Journal of Applied Psychology*, 88 (2): 276–283.

Barney, J. (1991) 'Firm resources and sustained competitive advantage', *Journal of Management*, 17 (1): 99–120.

Barney, J.B. (1995) 'Looking inside for competitive advantage', *Academy of Management Executive*, 9 (4): 49–61.

Barney, J. and Wright, P.M. (1998) 'On becoming a strategic partner: The role of human resources in gaining competitive advantage', *Human Resource Management*, 37 (1): 31–46.

Batt, R. (2004) 'Who benefits from teams? Comparing workers, supervisors, and managers', *Industrial Relations*, 43 (1): 183–212.

Batt, R. and Valcour, P.M. (2003) 'Human resources practices as predictors of work–family outcomes and employee turnover', *Industrial Relations*, 42 (2): 189–220.

Becker, B.E. and Huselid, M.A. (1998) 'High performance work systems and firm performance: A synthesis of research and managerial implications', *Research in Personnel and Human Resource Management*, 16: 53–101.

Becker, B.E. and Huselid, M.A. (2006) 'Strategic human resource management: Where do we go from here?', *Journal of Management*, 32 (6): 898–925.

Blau, P.M. (1964) *Exchange and Power in Social Life*. New York: John Wiley and Sons, Inc.

Boselie, P., Dietz, G. and Boon, C. (2005) 'Commonalities and contradictions in HRM and performance research', *Human Resource Management Journal*, 15 (3): 67–94.

Bowen, D.E. and Ostroff, C. (2004) 'Understanding HRM-firm performance linkages: The role of the "strength" of the HRM system', *Academy of Management Review*, 29 (2): 203–221.

Browning, V. (2006) 'The relationship between HRM practices and service behaviour in South African service organizations', *The International Journal of Human Resource Management*, 17 (7): 1321–1338.

Cappelli, P. and Neumark, D. (2001) 'Do "high-performance" work practices improve establishment-level outcomes?', *Industrial and Labor Relations Review*, 54 (4): 737–775.

Cappelli, P. and Neumark, D. (2004) 'External churning and internal flexibility: Evidence on the functional flexibility and core-periphery hypotheses', *Industrial Relations*, 43 (1): 148–182.

Chen, S., Lawler, J.J. and Bae, J. (2005) 'Convergence in human resource systems: A comparison of locally owned and MNC subsidiaries in Taiwan', *Human Resource Management*, 44 (3): 237–256.

Collins, C.J. and Smith, K.G. (2006) 'Knowledge exchange and combination: The role of human resource practices in the performance of high technology firms', *Academy of Management Journal*, 49 (3): 544–560.

Collis, D.J. and Montgomery, C.A. (1995) 'Competing on resources: Strategy for the 1990s', *Harvard Business Review*, July/August, 73 (4): 118–128.

Colvin, A.J.S. (2004) 'The relationship between employee involvement and workplace dispute resolution', *Industrial Relations*, 59 (4): 681–704.

Combs, J., Liu, Y., Hall, A. and Ketchen, D. (2006) 'How much do high-performance work practices matter? A meta-analysis of their effects on organizational performance', *Personnel Psychology*, 59 (3): 501–528.

Coyle-Shapiro, J.A-M. and Conway, N. (2005) 'The employment relationship through the lens of social exchange', in J.A-M. Coyle-Shapiro, L.M. Shore, M.S. Taylor and L.E. Tetrick (eds), *The Employment Relationship: Examining Psychological and Contextual Perspectives*. Oxford University Press, pp. 5–28.

Datta, D.K., Guthrie, J.P. and Wright, P.M. (2005) 'Human resource management and labor productivity: Does industry matter?', *Academy of Management Journal*, 48 (1): 135–145.

Deery, S.J., Iverson, R.D. and Walsh, J. (2006) 'Towards a better understanding of psychological contract violation: A study of customer service employees', *Journal of Applied Psychology*, 91 (1): 166–175.

Delery, J.E. and Doty, D.H. (1996) 'Modes of theorizing in strategic human resource management: Tests of universalistic, contingency, and configurational performance predictions', *Academy of Management Journal*, 39 (4): 802–835.

Deming, W.E. (1986) *Out of the Crisis*. Cambridge, MA: MIT Press.

de Saá–Pérez, P. and García–Falcón, J.M. (2002) 'A resource-based view of human resource management and organizational capabilities development', *International Journal of Human Resource Management*, 13 (1): 123–140.

Farrell, D. and Rusbult, C.E. (1981) 'Exchange variables as predictors of job satisfaction, job commitment and turnover: The impact of rewards, costs, alternatives and investments', *Organizational Behavior and Human Performance*, 28 (1): 78–95.

Gerhart, B., Wright, P.M., McMahan, G.C. and Snell, S.A. (2000) 'Measurement error in research on human resources and firm performance: How much error is there and how does in influence effect size estimates?', *Personnel Psychology*, 53 (4): 803–834.

Godard, J. (2001) 'High performance and the transformation of work? The implications of alternative work practices for the experience and outcomes of work', *Industrial and Labor Relations Review*, 54 (4): 776–805.

Green, F. and McIntosh, S. (1998) 'Union power, cost of job loss, and workers' effort', *Industrial and Labor Relations Review*, 51 (3): 363–383.

Guest, D.E. (1987) 'Human resource management and industrial relations', *Journal of Management Studies*, 24 (5): 503–521.

Guest, D.E. (1997) 'Human resource management and performance: A review and research agenda', *International Journal of Human Resource Management*, 8 (3): 263–276.

Guest, D.E., Michie, J., Conway, N. and Sheehan, M. (2003) 'Human resource management and corporate performance in the UK', *British Journal of Industrial Relations*, 41 (2): 291–314.

Guthrie, J.P. (2001) 'High involvement work practices, turnover and productivity: Evidence from New Zealand', *Academy of Management Journal*, 44 (1): 180–190.

Handel, M.J. and Levine, D. (2004) 'Editors' introduction: The effects of new work practices on workers', *Industrial Relations*, 43 (1): 1–43.

Hannah, M. and Freeman, J. (1984) 'Structural inertia and organizational change', *American Sociological Review*, 49 (2): 149–164.

Hannah, D. and Iverson, R.D. (2004) 'Employment relationships in context: Implications for policy and practice', in J.A-M. Coyle-Shapiro, L.M. Shore, M.S. Taylor and L.E. Tetrick (eds), *The Employment Relationship: Examining Psychological and Contextual Perspectives*. Oxford University Press, pp. 332–350.

Helper, S., Levine, D.I. and Bendoly, E. (2002) 'Employee involvement and pay at us and Canadian auto suppliers', *Journal of Economics and Management Strategy*, 11 (2): 329–377.

Homans, G.C. (1961) *Social Behavior: Its Elementary Forms*. New York: Harcourt, Brace & World.

Hoopes, D.G., Madsen, T.L. and Walker, G. (2003) 'Guest editors' introduction to the special issue: Why is there a resource-based view? Toward a theory of competitive heterogeneity', *Strategic Management Journal*, 24 (10): 889–902.

Hoque, K. (1999) 'Human resource management and performance in the UK hotel industry', *British Journal of Industrial Relations*, 37 (3): 419–443.

Hunter, L.W., Macduffie, J.P. and Doucet, L. (2002) 'What makes teams take? Employee reactions to work reforms', *Industrial and Labor Relations Review*, 55 (3): 448–472.

Huselid, M.A. (1995) 'The impact of human resource practices on turnover, productivity, and corporate financial performance', *Academy of Management Journal*, 38 (3): 635–672.

Ichniowski, C., Shaw, K. and Prennushi, G. (1997) 'The effects of human resource management practices on productivity: A study of steel finishing lines', *American Economic Review*, 87 (3): 291–313.

Iverson, R.D. and Zatzick, C.D. (2007) High-commitment work practices and downsizing harshness in Australian workplaces. *Industrial Relations*, 46 (3): 456–480.

Jackson, S.E. and Schuler, R.S. (1995) 'Understanding human resource management in the context of organizations and their environments', in J.T. Spence, J.M. Darley, and J. Foss (eds), *Annual Review of Psychology*. Palo Alto, CA: Annual Reviews, pp. 237–264.

Jones, G.R. and Wright, P.M. (1992) 'An economic approach to conceptualizing the utility of human resource management practices', in K. Rowland and G. Ferris (eds), *Research in Personnel and Human Resources Management*. Greewich, CT: JAI Press. Volume 10: pp. 271–299.

Katz, H.C. and Darbishire, O. (1999) *Converging Divergences: Worldwide Changes in Employment Systems*. Ithaca: ILR Press.

Katz, H.C., Kochan, T.A. and Gobielle, K.R. (1983) 'Industrial relations performance, economic performance, and QWI Programs: An interplant analysis', *Industrial and Labor Relations Review*, 37 (1): 3–17.

Katz, H.C., Kochan, T.A. and Weber, M.A. (1985) 'Assessing the effects of industrial relations systems and efforts to improve the quality of working life on organizational effectiveness', *Academy of Management Journal*, 28 (3): 509–526.

Kintana, M.L., Alonso, A.U. and Olaverri, C.G. (2006) 'High-performance work systems and firms' operational performance: The moderating role of technology', *International Journal of Human Resource Management*, 17 (1): 70–85.

Kramer, R.M. (1999) 'Trust and distrust in organizations: Emerging perspectives, enduring questions', *Annual Review of Psychology*, 50: 569–598.

Lawler, E. (1992) *The Ultimate Advantage: Creating the High-Involvement Organization*. San Francisco: Jossey-Bass.

Lepak, D.P. and Snell, S.A. (1999) 'The human resource architecture: Toward a theory of human capital allocation and development', *Academy of Management Review*, 24 (1): 31–48.

Levinson, H. (1962) *Men, Management, and Mental Health*. Cambridge, MA: Harvard University Press.

MacDuffie, J.P. (1995) 'Human resource bundles and manufacturing performance: Organizational logic

and flexible production systems in the world auto industry', *Industrial and Labor Relations Review*, 48 (2): 197–221.

Miles, R.E. and Snow, C.C. (1978) *Organizational Strategy, Structure, and Process*. New York: McGraw-Hill.

Orlitzky, M. and Frenkel, S.J. (2005) 'Alternative pathways to high-performance workplaces', *International Journal of Human Resource Management*, 16 (8): 1325–1348.

Ouchi, W.G. (1981) 'Organizational paradigms: A commentary on Japanese management and theory z organizations', *Organizational Dynamics*, 9 (4): 36–43.

Osterman, P. (2000) 'Work reorganization in an era of restructuring: Trends in diffusion and effects on employee welfare', *Industrial and Labor Relations Review*, 53 (2): 179–196.

Osterman, P. (2006) 'The wage effects of high performance work organization in manufacturing', *Industrial and Labor Relations Review*, 59 (2): 187–204.

Pascale, R.T. and Athos, A.G. (1981) *The Art of Japanese Management*. New York: Simon and Schuster.

Peters, T.J. and Waterman, R.H. (1982) *In Search of Excellence*. New York: Harper Row.

Podsakoff, P.M., MacKenzie, S.B., Lee, J. and Podsakoff, N.P. (2003) 'Common method biases in behavioral research: A critical review of the literature and recommended remedies', *Journal of Applied Psychology*, 88 (5): 879–903.

Ramsay, H., Scholarios, D. and Harley, B. (2000) 'Employees and high-performance work systems: Testing inside the black box', *British Journal of Industrial Relations*, 38 (4): 501–531.

Rousseau, D.M. (1989) 'Psychological and implied contracts in organizations', *Employee Responsibilities and Rights Journal*, 2 (2): 121–139.

Rowley, C. and Benson, J. (2002) 'Convergence and divergence in Asian human resource management', *California Management Review*, 44 (2): 90–109.

Schein, E.H. (1965) *Organizational Psychology*. Englewood Cliffs, NJ: Prentice-Hall Inc.

Schuler, R.S. (1992) 'Strategic human resource management: Linking people with the strategic needs of a business', *Organizational Dynamics*, 21 (2): 18–31.

Schuler, R.S. and Jackson, S.E. (1987) 'Linking competitive strategies with human resource management practices', *Academy of Management Executive*, 1 (3): 207–219.

Shih, H., Chiang, Y. and Hsu, C. (2006) 'Can high performance work systems really lead to better performance?', *International Journal of Manpower*, 27 (8): 741–763.

Snell, S.A. and Dean, J.W., Jr. (1994) 'Strategic compensation for integrated manufacturing: The moderating effects of jobs and organizational inertia', *Academy of Management Journal*, 37 (5): 1109–1140.

Sung-Choon, K., Morris, S.S. and Snell, S.A. (2007) 'Relational archetypes, organizational learning, and value creation: Extending the human resource architecture', *Academy of Management Review*, 32 (1): 236–256.

Teece, D.J., Pisano, G. and Shuen, A.A. (1997) 'Dynamic capabilities and strategic management', *Strategic Management Journal*, 18 (7): 504–534.

Tsai, C. (2006) 'High performance work systems and organizational performance: An empirical study of Taiwan's semiconductor design firms', *International Journal of Human Resource Management*, 17 (9): 1512–1530.

Tsui, A.S., Pearce, J.L., Porter, L.W. and Tripoli, A.M. (1997) 'Alternative approaches to the employee-organization relationship: Does investment in employees pay off?', *Academy of Management Journal*, 40 (5): 1089–1121.

Wall, T.D., Michie, J., Patterson, M., Wood, S.J., Sheehan, M., Clegg, C.W. and West, M. (2004) 'On the validity of subjective measures of company performance', *Personnel Psychology*, 57 (1): 95–118.

Whitener, E.M. (2001) 'Do "high commitment" human resource practices affect employee commitment? A cross-level analysis using hierarchical linear modeling', *Journal of Management*, 27 (5): 515–535.

Womack, J.P., Jones, D.T. and Roos, D. (1990) *The Machine That Changed the World*. New York: Rawson Associates.

Wood, S.J. and de Menezes, L. (1998) 'High commitment management in the UK: Evidence from the workplace industrial relations survey and employers' manpower and skills practices survey', *Human Relations*, 51 (4): 485–515.

Wood, S.J. and Wall, T.D. (2002) 'Human resource management and business performance', in P. Warr (ed.), *Psychology at Work*. London: Penguin, pp. 351–374.

Wright, P.M., Dunford, B.B. and Snell, S.A. (2001) 'Human resources and the resource-based view of the firm', *Journal of Management*, 27 (6): 701–721.

Wright, P.M., Gardner, T.M., Moynihan, L.M., Allen, M.R. (2005) 'The relationship between HR practices and firm performance: Examining causal order', *Personnel Psychology*, 58 (2): 409–446.

Wright, P.M. and McMahan, G.C. (1992) 'Theoretical perspectives for strategic human resource management', *Journal of Management*, 18 (2): 295–320.

Youndt, M.A., Snell, S.A., Dean, J.W. and Lepak, D.P. (1996) 'Human resource management, manufacturing strategy, and firm performance', *Academy of Management Journal*, 39 (4): 836–866.

Zacharatos, A., Barling, J. and Iverson, R.D. (2005) 'High-performance work systems and occupational safety', *Journal of Applied Psychology*, 90 (1): 77–93.

Zatzick, C.D. and Iverson, R.D. (2006) 'High-commitment management and workforce reduction: Competitive advantage or disadvantage?', *Academy of Management Journal*, 49 (5): 999–1015.

Zatzick, C.D., Fang, T. and Moliterno, T. (2007) 'Revisiting the Change/Performance Relationship: The Moderating Role of Strategic Alignment'. *Presented at the Academy of Management Meetings*, Philadelphia, P.A.

22

Work Design: Still Going Strong

Heather C. Vough and
Sharon K. Parker

The basic tenet of traditional industrial engineering is that a factory worker can be manipulated, through time and motion study procedures and other techniques, into enriching his company at the expense of himself. The truth is that a man on the job can outfox the company almost every time. Nobody is going to work faster or better if it means cutting his own throat .... People – and their brains – are the most precious resource we have in our shop ... Our most valuable partners in cutting waste are the people on the production floor, who know their jobs better than anyone.

The above quotation comes from Clair Vough's (Vough and Asbell, 1975: 6–7) introduction to a book about increasing productivity through redesigning the assembly lines at IBM in the 1950s and 1960s. At the time that this redesign was being implemented, the Taylorism and job simplification prevalent in the early 1900s was giving way to a new philosophy on jobs; one that emphasized how employees experienced their work and recognized that the way work was designed mattered to them, and should therefore matter to the organization. The understanding of

how people experience and shape their jobs remains a salient issue today, especially given the multitude of management practices that have work design issues at their core, such as just-in-time inventory control, total quality management, integrated management, lean production, concurrent engineering, empowerment, job enrichment, job enlargement, and self-managing teams.

The changing nature of organizations makes such understanding even more important. Work design theory and practice must keep pace with the greater number of employees employed in the service sector, an increase in the use of contingent work, preferences by many for a more boundaryless career, a knowledge-based economy with increased competition over human resources, and other changes (Mirvis and Hall, 1994). Responses to the new organizational environment include expanding the core characteristics of work that are considered, identifying ways to design work to achieve broader outcomes, and recognizing that employees affect how work is designed as much as work design influences employees. Work design research is also beginning to widen its focus away from the task and towards the situated and social context in which the task exists. We discuss these and other important developments in work design theory and research later in this chapter.

First, however, we review classic studies and existing models of work design. Because work design is a vast and heavily studied field, any review must be partial. Here we place emphasis on the characteristics of the job, the outcomes of these job characteristics, and the mediators and moderators to the relationship between characteristics and outcomes. In-depth discussions of many other important topics, such as antecedents of work design, can be found elsewhere (e.g. Morgeson and Campion, 2003; Parker et al., 2001; Torraco, 2005).

CLASSIC WORK DESIGN STUDIES AND WORK DESIGN MODELS

Scholars have long recognized the importance of work design in relation to both individuals and groups; a multi-level focus that continues today. While the individual and group level research often overlap and draw from each other, we address them separately here.

Individual level work design

At the dawn of the Industrial Revolution, early attempts to design jobs for optimal performance focused on simplifying jobs by dividing labor amongst workers so that each job required less skill on the part of the worker (Babbage, 1835; Smith, 1776). Empirical work on the impact of these simplified jobs, designed according to principles of 'scientific management' (Taylor, 1911), showed that they were experienced as dissatisfying, tiring, and boring, and that they reduced mental health and increased employee turnover and absence (Fraser, 1947; Walker and Guest, 1952).

Researchers then began focusing on what employees brought to their jobs and how to jointly optimize employees' working experiences and organizational productivity. One theory concerned with how employees respond to their working conditions was Herzberg's Two-Factor theory (Herzberg, 1968; Herzberg et al., 1959). According to this theory, the elements of the job that could be satisfying and motivating ('motivators') were different than the factors that could be dissatisfying and demotivating ('hygiene factors'). While subsequent research has provided disconfirming evidence for the two-factor theory (e.g. King, 1970; Schneider and Locke, 1971), the focus on how employees respond to their working conditions paved the path for later work on job enrichment that remains relevant.

The next wave of interest in work design was in response to Hackman and Oldham's (1976) job characteristics model (JCM). In the JCM, the authors identified five job characteristics (skill variety, task significance, task identity, feedback, and autonomy) that constitute enriched jobs, and proposed that these affect outcomes such as motivation, performance, satisfaction, absenteeism, and turnover. By averaging the first three job characteristics then multiplying by the last two, the job characteristics can be aggregated into a 'motivating potential score' (MPS) for each job. The authors further predicted that employees high in growth need strength would respond more positively to the job characteristics than those low in growth need strength. Despite some inconsistencies with the model (Johns et al., 1992; Parker and Wall, 1998), much of the JCM has received ample support (Fried and Ferris, 1987), and it remains one of the most influential work design models. It has even been elaborated to better align its core aspects to the changes occurring in the wider organizational context (Parker et al., 2001).

Much research has also been stimulated by related theoretical models of individual work design from the stress literature, most notably the demand-control model of strain (Karasek, 1979). This model proposes that high job demands and low control cause strain, and, in the long-term, stress-related illnesses such as heart disease. Many studies have tested, with mixed support (e.g. de Jonge and Kompier, 1997), the buffering role of job control; if high demands occur in the presence of high control, then strain will not accrue. The core model has also been elaborated by adding social support as an influence on strain, and proposing that work design affects strain via dynamic spirals of learning and behavior (Karasek and Theorell, 1990). For example, over time, the learning experiences that arise from an active job promote a sense of mastery and confidence, which in turn helps people to cope with further strain, thereby freeing up their capacity to accept even more challenging situations that promote yet more learning.

Several other models with distinct contributions can be identified. First, the job demands-resources model of burnout (Demerouti et al., 2001) proposes that job demands lead to exhaustion, whereas a lack of job resources (e.g., job control and social support) leads to disengagement. Second, Warr's (1987) vitamin model of the work environment's influences on well-being is unique in proposing non-linear relationships between job characteristics and well-being outcomes. It suggests that some characteristics of work (e.g. physical security), like vitamins C and E, are damaging in their absence, but beyond a certain level add no benefit. In contrast, other job characteristics (e.g. opportunity for personal control and externally generated goals), like vitamins A and D, as well as being damaging in their absence, can be toxic in very large quantities. Finally, the research on psychological empowerment has embraced similar mediating mechanisms to the JCM (meaning, impact, competence, and choice), although it does not posit these experiences as mediators per se but rather as the defining features of empowerment (Thomas and Velthouse, 1990).

Group level work design

Since the onset of research and thinking on work design, scholars have been interested in how work can be redesigned not only for individuals, but for groups of employees. Drawing on socio-technical systems approach, which originated at the Tavistock Institute of Human Relations in London during the 1950s, Trist and Bamforth (1951) investigated 'long-wall' coal mining methods in Durham, England. They studied how redesigning the group structure in a coalmine from autonomous groups to large, disconnected departments lowered the morale of the workers. In the new structure, employees had difficulty communicating, and the high level of task interdependence led to rigid performance constraints. The redesign led to a decrease in productivity, although interestingly, over time, employees learned to cope with the new conditions and morale and performance improved.

Most of the work that followed this early research on group work design focused on the impact of introducing autonomous workgroups. Autonomous work groups were thought to be ideal for meeting socio-technical design criteria (Cherns, 1976) that were developed at Tavistock. Criteria include, for example, that methods of working should be minimally specified and that variances in work processes should be handled at the source. Wall and Clegg (1981) found that when two previously segregated teams were integrated, with a consequent increase in autonomy and task identity, there were increases in motivation, satisfaction, performance, mental health, and retention. Reviews of other such studies (e.g., see the study by Cordery et al., 1991) typically conclude that autonomous work groups consistently enhance job satisfaction and related attitudinal outcomes, but the effects on behavioral outcomes such as performance and absence are less consistently demonstrated (Parker and Wall, 1998).

In contrast to these studies showing mostly benefits of group work design, Barker's (1993) ethnographic study of self-managed teams demonstrated some drawbacks. In the case investigated, the self-managed teams that replaced the hierarchical structure developed sets of normative rules that actually meant stricter control over employee behaviors due to the monitoring of teammates. Barker's research suggests that it is important to understand not only the group structure but also the group dynamics. This premise is reflected in team effectiveness models which, as well as highlighting group work design elements as important for team performance and morale, also identify aspects such as group processes, group synergy, and group norms (e.g., Cohen and Ledford, 1994; Hackman, 1987).

Other work design models

Up to this point, our review has primarily emphasized motivational approaches to work design which focus on how to design jobs in order to promote optimal motivation on the part of employees. However, there are a variety of other perspectives on work design that come from different disciplines (Campion and McClelland, 1991, 1993). A second approach, the mechanistic perspective – a product of both Taylor's scientific management and industrial engineering – focuses on simplifying tasks. This perspective has the purported benefit of facilitating staffing and training. The biological model, stemming from ergonomics, is a third perspective that emphasizes how tasks can be designed in order to maximize employees' comfort and physical health. Fourth, the perceptual-motor model of work design, derived from experimental psychology and human factors, takes into consideration the attentional and informational demands that employees can handle in their work.

Campion and McClelland's (1991) interdisciplinary framework is helpful in practice because it highlights contrasting professionals' assumptions about how to design jobs. It can also be used to evaluate work designs from multiple perspectives (e.g. see Campion and McClelland, 1993). Nevertheless, it might be most useful to view these disciplines as categories and focus on the dimensions within them rather than the perspectives as a whole. Edwards et al. (2000) showed that work design was best characterized by ten factors, rather than the four used by Campion and McClelland, and that these different dimensions were differentially related to

job satisfaction, efficiency, comfort, and reliability. In a similar vein, Parker and Wall (1998) suggested that the interdisciplinary approach to work design results in a somewhat oversimplified characterization of the motivational approach and its outcomes.

CHARACTERISTICS, OUTCOMES, MEDIATORS AND MODERATORS

In this section we discuss the core elements of the job characteristics approach to work design.[1] Thus, we consider the key job characteristics, outcomes, mediating processes, and moderators or contingencies.

Job characteristics

Job characteristics are the heart of work design research and practice, so it is important to identify those that are most important for the situation and measure them effectively.

In terms of identifying key characteristics, there are many to consider beyond the five originally identified in the Job Characteristics Model. In Edwards et al. (2000), the ten featured factors were:

- feedback;
- skill;
- rewards;
- specialization;
- task simplicity;
- physical ease;
- work scheduling;
- work conditions;
- ergonomic design; and
- cognitive simplicity.

In their meta-analysis, Morgeson and Humphrey (2006) identified 21 distinct job characteristics within four broad categories:

- task motivation work characteristics (e.g., autonomy);
- knowledge motivation characteristics (e.g., job complexity, problem solving);
- social work characteristics (e.g., interdependence, feedback); and
- contextual characteristics (e.g., work conditions).

Time pressure, role conflict, role ambiguity, and work load can be added to this list, as can characteristics that are more salient in the changing work context, such as emotional demands and electronic performance monitoring. To ascertain which characteristics are most relevant to a particular study or intervention, Parker et al. (2001: 433) recommended considering both theory and context.

> … In some contexts, some variables will vary little, so the explanatory power will lie in other variables. For example, social interaction might not vary much in most jobs, but might assume especial significance for certain forms of work such as teleworking … Generally, the choice of variables will be guided by the overall theory as well as an understanding and analysis of the context. Rather like the premise of traditional work design theory, researchers and practitioners need to be afforded autonomy and minimal critical specification if the full potential of their contribution is to be realised.

A further important issue in regard to job characteristics is their measurement. Self-perceptions of job characteristics are most commonly used as indicators of objective job characteristics, but these can be affected by mood, personality, and social processes (Salancik and Pfeffer, 1978). When the outcome variable is also assessed via self-perceptions, such as measures of well-being, the link between job characteristics and the outcome can be inflated by common method variance.

These concerns have led to the use of complementary approaches to assess objective job characteristics, such as using others' perceptions (e.g. managers, researchers), aggregating measures of job perceptions to the group or job level, and using data bases of occupations such as the Dictionary of Occupational Titles or O*NET. Unfortunately, none of these additional methods are problem-free. Another person's rating of the job is not necessarily appropriate, or sufficiently nuanced, to capture real variations in job content or its meaning for individuals. Further, aggregated measures do not allow for the possibility that individuals within groups can have different job characteristics, and data bases such as O*NET only give information

on the characteristics of occupations rather than specific jobs. Using more 'objective' indicators, such as the presence of machine-pacing to indicate low job control, can oversimplify job content and they are not helpful for assessing more subjective aspects like role conflict. In contrast, subjective measures allow for the role of social cues and personal meaning in determining job characteristics (Salancik and Pfeffer, 1978; Wrzesniewski et al., 2003).

In fact, despite the concerns about them, there are several sources of evidence that employee self-ratings can closely match objective job features (Oldham, 1996). First, meta-analyses show relatively high convergence between self-ratings and ratings from external observers, especially for the more observable job characteristics like job control (Fried and Ferris, 1987). Studies also show convergence between surveys of relevant job characteristics and occupations classified via DOT and O*NET (Morgeson and Humphrey, 2006). Second, studies show that, if there are objective changes in job characteristics, there is a parallel change in job holders' self-rating (see Taber and Taylor, 1990). Third, although studies based on the social information processing approach have shown that social information does indeed affect employee job ratings, these studies also suggest the effects are weaker than those of objective job features (Taber and Taylor, 1990). Therefore, there are good reasons for the continued use of self-report measures of job characteristics, albeit with the recognition that they likely reflect more than 'objective' job characteristics and with due caution about common method variance. At the same time, using multilevel approaches to analyze self-report date can also be insightful (see de Jonge et al., 1999 and Van Yperen and Snijders, 2000 for two contrasting multilevel approaches), and we recommend complementing self-report measures with others' reports.

Most important, one must think about exactly what it is one is trying to assess and design the measurement strategy accordingly. To assist in this process, Daniels (2006) distinguished global perceptions of jobs (best assessed through self or other reports) from enacted and emergent job characteristics (best assessed through self-reports within specific time frames, such as daily diary methods) and from latent job characteristics (best assessed by data bases, analysis of job descriptions, or inferred from interventions that change structures, processes or technology). Daniels' (2006) approach may help to achieve a better match between the theoretical construct and its measurement. One should also bear in mind that some research questions will be usefully addressed with more interpretivist approaches, and ethnographic methodologies, that focus on how jobs are understood and experienced by the incumbent.

Outcomes

The importance of work design lies in its ability to predict valuable individual and organizational outcomes. In Fried and Ferris's (1987) meta-analysis of the JCM, they found consistently strong relationships between the five job characteristics and satisfaction and motivation, as well as weaker relationships with performance and absenteeism (see also Loher et al., 1985; Rentsch and Steel, 1998), although other research has not found support for the relationship between job characteristics and performance (Kelly, 1992). More recently, Humphrey et al. (2007) performed an extended meta-analysis and found even stronger relationships between job characteristics and attitudinal outcomes. They also demonstrated that the job characteristics predicted organizational commitment, job involvement, and role conflict.

Some of the most intriguing results regarding these traditional outcomes of work redesign come from longitudinal studies. In Wall and Clegg's (1981) study of autonomous work groups, the positive effects on performance, retention, and motivation lasted throughout the 33-month study, whereas the positive impact on satisfaction and mental health was only evident one year after the work redesign. In contrast, in a study of job enrichment of bank tellers that consisted

of four measurement periods, Griffin (1991) found an increase in satisfaction and commitment in the first six months after the redesign, but a drop back to original levels in these job attitudes after 24 months. Performance, in contrast, showed significant increases between 6 and 24 months and stayed at that high level until the end of the study at 48 months. Clearly, these two studies show different patterns of change, which might stem from differences in the two samples (blue collar employees vs. bank tellers) or the different level of analysis (groups vs. individuals) or some other factor. Clearly there is a need for additional research into the longitudinal effects of work design because, as these studies indicate, some of the initially positive outcomes might not be enduring, perhaps because employees adapt to the work redesign. Longitudinal designs also remain important for establishing causality.

Other important outcomes of work design are mental and physical health. Karasek (1979; see also Karasek, 1990) demonstrated that when employees have high job demands and low job latitude they are more likely to be depressed, exhausted, absent, dissatisfied, and take pills than employees in other job conditions. Le Blanc et al. (2007) attributed the success of a team-based burnout intervention amongst oncology care providers to improvements in job control, social support, and reduced job demands. Both social support and job demands were also shown to be important in a longitudinal analysis of UK civil servants (Stansfeld et al., 1997). Overall, when rigorous work designs are implemented, there is consistent evidence of the negative effects of excess demands on mental health outcomes (Frese, 1985; Parkes, 1995). However, the positive mental health effects of job control are more mixed (e.g. Dwyer and Fox, 2000; Sargent and Terry, 1998).

Research is also increasingly highlighting the potential role of work design for physical health and safety (Parker et al., 2003). In their review, Theorell and Karasek (1996) reported that 16 out of 22 studies showed significant associations between high demand-low control jobs and cardiovascular disease (CVD) or CVD symptoms. As another example, Sprigg et al. (2007) found that, for call center employees, higher work load was associated with upper body and lower back musculoskeletal disorders, and this relationship was largely accounted for by job-related strain. The effect of work design might affect safety through a number of mechanisms. For example, job variety might alleviate boredom and increase attentiveness, thereby reducing risks, whereas excess job demands might cause short cuts to be taken, thereby increasing the chance of injuries. However, so far, few studies have investigated how work design affects accidents or injuries, and the studies that exist show diverse findings (Parker et al., 2003). Overall, although promising, research on the effects of work design on physical health remains relatively underdeveloped.

Researchers have also investigated how work design influences employees' self-efficacy and proactivity. These two outcomes are important because they relate to employee motivation (Gist and Mitchell, 1992) and organizational effectiveness (Hisrich, 1990). Parker (1998) defined role based self-efficacy as the degree to which people believe they can take on a broader array of interpersonal, integrative, and proactive tasks rather than just fulfil technical requirements. In one longitudinal study of a manufacturing company, she found that participation in improvement circles and job enrichment promoted role-based self-efficacy (Parker, 1998) and, in the reverse situation when jobs were deskilled due to introducing lean assembly lines, role based self-efficacy decreased (Parker, 2003). In a related vein, in a study of East and West Germany, Frese et al. (1996) demonstrated that the lower control and complexity that was characteristic of the East led to less personal initiative for the East German employees. These results were further substantiated with evidence showing that self-efficacy both mediates and moderates job complexity and control's relationship with initiative (Speier and Frese, 1997).

Parker et al. (2006) similarly showed that job autonomy was associated with more proactive problem-solving as well as self-implementation of ideas; a relationship that was partially mediated by role breadth self-efficacy and flexible role orientation.

Although researchers have investigated the effects of job characteristics on outcomes for nearly half a decade, the influence of job characteristics on specific emotions is still in its infancy. We know that job characteristics impact both positive and negative moods and that the five job characteristics differentially affect enthusiasm, fatigue, nervousness, and relaxation (Saavedra and Kwun, 2000). Certain job characteristics (e.g. interactions with others) can also lead to emotional labor (Schaubroeck and Jones, 2000). Due to the importance many employees place on social interactions in the workplace (Tschanh et al., 2005), social work design models may be especially crucial to understanding how job characteristics impact emotion.

Mediators

In addition to a focus on the outcomes of work design, there has been substantial work exploring the mechanisms that mediate this relationship. In the JCM, it was proposed that skill variety, task identity, and task significance would influence experienced meaningfulness, autonomy would influence experienced responsibility, and feedback would influence knowledge of results and that these three psychological states would, in turn, drive attitudinal and behavioral outcomes. While there is evidence that these states do mediate the job characteristics-outcomes relationship (Humphrey et al., 2007), the psychological states may not only mediate the specified relationships (Fried and Ferris, 1987) and may not all be necessary (Johns et al., 1992).

In an effort to provide a more detailed analysis of the mediating role of motivation, Parker and Ohly (in press) proposed that job characteristics can affect motivation in ways beyond their effect on traditional states. For example, they proposed that, because they enhance feelings of internal control, enriched jobs will lead to a promotion vs. prevention regulatory focus (Higgins, 1996), in which employees focus on growth and accomplishment rather than security and obligation. In turn, employees will demonstrate more creativity and discretionary behavior (Friedman and Foerster, 2005). Integrating work design theory with Kanfer's (1990) task specific motivation theory, the authors also proposed that job characteristics can affect the kinds of goals employee choose (goal generation) as well as their persistence in achieving them (goal striving). For example, job enrichment might lead employees to generate more difficult goals with longer-time frames because autonomy increases the sense of ownership one has for a broader range of goals (Parker et al., 1997).

Job characteristics not only affect outcomes through influencing motivation, but also through improved logistics and learning. When employees are given increased autonomy and responsibility for their work they can often respond to problems faster (Wall et al., 1992) and use their knowledge to anticipate and fix problems more effectively (Miller and Monge, 1986). In a novel demonstration of this point, Wall et al. (1992) investigated employees on an assembly line where the rate of production is fixed and, therefore, not a matter of motivation. They found that the positive relationship between work redesign and performance was a result of the fact that when employees were given greater control over their jobs, as well as performance contingent compensation, they were able to respond to technological problems faster and they could anticipate and prevent potential problems.

The role of knowledge is not limited to its utility for quickly remedying or preventing problems. Individuals with enriched jobs are more likely to empathize with the perspective of others in their work environment, and to have 'big picture' understanding of how the whole department works (Parker et al., 2001). Likewise, at the team level, it has been suggested that autonomous work group members learn from each other (Pearce and Ravlin, 1987) and, because they assume more

responsibility for external coordination with others in other organizations, they gain more understanding of the broader work process (Batt, 1999).

Of course, by expanding the range of outcomes considered, one also ultimately needs to expand the range of mechanisms that are considered. For example, job enrichment might promote more active coping, which explains why it can enhance mental health; whereas high work load in a call center might cause musculoskeletal damage because it 'ties' individuals to their work station thereby creating biomechanical strain. By understanding why a given work characteristic or form of work design affects outcomes, one can better identify the circumstances under which it will and will not be effective.

Moderators

The research on moderators to the JCM has focused mostly on individual differences and has been plagued with inconsistent findings. For example, White (1978) found that none of 73 potential moderators consistently moderated the relationship between participation in decision making and employee attitudes across 14 research sites. Most studies of individual moderators have focused on the role of growth need strength (GNS) that was proposed in the original JCM. Some studies have supported its moderating role (e.g. Loher et al., 1985); others have not (Tiegs et al., 1992). In a more comprehensive examination of moderators, Johns et al. (1992) found that personal characteristics (GNS, educational level, and job tenure) primarily moderated the relationship between psychological states and outcomes, whereas contextual moderators (social supervisory security and pay satisfaction) primarily moderated the relationship between job characteristics and psychological states.

Another individual difference that has often been related to work design is cognitive ability. Employees with higher cognitive abilities should be able to handle the additional pressures and knowledge requirements when autonomy is increased. In contrast, employees with lower levels of cognitive ability will feel overloaded and stressed when they are faced with increased autonomy (Dunham, 1977; Schneider et al., 1982). Using the interdisciplinary approach, Campion (1989) found that motivational job characteristics are positively related to mental ability requirements, while the other approaches (mechanistic, biological, and perceptual-motor) are negatively related to ability requirements. Cognitive ability therefore does appear to be relevant to work design, although its specific moderating effect warrants further investigated.

There is initial support for the notion that people differ in their propensity to be proactive and that this difference moderates the job characteristics to outcomes relationship (Parker and Sprigg, 1998). Specifically, Parker and Sprigg (1998) found that when employees faced jobs with high autonomy as well as high demands, proactive employees took advantage of the opportunity to reduce demand and avoid strain, while less proactive employees felt higher degrees of strain, presumably because they did not act on the greater autonomy afforded them. Further, it has been demonstrated that the impact of access to resources and strategy-related information on felt responsibility for constructive change depends on employees' proactive personality (Fuller et al., 2006).

The relationship between job characteristics and outcomes can also be affected by group and organizational variables. Most of the attention to this issue has been given to interdependence and uncertainty. In regard to interdependence, some studies suggest interdependence is necessary for teamwork to be of benefit (e.g., Sprigg et al., 2000) whereas others show benefits of teamwork even if interdependence is low (Batt, 1999). For uncertainty, the evidence is quite consistent: job enrichment, particularly job control, is most powerful in enhancing performance when uncertainty is high (e.g., Wall et al., 1990; Wright and Cordery, 1999), probably because autonomy promotes the learning needed to be successful in such contexts.

Beyond uncertainty and interdependence, many other organizational factors are likely to affect whether work redesign leads to the predicted outcomes, such as how well the change process is introduced, the organization's readiness for work redesign, the level of employee job security, and national culture. Regarding the latter, Robert et al. (2000) found that empowerment was associated with lower job satisfaction in India, which they attributed to cultural deference to hierarchy and status. However, this contrasts with early studies of autonomous work groups in Indian textile companies, in which Rice (1958) described how autonomous work groups emerged relatively spontaneously, on the basis of workers' 'intuitive recognition' (p. 81). Another pertinent avenue for exploration is whether broader work organization variables (e.g. reward, training, information systems) need to align with the work design in order for it to be effective, as proposed by Cordery and Parker (2007). Interestingly, in contrast to the idea of alignment, Morgeson et al. (2006) found that work redesign into autonomous work groups only had a positive effect on self-reported performance when reward, feedback, and information systems were poor.

Again, as the range of job characteristics and outcomes expand, a wider set of moderators becomes relevant. For example, a study of service workers showed that emotional demands were only negative for employee well-being when individuals lacked emotional competence. For those who had emotional competence to deal with their own and others' affect, emotional demands was not detrimental to well-being (Giardini and Frese, 2006).

In this section we have addressed some of the theories and findings concerning work design. We now turn to where we believe work design is headed.

CURRENT AND FUTURE TRENDS

We focus here on four areas that are increasingly taking shape in the work design arena: the role of context, social influence, job crafting, and meaning of work. We also briefly discuss the current state of practice regarding work design.

Context

A theme throughout this review concerns how changes in the wider context shape the job characteristics that are relevant, as well as give rise to interest in different outcomes, underpinning mechanisms, and contingencies. Fuller theoretical development in regard to context, such as along the lines proposed by Johns (2006) is now important. One contextual issue we have not yet explicitly addressed concerns the 'who' of work design. When one thinks of work design research, many studies are in manufacturing contexts (e.g. Dean and Snell, 1991; Kemp et al., 1983; Parker, 2003) or call centers (e.g. Frenkel et al., 1998), both traditionally characterized by poor quality work design. However, increasingly, studies are investigating work design in white-collar, service, or professional settings. Using a sample that included members of a broad array of white collar professions in Sweden, Karasek (1990) found that increased control over work had health benefits. Additionally, Janz et al. (1997) demonstrated the important role that autonomy and interdependence played for effectiveness in groups of knowledge workers.

These studies point to the need for additional research into work design in professional and knowledge-based jobs. The argument could be made that autonomy is the foundation of most work design research and because professionals, by definition, typically have high autonomy, work design is less relevant to them. From a different perspective, the fact that professionals are often given high autonomy can make them ideal for learning how autonomy interacts with the other job characteristics to influence outcomes. For instance, a young lawyer may be given a great deal of autonomy in assisting clients, but she may be given only minimal feedback because her job relies on providing services to clients, who may not be willing or knowledgeable enough to give her information

about her performance. Thus, in this context, feedback may become the most influential job characteristics in influencing outcomes. Because professional jobs have different job characteristics than the most commonly researched contexts, it is unlikely that the findings from non-professional contexts will apply equally to them.

Social influences

The influence of the social context can be viewed from at least two perspectives. First, the social context influences how employees perceive their working situations. Salancik and Pfeffer (1978) proposed that work design can be best understood from a social information processing approach in which employees take into consideration social information and use social reality construction processes in order to understand their job characteristics. More recently, Wrzesniewski and colleagues (2003) described how interactions with other people at work provide employees with information about the nature and value of their jobs, roles, and selves. For example, Griffin (1983) showed how employees' perceptions of their jobs, and their job satisfaction, were more positive as a result of supervisors repeatedly drawing attention to the variety, autonomy and other positive work design aspects present in employees' jobs. One might extend this research to consider how emotional contagion processes from others influence work perceptions.

A second way in which the social context is relevant to work design is more direct. Rather than being viewed as a perceptual filter, the social context itself can be considered a job characteristic to be designed. Variables such as social support have long been acknowledged as important job characteristics, especially in stress-related work design research. However, perhaps because of a broader interest within organizational behavior on topics like social networks and positive relationships, social processes are now being highlighted within mainstream work design research. For example, in their meta-analytical tests, Humphrey et al. (2007)

found that the social environment variables explained an additional 40 per cent of the variance above motivational factors when predicting organizational commitment, and an additional 24 per cent of the variance on job satisfaction. As part of this renewed interest in social processes, it has been proposed that jobs can be designed in order to increase employees' understanding of how their work makes a prosocial difference (Grant, 2007). Work that involves contact with beneficiaries of the work and provides feedback about its impact on beneficiaries is predicted to lead to greater effort, persistence, and helping behavior towards beneficiaries.

Crafting/proactivity

An exciting realm of new work design research is the role that employees themselves play in creating and crafting their jobs. Extending earlier work on constructs like task revision (Staw and Boettger, 1990) and flexible role orientation (Parker et al., 1997), Wrzesniewski and Dutton (2001) argued that employees do not passively accept their work context but proactively craft their work by cognitively or behaviorally altering their tasks or work interactions in order to change their work identities and work meaning. These authors give the examples of hospital cleaners who had the same objective tasks but varied greatly on their perceptions of the necessary tasks, skill levels, and social interactions. Thus, some of the cleaners had crafted their jobs to have greater boundaries while others had confined their tasks to relatively few activities.

This more dynamic perspective on work design has also been captured in the current emphasis on self-efficacy and proactivity in the work design literature because, as employees' self-efficacy increases, their beliefs about what can be done on the job and, subsequently, their actions on the job, may actually lead them to change the characteristics of the job. In an excellent four wave study of East German employees during transition to reunification, Frese et al. (2007) demonstrated this reciprocity between people and their work.

Job control and job complexity were associated with greater personal initiative, which led, in the longer term, to even higher levels of job control and job complexity. Both causal pathways were mediated by control orientations, a concept that encapsulates self efficacy.

In sum, as people find that they are not satisfied with their work or that their work is not meeting their needs, they may actively change the job characteristics to get what they want out of the job. We hope to see future research embrace this approach. Of course, this recommendation also comes with a caveat; which is that the possibility of crafting does not absolve organizations from the responsibility of designing good quality work.

Meaning as a key mechanism

One set of relationships that we believe warrants special attention is that between the job characteristics and experienced meaningfulness. Experienced meaningfulness has been repeatedly shown to be a strong mediator between job characteristics and outcomes (Fried, 1991; Humphrey et al., 2007). However, because the meaning of work literature and the work design literature have evolved in parallel with little dialogue, it is not clear what 'experienced meaningfulness' really means. In the original conceptualization, experienced meaningfulness is defined as 'The degree to which the individual experiences the job as one which is generally meaningful, valuable, and worthwhile' (Hackman and Oldham, 1976: 256). Researchers studying meaning of work have recently begun focusing on the self-concept and the notions of significance and purpose as the defining characteristics of meaningfulness (e.g. Chalofsky, 2003; Pratt and Ashforth, 2003; Wrzesniewski et al., 2003), therefore further specifying the conditions under which work is experienced as meaningful. Thus, it may be possible to borrow from the meaning of work literature in order to understand how the job characteristics influence employees' sense of self, significance, and purpose, and consequently how they find their work to be meaningful. Such research will likely benefit from an interpretivist approach that focuses on subjective experiences and how individuals create and maintain the world through their own actions and those of others.

Another way in which the job characteristics model may be further integrated with the meaning of work research is by investigating the moderating role of employees' orientation to their work as a job, career, or calling (Bellah et al., 1985; Wrzesniewski et al., 1997). Employees who are job oriented focus on financial rewards, career oriented employees emphasize the advancement opportunities available to them at work, and calling oriented employees derive enjoyment from doing socially useful and fulfilling work. These orientations are likely to affect how employees respond when their tasks are redesigned. For example, employees who are job oriented might react to job enrichment with concerns that they are being given added responsibilities without additional pay. The career-oriented employee may worry that enrichment is occurring in lieu of her getting the opportunity to move into a more managerial position. Finally, the calling-oriented employee may be positive about increased control and variety because he views this as an opportunity to be even more involved in the already fulfilling job.

It is also possible that work orientations might be influenced by work design through a process of adaptation. One might expect that long-term exposure to deskilled jobs with little opportunity to make a difference will lead individuals to define their work as a 'job', whereas exposure to enriched jobs will increase the likelihood that individuals will define their work as a calling. The idea that individuals adapt to their jobs has been suggested in other related research. For example, Parker et al. (1997) showed that, as a result of enriched work design, employees develop broader and more flexible role orientations, in which they feel ownership for longer-term goals (e.g. customer satisfaction). At the same time, deskilled work can lower one's aspirations (Parker, 2003) and engender inflexible role orientations. The idea is that job characteristics can, over the long term, shape and influence the meaning employees give to their work through changing their orientation.

Practice

An important but rarely addressed issue in the work design literature is whether the ideas and suggestions from work design research have been successfully mined and integrated into practice. Or, in contrast, have practicing managers continued to work in parallel with existing research, preferring management fads over academic findings? For example, the autonomous workgroup has purportedly been embraced across industries (Druskat and Wheeler, 2004), but are organizations implementing these teams in a way that allows for the potential benefits (Kemp et al., 1983; Wall and Clegg, 1981) or are they instead actually exerting more control over their employees, albeit in a less conspicuous manner (Barker, 1993)? Certainly evidence would suggest that positive work designs exist more readily in rhetoric than reality. For example, many management initiatives fail to meet their objectives, which are, in turn, often attributed to a failure to adequately address issues of work design (e.g. Storey, 1994). Therefore, more effort developing and promoting tools and methods, coaching leaders, and changing policy to have an impact on work design is needed.

In this respect, it is useful to consider how researchers can best influence the practices managers (and others) choose to adopt. Harkening back to the opening quotation, Clair Vough claimed that he could explain his work design philosophy to other managers, but rarely were these other managers able to implement it properly in their respective organizations. Thus, researchers may face an uphill battle when trying to influence work design practices. The traditional outlet of academic publications is clearly underperforming, as is evident in the Academy of Management's current attempts to find new ways to bridge academia and practice.

Teaching work design in MBA classes is one potential source of influence, but there are a number of intermediate events that have to occur before an MBA student can influence an organization.

Thus, the world of academia needs to find better ways of influencing work design practice and policy. Regarding the former, action research is one way a researcher learns about a work context and gains data through their experiences, while simultaneously helping the organization move in a desired direction (e.g. Wall and Clegg, 1981). Also important is the development of evidence-based tools, processes, and guidance to analyze work design and facilitate its redesign, as well as tools that can be used to incorporate work design principles when introducing changes to work practices and/or new technologies (e.g., Nadin et al., 2001). In the development of such practical guidance, it is important to include the politics of change, which have often been considered in interpretivist approaches to work design (e.g. Badham et al., 1996). In this way, by influencing practice and policy, academics can not only respond to changes in work design, but shape them.

CONCLUSION

While in the 1950s and 1960s, when Vough was redesigning IBM's typewriter assembly lines, he did not face the rapid change and limited employee commitment employers face today, he did understand that people were the core of any business and that people shaped the tasks just as much as the tasks shaped the people. Although the job characteristics model has remained the dominant model for 30 years, new models are emerging that increasingly acknowledge the role of the employee. These models propose that jobs should be designed to allow for social interactions, individual initiative, self-efficacy, and an understanding of the impact the work has on others. Researchers within these perspectives have recognized the changing working context, characterized by rapid technological development, and have

responded with an emphasis on dynamism and reciprocity, where employees themselves influence and craft the nature and meaning of work design. Thus, work design research has come a long way since its inception and it is now coming into its own in terms of the social and enacted environments in which jobs are embedded.

NOTES

1 Note that most of the research we review here can be characterized as deriving from a functionalist paradigm. For consideration of work design from other paradigms, see Holman et al. (2002).

REFERENCES

Babbage, C. (1835) *On the Economy of Machinery and Manufacturers*. London: Charles Knight.

Badham, R, Couchman, R.P. and Selden, D. (1996) 'Winning the Socio-Technical Wager: Change Roles and the Implementation of Self-Managing Work Cells', in R.J. Koubek and W. Karwowski (eds), *Manufacturing Agility and Hybrid Automation – I*. Louisville: IEA Press, pp. 339–343.

Barker, J.R. (1993) 'Tightening the iron cage: Concertive control in self-managing teams', *Administrative Science Quarterly*, 38 (3): 408–437.

Batt, R. (1999) 'Work organization, technology, and performance in customer service and sales', *Industrial and Labor Relations Review*, 52 (4): 539–564.

Bellah, R.N., Madsen, R., Sullivan, W.M., Swidler, A. and Tipton, S.M. (1985) *Habits of the Heart: Individualism and Commitment in American Life*. New York: Harper & Row.

Campion, M.A. (1989) 'Ability requirement implications of job design: An interdisciplinary perspective', *Personnel Psychology*, 42 (1): 1–24.

Campion, M.A. and McClelland, C.L. (1991) 'Interdisciplinary examination of costs and benefits of enlarged jobs: A job design quasi-experiment', *Journal of Applied Psychology*, 76 (2): 186–198.

Campion, M.A. and McClelland, C.L. (1993) 'Follow-up and extension of the interdisciplinary costs and benefits of enlarged jobs', *Journal of Applied Psychology*, 78 (3): 339–351.

Chalofsky, N. (2003) 'An emerging construct of meaning of work', *Human Resource Development International*, 6 (1): 69–83.

Cherns, A.B. (1976) 'The principles of socio-technical design', *Human Relations*, 29 (8): 783–792.

Cohen, S.G. and Ledford, G.E. (1994) 'The effectiveness of self-managing teams: A quasi-experiment', *Human Relations*, 47 (1): 13–43.

Cordery, J.L., Mueller, W.S. and Smith, L.M. (1991) 'Attitudinal and behavioural effects of autonomous group working: A longitudinal field study', *Academy of Management Journal*, 43 (2): 464–476.

Cordery, J. and Parker, S.K. (2007) 'Work Organization', in P. Boxall, J. Purcell and P. Wright (eds), *Oxford Handbook of Human Resource Management*. Oxford: Oxford University Press, pp. 187–209.

Daniels, K. (2006) 'Rethinking job characteristics in work stress research', *Human Relations*, 59 (3): 267–290.

Dean, J.W.J. and Snell, S.A. (1991) 'Integrated manufacturing and job design: Moderating effects of organizational inertia', *Academy of Management Journal*, 34 (4): 776–804.

de Jonge, J., van Breukelen, G.J.P., Landeweerd, J.A. and Nijhuis, F.J.N. (1999) 'Comparing group and individual level assessments of job characteristics in testing the job demand-control model: A multi-level approach', *Human Relations*, 52 (1): 95–122.

de Jonge, J. and Kompier, M.A.J. (1997) 'A critical examination of the Demand-Control-Support model from a work psychological perspective', *International Journal of Stress Management*, 4 (4): 235–258.

Demerouti, E., Nachreiner, F., Baker, A.B. and Schaufeli, W.B. (2001) 'The job demands-resources model of burnout', *Journal of Applied Psychology*, 86 (3): 499–512.

Druskat, V.U. and Wheeler, J.V. (2004) 'How to lead a self-managing team', *Sloan Management Review*, 45 (4): 65–71.

Dunham, R.B. (1977) 'Relationships of perceived job design characteristics to job ability requirements and job value', *Journal of Applied Psychology*, 62 (6): 760–763.

Dwyer, D. and Fox, M.L. (2000) 'The moderating role of hostility in the relationship between enriched jobs and health', *Academy of Management Journal*, 43 (6): 1086–1096.

Edwards, J.R., Scully, J.A. and Brtek, M.D. (2000) 'The nature and outcomes of work: A replication and extension of interdisciplinary work-design research', *Journal of Applied Psychology*, 85 (6): 860–868.

Fraser, R. (1947) *The Incidence of Neurosis Among Factory Workers. Report no. 90, Industrial Health Research Board*. London: HMSO.

Frenkel, S.J., Tam, M., Korczynski, M. and Shire, K. (1998) 'Beyond bureaucracy? Work organization in call centres', *The International Journal of Human Resource Management*, 9 (6): 957–979.

Frese, M. (1985) 'Stress at work and psychosomatic complaints: A causal interpretation', *Journal of Applied Psychology*, 70 (2): 314–328.

Frese, M., Garst, H. and Fay, D. (2007) 'Making things happen: Reciprocal relationships between work characteristics and personal initiative in a four-wave longitudinal structural equation model', *Journal of Applied Psychology*, 92 (4): 1084–1102.

Frese, M., Kring, W., Soose, A. and Zempel, J. (1996) 'Personal initiative at work: Differences between East and West Germany', *Academy of Management Journal*, 39 (1): 37–63.

Fried, Y. (1991) 'Meta-analytic comparison of the Job Diagnostic Survey and Job Characteristics Inventory as correlates of work satisfaction and performance', *Journal of Applied Psychology*, 76 (5): 690–697.

Fried, Y. and Ferris, G.R. (1987) 'The validity of the job characteristics model: A review and meta-analysis', *Personnel Psychology*, 40 (2): 287–322.

Friedman, R.S. and Foerster, J. (2005) 'Effects of motivational cues on perceptual asymmetry: Implications for creativity and analytical problem solving', *Journal of Personality and Social Psychology*, 88 (2): 263–275.

Fuller, J.B., Marler, L.E., and Hester, K. (2006) 'Promoting felt responsibility for constructive change and proactive behavior: Exploring aspects of an elaborated model of work design', *Journal of Organizational Behavior*, 27 (8): 1089–1120.

Gerhart, B. (1987) 'How important are dispositional factors as determinants of job satisfaction? Implications for job design and other personnel programs', *Journal of Applied Psychology*, 72 (3): 366–373.

Giardini, A. and Frese, M. (2006) 'Reducing the negative effects of emotion work in service occupations: Emotional competence as a psychological resource', *Journal of Occupational Health Psychology*, 11 (1): 63–75.

Gist, M.E. and Mitchell, T.R. (1992) 'Self-efficacy: A theoretical analysis of its determinants and malleability', *Academy of Management Review*, 17 (2): 183–211.

Grant, A.M. (2007) 'Relational job design and the motivation to make prosocial difference', *Academy of Management Review*, 32 (2): 393–417.

Griffin, R.W. (1991) 'Effects of work redesign on employee perceptions, attitudes, and behaviors: A long-term investigation', *Academy of Management Journal*, 34 (2): 425–435.

Griffin, R.W. (1983) 'Objective and social sources of information in task design: A field experiment', *Administrative Science Quarterly*, 28 (2): 184–200.

Hackman, J.R. (1987) 'The Design of Effective Work Teams', in J.W. Lorsch (ed.), *Handbook of Organizational Behavior.* Englewood Cliffs, NJ: Prentice-Hall, pp. 316–341.

Hackman, J.R. and Oldham, G.R. (1976) 'Motivation through the design of work: Test of a theory', *Organizational Behavior and Human Decision Processes*, 16 (2): 250–279.

Herzberg, F. (1968) 'One more time: How do you motivate employees?', *Harvard Business Review*, 46 (1): 53–62.

Herzberg, F., Mausner, B. and Snyderman, B.B. (1959) *The Motivation to Work.* New York: Wiley.

Higgins, E.T. (1996) 'Ideals, oughts, and regulatory focus', in P. M. Gollwitzer, and J.A. Bargh (eds), *The Psychology of Action: Linking Motivation to Behavior.* New York: The Guilford Press, pp. 91–114.

Hisrich, R.D. (1990) 'Entrepreneurship/ intrapreneurship', *American Psychologist*, 45 (2): 209–222.

Holman, D., Clegg, C. and Waterson, P. (2002) 'Navigating the territory of job design: current maps and future directions', *Applied Ergonomics*, 33 (3): 197–205.

Humphrey, S.E., Nahrgang, J.D. and Morgeson, F.P. (2007) 'Integrating motivational, social, and contextual work design features: A meta-analytic summary and theoretical extension of the work design literature', *Journal of Applied Psychology*, 92 (5): 1332–1356.

Janz, B.D., Colquitt, J.A. and Noe, R.A. (1997) 'Knowledge worker team effectiveness: The role of autonomy, interdependence, team development, and contextual support variables', *Personnel Psychology*, 50 (4): 877–904.

Johns, G. (2006) 'The essential impact of context on organizational behavior', *Academy of Management Review*, 31 (2): 386–408.

Johns, G., Xie, J.L. and Fang, Y. (1992) 'Mediating and moderating effects in job design', *Journal of Management*, 18 (4): 657–676.

Kanfer, R. (1990) 'Motivation theory and industrial and organizational psychology', in M.D. Dunnette and L.M. Hough (eds), *Handbook of Industrial and Organizational Psychology* (2nd edn). Palo Alto, CA: Consulting Psychologists Press, pp. 75–170.

Karasek, R.A.J. (1979) 'Job demands, job decision latitude, and mental strain: Implications for job redesign', *Administrative Science Quarterly*, 24 (2): 285–308.

Karasek, R.A.J. (1990) 'Lower health risk with increased job control among white collar workers', *Journal of Organizational Behavior*, 11 (3): 171–185.

Karasek, R.A. and Theorell, T. (1990) *Healthy Work: Stress, Productivity, and the Reconstruction of Working Life.* New York: Basic Books.

Kelly, J. (1992) 'Does job re-design theory explain job re-design outcomes?', *Human Relations*, 45 (8): 753–774.

Kemp, N.J., Wall, T.D., Clegg, C.W. and Cordery, J.L. (1983) 'Autonomous work groups in a greenfield site: A comparative study', *Journal of Occupational Psychology*, 56 (4): 271–288.

King, N.A. (1970) 'A clarification and evaluation of the two-factor theory of job satisfaction', *Psychological Bulletin*, 74 (1): 18–30.

Le Blanc, P.M., Hox, J.J., Schaufeli, W.B., Taris, T.W. and Peeters, M.C.W. (2007) 'Take care! The evaluation of a team–based burnout intervention program for oncology care providers', *Journal of Applied Psychology*, 92 (1): 213–227.

Loher, B.T., Noe, R.A., Moeller, N.L. and Fitzgerald, M.P. (1985) 'A meta-analysis of the relation of job characteristics to job satisfaction', *Journal of Applied Psychology*, 70 (2): 280–289.

Miller, K.L. and Monge, P.R. (1986) 'Participation, satisfaction, and productivity: A meta-analytic review', *Academy of Management Journal*, 29 (4): 727–753.

Mirvis, P.H. and Hall, D.T. (1994) 'Psychological success and the boundaryless career', *Journal of Organizational Behavior*, 15 (4): 365–380.

Morgeson, F.P., Johnson, M.D., Campion, M.A., Medsker, G.J. and Mumford, T.V. (2006) 'Understanding reactions to job redesign: A quasi-experimental investigation of the moderating effects of organizational context on perceptions of performance behavior', *Personnel Psychology*, 59 (2): 333–363.

Morgeson, F.P. and Campion, M.A. (2003) 'Work Design', in R.J. Klimoski and D.R. Ilgen (eds), *Handbook of Psychology: Industrial and Organizational Psychology.* New York: John Wiley. Vol. 12: pp. 423–452.

Morgeson, F.P. and Humphrey, S.E. (2006) 'The Work Design Questionnaire (WDG): Developing and validating a comprehensive measure for assessing job design and the nature of work', *Journal of Applied Psychology*, 91 (6): 1321–1339.

Nadin, S.J, Waterson, P.E, and Parker, S.K. (2001) 'Participation in job redesign: An evaluation of the use of a socio-technical tool and its impact', *Human Factors and Ergonomics in Manufacturing*, 11 (1): 53–69.

Oldham, G.R. (1996) 'Job design', in C.L. Cooper and I.T. Robertson (eds.), *International Review of Industrial and Organizational Psychology.* Chichester: Wiley, pp. 33–60.

Parker, S.K. (1998) 'Enhancing role breadth self-efficacy: The roles of job enrichment and other organizational interventions', *Journal of Applied Psychology*, 83 (6): 835–852.

Parker, S.K. (2003) 'Longitudinal effects of lean production on employee outcomes and the mediating role of work characteristics', *Journal of Applied Psychology*, 88 (4): 620–634.

Parker, S.K. and Ohly, S. (in press) 'Designing motivating jobs', in R. Kanfer, G. Chen, and R. Pritchard (eds.), *Work Motivation: Past, Present, and Future*. New York: Psychology Press.

Parker, S.K. and Sprigg, C.A. (1998) 'A Move Backwards? The Introduction of a Moving Assembly Line', *Proceedings of the Occupational Psychology Conference, Eastbourne, UK*. Leicester: British Psychological Society, pp. 139–144.

Parker, S.K., Turner, N. and Griffin, M.A. (2003) 'Designing Healthy Work', in D.A. Hofmann and L.E. Tetrick (eds.), *Health and Safety in Organizations: A Multi-Level Perspective*. California: Jossey-Bass, pp. 91–130.

Parker, S.K. and Wall, T.D. (1998) *Job and Work Design: Organizing Work to Promote Well-being and Effectiveness*. San Francisco, CA: Sage.

Parker, S.K., Wall, T.D. and Cordery, J.L. (2001) 'Future work design research and practice: Towards an elaborated model of work design', *Journal of Occupational and Organizational Psychology*, 74 (4): 413–440.

Parker, S.K., Wall, T.D. and Jackson, P.R. (1997) '"That's not my job": Developing flexible employee work orientations', *Academy of Management Journal*, 40 (4): 899–929.

Parker, S.K., Williams, H.M. and Turner, N. (2006) 'Modeling the antecedents of proactive behavior at work', *Journal of Applied Psychology*, 91 (3): 636–652.

Parkes, K.R. (1995) 'The effects of objective workload on cognitive performance in a field setting: A two-period cross-over trial', *Applied Cognitive Psychology*, 9 (Special): S153–S157.

Pearce, J.A. II and Ravlin, E.C. (1987) 'The design and activation of self-regulating work groups', *Human Relations*, 40 (11): 751–782.

Pratt, M.G. and Ashforth, B.E. (2003) 'Fostering Meaningfulness in Working and Meaningfulness at Work: An Identity Perspective', in K. Cameron, J.E.Dutton and R.E. Quinn (eds.), *Positive Organizational Scholarship*. San Francisco: Berrett-Koehler, pp. 309–327.

Rentsch, J.R. and Steel, R.P. (1998) 'Testing the durability of job characteristics as predictors of absenteeism over a six-year period', *Personnel Psychology*, 51 (1): 165–190.

Rice, A.K. (1958) *Productivity and Social Organization*. London: Tavistock.

Robert, C., Probst, T.M., Martocchio, J.J., Drasgow, F. and Lawler, J.J. (2000) 'Empowerment and continuous improvement in the United States, Mexico, Poland, and India: Predicting fit on the basis of the dimensions of power distance and individualism', *Journal of Applied Psychology*, 85 (5): 643–658.

Saavedra, R. and Kwun, S.K. (2000) 'Affective states in job characteristics theory', *Journal of Organizational Behavior*, 21 (2): 131–146.

Salancik, G.R. and Pfeffer, J. (1978) 'A social information processing approach to job attitudes and task design', *Administrative Science Quarterly*, 23 (2): 224–253.

Sargent, L.D. and Terry, D.J. (1998) 'The effects of work control and job demands on employee adjustment and work performance', *Journal of Occupational and Organizational Psychology*, 71 (3): 219–236.

Schaubroeck, J. and Jones, J.R. (2000) 'Antecedents of workplace emotional labor dimensions and moderators of their effects on physical symptoms', *Journal of Organizational Behavior*, 21 (2): 163–183.

Schneider, B., Reichers, A.E. and Mitchell, T.M. (1982) 'A note on some relationships between the aptitude requirements and reward attributes of tasks', *Academy of Management Journal*, 25 (3): 567–574.

Schneider, J. and Locke, E.A. (1971) 'A critique of Herzberg's incident classification system and a suggested revision', *Organizational Behavior and Human Performance*, 6 (4): 441–457.

Smith, A. (1776) *The Wealth of Nations* (Republished in 1974 ed.). Harmondsworth: Penguin.

Speier, C. and Frese, M. (1997) 'Generalized self-efficacy as a mediator and moderator between control and complexity at work and personal initiative: A longitudinal field study in East Germany', *Human Performance*, 10 (2): 171–192.

Sprigg, C.A., Jackson, P.R. and Parker, S.K. (2000) 'Production teamworking: The importance of interdependence and autonomy for employee strain and satisfaction', *Human Relations*, 53 (11): 1519–1543.

Sprigg, C.A., Stride, C.B., Wall, T.D. and Holman, D.J. (2007) 'Work characteristics, musculoskeletal disorders, and the mediating role of psychological strain: A study of call center employees', *Journal of Applied Psychology*, 92 (5): 1456–1466.

Stansfeld, S.A., Fuhrer, R., Head, J., Ferrie, J. and Shipley, M. (1997) 'Work and psychiatric disorder in the Whitehall II study', *Journal of Psychosomatic Research*, 43 (1): 73–81.

Staw, B.M. and Boettger, R.D. (1990) 'Task revision: A neglected form of work performance', *Academy of Management Journal*, 33 (3): 534–559.

Storey, J. (1994) *New Wave Manufacturing Practices: Organizational and Human Resources Management Dimensions.* London: Chapman & Hall.

Taber, T.D. and Taylor, E. (1990) 'A review and evaluation of the psychometric properties of the job diagnostic survey', *Personnel Psychology*, 43 (3): 467–500.

Taylor, F.W. (1911) *The Principles of Scientific Management.* New York: Harper.

Theorell, T. and Karasek, R.A. (1996) 'Current issues relating to psychosocial job strain and cardiovascular disease research', *Journal of Occupational Health Psychology*, 1 (1): 9–26.

Thomas, K.W. and Velthouse, B.A. (1990) 'Cognitive elements of empowerment: An "interpretive" model of intrinsic task motivation', *Academy of Management Review*, 15 (4): 666–681.

Tiegs, R.B., Tetrick, L.E. and Fried, Y. (1992) 'Growth need strength and context satisfactions as moderators of the relations of the job characteristics model', *Journal of Management*, 18 (3): 575–593.

Torraco, R.J. (2005) 'Work design theory: A review and critique with implications for human resource development', *Human Resource Development Quarterly*, 16 (1): 85–109.

Trist, E.L. and Bamforth, K.W. (1951) 'Some social and psychological consequences of the Longwall method of coal-getting', *Human Relations*, 4 (3): 3–38.

Tschanh, F., Rochat, S. and Zapf, D. (2005) 'It's not only clients: Studying emotion work with clients and co-workers with an event-sampling approach', *Journal of Occupational and Organizational Psychology*, 78 (2): 195–220.

Van Yperen, N.W. and Snijders, T.A.B. (2000) 'A multi-level analysis of the demands-control model: Is stress at work determined by factors at the group level or the individual level?', *Journal of Occupational Health Psychology*, 5 (1): 182–190.

Vough, C. and Asbell, B. (1975) *Productivity: A Practical Program for Improving Efficiency.* Melrose, MA: Productivity Research International.

Walker, C.R. and Guest, R. (1952) *The Man on the Assembly Line.* Cambridge, MA: Harvard University Press.

Wall, T.D. and Clegg, C.W. (1981) 'A longitudinal field study of group work redesign', *Journal of Occupational Behaviour*, 2 (1): 31–49.

Wall, T.D., Corbett, M.J., Martin, R., Clegg, C.W. and Jackson, P.R. (1990) 'Advanced manufacturing technology, work design and performance: A change study', *Journal of Applied Psychology*, 75 (6): 691–697.

Wall, T.D., Jackson, P.R. and Davids, K. (1992) 'Operator work design and robotics system performance: A serendipitous field study', *Journal of Applied Psychology*, 77 (3): 353–362.

Warr, P. (1987) *Work, Unemployment, and Mental Health.* Oxford: Clarendon Press.

White, J.K. (1978) 'Generalizability of individual difference moderators of the participation in decision making-employee response relationship', *Academy of Management Journal*, 21 (1): 36–43.

Wright, B.M. and Cordery, J.L. (1999) 'Production uncertainty as a contextual moderator of employee reactions to job design', *Journal of Applied Psychology*, 84 (3): 456–463.

Wrzesniewski, A. and Dutton, J.E. (2001) 'Crafting a job: Revisioning employees as active crafters of their work', *Academy of Management Review*, 26 (2): 179–201.

Wrzesniewski, A., Dutton, J.E. and Debebe, G. (2003) 'Interpersonal Sensemaking and the Meaning of Work', in R.M. Kramer and B.M. Staw (eds), *Research in Organizational Behavior.* Amsterdam: Elsevier. Vol. 25: pp. 93–136.

Wrzesniewski, A., McCauley, C., Rozin, P. and Schwartz, B. (1997) 'Jobs, careers, and callings: People's relations to their work', *Journal of Research in Personality*, 31 (1): 21–33.

23

Job Performance

Sabine Sonnentag, Judith Volmer and
Anne Spychala

Individual performance is of high relevance for organizations and individuals alike. Showing high performance when accomplishing tasks results in satisfaction, feelings of self-efficacy and mastery (Bandura, 1997; Kanfer et al., 2005). Moreover, high performing individuals get promoted, awarded and honored. Career opportunities for individuals who perform well are much better than those of moderate or low performing individuals (Van Scotter et al., 2000).

This chapter summarizes research on individual performance and addresses performance as a multi-dimensional and dynamic concept. First, we define the concept of performance, next we discuss antecedents of between-individual variation of performance, and describe intraindividual change and variability in performance, and finally, we present a research agenda for future research.

JOB PERFORMANCE AS A MULTI-DIMENSIONAL CONCEPT

The concept and definition of individual performance has received considerable scholarly research attention over the past 15 to 20 years.

Researchers agree that performance has to be considered as a multi-dimensional concept. On the most basic level one can distinguish between a process aspect (i.e., behavioral) and an outcome aspect of performance (Borman and Motowidlo, 1993; Campbell, McCloy, Oppler, and Sager, 1993; Roe, 1999).

The behavioral aspect refers to what people do while at work, the action itself (Campbell, 1990). Performance encompasses specific behavior (e.g., sales conversations with customers, teaching statistics to undergraduate students, programming computer software, assembling parts of a product). This conceptualization implies that only actions that can be scaled (i.e., counted) are regarded as performance (Campbell et al., 1993). Moreover, this performance concept explicitly only describes behavior which is goal-oriented, i.e. behavior which the organization hires the employee to do well as performance (Campbell et al., 1993).

The outcome aspect in turn refers to the result of the individual's behavior. The actions described above might result in contracts or selling numbers, students' knowledge in statistical procedures, a software product, or numbers of products assembled. Empirically, the behavioral and outcome aspect are related. However, there is no complete overlap, as the outcome aspect is affected by other determinants than the behavioral aspect. Imagine a car retailer who communicates the preferences of a product (behavioral aspect) excellently, but who nevertheless achieves low sales figures (outcome aspect) due to low demand of this specific type of cars. Similarly, a teacher who provides an excellent statistics lesson which fulfills all learning requirements (behavioral aspect) might not provide students with knowledge (outcome aspect) if students' lack motivation or cognitive abilities.

Moreover, performance must be distinguished from effectiveness and from productivity or efficiency (Campbell et al., 1993; Pritchard et al., 1992). Effectiveness refers to the evaluations of the results of performance (i.e., financial value of sales). In comparison, productivity is the ratio of effectiveness to the cost of attaining the outcome. For example, the ratio of hours of work (input) in relation to products assembled (outcome) describes productivity.

A great deal of attention has been paid to the distinction between task and contextual performance. There are three basic differences between task and contextual performance (Borman and Motowidlo, 1997; Motowidlo et al., 1997; Motowidlo and Schmit, 1999):

(1) contextual performance activities are comparable for almost all jobs, whereas task performance is job specific;
(2) task performance is predicted mainly by ability, whereas contextual performance is mainly predicted by motivation and personality;
(3) task performance is in-role behavior and part of the formal job-description, whereas contextual performance is extra-role behavior and discretionary (i.e. not enforceable), and often not rewarded by formal reward systems or directly or indirectly considered by the management.

Task performance

Task performance covers a person's contribution to organizational performance, refers to actions that are part of the formal reward system (i.e., technical core), and addresses the requirements as specified in job descriptions (Williams and Karau, 1991). At a general level, task performance consists of activities that transform materials into the goods and services produced by the organization or to allow for efficient functioning of the organization (Motowidlo et al., 1997). Thus, task performance covers the fulfillment of the requirements that are part of the contract between the employer and employee.

Moreover, task performance in itself can be described as a multi-dimensional construct. Campbell (1990) proposed a hierarchical model of eight performance factors. Among these eight factors, five refer to task performance:

(1) job-specific task proficiency;
(2) non-job-specific task proficiency;
(3) written and oral communication proficiency;
(4) supervision, in case of leadership position; and partly
(5) management/administration.

Each of these five factors itself consists of subfactors which are differently important for various jobs. For example, the supervision factor includes (1) guiding, directing, and motivating subordinates and providing feedback, (2) maintaining good working relationships, and (3) coordinating subordinates and others resources to get the job done (Borman and Brush, 1993).

Contextual performance

Often it is not sufficient to comply with the formal job requirements, one needs to go beyond what is formally required (Parker et al., 2006; Sonnentag and Frese, 2002). Contextual performance consists of behavior that does not directly contribute to organizational performance but supports the organizational, social and psychological environment. Contextual performance is different from task performance as it includes activities that are not formally part of the job description. It indirectly contributes to an organization's performance by facilitating task performance.

Borman and Motowidlo (1993) enumerate five categories of contextual performance:

(1) volunteering for activities beyond a person's formal job requirements;
(2) persistence of enthusiasm and application when needed to complete important task requirements;
(3) assistance to others;
(4) following rules and prescribed procedures even when it is inconvenient; and
(5) openly defending organization objectives.

Examples of contextual performance are demonstrating extra effort, following organizational rules and policies, helping and cooperating with others, or alerting colleagues about work-related problems (Borman and Motowidlo, 1993; Motowidlo et al., 1997).

In the past, contextual performance was conceptualized and measured in numerous ways. On a very general level, these different conceptualizations can be identified that aim at the effective functioning of an organization as it does at a certain time ('stabilizing' contextual performance), and proactive behaviors which intend to implement new and innovative procedures and processes in an organization, thus changing the organization ('proactive' contextual performance; Sonnentag and Frese, 2002).

The 'stabilizing' contextual performance comprises organizational citizenship behavior (OCB; Organ, 1988), and some aspects of prosocial organizational behavior (Brief and Motowidlo, 1986). OCB describes discretionary behavior which is not necessarily recognized and rewarded by the formal reward system. Discretionary means that the behavior is not enforceable and not part of the formal role in terms of the person's contract with the organization. Furthermore, Organ (1988) explains that not every single discrete instance of OCB is expected to make a difference in organizational outcomes, but that the aggregate promotes the effective functioning of an organization

(Organ, 1988; 1997). OCB consists of five components:

- altruism (i.e. helping others);
- conscientiousness (i.e., compliance to the organization);
- civic virtue (e.g., keeping up with matters that affect the organization);
- courtesy (e.g., consulting with others before taking action); and
- sportsmanship (e.g., not complaining about trivial matters)

(LePine et al., 2002; Organ, 1988).

The more 'proactive' view on contextual performance includes concepts such as personal initiative (Frese et al., 1996), taking charge (Morrison and Phelps, 1999), and proactive behavior (Crant, 1995). Personal initiative is characterized as a self-starting and active approach to work and comprises activities that go beyond what is formally required. Consequently, employees show personal initiative when their behavior fits to an organization's mission, when their goals have a long-term focus, and when they are capable of finding solutions for challenging situations. Similarly, taking charge implies that employees accomplish voluntary and constructive efforts which effect organizationally functional change. Proactive behavior refers to showing self-initiated and future-oriented action that aims to challenge the status quo and improve the current situation (Crant, 1995; Parker et al., 2006). In sum, contextual performance is not a single set of uniform behaviors, but is multidimensional in nature (Van Dyne and LePine, 1998).

Adaptive performance

Campbell et al.'s (1993) taxonomy of work performance did not initially include adaptive performance. However, due to changing and dynamic work environments, the need for adaptive employees has become increasingly important (Pulakos et al., 2000; Smith et al., 1997). Numerous authors refer to adaptability using different names. Hesketh and Neal (1999) referred to adaptive performance,

Murphy and Jackson (1999) discussed role flexibility, and London and Mone (1999) wrote about the proficiency of integrating new learning experiences. As a result of extensive literature review and factor analyses, Pulakos et al. (2000) presented an eight-dimensional taxonomy of adaptive performance:

(1) handling emergencies or crisis situations;
(2) handling work stress;
(3) solving problems creatively;
(4) dealing with uncertain and unpredictable work situations;
(5) learning work tasks, technologies and procedures;
(6) demonstrating interpersonal adaptability;
(7) demonstrating cultural adaptability; and
(8) demonstrating physically oriented adaptability.

These dimensions of adaptive performance were shown to exist across many different types of jobs (Pulakos et al., 2000).

Like task and contextual performance, adaptive performance also appears to be a multidimensional construct. However, future research is needed to specify, for example, the antecedents and consequences of adaptive performance and the generalizability of the adaptive performance taxonomy suggested by Pulakos and her co-workers (2000). Given the increased importance of adaptive performance, more empirical research is needed.

Relationship between task, contextual and adaptive performance

One can distinguish conceptually between task, contextual, and adaptive performance; and task and contextual performance can be separated empirically (Griffin et al., 2000, Motowidlo and Van Scotter, 1994). Additionally, there is evidence that task and contextual performance are differently important for outcome variables (Conway, 1999; Johnson, 2001). In a meta-analysis of managerial jobs, Conway (1999) found that task and contextual performance (job dedication, interpersonal facilitation) contributed

uniquely to overall managerial performance. Moreover, Johnson (2001) showed that raters vary the relative weight they put on different aspects of performance speaking in favor of raters' implicit models of performance dimensions.

Recently, Griffin et al. (2007) presented and tested a model that aimed at integrating major performance concepts. These authors argued that two principle changes (i.e., increasing interdependence and uncertainty of work systems) require an integrative model of different performance dimensions. They defined three core performance dimensions, namely proficiency, adaptivity, and proactivity which they classified at three levels (individual, team and organization). Proficiency covers the fulfillment of role requirements that can be formalized, adaptivity refers to the extent of adaptation to changes at the workplace and proactivity describes the extent of self-directed action necessary to adapt to changes. Griffin et al. (2007) regarded individual task proficiency to be comparable to task performance, and adaptivity and proactivity to be especially important in uncertain situations. Furthermore, these different types of behavior are not considered to be mutually exclusive but their importance should vary depending on the uncertainty of the environment.

In sum, performance should be seen as a multidimensional construct with the dimensions being multidimensional themselves. Moreover, each performance dimension is related to different aspects of organizational success (e.g., task performance helps to satisfy technical core requirements). The ongoing rapid changes in technology (Burke and Ng, 2006), mergers and fusions (Pike, 2006), and the globalization of many firms (Black et al., 1991) require workers to be increasingly tolerant of uncertainty (Pulakos et al., 2000).

Measurement of performance

Given the centrality of job performance in organizations, it becomes clear that the measurement of individual performance should capture job performance as reliable and valid as possible.

A variety of measures of job performance has been used over the past decades (Campbell et al., 1990; Viswesvaran et al., 1996). For example, rating scales, tests of job knowledge, hands-on job samples, and archival records have been used to assess job performance (Campbell et al., 1990). From these measurement options, performance ratings (e.g. peer ratings and supervisor ratings) are the most frequent way of measuring job performance (Viswesvaran et al., 1996). Often, 'objective' criteria such as sales figures and production records are requested. However, even these criteria involve subjective judgments of which specific type of criteria pictures performance (Campbell, 1990) and are, like other performance measures, not perfect.

Several studies have focused on the degree of convergence across various sources of performance ratings (Conway and Huffcutt, 1997; Harris and Schaubroeck, 1988; Mabe and West, 1982; Viswesvaran et al., 1996). Using meta-analysis, Viswesvaran et al., (1996) compared the reliability of supervisor ratings and peer ratings. They concluded that supervisory ratings showed higher interrater reliability than peer ratings. Another meta-analytic review (Harris and Schaubroeck, 1988) revealed that self and supervisor ratings correlated moderately ($r = 0.35$) as did self and peer ratings ($r = 0.36$), whereas correlations between peer and supervisory ratings were higher ($r = 0.62$). Comparing the reliability of peer and supervisor ratings, findings yield higher correlations of different supervisors ratings assessing the same individual compared to different peers ratings evaluating the same individual (Conway and Huffcutt, 1997; Mount et al., 1998).

Woehr et al. (2005) investigated the impact of the performance dimension (e.g., technical knowledge, integrity, and leadership) and rating source (i.e., peer, self, and supervisor) as well as the degree of measurement equivalence across sources. Results suggest that the impact of the underlying performance dimension is comparable across different rating sources. Woehr et al. (2005) also found that, in terms of a multi-trait multi-method approach, trait effects (source) were larger than method (source) effects. Thus, Woehr et al. (2005) concluded that ratings from different sources are to some extent comparable. However, there is no perfect convergence of ratings across sources and at present it is not clear if this is attributable to systematic or random error components.

Literature examining the effect of contextual performance on managerial evaluations (Conway, 1999; Van Scotter and Motowidlo, 1996; Werner, 1994) suggests that manager ratings should, aside from evaluations of task performance, incorporate ratings of contextual performance and that the effects of contextual performance on organizational performance and success are at least as great as those of task performance (Podsakoff et al., 2000).

As it is not always possible to assess multiple performance dimensions in practice, it is valuable to know if there is one general factor in ratings of job performance. Viswesvaran et al. (2005) addressed this question using a meta-analytic framework, and their results suggest that there is one large general factor. This finding implies that the practice of generating a composite measure of various performance dimensions seems to be justifiable as long as it is theoretically satisfying.

Summary and conclusion

The overview of the major performance dimensions views individual performance as a multi-dimensional concept. At the most basic level, performance can be differentiated in terms of process and outcome. Moreover, one can distinguish between task, contextual, and adaptive performance and each of these types in itself is multidimensional. These performance types differ with respect to their antecedents and consequences and can be conceptually and empirically separated. Measurement of performance is central as important organizational decisions are based on individual performance. Future research is needed to clarify the interplay of the different performance types.

PREDICTORS OF INTERINDIVIDUAL DIFFERENCES IN JOB PERFORMANCE

Both theoretically and practically, it is critical to identify predictors of job performance. Most generally, one can differentiate between person-specific and situation-specific predictor variables. Person-specific variables are individual difference variables, that is, variables that differ between individuals, but are expected to be rather stable within individuals. Situation-specific variables characterize the work situation or the organizational context, but not the individual person.

Person-specific variables

Individuals differ considerably in job performance level. In jobs with low difficulty, the performance of the highest performer exceeds the lowest performers between two to four times, whereas in jobs with high difficulty, highest performers may exceed the lowest performers by even a greater ratio (Campbell et al., 1996). What predicts these differences? Most research on person-specific predictors of job performance focused on abilities, knowledge, experience, and non-cognitive traits.

Cognitive abilities

Ability refers to 'the power or capacity to act financially, legally, mentally, physically, or in some other way' (Ree et al., 2001: 21). Cognitive ability refers to qualifications or capacity with respect to mental tasks. Substantive research efforts have been undertaken to examine whether general mental ability (GMA), also referred to as 'g' (Spearman, 1904), is related to job performance. Meta-analyses show that GMA is a strong predictor of job performance. For example, in a comprehensive meta-analysis based on data from 425 studies (N = 32,124) Hunter and Hunter (1984) reported a corrected mean correlation of 0.51 (corrected for range restriction and criterion unreliability) between measures of GMA and job performance, a finding replicated from data in the US and Canada (for summaries, see Salgado et al., 2001; Schmidt

and Hunter, 2004). More recent meta-analyses based on UK and other European samples reported corrected mean correlations between GMA and job performance of 0.48 (Bertua et al., 2005) and 0.62 (Salgado et al., 2003) suggesting that the association between GMA and job performance is culturally invariant, at least within Western cultures. Additional analyses based on meta-analytic data showed that the correlations between GMA and job performance differ across job types. Generally, the correlations are higher for more complex jobs; but also for less complex jobs GMA remains substantially related to job performance.

Studies examining the association between more specific abilities also found substantive correlations between these abilities and indicators of job performance. For example, Bertua et al. (2005) reported corrected correlations between verbal, numerical, perceptual, and special abilities on the one hand and job performance on the other hand of 0.39, 0.42, 0.50, 0.35 respectively. Thus, these specific abilities were nearly as strong predictors of job performance as is GMA.

An important question in this research area is whether specific cognitive abilities contribute to the prediction of job performance beyond the predictive power of GMA. Based on data from 1,036 enlistees from the US Air Force working in seven different jobs, Ree et al. (1994) concluded that specific abilities added significantly to the prediction of job performance, but that this incremental contribution was small in practical terms (cf. Olea and Ree, 1994). Ree et al.'s conclusion that, in the prediction of job performance, there is 'not much more than g' was and still is heavily debated in the field of personnel selection and beyond (Brown et al., 2006; Reeve, 2004; Sternberg and Wagner, 1993). For example, at least in some types of jobs, social skills add to the prediction of job performance (Ferris et al., 2001).

Most meta-analyses examining the association between cognitive abilities and job performance did not differentiate between various types of job performance, leaving the question of whether cognitive abilities are uniformly related to all types of job performance largely unanswered. Motowidlo et al. (1997) have argued that cognitive ability is mainly related to task performance by impacting on task habits, task skills, and task knowledge. According to these authors, the relationship between cognitive ability and contextual performance should be weaker because cognitive ability should be only related to contextual knowledge, but not to contextual habits or contextual skills.

Empirical research largely supports this assumption. In most studies, the associations between cognitive ability and organizational citizenship behavior or related contextual performance constructs were weak and mostly non-significant (Chan and Schmitt, 2002; Hattrup et al., 1998; LePine and VanDyne, 2001; VanScotter and Motowidlo, 1996; for contrary findings, see Allworth and Hesketh, 1999; Motowidlo and VanScotter, 1994).

With respect to more proactive types of contextual performance, research evidence remains inconclusive. Whereas Fay and Frese (2001) reported a positive relationship between cognitive ability and personal initiative, Le Pine and Van Dyne (2001) showed that cognitive ability was not related to voice behavior as one specific aspect of proactive behavior. Clearly more studies are needed that also take the type of job into account.

Research evidence remains scarce regarding the relationship between cognitive ability and adaptive performance. The few studies that did examine the association between cognitive ability and adaptive performance, however, largely converge in their findings, inasmuch as cognitive ability was found to be positively related to adaptive performance (Allworth and Hesketh, 1999; LePine, 2003; Pulakos et al., 2002).

Thus, there is convincing empirical evidence that cognitive abilities, particularly GMA, are substantially related to overall job performance in general, and to task performance in particular. Cognitive abilities do not seem to be a strong and consistent predictor of contextual performance, but they are associated with adaptive performance.

Knowledge

Campbell et al.'s performance model (1993) proposed declarative and procedural knowledge as core performance determinants. Meta-analytic evidence suggests that job knowledge (i.e., declarative knowledge) is related to job performance. For example, Hunter and Hunter (1984) reported average correlations between job content knowledge tests and performance ratings of 0.48. A more recent meta-analysis examining the relationship between written knowledge tests and job performance resulted in an effect size (corrected for the effects of sampling error, range restriction and criterion unreliability) of 0.45. Moderator analysis indicated that the relationship was higher for more complex jobs (Dye et al., 1993).

Studies assessing more procedural aspects of knowledge reported that the correlations between tacit knowledge and job performance ranged between 0.20 and 0.40 (Sternberg, 1997). A meta-analysis that used situational judgement tests as measures for procedural knowledge found a mean estimated population correlation of 0.34 between these knowledge measures and job performance (McDaniel et al., 2001).

Generally, it is argued that job knowledge mediates between individual dispositions (e.g., cognitive ability and personality) and job performance. Using path-analysis, Schmidt et al. (1986) demonstrated that job knowledge mediates the relationship between general mental ability and job performance, suggesting that individuals high on cognitive ability are more successful in acquiring job-relevant knowledge that in turn helps them to accomplish their work tasks.

Chan and Schmitt (2002) examined the relationship between situational judgement test measures and various aspects of job performance. In a study based on data from 160 civil service employees the authors found that the situational judgement test score predicted task performance as well as contextual performance (job dedication, interpersonal facilitation). Interestingly, the situational judgement test predicted task and contextual performance beyond cognitive abilities, personality factors, and job experience (for a similar finding see also Clevenger et al., 2001).

Knowledge might not only be related to task performance but also to proactive and adaptive performance. For example, Fay and Frese (2001) have argued that knowledge helps in showing proactive behavior. Parker et al. (1997) conceptualized the subjective importance of production knowledge as one core facet of a flexible work orientation (i.e., an individual's propensity to show proactive performance). In addition, research has shown that knowledge can also be beneficial for adaptive performance (Chen et al., 2005).

Taken together, there is convincing evidence that knowledge is related to various aspects of job performance. However knowledge may not only affect performance, but specific facets of performance may help in increasing knowledge (cf., Seibert et al., 2001).

Experience

Job experience is also relevant for performance. Hunter and Hunter (1984) reported a mean corrected correlation between job experience and job performance of 0.18 (corrected for measurement error in job performance ratings). Another meta-analysis (McDaniel et al., 1988) reported a higher estimate of the population estimate and further indicated that the relationship between job experience and job performance decreases with age. A more recent meta-analysis resulting in an overall effect size of 0.13 suggests the relationship between job experience and performance might be also contingent on job complexity and type of performance measurement (Sturman, 2003).

Another meta-analysis on the relationship between experience and job performance differentiated between diverse performance measures (soft vs. hard), measurement mode (amount, i.e. number of times having performed a particular task, time, and type), and level of specificity (task experience, job experience, organizational experience; Quiñones et al., 1995), with an overall mean estimated population correlation, of 0.27. Correlations were higher for hard as opposed to soft performance measures, for amount of experience compared to time and type, and for task experience, compared to job or organizational experience. This meta-analytic finding suggests that experience is a complex construct and the time aspect of job experience might not be most relevant for job performance.

To advance knowledge on the role of experience, Tesluk and Jacobs (1998) suggested a comprehensive model that includes qualitative aspects of experience, particularly type of experience including variety, challenge and complexity. Also, research on managerial learning suggests that specific experiences and individuals' reactions to these experiences might matter more for subsequent performance than simple quantitative indicators of experience (McCauley et al., 1994).

Meta-analytic findings on the role of experience mostly refer to task performance or overall job performance. Research evidence on the relationship between job experience and contextual performance is relatively scarce, and mostly yields weak correlations between job experience and contextual performance, particularly OCB-related indicators (Chan and Schmitt, 2002; Motowidlo and VanScotter, 1994; VanScotter and Motowidlo, 1996). With respect to adaptive performance, research showed a weak positive correlation between experience with change and this performance aspect (Allworth and Hesketh, 1999).

Thus, quantitative aspects of job experience show weak to moderate associations with task performance, and rather low correlations with contextual and adaptive performance. Moderator variables probably play a substantial role in the relationship between job experiences and performance.

Non-cognitive predictors

In addition to cognitive factors (e.g., general mental ability and knowledge) and experience, non-cognitive traits have also received considerable research attention as potential person-specific predictors of job performance. These non-cognitive traits include personality factors such as proposed by the Five Factor

Model (Digman, 1990; McCrae and Costa, 1989), more narrow traits (Dudley et al., 2006), the proactive personality concept (Crant, 1995), and core self-evaluations (Judge and Bono, 2001).

The Five Factor Model differentiates five distinct dimensions of personality:

- emotional stability;
- extraversion:
- openness to experience;
- agreeableness;
- conscientiousness.

Individuals high on emotional stability (i.e., low neuroticism) are characterized by low negative affectivity and tend to respond with less subjective distress to negative events than do individuals low on emotional stability. Extraversion refers to individuals' propensity to experience positive affect and to be sociable, assertive, and energized by social interactions. Openness to experience characterizes an individual's tendency to be creative, flexible, imaginative and willing to take risks. Agreeableness describes individuals who are kind, gentle, likable, cooperative, and considerate. Conscientiousness refers to an individual's degree of being orderly, self-disciplined, achievement-oriented, reliable and perseverant.

An early meta-analysis on the relationship between these Big Five personality factors and job performance (based on 162 samples from 117 studies) showed generally low correlations between personality factors and performance measures. Specifically, the estimated true correlations were 0.08 for emotional stability, 0.13 for extraversion, 0.04 for openness to experience, 0.07 for agreeableness and between 0.22 for conscientiousness (Barrick and Mount, 1991).

Kanfer and Kantrowitz (2002) summarized the findings from 11 meta-analytic studies published between 1990 and 2000 that addressed the relationship between personality and job performance. The estimated true-score correlations between personality and overall job performance ranged between 0.08 and 0.22 for emotional stability, 0.09 and 0.16 for extraversion, −0.03 and 0.27 for openness to experience, −0.01 and 0.33 for agreeableness and 0.12 and 0.31 for conscientiousness.

When differentiating between diverse aspects of job performance, the pattern of overall findings picture does not change substantially. Meta-analyses on the relationship between dimensions of the Five Factor Model of personality and OCB resulted in estimated true correlations ranging between 0.23 and 0.30 for conscientiousness (Dalal, 2005; LePine et al., 2002; Organ and Ryan, 1995). The estimated true correlation between emotional stability (low negative affect) and OCB was 0.10 (Dalal, 2005; Organ and Ryan, 1995) and between agreeableness and OCB it was 0.12 (Organ and Ryan, 1995).

It has been suggested that proactive performance is predicted by a specific personality concept, namely proactive personality (Crant, 1995). Not surprisingly, proactive personality predicts proactive performance (Parker et al., 2006; Thompson, 2005). More interestingly, proactive personality was also significantly related to task performance (Crant, 1995; Thompson, 2005). In addition, there is some evidence that personality predicts adaptive performance (Pulakos et al., 2002; but see also Griffin and Hesketh, 2003, 2004).

Broad personality traits such as global conscientiousness might not be the best predictors of job performance (Dudley et al., 2006). Meta-analysis showed that more narrow personality traits (achievement, dependability, order, and cautiousness) contribute to the prediction of performance beyond the predictive power of global conscientiousness. The amount of additional variance explained varied across performance criteria with the largest increase of more than 25 per cent of the variance for job dedication and much smaller increases for other performance facets such as overall job performance and task performance (Dudley et al., 2006).

One personality-related framework that received increasing research attention during the past decade refers to individuals' core self-evaluations. Judge et al. (1998) characterized core self-evaluations as 'fundamental, subconscious conclusions individuals reach about themselves, other people, and the world' (Judge et al., 1998: 18; cf. also Judge et al., 1997). Core self-evaluations comprise an individual's self-esteem, generalized self-efficacy, locus of control, and emotional stability. Meta-analytic evidence suggests that these core self-evaluations are related to job performance (Judge and Bono, 2001). More specifically, self-esteem showed a corrected correlation of 0.26 with job performance. For generalized self-efficacy, locus of control and emotional stability the corrected correlations were 0.23, 0.22, and 0.19 respectively.

Thus, empirical data show that personality is related to job performance. However, overall the effect sizes are relatively small, particularly in comparison to cognitive ability predictors.

Situation-specific variables: work characteristics and job design

Job performance is not only influenced by person-specific variables such as general mental abilities, but also by characteristics of the situation in which the performance occurs. Research on situational antecedents of job performance addresses workplace factors that enhance as well as potentially hinder performance, and includes research on leadership and reward systems (e.g. Gerstner and Day, 1997; Podsakoff et al., 2006). We now concentrate on workplace factors and their relationships to job performance.

The Job Characteristics Model (JCM) is a major approach that deals with workplace factors that enhance performance (Hackman and Oldham, 1976). The JCM describes the relationships between core job characteristics, critical psychological states and personal and work outcomes. Hackman and Oldham (1976) assumed that core job characteristics (i.e., skill variety, task identity, task significance, autonomy, and feedback) support the quality of job performance as well as other outcomes such as internal work motivation, job satisfaction, absenteeism, or turnover by enhancing critical psychological states (i.e., experienced meaningfulness of the work, experienced

responsibility for outcomes of the work, and knowledge of the actual results of the work activities). Additionally, they proposed that individual growth need strength moderates these relationships.

Most of the empirical work based on the JCM focused on task performance and overall job performance. Meta-analytic findings showed small, but positive associations between job characteristics and job performance. Fried and Ferris (1987) reported corrected mean correlations between job performance and feedback, autonomy, task identity, and skill variety of 0.22, 0.18, 0.13, and 0.09 respectively, based on data from eight studies (N = 1,091) and between job performance and task significance of 0.14 based on seven studies (N = 1,031). However, the data also suggested the existence of moderators between autonomy and task significance on the one hand and job performance on the other hand. In a meta-analysis based on data from 18 studies (N = 6,291), Spector (1986) reported an adjusted mean correlation of 0.26 (corrected for unreliability of the measures) between autonomy and job performance. Concerning mediating effects of the assumed psychological states in the job characteristics-performance relationships inconclusive results were reported in the mentioned meta-analyses. Additionally, in a review of 26 studies, only weak support was found for the assumed moderator effect of individual growth need strength on the relationships between job characteristics and job performance (Graen et al., 1986). Because of the cross-sectional character of many studies, causal interpretations are not warranted, and it remains unclear whether better jobs foster high performance, or vice versa. However, intervention studies showed that job redesign had positive effects on job performance (Guzzo et al., 1985; Parker and Turner, 2002), lending some support to the interpretation that well-designed jobs increase performance (for the most recent meta-analysis see Humphrey et al., 2007).

Although there is empirical evidence for a positive relationship between particular job characteristics and task performance, the specific mechanisms are not yet fully understood. Exemplary for the relationship between task autonomy and job performance Langfred and Moye (2004) discussed motivational, informational, and structural mechanisms with some mechanisms enhancing but other mechanisms impeding performance.

Research on relationships between job characteristics and contextual or adaptive performance is very scarce. However, Chiu and Chen (2005) reported significant associations between particular job characteristics (i.e., skill variety and task significance) and OCB, which were partially mediated by intrinsic job satisfaction. Furthermore, significant relationships were found between autonomy or job control and proactive behavior (Ohly et al., 2006; Parker, 2003; Parker et al., 1997), which were mediated by psychological states such as control orientation and self-efficacy (Frese et al., 2007; Parker et al., 2006; Speier and Frese, 1997).

Regarding workplace factors that potentially hinder job performance (often called stressors), much research has focused on role stressors. Role theory suggests that role ambiguity and role conflict deplete job performance (Kahn et al., 1964; see the Chapter by Jex in this volume). Meta-analytic findings revealed a negative, non-significant relationship between role ambiguity and job performance (corrected mean correlations with various performance measures ranging between −0.04 and −0.28; Tubre and Collins, 2000). The relationship between role conflict and job performance was also negative, but much smaller than between role ambiguity and performance (corrected mean correlations between −0.12 and 0.03 depending on the performance measure; Tubre and Collins, 2000).

Situational constraints are also negatively related to job performance (Bacharach and Bamberger, 1995; Peters and O'Connor, 1980). Situational constraints refer to problems with machines, incomplete materials or lack of necessary information, and these stressors impede job performance directly and indirectly: For example, problems with machines directly hinder the accomplishment

of a task and can additionally reduce effort-to-performance expectancies. In a meta-analysis Villanova and Roman (1993) reported a negative, non-significant relationship between situational constraints and job performance (mean correlation of −0.14 based on 11 studies with N = 9,273).

In their meta-analysis, LePine et al. (2005) summarized relationships between various stressors and job performance by classifying different stressors as hindrance versus challenge. Hindrance stressors included role stressors and situational constraints and were negatively related to job performance (corrected mean correlation of −0.20 based on 73 studies with N = 14,943). Challenge stressors on the other hand (e.g., demands, pressure, time urgency, and workload) were positively related to performance (corrected mean correlation of 0.12 based on 20 studies, N = 3,465). Thus, some stressors hinder job performance, but others enhance job performance.

Importantly, these results refer mainly to task or global performance. Initial studies on the relationships between stressors and contextual performance (namely proactive behavior) reported positive relationships between time pressure and personal initiative (Fay and Sonnentag, 2002; Sonnentag, 2003), which is consistent with the results of LePine et al. (2005) on challenge stressors. Furthermore, Fay and Sonnentag (2002) reported a positive relationship between situational constraints (a hindrance stressor) and personal initiative. Thus, whereas hindrance stressors seem to impede task performance, this does not have to be true for specific aspects of contextual performance. Perhaps situational constraints point to sub-optimalities in the work organization that elicit attempts for improving the situation (Fay et al., 1998).

Overall, challenge stressors (e.g. time pressure, demands) seem to be positively associated with task performance and also with proactive behavior, whereas hindrance stressors (e.g. role stressors and situational constraints) seem to be negatively associated with task performance but possibly positively with proactive behavior.

INTRAINDIVIDUAL CHANGE AND VARIABILITY IN PERFORMANCE

Most research discussed in earlier sections of this chapter adopted a between-person perspective on performance, assuming that individual performance is rather stable – at least as long as the work situation does not change and as long as no learning occurs. However, researchers have long recognized that performance is not a stable construct and that within-individual performance variability is large (e.g., Ghiselli and Haire, 1960). During the past 10 to 20 years, questions regarding within-person performance variability and change received increased research attention – a trend that may be, at least partially – attributed to the increased availability of statistical methods and software programs that allow for analyzing within-person variability and change. Research in intraindividual change and variability of performance is important and interesting for a number of reasons. First, it promises a more thorough understanding of the performance phenomenon itself. Second, it examines if performance predictors such as cognitive ability are uniformly relevant and powerful across various levels of job experience. Third, it points to additional, more transient predictors of performance that can not be captured when approaching performance only from an individual difference or a job design perspective.

Research on intra-individual variability and change of performance addressed a number of issues. A basic issue is whether individual performance itself is stable over time (Henry and Hulin, 1987). Empirical evidence suggests that individual performance does not only change contingent on job tenure (McDaniel et al., 1988) and – to a small extent – ageing processes (Waldman and Avolio, 1986), but also that individuals' rank order with respect to performance changes over time (Hanges et al., 1990; Hofmann et al., 1992): The best performers at a given point in time might not be the best performers five or ten years later.

A related line of research aims at describing the patterns of change, and identifying predictors of intraindividual change over time. In other words, the core question is which variables account for increases (or decreases) in performance over time – relative to the performance of other individuals working under similar conditions. Interindividual differences relevant for skill acquisition are one core reason for intraindividual change over time (Ackerman, 1987; Fleishman, 1972).

Murphy (1989) suggested that cognitive abilities and other dispositional variables are not uniformly important at all levels of job tenure. Murphy differentiated between a transition stage (e.g., times when an employee is new to a job or when major aspects of the job change) and a maintenance stage (i.e., times when an employee has well learned his or her major tasks). During the transition stage, when new skills must be learned, cognitive abilities are important for performing well, whereas during maintenance stage, cognitive abilities will not play a major role for job performance any more, and personality and motivational factors become more important. Using meta-analyses, Keil and Cortina (2001) showed that the relationship between cognitive ability and job performance decreases over time spent on a task, supporting the proposition that cognitive ability loses its predictive validity as experience increases (Ackerman, 1987; Murphy, 1989).

Several studies focusing primarily on sales personnel (for an exception, see Zickar and Slaughter, 1999) showed that there is substantial interindividual difference in intraindividual change in performance over time (Hofmann et al., 1993; Ployhard and Hakel, 1998; Thoresen et al., 2004). A few studies tried to identify predictors of intraindividual change. For example, Ployhart and Hakel (1998) found that initial performance levels and person-specific predictor variables were related to increases in performance over a two-year period: Individuals with higher performance in the first year tended to increase their sales performance more quickly. Similarly, persuasion and empathy (self-report measures of others' perceptions) were positively related to the *increase* in performance increase. Zickar and Slaughter's (1999) study on film directors revealed that those who directed more films per year showed a higher increase in performance (as rated by external film critics) over time, and also demonstrated performance trajectories that were more strongly accelerating. In a study with pharmaceutical sales representative, Thoresen et al. (2004) differentiated between employees working on a maintenance stage and those working on a transitional stage. In the maintenance stage, personality factors were not related to changes in performance over time. In the transition stage, sales representatives high on agreeableness and low on emotional stability were more likely to increase their performance over time. One explanation for this finding is that individuals low on emotional stability will be more concerned in a transitional situation, and therefore might invest more effort that will lead to better performance.

As a whole, empirical research demonstrated that individuals differ in their performance trajectories, with some individuals increasing their performance at a faster rate than others. With respect to predictors of intraindividual changes, recent studies are promising. However, compared to the vast amount of studies on person-specific and situation-specific predictors of interindividual differences in performance, research evidence on predictors of intra-individual change in performance remains limited and not yet well-integrated. Clearly, more studies are needed that include a broader range of predictors and that systematically address cognitive, non-cognitive, experience-related and situational variables and their relative importance. In addition, it appears to be helpful to differentiate between maintenance and transition stages as predictors of the performance change probably differ between these stages.

Most studies on intraindividual change in performance summarized so far refer to changes over longer periods of time (mostly months or years – for an exception see Deadrick et al., 1997). However, performance may also vary within shorter periods of time. For example, Stewart and Nandkeolyar (2006) demonstrated substantial weekly performance

variation in a sample of sales representatives. Thus, it is not only important to identify variables that predict performance change over longer times, it is also interesting to address performance variability within shorter time frames. Beal et al. (2005) recently offered a theoretical approach to intraindividual performance variability that addresses within-person fluctuations of performance within relatively short periods of time (e.g., over the course of a working day). They presented a model of episodic performance to describe how immediate affective experiences are linked to within-person variations of performance. They defined performance episodes as 'behavioral segments that are thematically organized around organizationally relevant goals and objectives' (p. 1055). This model suggests that performance within each performance episode is influenced by a person's general resource level (e.g., cognitive ability, task-relevant skills) and the momentary allocation of resources. Beal et al. argued that performance within an episode is impeded when the person does not succeed in allocating all resources to the primary work task and when attention is diverted by off-task demands. The authors assumed that affective experiences – along with distractions and interruptions that cause specific affective states – are a core source of attentional demands that interfere with the attentional demands of the primary work tasks. A recent empirical study related to this model provided promising results (Beal et al., 2006).

Taken together, the literature summarized in this section suggests that individual performance is not necessarily stable over time. We anticipate that with the advance of available software that can analyze change, more research will be conducted addressing performance variability and change over time.

RESEARCH AGENDA

During the past decades research on job performance has made substantial progress. Core accomplishments are certainly the differentiation between task performance and contextual performance, the differentiation between various contextual performance constructs with a particular focus on proactive performance, the emergence of the adaptive performance concept, new insights on the dynamic nature of performance, and the understanding of the predictors of performance, particularly person-specific predictors. Nonetheless, many questions still remain unanswered. In this section, we suggest some avenues for future research.

Adaptive performance is an interesting concept that receives increasing research attention (Griffin et al., 2007; Pulakos et al., 2000). Conceptual refinements and improved measures are important: Compared to other aspects of job performance (particularly task performance), little is known about predictors of adaptive performance. This applies both to person-specific and situation-specific predictors.

With respect to situational variables as predictors of job performance, future research may address several issues. First, more research is needed on the processes by which specific features of the work situation (e.g., job control) translate into various aspects of job performance (Langfred and Moye, 2004). Second, more focus on job design studies would be helpful in learning about the causal link between situational variables and job performance. Although there is evidence (e.g., Wall and Clegg, 1981) that job design results in performance improvement, more studies are needed that take the recent changes on the nature of work and the context in which work occurs (e.g., globalization) into account when testing the impact of job design interventions (Holman et al., 2003). Third, there is increasing evidence that job stressors do not necessarily impair job performance (LePine et al., 2005), and this is particularly true for proactive performance (e.g., Fay and Sonnentag, 2002). More research is now required that examines how and under what conditions job stressors facilitate performance – without compromising employee health and well-being.

Most studies examining job performance investigated how person-specific and situation-specific variables affect performance. Nevertheless, an interesting avenue for future research would be to examine how performance affects other organizational phenomena and processes. The core underlying assumption here is that showing specific performance behaviors may predict individual orientations, behaviors, or even knowledge (Seibert et al., 2001). Similarly, experiencing oneself as someone who performs well, or being perceived as demonstrating high performance levels, may also influence specific behaviors (Sonnentag and Volmer, in press). More theoretical work is needed that specifies how objective performance levels, as well as subjective perceptions of performance, influence other organizationally relevant processes.

A related question concerns possible effects of task performance on contextual and adaptive performance. As past research has aimed at a differentiation between these three performance aspects (Griffin et al., 2007), the question how task performance might influence contextual and adaptive performance – and vice versa – has received little research attention so far.

Research demonstrated that performance is a dynamic construct and that performance fluctuates within individuals and changes over time. Comprehensive studies are needed that systematically examine the time frames of such fluctuations and changes (Mitchell and James, 2001). Moreover, research on within-individual variability and change focused on task performance (for an exception, Sonnentag, 2003). Future studies may also investigate how contextual and adaptive performance fluctuate and change over time (Grant and Ashford, in press). In addition, as performance in general is predicted by person-specific and situation-specific variables, it seems to be promising to include both person-specific and situation-specific constructs in the prediction of performance fluctuations and change.

Long-term changes in performance levels are at least partially caused by learning processes. While there is a tremendous amount of research examining training and learning processes, resulting in improved task performance (Colquitt et al., 2000; Sonnentag et al., 2004), little is known about how training impacts contextual and adaptive performance. Because it is increasingly important that employees show proactive and adaptive performance at work, opportunities associated with training approaches should be explored (Frese et al., 2002), as investing in training and learning is likely a promising avenue for increasing contextual and adaptive performance.

Although many researchers agree that performance is a process (Campbell, 1990; Grant and Ashford, in press), the performance *process* itself remains a 'grey box.' There are few attempts to disentangle the various aspects of the performance process (Frese, 2007; Marks et al., 2001; Sonnentag and Frese, 2002). For example, such approaches specify how the performance process evolves from goal development, via planning, analysis of the situation, performance execution and monitoring to feedback processing. Much more research is needed to arrive at a more comprehensive understanding of what happens while individuals are performing.

CONCLUSION

Research on job performance has come a long way. Numerous studies have been conducted that have resulted in a solid knowledge base, for example when it comes to the differentiation between different aspects of job performance and person-specific predictors of job performance in general, and task performance in particular. Other areas received comparably less attention but scholars have demonstrated that there are great opportunities for better understanding and predicting job performance. For example, situational variables must not be neglected when predicting job performance. In addition, researchers increasingly challenge the view that job performance is stable over time. These different lines of research provide a set of different approaches that scholars may pursue to ensure a greater knowledge of the nature and predictors of job

performance, that in turn is predicted to facilitate, and high performance in organizational contexts.

REFERENCES

Ackerman, P. L. (1987) 'Individual differences in skill learning: An integration of psychometric and information processing perspectives', *Psychological Bulletin*, 102: 3–27.

Allworth, E. and Hesketh, B. (1999) 'Construct–oriented biodata: Capturing change–related and contextually relevant future performance', *International Journal of Selection and Assessment*, 7: 97–111.

Bandura, A. (1997) *Self-Efficacy: The Exercise of Control*. New York: Freeman.

Bacharach, S. B. and Bamberger, P. (1995) 'Beyond situational constraints: Job resources inadequacy and individual performance at work', *Human Resource Management Review*, 5: 79–102.

Barrick, M. R. and Mount, M. K. (1991) 'The big five personality dimensions and job performance: A meta-analysis', *Personnel Psychology*, 44: 1–26.

Beal, D. J. Weiss, H. M. Barros, E. and MacDermid, S. M. (2005) 'An episodic process model of affective influences on performance', *Journal of Applied Psychology*, 90: 1054–1068.

Beal, D. J., Trougakos, J. P., Weiss, H. M. and Green, S. G. (2006) 'Episodic processes in emotional labor: Perceptions of affective delivery and regulation strategies', *Journal of Applied Psychology*, 91: 1053–1065

Bertua, C., Anderson, N. and Salgado, S. R. (2005) 'The predictive validity of cognitive ability tests: A UK meta-analysis', *Journal of Occupational and Organizational Psychology*, 78: 387–409.

Black, J. S., Mendenhall, M. and Oddou, G. (1991) 'Toward a comprehensive model of international adjustment: An integration of multiple theoretical perspectives', *Academy of Management Review*, 16: 291–317.

Borman, W. C. and Brush, D. H. (1993) 'More progress toward a taxonomy of managerial performance requirements', *Human Performance*, 6: 1–21.

Borman, W. C. and Motowidlo, S. J. (1993) 'Expanding the Criterion Domain to Include Elements of Contextual Performance', in N. Schmitt and W. Borman (eds), *Personnel Selection in Organizations*. New York: Jossey-Bass, pp. 71–98.

Borman, W. C. and Motowidlo, S. J. (1997) 'Task performance and contextual performance: The meaning for personnel selection research', *Human Performance*, 10: 99–109.

Brief, A. P. and Motowidlo, S. J. (1986) 'Prosocial organizational behaviors', *Academy of Management Review*, 11: 710–725.

Brown, K. G., Le, H. and Schmidt, F. L. (2006) 'Specific aptitude theory revisited: Is there incremental validity for training performance?', *International Journal of Selection and Assessment*, 14: 87–100.

Burke, R. J. and Ng, E. (2006) 'The changing nature of work and organizations: Implications for human resource management', *Human Resource Management Review*, 16: 86–94.

Campbell, J. P., Glaser, M. B. and Oswald, F. L. (1996) 'The substantive nature of job performance variability', in K. R. Murphy (ed.), *Individual Differences and Behavior in Organizations*. San Francisco: Jossey-Bass, pp. 258–299.

Campbell, C. H., Ford, P., Rumsey, M. G. and Pulakos, E. D. (1990) 'Development of multiple job performance measures in a representative sample of jobs', *Personnel Psychology*, 43: 277–300.

Campbell, J. P. (1990) 'Modeling the Performance Prediction Problem in Industrial and Organizational Psychology', in M. D. Dunnette and L. M. Hough (eds), *Handbook of Industrial and Organizational Psychology*. Palo Alto: Consulting Psychologists Press. Vol. 1: pp. 687–732.

Campbell, J. P., McCloy, R. A., Oppler, S. H. and Sager, C. E. (1993) 'A theory of performance', in C. W. Schmitt and W. C. A. Borman (eds), *Personnel Selection in Organizations*. San Francisco: Jossey-Bass, pp. 35–70.

Chan, D. and Schmitt, N. (2002) 'Situational judgement and job performance', *Human Performance*, 15: 233–254.

Chen, G., Thomas, B. and Wallace, J. C. (2005) 'A multilevel examination of the relationships among training outcomes, mediating regulatory processes, and adaptive performance', *Journal of Applied Psychology*, 90: 827–841.

Chiu, S.-F. and Chen, H.-L. (2005) 'Relationship between job characteristics and organizational citizenship behavior: The mediational role of job satisfaction', *Social Behavior and Personality*, 33, 523–540

Clevenger, J., Pereira, G. M. and Wiechmann, D. (2001) 'Incremental validity of situational judgment tests', *Journal of Applied Psychology*, 86: 410–417.

Colquitt, J. A., LePine, J. A. and Noe, R. A. (2000) 'Toward an integrative theory of training motivation: A meta-analytic path analysis of 20 years of research', *Journal of Applied Psychology*, 85: 678–707.

Conway, J. M. (1999) 'Distinguishing contextual performance from task performance for managerial jobs', *Journal of Applied Psychology*, 84, 3–13.

Conway, J. M. and Huffcutt, A. I. (1997) 'Psychometric properties of multisource performance ratings: A meta-analysis of subordinate, supervisor, peer, and self-ratings', *Human Performance*, 10: 331–360.

Crant, J. M. (1995) 'The Proactive Personality Scale and objective job performance among real estate agents', *Journal of Applied Psychology*, 80: 532–537.

Dalal, R. S. (2005) 'A meta-analysis of the relationship between organizational citizenship behavior and counterproductive work behavior', *Journal of Applied Psychology*, 90: 1241–1255.

Deadrick, D. L., Bennett, N. and Russell, C. J. (1997) 'Using hierarchical linear modelling to examine dynamic performance criteria over time', *Journal of Management*, 23, 745–757.

Digman, J. M. (1990) 'Personality structure: Emergence of the five-factor model', *Annual Review of Psychology*, 41: 417–440.

Dudley, N. M., Orvis, K. A., Lebiecke, J. E. and Cortina, J. M. (2006) 'A meta-analytic investigation of conscientiousness in the prediction of job performance: Examining the intercorrelations and the incremental validity of narrow traits', *Journal of Applied Psychology*, 91, 40–57.

Dye, A. D., Reck, M. and McDaniel, M. A. (1993) 'The validity of job knowledge measures', *International Journal of Selection and Assessment*, 1, 153–157.

Fay, D. and Frese, M. (2001) 'The concepts of personal initiative (PI): An overview of validity studies', *Human Performance*, 14, 97–124.

Fay, D. and Sonnentag, S. (2002) 'Rethinking the effects of stressors: A longitudinal study on personal initiative', *Journal of Occupational Health Psychology*, 7, 221–234.

Fay, D., Sonnentag, S. and Frese, M. (1998) 'Stressors, Innovation, and Personal Initiative: Are Stressors Always Detrimental?', in C. L. Cooper (ed.), *Theories of Organizational Stress*. Oxford: Oxford University Press, pp. 170–189.

Ferris, G. R. Witt, L. A. and Hochwarter, W. A. (2001) 'Interaction of social skill and general mental ability on job performance and salary', *Journal of Applied Psychology*, 86, 1075–1082.

Fleishman, E. A. (1972) 'On the relation between abilities, learning, and human performance', *American Psychologist*, 27, 1017–1032.

Frese, M. (2007) 'The Psychological Actions and Entrepreneurial Success: An Action Theory Approach', in J. R. Baum, M. Frese and R. A. Baron (eds), *Siop Organizational Frontiers Series: The Psychology of Entrepreneurship*. Mahwah, NJ: Lawrence Erlbaum, pp. 151–188.

Frese, M., Garman, G., Garmeister, K., Halemba, K., Hortig, A., Pulwitt, T. et al. (2002) Training zur Erhöhung der Eigeninitiative bei Arbeitslosen: Bericht über einen Pilotversuch [Training for increasing personal initiative in unemployed individuals: Report on a pilot study]. *Zeitschrift für Arbeits- und Organisationspsychologie*, 46, 89–97.

Frese, M., Garst, H. and Fay, D. (2007) 'Making Things Happen: Reciprocal Relationships Between Work Characteristics and Personal Initiative in a four-wave longitudinal structural equation model', *Journal of Applied Psychology*, 92: 1084–1102.

Frese, M., Kring, W., Soose, A. and Zempel, J. (1996) 'Personal initiative at work: Differences between East and West Germany', *Academy of Management Journal*, 39: 37–63.

Fried, Y. and Ferris, G. R. (1987) 'The validity of the job characteristics model: A review and meta-analysis', *Personnel Psychology*, 40: 287–322.

Gerstner, C. R. and Day, D. V. (1997) 'Meta-analytic review of leader-member exchange theory: Correlates and construct issues', *Journal of Applied Psychology*, 82: 827–844.

Ghiselli, E. E. and Haire, M. (1960) 'The validation of selection tests in the light of the dynamic character of criteria', *Personnel Psychology*, 13: 225–231.

Graen, G. B., Scandura, T. A. and Graen, M. R. (1986) 'A field experimental test of the moderating effects of growth need strength on productivity', *Journal of Applied Psychology*, 71: 484–491.

Grant, A. M. and Ashford, S. J. (in press) 'The Dynamics of Proactivity at Work', *Research in Organizational Behavior*.

Griffin, M. A., Neal, A. and Neale, M. (2000) 'The contribution of task performance and contextual performance to effectiveness: Investigating the role of situational constraints', *Applied Psychology: An International Review*, 49: 479–497.

Griffin, M. A., Neal, A. and Parker, S. K. (2007) 'A new model of work role performance: Positive behavior in uncertain and interdependent contexts', *Academy of Management Journal*, 50: 327–347.

Griffin, B. and Hesketh, B. (2003) 'Adaptable behaviours for successful work and career adjustment', *Australian Journal of Psychology*, 55: 65–73.

Griffin, B. and Hesketh, B. (2004) 'Why openness to experience is not a good predictor of job performance', *International Journal of Selection and Assessment*, 12: 243–251.

Guzzo, R. A., Jette, R. D. and Katzell, R. A. (1985) 'The effects of psychologically based intervention programs on worker productivity: A meta-analysis', *Personnel Psychology*, 38: 275–291.

Hackman, J. R. and Oldham, G. R. (1976) 'Motivation through the design of work: Test of a theory', *Organizational Behavior and Human Performance*, 16: 250–279.

Hanges, P. J., Schneider, B. and Niles, K. (1990) 'Stability of performance: An interactionist perspective', *Journal of Applied Psychology*, 75: 658–667.

Harris, M. M. and Schaubroeck, J. (1988) 'A meta-analysis of self-supervisor, self-peer, and peer-supervisor ratings', *Personnel Psychology*, 41: 43–62.

Hattrup, K., O'Connell, M. S. and Wingate, P. H. (1998) 'Prediction of multidimensional criteria: Distinguishing task and contextual performance. *Human Performance*, 11: 305–319.

Henry, R. A. and Hulin, C. L. (1987) 'Stability of skilled performance across time: Some generalizations and limitations on utilities', *Journal of Applied Psychology*, 72: 457–462.

Hesketh, B. and Neal, A. (1999) 'Technology and Performance', in D. R. Ilgen and E. D. Pulakos (eds), *The Changing Nature of Performance: Implications for Staffing, Motivation, and Development*. San Francisco: Jossey-Bass, pp. 21–55.

Hofmann, D. A., Jacobs, R. and Baratta, J. E. (1993) 'Dynamic criteria and the measurement of change', *Journal of Applied Psychology*, 78: 194–204.

Hofmann, D. A., Jacobs, R. and Gerras, S. J. (1992) 'Mapping individual performance over time', *Journal of Applied Psychology*, 77: 185–195.

Holman, D., Wall, T. D., Clegg, C. W., Sparrow, P. and Howard, A. (2003) *The New Workplace: A Guide to the Human Impact of Modern Working Practices*. Chichester: Wiley.

Hunter, J. E. and Hunter, R. F. (1984) 'Validity and utility of alternative predictors of job performance', *Psychological Bulletin*, 96: 72–98.

Johnson, J. W. (2001) 'The relative importance of task and contextual performance dimensions to supervisor judgments of overall performance', *Journal of Applied Psychology*, 86: 984–996.

Judge, T. A. and Bono, J. E. (2001) 'Relationship of core self-evaluation traits — self-esteem, generalized self–efficacy, locus of control, and emotional stability — with job satisfaction and job performance: A meta-analysis', *Journal of Applied Psychology*, 86: 80–92.

Judge, T. A., Locke, E. A. and Durham, C. C. (1997) 'The dispositional causes of job satisfaction: A core evaluations approach', *Research in Organizational Behavior*, 19: 151–188.

Judge, T. A., Locke, E. A., Durham, C. C. and Kluger, A. N. (1998) 'Dispositional effects on job and life satisfaction: The role of core evaluations', *Journal of Applied Psychology*, 83: 17–34.

Kahn, R. L., Wolfe, D. M., Quinn, R. P., Snoek, J. D. and Rosenthal, R. A. (1964) *Organizational stress: Studies in role conflict and ambiguity*. New York: Wiley.

Kanfer, R. and Ackerman, P. L. (2005) 'Work competence: A Person-Oriented Perspective', in A. J. Elliot and C. S. Dweck (eds), *Handbook of Competence and Motivation*. Guilford Publications, pp. 336–353.

Kanfer, R. and Kantrowitz, T. M. (2002) 'Ability and Non-Ability Predictors of Performance', in S. Sonnentag (ed.), *Psychological Management of Individual Performance*. Chichester: Wiley, pp. 27–50.

Keil, C. T. and Cortina, J. M. (2001) 'Degradation of validity over time: A test and extension of Ackerman's model', *Psychological Bulletin*, 127: 673–697.

Langfred, C. W. and Moye, N. A. (2004) 'Effects of task autonomy on performance: An extended model considering motivational, informational, and structural mechanisms', *Journal of Applied Psychology*, 89: 934–945.

LePine, J. A. (2003) 'Team adaptation and postchange performance: Effects of team composition in terms of members' cognitive ability and personality', *Journal of Applied Psychology*, 88: 27–39.

LePine, J. A., Erez, A. and Johnson, D. E. (2002) 'The nature and dimensionality of organizational citizenship behavior: A critical review and meta-analysis', *Journal of Applied Psychology*, 87: 52–65.

LePine, J. A., Podsakoff, N. P. and LePine, M. A. (2005) 'A meta-analytic test of the challenge stressor-hindrance stressor framework: An explanation for inconsistent relationships among stressors and performance', *Academy of Management Journal*, 48: 764–775.

LePine, J. A. and VanDyne, L. (2001) 'Voice and cooperative behavior as contrasting forms of contextual performance: Evidence of differential relationships with big five personality characteristics and cognitive ability', *Journal of Applied Psychology*, 86: 326–336.

London, M. and Mone, E. M. (1999) 'Continuous Learning', in D. R. Ilgen and E. D. Pulakos (eds), *The Changing Nature of Performance: Implications for Staffing, Motivation, and Development*. San Francisco: Jossey-Bass, pp. 119–153.

Mabe, P. A. and West, S. G. (1982) 'Validity of self–evaluation of ability: A review and meta-analysis', *Journal of Applied Psychology*, 67: 280–296.

Marks, M. A., Mathieu, J. E. and Zaccaro, S. J. (2001) 'A temporally based framework and taxonomy of team processes', *Academy of Management Review*, 26: 356–376.

McCauley, C. D., Ruderman, M. N., Ohlott, P. J. and Morrow, J. E. (1994) 'Assessing the developmental components of managerial jobs', *Journal of Applied Psychology*, 79, 544–560.

McCrae, R. R. and Costa, P. T. Jr. (1989) 'The structure of interpersonal traits: Wiggins's circumplex and the five-factor model', *Journal of Personality and Social Psychology*, 56: 586–595.

McDaniel, M. A., Morgeson, F. P. and Finnegan, F. B. (2001) 'Use of situational judgment tests to predict job performance: A clarification of the literature', *Journal of Applied Psychology*, 86: 730–740.

McDaniel, M. A., Schmidt, F. L. and Hunter, J. E. (1988) 'Job experience correlates of job performance', *Journal of Applied Psychology*, 73: 327–330.

Mitchell, T. R. and James, L. R. (2001) 'Building better theory: Time and the specification of when things happen', *Academy of Management Review*, 26: 530–547.

Morrison, E. W. and Phelps, C. C. (1999) 'Taking charge at work: Extrarole efforts to initiate workplace change', *Academy of Management Journal*, 42: 403–419.

Motowidlo, S. J., Borman, W. C. and Schmit, M. J. (1997) 'A theory of individual differences in task and contextual performance', *Human Performance*, 10: 71–83.

Motowidlo, S. J. and Schmit, M. J. (1999) 'Performance Assessment in Unique Jobs', in D. R. Ilgen and E. D. Pulakos (eds), *The Changing Nature of Job Performance: Implications for Staffing, Motivation, and Development*. San Francisco, CA: Jossey-Bass, pp. 56–86.

Motowidlo, S. J. and Van Scotter, J. R. (1994) 'Evidence that task performance should be distinguished from contextual performance', *Journal of Applied Psychology*, 79: 475–480.

Mount, M. K., Judge, T. A., Scullen, S. E., Sytsma, M. R. and Hezlett, S. A. (1998) 'Trait, rater and level effects in 360-degree performance ratings', *Personnel Psychology*, 51: 557–576.

Murphy, K. R. (1989) 'Is the relationship between cognitive ability and job performance stable over time?', *Human Performance*, 2: 183–200.

Murphy, P. R. and Jackson, S. E. (1999) 'Managing Work Role Performance. Challenging the Twenty-First Century Organizations and Their Employees', in D. R. Ilgen and E. D. Pulakos (eds), *The Changing Nature of Performance: Implications for Staffing, Motivations, and Development*. San Francisco: Jossey-Bass, pp. 325–365.

Ohly, S., Sonnentag, S. and Pluntke, F. (2006) 'Routinization, work characteristics and their relationships with creative and proactive behaviors', *Journal of Organizational Behavior*, 27: 257–279.

Olea, M. M. and Ree, M. J. (1994) 'Predicting pilot and navigator criteria: Not much more than g', *Journal of Applied Psychology*, 79: 845–851.

Organ, D. W. (1988) *Organizational citizenship behavior: The Good Soldier Syndrome*. Lexington, MA: Lexington.

Organ, D. W. (1997) 'Organizational citizenship behavior: It's construct clean-up time', *Human Performance*, 10: 85–97.

Organ, D. W. and Ryan, K. (1995) 'A meta-analytic review of attitudinal and dispositional predictors of organizational citizenship behavior', *Personnel Psychology*, 48: 775–802.

Parker, S. K. (2003) 'Longitudinal effects of lean production on employee outcomes and the mediating role of work characteristics', *Journal of Applied Psychology*, 88: 620–634.

Parker, S. K. and Turner, N. (2002) 'Work design and individual work performance: Research findings and an agenda for future inquiry', in S. Sonnentag (ed.), *The Psychological Management of Individual Performance: A Handbook in the Psychology of the Management of Organizations*. Chichester: Erlbaum, pp. 69–93.

Parker, S. K., Wall, T. D. and Jackson, P. R. (1997) ' "That's not my job": Developing flexible employee work orientations', *Academy of Management Journal*, 40: 899–929.

Parker, S. K., Williams, H. M. and Turner, N. (2006) 'Modelling the antecedents of proactive behavior at work', *Journal of Applied Psychology*, 91: 636–652.

Peters, L. H. and O'Connor, E. J. (1980) 'Situational constraints and work outcomes: The influences of a frequently overlooked construct', *Academy of Management Review*, 5: 391–397.

Pike, C. (2006) 'Mergers and acquisitions: Managing culture and human resources', *Personnel Psychology*, 59: 480–484.

Ployhard, R. E. and Hakel, M. D. (1998) 'The substantive nature of performance variability: Predicting interindividual differences in intraindividual performance', *Personnel Psychology*, 51: 859–901.

Podsakoff, P. M., Bommer, W. H., Podsakoff, N. P. and MacKenzie, S. B. (2006) 'Relationships between leader reward and punishment behavior and subordinate attitudes, perceptions, and behaviors: A meta-analytic review of existing and new research', *Organizational Behavior and Human Decision Processes*, 99: 113–142.

Podsakoff, P. M., MacKenzie, S. B., Paine, J. B. and Bachrach, D. G. (2000) 'Organizational citizenship behaviors: A critical review of the theoretical and empirical literature and suggestions for future research', *Journal of Management*, 26: 513–563.

Pritchard, R. D. (1992) 'Organizational Productivity', in M. D. Dunnette and L. M. Hough (eds), *Handbook of Industrial and Organizational Psychology*, Vol. 3 (2nd ed.). Palo Alto: Consulting Psychologists Press, pp. 443–471.

Pulakos, E. D., Arad, S., Donovan, M. A. and Plamondon, K. E. (2000) 'Adaptability in the workplace: Development of a taxonomy of adaptive performance', *Journal of Applied Psychology*, 85: 612–624.

Pulakos, E. D., Schmitt, N., Dorsey, D. W., Arad, S., Hedge, J. W. and Borman, W. C. (2002) 'Predicting adaptive performance: Further tests of a model of adaptability', *Human Performance*, 15: 299–323.

Quiñones, M. A., Ford, J. K. and Teachout, M. S. (1995) 'The relationship between work experience and job performance: A conceptual and meta-analytic review', *Personnel Psychology*, 48: 887–910.

Ree, M. J., Carretta, T. R. and Steindl, J. R. (2001) 'Cognitive ability', in D. S. O. N. Anderson, H. K. Sinangil and C. Viswesvaran (eds), *Handbook of Industrial, Work, and Organizational Psychology*. London: Sage. Vol. 1: pp. 219–232.

Ree, M. J., Earles, J. A. and Teachout, M. S. (1994) 'Predicting job performance: Not much more than g', *Journal of Applied Psychology*, 79: 518–524.

Reeve, C. L. (2004) 'Differential ability antecedents of general and specific dimensions of declarative knowledge', *Intelligence*, 32: 621–652.

Roe, R. A. (1999) 'Work performance: A multiple regulation perspective', in C. L. Cooper and I. T. Robertson (eds), *International Review of Industrial and Organizational Psychology*. Chichester: Wiley. Vol. 14: pp. 231–335.

Salgado, J. F., Anderson, N., Moscoso, S., Bertua, C., de Fruyt, F. and Rolland, J. P. (2003) 'A meta-analytic study of general mental ability validity for different occupations in the European community', *Journal of Applied Psychology*, 88: 1068–1081.

Salgado, J. F., Viswesvaran, C. and Ones, D. S. (2001) 'Predictors Used for Personnel Selection: An Overview of Constructs, Methods and Techniques', in N. Anderson, D. S. Ones, H. K. Sinangil and C. Viswesvaran (eds), *Handbook of Industrial, Work and Organizational Psychology*. London: Sage. Vol. 1: pp. 165–199.

Salgado, S. R., Anderson, N., Moscoso, S., Bertua, C. and DeFruyt, F. (2003) 'International validity generalization of GMA and cognitive abilities: A European community meta-analysis', *Personnel Psychology*, 56: 573–605.

Schmidt, F. L. and Hunter, J. (2004) 'General mental ability in the work of work: Occupational attainment and job performance', *Journal of Personality and Social Psychology*, 86: 162–173.

Schmidt, F. L., Hunter, J. E. and Outerbridge, A. N. (1986) 'Impact of job experience and ability on job knowledge, work sample performance, and supervisory ratings of job performance', *Journal of Applied Psychology*, 71: 432–439.

Seibert, S. E., Kraimer, M. L. and Crant, J. M. (2001) 'What do proactive people do? A longitudinal model linking proactive personality and career success', *Personnel Psychology*, 54: 845–874.

Smith, E. M., Ford, J. K., Kozlowski, S. W. J., Quinones, M. A. and Ehrenstein, A. (1997) 'Building Adaptive Expertise: Implications for Training Design Strategies', in *Training for a Rapidly Changing Workplace: Applications of Psychological Research.* Washington, D.C.: American Psychological Association, pp. 89–118.

Sonnentag, S. (2003) 'Recovery, work engagement, and proactive behavior: A new look at the interface between nonwork and work', *Journal of Applied Psychology*, 88: 518–528.

Sonnentag, S. and Frese, M. (2002) 'Performance concepts and performance theory', in S. Sonnentag (ed.), *Psychological Management of Individual Performance.* Chichester: Wiley, pp. 3–25.

Sonnentag, S., Niessen, C. and Ohly, S. (2004) 'Learning at work: Training and development', in C. L. Cooper and I. T. Robertson (eds), *International Review of Industrial and Organizational Psychology.* Chichester: Wiley, Vol. 19: pp. 249–289.

Sonnentag, S. and Volmer, J. (in press) 'Individual-level predictors of task-related teamwork processes: The role of expertise and self-efficacy in team meetings', *Group and Organization Management.*

Spearman, C. (1904) 'General intelligence, objectively determined and measured', *American Journal of Psychology*, 15: 201–293.

Spector, P. E. (1986) 'Perceived control by employees: A meta-analysis of studies concerning autonomy and participation at work', *Human Relations*, 39: 1005–1016.

Speier, C. and Frese, M. (1997) 'Generalized self–efficacy as a mediator and moderator between control and complexity at work and personal initiative: A longitudinal field study in East Germany', *Human Performance*, 10: 171–192.

Sternberg, R. J. (1997) 'Tacit knowledge and job success', in N. Anderson and P. Herriot (eds), *International Handbook of Selection and Assessment.* London: Wiley, pp. 201–213.

Sternberg, R. J. and Wagner, R. K. (1993) 'The g-ocentric view of intelligence and job performance is wrong', *Current Directions in Psychological Science*, 2: 1–5.

Stewart, G. L. and Nandkeolyar, A. K. (2006) 'Adaptation and intraindividual variation in sales outcomes: Exploring the interactive effect of personality and environmental opportunity', *Personnel Psychology*, 59: 307–332.

Sturman, M. C. (2003) 'Searching for the inverted u-shaped relationship between time and performance: Meta-analyses of the experience/performance, tenure/performance, and age/performance relationships', *Journal of Management*, 29: 609–640.

Tesluk, P. E. and Jacobs, R. R. (1998) 'Towards an integrated model of work experience', *Personnel Psychology*, 51: 321–355.

Thompson, J. A. (2005) 'Proactive personality and job performance: A social capital perspective', *Journal of Applied Psychology*, 90: 1011–1017.

Thoresen, C. J., Bradley, J. C., Bliese, P. B. and Thoreson, J. D. (2004) 'The big five personality traits and individual job performance growth trajectories in maintenance and transitional job stages', *Journal of Applied Psychology*, 89: 835–853.

Tubre, T. C. and Collins, J. M. (2000) 'Jackson and Schuler (1985) revisited: A meta-analysis of the relationships between role ambiguity, role conflict, and job performance', *Journal of Management*, 26: 155–169.

Van Dyne, L. and LePine, J. A. (1998) 'Helping and voice extra-role behaviors: Evidence of construct and predictive validity', *Academy of Management Journal*, 41: 108–119.

Van Scotter, J. R. and Motowidlo, S. J. (1996) 'Interpersonal facilitation and job dedication as separate facets of contextual performance', *Journal of Applied Psychology*, 81: 525–531.

Van Scotter, J. R., Motowidlo, S. J. and Cross, T. C. (2000) 'Effects of task performance and contextual performance on systemic rewards', *Journal of Applied Psychology*, 85: 526–535.

Villanova, P. and Roman, M. A. (1993) 'A meta-analytic review of situational constraints and work-related outcomes: Alternative approaches to conceptualization', *Human Resource Management Review*, 3: 147–175.

Viswesvaran, C., Ones, D. S. and Schmidt, F. L. (1996) 'Comparative analysis of the reliability of job performance ratings', *Journal of Applied Psychology*, 81: 557–574.

Viswesvaran, C., Schmidt, F. L. and Ones, D. S. (2005) 'Is there a general factor in ratings of job performance? A meta-analytic framework for disentangling substantive and error influences', *Journal of Applied Psychology*, 90: 108–131.

Waldman, D. A. and Avolio, B. J. (1986) 'A meta-analysis of age differences in job performance', *Journal of Applied Psychology*, 71: 33–38.

Wall, T. D. and Clegg, C. W. (1981) 'A longitudinal field study of group work redesign', *Journal of Occupational Behavior*, 2: 31–49.

Werner, J. (1994) 'Dimensions that make a difference: Examining the impact of in-role and extra-role behaviors on supervisory ratings', *Journal of Applied Psychology*, 79: 98–107.

Williams, K. D. and Karau, S. J. (1991) 'Social loafing and social compensation: The effects of expectations of co-worker performance', *Journal of Personality and Social Psychology*, 61: 570–581.

Woehr, D. J., Sheehan, M. K. and Bennett, W. (2005) 'Assessing measurement equivalence across rating sources: A multitrait-multirater approach', *Journal of Applied Psychology*, 90: 592–600.

Zickar, M. J. and Slaughter, J. E. (1999) 'Examining creative performance over time using hierarchical linear modelling: An illustration using film directors', *Human Performance*, 12: 211–230.

PART THREE

Work, Stress and Well-Being

24

Work–Family Conflict

Joseph G. Grzywacz and Adam B. Butler

Work–family conflict, defined as the degree to which an individual's work and family lives are incompatible, is a significant problem in organizations. Evidence suggests that work–family conflict is associated with increased turnover, poor performance, and poor employee and family health (Allen et al., 2000; Greenhaus et al., 2006). All of these issues raise 'bottom-line' concerns in organizations. Moreover, given that work–family conflict is fundamentally rooted in societal changes related to women's large scale entrance in to the labor-force, the problem arising from work–family conflict are widespread and likely to persist. Given both the extent and importance of the problem, the work–family conflict literature has burgeoned in the past decade, and researchers have made substantial gains in understanding both work–family conflict and organizational attempts to manage it.

Our goal in the chapter is to advance work–family conflict research. To accomplish this goal, we focus on two primary specific aims. First, we will document what is known about work–family conflict as it relates to organizational behavior by critically reviewing existing research. Second, we will outline a

high-priority agenda for future organizational behavior research. The chapter is organized chronologically with the first section describing work–family conflict research in the past. 'The past' section begins with an overview of theoretical origins of the work–family conflict construct, and it continues with a brief discussion of the phases of work–family conflict research including influential papers. Our discussion of the evolution of work–family conflict is brief because the progression of this literature has been described (Frone, 2003), and there are several reviews of the work–family conflict literature (Bellavia and Frone, 2005; Eby et al., 2005; Geurts and Demerouti, 2003) as well as chapters on work–family conflict (Carlson and Grzywacz, 2008; MacDermid, 2005; Tetrick and Buffardi, 2006), and numerous edited volumes on work and family (Jones et al., 2006; Kossek and Lambert, 2005; Pitt-Catsouphes et al., 2006). In the section focused on 'the present,' we describe several key debates in the work–family conflict literature and we characterize current research (i.e., dated 2000–2006) informing these debates. We then highlight several emerging issues in the work–family conflict literature. In the final section of the chapter, we conclude by articulating several key areas for future research.

WORK–FAMILY CONFLICT RESEARCH: PAST

Theoretical origins

Work–family conflict is typically defined using Greenhaus and Beutell's (1985) definition: 'work–family conflict is a form of interrole conflict in which role pressures from work and family domains are mutually incompatible in some respect' (p. 77). This definition was influenced directly by Kahn and colleagues (Kahn et al., 1964) theory of role dynamics within organizations and their conceptualization of interrole conflict. In order to interpret and understand the work–family conflict literature, both inside and outside the organizational behavior (OB) literature, it is important for researchers to be familiar with the basic elements of this theory.

At the most general level, Kahn and colleagues (1964) conceptualized organizations as social systems comprised of interdependent sub-units designed and structured to maintain organizational functioning. The 'office' is the basic building block of the organization and is described as a unique space within an organization that is defined relationally by its interrelationship with other offices in the organization. Roles, in essence, are the behavioral manifestations of the interrelationships among various offices within the organization.

Pressure within a role is conceptualized as a transactional phenomenon resulting from environmental circumstances and individuals' appraisals of these circumstances. Activities performed by the occupant of a focal office (roles) are regulated by individuals occupying adjacent or connected offices, in part because their own activities are influenced by the individual in the focal office. Communicated expectations of occupants in other offices, or 'sent roles,' have the potential to elicit psychological pressure or strain. However, the potential of sent roles to elicit pressure depends on how they are received by the focal office's occupant. If a sent role is interpreted as having sufficient motive force, either in terms of incentive or sanction, it elicits pressure in the individual to whom it was directed.

Focus of past work–family conflict research

Although the preceding discussion only hints at the complexity of Kahn and colleagues' theory, it is sufficient to foreshadow the historical approach to and focus of work–family conflict research within the OB literature. Consistent with the idea that activities within any given office are institutionally set, there is a substantial body of research examining the putative effects of job-related characteristics such as flexibility or the pace of work on work–family conflict. This body of research is sometimes referred to as the 'demands' perspective (Pleck, 1995). However, recognizing that the experience of role-related pressure is transactional in nature, there is also a substantial body of research focusing on the psychological processes involved in the manifestation of work–family conflict. For example, some researchers suggest that the relative salience of work and family to an individual's core identity shapes the extent to which work-related demands elicit work–family conflict (e.g., Frone et al., 1995; Lobel, 1991).

The last several years have seen no fewer than ten narrative reviews of the work–family literature relevant to organizational researchers. Most of these reviews provide summaries of the putative antecedents and consequences of work–family conflict (Bellavia and Frone, 2005; Eby et al., 2005; Frone, 2003; Geurts and Demerouti, 2003; Greenhaus and Powell, 2006). Others provide a detailed description and critique of attempts to measure the work–family interface (Bellavia and Frone, 2005; MacDermid, 2005; Tetrick and Buffardi, 2006). Still other reviews are unique in their focus, spotlighting the little researched construct of work–family balance (Greenhaus and Allen, 2006; Grzywacz and Carlson, 2007) or organizational attempts to reduce work–family conflict (Roman and Blum, 2001).

There is agreement on some central issues. First, although much of the work–family literature is based on role theory, research is beginning to explore other theoretical paradigms like ecological systems theory (Bronfenbrenner, 1979) or conservation of resources theory (Hobfoll, 1989, 1998) for understanding work–family conflict, as well as other linkages between work and family (e.g., Bellavia and Frone, 2005; Geurts and Demerouti, 2003). Despite this expansion, concern remains that current theories of work–family conflict lack specificity, that mechanisms linking work and family are not well known, and that the literature is more empirically- than theoretically-based (Eby et al., 2005; Geurts and Demerouti, 2003; MacDermid and Harvey, 2006). Second, there is agreement that, in addition to creating conflict, work and family can be mutually beneficial, and that more research is necessary describing what these benefits may look like, how they arise, and how they combine with work–family conflict in shaping broader experiences like balance (e.g., Bellavia and Frone, 2005; Greenhaus and Allen, 2006). Third, although many of the reviews devote significant space to the issue of gender, there are disagreements regarding its primacy in the work–family equation (Eby et al., 2005; Frone, 2003; Greenhaus and Parasuraman, 1999). Finally, the mere existence of these reviews suggests that the work–family literature is mature, vast, and complex.

Phases of work–family conflict research

The progression of work–family conflict research has been described. In particular, Bellavia and Frone (2005) suggest there are two generations of work–family conflict research. The first generation of research, according to Bellavia and Frone (2005), conceptualized work–family conflict as a mediator between work- and family-related demands and work- and family-related outcomes such as satisfaction. This research,

ushered in by a few influential papers (Kopelman et al., 1983; Greenhaus and Parasuraman, 1986), demonstrated the interconnections between work and family, thereby providing evidence that work and family are not 'separate spheres' (Kanter, 1977). In the second generation of work–family conflict research, researchers focused on the distinction between work-to-family and family-to-work conflict and delineated the unique antecedents and consequences of each. Frone and colleagues' research (Frone et al., 1992; Frone et al., 1997b) was instrumental in this arena, and it is now firmly established that work-to-family and family-to-work conflict are distinct, bidirectional related phenomenon (Byron, 2005; Mesmer-Magnus and Viswesvaran, 2005); and that work-related demands are the primary antecedents of work-to-family conflict, whereas family-related demands are the primary antecedents of family-to-work conflict (Bellavia and Frone, 2005; Eby et al., 2005).

It appears as though work–family conflict research is entering a third phase. This emerging phase of research considers the work–family interface more broadly, and grapples with the distinctions and inter-relationships between work–family conflict and more positive experiences like work–family enrichment. Some studies have documented that combining work and family yields both conflicts and synergies (e.g., Barnett et al., 1992; Crouter, 1984; Kirchmeyer 1992), however, only recently have positive experiences become a focus of systematic research. Grzywacz and Marks (2000) illustrated the apparent uniqueness of negative and positive experiences at the work–family interface, and others have since replicated these findings (e.g., Kinnunen et al., 2006). Voydanoff (2004) and Grzywacz and Butler (2005) demonstrated that positive experiences at the work–family interface are shaped primarily by resources like autonomy or skill variety, whereas work–family conflict is shaped primarily by demands. Evidence is also emerging suggesting that positive experiences at the work–family interface may offset the negative consequences of work–family conflict (Grzywacz and Bass, 2003), that they are stronger predictors of mental health (Hammer et al., 2005a), and that they are correlated with valued organizational outcomes such as job satisfaction or engagement (Aryee et al., 2005; Wayne et al., 2004).

An increased focus on broader experiences like 'balance' and 'fit' have coincided with an expanded view of the work–family interface that incorporates both negative and positive experiences. Frone (2003) argued that work–family balance is characterized by low levels of work–family conflict and high levels of work–family facilitation. Similarly, Barnett (1998) argued that the combination of conflict and compatibility contributed to better 'fit' between work and family. Drawing on person-environment fit theory, Voydanoff (2005) differentiated 'job resources-family demand fit' and 'family-resources-job demand fit' to highlight the extent to which resources in one domain were sufficient to meet the demands in another domain. She argued that the two types of fit, which are akin to negative (demands exceed resources) and positive (resources exceed demands) experiences at the work–family interface, combine to create 'balance.' These and more recent papers (Greenhaus and Allen, 2006; Grzywacz and Carlson, 2007) suggest that a solitary focus on work–family conflict may be inappropriate.

WORK–FAMILY CONFLICT RESEARCH: PRESENT

Current work–family conflict research is multifaceted; nonetheless, much of this research revolves around a discrete number of issues. One major issue motivating much research is the need to make the 'business case' for work–family conflict. This research is focused primarily on documenting the putative consequences of work–family conflict for organizations, presumably with the goal of persuading businesses to attend to and better manage employees' work–family conflict. A related issue focuses on the utility of implementing 'family-friendly' policies for minimizing

conflicts between work and family. Still other issues underlying the work–family conflict literature include the role of gender in work–family conflict research, and whether or not work–family conflict sufficiently captures the interrelationship between work and family. We now turn to each of these issues. In the following paragraphs we summarize each of these issues and we highlight research characterizing these issues.

The business case for reducing work–family conflict

There is a substantial body of research examining outcomes of work–family conflict within organizations. Although individuals bear some responsibility for managing the competing demands in their life, some might argue that organizations only incur responsibility for reducing work–family conflict if a firm link is established between conflict and valued organizational outcomes. In this section, we characterize research linking work–family conflict to three such outcomes, withdrawal behaviors, performance, and worker health.

Withdrawal behaviors are those that produce a physical or psychological separation from one's work, including tardiness, absence, and turnover (Hulin, 1991). Two of those withdrawal constructs, tardiness and absence, could be expected to increase as an individual experiences greater family conflict with work (Frone et al., 1992). In fact, research suggests that the relationships between work-to-family conflict and tardiness or absenteeism are complex and dependent on other variables. For example, Hammer et al. (2003) showed that family-to-work conflict predicted absence for men only, whereas Boyar et al. (2005) found that work-to-family conflict predicted absence for women only. Studies using a bidirectional conflict measure find weak or non-significant relationships with absenteeism (Goff et al., 1990; Thomas and Ganster, 1995). A meta-analysis of these two studies reported a weighted r of -0.06 with a 95 per cent confidence interval that included zero (Allen et al., 2000). However, a large sample longitudinal study found that both work-to-family and family-to-work conflict were related to sickness absence six months later (Jansen et al., 2006). There is no evidence of a direct relationship between work-to-family or family-to-work conflict and tardiness (Boyar et al., 2005; Hammer et al., 2003), although Hammer et al. found a crossover effect in that husbands' family-to-work conflict predicted wives' tardiness. In short, compelling empirical evidence of a link between work–family conflict and two withdrawal behaviors, absence and tardiness, is lacking. A simple explanation for the lack of relationships between work–family conflict and these forms of withdrawal may be due to organizational policies that constrain these behaviors (e.g., Kohler and Mathieu, 1993). In other words, the consequences of work–family conflict are not manifest in absence or tardiness because organizational policy does not permit it.

In contrast to tardiness and absence, turnover could be expected to increase as individuals experience greater work conflict with family. In fact, leaving an organization for another job may be one of the few strategies available to reduce conflicts stemming from job demands. Again, however, empirical studies suggest that the relationship between work–family conflict and turnover is complex and perhaps dependent on other variables. In the only study of actual turnover of which we are aware, work-to-family conflict predicted quitting only when career involvement was low (Greenhaus et al., 2001). There are numerous studies examining turnover intentions – an easier construct to measure – but the results are mixed, again suggesting the potential for moderators. Some of these studies find a relationship between turnover intentions and both work-to-family and family-to-work conflict (e.g., Netemeyer et al., 1996), others find a relationship only with work-to-family conflict (e.g., Grandey and Cropanzano, 1999), and at least one study found no relationship with either work-to-family or family-to-work conflict (Bhuian et al., 2005). Nevertheless, meta-analyses of research published prior to 2000 found weighted r's of 0.29 and 0.32

between turnover intentions and work-to-family conflict (Allen et al., 2000; Kossek and Ozeki, 1999), and a somewhat weaker relationship between turnover intentions and family-to-work conflict, with a weighted r of 0.17 (Kossek and Ozeki, 1999).

Among all of the constructs investigated by organizational behavior researchers, few are more central to bottom-line concerns in business than job performance. Although it has been argued that family-to-work conflict is likely to be associated with decreased job performance (Frone et al., 1992), it might be argued that either direction of conflict may disrupt performance by diverting attentional resources necessary for quality performance or by creating strain, such as exhaustion, that reduces performance quality and quantity. Unfortunately, there are few studies examining the relationship between conflict and performance, and those that do predominantly rely on self-reported performance levels. Studies have shown that both work-to-family and family-to-work conflict are negatively related to self-reported performance (e.g., Frone et al., 1997b). Two meta-analyses examined the relationship of work-to-family conflict with performance, and both report small effects with 95 per cent confidence intervals that include zero (Allen et al., 2000; Kossek and Ozeki, 1999). One study that did not rely on self-reported performance showed that family-to-work but not work-to-family conflict was negatively related to supervisory performance ratings, and the relationship was stronger for workers with higher levels of conscientiousness and lower levels of perceived organizational support (Witt and Carlson, 2006). Finally, preliminary data suggest that higher levels of work–family conflict are related to lower rates of organizational citizenship behavior (Bragger et al., 2005).

Partly because of the business costs associated with poor worker health, there has been increased attention to the health-related implications of work–family conflict. Unlike some of the business consequences reviewed above, there is little evidence suggesting that the directionality of conflict results in differential relationships with health (Frone et al., 1997a). A substantial body of research suggests a link between work–family conflict and adult health (see Greenhaus et al., 2006). Higher levels of work–family conflict are associated with several indicators of physical health including hypertension, comorbid physical conditions, and self-reported somatic complaints (e.g., Adams and Jex, 1999; Frone et al., 1997a; Grzywacz, 2000; Thomas and Ganster, 1995). Likewise, higher levels of work–family conflict are associated with general distress, depressive symptomatology, psychiatric disorders including depression, anxiety disorder and behavior patterns indicative of alcoholism (e.g., Frone, 2000; Grzywacz and Bass, 2003; Hammer et al., 2005). Moreover, levels of work–family conflict are predictive of health six months later, a finding that is consistent with a causal mechanism (Grant Vallone and Donaldson, 2001). Overall, despite the fact that most health research is cross-sectional in nature, there is a coherent body of research suggesting that work–family conflict may have a deleterious impact on the physical and mental health of employees.

Family-friendly benefits

An important question regarding the business case for work–family conflict involves organizational responsibility for alleviating it. Given the potential negative consequences of work–family conflict for individuals and organizations, one could argue there is an organizational imperative to help employees better manage their work and family lives. One way in which organizations have attempted to alleviate work–family conflict is by offering family-friendly benefits. In this section, we describe family-friendly benefits and their use within organizations. We also review the literature on consequences associated with family-friendly benefits, as well as consider the potential for backlash from workers without dependents who may not qualify to use such benefits.

Although there is no consensual list of family-friendly benefits, they generally

include alternative work arrangements and dependent care support (Parker and Allen, 2001). Alternative work arrangements allow work to be conducted at atypical locations or times and include benefits such as flexible schedules, telecommuting, and job sharing. Dependent care support facilitates an employee's family caretaking responsibilities and includes benefits such as paid leave, on-site childcare, and childcare or eldercare subsidies. One dependent care benefit in the US, the Family and Medical Leave Act, is federally (US) mandated for organizations with 50 or more employees. The law provides up to 12 weeks of unpaid leave annually for personal or family health issues (Nowicki, 2003). Often, the extent to which organizations offer these benefits is considered a sign of commitment to creating a family-friendly workplace. The Families and Work Institute developed a measure called the Family-Friendly Index assessing the degree to which organizations have implemented many of these benefits (Galinsky et al., 1991). More well-known family-friendly benchmarks are provided by popular magazines such as *Working Mother* or *Fortune* that provide annual rankings of desirable places to work partly based on benefit offerings.

Despite popular attention paid to family-friendly organizations, family-friendly benefits remain rare in corporate America. According to the Bureau of Labor Statistics (2006), the percentage of workers in private firms with access to family-friendly benefits is typically less than 10 per cent (e.g., 8 per cent had access to paid family leave, 5 per cent had access to on-site or off-site childcare, and 4 per cent had access to a flexible workplace). These benefits are more likely to be available to white collar than blue collar or service workers. Cross-national comparisons are difficult, but it appears that family-friendly benefits are also rare in Britain; for example, 5.9 per cent of British workers reported access to on-site childcare (Budd and Mumford, 2006). A nationally representative survey of US employers by the Families and Work Institute suggests higher rates in the availability of workplace flexibility programs.

For example, 60 per cent of employers allow most employees to take time off for family needs, and 33 per cent allow most employees to periodically change start and stop times (Bond et al., 2005). The same survey showed that the availability of flexibility programs increased from 1998 to 2005.

External and internal environmental factors are related to organizational offerings of family-friendly benefits, and research suggests that particular environmental pressures are uniquely associated with particular benefits. Organizations characterized by high performance work practices (e.g., quality programs, enriched jobs, autonomous teams), and a greater proportion of women employees, are more likely to offer family-friendly benefits (e.g., flexible scheduling and dependent care support; Davis and Kalleberg, 2006). However, organizations with recruitment problems, a principally white-collar workforce, and benchmarked training practices are more likely to offer flexible scheduling and paid leave (Davis and Kalleberg, 2006). The association between family-friendly benefits and high performance work practices may reflect the influence of a third variable, a progressive corporate culture attuned to developments in job design and organizational policy. The associations between benefit offerings and internal labor constituencies, such as women and professionals, may reflect a rational response to the identification of work–family conflict as an organizational problem (Osterman, 1995). Moreover, these benefits serve as powerful recruitment and retention tools for talented workers in a tight labor market (Casper and Buffardi, 2004).

Numerous cross-sectional studies find that employee use of family-friendly benefits is associated with reduced work–family conflict (e.g., Anderson et al., 2002; Thompson et al., 1999), although not all studies find a positive effect (Batt and Valcour, 2003; Butler et al., 2004; Hammer et al., 2005b). To date, only one study has examined the impact of family-friendly benefits on work–family conflict using a prospective longitudinal design. Hammer et al. (2005b) found that use of alternative work arrangements and dependent care support was not related to husbands' or wives' work-to-family conflict one year later or husbands' family-to-work conflict one year later, but use of these benefits was associated with an unexpected increase in wives' family-to-work conflict one year later. The authors reasoned that women who use these benefits may take on additional family caretaking responsibilities, increasing their experience of family-to-work conflict. Other putative consequences associated with the use of family-friendly benefits include increased commitment (e.g., Kopelman et al., 2006; Thompson et al., 1999), increased job satisfaction (Allen, 2001; Baltes et al., 1999), and increased intentions to pursue employment with the organization (Casper and Buffardi, 2004). Finally, some argue that being family-friendly positively impacts productivity, cost savings, and company stock price (Cascio and Young, 2005; Corporate Voices for Working Families, 2005).

Although there appear to be clear organizational benefits associated with family-friendly benefits, it may be more important for organizations to foster a supportive organizational climate. Friedman and Johnson (1997) argued that family-friendly benefits are most effective when delivered within a corporate culture that respects individual well-being and treats workers as whole people. When supervisors or organizations are family supportive, employees report lower levels of work-to-family conflict, greater commitment, and weaker intentions to leave the organization (e.g., Thompson et al., 2004). Allen (2001) found that the extent to which an organization was perceived as family supportive predicted work-to-family conflict and turnover intentions over and above supervisor support and the availability of family-friendly programs. These results illustrate that it is important for organizations to move beyond merely offering benefit programs to also include organizational culture change regarding the way employees are viewed, valued, and rewarded.

A frequent concern with making family-friendly benefits available to workers is that single or older employees may feel such expenditures constitute an unfair distribution of rewards because they are less likely to use them. However, there is little empirical evidence of 'backlash' from these employees. Although one study found that workers currently using an on-site childcare center were more likely to have positive attitudes toward the benefit, there was no relationship between care center use and more general organizational attitudes (Rothausen et al., 1998). In fact, any backlash effect may be limited to employees who would like to use an existing benefit but are prohibited from doing so, such as when there is a long waiting list for a childcare program (Kossek and Nichol, 1992). In general, attachment to an organization is likely to be greater if one can use a family-friendly benefit, but not being able to use the benefit does not reduce attachment (Grover and Crooker, 1995).

Summary

In summary, there is a substantial body of research on the relationship between work–family conflict and business-related outcomes. Although there is a positive relationship between work–family conflict and turnover, evidence of an association between conflict and absence or tardiness is lacking. Likewise, there is no conclusive evidence of an association between work–family conflict and performance. In contrast, the negative health consequences associated with work–family conflict are more firmly established, although there is a clear need for longitudinal research. Offering family-friendly benefits appears to be an effective organizational response to the problem of work–family conflict. Yet, organizations may reduce work–family conflict further by moving beyond benefits to produce a more family supportive organizational culture.

The role of gender in work–family conflict research

Gender plays a persistent and central role in work–family conflict research for several reasons. First, the work–family conflict literature is historically rooted in the surge of women's labor force participation during World War II and again the 1970s, and the assumption that it would lead to problems, particularly for women. Second, a variety of theories suggest that gender is central to work–family conflict. Functionalist theories, for example, suggest that socialization patterns assign greater responsibility for family to women and that these elevated responsibilities would contribute to greater opportunities for work–family conflict (Duxbury et al., 1994). Similarly, other theories suggest that work-to-family conflict has greater significance for women than men because family has greater psychological meaning for women; likewise, family-to-work conflict has more significance for men than women because work has greater meaning for men (Eagly, 1987; Lobel, 1991; Pleck, 1977). Finally, there is evidence suggesting that men and women interpret experiences in their work and family domains differently (Larson et al., 1994).

Evidence regarding the effect of gender in work–family conflict is mixed. Bellavia and Frone (2005) conclude, '...we note that there is little support for differences across basic characteristics that are typically examined such as gender...' (p. 118). By contrast, Eby and colleagues (2005) conclude that 'gender is deeply engrained in work–family relationships' (p.181) although they recognize that 'there is no clear pattern in terms of the relative importance of work or family domain predictors for men's and women's work–family conflict.' (p. 181). A meta-analysis concluded that there was little evidence suggesting that work–family conflict differs by gender (Byron, 2005). The inconsistent pattern of results by gender is likely driven by multiple factors, including wide variability in sampling strategies and measures used to study work–family conflict. Nevertheless, the frequency with which gender differences are examined in studies of work–family conflict suggests that it is widely assumed that work–family conflict is inherently gendered.

The work–family interrelationship: Is work–family conflict enough?

An emerging, or more appropriately re-emerging, issue in the work–family literature is whether work–family conflict alone adequately characterizes the quality of the interrelationship between an individual's work and family lives. Research has focused on work–family conflict for the past 25 years (Barnett, 1998; Eby et al., 2005; Frone, 2003; Parasuraman and Greenhaus, 2002; Werbel and Walter, 2002), despite longstanding evidence suggesting that work and family can benefit each other (Barnett et al., 1992; Crouter, 1984; Kirchmeyer, 1992), and the focus on positive aspects of organizational life (see the Chapter in this volume by Dutton and Glynn). Researchers are now increasingly pointing out that, while individuals may encounter conflict as they navigate their work and family lives, they also experience substantial synergies. They further suggest that work–family conflict does not capture these synergies and that an exclusive focus on work–family conflict portrays adults' daily work and family lives in an overly negative fashion.

Evidence is accumulating suggesting that work–family conflict may not fully characterize the quality of the interrelationship between work and family for most adults. Consistent with early research, evidence from both nationally representative samples as well as samples reflective of narrower populations indicates that adults can recognize both conflicts and synergies between work and family (Grzywacz and Marks, 2000; Ruderman et al., 2002; Stephens and Townsend, 1997). Evidence indicates that both work–family conflict and variables reflecting the positive side of the work–family interface contribute meaningfully to predictions of desirable outcomes such as individual health (Grzywacz, 2000; Grzywacz and Bass, 2003; Hammer et al., 2005a), as well as job-related outcomes like satisfaction and effort (Wayne et al., 2004). Collectively, this evidence suggests that work–family conflict alone may be insufficient to describe the interrelationship between work and family.

However, several limitations undermine a definitive conclusion about the added value of the positive side of the work–family interface. Research into the positive side of the work–family interface is still nascent. Several concepts like positive spillover, facilitation, enrichment, and compatibility have emerged in the literature (Barnett, 1998; Frone, 2003; Greenhaus and Powell, 2006; Grzywacz and Butler, 2005; Grzywacz and Marks, 2000; Wayne et al., 2004), and there has been little explicit discussion regarding what these concepts represent, whether they reflect isomorphic phenomena and, if not, how they differ from each other. This problem is further exacerbated by the use of the same items to operationalize different concepts (e.g., Grzywacz and Marks, 2000; Wayne et al., 2004). The proliferation of these concepts creates substantial confusion which undermines the ability to determine if these concepts add value to the literature. There is also little theorizing about the positive synergies that characterize individuals' work and family lives. The absence of coherent theory makes it difficult to determine if these positive experiences are distinct from work–family conflict (or the absence thereof). Connected to the absence of theory, the literature began developing without strong measures of the positive experiences.

Many of these issues are beginning to be addressed. Greenhaus and Powell's (2006) work–family enrichment theory considers the processes that give rise to work–family enrichment. Grzywacz and colleagues (2007b) differentiated work–family enrichment and facilitation as a 'levels' issue and encouraged researchers to use the enrichment concept when focusing on individual-level phenomenon (e.g., does an individual's work experiences benefit the individual's quality of family life?) and use facilitation when focusing on family phenomenon (does a family member's work benefit family functioning?). Grzywacz and colleagues (2007b) and Powell and Greenhaus (2006a) explicitly address how positive experiences differ from work–family conflict at the conceptual level, and other papers have begun to address these issues at the empirical level (Grzywacz and Butler, 2005; Kinnunen et al., 2006; Voydanoff, 2004). Researchers have created theoretically based instruments to assess work–family enrichment (Carlson et al., 2006) and positive spillover (Hanson et al., 2006). These and other advancements, which can be situated in broader movements such as Positive Organizational Scholarship (Wayne et al., 2007), will enable researchers to determine if work–family conflict sufficiently characterizes the quality of the interrelationship between work and family.

Emerging issues

In addition to these debates, there are several emerging issues in the work–family conflict literature. The first is whether work–family conflict can be viewed as distinct from its directional counterparts of work interference with family and family interference with work. Work–family conflict arises when individuals simultaneously confront mutually incompatible pressures from both work and family (Greenhaus and Beutell, 1985). Greenhaus and Beutell clearly argued that work–family conflict is inherently non-directional until a decision is made to resolve one of the pressures contributing to the conflict, at which point directionality takes form. Being asked to work during a time when an individual already has a family obligation illustrates work–family conflict (see Greenhaus and Powell, 2003). This situation does not have implications for work or family until the individual makes and follows through on a decision. If the individual resolves the work-related pressure by working the unscheduled time, work has interfered with the individual's family responsibility. By contrast, if the individual resolves the family-related pressure by attending the family event, family has interfered with work responsibilities. Carlson and Grzywacz (2008) were critical of researchers' tendency to use work–family conflict and work–family interference interchangeably. In particular, they argued that the confluence of these concepts undermines interpretation of observed

associations because researchers cannot determine if presumed antecedents create mutually incompatible pressures in work and family (i.e., work–family conflict), or if they shape the decision processes that dictates whether work will interfere with family or family will interfere with work. They further suggest that more research is needed that differentiates work–family conflict from work–family interference, and that studies are needed showing how and under what circumstances work–family conflict translates into interference (Powell and Greenhaus, 2006b).

A related issue is the temporal nature of work–family conflict. Original formulations suggested that work–family conflict is mainly episodic in nature. Pressures emanating from work and family take acute and chronic forms (Greenhaus and Parasuraman, 1994). Acute pressures are those arising from discrete events such as weather-related school closures, sick family members, computer problems at the office, or unexpected deadlines at work. Chronic pressures, by contrast, are open-ended and enduring circumstances such as family dysfunction, poor intra-family relationships, inflexible and highly structured work schedules, work-role ambiguity, or unattainable productivity goals.

The acute vs. chronic distinction of pressures arising from work and family can be situated in a two-by-two table to represent simultaneous presentation of role pressures, a prerequisite for arousing work–family conflict according to Greenhaus and Beutell's first proposition. When depicted in this way, it is clear that three of the four combinations of possible work and family pressures would yield episodes of work–family conflict, assuming that acute pressures have definable start and end points (see Table 1).

Table 1   Temporal underpinning of work–family conflict based on types of work and family pressures

	Work pressure	
	Acute	Chronic
Family pressure		
Acute	Episodic	Episodic
Chronic	Episodic	Chronic

If work–family conflict is comprised primarily of circumscribed episodes, then the immediate downstream consequences of work interference with family (or work-to-family conflict) and family interference with work (or family-to-work conflict) must also be primarily episodic in nature. Greenhaus and Parasuraman (1994) urged researchers to view work–family interference episodically and to document the factors shaping the onset, duration, and consequences of distinct types of incidences of work–family interference. Zerubaval (1985) cogently argues that both work and family responsibilities follow a seven day cycle, suggesting that the potential for work–family and family-work interference waxes and wanes. Morehead (2001) likewise argued that the routines of daily work and family life are heavily synchronized, in part, to minimize the potential for work–family interference. Kirkcaldy and Martin (2000) invoked the concept of punctuated equilibrium in describing intense periods of work–family interference in the wake of specific work or family episodes. These periods are then followed by periods of relative calm when new family adaptive strategies take hold and contribute to relative balance between work and family. Evidence based on a national sample of registered nurses indicated that the majority (52 per cent) of participants experienced family-to-work conflict episodically, and over 40 per cent experienced work-to-family conflict episodically (Grzywacz et al., 2006). Future research will need to give this issue greater attention.

A third issue is the cross-cultural meaning of work–family conflict (and see the chapter by Gardner and Early in this volume). Emerging theoretical models argue that the inherent meaning of 'work' and 'family' is shaped by shared values and beliefs (i.e., culture), and that variation in cultural beliefs will create differences in experiences of work–family conflict (Joplin et al., 2003; Korabik et al., 2003). Although there is relatively little cross-cultural work–family conflict research, there is evidence suggesting that cultural attributes like collectivism and adherence to sharp distinctions in men's and women's responsibilities may shape how frequently work–family is reported, as well as associations with presumed antecedents and consequences of work–family conflict (Aryee et al., 1999; Grzywacz et al., 2007a; Spector et al., 2004; Yang et al., 2000). As globalization continues to unfold with corresponding growth in trans-national companies and greater exchanges of labor through immigration, researchers will need to give greater attention to the cultural meaning of work–family conflict.

A final emerging issue is the relative value of differentiating distinct types of work–family conflict. Greenhaus and Beutell (1985) originally argued that there were three major types of work–family conflict. More recently, Greenhaus and colleagues (2006) differentiated 'energy-based' and 'strain-based' conflict, whereby the former reflects physical or emotional exhaustion and the latter reflects the transfer of negative emotions or feeling states (e.g., stressed, cranky). Conclusions from two literature reviews frame the basis for this issue. On one hand, Geurts and colleagues (2003) suggest there is little evidence for the existence of 'behavior-based' conflict, but useful evidence supporting the distinction of time and strain-based conflict. On the other hand, Bellavia and Frone (2005) were less sanguine and argued that the often cited taxonomy of time-, strain-, and behavior-based conflict confounds the cause of work–family conflict with the experience of work–family conflict.

FUTURE DIRECTIONS

Having laid out the past and present, we are ideally situated to highlight high-priority areas for work–family conflict research. The first high priority area is more quantitative reviews of the literature. Two decades ago, Greenhaus and Beutell (1985) introduced the term work–family conflict to organizational behavior researchers. Hundreds of published articles later, the work–family conflict literature could only be characterized as vast and mature; the large number of narrative reviews and the proliferation of edited volumes and 'handbooks' devoted to work and family are a testament to that fact. Yet, there are few quantitative reviews of this burgeoning literature, and two of the most cited work–family conflict meta-analyses were published a number of years ago (Allen et al., 2000; Kossek and Ozeki, 1999). Two other meta-analyses (Byron, 2005; Mesmer-Magnus and Viswesvaran, 2005) evaluate antecedents and consequences with work–family conflict. However, more meta-analyses focusing on specific associations, particularly associations with specific domains of health (e.g., depression, physical symptoms), are needed. Given the relatively small and non-random samples characteristic of most work–family research, meta-analyses would provide a more accurate estimate of effect sizes as well as indicate the presence of potential moderators. Still, as the input to any meta-analysis will be dominated by cross-sectional studies, the results will be unable to answer pressing questions regarding the causal ordering of effects in the work–family literature.

The next high priority need is an expansion of research designs used to study work–family conflict (see Casper et al., 2007). In particular, there is a desperate need for research using designs that allow greater causal inference. Work–family conflict research using longitudinal designs is sorely needed. However, we suggest that researchers experiment with various time horizons when designing longitudinal studies. The expansion of daily diary designs (e.g., Butler et al., 2005), as well as designs with data collection points separated by weeks, months, quarters, or years would be invaluable (MacDermid, 2005) that might delineate the temporal ordering of putative antecedents and consequences of work–family conflict, thereby providing more relevant data to the business case for work–family conflict. Further, longitudinal study designs that document within-person variation in work–family conflict over different time horizons would offer important insight into determining whether work–family conflict is chronic or episodic in nature. Greater use of experimental or quasi-experimental designs

that manipulate job-related antecedents of work–family conflict (e.g., schedule flexibility), or potential interventions to help minimize work–family conflict (e.g., positive parenting; Martin and Sanders, 2003) would be invaluable for advancing understanding of work–family conflict, as well as provide practical tools to individuals and organizations.

In addition to designs that capture temporal variations in conflict, there is a need for more cross-level research. Despite the fact that individual employees are nested within workgroups and organizations on the one hand, and within families on the other, there is little research examining linkages between work–family conflict and group-level constructs (cf. Bliese and Jex, 2002). Although it is reasonable to expect, given interdependencies at work, that an individual's experience of conflict between work and family is likely to affect group-level variables, there is little research addressing these questions. There is a growing body of research examining relationships among group-level perceptions of support, as an indicator of a family-supportive climate, and individual outcomes (Kopelman et al., 2006; Thompson et al., 2004), yet these cross-level analyses remain unique. We believe such studies are valuable for making the case that work–family conflict affects more than just the individual who experiences it, as well as for justifying organizational changes toward a more family-friendly culture.

Movement beyond self-report measures is a fourth high priority area for work–family conflict researchers. Researchers should use 'objective' indicators of outcomes of interest. Work–family conflict and performance research that uses supervisors' performance appraisals or the results of 360-feedback as the outcome variable would be invaluable. Likewise, research that operationalizes withdrawal behaviors based on absence or tardiness records or that focuses on job departures rather than turnover intentions is needed. Researchers interested in health outcomes need to expand measurement to physical assessments (e.g., blood pressure, blood glucose), clinical evaluations (e.g., health records), or biologic processes indicative of potential disease (e.g., cortisol dysregulation). Of course, there are significant threats to measurement validity associated with these 'objective' measures as well as significant data collection challenges. Nonetheless, carefully designed studies that use these types of measures would make a significant contribution to the literature.

Another high priority area for research is a focus on basic conceptual issues related to work–family conflict. Research should determine if the distinction between work–family conflict and work–family interference (Carlson and Grzywacz, 2008) is useful or simply academic fodder. Researchers need to delineate whether work–family conflict is a psychological (i.e., appraisal that work and family demands incompatible) or social (i.e., externally observable incompatible work and family demands) construct. The temporal nature of work–family conflict or the degree to which it is a chronic or episodic phenomenon requires attention. Each of these conceptual issues has substantial implications for theory development, research design, and practical application. To illustrate, suppose that work–family conflict were an episodic phenomenon. Measures would need to be designed to capture the waxing and waning of typical work–family conflict experiences. Studies would need to rely on dynamic as opposed to static theories. Finally, if work–family conflict were episodic, organizational interventions that help workers adapt to periods of conflict may be the most useful.

CONCLUSION

The work–family conflict literature has blossomed and matured since the concept was formally introduced. Over the past 25 years hundreds of articles and chapters have been published, and this research has produced several consistent findings that highlight the potential influence of work–family conflict on organizations. This research provides a foundation for an exciting new phase of work–family conflict research: one that uses a variety of research designs and measurement strategies so that work–family conflict can be placed in its temporal and situational context that recognizes synergies between work and family. This new phase of research coupled with existing evidence will produce definitive evidence of the significance of work–family conflict for organizations, as well as serve as a guide for creating strategic interventions that benefit workers, their families, and organizations.

REFERENCES

Adams, G.A. and Jex, S.M. (1999) 'Relationships between time management, control, work-family conflict, and strain', *Journal of Occupational Health Psychology*, 4: 72–77.

Allen, T.D. (2001) 'Family-supportive work environments: The role of organizational perceptions', *Journal of Vocational Behavior*, 58: 414–435.

Allen, T.D., Herst, D.E., Bruck, C.S. and Sutton, M. (2000) 'Consequences associated with work-to family conflict: A review and agenda for future research', *Journal of Occupational Health Psychology*, 5: 278–308.

Anderson, S.E., Coffey, B.S. and Byerly, R.T. (2002) 'Formal organizational initiatives and informal workplace tactics: Links to work-family conflict and job-related outcomes', *Journal of Management*, 28: 7887–810.

Aryee, S., Fields, D. and Luk, V. (1999) 'A cross-cultural test of a model of the work-family interface', *Journal of Management*, 25: 491–511.

Aryee, S., Srinivas, E.S. and Tan, H.H. (2005) 'Rhythms of life: Antecedent and outcomes of work-family balance in employed parents', *Journal of Applied Psychology*, 90: 132–146.

Baltes, B.B., Briggs, T.E., Huff, J.W., Wright, J.A. and Neuman, G.A. (1999) 'Flexible and compressed workweek schedules: A meta-analysis of their effects on work-related criteria', *Journal of Applied Psychology*, 84: 496–513.

Barnett, R.C. (1998) 'Toward a review and reconceptualization of the work/family literature', *Genetic, Social and General Psychology Monographs*, 124: 125–182.

Barnett, R.C., Marshall, N.L. and Sayer, A. (1992) 'Positive-spillover effects from job to home: A closer look', *Women and Health*, 19: 13–41.

Batt, R. and Valcour, P.M. (2003) 'Human resources practices as predictors of work-family outcomes and employee turnover', *Industrial Relations*, 42: 189–220.

Bellavia, G. and Frone, M.R. (2005) 'Work-family conflict', in J. Barling, E.K. Kelloway and M.R. Frone (eds), *Handbook of Work Stress*. Thousand Oaks, CA: Sage, pp. 113–147.

Bhuian, S.N., Menguc, B. and Borsboom, R. (2005) 'Stressors and job outcomes in sales: A triphasic model versus a linear-quadratic-interactive model', *Journal of Business Research*, 58: 141–150.

Bliese, P.D. and Jex, S.M. (2002) 'Incorporating a multilevel perspective into occupational stress research: Theoretical, methodological, and practical implications', *Journal of Occupational Health Psychology*, 7: 265–276.

Bond, J.T., Galinsky, E., Kim, S.S. and Brownfield, E. (2005) *National Study of Employers*. New York: Families and Work Institute. Available: http://www.familiesandwork.org/.

Boyar, S.L., Maertz, C.P., Pearson, A.W. and Keough, S. (2003) 'Work-family conflict: A model of linkages between work and family domain variables and turnover intentions', *Journal of Managerial Issues*, 15: 175–190.

Bragger, J.D., Rodriguez-Srednicki, O., Kutcher, E.J., Indovino, L. and Rosner, E. (2005) 'Work-family conflict, work-family culture, and organizational citizenship behavior among teachers', *Journal of Business and Psychology*, 20: 303–324.

Bronfenbrenner, U. (1979) *The Ecology of Human Development: Experiments by Nature and Design*. Cambridge, MA: Harvard University Press.

Budd, J.W. and Mumford, K.A. (2006) 'Family-friendly work practices in Britain: Availability and perceived accessibility', *Human Resource Management*, 45: 23–42.

Bureau of Labor Statistics (2006) *National compensation survey: Employee benefits in private industry in the United States, March 2006*. Washington, DC: US Department of Labor. Available: http://www.bls.gov/ncs/ebs/home.htm.

Butler, A.B., Grzywacz, J.G., Bass, B.L. and Linney, K.D. (2005) 'Extending the demands-control model: A daily diary study of job characteristics, work-family conflict and work-family facilitation', *Journal of Occupational and Organizational Psychology*, 78: 155–169.

Butler, A., Gasser, M. and Smart, L. (2004) 'A social-cognitive perspective on the use of family-friendly benefits', *Journal of Vocational Behavior*, 65: 57–70.

Byron, K. (2005) 'A meta-analytic review of work-family conflict and its antecedents', *Journal of Vocational Behavior*, 67: 169–198.

Carlson, D.S. and Grzywacz, J.G. (2008) 'Reflections and future directions on measurement in work-family research', in K. Korabik, D.S. Lero, and D.L. Whitehead (eds) *The Handbook of Work-Family Integration: Theories, Perspectives, and Best Practices*. Elsevier. In press.

Carlson, D.S., Kacmar, K.M., Wayne, J.H. and Grzywacz, J.G. (2006) 'Measuring the positive side of the work-family interface: Development and validation of a work-family enrichment scale', *Journal of Vocational Behavior*, 68: 131–164.

Cascio, W.F. and Young, C.E. (2005) 'Work-family balance: Does the market reward firms that respect it?', in D.F. Halpern, and S.E. Murphy (eds), *From Work-Family Balance to Work-Family Interaction: Changing the Metaphor*. Mahwah, NJ: Lawrence Erlbaum, pp. 49–63.

Casper, W.J. and Buffardi, L.C. (2004) 'Work-life benefits and job pursuit intentions: The role of anticipated organizational support', *Journal of Vocational Behavior*, 65: 391–410.

Casper, W.J., Eby, L.T., Bordeaux, C., Lockwood, A. and Lambert, D. (2007) 'A review of research methods in IO/OB work-family research', *Journal of Applied Psychology*, 92: 28–43.

Corporate Voices for Working Families (2005) *Business Impacts of Flexibility: An Imperative for Expansion*. Washington, DC: Available http://www.cvworkingfamilies.org.

Crouter, A.C. (1984) 'Spillover from family to work: The neglected side of the work-family interface', *Human Relations*, 37: 425–442.

Davis, A.E. and Kalleberg, A.L. (2006) 'Family-friendly organizations: Work and family programs in the 1990's', *Work and Occupations*, 33: 191–223.

Duxbury, L., Higgins, C. and Lee, C. (1994) 'Work-family conflict: A comparison by gender, family type, and perceived control', *Journal of Family Issues*, 15: 449–466.

Eagly, A.H. (1987) *Sex Differences in Social Behavior: A Social-Role Interpretation*. Hillsdale, NJ: Lawrence Erlbaum Associates.

Eby, L.T., Casper, W.J., Lockwood, A., Bordeaux, C. and Brinley, A. (2005) 'Work and family research in IO/OB: Content analysis and review of the literature (1980–2002)', *Journal of Vocational Behavior*, 66: 127–197.

Friedman, D.E. and Johnson, A.A. (1997) 'Moving from programs to culture change: The next stage for the corporate work-family agenda', in S. Parasuraman and J.H. Greenhaus (eds), *Integrating Work and Family: Challenges and Choices for a Changing World*. Westport, CT: Quorom Books, pp. 192–208.

Frone, M.R. (2000) 'Work-family conflict and employee psychiatric disorders: The National Comorbidity Survey', *Journal of Applied Psychology*, 85: 888–895.

Frone, M.R. (2003) 'Work-family balance', in J.C. Quick and L. E. Tetrick (eds), *Handbook of Occupational Health Psychology*. Washington, DC: American Psychological Association, pp. 143–162.

Frone, M.R., Russell, M., and Cooper, M.L. (1992) 'Antecedents and outcomes of work-family conflict: Testing a model of the work-family interface', *Journal of Applied Psychology*, 77: 65–78.

Frone, M.R., Russell, M. and Cooper, M.L. (1995) 'Job stressors, job involvement and employee health: A test of identity theory', *Journal of Occupational and Organizational Psychology*, 68: 1–11.

Frone, M.R., Russell, M. and Cooper, M.L. (1997a) 'Relation of work-family conflict to health outcomes: A four-year longitudinal study of employed parents', *Journal of Occupational and Organizational Psychology*, 70: 325–335.

Frone, M.R., Yardley, J.K. and Markel, K.S. (1997b) 'Developing and testing an integrative model of the work-family interface', *Journal of Vocational Behavior*, 50: 145–167.

Galinsky, E., Friedman, D.E. and Hernandez, C.A. (1991) *The corporate reference guide to work-family programs*. New York: The Families and Work Institute.

Geurts, S.A.E. and Demerouti, E. (2003) 'Work/nonwork interface: A review of theories and findings', in M.J. Schabracq, J.A.M. Winnubst, and C.L. Cooper (eds), *The Handbook of Work and Health Psychology*. New York: John Wiley and Sons, pp. 279–312.

Goff, S.J., Mount, M.K. and Jamison, R.L. (1990) 'Employer supported child care, work/family conflict, and absenteeism: A field study', *Personnel Psychology*, 43: 793–809.

Grandey, A.A. and Cropanzano, R. (1999) 'The conservation of resources model applied to work-family conflict and strain', *Journal of Vocational Behavior*, 54: 350–370.

Grant Vallone, E.J. and Donaldson, S.I. (2001) 'Consequences of work-family conflict on employee well-being over time', *Work and Stress*, 15: 214–226.

Greenhaus, J.H. and Allen, T.D. (2006) 'Work-family balance: Exploration of a concept'. Paper presentation, *Families and Work Conference*. (March) Provo, UT.

Greenhaus, J.H. and Beutell, N.J. (1985) 'Sources of conflict between work and family roles', *Academy of Management Review*, 10: 76–88.

Greenhaus, J.H. and Parasuraman, S. (1986) 'A work-nonwork interactive perspective of stress and its consequences', *Journal of Organizational Behavior Management*, 8: 37–60.

Greenhaus, J.H. and Parasuraman, S. (1994) 'Work-family conflict, social support and well-being', in M.J. Davidson, and R.J. Burke (eds), *Women in Management: Current Research Issues*. London: Paul Chapman Publishing, pp. 213–229.

Greenhaus, J.H. and Parasuraman, S. (1999) 'Research on work, family, and gender: Current status and future directions', in G. N. Powell (ed.), *Handbook of Gender and Work*. Thousand Oaks, CA: Sage Publications, Inc., pp. 391–412.

Greenhaus, J.H., Parasuraman, S. and Collins, K.M. (2001) 'Career involvement and family involvement as moderators of relationships between work-family conflict and withdrawal from a profession', *Journal of Occupational Health Psychology*, 6: 91–100.

Greenhaus, J.H. and Powell, G.N. (2003) 'When work and family collide: Deciding between competing role demands', *Organizational Behavior and Human Decision Processes*, 90: 291–303.

Greenhaus, J.H. and Powell, G.N. (2006) 'When work and family are allies: A theory of work-family enrichment', *Academy of Management Review*, 31: 72–92.

Greenhaus, J.H., Allen, T.D. and Spector, P.E. (2006) 'Health consequences of work-family conflict: The dark side of the work-family interface', in P.L. Perrewe and D.C. Ganster (eds) *Research in Occupational Stress and Well-Being*. Amsterdam: JAI Press: Elsevier. Vol. 5: pp. 61–98.

Grover, S.L. and Crooker, K.J. (1995) 'Who appreciates family-responsive human resource policies: The impact of family-friendly policies on the organizational attachment of parents and non-parents', *Personnel Psychology*, 48: 271–288.

Grzywacz, J.G. (2000) 'Work-family spillover and health during midlife: Is managing conflict everything?', *American Journal of Health Promotion*, 14: 236–243.

Grzywacz, J.G., Arcury, T.A., Marín, A. Carrillo, L., Burke, B., Coates, M.L. and Quandt, S.A. (2007a) 'Work-family Conflict: Experiences and Health Implications among Immigrant Latinos', *Journal of Applied Psychology*, 92 (4): 1119–1130.

Grzywacz, J.G. and Bass, B.L. (2003) 'Work, family, and mental health: Testing different models of work-family fit', *Journal of Marriage and Family*, 65: 248–261.

Grzywacz, J.G. and Butler, A.B. (2005) 'The impact of job characteristics on work-to-family facilitation: Testing a theory and distinguishing a construct', *Journal of Occupational Health Psychology*, 10: 97–109.

Grzywacz, J.G. and Carlson, D.S. (2007) 'Conceptualizing work-family balance: Implications for practice and future research', *Advances in Human Resource Development*, 9 (4): 455–471.

Grzywacz, J.G., Carlson, D.S., Kacmar, K.M. and Wayne, J.H. (2007b) 'Work-family facilitation: A multilevel perspective on the synergies between work and family', *Journal of Occupational and Organizational Psychology*, 80 (4): 559–574.

Grzywacz, J.G. and Marks, N.F. (2000) 'Reconceptualizing the work-family interface: An ecological perspective on the correlates of positive and negative spillover between work and family', *Journal of Occupational Health Psychology*, 5: 111–126.

Grzywacz, J.G., Frone, M.R., Brewer, C.S. and Kovner, C.T. (2006) 'Quantifying work-family conflict among registered nurses', *Research in Nursing and Health*, 29: 414–426.

Hammer, L.B., Bauer, T.N. and Grandey, A.A. (2003) 'Work-family conflict and work-related withdrawal behaviors', *Journal of Business and Psychology*, 17: 419–436.

Hammer, L.B., Cullen, J.C., Neal, M.B., Sinclair, R.R. and Shafiro, M.V. (2005a) 'The longitudinal effects of work-family conflict and positive spillover on depressive symptoms among dual-earner couples', *Journal of Occupational Health Psychology*, 10: 138–154.

Hammer, L.B., Neal, M.B., Newsom, J.T., Brockwood, K.J. and Colton, C.L. (2005b) 'A longitudinal study of the effects of dual-earner couples' utilization of family-friendly workplace supports on work and family outcomes', *Journal of Applied Psychology*, 90: 799–810.

Hanson, G.C., Hammer, L.B. and Colton, C.L. (2006) 'Development and validation of a multidimensional scale of perceived work-family positive spillover', *Journal of Occupational Health Psychology*, 11: 249–265.

Hobfoll, S.E. (1989) 'Conservation of resources: A new attempt at conceptualizing stress', *American Psychologist*, 44: 513–524.

Hobfoll, S.E. (1998) *Stress, Culture, and Community: The Psychology and Philosophy of Stress*. (The Plenum series on stress and coping.) New York: Plenum.

Hulin, C.L. (1991) 'Adaptation, persistence, and commitment in organizations', in M.D. Dunnette and L.M. Hough (eds), *Handbook of Industrial and Organizational Psychology* (2nd edn). Palo Alto, CA: Consulting Psychologists Press. Vol. 2: pp. 445–505.

Jansen, N.W.H., Kant, J.J., van Amelsvoort, L.G.P.M., Kristensen, T.S., Swaen, G.M.H. and Nijhuis, F.J.N. (2006) 'Work-family conflict as a risk factor for sickness absence', *Journal of Occupational and Environmental Medicine*, 63: 488–494.

Jones, J., Burke, R.J. and Westman, M. (eds) (2006) *Work-life Balance: A Psychological Perspective*. New York: Psychology Press.

Joplin, J.R.W., Shaffer, M.A., Francesco, A.M. and Lau, T. (2003) 'The macro-environment and work-family conflict: Development of a cross-cultural comparative framework', *International Journal of Cross Cultural Management*, 3: 305–328.

Kahn, R.L., Wolfe, D.M., Quinn, R.P., Snoek, J.D. and Rosenthal, R.A. (1964) *Organizational Stress: Studies in Role Conflict and Ambiguity*. New York: John Wiley and Sons.

Kanter, R.M. (1977) *Work and Family in the United States: A Critical Review and Agenda for Research and Policy*. New York: Russell Sage Foundation.

Kinnunen, U., Feldt, T., Geurts, S. and Pulkkinen, L. (2006) 'Types of work-family interface: Well-being correlates of negative and positive spillover between work and family', *Scandinavian Journal of Psychology*, 47: 149–162.

Kirchmeyer, C. (1992) 'Nonwork participation and work attitudes: A test of scarcity vs. expansion models of personal resources', *Human Relations*, 45: 775–795.

Kirkcaldy, B.D. and Martin, T. (2000) 'Job stress and satisfaction among nurses: Individual differences', *Stress Medicine*, 16: 77–89.

Kohler, S.S. and Mathieu, J.E. (1993) 'Individual characteristics, work perceptions, and affective reactions influences on differentiated absence criteria', *Journal of Organizational Behavior*, 14: 515–530.

Kopelman, R.E., Greenhaus, J.H. and Connolly, T.F. (1983) 'A model of work, family, and interrole conflict: A construct validation study', *Organizational Behavior and Human Performance*, 32: 198–215.

Kopelman, R.E., Prottas, D.J., Thompson, C.A. and Jahn, E.W. (2006) 'A multilevel examination of work-life practices: Is more always better?', *Journal of Managerial Issues*, 18: 232–253.

Korabik, K., Lero, D.S. and Ayman, R. (2003) 'A multi-level approach to cross-cultural work-family research', *International Journal of Cross Cultural Management*, 3: 289–303.

Kossek, E.E. and Lambert, S.J. (eds) (2005) *Work and Life Integration: Organizational, Cultural, and Individual Perspectives*. Mahwah, NJ: Lawrence Erlbaum Associates.

Kossek, E.E. and Nichol, V. (1992) 'The effects of on-site child care on employee attitudes and performance', *Personnel Psychology*, 45: 485–509.

Kossek, E.E. and Ozeki, C. (1999) 'Bridging the work-family policy and productivity gap: A literature review', *Community, Work and Family*, 2: 7–32.

Kossek, E.E., Lautsch, B.A. and Eaton, S.C. (2006) 'Telecommuting, control, and boundary management: Correlates of policy use and practice, job control, and work-family effectiveness', *Journal of Vocational Behavior*, 68: 347–367.

Larson, R.W., Richards, M.H. and Perry-Jenkins, M. (1994) 'Divergent worlds: The daily emotional experience of mothers and fathers in the domestic and public spheres', *Journal of Personality and Social Psychology*, 67: 1034–1046.

Lobel, S.A. (1991) 'Allocation of investment in work and family roles: Alternative theories and implications for research', *Academy of Management Review*, 16: 507–521.

MacDermid, S.M. (2005) '(Re)Considering conflict between work and family', in E.E. Kossek, and S. Lambert (eds), *Work and Family Integration in Organizations: New Directions for Theory and Practice*. Mahwah, NJ: Lawrence Earlbaum Associates, pp. 19–40.

MacDermid, S.M. and Harvey, A. (2006) 'The work-family conflict construct: Methodological implications', in M. Pitt-Catsouphes, E.E. Kossek and S. Sweet (eds), *The Work and Family Handbook: Multi-Disciplinary Perspectives, Methods, and Approaches*. Mahwah, NJ: Lawrence Erlbaum Associates, pp. 567–586.

Martin, A.J. and Sanders, M.R. (2003) 'Balancing work and family: A controlled evaluation of the Triple P–Positive Parenting Program as a work-site intervention', *Child and Adolescent Mental Health*, 8: 161–169.

Mesmer-Magnus, J.R. and Viswesvaran, C. (2005) 'Convergence between measures of work-to-family and family-to-work conflict: A meta-analytic examination', *Journal of Vocational Behavior*, 67: 215–232.

Morehead, A. (2001) 'Synchronizing time for work and family: Preliminary insights from qualitative research with mothers', *Journal of Sociology*, 37: 355–369.

Netemeyer, R.G., Boles, J.S. and McMurrian, R. (1996) 'Development and validation of work-family conflict and family-work conflict scales', *Journal of Applied Psychology*, 81: 400–410.

Nowicki, C. (2003) *Family and Medical Leave Act: A Sloan Work and Family Encyclopedia Entry*. Available: http://wfnetwork.bc.edu/encyclopedia_entry.php?id=234&area=academics.

Osterman, P. (1995) 'Work family programs and the employment relationship', *Administrative Science Quarterly*, 40: 681–700.

Parasuraman, S. and Greenhaus, J.H. (2002) 'Toward reducing some critical gaps in work-family research', *Human Resource Management Review*, 12: 299–312.

Parker, L. and Allen, T.D. (2001) 'Work/family benefits: Variables related to employees' fairness perceptions', *Journal of Vocational Behavior*, 58: 453–468.

Pitt-Catsouphes, M., Kossek, E.E. and Sweet, S. (eds) (2006) *The Work and Family Handbook: Multi-Disciplinary Perspectives, Methods, and Approaches*. Mahwah, NJ: Lawrence Erlbaum Associates.

Pleck, J.H. (1977) 'The work-family role system', *Social Problems*, 24: 417–442.

Pleck, J.H. (1995) 'Work roles, family roles and well-being: Current conceptual perspectives', in G.L. Bowen and J.F. Pittman (eds), *The Work and Family Interface: Toward a Contextual Effects Perspective*. Minneapolis, MN: National Council on Family Relations, pp. 17–22.

Powell, G.N. and Greenhaus, J.H. (2006b) 'Managing incidents of work-family conflict: A decision making perspective', *Human Relations*, 59: 1179–1212.

Powell, G.N. and Greenhaus, J.H. (2006a) 'Is the opposite of positive negative: Untangling the complex relationship between work-family enrichment and conflict', *Career Development International*, 11 (7): 650–659.

Roman, P.M. and Blum, T.C. (2001) 'Work-family role conflict and employer responsibility: An organizational analysis of workplace responses to a social problem', in R.T. Golembiewski (ed.), *Handbook of Organizational Behavior* (2nd edn). New York: Marcel Dekker, pp. 415–444.

Rothausen, T.J., Gonzalez, J.A., Clarke, N.E. and O'Dell, L.L. (1998) 'Family-friendly backlash—fact or fiction: The case of organizations' on-site child care centers', *Personnel Psychology*, 51: 685–706.

Ruderman, M.N., Ohlott, P.J., Panzer, K. and King, S.N. (2002) 'Benefits of multiple roles for managerial women', *Academy of Management Journal*, 45: 369–386.

Spector, P.E., Cooper, C.L., Poelmans, S., Allen, T.D., O'Driscoll, M., Sanchez, J.I., Siu, O.L., Dewe, P., Hart, P., Lu, L., De Moreas, L.F.R., Ostrognay, G.M., Sparks, K., Wong, P. and Yu, S. (2004) 'A cross-national comparative study of work-family stressors, working hours, and well-being: China and Latin America versus the Anglo World', *Personnel Psychology*, 57: 119–142.

Stephens, M.A. and Townsend, A.L. (1997) 'Stress of parent care: Positive and negative effects of women's other roles', *Psychology and Aging*, 12: 376–386.

Tetrick, L.E. and Buffardi, L.C. (2006) 'Measurement issues in research on the work-home interface', in F. Jones, R.J. Burke, and M. Westman (eds), *Work-Life Balance: A Psychological Perspective*. Hove, East Sussex: Psychology Press, pp. 90–114.

Thomas, L.T. and Ganster, D.C. (1995) 'Impact of family supportive work variables on work-family conflict and strain: A control perspective', *Journal of Applied Psychology*, 80: 6–15.

Thompson, C.A., Beauvais, L.L. and Lyness, K.S. (1999) 'When work-family benefits are not enough: The influence of work-family culture on benefit utilization, organizational attachment, and work-family conflict', *Journal of Vocational Behavior*, 54: 392–415.

Thompson, C., Jahn, A., White, E., Kopelman, R.E. and Prottas, D.J. (2004) 'Perceived organizational family support: A longitudinal and multilevel analysis', *Journal of Managerial Issues*, 16: 545–565.

Voydanoff, P. (2004) 'The effects of work demands and resources on work-to-family conflict and facilitation', *Journal of Marriage and Family*, 66: 398–412.

Voydanoff, P. (2005) 'Toward a conceptualization of perceived work-family fit and balance: A demands and resources approach', *Journal of Marriage and Family*, 67: 822–836.

Wayne, J.H., Grzywacz, J.G., Carlson, D.S. and Kacmar, K.M. (2007) 'Work-family facilitation: A theoretical explanation and model of primary antecedents and consequences', *Human Resource Management Review*, 17: 63–76.

Wayne, J.H., Musisca, N. and Fleeson, W. (2004) 'Considering the role of personality in the work-family experience: Relationships of the big five to work-family conflict and facilitation', *Journal of Vocational Behavior*, 64: 108–130.

Werbel, J. and Walter, M.H. (2002) 'Changing views of work and family roles: A symbiotic perspective', *Human Resource Management Review*, 12: 293–298.

Witt, L.A. and Carlson, D.S. (2006) 'The work family interface and job performance: Moderating effects of conscientiousness and perceived organizational support', *Journal of Occupational Health Psychology*, 11: 343–357.

Yang, N., Chen, C.C., Choi, J. and Zou, Y. (2000) 'Sources of work-family conflict: A Sino-U.S. comparison of the effects of work and family demands', *Academy of Management Journal*, 43: 113–123.

Zerubaval, E. (1985) *The Seven Day Circle: The History and Meaning of the Week*. New York: Free Press.

25

Sexual Harassment in Organizations: A Decade of Research in Review

Lilia M. Cortina and Jennifer L. Berdahl

For 30 years, sexual harassment has been recognized as a serious organizational problem and a violation of US law. The Navy Tailhook scandal and Clarence Thomas hearings in 1991 launched sexual harassment to the forefront of public attention. This was followed by a virtual explosion of research on the topic, leading to the estimate that one out of every two women is harassed at some point in her working life. We review this scholarship in the current chapter, concentrating on the last decade of work.

Our principal focus is sexual harassment in the workplace. Although sexual harassment also occurs elsewhere, other domains are beyond the scope of this chapter. This chapter also primarily covers research since the mid-1990s (except for brief historical overviews). Sexual harassment scholarship began in the late 1970s, and several large-scale surveys in the 1980s (Gutek, 1985; USMSPB, 1981, 1988; Martindale, 1990) influenced work that followed. Since then, however, the workforce has become more educated about

sexual harassment, organizational methods of combating sexual harassment have evolved, and sexual-harassment research methodologies have become increasingly advanced. We therefore concentrate on the most recent, methodologically sophisticated work. Finally, research on this topic largely addresses men's harassment of women, so this will be the main focus of our review.

We organize this chapter around the following questions: What is sexual harassment? Why does it happen? Who harasses whom? What are its effects? Finally, how do and how should individuals and organizations respond to sexual harassment? Each of these sections provides a brief historical recap of early work on the topic, followed by a detailed review of recent scholarship. Throughout, we address relevant issues in US law but maintain a focus on theory and findings from social science (particularly psychology). The chapter will close with a discussion of the future of sexual harassment scholarship.

DEFINING SEXUAL HARASSMENT

There are two main approaches to defining sexual harassment: One from a legal perspective and the other from a social-psychological perspective. In general, social-psychological definitions are broader than legal ones, though recent exceptions exist. A third perspective on sexual harassment – the public, or lay perspective – preceded legal and social-psychological ones but now lags well behind each in understanding the scope, nature, and impact of the phenomenon. We review each in turn below.

Legal definitions

According to historical writings, sexually harassing behavior has long been a problem (e.g., Segrave, 1994). The term 'sexual harassment,' however, only emerged in the 1970s, when feminists argued that sexual threats, bribes, and objectification presented odious conditions of employment often faced by women, but rarely by men, and therefore constitute unlawful sex discrimination (Farley, 1978; MacKinnon, 1979). The historical pervasiveness of this behavior made it so taken-for-granted that courts initially balked at the idea of calling it discrimination, and early cases were denied or decided in favor of defendants. Organizations saw sexual harassment as a 'private' issue between the harasser and victim, beyond the scope of organizational responsibility (MacKinnon, 1979).

This changed in the late 1970s when US courts finally decided that women who lost jobs for failing to comply with their employers' sexual demands were discriminated against based on sex (beginning with Williams v. Saxbe, 1976). Courts used Title VII of the 1964 Civil Rights Act to reason that quid pro quo sexual harassment (the loss/denial of a job-related benefit for refusal to cooperate sexually) was illegal sex discrimination. The legal definition of sexual harassment was expanded in the 1980s to include hostile environment harassment: Unwanted sexual attention and requests that

do not necessarily come from a supervisor or result in the loss/denial of a job-related benefit, but that create a hostile work environment (Bundy v. Jackson, 1981; Meritor Savings Bank v. Vinson, 1986). Unlike quid pro quo harassment, which typically involves one perpetrator and victim, hostile environment harassment can involve multiple perpetrators and victims. Some acts (e.g., posting pornography, telling sexist jokes) may be experienced by many employees but create a hostile environment for only a few. Recognizing hostile environment harassment meant recognizing that sexual behavior itself can be hostile and demeaning, particularly to women, who constitute the main targets of sexual objectification, exploitation, and violence in the world. Sexual behavior at work can therefore remind men and women of their unequal status in society more broadly and reinforce their inequality at work.

In 1980 the US Equal Employment Opportunity Commission (EEOC; the legal entity charged with enforcing federal sex discrimination law) developed the following definition of sexual harassment, still used today:

> Unwelcome sexual advances, requests for sexual favors, and other verbal or physical conduct of a sexual nature constitute sexual harassment when this conduct explicitly or implicitly affects an individual's employment, unreasonably interferes with an individual's work performance, or creates an intimidating, hostile, or offensive work environment. (p. 74677)

The EEOC has since offered more specific guidelines for identifying sexual harassment. Prompted by court rulings, these include that the victim and harasser can be of the same sex, that the harasser need not be employed by the victim's organization, and that the victim can be anyone affected by the conduct (including those not directly targeted).

As awareness of sexual harassment and the breadth of behavior covered by law have grown, so too have the number of grievances filed. In 1980, the EEOC received one sexual harassment complaint. By 1989, nearly 6,000 new cases had been filed, and between 1990 and 1999 this number soared to 37,725. The number of new complaints filed annually peaked at 5,332 in the year 2000, and has declined slightly each year since (http://www.eeoc.gov/stats/harassment.html).

Social-psychological definitions

Unlike legal definitions, social-psychological perspectives on sexual harassment do not require negative work outcomes and therefore tend to be broader. The focus instead is on specific behaviors and the victim's subjective experience of those behaviors. Illustrating this perspective, Fitzgerald et al. (1997: 15) define sexual harassment as 'unwanted sex-related behavior at work that is appraised by the recipient as offensive, exceeding her resources, or threatening her well-being.'

Psychologists have concentrated on developing operational definitions of sexual harassment. In a now-classic study, Till (1980) collected descriptive anecdotes and classified sexually harassing conduct into five categories:

(1) generalized sexist remarks or behavior;
(2) inappropriate and offensive (but essentially sanction-free) sexual advances;
(3) solicitation of sexual activity or other sex-linked behavior by promise of rewards;
(4) coercion of sexual activity by threat of punishments; and
(5) sexual assaults.

Fitzgerald and colleagues (1988) developed a list of behaviors to reflect these five categories and asked women students and employees how often they experienced each. Factor-analysis revealed a three-factor structure:

(1) gender harassment (Till's category 1, sexist remarks and behavior);
(2) unwanted sexual attention (Till's categories 2 and 5, sexual attention and force); and
(3) sexual coercion (Till's categories 3 and 4, threats and bribes).

Gender harassment and unwanted sexual attention correspond to the legal definition of hostile environment harassment, while sexual coercion parallels illegal quid pro quo harassment (Fitzgerald et al., 1988; Fitzgerald et al., 1995a). Based on this work, Fitzgerald and colleagues developed the Sexual Experiences Questionnaire (SEQ), the most widely-used and validated measure of sexual harassment to date.

Lay definitions

It is important to consider opinions about sexual harassment in the general public. Lay perceptions have a profound influence on managerial policy and employee ideas about what constitutes 'appropriate' behavior at work and what justifies a complaint. More research has examined lay perceptions than any other aspect of sexual harassment (over 300 studies to date, according to the PsycINFO database), perhaps due to the ease and speed with which such research can be conducted.

Not surprisingly, lay perceptions of sexual harassment have differed over time, between men and women, and across cultures. The US Merit Systems Protection Board (USMSPB) asked federal employees in 1980, 1987, and 1994 to indicate whether they thought each of six different types of behavior (from sexual teasing to sexual pressure) constituted sexual harassment. In each successive survey, a greater proportion of employees judged each type of behavior as harassing. Other studies have consistently shown that women are more likely than men to view sexual behaviors as harassing. The gap between men's and women's perceptions is quite small for sexual pressure and coercion, especially from a supervisor, but is greater for gender harassment (USMSPB, 1994; Blumenthal, 1998; Rotundo, Nguyen, and Sackett, 2001). It is important to note, however, that a majority of men and women consider gender-harassing behaviors to be sexual harassment (77–88 per cent of women, and 64–70 per cent of men, USMSPB, 1994). In studies asking participants to evaluate how offended or bothered they would be (or have been) by specific behaviors, the gender gap widens: Men often report not being upset by, and even enjoying, a variety of behaviors that women find harassing (Berdahl, 2007a; Berdahl et al., 1996; Gutek, 1985).

Emerging developments and debates about definitions of sexual harassment

Although sexual harassment is now a well-established construct in both law and psychology, questions remain about how best to define and assess this behavior.

Which definition should researchers adopt?

There has been some debate about whether researchers should use legal or social-psychological definitions of sexual harassment to study its prevalence (Fitzgerald et al., 1997; Gutek et al., 2004). Because social-psychological definitions are broader than legal ones, measuring sexual harassment according to the former yields higher prevalence estimates. This may pose a problem in legal contexts if the focus of the assessment is strictly limited to unlawful behavior. On the other hand, if researchers are interested in studying and understanding sexual harassment as a social and psychological phenomenon, using definitions derived from social-psychological theories makes the most sense. Confining measures to current legal definitions risks studying a narrow and moving target. It would make cross-temporal and cross-cultural comparisons difficult because sexual harassment law has evolved over time and differs widely across countries (some of which have no laws against sexual harassment). Restricting studies of sexual harassment to legal definitions implicitly argues that sexual harassment should not have been studied prior to the late 1970s in the US and should not be studied in many parts of the world today. As social scientists, our charge is to shed light on social phenomena, not to limit our attention to phenomena currently deemed illegal.

There is also debate about whether lay perceptions of sexual harassment should be used to inform definitions of the construct. This is a complicated issue. On the one hand, the general public is usually much less informed about sexual harassment than the lawyers, judges, policy experts, and social scientists who study it. During some eras, and among some people and cultures, behaviors that we now consider to be the most heinous examples of harassment were considered justified (Segrave, 1994). Had the courts and social scientists relied on majority public opinion polls, sexual harassment probably would have never been identified as a form of sex discrimination. After all, these behaviors were tolerated – even condoned – for centuries.

On the other hand, if sexual harassment is partially defined by the subjective experience of its victim, then *how* the victim experiences these behaviors must be taken into account. If someone reports *enjoying* sexual attention at work – even uninvited sexual attention – then it is probably inappropriate to label that person's experience 'harassing.' Research shows that many victims do not label their own experiences as harassment (Arvey and Cavanaugh, 1995; Magley et al., 1999a). Thus, rather than having respondents categorize it as such, researchers should instead define sexual harassment and use those guidelines to measure harassment.

Considering non-sexual forms of harassment

Research has increasingly identified forms of harassment that discriminate based on sex but do not necessarily entail sexual advances. For example, professional women compared to men report significantly more incivility and aggression – behaviors that alienate the victim rather than approach them sexually (Berdahl, 2007c; Cortina, 2008). Moreover, when men are harassed, it often involves punishment for deviating from traditional masculine gender roles (Berdahl et al., 1996; Oncale v. Sundowner Offshore Services, 1998; Waldo et al., 1998). Examples include teasing a man about his role in the home; deriding him for failing to participate in the objectification of women; and calling him derogatory names that challenge his masculinity. Consistent with this, legal theorists argue that sex-based harassment often entails behaviors that undermine the victim but make no explicit reference to sexuality (Franke, 1997; Schultz, 1998). That is, 'much of the time, harassment assumes a form that has little or nothing to do with sexuality but everything to do with gender' (Schultz, 1998: 1687). Capturing the notion sexual harassment can be *based on sex* but not necessarily *sexual*, Berdahl (2007b) offers a new definition of sexual harassment as 'behavior that derogates, demeans, or humiliates an individual based on that individual's sex.'

Considering perspectives beyond mainstream White America

Despite the fact that some of the most prominent sexual harassment cases in the US have involved ethnic-minority victims (e.g., Anita Hill in the Senate confirmation hearings of Clarence Thomas; Mechelle Vinson in Meritor Savings Bank v. Vinson, 1986), the most prominent sexual harassment research has focused on White/European American women. Questions remain about whether and how models of sexual harassment extend to women from other ethnic and cultural backgrounds.

One manifestation of harassment that may be more salient to ethnic minority women is *sexual racism*. This refers to harassment that combines sexism and racism to create a simultaneous manifestation of sex and race discrimination. These are '…forms of sexual aggression [that] are embedded in a system of interlocking race, gender, ethnicity, and class oppression' (Murrell, 1996: 56). Behaviors falling into this category include not only those that disproportionately target minority women, but also conduct that reflects and perpetuates stereotypes about particular genders in particular ethnic groups (e.g., Adams, 1997; Buchanan and Ormerod, 2002; Cortina, 2001). To date, this concept has primarily been the focus of theory and commentary, so it remains unclear how sexual racism might fit into empirical models. Given that sexual harassment transcends boundaries of race, class, and country (e.g., Barak, 1997), definitions and assessments of this phenomenon

must begin considering perspectives beyond mainstream White America.

Evolving measures of sexual harassment

Operational definitions of sexual harassment have varied over the past 20 years, for good reason: Criteria for what constitutes sexual harassment have expanded (e.g., to include same-sex harassment); research has shown that groups differ on which behaviors they consider to be harassing (e.g., unlike women, many men do not experience uninvited sexual attention as harassing); and scholars have come to recognize that sexual harassment involves different language, insinuation, and reference by context (e.g., the military vs. a law firm; one culture vs. another). This poses a problem for comparative research purposes (Gutek et al., 2004). The USMSPB studies spanning 14 years used the same six items assessing 'socio-sexual behavior;' this facilitated comparisons across survey administrations, but ignored developments in understanding sexual harassment, such as its frequent non-sexual forms and the important qualification that it be unpleasant or offensive to the victim.

The SEQ has been adapted over time to reflect the particular styles of sexual harassment in different contexts and against different groups, such as the military (Fitzgerald et al., 1999b), Latinas (Cortina, 2001), Turkish women (Wasti et al., 2000), and men (Waldo et al., 1998; Berdahl and Moore, 2006). At the same time, the factor structure of the SEQ (gender harassment, unwanted sexual attention, and sexual coercion) has remained stable across time, culture, and occupational sector, despite variations in the specific items assessing each construct (Gelfand et al., 1995; Lee and Ormerod, 2003).[1] Lee and Ormerod (2003: 6) argued that, 'similar to aptitude testing … it is the dimensions, rather than any particular items, that form the core construct … The dimensions are considered finite, whereas infinite items can be sampled as needed for the assessment of particular populations.' In addition to this structural robustness, the SEQ consistently predicts various professional, psychological, and physical health outcomes (see Hershcovis and Barling, under review). Moreover, all SEQ items were developed to meet the highest psychometric standards (e.g., using clear behavioral language; avoiding 'double-barreled' items or those with multiple components; including multiple items to assess each latent construct; e.g., Dillman, 2000). As such, the SEQ presents a flexible but highly reliable and valid approach to assessing unwanted sex-related behavior at work.

THEORIZING SEXUAL HARASSMENT

Why does sexual harassment occur? Below we discuss four viewpoints:

(1) The 'nature' perspective, which sees sexual harassment as the result of biological sex differences;
(2) The 'nurture' perspective, which conceptualizes sexual harassment as a consequence of socialized sex roles and stereotypes;
(3) The 'power' perspective, which views sexual harassment as emerging from sex differences in power; and
(4) the 'nurture x power' perspective, which regards sexual harassment as a means of protecting valued social identities (for other reviews, see Tangri and Hayes, 1997; Welsh, 1999).

The nature perspective: Physical design

Within the nature perspective, sexual harassment is viewed as the inevitable and natural result of biological sexual urges. The most common pattern of male perpetrators harassing female victims is attributed to assumed sex differences in sexual drive and function (Studd and Gattiker, 1991). This explanation fails to predict most sexual harassment, however, which constitutes hostile acts aimed not at sexual intimacy but rather at degradation and alienation of the victim. It also fails to explain why sexual harassment is usually targeted at individuals who violate gender ideals rather than those who meet them (Berdahl, 2007b). Thus, despite its ready acceptance among the lay public, most sexual

harassment scholars have dismissed the nature perspective. Some have also rejected it for its pessimistic implications. As one scholar noted, 'linking sexual harassment with libido laid the groundwork for excusing, accepting, and forgiving male violence against women ... If it is libido, then nature is the culprit, and what can be done about nature?' (Segrave, 1994: 2).

The nurture perspective: Cognitive design

Within the nurture perspective, sexual harassment is viewed as the result of sex roles and stereotypes. One version of this theory views cognitive biases as the main cause of sexual harassment. A second accords this role to negative attitudes toward women, or misogyny. A third version considers both cognitive and attitudinal biases to play important roles.

Representing the cognitive-bias perspective is sex-role spillover theory (Gutek, 1985; Gutek and Morasch, 1982), which regards sexual harassment as behavior guided by socialized roles of men as sexual agents and women as sexual objects. When the ratio of men to women in an occupational context is highly skewed, these sex roles are confounded with the job. Thus, secretaries, elementary school teachers, and nurses are viewed as sexual objects, whereas construction workers, fire fighters, and engineers are seen as sexual agents. Sex-role spillover theory predicts that women should experience equally high levels of sexual harassment in both male- and female-dominated occupations. However, research shows that women are sexually harassed more in male-dominated than female-dominated work contexts (Berdahl, 2007a; Fitzgerald et al., 1997; Glomb et al., 1999; Gruber, 1998; Mansfield et al., 1991). It might be the amount of contact a woman has with men, rather than occupational sex ratios, that best predict women's likelihood to be sexually harassed (Gutek et al., 1990; Gruber, 1998).

A second perspective is that negative attitudes toward women drive sexual harassment.

Theorists have long argued that sexual harassment is a form of hostility and aggression toward women in the workplace (e.g., Farley, 1978; Franke, 1997; MacKinnon, 1979; Schultz, 1998). In a now-classic study, Pryor (1987) demonstrated that men who held negative attitudes toward women, and who admitted to being likely to rape a woman if they could get away with it, were more likely to sexually harass a woman when given the chance.

A third perspective offers a combination of the first two: Sexual harassers are motivated by sex roles and sexist hostility (Fiske and Glick, 1995). Based on their theory of ambivalent sexism, Fiske and Glick (1995) suggested that:

(1) unwanted sexual attention is mainly motivated by romantic interest and 'benevolent' sexist beliefs (i.e., those assuming heterosexual interdependence and complementarity);
(2) gender harassment is mainly motivated by inter-gender competition and hostile sexist beliefs (i.e., those assuming female malevolence and inferiority); and
(3) most episodes of sexual harassment include some combination of these behaviors and motives.

The fact that sexual coercion, unwanted sexual attention, and gender harassment are highly correlated (e.g., Fitzgerald et al., 1995a; Schneider et al., 1997) supports this assertion as well as the possibility that all forms of sexual harassment share a common root.

The power perspective: Structural design

The power perspective views sexual harassment as the result of power inequality that enables harassers to sexually coerce and objectify those 'beneath' them in a hierarchy (e.g., Farley, 1978; MacKinnon, 1979). Power inequality facilitates sexual harassment, and sexual harassment reinforces power inequality. Advocates of this perspective rarely articulate the direct motives of harassers, but usually assume that harassers are motivated by sexual desire, a desire to dominate the victim, or both. As Farley (1978: 207) argued,

[F]emale oppression at work is the result of nearly universal male power to hire and fire. Men control the means of economic survival. This control, however, is also used to coerce working women sexually. Institutionalized male power has thus created its own means of maintaining its superior position.

Different types of power may enable sexual harassment (Berdahl et al., 1996; Cleveland and Kerst, 1993; Farley, 1978; MacKinnon, 1979). A frequent argument is that harassers use their organizational power to impose their sexual will on victims, as in quid pro quo harassment. This is a limited view of power, however. A broader view considers power relationships outside the organization. Women are usually more economically dependent on men than vice-versa. Thus, if a woman does not please her male boss (sexually or otherwise), she is less able to support herself and must depend on a man at home; if a woman does not please a man at home, she is made more dependent on her male boss, and so on. This pervasive economic power yields another type that enables men to sexually harass women: Social power, upheld by societal values and beliefs about men and women's appropriate status, roles, and inherent worthiness. With social power, a man can act as a sexual agent and treat a woman as a sexual object even when he lacks organizational or economic power over her.

Finally, physical power, or the ability to physically intimidate and dominate someone, enables men to sexually harass women. Physical power often seems so obvious that it gets overlooked, but it may be the original source of men's economic and social power over women (Engels, 1884), and clearly plays a role in sexual violence.

Nurture x power: The social identity perspective

Combining the nurture and power perspectives, social identity theories of sexual harassment emphasize prescriptive stereotypes (beliefs about how men and women *should* differ, rather than how they *do* differ) and their motives. According to this viewpoint, sexual harassment is a mechanism for punishing those who threaten a harasser's gender identity and the benefits derived from it (Berdahl, 2007b; Berdahl et al., 1996; Dall'Ara and Maass, 1999; Franke, 1997; Maass et al., 2003; Schultz, 1998). Berdahl (2007b) proposes that sexual harassment is triggered by the harasser's desire to protect or enhance his or her sex-based social status in a system of gender hierarchy. Sexual harassers are more likely to be men, because men compared to women have more to gain from protecting their sex-based status. Harassers can protect or define their status by derogating another's in a variety of ways, including sexual and non-sexual harassment targeted at members of both sexes.

We have considered different explanations for what motivates harassment, from nature to nurture to power to social identity. Different explanations have different implications for who harasses whom.

WHO HARASSES WHOM?

Because the first court cases of sexual harassment involved male bosses making sexual cooperation a condition of women's employment, this became the prototype of sexual harassment. We now know, however, that this scenario represents a small minority of incidents: Co-workers, subordinates, customers, and clients are often the harassment perpetrators; men are harassed based on sex; and same-sex harassment is surprisingly common.

Gender

Most sexual harassment is targeted against women. Only 10–14 per cent of sexual harassment cases filed with the EEOC are filed by men. The 1994 USMSPB study of federal workers found that more women (44 per cent) than men (19 per cent) had experienced any of seven types of sexual behavior in

the past two years at work. Perpetrators of these sexual behaviors toward women were almost exclusively men (93 per cent). In contrast, men were targeted by both women (65 per cent) and men (21 per cent). In more recent research assessing not just sexual behavior but sexual behavior that is offensive, or unwanted, a similar pattern has emerged. Women are sexually harassed more than men (e.g., Cortina et al., 2002; Magley et al., 1999), especially when researchers only count negatively-appraised behaviors (e.g., Berdahl, 2007a). Without such adjustments, some studies have found men and women report similar amounts of sexual experiences at work (e.g., Berdahl, 2007a; Konik and Cortina, in press).

Systematic research into the gender of both harassers and victims has been rare, however. Many studies only investigate women's experiences, and until the late 1990s, most surveys only asked about behaviors instigated by men. More research is needed to understand same-sex sexual harassment as well as non-sexual forms of gender harassment. 'Not man enough' harassment, for example, first identified in male samples, has recently been studied in women as well. It appears that women too are teased for being 'not tough enough' or 'overly sensitive' in male-dominated jobs (Berdahl and Moore, 2006). Berdahl (2007b) predicts that when different forms of harassment based on sex are considered, the most common pattern should be men harassing women, followed by men harassing men and women harassing women; women harassing men should be the least common. These and other questions require further exploration.

Status

Early research into sexual harassment focused on sexual attention and coercion from bosses and supervisors. Co-workers were included when hostile environment harassment was recognized. The stem used in the SEQ was limited to 'supervisors or co-workers' until recently, when researchers included subordinates, customers, and anyone else in the work environment (e.g., Berdahl, 2003; Konik and Cortina, in press). In service-oriented jobs and organizations, customers and clients are common sources of sexual harassment (Barling et al., 2001; Berdahl, 2003; Gettman and Gelfand, 2007). Research has demonstrated that subordinates sometimes sexually harass their superiors, though rarely. This type of 'contrapower' harassment has mainly been studied among female professors who experience it from their male students (e.g., DeSouza and Fansler, 2003). More research is needed on harassment from subordinates and those outside the organization.

Race/ethnicity

To date, sexual harassment research has paid only limited attention to issues of race and ethnicity. Ethnic stereotypes, numerical minority status, cultural marginality, and economic vulnerability should theoretically increase the risk of sexual harassment for ethnic minority women (e.g., MacKinnon, 1979; Murrell, 1996). That said, most empirical research on sexual harassment has focused on White/European American women. When ethnic differences have been examined, findings have been mixed. Earlier large-scale studies yielded no differences in the harassment rates of White and non-White women (Gutek, 1985; USMBSP, 1987). More recent research reports higher rates of sexual harassment against ethnic minority women compared to White women (Berdahl and Moore, 2006; Bergman and Drasgow, 2003; Cortina et al., 1998; Mansfield et al., 1991) and men (Berdahl and Moore, 2006). In contrast, some surveys found Latina and Black women to report significantly lower rates of harassment than their non-Latina White counterparts (Shupe et al., 2002; Wyatt and Riederle, 1995). Each of these studies followed a different approach to assessing sexual harassment, making comparisons and conclusions difficult.

The empirical literature is virtually silent about the race and ethnicity of sexual harassers, possibly due to the intricacy of this issue. Perpetrators can be members of the victim's own ethnic group, or numerous other groups of varying social class and organizational power, which can change the victim's subjective experience For example, from the perspective of a Black woman, the experience of being harassed likely 'feels' very different, depending on whether it comes from White men in power, Black men in power, Black men of lower organizational status, or male members of other low-status ethnic groups. More studies are warranted to disentangle the complexity of race, class, and power in sexual harassment.

OUTCOMES OF SEXUAL HARASSMENT

In the early 1990s, researchers lamented the 'appalling' lack of systematic empirical attention to sexual harassment outcomes (Gutek and Koss, 1993: 43). This situation changed dramatically over the decade that followed, as scientists documented myriad links between sexual harassment and victims' occupational functioning, psychological/behavioral health, and physical health. Such outcome relationships remained significant even when controlling for the experience of other stressors (e.g., general job stress, trauma outside of the workplace), other features of the job (occupational level, organizational tenure, workload), personality (negative affectivity, neuroticism, narcissism), and other demographic factors (age, education level, race). Table 1 summarizes findings of this scholarship, reviewed below.

Occupational outcomes

Not surprisingly, the organizational psychology literature has focused primarily on associations between sexual harassment and victims' occupational well-being (see Table 1). In particular, over 20 articles report that sexual harassment is associated with job dissatisfaction (for a meta-analytic review, see Lapierre et al., 2005). This finding applies to not only White American civilians, but also US military personnel, ethnic minority women in the US, and women in other nations

Table 1 Summary of research (from the mid-1990s to the present) on outcomes of sexual harassment. An 'X' indicates that a significant relationship was found between sexual harassment and that outcome. When the harassment-outcome relationship was indirect (i.e., mediated through other variables), this is noted in parentheses

Key

Job outcomes
A Job satisfaction
B Actual and intended turnover
C Work withdrawal or neglect
D Organizational commitment
E Productivity or performance
F Job stress
G Other

Psychological outcomes
H Depression, anxiety, or general distress
I Post traumatic stress disorder
J Other psychological outcomes

Study	Job outcomes							Psychological outcomes			Health	
	A	B	C	D	E	F	G	H	I	J		Health
Barling et al. (1996)	X (indirect)	X (indirect)								negative mood		X (indirect)
Barling et al. (2001)			X (indirect)	X (indirect)	X		justice perceptions and cognitive difficulties			fear (direct) and negative mood (indirect)		
Bergman and Drasgow (2003)	X			X (indirect)	X (indirect)			X				X
Bond et al. (2004)	X							X				
Chan et al. (1999)	X											
Cortina, Fitzgerald and Drasgow (2002)	X	X (indirect)	X (indirect)					X		life satisfaction (indirect)		X
Cortina, Lonsway et al. (2002)	X	X (indirect)				X						
Culbertson and Rosenfeld (1994)			X					X		anger, disgust, fear, self-blame, and low self-esteem		X

Study										
Dansky and Kilpatrick (1997)	X	X (indirect)					X	X		
Fitzgerald et al. (1997)	X	X (indirect)	X (indirect)				X	X	life satisfaction	X (indirect)
Fitzgerald et al. (1999)	X	X (indirect)		X (indirect)			X			X (indirect and direct)
Fontana and Rosenheck (1998)								X	problem drinking	
Freels et al. (2005)	X									
Glomb et al. (1999)	X	X (indirect)	X (indirect)				X	X	life satisfaction	
Harned and Fitzgerald (2002)	X	X (indirect)					X	X	disordered eating (indirect), self-esteem and self-blame (direct)	X (indirect)
Harned et al (2002)	X		X (indirect)	X (indirect)			X			X (indirect and direct)
Langhout et al. (2005)	X		X (indirect)	X (indirect)			X	X		X
Lim and Cortina (2005)	X	X			X		X		life satisfaction	X
Magley et al. (2005)	X	X			X	job burnout	X	X		
Magley et al. (1999)	X	X		X			X	X		X
Morrow et al. (1994)	X	X			X	role ambiguity, role conflict				
Munson et al. (2000)	X	X						X	life satisfaction	
O'Connell and Korabik (2000)	X	X			X			X	negative mood	
Parker and Griffin (2002)	X				X	over-performance demands		X		
Piotrkowski (1998)	X	X						X		
Ragins and Scandura (1995)	X	X						X		

(continued)

Table 1 Cont'd

Study	Job outcomes							Psychological outcomes			Health
	A	B	C	D	E	F	G	H	I	J	Health
Raver and Gelfand (2005)					X		impaired team relationships and cohesion; increased team conflict				
Richman et al. (1999)								X		prescription drug use; problem drinking	
Richman et al. (2002)								X		problem drinking	
Richman et al. (2006)										problem drinking	
Rospenda et al. (2005)											X
Schneider et al. (1997)	X	X	X	X				X	X	life satisfaction	
Schneider et al. (2001)								X			X
Shaffer et al. (2000)	X	X		X				X			
Shupe et al. (2002)	X	X									
Sims et al. (2005)		X									
USMSPB (1994)		X	X		X						X
Vogt et al. (2005)								X	X		
Wasti et al. (2000)	X	X (indirect)	X (indirect)					X	X	life satisfaction	
Wislar et al. (2002)										problem drinking	
Wolfe et al. (1998)									X		X (indirect)
Woodzicka and LaFrance (2005)					X						

(e.g., Canada, Mainland China, Hong Kong, Turkey).

Over 15 studies have addressed organizational withdrawal as an outcome of sexual harassment. Some harassed personnel engage in work withdrawal, remaining in the organization but disengaging from work (e.g., through absenteeism, tardiness, work neglect). Others manifest more complete forms of withdrawal, through turnover thoughts and intentions or actual turnover. Organizational withdrawal is often conceptualized as a way of avoiding further exposure to sexual harassment at work.

Sexual harassment is also associated with decrements in employees' organizational commitment, performance, and productivity. Other job-related correlates include impaired team relationships, increased team conflicts, lowered team financial performance, lowered justice perceptions, cognitive difficulties (e.g., distraction), and over-performance demands (i.e., the 'need to overperform to gain acceptance and recognition within the workplace'; Parker and Griffin, 2002). These studies often include job stress as a covariate; when researchers instead conceptualize job stress as an outcome in its own right, they invariably uncover significant direct relationships with sexual harassment.

Organizations pay a price for these outcomes. The USMSPB used a 'behavioral costing approach' to attach a dollar value to sexual harassment, based on its large-scale surveys of federal employees. The most recent figures, extrapolated to the entire federal workforce, estimated the annual cost of sexual harassment for the US government to be $327 million (in 1994 dollars). This includes costs related to employee turnover, employees' self-reported use of sick leave due to harassment, self-reported individual productivity losses, and estimated workgroup productivity losses (USMSPB, 1994). Costs related to the harasser's lost time or productivity, complaint processing, litigation, or medical and counseling services for the victim are excluded from this figure, thereby underestimating the cost of sexual harassment to the federal government.

Psychological and physical health outcomes

Many studies (detailed in Table 1) of sexual harassment outcomes have appeared in the clinical and psychiatric literatures. The more that employees experience sexual harassment, the more that they report symptoms of depression, general stress and anxiety, posttraumatic stress disorder, and overall impaired psychological well-being. In a series of articles based on a 4-wave longitudinal survey, Richman and colleagues documented associations between earlier sexual harassment and later alcohol use and misuse. Other psychological and behavioral correlates include negative mood, disordered eating, self-blame, lowered self-esteem, increased prescription drug use, anger, disgust, and lowered satisfaction with life in general.

Less research has addressed relationships between sexual harassment and physical health. Such effects are often indirect, mediated through mental health. Some research has documented links to overall health perceptions or satisfaction. Others have identified specific somatic complaints (headaches, exhaustion, sleep problems, gastric problems, nausea, respiratory complaints, musculoskeletal pain, and weight loss/gain) associated with experiencing harassment. In the only experiment of its kind, Schneider et al. (2001) showed that exposure to mild gender harassment leads to increased cardiovascular reactivity.

What mitigates or exacerbates the harm?

Employees report considerable variability in the outcomes they experience from sexual harassment, prompting research on person and situation factors that moderate these outcomes. Searching for moderators of this relationship has both theoretical and applied significance, isolating which populations are most at risk for harm, under which circumstances, and what might be done to reduce that harm.

Victim gender

The moderator that has received the most empirical attention is gender: when sexually harassed, do women and men experience comparable consequences? Male targets of unwanted sex-related behaviors often report that these experiences were not anxiety-provoking (Berdahl, Magley, and Waldo, 1996), 'bothersome,' 'stressful' (Berdahl, 2007b), or 'upsetting' (Cochran et al., 1997). In fact, some men describe these behaviors as 'welcomed' and even 'fun and flattering' (Berdahl, 2007b; Gutek, 1985). Moreover, studies find harassed women vs. men to report worse outcomes, in terms of negative mood and turnover intentions (Barling et al., 1996), disordered eating (Harned and Fitzgerald, 2002), over-performance demands (Parker and Griffin, 2002), and longitudinal effects on anxiety, problem drinking, job stress, job burnout, and turnover intentions (Freels et al., 2005, Magley, Cortina and Kath, 2005). In stark contrast with this prior work, Vogt et al. (2005) reported sexual harassment to be a stronger depression and anxiety risk factor for men compared to women.

Other research reports that, when women and men experience similar rates of sexual harassment, the impact is comparable. For instance, no sex differences were found in the relationship between sexual harassment and various job outcomes (Cortina et al., 2002; Morrow et al., 1994), psychological and physical health outcomes (Magley et al., 1999), and longitudinal links to depression, anxiety, hostility, prescription drug use, and problem drinking (Richman et al., 1999, 2002, 2006). Morrow et al. (1994) also described sex similarities in relationships between supervisor harassment and victims' occupational stress and satisfaction.

Despite these mixed findings, the weight of the research evidence suggests that women face greater harm from sexual harassment than men. Even studies that report sex similarities acknowledge that women are far more likely than men to be sexually harassed, 'thus making sexual harassment a bigger and more harmful problem for women as a group' (Magley et al., 1999: 299). Other research

(e.g., Berdahl et al., 1996; Waldo et al., 1998) shows sexual harassment to be a qualitatively different phenomenon for women and men, questioning whether sex comparisons in outcomes should be conducted at all.

Victim race, ethnicity, and culture

Various writers have suggested that minority ethnicity should amplify the negative impact of sexual harassment (e.g., Fitzgerald et al., 1995b; Murrell, 1996; Shupe et al., 2002). The rationale for this expectation is that minorities face additional stressors beyond sexual harassment, such as racism and racial harassment, economic hardship, and (for recent immigrants) lack of adequate support networks.

To date, however, little research has directly compared outcomes for minority and non-minority women, and findings have been mixed. In comparing the experiences of Latina and non-Latina White women, Shupe et al. (2002) reported that Latinas fared worse in terms of work and coworker satisfaction, whereas effects on turnover intentions were stronger for Whites; culture did not moderate relationship between harassment and supervisor satisfaction, psychological distress, or psychological well-being. Bergman and Drasgow (2003) compared harassment outcomes across members of five different ethnic groups in the US Armed Forces, finding no evidence that ethnicity moderates relationships between sexual harassment and occupational, psychological, or health-related outcomes. Likewise, Piotrkowski (1998) reported no moderating influence of minority status on effects of gender harassment on job satisfaction and 'distress.' It is difficult to draw definitive conclusions from these limited, divergent findings on ethnic differences in sexual harassment outcomes.

Even less is known about cross-national differences (or similarities) in the experience of sexual harassment outcomes. Wasti and colleagues (2000) compared employed women in Turkey and the US, reporting a similar pattern of harassment outcomes in both populations. Shaffer et al. (2000) found no differences among US, Chinese

Mainland, and Hong Kong Chinese women in the impact of harassment on job satisfaction and turnover intentions, but culture did moderate relationships with organizational commitment. Beyond these two studies, we could locate no other recent, rigorous research that directly compares harassment-outcome relationships across nations, so this remains an area ripe for further research.

Victim self-labeling

Among women who report unwanted sex-related behavior in the workplace, fewer than 20 per cent typically label their experiences as 'sexual harassment' per se (Magley et al., 1999). Nevertheless, regardless of whether victims self-label or not, they report a similar pattern of negative occupational, psychological, and physical outcomes (Magley et al., 1999; Munson et al., 2001). In an experimental study, Woodzicka and LaFrance (2005) demonstrated that even brief, subtly sexually harassing behaviors lead to impaired performance in victims, irrespective of what they call these behaviors. These studies suggest that labeling does not moderate the link between sexual harassment and outcomes.

Perpetrator power

Although sexual harassment has adverse effects whether perpetrated by peers or superiors (e.g. Morrow et al., 1994), research suggests that harassment 'from above' is more harmful. Cortina et al. (2002) and Langhout and colleagues (2005) found significant correlations between perpetrator power/status and victim perceptions that the harassment was severe, upsetting, and frightening. In addition, O'Connell and Korabik (2000) and Morrow et al. (1994) analyzed outcomes of harassment from higher- and equal-level perpetrators separately; they reported more numerous negative effects of the former. O'Connell and Korabik (2000) also investigated women's experiences of sexual harassment from lower-status men ('contrapower harassment'), finding no negative outcomes at all. Explanations for the greater consequences associated with top-down sexual harassment emphasize the victim's heightened experience

of helplessness and fear (e.g., Cortina et al., 2002; Langhout et al., 2005).

Support of the victim

To generate practical recommendations for organizations, some studies have investigated whether social and organizational supports mitigate the impact of sexual harassment. Several studies have found that military women's perceptions of leaders as fair, supportive, trustworthy, and intolerant of sexual harassment were related to higher job satisfaction and organizational commitment and lower turnover intentions (Murry et al., 2001; Offerman and Malamut, 2002; Williams et al., 1999). Likewise, Bond and colleagues (2004) and Cortina (2004) reported that positive social support from leaders, co-workers, friends, and family attenuates effects of sexual harassment on women's job satisfaction.

Mixed results have emerged regarding the benefits of social support for victims' mental health. Cortina (2004) found no moderating impact of positive support on victims' anxiety and depression, whereas Bond and colleagues (2004) did find such an effect. The divergent findings could result from disparate methodologies (e.g., sample composition, measurement of harassment, operationalization of support). More research is clearly needed to understand what types of support can benefit which harassment victims, and under what conditions.

COPING WITH SEXUAL HARASSMENT

Compared to the 1980s, studies of coping with sexual harassment have been relatively scarce in the past decade. We summarize this research below and in Table 2. Excluded from this review are 'analogue' studies, in which participants (often college students with limited work experience) read brief harassing scenarios and report how they *would* respond *if* confronted with such a situation. This method is known to be highly flawed: how individuals say they would think, feel or behave in response to hypothetical sexual harassment fails to reflect the reality of how sexually harassed individuals actually respond in real life. In particular, the analogue method yields inflated estimates of assertive or confrontational coping (e.g., Fitzgerald et al., 1995c; Gutek and Koss, 1993; Woodzicka and LaFrance, 2001).

The nature and antecedents of harassment coping

Reporting

Of all potential responses to sexual harassment, intra-organizational reporting has received most research attention, reflecting increasing emphases by American employers and courts on organizational reporting as *the* key mechanism for eliminating workplace sexual harassment (Burlington Industries v. Ellereth, 1998; Faragher v. City of Boca Raton, 1998). Some social scientists allege that reporting is the most appropriate or effective means of coping with sexual harassment (e.g., Knapp et al., 1997; Reese and Lindenberg, 1997). This claim, however, has little empirical basis. On the contrary, various studies (described below) have revealed that harassment reporting can give rise to additional problems that exacerbate the situation for the victim.

According to victims' accounts of how they responded to previous experiences of sexual harassment, fewer than one-third of victims informally discuss sexual harassment with supervisors, and less than 25 per cent file formal sexual harassment complaints with their employers (see Table 2). Moreover, only a tiny minority of victims take their complaints to court. Victims typically only turn to formal reporting (internal or external to the organization) after they have exhausted all other response options. Employees' reluctance to report experiences of sexual harassment is primarily attributed to fear – fear of blame, disbelief, inaction, retaliation, humiliation, ostracism, and damage to one's career and reputation (e.g., Cortina, 2004; Fitzgerald et al., 1995c; Wasti and Cortina, 2003).

Victims' fears of reporting are well-founded. Cortina and Magley (2003) learned

that two-thirds of employees who spoke out against workplace mistreatment then faced some form of retaliation. Others have found that sexual harassment reporting is often followed by organizational indifference or trivialization of the harassment complaint as well as hostility and reprisals against the victim (Bergman et al., 2002; Lee et al., 2004). Perhaps it comes as no surprise, then, that victims often leave the complaint process with a greater perception of organizational injustice (Adams-Roy and Barling, 1998).

Confrontation

Confronting the harasser is less common that popular wisdom suggests. Woodzicka and LaFrance (2001) conducted an experiment in which 50 job applicants were asked questions by a male interviewer that were mildly harassing and clearly inappropriate in a job interview (e.g., 'Do you have a boyfriend?', 'Do people find you desirable?'). *Not a single woman* challenged the interviewer about the inappropriate questions or refused to answer them. Among the harassed women in civilian organizations described in Table 2, an average of 39 per cent had confronted their harassers in some way. This coping strategy may be more prevalent in the military, where Culbertson and Rosenfeld (1994) found 72 per cent of enlisted women and 54 per cent of female officers confronting their perpetrators.

Social-support seeking

A more typical response to sexual harassment is to rely on informal social support from colleagues, friends, and family members. In the research detailed in Table 2, an average of one-third of victims had discussed the harassing situation with family members, and approximately 50–70 per cent had sought support from friends or trusted others.

Avoidance, denial, and endurance

Illustrating what might be the most prevalent response to sexual harassment in the workplace (e.g., Fitzgerald et al., 1995; Gutek and Koss, 1993), harassed employees frequently try to avoid the perpetrator or the harassing context, deny or downplay the seriousness

Table 2 Summary of research (from the mid-1990s to the present) on the prevalence of specific harassment coping strategies

Key

Coping strategy
1   Filed formal complaint or grievance
2   Talked with supervisor, manager or union representative
3   'Reported' the harassment
4   Confronted the harasser in some way
5   Talked with friend or trusted other
6   Talked with family
7   Avoided harasser
8   Denied or downplayed gravity of situation
9   Attempted to ignore, forget or endure

Note on population of study
Cochran et al. (1997) – University staff and students (male and female)
Cortina (2004) – Working Latinas (different companies)
Culbertson and Rosenfeld (1994) – Navy women
Schneider et al. (1997) – Working women (different companies)
USMSPB (1994) – Federal workers (male and female)

Study	Coping strategy								
	1	2	3	4	5	6	7	8	9
Cochran et al. (1997)	2%			25%			45%		60%
Cortina (2004)	17–20%	26%	21%		49–64%	27–37%			
Culbertson and Rosenfeld (1994)	6–8%		24% of enlisted, 19% of officers	72% of enlisted, 54% of officers			75% of enlisted, 54% of officers		
Schneider et al. (1997)	6–13%	17–36%		33–57%	53–70%		54–74%	54–73%	49–70%
USMSPB (1994)			13% of women, 8% of men	41% of women, 23% of men			33% of women, 20% of men		45% of women, 44% of men

of the situation, or simply ignore or endure it if possible (see Table 2). Women in these circumstances often hope that if they evade the harasser or fail to show any reaction, he will lose interest and leave them alone. Note that this research only represents individuals who remain in their jobs despite being harassed, typically excluding those who quit or retire due to the harassment.

Some writers have criticized avoidance, denial, and endurance as passive, unassertive, or otherwise undesirable reactions to sexual harassment (e.g., Knapp et al., 1997; Gruber and Smith, 1995). Judges, juries, and the media and lay public often interpret the lack of vocal protest (preferably, a formal complaint) as evidence that the woman consented to, 'welcomed,' or fabricated the inappropriate conduct. This was clear in the case of Anita Hill, whose credibility was assailed because she had not formally complained about Clarence Thomas at the time of the alleged harassment. If the harassment had really happened, Senators reasoned, she would have reported it.

However, avoidance, denial and 'doing nothing' often reflect deliberate attempts to extinguish the harasser's behavior by refusing to reinforce it. Such reactions appear quite reasonable when a woman fears for herself or her job, has no other effective response options available, or seeks to bring an end to the harassment without 'rocking the boat' (Fitzgerald et al., 1995c; Magley, 2002). Thus, these behaviors represent a common, albeit quiet method of resisting sexual harassment; they are the only coping responses available to some women in some situations.

Antecedents of coping

Generally speaking, as sexual harassment becomes more severe (i.e., upsetting, disruptive, enduring, frequent), attempts to ignore it decrease while efforts to avoid, confront, report, and seek social support increase (Bergman et al., 2002; Cochran et al., 1997; Cortina, 2004; Malamut and Offermann, 2001; Wasti and Cortina, 2003). Victims are also more likely to report the situation and seek social support when being harassed by

an authority figure (Bergman et al., 2002; Cochran et al., 1997; Cortina, 2004; Malamut and Offermann, 2001). Reporting and confrontation are more common among victims who are lower in occupational status, female, or White/European American (Malamut and Offermann, 2001; Rudman et al., 1995; Wasti and Cortina, 2003), whereas avoidance and denial are more frequent among women from traditional, patriarchal, collectivist cultures (Wasti and Cortina, 2003).

ELIMINATING SEXUAL HARASSMENT IN ORGANIZATIONS

Given the negative consequences – personal, legal, and financial – that accompany sexual harassment, many organizations have taken steps to eliminate harassment where possible, and correct it where necessary. We now review and critique harassment policies, procedures, and training programs implemented by organizations.

Sexual harassment policies

Today, most large US organizations and many smaller ones have policies prohibiting sexual harassment and specifying reporting procedures. The policies vary with respect to content, but often include language from the EEOC's (1980) definition of sexual harassment, quoted earlier. This definition, however, has been criticized as overly vague (Gutek, 1997), and it privileges *sexualized* actions while neglecting the more common, *sexist* forms of hostility (Schultz, 1998; 2003).

Experts agree that sexual harassment policies should clearly delineate grievance procedures. Some add that policies should explain disciplinary actions that harassers might face; prohibit retaliation against complainants; and provide safeguards for the confidentiality of all parties. Several scholars emphasize that supervisors and top management must be committed to and well-trained on these policies for them to be effective (Gutek, 1997; Gruber, 1998; Reese and Lindenberg, 1997; Riger, 1991; Rowe, 1996; Stokes et al., 2000).

Few empirical studies have evaluated the impact of such policy-making. One notable exception is Gruber (1998), who found that employees reported the lowest rates of sexual harassment when they worked for organizations that proactively developed, disseminated, and enforced the sexual harassment policy (e.g., by training all employees, creating official complaint procedures, designating a specialist to receive complaints). Significantly more harassment was reported by personnel whose companies only used informational approaches to policy dissemination (e.g., posting it in the workplace or employee handbook), and individuals in workplaces with no policy at all described the most sexual harassment. In a unique study of factors related to men's reports of harassment perpetration, Dekker and Barling (1998) found that men who perceived strong sanctions against sexual harassment in their organization reported engaging in less frequent harassment of others.

Sexual harassment complaint procedures

In some workplaces, the only procedures available for reporting sexual harassment are formal, requiring victims to lodge written, signed complaints against their harassers; the organization then typically notifies the harasser of the complaint and conducts an investigation. Some companies have specialized personnel for these investigations; many do not. Organizations also differ in the standard of proof used to determine whether sexual harassment has taken place. Some rely on the civil standard of 'preponderance of evidence' (i.e., is it 'more likely than not' that harassment occurred), the standard used by the courts in Title VII cases. Other companies use the more stringent criminal standard of 'beyond a reasonable doubt,' the highest level of proof required to win a case in court; because sexual harassment is not considered a criminal offense under US law, it is peculiar to apply this criminal standard to these investigations. Penalties imposed on employees found guilty of sexual harassment

also vary widely across organizations. Some grievance procedures offer the possibility of appeal, others do not. Companies typically maintain formal records of the complaint and outcome, including names of all parties involved (Gutek, 1997; Riger, 1991; Rowe, 1996).

Formal grievance mechanisms have distinct advantages, allowing for official sanctions to be imposed, repeat offenders to be tracked, and managers to be held accountable (Rowe, 1996). However, these procedures are often adversarial, with the complainant's perspective potentially competing against that of the accused, his union representatives, and management. Such procedures frequently fail to end the harassment, sometimes worsen the situation, and rarely protect the complainant's privacy (e.g., Cortina and Magley, 2003; Gutek, 1997; Riger, 1991).

Because of these drawbacks, some experts recommend that informal dispute resolution also be available to sexually harassed employees (Gutek, 1997; Riger, 1991; Rowe, 1996). Many victims do not want to lodge a formal complaint, set an investigation into motion, or see their harasser punished; they simply want the offensive behavior to end (Fitzgerald et al., 1995c). Informal dispute resolution could involve, for example, someone speaking with the offender on behalf of the complainant or a neutral third party mediating discussions between them. The goal is generally not to determine guilt or impose punishment, but rather to restore peaceful co-existence between the parties. Often no formal records are kept, and participation is purely voluntary (Riger, 1991; Rowe, 1996). Outcomes can include an agreement to change behavior, an apology, a voluntary transfer or resignation of either party, or nothing at all (Gutek, 1997).

Opinions of informal methods for handling sexual harassment have been mixed. Informal processes provide a more accessible and realistic option for harassment victims who wish to avoid formal investigation and adjudication (Riger, 1991; Rowe, 1996), and they tend to be less public, confrontational, and litigious (Gutek, 1997). However, if the aim of informal procedures is not to establish guilt or punish the offender, this process will not necessarily deter would-be harassers. If a third party mediator is involved, that person typically must remain neutral, lacks authority over the harasser, and cannot protect the victim from retaliation (Riger, 1991).

A general recommendation about harassment complaint procedures is that choices be available to complainants, including a choice among multiple procedures (both informal and formal), and choices among multiple 'complaint handlers' with different ethnicities, sexes, and positions in the organization (Gutek, 1997; Reese and Lindenberg, 2004; Riger, 1991; Rowe, 1996; Stokes et al., 2000).

Sexual harassment training

As with reporting procedures, sexual harassment training initiatives also vary tremendously. Some organizations mandate training for all employees; others train only managers, supervisors, complaint handlers, or employees found guilty of sexual harassment; still others offer no training at all. The trainer may be a manager, HR employee, compliance officer, EEO specialist, sexual harassment expert, or attorney. Different training programs use different formats, including lectures, speeches from organizational leaders, skits or plays with professional actors, behavioral modeling, role-plays and other experiential exercises, computer-based programs, films, readings, and case-studies. The length of these different programs ranges from minutes to hours to days (e.g., Bingham and Scherer, 2001; Gutek, 1997). In a recent survey of 1,277 working adults in the US, Magley and colleagues (2004) found that only 46 per cent of respondents had received any training at all on sexual harassment, which was more common in larger organizations and lasted an average of 1.5 hours.

Content also differs across sexual harassment training programs. Many experts agree that training should include education about what constitutes harassing conduct and how employees can report such conduct. Some programs are oriented around awareness-raising or sensitivity-training,

whereas others focus more on legal issues and penalties for harassers (Bingham and Scherer, 2001; Gutek, 1997; Magley et al., 1997; Reese and Lindenberg, 1997). Some training uses 'rational-empirical' techniques (assuming that people are more likely to change behavior when given a rational justification), while others use 'power-coercive' strategies (assuming that a threat from a legitimate authority will promote behavior change). Yet another approach is 'normative re-educative,' the assumption being that substantive change requires the development of new norms, shared meanings, and transformations in attitudes, values, skills, and relational styles (Bingham and Scherer, 2001). The primary goal of such training is generally prevention, but little empirical evidence shows that training actually deters would-be harassers from abusing others. Another goal of training is to encourage employees to come forward with internal complaints of sexual harassment, but as noted earlier, such complaints are rare. One longitudinal study, however, did document an increase in internal sexual harassment complaints following company-wide training (Magley et al., 1997). What else do sexual harassment training programs accomplish?

Researchers have found that recipients of sexual harassment training (particularly men) report increased knowledge of sexual harassment definitions, legal regulations, and organizational policies (Antecol and Cobb-Clark, 2003; Bingham and Scherer, 2001). Other outcomes include satisfaction with the organization's harassment policy or complaint procedures (Magley et al., 2004; Reese and Lindenberg, 2004), lowered victim-blaming or harassment-trivializing attitudes (Lonsway et al., 2008; Magley et al., 2004), and greater belief that sexual behavior is inappropriate in the workplace (Bingham and Scherer, 2001). The USMSPB (1994) found that employees working in federal agencies providing sexual harassment training described less 'uninvited and unwanted sexual attention.' This effect was strongest for agencies that trained *all* employees.

We could locate only one study providing direct evidence that sexual harassment training affects men's behavior toward women, at least in the short run. Perry et al. (1998) showed male participants a training video on either sexual harassment or sign language, followed by a golf training video. Participants then trained a female confederate on how to putt. The researchers found that harassment training increased knowledge and reduced inappropriate touching for men with a prior propensity to sexually harass women.

Some research, however, has found sexual harassment training programs to have either null effects (e.g., Magley et al., 1997, 2004) or adverse effects on employees. Magley and colleagues (1997) and Antecol and Cobb-Clark (2003) reported that some trained employees became more cynical about their organization's ability or commitment to prevent sexual harassment, and Bingham and Scherer (2001) found male trainees to report *greater* victim-blaming attitudes and *less* willingness to file a complaint of sexual harassment, compared to women and non-trained men. Moreover, the short-term attitudinal changes reported by Perry et al. (1998) did not persist over the long term.

It is important to note, however, that each of these studies evaluated different sexual harassment training programs. Moreover, the methodological quality of this research varied (Magley et al., 1997), often lacking control groups, utilizing small samples, failing to take into account pre-training assessment effects, or lacking pre-training assessment altogether. Most post-training assessments were conducted immediately after the training, making it impossible to know whether the training has any lasting effects. More research is clearly warranted to demonstrate empirically the effectiveness of sexual harassment training interventions.

THE FUTURE OF SEXUAL HARASSMENT RESEARCH

As this chapter makes clear, sexual harassment remains a serious problem that takes a toll on employees, workgroups, and their organizations. Notably, the bulk of research on this topic has appeared outside of the mainstream organizational literature. Conducting searches on the keyword 'sexual harassment' in all issues published through 2006 of the top five OB and I/O journals, we found only 31 sexual harassment articles:

- *Journal of Applied Psychology* (18 articles);
- *Organizational Behavior and Human Decision Processes* (3 articles);
- *Academy of Management Journal* (6 articles);
- *Academy of Management Review* (3 articles); and
- *Administrative Sciences Quarterly* (1 article).

By contrast, 183 articles on workplace sexual harassment have appeared in five social science journals that do not specialize in organizational behavior:

- *Sex Roles* (100 articles);
- *Psychology of Women Quarterly* (31 articles);
- *Journal of Social Issues* (24 articles);
- *Gender and Society* (19 articles); and
- *Signs: The Journal of Women in Culture and Society* (9 articles).

The topic of workplace sexual harassment clearly deserves greater attention from organizational scientists. Below, we propose three questions that warrant further research, and conclude with methodological suggestions to enrich this literature.

What constitutes 'sexual harassment'?

After three decades of legal decisions and social science on sexual harassment, an explicit definition remains elusive. We continue to discover 'new' forms of harassment, which have long occurred but seldom been studied. One such form is extra-organizational sexual harassment, i.e., harassment from customers, clients, or members of the public. These organizational outsiders can easily target an employee with sex-based disparagement and unwanted sexual advances, interfering with that person's work and well-being

(Barling et al., 2001; Gettman and Gelfand, 2007). With the recent expansion of the service professions, 'outsider sexual harassment' deserves more empirical attention.

Non-sexual forms of harassment are also being increasingly recognized. Sexist behaviors directed at women, such as jokes about women's intelligence and comments about women 'not belonging' in certain jobs, represent the most common manifestations of sex-based harassment; these behaviors, however, are often overlooked in research, the law, and organizational policy. Likewise, sexist conduct directed against men (e.g., 'not man enough' harassment) is rarely studied. Not only should science focus more on these sexist but non-sexualized behaviors, it should also examine sex-based harassment that makes no explicit reference to gender, such as incivility, sabotage, and threats directed disproportionately at women (and some men) in the workplace (Berdahl, 2007b; Berdahl, 2007c; Cortina, 2008).

More sexual harassment research should also consider how gender intersects with other social identities. Having a low-status identity, such as being ethnic minority, poor, or gay, may increase an individual's risk for sex-based harassment (e.g., Berdahl and Moore, 2006; Konik and Cortina, in press). These identities may also affect the *type* of harassment experienced, because sex-based disparagements can take different forms and meanings specific to one's ethnicity, sexual orientation, or other social dimension. Research addressing these intersections can further our understanding of sexual harassment as a tool that reinforces social hierarchies in the workplace.

What motivates (or inhibits) sexual harassment?

Sexual harassers were originally assumed to be driven by a desire for sexual expression or gratification. Men's wish to dominate or control women was later proposed to motivate sexual harassment. Research now considers a more basic motive: The desire to retain a valued social identity and attendant benefits in a system of gender hierarchy. Given that this theorizing has continued for several decades, it is striking to see how little *empirical* research has focused explicitly on harassers (exceptions include Bargh et al., 1995; Dekker and Barling, 1998; Perry et al., 1998; Pryor, 1987; Pryor et al., 1993). This is an important direction for future studies.

How can organizations eliminate sexual harassment?

Sexual harassment grievance mechanisms have limited effectiveness and efficiency, as they attempt to correct harassment by rooting out and punishing individual harassers, and place the burden of managing misbehavior on individual victims. Moreover, grievance procedures typically fail to address broader problems that fuel hostile work environments. Experts therefore emphasize the futility of relying primarily or solely on formal victim complaints to correct workplace harassment (e.g., Fitzgerald et al., 1995c; Magley, 2002; Shultz, 2003). Instead, innovative harassment-prevention and control mechanisms are badly needed; below are several examples.

One novel approach to managing sexual harassment is bystander intervention (Bowes-Sperry and O'Leary-Kelly, 2005; Rowe, 1996). As Bowes-Sperry and O'Leary-Kelly (2005) explain, this can take a variety of forms. Employees who witness the harassment of a co-worker can redirect the harasser, remove the victim, or otherwise interrupt the situation. Further, bystanders can provide support to the victim, bolstering the victim's resources and sense of clarity and control. Bystanders can also take it upon themselves to confront or report the harasser, as such responses may be easier for nonvictims. These possibilities suggest that organizations should train employees on how to respond not only when they personally experience harassment, but also when they witness the harassment of others.

Sexual harassment interventions might also be embedded in broader initiatives to establish a civil, respectful workplace. For instance, to promote civility, experts (e.g., Pearson and Porath, 2004) recommend that senior management model appropriate, respectful workplace behavior; clearly state expectations of civility in mission statements or policy manuals; and educate all employees on civility expectations. Cortina (2008) adds that organizational practices to set norms of civility should explicitly discuss equitable respect toward women and men (and Whites, gays, ethnic minorities, etc.). Leaders should also emphasize that unacceptable conduct includes not just overt acts of misogyny, obscenity, and sexual aggression, but also subtle devaluation and derision of members of either sex. This integrated strategy of embedding harassment-prevention efforts into larger civility-promotion programs would attract broader audiences, being relevant to all employees (female and male) and avoiding the resistance met by interventions that exclusively target sexual harassment (Cortina, 2008; Cortina et al., 2002; Lim and Cortina, 2005).

A final intervention aims to prevent sexual harassment by overhauling the structures that support it. The recommendation itself is quite simple: employ more women, promote more women, and integrate more women into every level of the organization. The goal should be a 'well-integrated, structurally egalitarian workplace,' in which women and men equally share power and authority (Schultz, 2003: 2071). Supporting this recommendation is empirical research linking male-skewed sex ratios to sexual harassment (e.g., Berdahl, 2007a; Fitzgerald et al., 1997; Gruber, 1998), stereotyping, and discrimination (see Kanter, 1977; Whitley and Kite, 2006). Organizational 'desegregation' may not eradicate sexual harassment entirely, but it can reduce the culture of hypermasculinity that promotes objectification, devaluation, and aggression toward women and gender-nonconforming men.

Methodological recommendations for sexual harassment research

Most sexual harassment research relies on cross-sectional, self-report surveys, with findings restricted to a single level of analysis. The importance of this work cannot be overstated, but it is time to broaden the range of methods employed in this domain.

With some notable exceptions (Glomb et al., 1999; Magley et al., 2005; Rospenda et al., 2006), few have investigated sexual harassment longitudinally. Longitudinal methods can address questions about causality, temporal patterning, and the persistence of negative outcomes. These approaches also allow researchers to conceptualize harassment as a dynamic process that 'unfolds' or has 'cascading effects' over time. Moreover, when self-report research temporally separates assessment of the predictor (harassment) and criterion (outcome) variables, concerns about mono-method bias are lessened.

We also encourage more experimental studies of sexual harassment. However, we do not advocate vignette-based paradigms in which students imagine how they might interpret or respond to a hypothetical scenario (if anything, such studies should be discontinued, given that their data have questionable validity). Instead, more fruitful and interesting possibilities lie in simulations of harassing behavior in the laboratory. There are ethical limits to such studies, but they are possible (see Maass et al., 2003; Pryor, 1987; Schneider et al., 2001; Woodzicka and LaFrance, 2001) and can yield unique contributions to the field.

Sexual harassment research should also incorporate multiple levels of analysis. Most studies have revolved around individual self-reports of perceptions, experiences, responses, etc. Not only does this approach have potential problems with mono-method bias, it typically misses group- or organizational-level antecedents (e.g., work-group gender attitudes) and outcomes (e.g., declines in unit productivity; see Raver and Gelfand, 2005, for a notable exception). We therefore recommend that multilevel methods become more customary in sexual harassment research, addressing processes at the level of the individual, team, organization, and society.

CONCLUSION

The past decade has witnessed great strides in research on sexual harassment. Much has been learned about its different forms, perpetrators, and victims, the contexts that promote it, and its effects on individuals and organizations. No longer seen as 'just' a 'women's issue,' sexual harassment is now recognized as illegal and immoral behavior that harms women, men, and the 'bottom line.' Despite these knowledge gains and the organizational changes that have accompanied them, harassment based on sex remains all too common. More research is clearly needed to better understand and prevent sexual harassment, helping organizations to foster vibrant, healthy, and respectful work environments.

NOTES

1 Some might wonder about the division between sexist and sexual hostility (Cortina, 2001; Fitzgerald et al., 1999b), or the gender-role-deviation harassment (e.g., Berdahl and Moore, 2006; Konik and Cortina, in press) identified in some administrations of the SEQ. Readers should note, however, that these are all subdimensions of gender harassment that emerged with the addition of new items. Thus, the higher-order tripartite factor structure of the SEQ has remained quite constant for over a decade.

REFERENCES

Adams, J.H. (1997) 'Sexual Harassment and Black Women: A Historical Perspective', in W. O'Donahue (ed.), *Sexual Harassment: Theory, Research, and Treatment.* Boston, MA: Allyn & Bacon, pp. 213–224.

Adams-Roy, J. and Barling, J. (1998) 'Predicting the decision to confront or report sexual harassment', *Journal of Organizational Behavior*, 19 (4): 329–336.

Antecol, H. and Cobb-Clark, D. (2003) 'Does sexual harassment training change attitudes? A view from the federal level', *Social Science Quarterly*, 84 (4): 826–842.

Arvey, R.D. and Cavanaugh, M.A. (1995) 'Using surveys to assess the prevalence of sexual harassment: Some methodological problems', *Journal of Social Issues*, 51 (1): 39–52.

Barak, A. (1997) 'Cross-cultural Perspectives on Sexual Harassment', in W. O'Donahue (ed.), *Sexual Harassment: Theory, Research, and Treatment.* Boston, MA: Allyn & Bacon, pp. 263–300.

Bargh, J.A., Raymond, P., Pryor, J.B., Strack, F. (1995) 'Attractiveness of the underling: An automatic power → sex association and its consequences for sexual harassment and aggression', *Journal of Personality and Social Psychology*, 68 (5): 768–781.

Barling, J., Dekker, I., Loughlin, C., Kelloway, E., Fullagar, C. and Johnson, D. (1996) 'Prediction and replication of the organizational and personal consequences of workplace sexual harassment', *Journal of Managerial Psychology*, 11 (5): 4–25.

Barling, J., Rogers, A. and Kelloway, E. (2001) 'Behind closed doors: In-home workers' experience of sexual harassment and workplace violence', *Journal of Occupational Health Psychology*, 6 (3): 255–269.

Berdahl, J.L. (2003) 'The Dark Side of Gender and the Lighter Side of Sex: Exploring Unchartered Waters in Sexual Harassment Research'. Paper Presented at the Annual Meeting of the Academy of Management, Seattle, WA.

Berdahl, J.L. (2007a) 'The sexual harassment of uppity women', *Journal of Applied Psychology*, 92 (2): 425–437.

Berdahl, J.L. (2007b) 'Harassment based on sex: Protecting social status in the context of gender hierarchy', *Academy of Management Review*, 22 (2): 641–658.

Berdahl, J.L. (2007c) 'Gender and social undermining in the workplace'. Paper presented at the 22nd Annual Meeting of the Society of Industrial and Organizational Psychology, 2007.

Berdahl, J.L., Magley, V.J. and Waldo, C.R. (1996) 'The sexual harassment of men: Exploring the concept with theory and data', *Psychology of Women Quarterly*, 20 (4): 527–547.

Berdahl, J.L. and Moore, C. (2006) 'Workplace harassment: Double-jeopardy for minority women', *Journal of Applied Psychology*, 91 (2): 426–436.

Bergman, M. and Drasgow, F. (2003) 'Race as a moderator in a model of sexual harassment: An empirical test', *Journal of Occupational Health Psychology*, 8 (2): 131–145.

Bergman, M., Langhout, R., Palmieri, P., Cortina, L. and Fitzgerald, L. (2002) 'The (un) reasonableness of reporting: Antecedents and consequences of reporting sexual harassment', *Journal of Applied Psychology*, 87 (2): 230–242.

Bingham, S. and Scherer, L. (2001) 'The unexpected effects of a sexual harassment educational program', *The Journal of Applied Behavioral Science*, 37 (2): 125–153.

Blumenthal, J.A. (1998) 'The reasonable woman standard: A meta-analytic review of gender differences in perceptions of sexual harassment', *Law and Human Behavior*, 22 (1): 33–57.

Buchanan, N.T. and Ormerod, A.J. (2002) 'Racialized sexual harassment in the lives of Black women', *Women and Therapy*, 25 (3–4): 107–124.

Bond, M., Punnett, L., Pyle, J., Cazeca, D. and Cooperman, M. (2004) 'Gendered work conditions, health, and work outcomes', *Journal of Occupational Health Psychoology*, 9 (1): 28–45.

Bowes-Sperry, L. and O'Leary-Kelly, A. (2005) 'To act or not to act: The dilemma faced by sexual harassment observers', *Academy of Management Review*, 30 (2): 288–306.

Bundy v. Jackson, 205 U.S. App. D.C. 444, 641 F.2d 934 (1981).

Burgess, D. and Borgida, E. (1999) 'Who women are, who women should be: Descriptive and prescriptive gender stereotyping in sex discrimination', *Psychology, Public Policy, and Law*, 5 (1): 665–692.

Burlington Industries v. Ellereth, *524 U.S. 742* (Supreme Court of the United States 1998)

Chan, D., Tang, C. and Chan, W. (1999) 'Sexual harassment: A preliminary analysis of its effects on Hong Kong Chinese women in the workplace and academia', *Psychology of Women Quarterly*, 23 (4): 661–672.

Cleveland, J.N. and Kerst, M.E. (1993) 'Sexual harassment and perceptions of power: An under-articulated relationship', *Journal of Vocational Behavior*, 42 (2): 49–67.

Cochran, C., Frazier, P. and Olson, A. (1997) 'Predictors of responses to unwanted sexual attention', *Psychology of Women Quarterly*, 21 (1): 207–226.

Cortina, L.M. (2008) 'Unseen injustice: Incivility as modern discrimination in organizations', *Academy of Management Review*, 33 (1): 55–75.

Cortina, L.M. (2001) 'Assessing sexual harassment among Latinas: Development of an instrument', *Cultural Diversity and Ethnic Minority Psychology*, 7 (2): 164–181.

Cortina, L. (2004) 'Hispanic perspectives on sexual harassment and social support', *Personality and Social Psychology Bulletin*, 30 (5): 570–584.

Cortina, L., Fitzgerald, L. and Drasgow, F. (2002) 'Contextualizing Latina experiences of sexual harassment: Preliminary tests of a structural model', *Basic and Applied Social Psychology*, 24 (4): 295–311.

Cortina, L.M., Lonsway, K.L., Magley, V.J., Freeman, L.V., Collinsworth, L.L., Hunter, M. and Fitzgerald, L.F. (2002) 'What's gender got to do with it? Incivility in the federal courts', *Law and Social Inquiry*, 27 (2): 235–270.

Cortina, L. and Magley, V. (2003) 'Raising voice, risking retaliation: Events following interpersonal mistreatment in the workplace', *Journal of Occupational Health Psychology*, 8 (4): 247–265.

Cortina, L.M., Swan, S., Fitzgerald, L.F. and Waldo, C.R. (1998) 'Sexual harassment and assault: Chilling the climate for women in academia', *Psychology of Women Quarterly*, 22 (3): 419–441.

Cortina, L. and Wasti, S. (2005) 'Profiles in coping: responses to sexual harassment across persons, organizations, and cultures', *Journal of Applied Psychology*, 90 (1): 182–192.

Culbertson, A. and Rosenfeld, P. (1994) 'Assessment of sexual harassment in the active-duty Navy', *Military Psychology*, 6 (2): 69–93.

Dall'Ara, E. and Maass, A. (1999) 'Studying sexual harassment in the laboratory: Are egalitarian women at higher risk?' *Sex Roles*, 41 (9–10): 681–704.

Dansky, B. and Kilpatrick, D. (1997) 'Effects of Sexual Harassment', in W. O'Donohue (ed.) *Sexual Harassment: Theory, Research, and Treatment*. Needham Heights, MA: Allyn & Bacon, pp. 152–174.

Dekker, I. and Barling, J. (1998) 'Personal and organizational predictors of workplace sexual harassment of women by men', *Journal of Occupational Health Psychology*, 3 (1): 7–18.

DeSouza, E. and Fansler, A.G. (2003) 'Contrapower sexual harassment: A survey of students and faculty members', *Sex Roles*, 48 (11–12): 519–542.

Dillman, D.A. (2000) *Mail and Internet Surveys: The Tailored Design Method*. New York: Wiley-Interscience.

Engels, F. (1884) 'The origins of family, private property, and the state', in A. Jaggar and P.R. Struhl (eds) *Feminist Frameworks: Alternative Theoretical Accounts of the Relations between Women and Men*, 1978. McGraw-Hill.

Equal Employment Opportunity Commission (1980) Guidelines on discrimination because of sex (Sect. 1604.11) *Federal Register, 45*, 74676–74677.

Faragher vs. City of Boca Raton, *524 U.S. 775* (Supreme Court of the United States 1998)

Farley, L. (1978) *Sexual Shakedown: The Sexual Harassment of Women on the Job*. New York: McGraw-Hill.

Fiske, S.T. and Glick, P. (1995) 'Ambivalence and stereotypes cause sexual harassment: A theory with implications for organizational change', *Journal of Social Issues*, 51 (1): 97–115.

Fitzgerald, L.F., Drasgow, F. and Magley, V.J. (1999a) 'Sexual harassment in the armed forces: A test of an integrated model', *Military Psychology*, 11 (3): 329–343.

Fitzgerald, L.F., Drasgow, F., Hulin, C.L., Gelfand, M.J. and Magley, V.J. (1997) 'Antecedents and consequences of sexual harassment in organizations: A test of an integrated model', *Journal of Applied Psychology*, 82 (4): 578–589.

Fitzgerald, L.F., Gelfand, M.J. and Drasgow, F. (1995a) 'Measuring sexual harassment: Theoretical and psychometric advances', *Basic and Applied Social Psychology*, 17 (3): 425–445.

Fitzgerald, L.F., Hulin, C.L. and Drasgow, F. (1995b) 'The Antecedents and Consequences of Sexual Harassment in Organizations: An Integrated Model', in G.P. Keita and J.J. Hurell (eds), *Job Stress in a Changing Workforce: Investigating Gender, Diversity, and Family Issues*. Washington, DC: American Psychological Association, pp. 55–73.

Fitzgerald, L.F., Magley, V.J., Drasgow, F. and Waldo, C.R. (1999b) 'Measuring Sexual Harassment in the Military: The sexual experiences questionnaire (SEQ—-DoD)', *Military Psychology. Special Issue: Sexual harassment*, 11 (2): 243–263.

Fitzgerald, L.F., Shullman, S.L., Bailey, N., Richards, M., Swecker, J., Gold, A., Ormerod, A.J. and Weitzman, L. (1988) 'The incidence and dimensions of sexual harassment in academia and the workplace', *Journal of Vocational Behavior*, 32 (4): 152–175.

Fitzgerald, L., Swan, S. and Fischer, K. (1995c) 'Why didn't she just report him? The psychological and legal implications of women's responses to sexual harassment', *Journal of Social Issues*, 51 (1): 117–138.

Fitzgerald, L.F., Swan, S. and Magley, V.J. (1997) 'But was it Really Sexual Harassment? Legal, Behavioral, and Psychological Definitions of the Workplace Victimization of Women', in W. O'Donohue (ed.), *Sexual Harassment: Theory, Research, and Treatment*. Needham Heights, MA: Allyn & Bacon, pp. 5–28.

Fontana, A. and Rosenheck, R. (1998) 'Duty-related and sexual stress in the etiology of PTSD among women veterans who seek treatment', *Psychiatric Services*, 49 (5): 658–662.

Franke, K.M. (1997) 'What's wrong with sexual harassment?', *Stanford Law Review*, 49 (4): 691–772.

Freels, S., Richman, J. and Rospenda, K. (2005) 'Gender differences in the causal direction between workplace harassment and drinking', *Addictive Behaviors*, 30 (7): 1454–1458.

Gelfand, M., Fitzgerald, L. and Drasgow, F. (1995) 'The structure of sexual harassment: A confirmatory analysis across cultures and settings', *Journal of Vocational Behavior*, 47 (2): 164–177.

Gettman, H.J. and Gelfand, M.J. (2007) 'When the customer shouldn't be king: Antecedents and consequences of sexual harassment by clients and customers', *Journal of Applied Psychology*, 92 (3): 757–770.

Glomb, T.M., Munson, L.J., Hulin, C.L., Bergman, M.E. and Drasgow, F. (1999) 'Structural equation models of sexual harassment: Longitudinal explorations and cross-sectional generalizations', *Journal of Applied Psychology*, 84 (1): 14–28.

Gruber, J.E. (1998) 'The impact of male work environments and organizational policies on women's experiences of sexual harassment', *Gender and Society*, 12 (3): 301–320.

Gruber, J. and Smith, M. (1995) 'Women's responses to sexual harassment: A multivariate analysis', *Basic and Applied Social Psychology*, 17 (4): 543–562.

Gutek, B.A. (1985) *Sex and the Workplace: The Impact of Sexual Behavior and Harassment on Women, Men, and Organizations*. San Francisco: Jossey-Bass.

Gutek, B., Cohen, A.G. and Konrad, A.M. (1990) 'Predicting social-sexual behavior at work: A contact hypothesis', *Academy of Management Journal*, 3 (4): 560–577.

Gutek, B. and Koss, M. (1993) 'Changed women and changed organizations: Consequences of and coping with sexual harassment', *Journal of Vocational Behavior*, 42 (1): 28–48.

Gutek, B.A. and Morasch, B. (1982) 'Sex-ratios, sex-role spillover, and sexual harassment of women at work', *Journal of Social Issues*, 38 (3): 55–74.

Gutek, B.A., Murphy, R.O. and Douma, B. (2004) 'A review and critique of the Sexual Experiences Questionnaire (SEQ)', *Law and Human Behavior*, 28 (4): 457–482.

Harned, M. and Fitzgerald, L. (2002) 'Understanding a link between sexual harassment and eating disorder symptoms: A mediational analysis', *Journal of Consulting and Clinical Psychology*, 70 (5): 1170–1181.

Harned, M.S., Ormerod, A.J. and Palmieri, P.A. (2002) 'Sexual assault and other types of sexual harassment by workplace personnel: A comparison of antecedents and consequences', *Journal of Occupational Health Psychology*, 7 (2): 174–188.

Hershcovis, M.S. and Barling, J. (under review) 'Comparing the outcomes of workplace aggression and sexual harassment: A meta-analysis'.

Kanter, R.M. (1977) *Men and Women of the Corporation*. New York: Basic Books.

Knapp, D., Faley, R., Ekeberg, S. and Dubois, C. (1997) 'Determinants of Target Responses to Sexual Harassment: A Conceptual Framework', *Academy of Management Review*, 22 (3): 687–729.

Konik, J. and Cortina, L.M. (in press) 'Policing gender at work: Intersections of harassment based on sex and sexuality', *Social Justice Research: Special Issue on Social Behavior and Inequality.*

Langhout, R., Bergman, M., Cortina, L., Fitzgerald, L., Drasgow, F. and Williams, J.H. (2005) 'Sexual harassment severity: Assessing situational and personal determinants and outcomes', *Journal of Applied Social Psychology,* 35 (5): 975–1007.

Lapierre, L.M., Spector, P.E. and Leck, J.D. (2005) 'Sexual versus nonsexual workplace aggression and victims' overall job satisfaction: A meta-analysis', *Journal of Occupational Health Psychology,* 10 (3): 155–169.

Lee, J., Heilmann, S. and Near, J. (2004) 'Blowing the whistle on sexual harassment: Test of a model of predictors and outcomes', *Human Relations,* 57 (3): 297–322.

Lee, W. and Ormerod, A. (2003, August) '"Constructing" the SEQ: A Multiple-group analysis across samples and versions of the SEQ'. Paper presented at the Annual Meeting of the American Psychological Association, Toronto, Canada.

Lim, S. and Cortina, L.M. (2005) 'Interpersonal mistreatment in the workplace: The interface and impact of general incivility and sexual harassment', *Journal of Applied Psychology,* 90 (5): 483–496.

Lonsway, K.A., Cortina, L.M. and Magley, V.J. (2008) 'Sexual harassment mythology: Definition, conceptualization, and measurement', *Sex Roles,* 58 (9): 599–615.

Maass, A. Cadinu, M, Guarnieri, G. and Grasselli, A. (2003) 'Sexual harassment under social identity threat: The computer harassment paradigm', *Journal of Personality and Social Psychology,* 85 (5): 853–780.

MacKinnon, C.A. (1979) *Sexual Harassment of Working Women.* New Haven: Yale University Press.

Magley, V. (2002) 'Coping with sexual harassment: Reconceptualizing women's resistance', *Journal of Personality and Social Psychology,* 83 (4): 930–946.

Magley, V.J., Cortina, L.M. and Kath, L.M. (2005) *Stress, Withdrawal, and Gender in the Context of Sexual Harassment: A Longitudinal Analysis.* Paper presented at the Annual Meeting of the American Psychological Association, Washington, DC.

Magley, V., Grossman, J. and Kath, L. (2004) *First Steps First: Understanding What Are Employers Doing About Sexual Harassment?* Paper presented at the Annual Meeting of the Academy of Management, New Orleans, LA.

Magley, V., Hulin, C., Fitzgerald, L. and DeNardo, M. (1999) 'Outcomes of self-labeling sexual harassment', *Journal of Applied Psychology,* 84 (3): 390–402.

Magley, V., Waldo, C., Drasgow, F. and Fitzgerald, L. (1999) 'The impact of sexual harassment on military personnel: Is it the same for men and women?', *Military Psychology,* 11 (3): 283–302.

Magley, V., Zickar, M., Salisbury, J., Drasgow, F. and Fitzgerald, L. (1997) *Evaluating the Effectiveness of Sexual Harassment Training.* Paper presented at the Annual Meeting of the Society for Industrial and Organizational Psychology, St. Louis, MO.

Malamut, A.B. and Offermann, L.R. (2001) 'Coping with sexual harassment: Personal, environmental, and cognitive determinants', *Journal of Applied Psychology,* 86 (6): 1152–1166.

Mansfield, P.K., Koch, P.B. and Henderson, J. (1991) 'The job climate for women in traditionally male blue-collar occupations', *Sex Roles,* 25 (1–2): 63–79.

Martindale, M. (1990) *Sexual Harassment in the Military: 1988.* Washington, DC: Defense Manpower Data Center.

Meritor Savings Bank v. Vinson, 477 U.S. 57 (1986).

Morrow, P., McElroy, J. and Phillips, C. (1994) 'Sexual harassment behaviors and work related perceptions and attitudes', *Journal of Vocational Behavior,* 45 (3): 295–309.

Munson, L.J., Hulin, C. and Drasgow, F. (2000) 'Longitudinal analysis of dispositional influences and sexual harassment: Effects on job and psychological outcomes', *Personnel Psychology,* 53 (1): 21–46.

Munson, L., Miner, A. and Hulin, C. (2001) 'Labeling sexual harassment in the military: An extension and replication', *Journal of Applied Psychology,* 86 (2): 293–303.

Murrell, A. (1996) 'Sexual harassment and women of color', in M.S. Stockdale (ed.) *Sexual Harassment in the Workplace: Perspectives, Frontiers and Response Strategies.* Thousand Oaks, CA: Sage, pp. 51–67.

Murry, W.D., Sivasubramaniam, N. and Jacques, P.H. (2001) 'Supervisory support, social exchange relationships, and sexual harassment consequences: A test of competing models', *Leadership Quarterly,* 12 (1): 1–29.

O'Connell, C. and Korabik, K. (2000) 'Sexual harassment: The relationship of personal vulnerability, work context, perpetrator status, and type of harassment to outcomes', *Journal of Vocational Behavior,* 56 (3): 299–329.

Offermann, L. and Malamut, A. (2002) 'When leaders harass: The impact of target perceptions of organizational leadership and climate on harassment reporting and outcomes', *Journal of Applied Psychology,* 87 (5): 885–893.

O'Leary-Kelly, A.M., Paetzold, R.L. and Griffin, R.W. (2000) 'Sexual harassment as aggressive behavior: An actor-based perspective', *Academy of Management Review,* 25: 372–388.

Oncale v. Sundowner Offshore Services, Inc. 118 S. Ct. 998 (1998)

Parker, S. and Griffin, M. (2002) 'What is so bad about a little name-calling? Negative consequences of gender harassment for overperformance demands and distress', *Journal of Occupational Health Psychology*, 7 (3): 195–210.

Pearson, C.M. and Porath, C.L. (2004) 'On incivility, its impact, and directions for future research', in R.W. Griffin and A.M. O'Leary–Kelly (eds), *The Dark Side of Organizational Behavior*. San Francisco: Jossey-Bass, pp. 403–425.

Perry, E., Kulik, C. and Schmidtke, J. (1998) 'Individual differences in the effectiveness of sexual harassment awareness training', *Journal of Applied Social Psychology*, 28 (8): 698–723.

Piotrkowski, C. (1998) 'Gender harassment, job satisfaction, and distress among employed white and minority women', *Journal of Occupational Health Psychology*, 3 (1): 33–43.

Pryor, J.B. (1987) 'Sexual harassment proclivities in men', *Sex Roles*, 17 (5–6): 269–290.

Pryor, J.B., La Vite, C. and Stoller, L. (1993) 'A social psychological analysis of sexual harassment: The person/situation interaction', *Journal of Vocational Behavior*, 42 (1): 68–83.

Ragins, B.R. and Scandura, T.A. (1995) 'Antecedents and work-related correlates of reported sexual harassment: An empirical investigation of competing hypotheses', *Sex Roles*, 32 (7–8): 429–455.

Raver, J.L. and Gelfand, M.J. (2005) 'Beyond the individual victim: Linking sexual harassment, team processes, and team performance', *Academy of Management Journal*, 48 (3): 387–400.

Reese, L. and Lindenberg, K. (1997) '"Victimhood" and the implementation of sexual harassment policy', *Review of Public Personnel Administration*, 17 (1): 37.

Richman, J., Rospenda, K., Nawyn, S., Flaherty, J., Fendrich, M., Drum, M.L. and Johnson, T.P. (1999) 'Sexual harassment and generalized workplace abuse among university employees: Prevalence and mental health correlates', *American Journal of Public Health*, 89 (3): 358–363.

Richman, J., Shinsako, S., Rospenda, K., Flaherty, J. and Freels, S. (2002) 'Workplace harassment/abuse and alcohol-related outcomes: The mediating role of psychological distress', *Journal of Studies on Alcohol*, 63 (4): 412–419.

Richman, J., Zlatoper, K., Ehmke, J.L.Z. and Rospenda, K.M. (2006) 'Retirement and drinking outcomes: Lingering effects of workplace stress?', *Addictive Behaviors*, 31 (5): 767–776.

Riger, S. (1991) 'Gender dilemmas in sexual harassment policies and procedures', *American Psychologist*, 46 (5): 497–505.

Rospenda, K.M., Richman, J.A. and Ehmke, J.L.Z. (2005) 'Is workplace harassment hazardous to your health?', *Journal of Business and Psychology*, 20 (1): 95–110.

Rospenda, K., Richman, J., Wislar, J. and Flaherty, J. (2000) 'Chronicity of sexual harassment and generalized work-place abuse: Effects on drinking outcomes', *Addiction*, 95 (12): 1805–1820.

Rotundo, M., Nguyen, D. and Sackett, P.R. (2001) 'A meta-analytic review of gender differences in perceptions of sexual harassment', *Journal of Applied Psychology*, 86 (5): 914–922.

Rowe, M. (1996) 'Dealing with harassment: A systems approach', in M. Stockdale (ed.), *Sexual Harassment in the Workplace: Perspectives, Frontiers, and Response Strategies*. Thousand Oaks: Sage, pp. 241–271.

Rudman, L., Borgida, E. and Robertson, B. (1995) 'Suffering in silence: Procedural justice versus gender socialization issues in university sexual harassment grievance procedures', *Basic and Applied Social Psychology*, 17: 519–541.

Schneider, K., Swan, S. and Fitzgerald, L. (1997) 'Job-related and psychological effects of sexual harassment in the workplace: Empirical evidence from two organizations', *Journal of Applied Psychology*, 82 (4): 401–415.

Schneider, K., Tomaka, J. and Palacios, R. (2001) 'Women's cognitive, affective, and physiological reactions to a male co-worker's sexist behavior', *Journal of Applied Social Psychology*, 31 (3): 1995–2018.

Schultz, V. (1998) 'Reconceptualizing sexual harassment', *Yale Law Journal*, 107: 1683–1796.

Schultz, V. (2003) 'The sanitized workplace', *Yale Law Journal*, 112 (8): 2061–2197.

Segrave, K. (1994) *The Sexual Harassment of Women in the Workplace, 1600 to 1993*. Jefferson, NC: McFarland and Co. Inc.

Shaffer, M., Joplin, J., Bell, M., Lau, T. and Oguz, C. (2000) 'Gender discrimination and job-related outcomes: A cross-cultural comparison of working women in the United States and China', *Journal of Vocational Behavior*, 57 (3): 395–427.

Shupe, E., Cortina, L., Ramos, A., Fitzgerald, L. and Salisbury, J. (2002) 'The incidence and outcomes of sexual harassment among Hispanic and non-Hispanic White women: A comparison across levels of cultural affiliation', *Psychology of Women Quarterly*, 26: 298–308.

Sims, C., Drasgow, F. and Fitzgerald, L. (2005) 'The effects of sexual harassment on turnover in the military: Time-dependent modeling', *Journal of Applied Psychology*, 90: 1141–1152.

Stokes, P., Stewart-Belle, S. and Barnes, J. (2000) 'The supreme court holds class on sexual harassment: How to avoid a failing grade', *Employee Responsibilities and Rights Journal*, 12 (2): 79–91.

Studd, M.V. and Gattiker, U.E. (1991) 'The evolutionary psychology of sexual harassment in organizations', *Ethology and Sociobiology*, 12: 249–290.

Tangri, S. and Hayes, S.M. (1997) 'Theories of sexual harassment', in W. O'Donohue (ed.), *Sexual Harassment: Theory, Research, and Treatment*. New York: Praeger, pp. 99–111.

Till, F. (1980) *Sexual Harassment: A Report on the Sexual Harassment of Students*. Washington: National Advisory Council on Women's Educational Programs.

U.S. Merit Systems Protection Board (1981) *Sexual Harassment in the Federal Workplace: Is it a Problem?* Washington, DC: U.S. Government Printing Office.

U.S. Merit Systems Protection Board (1988) *Sexual Harassment in the Federal Government: An Update.* Washington, DC: U.S. Government Printing Office.

U.S. Merit Systems Protection Board (1994) *Sexual Harassment in the Federal Workplace: Trends, Progress, Continuing Challenges*. Washington, DC: U.S. Government Printing Office.

Vogt, D., Pless, A., King, L. and King, D. (2005) 'Deployment stressors, gender, and mental health outcomes among Gulf War I veterans', *Journal of Traumatic Stress*, 18 (2): 115–127.

Waldo, C.R., Berdahl J.L. and Fitzgerald, L.F. (1998) 'Are men sexually harassed? If so, by whom?', *Law and Human Behavior*, 22: 59–79.

Wasti, S., Bergman, M., Glomb, T. and Drasgow, F. (2000) 'Test of the cross-cultural generalizability of a model of sexual harassment', *Journal of Applied Psychology*, 85 (5): 766–778.

Wasti, S.A. and Cortina, L.M. (2002) 'Coping in context: Sociocultural determinants of responses to sexual harassment', *Journal of Personality and Social Psychology*, 83: 394–405.

Welsh, S. (1999) 'Gender and sexual harassment', *Annual Review of Sociology*, 25: 169–190.

Whitley, B.E. and Kite, M.E. (2006) *The Psychology of Prejudice and Discrimination*. Belmont, CA: Wadsworth Publishing.

Williams v. Saxbe, 413 F. Supp. 665, 11EPD 10,840 (D.D.C. 1976).

Williams, J.H., Fitzgerald, L. and Drasgow, F. (1999) 'The effects of organizational practices on sexual harassment and individual outcomes in the military', *Military Psychology*, 11 (3): 303–328.

Wislar, J., Richman, J., Fendrich, M. and Flaherty, J. (2002) 'Sexual harassment, generalized workplace abuse and drinking outcomes: The role of personality vulnerability', *Journal of Drug Issues*, 32 (4): 1071–1088.

Wolfe, J., Sharkansky, E.J. and Read, J.P. (1998) 'Sexual harassment and assault as predictors of PTSD symptomatology among U.S. female Persian Gulf War military personnel', *Journal of Interpersonal Violence*, 13 (1): 40–57.

Woodzicka, J. and LaFrance, M. (2001) 'Real versus imagined gender harassment', *Journal of Social Issues*, 57 (1): 15–30.

Woodzicka, J. and LaFrance, M. (2005) 'The effects of subtle sexual harassment on women's performance in a job interview', *Sex Roles*, 53 (1): 67–77.

Wyatt, G.E. and Riederle, M. (1995) 'The prevalence and context of sexual harassmen among African American and White American women', *Journal of Interpersonal Violence*, 10 (3): 309–321.

26

Work Stress

Steve M. Jex and Maya Yankelevich

INTRODUCTION

In the broadest sense, work stress represents the study of the impact of jobs and organizational conditions on the health and well-being of employees. Work stress researchers typically investigate the relationship between stressful jobs and organizational conditions (termed 'stressors') and employees' reactions to these conditions (termed 'strains'). According to Cooper and Dewe (2004) work stress research has existed for nearly a half century, and along the way, volumes of research findings have been accumulated.

Fortunately, several excellent and comprehensive reviews of the work stress literature have appeared during this period. Why, then, do we need yet another review of the work stress literature? We believe there are four reasons. First, given the sheer volume of work stress research that has been conducted to date, some consistent themes of both theoretical and practical significance have emerged. Stated differently, we believe there are some definitive conclusions that can be drawn about stress in the workplace.

Second, recent changes in the workplace have and will continue to impact work

stress research. That is not to deny that some of the previous findings have a timeless quality; rather, it acknowledges that the work world today is different in many respects than it was in the 1960s and 1970s when a great deal of groundbreaking work stress research took place (e.g., Beehr and Newman, 1978; Kahn et al., 1964).

Third, research on work stress has become much more methodologically sophisticated in the last 10 years. Fewer studies, for example, are using same-source data, and more researchers are making use of longitudinal designs. This is an extremely positive trend that has not been systematically documented in recent reviews. However, more sophisticated methods are not without their drawbacks and that there has not been a critical review of new methods in work stress research to date.

Finally, a recent trend that has not been captured in reviews of the work stress literature investigates the positive impact of stress in work settings. While it is true that Selye (1956) wrote about possible positive effects many years ago, and even introduced the term *eustress*, only very recently have work stress researchers systematically investigated this possibility. The results of this 'positive psychology' approach to work stress are provocative, and represent a fruitful avenue for future work stress researchers.

WORK STRESS RESEARCH: THE BIGGER PICTURE

Before diving headlong into work stress research, we first examine where work stress fits with other research in organizational settings. As other work stress reviews have pointed out (e.g., Beehr and Franz, 1987; Jex and Beehr, 1991; Jex, 1998), work stress is a multidisciplinary field. Beehr and Franz (1987) express this most clearly by listing four disciplinary approaches:

- medicine;
- clinical psychology;
- engineering psychology; and
- organizational psychology.

It is not coincidental that the vast majority of work stress research has been conducted by individuals in these four disciplines.

Despite the advantages of studying work stress from a multidisciplinary approach, the field that ultimately staked the greatest claim to work stress research was organizational psychology, or more specifically industrial/organizational (I/O) psychology. Work stress became a popular topic of study among I/O psychology in the early 1980s and continues unabated.

In some respects, the fact that work stress became an area within I/O psychology seems quite natural. I/O psychology has been focused for many years on social processes in organizational settings, many of which are highly relevant to stress research (e.g., role sending, fairness). I/O psychologists have also been interested in using selection methods to maximize the fit between characteristics of employees and aspects of jobs and organizations (Kristof, 1996); it is not surprising, therefore, that a lack of fit is seen as a major stressor and Person-Environment Fit is a very commonly used stress model.

Despite the natural fit of work stress into the broader field of I/O psychology, this has not always been the *best* fit. From it's beginning, I/O psychology has primarily been concerned with enhancing the effectiveness of organizations. Most work stress research, however, is concerned with enhancing the health and well-being of employees. While these two aims are not necessarily incompatible (e.g., Murphy, 1996), they are often viewed this way. Some commentators (e.g., Zickar, 2003) have noted that throughout the history of I/O psychology, research into worker well-being and health typically has not been deemed to be as important as research aimed at enhancing employee performance.

The field of Occupational Health Psychology (OHP) has emerged in recent years in response to a perceived void in the occupational health community (Barling and Griffiths, 2003). OHP reflects the application of the theories and methods of psychology to occupational health (Tetrick and Quick, 2003). The growth of the field of OHP has been quite rapid; journals devoted exclusively to OHP-related topics (*Journal of Occupational Health Psychology* and *Work and Stress*) have emerged, and a professional organization has recently been formed (Society for Occupational Health Psychology) to represent those in this field.

For researchers interested in work stress, the emergence of OHP is a very positive development. While OHP is not synonomous with work stress research (as some mistakenly believe), it is true that work stress does have a strong impact on employee health and well-being, and for this reason, work stress is considered an important core area of OHP. Of course, because many who are involved in OHP are also I/O psychologists, the study of work stress will always have some ties to the profession of I/O psychology and other related fields such as organizational behavior.

What are the advantages of work stress being a part of the emerging field of OHP? One is the multidisciplinary nature of OHP. Despite the term 'psychology' in the title, the field of OHP has welcomed those from other professions such as ergonomics, occupational medicine, occupational health nursing, and public health, to name a few. This inclusion of multiple disciplines has led to productive collaborations, as well as exciting cross-disciplinary research.

A second advantage is that work stress researchers now appear more often in forums with other researchers who view employee health and well-being as an end in itself. Within I/O psychology, employee health and well-being is often viewed as a means to an end; that is, employees should be concerned about employee health because it might have an impact on the performance of the organization. This view often leaves work stress researchers in the precarious position of having to relate their findings to organizational performance (e.g., Jex and Crossley, 2005). It also subtly suggests that work stress is less 'central' of a topic in comparison to ones that contribute more directly to the 'bottom line' (e.g., selection, training).

WORK STRESS RESEARCH: SOME 'BASIC TRUTHS'

As stated earlier, systematic research on work stress has been conducted for over half a century (Cooper and Dewe, 2004) and continues unabated. Given the sheer volume of research, it is obviously difficult to summarize all of the major findings from this vast literature, and we do not attempt to do so in this chapter. Nevertheless, it is possible to draw some definitive conclusions about stress in the workplace, and we refer to these as 'basic truths' about stress in the workplace. These conclusions are based on much research that there is little need for additional research to further support them.

Stressor–strain relationships

Much work stress research has been aimed at investigating the relationship between work-related stressors and employee strains (Jex and Crossley, 2005). The most common

workplace stressors investigated have been thing such as role stressors, workload, interpersonal conflict, and lack of personal control (Jex, 1988). Less research has focused on organizational constraints, yet this has also been found to be an important stressor (Spector et al., 1988; Spector and Jex, 1998).

If one considers research on all of these stressors collectively (see Barling, Kelloway, and Frone, 2005), it is evident that they all are associated with employee strain. More specifically, these stressors are all positively associated with maladaptive psychological, physical, and behavioral responses in employees. Granted, a good deal of this research has been cross-sectional, leaving conclusions regarding causality tentative (Cook and Campbell, 1979). Yet, at the same time, the sheer weight of the evidence allows one to make the following conclusion: Employees who perceive high levels of stressors in their work environment tend to react in maladaptive ways.

Having made this general statement, research has also shown that all strains are not equally likely to occur. In general, for example, employees' maladaptive responses to stressors are more likely to be psychological in nature than they are physical or behavioral (e.g., Bowling and Beehr, 2006; Jackson and Schuler, 1985; Spector, 1986; Spector and Jex, 1998; Tubre et al., 2000).

What is less clear, however, is *why* stressors are more strongly linked to psychological strains than to other types. One explanation is that this is due to the fact that stressors and psychological strains are both self-reported; thus, relationships with psychological strains are inflated due to common method bias (Podsakoff et al., 2003). While this is plausible, empirical research over the years has not strongly supported this argument (e.g., Crampton and Wagner, 1994), so there are likely to be other reasons as well.

One alternative to the method bias argument is that physical and behavioral strains are affected more than are psychological strains. Sonnentag and Fritz (2006), for example, describe the many extraneous variables that impact employees' hormonal levels; thus, stressors may simply not have as much variance to explain. This same argument has been made for behavioral outcomes such as job performance (Jex, Adams, Bachrach and Rosol, 2003), accidents (Neal and Griffith, 2006), and substance use (Frone, 2006).

Moderators of stressor–strain relationships

Most models of occupational stress (see Jex, 2002) highlight the role of moderator variables (see Baron and Kenny, 1986), variables that change or alter the relationship between two other variables, such that the relationship between two variables may be stronger, weaker or non-existent at different levels of the moderator. In occupational stress research, numerous moderator variables have been proposed yet researchers have tended to focus largely on individual differences such as demographics (Mayes et al., 1991), personality (Richard and Jex, 1995), and others such as beliefs about the self (Ganster and Schaubroeck, 1991; Jex and Bliese, 1999; Jex and Elacqua, 1999) and personal control (Theorell, 2003). There have also been attempts to focus on aspects of the social environment, such as social support (Beehr, 1995).

Over the years, findings bearing on moderator effects have been quite mixed. This variability in research support can be attributed to both methodological and conceptual factors. Methodologically, statistical tests of moderator effects are notoriously underpowered (Aguinis and Stone-Romero, 1997) so it remains possible that many moderator effects have gone undetected over the years due to Type II error. Another methodological consideration is that the vast majority of occupational stress studies have used cross-sectional designs, even though moderator effects are more likely to surface in longitudinal designs because the stressor precedes the strain or outcome (Zapf et al., 1996).

The major conceptual reason that empirical evidence for moderators is so mixed is that many moderator hypotheses are misspecified. It is often hypothesized, for example, that a particular variable (i.e. self-esteem) moderates the relationship between 'stressors and strains'; that is, many moderator hypotheses are proposed at a general level rather than for specific stressor–strain combinations. In their widely-cited review of social support research, Cohen and Wills (1985) proposed what some have termed the 'matching hypothesis' with respect to social support as a moderator variable. What this means is that for a moderator effect to occur, the form of social support (moderator) must match the stressor one is experiencing for it to function as a moderator. As one example, if one is experiencing work overload, support from a supervisor would likely be more helpful than would support from a family member.

Despite Cohen and Wills' (1985) proposition, occupational stress researchers have been slow to consider the matching hypothesis when examining moderator variables other than social support. Recently, however, de Jonge and Dormann (2006) showed empirically that the odds of uncovering moderator effects were in fact proportional to the match between stressors, the moderator, and the strain being measured.

What, then, can be concluded about moderators? One conclusion is that moderators are likely to be highly situation dependent, and require careful conceptual specification and methodological planning. Is there such a thing as a universal moderator of stressor–stain relations? In our opinion the variable that comes closest to fitting in this category is *perceived control*. Many studies have shown that stressors are more strongly related to strains when employees perceive that they have low levels of control over their job tasks and job-related decision making (Theorell, 2003).

Even perceived control, however, may have limited value as a moderator variable. Liu and Spector (2005) aptly pointed out that control may not have the same meaning across cultures (e.g., Spector et al., 2004). Therefore, researchers examining stress moderators should pay more careful attention to the meaning of the moderator variables across cultures (and see the Chapter by Gardner and Early, in this volume, for a more extensive discussion).

Reducing the effects of stressors

Since stress research began, researchers and organizations have been interested in ways to decrease employee stress. While a comprehensive treatment of stress reduction techniques is beyond the scope of this chapter (see Cartwright and Cooper, 2005 and Hurrell, 2005 for comprehensive summaries), it is nevertheless possible to describe general approaches to stress reduction, and derive some general conclusions regarding their efficacy.

A common distinction is made between *primary*, *secondary*, and *tertiary* interventions for stress reduction. Primary interventions, which tend to be favored by public health professionals (Tetrick and Quick, 2003), involve changing the work environment to decrease work-related stressors. Secondary interventions, which have been the focus of a great deal of work stress research, involve training employees to cope more effectively with stressors in the work environment (Beehr, Jex, and Ghosh, 2001). Finally, tertiary interventions involve providing more serious forms of intervention such as mental health counseling or employee assistance. As one might expect, tertiary prevention tends to be the major focus of those studying work stress from a clinical psychology perspective.

Which, then, is the optimal approach to stress reduction in organizations? This is a difficult question because all three forms of intervention have received varying levels of empirical support (Cartwright and Cooper, 2005; Hurrell, 2005). However, we suggest that the weight of the evidence favors a primary intervention approach to workplace stress reduction. The rationale for this is that the other two intervention approaches, while in some cases effective, do not address the root causes of stress in organizations. For example, an organization may teach

employees relaxation techniques, yet this does not change the fact that the environment is stressful, and the organization would therefore have to continually address the negative consequences of the stress.

Despite the inherent value of primary interventions, primary interventions may not always be possible. Some stressors, by their very nature, may not be amenable to primary prevention efforts. For example, employees' workload may at times be influenced by factors beyond an organization's control (e.g., an unanticipated increase in customer demand). In such cases, having the capability to develop both secondary and tertiary interventions would obviously be useful.

THEORETICAL ADVANCES IN OCCUPATIONAL STRESS

Having reviewed what we see as the strongest conclusions from work stress research, we now shift to work stress theory. As many readers will note, it is common for reviews of the work stress literature (e.g., Jex and Britt, forthcoming) to review theories that have guided research over the years. Such theories typically include the Institute for Social Research (ISR) Model (Katz and Kahn, 1978), McGrath's process model (McGrath, 1976), Beehr and Newman's (1978) process model, and perhaps the most widely studied recent theory, the Karasek's Demands-Control Model (deLange et al., 2003). Given the extent to which these theories have been reviewed, we will not do so here. Rather, we now describe what we believe to be the most important theoretical advances in the past 20 years.

Siegrist's effort-reward imbalance model

Siegrist (1996) proposed that stress stems from employees' comparisons of the rewards (e.g., rewards, praise) they receive in the workplace relative to the effort (both physical and psychological) they expend. When the ratio of effort to rewards is relatively equal, employees are happy and fulfilled. An unbalanced ratio, such that employees perceive that the rewards received do not reflect the effort expended, is the most stressful situation for employees and is the major proposition of the Effort-Reward (E-R) Imbalance model.

A secondary component of this model is the notion of *overcommitment*. Siegrist proposed that some individuals tend to be overly committed to their work, and to their employing organization. For these individuals, it is more likely that the ratio of efforts to rewards will be out of balance compared to individuals who are less committed. Perhaps not surprisingly, much research examining this has focused on components of burnout (usually, emotional exhaustion) as the consequences of effort-reward imbalance.

A positive feature of the E-R Imbalance model, and one that we believe is important, is that it is consistent with what has long been know about equity (e.g., Adams, 1965), and more recently organizational justice (Colquitt, 2001). In essence, employees evaluate a good deal of their work experiences with regard to equity, fairness, and justice. This theory is also consistent with recent work which has directly linked justice and work stress (e.g., Judge and Colquitt, 2004). Empirical research has also shown that feelings of effort-reward imbalance are associated with decreased psychological and physical well-being (Peter, Geisler, and Siegrist, 1998; Siegrist et al., 2004), though more tests of this theory are needed. This is particularly true because most tests solely use self-report measures and cross-sectional designs. Perhaps the biggest drawback of the Effort-Reward Imbalance model is not with the model itself, per se, but with measures of important constructs. Siegrist (1996) developed and used a measure which is consistent with the major premise of the theory – it is actually a ratio of one's perceived rewards relative to their efforts. Unfortunately, such measures are problematic from a psychometric point of view (Nunnally and Bernstein, 1994) so it is difficult to evaluate this theory apart from this measure. We hasten to add that the measures developed by Siegrist and colleagues derive from an epidemiological research tradition, which tends to emphasize discrete categorical measures as opposed to those of a continuous nature. Thus, many of the criticisms of this measure may be based more on unfamiliarity than the technical inadequacy of the measures.

Conservation of resources theory

Another relatively recent theoretical development in occupational stress is Hobfoll's Conservation of Resources (COR) Theory (Hobfoll, 1998; Hobfoll and Freedy, 1993). The basic premise of this theory is that people are motivated to conserve cognitive and emotional resources in their work lives and daily transactions with others. Having to cope with stressors is a resource depleting activity, which explains why those who experience stressors tend to experience states such as emotional exhaustion and depression.

While resource depletion explains why stressors have negative effects, COR theory is also particularly useful for explaining coping responses. According to Hobfoll (1998), people cope in ways that deplete the least amount of their limited physical, cognitive, emotional resources. Thus, problem-focused coping (e.g., trying to change the stressful situation) is often not used because of the high resource demands. On the other hand, appraisal-focused coping is often preferred because it requires fewer resources compared to problem-focused coping.

Like Siegrist's model, COR Theory has been subject to a limited amount of empirical testing, though it has been supported (e.g., Ito and Brotheridge, 2003). One of the positive features of COR Theory is that it incorporates recent work on self-regulation or control theory (e.g., Lord and Hanges, 1987), recognizing that humans have a finite supply of mental, physical, and emotional resource to use when confronted with stressors. Furthermore, a major issue for people is to strike a balance between confronting stressors, yet at the same time conserving those limited resources.

Arguably, the primary disadvantage of COR theory is the difficulty in testing it properly. Given the central premise of the theory, namely that stressors deplete individuals' cognitive and emotional resources over time, it would seem to require a longitudinal or even experience sampling methodology. These methods, and perhaps laboratory experimentation, may be the most appropriate ways to describe situations that lead to resource depletion or conservation.

RECENT CHANGES IN THE WORKPLACE

The workplace has changed in numerous ways over the past 20 years, and many of these changes have important implications for work stress research, and the design of interventions to reduce employee stress. A comprehensive review of these changes is well beyond the scope of this chapter, and we focus on three changes that have had the biggest impact to date and for the future. These include: Increased Permeability of Role Boundaries, Continued Growth of the Service Sector, and finally Globalization.

Increased permeability of role boundaries

Perhaps one of the most misleading phrases in the work world today is 'I'm leaving work and going home.' It is common for people to respond to e-mails when they are at home, combine vacations with business trips, respond to work-related phone calls while driving, and even spend a portion of their week working at a home office (i.e., telecommuting). This trend is facilitated by advances in both information and communication technology. Computer technology, in particular, has advanced to the point where people can communicate and even engage in business transactions when they are separated by great distances.

This trend, however, is not completely driven by technology. Many organizations

allow employees greater flexibility in deciding their schedules and how they do their work. In some cases, organizations even allow employees to work in a separate location if the job does not require the employee to be present. For most employees, this greater level of flexibility is appreciated because it helps them balance the demands of their personal and professional lives (La Pierre and Allen, 2006).

In our opinion, this enhanced flexibility is not without its cost; namely, that work is nearly a 24 hour activity. A good example of this can be seen in recent research on telecommuting. La Pierre and Allen (2006) found that telecommuting was associated with lower levels of work-to-family conflict. At the same time, however, it was associated with higher levels of family-to-work conflict, in a sense, trading one problem for another. Other recent research on telecommuting has supported these findings (e.g., Golden et al., 2006).

Another issue to consider is that the existence of enhanced computer and communication technology implies that people should use it. When a university allows faculty to access their e-mail accounts through the university's web page, there would seem to be an implicit assumption that they should respond to students' questions and take care of other professional issues during times that are traditionally considered to be 'non-working' hours. The same can be said when one carries a cellular phone at all times.

For work stress research, increased permeability of role boundaries has important and interesting implications. The extent to which work and non-work roles influence each other will continue to be viewed as a stressor. At the same time, permeability may serve as a way to decrease the effects of some stressors. Perhaps the challenge in research is in finding the optimal way for people to smoothly transition between roles. It may be, for example, that people who have greater control over the timing of role transitions respond more favorably than those who are forced to do so by outside demands.

Continued growth of the service sector

For over 20 years, we have continued to witness the growth of the service sector and a reduction in heavy manufacturing. In the mid-1980s, there was a flurry of research examining customer service (e.g., Schneider and Bowen, 1985) and emotional labor (e.g., Hochschild, 1983). Customer service research was largely focused on uncovering ways that organizations could enhance service levels, while research on emotional labor focused on the emotional demands of customer service work.

While research on customer service has slowed somewhat, emotional labor research has grown tremendously (Grandey, 2000). Much of the research now focuses on the way in which employees regulate or change their emotions to fit job requirements, as well as the consequences of doing so (Grandey, 2003). In our opinion this has essentially become an area of occupational stress research, and a very important one at that.

This growth in emotional labor research has helped clarify the effects of other stressors. Interpersonal conflict, for example, has long been studied as a stressor (Spector and Jex, 1998) and more recently the focus has been on other forms of mistreatment (Bowling and Beehr, 2006). The focus of this research has largely been on conflict or mistreatment at the hands of co-workers and supervisors. What has now become apparent, however, is that for many employees the most important, and potentially stressful mistreatment, emanates from customers or clients (Grandey et al., 2007). As the service sector continues to expand, research on the impact of service work will also undoubtedly grow as well.

Globalization

Like the growth of the service sector, increased globalization is a trend that has been in motion for many years (and see the Chapter by Sparrow in this volume). Most large organizations cross international boundaries, and must confront challenging issues such as adjusting to different cultures, and expatriation. With regard to work stress research, increased globalization has motivated researchers to assess the frequency of stressors in different cultures (e.g., Spector et al., 2004), the validity of some theories across cultures (e.g., Xie, 1996), and the meaning of different stress moderators in different cultures (e.g., Spector et al., 2004).

Despite the progress that has been made in cross-cultural occupational stress research, there is obviously more that needs to be done. More specifically, we need to gain a better understanding of the generalizability of work stress theories and research findings across cultures. There is also a need to understand stressors and coping methods that may be unique to a particular cultural context.

METHODOLOGICAL ADVANCES

The 1950s and 1960s presented an important shift in stress research, going from behaviorism to a more relational framework (Cooper and Dewe, 2004); both the person and the environment were now part of the stress and coping relationship (Lazarus, 1991). As a result, the stress research that followed is, 'as much a debate about methods and approaches as they are about advancing our understanding of stress,' (Cooper and Dewe, 2004: 59), with methodological advances in stress research occurring frequently. In this section we will briefly cover the main methodological techniques employed in stress research, as well as the methodological advances achieved in recent years.

Self-report measures

Surveys remain the most common approach to stress research (Jones and Kinman, 2001), with the primary source of data based on self-report measures. However, while self-report measures are a particularly efficient way of gathering information, the results they provide can be affected by socially desirable responding (Moorman and Podsakoff, 1992), and more broadly, common method variance, defined as variance due to the measurement method rather than the construct being measured (Podsakoff et al., 2003; Spector, 1994).

One way to reduce common method variance is by using different sources to obtain measures of the predictor and criterion (Podsakoff, et al., 2003); otherwise referred to as significant other or co-worker reports (Jex and Crossley, 2005). When researching the effects of work-family conflict on employees' well-being, Grant-Vallone and Donaldson (2001) collected co-worker and self-report data. Sonnentag and Kruel (2006) used significant other reports of psychological detachment when studying the role of job stressors, job involvement, and recovery-related self-efficacy on psychological detachment from work. The major benefit of alternative data sources is that they introduce a level of objectivity not possible with self-report data (Connell et al., 2004), and reduce common method variance.

Objective measures of stress (e.g., physiological symptoms) (Grant-Vallone and Donaldson, 2001; Jex and Crossley, 2005) also reduce biases due to common method variance (to be discussed later in the chapter). Furthermore, because of the varying meaning of stress to each individual, to maintain the integrity of the measurement it is recommended that the use of the word 'stress' be eliminated (Jex et al., 1992); instead, work stress can be measured indirectly through workload, job ambiguity, or role conflict.

Cross-sectional studies

Cross-sectional studies, which gather all the data in one survey at one time are frequently used in work stress research, probably because it is the easiest way of collecting data in an applied setting (Jones and Kinman, 2001). However, a disadvantage and criticism of this method is that it assumes that work stressors cause strains, or the other outcomes being measured (Hart and Cooper, 2002; Zapf et al., 1996). Because cross-sectional studies cannot determine causation, longitudinal studies are preferred. Unlike with the use of longitudinal studies, cross-sectional research does not provide the same ability to formulate causal conclusions.

Longitudinal studies

Although longitudinal studies cannot prove causation, they do allow researchers to demonstrate *temporal continuity*, or that stressors emerge before strains (Jones and Kinman, 2001). Additionally, even though longitudinal studies do not solve all methodological concerns (Zapf et al., 1996), they allow researchers to exclude alternative causal hypotheses. For example, cross-sectional data may leave results vulnerable to the influence of third variables, which produce false relationships between job stressors, job strains, or the particular variable being investigated (Spector et al., 2000). However, longitudinal designs allow researchers to test models in which effects do not occur just concurrently, but also are lagged, or are in reverse (Sonnentag and Frese, 2003), and allow for the control of third variables.

In their study of the effects of work stressors, Fay and Sonnentag (2002) hypothesized that stressors at work would be related to future levels of personal initiative. To test this assumption they used a longitudinal study with four waves of data collection over five years, and found that on-the-job stressors were related to subsequent changes in personal initiative.

Although traditional longitudinal studies, consisting of multiple data waves collected over a few months or years, are useful for examining prolonged effects of occupational stress, studies measuring many data points separated by much smaller time lags (i.e. days or even hours) provide a better understanding of within-person variance (Fuller et al., 2003) (and see the chapter by Carson and Barling in this volume). Unlike longitudinal studies, which usually obtain measurements on average two to four times in the span of a few months or even years (Sonnentag and Frese, 2003), *diary studies* obtain measurements daily for an average of one to four weeks (Fuller, et al., 2003). While still relatively infrequent, diary studies are particularly helpful in stress research because they allow close examination of stressor–strain relationships (Jones and Kinman, 2001).

The benefit of examining within-person variation is also evident. In one study researchers found that pre-work pain accounted for only 47 per cent of the within-person variance in midday pain compared to the 97 per cent shared variance in the between-person aggregate level (Fifield et al., 2004). Additionally, neither work demands, nor control, or undesirable daily events were related to chronic pain at the between-subjects level. Conversely, examining the within-subject effects showed that undesirable work events were related to both pain and negative mood during the day. Diary studies are also advantageous because they reduce some biases inherent in regular self-report and recall studies (Hahn, 2000). Hahn (2000) argues that studies which ask participants to either report on their general level of stress, or on a particularly stressful event, are subject to retrospective recall biases that may potentially misrepresent the participants' reports. Using a diary methodology reduces recall bias by capturing responses within hours of experiencing a stressor or a stressful situation.

Another complex longitudinal methodology is experience-sampling (ESM). Similar to diary studies, ESM studies gather data in a shorter period of time (a few days) and multiple times (with exact times randomly selected) throughout the day, not just once. ESM studies are particularly useful in capturing the effect of stressful events on mood changes and emotions (Fisher, 2002; Teuchmann et al., 1999; van Eck et al., 1998). An advantage of ESM studies over diary studies is that they rely even less on retrospection by capturing momentary states (e.g. mood) (Fisher, 2000). Finally, the benefit of both diary studies and ESM studies is that they allow for data collection within an individual's natural environment (Ilies and Judge, 2002).

Nevertheless, some caution is advisable. These methodologies produce complex data that are difficult to interpret in the absence of concrete theories and hypotheses, as well as a proficiency in statistical analysis. Multi-level modeling (MLM) is a statistical approach which facilitates the analysis of diary and ESM data. MLM takes into account the fact that (1) these data are nested within an individual and (2) that data from proximate time points is more similar than data from more distal time points. Thus, because MLM usually requires aggregation of data, it is important that it be guided by theory; otherwise the aggregation might not make any sense. Finally, application of MLM requires a large number of participants and meaningful higher-order groupings.

Physical strain measures

In work stress measures there are typically two different types of physical strain measures: self-report and physiological. Self-report measures assess either an individual's physical or psychological status, or both, usually in the form of a checklist of physical symptoms. The Subjective Health Complaints Inventory (SHC; Eriksen et al., 1999) and the Cornell Medical Index (CMI; Brodman et al., 1949) are examples of such measures. The CMI contains 195 yes/no items, and measures 18 different symptom subgroups. Not only can these measures be used as indicators of stress levels, but also as indicators of whether stress levels change over time (Eriksen et al., 2002). However, some researchers question their accuracy because they are subject to the influences of other variables. For instance, individuals high in neuroticism are prone to reporting more complaints (Costa and McRae, 1987), while positive individuals, or those low in neuroticism, report fewer complaints (O'Brien, Vangeren, and Mumby, 1995).

Because self-report can result in shared response bias, due to common method variance (Ganster and Schaubroeck, 1991; Kasl, 1987), which increases the possibility of conceptual overlap in the measures (Hurrell et al., 1998), objective physiological measures are often advocated.

Physiological measurement of stress focuses on the internal reaction to a situation, rather than the situation itself (Clow, 2001). There are a number of physiological measures that have been used in stress research. Mainly, they consist of cardiovascular and biochemical symptoms (Fried et al., 1984). Blood pressure, heartbeat, number and activity of circulating immune cells (Clow, 2001), serum cholesterol levels, catecholamine, cortisol, and uric acid (Fried et al., 1984) can all be used as indicators of stress (see Sonnentag and Fritz, 2006; Clow, 2001).

Many studies within the work environment measure endocrinological processes, blood pressure, and heart rate (e.g. Grossi et al., 2005; Nettersrom and Hansen, 2000). One of the problems with physiological measures is how such they might be obtained in an unobtrusive and noninvasive manner. Catecholamine levels can be measured through blood or urine (Sonnentag and Fritz, 2006), while cortisol can be measured through saliva (Kirschbaum and Hellhammer, 1989). Particularly in field studies, salivary and urine testing are preferred to blood testing because they can be obtained through less invasive methods (Sonnentag and Fritz, 2006).

Catecholamine studies have shown that adrenaline and noradrenalin levels were elevated during work compared to rest periods (Lundberg et al., 1999) and even more elevated compared to evening measures during non-work time (Brown and James, 2000; Lundberg et al., 1999; James et al., 1993). Catecholamine excretion was also found to be higher during working days compared to non-work days (Goldstein et al., 1999; Sluiter et al., 2001). On the other hand, some studies have found adrenaline, but not noradrenalin levels, to be higher during work compared to non-work times (Frankhaeuser et al., 1989; Johansson and Aaronsson, 1984). Overall however, the majority of the findings indicate that catecholamine excretion differs during work and non-work time, which suggests that this is a meaningful stress indicator.

Unlike studies of catecholamine levels, findings from studies examining cortisol responses are mixed. Pollard et al. (1996) examined cortisol levels on Sunday, Monday, and Tuesday of a given work week. They found no differences in cortisol secretion between Sunday and the two work days. Similarly, Raggart and Morrissey (1997) tested bus drivers' cortisol levels three times a day on work and non-work days and found no difference in cortisol levels.

Recent research suggests that cortisol response is dependent on the time of day it is measured (Kunz-Ebrecht et al., 2003; Schlotz et al., 2004). Grossi et al. (2005) found that morning cortisol levels were increased for individuals with higher levels of burnout compared to individuals with lower levels of burnout. These findings might indicate that it is the morning period that reflects a physiological stress response during work days compared to non-work days (Sonnentag and Fritz, 2006).

A number of studies have also used ESM to measure the effect of daily stressful events on cortisol levels. The findings of these studies are also mixed. Van Eck et al. (1996) collected salivary cortisol samples 10 times during the day for 5 days and found that increased cortisol levels were significantly related to the occurrence of a stressful event. Conversely, two similar studies found no relation between stressful events and cortisol levels (Hanson et al., 2000; Smyth et al., 1998).

Blood pressure (BP) and heart rate (HR) have also been used as physiological measures of stress. Collins (2001) indicates that heart rate alone should not be used as a stress indicator, as there is insufficient information to really understand what is causing the response. While some studies have used HR as a measure (Gallo et al., 2004; Kozena and Frantik, 2001) the findings are not clear. Similarly, significant relationships between BP and subjective stress have been found in some studies (e.g., Kozena and Frantik, 2001), but not in others (Carrere et al., 1991).

Although physiological measures may be preferred to self-report measures of physical strain, Fried et al. (1984) identified three confounds inherent in physiological assessment: stable or permanent factors (e.g. age or genetic tendencies), transitory factors (e.g. room temperature, prior exertion, time of day), and procedural factors (e.g. number of times the measurements are taken or time between measurements). For example, Folger and Belew (1985) indicated that it is sometimes difficult to determine whether accelerated heart rate is due to physical exertion, activation due to stress, or even positive emotional states (e.g., excitement over a positive event). Also, cardiovascular variables are highly affected by transient events, such as speaking or touching (Hurrell et al., 1998), and may vary widely across individuals (Hurrell et al., 1998).

The issues of sensitivity and specificity can be problematic when using physiological measures of strain. Sensitivity refers to the extent to which a test identifies people with a given condition. For example, hormonal measures vary in how they respond to stress. Catecholamines, in particular, are less sensitive to transient event (Hurrell et al., 1998). Other measures respond quickly to the same transient occurrences, but might recover slowly. Thus, it is important to know the differences in responsiveness when using a physiological measure.

Specificity refers to a measure's ability to separate individuals with a particular condition from those who do not have it. Cardiovascular measures, particularly heart rate, are prone to specificity problems. For instance, heart rate is extremely variable, and is easily influenced by a variety of temporary events, and thus lacks specificity. Catecholamine levels are also confounded by a number of different factors, such as illness, drugs, and daily diet (Hurrell et al., 1998).

STRESS AND POSITIVE PSYCHOLOGY

To date, work stress research has mainly focused on the negative consequences of stress. However, recently there has been a movement to explore the more positive side of life (Seligman and Csiksentmihalyi, 2000) in general and work (Turner, Barling, and Zacharatos, 2002), in particular. With this

movement in mind, we now explore the role positive psychology has played in work stress research.

Positive psychology is 'a science of positive subjective experience, positive individual traits, and positive promises to improve quality of life and prevent the pathologies that arise when life is barren and meaningless' (Seligman and Csiksentmihalyi, 2000: 5). In line with the tenets of positive psychology, Nelson and Simmons (2004) propose that positive outcomes like health and performance should be more the focus of work stress research, instead of the negative outcomes, which have been the core of stress research to date. However, 'before throwing the baby out with the bathwater,' we need to keep remembering that work stress and its effects on so-called 'negative' outcomes helped to reorganize the work environment and develop interventions to address some of the problems causing the psychological, behavioral, and physical symptoms. Thus, while stress research has been referred to as negative psychology, for a number of reasons, we and other scholars (Lazarus, 2003) find this to be misleading.

Eustress

Selye (1964; 1987) first defined and used the term eustress as 'good stress.' He explained that stress was any response of the body to any demand placed upon it, and that stress can be differentiated between distress and eustress, where distress is a result of a negative perception of the demand placed upon a person, and eustress is the result of a positive perception of the demand. Selye (1987) emphasized that learning to react to stress with positive emotions, while decreasing negative ones, would increase the likelihood of experiencing eustress. Applying this theory empirically, Simmons and Nelson (2001) used the positive psychological states of hope, positive affect, and meaningfulness as indicators of eustress in their study of nurses, and showed that despite the stressful situations the nurses were in, they still reported a high degree of hope; their positive responses to stressful situations displayed a significant relationship with well-being.

Also fundamental to Selye's treatment of stress is the concept of demand, and how much demand is placed on the body as a result of stress. If the stress exceeds the body's physical and psychological capacity, distress will result. Likewise, distress will occur if insufficient demand is placed on the body. The concept of an optimal level of stress is best explained by the Yerkes-Dodson Law, which states that performance will increase with an increase of stress until the optimal level of stress is reached, after which performance will begin to decline (Benson and Allen, 1980; Yerkes and Dodson, 1908). The Yerke-Dodson Law does not, however, distinguish between positive and negative perceptions of stress, as Selye does, but only claims that a certain amount of stress is desirable.

Flow

Csikszentmihalyi discovered that under certain conditions, individuals become so involved in work that they can persist single-mindedly while also operating under full capacity and experiencing great pleasure (Csikszentmihalyi and Csikszentmihalyi, 1988; Nakamura and Csikszentmihalyi, 2002). To experience flow, two conditions must be met: (1) individuals must feel that the task will be challenging enough to stretch their abilities but not so much that it will be impossible to complete and (2) clear goals and immediate feedback must exist (Nakamura and Csikszentmihalyi, 2002). However, some of the flow research has not focused on work experiences, instead concentrating on different activities, including art and science (Csikszentmihalyi, 1996), aesthetic experiences (Csikszentmihalyi and Robinson, 1990), sports (Jackson, 1995, 1996), and literary writing (Perry, 1999).

Researchers have developed a number of different methods for measuring flow both intraindividually and interindividually. Jackson (1995) and Perry (1999) used interviews to measure flow experiences in athletes and writers, respectively.

Csikszentmihalyi and Csikszentmihalyi (1988) developed the Flow Questionnaire and Mayers (1978) developed the Flow Scale. More specific flow scales have also been designed, particularly for sports (Jackson and Marsh, 1996). Finally, flow research has even used ESM (Moneta and Csikszentmihalyi, 1996).

Although some research has examined flow in work experiences (Allison and Duncan, 1988), there has been a lack of focus on organizational stress and how flow can alleviate it. Cranwell-Ward and Abbey (2005) suggested that operating in the flow within an organizational context is a form of positive stress. They explain that the best and most creative work is conducted when individuals are in a state of flow. To further examine this statement, research needs to be conducted on the relationship between flow and work stress.

Coping

Coping is an area of positive psychology that should be included in discussions of work stress. There is research examining how coping strategies alleviate stress and lead to a better work life (Greenglass, 2005). Two general types of coping styles have been identified: problem and emotion focused (Lazarus and Folkman, 1984). Decades of research on coping with work stress has focused more on developing a taxonomy of approaches, as opposed to examining the process and outcomes of coping (Cooper and Dewe, 2004).

Coping strategies involving problem solving or mastery lead to more positive outcomes and decreased distress, more so than coping strategies of escape or passivity (Armstrong-Stassen, 1994; Leiter, 1991). Lee and Lee (2001) found that direct action coping positively influenced stressors. That is, individuals did not perceive the job stressor as harmful when they used the direct action coping strategy. Similarly, Fortes-Ferreira et al. (2006) found a relationship between direct action coping and psychological well-being. Specifically, individuals using direct action coping were more satisfied with their work and experienced less psychological distress.

The extent to which individuals take control and initiative in coping contributes to positive outcomes (e.g. feelings of professional competence; Greenglass, 2005). Focusing on proactive coping is consistent with positive psychology (Seligman and Csikszentmihalyi, 2000). Coping is a strategy that people can enact before a stressful event. Proactive coping integrates autonomous goal-setting, self-regulatory goal attainment cognitions, and processes of personal quality of life management (Greenglass et al., 1999), and differs from traditional reactive coping (which focuses on stressful events which have already occurred), because it is more future-oriented in its design. Instead of perceiving difficult situations as threats or losses, proactive coping frames demands as opportunities. Thus, people anticipate potential stressors and act in advance to prevent them. This promotes personal growth and the achievement of challenging goals (Greenglass, 2005: Schwarzer and Taubert, 2002).

Optimism

Optimism refers to how people assess or anticipates outcomes (Scheier and Carver, 1985) with a generalized expectation of positive outcomes (Scheier et al., 2001). Recent stress research has indicated that individual characteristics are, in part, responsible for how one perceives job circumstances (Mäkikangas and Kinnunen, 2003). Optimists make use of better coping strategies and have better physical and psychological health than pessimists (Carver and Scheier, 1999; Chang and Farrehi, 2001; Scheier and Carver, 1992; Scheier et al., 1986). Findings of all studies indicate that regardless of the stressful situation, an optimistic orientation minimizes the disabling perception of stress (Tuten and Neidermeyer, 2004).

Mäkikangas and Kinnunen (2003) conducted a longitudinal study of Finish workers to examine the moderating effects of optimism and self-esteem on work stress. They found that optimism had a buffering effect on psychosocial stressors. For female employees, optimism reduced the effect of time pressure, job insecurity, and organizational climate on mental distress. The relationship between optimism and job insecurity was less clear. Negative effects of job insecurity were worse for individuals high, rather than low, in optimism. The authors believe such prolonged threat might be worse for optimists because of their different expectations and outlook.

Tuten and Neidermeyer (2004) studied call center employees and the effect of stress and optimism on performance, satisfaction, and turnover. They showed that optimists reported significantly lower perceptions of stress and work/nonwork conflict than pessimists. In a sample of palliative care providers, Hulbert and Morrison (2006) found that optimism was strongly and consistently related to lower levels of perceived stress, and that while satisfaction with social support was related to reduced perceptions of stress, it was mediated by optimism. These findings indicate a need for further research into the relationship between optimism and work stress, and that interventions directed at optimism might be particularly useful.

CONCLUSIONS

Our major objective in this chapter was to review what is currently known about stress in organizations, highlight recent theoretical and methodological advances, and describe some trends which will likely impact this research domain in the future. Occupational stress researchers should be proud of the progress that has been made in understanding stress in organizations; we have reached the point where definitive statements about a number of stressor–strain relationships in organizational settings are in order. Also, given the increased methodological sophistication of this research, statements about causality are more plausible. It is also evident that work stress theories based on other organizational sciences are being developed, and these are providing more testable hypotheses that will advance our knowledge.

Work stress researchers have also begun to recognize that not all of the effects of stressors are negative. This reflects a more general trend in psychology and organizational behavior (see the Chapter by Dutton and Glyn in this volume), and is also important in work stress research. Future research that addresses recent trends in the workplace focuses more on role boundaries and the stressors inherent in service work, and assumes a cross-cultural approach will strengthen the many lessons already learned about the nature, predictors and consequences of work stress.

REFERENCES

Adams, J.S. (1965) 'Inequity in social exchange', in L. Berkowitz (ed.), *Advances in Experimental Social Psychology.* San Diego, CA: Academic Press. Vol. 2, pp. 267–299.

Aguinis, H. and Stone–Romero, E.F. (1997) 'Methodological artifacts in moderated multiple regression and their effects on statistical power', *Journal of Applied Psychology*, 82: 192–206.

Allison, M.T. and Duncan, M.C. (1988) 'Women, work, and flow', in M. Csikszentmihalyi and I.S. Csikszentmihalyi (eds), *Optimal Experience: Psychological Studies of Flow in Consciousness.* New York: Cambridge University Press, pp. 118–137.

Armstrong-Stassen, M. (1994) 'Coping with transition: A study of layoff and proactive coping', *Psychological Behavior*, 15: 597–621.

Barling, J. and Griffiths, A. (2003) 'A history of occupational health psychology', in J.C. Quick and L.E. Tetrick (eds), *Handbook of Occupational Health Psychology.* Washington, DC: American Psychological Association, pp. 19–34.

Barling, J., Kelloway, E.K. and Frone, M.R. (eds) (2005) *Handbook of Work Stress.* Thousand Oaks, CA: Sage.

Baron, R.M. and Kenny, D.A. (1986) 'The moderator-mediator distinction in social psychological research: Conceptual, strategic and statistical considerations', *Journal of Personality and Social Psychology*, 51: 1173–1182.

Beehr, T.A. (1995) *Psychological Stress in the Workplace.* London: Routledge.

Beehr, T.A. and Franz, T.M. (1987) 'The current debate about the meaning of job stress', in J.M. Ivancevich and D.C. Ganster (eds), *Job Stress: From Theory to Suggestion.* New York: Haworth Press, pp. 5–18.

Beehr, T.A. and Newman, J.E. (1978) 'Job stress, employee health, and organizational effectiveness: A facet analysis, model, and literature review', *Personnel Psychology*, 31: 665–699.

Beehr, T.A., Jex, S.M. and Ghosh, P. (2001) 'The management of occupational stress', in C.M. Johnson, W.K. Redmon, and T.C. Mawhinney (eds), *Handbook of Organizational Performance.* New York: The Haworth Press, pp. 225–254.

Benson, H. and Allen, R.L. (1980) 'How much stress is too much?', *Harvard Business Review*, 58: 86–92.

Bowling, N.A. and Beehr, T.A. (2006) 'Workplace harassment from the victim's perspective: A theoretical model and meta-analysis', *Journal of Applied Psychology*, 91: 998–1012.

Brodman, K., Erdmann, A.J., Jr., Lorge, I. and Wolff, H.G. (1949) 'The Cornell medical index', *Journal of the American Medical Association*, 140: 530–534.

Brown, D.E. and James, G.D. (2000) 'Physiological stress responses in Filipino-American immigrant nurses: The effects of residence on time, life-style, and job strain', *Psychosomatic Medicine*, 62: 394–400.

Carrere, S., Evans, G.W., Palsane, M.N. and Rivas, M. (1991) 'Job strain and occupational stress among urban public transit operators', *Journal of Occupational Psychology*, 64: 305–316.

Cartwright, S. and Cooper, C.L. (2005) 'Individually targeted interventions', in J. Barling, K. Kelloway and M.R. Frone (eds), *Handbook of Work Stress.* Thousand Oaks, CA: Sage, pp. 607–622.

Carver, C. and Scheier, M. (1999) 'Optimism', in C.R. Snyder (ed.), *The Psychology of What Works.* New York: Oxford University Press, pp. 182–204.

Chang, E.C. and Farrehi, A.S. (2001) 'Optimism/pessimism and information-processing styles: Can their influence be distinguished in predicting psychological adjustment?', *Personality and Individual Differences*, 31: 555–563.

Clow, A. (2001) 'Physiology of stress', in F. Jones and J. Bright (eds), *Stress: Myth, Theory and Research.* England: Pearson Education Limited, pp. 47–61.

Cohen, S. and Wills, T.A. (1985) 'Stress, social support, and the buffering hypothesis', *Psychological Bulletin*, 98: 310–357.

Collins, S.M. (2001) 'Emerging methods for the physiological assessment of occupational stress', *Work*, 17: 209–219.

Colquitt, J.A. (2001) 'On the dimensionality of organizational justice: A construct validation of a measure', *Journal of Applied Psychology*, 86: 386–400.

Connell, P., Bruk Lee, V. and Spector, P. (2004) 'Job stress assessment methods', in J.C. Thomas and M. Hersen (eds), *Comprehensive Handbook of Psychological Assessment*. Hoboken, NJ: John Wiley and Sons, Inc. Vol. 4, pp. 455–469.

Cook, T.D. and Campbell, D.T. (1979) *Quasi-experimentation: Design and Analysis Issues for Field Settings*. Chicago: Rand McNally College Pub.

Cooper, C.L. and Dewe, P. (2004) *Stress: A Brief History*. Malden, MA: Blackwell Publishing.

Costa, P.T. and McRae, R.R. (1987) 'Neuroticism, somatic complaints and disease: Is the bark worse than the bite?', *Journal of Personality*, 55: 299–316.

Crampton, S.M. and Wagner, J.A., III (1994) 'Percept-percept inflation in micro organizational research: An investigation of prevalence and effect', *Journal of Applied Psychology*, 79: 67–76.

Cranwell-Ward, J. and Abbey, A. (2005) *Organizational Stress*. New York: Palgrave McMillan.

Csikszentmihalyi, M. (1996) *Creativity*. New York: HarperCollins.

Csikszentmihalyi, M. and Csikszentmihalyi, I. (1988) *Optimal Experience: Psychological Studies of Flow and Consciousness*. Cambridge: Cambridge University Press.

Csikszentmihalyi, M. and Robinson, R. (1990) *The Art of Seeing*. Maliby, CA: J. Paul Getty Museum and the Getty Center for Education in the Arts.

De Jonge, J. and Dormann, C. (2006) 'Stressors, resources, and strain at work: A longitudinal test of the triple-match hypothesis', *Journal of Applied Psychology*, 91: 1359–1374.

De Lange, A.H., Taris, T.W., Kompier, M.A., Houtman, I.L.D. and Bongers, P.M. (2003) ' "The very best of the millennium": Longitudinal research and the demands-control-support model', *Journal of Occupational Health Psychology*, 8: 282–305.

Eriksen, H., Ihlenbaek, C., Mikkelsen, A., Gronningsaeter, H., Sandal, G.M. and Ursin, H. (2002) 'Improving subjective health at the worksite: A randomized controlled trial of stress management training, physical exercise and an integrated health programme', *Occupational Medicine*, 52: 383–391.

Eriksen, H., Ihlebaek, C. and Ursin, H. (1999) 'A scoring system for subjective health complaints (SHC): Original article', *Scandinavian Journal of Public Health*, 27: 63–72.

Fay, D. and Sonnentag, S. (2002) 'Rethinking the effects of stressors: A longitudinal study on personal initiative', *Journal of Occupational Health Psychology*, 7: 221–234.

Fifield, J., McQuillan, J., Armeli, S., Tennen, H., Reisine, S. and Affleck, G. (2004) 'Chronic strain, daily work stress and pain among workers with rheumatoid arthritis: Does job stress make a bad day worse?', *Work and Stress*, 18: 275–291.

Fisher, C.D. (2000) 'Mood and emotions while working: Missing pieces of job satisfaction?', *Journal of Organizational Behavior*, 21: 185–202.

Fisher, C.D. (2002) 'Antecedents and consequences of real-time affective reactions at work', *Motivation and Emotion*, 26: 3–30.

Folger, R. and Belew, J. (1985) 'Nonreactive measurement: A focus for research on absenteeism and occupational stress', *Research in Organizational Behavior*, 7: 129–170.

Fortes-Ferreira, L., Peiró, J. M., González-Morales, M. G. and Martín, I. (2006) 'Work-related stress and well-being: The roles of direct action coping and palliative coping', *Scandinavian Journal of Psychology*, 47: 293–302.

Frankhaeuser, M., Lundberg, U., Fredrikson, M., Melin, B., Tuomisto, M. and Myrsten, A.L. (1989) 'Stress on and off the job as related to sex and occupational status in white-collar workers', *Journal of Organizational Behavior*, 10: 321–346.

Fried, Y., Rowland, K.M. and Ferris, G.R. (1984) 'The physiological measurement of work stress: A critique', *Personnel Psychology*, 37: 583–615.

Frone, M.R. (2006) 'Prevalence and distribution of illicit drug use in the workforce and in the workplace: Findings and implications from a U.S. national survey', *Journal of Applied Psychology*, 91: 856–869.

Fuller, J.A., Stanton, J.M., Fisher, G.G., Spitzmuller, C., Russell, S.S. and Smith, P.C., (2003) 'A lengthy look at the daily grind: Time series analysis of events, mood, stress, and satisfaction', *Journal of Applied Psychology*, 88: 1019–1033.

Gallo, L.C., Bogart, L.M., Vrnceanu, A. and Walt, L.C. (2004) 'Job characteristics, occupational status, and ambulatory cardiovascular activity in women', *Annuals of Behavioral Medicine*, 28: 62–73.

Ganster, D.C. and Schaubroeck, J. (1991) 'Role stress and worker health: An extension of the plasticity hypothesis of self-esteem', *Journal of Social Behavior and Personality*, 6: 349–360.

Golden, T.D., Veiga, J. and Simsek, Z. (2006) 'Telecommuting's differential impact on work-family conflict: Is there no place like home?', *Journal of Applied Psychology*, 91: 1340–1350.

Goldstein, I.B., Shapiro, D.L., Chicz-DeMet, A. and Guthric, D. (1999) 'Ambulatory blood pressure, heart rate, and neuroendocrine responses in women nurses during work and off work days', *Psychosomatic Medicine*, 61: 387–396.

Grandey, A.A. (2000) 'Emotion regulation in the workplace: A new way to conceptualize emotional labor', *Journal of Occupational Health Psychology*, 5: 95–110.

Grandey, A.A. (2003) 'When "the show must go on": Surface and deep acting as predictors of emotional exhaustion and service delivery', *Academy of Management Journal*, 46: 86–96.

Grandey, A.A., Kern, J.H. and Frone, M.R. (2007) 'Verbal abuse from insiders versus outsiders: Comparing frequency, impact on emotional exhaustion, and the role of emotional labor', *Journal of Occupational Health Psychology*, 12: 63–79.

Grant-Vallone, E.J. and Donaldson, S. (2001) 'Consequences of work-family conflict on employee well-being over time', *Work and Stress*, 15: 214–226.

Greenglass, E.R. (2005) 'Proactive coping, resources and burnout: Implication for occupational stress', in A.G. Antoniou and C.L. Cooper (eds), *Research Companion to Organizational Health Psychology*. Cheltenham: Edward Elgar, pp. 503–515.

Greenglass, E.R., Schwarzer, R., Jakubiec, D., Fiksenbaum, L. and Taubert, S. (1999) *The Proactive Coping Inventory (PCI): A Multidimensional Research Instrument*. Paper presented at the 20th International Conference of the Stress and Anxiety Research Society (STAR), Cracow, Poland, 12–14 July.

Grossi, G., Perski, A., Ekstedt, M., Johansson, T., Lindstrom, M. and Holm, K. (2005) 'The morning salivary costisol response in burnout', *Journal of Psychosomatic Research*, 59: 103–111.

Hahn, S.E. (2000) 'The effects of locus of control on daily exposure, coping and reactivity to work interpersonal stressors: A diary study', *Personality and Individual Differences*, 29: 729–748.

Hanson, E.K.S., Maas, C.J.M., Meijman, T.F. and Godaert, G.L.R. (2000) 'Cortisol secretion throughout the day, perceptions of the work environment, and negative affect', *Annals of Behavioral Medicine*, 22: 316–324.

Hart, P. and Cooper, C.L. (2002) 'Occupational stress: Toward a more integrated framework', in N. Anderson, D.S. Ones, H.K. Sinangil, and C. Viswesvaran (eds), *Handbook of Industrial, Work, and Organizational Psychology*. London: Sage. Vol. 1, pp. 93–114.

Hobfoll, S.E. (1998) *Stress, Culture, and Community: The Psychology and Philosophy of Stress*. New York: Plenum Press.

Hobfoll, S.E. and Freedy, J. (1993) 'Conservation of resources: A general stress theory applied to burnout', in W. Schaufeli, C. Maslach, and T. Marek (eds), *Professional Burnout: Recent Developments in Theory and Research*. Washington, DC: Taylor and Francis, pp. 115–129.

Hochschild, A.R. (1983) *The Managed Heart: The Commercialization of Human Feeling*. Berkeley, CA: University of California Press.

Hulbert, N.J. and Morrison, V.L. (2006) 'A preliminary study into stress in palliative care: Optimism, self–efficacy and social support', *Psychology, Health and Medicine*, 11: 246–254.

Hurrell, J.J. (2005) 'Organizational stress interventions', in J. Barling, K. Kelloway, & M.R. Frone (eds), *Handbook of Work Stress* Thousand Oaks, CA: Sage, pp. 623–645.

Hurrell, J.J., Nelson, D.L. and Simmons, B.L. (1998) 'Measuring job stressors and strains: Where we have been, where we are, and where we need to go', *Journal of Occupational Health Psychology*, 3: 368–389.

Ilies, R. and Judge, T.A. (2002) 'Understanding the dynamic relationships among personality, mood, and job satisfaction: A field experience sampling study', *Organizational Behavior and Human Decision Making Processes*, 89: 1119–1139.

Ito, J.K., and Brotheridge, C.M. (2003) 'Resources, coping strategies, and emotional exhaustion: A conservation of resources perspective', *Journal of Vocational Behavior*, 63: 490–509.

Jackson, S. (1995) 'Factors influencing the occurrence of the flow experience in elite athletes', *Journal of Applied Sports Psychology*, 7: 138–166.

Jackson, S. (1996) 'Toward a conceptual understanding of the flow experience in elite athletes', *Research Quarterly for Exercise and Sport*, 67: 16–90.

Jackson, S.E. and Schuler, R.S. (1985) 'A meta-analysis and conceptual critique of research on role ambiguity and role conflict in work settings', *Organizational Behavior and Human Decision Processes*, 36: 16–78.

Jackson, S.A. and Marsh, H. (1996) 'Development and validation of a scale to measure optimal experience: The Flow State Scale', *Journal of Sport and Exercise Psychology*, 18: 17–35.

James, G.D., Schlussel, Y.R. and Pickering, T.G. (1993) 'The association between daily blood pressure and catecholamine variability in nomotensive working women', *Psychosomatic Medicine*, 55: 55–60.

Jex, S.M. (1998) *Stress and Job Performance: Theory, Research, and Implications for Managerial Practice*. Thousand Oaks, CA: Sage.

Jex, S.M. (2002) *Organizational Psychology: A Scientist-Practitioner Approach*. New York: John Wiley & Sons.

Jex, S.M., and Beehr, T.A. (1991). 'Emerging theoretical and methodological issues in the study of work-related stress', in K. Rowland and G. Ferris (eds), *Research in Personnel and Human Resources Management*. Greenwich, CT: JAI Press, (Vol. 9), pp. 311–365.

Jex, S.M. and Bliese, P.D. (1999) 'Efficacy beliefs as a moderator of the effects of work-related stressors: A multilevel study', *Journal of Applied Psychology*, 84: 349–361.

Jex, S.M. and Britt, T.D. (2008) *Organizational Psychology: A Scientist–Practitioner Approach* (2nd edn). New York: John Wiley & Sons.

Jex, S.M. and Crossley, C.D. (2005) 'Organizational consequences', in J. Barling, K. Kelloway and M.R. Frone (eds), *Handbook of Work Stress*. Thousand Oaks, CA: Sage, pp. 575–599.

Jex, S.M. and Elacqua, T.C. (1999) 'Self-esteem as a moderator: A comparison of global and organization-based measures', *Journal of Occupational and Organizational Psychology*, 72: 71–81.

Jex, S.M., Beehr, T.A. and Roberts, C.K. (1992) 'The meaning of occupational stress items to survey respondents', *Journal of Applied Psychology*, 77: 623–628.

Jex, S.M., Adams, G.A., Bachrach, D.G. and Rosol, S. (2003) 'The impact of situational constraints, role stressors, and commitment on employee altruism', *Journal of Occupational Health Psychology*, 8: 171–180.

Johansson, G. and Aronsson, G. (1984) 'Stress reactions in computerized administrative work', *Journal of Occupational Behavior*, 5: 159–181.

Jones, F. and Kinman, G. (2001) 'Approaches to studying stress', in F. Jones and J. Bright (eds), *Stress: Myth, Theory and Research*. Harlow, England: Prentice-Hall, pp. 17–45.

Judge, T.A., and Colquitt, J.A. (2004) 'Organizational justice and stress: The mediating role of work-family conflict', *Journal of Applied Psychology*, 89(3): 395–404.

Kahn, R.L., Wolfe, D.M., Quinn, R.P., Snoeck, J.D. and Rosenthal, R.A. (1964). *Organizational Stress: Studies in Role Conflict and Ambiguity*. New York: Wiley.

Karasek, R.A. (1979) 'Job demands, job decision latitude, and mental strain: Implications for job redesign', *Administrative Science Quarterly*, 24: 285–308.

Kasl, S.V. (1987) 'Methodologies in stress and health: Past difficulties, present dilemmas, future directions', in S.V. Kasl and C.L. Cooper (eds), *Stress and Health: Issues in Research Methodology*. Chichester: Wiley, pp. 307–318.

Katz, D. and Kahn, R.L. (1978) *The Social Psychology of Organizations* (2nd edn). New York: Wiley.

Kirschbaum, C. and Hellhammer, D.H. (1989) 'Salivary cortisol in psychoneuroendocrine research: Recent developments and applications', *Psychoendocrinology*, 19: 313–333.

Kozena, L. and Frantik, E. (2001) 'Psychological and physiological response to job stress in emergency ambulance personnel', *Homeostasis in Health and Disease*, 41: 121–122.

Kristof, A.L. (1996) 'Person-organization fit: An integrative review of its conceptualization, measurement, and implications', *Personnel Psychology*, 49: 1–50.

Kunz-Ebrecht, S.R., Kirshcbaum, C., Marmot, M. and Steptoe, A. (2003) 'Differences in cortisol awakening response on work days and weekends in women and men from Whitehall II cohort', *Psychoneuroendocrinology*, 29: 516–528.

Lapierre, L.M. and Allen, T.D. (2006) 'Work-supportive family, family-supportive supervision, use of organizational benefits, and problem-focused coping: Implications for work-family conflict and employee well-being', *Journal of Occupational Health Psychology*, 11: 169–181.

Lazarus, R.S. (1991) *Emotion and Adaptation*. New York: Oxford University Press.

Lazarus, R.S. (2003) 'Does the positive psychology movement have legs?', *Psychological Inquiry*, 14: 93–109.

Lazarus, R.S. and Folkman, S. (1984) *Stress, Appraisal and Coping*. New York: Springer.

Lee, S. and Lee, W. (2001) 'Coping with job stress in industries: A cognitive approach', *Human Factors and Ergonomics in Manufacturing*, 11: 255–268.

Leiter, M.P. (1991) 'Coping patterns as predictors of burnout: The function of control and escapist coping patterns', *Journal of Organizational Behavior*, 12: 123–144.

Liu, C. and Spector, P.E. (2005) 'International and cross-cultural issues', in J. Barling, E.K. Kelloway, and M.R. Frone (eds), *Handbook of Work Stress*. Thousand Oaks, CA: Sage, pp. 487–516.

Lord, R.G. and Hanges, P.J. (1987) 'A control system model of organizational motivation: Theoretical development and applied implications', *Behavioral Science*, 32: 161–178.

Lundberg, U., Elfsberg Dohns, I., Melin, B., Sandsjo, L., Palmerud, G., Kadefors, R., Ekstrom, M. and Parr, D. (1999) 'Psychophysiological stress responses, muscle tension, and neck and shoulder pain among supermarket cashiers', *Journal of Occupational Health Psychology*, 4: 245–255.

Mäkikangas, A. and Kinnunen, U. (2003) 'Psychosocial work stressors and well-being: Self-esteem and optimism as moderators in a one-year longitudinal sample', *Personality and Individual Differences*, 35: 537–557.

Mayers, P. (1978) *Flow in Adolescence and its Relation to School Experience*. Unpublished doctoral dissertation, University of Chicago.

Mayes, B.T., Barton, M.E. and Ganster, D.C. (1991) 'An exploration of the moderating effect of age on job stressor-employee strain relationships', *Journal of Social Behavior and Personality*, 6: 289–308.

McGrath, J.E. (1976) 'Stress and behavior in organizations', in M.D. Dunnette (ed.), *Handbook of Industrial and Organizational Psychology*. Chicago: Rand McNally, pp. 1351–1396.

McGrath, J.E. and Beehr, T.A. (1990) 'Time and the stress process: Some temporal issues in the conceptualization and measurement of stress', *Stress Medicine*, 6: 93–104.

Moneta, G. and Csikszentmihalyi, M. (1996) 'The effect of perceived challenges and skills on the quality of subjective experience', *Journal of personality*, 64: 275–310.

Moorman, R.H. and Podsakoff, P.M. (1992) 'A meta-analytic review and empirical test of the potential confounding effects of social desirability response sets in organizational behavior research', *Journal of Occupational and Organizational Behavior*, 12: 565–579.

Murphy, L.R. (1996) '*Future directions for job stress research and practice: Expanding the focus from worker health to organizational health*', Opening keynote speech at the 2nd National Occupational Stress Conference 1996, Brisbane, Queensland, Australia.

Nakamura, J. and Csikszentmihalyi, M. (2002) 'The concept of flow', in C.R. Dnyder and S.J. Lopez (eds), *Handbook of Positive Psychology*. Oxford: Oxford University Press, pp. 89–105.

Neal, A. and Griffin, M.A. (2006) 'A study of the lagged relationship among safety climate, safety motivation, safety behavior, and accidents at the individual and group levels', *Journal of Applied Psychology*, 91: 946–953.

Nelson, D.L. and Simmons B.L. (2004) 'Eustress: An elusive construct, an engaging pursuit', in P.L. Perrewe and D.C. Ganster (eds), *Research in Occupational Stress and Well Being: Emotional and Physiological Processes and Positive Intervention Strategies*. Oxford: Elsevier. Vol. 3, pp. 265–322.

Nelson, D.L. and Simmons B.L. (2006) 'Eustress and hope at work', in A.M. Rossi, P.L. Perrewe, and S.L. Sauter (eds), *Stress and Quality of Working Life: Current Perspectives in Occupational Health*. Greenwich, CT: Information Age Publishing, pp. 121–135.

Nettersrom, B. and Hansen, A.M. (2000) 'Outsourcing and stress: Physiological effects on bus drivers', *Stress Medicine*, 16: 149–160.

Nunnally, J.C. and Bernstein, I.H. (1994) *Psychometric Theory* (3rd edn). New York: McGraw–Hill.

O'Brien, W.H., Vanegeren, L. and Mumby, P.B. (1995) 'Predicting health behaviors using measures of optimism and risk', *Health Values*, 19: 21–28.

Perry, S.K. (1999) *Writing in Flow*. Cincinnati, OH: Writer's Digest Books.

Peter, R., Geisler, H. and Seigrist, J. (1998) 'Associations of effort-reward imbalance at work and self-reported symptoms in different groups of male and female public transport workers', *Stress Medicine*, 14: 175–182.

Pollard, T.M., Ungpakorn, G., Harrison, G.A. and Parkes, K.R. (1996) 'Epinephrine and cortisol responses to work: A test of the models of Frankenhaeuser and Karasek', *Annals of Behavioral Medicine*, 18: 229–237.

Podsakoff, P.M., McKenzie, S.B., Lee, J. and Podsakoff, N.P. (2003) 'Common method biases in behavioral research: A critical review of the literature and recommended remedies', *Journal of Applied Psychology*, 88: 879–903.

Raggartt, P.T.F. and Morrissey, S.A. (1997) 'A field study of stress and fatigue in long-distance bus drivers', *Behavioral Medicine*, 23: 122–129.

Richard, R.L. and Jex, S.M. (1995) 'The relationship between the Type A Behavior Pattern (TABP) and in-basket performance: Recognition as a moderator', *Work and Stress*, 9: 77–87.

Scheier, M.F. and Carver, C.S. (1985) 'Optimism, coping, and health: Assessment and implications of generalized outcome expectancies', *Health Psychology*, 4: 219–247.

Scheier, M.F. and Carver, C.S. (1992) 'Effects of optimism on psychological and physical well-being: theoretical overview ad empirical update', *Cognitive Therapy and Research*, 16: 565–582.

Scheier, M.F., Carver, C.S. and Bridges, M.W. (2001) 'Optimism, pessimism and psychological well-being', in E.C. Change (ed.), *Optimism and pessimism. Implications for Theory, Research, and Practice*. Washington, DC: American Psychological Association, pp. 189–216.

Scheier, M.F., Weintraub, J.K. and Carver, C.S. (1986) 'Coping with stress: Divergent strategies of optimists and pessimists', *Journal of Personality and Social Psychology*, 51: 1257–1264.

Schneider, B. and Bowen, D.E. (1985) 'Employee and customer perceptions of service in banks: Replication and extension', *Journal of Applied Psychology*, 70(3): 423–433.

Schlotz, W., Hellhammer, J., Schulz, P. and Stone, A.A. (2004) 'Perceived work overload and chronic worrying predict weekend-weekday differences in the Cortisol

Awakening Response', *Psychosomatic Medicine*, 66: 207–214.

Schwarzer, R. and Taubert S. (2002) 'Tenacious goal pursuits and striving toward personal growth: Proactive coping', in E. Frydenberg (ed.), *Beyond Coping: Meeting Goals, Visions and Challenges.* London: Oxford University Press, pp. 19–35.

Seligman, M.E.P and Csikszentmihalyi, M. (2000) 'Positive psychology', *American Psychologist*, 55: 5–14.

Selye, H. (1956) *The Stress of Life.* New York: McGraw-Hill.

Selye, H. (1964) *From Dream to Discovery.* New York: McGraw-Hill.

Selye, H. (1987) *Stress Without Distress.* London: Transworld.

Siegrist, J. (1996) 'Adverse health effects of high-effort/low-reward conditions', *Journal of Occupational Health Psychology*, 1: 27–41.

Siegrist, J., Starke, D., Chandola, T., Godin, I., Marmot, M., Niedhammer, I. and Peter, R. (2004) 'The measurement of effort-reward imbalance at work: European comparisons', *Social Sciences and Medicine*, 58: 1483–1499.

Simmons, B.L. and Nelson, D.L. (2001) 'Eustress at work: The relationship between hope and health in hospital nurses', *Health Care Manager Review*, 26: 7–18.

Sluiter, J.K., Frings-Dresen, M.H., van der Beek, A.J. and Meijman, T.F. (2001) 'The relation between work-induced neuroendocrine reactivity and recover, subjective need for recovery, and health status', *Journal of Psychosomatic Research*, 50: 29–37.

Smyth, J., Ockenfels, M.C., Porter, L., Kirschbaum, C., Hellhammer, D.H. and Stone, A.A. (1998) 'Stressors and mood measures on a momentary basis are associated with salivary cortisol secretion', *Psychoendocrinology*, 23: 353–370.

Sonnentag, S. and Frese, M. (2003) 'Stress in Organizations', in W.C. Borman, D.R. Ilgen, and R.J. Klimoski (eds), *Handbook of Psychology: Industrial and Organizational Psychology.* Hoboken, NJ: John Wiley and Sons, Inc. Vol. 12, pp. 453–491.

Sonnentag, S. and Fritz, C. (2006) 'Endocrinological processes associated with job stress: Catecholamine and cortisol responses to acute and chronic stressors', in P.L. Perrewé and D.C. Ganster (eds), *Research in Occupational Stress and Well Being: Employee Health, Coping, and Methodologies.* Oxford: Elsevier Ltd, pp. 1–60.

Sonnentag, S. and Kruel, U. (2006) 'Psychological detachment from work during off-job time: The role of job stressors, job involvement, and recovery-related self-efficacy', *European Journal of Work and Organizational Psychology*, 15: 197–217.

Spector, P.E. (1986) 'Perceived control by employees: A meta-analysis of studies concerning autonomy and participation at work', *Human Relations*, 11, 1005–1016.

Spector, P.E. (1994) 'Using self-report questionnaires in OB research: A comment on the use of a controversial method', *Journal of Organizational Behavior*, 15: 385–392.

Spector, P.E., Chen, P.Y. and O'Connell, B.J. (2000) 'A longitudinal study of relations between job stressors and job strains while controlling for prior negative affectivity and strains', *Journal of Applied Psychology*, 85: 211–218.

Spector, P.E., Dwyer, D.J. and Jex, S.M. (1988) 'Relation of job stressors to affective, health, and performance outcomes: A comparison of multiple data sources', *Journal of Applied Psychology*, 73: 11–19.

Spector, P.E. and Jex, S.M. (1998) 'Development of four self-report measures of job stressors and strain: Interpersonal conflict at work scale, organizational constraints scale, quantitative workload inventory, and physical symptoms inventory', *Journal of Occupational Health Psychology*, 3: 356–367.

Spector, P.E., Sanchez, J.I., Siu, O.L., Salgado, J. and Ma, J. (2004) 'Eastern versus Western control beliefs at work: An investigation of secondary control, socioinstrumental control, and work locus of control in China and in the U.S', *Applied Psychology: An International Review*, 55: 38–60.

Tetrick, L.E. and Quick, J.C. (2003) 'Prevention at work: Public health in occupational settings', in J.C. Quick and L.E. Tetrick (eds), *Handbook of Occupational Health Psychology.* Washington, DC: American Psychological Association, pp. 3–18.

Teuchmann, K., Totterdell, P. and Parker, S.K. (1999) 'Rushed, unhappy, and drained: An experience sampling stuffy relations between time pressure, perceived control, mood and emotional exhaustion in a group of accountants', *Journal of Organizational Health Psychology*, 4: 37–54.

Theorell, T. (2003) 'To be able to exert control over one's own situation: A necessary condition for coping with stressors', in J.C. Quick and L.E. Tetrick (eds), *Handbook of Occupational Health Psychology.* Washington, DC: American Psychological Association, pp. 201–220.

Tubre, T.C. and Collins, J.M. (2000) 'Jackson and Schuler (1985) revisited: A meta-analysis of the relationships between role ambiguity, role conflict, and job performance', *Journal of Management*, 26(1): 155–189.

Turner, N., Barling, J. and Zacharatos, A. (2002) 'Positive psychology at work', in C.R. Snyder and S.J. Lopez (eds), *Handbook of Positive Psychology*. New York: Oxford University Press, pp. 715–728.

Tuten, T.L. and Neidermeyer, P.E. (2004) 'Performance, satisfaction and turnover in call centers: The effects of stress and optimism', *Journal of Business Research*, 57: 26–34.

van Eck, M., Berkhof, J., Nicolson, N.A. and Sulon, J. (1996) 'The effect of perceived stress, traits, mood states, and stressful events on salivary cortisol', *Psychosomatic Medicine*, 58: 447–458.

van Eck, M. Nicolson, N.A. and Berkhof, J. (1998) 'Effects of stressful daily events on mood states: Relationship to global perceived stress', *Journal of Personality and Social Psychology*, 75: 1572–1585.

Yerkes, R.M. and Dodson, J.D. (1908) 'The relation of strength of stimulus to rapidity of habit-formation', *Journal of Comparative Neurology and Psychology*, 18: 459.

Xie, J.L. (1996) 'Karasek's model in the People's Republic of China: Effects of job demands, control, and individual differences', *Academy of Management Journal*, 39: 1594–1618.

Zapf, D., Dormann, C. and Frese, M. (1996) 'Longitudinal studies in organizational stress research: A review of the literature with reference to methodological issues', *Journal of Occupational Health Psychology*, 1: 145–169.

Zickar, M.J. (2003) 'Remember Arthur Kornhauser: Industrial psychology's advocate for worker well-being', *Journal of Applied Psychology*, 88: 363–369.

27

Employee Alcohol and Illicit Drug Use: Scope, Causes, and Organizational Consequences

Michael R. Frone

Employee alcohol and illicit drug use is an issue that is important to and has received attention from managers, unions, policymakers, politicians, researchers, and the media. There are several reasons for this attention. First, use of alcohol and illicit drugs may undermine employee health, productivity, and safety, which leads to costs being incurred by employers. Second, in the US, passage of the Drug-Free Workplace Act of 1988 made employee substance use a salient issue for certain employers. Third, a large industry has developed around the issue of testing employees for the use of illicit drugs, and in some cases for alcohol use.

Although research on employee alcohol use can be traced back at least to the early 1940s, systematic empirical research has grown considerably over the last 15–20 years. Nonetheless, many research findings have not

found their way to relevant stakeholders, (e.g., managers, unions, policymakers, politicians, researchers, and the media) and many gaps exist in what we know. Consequently, it is not uncommon for the issue of employee substance use to produce erroneous commentary on its scope, causes, and organizational outcomes. Such commentary is often based on speculation, vested interests, and pseudo-science rather than on objective interpretation of all available scientific data (e.g., Costa e Silva, 2002; Maltby, 1999).

The goal of this chapter, therefore, is to summarize what we know and do not know about the scope, causes, and organizational consequences of employee substance use. The first section of this chapter explores the scope of alcohol and illicit drug use among employees in the US and in other national contexts. The second section summarizes the causes of employee substance use, and the third section looks at organizational consequences of employee substance use. Each of these three sections ends with suggestions for future research. The final section provides an integrative summary and concluding thoughts.

SCOPE OF EMPLOYEE SUBSTANCE USE AND IMPAIRMENT

Before summarizing research on the scope of employee substance use, it is important to point out that past research on this issue has failed to address adequately several issues (e.g., Frone, 2004, 2006a, 2006b; Normand et al., 1994). The first issue involves differentiating between substance use and impairment. Measures of substance use reflect the mere use of a substance – that is, the prevalence or frequency of using a substance over some fixed period of time or the quantity of a substance consumed on a typical occasion of use. Substance impairment has two dimensions: intoxication and withdrawal. Intoxication refers to reversible central nervous system impairment due to the direct pharmacological action of a substance, which results in various behavioral, cognitive, and affective changes (e.g., American Psychiatric Association, 1994). In contrast, among individuals who have developed pharmacodynamic tolerance to a substance, withdrawal refers to central nervous system impairment due to cessation or reduction in substance use, which results in various behavioral, cognitive, and affective changes (e.g., American Psychiatric Association, 1994; Saitz, 1998). Also included in the definition of withdrawal is the 'hangover' syndrome associated with alcohol use. An alcohol hangover refers to disagreeable physical and mental symptoms that begin while blood alcohol level is dropping and remain after blood alcohol level returns to zero. Alcohol hangovers are believed to partially reflect a mild form of acute alcohol withdrawal (e.g., Moore, 1998; Swift and Davidson, 1998). When one

considers substance use and impairment, it is the latter that may be the more proximal cause of poor workplace productivity outcomes (Frone, 2004).

A second overlooked issue is the context of employee substance use and impairment. Researchers have typically only assessed employees' overall use of and impairment from alcohol or illicit drugs. Overall substance use represents the consumption of alcohol or illicit drugs across all contexts. Overall substance impairment represents impairment (intoxication or withdrawal) due to alcohol or illicit drug use across all contexts. Thus, past research has primarily explored substance use and impairment in the workforce, which largely reflects use and impairment away from work and outside an employed individual's normal work hours. In contrast, little research has focused on alcohol and illicit drug use in the workplace even though such information is important to employers and policymakers. Substance use in the workplace represents the consumption of alcohol or illicit drugs at times that occur just before or during formal work hours (Ames et al., 1997; Frone, 2004, 2006a, 2006b). Specifically, workplace substance use refers to the consumption of alcohol or illicit drugs:

(a) within two hours of starting one's work shift;
(b) during a lunch break;
(c) during other work breaks; and
(d) while performing one's job.

Workplace substance impairment represents impairment (intoxication or withdrawal) due to alcohol or illicit drug use experienced during work hours.

The third issue is the failure of past research to provide information on the frequency of substance use. In most cases, 12 month or 30 day prevalence rates are reported. For example, a 12 month prevalence rate for overall alcohol use represents the proportion of employees who have used alcohol in any context at least once during the preceding 12 months. However, a strong understanding of the scope of employee substance use requires information on the frequency with which employees use or are impaired by alcohol or illicit drugs.

Substance use in the workforce

US data

In the US, data from the annual National Household Survey on Drug Abuse reveal that among employed adults (ages 18–49) who work full-time, approximately 78 per cent have used alcohol and 15 per cent have used an illicit drug (marijuana: 9 per cent, other illicit drugs: 5 per cent) during the preceding 12 months. Furthermore, within the preceding 30 days, 64 per cent have used alcohol, 35 per cent have engaged in binge drinking (a single occasion where five or more drinks were consumed), 12 per cent reported heavy drinking (at least five occasions of binge drinking), 5 per cent used marijuana, and 2 per cent used other illicit drugs (e.g., US Department of Health and Human Services, 1999; Hoffmann et al., 1996).

Using a national probability sample of the US workforce (ages 18–65), a subsequent study by Frone (2003a, 2006b) explored the prevalence, frequency, and distribution of alcohol and illicit drug use during the preceding 12 months. Frone (2003a) found that 73.6 per cent of the workforce (92.5 million workers) used alcohol, 30.6 per cent (38.4 million workers) drank enough to become intoxicated, and 22.6 per cent (28.4 million workers) experienced a hangover. Looking at the frequency of alcohol use in the workforce showed that weekly alcohol use was reported by 32.7 per cent of workers; monthly use was reported by 19.5 per cent of workers; and less than monthly use was reported by 21.4 per cent of workers. Drinking to intoxication on a weekly basis was reported by 3.4 per cent of the workforce; monthly intoxication was reported by 6.4 per cent of the workforce; and less than monthly intoxication was reported by 20.9 per cent of the workforce. Experiencing a hangover on a weekly basis was reported by 1.4 per cent of the workforce; monthly hangover was

reported by 3.6 per cent of the workforce; and less than monthly hangover was reported by 17.6 per cent of the workforce.

The prevalence rates for overall illicit drug use (Frone, 2006b) showed that 14.1 per cent (17.7 million workers) used at least one illicit drug during the preceding 12 months. Categorized by type of drug, 11.3 per cent of the workforce (14.2 million workers) used marijuana, 1.0 per cent (1.3 million workers) used cocaine, and 4.9 per cent (6.2 million workers) illicitly used a prescription drug (stimulants, sedatives, tranquilizers, or analgesics). The prevalence rates for using enough of each type of drug to get high or stoned showed that 11.2 per cent (14.1 million workers) were impaired by any illicit drug, 10.6 per cent (13.3 million workers) were impaired by marijuana, 0.9 per cent (1.2 million workers) were impaired by cocaine, and 2.2 per cent (2.8 million workers) were impaired by the illicit use of a prescription drug.

The frequency of illicit drug use showed that weekly use of any illicit drug was reported by 4.5 per cent of the workforce; monthly use was reported by 2.5 per cent of the workforce; and less than monthly use was reported by 7.1 per cent of the workforce. Impairment from any illicit drug on a weekly basis was reported by 3.6 per cent of the workforce; monthly drug impairment was reported by 1.9 per cent of the workforce; and less than monthly drug impairment was reported by 5.7 per cent of the workforce.

Finally, three groups of vulnerable workers were identified by cross-classifying gender (male vs. female), age (18–30 vs. 31–65), and occupation (low vs. high risk) (see Frone, 2006b, for a detailed discussion). Among young women in the high risk occupations (legal occupations; arts, design, entertainment, sports, and media occupations; food preparation and serving related occupations; and building and grounds cleaning and maintenance occupations), 43.2 per cent reported using an illicit drug in the past 12 months and 42.6 per cent reported being impaired by an illicit drug. Among young men in the high risk occupations, 55.8 per cent reported using an illicit drug and 37.8 per cent reported being impaired by an illicit drug. Also, young men in the low risk occupations showed elevated prevalence rates, with 24.7 per cent reporting illicit drug use and 20.9 per cent reporting substance use impairment. Despite these high prevalence rates, it is important to point out that that the estimated population of individuals in these three subgroups reporting overall illicit drug use represents 5.5 per cent of the US workforce.

International data

Published data also exist for overall employee substance use in other countries. Based on a large probability sample of the Australian workforce, Pidd et al. (2006) reported that 89.4 per cent of Australian workers used alcohol in the past 12 months and 43.9 per cent drank at levels defined as risky. The same study found that the 12 month prevalence rate for illicit drug use in the Australian workforce was 17.3 per cent (Bywood et al., 2006). Smith et al. (2004) used a large regional probability sample from the UK and reported that 13 per cent of the workforce used an illicit drug during the preceding 12 months and 7 per cent reported use during the preceding month. Finally, based on a large probability sample of the workforce in Alberta, Canada, 81 per cent of Alberta workers reported using alcohol during the preceding 12 months and 10 per cent reported using an illicit drug (Alberta Alcohol and Drug Abuse Commission [AADAC], 2003).

Substance use in the workplace

US data

Two reviews conducted in the mid-1990s summarized what was known about the prevalence of workplace substance use and impairment in the US from available empirical studies (Ames, 1993; Newcomb, 1994). The prevalence rates revealed wide inconsistency for workplace substance use or impairment, ranging from less than 1 per cent to about 39 per cent. These inconsistencies result from the fact that these studies differed widely on several critical dimensions:

(a) the nature and quality of the sample used (unrestricted samples vs. samples of specific subgroups; convenience vs. probability samples);
(b) the time frame evaluated (past month, past 6 months, past year);
(c) the specific substance under investigation (e.g., alcohol, marijuana, cocaine); and
(d) the dimension of workplace substance use and impairment assessed (e.g., use just before work, use during lunch, use while working, use during breaks, being at work impaired, or some unknown combination).

A subsequent study by Frone (2006a, 2006b) used a national probability sample of the US workforce to explore the prevalence, frequency, and distribution of workplace alcohol and illicit drug use during the preceding 12 months. Frone (2006a) reported that workplace alcohol use and impairment directly affected an estimated 15.3 per cent of the US workforce (19.2 million workers). Specifically, an estimated 1.8 per cent (2.3 million workers) drank before work, 7.1 per cent (8.9 million workers) drank during the workday (i.e., during lunch breaks, during other breaks, or while working), 1.7 per cent (2.1 million workers) worked under the influence of alcohol, and 9.2 per cent (11.6 million workers) worked with a hangover.

Frone (2006a) also provided information on the frequency of workplace alcohol use and impairment. Turning to the frequency of drinking before work, weekly use was reported by 0.1 per cent of the workforce; monthly use was reported by 0.5 per cent of the workforce; and less than monthly use was reported by 1.3 per cent of the workforce. Drinking during the workday was reported to occur weekly by 1.0 per cent of the workforce; monthly by 1.7 per cent of the workforce; and less than monthly by 4.4 per cent of the workforce. Working while under the influence of alcohol was reported to occur weekly by 0.3 per cent of the workforce; monthly by 0.4 per cent of the workforce; and less than monthly by 1.0 per cent of the workforce. Finally, working with a hangover was reported to occur weekly by 0.5 per cent of the workforce; monthly by 1.4 per cent of the workforce; and less than monthly by 7.3 per cent of the workforce.

Logistic regression analyses revealed that the prevalence of alcohol use or impairment at work was highest among males, younger workers, Whites, and unmarried workers. Also, compared with the low-risk occupations, the prevalence of workplace alcohol use and impairment was elevated among the arts/entertainment/sports/media occupations, food preparation and serving occupations, and building and grounds maintenance occupations.

Moving to illicit drug use in the workplace, Frone (2006b) found that 3.1 per cent of the workforce (3.9 million workers) used at least one illicit drug in the workplace – 1.6 per cent (2 million workers) used marijuana, 0.1 per cent (169,000 workers) used cocaine, and 1.8 per cent (2.3 million workers) used prescription drugs. In terms of being at work under the influence of an illicit drug, 2.9 per cent (3.6 million workers) were impaired by an illicit drug – 1.7 per cent (2.2 million workers) were impaired by marijuana, 0.2 per cent (233,000 workers) were impaired by cocaine, and 1.4 per cent (1.8 million workers) were impaired by prescription drugs.

Frone (2006b) also provided information on the frequency of use or impairment and the prevalence of use in specific workplace contexts. Turning to the frequency of workplace illicit drug use, weekly use was reported by 1.8 per cent of the workforce; monthly use was reported by 0.5 per cent of the workforce; and less than monthly use was reported by 0.9 per cent of the workforce. Workplace illicit drug impairment was reported to occur weekly by 1.2 per cent of the workforce; monthly by 0.6 per cent of the workforce; and less than monthly by 1.0 per cent of the workforce. In terms of temporal context, 2.7 per cent of the workforce (3.4 million workers) used illicit drugs within two hours of reporting to work, 1.8 per cent (2.3 million workers) used during lunch breaks, 1.2 per cent (1.5 million workers) used during other work breaks, and 1.7 per cent (2.2 million workers) used while working.

Finally, as noted earlier, three groups of vulnerable workers were identified by cross-classifying gender, age, and occupation. Among young women in the high risk occupations, 10.6 per cent reported workplace illicit drug use in the past 12 months and 11.4 per cent reported workplace drug impairment. Among young men in the high risk occupations, 28.0 per cent reported workplace illicit drug use and 26.3 per cent reported workplace drug impairment. Also, young men in the low risk occupations showed somewhat elevated prevalence rates, with 7.7 per cent reporting workplace illicit drug use and 6.8 per cent reporting workplace drug impairment. Despite the high prevalence rates in these three subgroups, it is again important to point out that that the estimated population of individuals in these three subgroups reporting workplace illicit drug use represents 1.9 per cent of the US workforce.

International data

Some data also exist on substance use in the workplace from other countries. Based on reports from 100 Israeli employers with a total workforce of 32,500 employees, Bamberger and Biron (2006) reported a 12-month prevalence rate for workplace substance use of 0.16 per cent. Pidd et al. (2006) summarized several published and unpublished findings on Australian workers. Among 337 Australian urban train drivers, 3.1 per cent drank within 3 hours of coming to work and 2 per cent drank during actual work hours. Among 4,193 Australian police officers, 26 per cent reported occasionally drinking at work. Among 319 Australian construction apprentices, 29.3 per cent (2.6 per cent at least weekly and 26.7 per cent less than weekly) drank during work hours. Also, a regional sample of 1,200 Australian workers found that 4 per cent reported drinking at work. Finally, using data from a large probability sample of the Australian workforce, Bywood et al. (2006) reported that 2.5 per cent reported going to work under the influence of illicit drugs.

A study of the workforce in Alberta, Canada (AADAC, 2003) found that 4 per cent of workers reported drinking alcohol within 4 hours of coming to work and 11 per cent reported drinking while at work. Drinking before work was reported to occur weekly by 0.4 per cent of the workforce, monthly by 0.6 per cent of the workforce; and less than monthly by 3 per cent of the workforce. Drinking while at work was reported to occur weekly by 2 per cent of the workforce, monthly by 1.0 per cent of the workforce, and less than monthly by 8 per cent of the workforce. In this same study of Alberta workers, 2 per cent of workers reported using an illicit drug within 4 hours of coming to work and 1 per cent reported using an illicit drug while at work. Illicit drug use before work was reported to occur weekly by 0.7 per cent of the workforce, monthly by 0.2 per cent of the workforce, and less than monthly by 1.1 per cent of the workforce. Illicit drug use while at work was reported to occur weekly by 0.4 per cent of the workforce; monthly by 0.3 per cent of the workforce; and less than monthly by 0.3 per cent of the workforce.

Future research

Additional research on the scope of employee substance use and impairment is needed in several areas. The first area is the scope of employee substance use in specific occupations. Most high quality research on the prevalence of substance use in the workforce and in the workplace is based on national probability samples. Despite their size, the heterogeneity of national samples usually limits the study of employee substance use to broad occupation categories. Exploring the scope of employee substance use and impairment within specific occupations will help focus research on predictors and outcomes in those occupations at greatest risk. The second area is the need for repeated cross-sectional surveys in order to track trends in the scope of employee substance use and impairment over time. Repeated surveys, which differ from panel studies (Firebaugh, 1997), can

be used to track changes in the prevalence of employee substance use, changes in the demographic characteristics of users, and changes in the patterns of use. In the US, data from the National Survey on Drug Use and Health (formerly called the National Household Survey on Drug Abuse) provides several decades of data on the scope of overall alcohol and illicit drug use in the US workforce. However, no national study in the US has tracked alcohol and drug use in the workplace over time. A study in Alberta, Canada investigated changes in overall and workplace alcohol and drug use based on data collected in 1992 and 2002 (AADAC, 2003). Unfortunately, differences in measures and methods make direct comparisons across time difficult. The third area for future research involves cross-national research. Although relatively little published data on the scope of workforce and workplace substance use exists in the US, even less published research exists in other national contexts. Cross-national comparisons may help delineate the role culture may play in promoting or inhibiting employee substance use and impairment, especially use and impairment in the workplace. Finally, it is important to point out that tracking alcohol and illicit drug use across time or making comparisons across nations will require studies using similar methods, definitions, and measures to make such comparisons valid.

CAUSES OF EMPLOYEE SUBSTANCE USE

The potential causes of employee substance use can be classified along two primary dimensions: Causes that are external to the workplace (i.e., genetics, demographics, personality characteristics, socialization, and environmental factors) and causes internal to the workplace (i.e., socialization, experiences, and environmental exposures at work). Although many factors external to the workplace may influence employee substance use, three categories of predictors or causes from the external dimension may be particularly

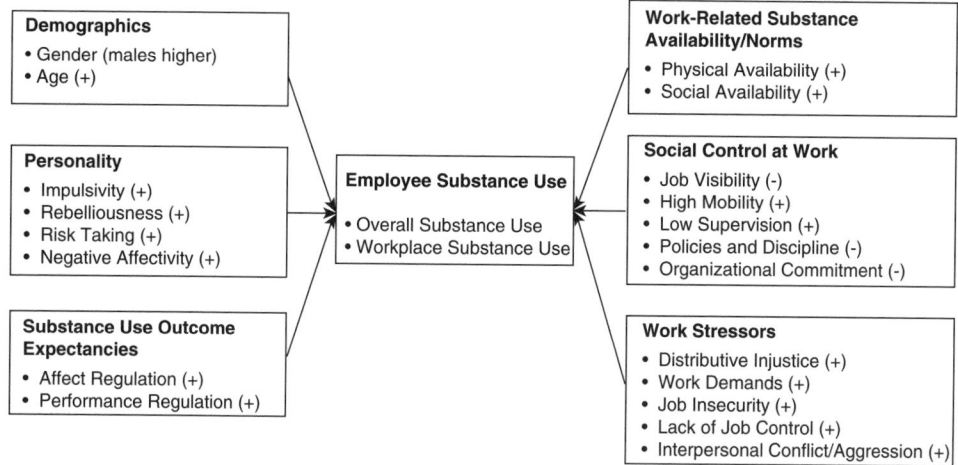

Figure 1   Predictors of employee substance use. Adapted with permission from Frone, M. R. (2003). Predictors of overall and on-the-job substance use among young workers. *Journal of Occupational Health Psychology*, 8, 39–54. Copyright ©2003 by the American Psychological Association.

salient to employee substance use. Also, researchers have identified three categories of predictors internal to the workplace that are relevant to workforce and workplace substance use. Figure 1 presents the major categories of causes that will be reviewed. The three categories of predictors on the left of the figure represent the external dimension and the three categories of predictors on the right represent the internal dimension. For each category, examples of specific predictors are provided as well as the hypothesized direction of their relation to employee substance use.

Demographics

Prior research demonstrates that gender and age are related to substance use in the general population and among workers. Employed adolescent and adult males report higher levels of overall alcohol and illicit drug use than employed adolescent and adult females, respectively (e.g., Bacharach, Bamberger, and Sonnenstuhl, 2002; Frone, 2003b, 2006b; Frone et al., 1996; Frone et al., 1995; Hoffmann et al., 1997; Newcomb, 1994). Moreover, past research among employed adolescents and adults reveals that males are more likely than females to engage in

workplace substance use (e.g., Frone, 2003b, 2006a, 2006b; Newcomb, 1994). Regarding age, general substance use research shows that the prevalence of alcohol and illicit drug use increases from early adolescence until it peaks and begins to drop during the latter part of early adulthood (e.g., Anthony and Arria, 1999; O'Malley et al., 1999). Therefore, among employed adolescents, age is positively related to overall and workplace substance use (e.g., Frone, 2003b). In contrast, among employed adults, age is negatively related to overall and workplace substance use (e.g., Bacharach et al., 2002; Frone, 2006a, 2006b; Hoffmann et al., 1997).

Personality

A number of personality characteristics could cause employee substance use. Research suggests that two domains of personality are consistently related to substance use – behavioral undercontrol and negative affectivity. Behavioral undercontrol represents a tendency to focus on short-term incentives and to inhibit behavioral responses to cues of impending or possible punishment. Impulsivity, rebelliousness or intolerance of rules, and risk taking propensity are distinct dimensions of behavioral undercontrol that are positively associated with overall substance use among adolescents (e.g., Colder and Chassin, 1997; King and Chassin, 2004) and adults (Elkins et al., 2006; Jackson and Sher, 2003). Negative affectivity, or the propensity to experience negative mood states and psychological distress, also has been identified as a vulnerability factor for substance use among adolescents and adults (e.g., Colder and Chassin, 1997; Cooper et al., 1995; Elkins et al., 2006). However, few studies have explored the relation of negative affectivity and behavioral undercontrol to workforce or workplace substance use. Grant and Langan-Fox (2007) explored the relation of the Big Five personality traits to overall employee substance use. They found that only negative affectivity predicted overall substance use. Although Frone (2003b) failed to find a relation of negative affectivity to overall and workplace substance use among young workers, several dimensions of behavioral undercontrol were related to employee substance use. Impulsivity and risk taking were positively related to overall alcohol and marijuana use, and rebelliousness (i.e., intolerance of rules) was positively related to workplace alcohol use.

Substance use outcome expectancies

Outcome expectancies are 'anticipations of one's own automatic reactions to various situations and behaviors' (Kirsch, 1999: 4). As such, outcome expectancies act as determinants of behavior. For example, during a stressful episode, individuals may consume alcohol if they expect to be more relaxed after consuming alcohol. In fact, individuals can hold a number of different expectancies regarding the outcomes of using psychoactive substances. For instance, alcohol and drugs are regarded as powerful transforming agents that might enhance or impede social behavior and cognitive and motor functioning, enhance sexuality and increase arousal, and promote relaxation and reduce tension (e.g., George et al., 1995; Goldman et al., 1987; Schafer and Brown, 1991). One important

anticipated effect of many psychoactive substances with relevance to organizational research is affect regulation – the reduction of negative emotions and the augmentation of positive emotions (e.g., Cooper et al., 1995; Goldman et al., 1987; Schafer and Brown, 1991). Thus, it is not surprising that many studies have examined and documented a positive relation between affect regulation expectancies and overall levels of alcohol use in samples of adolescents and adults (e.g., Cooper et al., 1995). Although few studies have focused on the substance use of employed individuals, research shows that affect regulation expectancies are positively related to overall alcohol and marijuana use among employees (Frone, 2003b; Frone et al., 1993). However, the only study to explore the relation of affect regulation expectancies to workplace alcohol and marijuana use failed to find significant relations in a sample of young workers (Frone, 2003b).

A second, but much less studied, anticipated effect of psychoactive substances with relevance to organizational research is performance regulation – the impairment or improvement of cognitive and motor performance (e.g., Goldman et al., 1987; Schafer and Brown, 1991). For example, individuals who believe that alcohol will improve their ability to think and function are more likely to report heavy drinking (e.g., Christiansen and Goldman, 1983). The only study to explore this issue among employed individuals found that performance regulation expectancies were positively related to overall alcohol and marijuana use and to workplace alcohol and marijuana use in a sample of young workers (Frone, 2003b).

Workplace availability

The workplace availability paradigm represents the notion that work settings where alcohol and other drugs are available may promote substance use among employees (Ames and Grube, 1999; Ames and Janes, 1992; Trice and Sonnenstuhl, 1990). There are two dimensions of availability related to the workplace: physical availability and social availability. Workplace physical availability of alcohol and drugs represents the ease of obtaining or using alcohol and other drugs during work hours, during breaks, and at work-related events (Ames and Grube, 1999). Findings from the few studies that have assessed workplace physical availability are mixed. Controlling for a number of demographic covariates, MacDonald et al. (1999) found that reports of drugs being easily available from coworkers were positively related to having an alcohol use problem. However, after controlling for social availability, Ames and Grube (1999) failed to find a relation between physical availability of alcohol at work and an individual's drinking at work. Similarly, Frone (2003b) found that after controlling for demographics, personality, and social availability, physical availability of alcohol or marijuana at work was unrelated to both overall and workplace alcohol and marijuana use.

Workplace social availability reflects the normative support within one's work environment for the use of alcohol or drugs (Ames and Grube, 1999; Ames and Janes, 1992; Trice and Sonnenstuhl, 1990). Workplace social availability has two components – use of substances by members of one's social network at work (i.e., descriptive norms) and normative approval or disapproval of substance use by members of one's workplace social network (i.e., injunctive norms). Although few studies have explored workplace social availability, their results generally support a positive relation to overall and workplace substance use (e.g., Ames and Grube, 1999; Bacharach et al., 2002; Frone, 2003b; Kjærheim et al., 1995; MacDonald et al., 1999). Nonetheless, the measures used in past research have been narrow and provide a limited test of the relation of physical and social availability to employee substance use, either overall or in the workplace.

Workplace social control

The social control paradigm posits that substance use may be higher among employees who are not integrated into or regulated by the work organization (Ames et al., 2000; Trice and Sonnenstuhl, 1990). The specific work conditions that put employees at risk of alcohol and illicit drug use include low levels of commitment or attachment to an organization, high mobility during work hours, low visibility of work behaviors, working in isolation, low levels of supervision, and a lack of formal and informal policies and disciplinary actions regarding substance use. A few studies have assessed workplace social control, focusing primarily on supervisor monitoring and job visibility. Some research supports a relation between workplace social control and overall and workplace substance use (Frone, 2003b; Trice and Sonnenstuhl, 1990), whereas other research fails to support this relation (MacDonald et al., 1999). Because the measures used have not assessed all dimensions of social control, prior research provides a limited test of the relation of social control to employee substance use.

Workplace stress

The workplace stress paradigm has received much more empirical attention, and posits that employee alcohol and other drug use represents a strategy to cope with negative emotions resulting from exposure to aversive physical and psychosocial qualities of the work environment (Ames and Janes, 1992; Frone, 1999; Trice and Sonnenstuhl, 1990). This paradigm derives from the notion of tension reduction developed in the literature on alcohol use. First introduced by Conger (1956), the tension-reduction hypothesis has two general propositions. The stress-response dampening proposition states that substance use will reduce tension or strain resulting from exposure to stressors (e.g., Sayette, 1993, 1999). The stress-induced drinking proposition states that exposure to stressors will induce substance use as a means of mitigating experienced tension and strain (e.g., Frone, 1999; Sayette, 1993, 1999). Most work stress research has tested the stress-induced substance use proposition that more frequent exposure to work stressors is expected to cause more frequent use of alcohol and drugs. The workplace stress paradigm also is consistent with a broader literature that supports the use of substances for affect regulation (e.g., Cooper et al., 1995; Peirce et al., 2000).

Research on work stress and substance use has focused primarily on alcohol use, with relatively little attention devoted to illicit drug use. Frone (1999) categorized the available studies along two dimensions. The first dimension reflected two general categories of work stressors. The work stressors either represented those that occur within the work role (within-role work stressors, such as work demands) or those that occur at the interface of work and family life, such as work-to-family and family-to-work conflict, collectively referred to as work-family conflict (e.g., Bellavia and Frone, 2005; Frone, 2003c).

The second dimension reflected the four types of conceptual models employed. The first model is the simple cause-effect model, which simply postulates an overall direct relation between work stressors and alcohol use. The second model is the mediation model, which explicitly incorporates the intervening variables thought to link work stressors to alcohol use. Thus, the mediation model goes beyond the simple cause-effect model by trying to explain *why* or *by what mechanism* work stressors are related to alcohol use. The third model is the moderation model, which explicitly includes variables that moderate the relation between work stressors and alcohol use. This model is interactional in that work stressors interact with certain characteristics that place a worker at increased risk for alcohol use and misuse in response to work stressors. The moderator model, therefore, goes beyond the simple cause-effect model by trying to explain *when* or *under what conditions* work stressors are related to alcohol use. The fourth model is the moderated mediation model, which combines the features of the mediation and the moderation models. By explicitly including both mediating and moderating variables, the moderated mediation model goes beyond each of the other three models by simultaneously

trying to explain *how* as well as *when* work stressors are related to alcohol use.

Most research on work stress and alcohol use has tested the simple cause-effect model. However, little support exists for this model in relation to within-role work stressors (Frone, 1999), which is also consistent with subsequent research (e.g., Kouvonen et al., 2005; Weisner et al., 2005). In contrast, research assessing the between-role stressor of work-family conflict has provided more consistent support for the simple cause-effect model (Frone, 1999). Although one study failed to find a relation between work-family conflict and substance use (Steptoe et al., 1998), five studies collectively provide both cross-sectional (Bromet et al., 1990; Frone, 2000; Frone et al., 1996; Roos et al., 2006) and longitudinal (Frone et al., 1997) support for this relation.

Several studies have explored mediational models linking work stressors to substance use. Although some studies of within-role work stressors failed to support the mediating role of negative affect (Cooper et al., 1990; Kawakami et al., 1993; Richman et al., 2002), others support the mediating role of negative affect (Greenburg and Grunberg, 1995; Martin et al., 1992; Vasse et al., 1998). In addition to negative affect, Delaney et al. (2002) found that inability to unwind after work mediated the relation between job problems and alcohol use. Turning to between-role work stressors, two studies supported the mediating role of negative affect in the relation between work-family conflict and alcohol use (Frone et al., 1994; Vasse et al., 1998).

Three studies tested and provided support for the moderation model of work stress and alcohol use in relation to within-role work stressors (Bacharach et al., 2002; Frone et al., 1995; Grunberg et al., 1999). For example, building from identity theory, Frone et al. (1995) found that both job demands and role ambiguity were positively related to heavy drinking only among employees who reported that their work role was psychologically important for self-definition. One study explored and supported the moderation model with the between-role stressor of work-family conflict. Frone and colleagues (1993) found that work-family conflict was positively related to problem drinking only among people with strong affect regulation expectancies.

Two studies have tested and provided support for a moderated mediation model of work stress and alcohol use using within-role work stressors (Cooper et al., 1990; Grunberg et al., 1998). For example, Grunberg and colleagues (1998) found that work demands, interpersonal criticism from supervisors and co-workers, and feeling stuck in one's job were positively related to job dissatisfaction. Furthermore, they found that job dissatisfaction was related to problem drinking only among those who reported that they drank to reduce negative emotions. No studies have tested the moderated mediation model with respect to work-family conflict.

Although research on work stress and alcohol use has become increasingly sophisticated, it remains difficult to draw firm conclusions from this body of research and a number of issues need to be addressed (Frone, 1999). For example, prior research focused exclusively on measures of overall substance use. Thus, many nonsignificant and inconsistent results may result from the fact that measures of overall substance use primarily assess consumption that occurs at times and in settings far removed from the workday. Contextualized measures of substance use may provide a more consistent link to work stressors. To explore this possibility, Frone (2008) examined the relation of work overload and job insecurity to overall and contextualized measures of alcohol and illicit drug use in a national sample of the US workforce. The contextualized measures assessed alcohol and drug use within two hours of starting work, during the workday, and within two hours of leaving work. Consistent with past research, the results failed to support a link between the within-role work stressors and measures of overall alcohol and illicit drug use. However, the results provided consistent support for the relations of work stressors to alcohol and illicit drug use before work, during the workday, and

after work. In addition, the temporal assessment of substance use allowed tests of and provided support for both the stress-response dampening (substance use before work) and stress-induced substance use (substance use during and after work) propositions of the tension reduction hypothesis.

Future research

Regarding the work-related causes of employee substance use, several issues need more attention. First, more effort needs to be devoted to the development of measures of workplace physical availability and social availability (i.e., descriptive and injunctive norms). Available measures were developed for specific studies and therefore evidence of construct validity and cross-study comparisons of findings and conclusions remain tenuous. Second, research has not assessed all the different dimensions of workplace social control. Moreover, rarely are multiple dimensions of social control explored simultaneously to see which dimensions are uniquely predictive of employee substance use. In addition, research exploring the dimensionality of workplace social control is important. Third, studies of work stress have failed to explore systematically the various sources of work stress. Thus, we do not know which work stressors are the most important causes of employee substance use (see Barling et al., 2005, for recent reviews of established and emerging work stressors). Also, more research needs to explore the variables that mediate and moderate the relations between work stressors and employee substance use (Frone, 1999). Finally, future research on the causes of employee substance use needs to take a more sophisticated and more integrated approach that includes (a) the simultaneous main and interactive effects of several domains of predictors (demographics, personality, substance use expectancies, workplace availability, workplace social control, and work stressors) and (b) a broader assessment of employee substance use that explores specific classes of substances (alcohol, marijuana, depressants, stimulants) and takes into account the temporal context of substance use.

ORGANIZATIONAL CONSEQUENCES OF EMPLOYEE SUBSTANCE USE

The organizational consequences of employee substance use have received much attention and speculation. Despite the widely held belief that the use of alcohol and other psychoactive drugs among employees may have a strong and consistent negative relation to employee productivity, past research suggests that these relations are neither consistent nor robust. For example, a panel convened by the National Research Council-Institute of Medicine (NRC-IOM) concluded that 'Research support is most consistent … with absenteeism. For other types of outcomes, there is mixed or weak support, with very little support from better-designed studies' (Normand et al., 1994: 134).

In this section, I summarize research exploring the relation of employee alcohol and illicit drug use to three categories of organizational consequences:

(a) attendance outcomes;
(b) task performance and other on-the-job behaviors; and
(c) job accidents and injury outcomes.

Although a detailed review of this of literature cannot be provided in this chapter, the interested reader is referred to Frone (2004) and Normand et al. (1994) for additional information. I will then summarize a general model of substance use and employee productivity that begins to highlight the complexity of these relations (Frone, 2004).

Organizational consequences

Attendance outcomes

A general consensus exists across several older literature reviews that absenteeism is the most consistently documented organizational outcome related to employee substance use

(e.g., Martin et al., 1994; Normand et al., 1994; Zwerling, 1993). However, these conclusions were based on a small set of studies. More recent research suggests that some studies support a positive relation between employee substance use and poor attendance (e.g., Cunradi et al., 2005; McFarlin and Fals-Stewart, 2002) and some studies fail to support this relation (e.g., Boles et al., 2004; Moore et al., 2000; Vasse et al., 1998).

Given these inconsistent findings, a particularly interesting study was conducted by McFarlin and Fals-Stewart (2002). Using a sample of 280 employees from three organizations, each employee reported their use of alcohol during the preceding four weeks. A timeline follow-back measure of alcohol use was used where individuals initially reported the days on which they drank alcohol over the prior two weeks with the help of an interviewer. Two weeks later the measure was repeated. Company records were then used to identify the days absent during the same four week reporting period. A sequential analysis was conducted that allowed for lags of different lengths between alcohol use and being absent. Alcohol use was related to being absent the next day (Lag 1). Specifically, workers were approximately two times more likely to be absent from work the day after alcohol was consumed. However, alcohol use was not related to same day absenteeism (Lag 0) or to being absent two or more days (Lags 2 and greater) after drinking. Notwithstanding this study's strengths, the quantity of alcohol consumed was not assessed. As discussed later, being absent is likely the outcome of impairment (intoxication or hangover) due to heavy alcohol use and not the mere use of alcohol on a given day. The fact that the sample was primarily comprised of young men, who generally drink more heavily than other groups of workers, might explain the relation they found between the dichotomous alcohol measure (drank vs. did not drink) and absenteeism. However, to understand the underlying process that links alcohol use to absenteeism, failing to assess quantity consumed may (a) lead to the misleading conclusion that any alcohol use is related to absenteeism and (b) underestimate the size of the relation between dimensions of alcohol impairment and absenteeism.

Task performance and other on-the-job behaviors

Basic laboratory research on the acute effects of substance use generally shows that alcohol, marijuana, opioid analgesics, tranquilizers, and sedatives either have no effect or impair performance on a variety of tasks, such as time estimation, divided attention, tracking, vigilance, postural stability, and complex reaction time (e.g., Adams and Martin, 1996; Coambs and McAndrews, 1994; Folton and Evans, 1993; Heishman, 1998; MacDonald et al., 2003; Martin, 1998; Normand et al., 1994). In contrast, stimulants (which include cocaine) either have no effect or improve performance in laboratory settings (e.g., Coambs and McAndrews, 1994; Folton and Evans, 1993; Heishman, 1998; MacDonald et al., 2003; Normand et al., 1994).

Several laboratory studies have explored the acute effect of alcohol use on performance using work-related simulations. Even at low levels (e.g., blood-alcohol concentrations of 0.04 per cent to 0.09 per cent), acute exposure to alcohol can impair various dimensions of cognitive and psychomotor performance used for many jobs, such as drill press operation, punch press operation, assembly tasks, welding, maintaining a power plant on a merchant ship, piloting a merchant ship, and managerial performance (see Hahn and Price, 1994; Howland et al., 2001; Howland et al., 2000; Streufert et al., 1994). In contrast, work-related simulations have failed to find an effect of alcohol hangover on managerial performance (Streufert et al., 1995) and ship power plant operation (Rohsenow et al., 2006). Work simulation studies have not explored the acute effect of illicit psychoactive drugs or illicit use of prescription drugs on cognitive and psychomotor performance.

Although laboratory studies have strong internal validity, the statistically significant cognitive and psychomotor deficits are often weak in practical terms. Moreover, because laboratory studies and work simulations have weak external validity, it is not yet clear whether and how strongly they translate into actual changes in on-the-job behavior and performance (e.g., Heishman, 1998; MacDonald et al., 2003). Compared to laboratory research, field research has stronger external validity (though weaker internal validity) and has explored a broader set of performance and on-the-job behavioral outcomes. Several studies have reported that employee alcohol or illicit drug use is related to poorer job performance (e.g., Ames et al., 1997; Blum et al., 1993; Burton et al., 2005), whereas other research has failed to support such a relation (e.g., Boles et al., 2004; Burton et al. 2005; Moore et al., 2000). Research also has found that alcohol and drug use are related to lower levels of positive contextual performance, such as working overtime, volunteering for additional work, or trying to improve the job (Lehman and Simpson, 1992), and to higher levels of counterproductive behavior, such as psychological and physical withdrawal at work and the perpetration of aggression and antagonistic behaviors at work (e.g., Ames et al., 1997; Lehman and Simpson, 1992; McFarlin et al., 2001; Moore et al., 2000).

Accident and injury outcomes

Two sources of data address the relation between employee substance use and workplace accidents and injuries. The first source is data from coroner and medical examiner records and from emergency room visits. Zwerling (1993) estimated that acute alcohol impairment is present in approximately 10 per cent of fatal work injuries and 5 per cent of nonfatal work injuries. Based on the average positivity rates for over 35 million employee drug tests over a five year period (2002–2006), conducted by Quest Diagnostics Incorporated (2007), 3.0 per cent of post-accident drug tests were positive for at least one illicit drug in the federally mandated safety-sensitive workforce and 5.8 per cent of post-accident drug tests were positive in the general workforce. However, to conclude that an accident or injury was 'drug related' because some level of inactive metabolites are present in a person's urine is insufficient evidence that the substance played a causal role in the accident or injury. The primary problems with studies that report the proportion of drug-related injuries are the lack of a control condition and the inability of urine tests to discern the timing of substance use relative to the injury or accident and level of impairment. Nonetheless, the causal role of overall illicit drug use can be addressed by comparing the positivity rate from post-accident drug tests to the positivity rate from random drug tests. If employee drug use plays a major role in workplace accidents and injuries, the positivity rate for post-accident drug tests (3.0 per cent in the safety-sensitive workforce; 5.8 per cent in the general workforce) would be substantially higher than the positivity rate for random drug tests (1.8 per cent in the safety-sensitive workforce; 6.3 per cent in the general workforce). Thus, these comparisons do not support a causal role for overall employee drug use in workplace accidents and injuries.

The second source of data comes from epidemiologic field studies that attempt to estimate the relation between employee substance use and work accidents or injuries. Several reviews conducted during the 1990s concluded that there was no consistent and robust relation between employee substance use and workplace accidents or injuries (e.g., Feinauer, 1990; Macdonald, 1997; Normand et al., 1994; Stallones and Kraus, 1993; Webb et al., 1994; Zwerling, 1993). Nonetheless, because of various methodological weaknesses, earlier reviews also suggested that it was premature to conclude that employee substance use plays no causal role in the etiology of workplace injuries and accidents. More recent field studies show that with few exceptions (Fan et al., 2006; Ragland et al., 2002), overall employee alcohol and illicit drug use are not significantly related to workplace injuries (Chau et al., 2004; Craig et al., 2006; Frone, 1998; Spicer et al., 2003; Veazie and Smith, 2000; Wadsworth et al., 2003, 2006a,

2006b), but see the discussion in the next section.

A general model of employee substance use and productivity

Considerable inconsistency exists in research findings relating employee substance use to several dimensions of organizational outcomes. Some of the inconsistency is found across field studies exploring different outcomes (e.g., injuries, attendance, and task performance) and some is found comparing laboratory studies exploring cognitive and psychomotor impairment to field studies of various productivity outcomes. These inconsistencies may not be surprising because most researchers have set out to test a simple and perhaps misguided hypothesis: Employee substance use is related to unfavorable productivity outcomes (Frone, 2004). Although its simplicity is appealing, this hypothesis is based on the often unrecognized assumption of causal homogeneity. In other words, it is assumed that the mere consumption of a psychoactive substance will have the same effect across all productivity outcomes for all employees. The general alcohol and drug literature, however, suggests that the underlying process linking employee substance use to workplace productivity may be more complicated. Failing to account for this complexity may explain much of the incongruity in past research findings.

To account for these inconsistencies and to highlight the underlying complexity in the relations between employee substance use and productivity, Frone (2004) developed the conceptual model depicted in Figure 2. I will briefly summarize the major features of this model, though the reader is referred to the original source for a detailed discussion of the development this conceptual model. The first general feature of the model is that the context of substance use is matched to specific organizational outcomes. In past research, researchers have typically assessed employees' overall alcohol and drug use, which largely reflects substance use off the job (i.e., use away from work and

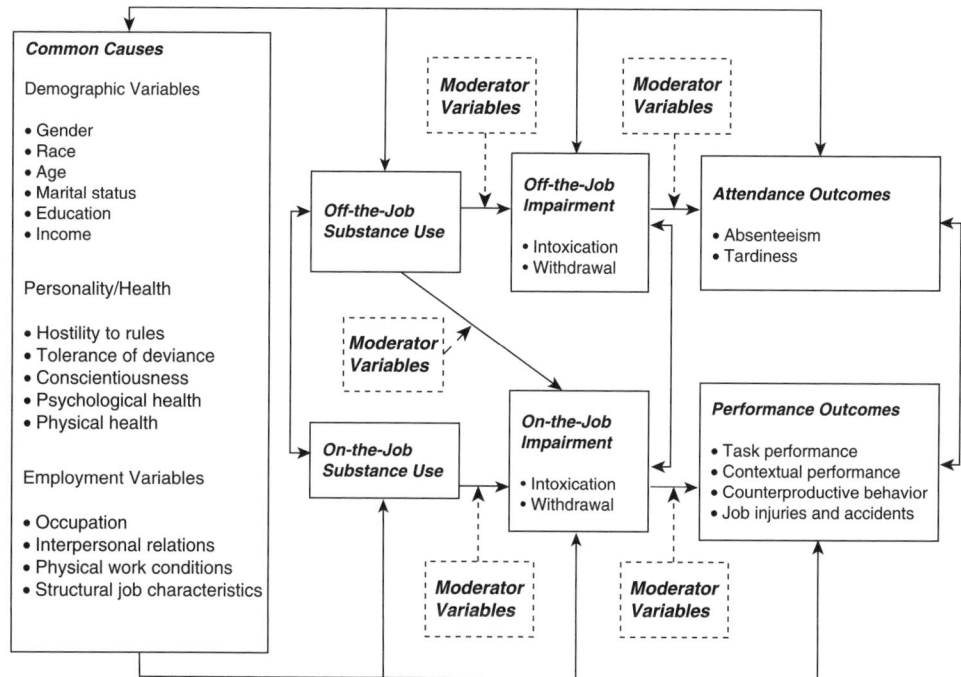

Figure 2   Predictors of employee substance use. Reprinted with permission from Frone, M. R. (2004). Alcohol, drugs, and workplace safety outcomes: A view from a general model of employee substance use and productivity. In J. Barling and M. R. Frone (eds), *The Psychology of Workplace Safety.* **Washington, DC: American Psychological Association. Copyright ©2004 by the American Psychological Association.**

outside an individual's normal work hours). Thus, it is important to explicitly distinguish between off-the-job and on-the-job substance use and impairment. It is also important to distinguish between attendance and performance outcomes. Attendance outcomes represent the failure to come to work on time (tardiness) or the failure to come to work at all (absenteeism). Performance outcomes represent behaviors and outcomes that occur on the job, such as accidents and injuries, task performance, contextual performance, and counterproductive behaviors. As shown in Figure 2, the model proposes that there is a correspondence between the context of employee substance use and impairment and the type of productivity outcomes affected. In other words, off-the-job substance use and impairment primarily predict attendance outcomes and on-the-job substance use and impairment predict performance outcomes. To the extent that

the overall substance use measures used in prior studies differed in the degree to which they indirectly captured workplace substance use, inconsistencies across studies exploring the relation of employee substance use to the performance outcomes would be expected.

The second general feature of the model is that it distinguishes between substance use and substance impairment (see definitions provided earlier). The model proposes that substance impairment is the proximal cause of poor productivity outcomes and mediates the more distal effect of substance use. Specifically, increasing levels of off-the-job substance use are expected to cause higher levels of intoxication and more severe withdrawal (when substance use is decreased) off the job, which then causes poor attendance. Likewise, higher levels of off-the-job substance use may be related to intoxication at work because individuals may still have a non-zero blood level when they arrive at work, and withdrawal symptoms at work may be more severe among chronic heavy off-the-job substance users if they do not consume the substance during their work shift. Also, higher levels of on-the-job substance use are expected to cause higher levels of on-the-job intoxication. In turn, on-the-job intoxication and withdrawal are expected to negatively affect performance outcomes.

Thus, the distinction between substance use and substance impairment may help explain inconsistencies in prior research. For example, as discussed earlier, past reviewers concluded that employee substance use had the most consistent relation to attendance outcomes. However, a broader review of more recent studies shows a fair amount of inconsistency regarding this relation. To explain this inconsistency, one must consider that some studies merely compare the attendance behaviors of substance users to non-users. Also, even studies that used measures of overall frequency and quantity of use may have differed substantially in the proportion of subjects at the higher end of the frequency and quantity distributions. To the extent that past studies differed in the degree to which the measures of substance use captured meaningful substance impairment off the job, one would expect between-study variation in support for a relation between employee substance use and attendance outcomes. Parallel explanations also can be developed for inconsistencies in results involving the other productivity outcomes.

The third general feature of the model is that it calls attention to the need to control for common causes of employee substance use and the various productivity outcomes. Care must be taken in the interpretation of some prior studies that have supported relations between employee substance use and the various organizational outcomes. Much of this research has lacked adequate controls for common causes of substance use, substance impairment, and productivity. Differences across studies in the potential confounding variables that were modeled may partly explain inconsistencies across studies

in the extent to which employee substance use was related to specific outcomes.

The final general feature of the model is that it highlights the need to consider variables that may moderate the various relations involving substance use, substance impairment, and the organizational outcomes. Frone (2004) discussed various moderating processes that included pharmacological, dispositional, motivational, and situational influences. As shown in Figure 2, variables may moderate the relation between substance use and substance impairment and between substance impairment and the productivity outcomes. For example, the relation between substance use and substance intoxication may be affected by between-person differences in the physiological processes of absorption, distribution, and metabolism and elimination. These physiological processes influence the concentration of a substance in blood for a given dose. Specific moderators that influence these processes include mode of administration (e.g., oral, injection, inhalation, intranasal and sublingual), first-pass metabolism, biochemical properties of the drug (e.g., water or fat solubility and binding properties), physiological factors (e.g., diffusibility of membranes and tissues, amount of body water or amount of body fat), gender, age, pharmacokinetic tolerance (i.e., dispositional tolerance or metabolic tolerance), and pharmacodynamic tolerance (i.e., functional tolerance or cellular tolerance). The relation between substance intoxication and productivity may be moderated by behavioral (or learned) tolerance, latent potential for workplace injuries, age, and propensity for risk-taking.

Future research

The conceptual model presents a detailed guide to help future research gain a more comprehensive understanding of the impact of employee substance use on workplace productivity. To date, little research has directly tested the various processes outlined in the model and no research has attempted a full test of the proposed model. Nonetheless, a few studies have provided partial support for the model. For example, Hoffman et al. (1997) examined the relation of overall drug use and heavy drinking to absenteeism and workplace accidents. They found that overall (i.e., off-the-job) drug use and heavy drinking were related to higher absenteeism but were unrelated to workplace accidents. Similarly, an evaluation study of pre-employment drug testing found that positive test results were related to higher levels of absenteeism, but were unrelated to workplace injuries and accidents (Normand et al., 1990). Frone (1998) examined the relation of overall (i.e., off-the-job) and on-the-job substance use (combined use of alcohol and marijuana) to job injuries in a sample of young workers. At the bivariate level, both overall and on-the-job substance use were related to an elevated rate of job injuries. However, after controlling for 18 potential common causes of employee substance use and work injuries (demographics, personality variables, work characteristics, and health variables), when both substance use measures were analyzed simultaneously, only on-the-job substance use predicted injuries. Ames et al. (1997) examined the simultaneous relation of on-the-job alcohol use and overall alcohol use to several dimensions of work performance in a sample of manufacturing employees. In a multiple regression analysis that controlled for several demographic and employment covariates, only on-the-job alcohol use was related to poor performance.

CONCLUSION

The goal of this chapter was to review what we know and do not know about the scope, causes, and organizational consequences of employee substance use. Recommendations for future research were also presented. Regarding the scope of alcohol and illicit drug use in the workforce and in the workplace, detailed data are beginning to be published in the US. However, detailed published data for other countries are scarce. Data from the US support several general conclusions.

First, despite the attention devoted to illicit drug use, alcohol is likely to be more problematic for employers than illicit drugs. Alcohol use and impairment in the workforce and workplace are much more prevalent than illicit drug use and impairment in the workforce and workplace. Second, illicit drug use primarily reflects the use of marijuana. Third, comparing the prevalence of workforce and workplace substance use shows that most substance use and impairment occurs outside the workplace. In other words, 79 per cent of employees who use alcohol do not report any workplace alcohol use and 78 per cent of those who report illicit drug use do not report any workplace illicit drug use. Finally, alcohol and illicit drug use in the workforce and in the workplace are not distributed uniformly in the working population. The primary factors related to the distribution of substance use are gender, age, and occupation. This means that not all employers are affected equally and that substance use, especially illicit drug use, is not a major issue for most employers. Nonetheless, those employers who draw from the three high-risk segments of the workforce identified earlier may be more likely to deal with problems related to overall and workplace substance use.

Research findings on the causes and outcomes of employee substance use are inconsistent and inconclusive. This is partly due to a lack of research in some areas and partly due to conceptual and measurement shortcomings. As discussed throughout this review, future research needs to be much more sophisticated and integrated if we are to (a) better understand the role of causes that are external (e.g., demographics, personality, substance use outcome expectancies) and internal (social control, physical and social availability, and work stressors) to the workplace and (b) better understand the complex relation of employee substance use to organizational outcomes. The ability of relevant stakeholders to develop defensible and effective evidence-based policies and interventions regarding employee substance will require increasing the quantity and improving the quality of research being conducted. It is hoped that this review will motivate additional research on the scope of substance use in the workforce and in the workplace and a new generation of integrative theoretical research on the causes and organizational outcomes of employee substance use.

REFERENCES

Alberta Alcohol and Drug Abuse Commission (2003) *Substance Use and Gambling in the Alberta Workplace, 2002: A Replication Study* (technical report) Alberta, Canada: Author.

Adams, I.B. and Martin, B. (1996) 'Cannabis: Pharmacology and toxicology in animals and humans', *Addiction*, 91: 1585–1614.

American Psychiatric Association (1994) *Diagnostic and Statistical Manual of Mental Disorders* (4th edn). Washington, DC: Author.

Ames, G.M. (1993) 'Research strategies for the primary prevention of workplace alcohol problems', *Alcohol Health and Research World*, 7: 19–27.

Ames, G. and Janes, C.J. (1992) 'A cultural approach to conceptualizing alcohol and the workplace', *Alcohol Health and Research World*, 16: 112–119.

Ames, G.M. and Grube, J.W. (1999) 'Alcohol availability and workplace drinking: Mixed method analyses', *Journal of Studies on Alcohol*, 60: 383–393.

Ames, G.M., Grube, J.W. and Moore, R.S. (2000) 'Social control and workplace drinking norms: A comparison of two organizational cultures', *Journal of Studies on Alcohol*, 61: 203–219.

Ames, G.M., Grube, J.W. and Moore, R.S. (1997) 'The relationship of drinking and hangovers to workplace problems: An empirical study', *Journal of Studies on Alcohol*, 58: 37–47.

Anthony, J.C. and Arria, A.M. (1999) 'Epidemiology of substance abuse in Adulthood', in P.J. Ott, R.E. Tarter and R.T. Ammerman (eds), *Sourcebook on Substance Abuse: Etiology, Epidemiology, Assessment, and Treatment*. Boston: Allyn & Bacon, pp. 32–49.

Bacharach, S.B., Bamberger, P.A. and Sonnenstuhl, W.J. (2002) 'Driven to drink: Managerial control, work-related risk factors, and employee problem drinking', *Academy of Management Journal*, 45: 637–658.

Bamberger, P. and Biron, M. (2006) 'The prevalence and distribution of employee substance-related problems and programs in the Israeli workplace', *Journal of Drug Issues*, 36: 755–786.

Barling, J., Kelloway, E.K. and Frone, M.R. (eds) (2005) *Handbook of Work Stress*. Thousand Oaks, CA: Sage.

Bellavia, G, and Frone, M.R. (2005) 'Work-family conflict', in J. Barling, E.K. Kelloway, and M.R. Frone (eds), *Handbook of Work Stress*. Thousand Oaks, CA: Sage.

Blum, T.C., Roman, P.M. and Martin, J.K. (1993) 'Alcohol consumption and work performance', *Journal of Studies on Alcohol*, 54: 61–70.

Boles, M., Pelletier, B. and Lynch, W. (2004) 'The relationship between health risks and work productivity', *Journal of Occupational and Environmental Medicine*, 46: 737–745.

Bromet, E.J., Dew, M.A. and Parkinson, D.K. (1990) 'Spillover between work and family: A study of blue-collar working women', in J. Eckenrode, and S. Gore (eds), *Stress Between Work and Family*. New York: Plenum Press, pp. 133–151.

Burton, W.N., Chen, C.-Y., Conti, D.J., Schultz, A.B., Pransky, G. and Edington, D.W. (2005) 'The association of health risks with on-the-job productivity', *Journal of Occupational and Environmental Medicine*, 47: 769–777.

Bywood, P., Pidd, K. and Roche, A. (2006) *Illicit Drugs in the Australian Workforce: Prevalence and Patterns of Use*. Canberra, Australia: National Centre for Education and Training on Addiction.

Chau, N., Mur, J.M., Touron, C., Benamghar, L. and Dehaene, D. (2004) 'Correlates of occupational injuries for various jobs in railway workers', *Journal of Occupational Health*, 46: 272–280.

Christiansen, B.A. and Goldman, M.S. (1983) 'Alcohol related expectancies vs. demographic/background variables in the prediction of adolescent drinking', *Journal of Consulting and Clinical Psychology*, 51: 249–257.

Coambs, R.B. and McAndrews, M.P. (1994) 'The effects of psychoactive substances on workplace performance', in S. Macdonald and P.M. Roman (eds), *Research Advances in Alcohol and Drug Problems: Vol. 4. Drug Testing in the Workplace*. New York: Plenum.

Colder, C.R. and Chassin, L. (1997) 'Affectivity and impulsivity: Temperament risk for adolescent alcohol involvement', *Psychology of Addictive Behaviors*, 11: 83–97.

Conger, J. (1956) 'Reinforcement theory and the dynamics of alcoholism', *Quarterly Journal of Studies on Alcohol*, 17: 296–305.

Cooper, M.L., Frone, M.R., Russell, M. and Mudar, P. (1995) 'Drinking to regulate positive and negative emotions: A motivational model of alcohol use', *Journal of Personality and Social Psychology*, 69: 990–1005.

Cooper, M.L., Russell, M. and Frone, M.R. (1990) 'Work stress and alcohol effects: A test of stress-induced drinking', *Journal of Health and Social Behavior*, 31: 260–276.

Costa e Silva, J.A. (2002) 'Evidence-based analysis of the worldwide abuse of licit and illicit drugs', *Human Psychopharmacology*, 17: 131–140.

Craig, B.N., Congleton, J.J., Kerk, C.J., Amendola, A.A. and Gaines, W.G. (2006) Personal and non-occupational risk factors and occupational injury/illness', *American Journal of Industrial Medicine*, 49: 249–260.

Cunradi, C.B., Greiner, B.A., Ragland, D.R. and Fisher, J. (2005) 'Alcohol, stress-related factors, and short-term absenteeism among urban transit operators', *Journal of Urban Health*, 82: 43–57.

Delaney, W.P., Grube, J.W., Greiner, B., Fisher, J.M, and Ragland, D.R. (2002) 'Job stress, unwinding and drinking in transit operators', *Journal of Studies on Alcohol*, 63: 420–429.

Elkins, I.J., King, S.M., McGue, M. and Iacono, W.G. (2006) 'Personality traits and the development of nicotine, alcohol, and illicit drug disorders: Prospective links from adolescence to young adulthood', *Journal of Abnormal Psychology*, 115: 26–39.

Fan, Z.J., Bonauto, D.K., Foley, M.P. and Silverstein, B.A. (2006) 'Underreporting of work-related injury or illness to workers' compensation: Individual and industry factors', *Journal of Occupational and Environmental Medicine*, 48: 914–922.

Feinauer, D.M. (1990) 'The relationship between workplace accident rates and drug and alcohol abuse: The unproven hypothesis', *Labor Studies Journal*, 15: 3–15.

Firebaugh, G. (1997) *Analyzing Repeated Surveys*. Thousand Oaks, CA: Sage.

Folton, R.W. and Evans, S.M. (1993) 'Performance effects of drugs of abuse: A methodological survey', *Human Psychopharmacology*, 8: 9–19.

French, M.T, Zarkin, G.A. and. Dunlap, L.J. (1998) 'Illicit drug use, absenteeism, and earnings at six US worksites', *Contemporary Economic Policy*, 16: 334–346.

Frone, M.R. (1998) 'Predictors of work injuries among employed adolescents', *Journal of Applied Psychology*, 83: 565–576.

Frone, M.R. (1999) 'Work stress and alcohol use', *Alcohol Research and Health*, 23: 284–291. Available at: http://pubs.niaaa.nih.gov/publications/arh23–4/284–291.pdf

Frone, M.R. (2000) 'Work-family conflict and employee psychiatric disorders: The national comorbidity survey', *Journal of Applied Psychology*, 85: 888–895.

Frone, M.R. (2003a) *The National Survey of Workplace Health and Safety*. Unpublished survey data.

Frone, M.R. (2003b) 'Predictors of overall and on-the-job substance use among young workers', *Journal of Occupational Health Psychology*, 8: 39–54.

Frone, M.R. (2003c) 'Work-family balance', in J.C. Quick and L.E. Tetrick (eds), *Handbook of Occupational Health Psychology*. Washington, DC: American Psychological Association, pp. 143–162.

Frone, M.R. (2004) 'Alcohol, Drugs, and Workplace Safety Outcomes: A View from a General Model of Employee Substance Use and Productivity', in J. Barling and M.R. Frone (eds), *The Psychology of Workplace Safety*. Washington, DC: American Psychological Association, pp. 127–156.

Frone, M.R. (2006a) 'Prevalence and distribution of alcohol use and impairment in the workplace: A US national survey', *Journal of Studies on Alcohol*, 76: 147–156.

Frone, M.R. (2006b) 'Prevalence and distribution of illicit drug use in the workforce and in the workplace: Findings and implications from a US national survey', *Journal of Applied Psychology*, 91: 856–869.

Frone, M.R. (2008) 'Are work stressors related to employee substance use? The importance of temporal context in assessments of alcohol and illicit drug use', *Journal of Applied Psychology*, 93: 199–206.

Frone, M.R., Barnes, G.M. and Farrell, M.P. (1994) 'Relationship of work-family conflict to substance use among employed mothers: The role of negative affect', *Journal of Marriage and the Family*, 56: 1019–1030.

Frone, M.R., Russell, M. and Barnes, G.M. (1996) 'Work-family conflict, gender, and health-related outcomes: A study of employed parents in two community samples', *Journal of Occupational Health Psychology*, 1: 57–69.

Frone, M.R., Russell, M. and Cooper, M.L. (1993) 'Relationship of work-family conflict, gender, and alcohol expectancies to alcohol use/abuse', *Journal of Organizational Behavior*, 14:, 545–558.

Frone, M.R., Russell, M. and Cooper, M.L. (1995) 'Job stressors, job involvement, and employee health: A test of identity theory', *Journal of Occupational and Organizational Psychology*, 68: 1–11.

Frone, M.R., Russell, M. and Cooper, M.L. (1997) 'Relation of work-family conflict to health outcomes: A four-year longitudinal study of employed parents', *Journal of Occupational and Organizational Psychology*, 70: 325–336.

George, W.H., Frone, M.R., Cooper, M.L., Russell, M., Skinner, J.B. and Windle, M. (1995) 'A revised alcohol expectancy questionnaire: Factor structure confirmation and invariance in a general population sample', *Journal of Studies on Alcohol*, 56: 177–185.

Goldman, M.S., Brown, S.A. and Christiansen, B.A. (1987) 'Expectancy Theory: Thinking About Drinking', in H.T. Blane and K.E. Leonard (eds), *Psychological Theories of Drinking and Alcoholism*. New York: Guilford Press, pp. 181–226.

Grant, S. and Langan–Fox, J. (2007) 'Personality and the occupational stressor–strain relationship: The role of the big five', *Journal of Occupational Health Psychology*, 12: 20–33.

Greenberg, E.S. and Grunberg, L. (1995) 'Work alienation and problem alcohol behavior', *Journal of Health and Social Behavior*, 36: 83–102.

Grunberg, L., Moore, S. and Greenberg, E.S. (1998) 'Work stress and problem alcohol behavior: A test of the spill-over model', *Journal of Organizational Behavior*, 19: 487–502.

Grunberg, L., Moore, S., Anderson-Connolly, R. and Greenberg, E.S. (1999) 'Work stress and self-reported alcohol use: The moderating role of escapist reasons for drinking', *Journal of Occupational Health Psychology*, 4: 29–36.

Hahn, H.A. and Price, D.L. (1994) 'Assessment of the relative effects of alcohol on different types of job behavior', *Ergonomics*, 37: 435–448.

Heishman, S.J. (1998) 'Effects of abused drugs on human performance: Laboratory assessment', in S.B. Karach (ed.), *Drug Abuse Handbook*. New York: CRC Press, pp. 206–235.

Hoffmann, J.P., Brittingham, A. and Larison, C. (1996) *Drug Use among US Workers: Prevalence and Trends by Occupation and Industry Categories* (DHHS Pub. No. SMA 96–3089) Washington, DC: US Government Printing Office.

Hoffmann, J.P., Larison, C. and Sanderson, A. (1997) *An Analysis of Worker Drug Use and Workplace Policies and Programs* (DHHS Pub. No. SMA 97–3142) Washington, DC: US Government Printing Office.

Howland, J., Rohsenow, D.J., Cote, J., Gomez, B., Mangione, T.W. and Laramie, A.K. (2001) 'Effects of low-dose alcohol exposure on simulated merchant ship piloting by maritime cadets', *Accident Analysis and Prevention*, 33: 257–265.

Howland, J., Rohsenow, D.J., Cote, J., Siegel, M. and Mangione, T.W. (2000) 'Effects of low-dose alcohol exposure on simulated merchant ship handling power plant operations by maritime cadets', *Addiction*, 95: 719–726.

Jackson, K.M. and Sher, K.J. (2003) 'Alcohol use disorders and psychological distress: A prospective state–trait analysis', *Journal of Abnormal Psychology*, 112: 599–613.

Kawakami, N., Araki, S., Haratani, T. and Hemmi, T. (1993) 'Relations of work stress to alcohol use and drinking problems in male and female employees of a computer factory', *Environmental Research*, 62: 314–324.

King, K.M. and Chassin, L. (2004) 'Mediating and moderating effects of adolescent behavioral undercontrol and parenting in the prediction of drug use disorders in emerging adulthood', *Psychology of Addictive Behaviors*, 18: 239–249.

Kirsch, I. (1999) 'Response expectancy: An introduction', in I. Kirsch (ed.), *How Expectancies Shape Experience*. Washington, DC: American Psychological Association, pp. 3–13.

Kjærheim, K., Mykletun, R., Aasland, O.G., Haldorsen, T. and Andersen, A. (1995) 'Heavy drinking in the restaurant business: The role of social modeling and structural factors of the work-place', *Addiction*, 90: 1487–1495.

Kouvonen, A., Kivimaki, M., Cox, S., Poikolainen, K., Cox, T. and Vahtera, J. (2005) 'Job strain, effort–reward imbalance, and heavy drinking: A study in 40,851 employees', *Journal of Occupational and Environmental Medicine*, 47: 503–515.

Lehman, W.E.K. and. Simpson, D.D. (1992) 'Employee substance use and on-the-job behaviors', *Journal of Applied Psychology*, 77: 308–321.

Macdonald, S. (1997) 'Work-place alcohol and drug testing: A review of the scientific evidence', *Drug and Alcohol Review*, 16: 251–259.

MacDonald, S., Anglin-Bodrug, K., Mann, R.E., Erickson, P., Hathaway, A., Chipman, M, and Rylett, M. (2003) 'Injury risk associated with cannabis and cocaine use', *Drug and Alcohol Dependence*, 72: 99–115.

MacDonald, S., Wells, S. and Wild, T.C. (1999) 'Occupational risk factors associated with alcohol and drug problems', *American Journal of Drug and Alcohol Abuse*, 25: 351–369.

Maltby, L.L. (1999) *Drug Testing: A Bad Investment*. New York: American Civil Liberties Union.

Martin, C.S. (1998) 'Measuring acute alcohol impairment', in S.B. Karach (ed.), *Drug Abuse Handbook*. New York: CRC Press, pp. 309–326.

Martin, J.K., Blum, T.C. and Roman, P.M. (1992) 'Drinking to cope and self-medication: Characteristics of jobs in relation to workers' drinking behavior', *Journal of Organizational Behavior*, 13: 55–71.

Martin, J.K., Kraft, J.M. and Roman, P.M. (1994) 'Extent and impact of alcohol and drug use problems in the workplace: A review of empirical evidence', in S. Macdonald and P.M. Roman (eds), *Research Advances in Alcohol and Drug Problems: Vol. 2. Drug Testing in the Workplace*. New York: Plenum.

McFarlin, S.K. and Fals-Stewart, W. (2002) 'Workplace absenteeism and alcohol use: A sequential analysis', *Psychology of Addictive Behaviors*, 16: 17–21.

McFarlin, S.K., Fals-Stewart, W, Major, D.A. and Justice, E.M. (2001) 'Alcohol use and workplace aggression: An examination of perpetration and victimization', *Journal of Substance Abuse*, 13: 303–321.

Moore, R.S. (1998) 'The hangover: An ambiguous concept in workplace alcohol policy', *Contemporary Drug Problems*, 25: 49–63.

Moore, S., Grunberg, L. and Greenberg, E. (2000) 'The relationships between alcohol problems and well-being, work attitudes, and performance: Are they monotonic?', *Journal of Substance Abuse*, 11: 183–204.

Newcomb, M. (1994) 'Prevalence of alcohol and other drug use on the job: Cause for concern or irrational hysteria?', *Journal of Drug Issues*, 24: 403–416.

Normand, J., Lempert, R.O. and O'Brien, C.P. (1994) *Under the Influence? Drugs and the American Work Force*. Washington, DC: National Academy Press.

Normand, J., Salyards, S.D. and Mahoney, J.J. (1990) 'An evaluation of preemployment drug testing', *Journal of Applied Psychology*, 75: 629–639.

O'Malley, P.M., Johnston, L.D. and Bachman, J.G. (1999) 'Epidemiology of substance abuse in adolescence', in P.J. Ott, R.E. Tarter, and R.T. Ammerman (eds), *Sourcebook on Substance Abuse: Etiology, Epidemiology, Assessment, and Treatment*. Boston: Allyn & Bacon, pp. 14–31.

Peirce, R.S., Frone, M.R., Russell, M., Cooper, M.L. and Mudar, P. (2000) 'A longitudinal model of social contact, social support, depression, and alcohol use', *Health Psychology*, 19: 28–38.

Pidd, K., Berry, J.G., Harrison, J.E., Roche, A.M., Driscoll, T.R. and Newson, R.S. (2006) *Alcohol and Work: Patterns of Use, Workplace Culture and Safety*. Injury research and Statistics Series Number 28. (AIHW cat no. INJCAT 82) Adelaide, Australia: Australian Institute of Health and Welfare.

Quest Diagnostics Incorporated (2007) *The Drug Testing Index*. Lyndhurst, NJ: Author.

Ragland, D.R., Krause, N., Greiner, B.A., Holman, B.L., Fisher, J.M. and Cunradi, C.B. (2002) 'Alcohol consumption and incidence of workers' compensation claims: A 5-year prospective study of urban transit operators', *Alcoholism: Clinical and Experimental Research*, 26: 1388–1394.

Richman, J.A., Shinsako, S.A., Rospenda, K.M., Flaherty, J.A. and Freels, S. (2002) 'Workplace harassment/abuse and alcohol-related outcomes: The mediating role of psychological distress', *Journal of Studies on Alcohol*, 63: 412–419.

Rohsenow, D.J., Howland, J., Minsky, S.J. and Arnedt, J.T. (2006) 'Effects of heavy drinking by maritime academy cadets on hangover, perceived sleep, and next-day ship power plant operation', *Journal of Studies on Alcohol*, 67: 406–415.

Roos, E., Lahelma, E. and Rahkonen, O. (2006) 'Work-family conflicts and drinking behaviours among employed men and women', *Drug and Alcohol Dependence*, 83: 49–56.

Saitz, R. (1998) 'Introduction to alcohol withdrawal', *Alcohol Health and Research World*, 22: 5–12.

Sayette, M.A. (1993) 'An appraisal–disruption model of alcohol's effects on stress responses in social drinkers', *Psychological Bulletin*, 114: 459–476.

Sayette, M.A. (1999) 'Does drinking reduce stress?', *Alcohol Research and Health*, 23: 250–255.

Schafer, J., and Brown, S.A. (1991) 'Marijuana and cocaine effect expectancies and drug use patterns', *Journal of Consulting and Clinical Psychology, 59,* 558–565.

Smith, A., Wadsworth, E., Moss, S. and Simpson, S. (2004) *The Scale and Impact of Illegal Drug Use by Workers* (Research Report 193) London: Health and Safety Executive.

Spicer, R.S., Miller, T.R. and Smith, G.S. (2003) 'Worker substance use, workplace problems and the risk of occupational injury: A matched case-control study', *Journal of Studies on Alcohol*, 64: 570–578.

Stallones, L. and Kraus, J.F. (1993) 'The occurrence and epidemiologic features of alcohol-related occupational injuries', *Addiction*, 88: 945–951.

Steptoe, A., Wardle, J., Lipsey, Z., Mills, R., Oliver, G., Jarvis, M. and Kirschbaum, C.A. (1998) 'Longitudinal study of workload and variations in psychological well-being, cortisol, smoking, and alcohol consumption', *Annals of Behavioral Medicine*, 20: 84–91.

Streufert, S., Pogash, R., Briang, D., Gingrich, D., Kantner, A., Landis, R., Lonardi, L., Roache, J. and Severs, W. (1995) 'Alcohol hangover and managerial effectiveness', *Alcoholism: Clinical and Experimental Research*, 19: 1141–1146.

Streufert, S., Pogash, R., Roache, J., Severs, W., Gingrich, D., Landis, R., Lonardi, L. and Kantner, A. (1994) 'Alcohol and managerial performance', *Journal of Studies* on Alcohol, 55: 230–238.

Swift, R. and. Davidson, D. (1998) 'Alcohol hangover: Mechanisms and mediators', *Alcohol Health and Research World*, 22l: 73–80.

Trice, H.M. and Sonnenstuhl, W.J. (1990) 'On the construction of drinking norms in work organizations', *Journal of Studies on Alcohol*, 51: 201–220.

US Department of Health and Human Services (1999) *Substance Use and Mental Health Characteristics by Employment Status* (DHHS Publication No. SMA 99–3311) Washington, DC: US Government Printing Office.

Vasse, R.M., Nijhuis, F.J.N. and Kok, G. (1998) 'Associations between work stress, alcohol consumption, and sickness absence', *Addiction*, 93: 231–241.

Veazie, M.A. and Smith, G.S. (2000) 'Heavy drinking, alcohol dependence, and injuries at work among young workers in the united states labor force', *Alcoholism: Clinical and Experimental*, 24: 1811–1819.

Wadsworth, E.J.K., Moss, S.C., Simpson, S.A. and Smith, A.P. (2003) 'Preliminary investigation of the association between psychotropic medication use and accidents, minor injuries and cognitive failures', *Human Psychopharmacology*, 18: 535–540.

Wadsworth, E.J.K., Moss, S.C., Simpson, S.A. and Smith, A.P. (2006a) 'A community based investigation of the association between cannabis use, injuries and accidents', *Human Psychopharmacology*, 20: 5–13.

Wadsworth, E.J.K., Moss, S.C., Simpson, S.A. and Smith, A.P. (2006b) 'Cannabis use, cognitive performance and mood in a sample of workers', *Journal of Psychopharmacology*, 20: 14–23.

Webb, G.R., Redman, S., Hennrikus, D.J., Kelman, G.R., Gibberd, R.W. and Sanson-Fisher, R.W. (1994) 'The relationships between high-risk and problem drinking and the occurrence of work injuries and related absences', *Journal of Studies on Alcohol*, 55: 434–446.

Weisner, M., Windle, M. and Freeman, A. (2005) 'Work stress, substance use, and depression among young adult workers: An examination of main and moderator effect models', *Journal of Occupational Health Psychology*, 10: 83–96.

Zwerling, C. (1993) 'Current practice and experience in drug and alcohol testing', *Bulletin on Narcotics*, 45: 155–196.

28

Psychology of Workplace Safety: A Thematic Review and Some Possibilities[1]

Anthony E. Carroll and Nick Turner

The prevalence of workplace injuries and fatalities suggests that safety in organizations should be a primary concern for both organizational researchers and practitioners. In calculating occupational injuries in 175 countries worldwide, Hämäläinen and colleagues (2006) estimated that 264 million workplace injuries occurred in 1998, with more than 700,000 workers a day suffering a workplace injury causing absence of three days or more.

Given such overwhelming statistics, it is not surprising that workplace safety has captured the attention of researchers from a range of social scientific and biomedical disciplines connected to organizational behavior. For example, social and applied psychologists have examined how various individual, group, and organizational factors contribute to the prediction of workplace injuries and safety-related work behaviors (e.g., Barling and Frone, 2004; Hofmann and Tetrick, 2003). At an organizational level of analysis, organizational sociologists and industrial relations scholars have investigated the impact of work and employment practices and workforce characteristics on the incidence of work safety-related incidents (e.g., Brown, 2002; Robinson and Smallman, 2006). Similarly, epidemiologists and other health-related researchers interested in policy-level issues have examined the etiology of workplace injuries (e.g., Veazie et al., 1994), the risk and cost assessments of occupational injuries (e.g., McCall and Horwitz, 2006), and the prevalence of occupational injuries and fatalities in various geographical regions, industries, and professions (e.g., Bunn et al., 2006). From both a research and practice perspective, workplace safety has become an arena of interdisciplinary concern from a wide spectrum of scientific disciplines.

NATURE OF WORKPLACE SAFETY AND CHAPTER SCOPE

With such a range of perspectives, it is important to define the nature of workplace safety to delimit the scope of this chapter. In this chapter, we concentrate on workplace safety from a behavioral perspective, focusing on understanding workplace safety outcomes (e.g., injuries, and safety-related work behaviors) and the individual differences and situational/environmental factors that may be determinants of these outcomes.

We neither examine nor debate the economic or legislative issues surrounding safety in organizations, as there are other sources (e.g., Boone and van Ours, 2006; Breslin et al., 2006; Lambert, 2004; Wheelwright, 2005) that explore these issues in much greater depth and more comprehensively than we can here. Furthermore, although some researchers have conducted post-hoc assessments of workplace-related disasters (e.g., the destruction of World Trade Center buildings in New York on September 11, 2001; Ryan et al., 2003) that implicitly concern workplace safety, this chapter will not address crisis management (e.g., Mitroff and McWhinney, 1990) or sensemaking perspectives (e.g., Weick, 1993) on safety. Finally, although researchers and practitioners often linguistically connect occupational health with occupational safety (such as in 'occupational health and safety') and the connection between psychological and physical health is in effect indisputable, we necessarily limit the focus of this chapter on workplace safety as the acute failure, everyday maintenance, and longer-term promotion of *physical well-being* in the workplace.[2] That is, while we will discuss a range of psychological factors that have been associated with physical safety at work, our emphasis is on the prediction of workplace safety outcomes. As such, our custom in this chapter will be to refer to acute failures of physical safety as injuries rather than accidents,[3] due to the causal assumption we believe is embedded in the latter term.

In the following sections, we briefly summarize our interpretation of the past, the present, and what we believe are some possibilities for research into the psychological study of workplace safety. The perspective on the past outlines what can be broadly classified as 'accident proneness' research, with a shift in perspective in more contemporary research to the individual differences and situational determinants associated with workplace safety outcomes. The perspective on future possibilities includes conceptual and methodological observations that, if addressed, we believe could serve to further our understanding of the causes and consequences of workplace safety.

THE PAST

Much of the early research on the psychology of workplace safety published in English originated in the United Kingdom (UK) at the turn of the twentieth century and accelerated during times of war. Government-funded research on workers in munitions factories during World War I described 'accident prone' individuals as people who had a natural propensity to be injured on the job (Nichols, 1997). Researchers attributed this to inadaptability on the part of the worker, and went as far as suggesting that encouraging accident-prone workers to work more safely was a waste of time, perhaps even a source of unnecessary apprehension. With the enthusiastic uptake of scientific management at the time, the rather vague concept of accident proneness swept into mainstream industrial thinking and became a popular factor in selecting workers for manufacturing settings. Social scientific interest in workplace injuries after World War II explored possible motivations of 'accident-prone' workers. Hill and Trist, (1953) asserted that work-related injuries were a form of withdrawal, and found an association between able-bodied absences and absences due to injuries. A subsequent study by the same authors (Hill and Trist, 1955) examined absences and injuries of employees over a four-year period and argued that employees used absences as a means for remaining with an organization, with absences peaking toward the second year of employment, a change from unsanctioned absences to sanctioned absences, and a decline in injuries over time. They asserted that this was due to a 'progressive acceptance of responsibility and progressive internalization of the firm as a good employing authority' (Hill and Trist, 1955: 137). Consequently, the underlying assumption of this research was that workers were to blame for injuries in the workplace, and that this ultimately happens when employees fail to internalize organizational values of their employer.

The next phase of accident proneness research began to focus on a range of individual differences and situational factors that might be related to the experience of workplace injuries. For example, Davids and Mahoney (1957) compared two groups of employees (one group had a total of 47 injuries over a 2-year period and the other group was injury-free) on a number of socially-desirable and socially-undesirable characteristics. The authors concluded that there was a small positive association between accident proneness and egocentricity, resentment, and anxiety. Furthermore, they found that there was a significant association between accident proneness and a negative attitude towards employment. A subsequent study by Kunce (1967) indicated that high accident rates were associated with high accident proneness scores from a sample of 62 industrial employees. Ironically, Kunce also found a negative relationship between job tenure and accident proneness, and rates suggesting that injuries were related to job experience and training. Nichols (1997) has challenged the assumptions of these early accident proneness studies, arguing that although they emphasized a socially determined approach to workplace safety, they often engaged in blaming the victim through their dispositional and psychoanalytical attributions, and drew conclusions from particularly small samples of participants. To its credit, accident proneness research, as Nichols (1997) has also argued, gave rise to

initial examination of potential psychosocial correlates of workplace safety outcomes.

The geographic divide between the UK and the United States (US) also paralleled separate bodies of accident proneness research. It seems the US accident proneness research was more critical in nature, and concerned the validity of methods and criteria used to assess the experience of workplace injuries. For example, Cobb (1940) challenged the fruitfulness of using injury rates as a measure of accident proneness, and Mintz and Blum (1949) similarly criticized the methodology used in accident proneness studies, suggesting that this led to an oversimplified view of the concept.

The majority of the research on the psychology of workplace safety in the post-war period in both the UK and the US shifted focus from dispositional and individual differences in motivation to employer practices, employee behaviors, and the connection between the two. By the mid-twentieth century, positions such as those advocated by Crawford (1960) emphasized the similarities amongst employees on injury rates, arguing that a focus on hazard exposure would be a more fruitful avenue for psychology to pursue in learning how to prevent workplace injuries. Over a decade later, Cohen et al. (1975) argued that differences in workplace injury rates may not lie solely with employees, but with management involvement in safety. They compared low-injury companies to high-injury companies and found that, in low-injury companies, top management was more often personally involved in safety activities on a routine basis. These findings are consistent with other empirical findings on top management involvement in safety conducted around the same time (e.g., Cleveland et al., 1978; Shafai-Sahrai, 1971), and served as a precursor to what would become safety climate research (e.g., Zohar, 1980).

A related stream of research emerged around this time which proposed behavioral modification as a way of encouraging employee safety behaviors and organizational safety programs designed to prevent occupational injuries by reinforcing safe work behaviors. As an example, Komaki et al. (1978) applied a behavioral analysis intervention in two departments of a food manufacturing plant. Their behavioral analysis consisted of identifying desired employee safety practices, explaining and presenting desired behaviors, and reinforcing desired behaviors. They found a significant improvement in safety performance of employees in both departments as a result of the intervention.

There are three criticisms levelled at behavioral modification workplace safety research. First, evaluation of many of these interventions suggests that they are not sustainable over time (i.e., the effects dissipate over time). Second, the majority of assessments of these interventions are short term in nature and often without attention to superior research designs. (e.g., placebo control groups) (Tuncel et al., 2006). Third, although the post accident-prone research focused less on dispositional approaches and more on behavioral modification, this latter research has largely ignored the cognitive-behavioral orientation that more fully implicates psychosocial mechanisms linking organizational practices and employee safety-related behaviors (Hopkins, 2006). More specifically, by attributing safety outcomes to sustained behavior modification, there was little sense of the psychological processes (e.g., ability-related, opportunity-related) that might be associated with desirable safety performance. This dearth of exploring the psychological processes paralleled similar research on the determinants of other performance outcomes more generally (e.g., Campbell et al., 1993). In the last twenty five years, contemporary research on the psychology of workplace safety has begun to focus on these issues to a much greater extent (e.g., Barling and Frone, 2004; Hofmann and Tetrick, 2003), and we now turn to these issues.

THE PRESENT

Research on the psychology of workplace safety from the 1980's onwards has broadly converged on the importance of the interaction among numerous individual differences (e.g., cognitive failure, personality and age) and situational factors (i.e., work characteristics, leadership and safety climate) in predicting safety-related outcomes (e.g., safety-related behaviors and injuries). In this section, we briefly review some representative findings of workplace safety research investigating the role of individual differences and situational factors, as well as what emerged at the same time regarding the broader conceptualization of workplace safety-related outcomes.

Some individual differences

Cognitive failure and Big Five personality traits

One individual difference that has begun to show particular prominence in predicting workplace injuries and employee safety-related behaviors is cognitive failure. Cognitive failure is defined as a breakdown in mental functioning that results in a mistake or error in task execution that an individual should normally be capable of completing (Broadbent et al., 1982; Martin, 1983). Recent research suggests that cognitive failures are associated with several important safety outcomes. For example, Wallace and Vodanovich (2003a, 2003b) found that cognitive failure was associated with work injuries and unsafe work behavior.

While individual differences such as cognitive failure have been considered important determinants of organizational behavior, personality factors more generally (e.g., openness, agreeableness, conscientiousness, extraversion, and neuroticism) have also been shown to be associated with a range of work-related attitudes (e.g., organizational commitment, Chan, 2006; job satisfaction, Raja et al., 2004) as well as dimensions of work performance (Dudley et al., 2006). Within the safety domain, there is now moderate evidence regarding the links between personality and workplace safety-related attitudes and outcomes. As an example, conscientiousness is one of the five factors that comprise the Big Five model of personality and refers to the extent to which individuals are dependable and dutiful (Barrick and Mount, 1991). Wallace and Vodanovich (2003b) examined the influence of cognitive failure on the relationship between conscientiousness and unsafe work behavior in a sample of production workers; the data showed that cognitive failure moderated the relationship, such that levels of unsafe behavior were the highest when conscientiousness was low and cognitive failure was high. In a subsequent multi-level study, Wallace and Chen (2006) hypothesized that regulatory focus mechanisms (prevention and promotion) would explain the reason why group safety climate and individual differences in conscientiousness relate to individual productivity and safety performance. Based on regulatory focus theory, promotion focus is characterized by a concern for accomplishing a greater quantity of work more quickly, whereas prevention focus is characterized by a concern for adhering to work-related rules. They found that conscientiousness predicted a prevention and promotion focus which, in turn, mediated the relationships of conscientiousness and safety climate with productivity and safety performance. These findings highlight the importance of conscientiousness on safety performance through the mechanisms of promotion and prevention orientations.

With regards to a broader range of personality characteristics, Clarke and Robertson (2005) performed a meta-analysis of the Big Five personality dimensions and safety incidents. They found that individuals who were low in agreeableness and conscientiousness are more likely to be involved in safety incidents. They also found that low agreeableness and neuroticism were significant personality predictors of safety incidents in occupational settings. The associations between low agreeableness and low conscientiousness with safety incidents demonstrated validity generalization, indicating that there are possible moderators between these personality characteristics and workplace safety incidents. In a related study, Clarke (2006) conducted

a meta-analysis of perceptual, attitudinal, and dispositional predictors of workplace injuries. She found that low agreeableness was a strong predictor of safety incidents and had greater predictive validity across occupational settings than safety perceptions, suggesting that personality plays a vital role in safety in the workplace. In short, personality factors have been shown to be associated with workplace safety behaviors and incidents; however, the predictive power of personality traits such as cognitive failure and the Big Five personality range is modest at best.

Age as a proxy for individual experience

Another individual difference that has consistently been shown to be related to workplace safety outcomes is age, which functions as a proxy for work and life experience (Castillo, 1999; Dupre, 2000; Frone, 1998). Young workers are particularly vulnerable to being injured at work (Loughlin and Frone, 2004), with adolescent workers often more likely than older workers to be injured on the job. In reviewing research on young workers and safety, we suggest that young workers may differ from their older counterparts in two relevant ways. First, the risk-taking orientation of young workers often reflects limited work and life experience: knowledge of potential workplace hazards through either little work experience or accumulated formal training is often less than adult workers doing the same job, and this lack of experience has been linked to increased injuries among young workers (Westaby and Lowe, 2005). Second, young workers are more likely than older workers to be working under contingent employment conditions (Loughlin and Barling, 1999). Contingent employment has been associated with inferior occupation safety outcomes (Quinlan and Bohle, 2004), often due to the lack of safety training provided to contingent workers and the limited power possessed by these workers relative to their permanently-employed counterparts to refuse dangerous work and stand up to supervisors responsible for task allocation. In general, young employees are often working in disadvantaged circumstances and politically marginalized in the workplace. As such, future research needs to examine ways young workers can protect themselves from dangerous work (e.g., speaking out; Mullen, 2005) and potential on-the-job circumstances (e.g., psychological safety, openness of supervisor, perceived autonomy) that might moderate the extent to which young workers can raise concerns.

In summary, there is evidence to suggest that individual differences such as cognitive failure, personality factors, and age (as a proxy for task and interpersonal experience) are related to workplace injuries and other safety outcomes. Understanding how individual difference and characteristics of the work situation might interact or intercede in predicting safety outcomes is another focus of contemporary safety research.

Some situational factors

Research has identified a number of features of the work environment that have been associated with workplace safety outcomes. While it is beyond the scope of this chapter to cover a fuller range of situational factors related to workplace safety outcomes (see Barling and Frone, 2004, for a comprehensive review), we discuss here how particular aspects of work design, leadership, and safety climate are related to workplace safety outcomes.

Work design: Job demands and job control as exemplars

There are various ways in which aspects of work design might affect the likelihood of work injury. For instance, job variety might alleviate boredom, increase attentiveness, and minimize the likelihood of cognitive failure, thereby reducing the risk of workplace injuries. In contrast, excessive cognitive or physical demands might put strain on employees, causing short cuts to be taken and increasing the risk of cognitive failure, thereby increasing the risk of injuries. Despite the intuitive connection between the psychological experience of work and physical experience of work-related injuries,

relatively few studies have investigated this connection, as consistently noted by a number of researchers from a variety of disciplines (e.g., Frone, 1998; Veazie et al., 1994). The limited set of studies that do examine work design factors in relation to injuries are highly diverse and pose a number of challenges in reconciling findings. First, existing studies do not use consistent definitions of work design factors or safety outcomes, making systematic comparisons of effects across studies difficult. For example, a study by Holcom et al. (1993) examines 'job characteristics' in predicting injury potential. However, what these researchers operationalize as 'power' is termed elsewhere in the work design literature as job control or autonomy; similarly, a construct labelled 'job tension' confounds elements of role stressors and social support. While some studies (e.g., Frone, 1998; Iverson and Erwin, 1997) use distinct measures of work characteristics, other studies (e.g., Neal et al., 2000) use broader constructs such as organizational climate to capture perceptions of the work environment, and others (e.g., Hemingway and Smith, 1999) blur the two.

With these types of inconsistencies, it is difficult to establish which factors of work design are associated with injury occurrence. At the same time, the different types of safety outcomes assessed add to the diversity of findings. Some studies use self-reported injury measures of varying specificity (e.g., Frone, 1998; Hemingway and Smith, 1999), whereas others draw injury data from company safety records (e.g., Iverson and Erwin, 1997; Murata et al., 2000) that invariably collect and classify injuries in different ways. While each of these types of outcomes has its merits and problems, the inconsistency makes robust comparisons across studies difficult.

Despite these methodological and contextual variations, the existing research does suggest that certain work characteristics are associated with workplace safety outcomes. What is unclear, however, is what characteristics are important under what circumstances. For example, across a number of models on a sample of working adolescents, Frone (1998) found that workload, job boredom, and physical hazards were three predictors of injury occurrence among a comprehensive set of other situational factors. However, in a similar analysis of an adult sample, Iverson and Erwin (1997) did not find the same relationship for physical hazards and role demands, but found a significant effect for routinization.

Although safety research has traditionally used injury rates as a key indicator of workplace safety, there is emerging interest in using more positive and proximal measures of workplace safety. Similar to the distinction between task and contextual performance that has been made in relation to job performance literature (e.g., Borman and Motowidlo, 1993), safety researchers in organizational behavior have identified two types of correlated safety behavior dimensions (see Burke et al., 2002, for a contextually-specific multidimensional model). The safety compliance dimension (Griffin and Neal, 2000), also referred to as carefulness (Andriessen, 1978) or compliance-with-safety-rules (Marchand et al., 1998) is analogous to task performance, and refers to behaviors such as adhering to safety regulations, reporting safety-related incidents, and wearing protective equipment. A second dimension, variously labelled as safety participation (Griffin and Neal, 2000), safety citizenship (Hofmann et al., 2003), safety initiative (Andriessen, 1978), or propensity to actively care for safety (Geller et al., 1996) parallels contextual performance, focusing on self-directed, discretionary behaviors such as making suggestions or volunteering to carry out safety audits.

Existing evidence about what aspects of work design predict these safety behaviors remains limited. For example, DeJoy et al. (2000) found that job-related hindrances were related to higher levels of personal protective equipment use, suggesting a relationship between work demands and safety compliance. When employees face undue work pressure, such as heightened production goals, there is a risk that safety procedures are ignored or forgotten in an effort to get production tasks done. Consistent with this,

there is evidence for the negative association of workload on compliance-related safety outcomes from both qualitative studies (e.g., Collinson, 1999) and quantitative studies (Hofmann and Stetzer, 1996) in organizational behavior.

Although excessive job demands such as workload may hinder safety behaviors, aspects of work design can also provide employees ways to prevent or manage these demands, such as in the form of enhanced job control. For instance, Parker et al. (2001) found in a longitudinal investigation of manufacturing employees that job autonomy was indirectly related to safety compliance via organizational commitment. They argued that job autonomy exerted both instrumental and symbolic effects on workers' propensity to follow the rules: employees had the control to decide if the rules were relevant (instrumental) and this autonomy also imparted a sense that the organization valued their skilled judgment (symbolic). Evidence of job control as a predictor of more discretionary safety behaviors (e.g., safety initiative) is more prevalent. Simard and Marchand (1995) found that job control was positively related to workgroups' propensity to take safety initiatives, and Geller et al. (1996) found that higher levels of perceived job control positively were positively related to caring for safety, in terms of effort exerted to ensure the safety of themselves and their co-workers.

One particular model linking aspects of work design and worker health that has received more research attention than definitive empirical support (de Lange et al., 2003) is Karasek's (1979) Job Demands-Control (JD-C) model. The Karasek model asserts that strain-producing jobs are those which encompass high job demands and low job control over work tasks. Within the workplace safety domain, Turner et al. (2005) applied the JD-C model in the prediction of safety citizenship role definition (i.e., the extent to which employees perceived workplace safety to be an implicit part of their role orientation; Hofmann et al., 2003). Consistent with Karasek's strain hypothesis, the data showed that participants with high demand/low control jobs reported lower safety citizenship role definition than those in other jobs, yet there was no evidence that high demand/high control jobs were associated with enhanced safety citizenship. These findings suggest that high job demands are associated with employees less likely to consider effortful safety behaviors as part of their work roles, but that this detrimental effect may be tempered by the level of job control these employees have.

Leadership as a determinant of safety climate

Leadership has been investigated as a determinant of a range of organizational outcomes and research in the psychology of workplace safety is no exception. Two leadership theories in particular have been the focus of research on workplace safety. The first, transformational leadership (Bass, 1985; Bass and Riggio, 2006), asserts that leaders influence their followers with four types of behavior (idealized influence, inspirational motivation, intellectual stimulation, individualized consideration). Recent research on transformational leadership has shown that transformational leadership predicts higher safety consciousness (Barling et al., 2002; Kelloway et al., 2006), lower safety-related events (i.e., events that precede injuries; Barling et al., 2002), and lower workplace injuries (i.e., Barling et al., 2002).

The second leadership theory is leader-member exchange (LMX), asserting that leaders develop exchange relationships with their followers, and that the quality of these exchange relationships influence follower outcomes. Like transformational leadership, past research has shown that LMX is related to team potency (e.g., Boies and Howell, 2006), work values (e.g., Schyns, 2006), and a range of citizenship behaviors (e.g., Bhal, 2006). Within the safety domain, Hofmann and colleagues (Hofmann and Morgeson, 1999; Hofmann, Morgeson, and Gerras, 2003) have asserted and found that in high-quality LMX relationships, followers reciprocate the leader-follower relationship

by extending their roles beyond their normal job requirements and engaging in a broader range of safety activities. This broader safety citizenship role definition, in turn, would be positively related to forms of safety participation.

One of the most salient safety-related outcomes of leadership is safety climate (Narhgang et al., 2007). Safety climate refers to employees' shared perceptions about the extent to which working safely is valued by their supervisor, workgroup, or organization (Zohar, 1980, 2002; Zohar and Luria, 2003). Individual studies and meta-analytic evidence has shown that safety climate is related to safety attitudes of employees (Clarke, 2006), individual safety motivation (Neal and Griffin, 2006), employee safety behaviors such as safety compliance and safety participation (Clarke, 2006), and occupational safety incidents such as injuries (Wallace et al., 2006; Zohar, 2003). Consequently, there is now considerable evidence that the extent to which employees or workgroups perceive their supervisors and organizations as valuing their physical safety is highly related to employee attitudes and behaviors.

In reviewing existing safety climate research, we were struck by several issues regarding safety climate that remain relatively unexplored. First, despite the influence of safety climate on both employee and organizational outcomes, little safety climate research has focused on safety climate fostered among co-workers. With the exception of Zohar and Luria (2004), the predominant referents of safety climate have been the organization more generally (e.g., Wallace et al., 2006; Zohar, 1980) and the behaviors of local supervisors in particular (e.g., Zohar, 2002; Zohar and Luria, 2003). We argue that co-workers in work groups, for example, may provide a more salient influence on employee shared perceptions of workplace safety than either upper-management or local supervisors, with whom employees in many occupations may have little day-to-day contact or whom may have little relative impact on how work is conducted on a daily basis. The assumption in much safety climate research has been that authority figures such as supervisors exert the largest influence on employee attitudes and behaviors, and little research has tested alternative referents (e.g., co-workers) as anchors of safety climate perceptions. While we are not arguing that supervisors are insignificant in shaping perceptions of workplace safety, future research in this area could afford to test a more comprehensive set of on-the-job (e.g., co-workers; supervisors; and upper-management) and off-the-job social influences (e.g., parents in the case of young workers; prior supervisors and employers in the case of adult workers) in shaping safety climate. While some researchers have begun to explore a range of social influences, (e.g., Westaby and Lowe, 2005), it is our hope that this perspective will permeate interest in different sources of safety climate. This question among others may provide both academics and practitioners with much needed answers on how to develop a climate that promotes occupational safety.

SOME POSSIBILITIES

Thus far in this chapter, we have described some of the historical background of workplace safety research rooted in a psychological perspective, as well as some key contemporary themes of workplace safety research in organizational behavior. The current section identifies and describes a number of issues that we believe will serve to provide some conceptual clarification and empirical richness to our understanding of workplace safety.

Conceptual issues

Exploring mechanisms and moderators of key relationships

Much of the research described in the background and current research sections of this chapter focused on the main effects of individual differences and situational factors in predicting workplace safety outcomes. That is, researchers have been interested

in understanding how various individual differences (e.g., Clarke, 2006) and situational factors (e.g., Frone, 1998) compete to explain variance in safety performance (e.g., injuries and safety behaviors). As an extension, we believe that a greater emphasis on conceptualizing and testing the constructs through which individual differences and situational factors may potentially exert their effects on these outcomes, as well as the conditions under which the main effects of the determinants may differ, serve to provide richness to these findings.

Some recently published as well as some emerging research in the field provides some examples of the focus we are advocating. For example, Wallace and Chen (2006) tested the notion that motivational orientations of prevention and promotion orientations (attitudinally similar to compliance and participation distinctions of safety behavior) mediate the relationship between safety climate and aspects of safety performance. Understanding how the individual makes sense of safety climate helps to explain why safety climate should affect safety performance. Similarly, understanding the circumstances under which situational factors such as work characteristics relate to safety outcomes may illustrate the boundary conditions of more common main effects. For example, Grote (2007) argues that job autonomy will be more strongly related to safety outcomes such as injuries under conditions of higher technical uncertainty (e.g., equipment breaking down) than in a more stable technical environment (e.g., a reliable production process). The idea here is that variance in the environment provides challenges (i.e., skill/ability), activates the need for control (i.e., motivation), as well as chances (i.e., opportunities) for employees to use the autonomy afforded to them – all to help ensure safe work. In a more certain environment, there is less challenge, less need to engage autonomy, and less opportunity to use the autonomy provided. Taken together, defining the ways or the circumstances under which individual differences (e.g., cognitive failure) and situational factors (e.g., job autonomy) are related to workplace safety provides a more thorough understanding of how employees and their organizations can create safe work.

Avoiding the 'safety fallacy' by taking care in theory building

One observation we have noted in reviewing the literature on workplace safety is that researchers (including ourselves) are often careless in how we scaffold our research with prior evidence. That is, it is quite common to make claims about determinants of safety outcomes as if workplace safety was a unitary construct: as if injuries, safety-related behaviors, near-misses, and an assortment of safety-related attitudes all shared common determinants because they concern workplace safety. In reading a range of research on workplace safety, we noticed that this is a frequent fallacy. We draw on our own work-in-progress to illustrate specifically what we mean. In one current project (Turner et al., 2007), we are interested in understanding how job control and job demands measured at three annual time points predict two types of safety behaviors (safety compliance and safety participation) contemporaneously and in lagged ways. In earlier drafts, we found ourselves using evidence of the determinants of injuries to bolster arguments about predictors of safety behaviors, perpetuating the assumption that all safety criterion variables share common correlates. We are concerned about this 'safety fallacy' for several reasons. First, misappropriating existing safety-related evidence to substantiate claims about safety-related research more generally is not considered robust practice in any area interested in building strong theory (Sutton and Staw, 1995). To draw a parallel in the organization sciences more generally, researchers would not tolerate claims that all organizationally-focused attitudinal constructs (e.g., organizational commitment, organizational based self-esteem) are unitary, thus treating all safety-focused outcomes in the same way (e.g., injuries, safety behaviors, near misses) seems similarly amiss. Second, many of the items we use in operationalizing safety constructs contain the words 'safety' or

'safe'; the methodological concern is the need to ensure that safety-related constructs do not covary solely on the basis of common item wording. Third and finally, there is a moral weight associated with research that strives to protect human safety, and thus questioning research that intends to promote safety without robust conceptual underpinning becomes tricky. While we are clearly advocates of research that aims to promote workplace safety, we also advocate using prior evidence appropriately in a domain in which socially desirable practical concerns (human safety) can sometimes blind the need to build strong theory.

Connection with growing literatures

Connecting social scientific research on workplace safety to other growing parts of the field is important for a number of reasons. First, many of the frameworks used in existing workplace safety research borrow from more well-established perspectives in other areas of social and organizational psychology. For example, a range of recent research (e.g., Neal and Griffin, 2006; Zohar and Luria, 2004) has transplanted commonly-used work performance frameworks and cost-benefit/utility theory into the study of types of safety-related behavior. Second, certain organizations face issues of safety across a number of domains; for example, in healthcare settings, understanding the connection between workplace and patient safety becomes important. Located within a diverse field like organizational behavior, which itself draws on many disciplines, means that research focused on workplace safety has the potential to learn from and contribute to a number of emerging areas. As an example, the concept of safety climate has recently been extended into understanding patient safety climates in healthcare organizations (e.g., Hofmann and Mark, 2006; Katz-Navon et al., 2005), with safety climates in hospital settings associated with post-operative infection rates and other medical errors. One of the key opportunities for safety climate research focused on non-healthcare organizations will be to translate lessons learned from research in healthcare settings back into, tested in, and applied within other organizational contexts. The parallels between the work of Edmondson and her colleagues (e.g., Edmondson, 1999; Edmondson, 2004; Nembhard and Edmondson, 2006) on the importance of psychological safety in identifying and learning from errors in medical settings, and recent work on the social construction and dynamic nature of safety climate in tank units (Zohar and Luria, 2004) serve as a prime example of the potential for cross-fertilization. Similarly, in thinking about more sophisticated models of work performance (e.g., Griffin et al., 2007), and particularly on the conceptualization of proactive work behaviors (Grant and Ashford, in press; Parker et al., 2006), we believe there is room to extend and operationalize models of safety behavior beyond the bi-dimensional task-compliance/contextual-participation framework described earlier in the chapter.

METHODOLOGICAL ISSUES

Analytical treatment of the outcome variable

We believe that there are several methodological issues that need to be considered when operationalizing and analyzing safety outcomes in organizational behavior research. These issues include appropriate statistical treatment of infrequently occurring data such as injuries, the questionable nature of other-source safety data, and the assumption that injuries are the ultimate safety outcome. We deal with each of these issues in turn.

Statistical treatment of infrequently occurring data

The statistical distribution of workplace injuries in most organizational settings is rarely normal, and is often severely positively skewed. Two recent reports of safety research illustrate this well. Zacharatos et al. (2005) reported that only 2.8 per cent of employees sampled reported experiencing

a lost-time injury in the year previous to their cross-sectional study. In a longitudinal design, Neal and Griffin (2006) reported a mean of 0.5 lost-time injuries in a sample of workgroups in Australian healthcare over a five year period. Other studies published in organizational behavior journals examining workplace injuries have also reported and transformed positively-skewed data (e.g., Hofmann and Morgeson, 1999; Probst and Brubaker, 2001; Wallace et al., 2006).

The error properties of these distributions often complicate treatment of workplace injury data as they ask researchers to reach outside their comfort zones of analytical techniques grounded in the general linear model to non-parametric techniques. Although most applications of linear regression remain fairly robust in the face of data that deviate modestly from a normal distribution, workplace injury distributions are often skewed quite severely. Researchers have addressed the normality issue in various ways. Zacharatos et al. (2005) dropped the most severely skewed criterion (number of lost time injuries) from further analyses, while a host of others (e.g., Hofmann and Morgeson, 1999; Hofmann and Stetzer, 1996; Probst and Brubaker, 2001; Wallace et al., 2006; Zohar, 2000) transformed the injury data via a square-root transformation, often suggested by other researchers studying skewed workplace phenomena, such as absenteeism (e.g., Harrison and Hulin, 1989), which has similar distributional properties. While these approaches certainly help to mitigate non-normal distributions, they serve to fundamentally change the interpretation of the data. Exploring the possibility of using techniques that do not rely on the assumption of normality (e.g., partial least squares) or operationalizing the criterion in a manner more consistent with the distribution of the phenomenon (e.g., negative binomial distributions; Harrison and Hulin, 1989; Lord, 2006) becomes important.

Questionable nature of other-source safety data

While most researchers and journal editors and reviewers often request other-source data to enhance construct validity and eliminate same-source or mono-operation biases, there are often unstated issues about the validity of safety data from commonly-used 'other' sources. An examination of studies conducted on safety-related incidents (i.e., injuries, near-misses) shows that many studies in the field have relied on data obtained either from company records or regulatory databases (Clarke, 2006). Nevertheless, issues arise about the construct and convergent validity of such measures. Very often, these statistics are derived from systems that rely on employees to report these incidents, either themselves or via a supervisor, and such safety incident reports are subject to differences among organizational members' perceptions about what actually happened (Kelloway et al., 2004). More generally, different mental models of what constitutes an injury or safe work (e.g., Prussia et al., 2003) and organizational climates which encourage employees to keep safety incidents hidden (e.g., Collinson, 1999) further complicate how other-source data is created and interpreted. This concern is not unique to safety-related data but to other socially sensitive phenomena in organizational behavior such as absenteeism (Johns, 1994) and employee lateness (Koslowsky and Dishon-Berkovits, 2001). A consequence of relying on safety incident data is an underestimation of experienced incidents that required self-administered or slightly more substantial medical attention (e.g., casual first aid) than the more serious injuries requiring hospitalization or time away from work. While the call for researchers to use multi-source, multi-method data is now almost a ritualistic refrain, we urge particular attention to the reliability and validity of other-source safety data.

Injuries as the dependent variable

One of the major assumptions we noted in reviewing models tested in the workplace safety literature is that attitudes precede behavior, and that behavior precedes injuries. Yet, this assumption precludes the possibility that workplace injuries may have a reciprocal influence on employee safety attitudes and behaviors. Although much research has focused on what factors predict workplace injuries, relatively little is known about the attitudinal and behavioral consequences of workplace injuries. A study by Barling et al. (2003) suggests injuries in the workplace could have negative effects on employee attitudes towards management and one's job. Analyzing almost ten thousand employees who participated in the 1995 Australian Workplace Industrial Relations Survey, Barling et al. found that injury occurrence predicted both employee perceptions of distrust in management and lack of influence which both, in turn, predicted employee job dissatisfaction. By extension, an exclusive focus on the determinants of safety behaviors does not incorporate vicarious effects on employees who witness others getting injured (Kelloway et al., 2004) or the families of workers injured who may reassess their own attitudes about work and occupational safety.

CONCLUSION

In this chapter, we have highlighted the beginnings of safety research on accident proneness and followed through to current research on individual and situational predictors of safety behaviors and other safety-related outcomes (e.g., injuries). While our review was by no means exhaustive, it should provide the reader with a comprehensive overview of major strands of psychological research on workplace safety.

Workplace safety needs to remain a vital concern for organizational researchers and practitioners. It will only be through continual refinement of safety constructs and careful examination of potential individual and situational determinants that psychology will contribute workable ways of achieving safety on-the-job. Research has evolved from blaming employees for safety incidents in the early part of the twentieth century to exploring how various individual and situational influences interact to predict safety outcomes. In this chapter, we have outlined various conceptual and methodological issues that will serve to provide a clearer understanding of the human dimensions of occupational safety.

NOTES

1 Funding from the Social Sciences and Humanities Research Council of Canada supported collaboration on this chapter.

2 See Carson and Barling's chapter in this volume for a review of workplace well-being, including mental health, and Robinson's review in this volume of counterproductive behaviors, including the health consequences of workplace aggression and violence.

3 Some psychological research has focused on 'accident proneness' and we have used the term 'accident' when discussing this literature to remain true to both the label and the assumption about injury causation inherent in this approach.

REFERENCES

Andriessen, J.H.T.H. (1978) 'Safe behaviour and safety motivation', *Journal of Occupational Accidents*, 1: 368–376.

Barling, J. and Frone, M.R. (eds) (2004) *Psychology of Workplace Safety*. Washington, DC: American Psychological Association.

Barling, J., Kelloway, E.K. and Iverson, R. (2003) 'Accidental outcomes: Attitudinal consequences of workplace injuries', *Journal of Occupational Health Psychology*, 8: 74–85.

Barling, J., Loughlin, C. and Kelloway, E.K. (2002) 'Development and test of a model linking transformational leadership and occupational safety', *Journal of Applied Psychology*, 87: 488–496.

Barrick, R.M. and Mount, M.K. (1991) 'The Big Five personality dimensions and job performance: A meta-analysis', *Personnel Psychology*, 44: 1–26.

Bass, B.M. (1985) *Leadership and Performance Beyond Expectations*. New York: Free Press.

Bass, B.M. and Riggio, R.E. (2006) *Transformational Leadership* (2nd edn) Mahwah, NJ: Lawrence Erlbaum Associates Publishers.

Bhal, K.T. (2006) 'LMX-citizenship behavior relationship: Justice as a mediator', *Leadership and Organization Development Journal*, 27: 106–117.

Boies, K. and Howell, J.M. (2006) 'Leader-member exchange in teams: An examination of the interaction between relationship differentiation and mean *LMX* in explaining team-level outcomes', *Leadership Quarterly*, 17: 246–257.

Boone, J. and van Ours, J.C. (2006) 'Are recessions good for workplace safety?' *Journal of Health Economics*, 25: 1069–1093.

Borman, W.C. and Motowidlo, S.J. (1993) 'Expanding the criterion domain to include elements of contextual performance', in N. Schmitt, W.C. Borman, and Associates, *Personnel Selection in Organizations*, San Francisco: Jossey-Bass, pp. 71–98.

Breslin, F.C., Smith, P., Koehoorn, M. and Lee, H. (2006) 'Is the workplace becoming safer?', *Perspectives on Labor and Income*, 18: 36–41.

Broadbent, D.E., Cooper, P.R., Fitzgerald, P. and Parkes, K.R. (1982) 'The cognitive failures questionnaire (CFQ) and its correlates', *British Journal of Clinical Psychology*, 21: 1–16.

Brown, G.D. (2002) 'The global threats to workers' health and safety on the job', *Social Justice*, 29: 12–25.

Bunn, T., Costich, J. and Slavova, S. (2006) 'Identification and characterization of Kentucky self-employed occupational injury fatalities using multiple sources, 1995–2004', *American Journal of Industrial Medicine*, 49: 1005–1012.

Burke, M.J., Sarpy, S.A., Tesluk, P.E., Smith-Crowe, K. (2002) 'General safety performance: A test of a grounded theoretical model', *Personnel Psychology*, 55: 429–457.

Campbell, J.P., McCloy, R.A., Oppler, S.H. and Sager, C.E. (1993) 'A theory of performance', in N. Schmitt, W.C. Borman, and Associates (eds), *Personnel Selection in Organizations*. San Francisco: Jossey-Bass, pp. 35–70.

Castillo, D.N. (1999) 'Occupational safety and health in young people', in J. Barling and E.K. Kelloway (eds), *Young Workers: Varieties of Experience*. Washington, DC: American Psychological Association, pp. 159–200.

Chan, D. (2006) 'Interactive effects of situational judgment effectiveness and proactive personality on work perceptions and work outcomes', *Journal of Applied Psychology*, 91: 475–481.

Clarke, S. (2006) 'Contrasting perceptual, attitudinal and dispositional approaches to accident involvement in the workplace', *Safety Science*, 44: 537–550.

Clarke, S. and Robertson, I.T. (2005) 'A meta-analytic review of the big five personality factors and accident involvement in occupational and non-occupational settings', *Journal of Occupational and Organisational Psychology*, 78: 355–376.

Cleveland, R.J., Cohen, H.H., Smith, M.J. and Cohen, A. (1978) *Safety Program Practices in Record Holding Plants*. Cincinnati, OH: National Institute for Occupational Safety and Health.

Cobb, P.W. (1940) 'The limit of usefulness of accident rate as a measure of accident proneness', *Journal of Applied Psychology*, 24: 154–159.

Cohen, A., Smith, M. and Cohen, H.H. (1975) 'Safety program practices in high vs. low accident rate companies—An interim report (U.S. Department of Health, Education and Welfare Publication No. 75–185).' Cincinnati, OH: National Institute for Occupational Safety and Health.

Collinson, D.L. (1999) ' "Surviving the rigs": Safety and surveillance on North Sea oil installations', *Organizational Studies*, 20: 579–600.

Crawford, P. (1960) 'Hazard exposure differentiation necessary for the identification of the accident prone employee', *Journal of Applied Psychology*, 44: 192–194.

Davids, A. and Mahoney, J.T. (1957) 'Personality dynamics and accident proneness in an industrial setting', *Journal of Applied Psychology*, 41: 303–306.

DeJoy, D.M., Searcy, C.A., Murphy, L.R. and Gershon, R.R.M (2000) 'Behavior-diagnostic analysis of compliance with universal precautions among nurses', *Journal of Occupational Health Psychology*, 5: 127–141.

de Lange, A.H., Taris, T.W., Kompier, M.A.J., Houtman, I.L.D. and Bongers, P.M. (2003) ' "The very best of the millennium": Longitudinal research and the demand-control-support) model', *Journal of Occupational Health Psychology*, 8: 282–305.

Dudley, N.M., Orvis, K.A., Lebiecki, J.E. and Cortina, J.M. (2006) 'A meta-analytic investigation of conscientiousness in the prediction of job performance: Examining the intercorrelations and the incremental validity of narrow traits', *Journal of Applied Psychology*, 91: 40–57.

Dupre, D. (2000) 'Injuries at work in the EU', *Statistics in Focus: Population and Social Conditions* (Catalogue Number: CA-NK-00-004-EN-I) Luxembourg: Eurostat.

Edmondson, A. (2004) 'Psychological safety, trust, and learning in organizations: A group-level lens', in R.M. Kramer and K.S. Cook (eds), *Trust and Distrust in Organizations: Dilemmas and Approaches*. New York: Russell Sage Foundation.

Edmondson, A. (1999) 'Psychological safety and learning behavior in work teams', *Administrative Science Quarterly*, 44: 350–383.

Frone, M.R. (1998) 'Predictors of work injuries among employed adolescents', *Journal of Applied Psychology*, 83: 565–576.

Geller, E.S., Roberts, D.S. and Gilmore, M.R. (1996) 'Predicting propensity to actively care for occupational safety', *Journal of Safety Research*, 27: 1–8.

Grant, A.M. and Ashford, S.J. (in press) 'The dynamics of proactivity at work', *Research in Organizational Behavior*, 28.

Griffin, M.A. and Neal, A. (2000) 'Perceptions of safety at work: A framework for linking safety climate to safety performance, knowledge, and motivation', *Journal of Occupational Health Psychology*, 5: 347–358.

Griffin, M.A., Neal, A. and Parker.S.K. (2007) 'A new model of work performance: Positive behaviour in uncertain and interdependent contexts', *Academy of Management Journal*, 50: 327–347.

Grote, G. (2007) 'Understanding and assessing safety culture through the lens of organizational management of uncertainty', *Safety Science*, 45: 637–652.

Hämäläinen, P., Takala, J. and Saarela, K.L. (2006) 'Global estimates of occupational accidents', *Safety Science*, 44: 137–156.

Harrison, D.A. and Hulin, C.L. (1989) 'Investigations of absenteeism: Using event history models to study the absence-taking process', *Journal of Applied Psychology*, 74: 300–316.

Hemingway, M.A. and· Smith, C.S. (1999) 'Organizational climate and occupational stressors as predictors of withdrawal behaviours and injuries in nurses', *Journal of Occupational and Organizational Psychology*, 72: 285–299.

Hill, J.M.M. and Trist, E.L. (1953) 'A consideration of industrial injuries as a means of withdrawal from the work situation', *Human Relations*, 6: 357–380.

Hill, J.M.M. and Trist, E.L. (1955) 'Changes in injuries and other absences with length of service', *Human Relations*, 8: 121–152.

Hofmann, D.A. and Mark, B. (2006) 'An investigation of the relationship between safety climate and medication errors as well as other nurse and patient outcomes', *Personnel Psychology*, 59, 847–869.

Hofmann, D.A. and Morgeson, F.P. (1999) 'Safety related behavior as a social exchange: The role of perceived organizational support and leader-member exchange', *Journal of Applied Psychology*, 84: 286–296.

Hofmann, D.A., Morgeson, F.P. and Gerras, S.J. (2003) 'Climate as a moderator of the relationship between leader-member exchange and content specific citizenship: Safety climate as an exemplar', *Journal of Applied Psychology*, 88: 170–178.

Hofmann, D.A. and Stetzer, A. (1996) 'A cross-level investigation of factors influencing unsafe behaviors and injuries', *Personnel Psychology*, 49: 307–339.

Hofmann, D. and Tetrick, L.E. (eds) (2003) *Health and Safety in Organizations: A Multilevel Perspective*. San Francisco: Jossey-Bass.

Holcom, M.L., Lehman, W.E.K. and Simpson, D.D. (1993) 'Employee accidents: Influences of personal characteristics, job characteristics, and substance use in jobs differing in accident potential', *Journal of Safety Research*, 24: 205–221.

Hopkins, A. (2006) 'What are we to make of safe behaviour programs?', *Safety Science*, 44: 583–597.

Iverson, R.D. andErwin, P.J. (1997) 'Predicting occupational injury: The role of affectivity', *Journal of Occupational and Organizational Psychology*, 70: 113–128.

Johns, G. (1994) 'How often were you absent? A review of the use of self-reported absence data', *Journal of Applied Psychology*, 79: 574–591.

Karasek, R.A. (1979) 'Job demands, job decision latitude and mental strain: Implications for job design', *Administrative Science Quarterly*, 24: 285–308.

Katz-Navon, T., Naveh, E. and Stern, Z. (2005) 'Safety climate in health care organizations: A multidimensional approach', *Academy of Management Journal*, 48: 1075–1089.

Kelloway, E.K., Mullen, J. and Francis, L. (2006) 'Divergent effects of transformational and passive leadership on employee safety', *Journal of Occupational Health Psychology*, 11: 76–86.

Kelloway, E.K., Stinson, V. and MacLean, C. (2004) 'Eyewitness testimony in occupational accident investigations: Towards a research agenda', *Law and Human Behavior*, 28: 115–132.

Komaki, J., Barwick, K.D. and Scott, L.R. (1978) 'A behavioral approach to occupational safety: Pinpointing and reinforcing safe performance in a food manufacturing plant', *Journal of Applied Psychology*, 63: 434–445.

Koslowsky, M. and Dishon–Berkovits, M. (2001) 'Self-report measures of employee lateness: Conceptual and methodological issues', *European Journal of Work and Organizational Psychology*, 10: 145–159.

Kunce, J.T. (1967) 'Vocational interests and accident proneness', *Journal of Applied Psychology*, 51: 223–225.

Lambert, T.A. (2004) 'Avoiding regulatory mismatch in the workplace. An informational approach to workplace safety regulation', *Nebraska Law Review*, 82: 1006–1087.

Lord, D. (2006) 'Modeling motor vehicle crashes using Poisson-gamma models: Examining the effects of low sample mean values and small sample size on the estimation of the fixed dispersion parameter', *Accident Analysis and Prevention*, 38: 751–766.

Loughlin, C. and Barling, J. (1999) 'The nature of youth employment', in J. Barling and E.K. Kelloway (eds), *Young Workers: Varieties of Experience*. Washington, DC: American Psychological Association, pp. 17–36.

Loughlin, C. and Frone, M.R. (2004) 'Young workers' occupational safety', in J. Barling and M.R. Frone (eds), *The Psychology of Workplace Safety*. Washington, DC: American Psychological Association, pp. 107–125.

Marchand, A., Simard, M., Carpentier-Roy, M.C., Ouellet, F. (1998) 'From a unidimensional to a bidimensional concept and measurement of workers' safety behaviour', *Scandinavian Journal of Work, Environment, and Health*, 24: 293–299.

Martin, M. (1983) 'Cognitive failure: Everyday and laboratory performance', *Bulletin of Psychonomic Society*, 21: 97–100.

McCall B.P. and Horwitz I.B. (2006) 'An assessment and quantification of the rates, costs, and risk factors of occupational amputations: Analysis of Kentucky workers' compensation claims, 1994–2003', *American Journal of Industrial Medicine*, 49: 1031–1038.

Mintz, A. and Blum, M.L. (1949) 'A re-examination of the accident proneness concept', *Journal of Applied Psychology*, 33: 195–211.

Mitroff, I.I. and McWhinney, W. (1990) 'Crisis creation by design', in F. Massarik (ed.), *Advances in Organizational Development*. Westport, CT: Ablex Publishing, pp. 105–114.

Mullen, J. (2005) 'Testing a model of employee willingness to raise safety issues', *Canadian Journal of Behavioural Science*, 37: 273–282.

Murata, K., Kawakami, N. and Amari, N. (2000) 'Does job stress affect injury due to labor accident in Japanese male and female blue-collar workers?', *Industrial Health*, 38: 246–251.

Nahrgang, J.D., Morgeson, F.P. and Hofmann, D.A. (2007) *Predicting Safety Performance: A Meta-analysis of Safety and Organizational Constructs*. Poster session presented at the 22nd Annual Conference of the Society for Industrial and Organizational Psychology, New York.

Neal, A. and Griffin, M.A. (2006) 'A study of the lagged relationships among safety climate, safety motivation, safety behavior, and injuries at the individual and group levels', *Journal of Applied Psychology*, 91: 946–953.

Neal, A., Griffin, M.A. and Hart, P.M. (2000) 'The impact of organizational climate on safety climate and individual behaviour', *Safety Science*, 34: 99–109.

Nembhard, I.M. andEdmondson, A.C. (2006) 'Making it safe: The effects of leader inclusiveness and professional status on psychological safety and improvement efforts in health care teams', *Journal of Organizational Behavior*, 27: 941–966.

Nichols, T. (1997) *Sociology of Industrial Injury*. London: Mansell.

Parker, S.K., Axtell, C.M. and Turner, N. (2001) 'Designing a safer workplace: Importance of job autonomy, communication quality, and supportive supervisors', *Journal of Occupational Health Psychology*, 6: 211–228.

Parker, S.K., Williams, H.M. and Turner, N. (2006) 'Modeling the antecedents of proactive behavior at work', *Journal of Applied Psychology*, 91: 636–652.

Probst, T.M. and Brubaker, T.L. (2001) 'The effects of job insecurity on employee safety outcomes: Cross-sectional and longitudinal explorations', *Journal of Occupational Health Psychology*, 6: 139–159.

Prussia, G.E., Brown, K.A. and Willis, P.G. (2003) 'Mental models of safety: Do managers and employees see eye to eye?', *Journal of Safety Research*, 34: 143–156.

Quinlan, M. and Bohle, P. (2004) 'Contingent work and occupational safety', in J. Barling and M.R. Frone (eds), *The Psychology of Workplace Safety*. Washington, DC: American Psychological Association, pp. 81–105.

Raja, U., Johns, G. and Ntalianis, F. (2004) 'The impact of personality on psychological contracts', *Academy of Management Journal*, 47: 350–367.

Robinson, A.M. and Smallman, C. (2006) 'The contemporary British workplace: A safer and healthier place?', *Work, Employment and Society*, 20: 87–107.

Ryan, A.M., West, B.J. and Carr, J.Z. (2003) 'Effects of the terrorist attacks of 9/11/01 on employee attitudes', *Journal of Applied Psychology*, 88: 647–659.

Schyns, B. (2006) 'Are group consensus in leader-member exchange (*LMX*) and shared work values related to organizational outcomes?'. *Small Group Research*, 37: 20–35.

Shafai-Sahrai, Y. (1971) *An Inquiry into Factors that Might Explain Differences in Occupational Accident Experience of Similar Size Firms in the Same Industry (Tech. rep.)* East Lansing, MI: Division of Research, Graduate School of Business Administration, Michigan State University Press.

Simard, M. and Marchand, A. (1995) 'A multilevel analysis of organisational factors related to the taking of safety initiatives by work groups', *Safety Science*, 21: 113–129.

Sutton, R.I. and Staw, B.M. (1995) 'What theory is not', *Administrative Science Quarterly*, 40: 371–384.

Tuncel, S., Lotlikar, H., Salem, S. and Daraiseh, N. (2006) 'Effectiveness of behaviour based safety interventions to reduce accidents and injuries in workplaces: Critical appraisal and meta-analysis', *Theoretical Issues in Ergonomics Science*, 7: 191–209.

Turner, N., Chmiel, N. and Walls, M. (2005) 'Railing for safety: Job demands, job control, and safety citizenship role definition', *Journal of Occupational Health Psychology*, 10: 504–512.

Turner, N., Stride, C.B., Carroll, A.E. and Carter, A.J. (2007) *Job Demands, Job Control, and Workplace Safety Behaviors: A Three–wave Longitudinal Model.* Working paper: University of Manitoba.

Veazie, M.A., Landen, D.D., Bender, T.R. and Amandus, H.E. (1994) 'Epidemiologic research on the etiology of injuries at work', *Annual Review of Public Health*, 15: 203–221.

Wallace, C. and Chen, G. (2006) 'A multilevel integration of personality, climate, self-regulation, and performance', *Personnel Psychology*, 59: 529–557.

Wallace, J.C., Popp, E. and Mondore, S. (2006) 'Safety climate as a mediator between foundation climates and occupational injuries: A group-level investigation', *Journal of Applied Psychology*, 87: 304–311.

Wallace, J.C. and Vodanovich, S.J. (2003a) 'Can injuries and industrial mishaps be predicted? Investigating workplace performance', *Journal of Business and Psychology*, 17: 503–514.

Wallace, J.C. and Vodanovich, S.J. (2003b) 'Workplace safety performance: Conscientiousness, cognitive failure, and their interaction', *Journal of Occupational Health Psychology*, 8: 316–327.

Weick, K.E. (1993) 'The collapse of sensemaking in organizations: The Mann Gulch disaster', *Administrative Science Quarterly*, 38: 628–652.

Westaby, J.D. and Lowe, J.K. (2005) 'Risk-taking orientation and injury among youth workers: Examining the social influence of supervisors, coworkers, and parents', *Journal of Applied Psychology*, 90: 1027–1035.

Wheelwright, K. (2005) 'Some care, little responsibility: Promoting directors' and managers' legal accountability for occupational health and safety in the workplace', *Dean Larkin Review*, 10: 470–497.

Zacharatos, A., Barling, J. and Iverson, R.D. (2005) 'High-performance work systems and occupational safety', *Journal of Applied Psychology*, 90: 77–84.

Zohar, D. (1980) 'Safety climate in industrial organizations: Theoretical and applied implications', *Journal of Applied Psychology*, 65: 96–102.

Zohar, D. (2000) 'A group-level model of safety climate: Testing the effect of group climate on microinjuries in manufacturing jobs', *Journal of Applied Psychology*, 85: 587–596.

Zohar, D. (2002) 'The effects of leadership dimensions, safety climate, and assigned priorities on minor injuries in work groups', *Journal of Organizational Behavior*, 23: 75–92.

Zohar, D. (2003) 'Modifying supervisory practices to improve subunit safety: A leadership–based intervention model', *Journal of Applied Psychology*, 87: 156–163.

Zohar, D. and Luria, G. (2003) 'The use of supervisory practices as leverage to improve safety behavior: A cross-level intervention model', *Journal of Safety Research*, 34: 567–577.

Zohar, D. and Luria, G. (2004) 'Climate as a social-cognitive construction of supervisory safety practices: Scripts as proxy of behavior patterns', *Journal of Applied Psychology*, 89: 322–333.

PART FOUR

Individuals, Organizations and Society

29

Cross-Cultural Issues in Organizational Behavior

Heidi K. Gardner and P. Christopher Earley

INTRODUCTION

Globalization and regionalization of business have increasingly compelled us to integrate the concept of cultural variation into business research and practice. Research covering these dynamics spans a wide array of academic disciplines, including international business, comparative management, and cross-cultural social, organizational and cognitive psychology. This chapter focuses on the field of cross-cultural organizational behavior, which Gelfand et al. (2007: 20.2) define as '... the study of cross-cultural similarities and differences in processes and behavior at work and the dynamics of cross-cultural interfaces in multicultural domestic and international contexts.' Cross-cultural organizational behavior covers several levels of analysis, examining how culture affects intra-individual phenomena (e.g., cognition, emotions), interpersonal phenomena (e.g., teams, communications, power) and firm-level phenomena (e.g., work practices,

organizational structure). A growing and important area of cross-cultural organizational behavior focuses on meso research – examining the interplay between these levels of analysis.

CHAPTER PREVIEW

This chapter addresses how culture links to organizational phenomena at the individual, group and firm levels. We first describe the chapter's two central themes: the need to specify the appropriate level at which culture affects the variable of interest, and the shift from proximal, intra-individual influences (i.e., cultural values) to distal influences that determine how culture shapes behavior and cognition. We then review key classic frameworks to understand the foundation for theorizing on these themes, followed with a focus on more recent research that elucidates specific mechanisms for how culture affects the actions of individuals, teams and organizations. Finally, we highlight recent advances in cross-cultural research, suggesting how new directions can shape future research.

DEFINITION OF CULTURE

Before we can examine any cross-cultural research, we must clarify what we mean by 'culture.' In the academic world, there is no single, widely accepted definition of culture. One school of thought sees culture as an explicit and implicit pattern of reactions – cognitive, affective and behavioral – to various situations and actions (e.g., Kluckhohn, 1954). Herskovits (1948: 17) provided another influential conceptualization of culture, defined as 'the man-made part of the human environment.' In contrast to the idea of culture as artifacts and visible manifestations, Hofstede (1991) calls culture the 'software of the mind.' Triandis (1994) distinguishes between the objective and the subjective elements of culture: Objective elements include, for example, tools and radio stations, while subjective elements include values, beliefs, norms, and categorizations. Rohner's (1984: 119–120) widely-cited definition of culture is '… *the totality of equivalent and complementary learned meanings maintained by a human population, or by identifiable segments of a population, and transmitted from one generation to the next*' [italics in original]. Three aspects of Rohner's (1984) conceptualization bear further elaboration:

- Meanings and values: more than just a behavioral manifestation, culture provides the underlying belief and value system that helps people interpret, understand and evaluate their environment. Although it is unlikely that any single individual in a given population knows the totality of meanings that define a culture, as long as a culture contains 'complementary meanings' people can interact in predictable, important ways.
- Transmitted and maintained: people shape and are shaped by culture. Culture is acquired and transmitted (albeit imperfectly) within and across generations mainly by symbols and their embodiment in artifacts.
- Segments of a human population: there are both cultural similarities and differences across populations. Even within a culture meanings are often not shared uniformly by all members of a society; any two members of a society are thus likely to hold similar – but not identical – meanings for the same event or action. Some researchers use 'ethnicity' as an explicit construct within their cultural research to explore distinct segments within any grouping.

In summary, we follow Rohner (1984) in viewing culture as the individual-level manifestations of shared meaning systems learned from others through socialization and common experiences. In contrast, 'society' refers to a geographically bounded and multigenerational group of people who share a common (albeit imperfectly shared) culture. Thus, a cross-cultural approach to organizational research must differentiate between individuals and the society in which they live (Earley and Mosakowski, 2002).

CENTRAL THEMES

This section previews the two central themes that run throughout the chapter: the need for researchers in cross-cultural organizational behavior to specify the appropriate level at which culture affects the variable of interest, and to shift their attention from proximal, intra-individual influences (i.e., cultural values) to other more proximal or more distal influences that determine how culture shapes human and organizational behavior.

Neither of these themes is novel. Scholars have long recognized the need for more precise theorizing and measurement of levels of analysis in cross-cultural research (Earley and Singh, 1995; Hofstede, Bond, and Luk, 1993; Triandis, 1994). Similarly, scholars have called for research to move beyond using values as the sole mechanism through which culture affects human behavior (Bond and Smith, 1996; Gelfand, Erez and Aycan, 2007) and to advance beyond the somewhat myopic emphasis on the values of individualism versus collectivism (Earley and Gibson, 1998). Despite these repeated and widespread appeals for changes, most research continues to focus primarily on individualism-collectivism to explain differences across cultures. Indeed, it is precisely this gap between existing research and the acknowledged needs for future research that prompts us to focus on multi-level research and distal influences of culture as the two primary themes of this chapter.

LEVELS OF ANALYSIS ISSUES IN CROSS-CULTURAL RESEARCH

Cross-cultural research in organizational behavior spans a wide spectrum of analysis, ranging from intra-individual to interpersonal, team, and organizational outcomes. By its very nature, research that examines (or assumes) an impact of culture on any of these types of variables is necessarily multi- or cross-level (Rousseau, 1985). Multi-level research in general faces several distinctive issues that call for sensitivity and care (e.g., Klein and Dansereau, 1994). The problem of specifying the appropriate level for variables in cross-cultural research is exacerbated because similar socio-cultural dimensions have also been conceptualized at the individual level.

One problem that is especially common to cross-cultural research is the 'ecological fallacy.' The ecological fallacy refers to a widely recognized error whereby inferences about less aggregate variables such as individual behavior are based solely upon aggregate statistics collected for the group to which those individuals belong. When a country scores higher on a particular value, such as individualism, it means that *on average* people in that country are more individualistic. Hofstede (1991) warns that data collected at a national level should not be used to predict individual behavior (for a recent debate see Earley, 2006; Smith, 2006), although he acknowledges that his data have been frequently misused in this way.

The 'reverse ecological fallacy' pertains to mistakes made when relationships identified at a lower level of analysis are assumed to hold at a higher level. Despite its prevalence in cross-cultural research, there is much less recognition of reverse ecological fallacy; Hofstede et al. (1993) speculate that the dominance of individualistic cultures (i.e., the US, Britain) within social science research legitimates data collected at the individual level, even when that data are then used (erroneously) to draw conclusions about higher levels of analysis.

Several scholars provide advice for dealing with the ecological fallacy (Bond, 1997; Hofstede et al., 1993; Van de Vijver and Leung, 1997). Consistent with prior theorizing (e.g., Earley and Mosakowski, 2002), we suggest that 'meso' research provides a clear approach for directing cross-cultural research in organizational behavior. Meso research refers to the simultaneous study of at least two levels of analysis that are linked through some specified intervening process or processes (Rousseau, 1985). Earley and Singh (1995) recommended a 'hybrid' research design to identify and isolate which of various alternative explanations accurately captures a given phenomenon by identifying specific aspects of nation or culture that are related to a given explanation. Finally, Gelfand et al. (2007) call for more work in the area of 'the cross-cultural interface,' meaning the role of culture in encounters where multiple cultures are present, pointing to the relative dearth of theory and empirical data concerning whether, how and to what extent culture affects these cross-cultural situations. We hope that by highlighting the issues and showing exemplary studies that attend to their resolution, our chapter will encourage future researchers to be mindful of carefully specifying, theorizing and measuring the influence of culture on organizational behavior.

MOVING BEYOND CULTURAL VALUES

One of the major trends in cross-cultural organizational behavior research is the shift from an exclusive focus on cultural values to the examination of other influences that determine how culture shapes human and organizational behavior.

A rich stream of research has examined cultural influence on individual values and beliefs, which in turn shape individual and collective behavior. Early comparative work such as Haire et al.'s (1966) study identified a set of values that underpin managerial actions in different cultural settings. An important extension of this work is Hofstede's (1984) now classic study, in which he sampled the values of organizational members from more than 40 countries. His empirical analysis resulted in a four-part typology of cultural dimensions (individualism-collectivism, power distance, uncertainty avoidance, and masculine-feminine); subsequent research (Hofstede and Bond, 1988) uncovered a fifth dimension relating to beliefs about time and fate. This typology has received enormous research attention with literally thousands of citations (see Kirkman et al., 2006). Other scholars and large-scale research projects have devoted significant attention to developing valid instruments and approaches to studying cultural values (Chinese Culture Connection, 1987; House et al., 1999; Schwartz, 1992).

There has, however, been a growing trend away from using cultural values as the sole indicators of cultural differences. Bond (1997), for example, called for cross-cultural researchers to move beyond an emphasis on values as if there were the only and best indicator of national differences. Management research has been especially guilty of this focus, not only on values, but on one specific dimension: individualism versus collectivism (Earley and Gibson, 1998). To understand other approaches for theorizing about culture's influence, we follow Poortinga (1992) and Bond and Smith (1996), who differentiated between two types of 'constraints' on individual behavior (i.e., cultural effects that limit members of a particular group from exhibiting otherwise universal behaviors): on the one hand, values and beliefs are *internal-proximal* constraints; on the other hand

external-distal constraints such as economic, social, political and developmental indicators also influence behavior.

Since the 1950s, social psychology has recognized that individual behavior cannot be explained merely by dispositional values or context; rather, researchers must understand how the individual subjectively constructs a representation of the context. One response has been to examine *proximate* variables such as cognitive structures as a link between culture and outcomes (e.g., Morris and Young, 2002). Another trend has been evolving in the opposite direction: explaining the 'why and how' of culture's influence on behavior by focusing on causal mechanisms that are more *distal* than intra-individual values. More than a decade ago, Bond and Smith (1996) noted that researchers in the psychological domain have typically eschewed variables like economic and political factors. Today, most models of cultural differences remain more proximal than distal. Yet there is some progress. Research on group composition within multinational teams, for instance, is helping to understand interpersonal – rather than intra-individual – cultural constraints on behavior.

FOUNDATIONAL FRAMEWORKS

This section examines several core cross-cultural frameworks to understand how various research traditions theorize on the link between cultural constructs and lower-level outcomes. This abbreviated historical account illustrates trends in the field's theoretical development, focusing on the themes of cross-level theorizing and the shift from cultural values towards other antecedents (behavioral and psychological) of culturally-based action. Table 1 summarizes the frameworks discussed below.

One of the earliest models of cultural values that still resonates in modern work is that of Kluckhohn and Strodtbeck (1961), who proposed that five basic value-orientations underlie cultures: human nature, man-nature, time, activity, and relational. *Human nature*

Table 1   Classic frameworks covered in Section 2

Authors (date)	Framework	Essential concepts
Kluckhohn and Strodtbeck (1961)	Value orientations underlying culture	Five basic value-orientations underlie cultures: human nature, man-nature, time, activity and relational
Triandis (1972)	Subjective culture	Links macro-societal elements to micro-individual behavior by assessing the relations among environment, social environment, values, and psychological process
Hofstede (1984, 1991)	Software of the mind	Culture can be viewed as a series of mental programs, with values and culture at the core
Markus and Kitayama (1991)	Independent versus interdependent self-construals	Seminal discussion concerning how culture and self can be integrated
Erez and Earley (1993)	Cultural self representation model	Three basic motives guide a person's self concept: enhancement, efficacy, and consistency
Earley (2002); Earley and Ang (2003)	Cultural intelligence (CQ)	CQ represents an individual's capability to adapt effectively across cultures and comprises four facets: meta-cognition, cognition, motivation and behavior

refers to the innate goodness of people. The *man-nature* aspect describes the individual's relationship with nature. The *time* orientation refers to the timeframe salient to a group. An *activity* orientation refers to self-expression in activity, contrasting Being with Being-in-Becoming societies. Finally, the *relational* orientation refers to an individual's relation to his or her collective.

Triandis (1972) presented one of the earliest models that explicitly linked macro-societal elements to micro-individual behavior. His model describes how people in different cultures perceive their social environment, as well as the impact of environmental factors on these processes. Perhaps the most notable aspect of Triandis' model is its breadth in assessing the relations among environment, social environment, values, and psychological process.

The distal antecedent of subjective culture is physical environment – resources as well as historical events. The physical environment has a direct impact on a society's economic activities that, in turn, influence more proximal antecedents such as occupations and labor structure. Historical events have an impact on the social and political organizations that evolve in a society as well as the more proximal aspects of

culture including language, religion, location, and feedback from own behavior. With regard to other effects, Triandis posits that proximal antecedents have an impact on pancultural psychological processes that, in turn, create subjective culture. For example, religion and language influence the types of categorizations that individuals make, the number of categories they use, as well as the consistency with which a particular label is assigned to a particular object. Occupations and social settings also influence roles that individuals enact as well as tasks they perform. For example, trades (e.g., carpentry) involve mentoring and apprenticeship, and thus encourage hierarchically differentiated roles within the context of a communal group (Van Maanen and Barley, 1984).

The determinants of action in Triandis' model are behavioral intentions and habits. The link from subjective culture to behavioral intentions provides an explicit relation that is lacking in value-based models. In a subjective culture approach, values influence behavioral intentions through an individual's affective states as well as cognitive structures (although values are reciprocally determined by cognitive structures). Triandis adds non-volitional antecedents of action not typically incorporated in others' models.

Habits represent the impact of repeated feedback concerning particular actions. Likewise, social behavior and protocol such as social distance reflect habit rather than cognition.

Thus, the core of Triandis' model is the specific action of behavioral patterns as a function of distal and proximal antecedents that impact subjective culture. His model captures the relation of macro, societal-level influences on individuals' responses through psychological process.

Hofstede's work on cultural values is perhaps the most widely cited work on culture developed for the study of organizations (1984; 1991). Hofstede developed a four dimension overview of cultural variation in values based on data from over 40 countries from a single multinational organization and over 100,000 questionnaires from individuals in a wide variety of occupations, ages, and other demographic backgrounds measured at two different time periods.

Hofstede's model of culture is based on the idea that culture can be viewed as a series of mental programs; culture is '… the collective programming of the mind which distinguishes the members of one human group from another' (1984: 21). These mental programs refer to prescribed ways of acting, and vary according to levels of uniqueness. At the least unique level are universal mental programs that are shared by all people, such as flight-or-fight oriented responses, emotional displays, and other parts of the human biological system. Slightly higher is the collective level that refers to mental programming shared among individuals belonging to a certain group or category, similar to Triandis' (1972) concept of subjective culture. Finally, the individual level of programming refers to those aspects of an individual that determine unique personalities. These mental programs are transferred through genetic linkages as well as learned by individuals through their cultural system, particularly during childhood and early development. The middle, or collective, level, refers to the programming that is most often transferred via socialization mechanisms.

At the core of mental programs are values and culture. Values are defined as '… a broad tendency to prefer certain states of affairs over others' (Hofstede, 1984: 18) and are an attribute of individuals as well as collectivities. Hofstede's research on cultural values was framed within a general model of forces on cultural patterns. His model begins with exogenous influences (e.g., forces of nature, trade and conquest) that affect cultural origins (e.g., historical, technological, and urbanization effects). Origins, in turn, influence societal norms (e.g., value systems of major groups in the population) followed by consequences (e.g., education, religion and family patterns), and these consequences reinforce the origins and societal norms. Hofstede argues that outside influences rarely have a direct impact on norms; rather, they influence norms through cultural origins such as technology. Values play a key role by regulating the impact of these origins on consequences such as institutional practices.

Markus and Kitayama (1991) present a significant view of self concept from a cultural perspective. Together with Triandis (1990), they provided the initial discussion of how culture and self can be integrated. Within this approach, self concept is represented by a collection of associations of memberships and activities. Using the metaphor of Venn diagrams, these associations vary in their relative size, degree of inclusiveness, and overlap with other associations.

According to Erez and Earley's (1993) Cultural Self Representation Model, people have the capacity for self evaluation, which necessitates the preservation of a positive self esteem. Self regulatory processes ensure that people maintain a positive self view in a variety of operating environments. Individuals' self concept, then, is partly of its own origins. Erez and Earley argue that three basic motives guide self concept, namely, enhancement, efficacy, and consistency. Self enhancement refers to the desire to feel positively, and is affected by environmental influences, and psychological processes of sampling, assessing, and interpreting the environment.

The model's second motive is self efficacy (Bandura, 1986: 391), 'a judgment of one's capability to accomplish a certain level of performance.' Efficacy judgments promote the choice of situations and tasks with high likelihood of success, and eliminate the choice of tasks that exceed one's capabilities. Erez and Early's final motive is self consistency. Self consistency leads to the active construction of memories and selective perceptions in line with previous events, and directs people to behave according to their values and norms.

The concept of 'cultural intelligence' (Earley, 2002; Earley and Ang, 2003; Thomas and Inkson, 2004) takes cross-cultural research in a somewhat different direction. The cultural intelligence perspective explains and describes individuals' cultural adjustment based on a faceted model of intelligence, rather than on commonly-held cultural values or beliefs. In contrast to traditional acculturation and adjustment literature that tends to consist of atheoretical groupings of effects and predictors, cultural intelligence integrates a multi-faceted approach through the general construct of intelligence.[1]

Cultural intelligence (CQ) reflects an individual's capability to adapt effectively across cultures (Earley, 2002; Earley and Ang, 2003), and seeks to understand inter-individual differences in the ability to adapt effectively to new cultural settings (Earley and Ang, 2003; Thomas and Inkson, 2004). In Earley and Ang's (2003) theory, CQ comprises four facets: meta-cognition (cognitive strategies to acquire and develop coping strategies), cognition (knowledge about different cultures), motivation (desire and self-efficacy), and behavior (repertoire of culturally-appropriate behaviors).

A review of intercultural competence research reveals various predictors of effectiveness (Dinges and Baldwin, 1996) that can be classified as either *individual difference factors* (ranging from demographic variables such as previous experience, to general personality traits, to more specific variables involving cross-cultural attitudes and communicative behaviors) or *situational factors* (e.g., pre-departure training, cultural distance). CQ clearly fits into the first category of individual difference variables. Unlike general personality traits that are relatively enduring, however, CQ can be developed and enhanced through intervention. CQ also differs from communicative behavior, in that it is a broader concept that includes, but is not limited to, behavioral competency; it implies a broad repertoire of verbal and non-verbal behaviors that may be exhibited appropriately according to the cultural context.

Is CQ an indicator or a predictor of cross-cultural effectiveness? Akin to theories of human intelligence, CQ is a capability that is posited to predict, but is distinct from, the actual outcome arising from a specific situation or episode of interaction. In other words, we expect that individuals with high CQ are likely to adapt faster and more effectively, although the presence (or absence) of other factors may alter this relationship. Nevertheless, individuals who are effective in a particular cross-cultural situation should not be presumed to have high CQ, as such a judgment is based purely on the outcome of effectiveness, and not from an analysis of the individual's relevant capabilities.

In summary, our review of these core frameworks shows some that there has been a trend away from a focus on cultural values towards other antecedents of culturally-based action and that researchers are returning to the cross-level work that was outlined nearly forty years ago by scholars such as Triandis. The next section shows how recent work builds on these trends to address core theoretical challenges in cross-cultural research.

RECENT RESEARCH

We now focus on recent research that isolates specific mechanisms for how culture affects individuals, teams and organizations. Because many of the early cross-cultural studies focused on discovering average differences in focal variables between national samples, there were abundant research findings on the main effects of culture. Chen (2006) notes that cross-cultural researchers are now finding that direct comparisons of mean differences can be problematic (Van de Vijver and Leung, 1997). Consequently, researchers examining the interplay between culture and various other constructs have begun examining more complex, dynamic interactional models to try to uncover the relationships between culture and myriad outcomes (see Hong et al., 2000; Erez and Gati, 2004). In other words, an evolution is taking shape, moving from a focus on comparative research (i.e., 'What happens') to an emphasis on uncovering the explanatory mechanisms and underlying theoretical relationships (i.e., 'How and why does it work?').

In general, researchers seeking to answer these 'how and why' questions can theorize about two kinds[2] of causal relationships linking culture to lower-level outcomes, namely main effects (including mediation) or moderation (Lytle et al., 1995). In main-effect models, culture is posited to affect organizational behavior either directly or via another (sometimes unspecified) variable. Morris and Young (2002) make an important observation: to measure a mediating process, such as culture's influence on behavior via knowledge structures, researchers must not only determine whether the cognitive structure is *available* to the individual, but also whether it has been *activated* in relation to the task. Therefore, to understand how culture influences organizational behavior, researchers must pay attention to the processes and contextual factors that trigger individuals to apply their culturally conferred knowledge in any given situation. In many of the studies we review below, researchers use explicit theorizing and careful designs and analysis in order to investigate culture's impact on mediating variables.

In contrast, culture can be conceived as moderating a relationship between two other variables. Given that much of the organizational behavior research in the twentieth century was generated from a Western perspective, the field is ripe for

studies that show how culture changes (strengthens, weakens, reverses) previously 'known' relationships. In the more rigorous of these studies, culture itself is directly measured, rather than offered as a post hoc explanation for different outcomes in a comparative study.

The remainder of this section focuses on more recent work, both empirical and theoretical, that aims to uncover *how* culture affects organizational behavior. We base the review on two factors: the type of relationship posited between culture and outcome variables (main effects/mediation or moderation), and the basic level of analysis used for theorizing (individual, group or organization).[3] We further divide some of the longer subsections based on thematic similarities. Table 2 provides an overview of the studies in this review.

Mediation studies – individual level

A long history of research, especially in cross-cultural psychology, has examined the role of culture at an individual level, seeking to understand how various aspects of a person's native culture influence individual-level outcomes (see Kirkman et al., 2006). Recent theoretical and empirical work is beginning to uncover the *mechanisms* through which culture affects individuals. One approach draws on theory from social cognition and suggests how culture affects individuals' perceptions, framing and other cognitive functioning. This stream typifies the move away from cultural values toward other internal, proximal mechanisms outlined above. A second approach draws more on industrial-organizational psychology to posit culture's effects via organizational factors such as work practices. Recognizing the heterogeneity existing at the national level, a substream of this research considers the role of ethnic culture on individual outcomes. This sort of research represents the move toward examining culture's influence via external, distal mechanisms. We examine these two approaches with some exemplary recent work.

Table 2 Overview of key studies in Section 3, classified by culture's causal role, primary level of analysis, and type of research

	Individual level	Group level	Organisational level
Main effects	• Choi and Nisbett, 1998 (E) • Choi, Nisbett, and Norenzayan, 1999(E) • Fischer et al., 2005 (T) • Gelfand et al., 2001 (E) • Gelfand et al., 2006 (T) • Gibson, Maznevski and Kirkman, forthcoming (T) • Hanges et al., 2000 (T) • Heine et al., 2002 (E) • Kirkman, Lowe, and Gibson, 2006 (R) • Morris and Peng, 1994 (E) • Nisbett, Peng, Choi and Norenzayan, 2001 (T) • Pineda and Whitehead, 1997 (E) • Sullivan and Transue, 1999 (R)	• Adair, Tinsley and Taylor, 2006 (T) • Behfar, Kern and Brett, 2006 (T) • Dahlin, Weingart and Hinds, 2005 (E) • Earley and Mosakowski, 2000 (E) • Gibson and Zellmer-Bruhn, 2001 (E) • Haas, 2006 (E) • Kirkman and Shapiro, 1997 (T) • Kirkman and Shapiro, 2001 (E) • Moynihan, Peterson and Earley, 2006 (E) • Randel, 2003 (E) • Ravlin, Thomas and Ilsev, 2000 (T) • Sanchez-Burks, Nisbett and Ybarra, 2000 (E)	• Aycan, Kanungo, et al., 2000 (E) • Fischer et al., 2007 (E) • Kanungo and Jaeger 1990 (T) • Mathur, Aycan, et al., 1996 (E) • Mendonce and Kanungo, 1994 (T) • Sagie and Aycan, 2003 (T)
Moderating effects	• Fischer and Smith, 2006 (E) • Gelfand, Erez and Aycan, 2006 (R) • Zhong et al., 2006 (E)	• Earley and Gardner, 2005 (T) • Elfenbein and Shirako, 2006 (T) • Wang, Doucet and Northcraft, 2006 (T)	• Fischer et al., 2005 (T)

Notes:
(R) Review.
(T) Theoretical/conceptual, without empirical data.
(E) Empirical (studies may develop and/or test theory, but all include empirical data).

Cognitive approach

The basic thesis underlying the cognitive approach is that processing frameworks acquired in one culture persist and influence individual behavior, even when circumstances change (Walsh, 1995). One important finding from the cognitive stream of research concerns the fundamental attribution error (FAE), the tendency to attribute people's behavior to their fixed characteristics (i.e., personality) rather than to the situation. For decades, the psychological literature indicated that the FAE was a universal principle, invariant across cultures (see Morris and Peng, 1994). More recently, however, psychological research confirms that Asians are much less likely to commit the FAE than Americans; instead, Asians tend to attribute behavior much more to the situation and context (Choi and Nisbett, 1998; Morris and Peng, 1994).

This line of research is even more important, in our view, because it begins to uncover some of the underlying reasons for these differences, rather than simply cataloging cross-cultural variation. Morris and Peng (1994), for example, propose and test a theory that culture affects cognitions via individuals' implicit theory of human behavior, acquired through induction and socialization in their native culture. Accordingly, the person-centered theory (i.e., social behavior expresses mainly stable, global, internal dispositions) is posited as more widespread in cultures influenced by Judeo-Christian notions of individualism. The situation-centered theory (i.e., social behavior is shaped by relationships and context) is more prevalent in collectivistic cultures where people are steeped in Confucian beliefs about the primacy of social relations.

Nisbett et al. (2001) posit two distinct mechanisms through which culture affects cognitive processes: first, indirectly by focusing attention on specific parts of the environment and second, directly by making some kinds of social patterns more acceptable than others. In brief, they trace Westerners' *analytic* cognitive style (i.e., focused on the object, the categories to which it belongs and the rules /logic that govern its behavior) to ancient Greek society where beliefs about individuals' autonomy focused attention on the object in isolation from its context. In contrast, because ancient Chinese society directed people's attention toward the social field, today East Asians tend to prefer a *holistic* cognitive style. In addition, Nisbett et al. propose that cognitive systems and social practices mutually support and reinforce one another, identifying numerous practices (e.g., fêng shui, legal contracts, language acquisition) that could act as links between culture and cognitive systems over long time periods. In general terms, this research develops a mediation model that links culture's effects on cognitive functioning via specific mechanisms that are theoretically justified and empirically testable.

Gelfand and colleagues have conducted research to show how culture affects cognitive representations related to conflict and negotiation. Gelfand et al. (2001) propose that disputants' cognitive representations are influenced by the perception of the self that is dominant in the surrounding culture (i.e., individualistic vs. collectivistic). Consistent with this supposition, they found that Americans framed particular conflicts as an issue of winning and violations to individual rights, whereas Japanese perceived the same conflict to be about compromise and violations of duty. Gelfand et al. (2006) develop a complex theoretical model linking culture (among other factors) to negotiation behaviors and outcomes. Briefly, they build on research showing that people from different national cultures vary in the degree to which they are and perceive themselves

to be relational. The accessibility of the relational self-construal affects its strength, in turn affecting pre-negotiation psychological states (i.e., frames, judgments, goals), behaviors and outcomes. This research furthers our understanding of mediating mechanisms that link culture with specific behavioral outcomes; in particular, it shows the value of considering internal, proximal mechanisms aside from cultural values.

Finally, Hanges et al. (2000) develop an information-processing model that connects culture with leadership and follower reactions and behaviors. In their framework, cultural meaning systems generate cognitive components such as affect, values, and self-concept. In turn, these elements influence scripts and beliefs, which people use to interpret leadership behaviors. The authors' use of a connectionist architecture helps to develop an explicit meditation model that accounts for specific cognitive mechanisms intervening between culture and behavior.

Behavioral approach

Alongside the information-processing or cognitive approach, a body of research draws on industrial-organizational psychology to seek mechanisms through which culture affects individual behaviors and motivation. Much of this work builds, explicitly or implicitly, on what Chen et al. (1998: 287) call the 'layers model of culture,' derived from Hofstede (Hofstede et al., 1990). This model presumes that cultural values, assumptions and beliefs constitute the foundational elements of culture. Tangible artifacts and patterns of activities and behaviors are culture's outwardly visible manifestations, constituting the top of the pyramid. The intervening mechanisms make up the mid-level of the pyramid, and it is these specific constructs that researchers must identify through rigorous theorizing and empirical testing.

Few studies using the behavioral approach move beyond cultural values to investigate culture as a system of external-proximal influences on individual behavior. This approach, which requires interdisciplinary thinking, is certainly under-explored. We agree with Singelis (2000: 87) who writes, 'although it is difficult, connecting institutions and social interactions with the transmission of culture and, subsequently, with psychological and behavioral outcomes is well worth the effort.'

Sullivan and Transue's (1999) review of democracy and its psychological underpinnings sheds some light on the link between institutional influences and individual outcomes, with their section focusing on cross-national studies of political participation most relevant here. They cogently review Inglehart's (1977, 1990, 1997) work, linking economic development with psychological variables (e.g., interpersonal trust, cognitive motivation) that underpin citizens' participation in political processes. Sullivan and Transue also review institutional effects on interpersonal trust (i.e., Putnam, 1993) and social capital (i.e., Brehm and Rahm, 1997; Stolle, 1998). While some of these works are limited in their explicit discussion of national culture, they could inspire researchers investigating cross-cultural differences in organizational behavior.

Turning to work within the cross-cultural field, Fischer et al. (2005) build on work by Aycan and colleagues (see below) to offer a multi-level theoretical model linking national culture with individual-level behaviors. Specifically, their model links four cultural values (power distance, fatalism, individualism, and paternalism) with four work practices (participation, communications, innovation, and support), ultimately leading to two types of extra-role behaviors (voice and helping).

Gibson et al. (forthcoming) contribute an important theoretical piece that not only delineates specific mechanisms for culture's influence on four types of individual-level work outcomes (perceptions, beliefs, values and behaviors), but also suggests moderators at the individual, group and contextual levels that delimit culture's impact on each of these effects. For example, in considering how personality moderates the propensity to behave in accordance with culture, the authors propose that culture will be a stronger predictor of *perceptions* when the trait *openness* is low, whereas culture will be a stronger predictor of *behavior* when *conscientiousness* is high. They also address more macro constructs that have been ignored in cross-cultural research (e.g., the effects of economic uncertainty and strong vs. weak technological environments).

While most of the research examining culture's effects on OB has used national culture as the focal level of analysis, there is a growing recognition that other cultural systems have significant effects on organizational phenomena (Earley and Singh, 1995). Pineda and Whitehead (1997) highlight the importance of considering ethnic groups, particularly in multicultural societies. Ethnic groups differ from other sub-group populations in their desire to maintain distinct values and behaviors, rather than assimilate, as for example immigrants might. Two studies (Heine et al., 2002; Pineda and Whitehead, 1997) demonstrate that differences between two ethnic sub-groups within the same culture (Asian Canadians vs. European Canadians; ethnic Chinese versus Filipinos in the Philippines) were more pronounced than when those two cultures were compared at the national levels. Such findings highlight the caution researchers must take in measuring cultural values at the appropriate level and considering the effects of sub-culture within a single nation.

Mediation studies – group/team level

A growing body of work investigates culture's impact on teams and teamwork. We classify this literature into two categories: research examining how culture affects people's perceptions about teams (i.e., what is the meaning of 'team,' what constitutes success for a team) and research focusing on group process and outcomes within multicultural teams. In many ways these two streams parallel the breakdown between 'cognitive' and 'behavioral' traditions covered above, although each encompasses somewhat broader perspectives and draws on a wider range of literature than their respective segments in the individual-level research.

Perceptions about teams

This first area of research concerns culture's effects on people's understanding of teams and teamwork, and tends to contrast cognition between different cultures. Gibson and Zellmer-Bruhn (2001), for example, draw on linguistic theory to develop a conceptual framework to explain how the meaning of teamwork varies across national and organizational cultures. The authors argue that knowledge of the categories that workers use to comprehend their environment can be used to clarify their behaviors. In-depth interviews of workers in six firms across four countries indicated that employees in different national and organizational cultures construe teamwork through five metaphors: family, sports, community, associates and military. They found that the use of each metaphor leads to different expectations of team roles, scope, membership and objectives. Gibson and Zellmer-Bruhn's study shows how cognitive frames act as mechanisms through which the cultural context (national and organizational) influences teams.

Sanchez-Burks et al. (2000) also examined how schemas about successful workgroups differ across cultures, using the concept of relational schemas. These cognitive structures provide goals about what can be expected to occur in a given situation, what behaviors are and are not appropriate, and which elements in the situation should be attended to (Fiske and Taylor, 1991). Sanchez-Burks et al. suggest that two types of relational schemas (task and socio-emotional) act as the mechanisms through which culture affects people's view of what factors inhibit or facilitate workgroup success. They theorize that those people whose culture emphasizes *sympatía* (Triandis and Berry, 1980), a value of personal charm, graciousness and hospitality, are likely to hold positive socio-emotional schemas regarding appropriate and successful workgroup interactions; in contrast, those people whose culture stems from Protestantism, which

historically emphasizes a strict distinction between work and social events, are likely to judge group work with schemas that accentuate task behaviors and minimize socioemotional displays. Consistent with their theorizing, the authors find in both lab- and field-based studies that Latins (Mexicans and Mexican-American) perceive socioemotional behaviors (i.e., discussing leisure activities) to be important for group success, whereas Anglo-Americans believe that high task orientation and low socioemotional displays were valuable for group success.

Kirkman and Shapiro (1997, 2001) have developed and tested a theoretical model positing an attitudinal mediator – resistance to self-managing work teams (SMWTs) – as the link between members' cultural values and team effectiveness. Kirkman and Shapiro (1997) initially suggested that individualism generates resistance to teams, while a 'being orientation' (e.g., value on minimizing work), power distance and determinism increase members' resistance to self-management. Their model further suggested that resistance to teams and to self-management would detract from team outcomes (e.g., productivity, cooperation and empowerment). In a follow-on field study of 81 SMWTs in Belgium, Finland, the Philippines and United States, Kirkman and Shapiro (2001) found that resistance to SMWT's did indeed mediate between members' cultural values and team effectiveness. It should be noted that Kirkman and Shapiro theorize and analyze their data at the group level; although they measured items at the individual level and aggregated them to the team, they did take careful steps to ensure that there was sufficient within-group agreement and between-group variance.

Multicultural team interaction and outcomes

Beyond the work focusing on between-culture comparisons, a body of work on multicultural teams begins to address Gelfand, et al.'s (2007) call for more research focusing on the dynamics of culture in inter-cultural encounters, or what they call 'the cross-cultural interface.' Given the pace and scope of globalization, organizations increasingly turn to multicultural teams as sources of innovation, problem solving, and general management (Earley and Gibson, 2002). Interestingly, it seems that the preponderance of these studies so far have focused on the challenges experienced by multicultural teams, such as conflict and challenges in learning.

In general, two theoretical domains inform cross-cultural research examining these challenges faced by multicultural teams (Earley and Gibson, 2002): (1) team composition and (2) team cognition and process. We include research on diversity and composition in our review of mediation studies because these studies typically posit culture as an initial input that affects team output via its impact on an interim (mediating) variable. The second area, team cognition and process, is fairly wide-ranging, covering the main (often mediated) effects of culture on areas such as conflict, communications, and shared belief systems. Our review also includes an emerging body of work examining the development of team-specific cultures (also called 'hybrid' or 'third' cultures). Early research in this area drew on team composition literature to examine the emergence of hybrid cultures, and recent work now uses this established construct to understand multicultural team processes and outcomes (Earley and Mosakowski, 2000).

Multicultural team composition

This approach draws on cultural diversity research (e.g., Watson et al., 1993) relating particular demographic characteristics to cultural attributes, values and perceptions. This approach also draws from a long history of research on team composition and its effect on team process and performance (i.e., McGrath, 1984). In general, the benefits of diversity stem from the variety of skills, experience and attributes offered by different team members. The downside of diversity, however, is that it is often more difficult for heterogeneous teams to develop effective group process. Overall, then, this literature suggests that the impact of

cultural diversity on team performance will be mixed, and likely subject to a number of contextual constraints.

Ravlin et al. (2000) develop a mediation model with a 'focus on the collision of different cultural value systems' and its impact on conflict (p. 23). They suggest that individuals in multicultural groups use culture as a way to categorize others, thereby highlighting members' different beliefs. This confrontation with opposing values challenges an individual's self-perceived legitimacy, in turn leading to negative affect and conflict. Given that different traits, behaviors and characteristics are valued more or less across different cultures, it is likely that members of multicultural groups will not necessarily agree on others' implicit ranking based on prestige. Such disagreement affects members' self-perceived legitimacy, and moderates the link between negative affect and open conflict within the group. In summary, the theoretical model developed by Ravlin et al. (2000) suggests that the mere presence of multiple cultures within a work group is a trigger for a host of group processes.

Earley and Mosakowski (2000) examined the effects of teams' nationality heterogeneity on performance. They hypothesized a curvilinear relationship between team heterogeneity and nationality and team performance, with effects depending on the time frame. Through a qualitative field study the authors develop a mediation model, positing that the effects of team composition on performance would be mediated by members' shared identity, team efficacy, expectations and intrateam communications. In the short term, all levels of heterogeneity had a detrimental effect on team functioning. Over time, however, highly heterogeneous teams appeared to develop a hybrid culture; these shared expectations and beliefs allowed them to exchange information and coordinate effectively. An important inference from Earley and Mosakowski's (2000) work is that multicultural team members do pay attention to one another's nationality and use this information to categorize others and interpret their behaviors.

Randel's (2003) study further isolates the conditions under which national culture becomes salient and influences the dynamics in multicultural teams. By measuring cultural identity salience at the individual level, Randel explored how team composition differently affects each team member's perception of how conspicuous or prominent members' nationalities are. This approach, which measures rather than assumes the salience of culture for individual team members, is an important step toward understanding how and when differences in cultural backgrounds will affect multicultural team dynamics.

Dahlin et al. (2005) found a curvilinear relationship between teams' nationality diversity and three stages of information use. As teams' national diversity increased from moderate to low, they used narrower ranges of information but considered that information more deeply and integrated it more completely into their project reports. As team diversity increased from moderate to high levels, however, the range of information use increased while depth and integration declined. Their results on information variety correspond to Earley and Mosakowski's (2000) findings that moderate levels of heterogeneity interfere with information use, while their findings on depth and integration contradict the prior study. One explanation suggests that the salience of team members' nationality varies over time, thereby determining how much nationality diversity will impact different stages of a team's information processing. In particular, if nationality salience is high in the initial stages of team formation, then diversity may negatively affect the search for new ideas and hamper a team's range of information used. If nationality salience declines over time, diversity's negative impact will lessen as the team moves on to processing and integrating the information. Like Randel (2003), the authors point out the need to measure salience rather than assume that nationality will affect team process and outcomes.

Finally, Haas (2006) addresses a question with both theoretical and practical significance: how does the mix of team members' national and international experience affect performance in multinational teams? Haas examines the roles of cosmopolitans (individuals with broad experience in many countries) and locals (those with deep experience in the project country) in multinational teams that work on knowledge-intensive projects, and finds that composition affects the acquisition and application of knowledge, in turn affecting project quality. This approach, while not explicitly linked to culture per se, represents an important step toward understanding influences and constraints within culture-bound situations.

Multicultural team process and outcomes

Researchers of multicultural teams also draw on work from social and industrial-organizational psychology that examines cognition and process within teams. When applied to multicultural teams, researchers tend to study how different cultural values or orientations affect team members' collective cognitions or their preference for group process. As one example, Behfar et al. (2006) conducted two studies to contrast culturally homogenous teams with multicultural teams to identify a set of problems that are unique to multicultural teams. They found that multicultural teams in particular must grapple with issues of explicit versus implicit communication, especially concerning the degree to which they have reached agreement and/or consensus. While not directly measuring cultural values, the authors propose that the reasons for such differences stem from members' different national origins. In general, Behfar et al. suggest that the challenges faced by multicultural teams were more complex and often invoked more serious consequences than those encountered in same-culture teams.

Moynihan et al. (2006) develop and test a model that blends theory of both cultural and compositional effects on team process. They suggest that experience working in a multicultural team will enhance members' CQ, especially in teams with strong norms and open communication. They argue that the team's mean level of CQ predicts team relational processes (trust, cohesion), because CQ is a predictive composition variable that should become more evident to team members with increasing familiarity. In a longitudinal study of 48 multinational teams, Moynihan et al. found that higher levels of team CQ were indeed correlated with group trust and cohesion three months later. They also found that teams higher in CQ were more effective on group projects. Although they did not provide a complete test of their mediation model, they presume that team CQ improves group effectiveness via its impact on the group process.

Hybrid culture

Scholars now recognize that culturally diverse teams do not begin with shared meaning systems; rather, over time multicultural teams develop a unique set of shared beliefs through their interactions. To indicate that this team-specific culture represents a composite of members' native cultural elements, Earley and Mosakowski (2002: 27) term this construct a 'hybrid culture' and define it as 'an emergent and simplified set of rules, norms, expectations, and roles that team members share and "enact".' As discussed above, Earley and Mosakowski theorize on the effects of varying levels of heterogeneity on the emergence of team culture, and demonstrate that these effects vary over time.

Adair et al. (2006) refer to the emergent shared schemas within multicultural teams as 'third cultures,' and they identify three specific ways in which cultural elements can be combined to generate a unique team culture. In the *union* model, aspects of team members' national cultures may be combined additively. In contrast, the *intersection* model implies that only the overlapping elements of each member's national culture will combine to form the third culture. Finally, the *emergent* third culture contains novel aspects that do not originate from any of the native cultures; these new elements arise perhaps in response to the need to negotiate differences in values, perceptions and expectation amongst culturally diverse team members. Similar to Earley and Mosakowski's (2000) findings on

hybrid cultures, Adair et al. argue that the successful negotiation of a third culture is essential to the process of sensemaking and group identity-building that in turn enhance group performance and outcomes.

Mediation studies – organizational level

A great deal of comparative research has focused on identifying cross-cultural differences on firm-level variables such as human resource practices (i.e., Geringer et al., 2002). Scholars have devoted considerably less attention, however, to understanding why and how culture shapes organizational outcomes. Given that cultural factors are only one of many variables to influence organizational choices, models that incorporate some degree of this complexity allow us to start parsing cultural effects from other environmental contingencies. One research stream investigated the relative influence of culture, and found that whereas contingencies like a company's development stage or technology influence formal characteristics of organization (e.g., centralization, span of control), cultural variables influence interpersonal aspects such as power and authority structure, delegation, communications, etc. (Tayeb, 1988). Others suggest that culture can be expected to influence organizational processes (i.e., the way organizations function) rather than formal characteristics (Drenth and Groenendijk, 1984) or that culture affects the choice of practices while institutional factors (e.g., size, industry) affect how practices are designed and implemented (Aycan, 2005). In short, research tells us that culture's effects will most likely arise where agents apply culturally-induced knowledge to make organizational decisions.

Kanungo, Aycan and colleagues have developed an important stream of meso-level theories linking culture to organizational behavior via its impact on an organization's work practices. Initially, they (Kanungo and Jaeger, 1990; Mendonca and Kanungo, 1994) propose a model linking cultural values (i.e., individualism-collectivism, power distance) to an organization's internal culture, which in turn is theorized to influence human resource practices such as work design, performance management and reward systems. Several empirical studies have tested this 'Model of Cultural Fit' with samples ranging between one (Mathur et al., 1996) and ten (Aycan et al., 2000) cultures. The latter study measured organizational culture as individual managerial assumptions about employee nature and behavior, such as malleability (i.e., belief that employees can change and improve their skills given the right training). The authors argue that different cultural values guide managers' interpretation of the environment, resulting in different sets of assumptions about people in the organization. In contrast, institutional differences (i.e., size, ownership structure, industry) shape managers' task-related assumptions. Together, these assumptions constitute differing organizational cultures. This study confirmed that organizational culture mediates between national cultural values and work practices (job design, supervisory practices and reward allocation).

Fischer et al. (2007) offer a rare study that includes macro-economic variables (national unemployment levels and income inequality) as predictors of organizational reward allocation practices. They found these variables, as well as Schwarz's nation-level values and organizational factor (e.g., performance) to be significant predictors of organizations' allocating rewards based on equity, equality or need.

Moderation studies – individual level

A different set of relationships are postulated in cross-cultural research examining culture as a moderator of previously established relationships. In these studies, culture acts to dampen, enhance or even change the nature of the link between two other variables. Much recent research focuses on understanding how culture affects individual level relationships that were previously established in a single (often Western, typically American) culture. Gelfand et al. (2007) comprehensively review recent studies in which culture is theorized

or empirically demonstrated to moderate a host of relationships between the individual and the organization, including organizational commitment, psychological contract, organizational justice, and organizational citizenship behaviors. Given this recent review, we highlight a single recent study illustrating how investigating national culture as a moderator can enhance our knowledge of individual behaviors.

Zhong et al. (2006) develop a framework to explain how culture moderates the previously established positive relationship between power and assertive action. The original model, developed in the context of Western societies, suggested that high power is associated with a greater action orientation. In Eastern cultures, however, high power is associated with greater caution and restraint. This apparent contradiction led Zhong et al. to restate the original theory in more general terms: power activates *culturally valued goals* that in turn have behavioral consequences. Preliminary testing of their model suggests that Asians (or Asian-Americans) are likely to behave differently than Americans when primed with high power. Despite the lack of strong empirical support thus far, this paper is interesting because it suggests that culture affects not only the norms for how people consciously believe they should behave but also individuals' unconscious responses to everyday cues.

Moderation studies – team level

Compared with research at the individual level, relatively little attention has been paid to culture as a moderator of groups or teams. Earley and Gardner (2005) develop a conceptual framework to explain variance in multi-national teams (MNTs), incorporating CQ as a moderator of core team dynamics. The authors propose that team composition (i.e., the number/proportion of members with high CQ) will influence groups' problem solving effectiveness. Drawing on group decision making literature (i.e., McGrath, 1984) the authors offer two competing hypotheses for predicting the optimal level of CQ in a team.

Expanding on this idea, Earley and Gardner examine which facets of CQ (i.e., metacognition versus motivational) are most critical for success in multinational teams and elaborate on how a CQ perspective could modify prior empirical findings concerning MNTs.

Aside from this compositional perspective, research using culture as a moderator can follow what Brewer (2006: 354) called a 'culturally infused' model of group process: authors take an existing theoretical model and 'plug in' cultural influences at various stages to see how culture affects prior relationships. In one study, Wang et al. (2006) explore how a set of cultural values (individualism-collectivism, power distance) moderate links in their model of affect and social influence in multicultural decision-making groups. In particular, they argue that individual-level cultural values will affect how much attention group members pay to others' nonverbal affective expressions, to whom they pay attention, and how accurate are their perceptions of those others. Elfenbein and Shirako (2006) also develop an integrated process model of emotion in teams, suggesting how teammates' cultural differences can affect each stage of the process. It is interesting to note that the key cultural difference these authors explore is emotional expressiveness – a variable that is somewhat less studied in cross-cultural research, but that clearly has important implications for multicultural teams.

Moderation studies – organizational level

Fischer et al. (2005) develop a multi-level theory for the effects of national culture on organizational work practices and individual employee attitudes and behaviors, and propose moderators that could strengthen or weaken these links. They suggest, for example, that the effect of national culture on organizational practices will be weakened when sizeable subcultures exist and employees do not agree on the values of the dominant subculture. They also argue that employees of multinational companies are exposed both to the local national culture and to the socio-cultural effects of the employing organization's home culture, as transmitted by expatriate managers, organizational structures, etc. In contrast, employees of indigenous organizations (owned and operated by nationals) will be affected only by the local culture. They propose, therefore, that the effects of national culture on organizational practices will be stronger for indigenous organizations compared with multinational organizations.

CONCLUSION

More than a decade ago, Earley and Singh (1995: 333) highlighted a nascent trend in intercultural research as '... the critical question shifts from, "Will it work here?" to "How and why does it work?".' Since then, the movement away from comparative research toward unpacking the underlying theoretical relationships has developed perhaps more slowly than anticipated (and hoped for). Yet this chapter shows that considerable progress has been made, and we now conclude by highlighting these recent advances and emerging directions in the arena of cross-cultural research.

First, researchers are confronting cross-level issues in their work, often using increasingly sophisticated theorizing and analyses to do so. Recent theorizing by Erez and Gati (2004) exemplifies one approach to understanding the reciprocal influences of culture across five nested levels: individual, group, organizational, national and global cultures. Their model suggests that *top-down* processes convey on lower levels the effects of higher-level constructs such as migration, historical events, technological advance, etc. In their model, *bottom-up* processes describe how phenomena with origins at the lower level emerge to become higher level properties (e.g., team performance from individuals' behaviors, team mental models from individuals' cognitions). Erez and Gati's model provides an important foundation for cross-cultural research that empirically tests mechanisms that transfer and shape culture across multiple levels. Gibson, et al. (forthcoming) develop a multi-level contingency model to address the research question, 'What are the conditions that increase an individual's propensity to think, feel, value or behave in accordance with culture?' Investigating moderating factors at the individual, group and contextual levels thus underscores the complexity of culture's effects on individual outcomes.

Clearly, then, cutting-edge research in cross-cultural organizational behavior focuses on explicit recognition and theorizing about the level(s) of analysis under investigation. While the preponderance of cross-cultural research still examines individual-level phenomena (often without due regard for identifying how culture affects lower levels), important new work focuses on culture's effects on teams and groups (e.g., Behfar et al., 2006; Moynihan et al., 2006). Two recent studies (Dahlin et al., 2005; Haas, 2006) with both theoretical and practical value have connected the important areas of cross-cultural issues and knowledge use in teams. To date, however, scholars have devoted far too little attention on developing or testing cross-level theories in cross-cultural OB research, which presents a clear opportunity for the future.

A second major development in cross-cultural research involves moving beyond cultural values to uncover and explore alternative mechanisms that explain how culture affects organizational behavior. As we discussed, researchers can conceptualize two types of cultural effects that constrain people from exhibiting otherwise universal behaviors: *internal-proximal* constraints such as cognitive structures, or *external-distal* constraints such as economic, social, political and developmental indicators that influence behavior.

The cultural intelligence (CQ) approach integrates cognitive process, motivation and behavior, thereby offering a theoretically grounded alternative to cultural values as an antecedent to culturally-induced outcomes. Ng and Earley (2006), for example,

develop a multi-level model of CQ, linking individual- and team-level CQ with performance outcomes at the individual, group and organizational levels. Such studies offer a potentially rich jumping-off point for future cross-cultural research that seeks to address both challenges outlined in this chapter: multi-level issues and alternative (non-values) antecedents to culturally-based outcomes.

Our chapter also highlights some of the foundational and emerging work that incorporates more distal antecedents of culturally-based behavior. Research on composition within multinational teams is helping us to understand inter-personal – rather than intra-individual – cultural constraints on behavior. Macro-level variables are another source of variance in organizational behavior. For example, Leung et al. (2005) review several pieces from the disciplines of economics, anthropology and sociology that examine how socio-political-economic variables moderate or mediate the effects of culture on individual and organizational behavior. Drawing attention to these variables will inspire future cross-cultural research that goes well beyond examining cultural values as the sole source of intercultural differences.

In conclusion, an evolution is taking shape, moving from a focus on comparative (or descriptive) research to an emphasis on uncovering the explanatory mechanisms and underlying theoretical relationships. Like all evolutions, early developments are slow in occurring; the goal of this chapter has been to enable more rapid and comprehensive growth of this fascinating and critical field.

NOTES

1 A notable exception to this atheoretic approach is reflected by Bhawuk and Brislin (1992). Instead of focusing on a particular target country the authors emphasize a target cultural value that can be shared across countries.

2 Lytle et al. (1995) propose a third approach to theorizing about culture, namely when researchers use culture as a source of emic meanings

and constructs. This approach is outside the scope of the present chapter.

3 As not all studies fall neatly into this categorization scheme (i.e., cross-level research) we classified studies based on our judgment of the primary purpose or most novel and interesting findings.

REFERENCES

Adair, W.L., Tinsley, C.H. and Taylor, M. (2006) 'Managing the intercultural interface: Third cultures, antecedents, and consequences', in Ya-Ru Chen, (ed.), *Research on Managing Groups and Teams: National Culture and Groups*. Greenwich, CT: JAI, pp. 205–232.

Aycan, Z. (2005) 'The interplay between cultural and institutional/structural contingencies in human resource management practices', *International Journal of Human Resource Management*, 16 (7): 1083–1119.

Aycan, Z., Kanungo, R.N., Mendonca, M., Yu, K., Deller, J., Stahl, G. and Kurshid, A. (2000) 'Impact of culture on human resources management practices: A 10-country comparison', *Applied Psychology: An International Review*, 49 (1): 192–221.

Bandura, A. (1986) *Social Foundations of Thoughts and Action: A Social Cognitive Theory*. Englewood Cliffs, NJ: Prentice-Hall.

Behfar, K., Kern, M. and Brett, J. (2006) 'Managing challenges in multicultural teams', in Ya-Ru Chen, (ed.), *Research on Managing Groups and Teams: National Culture and Groups*. Greenwich, CT: JAI, pp. 233–262.

Bhawuk, D.P. and Brislin, R.W. (1992) 'The measurement of intercultural sensitivity using the concepts of individualism and collectivism', *International Journal of Intercultural Relations*, 16: 413–446.

Bond, M. (1997) 'Adding value to the cross-cultural study of organizational behavior: Reculer pour mieux sauter', in P.C. Earley and M. Erez (eds), *New Perspectives on International Industrial and Organizational Psychology*. San Francisco: Jossey-Bass, pp. 256–275.

Bond, M.H. and Smith, P.B. (1996) 'Cross-cultural social and organizational psychology', *Annual Review of Psychology*, 47: 205–235.

Brehm, J. and Rahm, W. (1997) 'Individual-level evidence for the causes and consequences of social capital', *American Journal of Political Science*, 41: 999–1023.

Brewer, M.B. (2006) 'Bringing culture to the table', in Ya-Ru Chen (ed.), *Research on Managing Groups and Teams: National Culture and Groups*. Greenwich, CT: JAI, pp. 353–365.

Chen, C.C., Chen, X.-P. and Meindl, J.R. (1998) 'How can cooperation be fostered? The cultural effects of individualism-collectivism', *Academy of Management Review*, 23 (2): 285–304.

Chen, Y.-R. (2006) 'National culture and groups: An introduction', in Ya-Ru Chen (ed.), *Research on Managing Groups and Teams: National Culture and Groups*. Greenwich, CT: JAI, pp. xiii–xvi.

Chinese Culture Connection (1987) 'Chinese values and the search for culture-free dimensions of culture', *Journal of Cross-Cultural Psychology*, 18 (2): 143–164.

Choi, I. and Nisbett, R.E. (1998) 'Situational salience and cultural differences in the correspondence bias and actor-observer bias', *Personality and Social Psychological Bulletin*, 24 (9): 949–960.

Choi, I., Nisbett, R.E. and Norenzayan, A. (1999) 'Causal attribution across cultures: Variation and universality', *Psychological Bulletin*, 125: 47–63.

Dahlin, K.B., Weingart, L.R. and Hinds, P.J. (2005) 'Team diversity and information use', *Academy of Management Journal*, 48 (6): 1107–1123.

Dinges, N.G. and Baldwin, K.D. (1996) 'Intercultural competence', in D. Landis and R.S. Bhagat (eds), *Handbook of Intercultural Training* (2nd edn). Thousand Oaks: Sage, pp. 106–123.

Drenth P.J.D. and Groenendijk, B. (1984) 'Work and organizational psychology in cross-cultural perspective', in P.J.D. Drenth, H. Thierry, P.J. Willems and C.J. de Wolff (eds), *Handbook of Work and Organizational Psychology*. New York: Wiley, pp. 1197–1230.

Earley, P.C. and Singh, H. (1995) 'International and intercultural management research – What's next', *Academy of Management Journal*, 38 (2): 327–340.

Earley, P.C. and Mosakowski, E. (1996) 'Experimental International Management Research', in B.J. Punnett and O. Shenkar (eds), *Handbook of International Management Research*. London: Blackwell Publishers, pp. 83–114.

Earley, P.C. and Gibson, C.B. (1998) 'Taking stock in our progress on Individualism-Collectivism: 100 years of solidarity and community', *Journal of Management*, 24 (3): 265–304.

Earley, P.C. and Mosakowski, E. (2000) 'Creating hydrid team cultures: An empirical test of transitional team functioning', *Academy of Management Journal*, 43 (1): 26–49.

Earley, P.C. (2002) 'A theory of cultural intelligence in organizations', in B.M. Staw and R. Kramer (eds), *Research in Organizational Behavior*. Greenwich, CT: JAI Press, pp. 271–299.

Earley, P.C. and Gibson, C.B. (2002) *Multinational Work Teams: A New Perspective*. Mahwah, NJ: Lawrence Erlbaum Associates.

Earley, P.C. and Mosakowski, E. (2002) 'Linking culture and behavior in organizations: Suggestions for theory development and research methodology', in F.J. Yammarino and F. Dansereau (eds), *The Many Faces of Multi-Level Issues*. London: Elsevier, pp. 297–319.

Earley, P.C. and Ang, S. (2003) *Cultural Intelligence: Individual Interactions Across Cultures*. Stanford: Stanford University Press.

Earley, P.C. and Gardner, H.K. (2005) 'Internal dynamics and cultural intelligence in multinational teams', in D.L. Shapiro, M.A. Von Glinow and J.C. Cheng (eds), *Managing Multinational Teams: Global Perspectives*. London: Elsevier, pp. 1–31.

Earley, P.C. (2006) 'Leading cultural research in the future: A matter of paradigms and taste', *Journal of International Business Studies*, 37 (6): 922–931.

Elfenbein, H.A. and Shirako, A. (2006) 'An emotion process model for multicultural teams', in Ya-Ru Chen (ed.), *Research on Managing Groups and Teams: National Culture and Groups*. Greenwich, CT: JAI, pp. 263–297.

Erez, M. and Earley, P.C. (1993) *Culture, Self-Identity, and Work*. New York: Oxford University Press.

Erez, M. and Gati, E. (2004) 'A dynamic, multi-level model of culture: From the micro level of the individual to the macro level of a global culture', *Applied Psychology: An International Review*, 53 (4): 583–598.

Fischer, R., Ferreira, M.C., Assmar, E.M.L., Redford, P. and Harb, C. (2005) 'Organizational behaviour across cultures: Theoretical and methodological issues for developing multi-level frameworks involving culture', *International Journal of Cross Cultural Management*, 5 (1): 27–48.

Fischer, R., Smith, P.B., Richey, B., Ferreira, M.C., Assmar, E.M.L., Maes, J. and Stumpf, S. (2007) 'How do organizations allocate rewards? The predictive validity of national values, economic and organizational factors across six nations', *Journal of Cross-Cultural Psychology*, 38: 3–18.

Fiske, S.T. and Taylor, S.E. (1991) *Social Cognition*. 2nd edn. New York: McGraw-Hill.

Gelfand, M.J., Erez, M. and Aycan, Z. (2007) 'Cross-cultural organizational behaviour', *Annual Review of Psychology*, 58: 479–514.

Gelfand, M.J., Major, V.S., Raver, J.L., Nishii, L.H. and O'Brien, K. (2006) 'Negotiating relationally: The dynamics of the relational self in negotiations', *Academy of Management Review*, 31 (2): 427–451.

Gelfand, M.J., Nishii, L.H., Holcombe, K.M., Dyer, N., Ohbuchi, K.-I. and Fukuno, M. (2001) 'Cultural influences on cognitive representations of conflict: Interpretations of conflict episodes in the United States and Japan', *Journal of Applied Psychology*, 86 (6): 1059–1074.

Geringer, J.M., Frayne, C.A. and Milliman, J.F. (2002) 'In search of "best practices" in international human resource management: Research design and methodology', *Human Resource Management*, 41 (1): 5.

Gibson, C.B. and Zellmer-Bruhn, M.E. (2001) 'Metaphors and meaning: An intercultural analysis of the concept of teamwork', *Administrative Science Quarterly*, 46 (2): 274–303.

Gibson, C.B., Maznevski, M.L. and Kirkman, B.L. (Forthcoming) 'When does culture matter?', in A. Lewin (ed.), *Emerging Research in International Business*.

Haas, M.R. (2006) 'Acquiring and applying knowledge in transnational teams: The roles of cosmopolitans and locals', *Organization Science*, 17 (3): 367–384.

Haire, M., Ghiselli, E.E. and Porter, L. (1966) *Managerial Thinking: An International Study*. New York: John Wiley.

Hanges, P.J., Lord, R.G. and Dickson, M.W. (2000) 'An information-processing perspective on leadership and culture: A case for connectionist architecture', *Applied Psychology – an International Review – Psychologie Appliquee-Revue Internationale*, 49 (1): 133–161.

Heine, S.J., Lehman, D.R., Peng, K. and Greenholtz, J. (2002) 'What's wrong with cross-cultural comparisons of subjective Likert scales?: The reference-group effect', *Journal of Personality and Social Psychology*, 82: 903–918.

Herskovits, M.J. (1948) *Man and His Works: The Science of Cultural Anthropology*. New York: Knopf.

Hofstede, G. (1984) *Culture's Consequences: International Differences in Work Related Values*. Thousand Oaks, CA: Sage.

Hofstede, G. and Bond, M.H. (1988) 'The Confucius connection: From cultural roots to economic growth', *Organizational Dynamics*, 16: 4–21.

Hofstede, G. (1991) *Cultures and Organizations: Software of the Mind*. London: McGraw-Hill.

Hofstede, G., Neuijen, B., Ohayv, D. and Sanders, G. (1990) 'Measuring organizational cultures: A qualitative and quantitative study across twenty cases', *Administrative Science Quarterly*, 35: 286–316.

Hofstede, G., Bond, M.H. and Luk, C. (1993) 'Individual perceptions of organizational cultures: A methodological treatise on levels of analysis', *Organization Studies*, 14 (4): 483–503.

Hong, Y., Morris, M.W., Chiu, C. and Benet-Martinez, V. (2000) 'Multicultural minds: A dynamic constructive approach to culture and cognition', *American Psychologist*, 55: 709–720.

House, R.J., Hanges, P.J., Ruiz-Quintanilla, S.A., Dorfman, P.W., Javidan, M., Dickson, M. , Gupta, V. and Associates (1999) 'Cultural influences on leadership and organizations: Project GLOBE', in W. Mobley, M.J. Gessner and V. Arnold (eds), *Advances in Global Leadership*. Greenwich, CT: JAI Press, pp. 171–233.

Inglehart, R. (1977) *The Silent Revolution: Changing Values and Political Styles Among Western Publics*. Princeton, NJ: Princeton University Press.

Inglehart, R. (1990) *Culture Shift in Advanced Industrial Society*. Princeton, NJ: Princeton University Press.

Inglehart, R. (1997) *Modernization and Postmodernization. Cultural, Economic and Political Change in 43 Societies*. Princeton, NJ: Princeton University Press.

Iyengar, S.S. and Lepper, M.R. (1999) 'Rethinking the value of choice: A cultural perspective on intrinsic motivation', *Journal of Personality and Social Psychology*, 76: 349–366.

Kanungo, R.N. and Jaeger, A.M. (1990) 'Introduction: The need for indigenous management in developing countries', in A.M. Jaeger and R.N. Kanungo (eds), *Management in Developing Countries*. London: Routledge, pp. 1–23.

Kirkman, B.L. and Shapiro, D.L. (2001) 'The impact of team members' cultural values on productivity, cooperation, and empowerment in self-managing work teams', *Journal of Cross-Cultural Psychology*, 32 (5): 597–617.

Kirkman, B.L., Lowe, K.B. and Gibson, C.B. (2006) 'A quarter century of culture's consequences: A review of empirical research incorporating Hofstede's cultural values framework', *Journal of International Business Studies*, 37 (3): 285–320.

Kirkman, B.L. and Shapiro, D.L. (1997) 'The impact of cultural values on employee resistance to teams: Toward a model of globalized self-managing work team effectiveness', *Academy of Management Review*, 22 (3): 730–757.

Klein, K.J. and Dansereau, F. (1994) 'Levels issues in theory development, data collection, and analysis', *Academy of Management Review*, 19 (2): 195–229.

Kluckhohn, C. (1954) *Culture and Behavior*. New York: Free Press.

Kluckhohn, F. and Strodtbeck, F. (1961) *Variations in Value Orientation*. Westport, CT: Greenwood Press.

Leung, K., Bhagat, R.S., Buchan, N.R., Erez, M. and Gibson, C.B. (2005) 'Culture and international business: Recent advances and their implications for future research', *Journal of International Business Studies*, 36 (4): 357–378.

Lytle, A.L., Brett, J.M., Barsness, Z.I., Tinsley, C.H. and Janssens, M. (1995) 'A paradigm for confirmatory cross-cultural research in organizational behaviour', in L.L. Cummings and B.M. Shaw (eds), *Research in Organizational Behaviour*, 17: 167–214.

Markus H.R. and Kitayama, S. (1991) 'Culture and the self: Implications for cognition, emotion, and motivation', *Psychological Review*, 98: 224–253.

Mathur, P., Aycan, Z. and Kanungo, R.N. (1996) 'Work cultures in Indian organizations: A comparison between public and private sector', *Psychology and Developing Society*, 8 (2): 199–222.

McGrath, J.E. (1984) *Groups: Interaction and Performance*. Englewood Cliffs, NJ: Prentice-Hall.

Mendonca, M. and Kanungo, R.N. (1994) 'Managing human resources: This issue of cultural fit', *Journal of Management Inquiry*, 3 (2): 189–205.

Morris, M.W. and Peng, K. (1994) 'Culture and Cause: American and Chinese Attributions for Social and Physical Events', *Journal of Personality and Social Psychology*, 67 (6): 949–971.

Morris, M.W. and Young, M.J. (2002) 'Linking culture to behaviour: Focusing more proximate cognitive mechanisms', in F.J. Yammarino and F. Dansereau (eds), *Research in Multi-Level Issues: The Many Faces of Multi-Level Issues*. London: Elsevier, pp. 327–341.

Moynihan, L.M., Peterson, R.S. and Earley, P.C. (2006) 'Cultural intelligence and the multinational team experience: Does the experience of working in a multinational team improve cultural intelligence?', in Ya-Ru Chen (ed.), *Research on Managing Groups and Teams: National Culture and Groups*. Greenwich, CT: JAI, pp. 299–323.

Ng, K.Y. and Earley, P.C. (2006) 'Culture plus intelligence – old constructs, New Frontiers', *Group and Organization Management*, 31 (1): 4–19.

Nisbett, R.E., Peng, K., Choi, I. and Norenzayan, A. (2001) 'Culture and systems of thought : Holistic versus analytic cognition', *Psychological Review*, 108 (2): 291–310.

Pineda, R.C. and Whitehead, C.J. (1997) 'The effects of ethnic group culture on managerial task activities', *Group and Organization Management*, 22 (1): 31–52.

Poortinga, Y. (1992) 'Towards a conceptualization of culture for psychology', in S. Iwawaki, Y. Kashima and K. Leung (eds), *Innovations in Cross-Cultural Psychology*. Amsterdam: Swets and Zeitlinger, pp. 3–17.

Putnam, R. (1993) *Making Democracy Work: Civic Traditions in Modern Italy*. Princeton, NJ: Princeton University Press.

Randel, A.E. (2003) 'The salience of culture in multinational teams and its relation to team citizenship behavior', *International Journal of Cross Cultural Management*, 3 (1): 27–45.

Ravlin, E.C., Thomas, D.C. and Ilsev, A. (2000) 'Beliefs about values, status and legitimacy in multicultural groups: Influences on intragroup conflict', in P.C. Earley and H. Singh (eds), *Innovations in International and Cross-Cultural Management.* Thousand Oaks, CA: Sage, pp. 17–51.

Rohner, R.P. (1984) 'Toward a conception of culture for cross-cultural psychology', *Journal of Cross-Cultural Psychology*, 15: 111–138.

Rousseau, D.M. (1985) 'Issues of level in organizational research: Multi-level and cross-level perspectives', *Research in Organizational Behavior*, 7: 1.

Sagie, A. and Aycan, Z. (2003) 'A cross-cultural analysis of participative decision-making in organizations', *Human Relations*, 56: 453–473.

Sanchez-Burks, J., Nisbett, R.E. and Ybarra, O. (2000) 'Cultural styles, relational schema and prejudice against out-groups', *Journal of Personality and Social Psychology*, 79 (2): 174–189.

Schwartz, S.H. (1992) 'The universal content and structure of values: Theoretical advances and empirical tests in 20 countries', in M.P. Zanna, (ed.), *Advances in Experimental Social Psychology.* New York: Academic, pp. 1–65.

Singelis, T.M. (2000) 'Some thoughts on the future of cross-cultural social psychology', *Journal of Cross-Cultural Psychology*, 31 (1): 76–91.

Smith, P.B. (2006) 'When elephants fight, the grass gets trampled: The GLOBE and Hofstede projects', *Journal of International Business Studies*, 37: 915–921.

Stolle, D. (1998) 'Bowling together, bowling alone: The development of generalized trust in voluntary societies', *Political Psychology*, 19: 497–525.

Sullivan, J.L. and Transue, J.E. (1999) 'The psychological underpinnings of democracy: A selective review of research on political', *Annual Review of Psychology*, 50 (1): 625–650.

Tayeb, M. (1988) *Organizations and National Culture.* London: Sage.

Thomas, D.C. and Inkson, K.(2004) *Cultural Intelligence: People Skills for Global Business.* San Francisco: Berrett-Koehler.

Triandis H. C. (1972) *The Analysis of Subjective Culture.* New York: Wiley Interscience.

Triandis, H.C. (1994) *Culture and Social Behavior.* New York: McGraw–Hill.

Triandis, H.C. and Berry, J. (1980) 'Introduction', in H.C. Triandis and J. Berry (eds), *Handbook of Cross-cultural Psychology.* New York: Allyn and Bacon, pp. 1–28.

Van de Vijver, F. and Leung, K. (1997) *Methods and Data Analysis for Cross–Cultural Research.* Beverly Hills, CA: Sage.

Van Maanen, J. and Barley, S.R. (1984) 'Occupational communities: Culture and control in organizations', in B.M.Staw and L.L.Cummings (eds), *Research in Organizational Behavior.* Greenwich, CT: JAI Press. Vol. 6, pp. 287–365.

Walsh, J.P. (1995) 'Managerial and organizational cognition: Notes from a trip down memory lane', *Organization Science*, 6 (3): 280–321.

Wang, L., Doucet, L. and Northcraft, G. (2006) 'Culture, affect, and social influence in decision-making groups', in Ya-Ru Chen (ed.), *Research on Managing Groups and Teams: National Culture and Groups.* Greenwich, CT: JAI, pp. 147–172.

Watson, W.E., Kumar, K. and Michaelsen, L.K. (1993) 'Cultural diversity's impact on interaction process and performance: Comparing homogeneous and diverse task groups', *Academy of Management Journal*, 36 (3): 590–602.

Zhong, C.-B., Magee, J.C., Maddux, W.W. and Galinsky, A.D. (2006) 'Power, culture, and action: Considerations in the expression and enactment of power in East Asian and Western societies', in Ya–Ru Chen (ed.), *Research on Managing Groups and Teams: National Culture and Groups.* Greenwich, CT: JAI, pp. 53–73.

30

Mergers and Acquisitions: Why 2 + 2 Does Not Always Make 5

Susan Cartwright

A high level of merger and acquisition (M&A) activity has been an enduring feature of both domestic and international business for several decades. In 2004 alone, over 30,000 M&As were completed, equivalent globally to one transaction every 18 minutes (Cartwright and Schoenberg, 2006). M&As represent a means by which organizations can achieve diversity, growth and rationalization and so more rapidly respond to the demands of a changing global environment (Cartwright and Cooper, 1997). M&As also provide an opportunity for developing market economies, such as Central, Eastern Europe and China to attract much-needed foreign direct investment (Cooke, 2006).

Over 30 years ago, Hovers (1973) outlined the alchemy of M&A as being the ability to some way make the two elements worth significantly more when combined, than if they were to continue independently. This became known as 'the $2 + 2 = 5$ effect,' which over time has proven to be an enticing

formula and trigger for action amongst senior managers, dealmakers and investors. However, the expected gains to be made from M&A activity have often been very different from the reality.

M&A performance is notoriously difficult to assess (Sudarsanam, 2003). Whereas some studies have shown that approximately 40 per cent of acquirers experience positive returns in the first two or three years post acquisition (e.g., Conn, et al., 2001), the vast majority of research evidence presents a more gloomy picture in suggesting that many M&As destroy wealth rather than create it (Larsson, 2005).

In an early study of European acquisitions, Kitching (1974) reported failure rates of between 46–50 per cent, based on managerial assessments. More recently, using a comparable methodology, Rostand (1994) reported similarly poor failure rates of around 44–45 per cent. Whereas target firm shareholders experience positive and statistically significant wealth gains at the time of the bid (Sudarsanam and Mahate, 2006), many studies report value losses and negative abnormal returns (Agrawal and Jaffe, 2000), with failure rates ranging from 50 per cent (Cartwright and Cooper, 1997; Weber, 1996) to a high of 80 per cent (KPMG 2000; Marks 1988). More recently, a study by McKinsey and Co. (Frieswick, 2005) showed that 70 per cent of mergers failed to achieve anticipated revenue synergies, and 40 per cent did not meet cost synergies goals. A study of the largest cross-border M&As completed between 1996 and 1998 found that 83 per cent did not result in any increase in shareholder wealth (Kearney, 1999). Adding to these woes, Hitt et al. (1991) have also shown that M&As have a negative impact on research and development (R&D) investment and output.

The drive to understand the factors which explain the variance in M&A performance has traditionally been the dominant goal and focus of the financial and strategic management literature. Within the financial literature, studies have investigated the link between financial performance and factors such as target company attributes, price paid, acquisition type and bid circumstances, that is, whether the bidder is regarded as friendly or hostile (Gregory, 1997; Sudarsanam and Mahate, 2006). From the perspective of the strategic management literature, the focus of research enquiry has mainly centered around the link between performance and 'the goodness of the strategic fit' between the combining organizations (King et al., 2004; Seth, 1990). However, such lines of enquiry have failed to demonstrate a consistent relationship between strategic fit and performance (Chatterjee, 1992; Schoenberg, 2003). Indeed, in a recent meta-analysis of 93 studies, King et al. (2004) concluded that 'poor acquisition performance is modified by variables unspecified in existing research' (p.188). Stahl et al. (2005) suggest that the limitations of the financial and strategy literature reflect a preoccupation with the necessary 'conditioning factors' without taking account of the integration process variables

which affect performance and subsequent merger outcomes. In short, conditioning factors are important in determining the synergistic potential of the combination, but the extent to which this potential is realized and released is dependent upon the success and/or appropriateness of the integration process, and the way it is managed. For M&As to be successful, there needs to be both task and human integration and so highlights the potential convergence between the strategic management and the OB literatures (Birkinshaw et al., 2000).

In a recent article, Larsson (2005) briefly summarized the determinants of M&A success as selecting high strategic potential, managing high organizational integration and maintaining low employee resistance during the post combination process. And herein lies the challenge for M&A success: Meyer and Lieb-Doczy (2003) argue that the transformation and integration required of M&As produces inherent tensions between implementing radical change to match the strategy and corporate culture of the acquirer, and at the same time, promoting what is valuable in terms of resources and cultural attributes of the acquired organization.

In placing a greater emphasis on the M&A process and its behavioral aspects, contemporary research has increased the prominence and potential contribution of OB scholars. Previous reviews (Cartwright, 2005; Hogan and Overmeyer-Day, 1994) have tended to organize existing research studies into four broad categories: studies that focus on

(1) inputs or pre-merger characteristics;
(2) process variables:
(3) employee impact; and
(4) performance outcomes.

In this review, a broad distinction is made between research which is firmly rooted in a change perspective and research which examines the extent to which the process is managed to ensure the fair treatment of employees and the transfer of knowledge and resources. Within these perspectives, a variety of emergent themes will then be discussed.

The change perspective

A dominant theme within the OB literature has been explanations of M&A underperformance in terms of the adverse and disruptive impact that major organizational change has on the individuals involved, particularly those within the acquired company (Very et al., 1997), or the smaller merger partner (Cartwright and Cooper, 1993a). There is a substantial and growing body of research evidence showing that organizational change invariably leads to employee frustration, anxiety and stress (Ashford, 1988; Bovey and Hede, 2001; Nelson et al., 1995), lowered productivity and increased workloads (Abrahamson, 2004). However, M&As differ from other forms of organizational change regarding the speed of change, the scale of change and the critical mass of the unknown they present for both parties (Marks, 1988). Thus, the high levels of uncertainty, the wide scale adjustment required of employees and the increased stress associated with M&As are considered to have a cumulative and negative effect on merger performance.

The literature on M&As is diverse as researchers have focused on different aspects of change at the organizational, group and individual level within the context of M&A. Differences in the organizational and national cultures of the combining organizations and the enforced process of interaction which follows has become the dominant focus of much M&A research (Cartwright and Cooper, 1997; Schreyogg, 2005). Within this framework, researchers have argued that better merger outcomes could be achieved if acquiring organizations paid more attention to the degree of culture fit between the combining companies, and extended the process of due diligence to include some form of culture profiling (Cartwright and McCarthy, 2005; Sudarsanam, 2003; Hunt et al., 1987). At the group level, research has increasingly focused on issues of identity and whether employee groups can put aside old loyalties and rivalries, and form attachments with the new organization post-merger (Kleppesto, 1998; Gertsen and Soderberg, 1998). At the individual level, research has centered around the sense of loss, disruption, and uncertainty associated with M&As, the way in which individuals cope and adjust to these changes (Bruckman and Peters, 1987; Marks and Mirvis, 2001), and their impact on employee health and wellbeing. As well as studying M&As within a change perspective, the research focus has increasingly centered upon equity issues and the fair treatment of employees.

The fairness perspective

According to Schweiger and Lippert (2005), there must be an appropriate balance between making tough decisions and fair and compassionate management practices to realize value from M&As. Numerous studies have shown that M&As often result in higher levels of turnover, particularly at executive levels, compared with matched non-acquired organizations (Buchholtz et al., 2003; Cannella and Hambrick, 1993; Krug and Hegarty, 1997). In a nine year longitudinal study, Krug (2002) found that executive turnover rate in acquired organizations averaged 19 per cent per year – twice as high as a matched control group. Cartwright and Cooper (1997) reported employee turnover rates as high as 60 per cent in the first year post acquisition, and earlier British evidence (Graves, 1981) found that a third of all employees voluntarily left the merged organization within two years. The loss of acquired talent not only leads to increased recruitment and training costs but can also adversely affect performance (Zollo and Singh, 2004). However, fairness of treatment, the process of role re-allocation and the quality of leadership are critical factors in the retention and motivation of employees in acquired or merged companies. Consequently, there have been a small but growing umber of studies which have looked at M&As within the framework of organizational justice theories and shown that employee perceptions of unfair treatment are predictive of stress (Very et al., 1998). Other studies have investigated how factors such as communication effort contribute to build organizational trust (Stahl et al., 2006).

Employee response to mergers

Mergers have been described as 'a time of great organizational upheaval' (Corwin et al., 1991). Comparisons have been drawn between the experience of acquisition and bereavement, in that employees mourn the loss of their organization and its identity (Mirvis, 1985; Schweiger et al., 1987). Both Hunsaker and Coombs (1988) and Mirvis (1985) have developed stage models to describe the way in which employees respond and adjust to the organizational loss experience.

Such studies have highlighted the high levels of uncertainty and fear of the unknown experienced by employees in M&A situations, and the resultant psychological distress. Based on case studies from three US acquisitions, Bastian (1987) suggests this fear alternates with strong feelings of resentment consistent with the stress-related fight or flight response (Marks and Mirvis, 1985). The manifestation of the fight response often results in a collective attempt to resist, or possibly actively sabotage any changes proposed or introduced. In contrast, the 'flight response' i.e., the decision to psychologically withdraw or to leave the organization is an individual action.

The link between M&A and stress has been confirmed by a number of cross-sectional studies (e.g., Begley, 1998; Gibbons, 1998; Very et al., 1998). In one post merger study of managers, Cartwright and Cooper (1993a) found that both managerial groups reported poorer than average mental health scores, with a more pronounced affect amongst managers from the smaller merger partner. McHugh (1995) also found abnormal mental health scores (Goldberg, 1972) among teachers who had experienced a school merger or were threatened with one. Indeed, consistent with Schweiger and Ivancevich (1987), she found that those under the threat of merger, had significantly poorer mental health compared to those that had merged, a tendency described by Mirvis (1985) as the 'fear the worst' or

merger syndrome. Sui et al. (1997) also found elevated stress levels relative to normative data amongst employees of an acquired television company in Hong Kong.

Although stress is often conceived to be the outcome of uncertainty about job future, changes in the work environment and work practices, policies and organizational culture, Allred et al. (2005) suggest that there may be other profound reasons for employee stress. Many have used the metaphor of marriage in describing mergers (Cartwright and Cooper, 1997) to emphasize the emotional intensity, the importance of the post-merger compatibility, and the potential problems which can result when one partner asserts dominance. However, Allred et al. (2005) assert that the metaphor of mergers as stepfamilies may better convey the impact that changes in organizational parentage has on organizational members. They liken organizations to families in that they are both dynamic, but at the same time provide ongoing stability. Furthermore, like families, organizations have hierarchical and reciprocal interrelationships. Allred et al. (2005) suggest that when two organizations merge to form a new relationship, employees acquire a new stepparent and stepsiblings. As in restructured families, organizational stepchildren may suffer adversely from discrimination by the new stepparent, i.e. one employee group favored over another in the allocation of roles and/or rewards (Flinn, 1988), confused by a lack of common rules and norms or what has been described as 'incomplete institutionalization' (Tolbert and Zucker, 1996), experiencing less security and resources available to them than before (Gamong and Coleman, 1984), and considering themselves emotionally or physically deficient compared to their previous situation. Allred et al. (2005) concluded that the stepfamily provides powerful insights in explaining the stress and poor mental health outcomes experienced by acquired and merged employees, and is consistent with the earlier notion (Cartwright, 1998) that merging organizations may benefit from professional help from an 'organizational marriage guidance counselor' to clarify and develop the new relationship.

Recent evidence on the negative impact of M&A on employees derives from Armstrong-Strassen and Cameron (2003) longitudinal study of a hospital merger of 111 nurses. Using pre- and post-amalgamation measures, they showed that job satisfaction declined and intention to quit increased post amalgamation. Such findings are significant because workplace wellbeing is linked to business performance (Hartner et al., 2005. However, whilst negative reactions to mergers have been shown to be commonplace (Buono et al., 1985; Panchal and Cartwright, 2001) there are occasions when employees in the acquired organization perceive the M&A event more positively than members of the acquiring organization. This is likely when employees perceive their acquirer to be more prestigious than their present organization, see the change as increasing their employment security, and/or likely to lead to greater opportunities for career and skill development. Reactions also differ across hierarchical levels (Lohrum, 1996) and differentially affect different employee groups (Costello et al., 1963). Matteson and Ivancevich (1990), for example, found that acquired mid-career employees were more likely to express negative attitudes and feel more threatened by increased organizational size than those at earlier or later career states. Also, increased organizational size is associated with a greater loss of status and autonomy, and influences decisions to leave acquired organizations (Hayes and Hoag, 1974; Humpal, 1971).

Whilst Krishnan et al. (1997) suggest that the degree of complementarity between the two senior management groups positively influences performance, cultural and managerial differences are often the reason why executives leave acquired companies. Bucholtz et al. (2003) found that middle-aged executives were less likely to voluntarily leave acquired organizations than their younger or older counterparts: Human capital theory (Phan and Lee, 1995) would posit that younger executives are more mobile and place less emphasis on money and security, and that older executives are less inclined to invest effort and time in their careers as they approach retirement age. Cartwright and Cooper (1997) suggest that individuals choose to leave merged organizations because they prefer to select the type of organizational culture within which they wish to work – rather than having a cultural change imposed upon them. Cartwright and Hudson (2000) found strong evidence that prior experience with mergers leads to greater psychological resilience to the negative emotional and health effects and more adaptive coping.

The role of positive emotions

The research has overwhelmingly focused on the negative emotions associated with what is described as the merger syndrome (Appelbaum et al., 2000; Cartwright and Cooper, 1997; Marks and Mirvis, 1986). Yet possible benefits do exist; for example increased size and enhanced corporate reputation and prestige may mean that mergers and acquisitions lead to increased job security and widening job opportunities. Kusstatscher (2006) is one of the few researchers to study both positive and negative emotions in an M&A context. In a qualitative study of four European mergers, she measured emotions over time using a projective technique she describes as a temperature curve. This involved asking interviewees to describe and explain the peaks and changes in their emotions, and the events which aroused these emotions. Although she found that negative emotions were mentioned twice as often as positive ones, some interviewees experienced predominately positive emotions and recalled feelings of joy and euphoria. Furthermore, these employees reported higher job satisfaction, perceived the company in a more positive way and the performance of the merged company as successful. Importantly, Kusstatscher points to the role of management: Optimistic line managers had a contagious effect on employees.

The role of social identity

Organizational identity is derived from a set of core beliefs that members have about what is central to the organization, what it represents and how it differentiates itself from others (Albert and Whetten, 1985). An important element of organizational identity is that it is perceived by its members as being enduring in connecting the organization's past with the present (Van Dick et al., 2004). Organizational identity, like culture, only becomes salient when it is threatened (Albert and Whetten, 1985). Mergers or acquisitions threaten and challenge identity, as core beliefs are often redefined, previous history is put aside and the differentiating aspects of the combining organizations are fused by the need to externally project one single common identity. Changes in organizational identity, in turn, impact upon the individual's identification with the organization (Ashforth and Mael, 1989). Because continuity of identity is important in maintaining a sense of 'self,' acquired employees will often cling to the symbols, rites and rituals which characterized their old organization and reject those of the new organization. From a social identity perspective, Van Dick et al. (2004) define a merger as the combining of an ingroup with a former outgroup to form a larger new unit.

Various researchers have studied the process of M&A integration within the framework of social identity theory (Tajfel and Turner, 1979). There is some resonance between the idea of social identity as concerning attachment and alignment with others with Allred et al.'s (2005) notion of the centrality of parental status and attachment discussed earlier. As mergers are rarely a marriage of equals, there is an invariably a status difference between merger partners, as well as between the acquiring and the acquired organization. In a series of stimulated studies presenting various possible on merger scenarios, Giessner et al. (2006) found that employees of the higher status partner favored an integration strategy that maintained their dominance, even though they considered that this was the least fair and legitimate approach to take. In contrast, those from the lower status organization preferred an integration approach that treated both groups equally and offered some protection from total domination. Compared to the high status group, they expressed greater outrage at the injustice of an approach of total absorption or assimilation. This response from the employees in the lower status organization occurred even in circumstances when it was clear that they could achieve significant personal gains from the merger. Other studies have shown that employees who strongly identify with the post-merger organization report higher job satisfaction, engage in more extra-role behavior and are less likely to leave or be absent (Terry, 2001, 2003; Haslam and Ellemers, 2005). In contrast, employee groups within the less dominant organization and hence the more threatened in terms of continuity of identity, were more inclined to assert their own distinctiveness in their responses to the questionnaire survey (Dackert et al., 2003).

Kleppesto (1998) argues that social identity theory explains why, in an M&A situation, actors tend to emphasize cultural differences as part of the natural process of creating and maintaining social identities, boundaries and social categories. In a laboratory-based experiment, Haunschild et al. (1994) demonstrated that groups with a previous history of working together and hence a common identity, displayed less resistance to the prospect of group merger than groups with no shared history. Studies by Van Knippenberg et al. (2002) suggest that employees are more likely to identify with the post-merger organization if they feel that there is a sense of continuity between the former organizational culture and the practices and those of the new company or if employees had a weak attachment to their previous employer and perceive that the benefits offered in the post-merger organization are significantly more attractive. However, as Van Dick et al. (2004) note, this sense of attachment and identity may not necessarily be related to the organization but to other subunits or groups within it and provided there is continuity at this level, organizational members are likely to develop a sense of identity towards the wider organization at the same time.

Several pre-merger factors might help explain post-merger functioning. Bartels et al. (2006) investigated a range of potential variables, including pre-merger identification in two Dutch police organizations, sense of continuity and perceived utility of the merger in determining employees' expected level of post-merger identification. Their results replicated other findings (e.g., Backmann, 1993; Van Knippenberg et al., 2002) in that pre-merger identification predicted post merger identification, and that expected utility was also a predictor of positive post merger identification. This finding confirms the value of managerial effort in emphasizing the potential benefits both individually and organizationally to be gained from the merger. Similarly, in a study of a German hospital merger Van Dick et al. (2006) found that communication was strongly linked to post merger identification and job satisfaction.

In summary, the important contribution of studies within the framework of social identity theory has been to emphasize the impact on M&A on social as well as security needs and its potential impact on social and not just psychological well being.

Culture

The link between culture and performance has been extensively studied since the 1980s, forms the dominant perspective on M&A research, and has become something of a scapegoat in explaining merger failure (Bligh, 2006). Within the cultural framework, M&As are considered unlikely to perform well if there is a poor cultural fit between the acquirer and the acquired company, and hence potential for 'culture clash.' Culture clashes lead to conflict and disunity within the newly acquired or merged organization.

According to Daly et al. (2004), most of the research from the cultural perspective has focused on three inter-related dimensions: degree of cultural compatibility (Cartwright and Cooper, 1993a), organizational resistance (Schweiger and de Nisi, 1991) and acculturation processes (Elsass and Veiga, 1994; Nahavandi and Malekzadeh, 1988).

To date, research evidence examining the role of culture within the context of M&As has produced mixed results. In the context of domestic M&As, Datta (1991) found that differences in culture and senior management styles had a negative impact on performance. Chatterjee (1992) found that perception of cultural similarity positively influenced share market expectations in the performance of 30 US acquisitions. Similarly Weber et al. (1996) found that differences in organizational culture resulted in lower commitment and co-operation from senior management. Cartwright and Cooper (1997) concluded that whilst it was possible for mergers between organizations with vastly different corporate cultures to be successful, the task of integration was much easier if the cultures were more similar. In a study of 59 M&As during a 7-year period Daly et al. (2004) found that similarity in espoused values between the combining organizations presented in public reports exerted a significant and positive influence on post merger performance.

However, research into international M&As suggest that the contribution of national culture is more complex, as it presents a double acculturation problem (Nahavandi and Malekzadeh, 1988). Weber et al. (1996) found that national cultural differences were more strongly associated with negative merger attitudes and stress than differences in organizational culture. Whereas other research evidence (Morosini et al., 1998; Schweiger and Goulet, 2000) suggests that the greater the cultural difference between the partners, the better the performance. Larsson and Risberg (1998) believe that this occurs because there is more sensitivity towards culture differences in international than domestic M&As. Also there is likely to be fewer requirements for the two workforces to integrate and work together.

Consistent with the analysis of the pattern of cross-border M&As conducted by Larsson and Risberg (1998), two surveys on managerial attitudes towards foreign acquisitions (Cartwright et al., 1995; Cartwright and Price, 2003) suggest that decision-makers are more attracted to deals with other national cultures which they perceive to be similar to their own. This would suggest that under conditions of choice, and in the absence of more specific company knowledge, M&A selection decisions are likely to be strongly shaped by cultural stereotypes (Cooper and Kirkcaldy, 1995).

The discrepancy in findings and lack of clear understanding as to the role of culture in M&A is the likely outcome of the failure to take account of the strategic intent and the agreement of the combining parties as to the desired integration strategy and mode of acculturation. According to Nahavandi and Malekzadeh (1988) there are four possible modes of acculturation:

- assimilation;
- integration;
- separation; and
- alienation (Haspeslagh and Jemison, 1991; Napier 1989).

Within the acculturation model, the success of the integration strategy depends upon the willingness of each party to abandon their own culture and their perceptions of the attractiveness of the culture of the other. Members of an acquired organization are only likely to accept and assimilate into the acquirer's culture if they find it more attractive than their own, and are prepared to relinquish their own values and practices in the process. What research has shown is that it is the direction of cultural change which is important in that employees will resist cultural change that reduces autonomy and respond positively to a change which increases it (Cartwright and Cooper, 1993b, 1997; Ashkansay and Holmes, 1995). Furthermore, differences in culture impede the transfer of knowledge (Empson, 2001). However, Larsson and Lubatkin's (2001) meta-analysis suggests that, even in

circumstances of reduced autonomy, that effective acculturation can be achieved if management invest a great deal of effort into co-ordination mechanisms such as transition teams and personnel exchanges and socialization activities as a means of engaging employee involvement.

The role of leadership

It has been widely argued that effective change requires the active engagement of the CEO and the executive team (Nadler et al., 2001; Kavanagh and Ashkansay, 2006) and the skills and exercise of transformational leadership. Indeed, many years ago, Searby (1969) suggested that because so much energy is expended in negotiating the actual deal, management is often too exhausted and apathetic to be able to lead and coordinate the integration process effectively. Moreover, studies have suggested that often managers are overconfident in their expectations of the synergies that can be realistically delivered in the post merger integration period and underestimate the difficult challenges that lie ahead (Xia and Pan, 2006).

In a longitudinal ethnographic study spanning eight years, Yu et al. (2005) examined the relative amount of time that senior managers involved in a domestic healthcare merger spent discussing the integration. In bi-weekly meetings from 1996 to 2002, they analyzed over 10,000 meeting minutes and found that most of the meeting time was spent discussing structuring issues (38 per cent), patient care (17 per cent), financial performance (15 per cent) and leadership and strategy (13 per cent). However, it was not until the fifth year that patient care became the focus of significant attention, even though improvement in patient care was the primary objective of the merger. Perhaps surprisingly, little time was devoted to the discussion of organizational culture (6 per cent), the wider integration of other business units within the merged organization (5 per cent) and issues relating to the external environment (6 per cent).

In another longitudinal study, Kavanagh and Ashkansay (2006) examined the impact of leadership and change management strategy on three Australian university mergers, over a seven year period. They found that the most successful change strategy was an incremental approach. Based on their study of 18 acquisitions in Hungary and East Germany, Meyer and Lieb-Doczy (2003) also advocated the benefit of a more evolutionary approach to change, that provides acquired organizations the autonomy and opportunity to learn and adapt to the practices of the acquirer over time. However, evidence from Nikandrou et al. (2000) cautions against the erosion of initial positivity which can occur if change is too slow.

Bligh (2006) investigated the role of cultural leadership in the context of a US healthcare merger. Based on recorded interviews with 42 managers and employees, she concluded that effective leaders in merger situations:

(1) recognize historical cultural differences and how they can be reconciled to create cultural unity;
(2) recognize the emotional aspects of merger and provide outlets for loss and renewal;
(3) foster realistic expectations of both the challenges and opportunities.

Cohen et al. (2006) studied conflict resolution within the context of a merger of software developers. Based on interview data, they found that leadership behavior (open communication, acknowledgement of the history and value of the acquired company and widespread consultation) could influence the level of conflict. Another qualitative study of mergers in the healthcare sector (Harwood and Ashleigh, 2005) highlighted the conflict that integration managers experience due to the necessity to maintain confidentiality about forthcoming changes. They found that some managers found the need to be constantly vigilant in their communications with those outside the 'confidentiality bubble' to be personally stressful, and were uncomfortable with the incongruence between their requirement to be secretive and the espoused organizational values of honesty and integrity.

COMMON AND EMERGENT THEMES WITHIN THE M&A LITERATURE

Organizational learning and transfer of knowledge

Some mergers or acquisitions occur specifically to acquire a knowledge-based resource. This knowledge may relate to a particular product or technology, sales relationships and customer knowledge or research and development. The success of such M&As is dependent on the retention of the key knowledge holders within the acquired company, followed by an effective transfer of knowledge between the combining organizations which it is expected will lead to further innovation and growth. For knowledge to be shared and exchanged, a learning culture has to exist within any organization (Barrett, 1995). According to Coopey and Burgoyne (2000), learning cultures are characterized by an openness towards diverse opinions, a high level of participative decision making and a climate of psychological safety. The focus on the process of organizational learning and knowledge transfer within M&As is a relatively recent development in the literature.

In a study of 75 high-tech acquisitions Ranft (2006) found that maintaining autonomy within the acquired organization preserved tacit knowledge, whereas rich communication and retention of key employees facilitated the transfer of knowledge. In addition to studying the process whereby knowledge is transferred between the combining organization, other research has investigated the extent to which prior experience of M&A has produced beneficial outcomes. Evidence to date on the impact of knowledge gained from previous acquisition experience has produced mixed results. In an early and small scale study of UK acquisitions, Hunt (1988) showed that experienced acquirers performed no better than those acquiring for the first time. However, whereas Bruton et al. (1994) did find a positive relationship, other research has found a negative (Gick and Holyoak, 1987) or no relationship (Baum and Ginsberg, 1997) between prior learning experience and M&A performance. Haleblian and Finkelstein (1999) argue for a U-shaped relationship between previous experience and performance, suggesting that learning gained from other M&A situations may initially be beneficial but that over time the tendency to apply previous experiences to new situations, regardless of the circumstances, can possibly be detrimental. More recently, Zollo and Singh (2004) examined the role of prior learning on the integration process as well as performance in a large sample of acquisitions in the US banking sector. They found that performance was very much influenced by the extent to which acquirers codified the knowledge accumulated through past experiences in manuals, systems and other acquisition-specific tools. This they described as a strategy of deliberate learning. Furthermore, it was found that replacing top managers in the acquired organization had a negative impact on performance.

According to Greenberg et al. (2005), differences in national language is also an obstacle to organizational learning in cross-border M&As; similarly, differences in specialist languages and corporate or sector backgrounds within the same national culture can impede shared understanding and communication (Schoenberg, 2000). In addition, Greenberg et al. (2005) highlight the role of geographic proximity, organizational structure and motivation to share as factors relating to organizational learning and informational flows, which are worthy of further research in this field.

The role of communication

Many commentators have suggested that communication plays an important role in shaping and managing employee response to M&As (Gertsen and Soderberg, 1998; Marks, 1997; Risberg, 1997). Characteristically, employees involved in M&A report dissatisfaction with the amount of communication they receive (Napier et al., 1993). Employees look for communication to reduce their uncertainty and address their predictive needs – what is going to happen next, as well

as their explanatory needs – why are things the way they are (Berger, 1987).

Seeking information is a means whereby individuals regain control, reduce their stress and improve their well being (Ganster and Fusiler, 1989). At times of high uncertainty and stress, the actions of acquiring management are viewed with considerable suspicion and the detail of any communication is meticulously scrutinized. Therefore, many advise that acquiring or merger management must 'over-communicate by making full use of all available formal and informal mechanisms (Appelbaum et al., 2000). Studies have also demonstrated that employees generally prefer to receive information from their immediate line manager (Hargie and Tourish, 2000) However, whilst advice is plentiful, there has been very little empirical research specifically focused on merger communication and its role in the integration process. In one study involving interview and focus group data, Bastian (1987) concluded that, as well as the quantity and collegiality of the communication, communication needs to be congruent with the perceived reality; otherwise rumors will develop to 'fill in the blanks.' However, the study offered little insight regarding the specific communication processes which are positively received, and so influence M&A success. A well-designed experimental study conducted by Schweiger and de Nisi (1991) offers some useful insight. They compared the reactions of acquired employees in two geographically remote engineering plants. In the experimental plant, employees received extensive information aimed at providing a 'realistic merger preview' (RMP); the organization even established a hotline to answer any employee queries. In contrast, employees in the control plant were given minimal information of the type typically provided by organizations in merger situations. The results demonstrated the value of extensive merger communication: Employees in the experimental condition reported significantly lower levels of uncertainty, greater job satisfaction and rated the organization as more trustworthy and caring than the employees in the control condition. However, the study was confined to a relatively short period of time, i.e. from the time of the announcement to a few months post merger.

Building on this study, Cornett-De Vito and Freidman (1995) attempted to identify the type of communication activities which distinguished more from less successful mergers in four financial institution mergers, over a longer time period. Their study showed that communication needs change over time dependent upon the stage in the integration process. At the time of the announcement, directive communication relating to the expectations of the merger and the new reporting relationships was more associated with success levels than any other communications behaviors. Contrary to expectations (Bordia et al., 2004; Manz et al., 1991), more participative communication was more prevalent in the less successful mergers. However, it could be that increased employee involvement and participation has beneficial individual outcomes (e.g., perceptions of control, well being) but no direct impact on organizational performance (Bordia et al., 2004). During the first year post acquisition, respondents in the more successful mergers reported more satisfaction with the amount of informative communication behaviors from their acquirer, suggesting that acquired employees' need is for realistic, timely and accurate communication which provides them with a clear understanding of the 'new rules of the game' (Corwin et al., 1991). After one year post merger, Cornett-de Vito and Friedman (1995) found that merger success was associated with a focus on supportive communication activities (e.g., the extent to which managers listened and provided help to employees in adjusting to the new organization). The study also showed that employee communication needs were influenced by geographical distance and location. Where merger sites were widely separated there was more desire for supportive behaviors than when the sites were in closer proximity. Rural sites were less critical of the merger communication they received than urban sites. This was attributed to their fact that rural employees had less alternative job opportunities and so

were grateful just to keep their jobs. This study makes some interesting contributions to the sparsely researched area of merger communication but is based on a small sample.

More recently, Jimmieson et al. (2004) found the amount of change-related information employees received was a significant predictor of well being, customer orientedness and job satisfaction during the three month post implementation. However, Backmann (1993) showed that management communication had no impact on strengthening employee identification with the merged organization, whereas Koonce (1991) found that almost half of all employees surveyed considered that communication had been a major contributor to maintaining employee morale. In a study of employees during the restructuring of a psychiatric hospital in Australia, Bordia et al. (2004) demonstrated that communication not only reduced uncertainty but led to increased job satisfaction and perceptions of control.

Merger opinions can also be shaped by external communication such as press coverage. Risberg et al. (2003) analyzed the popular media coverage of a Swedish-Finnish of transnational merger, and found that press coverage focused on presenting the superiority of the national identity of one merger partner (Swedish) over the other (Finnish). This, they considered reflected the history of colonization and the traditional power relationships which existed between the two countries.

Trust

Rousseau (1998) defines trust as 'a psychological state comprising the intention to accept vulnerability based upon positive expectations of the intentions and behavior of the other.' It is considered to be of critical importance in M&As because the change event alters the locus of control from within the individual in their known organizational context to an unknown external organizational context (Bastien, 1987) and so serves to heighten perceptions of vulnerability.

Several studies have been conducted to identify the factors which affect trust in

M&As and the role it plays in merger outcomes. Schweiger and de Nisi (1991) showed employee satisfaction with communication leads to increased perceptions of the trustworthiness of the acquiring or merger management. According to Stahl and Sitkin (2005), trust in M&As is affected by the characteristics of the takeover or merger situation, and factors relating to the way in which the integration process is implemented. Nikandrou et al. (2000) investigated the factors associated with trust in a study of 27 domestic and cross border acquisitions in Greece. As might be expected, trust was positively correlated with communication efforts and employee relations, but trust did reduce job uncertainty. In a study of Swedish hospital workers, Engstrom et al. (2002) found that lack of trust in management was a significant predictor of reduced employee commitment and involvement.

More recently, Stahl et al. (2006) devised a decision-making task based on a series of 16 merger-related scenarios to assess five hypothesized antecedents of trust, namely friendliness of the takeover, national cultural similarity, interaction history, retained autonomy and the attractiveness of the acquiring company's HR policies. All five factors were found to influence target firm members' trust in acquiring management in the expected direction. Members of the target firm tended to report higher levels of trust when the takeover was friendly, when the cultures were more similar, when there was a history of prior collaboration, more retained an autonomy and when the HR policies were attractive. However, some factors were more important than others. Specifically, the attractiveness of the acquiring company's HR policies was found to be by far the most powerful predictor of trust. Interestingly, cultural similarity was shown to have the least impact on respondents' decision to trust the organization.

Organizational justice

Post merger performance is likely to be adversely affected by lowered morale and so possibly linked with perceptions of unfair treatment (researchers Cartwright and Cooper, 2000; Gutknecht and Keys, 1993). Consequently, there has been some research conducted within the framework of organizational justice theory (Greenberg, 1990, 2001) which has its roots within equity theory (Adams, 1965). Organizational justice theory has three elements and is concerned with the perceptions of employees as to the fairness of an organization's policies and procedures (procedural justice) and distribution of rewards (distributive justice), as well as the perceived fairness of its communication process (interactional justice). Employees who feel that they are treated fairly and with respect have been shown to be more inclined to do things for the organization over and above their contractual obligations (Guest, 1998) and engage in a wide range of Organizational Citizenship Behaviors (OCB).

Meyer (2001) applied an organizational justice perspective to study the re-allocation of roles following two Norwegian mergers. Based on interviews, direct observation and archival data, she highlighted the difficulties that the organizations experienced in applying justice rules to satisfy the potentially conflicting demands of productivity and relationship goals within tight time deadlines. Citera (2001) conducted a simulation study to investigate the criteria on which judgments of fairness are likely to be made in M&A situations. Students were presented with four different types of acquisition scenarios and asked to make judgments: The higher the degree of expected integration the more likely individuals were to believe that they would be treated unfairly. In a study of European mergers Very et al. (1997) found that changes in the perceived objectiveness of the performance and reward procedures were significant predictors of employee stress.

CONCLUSIONS

The OB literature to date has provided valuable insights into the social, cultural and psychological aspects of M&As. However, it has provided less convincing answers regarding the direct link between psychological factors and financial performance of M&As. In this respect, the influence of OB research continues to be overshadowed by that of financial scholars.

The eclectic and diverse perspectives and methodologies which have been applied to this field of study have highlighted the complexity of M&A activity. Yet, at the same time the inherent differences in conceptual definitions, competing frameworks, research paradigms and values have resulted in fragmentation and a lack of theoretical integration. This suggests that there is a strong need to move towards more interdisciplinary research and more innovatively combined methodologies.

M&As provide a complex setting for research. Cross sectional studies provide a snapshot of limited value in a lengthy and unfolding process of change and adjustment, and results are likely dependent on who is studied, and when, in the M&A process. Many studies are retrospective and involve small samples. At the same time, research involving questionnaire surveys, although they may purport to be measuring similar constructs, rarely use common measures and so offer little basis for comparability. Clearly, there is a need for more longitudinal research and the development of more specific merger instruments, together with a greater use of mixed research methods and naturalistic experiments.

As OB researchers, we know a lot more about the emotional and behavioral aspects of M&As than we did thirty years ago (Cartwright and Schoenberg, 2006). However, the field still has some way to go before it reaches maturity. This makes it both a challenging and exciting area in which to conduct research, extend knowledge and, importantly, to influence practice.

REFERENCES

Abrahamson, E. (2004) 'Change without pain', *Harvard Business Review*, 76.

Adams, J.S. (1965) 'Inequity in social exchange', in L. Berkowitz (ed.) *Advances in Experimental Social Psychology*. New York: Academic Press. Vol. 2, pp. 267–299.

Agrawal, A. and Jaffe, J. (2000) 'The post merger performance puzzle', *Advances in Mergers and Acquisitions*, 1: 119–156.

Albert, S. and Whetten, D. (1985) 'Organizational identity', *Research in Organizational Behaviour*, 7: 263–295.

Allred, B.B., Boal, K.B. and Holstein, W.K. (2005) 'Corporations as stepfamilies: A new metaphor for explaining the fate of merged and acquired companies', *Academy of Management Executive*, 19 (3): 23–38.

Appelbaum, S.H., Gandell, J., Yortis, H., Proper, S. and Jobin, F. (2000) 'Anatomy of a merger: Behaviour of organizational factors and processes throughout the pre-during-post stages (part 1)', *Management Decision*, 38 (9): 649–662.

Armstrong-Strassen, M. and Cameron, S.J (2003) 'Nurses' job satisfaction and turnover intentions over a six year period of hospital downsizing and amalgamation', *International Journal of Public Administration*, 26 (14): 1607–120.

Ashford, S.J. (1988) 'Individual strategies for dealing with stress during organizational transitions', *Journal of Applied Behavioural Science*, 24: 19–36.

Ashforth, B.E. and Mael, F.A. (1989) 'Social identity theory and the organization', *Academy of Management Review*, 14: 20–39.

Ashkansay, N.M. and Holmes, S. (1995) 'Perceptions of organizational ideology following merger: A longitudinal study of merging accounting firms', *Accounting, Organizations and Society*, 20 (1): 19–34.

Backmann, B.A. (1993) 'An intergroup model of organizational mergers', Unpublished doctoral thesis, UMI No. 9419517.

Barrett, F.J. (1995) 'Creating appreciative learning cultures', *Organizational Dynamics*, 24 (1): 36–49.

Bartels, J., Douwes, R., de Jong, M. and Pruyn, A. (2006) 'Organizational identification during a merger: Determinants of employees expected identification with the new organization', *British Journal of Management*, 17 Special Issue, Perspectives on Mergers and Acquisition: S51–S69.

Bastien, D.T. (1987) 'Common patterns of behaviour and communication in corporate mergers and acquisitions', *Human Resource Management*, 26 (1): 17–33.

Baum, J.C. and Ginsberg, A. (1997) 'Acquisition experience and profitability: Exploring the value of learning by doing', Unpublished manuscript, New York University.

Begley, T.M. (1998) 'Coping strategies as predictors of employee distress and turnover after an organizational consolidation: A longitudinal analysis', *Journal of Occupational and Organizational Psychology*, 71 (4): 305–315.

Berger, C.R. (1987) 'Communication under uncertainty', in M. Roloff and G. Miller (eds) *Interpersonal Processes: New Directions in Communication Research*. London: Sage, pp. 39–62.

Birkinshaw, J., Bresman, H. and Hakanson, L. (2000) 'Managing the post acquisition process: How the human integration and task integration processes interact to foster value creation', *Journal of Management Studies*, 37 (3): 395–425.

Bligh, (2006) 'Surviving post-merger culture clash: Can cultural leadership lessen the casualties', *Leadership*, 2 (4): 395–426.

Bordia, P., Hunt, E., Paulsen, N., Tourish, D. and DiFonzo, N. (2004) 'Uncertainty during organizational change: Is it all about control?', *European Journal of Work and Organizational Psychology*, 13 (3): 345–365.

Bovey, W.H. and Hede, A. (2001) 'Resistance to organizational change: The role of cognitive and affective processes', *Leadership and Organization Development Journal*, 22 (8): 372–382.

Bruckman, J.C. and Peters, S.C. (1987) 'Mergers and acquisitions: The human equation employee relations', *Today*, 14, Spring: 55–63.

Bruton, G.D., Oviall, B.M. and White, M.A. (1994) 'Performance of acquisitions of distressed firms', *Academy of Management Journal*, 37: 972–989.

Buchholtz, A.K., Ribbens, B.A and Houle, I.T. (2003) 'The role of human capital in post acquisition CEO departure', *Academy of Management Journal*, 46 (4): 506–514.

Buono, A.F, Bowditch, J.L. and Lewis J.W. (1985) 'When cultures collide: The anatomy of a merger', *Human Relations*, 38: 477–500.

Cannella, A. and Hambrick, D. (1993) 'Effects of executive departure on the performance of acquired firms', *Strategic Management Journal*, 14 (Special Issue): 137–152.

Cartwright, S. (1998) 'Cultural compatibility in mergers and acquisitions: The case for an organizational marriage counselor', *Journal of Professional HRM*, 2 (3): 10–16.

Cartwright, S. (2005) 'Mergers and acquisitions: An update and appraisal', in G.P. Hodgkinson and J.K. Ford (eds) *International Review of Industrial and Organizational Psychology*. Chichester: John Wiley. Vol. 20, pp. 1–39.

Cartwright, S. and Cooper, C.L. (1993a) 'The psychological impact of merger and acquisition on the individual: A study of building society managers', *Human Relations*, 46: 327–347.

Cartwright, S. and Cooper, C.L. (1993b) 'The role of culture compatibility in successful organizational marriage', *Academy of Management Executive*, 7 (2): 57–70.

Cartwright, S. and Cooper, C.L. (1997) *Managing Mergers, Acquisitions and Strategic Alliances: Integrating People and Cultures*. Oxford: Butterworth Heinemann.

Cartwright, S. and Cooper, C.L. (2000) *HR Know How in Mergers and Acquisitions*. London: Chartered Institute of Personnel Development.

Cartwright, S., Cooper, C.L. and Jordan, J. (1995) 'Managerial preferences in international merger and acquisition partners', *Journal of Strategic Change*, 4: 263–269.

Cartwright, S. and Hudson, S.L. (2000) 'Coping with mergers and acquisitions', in R. Burke and C.L. Cooper (eds) *The Organization in Crisis: Downsizing, Restructuring and Renewal*. London: Basil Blackwell.

Cartwright, S. and McCarthy, S. (2005) 'Developing a framework for cultural due diligence in mergers and acquisitions: Issues and ideas', in G.K Stahl and M.E. Mendenhall (eds) *Mergers and Acquisitions: Managing Culture and Human Resources*. Stanford University, CA: Stanford Business Press.

Cartwright, S. and Price, F. (2003) 'Managerial preferences in international merger and acquisition partners revisited: How are they influenced', in C.L. Cooper and A. Gregory (eds) *Advances in Mergers and Acquisitions*. London: JAI press. Vol. 2, pp. 81–95.

Cartwright, S. and Schoenberg, R. (2006) 'Thirty years of mergers and acquisitions research: Recent advances and future opportunities', *British Journal of Management*, (17) Special Issue: S1–S5.

Chatterjee, S. (1992) 'Sources of value in takeovers: Synergy or restructuring implications for target and bidder firms', *Strategic Management Journal*, 13: 267–286.

Citera, M. (2001) 'A policy modelling approach to examining fairness judgements in organizational acquisitions', *Journal of Behavioural Decision Making*, 14 (4): 309–327.

Cohen, C.F, Birkin, S.J., Cohen, M.E., Garfield, M.J. and Webb, H.E. (2006) 'Managing conflict during an organizational acquisition', *Conflict Resolution Quarterly*, 23 (3): 317 –331.

Conn, C., Cosh, A., Guest, P. and Hughes, A. (2001) *Long Run Share Performance of UK Firms Engaging in Cross Border Acquisitions*. University of Cambridge, Centre for Business Research Working paper No. 214.

Cooke, F.L. (2006) 'Acquisitions of state owned enterprises by MNC's: Driving forces, barriers and implications for HRM', *British Journal of Management*, (17) Special Issue: S107–S123.

Cooper, C.L and Kirkcaldy, B.D. (1995) 'Executive stereotyping between cultures: The British v German manager', *Journal of Managerial Psychology*, 10 (1): 3–6.

Coopey, J. and Burgoyne, J. (2000) 'Politics and organizational learning', *Journal of Management Studies*, 37 (6): 869–886.

Cornett–De Vito, M.M. and Freidman, P.G. (1995) 'Communication processes and merger success: An exploratory study of four financial institution mergers', *Management Communication Quarterly*, 9 (1): 46–77.

Corwin, S., Weinstein, H. and Sweeney, P. (1991) 'Facing the people issue in M&As', *Management Review*, 80: 47–334.

Costello, T.W., Kubis, J.F. and Shaffer, C.L. (1963) 'An analysis of attitudes toward a planned merger', *Human Relations*, 8 (2): 235–249.

Dackert, I., Jackson, P.R., Brenner, S-O. and Johanson, C.R. (2003) 'Eliciting and analysing employees' expectations of a merger', *Human Relations*, 56 (6): 705–725.

Daly, J.P., Pounder, R.W. and Kabanoff, B. (2004) 'The effect of firms' espoused values on their post merger performance', *Journal of Applied Behavioural Science*, 40 (3): 323–353.

Datta, D. (1991) 'Organization fit and acquisition performance: Effects of post merger integration', *Strategic Management Journal*, 12: 281–298.

Elsass, P.M. and Veiga, J.F. (1994) 'Acculturation in acquired organizations: A force field analysis', *Human Relations*, 47 (4): 431–453.

Empson, L. (2001) 'Fear of exploitation and fear of contamination: Impediments to knowledge transfer in mergers between professional service firms', *Human Relations*, 54 (7) Special Issue: 839–862.

Engstrom, A.K., Rosengreen, K. and Hallberg, L.R.M. (2002) 'Balancing involvement: Employees' experience of merging hospitals in Sweden', *Journal of Advanced Nursing*, 38 (1): 11–18.

Flinn, M. (1988) 'Step and genetic parent/offspring relationships in a Caribbean village', *Ethology and Sociobiology*, 9: 335–369.

Frieswick, K. (2005) 'Fools Gold', *CFO*, February 2005: 27.

Gamong, L.H. and Coleman, M. (1984) 'Effects of re-marriage on children: A review of the empirical literature', *Family Relations*, 33: 389–406.

Ganster, D.C. and Fusiler, M.R. (1989) 'Control in the Workplace', in C.L.Cooper and I.T. Robertson (eds) *International Review of Industrial and Organizational Psychology*. New York: John Wiley, pp. 235–280.

Gertsen, M.C. and Soderberg, A.M. (1998) 'Foreign acquisitions in Denmark: Cultural and communicative dimensions', in M.C. Gertsen, A.M. Soderberg and J.E. Torps (eds) *Cultural Dimensions of International Mergers and Acquisitions*. Berlin: de Guyter, pp. 167–194.

Gibbons, C. (1998) 'An investigation into the effects of organizational change on occupational stress in further education lecturers', *Journal of Further and Higher Education*, 22 (3): 315–317.

Gick, M.L. and Holyoak, K.J. (1987) 'The cognitive basis of knowledge transfer', in S.M. Cornier and J.D. Hagman (eds) *Transfer of Learning: Contemporary Research and Applications*. New York: Academic Press, pp. 9–46.

Giessner, S.R., Viki, G.T., Otten, S., Terry, D.J. and Tauber, S. (2006) 'The challenge of merging: Merger patterns, premerger status and merger support', *Personality and Social Psychology Bulletin*, 32 (3): 339–352.

Goldberg, D. (1972) *The Detection of Psychiatric Illness by Questionnaire*. London: Oxford University Press.

Graves, R. (1981) 'Individual reactions to a merger of two small firms of brokers in the re-insurance industry: A total population survey', *Journal of Management Studies*, 18 (1): 89–113.

Greenberg, J. (1990) 'Organizational justice: Yesterday, today and tomorrow', *Journal of Management*, 16: 339–432.

Greenberg, J. (2001) 'Setting the justice agenda: Seven unanswered questions about "what, why and how"', *Journal of Vocational Behaviour*, 58: 210–219.

Greenberg, D.N, Lane, H.W. and Bahde, K. (2005) 'Organizational learning in cross border mergers and acquisitions', in G.K. Stahl and M.E. Mendenhall (eds) *Mergers and Acquisitions: Managing Culture and Human Resources*. Stanford University, CA: Stanford Business Books, pp. 53–76.

Gregory, A. (1997) 'An examination of the long run performance of UK acquiring firms', *Journal of Business, Finance and Accounting*, 24 (7/8): 871–1002.

Guest, D. (1998) 'Is the psychological contract worth taking seriously?', *Journal of Organizational Behaviour*, 19, Special Issue: 649–664.

Gutknecht, J.E. and Keys, J.B. (1993) 'Mergers, acquisitions and takeovers: Maintaining morale of survivors and protecting employees', *Academy of Management Executive*, 7 (3): 25–35.

Haleblian, J. and Finkelstein, S. (1999) 'The influence of organizational acquisition experience on acquisition performance', *Administrative Science Quarterly*, 44: 29–56.

Hargie, O. and Tourish, D. (2000) 'Charting communication performance in a healthcare organization', in O. Hargie and D. Tourish (eds) *Handbook of Communication Audits for Organizations*. London: Routledge, pp. 195–209.

Hartner, J.K., Schmidt, F.L. and Keyes, C.L.M. (2005) 'Well Being in the workplace and its relationship to business outcomes: A review of the Gallup studies', in C.L.M. Keyes and J. Haidt (eds) *Flourishing Positive Psychology and the Life Welt Lived*. Washington, DC: American Psychological Society.

Harwood, I. and Ashleigh, M. (2005) 'The impact of trust and confidentiality on strategic organizational change programmes: A case study of post-acquisition integration', *Strategic Change Journal*, 14: 63–75.

Haslam, S.A. and Ellemers, N. (2005) 'Social identity in industrial and organizational psychology: Concepts, controversies and contributions', in G.P Hodgkinson and J.K. Ford (eds) *International Review of Industrial and Organizational Psychology*. Chichester: John Wiley, 20, pp. 39–118.

Haspeslagh, P.C. and Jemison, D.B. (1991) *Managing Acquisitions: Creating Value Through Corporate Renewal*. New York: Free Press.

Haunschild, P.R., Moreland, R.L. and Murrell, A.J. (1994) 'Sources of resistance to mergers between groups', *Journal of Applied Social Psychology*, 24: 1150–1178.

Hayes, R.H. and Hoag, G.H. (1974) 'Post acquisition retention of top managers', *Mergers and Acquisitions*, 9: 8–18.

Hitt, M.A., Hoskisson, R.E., Ireland, R.D. and Harrison, J.S. (1991) 'Effects of acquisition on R & D inputs and outputs', *Academy of Management Journal*, 34 (3): 693–706.

Hogan, E. and Overmeyer–Day, L. (1994) 'The psychology of mergers and acquisitions', in C.L. Cooper and I.T. Robertson (eds) *International Review of Industrial and Organizational Psychology*. Chichester: John Wiley, pp. 247–281.

Hovers, J. (1973) *Expansion Through Acquisition*. London: Business Books.

Humpal, J.J. (1971) 'Organizational marriage counselling: A first step', *Journal of Applied Behavioural Science*, 7: 103–109.

Hunsaker, P.L. and Coombs, M.W. (1988) 'Mergers and acquisitions: Managing the emotional issues', *Personnel Journal*, 65: 56–63.

Hunt, J. (1988) 'Managing the successful acquisition: A people question', *London Business Journal*, Summer: 2–15.

Hunt, J., Lees, S., Grumbar, I.J. and Vivian, P.D. (1987) *Acquisitions: The Human Factor* (Working paper). London Business School.

Jimmieson, N.L., Terry, D.J. and Callan, V.J. (2004) 'A longitudinal study of employee adaptation to organizational change: The role of change related information and change related self-efficacy', *Journal of Occupational Health Psychology*, 9 (1): 11–27.

Kavanagh, M. and Ashkansay, N. (2006) 'The impact of leadership and change management strategy on organizational culture and individual acceptance of change during a merger', *British Journal of Management*, 17: S83–S105.

Kearney, A.T. (1999) *White Paper on Post Merger Integration*. Amsterdam: KPMG.

King, D., Dalton, D., Daily, C. and Covin, J. (2004) 'Meta-analyses of post acquisition performance: Indications of unidentified moderators', *Strategic Management Journal*, 25: 187–200.

Kitching, J. (1974) 'Winning and losing with European Acquisitions', *Harvard Business Review*, 52: 124–136.

Kleppesto, S. (1998) 'A quest for social identity: The pragmatics of communication in mergers and acquisitions', in M.C. Gertsen, A-M. Soderberg and J.E. Torps (eds) *Cultural Dimensions of International Mergers and Acquisitions*. Berlin: De Guyter, pp. 147–166.

Koonce, R. (1991) 'The people side of organizational change', *Credit*, 17 (6): 22–25.

KPMG (2000) *Dealwatch*. Amsterdam: KPMG.

Krishnan, H.A., Miller, A. and Judge, W.Q. (1997) 'Diversification and managing executive team complementarily: Is performance improved by merging similar or dissimilar teams?', *Strategic Management Journal*, 18: 361–374.

Krug, J.A. (2002) *Executive Turnover in Acquired Firms: A Longitudinal Analysis of Long Term Integration Effects*. Paper presented at the Annual Academy of Management meeting, Seattle.

Krug, J.A. and Hegarty, W.H. (1997) 'Post acquisition turnover amongst US top management teams: An analysis of the effects of foreign v domestic acquisitions of US targets', *Strategic Management Journal*, 18: 667–675.

Kusstatscher, V. (2006) 'Cultivating positive emotions in mergers and acquisitions', in C.L. Cooper and S. Finkelstein (eds) *Advances in Mergers and Acquisitions*. Vol. 5. Oxford: JAI, pp. 91–103.

Larsson, R. (2005) 'Synergy realization in mergers and acquisitions: A co–competence and motivational approach', in G.K. Stahl and M.E. Mendenhall (eds) *Mergers and Acquisitions: Managing Culture and Human Resources*. Stanford, CA: Stanford Business Books, pp. 183–201.

Larsson, R. and Lubatkin, M. (2001) 'Achieving acculturation in mergers and acquisitions: An international case survey', *Human Relations*, 54: 1573–1607.

Larsson, R. and Risberg, A. (1998) 'Cultural awareness and national versus corporate barriers to acculturation', in M.C. Gertsen, A-M. Soderberg and J.E. Torp (eds) *Cultural Dimensions of International Mergers and Acquisitions*. Berlin: De Guyter, pp. 39–56.

Lohrum, C. (1996) *Post Acquisition Integration: Towards an Understanding of Employee Reactions*. Publication Swedish School of Economics and Business Administration, No. 65. Sweden.

Manz, C., Bastien, D. and Hostager, T. (1991) 'Executive leadership during organizational change: A bi-cycle model', *Human Resources Planning*, 14: 275–287.

Marks, M. (1988) 'The Merger Syndrome: The human side of corporate combinations', *Journal of Buyouts and Acquisitions*, January/February: 18–23.

Marks, M. (1997) 'Consulting in mergers and acquisitions: Interventions spawned by recent trends', *Journal of Organizational Change Management*, 10 (3): 267–279.

Marks, M.L. and Mirvis, P. (1985) 'Merger syndrome: Stress and uncertainty', *Mergers and Acquisitions*, 19, Summer: 50–55.

Marks, M.L. and Mirvis, P. (1986) 'Merger syndrome: Management by crisis', *Mergers and Acquisitions*, 20: 70–76.

Marks, M.L. and Mirvis, P.H. (2001) 'Making mergers and acquisitions work: Strategic and psychological preparation', *Academy of Management Executive*, 15 (2): 80–94.

Matteson, M.T. and Ivancevich, J.M. (1990) 'Merger and acquisition stress: Fear and uncertainty at mid career prevention', *Human Sciences Journal*, 8 (1): 139–158.

McHugh, M. (1995) 'Organizational merger: A stressful challenge', *Review of employment Topics*, 3 (1). Belfast: Labour Relations Agency.

Meyer, C. B. (2001) 'Allocation processes in mergers and acquisitions: An organizational justice perspective', *British Journal of Management*, 12 (1): 47–67.

Meyer, K.E. and Lieb–Doczy, E. (2003) 'Post-acquisition re-structuring as an evolutionary process', *Journal of Management Studies*, 40 (2): 459–482.

Mirvis, P.H. (1985) 'Negotiations after the sale: The roots and ramifications of conflict in an acquisition', *Journal of Occupational Behaviour*, 6: 115–136.

Morosini, P. and Singh, H. (1994) 'Post cross border acquisitions: Implementing national culture compatible strategies to improve performance', *European Management Journal*, 12: 390–400.

Morosini, P., Scott, S. and Singh, H. (1998) 'National cultural distance and cross border acquisition performance', *Journal of International Business Studies*, 29 (1): 137–158.

Nadler, D.A., Thies, P.K. and Nadler, M.B. (2001) 'Culture Change in the strategic enterprise: Lessons from the field', in C.L. Cooper, S. Cartwright and P.C. Earley (eds) *The International Handbook of Organizational Culture and Climate*. Chichester: John Wiley, pp. 309–324.

Nahavandi, A. and Malekzadeh, A.R. (1988) 'Acculturation in mergers and acquisitions', *Academy of Management Review*, 13 (1): 79–90.

Napier, N.K. (1989) 'Mergers and acquisitions: Human resource issues and outcomes', *Journal of Management Studies*, 26: 271–287.

Napier, N.K., Schweiger, D.M. and Kosglow, J. (1993) 'Managing organizational diversity: Observations from cross border acquisitions', *Human Resource Management*, 32: 505–523.

Nelson, A., Cooper, C.L. and Jackson, P. (1995) 'Uncertainty amidst change: The impact of privatisation on employee job satisfaction and well being', *Journal of Occupational and Organizational Psychology*, 68: 57–71.

Nikandrou, I., Papalaxandis, N. and Bourantes, D. (2000) 'Gaining employee trust after acquisitions: Implications for managerial action', *Employee Relations*, 4: 334–345.

Panchal, S. and Cartwright, S. (2001) 'Group differences in post merger stress', *Journal of Managerial Psychology*, 16 (6): 424–434.

Phan, P. and Lee, S. (1995) 'Human capital or social networks: What constrains CEO dismissal', *Academy of Management Best Paper Proceedings*, 37–41.

Ranft, A.L (2006) 'Knowledge preservation and transfer during post acquisition integration', in C.L. Cooper and S. Finkelstein (eds) *Advances in Mergers and Acquisition*. Elsvier. Vol. 5. Oxford: JAI, pp. 51–67.

Risberg, A. (1997) 'Ambiguity and communication in cross cultural acquisitions: Towards a conceptual framework', *Leadership and Organization Development Journal*, 18 (5): 257–267.

Risberg, A., Tienari, J. and Vaara, E. (2003) 'Making sense of a transnational merger: Media texts and the (re)construction of power relations', *Culture and Organization*, 9 (2): 121–137.

Rostand, A. (1994) *Optimizing Managerial Decisions During the Acquisition Integration Process*. Paper presented at 14th Annual Strategic Management Society International Conference, Paris.

Rousseau, D.M. (1998) 'Why workers still identify with organizations', *Journal of Organizational Behaviour*, 19: 217–233.

Schoenberg, R. (2000) 'The influence of cultural compatibility within cross border acquisitions: A review', *Advances in Mergers and Acquisitions*, 1: 43–59.

Schoenberg, R. (2003) *Organizational Determinants of Resource Base Sharing in International Acquisitions*. Paper presented at the 23rd Annual International Conference of the Strategic Management Society, Washington, DC.

Schreyogg, G. (2005) 'The role of corporate cultural diversity in integrating mergers and acquisitions', in G.K. Stahl and M.E. Mendenhall (eds) *Mergers and Acquisitions: Managing Culture and Human Resources*. Stanford University, CA: Stanford Business Books, pp. 108–125.

Schweiger, D. and de Nisi, A. (1991) 'Communication with employees following a merger: A longitudinal field experiment', *Academy of Management Journal*, 34: 110–135.

Schweiger, D.M, and Goulet, P.K. (2000) 'Integrating mergers and acquisitions: An international research review', in C.L. Cooper and A. Gregory (eds) *Advances in Mergers and Acquisitions*. Amsterdam: JA1 Press. Vol. 1, pp. 61–91.

Schweiger, D.M and Ivancevich, J. (1987) 'Human resources: The forgotten factor in mergers and acquisitions', *Personnel Administrator*, November: 47–61.

Schweiger, D.M., Ivancevich, J. and Power, F. (1987) 'Executive action in managing human resources before and after being acquired', *Academy of Management*, 1: 127–138.

Schweiger, D.M. and Lippert, R.L. (2005) 'Integration: The critical link in M&A value creation', in G.K Stahl and M.E. Mendenhall (eds) *Mergers and Acquisitions: Managing Cultures and Human Resources*. Stanford University, CA: Stanford Business Books, pp. 17–45.

Searby, F. (1969) 'Control of postmerger change', *Harvard Business Review*, September–October, 47 (5): 4–11.

Seth, A. (1990) 'Value creation in acquisitions: A re–examination of performance issues', *Strategic Management Journal*, 11: 99–116.

Stahl, G.K. and Sitkin, S.B. (2005) 'Trust in mergers and acquisitions', in G.K. Stahl and M.E. Mendenhall (eds) *Mergers and Acquisitions: Managing Culture and Human Resources*. Stanford, CA: Stanford Business Books, pp. 82–102.

Stahl, G.K., Chei, H.C. and Pablo, A.L. (2006) 'Antecedents of target firm members' trust in the acquiring firm's management: A decision-making simulation', in C.L. Cooper and S. Finkelstein (eds) *Advances in Mergers and Acquisitions*. Vol. 5. Oxford: JAI, pp. 69–89.

Stahl, G.K., Mendenhall, M., Pablo, A. and Javidan, M. (2005) 'Sociocultural integration in mergers and acquisitions', in G.K. Stahl and M.E. Mendenhall (eds) *Mergers and Acquisitions: Managing Culture and Human Resources*. Stanford: Stanford University Press, pp. 3–16.

Sudarsanam, S. (2003) *Creating Value from Mergers and Acquisitions*. Harlow: Pearson Education.

Sudarsanam, S. and Mahate, A.A. (2006) 'Are friendly acquisitions too bad for shareholders and managers? Long term value creation and top management turnover in hostile and friendly acquirers', *British Journal of Management*, 17, Special Issue: S7–S30.

Sui, O., Cooper, C.L. and Donald, I. (1997) 'Occupational stress, job satisfaction and mental health amongst employees of an acquired TV company in Hong Kong', *Stress Medicine*, 13 (2): 99–107.

Tajfel, H. and Turner, J.C. (1979) 'An integrative theory of intergroup conflict', in W.G. Austin and S. Worchel (eds) *Psychology of Inter Group Relations*. Monterey, CA: Brookes Cole, pp. 33–47.

Terry, D.J. (2001) 'Intergroup relations and organizational mergers', in M.A. Hogg and D.J. Terry (eds) *Social Identity Processes in Organizational Contexts*. Philadelphia, PA: Psychology Press, pp. 229–248.

Terry, D.J. (2003) 'A social identity perspective on organizational mergers: The role of group status, permeability and similarity', in S.A. Haslam, D. Van Knippenberg, M.J. Platow and N. Ellemers (eds) *Social Identity at Work: Developing Theory for Organizational Practice*. Philadelphia, PA: Psychology Press, pp. 293–316.

Tolbert, P.S. and Zucker, L.G. (1996) 'The institutionalization of institutional theory', in S.R. Clegg, C. Hardy and W.R. Nord (eds) *Handbook of Organizational Studies*. London: Sage, pp. 175–190.

Van Dick, R. (2004) 'My job is my castle: Identification in organizational contexts', in C.L. Cooper and I.T. Robertson (eds) *International Review of Industrial and Organizational Psychology*. Chichester: John Wiley. Vol. 19, pp. 171–203.

Van Dick, R., Ullrich, J. and Tissington, P.A. (2006) 'Working under a black cloud: How to sustain organizational identification after a merger', *British Journal of Management*, Special Issue, 17: S69–79.

Van Dick, R., Wagner, U. and Lemmer, G. (2004) 'The winds of change: Multiple identifications in the case of organizational mergers', *European Journal of Work and Organizational Psychology*, 13 (2): 121–138.

Van Knippenberg, D., Van Knippenberg, B., Monden, L. and de Lima, F. (2002) 'Organizational identification after a merger: A social identity perspective', *British Journal of Social Psychology*, 41: 233–252.

Very, P., Lubatkin, M. and Calori, R. (1998) 'A cross national assessment of acculturative stress in European mergers', in M.C. Gertsen, A-M. Soderberg and J.E. Torps (eds) *Cultural Dimensions of International Mergers and Acquisitions*. Berlin: de Gruyter, pp. 85–110.

Very, P., Lubatkin, M. and Veiga, J. (1997) 'Relative standing and the performance of recently acquired European mergers', *Strategic Management Journal*, 18: 593–614.

Weber, Y. (1996) 'Corporate culture fit and performance in mergers and acquisitions', *Human Relations*, 49 (9): 1181–1202.

Weber, Y., Shenkar, O. and Raveh, A. (1996) 'National and corporate culture fit in mergers and acquisitions: An exploratory study', *Management Science*, 42 (8): 1215–1227.

Xia, X. and Pan, H. (2006) 'The dynamics of corporate takeovers based on managerial overconfidence', *Journal of American Academy of Business*, Cambridge, 10 (1): 378–386.

Yu, J., Engleman, R.M. and Van de Ven, A.H. (2005) 'The integration journey: An attention based view of the merger and acquisition integration process', *Organization Studies*, 26 (10): 1501–1528.

Zollo, M. and Singh, H. (2004) 'Deliberate learning in corporate acquisitions: Post acquisitions strategies and integration capability in US bank mergers', *Strategic Management Journal*, 25: 1233–1256.

31

Organizational Change

Alannah E. Rafferty and Mark A. Griffin

Organizational change is a topic of concern for many organizational scientists, and has been recognized as 'one of the great themes in the social sciences' (Pettigrew et al., 2001: 697). Diverse disciplines and theoretical models have been drawn on to explain change, development, and transformation in organizations, including strategy, economics, international business, organizational theory, psychology, and sociology, to name but a few. Indeed, one of the difficulties when reviewing the organizational change field is the sheer amount of material with which one is confronted. This diversity of perspectives and approaches has contributed to disagreements regarding the meaning of organizational change and how to study it.

We begin this review by examining the history of the change field. First, we examine several classic studies that have had a considerable influence on the field, including the Hawthorne Studies (Roethlisberger and Dickson, 1939), Kurt Lewin's Planned Approach to Change (1947, 1951, 1952), and Coch and French's (1948) study of resistance to change. These works have had an important influence on the emergence of organizational development (OD), which is the largest and

the most coherent body of work that has informed the change literature.

OD is concerned with the 'use of planned, behavioral science-based interventions in work settings for the purpose of improving organizational functioning and individual development' (Porras and Robertson, 1992: 721–722). As described by Mirvis (1988: 1990), OD has moved from being a broad philosophy about how one should interact in organizations as a change agent, to a complex approach for managing change that is informed by research from many fields.

Next, we focus on recent research and identify issues that have been the subject of growing interest in the field. Specifically, we identify the pace, linearity, and sequence of different types of organizational change as an important emerging issue. We examine a number of empirical studies addressing this issue (Amis et al., 2004; Brown and Eisenhardt, 1997; Rindova and Kotha, 2001). Another important emerging issue concerns different types of change. We focus on Weick and Quinn's (1999) distinction between 'episodic' and 'continuous change,' exploring the implications of different types of change for the models and approaches academics and practitioners adopt.

A third emerging issue we identify is that authors have begun to question traditional assumptions about change, inertia, and momentum at the organizational level (Howard-Grenville, 2005; Jansen, 2004). The final emerging issue identified concerns the recent recognition that individuals are active participants in change efforts. We examine work exploring the role of individuals' emotions in organizational change processes (Huy, 1999, 2002).

Thereafter, we identify a number of key debates in the organizational change field, and review arguments concerning the appropriateness of 'normal science' techniques when studying organizational change processes (Kuhn, 1970). We then explore the ongoing debate concerning the relationship between theory and practice in the organizational change field. This particular issue is tied up with the need to develop closer and more effective partnerships between scholars and practitioners.

Finally, we identify several emerging trends in the change field. We emphasize the importance of researchers continuing to develop multi-level models of organizational change processes (e.g., Caldwell et al., 2004; Huy, 1999; Whelan-Barry et al., 2003). We also focus on the need for researchers to continue to carefully examine the appropriateness of traditional change models in hyper-turbulent organizational environments (e.g., Burnes, 2004a, 2004b; Marshak, 2004). The emerging trends that we identify reflect the increased complexity of change theory and research, and provide a positive view of the future of the field.

CLASSIC STUDIES

One of the greatest influences on the change field is organizational development (OD). Indeed, many textbooks and authors discuss 'organizational change and development,' inextricably linking these two areas. OD emerged from five major backgrounds including Action Research and survey feedback, techniques that were developed by Kurt Lewin (Cummings and Worley, 1997). Action Research is characterized by data collection, data feedback, action planning, implementation, and follow-up data collection. Lewin and a number of his colleagues discovered that research needed to be closely linked to action if organization members were to use it to manage change. Among the pioneering Action Research studies is the 'Hawthorne Studies,' conducted at Western Electric's Hawthorne Works, a large plant outside of Chicago, and the work of Coch and French (1948) on overcoming resistance to change. We examine these classic studies below.

The Hawthorne Studies

One of the most influential set of studies conducted in the social sciences is the Hawthorne Studies (Roethlisberger and Dickson, 1939) which refer to a series of studies conducted from 1924 to 1932. These studies provided the impetus for research focused on psychological and social factors in the workplace, which contrasted with the scientific management principles in vogue at the time. Today, these studies are generally acknowledged as one of the starting points of the Human Relations school of thought and of the disciplines of social psychology, industrial relations, and organizational behavior. However, despite the popularity of these studies, they are commonly misreported and misrepresented (Adair, 1984; McQuarrie, 2005).

The Hawthorne Studies began in November 1924 at the Western Electric Company's Hawthorne plant in Chicago, Illinois. A team of staff engineers working in conjunction with the National Engineering Council undertook a study to examine the influence of illumination levels on employee efficiency. While the 'Illumination Studies' were not formally part of the 'Hawthorne Studies,' they paved the way for these studies and are often discussed as part of this research program (Adair, 1984).

The first illumination study involved increasing lighting levels at certain intervals and recording productivity after each change. The results of this and two subsequent experiments did not indicate any connection between illumination and productivity. The research team concluded that lighting was only a minor factor affecting productivity. At this time, Fritz J. Roethlisberger and Elton Mayo, both from Harvard University, and William Dickson, the chief of Human Relations at the Hawthorne plant, began to work on the project.

The new research team designed the 'Relay Assembly Test Room Study,' where a small group of workers were isolated in a single room. Five female workers were subjected to a variety of variables expected to influence worker fatigue, including the timing of rest breaks, the length of the working day, and the type of equipment used. As the experiment progressed, pay rates were included as a variable of interest. The experiment began in April 1927, continued for five years, and incorporated 13 separate periods during which different variables were manipulated.

The results of the Relay Assembly Test Room Study indicated a continual rise in productivity, even under conditions that might be expected to produce worker fatigue and reduce output. As the experiment progressed, employees' attitudes became more positive and social interaction amongst the workers increased. Importantly, before this study began, the researchers had been concerned that employees taken from their regular work and placed in a test room would be negative and resistant. To overcome this anticipated effect, supervision was removed, special privileges were allowed, and considerable attention and interest was expressed towards the workers. However, ultimately, the researchers concluded that it was these factors that had resulted in productivity improvements, and *not* the experimental manipulations of working conditions (Adair, 1984; Sonnenfeld, 1985).

The research team then conducted two additional experiments involving changes in wage structure and work schedules. The first of these experiments, the 'Second Relay Assembly Group Study,' involved a group of workers who first worked collectively and then returned to work in their departments. At the same time, a second experiment was conducted, the 'Mica Splitting Test Room Study,' with a group of workers that were being paid on an individual piecework basis with five experimental periods involving changes in work schedules. The results of both studies indicated that variations in output could not be clearly linked to changes in working conditions. The researchers attributed the positive results of their studies to the positive attention being paid to workers as experimental subjects. This effect became known as the 'Hawthorne effect' (Adair, 1984).

The final part of the Hawthorne Studies was an experiment designed to address a phenomenon noted in interviews: that of social interactions within groups affecting the output of the group. This experiment began in 1931 and was referred to as the 'Bank Wiring Observation Room Study.' In this study, a group of nine male workers performing interdependent tasks was placed in a separate room to perform their jobs, and an observer was assigned to watch them. Data from this study revealed that employees have a shared concept of a 'day's work' which involved a certain level of output. Workers adjusted their efforts to produce to that level, which could involve misreporting productivity levels, stopping work early, or making claims about inadequate resources.

A number of lessons were derived from the Hawthorne Studies (Adair, 1984; McQuarrie, 2005; Roethlisberger and Dickson, 1939; Sonnenfeld, 1985). First, it was concluded that individual work behavior is rarely a consequence of simple cause and effect relationships, but rather is determined by a complex set of factors. Second, work groups develop their own set of norms, which mediated between the needs of the individual and the work group. Third, the social structure of groups is maintained through job-related symbols of prestige and power. Fourth, supervisors need to listen to the personal context of employee complaints to understand the unique needs and satisfaction of each individual. Finally, awareness of employee sentiments and employee participation can reduce resistance to change.

Despite the influence of the Hawthorne Studies, this research has also attracted a great deal of criticism. Authors have been critical of the assumption that findings in a non-unionized workplace would generalize to all workplaces (Adair, 1984; McQuarrie, 2005). Other authors have focused on the lack of commentary on issues such as gender-based power differences in operation in the studies. There has also been considerable criticism regarding the methodology of the studies themselves, and the interpretation of the study data (McQuarrie, 2005).

Despite these criticisms, the Hawthorne Studies have had an enduring influence on the field of organizational change, as can be seen in researchers' continuing interest in participation in change, the influence of the social context during change processes, and recently, a recognition that individuals are not passive recipients of change but also play an active role in interpreting and creating change processes (e.g., George and Jones, 2001).

Kurt Lewin's planned approach to change

Kurt Lewin has had a profound impact on the organizational change field, and his work still guides thinking today. Lewin (1947, 1951, 1952) developed an integrated Approach to Planned Change that incorporated his work on Field Theory, Group Dynamics, and Action Research, together with his 3-Step model of change. While Lewin developed an interlinked, elaborate, and robust Approach to Planned Change, most researchers have focused on just one component of this approach – the 3-Step model, or the 'unfreeze-transition-refreeze' model (Burnes, 2004b). Below, we discuss each of the components of Lewin's Approach to Change.

Field theory

This has been characterized as an approach to understanding group behavior that involves mapping out the complexity of the field in which behavior takes place (Burnes, 2004a, 2004b). Lewin (1947: 14) suggested that force field analysis provides a 'system of analysis which permits the representation of social forces in a group setting.' He argued that the present situation – the status quo – is maintained by opposing and restraining forces in an individual's social field. An individual's social field is in a constant state of quasi-stationary equilibrium due to the ongoing changes to the forces that impinge on groups. Some authors (e.g., Burnes, 2004a) suggest that Field Theory is the least understood element of Lewin's work, although this work underpins his Approach to Planned Change.

Group dynamics

A second component of Kurt Lewin's approach was his focus on group dynamics (e.g., Lewin, 1952). In particular, he was concerned with the influence of groups in shaping their members' behavior. Lewin argued that individuals are constrained by the group pressures to conform and, therefore, change efforts should focus on modifying group norms, roles, and interactions (Burnes, 2004a).

Action research

The third component of Lewin's Approach to Planned Change, Action Research, emphasizes that change requires action. Specifically, Action Research is aimed at ensuring the appropriate actions are implemented after identifying all alternatives and choosing the most appropriate one for the situation at hand. This approach also recognizes that if change is to occur individuals must recognize that change is necessary. Action Research proceeds in a spiral of steps, each of which is composed of a circle of planning, action, and fact finding about the results of action.

3-Step model of change

The final aspect of Lewin's Approach to Planned Change was his 3-Step model of change, the unfreeze-transition-refreeze model. This model is well known and is often identified as Lewin's key contribution to the understanding of change (e.g., Burnes, 2004b). However, the increased emphasis on the importance of implementing transformational change has meant that this model has been criticized as being inappropriate in 'hyper-turbulent' environments (e.g., Kanter, et al., 1992; Marshak, 2004). Marshak proposed that Lewin's (1947) 3-Step model might be helpful in stable or moderately turbulent environments, and argued that new models are needed for highly turbulent and hyperactive environments. However, Burnes (2004a, 2004b) presents a contrary perspective, arguing for the continuing importance of Lewin's work. We explore this debate later in this chapter.

Coch and French (1948): Resistance to change

Coch and French (1948) conducted a classic study on participative decision-making (PDM), which has been described as 'one of the best designed field experiments on PDM ... [it] shows impressive evidence of the effectiveness of PDM in decreasing resistance to change' (Locke and Schweiger, 1979: 308–309). Despite this, there are a number of issues that need to be taken into account when considering the implications of Coch and French's work (Bartlem and Locke, 1981).

Conducting a study in the Harwood Manufacturing Company in Marion, Virginia, Coch and French (1948) examined why production employees resisted changes in their methods of working and jobs, and what could be done to overcome this resistance. Coch and French concluded that the slow rate of relearning after transfer to a new job compared to the faster rate of learning when first entering the organization indicated that motivational issues were in operation. Interviews suggested that employees reported feeling resentment against management for transferring them, felt frustrated, and reported a loss of hope of regaining their former level of proficiency. Based on their analysis, Coch and French argued that resistance to change is a combination of an individual's reaction to frustration and strong group-induced forces. As a result, they designed a

study to overcome resistance to change using group methods.

An experiment was designed that used two variations of democratic procedures in handling groups that were to undergo job transfer. The first condition, 'participation through representation', involved selecting group members to represent all of the workers when designing the changes to be made to their jobs. The second condition, the 'total participation condition,' involved all employees being involved in designing changes. The third condition was a control group, where group members were told that change would occur. Two experimental groups received the total participation treatment. The three experimental groups and the control group were all matched with respect to the efficiency ratings of the groups prior to transfer, the degree of change involved in the transfer, and the amount of 'we-feeling' observed in the groups.

The results of Coch and French's (1948) study suggested the control group improved little beyond their early efficiency ratings. In addition, resistance developed almost immediately after change was introduced, and 17 per cent of this group left in the first 40 days after changes were introduced. In contrast, the participation through representation group displayed an unusually good relearning curve after changes were introduced. During this time, attitudes were cooperative and permissive, and there was no turnover in the first 40 days after change. The two groups that received the total participation condition recovered faster than the participation through representation group. Specifically, after a slight drop on the first day after changes were introduced, efficiency ratings returned to a pre-change level and showed sustained progress to a level of 14 per cent higher than before the change.

Two and a half months after the breakup of the control group, which had initially performed very poorly, the 13 remaining members of this group were brought together. This second experiment involved transferring the control group to a new job using the total participation technique similar to that used in the first study. With the use of the total participation technique, this group recovered rapidly to their previous efficiency rating and continued on beyond it to a new high level of production.

Coch and French (1948) concluded that the second experiment provided strong support for the argument that the total participation condition has a stronger influence on outcomes than participation through representation. Specifically, Coch and French (p. 531) reported that 'it is possible for management to modify greatly or to remove completely group resistance to changes in methods of work and ensuing piece rates' through the use of group participation in change.

Despite the enduring influence of Coch and French's (1948) study, this work has been the subject of criticism (e.g., Bartlem and Locke, 1981; Gardner, 1977). Bartlem and Locke suggest that to separate the content of the changes made from the effect of participation in designing them, the changes proposed by the experimental groups should have been imposed on another control group. This design would have enabled the researchers to separate the informational or cognitive effects from the motivational effects, on resistance to change.

In addition, Bartlem and Locke (1981) suggest that Coch and French (1948) also added two additional elements for the experimental groups that were not a part of the intervention for the control group. Specifically, the experimental groups were involved in setting new piece rates and also received additional training. This procedure is likely to have influenced workers' perceptions of fairness and objectivity when setting piece rates, which may have had an impact on reducing resistance to job transfer and lessening the fear of change. In addition, in the experimental conditions, some, or all of the workers, received special training, which may have resulted in a more optimistic appraisal of the transfer situation by the experimental workers. Bartlem and Locke argue that the perceived fairness of the new pay rates is likely to have been the main factor responsible for the findings of Coch and French's study.

Gardner (1977) also raises a number of concerns about Coch and French's (1948) study. Specifically, Gardner suggests that the random selection of subjects to conditions was not possible, and notes no statistical tests were reported. Sampling was problematic as the subjects were all female. Other issues of concern were the nature of the job changes, the nature of the tasks performed by the groups, the different sizes of the groups, the supervisory styles adopted in the groups resulting from differences in group sizes. These issues are all potential explanations for Coch and French's results. Gardner also suggests that Coch and French made no allowance for the possibility that the 'dramatic presentation' style used in the experimental groups may have contributed to the effects that are claimed for employee participation.

Despite these criticisms, Coch and French's (1948) study has influenced the way in which researchers have conceptualized resistance to change. In particular, Coch and French were instrumental in focusing researchers' attention on individuals as the source of resistance to change in organizations (Dent and Goldberg, 1999). However, Lewin (1951) argued that resistance to change can emerge from anywhere within a social system, and it is only recently that authors have begun to look at the organizational context as a source of resistance to change.

In summary, in this section we reviewed classic studies that have a strong influence on thinking about organizational change today. Indeed, Kurt Lewin's (1947, 1951, 1952) work is still at the heart of all change theorizing and research (e.g., Porras and Robertson, 1992; Weick and Quinn, 1999), although a number of authors have begun to debate the appropriateness of Lewin's planned approach to change given the need to implement change on an ongoing basis.

RECENT RESEARCH: EMERGING ISSUES

In this section, we focus on recent research and identity four emerging issues being discussed in the change literature. We identify the pace and sequencing of organizational transformations as a theoretically important area of study (Pettigrew et al., 2001), that has recently been the subject of empirical research (Amis et al., 2004; Whelan-Barry et al., 2003). We also examine the theoretical distinction between episodic and continuous change (e.g., Weick and Quinn, 1999), an issue that has important consequences in terms of the models used to conceptualize change and the strategies used to implement change.

The third emerging issue that we examine concerns the nature of organizational inertia and momentum during change. A number of theorists have begun to question assumptions about change at the organizational level of analysis (e.g., Howard-Grenville, 2005; Jansen, 2004). Finally, we address concerns about the role of individuals in organizational change processes (e.g., George and Jones, 2001). Authors have begun to acknowledge that individuals are not just passive recipients of change (e.g., George and Jones, 2001; Huy, 2002), suggesting that individuals play a much more active role in change processes than has been acknowledged in the past.

The pace, sequence, and linearity of different types of organizational change

Authors have recently considered issues related to the pace, sequence, and linearity of organizational change (e.g., Amis et al., 2004; Hinings and Greenwood, 1988; Whelan-Barry et al., 2003). Amis et al. identified a number of assumptions that underlie research on large-scale organizational transformation. In particular, researchers have assumed that revolutionary organizational change must be implemented rapidly if it is to be successful, and that all elements of an organization should be changed simultaneously and in a linear manner. For example, Miller and Friesen's (1984) work suggests that firms that successfully introduce such change modify many elements of their structure in concert and also tend to change more dramatically than unsuccessful firms. However, there has

been a lack of theoretical discussion regarding these issues and, until recently, empirical evidence has been lacking.

Amis et al. (2004) conducted a 12-year longitudinal study with a set of 36 Canadian Olympic National Sport Organizations (NSO) which were encouraged to transform from informal organizations operated by volunteers with professional assistance, to professional bureaucracies controlled by professional staff, with volunteers reduced to a support role. The results of this study revealed that contrary to assumptions in the field, rapid change throughout organizations was not only insufficient to bring about radical change, it was even be detrimental to its outcome. The organizations that completed radical organizational change were characterized by initial bursts of activity followed by relatively sedate progress toward the desired endpoint. This process allowed opportunities for trust to be established and productive working relationships to be developed.

On the basis of their longitudinal study, Amis et al. (2004) argued that what was important was the *sequence* in which organizational elements were altered. It was important to modify high-impact decision making systems early in the change process because this sent a clear message that the changes to be implemented were substantive and likely to be enduring. In addition, linear transitions occurred almost exclusively in areas that were uncontroversial, easy to implement, and relatively insignificant with respect to the organizations' traditional operating methods. In contrast, implementing changes to decision making structures and the associated transfer of power from volunteers to professionals was much more difficult and contested. Changes in these areas were more likely to be characterized by delays and reversals as opposed to a linear adoption of change.

Amis et al.'s (2004) work is an important addition to the change literature, because these authors developed theoretical propositions relating to issues of major importance and concern to change practitioners. Also, these authors adopted a longitudinal methodology and used multiple sources of data to allow them to study the process of change over time. As advocated by Pettigrew et al. (2001: 698), these authors 'attempt[ed] to catch reality in flight' and studied long term change processes in context.

Different types of organizational change: Distinguishing 'episodic' and 'continuous' change

In the last two decades, authors have increasingly framed radical organizational change as a strategic imperative (e.g., Oswick et al., 2005), citing major modifications in government regulations, global competition, and technology as factors that contribute to the need to implement change on an ongoing basis. At the same time, researchers have also begun to pay attention to the importance of studying and measuring smaller-scale changes that, over time, result in ongoing adjustments in organizations, which may translate into larger scale organizational changes (e.g., Brown and Duguid, 1991; Orlikowski, 1996; Volberda, 1996; Weick and Quinn, 1999).

Weick and Quinn (1999) conducted a theoretical analysis of 'episodic' vs. 'continuous' organizational change. Specifically, they explored the tempo of change, which they defined as the 'characteristic rate, rhythm, or pattern of work or activity' (p. 365). The term 'episodic change' describes changes that are infrequent, discontinuous, and intentional. This type of change tends to occur during periods of organizational disequilibrium that are precipitated by external events such as declines in organizational performance. In contrast, 'continuous change' describes changes that are ongoing, evolving, and cumulative. These changes are 'emergent' in the sense that they occur in response to everyday contingencies and are an unplanned response to one's circumstances (Orlikowski, 1996). An underlying assumption of work on continuous change is that these small adjustments can create substantial change in organizations over time.

An important issue that emerges from the distinction between episodic and continuous change is that different types of interventions are required to bring about these different types of change. Episodic change has been the focus of a large body of change literature, and authors have argued that episodic change requires deliberate efforts on the part of change agents to establish conditions that are different to what they are now. Weick and Quinn (1999) suggest that Lewin's (1947, 1951) 3-Step change model of unfreeze-transition-refreeze is appropriate when managing episodic change because this model assumes that organizational inertia is the main impediment to change. That is, the 3-Step model implies that an important first task when managing change is to overcome inertia by creating employee readiness for change, which has been defined as individuals' 'beliefs, attitudes, and intentions regarding the extent to which changes are needed and the organization's capacity to successfully undertake those changes' (Armenakis et al., 1993: 681).

In contrast, Weick and Quinn (1999) argue that continuous change does not involve breaking organizational inertia to encourage change. Rather, in an environment of continuous change, Weick and Quinn suggest that a more appropriate intervention model is freeze-rebalance-unfreeze. The freeze-rebalance-unfreeze model requires events to be slowed down so that organizational members have time to reflect on the changes that have been occurring. Rebalancing involves reinterpreting and reorganizing patterns of activity in a given environment. Finally, unfreezing involves engaging in one's normal stream of activities again. When this occurs, individuals regain the capacity to change in response to environmental stimuli.

Weick and Quinn's (1999) work is important because it explicitly recognizes the multiplicity of changes that occur in organizations. This work provides a framework by which to systematically consider the implications of distinctly different types of organizational changes on the change models that we use, and the strategies adopted to implement and manage change. However, this work has been the subject of some criticism (e.g., Marshak, 2004; Purser and Petranker, 2005).

Purser and Petranker (2005) argue that Weick and Quinn (1999) do not address the temporal dynamics responsible for episodic and continuous change. These authors propose that although the idea of continuous change appears to be a 'new' way of thinking about change, conceptualizations of both episodic and continuous change are based on the assumption that one can take a position external to the experience of change and the ongoing flow of time. However, one cannot 'stop' change or step outside of change. Purser and Petranker suggest that to effectively intervene in an environment of continuous change, agents must rely less on planning and visioning, and more on creative action in real time. These authors identify a number of emerging disciplines that allow people to foster capabilities for deep innovation, including deconstructive contemplation, action inquiry, first-person methodology in consciousness studies, and creative inquiry. In summary, these authors argue that we do not yet possess an appropriate understanding of how to effectively intervene when dealing with continuous organizational change.

Change vs. inertia

Some theoretical perspectives, such as institutional theory (e.g., Greenwood and Hinings, 1996), stress that organizational inertia rather than change is the norm. Recently, researchers have begun to reexamine existing understandings of inertia (e.g., Jansen, 2004), and the factors that contribute to organizational inertia (e.g., Howard-Grenville, 2005). To date, inertia has been conceptualized as the tendency to repeat past actions and patterns of activity and, therefore, has been understood as the tendency of organizations to resist change (Kelly and Amburgey, 1991; Miller and Friesen, 1984).

Miller and Friesen (1984) conducted the seminal work on inertia, and suggested that organizations display a tendency to repeat previous directions of evolution in strategy and structure. Miller and Friesen identified

four major reasons why organizations repeat past actions. First, an organization's goals create narrow, self-affirming views that reinforce past behaviors. Second, existing procedures and strategies have survived because they have been successful and as a result tend to persist even when they are no longer effective. Third, political factors in organizations mean that certain groups have a vested interest in the continuation of existing strategies. Finally, the programs and procedures in an organization are the outcome of rather complex bargaining and reconciliation processes that develop over time and groups have an interest in the continuation of these programs.

In a refinement of the distinction between change and inertia, Jansen (2004) focused on the concept of momentum. Jansen defined momentum as the force or energy associated with a moving body, and distinguished between stasis-based momentum, the energy associated with persisting or extending a current trajectory, and change-based momentum, which captures the energy associated with pursuing a new trajectory. Jansen argues that stasis-based momentum relies on existing routines, while change-based momentum requires the creation of new routines and patterns of behavior. This distinction is important because it acknowledges that both 'inertia' and change are effortful. In particular, stasis-based momentum requires effort to ensure that no deviation from existing patterns and approaches occur. In contrast, change-based momentum represents the energy associated with movement along a new trajectory.

A number of different factors, including organizational routines, have traditionally been viewed as a source of organizational inertia (Howard-Grenville, 2005; Tushman and Romanelli, 1985). However, Howard-Grenville suggests that routines can be a source of both stability *and* change. That is, Howard-Grenville argues that, intentionally or not, individuals and groups depart from standard routines and when this occurs the 'same' routine allows a variety of performances, which may alter the routine over time.

Howard-Grenville (2005) conducted a nine-month ethnographic study of high technology manufacturing organizations to investigate organizational inertia and change, and reported that 'roadmapping,' or planning out one's future actions to achieve work-related goals was an important routine in the organization under study. Some individuals enacted the routine habitually while others found new uses for it, and thus, this routine was associated with both stability and change.

In summary, the reconceptualization of momentum is an important addition to the literature because it acknowledges that both 'inertia' and change are effortful. In addition, while authors have traditionally identified organizational routines as a source of inertia, the work of Howard-Grenville (2005) suggests that routines are the source of both stability and change. These works reflect the increased complexity of thinking in relation to organizational-level change.

The role of individuals in change: Sensemaking and emotions

Recently, theorists have begun to reconceptualize the role of individuals in change processes (e.g., Bartunek et al., 2006; George and Jones, 2001; Kiefer, 2005), acknowledging that people are not just passive recipients of change, but also play an active role in creating and reacting to change. Researchers have begun to examine individuals' sensemaking in response to change (e.g., Lau and Woodman, 1995; Weber and Manning, 2001). Following the broader organizational behavior literature (e.g., Brief and Weiss, 2002; Weiss and Cropanzano, 1996), researchers have begun to explore the role of emotions in change processes (George and Jones, 2001; Kiefer, 2005).

George and Jones (2001: 421) suggest that change involves 'an individual and group sensemaking process taking place in a social context that is a product of constant and ongoing human production and interaction in organizational settings.' George and Jones argue that change is an affectively-laden process, and that emotions play a central role in initiating the change process and directing organizational members' sensemaking

activities to pressing concerns, opportunities, and problems. George and Jones developed a theoretical model of the role of emotions in change.

Kiefer (2005) also emphasizes that individuals' emotional responses to change are important in understanding the success, or failure, of change efforts. Kiefer examined the influence of multiple, complementary and competing change events on individuals' emotions. Conducting a longitudinal empirical study, Kiefer reported that organizational change is often emotional and produces negative reactions. Specifically, findings indicated that the more changes a person experiences at work, the poorer the working conditions, the more negative individuals' assessment of their personal situation and future and their treatment by the organization, and the more negative emotions are reported on a daily basis. Negative emotions were found to have a negative influence on employee withdrawal and trust.

Bartunek and her colleagues (2006) conducted an empirical study in a large American hospital implementing a shared governance initiative. The results of this study revealed that nurses reported experiencing mild positive affect about the change. However, membership of a council designed to implement the change enhanced understanding of the intervention, and increased the perception that the change led to gains in the quality of patient care and in professional development. Unit-level pleasant affect was associated with perceived gains in professional development.

In summary, recent research has acknowledged that individuals are active participants in change processes and that it is important to systematically consider how individuals' thoughts, feelings, and emotions shape their reactions to change in the workplace. Empirical evidence suggests that individuals can experience both positive and negative emotions in response to change. Currently, however, researchers rarely acknowledge or study both positive and negative responses to change.

George and Jones (2001) make an important point when they argue that it is critical that models of change and inertia at the organizational level of analysis are informed by an understanding of change at the individual level of analysis. Thus, it is not sufficient to continue to consider organizational-level change issues without considering individuals and groups. Rather, there is a need to develop multi-level models of organizational change processes. We discuss this issue when we identify a number of emerging research agendas for the field.

KEY DEBATES

Several key debates are currently occurring in the organizational change literature. First, there has an ongoing debate as to the appropriateness of using methods from the physical sciences when studying organizational change processes (e.g., Beer and Walton, 1987; Van de Ven and Huber, 1990; Van de Ven and Poole, 2006; Woodman, 1989). Another area of debate is the link between change scholars and practitioners, with authors such as Woodman (p. 223) stating that 'the schism between research and practice – between theories of change and the art of changing – has been deeply embedded in the change and development area since its inception and may well be the single greatest threat to the continued viability and progress of OD.' The debate regarding the link between change theory and practice is associated with concerns about the definition and boundaries of the field of organizational change and development (e.g., Greiner and Cummings, 2004; Hornstein, 2001). Below, we explore these two issues in some detail.

The nature of organizational change: Methodological implications

Considerable debate exists regarding methodological issues relating to the study of organizational change (e.g., Van de Ven and Huber, 1990; Van de Ven and Poole, 2006; Woodman, 1989). Woodman (p. 211) stated that the organizational change field is struggling with 'the real and/or perceived incongruencies

between "normal" science and OD research.' Beer and Walton (1987) identified a number of issues with using a Kuhnian notion of 'normal science' in organizational change and development studies. In particular, Beer and Walton suggest that traditional quantitative methodologies aim to isolate causation by identifying the results of a single intervention. As a result, these approaches overlook the systemic nature of organizations.

Beer and Walton (1987) argue that standard scientific methodologies make assumptions that might be inappropriate in field research. For example, the use of control groups may halt an experiment altogether via the creation of issues such as control-group hostility. These authors also suggest that replication, essential to standard scientific methods, might be impossible in field research. Finally, these authors suggest that organizational change results from multi-causal events involving a constellation of causes. Thus, it is often impossible to identify the specific effect of a given action using standard research methodologies.

Another criticism of change research is that it often overlooks time by failing to include sufficient longitudinal features (Beer and Walton, 1987; Pettigrew et al., 2001). In addition, it has been argued that that while researchers are precise about methodology and instruments, they often provide insufficient depth and description of the intervention and situation (Pettigrew et al., 2001). Finally, Beer and Walton suggest that research often does not fit the needs of its users, or is slow to be translated into practice. The issue of the links between research and practice will be discussed below.

Van de Ven and Huber (1990) examined the methodologies traditionally used in change research. In particular, these authors argued that researchers have typically asked questions such as 'what are the antecedents or consequences of changes in organizational forms or practices?', when studying change. This type of question usually involves a variance theory explanation. The variance method focuses on variables that represent the important aspects or attributes of the subject under study. Explanations take the form of causal models that incorporate these constructs.

In contrast to variance explanations, process explanations emphasize how organizational changes emerge, develop, grow, or terminate over time. This type of research is concerned with understanding the process of change and requires a 'process theory' explanation of the temporal order and sequence in which a discrete set of events occurred based on a historical narrative (Van de Ven and Huber, 1990). Process explanations often involve identifying critical events and turning points in change processes, contextual factors and formative patterns and causal factors that influence the sequencing of events. Process-focused research often involves eclectic designs that identify or reconstruct change processes through direct observation, archival analysis or multiple case study analysis. With process methods, generalization depends on versatility, or the degree to which the theory can encompass a broad array of developmental patterns without modification of its essential character.

Van de Ven and Poole (2006) suggest that process theory is capable of tapping aspects of processes that variance research cannot. However, the process method has its own limitations. Specifically, process research is very labor intensive, and involves collecting a great deal of multifaceted data. In addition, processes are often very complex, so developing process explanations and discerning patterns can be difficult. The depth of process data and the complexity of the data also limit the generalizability of the conclusions of process research.

Van de Ven and Poole (1995) argue that the best approach for a particular study depends on the type of questions addressed, the researchers' assumptions about the nature of organizations and methodological predispositions, as well as the data to which they have access. Recent work increasingly recognizes that there are a variety of ways in which authors can ask and answer questions, and that these different approaches have strengths and weaknesses that complement

each other. Typologies of research such as that developed by Van de Ven and Poole (2006) can potentially reduce simple dichotomous debates concerning features such as the quantitative vs. qualitative data and lead to more constructive discussions concerning when different methodologies are appropriate given the research questions of interest and the data available.

The partnership between scholars and practitioners and the relevance of OD

Another ongoing debate in the organizational change literature concerns the relationship between theory and practice (Pettigrew et al., 2001). Woodman (1989) acknowledged that a duality exists in the organizational change field, stating that there is 'tension between the theory of change and the practice of changing, between the worlds of the academic and the manager, between research and action' (p. 206).

Interestingly, the separation between theory and practice did not exist in the early days of OD, as it was 'the action arm of basic social and organizational research' (Bunker et al., 1992: 404). At that time, there was continuous communication between researchers and practitioners, in many cases they were the same person. Today, however, the division between the practice and theory of organizational change is reflected in the fact that two types of change theory have developed; change process theory and implementation theory (Porras and Robertson, 1992). Change process theories tend to be the realm of academic researchers, while change implementation theories are often developed by practitioners.

Change process theories explain the dynamics through which organizations, groups, or individuals change. In contrast, implementation theories are oriented towards practice and focus on specific activities needed to implement change (Porras and Robertson, 1992). Change process theory is particularly underdeveloped, with Woodman (1989) arguing that this has served as a 'major constraint on the ability of OD to contribute substantially to the organizational sciences' (pp. 206–207).

While the disconnect between scholars and practitioners is not unique to the change field (e.g., Mohrman et al., 2001; Rynes et al., 2001), it is of concern because the management of change has enormous consequences for employee well-being (e.g., Ferrie et al., 1998; Nelson et al., 1995; Rafferty and Griffin, 2006; Vahtera et al., 2000) and organizational sustainability and performance (e.g., Greenwood and Hinings, 1996). Researchers have acknowledged that there are compelling ideas being developed in the academic community and new methods being developed by practitioners (Bunker et al., 2004). However, there is a shortage of people who communicate to both practitioner and academic audiences, and as such this knowledge is not being shared.

One reason for the divide between academics and practitioners is the different assumptions under which these groups operate (Shrivastava and Mitroff, 1984). The assumptions of researchers largely emphasize methodological issues while managers and practitioners emphasize developing solutions to organizational problems. In addition, Shrivastava and Mitroff argue that researchers and practitioners have different standards relating to the types of information that should be used in decision making, the type of problems examined, and the solutions generated.

Another problem is that practitioners and researchers often have stereotypical views of each other (Anderson et al., 2001). Practitioners view researchers as interested only in methodological rigor and as failing to address issues in the real world, while researchers criticize practitioners for embracing the latest fads regardless of theory or evidence.

An important reason for the divide between academics and practitioners is the differences in the modes of scientific inquiry that are generally adopted by these groups. Specifically, Anderson et al. (2001) suggest that academics use 'scientific inquiry,' which involves testing theoretical models against empirical data. In this approach, each successive study adds to the previous study. This mode of research corresponds to 'normal science' as characterized by Kuhn (1970).

In contrast, practitioners typically use a 'problem solution' approach. Here, the origin of the problem to be addressed is likely to be found in working life and experience rather than in the scientific literature. The process of knowledge creation involves continuous feedback between whatever theory is useful and the outcomes of various interventions. In addition, different stakeholder groups are important for academics and practitioners (Anderson et al., 2001). Governments and powerful academics are key stakeholders in the academic knowledge creation process. These groups increase the pressure on academics to produce 'pedantic science,' or research with high methodological rigor with less regard to practical relevance. In contrast, the primary stakeholders of practitioners, their clients, push practitioners towards 'popularist science,' or research that is high in topical relevance regardless of methodological rigor.

Several ways to bridge the perceived divide between academics and practitioners have been explored (e.g., Arnold, 2004; Mohrman et al., 2001). Mohrman et al. suggested that research findings are more likely to be seen as useful if there are opportunities for researchers and practitioners to take each others' perspectives, and to jointly participate in interpreting the results of research. These authors found that when organizational members felt that their views had been taken into account then they had much more positive views of the collaboration. In addition, findings support the importance of perspective taking, where researchers and practitioners come to recognize and understand each other's thought-worlds and develop forums where both groups came together to jointly reflect and interpret information.

In summary, while the divide between researchers and practitioners is an issue of concern in diverse fields, authors have argued that this divide is particularly evident in the field of organizational change. In this field, distinct approaches to address the theoretical issues associated with change and the practical implications and requirements when enacting change have been developed. Differences in values, the existence of stereotypical views, and strong external pressures that contribute to the use of different modes of inquiry contribute to the division between researchers and academics. Strategies that may help to overcome the divide between academics and practitioners include the provision of opportunities for researchers and practitioners to take each others' perspectives and to jointly participate in interpreting the results of research.

EMERGING RESEARCH AGENDAS

We identify a number of emerging research agendas in the change field. First, we argue that it is vital to continue to develop multi-level change models. Authors such as Whelan-Barry et al. (2003), Caldwell et al. (2004), and Huy (1999) have developed theoretical models and conducted empirical research that recognizes that organizational change is a multi-level phenomenon. A second emerging research agenda concerns the relevance of traditional change theories and models in 'hyper-turbulent' environments (e.g., Burnes, 2004a; Marshak, 2004). Below, we examine these issues and explore the implications of this work for the future of organizational change research.

Multi-level change models

Organizational change typically involves adoption of change across teams, departments, and divisions, as well as at the individual level (e.g., Caldwell et al., 2004; Whelan-Barry et al., 2003). Understanding these different aspects of change requires that authors develop multi-level change models as opposed to focusing on change at a single level of analysis (e.g., change at the individual or organizational level of analysis). Despite this, very few authors have developed such models. We review studies by Whelan-Barry et al.,

Caldwell et al. and Huy (1999), all of which are focused on developing a theoretical understanding of change processes at multiple levels of analysis.

Whelan-Barry et al. (2003) conducted a study to examine how to motivate and sustain momentum for change across levels of analysis and also focused on exploring how the pace of change varies across levels of analysis. This case study was conducted in a Corporate Audit department of a large bank in the US which was undergoing a major change. These authors found that the particular actions required to sustain momentum for change differ at the three levels of analysis. An important finding of this study is that the linkages between the organizational, group, and individual levels of a change process are critical for effective change. That is, while results suggested that, at the organizational level, planning processes for change were very important, they also indicated that it is important to distinguish planning from the process of managing the change transition at lower levels of analysis. Specifically, these authors suggest that a lack of planning at the organizational level meant that the group and individual processes required to ensure change occurred were not addressed.

Another finding of note from Whelan-Barry et al.'s (2003) study was that the pace of change across levels of analysis is critical. In particular, the same step in the change process at the organizational level often preceded, by a significant amount of time, the same step at the group and individual level of analysis. Whelan-Barry et al. concluded that as the timing of change at the different levels of analysis becomes less synchronous, the chance of conflict increases.

Caldwell et al. (2004) assessed change at the group and individual level. The characteristics of organizational change and a number of change process variables were assessed as group-level phenomena. Results of their study of 34 work units in 21 organizations indicated that the effect of change on a person's perception of 'fit' with their environment depends not only on work unit change processes such as fair procedures, but also on how these change processes interact with the perceived extent of change within the work unit and individual differences. For example, Caldwell et al. found that individuals with a high mastery orientation (i.e., those individuals that are focused on learning and development) responded more positively to change in their work unit, even when the fairness of procedures was low.

Huy (1999) developed a multi-level theory of emotion and change. At the individual level, he proposed that the ability to monitor one's own and others' feelings facilitated change and adaptation. At the organization level, norms and routines related to the capacity to monitor and attend to members' feelings contributed to successful adaptation. Huy suggests that an emotionally capable organization does not require that most of its members possess these capabilities. However, to the extent that people in the organization are trained and encouraged to enact emotion-attending behaviors, the likelihood of realizing radical change is increased.

In summary, while the works of Whelan-Barry et al. (2003), Caldwell et al. (2004), and Huy (1999) are quite different from each other, each of these works addresses the multi-level nature of organizational change processes. These studies have begun the process of building more sophisticated theoretical understandings of the complexity of change processes within organizations and the processes that link the dynamics of change across organizational levels.

The relevance of traditional change models in 'hyper-turbulent' environments

One of the key debates in the change field at present focuses on whether traditional models and theories are appropriate in a dynamic organizational environment where firms are being called on to implement continuous organizational changes (e.g., Burnes, 2004b; Marshak, 2004; Purser and Petranker, 2005). Authors such as Marshak have argued that traditional change models are inadequate in hyper-turbulent environments and, as a result,

that new approaches and models are needed. In contrast, Burnes (2004a, 2004b) suggests that classic models, such those of Lewin (1947), not only continue to be relevant but directly address the issues of managing continuous organizational change.

Marshak (2004) argues that there is an absence of theories and concepts to adequately describe and explain emerging types of change. Lewin's (1947) 3-Step model, which has been at the very core of OD and change management, has been the subject of recent criticism (e.g., Kanter et al., 1992; Marshak, 2004). For example, Kanter et al. argue that this model is 'quaintly linear and static conception is so wildly inappropriate that it is difficult to see why it has not only survived but prospered' (p. 10). Thus, theorists such as Bradford and Burke (2004) have raised concerns about the relevance and vitality of OD. As a result of the qualitatively different demands that are facing change agents today, researchers have begun to talk about 'change management' as opposed to OD (e.g., Oswick et al., 2005).

Oswick et al. (2005) argue that unlike traditional OD, 'change management' is not focused on tangible aspects of organizations such as procedures and policies. Rather, change management is concerned with intangibles such as culture, identity, and knowledge and does not deal with 'hard' change. These authors suggest that change management involves managing the meanings attached to change. Finally, Oswick et al. suggest that while OD is reactive and incremental, change management is proactive and emergent.

Marshak (2004) proposed the metaphor of 'morphing,' or rapid, seamless and comprehensive change, to understand change dynamics in highly turbulent environments. Marshak argued that in dynamic environments there is a need for organizations to develop and maintain the capability to be morphogenic, which means building fluid organizational structures, developing ongoing organizational learning, and selecting and retaining managers with morphing mindsets, rather than arriving at a planned end state and halting change efforts. Marshak proposed that concepts from the new sciences, such as chaos theory and complexity theory, as well as philosophies from other cultures such as Confucian and Taoist worldviews that assume change is continuous and cyclical, may be helpful in understanding change in today's workplaces.

The theoretical arguments proposed by Marshak (2004) regarding the factors that contribute to an ability to implement continuous change in hyper-dynamic environments have been supported empirically (e.g., Brown and Eisenhardt, 1997; Rindova and Kotha, 2001). For example, Brown and Eisenhardt conducted a study in the context of the highly dynamic computer industry. They reported that certain structural characteristics were evident in successful multiple-product innovation companies. In particular, managers in these organizations improvised current projects by combining clear responsibilities and priorities with extensive communication and freedom. In addition, managers 'probed into the future' with a variety of low cost experiments and linked current products to future ones, using predictable product intervals and transition procedures that allowed the development of 'new' products.

Rindova and Kotha (2001) also conducted an empirical study of the factors contributing to the successful introduction of continuous change in a study of two internet firms, Yahoo! and Excite. Analysis of the actions of the firms in the media, in financial articles, and as reported by the firms themselves revealed that these organizations remained competitive by engaging in 'continuous morphing.' That is, the firms continuously redefined their products and services and changed the resources and capabilities that they employed in order to maintain their competitive advantage in a hypercompetitive environment so as to be able to implement change on an ongoing basis. This was possible because these firms operated with a decentralized structure where individual autonomy was emphasised.

Burnes (2004a, 2004b) took a contrary view to Marshak's (2004), and argued for the continuing relevance of traditional change theories and models. Burnes' analysis focused on the continuing relevance of Kurt Lewin's (1947, 1951) Planned Approach to Change. Burnes suggests that Lewin's approach has a number of complementarities with complexity theories, which theorists have identified as important in highly dynamic environments where the laws of cause and effect appear not to apply.

In particular, Burnes (2004a) suggests that while Lewin's work (1947, 1951) has often been criticized as being based on a static, simplistic, and mechanistic view of organizational life, Lewin did not see organizations as rigid or fixed. Specifically, Lewin (1947: 14) explicitly stated that 'group life is never without change, merely differences in the amount and type of change exist.' Lewin also argued for the importance of democracy and participation in organization life, which theorists have identified as critical in ensuring that organizations possess the ability to engage in continuous change (e.g., Rindova and Kotha, 2001). In addition, Lewin located group learning at the center of the change process, which authors have identified as a critical mechanism for generating self-organization in complex systems (Burnes, 2004a, 2004b).

In summary, considerable debate has occurred regarding the appropriateness of traditional change models in highly dynamic environments where organizations need to implement change on an ongoing basis. Some theorists have suggested that Lewin's planned approach to change is no longer appropriate (e.g., Marshak, 2004). Others argue that it is important to look at all of the components of Lewin's planned approach to change and recognize those aspects that have been ignored yet remain relevant to the field (Burnes, 2004a, 2004b). Overall, it seems important to consider both our existing knowledge base and more recent approaches to understanding the nature of organizational change to develop a comprehensive picture of change in the current global context.

CONCLUSION

To survive and grow in the presence of uncertainty and complexity, organizations continually adapt and modify their strategies, structures, and operations. It is clear that organizations in modern economies are facing increasing pressure to adapt and change. A review of the change literature reveals that there is a growth in the theoretical and methodological sophistication characterizing thinking in the field. Researchers now question long-held assumptions about organizational momentum and inertia and are reexamining classic change models in the context of dynamic and uncertain environments. Simple research dichotomies such as quantitative vs. qualitative and stability vs. change are evolving into more complex representations of change in organizations. Nevertheless, barriers such as the gap between change researchers and practitioners continue to limit the growth and contribution of the field.

Despite this, the emerging trends that we have identified suggest that the field of organizational change is itself changing in adaptive and positive ways, and provide a positive view of the future of the field.

REFERENCES

Adair, J.G. (1984) 'The Hawthorne effect: A reconsideration of the methodological artifact', *Journal of Applied Psychology*, 69: 334–345.

Amis, J., Slack, T. and Hinings, C.R. (2004) 'The pace, sequence, and linearity of radical change', *Academy of Management Journal*, 47: 15–39.

Anderson, N., Herriot, P. and Hodgkinson, G.P. (2001) 'The practitioner-researcher divide in Industrial, Work and Organizational (IWO) psychology: Where are we now and where do we go from here?', *Journal of Occupational and Organizational Psychology*, 74: 391–411.

Armenakis, A.A., Harris, S.G. and Mossholder, K.W. (1993) 'Creating readiness for organizational change', *Human Relations*, 46: 681–703.

Arnold, J. (2004) 'Editorial', *Journal of Occupational and Organizational Psychology*, 77: 1–10.

Bartlem, C.S. and Locke, E.A. (1981) 'The Coch and French study: A critique and reinterpretation', *Human Relations*, 34: 555–566.

Bartunek, J.M., Rousseau, D.M., Rudolph, J.W. and DePalma, J.A. (2006) 'On the receiving end: Sensemaking, emotion, and assessments of an organizational change initiated by others', *The Journal of Applied Behavioral Science*, 42: 182–206.

Beer, M. and Walton, A.E. (1987) 'Organization change and development', *Annual Review of Psychology*, 38: 339–367.

Bradford, D.L. and Burke, W.W. (2004) 'Introduction: Is OD in crisis?', *Journal of Applied Behavioral Science*, 40: 369–373.

Brief, A.P. and Weiss, H.M. (2002) 'Organizational behavior: Affect in the workplace', *Annual Review of Psychology*, 53: 279–307.

Brown, J.S. and Duguid, P. (1991) 'Organizational learning and communities-of-practice: Toward a unified view of working, learning, and innovation', *Organization Science*, 2: 40–57.

Brown, S.L. and Eisenhardt, K.M. (1997) 'The art of continuous change: Linking complexity theory and time-paced evolution in relentlessly shifting organizations', *Administrative Science Quarterly*, 42: 1–34.

Bunker, B.B., Alban, B.T. and Lewicki, R.J. (2004) 'Ideas in currency and OD practice: Has the well gone dry?', *The Journal of Applied Behavioral Science*, 40: 403–422.

Burnes, B. (2004a) 'Kurt Lewin and complexity theories: Back to the future?', *Journal of Change Management*, 4: 309–325.

Burnes, B. (2004b) 'Kurt Lewin and the planned approach to change: A reappraisal', *Journal of Management Studies*, 41: 977–1002.

Caldwell, S.D., Herold, D.M. and Fedor, D.B. (2004) 'Toward an understanding of the relationships among organizational change, individual differences, and changes in person-environment fit: A cross-level study', *Journal of Applied Psychology*, 89: 868–882.

Coch, L. and French, J.R.P. (1948) 'Overcoming resistance to change', *Human Relations*, 1: 512–532.

Cummings, T.G. and Worley, C.G. (1997) *Organization Development and Change* (6th edn). Cincinnati, OH: South-Western College Publishing.

Dent, E.B. and Goldberg, S.G. (1999) 'Challenging "resistance to change"', *Journal of Applied Behavioral Science*, 35: 25–41.

Ferrie, J.E., Shipley, M.J., Marmot, M.G., Stansfeld, S. and Smith, G.D. (1998) 'The health effects of major organizational change and job insecurity', *Social Science and Medicine*, 46: 243–254.

Gardner, G. (1977) '"Workers" participation: A critical evaluation of Coch and French', *Human Relations*, 30: 1071–1078.

George, J.M. and Jones, G.R. (2001) 'Towards a process model of individual change in organizations', *Human Relations*, 54: 419–444.

Greenwood, R. and Hinings, C.R. (1996) 'Understanding radical organizational change: Bringing together the old and the new institutionalism', *Academy of Management Review*, 21: 1022–1054.

Greiner, L.E. and Cummings, L.L. (2004) 'Wanted: OD more alive than dead!', *Journal of Applied Behavioral Science*, 40: 374–391.

Hinings, C.R. and Greenwood, R. (1988) *The Dynamics of Strategic Change*. Oxford: T.J. Press.

Hornstein, H. (2001) 'Organizational development and change management: Don't throw the baby out with the bath water', *The Journal of Applied Behavioral Science*, 37: 223–226.

Howard-Grenville, J.A. (2005) 'The persistence of flexible organizational routines: The role of agency and organizational context', *Organization Science*, 16: 618–636.

Huy, Q.N. (1999) 'Emotional capability, emotional intelligence, and radical change', *Academy of Management Review*, 24: 325–345.

Huy, Q.N. (2002) 'Emotional balancing of organizational continuity and radical change: The contribution of middle managers', *Administrative Science Quarterly*, 47: 31–69.

Jansen, K.J. (2004) 'From persistence to pursuit: A longitudinal examination of momentum during the early stages of strategic change', *Organization Science*, 15: 276–294.

Kanter, R.M., Stein, B.A. and Jick, T.D. (1992) 'The "big three" model of change', in R.M. Kanter, B.A. Stein and T.D. Jick (eds), *The Challenge of Organizational Change: How Companies Experience it and Leaders Guide it*. New York: The Free Press, pp. 3–19.

Kelly, D., and Amburgey, T.L. (1991) 'Organizational inertia and momentum: A dynamic model of strategic change', *Academy of Management Review*, 34: 591–612.

Kiefer, T. (2005) 'Feeling bad: Antecedents and consequences of negative emotions in ongoing change', *Journal of Organizational Behavior*, 26: 875–897.

Kuhn, T.S. (1970) *The Structure of Scientific Revolutions* (2nd edn). Chicago: University of Chicago Press.

Lau, C., and Woodman, R.W. (1995) 'Understanding organizational change: A schematic perspective', *Academy of Management Journal*, 38: 537–554.

Lewin, K. (1947) 'Frontiers in group dynamics', *Human Relations*, 1: 5–41.

Lewin, K. (1951) *Field Theory in Social Science*. New York: Harper Row.

Lewin, K. (1952) 'Group decision and social change', in T.M.N.G.E. Swanson, and E.L. Hartley (eds), *The Nature of Creativity: Creative Psychological Perspectives*. New York: Cambridge University Press, pp. 177–201.

Locke, E.A. and Schweiger, D. (1979) 'Participation in decision–making: One more look', *Research in Organizational Behavior*, 1: 265–339.

Marshak, R.J. (2004) 'Morphing: The leading edge of organizational change in the twenty-first century', *Organization Development Journal*, 22: 8–21.

McQuarrie, F.A.E. (2005) 'How the past is present(ed): A comparison of information on the Hawthorne studies in Canadian management and organizational behavior textbooks', *Canadian Journal of Administrative Sciences*, 22: 230–242.

Miller, D. and Friesen, P.H. (1984) *Organizations: A Quantum View*. Engelwood Cliffs, NJ: Prentice Hall.

Mirvis, P.H. (1988) 'Organization development: Part I – An evolutionary perspective', *Research in Organizational Change and Development*, 2: 1–57.

Mirvis, P.H. (1990) 'Organization development: Part II – A revolutionary perspective', *Research in Organizational Change and Development*, 4: 1–66.

Mohrman, S.A., Gibson, C.B. and Mohrman Jr, A.M. (2001) 'Doing research that is useful to practice: A model and empirical extension', *Academy of Management Journal*, 44: 357–375.

Nelson, A., Cooper, C.L. and Jackson, P.R. (1995) 'Uncertainty amidst change: The impact of privatization on employee job satisfaction and well-being', *Journal of Occupational and Organizational Psychology*, 68: 57–71.

Orlikowski, W.J. (1996) 'Improvising organizational transformation over time: A situated change perspective', *Information Systems Research*, 7: 63–92.

Oswick, C., Grant, D., Michelson, G. and Wailes, N. (2005) 'Looking forwards: Discursive directions in organizational change', *Journal of Change Management*, 18: 383–390.

Pettigrew, A.M., Woodman, R.W. and Cameron, K.S. (2001) 'Studying organizational change and development: Challenges for future research', *Academy of Management Journal*, 44: 697–713.

Porras, J.I. and Robertson, P.J. (1992) 'Organizational development: Theory, practice and research', in M.D. Dunnette and L.M. Hough (eds), *Handbook of Industrial and Organizational Psychology*. Palo Alto, CA: Consulting Psychologists Press, pp. 719–822.

Purser, R.E. and Petranker, J. (2005) 'Unfreezing the future: Exploring the dynamic of time in organizational change', *The Journal of Applied Behavioral Science*, 41: 182–203.

Rafferty, A.E. and Griffin, M.A. (2006) 'Perceptions of organizational change: A stress and coping perspective', *Journal of Applied Psychology*, 91: 1154–1162.

Rindova, V.P. and Kotha, S. (2001) 'Continuous "morphing:" Competing through dynamic capabilities, form, and function', *Academy of Management Journal*, 44: 1263–1280.

Roethlisberger, F.J. and Dickson, W.J. (1939) *Management and the Worker: An Account of a Research Program Conducted by the Western Company, Hawthorne Works. Chicago.* Cambridge, MA: Harvard University Press.

Rynes, S.L., Bartunek, J.M. and Daft, R.L. (2001) 'Across the great divide: Knowledge creation and transfer between participants and academics', *Academy of Management Journal*, 44: 340–355.

Shrivastava, P. and Mitroff, I.I. (1984) 'Enhancing organizational research utilization: The role of decision makers' assumptions', *Academy of Management Review*, 9: 18–26.

Sonnenfeld, J.A. (1985) 'Shedding light on the Hawthorne studies', *Journal of Occupational Behavior*, 6: 111–130.

Tushman, M.L. and Romanelli, E. (1985) 'Organizational evolution: A metamorphosis model of convergence and reorientation', *Research in Organizational Behavior*, 7: 171–222.

Vahtera, J., Kivimaki, M., Pentti, J. and Theorell, T. (2000) 'Effect of change in the psychosocial work environment on sickness absence: A seven year follow up of initially healthy employees', *Journal of Epidemiological Community Health*, 54: 484–493.

Van de Ven, A.H. and Huber, G.P. (1990) 'Longitudinal field research methods for studying organizational change', *Organization Science*, 1: 213–219.

Van de Ven, A.H. and Poole, M.S. (1995) 'Explaining development and change in organizations', *Academy of Management Review*, 20: 510–540.

Van de Ven, A.H. and Poole, M.S. (2006) 'Alternative approaches for studying organizational change', *Organization Science*, 26: 1377–1404.

Volberda, H.W. (1996) 'Toward the flexible form: How to remain vital in hypercompetitive environments', *Organization Science*, 7: 359–374.

Weber, P.S. and Manning, M.R. (2001) 'Cause maps, sensemaking, and planned organizational change', *The Journal of Applied Behavioral Science*, 37: 227–251.

Weick, K.E. and Quinn, R.E. (1999) 'Organizational change and development', *Annual Review of Psychology*, 50: 361–380.

Weiss, H.M. and Cropanzano, R. (1996) 'Affective events theory: A theoretical discussion of the structure, causes and consequences of affective experiences at work', *Research in Organizational Behavior*, 18: 1–74.

Whelan-Barry, K.S., Gordon, J.R. and Hinings, C.R. (2003) 'Strengthening organizational change processes: Recommendations and implications from a multilevel analysis', *The Journal of Applied Behavioral Science*, 39: 186–207.

Woodman, R.W. (1989) 'Organizational change and development: New areas for inquiry and action', *Journal of Management*, 15: 205–228.

32

Nonstandard Work Arrangements: Meaning, Evidence, and Theoretical Perspectives

Daniel G. Gallagher and Catherine E. Connelly

In the introduction to their study of organizational identification among contract workers in the information technology field, George and Chattopadhyay (2005) noted that 'much of the theoretical and empirical work on organizational identification has either implicitly or explicitly focused on full-time employees, employed by and work within a single organization' (p. 50). This concern, albeit correct, is neither new nor limited to the study of organizational identification. In fact, over the past two decades attention has been repeatedly called to the changing nature of the employment contract and the relationship between organizations and workers (e.g., Beard and Edwards, 1995; Connelly and Coyle-Shapiro et al., 2004; Gallagher, 2004). Most notably there has been a gradual recognition among behavioral researchers that

not only has the structure and content of jobs changed, but individuals are increasingly engaged in work arrangements outside of the 'traditional' or 'standard' employment relationship (De Cuyper et al., 2005; Kalleberg, 2000; Kalleberg et al., 2003; Mauno et al., 2005). In a broad sense, nontraditional working relationships depart from the prevailing view of 'real' employment (performed on a full-time basis in the context of an ongoing or permanent arrangement with a single employer organization; Kalleberg, 2000). Interestingly, there is historical evidence to suggest that the 'standard' working relationship of most of the 20th century is in and of itself an artefact of organizational efforts to attract and maintain human resources through the development of more secure firm specific or internal labor markets and organizational structures more effectively (Cappelli, 1999; Pfeffer and Baron, 1988).

The primary objective of this chapter is to provide a fundamental overview of the study of organizational behavior (OB) in the particular realm of nonstandard or nontraditional employment relationships. In doing so, attention will be directed to the examination of five broad topical areas. First, and most obvious, will be the effort to define the meaning of the term and phenomenon of 'nonstandard' or 'nontraditional' work arrangements. Second, attention will be briefly directed to identifying major strategic factors which have been contributing to the growth of nonstandard employment relationships. More specifically, focus will be directed to demand and supply-based factors which enhance the viability of nonstandard or alternative work arrangements. Third, drawing in part from a recent review of the literature in the area of 'contingent employment' (Connelly and Gallagher, 2004), we will identify and analyze the topics which have garnered attention by behavioral researchers in the area of nonstandard or alternative work relationships. Fourth, and relatedly, attention will further be directed to understanding the theoretical frameworks which have driven behavioral research pertaining to employment arrangements which lie outside of the traditional or standard employment relationship, and offer some observations about the applicability of existing OB theories or frameworks to the research questions, which have been, and will need to be addressed by behavioral researchers. Finally, based on suggestions of researchers who have begun focusing on nonstandard or alternative employment relationships, as well as our own observations, we will conclude with some suggestions pertaining to a research agenda in need of further development and investigation.

NONTRADITIONAL WORK ARRANGEMENTS

The opening challenge in any nuanced discussion of nonstandard employment relationships is to establish definitional parameters and to identify the forms of contemporary employment arrangements which can be perceived as an alternative to standard employment.

A useful anchoring point is Kalleberg's (2000) suggestion that nonstandard employment and other frequently used labels (e.g., alternative work arrangements, nontraditional employment relations, atypical employment, vulnerable or precarious employment) represent a departure to some degree from the characteristics of the 'standard' employment contract which has been the norm in many nations for much of the twentieth century. According to Kalleberg, the four central identifying features of standard employment are:

(a) the performance of work on a full-time basis;
(b) the expectation that employment would continue indefinitely;
(c) the work is performed at the 'employer's' place of business; and
(d) under the employer's direction or supervision.

Such a definition carries a great deal of face validity, conjuring up a stereotypical image of the office or factory-based employment arrangement which has been the hallmark of employment for a large part of the twentieth century. It is important to note that employment arrangements which meet these criteria of standard work are still, in fact, the most prevalent form of employment in industrialized countries throughout the world. What is of particular relevance is that the rate of job growth in nonstandard or alternative employment arrangements is often found to surpass the rate of growth in standard jobs in many countries (Houseman and Osawa, 2003; Nollen, 1999).

Although the definitional guidelines used by Kalleberg (2000) are useful to understanding a commonly accepted perspective of what constitutes standard work, it is alternatively problematic to suggest that employment arrangements can readily be dichotomized into a standard or nonstandard classification scheme. In contrast, many researchers (Kalleberg, et al., 2003; McLean Parks et al., 1998; McLean Parks and smith, 2006; Pfeffer and Baron, 1998) emphasize the importance of viewing nonstandard or alternative work arrangements as a continuum which captures the level and nature of attachment which exists between organizations and workers. One frequent perspective is Atkinson's (1984) 'core-periphery' or 'core-ring' model of flexible organizations (Nollen and Axel, 1996).

Atkinson's (1984) model posits that most contemporary organizations approach staffing needs through a primary reliance upon a 'core' or internal workforce. A large part of this core is comprised of what Kalleberg (2000), Handy (1989) and others have defined as the standard workforce (i.e., full-time and on-going). But perhaps more appropriately, Atkinson also includes within the core many jobs that are regularly staffed on a part-time basis. This approach has face validity within the context of the retail and service industries, which are heavily reliant upon ongoing, part-time work arrangements. The suggestion that ongoing, part-time work should be included within the scope of standard employment arrangements is also supported by the sheer magnitude of their presence in the employment landscape. In many countries, particularly Europe, Australia, and North America, part-time work schedules generally represent 18–36 per cent of all available jobs (Delsen, 1999). Furthermore, as noted by Barling and Gallagher (1996), behavioral research is generally supportive of greater similarities than differences between full- and part-time workers, and those similarities increase as the number of hours worked on a part-time basis increase. Thus, ongoing, part-time work contracts are a long-standing or traditional working arrangement found in most economies.

Within the context of Atkinson's core-ring analogy, a more meaningful departure from Kalleberg's (2000) concept of standard work emerges when the employment contract ceases to be ongoing, and instead becomes explicitly fixed-term in nature. Illustrative of this level of externalization are workers who are hired on a seasonal basis to meet predictable variations in the demand for a firm's goods or services (resorts, retail trade and farm labor). Alternatively, organizations may also go about directly hiring workers on an ad hoc daily or weekly basis. A variation in this type of work arrangements is 'zero-hour' or roster-based hiring, where workers are serving on an on-call basis and employed only when employers require additional labor on a short-term or temporary basis. Similar to standard employment, workers hired under these seasonal or direct-hire contracts perform work under the immediate control of the organization and most often at the employer's place of business. However, the work is more 'contingent' or precarious in nature because there is no implicit or explicit guarantee of ongoing employment, and also little predictability as to when employment opportunities will be offered (Polivka and Nardone, 1989).

Another departure from the notion of the standard work arrangement can be found in hiring practices where the organization actually relinquishes their status as an employer and contracts to have workers supplied to the organization on a fixed-term basis. Perhaps the most common example of this arrangement is the use of temporary help services firms (THS) (e.g., Manpower, Addeco, Kelly Services, Accountemps). As with direct hire temporary employees, the work performed for the organization is fixed-term or contingent in nature, but more importantly, the work is being performed within the organization by a non-employee. This type of nonstandard work arrangement assumes the characteristics of a triangular relationship where the worker is an employee of the temporary help firm, but works at the location of the client organization. Variation in THS staffing also exists in terms of the extent to which the client organization exercises control over how the work is performed and the level of supervision exercised.

As noted by several authors (Barley and Kunda, 2004; Evans et al., 2004), a form of contingent or nonstandard employment that has grown dramatically over the past decade is organizational reliance on individuals employed as 'independent contractors.' Particularly in the area of information technology, organizations contract for a fixed-term or project-based arrangement for professional skills or services. Unlike direct hire temporary arrangements, independent contracting is not an employer-employee relationship but rather a client-contractor arrangement. Furthermore, unlike many standard employment contracts, independent contracting assumes that, within guidelines, the contractor, and not management, will control how the work is performed (Connelly and Gallagher, 2006). Independent contracting is also interesting from a behavioral perspective, because independent contractors can simultaneously contract with multiple clients (McLean Parks et al., 1998).

A further level of externalization of the employment contract, or what Atkinson (1984) characterizes as the outermost ring from the core or standard employment relationship, is where the organization essentially abandons any vestige of employer status by entering into subcontracting or outsourcing arrangements. Although outsourced work may be performed onsite, the organization is not technically an employer, but rather it is a customer of the subcontracting firm (e.g., Gilley and Rasheed, 2000). However, it is important to realize that although outsourcing may provide organizations with increased staffing options, the work performed is often done so in the context of a standard employment relationship. Most notably, rather than working on a fixed-term or contingent basis, employees of subcontractors are likely to hold standard or ongoing employment contracts with their own immediate employer organization.

In a broad sense, the core-periphery framework is a useful tool for thinking about the various staffing arrangements that can be used by an organization to achieve its goals. However, from the perspective of linking potential research questions to structural arrangements, a few additional points deserve commentary. First, while much overlap exists between the concepts of core and standard employment, they are not identical. In particular, due to developments

in communication technology, mean that it is increasingly possible for core employees to escape the physical employment confines and 'telecommute' to work from home, offsite locations, or in transit (Fairweather, 1999; Templer et al., 1999). However, although this location-based flexibility differentiates these workers from the traditional or core workforce, telecommuters have much in common with 'traditional' workers, in that their employment relationship is still with a single organization, and these workers would not experience more employment-related uncertainty than any other permanent employee.

Second, while maintaining a core work-force, organizations may follow an external-ization strategy that leaves the work contract more fixed-term or contingent in nature. In effect, the promise of an ongoing employer-employee relationship with the organization evaporates. Finally, the externalization of work may exist in the form of institutional arrangements where the location and man-agerial control over work is shifted to other contracting organizations. Both the levels of contingency and externalization create a wide range of behavioral issues which may uniquely be included by the specific nature of the particular nonstandard work arrangement under consideration.

FORCES DRIVING THE GROWTH OF NONTRADITIONAL WORK ARRANGEMENTS

Gaining a better understanding of the potential behavioral consequences associated with the growing use of workers on nonstandard employment contracts also requires that we consider factors which have in some way contributed to this emerging phenomenon on an international basis.

There is a considerable literature examining the growth of nonstandard and contingent work arrangements (e.g., Bergstrøm and Storrie, 2003; Brewster et al., 1997; Kalleberg et al., 2003; Quinlan and Bohle, 2004; Zeytinoğlu, 1999). Research also exists that questions the extent to which standard employment contracts are on the decline (Doogan, 2001). As suggested in the introduction, efforts to explain the growth of nonstandard employment have considered the importance of both demand and supply.

From a demand-side perspective, there is a body of literature suggesting that organizational interest in the use of workers on contingent or fixed-term contracts is primarily driven by efforts to maximize a competitive advantage by increasing flexibility in not only the number but also the types of workers hired on an 'as needed' basis (Nollen and Axel, 1996). Such adjustments have increasingly been executed through the direct hiring of fixed-term workers or through the use of THS staffing firms. Furthermore, organizational use of an increasingly contingent workforce also provides greater functional flexibility as characterized by the ability to adjust the types of skills employed within the organization without adding to the long-term cost of retaining them (Kalleberg and Marsden, 2005; Klein Hesselink and van Vuuren, 1999). As previously noted, in workplaces where technology is rapidly changing, organizations have turned to the hiring of independent contractors and highly specialized workers dispatched through the services of THS firms to meet immediate skill-set demand (Nishikawa, 2000; Matusik and Hill, 1998). Many organizations also seek to provide locational flexibility (Reilly, 1998) by allowing telecommuters to work from home or while serving the needs of clients or customers. This conceptualization fits with Kalleberg's (2000) notion of nonstandard employment in that the workers' tasks are potentially performed outside of the normal organizational environment. However, this represents a more subtle departure from traditional employment relationships than others we have described.

The growth of nonstandard employment arrangements has also been encouraged within models of strategic management advocating that organizations stay close to their 'core competencies,' and therefore externalize a variety of support functions (e.g., marketing, transportation and janitorial services; Hamel and Prahalad, 1994; Handy, 1989; Nesheim, 2003). As previously mentioned, this notion of a core-periphery staffing model not only advocates the hiring of workers on nonstandard or fixed-term contracts, but also encourages the outsourcing of internal organizational functions to third parties. However, this strategic movement to reduce the extent of direct organizational control over the workforce may, in practice, increase the number of standard employment opportunities among subcontractor firms.

There is also an argument that the growth of contingent or fixed-term contracts, particularly among European nations, exists as a response to governmental policies limiting the ability of employers to legally terminate employees at will, or that impose high economic costs associated with termination actions (Segal and Sullivan, 1997). Furthermore, in countries where governments mandate extensive minimum benefit levels (e.g., vacations, holidays and paid leaves of absences), contingent work may be a practical strategy for temporarily replacing workers who are exercising their right to paid absence from work (Olsen, 2003).

From the supply-side perspective, it may be argued that the growth of contingent employment arrangements are, to some degree, a function of the increasing number of people seeking work outside of the traditional employer-employee relationship (Marler et al., 2002). For some workers, the selection of fixed-term arrangements through direct hire staffing firms or independent contracting arrangements represents a deliberate career decision to adopt a more personally flexible work schedule that could facilitate a more satisfactory work-life balance (Pink, 2001). However, it is important to recognize that a voluntary supply-side decision to engage in nonstandard work may be manifest differentially among different categories of workers. For workers with skills that are in high demand (e.g., health care, accounting, engineering), independent contracting or work through specialized staffing firms can represent a financially lucrative career path that also potentially increases personal control over work schedules (Evans et al., 2004; Connelly and Gallagher, 2006). Among less skilled and younger workers, contingent work contracts may be a viable strategy for attaining diverse workplace experience or as a port of entry into more traditional or standard employment contracts (Gallagher, 2002). Alternatively, for many workers, fixed-term employment may simply be a result of an inability to secure a more traditional job given the conditions of the labor market (Appelbaum, 1992).

Thus, the term 'nonstandard job' should not be interpreted as a monolithic concept. Instead, what can be characterized as nonstandard or nontraditional work assumes a variety of contractual arrangements with varying degrees of attachment to employer or client organizations. Similarly, both the motivation for organizations to employ workers on a more fixed-term or contingent basis and the decision of workers themselves to engage in fixed-term work is found to vary. However, it appears that nonstandard work arrangements are becoming an increasing part of the employment landscape. We now turn our attention to examining the growing body of behavioral research literature which has focused on nonstandard or fixed-term employment contracts.

EMERGING RESEARCH ON NONTRADITIONAL WORK ARRANGEMENTS

We can examine the existing research involving nonstandard employment from two somewhat different perspectives. On the one hand are studies examining how mainstream OB and HR constructs are affected by 'contingency.' In many ways, this body of research mirrors that of part-time employment, which was frequently undertaken in the late 1980s and reached its ascendancy in the mid-1990s; and has largely focused on extending research on a particular topic into a new participant sample. On the other hand, research focuses more specifically on understanding contingent workers' experiences, emphasizing 'context' in more detail.

We broadly summarize the current empirical research on nonstandard employment, grouping studies according to the main issues examined, and highlighting the different forms of nonstandard employment relationships.

Commitment and identification

One of the more frequent topics in research on nontraditional work arrangement is organizational commitment (and see the Chapter on Organizational Commitment in this volume). This is understandable, considering its importance in the OB and HR literatures, and the ways in which it can be studied (e.g., short, self-report scales are meaningful). Furthermore, there are intuitively interesting questions relating to the loyalties of workers whose affiliation with an organization may be somewhat more tenuous than among the population where the construct was originally developed. In addition, when we consider that some contingent workers (e.g., contractors) hold serial affiliations with multiple client organizations, and other contingent workers hold simultaneous affiliations with both client organizations and their temporary agencies, the intricacies of the employment relationships become fertile grounds for study.

When comparing levels of commitment between contingent and permanent employees, the findings are mixed. In some studies, contingent worker commitment is significantly higher than that of permanent employees (e.g., McDonald and Makin, 2000), other studies find no differences (e.g., Pearce, 1993a), with some studies even suggesting that contingent workers are less committed (e.g., Van Dyne and Ang, 1998). Similarly mixed results emerge regarding telecommuters' organizational commitment (e.g., Golden, 2006; Igbaria and Guimares, 1999; Olson, 1989). It is therefore important to consider that the mechanisms underlying the development of organizational commitment would be similar across different forms of employment arrangements. Differences in commitment levels, therefore, are likely attributable to differences in how employees are treated by their organizations, rather than a simple function of the existence of an alternative work arrangement.

However, there may be some features of nonstandard employment that exert unique effects on commitment; indeed, 'commitment' may have different meanings for different types of contingent workers (Gallagher and McLean Parks, 2001). One such example is evident when we note the dual organizational commitment experienced by temporary workers towards their agencies and client organizations. One possibility is that these workers have 'divided loyalties,' and be more deeply connected to either the organization where they have a continuing relationship (i.e., their temporary help or staffing firm) or the organization where they have more social connections (i.e., the client organization), and studies yield a wide range of correlations between workers' affective commitment to their agencies and their clients (e.g., Connelly et al., 2007; Coyle-Shapiro and Morrow, 2006; Liden et al., 2003; Moorman and Harland, 2002). However, a weighted average (r = 0.59) that takes into account the reliability of the measures used, as well as the sample sizes as reported in these studies, suggests that temporary workers can indeed be simultaneously committed to two organizations .

Like the research on organizational commitment, studies examining nonstandard workers' organizational identification explicitly investigate the possibility and the implications of potentially divided allegiances. George and Chattopadhyay (2005) explain how the characteristics of the client organization (e.g., firm prestige) can lead contract workers to identify with the primary employer, while social relations with coworkers predict contractors' identification with their clients. A similar pattern among telecommuters is reported by Wiesenfeld et al. (2001), who indicate that virtual workers who received work-based social support experienced higher identification with the organization, even if they had a

lower innate need for affiliation. Koene and van Riemsdijk (2005) suggest that flexible workers' identification is affected by the corporate socialization process; when the company specifically tries to emphasize the visibility of the 'temps'' affiliation with the organization.

Given the possibility of nonstandard workers' identification and commitment to their organizations, additional research on other forms of work commitment is warranted. For example, when investigating determinants of individuals' decisions to pursue temporary employment, it would be interesting to consider the role of employment commitment in this choice. Furthermore, it is not yet clear how all contingent workers define their occupations; 'contractors' may consider their occupation to be the collection of job tasks that they perform at various client sites, or they may define their occupation as 'contracting' or consulting itself. These distinctions have important implications for the study of contractors' occupational commitment.

Satisfaction

Job satisfaction has also received considerable attention in the contingent worker literature; again, the research findings are mixed. Compared with permanent employees, contingent workers have been reported to be more satisfied (Galup et al., 1997; McDonald and Makin, 2000), or less satisfied (Bergman, 2002). Similarly, telecommuters are alternately reported to be more satisfied (e.g., Igbaria and Guimares, 1999), less satisfied (e.g., Olson, 1989) or equally satisfied (e.g., Belanger, 1999; DuBrin, 1991) as non-telecommuters, although a curvilinear relationship between the time spent telecommuting and job satisfaction has also been suggested (e.g., Golden, 2006).

However, as with research on standard workers, it is most likely that nonstandard workers' job satisfaction is due to a variety of situational factors, rather than solely a function of 'nonstandard' status. For example, there is evidence that contingent workers' motivations for pursuing this employment relationship will affect their job-related attitudes. When workers feel they must pursue any form of employment due to a lack of viable alternatives, their attitudes towards their temporary assignments tend to be less positive than when they have actively chosen this type of employment relationship (Krausz et al., 1995; Ellingson et al., 1998).

Although one might assume that all workers would necessarily prefer permanent employment, research suggests that some individuals voluntarily select contingent arrangements in order to develop new skills (Marler et al., 2002). However, given that contingent workers are sometimes unilaterally allocated this status by employers (e.g., when formerly 'permanent' employees are terminated and rehired as contractors; Ho et al., 2003) and given that temporary workers often use their assignments as an opportunity to transition into permanent employment (Feldman et al., 1994; 1995; Hardy and Walker, 2003), the reasons behind nonstandard workers' employment arrangements are indeed complex.

Like full-time employees (De Cuyper and De Witte, 2006), contingent workers' job satisfaction is also substantially affected by feelings of job insecurity (De Witte and Näswall, 2003). It would be erroneous to assume that all contingent workers are concerned about obtaining a steady stream of employment contracts. Due to individual skills or connections, some workers may be confident about their ability to secure subsequent assignments, while permanent employees with limited employability may, in fact, be more concerned with possible job loss. In this regard, it may be useful to consider the notion of 'psychological contingency,' where the workers' beliefs about their employability take precedence over their actual work status (Bergman, 2002).

Perceived organizational support and justice

The way in which nonstandard workers are treated by their employers, their client organizations, and their temporary staffing firms (where applicable) has received substantial attention in the research literature. Generally, findings mirror those of the literature involving permanent employees, in that the importance of perceived organizational support and organizational justice is reaffirmed. For example, Liden et al. (2003) demonstrates that procedural justice from a client organization affects temporary workers' perceptions of organizational support (POS) from the client, and that procedural justice from the THS firm leads to increased POS from the THS firm. Similarly, interpersonal fairness from either the temporary agency or the client organization can affect temporary workers' organizational citizenship behaviors and counterproductive workplace behaviors towards both the THS firm and the client (Connelly, 2004). A few studies have examined the effects of organizational justice (e.g., Feldman, et al., 1994; Rogers, 2000) but more systematic research on the effects of organizational justice is warranted, especially with a focus on other forms of nonstandard employment, such as independent contractors.

Research involving long-term contracted employees suggests that, like permanent employment relationships, POS predicts organizational commitment (Coyle-Shapiro et al., 2006). However, temporary workers' situations are complicated, as they may form perceptions regarding both their client organization and their temporary firm. There is evidence that the levels of POS from the temporary firm predict commitment to the agency, and that POS from the client organization predicts commitment to the client (Liden et al., 2003; Newton McClurg, 1999). Similarly, agency supportiveness has been linked to temporary workers' affective and continuance commitment towards the agency (Van Breugel et al., 2005). Building on these findings, other researchers have suggested POS from one organization (e.g., the THS or contractor) may have additional effects on the workers' commitment to another firm, such as the client (Coyle-Shapiro and Morrow, 2006), and vice versa (Connelly et al., 2007).

Although perceived organizational support has received far more research attention than the different forms of organizational justice, many questions remain unanswered. For example, when assessing nonstandard workers' treatment by their colleagues and supervisors, it remains important to consider how nonstandard workers are integrated into the organization. Whereas some organizations intentionally keep contingent workers separate from permanent employees by assigning them different tasks (e.g., Ang and Slaughter, 2001) or physically separating them from the 'standard' workforce, others minimize distinctions wherever possible (Lautsch, 2002). Also, there are often noticeable demographic differences between contingent workers and permanent employees; contingent workers are more likely to be female, nonwhite, and to have lower levels of education than permanent employees (e.g., Bellemore, 1998; Marler et al., 2002). As such, permanent and contingent workers may not naturally form cohesive work groups without intentional organizational intervention. These demographic dissimilarities may, in turn, reinforce differences in employment status, and interfere with any informal communication or extra-role helping behaviors between coworkers.

Successful organizational integration may not only be a question of having contingent workers and permanent employees work well together when they are placed in adjacent work areas. The use of contingent workers may negatively affect permanent employees' perceptions of the trustworthiness of their employer (e.g., Pearce, 1993a), and of the trustworthiness of the contingent workers in their organization (Ang and Slaughter, 2001). Because there is often a disconnect between the stated purpose of hiring contingent workers and what eventually transpires in the organization, this is perhaps not surprising. For example, organizations may claim that independent contractors have been hired to protect permanent or core employees from fluctuations in the demand for their services. However, when the firm experiences financial difficulty, contractors with necessary skills often continue to be employed, while 'permanent' employees are laid off (Bidwell, 2005). Furthermore, a higher proportion of nonstandard workers in the organization is associated with permanent employees having less favorable attitudes towards supervisors and peers, increased turnover intentions, and decreased interpersonal helping (Broschak and Davis-Blake, 2006). Permanent employees with high levels of job insecurity are more likely to see temporary workers as a threat to their jobs (Kraimer et al., 2005).

Thus, careful consideration must be given to how contingent workers are integrated into the organization. There is a tendency to allocate contingent workers tasks that do not require interdependence with other employees (e.g., Ang and Slaughter, 2001). However, this practice may place an additional burden on permanent employees who must maintain social ties and continuity among projects. This strategy bears some similarities to what Lautsch (2003) describes as 'segregation,' whereby contingent workers perform entirely different tasks than permanent employees, often in a separate location, and incidentally with a different pay structure (e.g., piecework, no benefits). Alternatively, other organizations prefer a more 'assimilationist' strategy, where contingent workers perform identical tasks alongside permanent employees. This would be a more common strategy among firms that engage contingent workers as part of a general extended probationary recruitment pattern for all permanent employees.

In addition to restricted or nonexistent socialization processes, contingent workers also have few opportunities for formal training. In some situations, this occurs because contractors who receive employer-sponsored training are at risk of being legally reclassified as employees (e.g., Church and Lambert, 1993; Fragoso and Kleiner, 2005). However, contingent workers often have multiple opportunities for informal learning on-the-job as they complete their assignments in a variety of work units, organizations, and industries that can assist them in the performance of their duties (Sias et al., 1997). These informal behaviors have additional ancillary benefits; their willingness to learn may be interpreted as extra-role or organizational citizenship behaviors by supervisors and co-workers (Kidder, 1995).

Information-seeking behavior may be more common among contingent workers than among permanent employees who have recently joined the organization. In a study of employee communication, Sias et al. (1997) found that temporary workers routinely asked for help because they not feel as though they would be penalized for a lack of knowledge. In contrast, the permanent employees in their study felt the need to demonstrate early competence, and did not seek assistance from co-workers, even when it would readily be forthcoming.

Because of potential incongruence between the actual and required levels of safety-related knowledge, occupational health and safety problems may arise when contingent workers are assumed to have levels of experience and training that are similar to those of permanent employees. Workplace-specific knowledge (e.g., the location of fire extinguishers) is as important as the more generally available task-specific knowledge (e.g., how to operate a fire extinguisher. A lack of knowledge may especially be an issue among low-skilled occupations where the workforce tends to have poor literacy skills. Contingent workers may also be reticent to refuse work or to report accidents, even though legally permitted to do so, because they may be concerned that they will be jeopardizing the possibility of receiving future work assignments (Collinson, 1999).

Performance

The issue of nonstandard workers' performance relative to other workers is of utmost interest to organizations considering implementing alternative work arrangements or engaging the services of nonstandard workers. Task performance, extra-role performance or organizational citizenship behaviors, and

counterproductive workplace behaviors have all received some attention from researchers. However, the findings are often somewhat contradictory. According to Ang and Slaughter (2001), contract workers' in-role performance is lower than that of permanent employees at the same organization, even though the contractors also experienced higher levels of perceived organizational support. Similarly, Ellingson et al. (1998) found no direct relationship between temporary workers' volition (e.g., reasons for pursuing temporary work) and their performance. However, there is also evidence that other attitudes, such as commitment, are more salient predictors of temporary workers' performance (Marler et al., 2002).

The issue of contingent workers' extra-role performance or organizational citizenship behaviors may be complicated by their tendency to have job duties that are more circumscribed than those of permanent employees in the same organization (e.g., Uzzi and Barsness, 1998). As such, both workers and their supervisors may be more likely to consider certain behaviors to be 'extra-role' when performed by contingent workers, but part of the normal job responsibilities if performed by a permanent employee. These inconsistent expectations, which may well vary in different organizational contexts, may explain why contingent workers are alternately reported to engage in either significantly more or significantly less citizenship behaviors than permanent employees (e.g., Pearce, 1993a; Van Dyne and Ang, 1998).

Considering the many studies on nonstandard workers' in-role and extra-role performance, it is surprising to see so little research about these workers' counterproductive workplace behaviors (e.g., theft, interpersonal aggression; see the chapter by Robinson in this volume), especially considering how nonstandard workers are often maligned in the popular press and media. While some qualitative studies describe contingent workers' counterproductive or retaliatory behaviors (e.g., Rogers, 2000), the prevalence and underlying reasons for such actions have not been widely investigated. However, research involving temporary workers suggests that interpersonally unjust treatment from either the THS firm or the client organization can predict counterproductive workplace behaviors towards both (Connelly, 2004). Other research suggests that temporary workers who were laid off from previous jobs from which they had enjoyed a long tenure are more likely to exhibit counterproductive behaviors in future assignments (Posthuma et al., 2005). Further investigation into inappropriate behaviors by nonstandard workers is certainly warranted.

THE ROLE OF THEORY

A discussion of the available research on nonstandard employment would be incomplete without an examination of the primary theoretical lenses used to explain and understand these workers' experiences. One of the early criticisms of nonstandard worker research was that it was atheoretical and focused on simply contrasting their experiences from those of permanent employees (e.g., Beard and Edwards, 1995; Pfeffer and Baron, 1988). However, researchers should not simply assume that all behavioral theories will apply equally well to nonstandard workers, or particularly to all types of nonstandard workers.

An examination of the available research shows that there are two broad categories of theoretically informed research involving nonstandard workers. The first group of micro-level based theories has sought to explain the experiences of contingent workers, especially their interactions with other organizational members. These theories include social exchange theory, social identity theory, and others that emphasize either the nonstandard workers' status as 'other,' or their interactions with 'others.' The second group of theories, including human capital theory and transaction cost economics, present a more macro-level perspective that seeks to explain why nonstandard workers are sought by various types of organizations. In turn,

we examine both micro- and macro-based theories.

Micro-level theoretical perspectives

Much of the empirical research on nonstandard work and nonstandard workers tends to be dominated by a small number of theoretical frameworks, such as social exchange theory. Social exchange theory is a process in which one individual who engages in positive behavior towards another person will implicitly invoke a similar yet unspecified reciprocal behavior (Blau, 1964). The nature of these mutually rewarding exchanges expands over time, as obligations are met and new ones created (Cropanzano and Mitchell, 2005). In the context of permanent or traditional employment, social exchange theory has been widely used to explain the relationship between worker attitudes or perceptions and their behaviors (e.g., Rupp and Cropanzano, 2002). Among research involving nonstandard employment arrangements, social exchange theory is the theoretical lens used most frequently (e.g., Ang and Slaughter, 2001; Coyle-Shapiro and Morrow, 2006; Liden et al., 2003; Van Dyne and Ang, 1998). As research on the linkages between nonstandard workers' perceptions and attitudes continues, social exchange theory is likely to be used even more frequently.

Because of the emphasis on reciprocal expectations, psychological contract theory bears many similarities to social exchange theory. As such, it is also suitable for explaining any worker's behaviors. For example, De Cuyper and De Witte (2006) use psychological contract theory to explain how job insecurity affects temporary and permanent employees differently. Kraimer et al. (2005) also focused on job insecurity, and used psychological contract theory to explain permanent employees' perceptions of temporary workers. Because job security is generally considered to be a component of a relational psychological contract, and because contingent workers, by definition, do not have job security, this is likely to be a fruitful area of investigation. However, future research might further consider the role of 'employment security,' or the likelihood that a replacement contract could be obtained, in predicting contingent workers' attitudes and behaviors.

Social identity theory suggests that individuals maintain a positive self image by categorizing themselves into 'in-groups' that they perceive more favorably than others who are categorized as members of 'out-groups' (Tajfel and Turner, 1986). Because the demographic profiles of nonstandard workers are different from employees with more traditional employment relationships, many researchers have used social identity theory to examine relationships between these two groups of workers. For example, Chattopadhyay and George (2001) suggest that 'internal' permanent employees' attitudes and behaviors towards their peers are negatively influenced by working in groups that are dominated by temporary workers. George and Chattopadhyay (2005) use social identity theory to explain how contract workers begin to identify with their client and employing organization. Also, because status as a nonstandard employee is a mutable category, temporary workers may actually manifest out-group favoritism as a mechanism to retain a positive sense of self (von Hippel, 2006).

A related body of research specifically addresses interactions between nonstandard workers and other employees in the organization. These studies are again predicated on the observable differences between these two groups, but they seek to understand how employment status differentials affect the way in which workers relate to each other. Social comparison theory suggests that proximity between two separate groups will trigger a biased assessment of how these two groups are rated, either by group members or by outsiders (e.g., Kruglanski and Mayseless, 1990). Ang and Slaughter (2001) use this theory to help explain why supervisors might perceive contractors' in-role and extra-role performance differently from those of permanent employees.

However, other theories are also relevant in this context. For example, Broschak and Davis-Blake (2006) use Blalock's (1967) theory of majority-minority group relations to explain why contact between minority (nonstandard workers) and majority group members (standard workers) is likely to evoke negative reactions towards minority group members, especially those who are more tangibly different from the majority (i.e., temporary workers rather than part-time employees).

Other authors also investigate the relationship between traditional and nonstandard workers; and apply social cognition theory, which suggests that the effect of workers' attitudes on their behaviors will be affected by the salience of these attitudes (Fiske and Taylor, 1991). For example, social cognition theory can be utilized to explain why job insecurity affects permanent employees' attitudes towards temporary workers (Kraimer et al., 2005), or be used to explain why supervisors may retain their previously established expectations of contractors who are former employees (Ho et al., 2003).

Macro-level perspectives

Macro-level theories have been utilized to explain why organizations use nonstandard employment arrangements. Lepak and Snell (1999) draw on multiple organizational theories (i.e., resource-based view of the firm, human capital theory, and transaction cost economics) to identify what types of nonstandard work arrangements would be most beneficial, depending on the value and uniqueness of the human capital in question. Human capital theory, among other things, suggests that firms will seek to protect themselves from the transfer of their human capital investments, especially with respect to generalizable skills (e.g., Schultz, 1961). Thus, this theory has been applied to explain why contingent workers were less likely to receive occupational training and career planning than their permanent counterparts (Virtanen et al., 2003). In contrast, Lepak and Snell (2002) use human capital theory to explain how organizations choose which functions can be performed by nonstandard or external workers, and how these individuals can best be managed.

Transaction cost theory is an alternative theoretical framework that explains why organizations might employ a nonstandard workforce. As explained by Wheeler and Buckley (2000), firms seek to find the 'most efficient mode of transactions between entities by reducing the uncertainty of the transactions and specifying the assets involved' (p. 345). For example, using the services of a temporary agency might reduce costs associated with recruiting and selecting appropriate employees. Galup et al.'s (1997) findings support this perspective, and indicate that firms may reduce the uncertainty related to its workforce management by avoiding long-term salary commitments.

Although a few studies use competing theoretical approaches to explain worker behaviors (e.g., Galup et al., 1997; Kraimer et al., 2005), this practice is not widespread. Indeed, most studies focus primarily on describing nonstandard workers' behaviors, rather than explaining it. Furthermore, although some studies simultaneously examine more than one form of nonstandard work arrangements (e.g., Broschak and Davis-Blake, 2006), most studies focus solely on one type of employment relationship (usually temporary workers). Finally, because of the inherent nature of the population being studied, few studies are longitudinal, although there are notable exceptions (e.g., Parker et al., 2002). Such rigorous studies are particularly valuable, because they present a more stringent test of the theories and hypotheses being presented.

FUTURE DIRECTIONS

Nonstandard employment contracts no longer suffer from academic invisibility. Since the mid-1990s, a sizeable body of international literature which has explored the broad range of economic, legal, and social factors which have contributed to the growth of the contingent workforce; more recently, the focus on the individual and organizationally-based consequences of these re-emerging forms of employment contracts has increased. Using the terminology of McLean Parks and smith (2006), nonstandard workers have become less and less the 'amorphous ghosts' of organizational research, but the results of this research have at times been contradictory or unexpected.

In moving forward, it is imperative that researchers recognize:

(a) that nonstandard working arrangements are diverse in their contractual structure;
(b) the rationale for which organizations use such contracts; and
(c) the reasons why people undertake such work outside of the scope of the traditional employment model.

Of particular importance is the need to avoid simple dichotomizations or comparisons of standard vs. nonstandard working arrangements. As research now shows, there are subtle and significant differences among nonstandard employment contracts which require consideration. Like the volumes of research devoted to the study of part-time workers, interesting research questions may more likely emerge within types of non-standard work arrangements, rather than in simple comparisons with the more traditional employment contracts.

Instead of 'simply' differentiating nonstandard from standard forms of employment, it may be more beneficial to begin exploring which underlying dimensions of both the explicit and psychological contracts help to explain differences among nonstandard arrangements and how such dimensions help to explain worker reactions and behaviors (McLean Parks et al., 1998). Beard and Edwards (1995) illustrate this in their classic essay of contingent workers which suggests that, for example, the absence of control is a characteristic of the 'psychological experience' of contingent work. However, as demonstrated in the case of many workers employed as ad hoc independent contractors, the presence of control over how the work is performed is both an operational and legal hallmark of the type of work they perform. Hence, the issue is less the presence or absence of control, but rather the level of control found among different nonstandard work arrangements. We suggest much more research is needed in building frameworks which can be useful in meaningful distinctions among and between different nonstandard employment contracts.

A unifying theory of nonstandard or contingent work has yet to emerge. It is possible that a theoretical framework exclusive to nonstandard work is neither possible nor necessary. Our review of the literature highlights the need for future researchers to evaluate whether existing theory, developed in the context of standard employment, is fully or partially relevant to the study of various forms of nonstandard employment. A nice illustration of this is contained in Boyce et al.'s (2007) theoretical model of stigmatization among temporary workers. Building heavily on social comparison and identity theory, their model is appealing but it is not theoretically unique to temporary workers. The real challenge may not be in the development of a new grand theory of contingent worker behavior, but rather in determining individual and contextual variables which affect the way in which existing theories apply to nonstandard workers. Similarly, as noted by Beard and Edwards (1995), the social comparison process helps us to understand how contingent workers evaluate their jobs. However, the challenge for researchers is to determine what are the relevant and salient referent others to include in both the theoretical and empirical modeling. We would suggest that in the case of different types of contingent workers, the referent group extends beyond core (standard) organizational members, and includes comparisons with previous temporary assignments, or comparisons of the contingent self to the formerly permanent self in the same organization (e.g., Ho et al., 2003). Again, this does not call for completely new theories, but rather the refinement of existing frameworks

to accommodate the introduction of other variables which had not attracted sufficient attention when examining worker attitudes and behaviors in the world of the traditional employment contract.

Making the step from theoretical to empirical investigation also requires the reconsideration of the applicability of existing behavioral constructs. As noted by Gallagher and McLean Parks (2001), the meaning of constructs such as 'job' or 'commitment' may vary among workers in different types of nonstandard employment contracts. For example, the question arises as to how a temporary worker, dispatched through the services of a THS firm, would mentally anchor references to their 'job'? Would 'job' be evaluated in terms of the immediate collection of tasks being performed for the client organization? Or could, in fact, the 'job' be viewed as the collective tasks of being a temporary worker? Similarly, organizational commitment may have a less than precise meaning or relevance to the dispatched temporary worker or a self-employed independent contractor. Future research involving workers in nonstandard employment relationships needs to give systematic attention toward the construct validity of long-established attitudinal measures.

Following the work of Lautsch (2002, 2003), a great deal of intellectual and practical value can be derived from better understanding the relative advantages and disadvantages of structurally integrating workers on both standard and nonstandard work contracts. From a theoretical perspective, the integration or segregation of workers may have potentially meaningful consequences in terms of how contingent workers use social comparisons to evaluate their employment status, their employer or client organization. Structural integration may also have the potential to influence the level of perceived organization support (POS) experienced by the contingent worker, to reduce status distinctions in the organization (Pfeffer, 1998) and ultimately affect job performance and organizational-based attitudes (Coyle-Shaprio and Morrow, 2006).

Related to this is the issue of knowledge flow within organizations, and its impact on organizational effectiveness. Matusik and Hill (1998) suggested that the effective use of contingent workers can provide an important source of knowledge, especially if organizations engage the services of independent contractors with specialized skills or temporary workers with a broad range of organizational experience. However, little is known about this critical phenomenon. Future research might assess what strategies associated with the management of contingent workers are most conducive for effective knowledge sharing (Kelloway and Barling, 2000). Similarly, in the context of increased global competition and corporate espionage, research might also question the extent to which reliance on workers with fixed-term contacts represents a threat to the security of organizational data and knowledge.

In recent years there has been a growing interest in the effects of contingent work contracts on worker well-being (Barling et al., 2002). To date, much of this research has been conducted in the context of European organizations (e.g., De Cuyper et al., 2005; Isaksson and Bellagh, 2002; Mauno et al., 2005; Silla et al., 2005) and has established links between levels of job insecurity inherent in different forms of contingent work and individual worker well-being. This research might also identify the role of individual and organizational-based characteristics which mediate the negative health consequences associated with different aspects of fixed-term contracts.

Understanding new working relationships must involve a willingness to go beyond the vantage point of the bureaucratic model and consider alternative paradigms such as a combination of contracts, production process, or shared culture perspectives, all of which take organizational membership beyond the immediate employer – standard worker arrangement (McLean Parks and smith, 2006).

A related topic which has received limited attention is an organization's use of volunteer workers, especially in human services industries (e.g., health care and education). The meager body of research on volunteers focuses primarily on describing the volunteers' individual characteristics (i.e., age, gender, marital status and religious background), identifying trends in volunteering rates (e.g., Selbee and Reed, 2001), volunteers' attitudes towards their organizations (e.g., Catano et al., 2001), the public's attitudes towards voluntary organizations in general (e.g., Fenton et al., 1999), and why people volunteer (e.g., Harrison, 1995). Generally, the focus has been on volunteers *before* they become affiliated with organizations, rather than on their experiences, attitudes, and behaviors within organizations (Pearce, 1993b).

Although these volunteer workers may have valuable skills and be performing 'core' tasks, they are generally viewed as distinct from the staff members who have a standard employment relationship (Pearce, 1993b). It would be interesting to understand how volunteers' work experiences mirror those of other nontraditional workers, particularly with respect to interactions with other staff members and supervisors (who may themselves have nontraditional work arrangements). Because volunteer retention is a major challenge for many nonprofit organizations, and because volunteers typically have tenuous links to their organizations, it would be useful to determine if strategies developed to manage contingent workers may also be useful for effectively managing temporary workers.

CONCLUSION

Drucker noted that 'every organization must take management responsibility for *all* the people whose productivity and performance it relies on – whether they're temps, part-timers, employees of the organization itself, or employees of its outsourcers, suppliers, and distributors' (2002: 75). Managers today have a difficult challenge; to manage workers who are internal, external, and perhaps tangential to the organization's traditional employment structure. In short, they must rely on workers who are not 'employees' in the traditional sense. As such, managers must consider collaborative ways to manage people who do not necessarily report to them. In this respect, future research should give serious attention to providing a comprehensive understanding of the array of experiences associated with non-standard employment relationships, and as such knowledge accumulates how to make the transition from evidence-based knowledge to practical advice for those managing outside the traditional employment contract.

REFERENCES

Ang, S. and Slaughter, S.A. (2001) 'Work outcomes and job design for contract versus permanent information systems professionals on software development teams', *MIS Quarterly*, 25 (3): 321–350.

Appelbaum, E. (1992) 'Structural change and the growth of part-time and temporary employment', in V. DuRivage (ed.), *New Policies for the Part-Time and Contingent Workforce*. Armonk, NY: M.E. Sharpe, pp. 1–14.

Atkinson, J. (1984) 'Manpower strategies for flexible organizations', *Personnel Management*, 16 (August): 28–31.

Barley, S.R. and Kunda, G. (2004) *Gurus, Hired Guns, and Warm Bodies: Itinerant Experts in the Knowledge Economy*. Princeton, NJ: Princeton University Press.

Barling, J. and Gallagher, D.G. (1996) 'Part-time employment', in C.L. Cooper and I.T. Robertson (eds), *International Review of Industrial and Organizational Psychology*. Chichester: Wiley, 11: 243–277.

Barling, J., Inness, M. and Gallagher, D.G. (2002) 'Alternative work arrangements and employee well being', in P.L. Perrewé and D.C. Ganster (eds), *Historical and Current Perspectives of Stress and Health*. Oxford: Elsevier, pp. 183–216.

Beard, K.M. and Edwards, J.R. (1995) 'Employees at risk: Contingent work and the experience of contingent workers', in C.L. Cooper and D.M. Rousseau (eds), *Trends in Organizational Behavior 2*. Chichester: Wiley, pp. 109–126.

Belanger, F. (1999) 'Workers' propensity to telecommute: An empirical study', *Information and Management*, 35 (3): 139–153.

Bellemore, F.A. (1998) 'Temporary employment decisions of registered nurses', *Eastern Economic Journal*, 24 (3): 265–279.

Bergman, M.E. (2002) *Psychological and Objective Contingency as Predictors of Work Attitudes and Behavior*. Paper presentation at the Academy of Management Meeting, August, 2002, Denver, Colorado.

Bergstrøm, O. and Storrie, D. (2003) *Contingent Employment in Europe and the United States*. Cheltenham: Edward Elgar.

Bidwell, M. (2005) *Reworking Contingent Employment*. Presented at Academy of Management meeting in Honolulu, HI.

Blalock, H.M (1967) *Toward a Theory of Minority–Group Relations*. New York: Wiley.

Blau, P.M. (1964) *Exchange and Power in Social Life*. New Brunswick, NJ: Transaction Publishers.

Boyce, A.S., Ryan, A.M., Imus, A.L. and Morgeson, F.P. (2007) 'Temporary worker, permanent loser? A model of the stigmatization of temporary workers', *Journal of Management*, 33: 5–29.

Brewster, C., Mayne, L. and Tregaskis, O. (1997) 'Flexible working in Europe: A review of the evidence', *Management International Review*, 37 (2): 85–103.

Broschak, J.P. and Davis-Blake, A. (2006) 'Mixing standard work and nonstandard deals: The consequences of heterogeneity in employment arrangements', *Academy of Management Journal*, 49 (2): 371–393.

Cappelli, P. (1999) *The New Deal at Work*. Boston, MA: Harvard Business School Press.

Catano, V.M., Pond, M. and Kelloway, E.K. (2001) 'Exploring commitment and leadership in volunteer organizations', *Leadership and Organization Development Journal*, 22 (6): 256–263.

Chattopadhyay, P. and George, E. (2001) 'Examining work externalization through the lens of social identity theory', *Journal of Applied Psychology*, 86 (4): 781–788.

Church, P.H. and Lambert, K.R. (1993) 'Employee or independent contractor?', *Management Accounting*, 74: 52–55.

Collinson, D.L. (1999) ' "Surviving the rigs": Safety and surveillance on north sea oil installations', *Organization Studies*, 20 (4): 579–600.

Connelly, C.E. (2004) *Temporary Workers, Permanent Consequences: Behavioral Implications of the Triangular Employment Relationship*. Unpublished Ph.D. Thesis. Queen's University.

Connelly, C.E. and Gallagher, D.G. (2004) 'Emerging trends in contingent work research', *Journal of Management*, 30 (6): 959–983.

Connelly, C.E. and Gallagher, D.G. (2006) 'Independent and dependent contracting: Meaning and implications', *Human Resource Management Review*, 16 (2): 95–106.

Connelly, C.E., Gallagher, D.G. and Gilley, K.M. (2007) 'Organizational commitment among contracted employees: A replication and extension with temporary workers', *Journal of Vocational Behavior*, 70 (2): 326–335.

Coyle-Shapiro, J.A.-M, and Morrow, P.C. (2006) 'Organizational and client commitment among contracted employees', *Journal of Vocational Behavior*, 68 (3): 416–431.

Coyle-Shapiro, J.A.-M., Morrow, P.C. and Kessler, I. (2006) 'Serving two organizations: Exploring the employment relationship of contracted employees', *Human Resource Management*, 45 (1): 561–583.

Coyle-Shapiro, J.A, Shore, L.M., Taylor, M.S. and Tetrick, L.E. (eds) (2004) *The Employment Relationship: Examining Psychological and Contextual Perspectives.* Oxford: Oxford University Press.

Cropanzano, R. and Mitchell, M.S. (2005) 'Social exchange theory: An interdisciplinary review', *Journal of Management*, 31: 874–900.

De Cuyper, N. and De Witte, H. (2006) 'The impact of job insecurity and contract type on attitudes, well-being and behavioural reports: A psychological contract perspective', *Journal of Occupational and Organizational Psychology*, 79 (3): 395–409.

De Cuyper, N., Isaksson, K. and De Witte (eds) (2005) *Employment Contracts and Well-Being among European Workers.* Aldershot, UK: Ashgate.

De Witte, H. and Näswall, K. (2003) ' "Objective" vs "subjective" jobs insecurity: Consequences of temporary work for job satisfaction and organizational commitment in four European countries', *Economic and Industrial Democracy*, 24 (2): 149–188.

Delsen L. (1999) 'Changing work relationships in the European Union', in I.U. Zeytinoğlu (ed.), *Changing Work Relationships in Industrialized Economies.* Amsterdam: John Benjamins Publishing, pp. 99–114.

Doogan, K. (2001) 'Insecurity and long-term employment', *Work, Employment and Society*, 15 (3): 419–441.

Drucker, P.F. (2002) 'They're not employees, they're people', *Harvard Business Review*, February, 80 (2): 70–77.

DuBrin, A.J. (1991) 'Comparison of the job satisfaction and productivity of telecommuters versus in-house employees: A research note on work in progress', *Psychological Reports*, 68 (2): 1223–1234.

Ellingson, J.E., Gruys, M.L. and Sackett, P.R. (1998) 'Factors related to the satisfaction and performance of temporary employees', *Journal of Applied Psychology*, 83 (6): 913–921.

Evans, J.A., Kunda, G. and Barley, S.R. (2004) 'Beach time, Bridge time, and billable hours: The temporal structure of technical contracting', *Administrative Science Quarterly*, 49: 1–38.

Fairweather, N.B. (1999) 'Surveillance in employment: The case of teleworking', *Journal of Business Ethics*, 22 (1): 39–49.

Feldman, D.C., Doerpinghaus, H.I. and Turnley, W.H. (1994) 'Managing temporary workers: A permanent HRM challenge', *Organizational Dynamics*, 13 (2): 49–62.

Feldman, D.C., Doerpinghaus, H.I. and Turnley, W.H. (1995) 'Employee reactions to temporary jobs', *Journal of Managerial Issues*, 7 (2): 127–141.

Fenton, N., Passey, A. and Hems, L. (1999) 'Trust, the voluntary sector and civil society', *International Journal of Sociology and Social Policy*, 19 (7/8): 21–42.

Fiske, S.T. and Taylor, S.E. (1991) *Social Cognition.* New York: McGraw-Hill, Inc.

Fragoso, J.L. and Kleiner, B.H. (2005) 'How to distinguish between independent contractors and employees', *Management Research News*, 28 (2/3): 136–149.

Gallagher, D.G. (2002) 'Contingent work contracts: Practice and theory', in C.L. Cooper and R.J. Burke (eds), *The New World of Work.* Oxford: Blackwell, pp. 115–136.

Gallagher, D.G. and McLean Parks, J. (2001) 'I pledge thee my troth… contingently: Commitment and the contingent work relationship', *Human Resource Management Review*, 11 (3): 181–208.

Gallagher, D.G. and Sverke, M. (2005) 'Contingent employment contracts: Are existing employment theories still relevant?', *Economic and Industrial Democracy*, 26 (2): 181–203.

Galup, S., Saunders, C. Nelson, R.E. and Cerveny, R. (1997) 'The use of temporary staff and managers in a local government environment', *Communication Research*, 24 (6): 698–730.

George, E. and Chattopadhyay, P. (2005) 'One foot in each camp: The dual identification of contract workers', *Administrative Science Quarterly*, 50: 68–99.

Gilley, K.M. and Rasheed, A. (2000) 'Making more by doing less: An analysis of outsourcing and its effects on firm performance', *Journal of Management*, 26 (4): 763–790.

Golden, T.D. (2006) 'The role of relationships in understanding telecommuter satisfaction', *Journal of Organizational Behavior*, 27 (3): 319–340.

Hardy, D.J. and Walker, R.J. (2003) 'Temporary but seeking permanence: A study of New Zealand temps', *Leadership and Organization Development Journal*, 24 (3): 141–152.

Harrison, D.A. (1995) 'Volunteer motivation and attendance decisions: Competitive theory testing in multiple samples from a homeless shelter', *Journal of Applied Psychology*, 80 (3): 371–385.

Hamel, G. and Prahalad, C.K. (1994) *Competing for the Future.* Boston, MA: Harvard Business School Press.

Handy, C. (1989). *The Age of Unreason.* Boston, MA: Harvard University Press.

Ho, V.T., Ang, S. and Straub, D. (2003) 'When subordinates become IT contractors: Persistent managerial expectations in IT outsourcing', *Information Systems Research*, 14: 66–86.

Houseman, S. and M. Osawa (eds) (2003) *Nonstandard Work in Developed Economies: Causes and Consequences*. Kellogg, MI: Upjohn Institute.

Igbaria, M. and Guimares, T. (1999) 'Exploring differences in employee turnover intentions and its determinants among telecommuters and non-telecommuters', *Journal of Management Information Systems*, 16 (1): 147–164.

Isaksson, K., and Bellagh, K. (2002) 'Health problems and quitting among female "temps"', *European Journal of Work and Organizational Psychology*, 11 (1): 27–45.

Kalleberg, A.L. (2000) 'Nonstandard employment relations: Part-time, temporary and contract work', *Annual Review of Sociology*, 26 (August): 341–365.

Kalleberg, A.L, and Marsden, P.V. (2005) 'Externalizing organizational activities: Where and how U.S. establishments use employment intermediaries', *Socio-Economic Review*, 3 (3): 389–415.

Kalleberg, A.L., Reynolds, J. and Marsden, P.V. (2003) 'Externalizing employment: Flexible staffing arrangements in US organizations', *Social Science Research*, 32 (9): 525–552.

Kelloway, K.E. and Barling, J. (2000) 'Knowledge work as organizational behavior', *International Journal of Management Reviews*, 2: 287–304.

Kidder, D. (1995) *On call or Answering a Calling: Temporary Nurses and Extra-Role Behaviors*. Paper presented at the Academy of Management Meeting, Vancouver, British Columbia.

Klein Hesselink, D.J. and van Vuuren, T. (1999) 'Job flexibility and job insecurity: The Dutch case', *European Journal of Work and Organizational Psychology*, 8 (2): 273–294.

Koene, B. and van Riemsdijk, M. (2005) 'Managing temporary workers: Work identity, diversity and operational HR choices', *Human Resource Management Journal*, 15 (1): 76–92.

Kraimer, M.L., Wayne, S.J., Liden, R.C. and Sparrowe, R.R. (2005) 'The role of job security in understanding the relationship between employees' perceptions of temporary workers and employees' performance', *Journal of Applied Psychology*, 90 (2): 389–398.

Krausz, M., Brandwein, T. and Fox, S. (1995) 'Work attitudes and emotional responses of permanent , voluntary, and involuntary temporary-help employees: An exploratory study', *Applied Psychology: An International Review*, 44 (3): 217–232.

Kruglanski, A.W. and Mayseless, O. (1990) 'Classic and current social comparison research: Expanding the perspective', *Psychological Bulletin*, 108 (2): 195–208.

Lautsch, B.A. (2002) 'Uncovering and explaining variance in the features and outcomes of contingent work', *Industrial and Labor Relations Review*, 56 (1): 23–43.

Lautsch, B.A. (2003) 'The influence of regular work systems on compensation for contingent workers', *Industrial Relations*, 42 (4): 565–588.

Lepak, D.P. and Snell, S.A. (1999) 'The human resource architecture: Toward a theory of human capital allocation and development', *Academy of Management Review*, 24 (1): 331–48.

Lepak, D.P. and Snell, S.A. (2002) 'Examining the human resource architecture: The relationships among human capital, employment, and human resource configurations', *Journal of Management*, 28 (4): 517–543.

Liden, R.C., Wayne, S.J., Kraimer, M.L. and Sparrowe, R.T. (2003) 'The dual commitments of contingent workers: An examination of contingents' commitment to the agency and the organization', *Journal of Organizational Behavior*, 24 (5): 609–625.

Marler, J.H., Barringer, M.W. and Milkovich, G.T. (2002). 'Boundaryless and traditional contingent employees: Worlds apart', *Journal of Organizational Behavior*, 23 (4): 425–452.

Matusik, S.F. and Hill, C.W. (1998) 'The utilization of contingent work, knowledge creation, and competitive advantage', *Academy of Management Review*, 23 (4): 690–697.

Mauno, S., Kinnunen, U., Mäkikangas, A. and Nätti, J. (2005) 'Psychological consequences of fixed-term employment and perceived job insecurity among health care staff', *European Journal of Work and Organizational Psychology*, 14 (3): 209–237.

McDonald, D.J. and Makin, P.J. (2000) 'The psychological contract, organizational commitment and job satisfaction of temporary staff', *Leadership and Organizational Development Journal*, 21 (2): 84–91.

McLean Parks, J., Kidder, D.L. and Gallagher, D.G. (1998) 'Fitting square pegs into round holes: Mapping the domain of contingent work arrangements onto the psychological contract', *Journal of Organizational Behavior*, 19: 697–730.

McLean Parks, J. and smith, F. (2006) 'Ghost workers: Implications of new workforce realities for organizations and their workers', in P. Jackson and M. Shams (eds), *Developments in Work and Organizational Psychology: Implications for International Business*. Oxford: Elsevier Ltd, pp. 131–162.

Moorman, R.H. and Harland, L.K. (2002) 'Temporary employees as good citizens: Factors influencing their OCB performance', *Journal of Business and Psychology*, 17 (2): 171–187.

Nesheim, T. (2003) 'Using external work arrangements in core value-creation areas', *European Management Journal*, 21 (4): 528–537.

Newton McClurg, L. (1999) 'Organizational commitment in the temporary-help service industry', *Journal of Applied Management Studies*, 8 (1): 5–26.

Nishikawa, M. (2000) 'Diversification in the use of atypical workers in Japanese establishments', *Proceedings of the 12*th *World Congress of the International Industrial Relations Research Association*. Tokyo: Japan. Vol 1, 160–168.

Nollen, S. (1999) 'Flexible work arrangements', in I.U. Zeytinoğlu (ed.), *Changing Work Relationships in Industrialized Economies*. Amsterdam: John Benjamins Publishing, pp. 21–39.

Nollen, S. and Axel, H. (1996) *Managing Contingent Workers: How to Reap the Benefits and Reduce the Risks*. New York: AMACON.

Olsen, K.M. (2003) *Contingency Reversed: The Role of Agency Temporaries and Contractors in Client Organizations*. Paper presented at the Academy of Management meeting, Seattle, WA.

Olson, M.H. (1989) 'Work at home for computer professionals: Current attitudes and future prospects', *ACM Transactions on Office Information Systems*, 7 (4): 317–338.

Parker, S.K., Griffin, M.A., Sprigg, C.A. and Wall, T.D. (2002) 'Effect of temporary contracts on perceived work characteristics and job strain: A longitudinal study', *Personnel Psychology*, 55 (3): 689–719.

Pearce, J.L. (1993a) 'Toward an organizational behavior of contract laborers: Their psychological involvement and effects on employee co-workers', *Academy of Management Journal*, 36 (5): 1082–1096.

Pearce, J.L. (1993b) *Volunteers: The Organizational Behavior of Unpaid Workers*. London: Routledge.

Pfeffer, J. (1998) 'Seven practices of successful organizations', *California Management Review*, 40: 96–124.

Pfeffer, J. and Baron, N. (1988) 'Taking the work back out: Recent trends in the structures of employment', in B.M. Staw and L.L. Cummings (eds) *Research in Organizational Behavior*. Greenwich, CT: JAI Press, Vol. 10, pp. 257–303.

Pink, D.H. (2001) *Free Agent Nation*. New York: Time Warner.

Polivka, A.E. and Nardone, T. (1989) 'The definition of contingent work', *Monthly Labor Review*, 112 (12): 9–16.

Posthuma, R.A., Campion, M.A. and Vargas, A.L. (2005) 'Predicting counterproductive performance among temporary workers: A note', *Industrial Relations*, 44 (3): 550–554.

Quinlan, M. and Bohle, P. (2004) 'Contingent work and occupational safety', in J. Barling and M.R. Frone (eds), *The Psychology of Workplace Safety*. Washington: American Psychological Association, pp. 81–105.

Reilly, P.A. (1998) 'Balancing flexibility, meeting the interests of employer and employee', *European Journal of Work and Organizational Psychology*, 7 (1): 7–22.

Rogers, J.K. (2000) *Temps: The Many Faces of the Changing Workplace*. Ithaca, NY: Cornell University Press.

Rupp, D.E. and Cropanzano, R. (2002) 'The mediating effects of social exchange relationships in predicting workplace outcomes from multifoci organizational justice', *Organizational Behavior and Human Decision Processes*, 89 (1): 925–946.

Schultz, T.W. (1961) 'Investment in Human Capital', *The American Economic Review*, 1 (1): 1–17.

Segal, L.M. and Sullivan, D.G. (1997) 'The growth of temporary services workers', *Journal of Economic Perspectives*, 11 (2): 117–136.

Selbee, L.K. and Reed, P.B. (2001) *Patterns of Volunteering Over the Life Cycle*. Canadian Social Trends. Statistics Canada. Summer, 11–008.

Sias, P.M., Kramer, M.W. and Jenkins, E. (1997) 'A comparison of the communication behaviors of temporary employees and new hires', *Communication Research*, 24 (6): 731–754.

Silla, I., Gracia, F.J. and Peiró, J.M. (2005) 'Job insecurity and health-related outcomes among different types of temporary workers', *Economic and Industrial Democracy*, 26 (1): 89–117.

Tajfel, H. and Turner, J. (1986) 'The social identity theory of intergroup behavior', in S. Worchel, and W. Austin (eds), *Psychology of Intergroup Relations*. Chicago: Nelson-Hall, pp. 7–24.

Templer, A., Armstrong-Stassen, M., Devine, K. and Solomon, N. (1999) 'Telework and teleworkers', in I.U. Zeytinoglu (ed.) *Changing Work Relationship in Industrialized Economies*. Amsterdam: John Benjamin Publishing, pp. 77–95.

Uzzi, B. and Barsness, Z.I. (1998) 'Contingent employment in British establishments: Organizational determinants of the use of fixed-term hires and part-time workers', *Social Forces*, 76 (3): 967–1007.

Van Breugel, G., Van Olffen, W. and Olie, R. (2005) 'Temporary liaisons: The commitment of "temps" towards their agencies', *Journal of Management Studies*, 42 (3): 539–566.

Van Dyne, L. and Ang, S. (1998) 'Organizational citizenship behavior of contingent workers in Singapore', *Academy of Management Journal*, 41 (6): 692–703.

Virtanen, M., Kivimäki, M., Virtanen, P., Elovainio, M. and Vahtera, J. (2003) 'Disparity in occupational training and career planning between contingent and permanent employees', *European Journal of Work and Organizational Psychology*, 12 (1): 19–36.

von Hipple, C.D. (2006) 'When people would rather switch than fight: Out-group favoritism among temporary employees', *Group Processes and Intergroup Relations*, 9 (4): 533–546.

Wheeler, A.R. and Buckley, M.R. (2000) 'Examining the motivation process of temporary employees: A holistic model and research framework', *Journal of Managerial Psychology*, 16 (5): 339–354.

Wiesenfeld, B.M., Raghuram, S. and Garud, R. (2001) 'Organizational identification among virtual workers: The role of need for affiliation and perceived work-based social support', *Journal of Management*, 27 (2): 213–229.

Zeytinoğlu, I.U. (ed.) (1999) *Changing Work Relationships in Industrialized Economies* Amsterdam: John Benjamin Publishing.

33

Labor Organizations

Anthony R. Yue, E. Kevin Kelloway[1] and Lori Francis[1]

From the standpoint of organizational behavior, labor unions are particularly interesting organizations for at least two reasons. First, unions are organizations in their own right. As such they give rise to a unique context for, and forms of, organizational behavior. Participation in union governance, filing grievances and other forms of union behavior are unique in that they may be voluntary and allow the individual a voice that may be denied in employing organizations. Second, unions are inexorably linked to the workplace and influence multiple forms of organizational behavior in that context. Thus unions attempt to change organizational behavior directly by negotiating provisions that enhance workplace justice and improve working conditions. In doing so, unions create various secondary effects such as a decreased rate of turnover or an increased rate of absence relative to their non-union counterparts. To some extent, and particularly in North America, the pluralistic perspective of unions and the inherent conflict embedded in union-management relations (e.g., Francis and Kelloway, 2005) stands in stark contrast to the unitary perspective (Fox, 1973) that underlies modern approaches to Human Resource Management (Godard, 2004; Kelloway et al., 1998). In this chapter we examine both the unionization process and the consequences of unionization, and pinpoint a number of key areas of future research interest. First, however, we consider the prevalence of unionization.

UNION DENSITY

Unionization is a common feature of workplaces around the world. In the United States, union density in 2005 was 12.5 per cent (US Department of Labor, n.d.) while in Canada over 30 per cent of the workforce belongs to a union (Akyeampong, 2003). In Europe the rates of labor force unionization range rather dramatically from 26.2 per cent in the UK (Online, n.d.) to 74.1 per cent and 78 per cent in Finland and Sweden respectively (Visser, 2006). Outside of the North American and European context, Australia reports union density rates of 22.9 per cent, while Japan's union density rate is approximately 19.7 per cent of the working population (Visser, 2006).

Overall density rates may present a misleading picture because unionization varies by sector. For example, in Canada where the overall rate of unionization is 30.2 per cent, it rises to 72.5 per cent in the public sector (Akyeampong, 2003). In the US, where overall unionization is low and declining, 47 per cent of those who are unionized work in government (US Department of Labor, n.d.).

Union density has fluctuated over time. In the US, the 11.1 per cent decline of labor union density between 1970 and 2003 (Visser, 2006) has been partially attributed to changes in legislation in some states (Godard, 2004), as a result of which dramatic regional geographic differences in union density exist. Outside of the US, Canada, Australia, New Zealand, Japan and the European Union reported substantial declines in union density from 1970–2003 (Visser, 2006). Exceptions to this trend are noted in Finland, Sweden, Denmark, Belgium, and Spain, which all showed a meaningful increase in union density in this time frame (Visser, 2006).

THE UNIONIZATION PROCESS

While unions represent individuals collectively, it is ultimately individuals who join and comprise these labor organizations. To understand the unionization process better thus demands an examination of the critical elements relating to individuals and their intersection with labor unions. Barling et al. (1992) defined unionization not as a single decision but rather as a process that begins long before the individual enters the workforce and continues throughout the span of union involvement. Key events in this process can be placed within five broad categories: pre-joining, joining the union, committing to the union, participating in the union, and leaving the union. We examine each of these in turn.

Pre-joining

A psychological focus, with a strong reliance upon social learning theory (Bandura,

1977), has offered some insight into our understanding of how early in a person's life the precursors of unionization start. Research from this perspective has focused on the predictors of and influences on an individual's general attitudes toward labor unions. Building on the observations that [a] individual attitudes toward unions are relatively stable over time (Getman et al., 1976), [b] there are a wealth of data suggesting that parental work experiences affect children (e.g., Barling, 1990; Kelloway and Harvey, 1999) and [c] children can accurately report on parental job attitudes (Piotrkowski and Stark, 1987), researchers have proposed and tested a model of union attitude formation based on a process of family socialization.

Barling et al. (1991) found that young adults' union attitudes are significantly predicted by their perceptions of their parents' attitudes towards unions. Furthermore, their degree of both Marxist and humanistic work beliefs directly affected young people's union attitudes. These results are strengthened by research illustrating that young people can indeed correctly identify and report their parents' union beliefs (Kelloway and Watts, 1994).

The hypothesized role of family socialization processes on the development of union attitudes has largely been supported by a large body of empirical research (e.g., Hester and Fuller, 1999; Kelloway and Newton, 1996). Consistent with a family socialization model, the links between parental and children's attitudes are stronger when the child identifies with the parent in question (Kelloway et al., 1996). Further, family socialization influences on union attitudes may affect the views of potential managers (Pesek et al., 2006) suggesting that early family influences may impact on subsequent organizational behavior (Kelloway and Harvey, 1999). Perhaps most interestingly, family socialization processes appear to be a more important influence on young workers' union attitudes than their own job attitudes and experiences (Dekker et al., 1998).

Although most of the 'pre-joining' literature has focused on the effects of socialization processes within families on the formation of union attitudes, other investigators have considered a broader conceptualization of social influences. For example, both race and gender appear to affect union attitudes through their impact on economic hardship (Chang, 2003). Further, there is some evidence that personality characteristics influence union attitudes as anti-union attitudes among university students appear to be closely related to authoritarianism (Morand, 1998).

Summary

The available research is consistent with the view that individual attitudes toward unions are formed prior to entry into the workforce. The formation of union attitudes and perceptions of unions appears to be consistent with a model of economic socialization (Kelloway and Harvey, 1999) wherein children progressively acquire attitudes and perceptions through both direct and vicarious experiences of the work environment.

Joining

The question of why individuals join a union is arguably the single most researched topic relating to unions (Barling et al., 1992). Interest in this question stems both from unions who wish to expand their membership and employers who wish to prevent unionization of their workplaces. Acknowledging that many individuals become union members as a consequence of their employment (i.e., mandatory membership under a 'closed shop agreement') most of the research on union joining has focused on the predictors of pro-union voting in a certification election.

Three central models have dominated union joining research; frustration, social context and identity, and rational choice (Buttigieg et al., 2007). In other words, individuals are thought to join unions as a result of dissatisfaction (i.e., frustration), their identification with the union movement (context), or as a result of the perceptions that unionization would be instrumental (rational choice). Although most of the empirical evidence supports the rational choice model (e.g., Charlwood, 2002; Visser, 2002), it is more likely that these models are complementary rather than competing. For example, in her model of pro-union voting, Brett (1980) proposed that unionization is the combined result of job dissatisfaction (i.e., frustration), belief in the value of collective action (identification), and the perception of that joining a union would be instrumental in resolving the dissatisfaction (rational choice). Kelloway et al. (2007) noted the similarity between this view and models of participation in social protest (e.g., Klandermans, 1997, 2002; Opp, 1998).

There is little doubt that all three models are influential in shaping pro-union voting behavior in a certification election. With respect to frustration, a great deal of research confirms the importance of job dissatisfaction (see Barling et al., 1992; Davy and Shipper, 1993; Fiorito and Gallagher, 1986) or, more broadly, negative job attitudes (Friedman et al., 2006) as a trigger for pro-union voting. Perceptions of procedural injustice also predict union joining and union related protest (e.g., Buttigeig et al., 2007; Kelloway et al., 2007).

Regarding social context and identification, Brett (1980) proposed that a belief in collective action predicts union voting. These beliefs are most often operationalized as identification with the union or positive general attitudes toward unions (Kelloway et al., 1997). A distinction between pro- and anti-union attitudes has been made by LaHuis and Mellor (2001) who suggested that that the former are associated with a greater willingness to join the union and the latter with a resistance to union joining.

Hepburn and Barling (2001) examined the interesting and largely-ignored question of abstentions in union certification votes. Arguing that the decision to abstain from voting for or against certification is in itself a behavior of interest, they found that abstainers were generally more neutral in terms of attitudes towards unions and their job satisfaction. On the other hand, those who did vote had a greater belief in the instrumentality of their vote. In a second study, Hepburn and Barling (2001) manipulated, using a vignette design, several variables including voting utility, voting instrumentality, and responsibility to vote. Of particular note, they found that a particular emphasis upon responsibility to vote was related to an increased likelihood of voting rather than abstaining should there be an important issue present (e.g. wages). Thus, emphasizing the responsibility to vote (and thus identification with the union) and emphasizing the issues (i.e. the context of the vote) influenced union voting behaviour.

The perception that a union will be instrumental in resolving job dissatisfactions or injustice is also frequently identified as a predictor of union joining (e.g., Barling et al., 1992; Buttigieg et al. 2007; Charlwood, 2002; Visser, 2002). As a specific example consider the multi-level, vignette based, investigation conducted by Mellor et al. (2003). They found that the perceived costs and benefits of unionization, as well as contextual factors (i.e., whether individuals were asked to vote for or against a union, see also LaHuis and Mellor, 2001), were important predictors of individual voting decisions in a union representation election.

Summary

The empirical evidence is consistent with the view that union joining can be viewed as a form of protest behavior (e.g., Kelloway et al., 2007). Most of the literature on union joining has focused on the predictive role of job attitudes/satisfaction, identification with the union movement, and the perceived instrumentality of unionization. The body of evidence suggests that all three factors play an important role in union joining.

Committing to the union

In an explicit attempt to foster research on union-member relations, Gordon et al. (1980) developed a measure of union commitment. Defined 'as the binding of an individual to an organization' (Gordon et al., 1980: 480), commitment to the union was intended to serve as a criterion for future investigations.

In their classic 1980 study, Gordon et al. uncovered a four factor structure of union commitment comprised of union loyalty, responsibility to the union, willingness to work for the union, and belief in unionism. They found that the best predictor of both union loyalty and belief in unionism was past socialization, whereas past and present union activity correlated most strongly with a sense of responsibility and a willingness to work for the union.

Much of the early research on union commitment focused on the factor structure of the measure (e.g., Fullagar, 1986; Friedman and Harvey, 1986) with research eventually converging on a three factor solution representing union loyalty, responsibility to the union and willingness to work for the union (Kelloway et al., 1992; see also Bayazit et al., 2004).

Although early research on union commitment was largely sidetracked by a predominant focus on measurement issues, data also emerged suggesting the importance of a committed membership for attaining union goals. Thus, commitment surfaced as a predictor of participation in union activities (Kelloway and Barling, 1993), an antecedent of militancy and support for industrial action (Kelloway et al., 1992; Kelloway et al., 2000), and a correlate of strike propensity (Barling et al., 1992; Kelloway et al., 1992; Martin, 1986). Kelloway et al. (2002) found union shop stewards who are committed to and participate in the union are also more likely to take part in industrial action such as strike activities (e.g., picketing).

Research on the predictors of union commitment has largely confirmed Gordon et al.'s (1980) initial observations. Early socialization experience in the union (e.g., Fullagar et al., 1992; Fullagar et al., 1994; Fullagar et al., 1995) and experiences with the union leadership (Fullagar et al., 1994; Kelloway and Barling, 1993) emerge as important predictors of members' commitment to the union.

Moving beyond issues of factor structure, Bamberger et al. (1999) summarized the precursors and consequences of union commitment. They meta-analyzed 15 studies, and then examined four union commitment models (three from the literature, and one representing an integrative model) using structural equation modeling.

Their results supported an integrative model suggesting that both union (i.e., perceptions of instrumentality and union attitudes) and job attitudes (job satisfaction and organizational commitment) contribute to the prediction of union commitment and that these effects are both direct and indirect.

Interestingly, the meta and subsequent SEM analyses showed a weak association between job satisfaction and union commitment, although this observation is tempered by the acknowledgement that the studies included in the meta-analysis, particularly a rather large Japanese sample, may have resulted in mixed constructs being used.

Sjoberg and Sverke (2001) proposed and validated an alternate view of union commitment. They reported that two distinct factors, labeled instrumental and ideological commitment, were temporally stable over an 18 month period within the sample of 1170 unionized Swedish blue collar workers. The stability of separate ideology and instrumentality factors perhaps relates to research on the pre-joining phase regarding how attitudes towards unions and work beliefs are socialized.

To date, research on union-member relations has been largely limited to the notion of member commitment to the union. Although isolated studies have examined members' perceptions of union support (Shore et al., 1994) and psychological involvement in the union (Kelloway et al., 2000), the range of attitudinal measures available to researchers interested in union-member relations remains disappointingly small.

Summary

The publication of Gordon et al.'s (1980) measure of commitment to the union sparked a resurgence of interest in union member relations. Although much of the literature was focused on psychometric issues, commitment emerged as an important predictor of union-relevant criteria such as participation and militancy.

Participating

As voluntary organizations, labor unions are largely dependent on volunteers to take on the day-to-day tasks of running the union and administering the collective agreement. Thus the union's ability to attract and retain such volunteers is critical to its success (Barling et al., 1992). Not surprisingly, researchers have devoted considerable attention to the question of why some individuals choose to participate actively in the union (e.g., Kelloway and Barling, 1993).

Similar to the case with union commitment, early research on participation focused on the nature and measurement of this construct. McShane (1986) originally proposed a scale that purported to identify 'types' of participation. In contrast, Kelloway and Barling (1993) argued that such types did not exist, but were rather an artefact of limited opportunities to participate in some ways (e.g., holding union office), as a result of which participation is best viewed as a unidimensional and cumulative construct. Using a broader, more diverse, set of items, McLean-Parks et al. (1995) later suggested that participation can be conceptualized as administrative, intermittent, or supportive.

With respect to predictors of participation, we have already noted the role of union commitment. A recent longitudinal study of postal workers allows an examination of the temporal nature of the commitment/participation dyad (Fullagar et al., 2004). Using cross lagged regression techniques, the researchers demonstrated that, after controlling for the relationship between measures of union commitment across time, commitment emerges as a strong predictor of union participation, even after a 10 year time span. Likely of greater interest was the finding that union participation at time one was not predictive of such participation at time two 10 years hence, suggesting that that early union participation does not shape later behaviors of the same.

Redman and Snape (2004) explored the differences between affective and instrumental union commitment on the intent to participate in union activities in a sample of firefighters. The affective component of union commitment emerged as the main determinant of the intent to stand for union office, the intent to participate in rank-and-file activities, and the intent to engage in militant activities.

With the gender composition of workplaces changing over recent decades, an interest in how women participate in union activities has informed a number of studies (e.g., Mellor et al., 1994). Mellor (1995) studied how gender composition and representation impact women's participation in union activities and in office. Gender moderated the relationship between gender composition and participation. In union locals with higher female representation, female respondents reported both a higher competence level and greater opportunity to participate in local activities. This relationship was correspondingly non-significant for men.

Extending the work on women's union participation, Bulger and Mellor (1997) showed that union self-efficacy mediates the relationship between women's sense of union barriers and their participation in union activities. As the relationship was specific to union rather than community or family-based barriers, the researchers suggested that union barriers to participation primarily affect women with lower levels of union self-efficacy. In other words, women with a high sense of union self-efficacy participate in union activities regardless of the barriers to doing so. Given that women's participation is crucial to moving a union agenda towards greater consideration of women's needs, these findings point to the need to train women as a means to overcome low union self-efficacy.

Summary

Union participation is often viewed as a measure of union democracy and a reflection of members' support for the union. Union commitment has emerged as an important predictor of participation in the union and the

issue of women's participation in the union has been a focus of concern.

Leaving

Just as individuals may commit to a union, they may also choose to leave the labor organization (Klandermans, 1986). One can hypothesize that there are at least three ways in which a member can leave the union. In jurisdictions that allow for mandatory union membership (i.e., 'a closed shop'), individuals do not have the choice to leave and the only form of withdrawal from the union possible is to disengage and not be involved in union activities (see, for example, Kelloway and Barling, 1993). In the absence of closed shop provisions that mandate union membership, members may simply leave the union. To the extent that individuals can leave the union and maintain the benefits of union membership, instrumentality concerns may favor such a strategy. At the extreme, and even where closed shop provisions exist, the members of the union may vote to decertify in favor of another union or a lack of collective representation.

At the individual level, leaving the union has been considered in the limited literature on the process of leaving as the opposite of the joining process. Buttigieg et al. (2007) examined and refuted this construction of the leaving process using longitudinal data. They tracked the union membership and employment status of anonymous subjects over a five year period using data collected by an Australian organization. As a result of their analysis, the researchers challenged our conventional understanding of the process of leaving a union. They found that the presence of a union representative decreased the chance of an individual leaving the union by almost 50 per cent, and the more individualistic the workers, the more likely they were to leave the labor organization. Buttigieg et al. (2007) conclude that the decision to leave the union is influenced by different factors than those related to the decision to joining the union. A conclusion that was echoed by Friedman et al. (2006).

Summary

The available research suggests that union leaving is primarily associated with the ability of the union to address the individual concerns of the member. Thus, contrary to traditional treatment, the factors involved in one's decision to leave the union are more than the antithesis of those that predict union joining.

CONSEQUENCES OF UNIONIZATION

A primary reason to study unionization is that becoming involved in union activities has widespread implications for individuals, their organizations, and third parties. In this section we will first examine some of the consequences of unionization for individuals. We follow this with some discussion of broader organizational consequences of unionization, and finally consider how third parties are affected by labor organizations.

Effects of unionization on individuals

Industrial relations stress

Conflict, change (Bluen and Barling, 1988; Fried, 1993) and perceptions of injustice (Francis and Kelloway, 2005) are central dynamics of industrial relations. As such, it is not surprising that the practice of industrial relations is inherently stressful and adverse individual consequences have been associated with union membership (Shirom and Kirmeyer, 1988), union participation (Kelloway and Barling, 1994; Nandram and Klandermans, 1993), the assumption of leadership roles within the union (e.g., shop stewards, Martin and Berthiaume, 1993), participating in strikes (e.g., Barling and Milligan, 1987), and engaging in collective bargaining (e.g., Bluen and Jubiler-Lurie, 1990).

The stress-related adverse consequences of industrial relations practice include increased blood pressure (Bluen and Jubiler-Lurie, 1990), psychological indices of strain such as increased reports of anxiety and decreased psychological well-being (Bluen and Jubiler-Lurie, 1990), emotional exhaustion (Nandram

and Klandermans, 1993), and decreased job satisfaction (Kelloway et al., 1993). Acute stressors such as strikes and lockouts have been associated with short and long term stress responses such as withdrawal, exhaustion, psychological distress, decreased perceptions of health, and decreased general functioning (MacBride et al., 1981; Milburn et al., 1983). Moreover, strain resulting from strike participation does not necessarily end with the end of the strike (Barling and Milligan, 1987). Rather, symptoms such as psychological distress and psychosomatic complaints may persist up to six months following the strike in cases where there dispute was not settled at the end of the strike.

We would be remiss to focus on the occurrence of industrial relations stress without noting the potential for unionization to mitigate these, and other, organizational stressors. For instance, social support from the union is an important moderator of the relationship between exposure to industrial relations stressors and reports of stress and strain (Bluen and Edelstein, 1993; Bluen and Jubiler-Lurie, 1990; Fried and Tiegs, 1993). Such support could come from shop stewards (e.g., Fried and Tiegs, 1993) or from the union itself (Shore et al., 1994). For example, miners who witnessed a workplace disaster and who perceived their union as supportive of their emotional responses reported less psychological distress than did those who did not see the union as supportive (Bluen and Edelstein, 1993).

Industrial relations violence

With an increased interest in the phenomenon of workplace violence (Kelloway et al., 2006), there has been a renewed focus on the intersection of violence and industrial relations. Picket line violence in particular has been a key area of inquiry. This particular interest is not especially new in that there have been detailed reviews and case analyses of historical events of violence on the picket line (e.g. Baker, 2002; Snyder and Kelly, 1976).

Picket line violence has been defined as the 'non-privileged physical interference with the person or property of another, or the threat, expressed or implied, of such interference' (Thieblot and Haggard, 1983: 14). Thus, picket line violence includes both *physical* altercations as well as *psychologically* aggressive acts (e.g., threats and intimidation). There are also other dimensions along which picket line violence can be classified. It may be categorized as either *confrontational* (i.e. arising at the spur of the moment) or *purposeful* (i.e. deliberate and instrumental) in nature (Francis et al., 2006). Additionally, one must consider the target of the violence. Using data from the National Institute for Labor Relations Research (NILRR) in the United States, Francis et al. (2006) showed that 30 per cent of the strike related violence is directed at the *organization*, while 43 per cent of incidents involve *interpersonal* attacks. Although data are lacking, the literature on workplace violence suggests that violence from, or among, coworkers is extraordinarily rare (Schat et al., 2006) and has more direct effects on individual wellbeing than does violence from members of the public (LeBlanc and Kelloway, 2002). These observations highlight the need to understand, and prevent, picket line violence.

Although violence against coworkers is generally rare, violence is prevalent on picket lines. Based on National Institute for Labor Relations Research data, Thieblot et al. (1999) estimated that the annual average number of incidents of union and strike-related violence in the US was 432/year for the period from 1975 to 1995. Given the decrease in union density in general, and strike activity in particular, the data reported by Thieblot et al. (1999) reflects an increase in violent events on a per strike basis. Using the approach of surveying individuals who cross the picket line, Stennett-Brewer (1997) found that exposure to picket line violence is quite common. For example, 100 per cent of picket line crossers reported that they experienced verbal assaults, 40 per cent indicated that their vehicles were damaged and 11 per cent had gunshots fired at their vehicle or their property.

One of the most interesting features of violence associated with picketing relative to other types of workplace aggression and

violence is that it may acquire an aura of legitimacy attributable to the context. That is, many would suggest that aggression and violence are 'part and parcel' of picketing (Thieblot et al., 1999). The negotiation of back-to-work agreements that indemnify individuals who had committed violent or illegal acts during a strike is a common occurrence and legislation seems to be ineffective in dealing with the issue (Thieblot et al., 1999).

Most of the existing research has focused on violence that is perpetrated by the union members who are on strike against various parties (Francis et al., 2006). However, such members may be the targets of violence as well. A principal role of the picket line is to inhibit access to the workplace and both customers and other employees at times force their way across the picket line (e.g., by speeding toward the picket line in an automobile). In this sense, picket line violence may well be both an expression, and a cause, of the intense stress that is experienced by all parties in a strike.

Effects of unionization on organizational behavior

There is little doubt that unionization has been associated with a host of effects on organizational behavior (Freeman and Medoff, 1984). Kochan (1980, see also Barling et al., 1992) proposed a model in which unions were expected to have both primary and secondary effects in the workplace. Primary effects refer to the gains at the bargaining table (e.g., increased wages, benefits, changes in working conditions) achieved by the union, while secondary effects emerge indirectly as both unions and employers respond and react to these primary changes.

Primary effects

Perhaps the most obvious and well documented effect of unionization is the increase in wages and benefits that comes with unionization. The wage premium attributable to unionization can be substantial. For example, 2005 Canadian data suggest an average wage of $22.66/hour for unionized and $19.13 for non-unionized employees. As a result of wage differentials and increased work hours, unionized part-time workers earn almost double that earned by their non-unionized counterparts (Anonymous, 2006). The union wage effect extends to virtually all aspects of compensation (Dwayne et al., 2002) including fringe benefits and pension plans. Union members are more likely than are non-members to have pension plans, health plans and a variety of other fringe benefits (Marshall, 2003). Premium differentials are most likely when union bargaining coverage is high and unions are able to exert a monopolistic effect (e.g., Forth and Milward, 2002). Although increased wages may be associated with more adversarial relations with management (Bryson, 2005) they do contribute to members' satisfaction with union representation (Currall et al., 2005), and appear to be unrelated to the decline in unionization rates in the U.S. (Belman and Voos, 2006).

In addition to compensation rates, unionization also has an impact on compensation policy in the workplace (and see the Chapter by Bloom in this volume). Historically, unions prefer salary structures based on job classification and seniority (Barling et al., 1992) and oppose salary structures based on individual performance (e.g., Hanley and Nguyen, 2005). Despite this opposition, Mericle and Kim (1999) provided evidence that it was possible to transition to skill-based pay schemes in unionized environments and that such schemes need not be inconsistent with the principle of seniority that is enshrined in virtually all union contracts (Gordon and Johnson, 1982).

Unions also directly bargain for improvements in working conditions, including a specific focus on improving health and safety (Kelloway, 2003). Although there is little doubt that unions and management engage in adversarial collective bargaining around issues of safety (e.g., Gray et al., 1998) there is scant evidence that safety issues are used as bargaining weapons (Hebdon and Hyatt, 1998). Moreover, there is also considerable evidence that unions collaborate with management to promote health and safety in the workplace, leading Kelloway (2003) to describe the union-management relation as one of conflict and cooperation around issues of health and safety.

Secondary effects

Unionization has also been credited with a host of secondary effects on variables central to the study of organizational behavior. As Barling et al. (1992) noted, these effects are not a direct result of negotiations but, rather, emerge from the efforts of management and union members to accommodate the provisions of the collective agreement.

One of the most paradoxical secondary effects of unionization has been the observation that union members are more dissatisfied with their jobs than non-union members, but are concurrently more likely to indicate that they intend to stay with their present employer (Guest and Conway, 2004; Hammer and Avgar, 2005). This phenomenon likely results from the voice that unions provide for their members. That is, unions provide members with the potential to voice their dissatisfaction rather than to quit (Abraham et al., 2005; Guest and Conway, 2004; Iverson and Currivan, 2003).

Although the paradoxical effects of union membership on organizational behavior have been well documented, methodological difficulties limit the interpretability of the available data. The paradigm for 'union effects' research (e.g., the effect of unionization on wages, on safety, or on organizational attitudes, see Barling et al., 1992; Freeman and Medoff, 1984) usually comprises analyses conducted at the organizational level using archival data bases – most frequently large, nationally representative survey samples. With such an approach, individual differences are frequently confounded with organizational differences.

There are several empirical examples where teasing apart individual versus organizational differences have altered conclusions about union effects on organizational behavior. For instance, in an initial analysis Gordon and DeNisi (1995) showed that unionized workers were more dissatisfied with their job than were non-unionized workers, a result in keeping with the literature (for a review see Barling et al., 1992). However, they illustrated that this finding may be an artifact of the 'union effects' paradigm. When they examined union-nonunion differences within a workplace, the differences in job satisfaction disappeared. Similarly, after implementing statistical controls for endogeneity, Bryson et al. (2004) found that the initial relationship between unionization and job dissatisfaction disappeared. In a similar vein, Renaud (2002) observed that when statistically controlling for job quality, as unionized workers often work in lower quality jobs, the association between unionization and job dissatisfaction disappeared. It would appear, therefore, that the relationships among unionization, job satisfaction and turnover are complex.

The complexity of union effects is also illustrated when considering the relationship between unionization and absenteeism. Unionization is generally associated with greater absenteeism, presumably as a result of negotiating for paid sick leave (Barling et al., 1992). However, some recent research paints a more complex picture. Deery et al. (1999) found that the union-management climate moderates the relationship between unionization and absenteeism. That is, union members are more motivated to help the firm by reducing absenteeism when the union-management climate is positive than when it is negative (see also Deery and Iverson, 2005). Iverson et al. (2003) replicated these results and suggested that homogeneity in union member status within organizations may lead to a lowered absence culture. Thus, while much of the earlier research focused on unionization as the independent variable, more recent investigations suggest that the quality of union-management relations is critical to determining the nature and extent of any secondary effects of unionization.

Effects on third parties

The relationship between union members and the firm are far from isolated. Workers and managers are family members and part of their communities. The firms' representatives interact with suppliers and customers, and perhaps the media as well. In short there are likely many complex interactions between players in an industrial relations setting and other third parties. This has been a recent and growing area of interest in the literature concerning labor organizations.

Postulating a so called 'anger effect,' Block and Silver (2002) used surveys to gauge the effects of both the 1998 General Motors and Northwest Airlines strikes upon potential retail customers. Their descriptive statistical findings point to a persistent, negative intent to purchase based upon the strike action. The researchers suggest that the more commoditized the goods or services in question are the more distinctly possible such substitution on the part of the consumer becomes.

Day et al. (2006) considered the relationship between a threat of a labor disruption and individual experience of strain in relevant third parties (see also Amos et al., 1993; Grayson, 1999). Using a sample of students faced with the threat of a faculty strike against the university administration, they found that students who would be more affected by the potential strike action reported higher strain and a decreased sense of control. Interestingly, having more information regarding the dispute increased perceived control among the students (and see the chapter by Jex for a discussion of stress and perceived control). Perceived control in turn moderated the relationship between disruptions and strain.

Taking another approach, Kelloway et al. (in press) examined the predictors of third party support for strike action. Noting that third party support can be a critical determinant of the outcome of a labor dispute (Leung et al., 1993), they examined third party reactions and willingness to support the union in two widely-publicized strike actions. In both cases, individual attitudes toward unions and perceptions that the unions were being offered a distributively unfair contract emerged as predictors of willingness to support the union.

Future research directions

In his seminal review of the literature on union participation, Spinrad (1960) described the period from 1945 to 1960 as a 'Golden Age' of research on union governance. Perhaps fueled by a Cold War ideology that placed a premium on democratic procedures, a great deal of research accumulated on the nature and predictors of participation in union activities and, by extension, union governance. To some extent, Gordon et al.'s (1980) development of a criterion for union commitment met its stated goal of sparking a resurgence of interest in union-member relations and research on union commitment and union participation proliferated. While it would be overstating the case to claim that behavioral research on unionization is 'dead,' the intensity of the research effort does seem to have declined as we entered the new century.

In anticipating future research directions, we begin by looking backwards to identify some of the gaps that were left unexplored by research in the 1980s. In taking up the challenge laid down by Gordon et al., union researchers devoted a great deal of effort in exploring the dimensions, predictors and outcomes of union commitment. In doing so, however, they perpetuated a limited focus of research. Despite sporadic attempts to expand the repertoire of union attitudes available for research (e.g., union support, Shore et al., 1994) or union involvement (Kelloway et al., 2000), these efforts did not spark the same level of interest as did the development of a union commitment measure.

One potential reason for this sole focus was the early association between union commitment and members' participation in the union. The identification of participation as an important and valued criterion in the study of union-member relations gave impetus to behavioral research. It did so at the cost of limiting research to a sole focus. Indeed it is notable that Bamberger et al. (1999) identified only participation as a consequence of union commitment.

We suggest that any attempt to re-invigorate the study of union-member relations needs to move beyond studying these two variables. While recognizing the important contributions that have emerged from the commitment-participation line of research we note that there are a host of other issues that can be addressed in studying union-member relations. For example, beyond behavioral participation there are questions about militancy and members' support for union positions that are of interest. In jurisdictions where unions play an active political role, the translation of union support into political attitudes is of key interest.

Similarly, researchers could profitably move beyond the study of union member relations to examine third party attitudes. Unions, particularly in the public sector, rely on third party support to influence the outcomes of collective bargaining and strike activity (Kelloway et al., under review). How such support is obtained and used in the bargaining process is a critical issue for unions.

The decline of unionization, particularly in the United States, has undoubtedly influenced the rate at which behavioral research on unions is produced. However, claims that the union movement is 'over' have been around for most of the past century and unions are actively working to change public attitudes toward organized labour and to become more attractive to potential union members (e.g., Kelloway et al., 1998). The effectiveness of these strategies and the identification of key influences on attitudes toward unions would seem to be a natural extension of extant research on the unionization process.

Finally, we suggest that researchers need to expand their focus when conducting research on the collective bargaining process. Studies of grievance activity, strikes, and other industrial relations events have tended to focus exclusively on the impact on union members. While not denying the importance of this focus, we note that there are also other individuals that may be affected by industrial relations events and processes. Effects on customers, clients, third parties and managers all offer profitable lines of enquiry. Expanding the research focus in this way may bridge the gap between 'union' research and research in organizational behavior.

CONCLUSION

We are now beginning to understand the influence of organized labor on members, the firm, and upon third parties, but many issues remain to be explored. In this chapter we reviewed two lines of research. First, we considered the process of becoming attached to organized labor (Barling et al., 1992). In this view, unionization begins prior to the decision to join a union and continues through committing and participating until, ultimately, the individual makes a decision to retain membership or to leave the union. In this view, the union is an organization that gives rise to forms of organized behavior – some of these parallel behaviors found in employing organizations, while other are unique to the nature of labor unions.

Second, we examined the influence of unionization, the individual, the organization, and relevant third parties. The union influences both organizational behavior and those behaviors that occur in other domains. Although early research focused on documenting the existence of and describing these 'union effects' on organizational behavior and attitudes, more recent investigations have focused on the mechanisms through which unionization affects individual and organizational outcomes.

Whether viewed as organizations in and of themselves, or as influences on more traditional organizational variables, we suggest that the study of unions has much to contribute to the field of organizational behavior. We view it as unfortunate that a great deal of union research occurs outside of the mainstream of organizational behavior (i.e., in labor economics, labor studies or industrial relations) and advocate a greater integration of union issues into mainstream organizational behavior research.

NOTE

1 Preparation of this manuscript was supported by grants from the Social Sciences and Humanities Research Council of Canada to the 2nd and 3rd authors.

REFERENCES

Abraham, S.E., Friedman, B.A. and Thomas, R.K. (2005) 'The impact of unions on intent to leave: Additional evidence on the voice face of unions', *Employee Responsibilities and Rights Journal*, 17: 201–213.

Amos, M., Day, V. and Power, E. (1993) 'Students' reactions to a faculty strike', *Canadian Journal of Higher Education*, 26: 86–103.

Anonymous (2006) 'Unionization', *Perspectives on Labor and Income*, 18: 64–70.

Appleton, W.C. and Baker, J.G. (1984) 'The effect of unionization on safety in bituminous coal mines', *Journal of Labour Research*, 5: 139–147.

Akyeampong, E. B. (2003) 'Fact sheet on unionization', *Perspectives on Labor and Income*, 47 (7): 2–25.

Baker, D. (2002) '"You dirty bastards, are you fair dinkum?" Police and union confrontation on the wharf', *New Zealand Journal of Industrial Relations*, 27: 33–47.

Bamberger, P.A., Kluger, A.N. and Suchard, R. (1999) 'The antecedents and consequences of union commitment: A meta-analysis', *Academy of Management Journal*, 42 (3): 304–318.

Bandura, A. (1977) *Social Learning Theory*. Englewood Cliffs, NJ: Prentice-Hall.

Barling, J. (1988) 'Industrial relations–a "blind spot" in the teaching, research and practice of industrial/organizational psychology', *Canadian Psychology*, 29: 103–108.

Barling, J. (1990) *Employment Stress and Family Functioning*. Chichester: John Wiley and Sons.

Barling, J. and Milligan, J. (1987) 'Some psychological consequences of striking: A six month, longitudinal study', *Journal of Occupational Behavior*, 8: 127–138.

Barling, J., Fullagar, C. and Kelloway, E.K. (1992) *The Union and Its Members: A Psychological Approach*. New York: Oxford University Press.

Barling, J., Fullagar, C., Kelloway, E.K. and McElvie, L. (1992) 'Union loyalty and strike propensity', *Journal of Social Psychology*, 132: 581–590.

Barling, J., Kelloway, E.K. and Bremermann, E.H. (1991) 'Preemployment predictors of union attitudes: The role of family socialization and work beliefs', *Journal of Applied Psychology*, 76 (5): 725–731.

Bayazit, M., Hammer, T.H. and Wazeter, D.L. (2004) 'Methodological challenges in union commitment studies', *Journal of Applied Psychology*, 89 (4): 738–747.

Belman, D. and Voos, P.B. (2006) 'Union wages and union decline: Evidence from the construction industry', *Industrial and Labor Relations Review*, 60: 67–87.

Block, R.N. and Silver, B.D. (2002) *Post-strike Effects of Labor Conflict on Retail Consumers: Preliminary Evidence from the 1998 Northwest Airlines and General Motors Strikes.* Report for Institute for Public Policy and Social Research, Michigan State University.

Bluen, S.D. and Barling, J. (1988) 'Psychological Stressors Associated with Industrial Relations', in C.L. Cooper and R. Payne (eds), *Causes, Coping and Consequences of Stress at Work.* Chichester: John Wiley and Sons, pp. 175–205.

Bluen, S.D. and Edelstein, I. (1993) 'Trade union support following an underground explosion', *Journal of Organizational Behavior*, 14: 473–480.

Bluen, S.D. and Jubiler-Lurie, V.G. (1990) 'Some consequences of labor-management negotiations: Laboratory and field studies', *Journal of Organizational Behavior*, 11: 105–118.

Bluen, S.D. and Van Zwam, C. (1987) 'Trade union membership and job satisfaction', *South African Journal of Psychology*, 17: 160–164.

Brett, J.M. (1980) 'Why employees want unions', *Organizational Dynamics*, 8: 47–59.

Bryson, A. (2005) 'Union effects on employee relations in Britain', *Human Relations*, 58: 1111–1140.

Bryson, A., Cappellari, L. and Lucifora, C. (2004) 'Does union membership really reduce job satisfaction?', *British Journal of Industrial Relations*, 42 (3): 439–459.

Bulger, C.A. and Mellor, S. (1997) 'Self-efficacy as a mediator of the relationship between perceived union barriers and women's participation in union activities', *Journal of Applied Psychology*, 82 (6): 935–944.

Buttigieg, D.M., Deery, S.J. and Iverson, R.D. (2007) 'An event history analysis of union joining and leaving', *Journal of Applied Psychology*, 92 (3): 829–839.

Chang, T.F.H. (2003) 'A structural model of race, gender, class, and attitudes toward labor unions', *Social Science Journal*, 40 (2): 189–200.

Charlwood, A. (2002) 'Why do non-union employees want to unionize? Evidence from Britain', *British Journal of Industrial Relations*, 40: 463–491.

Currall, S.C., Towler, A.J., Judge, T.A. and Kohn, L. (2005) 'Pay satisfaction and organizational outcomes', *Personnel Psychology*, 58: 613–651.

Davy, J.A. and Shipper, F. (1993) 'Voter behavior in union certification elections: A longitudinal study', *Academy of Management Journal*, 36 (1): 187–199.

Day, A.L., Stinson, V., Catano, V.M. and Kelloway, E.K. (2006) 'Third-party attitudes and strain reactions to the threat of a labor strike', *Journal of Occupational Health Psychology*, 11 (1): 3–13.

Deery S.J., Erwin, P.J. and Iverson, R.D. (1999) 'Industrial relations climate, attendance behaviour and the role of trade unions', *British Journal of Industrial Relations*, 37 (4): 533–558.

Deery, S.J. and Iverson, R.D. (2005) 'Labor-management cooperation: Antecedents and impact on organizational performance', *Industrial and Labor Relations Review*, 58: 588.

Dekker, I., Greenberg, L. and Barling, J. (1998) 'Predicting union attitudes in student part-time workers', *Canadian Journal of Behavioural Science*, 30 (1): 49–55.

Dwayne, B., Gudnerson, M. and Riddell, C. (2002) *Labour Market Economics.* Toronto: McGraw-Hill Ryerson.

Fiorito, J. and Gallagher, D.G. (1986) 'Job content, job status, and unionism', in D.B. Lipsky and D. Lewin (eds), *Advances in Industrial and Labor Relations.* Greenwich, CT: JAI Press. Vol. 3, pp. 261–316.

Forth, J. and Millward, N. (2002) 'Union effects on pay levels in Britain', *Labour Economics*, 9: 547–561.

Fox, A. (1973) 'Industrial relations: A social critique of pluralist ideology', in J. Child (ed.), *Man and Organization.* London: Allen and Unwin, pp. 185–231.

Francis, L., Cameron, J.E. and Kelloway, E.K. (2006) 'Crossing the line: Violence on the picket line', in E.K. Kelloway, J. Barling, and J.J. Hurrell, Jr. (eds), *Handbook of Workplace Violence.* Thousand Oaks, CA: Sage, pp. 231–260.

Francis, L. and Kelloway, E.K. (2005) 'Industrial relations', in J. Barling, E.K. Kelloway and M.R. Frone (eds), *Handbook of Work Stress.* Thousand Oaks, CA: Sage, pp. 325–352.

Freeman, R.B. and Medoff, J.L. (1984) *What Do Unions Do?.* New York: Basic Books.

Fried, Y. (1993) 'Integrating domains of work stress and industrial relations: Introduction and overview', *Journal of Organizational Behavior*, 14: 397–399.

Fried, Y. and Tiegs, R.B. (1993) 'The main effect model versus the buffering model of shop steward social support: A study of rank-and-file auto worker in the U.S.A.' *Journal of Organizational Behavior*, 14: 481–493.

Friedman, B.A., Abraham, S.E. and Thomas, R.K. (2006) 'Factors related to employees' desire to join and leave unions', *Industrial Relations*, 45: 102–110.

Friedman, L. and Harvey, R.J. (1986) 'Factors of union commitment: The case for lower dimensionality', *Journal of Applied Psychology*, 71: 371–376.

Fullagar, C. (1986) 'A factor analytic study on the validity of a union commitment scale', *Journal of Applied Psychology*, 71: 129–137.

Fullagar, C., McCoy, D. and Shull, C. (1992) 'The socialization of union loyalty', *Journal of Organizational Behavior*, 13 (1): 13–26.

Fullagar, C., Clark, P., Gallagher, D. and Gordon, M.E. (1994) 'A model of the antecedents of early union commitment: The role of socialization experiences and steward characteristics', *Journal of Organizational Behavior*, 15 (6): 517–533.

Fullagar, C.J., Gallagher, D.G., Clark, P.F. and Carroll, A.E. (2004) 'Union commitment and participation: A 10-year longitudinal study', *Journal of Applied Psychology*, 89 (4): 730–737.

Fullagar, C.J.A., Gallagher, D.G., Gordon, M.E.E. and Clark, P.F. (1995) 'Impact of early socialization on union commitment and participation: A longitudinal study', *Journal of Applied Psychology*, 80 (1): 147–157.

Getman, J.G., Goldberg, S.B. and Herman, J.B. (1976) *Union Representation Elections: Law and Reality*, New York: Russell Sage.

Godard, J. (2004) 'A critical assessment of the high-performance paradigm', *British Journal of Industrial Relations*, 42 (2): 349–378.

Gordon, M.E. and DeNisi, A.S. (1995) 'A re-examination of the relationship between union membership and job satisfaction', *Industrial and Labor Relations Review*, 48: 222.

Gordon, M.E. and Johnson, W.A. (1982) 'Seniority: A review of its legal and scientific standing', *Personnel Psychology*, 35: 255–280.

Gordon, M.E., Philpot, J.W., Burt, R.E., Thompson, C.A. and Spiller, W.E. (1980) 'Commitment to the union: Development of a measure and an examination of its correlates', *Journal of Applied Psychology*, 64 (4): 479–499.

Gray, G.R., Myers, D.W. and Myers, P.S. (1998) 'Collective bargaining agreements: Safety and health provisions', *Monthly Labor Review*, (May): 13–35.

Grayson, J. P. (1999) 'Student hardship and support for a faculty strike', *Research in Higher Education*, 40: 589–611.

Guest, D.E. and Conway, N. (2004) 'Exploring the paradox of unionized workers' dissatisfaction', *Industrial Relations Journal*, 35:102–121.

Hackett, R.D. (1989) 'Work attitudes and employee absenteeism: A synthesis of the literature', *Journal of Occupational Psychology*, 62: 235–248.

Hammer, T.H. and Avgar, A. (2005) 'The impact of unions on job satisfaction, organizational commitment and turnover', *Journal of Labor Research*, 26: 241–266.

Hanley, G. and Nguyen, L. (2005) 'Right on the money: What do Australian unions think of performance related pay?', *Employee Relations*, 27: 141–160.

Hebdon, R. and Hyatt, D. (1998) 'The effects of industrial relations factors on health and safety conflict', *Industrial and Labor Relations Review*, 51: 579–593.

Hepburn, C.G. and Barling, J. (2001) 'To vote or not to vote: Abstaining from voting in union representation elections', *Journal of Organizational Behavior*, 22 (5): 569–591.

Hester, K. and Fuller, J.B. (1999) 'An extension of the family socialization model of union attitudes', *Journal of Social Psychology*, 139: 396–398.

Iverson, R.D., Buttigieg, D. and Maguire, C. (2003) 'Absence culture, the effects of union member status and union management climate', *Relations Industrielles*, 58: 483.

Iverson, R. D. and Currivan, D. B. (2003) 'Union participation, job satisfaction, and employee turnover: An event history analysis of the exit-voice hypothesis', *Industrial Relations*, 42: 101–105.

Kelloway, E.K. (2003) 'Labor unions and safety: Conflict and cooperation', in J. Barling and M. Frone (eds), *Psychology of Occupational Safety*. Washington, DC: APA Books, pp. 249–264.

Kelloway, E.K. and Barling, J. (1993) 'Members' participation in local union activities: Measurement, prediction, and replication', *Journal of Applied Psychology*, 78 (2): 262–279.

Kelloway, E.K. and Barling, J. (1994) 'Industrial relations stress and union activism: Costs and benefits of participation', *Proceedings of the 46th Annual Meeting of the Industrial Relations Research Association*. Boston, MA, pp. 442–451.

Kelloway, E.K., Barling, J. and Agar, S. (1996) 'Pre-employment predictors of union attitudes: The moderating role of parental identification', *Journal of Social Psychology*, 136: 413–415.

Kelloway, E.K., Barling, J. and Catano, V.M. (1997) 'Union attitudes as a perceptual filter', in M. Sverke (ed.), *The Future of Trade Unionism: International Perspectives on Emerging Union Structures*. London: Avebury, pp. 225–234.

Kelloway, E.K., Barling, J. and Harvey, S. (1998) 'Changing employment relations: What can unions do?', *Canadian Psychology*, 39: 124–132.

Kelloway, E.K., Barling, J. and Hurrell, J.J. (eds) (2006) *Handbook of Workplace Violence*. Thousand Oaks, CA: SAGE Publications.

Kelloway, E.K., Barling, J. and Shah, A. (1993) Industrial relations stress and job satisfaction: Concurrent effects and mediation', *Journal of Organizational Behavior*, 14: 447–457.

Kelloway, E.K., Catano, V.M. and Carroll, A.E. (2000) 'Psychological involvement in the union', *Canadian Journal of Behavioural Science*, 32 (3): 163–167.

Kelloway, E.K., Catano, V.M. and Southwell, R.R. (1992) 'The construct validity of union commitment: Development and dimensionality of a shorter scale', *Journal of Occupational and Organizational Psychology*, 65: 197–211.

Kelloway, E.K., Francis, L., Catano, V.M. and Dupre, K. (in press) 'Third party support for strike action', *Journal of Applied Psychology*.

Kelloway, E.K., Francis, L., Catano, V.M. and Teed, M. (2007) 'Predicting protest', *Basic and Applied Social Psychology*. 29: 13–22.

Kelloway, E.K., Francis, L. and Montgomery (2006) *Management of Occupational Health and Safety*, 3rd edn. Toronto, ON: Nelson.

Kelloway, E.K. and Harvey, S. (1999) 'Learning to Work', in J. Barling and E.K. Kelloway (eds), *Young Workers: Varieties of Experience*. Washington, DC: APA Books, pp. 37–57.

Kelloway, E.K. and Newton, T. (1996) 'Preemployment predictors of union attitudes: The effects of parental union and work experiences', *Canadian Journal of Behavioural Science*, 28 (2): 113–120.

Kelloway, E.K. and Watts, L. (1994) 'Preemployment predictors of union attitides: Replication and extension', *Journal of Applied psychology*, 79 (4): 631–634.

Klandermans, B. (1986) 'Psychology and trade union participation: Joining, acting, quitting', *Journal of Occupational Psychology*, 59: 189–204.

Klandermans, B. (1997) *The Social Psychology of Protest*. Oxford: Blackwell.

Klandermans, B. (2002) 'How group identification helps to overcome the dilemma of collective action', *The American Behavioral Scientist*, 45: 887–900.

Kochan, T.A. (1980) *Collective Bargaining and Industrial Relations: From Theory to Policy and Practice*. Homewood, IL: Richard D. Irwin.

LeBlanc, M. and Kelloway, E.K. (2002) 'Predictors and outcomes of workplace violence and aggression', *Journal of Applied Psychology*, 87: 444–453.

LaHuis, D.M. and Mellor, S. (2001) 'Antiunion and prounion attitudes as predictors of college students' willingness to join a union', *Journal of Psychology*, 135 (6): 661–681.

Leung, K., Chiu, W. and Au, Y. (1993) 'Sympathy and support for industrial actions: A justice analysis', *Journal of Applied Psychology*, 78: 781–787.

MacBride, A., Lancee, W. and Freeman, S.J.J. (1981) 'The psychosocial impact of a labor dispute', *Journal of Occupational Psychology*, 54: 125–133.

McLean-Parks, J., Gallagher, D.G. and Fullagar, C.J.A. (1995) 'Operationalizing the outcomes of union commitment: The dimensionality of participation', *Journal of Organizational Behavior*, 16: 533–555.

McShane, S.L. (1986) 'A path analysis of participation in union administration', *Industrial Relations*, 25: 72–80.

Marshall, K. (2003) 'Benefits of the job', *Perspectives on Labour and Income*, 4 (5): 5–12.

Martin, J.E. (1986) 'Predictors of individual propensity to strike', *Industrial and Labor Relations Review*, 39: 214–227.

Martin, J.E. and Berthiaume, R.D. (1993) 'Stress and the union steward's role', *Journal of Organizational Behavior*, 14: 433–466.

Mellor, S. (1995) 'Gender composition and gender representation in local unions: Relationships between women's participation in local office and women's participation in local activities', *Journal of Applied Psychology*, 80 (6): 706–720.

Mellor, S., Holzworth, R.J. and Conway, J.M. (2003) 'Individual unionization decisions: A multilevel model of cost-benefit influences', *Experimental Psychology*, 50 (2): 142–154.

Mellor, S., Mathieu, J.E. and Swim, J.K. (1994) 'Cross-level analysis of the influence of local union structure on women's and men's union commitment', *Journal of Applied Psychology*, 79 (2): 203–210.

Mericle, K. and Kim, D. (1999) 'From job-based pay to skill-based pay in unionized establishments: A three-plant comparative analysis', *Relations Industrielles*, 54 (3): 549–580.

Milburn, T.W., Schuler, R.S. and Watman, K.H. (1983) 'Organizational crisis. Part II: Strategies and responses', *Human Relations*, 36: 1161–1180.

Morand, D.A. (1998) 'Exploring the relationship between authoritarianism and attitudes toward unions', *Journal of Business and Psychology*, 12 (3): 343–353.

Nandram, S.S. and Klandermans, B. (1993) 'Stress experienced by active members of trade unions', *Journal of Organizational Behavior*, 14: 415–431.

Online, N. S. (n.d.) Union membership: Up slightly in 2005. Available; www.statistics.gov.uk/CCI/nugget.asp?ID=4andPos=1andColRank=2andRank=896

Opp, K.D. (1998) 'Does antiregime action under communist rule affect political protest after the fall? Results of a panel study in East Germany', *The Sociological Quarterly*, 39: 189–213.

Osborne, J.W. (2000) 'Advantages of hierarchical linear modeling', *Practical Assessment, Research and*

Evaluation, 7 (1). Available: http://PAREonline.net/getvn.asp?v=7andn=1.

Pesek, J.G., Raehsler, R.D. and Balough, R.S. (2006) 'Future professionals and managers: Their attitudes toward unions, organizational beliefs, and work ethic', *Journal of Applied Social Psychology*, 36 (6): 1569–1594.

Pinder, C.C. (1984) *Work Motivation: Theory, Issues and Applications*. Glenview, IL: Scott, Foresman and Co.

Piotrkowski, C.S. and Stark, E. (1987) 'Children and adolescents look at their parents' jobs', in J.H. Lewko (ed.), *How Children and Adolescents View the World of Work*. San Francisco: Jossey-Bass, pp. 3–19.

Redman, T. and Snape, E. (2004) 'Kindling activism? Union commitment and participation in the UK fire service', *Human Relations*, 57 (7): 845–869.

Renaud, S. (2002) 'Rethinking the union membership/job satisfaction relationship: Some empirical evidence from Canada', *International Journal of Manpower*, 2: 137–151.

Richey, B., Bernardin, H.J. and Tyler, C.L. (2001) 'The effect of arbitration program characteristics on applicants' intentions toward potential employers', *Journal of Applied Psychology*, 86 (5): 1006–1013.

Schat, A., Frone, M.R. and Kelloway, E.K. (2006) 'Prevalence of workplace aggression in the U.S. workforce: Findings from a national study', in E.K. Kelloway, J. Barling and J.J. Hurrell (eds), *Handbook of Workplace Violence*. Thousand Oaks, CA: Sage Publications, pp. 47–90.

Schwochau, S. (1987) 'Union effects on job attitudes', *Industrial and Labor Relations Review*, 10: 209–224.

Shirom, A. and Kirmeyer, S. (1988) 'The effects of unions on blue collar role stresses and somatic strains', *Journal of Organizational Behavior*, 9: 29–42.

Shore, L.M., Tetrick, L.E., Sinclair, R.R. and Newton, L.A. (1994) 'Validation of a measure of perceived union support', *Journal of Applied Psychology*, 79 (6): 971–977.

Sjoberg, A. and Sverke, M. (2001) 'Instrumental and ideological union commitment: Longitudinal assessment of construct validity', *European Journal of Psychological Assessment*, 17 (2): 98–111.

Snyder, D. and Kelly, W.R. (1976) 'Industrial violence in Italy, 1878–1903', *American Journal of Sociology*, 82: 131–163.

Spencer, D.G. (1986) 'Employee voice and employee retention', *Academy of Management Journal*, 29: 488–502.

Spinrad, W. (1960) 'Correlates of trade union participation: A summary of the literature', *American Sociological Review*, 25: 237–244.

Stennett-Brewer, L. (1997) *Trauma in the Workplace: The Book About Chronic Work Trauma*. Mount Zion, IL: Nepenthe Publications.

Summers, T.P., Betton, J.H. and DeCotiis, T.A. (1986) 'Voting for and against unions: A decision model', *Academy of Management Review*, 11: 643–655.

Tetrick, L.E. and Fried, Y. (1993) 'Industrial relations: Stress induction or stress reduction?', *Journal of Organizational Behavior*, 14: 511–514.

Thieblot, A.J. and Haggard, T.R. (1983) *Union Violence: The Record and the Response by the Courts, Legislatures, and the NLRB*. Philadelphia: Industrial Research Unit, Wharton School, University of Pennsylvania.

Thieblot, A.J., Haggard, T.R. and Northrup, H.R. (1999) *Union Violence: The Record and the Response by the Courts, Legislatures, and the NLRB* (Rev. Edn) Fairfax, VA: George Mason University, John M. Olin Institute of Employment Practice and Policy.

US Department of Labor, (n.d.) Trends in union membership. Available: http://www.aflcio.org/joinaunion/why/uniondifference/uniondiff11.cfm

Visser, J. (2002) 'Why fewer workers join unions in Europe: A social custom explanation of membership trends', *British Journal of Industrial Relations*, 40: 403–430.

Visser, J. (2006) 'Union membership statistics in 24 countries', *Monthly Labor Review* (Vol. 2006), Jan: 38–49.

34

Discrimination

Stella M. Nkomo

INTRODUCTION

The study of discrimination in organizational behavior has a long history (Dipboye and Halverson, 2004). Before tracing this history, it is important to locate the concept of discrimination in relationship to its corollary concepts: stereotyping and prejudice. In Gordon Allport's (1954) classic book, *The Nature of Prejudice*, he argued that an acceptable definition of prejudice had to include two essential elements. First, there must be an attitude of favor or disfavor; second, there had to be an over generalized, erroneous belief. The latter generally encompasses the concept of stereotypes, a term coined by Lippman (1922) and borrowed from printing lexicon to indicate its reference to a fixed, unchanging mental process. Discrimination captures the behavior element of Allport's classic conceptualization, and is typically defined as treating people differently from others based primarily on membership in a social group. It includes verbal and nonverbal acts, whether intended or unintended. Most theorists distinguish between discrimination at the individual level and institutional level (Dovidio et al., 1996). The former refers to actions carried out by individuals based on negative attitudes.

Institutional discrimination pertains to institutional norms, practices, and policies which help to create or perpetuate sets of advantages or privileges for dominant group members and to the exclusion or unequal access of subordinate groups (Dovidio et al., 1996).

The study of discrimination in organizational behavior has its roots in the classic work of a number of social psychologists, including Allport (1954), Merton (1949), and Mydral (1944). Their research centered upon explaining what caused people to discriminate. Merton (1949) argued that discrimination might be practiced by unprejudiced people who were afraid not to conform to the prejudices of others. In his seminal work, *The American Dilemma*, Mydral (1944) sought to explain the contradiction between continued discrimination in the US against African-Americans, and its democratic ideals of equality and justice. Adorno et al. (1950) searched for a relationship between personality and prejudice. They argued that prejudiced people differed from tolerant persons in central personality traits. Specifically, prejudiced people exhibited authoritarian personalities. In other words, discrimination and prejudice resulted from an aberrant personality (Nkomo, 1992). In contrast, Allport (1954) argued that prejudice was basically an antipathy based on faulty and inflexible generalizations directed toward a group or an individual of a group. Pettigrew (1979: 464) extended Allport's work drawing upon social attribution theory, which seeks to explain how different social groups explain the behavior and social conditions of members of their own group (ingroup) and other social groups (outgroups). He identified what he labelled the *ultimate attribution error* – 'a systematic patterning of intergroup misattributions shaped in part by prejudice.'

The influence of these early works is evident in the trajectories of the study of discrimination by organizational behavior scholars. Much of the interest in discrimination in the field emanates from the passage of equal employment legislation (particularly in the US), and the promotion of affirmative action. A notable exception is the pioneering work of Alderfer, which focused on diagnosing and changing race relations in the workplace (Alderfer et al., 1980).

A pervasive question that dominated early work was whether discrimination existed. One of the earliest articles focusing on this question appeared in the *Academy of Management Journal* in 1964. Kovarshy (1964) examined discrimination in a United States government apprentice programme. Other studies of this decade also focused on the issue of discrimination in the occupational distribution of jobs. However, the most significant volume of research on discrimination appeared after the amendment of Title VII of the Civil Rights Act that prohibited discrimination against individuals based upon race, color, religion, sex, age or national origin in employment. This amendment resulted in the Equal Opportunity Employment Equity Act of 1972 which strengthened enforcement of Title VII. The focus of the voluminous research that followed was on employment discrimination in terms of recruitment, selection, and performance evaluation. In the area of selection, much of this work was confined to racial discrimination, with an emphasis on differences in workplace outcomes for blacks and whites (e.g. Brown

and Ford, 1977; Newman and Kryztofiak, 1979; Terpstra and Larsen, 1980), as well as differential validity in employment tests (e.g. Arvey and Faley, 1988; Boehm, 1977; Hunter et al., 1979). Other scholars focused on bias and discrimination in performance ratings and evaluation (e.g. Dipboye, 1985; Kraiger and Ford, 1985; Landy and Farr, 1980; Schmitt and Lappin, 1980). The commonality among these studies was the search for objective evidence of discrimination. This search dominated organizational behavior research on discrimination through much of the 1980s and early 1990s.

There were only a few studies that attempted to probe deeper, and understand the factors contributing to discrimination and its effects on targets. For example, Ilgen and Youtz (1986) proposed a number of factors that contributed to the development and evaluation of black Americans in organizations relevant to understanding the ways in which organizational contexts influence the work performance of minorities. These factors were described as rater biases, lost opportunities effect, and self-limiting behavior. In essence, these factors offered a mix of individual explanations and organizational barriers as possible explanations for discrimination against black Americans in the workplace. Greenhaus et al. (1990) followed this line of research, and found the lower levels of performance of black Americans was related to differences in experience due to prejudice and discrimination.

CONTEMPORARY RESEARCH ON DISCRIMINATION IN ORGANIZATIONAL BEHAVIOR

In addition to reviewing the history of the study of workplace discrimination in the organization behavior literature for this chapter, seven major journals that typically publish organization behavior scholarship were reviewed, focusing on articles published in the last ten years from 1996 to 2006: *Academy of Management Journal, Academy* of *Management Review*, *Journal of Organizational Behavior*, *Journal of Applied Psychology*, *Journal of Applied Behavioral Science*, *Group and Organization Management*, and *Human Relations*. In addition, an effort was made to examine new theoretical and methodological currents in the study of discrimination emanating from related disciplines (e.g. social psychology, sociology and anthropology) and relevant books. Three electronic databases were also searched: ABI/Inform Global, Academic Search Premier, and Emerald. The goal was to offer a broad overview of how discrimination in organizations has been studied from 1996 and beyond.

This review revealed a continuation in traditional work testing for the existence of discrimination as well as identifying the forms discrimination takes in organizations. However, there was also a noticeable move towards understanding *how* discrimination affects what Deitch and colleagues (2003) refer to as the 'targets of discrimination.' Perhaps researchers heeded Brief's (1998) call for more research on understanding the experiences of discrimination and their causes. Finally, there has been a noticeable move from the primacy given to racial discrimination, to an inclusion gender discrimination and discrimination against other stigmatized groups, including gays, lesbians, older workers, and the physically disabled (Dietch et al., 2004). Significant research findings within each of these themes are explored in the sections that follow. However, there is now a significant reduction of research under the lexicon of 'discrimination,' with a notable shift towards the study of 'diversity' in organizations. There are fewer scholars who explicitly study so called 'traditional discrimination' (i.e. racism and sexism) in the workplace (Griffin and O'Leary-Kelly 2004). More is said about this change and its implications for the future study of discrimination at the conclusion to this chapter.

Racial discrimination

Cumulatively, studies in the organizational behavior field over the last decade support the persistence of racial discrimination at many points in the employment process (Goldman et al., 2006; Huffcutt and Roth, 1998; Roth et al., 2003; Thomas et al., 1998). For example, a review of 31 studies of racial group differences in employment interview outcomes found that, on average, whites received higher ratings than either blacks or Hispanics (Huffcutt and Roth, 1998). These differences were greater for low level jobs than for higher level jobs, and discrimination increased as the proportion of black applicants increased. The findings from studies on racial discrimination in performance evaluation and promotions are more complex (Roth et al., 2003; Thomas et al., 1998). Based on a review of 48 studies, Roth et al. (2003) showed that white employees received higher performance ratings than black employees although there were no differences in ratings between whites and Hispanics. These differences were found across job levels. Roberson and Block (2001) reported that this occurred especially when raters were white. Furthermore, some research indicates that even when ratings are similar, narrative comments made by supervisors may favor whites (Thomas et al., 1998). In a study conducted in the UK, Dewberry (2001) found that the tendency for whites to obtain better performance ratings than ethnic minorities is not confined to North America and to blacks (i.e. Caribbeans and Africans), but also to Asians and other non-whites. Tomkiewicz et al. (1998) found a strong correlation between the ratings of managers and whites but only a 0.17 correlation between ratings of managers and African-Americans, suggesting ratings of managerial performance may be affected by stereotypes about who fits the managerial role.

A difficult issue that must be confronted is whether there are objective differences in the work performance of black employees compared to whites. Roth and his colleagues (2003) did find that blacks had lower average ratings on objective measures of job performance compared to whites. However, caution is warranted because of the possible influence of methodology on results obtained.

Obtrusive studies of workplace discrimination (i.e. laboratory studies) have yielded contradictory results, with some studies showing blacks rated higher than whites. Field studies show more complicated effects of race on different workplace outcomes for blacks. Powell and Butterfield (1997) found applicant race did not directly affect promotion decisions for top management positions in a cabinet-level US government department with standardized promotion practices. However, race indirectly affected promotion decisions through key job relevant variables to the disadvantage of applicants of color. In particular, indirect effects were yielded of applicant race on both panel evaluations and referral decisions through two job-relevant variables, employment in the hiring department and years of work experience, favored white applicants. Analyzing results of 2 062 actual salary negotiations, Seidel et al. (2000) showed that members of racial minority groups negotiated significantly lower salary increases than majority members, but this effect was dramatically reduced when social ties to the organization were controlled. The authors suggest having social ties to the organization significantly increased salary negotiation outcomes and minorities were less likely than majority members to have such a social tie. Thus, the research examining discrimination against blacks in the workplace suggests it is important to design studies to uncover the more complex dynamics of differential treatment and outcomes related to race.

While much of the focus on traditional racial discrimination has been on African-Americans in the US, research has also examined the experiences of other racial ethnic minorities (e.g. Cheng, 1997; Sanchez and Brock, 1996). Cumulatively, research findings suggest these groups also experience discrimination and stereotyping, but that its form and intensity may differ. For instance, Asian-Americans are often stereotyped as the model minority (Cheng, 1997). However, they are also simultaneously subject to negative stereotyping, with one study reporting that whites believed Asian Americans have poor social skills and tend to be exclusionary

and insular (Lin et al., 2005). Asians have also been are described as lacking leadership and management potential because of a lack of assertiveness which could limit their placement in management positions (Prasad, 2001).

Targets of discrimination research

Beginning full scale in 2000, there appears to have been a turn to more research attempting to understand the experiences of targets of discrimination as well as the contexts in which discrimination occurs (Dietch et al., 2003). Indeed, a substantial body of research, primarily qualitative, chronicling the workplace experiences of blacks and other racial minorities has been published in recent years (e.g. Bell and Nkomo, 2001; Knouse et al., 2005; Livers and Caver, 2003; Thomas and Gabarro, 1999; Woo, 2000; Wu, 1997). These studies generally demonstrate the subtle and less-than subtle discriminatory barriers racial ethnic minorities experience in the workplace, and their detrimental effects. Prominent findings indicate promotional processes and opportunities for racial minorities are fundamentally different from those for white peers as is the daily experience of inequality (Bell and Nkomo, 2001; Knouse et al., 2005; Thomas and Gabarro, 1999; Woo, 2000). These findings themselves are perhaps not surprising: An important question, of course, is why?

Scholars have begun attempts to address this very issue. In line with theoretical developments in social psychology that indicate the nature of discrimination (especially in the US) has taken a new form in response to political and ideological shifts, organizational behavior scholars have utilized concepts of modern racism and everyday racism to better understand the persistence of racial discrimination in the work place. The latter concepts fall within a range of contemporary theories of prejudice that include modern racism, everyday racism (Essed, 1991), aversive racism (Dovidio and Gaertner, 2004), benevolent or ambivalent prejudice (Glick and Fiske, 2001), and subtle prejudice (Pettigrew and Meertens, 1995;

Pettigrew, 1998). While these theories may apply to discrimination against other stigmatized groups, they were primarily developed to explain racial discrimination (Whitely and Kite, 2006). Proponents of these theories argue discrimination has not disappeared; it has simply been replaced by less overt and direct forms.

McConahay (1983) developed the concept of modern racism (originally labelled symbolic racism) to emphasize the contemporary, post- civil-rights-movement nature of the tenets constituting the new ideology or belief system in the US. This belief system is characterized by five themes

(1) discrimination is no longer a problem because there is opportunity to compete in the marketplace;
(2) Blacks should work harder;
(3) claims of continued inequality are unjustified;
(4) Blacks demand too much and want special favors; and
(5) Blacks receive undeserved outcomes (Brief, 1998).

According to McConahay (1983), these belief systems allow people displaying modern racism views to maintain their self-images as unprejudiced, and to appear unprejudiced to others while engaging in discriminatory behavior. Thus, according to proponents of modern racism, racial discrimination has not disappeared; it has been replaced by less overt and direct forms (Dovidio and Gaertner, 2000). Using a laboratory study design, Brief et al. (2000) examined the role of modern racism in the selection of black and white job applicants. They found that when no justification had been given for not hiring a black candidate, respondents high and low in modern racism recommended black candidates at the same rate. However, when a business reason was provided for discrimination – in this case that the candidate would be interacting mainly with white customers – respondents scoring high in modern racism selected black applicants at a lower rate than those with low scores in modern racism. However, both groups altered their selection rates because of the business reason justifying discrimination. Brief et al. (2000) conclude that their study shows the existence of modern racism in the workplace, but also extends its role through their finding that justification of modern racist behavior need not be non-racial as posited by modern racism theory. This result warrants further study by organizational behavior scholars. Ziegert and Hanges (2005) attempted to replicate and extend Brief et al.'s (2000) findings. Although these authors were unable to replicate Brief et al.'s findings, they did demonstrate that implicit racist attitudes interacted with a climate for racial bias to predict discrimination. Both these studies suggest implicit attitudes may ultimately be more useful than explicit attitudes in explaining employment discrimination (Brief, 1998).

In another study, Dietch et al. (2003) used Essed's (1991) concept of *everyday racism* to provide evidence of everyday workplace discrimination against blacks. Essed (1991) defined everyday racism as a concept that connects structural forces of racism with routine situations in everyday life; it attempts to make visible the lived experience of racism, and more specifically explains black perceptions about racism in everyday life (Essed, 1991). Dietch et al. (2003) found race was significantly related to mistreatment, with blacks perceiving significantly more mistreatment on the job than whites. In addition, everyday discrimination partially accounted for lower job satisfaction on the part of black employees. Dietch et al. (2003) concluded that blacks appear to be experiencing an additional source of stress in the workplace, one with which whites do not have to cope (Cocchiara and Quick, 2004).

Discrimination has become a significant research issue in many countries in Europe where millions of ex-colonials, 'guest workers,' refugees and other immigrants from Africa, Asia, the Caribbean, the Middle East and South American have settled in Western European and Scandinavian countries in recent years. The research conducted has typically used the concept of *subtle prejudice* to understand the particular social and political ideologies that are different from the US context of white attitudes towards blacks (Pettigrew, 1998: 77). Pettigrew and Meertens (1995) argued that *subtle prejudice* differs in two ways. First, the emotional component of subtle prejudice is indifference, whereas the emotional component of modern racism consists of mild to moderate negative emotions. Second, people manifesting *subtle prejudice* tend to view differences between majority and minority group cultures as greater than their own, and strongly endorse the traditional values and norms of their own cultures. Research on discrimination in Western Europe, in particular, demonstrates the salience of a perceived threat to traditional cultural values, language and religion as justification for the exclusion of immigrants from Asian and North Africa from employment opportunities (Ogbonna and Harris, 2006). However, Pettigrew (1998)'s research demonstrates the complexity of immigrant discrimination across Europe. In France, he found less French prejudice against Asians than North Africans, with less discrimination towards Surinamers in the Netherlands than Turks. Thus, acceptance of immigrants was more closely related to cultural rather than racial similarities.

Gender discrimination

A significant body of work emerged in the mid to late-1990s examining gender discrimination in the workplace. There is less research on gender discrimination in areas such as recruiting, promotion and hiring compared to that on race. Although gender discrimination is prohibited by law in many countries around the world, research across the globe suggests discrimination against women in the workplace persists (Bell et al., 2002; Holst, 2006; Shaffer et al., 2000). Research on gender discrimination in organization behavior has coalesced around three areas: the glass ceiling as a barrier to upward mobility for women; discrimination in pay; and sexual harassment.

Glass ceiling

Stereotyping and discrimination have been offered as an explanation for the proverbial glass ceiling women encounter in their careers. While some of the research prior to the 1990s revealed direct bias against women in hiring, especially for male dominated jobs, recent studies (e.g. Bertrand and Mullainathan, 2003; Davison and Burke, 2000) report no evidence of blatant gender discrimination. However, there is a significant body of research that attributes the slow advancement of women into leadership and senior management positions to subtle discrimination (Eagly and Carli, 2007; Eagly and Karau, 2002; Goodman et al., 2004; Gutek, 2001). Eagly and Karau (2002) identified two types of subtle prejudice preventing women from breaking the glass ceiling, or succeeding when they do enter senior level positions. Drawing upon role congruity theory, they argue that one form of discrimination originates from the belief that women are less likely than men to succeed in a leadership role. This belief just does not affect male attitudes and behaviors where men are less likely to hire women but also affects women who may not seek a leadership role women – because they too are influenced by expectations of gender role congruity (Ritter and Yoder, 2004). Eagly and Karau (2002) further point out that even if women do manage to achieve leadership or non-traditional roles, a second form of discrimination emerges – women face a higher probability of negative evaluations of their performance and promotability.

Scholars have also examined gender discrimination in performance evaluations and hiring. However, the results are mixed. Heilman et al. (2004) found negative labeling of competent women in a laboratory study, when comparing evaluations of men and women with ambiguous performance levels. They concluded that such a result is more likely in employment areas that are typically male dominated. Other studies report men and women receive equal job performance ratings, while others report sex-stereotyping interacts with job ratings (Bowen et al., 2000). Bowen et al. (2000) reviewed 27 studies of gender differences in job performance ratings, and found that while men and women receive equal ratings, male evaluators tended to give higher ratings to women. Other researchers report men and women both receive slightly higher suitability ratings for sex-stereotyped positions (Davison and Burke, 2000). Even in studies where women scored higher on performance, they were not promoted faster, and some research even suggests a male advantage in female occupations (Maume, 1999) or what is referred to as *glass escalators*.

Biernat and Vescio (2002) offer the 'shifting standards' model of evaluation as an alternative explanation for the contradiction between the finding that while men and women may receive equal job performance ratings, women are still less likely to get promoted than men. They argue that when raters use subjective criteria to rate job performance, they are more likely to rate the person relative to the expectations the evaluator has for the person's group. If raters hold lower expectations for female employees than male employees, they may lower their standards for women, resulting in the assignment of a biased rating of women that can be higher or similar to men. However, they note that when the performance and men and women are assessed on objective criteria, women may be at a disadvantage. It is difficult for women in such circumstance to receive accurate feedback on their performance. The latter is prominently reported in qualitative studies of the experiences of women executives (e.g. Bell and Nkomo, 2001).

Gender discrimination in hiring decisions has been studied less than in the case of performance evaluation. Reviews of the extant research did not reveal discrimination (Bertrand and Mullainathan, 2003; Davison and Burke, 2000). For example, Davison and Burke (2000) reviewed 49 studies and found no differences in the suitability ratings of men and women as job applicants. In a study of the influence of decision-makers' race and gender on actual promotions to top management positions, Powell and Butterfield (2002) found overall decisions by

review panels of different race and gender compositions were to the advantage of female applicants, and to the disadvantage of African American and Hispanic male applicants. A recent body of research reveals a new form of discrimination experienced by women managers in organizations: Women are more likely than men to find themselves on a *glass cliff* – placed in positions of leadership associated with greater risk of failure (Ryan and Haslam, 2005).

Gender discrimination in pay

While studies show mixed results for performance evaluations and selection, studies of gender discrimination have demonstrated unequivocally the existence and persistence of gender-based wage differences in the labor market (Dreher and Cox, 1996; Hultin and Szulkin, 1999; Roos and Gatta, 2001). Recent studies have attempted to identify the underlying factors that result in gender based wage differentials. For example, Hultin and Szulkin (1999) found gender-differentiated access to power structures is essential in explaining women's relatively low wages. Lam and Dreher (2004) examined other job relevant variables and found that observed pay differentials between men and women had its origins in extra-firm mobility, not intra-firm gender discrimination.

Sexual harassment

The final area dominating the literature on gender discrimination is sexual harassment (and see the chapter by Cortina and Berdahl in this volume). Sexual harassment has been recognized as a form of overt sex discrimination by US courts, and this recognition has spurred a great deal of research to understand its effects and causes in the workplace (Gruber, 1997; Stockdale, 1997). Sexual harassment is also a workplace problem for women in other countries around the world (Barak, 1997). Explanations for the persistence of sexual harassment in the workplace include gender differences in perceptions of what constitutes harassment (Rotundo et al., 2001; Welsh, 1999) and differences in access to power and status.

In terms of the latter, sexual harassment appears to be a greater problem for women in blue-collar, lower paying occupations than for women in higher paying occupations as well as in situations where women occupy non-traditional jobs (Yoder and Aniakudo, 1996). Berdahl (2007a) found women who were perceived to be 'uppity' – challenging male dominance –also experienced greater sexual harassment.

Scholars point to three psychological dimensions of sexual harassment: sexual coercion, gender harassment and unwanted sexual attention (O'Leary-Kelly et al., 2000; Schneider et al., 1997; Shaffer et al., 2000; Williams et al., 1997). More recently, Berdahl (2007b) offers a different view of sexual harassment, arguing that the primary motive underlying all harassment is a desire to protect one's social status when it seems threatened, a desire held by both men and women. Consequently, sexual harassers derogate others based on sex to protect or enhance their own sex-based social status. Her theoretical framework also underscores the role that social context plays in the occurrence of sexual harassment, suggesting that harassers are motivated and able to harass by a social context that is pervasively and fundamentally stratified by a system of gender hierarchy. This more critical perspective differs sharply from most research that has viewed sexual harassment as inherently driven by sexual desire or a desire in men to dominate women.

As the above discussion highlights, organizational behavior researchers have followed three dominant approaches in studying gender discrimination. One approach has been a focus on identifying the direct effects of discrimination (i.e. differences in job outcomes like hiring rates, promotion rates, pay, and sexual harassment); another has been to look beyond intentional discrimination to study the indirect effect of discrimination through other job-relevant variables. The research incorporating other job relevant variables to understand discrimination against women has produced some interesting approaches and explanations. For example, Phillips (2005) examined

how organizational genealogies affect gender inequality. A parent firm's gender hierarchy is important to understanding the advancement of women in that firm's offspring. Phillips (2005) argued that traditional discrimination theory was not adequate to explain the persistence of gender inequality across generations of organizations.

The third approach is similar to the trajectory on race discrimination, and focuses on individual level psychological processes (e.g. stereotyping, modern sexism). A number of studies have focused on the manager-as-male stereotype as a major explanation for discrimination against women in the workplace. The pioneering work on this hypothesis was conducted by Schein (1973), although a number of scholars have studied the stereotype-fit hypothesis since that time (Eagly and Karau, 2002; Heilman, 2001; Powell and Butterfield, 2003). Schein's 1973 US research tested the relationship between sex role stereotypes and requisite management characteristics. She found the correlation between characteristics of successful middle managers and the characteristics ascribed to men was higher than that for women. Subsequently, Schein (2001) extended her earlier work to include studies in the UK, Germany, China, and Japan, and updated her US study. Her findings for the UK, Germany, China and Japan support her '*think manager-think male*' concept, while the US results were unchanged 20 years later from the male perspective. However, women's attitudes were found to have changed to the view that women are *equally* likely to possess management characteristics.

In a sample of male and female managers in South Africa, Booysen and Nkomo (2006) found men's attitudes were consistent with the '*think manager – think male*' hypothesis, while this was not true for the women in the study. They speculated that the government's emphasis on gender equity and women's empowerment may have influenced women's self-perceptions, but had less effect on the attitudes of men. The longitudinal research of Powell and Butterfield (2003) supports the persistence of the manager-as-male stereotype. They collected data from business students in 1976, 1989 and in 2002, and demonstrated that despite the considerable increase in women in management, as well as the call for feminine leadership, the expected change in managerial stereotypes did not occur. In a recent study, Lyness and Heilman (2006) examined the relationship between gender and type of position with performance evaluations of 448 upper level managers, and the relationship of performance evaluations to promotions during the subsequent two years. Consistent with the idea that there is a greater perceived lack of fit between stereotypical attributes of women and requirements of line jobs than staff jobs, women in line management jobs received lower performance ratings than women in staff jobs or men in either line or staff jobs. They also found women were held to stricter standards for promotion. These studies and others (e.g. Eagly and Carli, 2007; Cejka and Eagly, 1999; Martell et al., 1998) confirm the persistence of gender stereotyping as a form of discrimination limiting women's opportunities and progress in the workplace.

While the latter three perspectives have dominated the organizational behavior research on gender discrimination, some scholars have taken more critical and feminist perspectives of the reasons for the persistence of discrimination against women. These scholars point to the gendered nature of organizations, and the deep power structures that impede women's advancement in organizations (Acker, 2000; Alvesson and Billing, 1997; Appold et al., 1998; Benschop and Doorewaard, 1998; Calas and Smircich, 2006; Cockburn, 1991; Ely and Padavil, 2007). They argue that discrimination against women lingers in a plethora of work practices and cultural norms that appear on the surface to be gender neutral but produce inequities (e.g. see Ely and Meyerson, 2000; Flecther, 2001). As such they eschew what they see as an overemphasis on individual level and interpersonal factors in explaining gender discrimination in the workplace. Hence these feminist and critical perspectives call for greater attention to the role of structural antecedents and patriarchy in the continued discrimination against women in organizations.

Discrimination against other stigmatized groups

There is a modest amount of work in organizational behavior focusing on discrimination based on sexual orientation, age, and disability. Attention to discrimination based on sexual orientation has increased in the last few years, although it remains an area of research receiving little attention in organization behavior (Deitch et al., 2004). Scholars view discrimination against gay, lesbian, bisexual, and transgendered (GLBT) people as a form of stigma-based discrimination. Stigma based discrimination is aimed specifically at individuals who are perceived to possess (or are believed to possess) some attribute, or characteristic, that conveys a social identity that is devalued in a particular social context' (Crocker et al., 1998: 505). One of the salient aspects of research on the workplace discrimination faced by gays and lesbians is how revealing their sexual orientation affects their experiences and treatment by colleagues and organisations. Being gay, lesbian, bisexual or transgendered is viewed as a 'concealable stigma' unlike perhaps race. However, Deitch et al. (2004) note that prejudice against GLBT people is more socially acceptable than racism and sexism in many societies. Ragins and Cornwell (2001) argue that discrimination against GLBT groups is often the result of fear, stereotyping and misunderstanding. GLBT individuals who disclose their sexual orientation have been shown to be victims of negative attitudes, harassment, and lesser workplace outcomes compared to heterosexuals (Day and Schoenrade, 1997). Additionally, they experience job denial and loss, diminished mobility as well as ostracism and harassment (Crouteau, 1996), for the most part without legislative protection. It is important to note that, unlike the case with many other forms of discrimination, discrimination against GLBT persons is not prohibited nationally in the US (only a few states and local governments have anti-discrimination laws) as well as in many other countries.

The research conducted by Ragins and Cornwell (2001) showed that organizational context factors (e.g. gay-friendly policies and benefits, presence of other gays among staff, gays in supervisory and managerial ranks) greatly influence the quality of experience of gays in the workplace. The less hetero-sexist the workplace environment, the more likely gays are to report unbiased treatment. In general, the literature suggests anti-GLBT discrimination and prejudice is fuelled by a combination of organizational factors, gender role expectations, religious beliefs and the social dominance of heterosexism (Creed, 2006).

Much of the research on age discrimination in the workplace has focused on the role of stereotypes and their consequences for the perception of and suitability of older workers for recruitment, selection and pro-motion (Perry and Bourhis, 1998; Perry and Finkelstein, 1999; McCann and Giles, 2002). Most of the literature points to negative stereotyping of older workers, or what Perry and Parlaimis (2005) refer to as *ageism* in organizations. Older workers are often viewed as less effective, and less trainable with less performance capacity (Perry and Parlamis, 2005). Perry and Parlaimis' (2005) review of the existing literature on age stereotypes suggests that stereotypes about older worker are ubiquitous, and share a number of similarities across a variety of countries (see Chiu et al., 2001). Research suggests older works are also subject to covert discrimination and more subtle forms of discrimination. For example, unintentional code words are often used during selection interviews such as 'we are looking for "go-getters"' (Mujtaba et al., 2006). Bendick et al. (1999) found significant evidence of age discrimination in the hiring process. The evaluation and treatment of older workers was vastly different from that afforded younger applicants and heavily influenced by age-based stereotypes. Curiously, according to EEOC data, age discrimination charges against employers declined in the mid-1990s

but have increased again at the turn of the century (Grosch et al., 2004).

Discrimination against people with disabil-ities has received scant attention over the years. The research that does exist focuses on cognitive biases and stereotyping of people with disabilities (see Colella and Stone, 2005) as well as unfair treatment and differential out-comes in selection, performance evaluations, and procedural justice (e.g. Colella et al., 1998; Stone-Romero and Stone, 2005). People with disabilities are victims of stereotyping and employer negative attitudes towards accommodation. They are also perceived not to have the skills and abilities needed to perform their jobs, and to manifest low levels of emotional adjustment. Data show the employment of people with disabilities is declining (Stone-Romero et al., 2006). Some scholars argue people with disabilities are reluctant to request accommodation and many conceal their disabilities because of the stigma associated with disabilities (Baldridge and Veiga, 2001).

CONCLUSION

Two major conclusions are evident from this rather wide review of the extant research on discrimination in the workplace. First, discrimination against non-whites, women, ethnic minorities, individuals with physical disabilities, older employees, and GLBTs remains a stubborn feature of organizations. The prevalence of particular forms of dis-crimination (e.g. race, gender, ethnicity) or their manifestations may vary across countries and even within countries. Yet, even within countries with equal employment or anti-discrimination legislation, members of non-dominant or stigmatized groups continue to experience inequality (Tomei, 2003). In the US, class actions suits against US businesses rose more than 100 per cent in 2003 (Institute of Crisis Management, 2004). A study in Europe of sexism in the workplace concluded it is actually on the rise not the decline. Almost three out of the four female workers surveyed claimed they had been bullied because of their gender (Personnel Today, 2006). In South Africa, where the government has instituted aggressive employment equity legislation, progress remains slow in achieving equality at work (Booysen, 2007; Booysen and Nkomo, 2006). Australia's initial progressive efforts towards the elimination of discrimination have been virtually reversed by changes in government ideology towards indigenous Australians and migrant groups and refugees (Sinclair, 2006).

Second, from its initial trajectory focusing on the question of the existence of direct discrimination, organizational behavior research has begun to focus more on understanding the experiences of targets of discrimination in the last few years, as well as drawing more from newer theoretical currents in social psychology and other related disciplines (i.e. subtler forms of discrimination). Major tensions exist within the overall body of literature, however. There is a continuing pull between research focusing on individual explanations for discrimination versus structural and contextual forces. With few exceptions, scholars rely upon social identity theory, categorization, stereotyping and prejudice as the primary lens for explaining why discrimination occurs as well as the experiences of victims of discrimination Some scholars have criticized this intergroup paradigm approach as omitting the important influence of the social and historical positions of dominant and non-dominant groups on workplace discrimination (Prasad et al., 2006).

The inevitability of in-group favoritism and outgroup bias suggested by the minimal intergroup paradigm reveals another tension in the field. While OB research over the last ten years continues to document the occurrence of discrimination, there is relatively less research on how to *eliminate* discrimination. Few studies have explicitly examined or tested social psychological theories of discrimination reduction. For example, these theories include the contact hypothesis, stereotype suppression, self-regulation, and value confrontation (Whitely and Kite, 2006). Perhaps this has occurred because of the shift in the field to the study of diversity with its

purported aim of workplace inclusion. The shift towards the study of diversity reveals yet another tension in the current study of discrimination. Some scholars are concerned that diversity with its broad inclusion of 'everyone' distracts from the study of discrimination and oppression at work of groups who have been and continue to be systematically and historically disadvantaged (Linnehan and Konrad, 1999; Lorbiecki and Jack, 2000; Nkomo and Stewart, 2006; Prasad et al., 2006). Cleary more research is needed on how to eliminate discrimination in the workplace.

Still others drawing upon critical theory and postmodern perspectives view the shift towards the study of diversity in organizations as a *re*-writing project to maintain the status quo (Litivin, 1997). These scholars express skepticism that diversity management will produce real change in organizations, and argue how current diversity prescriptions maintain white male domination and superiority (Jones and Stabelin, 2006). Data on the increasing incidence of workplace discrimination suggests that approaches that value diversity in organizations have yet to yield significant benefits (James and Wooten, 2006). Critical management scholars would note that the effectiveness of diversity initiatives is largely inferred in terms of its 'bottom line' impact rather than the elimination of discrimination (Litvin, 2007). Still others take a more complex view, focusing on deconstructing the ways power is embedded in taken-for-granted understandings that result in privileging some actors, and disadvantaging others in the workplace (Dick and Nadin, 2006). Their concern is the effect of social practice, rather than the conscious intent of particular actors.

These tensions in and of themselves are not problematic. They all point to the complexity of the experience of, and study of discrimination in the workplace and the reality that its understanding is informed by a wide variety of theoretical perspectives. The embeddedness of workplace discrimination in the broader sociohistorical and organizational context cannot be ignored (Cooke, 2003; Dipboye and Halverson, 2004; Prasad, 2001).

Nor can organizational behavior scholars ignore the need for individuals in organizations to learn to value and embrace rather than exclude and reject those who are different from themselves (Litvin, 2007). Continued illumination will require multiple theoretical frameworks, attention to micro-, meso-, and macro-levels of analysis as well methodological variation in the study of discrimination.

REFERENCES

Acker, J. (2000) 'Gendered contradictions organizational equity projects', *Organization*, 7 (4): 625–632.

Adorno, T.W., Frenkel-Brunswick, E., Levinson, D.J., II, and Sanford, R.N. (1950) *The Authoritarian Personality*. New York: Harper & Row.

Alderfer, C.P., Alderfer, C.J., Tucker, L. and Tucker, R. (1980) 'Diagnosing race relations in management', *Journal of Applied Psychology*, 16: 135–166.

Allport, G.W. (1954) *The Nature of Prejudice*. New York: Perseus.

Alvesson, M. and Billing, Y.D. (1997) *Understanding Gender and Organizations*. London: Sage Publications.

Appold, S.J., Siengthai, S. and Kasarda, J.D. (1998) 'The employment of women managers and professionals in an emerging economy: Gender inequality as an organizational practice', *Administrative Science Quarterly*, 43: 538–565.

Arvey, R.D. and Faley, R.H. (1988) *Fairness in Selecting Employees*. Reading, MA: Addison-Wesley.

Baldridge, D.C. and Veiga, J.F. (2001) 'Toward a greater understanding of the willingness to request an accommodation: Can requesters' beliefs disable the Americans with disabilities act?', *Academy of Management Review*, 25: 85–99.

Barak, A. (1997) 'Cross-cultural perspectives on sexual harassment', in W. O'Donohue (ed.) *Sexual Harassment: Theory, Research and Treatment*. Boston: Allyn & Bacon, pp. 263–300.

Bell, E.E.L.J. and Nkomo, S.M. (2001) *Our Separate Ways: Black and White Women and the Struggle for Professional Identity*. Boston: Harvard Business School Press.

Bell, M.P., McLaughlin, M.E. and Sequeira, J.M. (2002) 'Discrimination, harassment, and the glass ceiling: Women executives as change agents', *Journal of Business Ethics*, 37: 65–76.

Bendick, M., Jr., Brown, L.E. and Wall, K. (1999) 'No foot in the door: An experimental study of employment discrimination against older workers', *Journal of Aging and Social Policy*, 10: 5–23.

Benschop, Y. and Doorewaard, H. (1998) 'Covered by equality: The gender subtext of organizations', *Organization Studies*, 19 (5): 787–805.

Berdahl, J.L. (2007a) 'The sexual harassment of uppity women', *Journal of Applied Psychology*, 92 (2): 425–437.

Berdahl, J.L. (2007b) 'Harassment based on sex: Protecting social status in the context of gender hierarchy', *Academy of Management Review*, 32: 641–658.

Bertrand, M. and Mullainathan, S. (2003) 'Are Emily and Greg more employable than Lakisha and Jamal? A field experiment on labor market discrimination'. (Working Paper 9873). Cambridge, MA: National Bureau of Economic Research.

Biernat, M. and Vescio, T.K. (2002) 'She swings, she hits, she's great, she's benched: Implications of gender-based shifting standards for judgment and behavior', *Personality and Social Psychology Bulletin*, 28: 66–77.

Boehm, V.R. (1977) 'Differential prediction—A methodological artifact', *Journal of Applied Psychology*, 62: 146–154.

Booysen, A.E. (2007) 'Societal power shifts and changing social identities in South Africa: Workplace implications', *South African Journal of Economic and Management Sciences,* 10: 1–20.

Booysen, A.E. and Nkomo, S.M. (2006) 'Think manager–Think female', *International Journal of Interdisciplinary Social Sciences*, 2 (1): 24–36.

Bowen, C.C., Swim, J. and Jacobs, R. (2000) 'Evaluating gender biases on actual job performance of real people: A meta-analysis', *Journal of Applied Social Psychology*, 30: 2195–2215.

Brief, A.P. (1998) *Attitudes In and Around Organizations*. Thousand Oaks, CA: Sage.

Brief, A.P., Dietch, E.A., Cohen, R.R., Pugh, S.D. and Vaslow, J.B. (2000) 'Just doing business: Modern racism and obedience to authority as explanations for employment discrimination', *Organization Behavior and Human Decision Processes*, 81: 72–97.

Brown, H.A. and Ford, D.L. (1977) 'An exploratory analysis of discrimination in the employment of black MBA graduates', *Journal of Applied Psychology*, 62: 50–56.

Calas, M. and Smircich, L. (2006) 'From the "Woman's Point of View" ten years later: Towards a feminist organization studies', in S.R Clegg, C. Hardy, T.B Lawrence and Nord, W.R. (eds), *The Sage Handbook of Organization Studies*. London: Sage Publications, pp. 284–346.

Ceijka, M.A. and Eagly, A.H. (1999) 'Gender-stereotypic images of occupations correspond to the sex segregation of employment', *Personality and Social Psychology Bulletin*, 25: 413–423.

Cheng, C. (1997) 'Are Asian American employees a model minority or just a minority?', *Journal of Applied Behavioral Science*, 33: 277–290.

Chiu, W.C., Chan, A.W., Snape, E. and Redman, T. (2001) 'Age stereotypes and discriminatory attitudes towards older workers: An East-West comparison', *Human Relations*, 54 (5): 629–61.

Cocchiara, F.K. and Quick, J.C. (2004) 'The negative effects of positive stereotypes: Ethnicity-related stressors and implications on organizational health', *Journal of Organizational Behavior*, 25: 781–785.

Cockburn, C. (1991) *In the Way of Women.* Ithaca, NY: ILR Press.

Colella, A., DeNisi, A.S. and Varma, A. (1998) 'The impact of ratee's disability on performance judgements and choice as partner: The role of disability-job fit stereotypes and interdependence of rewards', *Journal of Applied Psychology*, 83: 102–111.

Colella, A. and Stone, D.L. (2005) 'Workplace discrimination toward persons with disabilities: A call for some new research directions', in R. Dipboye and A. Colella (eds), *The Psychological and Organizational Bases of Discrimination at Work.* Mahwah, NJ: Lawrence Erlbaum, pp. 227–253.

Cooke, B. (2003) 'The denial of slavery in management studies', *Journal of Management Studies*, 40: 895–918.

Creed, W.E. (2006) 'Seven conversations about the same thing: Homophobia and heterosexism in the workplace', in A.M. Konrad, P. Prasad and J.K. Pringle (eds), *Handbook of Workplace Diversity.* London: Sage Publications, pp. 371–400.

Crocker, J., Major, B. and Steele, C. (1998) 'Social stigma', in D.T. Gilbert, S.T. Fiske, and G. Lindzey (eds), *The Handbook of Social Psychology.* Boston: McGraw-Hill, pp. 504–553.

Croteau, J.M. (1996) 'Research on the work experiences of lesbian, gay and bisexual people: An integrative view of the methodology and findings', *Journal of Vocational Behavior*, 48: 95–209.

Davison, R. and Burke, M.J. (2000) 'Sex discrimination in simulated employment contexts: A meta-analytic investigation', *Journal of Vocational Behavior*, 56: 225–248.

Day, N.E. and Schoenrade, P. (1997) 'Staying in the closet versus coming out: Relationships between communication about sexual orientation and work attitudes', *Personnel Psychology*, 50: 147–64.

Dewberry, C. (2001) 'Performance disparities between whites and ethnic minorities: Real difference or assessment bias', *Journal of Occupational and Organizational Psychology*, 74: 659–673.

Dick, P. and Nadin, S. (2006) 'Reproducing gender inequalities? A critique of realist assumptions underpinning personnel selection research and practice', *Journal of Occupational and Organizational Psychology*, 79: 481–498.

Dietch, E.A., Butz, R.M. and Brief, A.P. (2004) 'Out of the closet and out of a job? The nature, import and causes of sexual orientation discrimination', in R.W. Griffin and A.M. O'Leary (eds), *The Dark Side of Organizational Behavior.* San Francisco: Jossey-Bass, pp. 187–236.

Dietch, E.A., Barsky, A., Butz, R.M., Chan, S., Brief, A.P. and Bradley, J.C. (2003) 'Subtle yet significant: The existence and impact of everyday racial discrimination in the workplace', *Human Relations*, 56: 1299–1324.

Dipboye, R.L. (1985) 'Some neglected variables in research on discrimination in appraisals', *Academy of Management Review*, 10: 116–127.

Dipboye, R.L. and Halverson, S.K. (2004) 'Subtle (and not so subtle) discrimination in organizations', in R.W. Griffin and A. M. O'Leary (eds), *The Dark Side of Organizational Behavior.* San Francisco: Jossey-Bass, pp. 131–158.

Dreher, G.F. and Cox, T.H. Jr. (1996) 'Race, gender, and opportunity: A study of compensation attainment and the establishment of mentoring relationships', *Journal of Applied Psychology*, 81: 297–308.

Dovidio, J.F., Brigham, J.C., Johnson, B.T. and Gaertner, S.L. (1996) 'Stereotyping, prejudice, and discrimination. Another look', in C.N. Macrae, C. Stagnor, Y and M. Hewstone (eds) *Stereotypes and Stereotyping.* New York: Guilford, pp. 276–319.

Dovidio, J.F. and Gaertner, S.L. (2004) 'Aversive racism', *Advances in Experimental Social Psychology*, 36: 1–52.

Eagly, A.H. and Carli, L. (2007) *Through the Labyrinth: The Truth About How Women Become Leaders.* Boston: Harvard Business School Press.

Eagly, A.H. and Karau, S.J. (2002) 'Role congruity theory of prejudice towards female leaders', *Psychology Review*, 109: 573–598.

Ely, R. and Irene, P. (2007) 'A feminist analysis of organizational research on sex differences', *Academy of Management Review*, 32: 1121–1143.

Ely, R. and Meyerson, D.E. (2000) 'Theories of gender in organizations: A new approach to organizational analysis and change', in B. Staw and R. Sutton (eds), *Research in Organizational Behavior.* Greenwich, CT: JAI Press, pp. 103–151.

Essed, P. (1991) *Understanding Everyday Racism: An Interdisciplinary Theory.* Newbury Park: Sage Publications.

Fletcher, J.K. (2001) *Disappearing Acts: Gender, Power, and Relational Practice.* Boston: MIT Press.

Glick, P. and Fiske, S.T. (2001) 'Ambivalent stereotypes as legitimizing ideologies: Differing paternalistic and envious prejudice', in J.T. Jost and B. Major (eds), *The Psychology of Legitimacy.* New York: Cambridge University Press, pp. 278–306.

Goldman, B., Gutek, B., Stein, J. and Lewis, K. (2006) 'Employment discrimination in organizations: Antecedents and consequences', *Journal of Management,* 32: 786–830.

Goodman, J.S., Fields, D.L. and Blum, T.C. (2003) 'Cracks in the glass ceiling: In what kinds of organizations do women make it to the top?', *Group and Organization Management,* 28: 475–501.

Greenhaus, J., Parasuramen, S. and Wormley, W. (1990) 'Effects of race on organizational experiences, job performance evaluations, and career outcome', *Academy of Management Journal,* 33: 64–86.

Griffin, R.W. and O'Leary–Kelly, A.M. (2004) *The Dark Side of Organizational Behavior.* San Francisco: Jossey-Bass.

Grosch, J.W. , Roberts, R.K. and Grubb, P.L. (2004) *Workplace Discrimination After 25 Years: A Report on National Trends.* Paper presented at the America Psychological Association, Honolulu, HI.

Gruber, J.E. (1997) 'An epidemiology of sexual harassment: Evidence from North America and Europe', in W. O'Donohue (ed.) *Sexual Harassment: Theory, Research and Treatment.* Boston: Allyn & Bacon, pp. 84–98.

Gutek, B. (2001) 'Working environments', in J. Worell (ed.) *Encyclopedia of Women and Gender: Sex Similarities and the Impact of Society on Gender.* Vol. 2. San Diego: Academic Press, pp. 1191–1204.

Heilman, M.E. (2001) 'Description and prescription: How gender stereotypes prevent women's ascent up the organizational ladder', *Journal of Social Issues,* 57: 657–674.

Heilman, M.E., Wallen, A.S., Fuchs, D. and Tamkin, M.M. (2004) 'Penalties for success: Reactions to women who succeed at male gender-typed tasks', *Journal of Applied Psychology,* 89: 416–427.

Holst, E. (2006) 'Women in managerial positions in Europe: Focus on Germany', *Management Revue,* 17 (2): 122–142.

Huffcutt, A.I. and Roth, P.L. (1998) 'Racial group differences in employment interview evaluations', *Journal of Applied Psychology,* 83: 179–189.

Hultin, M. and Szulkin, R. (1999) 'Wages and unequal access to organizational power: An empirical test of gender discrimination', *Administrative Science Quarterly,* 44: 453–472.

Hunter, J.E., Schmidt, F.L. and Hunter, R. (1979) 'Differential validity of employment tests by race: A comprehensive review and analysis', *Psychological Bulletin,* 85: 721–735.

Ilgen, D.R. and Youtz, M.A. (1986) 'Factors affecting the evaluation and development of minorities in organizations', *Research in Personnel and Human Resources Management,* 4: 307–337.

Institute for Crisis Management (2004) *Annual ICM Crisis Report (research report),* vol 13:1. Louisville, KY: Institute for Crisis Management.

James, E.H. and Wooten, L. (2006) 'Diversity crises: How firms manage discrimination lawsuits', *Academy of Management Journal,* 49: 1103–1118.

Jones, D. and Stablein, R. (2006) 'Diversity as resistance and recuperation: Critical theory, post-structuralist perspectives and workplace diversity', in A.M. Konrad, P. Prasad and J.K. Pringle (eds), *Handbook of Workplace Diversity.* London: Sage Publications, pp. 145–166.

Kovarshy, I. (1964) 'Management, racial discrimination, and apprentice training programs', *Academy of Management Journal,* 7: 196–203.

Knouse, S.B., Rosenfeld, P. and Culberston, A. (eds) (2005) *Hispanics in the Workplace.* Thousand Oaks, CA: Sage Publications.

Kraiger, K. and Ford, J. (1985) 'A meta-analysis of ratee race effects in performance ratings', *Journal of Applied Psychology,* 70: 56–65.

Lam, S.K. and Dreher, G.F. (2004) 'Gender, extra-firm mobility, and compensation attainment in the United States and Hong Kong', *Journal of Organizational Behavior,* 25: 791–805.

Landy, F.J. and Farr, S.L. (1980) 'Performance rating', *Psychological Bulletin,* 87: 72–107.

Lin, M.H., Kwan, V.S.Y., Cheung, A. and Fiske, S.T. (2005) 'Stereotype content model explains prejudice for an envied outgroup: Scale of anti-Asian American stereotypes', *Personality and Social Psychology Bulletin,* 31: 34–47.

Linnehan, R. and Konrad, A.M. (1999) 'Diluting diversity: Implications for intergroup inequality in organizations', *Journal of Management Inquiry,* 8: 399–414.

Lippman, W. (1922) *Public Opinion.* New York: Harcourt.

Lorbiecki, A., and Jack, G. (2000) 'Critical turns in the evolution of diversity management', *British Journal of Management,* 11: 17–31.

Litvin, D.R. (1997) 'The discourse of diversity: From biology to management', *Organization,* 4: 187–210.

Litvin, D.R. (2007) 'Diversity: Making space for a better case', in A.M. Konrad, P. Prasad and J.K. Pringle (eds), *Handbook of Workplace Diversity.* London: Sage Publications, pp. 75–94.

Livers, A.B. and Caver, K.A. (2003) *Leading in Black and White: Working Across the Racial Divide in Corporate America*. San Francisco, CA: Jossey-Bass.

Lyness, K.S. and Heilman, M.E. (2006) 'When fit is fundamental: Performance evaluations and promotions of upper-level female and male managers', *Journal of Applied Psychology*, 91: 777–785.

Martell, R.F., Parker, C., Emrich, C.G. and Crawford, M.S. (1998) 'Sex stereotyping in the executive suite: "Much ado about something"', *Journal of Personality and Social Psychology*, 13: 127–138.

Maume, D.J., Jr. (1999) 'Glass ceilings and glass elevators: Occupational segregation and sex differences in managerial promotions', *Work and Occupations*, 26: 483–509.

McCann, R. and Giles, H. (2002) 'Ageism in the workplace', in T.D. Nelson (ed.), *Ageism: Stereotyping and Prejudice Against Older Persons*. Cambridge, MA: MIT Press, pp. 163–199.

McConahay, J.B. (1983) 'Modern racism and modern discrimination. The effects of race, racial attitudes and context on simulated hiring decisions', *Personality and Social Psychology Bulletin*, 9: 551–558.

Merton, R.K. (1949) 'Discrimination and the American creed', in R. MacIver (ed.), *Discrimination and National Welfare*. New York: Harper & Row, pp. 99–126.

Mydral, G. (1944) *An American Dilemma*. New York: Harper & Row.

Mujtaba, B.G., Cavico, F., Hinds, R.M. and Oskal, C. (2006) 'Age discrimination in the workplace: Cultural paradigms associated with age in Afghanistan, Jamaica, Turkey and the United States', *Journal of Applied Management Entrepreneurship*, 11: 17–35.

Newman, J.M. and Krzytofiak, F. (1979) 'Self-reports versus unobtrusive measures: Balancing method variance and ethical concerns in employment discrimination research', *Journal of Applied Psychology*, 64: 2–85.

Nkomo, S.M. (1992) 'The emperor has no clothes: "Rewriting race in organizations."' *Academy of Management Review*, 17: 487–513.

Nkomo, S.M. and Stewart, M. (2006) 'Diverse identities in organizations', in S.R Clegg, C. Hardy, T.B Lawrence, and W.R Nord (eds), *The Sage Handbook of Organization Studies*. London: Sage Publications, pp. 120–140.

Ogbonna, E. and Harris, L.C. (2006) 'The dynamics of employee relationships in an ethnically diverse workforce', *Human Relations*, 59: 379–407.

O'Leary-Kelly, A.M., Paetzold, R.L. and Griffin, R.W. (2000) 'Sexual harassment as aggressive behavior: An actor based perspective', *Academy of Management Review*, 25: 372–388.

Perry, E.L. and Bourhis, A.C. (1998) 'A closer look at the role of applicant age in selection decisions', *Journal of Applied Social Psychology*, 28: 1670–1697.

Perry, E.L. and Finkelstein, L.M. (1999) 'Toward a broader view of age discrimination in employment related decisions: A joint consideration of organizational factors and cognitive processes', *Human Resource Management Review*, 9: 21–49.

Perry, E.L. and Parlamis, J.D. (2005) 'Age and ageism in organizations: A review and consideration of national culture', in A.M. Konrad, P. Prasad, and J.K. Pringle (eds), *Handbook of Workplace Diversity*. London: Sage Publications, pp. 345–370.

Personnel Today. (9/12/2006) *Sexism on the Increase.*

Pettigrew, T.F. (1979) 'The ultimate attribution error: Extending Allport's cognitive analysis of prejudice', *Personality and Social Psychology Bulletin*, 5: 461–476.

Pettigrew, T.F. (1998) 'Reactions toward the new minorities of western Europe', *Annual Review of Sociology*, 24: 77–103.

Pettigrew T.F. and Meertens, R.W. (1995) 'Subtle and blatant prejudice in western Europe', *European Journal of Social Psychology*, 25: 57–75.

Phillips, D.J. (2005) 'Organizational genealogies and the persistence of gender inequality: The case of Silicon Valley law firms', *Administrative Science Quarterly*, 50: 440–472.

Powell, G.N. and Butterfield, A.D. (1997) 'Effect of race on promotions to top management in a federal department', *Academy of Management Journal*, 40: 112–128.

Powell, G.N. and Butterfield, A.D. (2002) 'Exploring the influence of decision makers' race and gender on actual promotions to top management', *Personnel Psychology*, 55: 397–428.

Powell, G.N. and Butterfield, A.D. (2003) 'Gender, gender identity, and aspirations to top management', *Women in Management Review*, 18, (1/2): 88–96.

Prasad, A. (2001) 'Understanding workplace empowerment as inclusion: A historical investigation of the discourse of difference in the United States', *Journal of Applied Behavioral Science*, 27: 33–50.

Prasad, P., Pringle, J.K. and Konrad, A.M. (2006) 'Examining the contours of workplace diversity: Concepts, contexts and challenges', in A.M. Konrad, P. Prasad and J.K. Pringle (eds), *Handbook of Workplace Diversity*. London: Sage Publications, pp. 1–22.

Ragins, B.R. and Cornwell, J.M. (2001) 'Pink triangles: Antecedents and consequences of perceived workplace discrimination against gay and lesbian employees', *Journal of Applied Psychology*, 86: 1244–61.

Ritter, B.A. and Yoder, J.D. (2004) 'Gender differences in leader emergence persist even for dominant women: An updated confirmation of role congruity theory', *Psychology of Women Quarterly*, 28: 187–193.

Roos, P.A. and Gatta, M.L. (2001) 'The gender gap in earnings: Trends, explanations and prospects', in G. Powell (ed.), *Handbook of Gender and Work*. Thousand Oaks, CA: Sage, pp. 95–123.

Roberson, L., and Block, C.J. (2001) 'Racioethnicity and job performance: A review and critique of theoretical perspectives on causes of group differences', in B. Staw (ed.), *Research In Organizational Behavior*. Oxford: JAI Press. Vol. 23, pp. 247–325.

Roth, P.L., Huffcutt, A.I. and Bobko, P. (2003) 'Ethnic group differences in measures of job performance: A new meta-analysis', *Journal of Applied Psychology*, 88: 694–706.

Rotundo, M., Nguyen, D. and Sackett, P.R. (2001) 'A meta-analytic review of gender differences in perceptions of sexual harassment', *Journal of Applied Psychology*, 86: 914–922.

Ryan, M.E. and Haslam, A.S. (2005) 'The glass cliff: Evidence that women are over-represented in precarious leadership positions', *British Journal of Management*, 16: 81–90.

Sanchez, J.I. and Brock, P. (1996) 'Outcomes of perceived discrimination among Hispanic employees: Is diversity management a luxury or necessity', *Academy of Management Journal*, 3: 704–719.

Schein, V.E. (1973) 'The relationship between sex role stereotypes and requisite management characteristics', *Journal of Applied Psychology*, 57: 95–105.

Schein, V.E. (2001) 'A global look at psychological barriers to women's progress in management', *Journal of Social Issues*, 57: 675–688.

Schmitt, N. and Lappin, M. (1980) 'Race and sex as determinants of the mean and variance of performance ratings', *Journal of Applied Psychology*, 65: 428–435.

Schneider, K.T., Swan, S. and Fitzgerald, L.F. (1997) 'Job-related and psychological effects of sexual harassment in the workplace: Empirical evidence from two organizations', *Journal of Applied Psychology*, 82: 401–415.

Shaffer, M.A., Joplin, J.R.W., Bell, M.P., Lau, T. and Oguz, C. (2000) 'Gender discrimination and job related outcomes: A cross-cultural comparison of working women in the United States and China', *Journal of Vocational Behavior*, 57 (4): 395–427.

Siedel, M.L., Polzer, J.T. and Stewart, K.J. (2000) 'Friends in high places: The effects of social networks on discrimination in salary negotiations', *Administrative Science Quarterly*, 45: 1–24.

Sinclair, A. (2006) 'Critical diversity management practice in Australia: Romanced or co-opted?', in

A.M. Konrad, P. Prasad and J.K Pringle (eds), *Handbook of Workplace Diversity*. London: Sage Publications, pp. 511–530.

Stockdale, M.S. (ed.) (1997) *Sexual Harassment in the Workplace*. Thousand Oaks, CA: Sage Publications. Vol. 5.

Stone-Romero, E.F., Stone, D.L. and Lukaszewski, K. (2006) 'The influence of disability on role-taking in organizations', in A.M. Konrad, P. Prasad and J.K. Pringle (eds), *Handbook of Workplace Diversity*. London: Sage Publications, pp. 401–425.

Stone-Romero, E.F. and Stone, D.L. (2005) 'How do organizational justice concepts relate to discrimination and prejudice?', in J. Greenberg and J.A. Colquitt (eds), *Handbook of Organizational Justice*. Mahwah, NJ: Lawrence Erlbaum, pp. 439–467.

Terpstra, D. and Larsen, M. (1980) 'A note on job type and applicant race as determinants of hiring decisions', *Journal of Occupational Psychology*, 53 (2): 117–119.

Thomas, P.J., Edwards, J.E., Perry, Z.A. and David, K.M. (1998) 'Racial differences in male navy officer fitness reports', *Military Psychology*, 10: 127–143.

Thomas, D.A. and Gabarro, J.J. (1999) *Breaking Through: The Making of Minority Executives in Corporate America*. Boston: Harvard Business School Press.

Tomei, M. (2003) 'Discrimination and equality at work: A review of the concepts', *International Labour Review*, 142: 401–412.

Tomkiewicz, J., Breenner, O.C. and Adeyemi–Bello, T. (1998) 'The impact of perceptions and stereotypes on the managerial mobility of African Americans', *Journal of Social Psychology*, 138: 88–92.

Welsh, S. (1999) 'Gender and sexual harassment', *Annual Review of Sociology*, 25: 169–190.

Whitley, Jr., B.E. and Kite, M.E. (2006) *The Psychology of Prejudice and Discrimination*. Belmont, CA: Thomson Wadsworth.

Williams, C., Brown, R., Lees-Haley, P. and Price, J. (1997) 'An atttirubtional (causal dimensional) analysis of perceptions of sexual harassment', *Journal of Applied Social Psychology*, 25: 1169–1183.

Woo, D. (2000) *Glass Ceilings and Asian-Americans: The New Face of Workplace Barriers*. Lanham, MD: Altamira Press.

Wu, D. (1997) *Asian Pacific Americans in the Workplace*. Lanham, MD: Altamira Press.

Yoder, J.D. and Aniakudo, P. (1996) 'When pranks become harassment: The Case of African American women firefighters', *Sex Roles*, 35: 253–270.

Ziegert, J.C. and Hanges, P.J. (2005) 'Employment discrimination: The role of implicit attitudes, motivation and a climate for racial bias', *Journal of Applied Psychology*, 90: 553–562.

PART FIVE

Future Directions

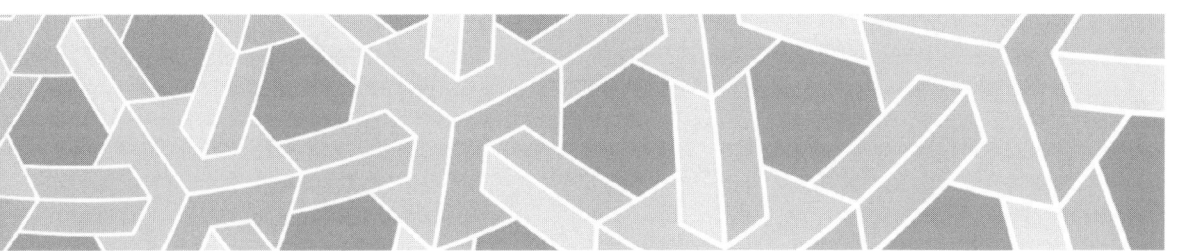

35

Work and Well-Being

Jennifer Carson and Julian Barling

For over a century, the question of how work affects individuals has attracted widespread attention. The changing nature of work-places following the industrial revolution, for example, captivated novelists and social and political theorists alike. This is also reflected by the number of authors (e.g., Franz Kafka, Charles Dickens) who chose to make this question a major topic of their works. The increasingly 'dehumanizing world of factories and offices' (Barling and Griffiths, 2002: 20) intrigued both Friedrich Engels (1845/1987) and Karl Marx (1867/1999). The result of this interest saw the appearance theories attempting to account for the 'dreadful' ways in which owners had begun to exploit their employees; theories that still have a direct and indirect influence today. Most recently, the intense public interest in how work might affect people negatively has been reflected in popular movies (e.g., *Office Space*, *The Devil wears Prada*) and TV shows (*The Office;* see Friend, 2006)

CLASSIC STUDIES ON WORK AND WELL-BEING

While acknowledging the critical historical role of social theorists and authors in trying to understand how work affects people, we limit this discussion to a brief review of sustained empirical attempts to address this question in the past century. In doing so, we note that three major patterns of research, differentiated by time and focus, can be discerned. These three trends will each be discussed, in succession, below.

The first trend, spanning several decades, was characterized by a positive focus; it began with the work of Arthur Kornhauser early in the 1920s, and ended with the work of Frederick Herzberg in the late 1950s. As early as the 1920s, Kornhauser was already devoted to understanding how work might influence what was then regarded as mental health. Not content to be a passive observer, Kornhauser was also a passionate advocate for the creation of work that might enhance well-being.

One example of this would be his alliance with unions in advocating for the well-being of workers (Zickar, 2003). Nonetheless, Kornhauser (1965) is remembered mostly because of his mammoth survey of 400, four-hour interviews of Detroit autoworkers. Many of Kornhauser's findings would be replicated repeatedly, such as the negative relationship between occupational status and mental health, and the role of job characteristics (e.g., task repetition, supervision, social interaction, job insecurity, financial stress and physical factors) in mental health. Kornhauser's contribution can be appreciated when seen against the prevailing zeitgeist, which was that work inevitably affects people negatively.

Then, stimulated primarily by the depravities of the World War II, Maslow (who was initially involved in animal research) turned his attention to the question of the upper positive limits of people's potential, resulting in his widely-known theory of self-actualization (Maslow, 1943). This hierarchical theory of needs suggested that given appropriate conditions such as freedom from social constraints, people satisfy their primary needs and ascend the hierarchy, getting ever closer to self-actualization, the only true state of mental health. It was only toward the end of his career that Maslow focused explicitly on the application of his need theory to the work context, resulting in *Eupsychian Management* (Maslow, 1965), a diary of his year-long experiences in a work organization while on sabbatical leave. However, Maslow's theory influenced many organizational thinkers and researchers (e.g., Argyris, MacGregor, Herzberg among others), and his work made a significant contribution to the literature on the positive effects of work on well-being.

Like Maslow, Herzberg was not an organizational psychologist; instead, his primary interest was in mental health. This was evident in his classic work (Herzberg, 1959), a study of the mental health of engineers and accountants, which produced many of the same findings as Kornhauser's (1965) extensive survey. However, as Herzberg's

'motivator-hygiene' or 'two factor' theory (which emphasized the role of autonomy and responsibility for well-being) gained in popularity, Herzberg explicitly extended his theory to work contexts (Herzberg, 1969). In the end, Herberg's contribution was to extend the positive area of organizational research.

Thus, this first trend occurred over several decades, and was characterized by a positive focus. Departing from the earlier focus of people such as Engels and Marx, Kornhauser, Maslow and Herzberg were all primarily interested in understanding how work affected people positively. In addition, while Kornhauser is typically identified with his survey of auto workers' mental health, what further characterizes these three is that they were all passionate advocates for more humane working conditions.

The second phase of research spans the 1960s and 1970s, is exclusively empirically based, and addressed the effects of work on ill-health – despite the fact that much of the research was couched in terms of 'work and health' (e.g., Kahn, 1981). The research of Robert Kahn and Michael Marmot – and their many colleagues, characterize this second trend.

Like Kornhauser, Kahn and his colleagues (Kahn et al., 1964) conducted a large scale survey of American workers, and in fact reported the results of his research a year before Kornhauser. Based on their large-scale national survey of the US labor force, Kahn et al. demonstrated the negative effects of three role stressors, namely role ambiguity, conflict and overload, on behavioral, attitudinal and health-related outcomes. Kahn (1981) extended these ideas almost 20 years later, and their enduring place in the study of work and health is evident from recent reviews (Beehr and Glaser, 2005).

Moreover, any discussion of Robert Kahn's seminal contribution would be incomplete without acknowledging his significant contributions in other areas: His classic *The social psychology of organizations* (Katz and Kahn, 1966) continues to exert a meaningful influence on the study of organizational psychology, and his interest in work and health-related issues continued well into his retirement, culminating with a book on 'aging well' (Rowe and Kahn, 1998). Thus, Kahn's contribution to work and health was to improve understanding around what factors increase the likelihood of illness.

It is now widely accepted that occupational status is monotonically related to health, and this is largely a function of the research of Sir Michael Marmot and his colleagues around the world (Marmot, 2004). Beginning with 'Whitehall 1,' an extensive study of approximately 18,000 male civil servants that included physiological markers of health, Marmot's findings consistently showed that illness, as well as mortality from all causes, were highest amongst men in the lowest employment grades. Whitehall II, which began in 1985 and includes 10,000 men *and* women employed in the British civil service, aimed to understand the factors that underlie the 'heath gradient.' Based on prospective data, variables frequently considered central within organizational behavior, such as procedural injustice, have been found to predict new instances of coronary heart disease (Kivimaki et al., 2005). There are now more than 250 published studies based on the Whitehall studies (http://www.ucl.ac.uk/whitehallII). The critical contribution of Marmot's research to our understanding of inequality at work and its invidious effects on health is acknowledged widely, and culminated in his receiving a knighthood in 2000. Clearly, Marmot's contribution to our understanding of illness at work has been profound.

The third phase of research is distinguished by its focus on the effects of unemployment (rather than employment itself) on health, and this research was stimulated by the large scale unemployment of the Great Depression. The research and theorizing of Marie Jahoda dominated this particular issue.

The first major study of unemployment focused on the Austrian community of Marienthal (Jahoda et al., 1933), and isolated its negative effects on mental health. That Jahoda's interest in this topic continued is remarkable given the obstacles she faced.

For instance, the Nazis attempted to burn all copies of the Jahoda et al. (1933) book because the authors were all Jewish. Despite this, in her 7th decade of publishing, Jahoda (1989) was still actively contributing to our understanding of unemployment, and her abiding interest in unemployment resulted in her theory of employment and unemployment (Jahoda, 1982). Still, today, her work is widely known; manuscripts on the psychological effects of unemployment invariably cite this book and a rock band even took its name from her theory, calling themselves NOJAHODA. Their name signified that they had none of the attributes of mental health that she identified, and their first recording was entitled 'Jahoda's witness.'

Jahoda's interests extended beyond the nature and effects of unemployment. A social activist all her life, she viewed her identities as psychologist and activist as intertwined (Jahoda, 1956). Overall, Jahoda offered a conceptual understanding of the nature of employment and unemployment (1982), and published well into her 90s, including translations of the sonnets of Louise Labe, a 16th century French proto-feminist poet (Jahoda, 1997).

In sum, just how work affects our health has been the focus of writers, social theorists and empirical researchers for more than a century. Initially, the focus of attention was on how work might positively influence psychological and physical well-being (e.g., Kornhauser, Maslow and Herzberg). Researchers then investigated workplace factors that might harm health (e.g., Kahn, Marmot). Throughout this period, researchers turned their attention to the effects of unemployment during sustained periods of high levels of unemployment (e.g., Jahoda).

In the sections that follow, we will discuss major conceptual, methodological and practical trends in current research on work and well-being. Thereafter, we present an agenda for future research; in doing so, we offer some thoughts on methodological issues that would enhance our understanding of work and well-being.

WHERE ARE WE TODAY?

To a large extent, research on work and health has come of age: There are journals devoted to the topic (*Journal of Occupational Health Psychology*, *Work and Stress*) and others that devote considerable focus to the effects of work on health (e.g., *Journal of Occupational Behavior*, *Scandinavian Journal of Work, Environment and Health*). Specialist international conferences take place regularly (e.g., the bi-annual meetings hosted by the America Psychological Association and NIOSH in North America, and the European Academy of Occupational Health Psychology in Europe) which provide a venue for an international community of scholars to debate theory and interpret data on the effects of work on the well-being of employees. Practical business implications of these data have been suggested, and in some cases (e.g., work fitness programs) implemented (Atlantis et al., 2007). This section will review the topics that dominate scholarly research today.

In the introduction, we identified unique trends in research and thinking about work and well-being over the past century. Continuing with that theme, research over the last 25 years has been strongly characterized by a focus on negative factors, namely, the study of the effects of harmful work experiences (e.g., long hours, work stress, precarious employment) on poor well-being (e.g., illness) and negative work outcomes (e.g., turnover). Underlying this approach is that after determining which work factors affect well-being negatively, ways to buffer against these factors and reduce harmful effects can be identified, and it is these different streams of research to which we now turn our attention. In the paragraphs that follow we will outline points of interest from five different areas of research in the work and well-being literature.

Overview of literature

Job stressors, resources and strains

One of the most frequent questions confronting both researchers and the lay public alike concerns the possible harmful effects of work stress on individuals. *Stressors* refer to characteristics in the environment that impinge on the individual's perceptual and cognitive processes (Pratt and Barling, 1988); *stress* reflects the individual's subjective interpretation of those events. *Resources* refer to coping mechanisms to defend against these stressors (Hobfoll, 2002). Finally, *strain* refers to the individual's response to the stress (Eden, 1982).

Within this theoretical framework, researchers have identified and studied specific work stressors. Such objective work stressors have included long work hours, alternative work arrangements, location flexibility, and job sharing; whereas, subjective stress has included job autonomy, and employee attitudes. Notwithstanding the intuitive appeal and widespread interest in this theory, research findings are mixed at best. While De Lange et al.'s (2004) comprehensive review of 45 longitudinal studies shows some support for the lagged effects of work characteristics on health and well-being (especially self-reported health and well-being), only modest support emerged for the central notion that high levels of control would buffer the effects of high demands. Within this framework, the demand-control-support model continues to stimulate considerable research, the findings of which have already added directly and indirectly to our understanding of work and well-being.

Alternative work arrangements and work design

Over the past two decades, the traditional idea of a 'full-time' job has been transformed into a variety of alternatives. In the organizational literature, this was initially reflected by a focus on the nature and consequences of *part-time work* (Barling and Gallagher, 1996). Subsequently, the range of alternative forms of employment multiplied, defying ready description; however, they vary on three dimensions, namely their temporal, numerical and functional flexibility (e.g., shift work, telecommuting). Despite early concerns that movements away from traditional forms of employment would generate poor physical and psychological well-being, empirical findings suggest that volitionality, or perceived control, is a critical moderator of any relationship between alternative work arrangements and well-being for job holders themselves (Barling et al., 2002), or any spillover effects on others (Barling et al., 1988). Findings like these again illustrate how personal resources, in this case, the choice to assume non-traditional work arrangements, might buffer against negative effects on well-being. Such resources are the focus of the next major area of research.

Work-related and personal resources

Consistent with most major theories of work stress, negative workplace experiences do not necessarily lead to negative outcomes; one explanation for this is the presence of organizational and/or personal resources buffers (or moderates) any negative effects of work stress on subsequent strain. This idea has received much empirical scrutiny over the past several decades. Two resources, namely perceived control and support, have been consistently studied as potential moderators in the work and well-being relationship.

First, the degree of perceived control is frequently studied as a moderator and this is consistent with the demand-control model (Karasek and Theorell, 1990), where high levels of demands, combined with a low level of control, results in work strain. When individuals believe they can exert some control, high demands need not result in negative outcomes (Tucker and Rutherford, 2005). Although this pattern has been reported in numerous studies, the interaction between demands and control as suggested in the theory has not received consistent support (Taris, 2006). Therefore, the role of autonomy as a moderator of the stressor-strain relationship remains unclear.

Second, social support is widely posited to moderate the relationship between job stressors and strains. Early studies showed that social support reduced somatic symptoms in the face of stressors (LaRocco et al., 1980). More recently, a lack of social support

has been associated with an increased risk of coronary heart disease, minor illnesses and impaired mental health (Cohen et al., 2003; Evans and Steptoe, 2001; Johnson and Hall, 1988; Stansfield et al., 1997). In fact, it has been included as part of a revised version of the JDC model (Johnson and Hall, 1988). In Johnson and Hall's study, perceived control was only found to have a negative effect on health symptoms when combined with social support. Similarly, Tucker and Rutherford (2005) found no direct effects of the number of hours worked on physical health symptoms, psychological health or chronic fatigue. However, they did find negative effects on physical health when a greater number of hours were combined with less control and lower social support.

However, findings on the effects of social support are not consistent, possibly because of the need to take account of how the nature (emotional, instrumental, material) and source (peer, supervisor, spouse, organization) of the support (Barling et al., 1988; Evans and Steptoe, 2001; MacEwen and Barling, 1988) interact with different job stressors and experiences (Tucker and Rutherford, 2005). This is consistent with the notion of the 'matching hypothesis': Cohen and McKay (1984) proposed that there are categories of stressors and resources, such that when the type of resources available corresponds to the nature of existing stressors (i.e. cognitive, emotional or physical), a buffering effect will occur. This hypothesis can help researchers determine which resources will be effective in a particular situation (Cutrona and Russell, 1990).

Recovery, leisure, vacation

Time away from work (e.g., leisure time, vacations) is commonly understood as a way of recovering from the rigors of everyday work experiences (e.g., Eden, 2001). But what empirical evidence is there for this? Overwork has been given much attention in the lay press, and a meta-analytic and qualitative review by Sparks et al. in 1997 concluded that work hours had a small (0.15) but positive and significant relationship with health complaints. However, a new trend in the work and well-being literature is to investigate not only the effects of work and overwork, but to consider the potential consequences of the absence of work (i.e. vacations and leisure time). This line of research was prompted by Sluiter et al. (1999), who proposed a model, in which unfavorable job characteristics (e.g., high job demands) increase an individual's need for recovery, which in turn increases health complaints.

Research now shows significant positive effects of vacations on well-being (e.g., Fritz and Sonnentag, 2006), albeit short term effects in some cases (Westman and Eden, 1997). More recent studies have extended this line of inquiry to the effects of vacations on work performance. Fritz and Sonnentag (2006) replicated findings that health complaints and exhaustion decline post-vacation, and also showed that vacations reduced the perceived effort required to complete the same level of workload. However, like earlier research (Westman and Eden, 1997), the effects of the vacation were subject to a fade-out over the next two weeks. Further, the effects were eliminated when individuals had negative thoughts about work while on vacation as this can actually cause exhaustion to increase.

This model was extended by Sonnentag and Zijlstra (2006) to include off-job (e.g., leisure, vacation) characteristics as predictors of need for recovery, fatigue and impaired well-being. Findings from two studies show that while leisure time predicted need for recovery, not all leisure activities had the same effect. Passive leisure activities were not related to need for recovery, whereas active activities (e.g., social activities, physical activities) resulted in a lower need for recovery. This effect is consistent with literature in the health sciences where physical activity has been found to reduce stress and anxiety, and increased positive affect, resulting in improved overall mood and cognitive function (Davranche and Audiffren, 2004; Fox, 1999; Giacobbi et al., 2005; Scully et al., 1998). In addition, the quality of self-reported experience was

related to need for recovery (Sonnentag and Zijlstra, 2006). These studies illustrate the importance of leisure time in buffering the negative health impacts of work stressors and provide additional support for the broader relationship between work, recovery and well-being.

Work and family

Another major area in the literature combines the research on work-family conflict with that of occupational health. Research has shown that work-family conflict can negatively impact job satisfaction (Allen et al., 2000), and psychological well-being (Frone, 2000). Recent research has further suggested that it may be beneficial to consider the formal organizational support for work-family culture as it has been found to negatively relate to stress, intentions to quit and work-family conflict (Thompson and Prottas, 2005). A comprehensive discussion of the nature and consequence of the intersection of work and family can be found in the Chapter in this volume by Grzywacz and Butler.

Negative organizational outcomes and poor well-being

As mentioned at the beginning of this section, and as can be seen from the research discussed above, much current research focuses on negative outcomes. Outcomes are typically studied in two ways. First, many studies measure well-being through aggregated organizational measures (e.g., absenteeism, turnover) perhaps because these data are easily identifiable and quantifiable: almost all HR departments have some data on employee sick days and exits. While acknowledging the difficulty in assigning costs to these measures, there are two additional problems to be considered. First, these types of measures potentially overestimate employee illness by assuming that employees are well unless they are absent. Second, these measures do not fully capture well-being, measuring only absence of well-being (i.e. illness) and not the positive aspects of well-being (e.g., positive affect). A second common method of measuring well-being is through individual, self-report measures that look at the presence or absence of psychological disorders, physical illness, or fatigue. However, these measures again invariably tell us more about illness or the absence of well-being. In contrast, assessing both negative and positive outcomes could provide a different and less truncated perspective of well-being and work performance.

TOWARDS A NEW AGENDA

Based on the above discussion, we believe that it is time to move to a new focus, one which emphasizes the positive aspects of both work and well-being. In the next section, we identify the roots of this movement and outline several directions that research might take that could benefit this alternative focus.

A positive focus

Positive psychology
The field of organizational behaviour may be experiencing a fundamental change. The dominance of the negative or 'deficit' based approach for understanding work and well-being is undergoing significant challenges from the new fields of positive psychology in general, and positive organizational scholarship and positive organizational behavior more specifically (see the Chapter by Dutton and Glynn in this volume).

As much as a century ago, Sigmund Freud summed up the goal of psychology as replacing 'neurotic misery with ordinary unhappiness', and although the statement may be a bit pessimistic, it was true inasmuch as the focus of psychology was on negative aspects of mental illness. Decades later, the work of psychologists such as Maslow (1965) focused on the possibilities of peak experience in organizations. Only in the late 1990s with the work of Martin Seligman, however, was there a sustained attempt to develop a research agenda on positive psychology (Roberts, 2006; Simonton and Baumiester,

2005). These calls for a positive psychology initially derived from observations that while psychology has made significant contributions to understanding dysfunction and illness, little was known about normal psychological functioning, much less the upper limits of human potential and experience (Roberts, 2006). Thus, the goal of positive psychology is to look at how individuals can be brought from 'ordinary unhappiness' to happiness, and by extension, from an emphasis on ill-health and psychological disorder to one of well-being and optimal functioning

Following the lead of Seligman, Snyder and Lopez (2002) suggested that the study of hedonic emotional states, such as happiness, satisfaction, joy, pleasure, and optimism would provide insight into virtuous acts, such as forgiveness, nurturance and wisdom. Broadening this conception, positive scholarship has involved three main components: positive subjective experiences (e.g., happiness, pleasure, joy, gratification), positive individual traits (e.g., capacity for love or vocation, courage, perseverance, self esteem), and the institutions and organizations that cultivate these experiences and enable these traits (Fineman, 2006). Positive psychological theory was perhaps applied initially to clinical practice. Outside of clinical psychology, the positive perspective has resulted in a paradigm shift across disciplines as it has been applied to health, education, political science, education and business (Roberts, 2006).

Positive organizational scholarship (POS)

One area in which positive psychology has had a significant impact is business research – articulated in depth in the Chapter in this volume by Dutton and Glynn – resulting in the approaches now known as positive organizational behavior (POB) or positive organizational scholarship (POS). Within the organizational realm, the positive emphasis was always present in initiatives to make employees' working lives better, dating back at least to the work of Kornhauser, Maslow and others.

In organizations, positive organizational scholarship attempts to understand and enable the full range of employee potential and capabilities by fostering high-quality relationships, and increasing positive emotions (Cameron et al., 2003). Creating positive emotions in employees and their co-workers is not an end goal of POB. Fredrickson (2003) asserts that 'people should consider cultivating positive emotions in themselves and others, not just as end-states in themselves, but also as a means to achieving individual and organizational transformation and optimal functioning over time' (p. 164). Therefore, within this field, old issues are being examined through a new lens (Roberts, 2006), new theory is being generated (Spreitzer et al., 2005), and applications for the workplace are being considered. Perhaps not surprisingly given the recent development of these initiatives, some critics however have suggested that the area lacks empirical data linking positive research to objective organizational performance (Fineman, 2006).

Positive organizational factors

Research has now begun to address organizational features that enable positive outcomes in the workplace (Turner et al., 2002). One of the earliest and most important lessons is that achieving positive well-being may not be straightforward. Simply removing stressors, as a traditional 'deficit' approach might suggest, may not be sufficient. As one example of this 'deficit' approach, Karasek's (1979) job demands and control model illustrates that a reduction in job demands or increase in autonomy results only in a corresponding reduction in job strain – there simply is no evidence that this results in *enhanced* well-being. Instead, enhancing well-being will require the presence of additional and different factors. Thus, as an example, positive organizational behavior seeks to identify the role of organizational climate in fostering positive well-being and performance outcomes (Roberts, 2006). Recent research has focused on how positive organizational factors such as transformational leadership,

work-life balance, climate and interpersonal relationships, may positively influence well-being.

Indeed, several of these overlapping factors have been investigated empirically. Still, most studies that have studied the relationship between climate or leadership and well-being have focused on the absence of well-being resulting from negative climates (e.g., Rose et al., 2006), or the negative relationship between leader behaviors and poor well-being (van Dierendonck et al., 2004; Gilbreath and Benson, 2004). However, several studies focusing on the positive effects should be noted. First, the role of leadership, in promoting positive well-being has recently been reported. A recent study by Arnold et al. (2007) examines the relationship between transformational leadership and positive psychological well-being. Using two measures of positive affective well-being – the first developed by Kelloway and Francis (Hess et al., 2005) and the second an adapted version of the General Health Questionnaire (GHQ) that used only six positively worded items (Mullarkey et al., 1999) – support emerged for the hypothesized relationship that transformational leadership exerts a positive influence on psychological well-being (Arnold et al., 2007).

In a separate study on the effects of leadership on well-being, Bono and Ilies (2006) found that leader emotions positively predicted followers' pleasant moods. Bridging research on climate and leadership, Nembhard and Edmondson (2006) investigated the effects of leadership and culture in health-care teams, and demonstrated that leader inclusiveness was positively related to both psychological safety and engagement at work. Finally, a meta-analysis of over 70 studies (Rhoades and Eisenberger, 2002) showed that perceived organizational support was significantly related to positive mood. As these examples illustrate, although the research in this area is still limited, early findings support the link between certain organizational features and positive employee outcomes.

Positive traits and behaviors

With the appearance of positive organizational scholarship, new constructs have emerged to describe and explain positive traits and behaviors in the workplace. One such construct, positive deviance, has been used to describe positive behaviors at both the individual and organizational level. In the organizational literature, deviance typically refers to intentional behaviors that go against organizational norms and that potentially threaten the well-being of the organization, its members, or both (Bennett and Robinson, 2000). Conversely, the term positive deviance reflects prosocial behaviors such as whistle-blowing, corporate social responsibility and creativity/innovation. Spreitzer and Sonenshein (2004) speculate that improved well-being is one of the possible outcomes of positive deviance.

Personal resilience has long been used to account for well-being in the face of considerable social and familial adversity (Rutter, 1987). As an example, while children exposed to family abuse are unlikely to thrive socially or educationally, some do, and resilience is an important explanatory factor (Rutter, 2002). Speculation now focuses on its possible extension to well-being in the organizational context (Cameron and Caza, 2004; Sutcliffe and Vogus, 2003).

Similarly, compassion at work has been identified as a process that occurs in response to suffering, and that can result in positive emotional outcomes – perhaps for both parties. Kanov and co-authors (2004) conceptualized compassion as a 'dynamic process, or a set of subprocesses, that may be found both in individuals and collectivities.' Thus, the compassion process comprises the subprocesses of 'noticing,' 'feeling' and 'responding.' Through a range of characteristics including culture, systems, leadership and technology, these authors theorized that compassion can be enabled at collective levels and stimulate positive organizational outcomes. Therefore, research in POS and POB has stimulated a renewed focus on positive traits and behaviors and these findings suggest these may influence well-being.

Positive employee outcomes

Pushing this new boundary even further, researchers have focused on specific positive outcomes at the individual level, such as happiness, flourishing, thriving and vigor in the workplace. First, the term 'happiness' is commonly used in everyday language, to connote bliss, pleasure or cheerfulness. Indeed, this term was used by Diener to describe subjective well-being. Generally speaking, happiness is a broad construct that refers to people's evaluations of their lives (Diener, 2000). A related concept is that of flourishing. Originally conceptualized by Keyes (2002) as the 'presence of mental health,' flourishing denotes the positive end of the well-being, both psychologically and socially (Keyes and Haidt, 2002). In fact, recent research by Keyes (2005) has supported a two factor model of mental health where one factor represents mental illness (e.g., anxiety, depression) and one represents mental health (i.e. flourishing). Further, employees who were mentally healthy according to both factors (absence of mental illness, presence of flourishing) had the lowest risk of cardiovascular disease, the lowest number of chronic diseases and the fewest daily health limitations (Keyes, 2007).

Spreitzer et al. (2005) suggested that thriving at work was important in predicting positive mental health. They defined thriving as a 'psychological state in which individuals experience both a sense of vitality and a sense of learning at work.' In this perspective, vitality describes a feeling of having available energy (Nix et al., 1999). Learning reflects the feeling of acquiring and applying new knowledge and skills (Elliott and Dweck, 1988). Unlike psychological disturbances which are reduced by decreasing workplace stressors, Spreitzer et al. (2005) suggested that thriving requires the presence of specific states, behaviors, resources and contexts. Their proposed model reflects a socially embedded process where contextual features (e.g., climate of trust and respect) and work resources (e.g., knowledge, positive meaning) predict individual thriving at work (i.e., vitality and learning) mediated by individual agentic work behaviors (e.g., task focus). Subsequently, thriving is proposed to result in positive development and health outcomes.

The last positive outcome to be discussed here is vigor, which has been frequently used in the sports literature (e.g., Reinboth and Duda, 2006) to describe a feeling often associated with physical activity. Recently, Shirom (2004) applied vigor to the organizational context. He suggested that vigor is the opposite of burnout and that it describes individuals' 'feelings that they possess physical strength, emotional energy and cognitive liveliness, a set of interconnected affective experiences …' (p. 3). Further, Shirom posits that vigor is not merely a mood state, but that it promotes specific goal-directed behaviors that could improve performance at work as well as positively impact well-being. Thus, vigor is a positive outcome that influences well-being in the workplace.

In sum, with the application of positive psychology to the organizational realm, new disciplines have emerged, namely positive organizational behavior and positive organizational scholarship. These new disciplines have given rise to special issues in established journals (e.g., *Journal of Organizational Behavior*), conferences (e.g., *Applied Positive Psychology Conference, International Positive Psychology Summit*), and a dedicated research center at the Ross School of Business at the University of Michigan. A wealth of new research investigating the positive aspects and outcomes of work have emerged from these initiatives. In working towards a new agenda, the influence of positive organizational scholarship will be instrumental in adding to a more complete understanding of the work and well-being relationship.

WHAT IS WELL-BEING?

Now that we have discussed past and present research on work and well-being, what exactly

is 'well-being'? In this section, we discuss how the construct is defined and applied in organizational research, and note some of the critiques of this approach.

Merriam-Webster's definition of well-being is 'the state of being happy, healthy or prosperous.' Part of this definition is captured in the organizational literature by Diener's (1984; 2000) definition of subjective well-being, which comprises people's affective and cognitive evaluations of their lives (i.e., 'happiness'). Diener then separates subjective well-being into three components, including: (1) life satisfaction (global judgment), (2) facet-specific satisfaction (e.g., work satisfaction), (3) positive affect (pleasant moods and emotions) and low levels of negative affects (unpleasant moods and emotions). In an integrative review (Ryan and Deci, 2000), well-being was organized into two distinct traditions: hedonic well-being (i.e., happiness) and eudaimonic well-being (i.e., human potential). Keyes et al. (2002) broadened these conceptualizations, including affective indicators of happiness (hedonic well-being), cognitive assessments of life satisfaction; psychological well-being included self-fulfillment (eudaimonic), but also relations with others and self-acceptance. Clearly, there is only limited agreement on the precise definition of well-being and its conceptualization continues to evolve.

Despite these conceptualizations, in empirical research, well-being continues to be measured largely as the absence of negative physical or psychological symptoms (e.g., Mattila et al., 2006; Rhoades and Eisenberger, 2002). Well-being is frequently operationalized as the absence of burnout (e.g., 'I often feel emotionally drained; leads to loss of motivation and energy), or the presence of health complaints (e.g., general health questionnaire) (Fritz and Sonnentag, 2006), anxiety or depression. Thus, although theory would suggest well-being is equated with positive affect (Keyes, 2002), most organizational research operationalizes well-being as the absence of these symptoms. This continued omission is all the more glaring because there are empirical examinations of context-free well-being (e.g., Diener et al., 2006; Kahneman et al., 2004), demonstrating that it is indeed possible to operationalize well-being both positively and negatively.

From this examination of the literature, therefore, it is apparent that there is a large gap between the conceptualization and operationalization of well-being. Our understanding of work and well-being would clearly benefit from greater consistency in this regard.

Physical and psychological health

From the definitions cited above, it is clear that most conceptualizations of well-being limit their focus to psychological outcomes. However, the experience of well-being in organizations often includes issues relating to physical health. In setting an agenda for future research, researchers might consider taking a more comprehensive view of well-being, including both psychological and physical health, as well as their reciprocal effects.

Evidence from outside of the organizational literature has long supported the interdependence between psychological and physical health (e.g. Hayes and Ross, 1986; Keyes, 2007). Empirical results from an epidemiological study by Von Korff and Simon (1996) showed a strong relationship between pain and psychological disorders (e.g., anxiety and depression). The relationship was strongest when the pain was diffuse and when it interfered with activities. Given these outcomes, Von Korff and Simon (1996) suggested that pain and psychological illness should be viewed as having both reciprocal and behavioral effects. The effects of chronic pain extend beyond physical harm, and have severe impacts on psychological well-being (Penny et al., 1999). Indeed, within the organizational domain, research suggests that physical and psychological well being are often related, and may be reciprocally caused (Jamal, 1999).

Similar findings have been noted for more global measures of well-being (e.g, life satisfaction) commonly used in the organizational literature. Correlations have been documented between life satisfaction and various objective and medical criteria (Kahneman and Krueger, 2006). As one example, Cohen et al. (2003) assessed respondents' life satisfaction after which they were exposed to a cold virus. Those with higher baseline ratings of life satisfaction were less likely to develop a cold, and in turn were quicker to recover if they became sick. In a similar study, Kiecolt-Glaser et al. (2002) subjected some participants to a deliberate wound; those who were more satisfied recovered more quickly from the wound. Given the support these findings provide for reciprocal relationships among psychological and physical health variables, researchers should extend their focus on well-being to include both physical and psychological aspects.

CRAFTING THE NEW AGENDA

We now turn our attention to some conceptual and empirical suggestions that might enhance both our understanding of work and well-being, and also enhance the likelihood that work might lead to well-being.

Defining and operationalizing the constructs

How should we define well-being? Currently, the prevailing conceptual definition is close to that of Diener's (1984; 2000); however, it is rarely measured as such. Current measures for well-being usually depict the absence of psychological and/or physical symptoms. Appropriate measures need to reflect the conceptual definitions of the construct; likewise, a construct definition is not useful unless we are able to measure it accurately. Method needs to follow theory, but in this case it is not clear this is occurring.

Diener's conceptualization, which includes affective and cognitive evaluation, can be reduced to its components – global, facet-specific and affective judgments – and would clearly be influenced by health. Although the WHO defines health as 'a state of complete physical, mental and social well-being and not merely the absence of disease or infirmity' (World Health Organization, 2006), the more commonly used definition views health as the absence of illness. This construct focuses on the absence of psychological (e.g., anxiety) and physical (e.g., headaches) health symptoms – negative symptoms. Following this definition, health would not be synonymous with well-being, but it would be a critical component.

An additional complexity is that both positive and negative aspects need to be understood. While well-being is a positive state, negative psychological or physical conditions can detract from well-being. Conversely, the removal of ill-health does not necessarily mean that well-being follows.

A renewed focus on positive outcomes

As we have already noted, while both the health and well-being constructs have positive and negative outcomes, the literature has overwhelmingly focused on the negative – a consistent trend across the broad spectrum of psychological research showing the greater effects of bad rather than good events (Baumeister et al., 2001). This is understandable given that illnesses (e.g., heart disease) tend to be more pressing, and sometimes more intriguing, than positive outcomes (e.g., increased energy). However, the emergence of positive organizational scholarship has shifted the focus from preventing illness to improving the lives of employees. Despite this, it would be premature to 'throw the baby out with the bathwater' and we now discuss the importance of focusing on both positive and negative aspects of well-being.

In a recent critique, Fineman (2006) suggested that in the emerging 'positive' literature, negative emotions have been unduly sidelined in order to study positive emotions with positive consequences. Fineman's (2006) is not the only voice questioning this approach; Lazarus (2003) also argues that positive emotions are inextricably linked with

negative ones. For example, happiness can trigger anxiety, or anger could be energizing.

However, the separation of positive and negative affect is hardly new. As early as 1965, researchers called for the separation of positive and negative affect after these two emotions, usually thought of as polar opposites, were shown to form separable factors that manifest divergent validity (Bradburn and Caplovitz, 1965). Subsequent research (Cacioppo et al., 1999) went further, indicating that separate biological processes were involved in creating positive and negative affect. Despite such findings, Diener (2000) reiterated the importance of studying positive and negative affect separately, because combining them could result in the loss of valuable information.

Research findings suggest that positive and negative emotions work in tandem. For example, positive emotions negate the impact of negative emotions on cardiovascular functioning (Fredrickson et al., 2000). One possibility is that the balance of positive and negative factors may be critical. Fredrickson and Losada (2005) found that optimal team functioning was achieved when the ratio of positive to negative experiences or emotions was 3:1. Clearly, research can no longer ignore the positive; equally clearly, even research on well-being needs to capture the experience of both positive and negative outcomes. As a result, we should not assume that positive affective states will only cause positive outcomes and vice versa; a sole look at positive or negative factors may result in a truncated perspective of work and well-being.

From a measurement perspective, the General Health Questionnaire (GHQ; Goldberg, 1972) was initially developed and intended to focus on minor psychiatric disturbance, but adaptations of the GHQ are commonly used in studying what is referred to as 'well-being' (e.g., Martin et al., 2005; van Dierendonck et al., 2004). In contrast, other measures of well-being are overly broad, for example, measuring overall life satisfaction (e.g., Satisfaction with Life Scale; Diener et al., 1985). The lack of a specific measure to appropriately assess well-being within organizations has no doubt hampered research about and understanding of work and well-being.

Acknowledging this methodological gap in the literature, Keyes (2002) created a mental health continuum that re-conceptualizes mental health. The scale conceptualizes the presence of mental health on one end of the spectrum as flourishing and the absence of mental health on the other end of the spectrum as languishing. Similarly, within an organizational context, Van Katwyk et al., 2000, created an affective well-being scale to overcome some these difficulties. These measures are clearly a step in the right direction.

Regarding methodology

Proposing the need for a new conceptual perspective presents an opportunity to question whether the methods that satisfied prior perspectives will still be sufficient. At least three issues warrant consideration in future research on work and well-being. First, consistent with the fact that questions about work and well-being first arose to understand 'what work did to people,' much of the research over the past has assumed (implicitly or explicitly) the existence of a one-way causality. This notion is challenged both conceptually and practically. Conceptually, it is clear that individuals are not simply passive responders to their environments. Instead, they actively participate in, and help to construct their environment (Bandura, 2005) – including their work environment. Practically, while research has focused extensively on whether work affects health (e.g., cardiovascular health), it is clear that health issues (suffering from heart disease) will affect work. Similarly, while it is commonly assumed that mothers' employment affects children, the reverse is just as plausible; for example, sick children will influence mothers' employment in many ways (Major et al., 2004). Thinking about work and well-being must now reflect this bi-directionality.

Second, while the best longitudinal studies will provide insight into issues of causal direction, such research will still be based on individuals' aggregated responses about work and well-being over some specified time period. Yet, these reports reflect nothing more that individuals' subjective aggregations of their daily experiences. Of critical importance in this respect is that daily experiences fluctuate; one can experience a wonderful workday on one day, but have negative experiences the next. Research needs to capture the meaning of daily work and well-being, and then to study the long-term effects of these daily experiences and fluctuations. Including studies of daily work experience with short-term and longitudinal studies may help unravel an additional issue that has bedeviled behavioral researchers, namely how long it takes for any effects (positive or negative) to emerge and how long that might persist.

Third, most existing research assumes that the relationship between work and well-being is linear. Yet Warr's (1987) vitamin model of mental health suggests that some thought must be given to the possibility of non-linear relationships in understanding work and well-being. As one example, it is possible that there are optimal benefits of work involvement and that after attaining a certain level, no additional benefits to well-being might accrue – or even that negative effects might emerge.

Regarding interventions

The extent to which any body of knowledge has been extended into well-designed interventions would be one indication of the maturity of that field. A review of specialist journals such as the *Journal of Occupational Health Psychology* and *Work and Stress* makes it all too clear that there are very few evaluations of personal and organizational interventions aimed at enhancing well-being. Acknowledging the practical and design difficulties associated with quasi-experimental research, if new findings are to be implemented by organizations, studies evaluating the effectiveness of interventions need to be conducted.

CONCLUSION

Understanding work and well-being has intrigued researchers, practitioners and the lay public for at least the past century, and empirical research has focused on work and well-being extensively over the past several decades. The recent reemergence of positive psychology and positive organizational scholarship have challenged the continual neglect of the positive aspects of work and well-being. In this chapter, we have focused on this tension between the negative and positive, identifying some issues that might help shape the on-going agenda for research on work and well-being. While the importance of considering positive influences and outcomes carefully is abundantly clear, this should not result in a pendulum swing away from the negative. The culmination of historical and current literature provides an excellent launching point for researchers to apply previous findings, examine both positive and negative influences and outcomes for well-being, and how these might interact. In effect, researchers not only have an opportunity to truly expand our understanding of work and well-being, but also to substantially influence the lives of working people.

ACKNOWLEDGEMENTS

Writing of this chapter was facilitated by separate grants from the Social Sciences and Humanities Research Council of Canada to both authors.

REFERENCES

Allen, T., Herst, D., Bruck, C. and Sutton, M. (2000) 'Consequences associated with work-to-family conflict: A review and agenda for future research', *Journal of Occupational Health Psychology*, 5: 278–308.

Arnold, K., Turner, N., Barling, J., Kelloway, E.K. and McKee, M.C. (2007) 'Transformational leadership and psychological well-being: The mediating role of meaningful work', *Journal of Occupational Health Psychology*, 12: 193–203.

Atlantis, E., Chow, C.M., Kirby, A. and Singh, M.A.F. (2007) 'Worksite intervention effects on sleep quality: A randomized controlled trial', *Journal of Occupational Health Psychology*, 11: 291–304.

Bandura, A. (2005) 'The evolution of social cognitive theory', in K.G. Smith and M.A. Hitt (eds), *Great Minds in Management: The Process of Theory Development.* New York: Oxford University Press, pp. 9–34.

Barling J., Fullagar, C. and Marchl-Dingel, J. (1988) 'Employment commitment as a moderator of the maternal employment/child behaviour relationship', *Journal of Organizational Behavior*, 9: 113–122.

Barling, J. and Gallagher, D.G. (1996) 'Part-time employment', in C.L. Cooper and I.T. Robertson (eds), *International Review of Industrial and Organizational Psychology.* London: Wiley and Sons. Vol II, pp. 243–277.

Barling, J. and Griffiths, A. (2002) 'The history of occupational health psychology', in L.E. Tetrick and J.C. Quick (eds), *Handbook of Occupational Health Psychology.* Washington, DC: American Psychological Association, pp. 19–33.

Barling, J., Inness, M. and Gallagher, D.G. (2002) 'Alternative work arrangements and employee-well-being', in P. Perrewe and D.C. Ganster (eds) *Research in Occupational Stress and Well-being.* New York: JAI Press, pp. 183–216.

Barling J., MacEwen, K.E. and Pratt, L. (1988) 'Manipulating the type and source of social support: An experimental investigation', *Canadian Journal of Behavioural Science*, 20: 140–154.

Baumeister, R.F., Bratslavsky, E., Finkenauer, C. and Vohs, K.D. (2001) 'Bad is stronger than good', *Review of General Psychology*, 5: 323–370.

Beehr, T.A. and Glaser, S. (2005) 'Organizational role stress', in J. Barling and E.K. Kelloway (eds), *Handbook of Work Stress.* Thousand Oaks, CA: Sage Publications, pp. 7–35.

Bennett, R. and Robinson, S. (2000) 'Development of a measure of workplace deviance', *Journal of Applied Psychology*, 85: 349–360.

Bono, J. and Ilies, R. (2006) 'Charisma, positive emotions and mood contagion', *The Leadership Quarterly*, 17: 317–334.

Bradburn, N. and Caplovitz, D. (1965) *Reports of Happiness.* Chicago: Aldine.

Cacioppo, J., Gardner, W. and Berntson, G. (1999) 'The affect system has parallel and integrative processing components: Form follows function', *Journal of Personality and Social Psychology*, 76: 839–855.

Cameron, K. and Caza, A. (2004) 'Contributions to the discipline of positive organizational scholarship', *American Behavioral Scientist*, 47: 731–739.

Cameron, K.S., Dutton, J.E. and Quinn, R.E. (eds) (2003) *Positive Organizational Scholarship*. San Francisco: Berrett-Koehler.

Cohen, S., Doyle, W., Tuner, R., Alper, C. and Skoner, D. (2003) 'Emotional state and susceptibility to the common cold', *Psychosomatic Medicine*, 65: 652–657.

Cohen, S. and McKay, G. (1984) 'Social support, stress and the buffering hypothesis; A theoretical analysis', in A. Baum, S.E. Taylor and J.E. Singer (eds), *Handbook of Psychology and Health*. Hillsdale, NJ: Erlbaum, pp. 253–267.

Cutrona, C. and McKay, G. (1990) 'Type of social support and specific stress: Toward a theory of optimal matching', in B.R. Sarason, I.G. Sarason and G.R. Pierce (eds), *Social Support: An Interactional View*. New York: Wiley, pp. 319–366.

Davranche, H. and Audiffren, M. (2004) 'Facilitating effects of exercise on information processing', *Journal of Sports Sciences*, 22: 419–428.

de Lange, A., Taris, T., Kompier, M., Houtman, I. and Bongers, P. (2003) '"The very best of the millennium": Longitudinal research and the demand-control (support) model', *Journal of Occupational Health Psychology*, 8: 282–305.

De Lange, A.H., Taris, T.W., Kompier, M.A.J., Houtman, I.L.D. and Bongers, P.M. (2004) 'The relationships between job characteristics and mental health: Examining normal, reversed and reciprocal relationships in a 4-wave study', *Work & Stress*, 18: 149–166.

Diener, E. (1984) 'Subjective well-being', *Psychological Bulletin*, 95: 542–575.

Diener, E. (2000) 'Subjective well-being: The science of happiness and a proposal for a national index', *American Psychologist*, 55: 34–43.

Diener, E., Lucas, R. and Scollon, C. (2006) 'Beyond the hedonic treadmill: Revising the Adaptation Theory of well-being', *American Psychologist*, 61: 305–314.

Diener, E., Emmons, R.A., Larsen, R.J. and Griffin, S. (1985) 'The satisfaction with life scale', *Journal of Personality Assessment*, 49: 71–75.

Dutton, J.E. and Glynn, M.A. (2007) 'Work-family conflict', in C.L. Cooper and J. Barling (eds), *Handbook of Organizational Behavior*. London: Wiley.

Eden, D. (1982) 'Critical job events, acute stress, and strain: A multiple interrupted time series', *Organizational Behaviour and Human Performance*, 30: 312–329.

Eden, D. (2001) 'Vacations and other respites: Studying stress on and off the job', in C.L. Cooper and I.T. Robertson (eds), *International Review of Industrial and Organizational Psychology*. New York: Wiley. Vol. 16, pp. 121–146.

Elliott, E. and Dweck, C. (1988) 'Goals: An approach to motivation and achievement', *Journal of Personality and Social Psychology*, 54: 5–12.

Evans, O. and Steptoe, A. (2001) 'Social support at work, heart rate, and cortisol: A self-monitoring study', *Journal of Occupational Health Psychology*, 6: 361–370.

Fineman, S. (2006) 'On being positive: Concerns and counterpoints', *Academy of Management Review*, 31: 270–291.

Fox, K. (1999) 'The influence of physical activity on mental well-being', *Public Health Nutrition*, 2 (3): 411–418.

Fredrickson, B. (2003) 'Positive emotions and upward spirals in organizations', in J.S. Cameron, J.E. Dutton, and R.E. Quinn (eds), *Positive Organizational Scholarship: Foundations of a New Discipline*. San Francisco: Berrett-Koehler, pp. 163–175.

Fredrickson, B. and Losada, M. (2005) 'Positive affect and the complex dynamics of human flourishing', *American Psychologist*, 60: 678–686.

Fredrickson, B., Mancuso, R., Branigan, C. and Tugade, M. (2000) 'The undoing effect of positive emotions', *Motivation and Emotion*, 24: 237–258.

Friend, T. (2006, December 11) The paper chase: Office life in two worlds. *New Yorker*, Available http://www.ucl.ac.uk/whitehallII.

Fritz, C. and Sonnentag, S. (2006) 'Recovery, well-being, and performance-related outcomes: The role of workload and vacation experiences', *Journal of Applied Psychology*, 91: 936–945.

Frone, M. (2000) 'Work-family conflict and employee psychiatric disorders: The national comorbidity survey', *Journal of Applied Psychology*, 85: 888–895.

Giacobbi, P., Hausenblas, H. and Frye, N. (2005) 'A naturalistic assessment of the relationship between personality, daily life events, leisure-time exercise, and mood', *Psychology of Sport and Exercise*, 6: 67–81.

Gilbreath, B. and Benson, P.G. (2004) 'The contribution of supervisor behaviour to employee psychological well-being', *Work and Stress*, 18: 255–266.

Goldberg, D.P. (1972) *The Detection of Psychiatric Illnesses by Questionnaire*. Oxford: Oxford University Press.

Grzywacz, J. and Butler, A. (2007) 'Work-family conflict', in C.L. Cooper and J. Barling (eds) (2008), *Handbook of Organizational Behavior*. London: Wiley.

Hayes, D. and Ross, C. E. (1986) 'Body and mind: The effect of exercise, overweight, and physical health on psychological well-being', *Journal of Health and Social Behavior*, 27: 387–400.

Herzberg, F. (1959) *The Motivation to Work*. New York: Wiley.

Hess, A., Kelloway, E.K. and Francis, L. (2005) *Development of the Positive Affective Well-being Scale*. Paper presented at the Convention of the Canadian Psychological Association, Montreal.

Hobfoll, S. (2002) 'Social and psychological resources and adaptation', *Review of General Psychology*, 6: 307–324.

Jahoda, M. (1956) 'Psychological issues in civil liberties', *American Psychologist*, 11: 99–120.

Jahoda, M. (1982) *Employment and Unemployment: A Social Psychological Analysis*. Cambridge: Cambridge University Press.

Jahoda, M. (1989) 'Economic recession and mental health: Some conceptual issues', *Journal of Social Issues*, 44 (4): 13–24.

Jahoda, M. (1997) *Louise Labe. Vierundzwanzig Sonette in drei Sprachen*. Munster: Johann Lang.

Jahoda, M., Lazarsfeld, P.F. and Zeisel, H. 91933) *Marienthal: The Sociography of an Unemployed Community* (English translation 1972). London: Tavistock Publications.

Jamal, M. (1999) 'Job stress and employee well being. A cross-cultural empirical study', *Stress Medicine*, 16: 153–158.

Johnson, J.V. and Hall, E.M. (1988) 'Job strain, work place social support, and cardiovascular disease: A cross-sectional study of a random sample of the Swedish working population', *American Journal of Public Health*, 78: 1336–1342.

Kahn, R.L. (1981) *Work and Health*. New York: Wiley.

Kahn, R.L., Wolfe, D.M., Quinn, R.P., Snoek, J.D. and Rosenthal, R.A. (1964) *Organizational Stress: Studies in Role Conflict and Ambiguity*. New York: Wiley.

Kahneman, D. and Krueger, A. (2006) 'Developments in the measurement of subjective well-being', *Journal of Economic Perspectives*, 20: 3–24.

Kahneman,D., Krueger, A., Schkade, D., Schwarz, N. and Stone, A. (2004) 'A survey method for characterizing daily life experience: The Day Reconstruction Method', *Science*, 306: 1776–1780.

Kanov, J., Maitlis, S., Worline, M., Dutton, J., Frost, P. and Lilius, J. (2004) 'Compassion in organizational life', *American Behavioral Scientist*, 47: 808–827.

Karasek, R. (1979) 'Job demands, job decision latitude, and mental strain: Implications for job redesign', *Administrative Science Quarterly*, 24: 285–308.

Karasek, R. and Theorell, T. (1990) *Healthy Work: Stress, Productivity, and the Reconstruction of Working Life*. New York: Basic Books.

Katz, D. and Kahn, R. (1966) *The Social Psychology of Organizations*. New York: Wiley.

Keyes, C.L.M. (2002) 'The mental health continuum: From languishing to flourishing in life', *Journal of Health and Social Behavior*, 43: 207–222.

Keyes, C. (2005) 'Mental illness and/or mental health? Investigating axioms of the complete state model of health', *Journal of Consulting and Clinical Psychology*, 73: 539–548.

Keyes, C. (2007) 'Promoting and protecting mental health as flourishing: A complementary strategy for improving national mental health', *American Psychologist*, 62: 95–108.

Keyes, C., Shmotkin, D. and Ryff, C. (2002) 'Optimizing well-being: The empirical encounter of two traditions', *Journal of Personality and Social Psychology*, 82: 1007–1022.

Keyes, C.L.M. and Haidt, J. (eds) (2002) *Flourishing: Positive Psychology and the Life Well-Lived*. Washington, DC: American Psychological Association.

Kiecolt-Glaser, J., McGuire, L., Robles, T. and Glaser, R. (2002) 'Psychoneuroimmunology: Psychological Influences on Immune Function and Health', *Journal of Consulting and Clinical Psychology*, 70: 537–547.

Kivimaki, M., Ferrie, J.E., Brunner, E., Head, J., Shipley, M.J., Vahtera, J. and Marmot, M.G. (2005) 'Justice at work and reduced risk of coronary heart disease among employees', *Archives of Internal Medicine*, 165: 2245–2251.

Kornhauser, A. (1965) *Mental Health of the Industrial Worker*. New York: Wiley.

LaRocco, J., House, J. and French, J. Jr. (1980) 'Social support, organizational stress, and health', *Journal of Health and Social Behavior*, 21: 202–218.

Lazarus, R. (2003) 'Does the positive psychology movement have legs?', *Psychological Inquiry*, 14: 93–109.

MacEwen, K.E. and Barling, J. (1988) 'Interrole conflict, family support and marital functioning in employed mothers: A short-term, longitudinal study', *Journal of Organizational Behavior*, 9: 241–250.

Major, D.A., Cardenas, R.A. and Allard, C.A. (2004) 'Child health: A legitimate business concern', *Journal of Occupational Health Psychology*, 9: 306–321.

Marmot, M. (2004) *The Status Syndrome: How Social Standing Affects Our Health and Longevity.* New York: Times Books.

Martin, A., Jones, E. and Callan, V. (2005) 'The role of psychological climate in facilitating employee adjustment during organizational change', *European Journal of Work and Organizational Psychology*, 14: 263–289.

Maslow, A. (1943) 'A Theory of Human Motivation', *Psychological Review*, 50: 370–396.

Maslow, A. (1965) *Eupsychian Management: A Journal.* Homewood, IL: Irwin–Dorsey.

Mattila, P., Elo, A., Kuosma, E. and Kylä-Setälä, E. (2006) 'Effect of participative work conference on psychosocial work environment and well-being', *European Journal of Work and Organizational Psychology*, 15: 459–476.

Merriam-Webster Online. Merriam-Webster's Online Dictionary. http://www.mw.com/dictionary/well% 20being January 25, 2007.

Mullarkey, S., Wall, T., Warr, P., Clegg, C. and Stride, C. (1999) *Measures of Job Satisfaction, Mental Health and Job-Related Well-Being: A Bench-marking Manual.* Sheffield: Institute of Work Psychology.

Nembhard, I.M. and Edmondson, A.C. (2006) 'Making it safe: The effects of leader inclusiveness and professional status on psychological safety and improvement efforts in health care teams', *Journal of Organizational Behavior*, 27: 941–966.

Nix, G., Ryan, R., Manly, J. and Deci, F. (1999) 'Revitalization through self-regulation. The effects of autonomous and controlled motivation on happiness and vitality', *Journal of Experimental Social Psychology*, 25: 266–284.

Penny, K., Purves, A., Smith, B. and Chambers, W. (1999) 'Relationship between the chronic pain grade and measures of physical, social and psychological well-being', *Pain*, 79: 275–279.

Pratt, L. and Barling, J. (1988) 'Differentiating daily hassles, acute and chronic stressors: A framework and its Implications', in J.R. Hurrell, L.R. Murphy, S.L. Sauter and C.L. Cooper (eds), *Occupational Stress: Issues and Developments in Research.* London: Taylor & Francis, pp. 41–53.

Reinboth, M. and Duda, J. (2006) 'Perceived motivational climate, need satisfaction and indices of well-being in team sports: A longitudinal perspective', *Psychology of Sport and Exercise*, 7: 269–286.

Rhoades, L. and Eisenberger, R. (2002) 'Perceived organizational support: A review of the literature', *Journal of Applied Psychology*, 87: 698–714.

Roberts, L. M. (2006) 'Shifting the lens on organizational life: The added value of positive scholarship', *Academy of Management Review*, 31: 292–305.

Rose, J., Ahuja, A. and Jones, C. (2006) 'Attitudes of direct care staff towards external professionals, team climate and psychological wellbeing', *Journal of Intellectual Disabilities*, 10: 105–120.

Rowe, J.W. and Kahn, R.L. (1998) *Successful Aging.* New York: Pantheon Books.

Rutter, M. (1987) 'Psychosocial resilience and protective mechanisms', *American Journal of Orthopsychiatry*, 57: 316–331.

Rutter, M. (2002) 'The interplay of nature, nurture, and developmental influences: The challenge ahead for mental health', *Archives of General Psychiatry*, 59: 996–1000.

Ryan, R. and Deci, E. (2001) 'On happiness and human potentials: A review of research on hedonic and eudaimonic well-being', *Annual Review of Psychology*, 52: 141–166.

Scully, D., Kremer, J., Meade, M., Graham, R. and Dudgeon, K. (1998) 'Physical exercise and psychological well being: A critical review', *British Journal of Sports Medicine*, 32: 111–120.

Shirom, A. (2004) 'Feeling vigorous at work? The construct of vigor and the study of positive affect in organizations', in D. Ganster and P.L. Perrewe (eds) *Research in Organizational Stress and Well-being.* Greenwich, CT: JAI Press. Vol. 3, pp. 135–165.

Simonton, D.K. and Baumeister, R.F. (2005) 'Positive psychology at the summit', *Review of General Psychology*, 9 (2): 99–102.

Sluiter, J., van der Beek, A. and Frings–Dresen, M. (1999) 'The influence of work characteristics on the need for recovery, and experienced health: A study on coach drivers', *Ergonomics*, 42: 573–583.

Snyder, C.R. and Lopez, S.J. (2002) *Handbook of Positive Psychology.* New York: Oxford University Press.

Sparks, K., Cooper, C., Fried, Y. and Shirom, A. (1997) 'The effects of hours of work on health: A meta-analytic review', *Journal of Occupational and Organizational Psychology*, 70: 391–408.

Spreitzer, G. and Sonenshein, S. (2004) 'Toward the construct definition of positive deviance', *American Behavioral Scientist*, 47: 828–847.

Spreitzer, G., Sutcliffe, K., Dutton, J., Sonenshein, S. and Grant, A. (2005) 'A socially embedded model of thriving at work', *Organization Science*, 16 (5): 537–549.

Sonnentag, S. and Zijlstra. (2006) 'Job characteristics and off-job activities as predictors of need for recovery, well-being and fatigue', *Journal of Applied Psychology*, 91: 330–350.

Stansfield, S., Fuhrer, R., Head, J., Ferrie, J. and Shipley, M. (1997) 'Work and psychiatric disorder in the Whitehall II study', *Journal of Psychosomatic Research*, 43: 73–81.

Sutcliffe, K.M. and Vogus, T.J. (2003) 'Organizing for resilience', in K.S. Cameron, J.E. Dutton and R.E. Quinn (eds), *Positive Organizational Scholarship: Foundations of a New Discipline*. San Francisco: Berrett-Koehler, pp. 94–110.

Taris, T. (2006) 'Bricks without clay: On urban myths in occupational health psychology', *Work and Stress*, 20: 99–104.

Thompson, C. and Prottas, D. (2005) 'Relationships among organizational family support, job autonomy, perceived control, and employee well-being', *Journal of Occupational Health Psychology*, 10: 100–118.

Tucker, P. and Rutherford, C. (2005) 'Moderators of the relationship between long work hours and health', *Journal of Occupational Health Psychology*, 10: 465–476.

Turner, N., Barling, J. and Zacharatos, A. (2002) 'Positive psychology at work', in C.R Snyder and S. Lopez. (eds), *The Handbook of Positive Psychology*. Oxford: Oxford University Press, pp. 715–730.

van Dierendonck, D., Haynes, C., Borrill C. and Stride, C. (2004) 'Leadership behavior and subordinate well-being', *Journal of Occupational Health Psychology*, 9: 165–175.

Van Katwyk, P.T., Fox, S., Spector, P.E. and Kelloway, E.K. (2000) 'Using the Job-related Affective Well-being Scale (JAWS) to investigate affective responses to work stressors', *Journal of Occupational Health Psychology*, 5: 219–230.

Von Korff, M. and Simon, G. (1996) 'The relationship between pain and depression', *British Journal of Psychiatry*, Suppl. 30: 101–108.

Warr, P. (1987) *Work, Unemployment and Mental Health*. London: Oxford Press.

Westman, M. and Eden, D. (1997) 'Effects of a respite from work on burnout: Vacation relief and fade-out', *Journal of Applied Psychology*, 82: 516–527.

WHO. *Constitution of the World Health Organization*, Geneva, 1946. Accessed October 30, 2006.

Zickar, M.J. (2003) 'Remembering Arthur Kornhauser: Industrial psychology's advocate for worker well-being', *Journal of Applied Psychology*, 88: 363–369.

36

Positive Organizational Scholarship

Jane E. Dutton and Mary Ann Glynn[1]

Positive Organizational Scholarship (POS) is a broad framework that seeks to explain behaviors in and of organizations. It focuses explicitly on the positive states and processes that arise from, and result in, life-giving dynamics, optimal functioning, or enhanced capabilities or strengths. There are three core aspects of a POS perspective:

(1) a concern with flourishing;
(2) a focus on the development of strengths or capabilities; and
(3) an emphasis on the generative, life-giving dynamics of organizing.

First, POS is concerned with conditions that foster flourishing at the individual, work group, and organizational levels. Although Positive Psychology is similarly interested in flourishing (e.g., Gable and Haidt, 2005; Keyes, 2002), a POS perspective focuses on these states and processes as they unfold in and between organizations (Cameron et al., 2003). For individuals in organizations, flourishing may be indicated by

generativity, growth, thriving or resilience (Fredrickson and Losada, 2005). For collectives, flourishing may be indicated by creativity, innovation, growth, resilience, or any other state or condition that indicates that a collective is operating in a healthy, (near) optimal state. Inquiries into the factors that foster moments of collective creativity (Hargadon and Bechky, 2006), organizational resilience (Gittell et al., 2006) illustrate these POS dynamics.

Second, POS focuses on the development and expression of strengths at multiple levels to understand the features (both unique and shared) that are sources of excellence or positive deviance (Cameron et al., 2003). This POS focus includes interest in individual virtues in organizations (e.g., Hornstein, 1986) and organizational virtuousness as a collective accomplishment (Cameron, 2003; Chun, 2005). A POS approach is evident in research on collective wisdom (Weick et al., 1999; Weick and Putnam, 2006) and, in empirical accounts of compassion-organizing (Dutton et al., 2006) and collective courage (Quinn and Worline, 2008).

Third, a POS lens looks at the generative (i.e., life-building, capability-enhancing, capacity–creating) dynamics in and of organizations that can explain flourishing and the cultivation of strengths across levels of analysis. For example, Glynn and Dutton (2007) identify the capability-building dynamics that characterized the improvised bricolage of NASA's Mission Control in enabling the rescue of the crippled Apollo 13 spacecraft and its astronauts (see also Useem, 1998). Sandelands (2003), Sandelands and Worline (2007) identify three 'moments' of social life in and of organizations (love, play and individuation) that lay the groundwork for understanding when and how capability and expressed vitality are likely to occur in organizations.

CORE ASSUMPTIONS OF THE POS PERSPECTIVE

Core POS assumptions include:

(1) human flourishing is contextually embedded;
(2) positive and negative states and processes are not necessarily asymmetrical but can be synergistic;
(3) organizational resources (e.g., human, social, administrative) are not fixed but dynamic (Feldman, 2004) and can be endogenously created through processes and actions; and
(4) normative aspects of organizational behavior (i.e., the 'good') are worthy of serious study.

We describe each of these.

First, POS assumes the contextual embed-dedness of flourishing in and of organizations (Cameron et al., 2003; Roberts, 2006). POS assumes that contexts are central in explaining the creation, development and change of individual and collective strengths in organizations; these might include the nested (or situated) embeddedness of contexts that shape action (Dacin et al., 1999). As a result, POS takes seriously the call by positive psychology to study the role of institutions in producing positive outcomes.

Second, a POS perspective assumes that negative states can occur alongside positive states, but that the two are not necessarily asymmetric. Roberts (2006: 296) explains that 'positive dynamics will not emerge' by simply reversing negative dynamics.' Questions about the potential asymmetry of the positive and negative are of interest to POS researchers, who might ask: Do the factors that underlie negative, problem-atic or undesirable conditions or states in organizations (e.g., organizational decline, corrosive relationships, injustice, social loaf-ing or stress) also explain (or relate to) flourishing or positively deviant states (e.g., growth, energized networks, high quality relationships, positive organizational justice, or connectivity in teams or thriving)?

Acknowledging that negative states are part of the organizational condition, POS seeks to complement the tendency to overweight the negative relative to the positive in the existing literature (Baumeister et al., 2001). Wang and Thompson (2006) point out that 'scholarly research makes more references to the shortcomings of leaders and groups rather than their successes' (p. 31). Greenhaus and Powell note a similar slant in work-family research, asserting that 'much of the work at the work-family interface continues to emphasize conflict, stress and enhanced well-being' (2006: 72). Although organiza-tional researchers have historically attended to key positive states such as employee satisfaction, employee health, and quality of life (as Fineman, 2006 points out), a POS perspective points to a wider set of constructs.

In spite of its explicit emphasis, however, POS does not focus on the positive to the exclusion of the negative. Often negative and positive conditions co-exist and interact to explain flourishing and capacity-building. For instance, Fredrickson and Losada (2005) show that flourishing dynamics (in individu-als, dyads, and groups) require the presence of both positive and negative expressions, roughly in a ratio of three (positive) to one (negative). This positivity ratio or 'appropriate negativity' (e.g., constructive conflict or the emotion of guilt) can redirect actions in ways that promote rather than diminish flourishing. Similarly, the cultivation of collective strengths such as organizational mindfulness (Weick et al., 1999) or collective resilience (Sutcliffe and Vogus, 2003) requires attention to negative conditions, thoughts, and feelings that can contribute to the dynamics underlying these strengths.

Third, a POS perspective assumes that new insights about organizational behavior are possible when we account for human and collective resourcefulness. Rather than assuming that organizational resources are always static or scarce, a POS perspective treats assets as potentially varied, expansive, and emergent. Resources can be produced, unlocked, expanded or innovatively bricolaged via multiple organizing dynamics. Some of these generative resources include energy, hope, trust, and knowledge. This POS assumption, captured in the notion of endogenous resourcefulness (Dutton et al., 2006; Feldman, 2004; Glynn and Dutton, 2007; Glynn and Wrobel, 2007; Spreitzer et al., 2005), makes concrete the basic idea that it is possible to unlock latent potential from within systems so as to expand resource capabilities and strength-based skills.

This POS assumption of endogenous resourcefulness anchors core ideas that have been central to humanistic psychology for individuals (e.g., Maslow, 1968) and extends it to social collectives. POS models how various types of resources can be activated by organizational structures, processes, systems, cultures or leaders to aid in the development of strengths and the cultivation of flourishing. For example, Heaphy and Dutton (2008) show how positive interactions with others at work foster employees' physiological resourcefulness by strengthening the immune system, reducing demand on the cardiovascular system, and producing a healthier hormone pattern. At the business unit level, Worline et al. (2006) document how clusters of practices used by a hospital billing department cultivate the resourcefulness of the unit so as to

explain patterns of unit-level resilience over time. And, at the organizational level, Glynn and Wrobel (2007) show how an organization's portrayal of family relationships in its identity claims enriches the social capital of the firm and enables strategic adaptation.

Fourth, a POS perspective is normative in that it focuses on manifestations of states and dynamics considered 'good' or affirmative in some way (Cameron et al., 2003). Such a view is consistent with other theoretical traditions which have taken an explicitly normative posture. Institutional theory, for one, explicitly attends to processes of infusing value in organizations (Selznick, 1957) as well as the cognitive guidance systems that may lead to such valuations (e.g., DiMaggio and Powell, 1991). Business ethics literature can substantially contribute to debate and discussion about the meaning of good as applied in POS (Sonenshein, 2005). In addition, there is a rich heritage of organizational work that considers 'good' topics such as health, satisfaction, learning, creativity and other positive or normatively-defined constructs.

In making normative assumptions, POS researchers recognize the cultural embeddedness (and inherent challenges) of defining what is 'good' (e.g., Fineman, 2006); this, however, is part of the POS agenda for study. A quest to understand the dynamics of how individuals in organizational contexts acquire and deepen certain strengths should not arrest serious exploration of the 'contingencies of positivity across cultures' (Roberts, 2006: 298). Although all values may not be universally perceived as 'good,' Dahsgaard et al. (2005) found convergence among philosophical and religious traditions in China, South Asia, and the West in valuing six core virtues: courage, justice, humanity, temperance, wisdom and transcendence. Although POS makes no claims about the universality of virtues, it does seek to investigate which values organizations embrace, to what degree, and how they affect collective strengths (Cameron, 2003; Cameron et al., 2004).

CONTRIBUTIONS OF THE POS PERSPECTIVE

The POS perspective contributes to organizational scholarship by supplying new constructs and processes for study, and by creating linkages among established (but often unrelated) constructs. Among the new constructs that POS implies are: compassionate organizing (Frost et al., 2006), cascading vitality (Feldman and Khademian, 2003), courageous collective action (Quinn and Worline, 2008), organizational healing (Powley and Cameron, 2006), organizational resilience (Sutcliffe and Vogus, 2003), peace-building (Spreitzer, 2007), thriving (Spreitzer et al., 2005) and virtuousness (Cameron, 2003).

As well, a POS lens offers explanatory mechanism for connecting previously disconnected topics in organizational studies. For example, a POS lens integrates traditional topics such as creativity or innovation (Drazin et al., 1999; Hargadon and Betchky, 2006), engagement (Kahn, 1990), health (Karasek and Theorell, 1990), justice (Greenberg and Colquitt, 2005), leadership (Selznick, 1957) prosocial behavior (Brief and Motowidlo, 1986), mindfulness (Weick et al., 1999), proactivity (Grant and Ashford, 2008), wisdom (Srivastva and Cooperrider, 1999), and well-being, among others. The underlying point of integration is an inquiry: Are there common processes or characteristics that help to explain these different forms of individual or collective flourishing and strength-building?

POS also deepens inquiry into veins of research that potentially explain flourishing and strength-building for individuals and collectives. For example, by focusing on positive relationships at work (sources, impacts, and manifestations at different levels of analysis), organizational researchers can theorize and research how the relational contexts and dynamics in organizations explain positive professional identities (Roberts, 2007), effective mentoring dynamics (Ragins and Verbos, 2007), learning across differences (Davidson and James, 2007), healthy teams (Ancona and Isaacs, 2007), attachment among temporary employees (Blatt and Camden, 2007), effective organizational change (Golden-Biddle et al., 2007) and a positive (i.e., attractive, legitimate or desirable) organizational identity (Glynn and Wrobel, 2007). Viewing relationships through a POS lens illuminates links between more durable research topics (like cooperation, developmental relationships, LMX theory, network research, social support, trust) and newer ones (e.g., energy networks (Baker et al., 2003), energy dynamics (Quinn, 2007; Quinn and Dutton, 2005), or human physiology (Heaphy, 2007), all of which are central for explaining the dynamics of flourishing and the creation of individual and collective strengths.

In weaving together unconnected ideas, POS often takes a cross-level approach. This is evident in the work of Feldman and Khademain (2003: 358) who examine how organizational empowerment can create 'dynamic potential in the relationship between the individual, organization, and community.' They model how factors at the individual level (e.g., employee involvement) influence the organizational level (e.g., job redesign), which in turn, affects positive individual-level outcomes (increased meaningfulness; Caza and Caza, forthcoming).

POS also creates an empirical basis for the domain of organizational change and development work that has been labeled 'Appreciative Inquiry' (AI; Cooperrider and Srivastiva, 1987). AI is built on assumptions that an organization has a positive core; that organizations are 'networks of relatedness'; and that these networks are 'alive' (Cooperrider and Sekerka, 2003). Moreover, appreciative inquiry assumes that a process, and set of practices around inquiry, can tap into, and build on, this positive core (Cooperrider et al., 2000) to enable a more positive future. As a research-focused perspective, POS helps to systematically integrate an understanding of the success of AI as a change practice with an understanding of why and when it works. For example, POS researchers indicate that energy networks in organizations can be meaningfully mapped and understood (e.g., Baker et al., 2003) and that understanding how these energy networks are activated and changed over time could provide insight into AI change and successes. In a recent analysis of 20 cases of the use of appreciative inquiry interventions, Bushe and Kassam (2005) found that appreciative inquiry created transformational outcomes 35 per cent of the time. A POS lens helps to unpack why and when these kinds of change practices may be particularly effective.

WHY POS? WHY NOW?

The emergence of the POS perspective in the early 21st century can be explained by a number of factors, including: an observed shift in the applied social sciences away from deficit-based to more strengths-based approaches, a return to organizational fundamentals and optimism in the wake of highly visible and significant organizational scandals, notably that of Enron, and a focus on healing, compassion, re-engagement, resilience and hope in the wake of tragic events like 9/11.

The POS perspective is part of a much broader shift in the applied social sciences that is motivated by a growing sense of dissatisfaction with the reliance on theories that are deficit-focused (Cooperrider, 1990). A turn towards understanding the cultivation of strengths and the creation of extraordinary conditions (positively deviant from normal) is evident in numerous fields. For example, political scientists seek to understand peace-building conditions to augment conflict-reduction approaches (e.g., peacecenter.berkeley.com). In social work, there is a turn toward considering asset-building in neighborhoods and communities that can augment the focus on addressing community deficits (http://www.northwestern.edu/ipr/abcd.html). In education, renewed interest in cultivating student character and assets shifts the focus of education toward building up the strengths of students and student communities (http://www.search-institute.org/). Psychotherapy has seen rapid growth of solution-based therapy which shifts the aim of the therapeutic intervention from diagnosing problems to finding workable solutions. The medical field more generally has witnessed a determined effort to focus on well-being and health–development rather than disease prevention. With escalating concerns about the costs of medical care by work organizations, there is likely to be an even more interest in wellness by business organizations.

Within the field of organizational research, there are several reasons why scholarly attention has turned POS, as well as Positive Organizational Behavior (Luthans, 2002; Wright, 2003), positive psychology and ethics (e.g., Giacalone et al., 2005), and positive perspectives on leadership (Avilio and Luthans, 2006; Hess and Cameron, 2005). First, POS (and other theoretical perspectives) may offer a natural corrective to the increasing concern with economics and financial considerations. Walsh et al. (2003) coded all articles published by the Academy of Management from about 1958–2001 and found a diminishing focus on social outcomes and a rising focus on economic outcomes over time. This emphasis on economic issues has also been observed in the leadership literature. For instance, Podolny et al. (2005) have decried the trajectory that leadership research has taken and urge a re-direction, because this shift has been problematic because 'we need to assess the importance of leadership in terms of its ability to infuse purpose and meaning into the organizational experience' (Podolny et al., 2005: 5). Consistent with these trends in the applied social sciences, POS re-emphasizes social and human-based strengths in processes and outcomes relevant to organizations.

Second, at a time when organizational scandals have become all too commonplace (Youssef and Luthans, 2005), there have been calls for relevance in organizational research. Some scholars have even suggested that current managerial theories contribute to unethical practices (e.g., Ghoshal, 2005). POS can suggest ways of addressing such problems and perhaps of preventing them; organizations grounded in virtuous and ethical actions by individuals and collectives may be less vulnerable to such corruption (Cameron, 2003; Sonenshein, 2005).

POS redounds in many ways to some of the foundational work in organizational research. Like 'old' institutional theory, which focused on the value-based aspects of leading and organizing (e.g., Selznick, 1957; DiMaggio and Powell, 1991; Podolny et al., 2005), POS takes a normative stance and returns to core questions about how organizations can be sites of human and collective flourishing. POS invites researchers to do likewise and reflect on our conduct and practices as organizational scholars, considering not only how our research impacts the field but also ourselves as researchers. POS emphasizes that professional practices of research and teaching can be ways that foster learning, creativity, growth or aspects of healthy functioning (Dutton, 2003).

Relevant recent research

In many ways, the POS perspective has long been embedded in organizational studies; several established domains of research have looked at manifestations of flourishing or the cultivation of strengths. These are as diverse as job satisfaction (e.g., Judge et al., 2001), empowerment (Spreitzer, 1995), individual and collective integrity, and individual and collective justice. What connects each of these topics is a common focus on flourishing or strengths, across different levels.

Although POS is in its infancy, emerging research has begun to map the domain, theoretically and empirically. We categorize POS research (to date) into two areas: one that re-examines existing research domains, and a second that generates new research domains. For the former, we focus on three research domains that illustrate the POS perspective within well-established organizational domains: well-being and health, engagement at work, and creativity (as an individual and collective topic). For the latter, we focus on new, POS-informed research frontiers by discussing, first, new outcome or dependent variables (indicating flourishing or strength-building) and next, key

explanatory mechanisms of generativity or dynamic capability-building processes.

Well-being and health

There is long-standing interest by organizational scholars in employee well-being and health which is a critical domain for POS scholars (Turner et al., 2002). In a review chapter focusing on applications of positive psychology at work, Turner et al. (2002) suggest that several bundles of organizational and job-related features are critical to explaining well-being on the job. They note that work on the job characteristics model (e.g., Hackman and Oldham, 1980), the demand/control model (e.g., Karasek and Theorell, 1990), role characteristics (e.g., Jackson and Schuler, 1985), team and group research (e.g., Sonnentag, 1996), and transformational leadership (e.g., Bass and Riggio, 2005) all contribute to an expanded model of how work contexts can foster healthy outcomes and particularly, individual well-being. This domain of research points to rich pockets of studies on POS-related themes that aid in identifying and explaining individual flourishing at work.

Engagement

Engagement as a psychological state had been studied in several different ways, each a potential indicator of some aspect of individual flourishing. Kahn (1990) defined engagement as the state of bringing one's full self to work; Rothbard (2001) extended this definition to study relative engagement in both work and family roles. Britt et al. (2005) have looked at how engagement modified the effect of stressors on performance, sometimes playing a buffering, but other times playing an amplifying role. Engagement has become central to several applied efforts to improve employees' psychological experiences at work. The Gallup Organization has shown that engagement, measured as the degree to which employees believe they have the opportunity to do what they do best at work, is related to both customer loyalty and employee productivity (Harter et al., 2002). Loehr and Schwartz (2003) developed the concept of full engagement at work to consider the important roles of replenishment, physical conditions, breaks and nutrition as important considerations, much like Sonnentag (2003).

Creativity and innovation

The hallmark of these twin processes is the production of novelty and usefulness; by their very nature, creativity and innovation result in expansive capacities for future action because they generate new resources or recombine old ones that can find new applications. Although earlier work on creativity and innovation in organizations tended to focus primarily on the production of creative outcomes, more recent approaches have focused on the organizational processes that undergird innovation; these involve positive states and processes. For instance, Drazin et al. (1999: 286) define creativity without regard to outcome, i.e., 'as the process of engagement in creative acts.' As such, it is intertwined with individuals' experience of engagement (Kahn, 1990), flow (Quinn, 2005) and intrinsic motivation (Amabile et al., 2005). Moreover, it is facilitated by the social relationships and networks in which individuals are embedded (Perry-Smith, 2006; Perry-Smith and Shalley, 2003), again pointing to the importance of context and connectedness in generativity.

In addition to informing traditional topics of organizational research, the POS perspective opens up (or re-activates) newer domains that center on outcome or dependent variables and on explanatory mechanisms of flourishing or strength-building in organizations. We discuss four examples of outcome variables at the individual level of analysis: thriving, flow, resilience and psychological capital. Given the relative newness of POS, most of these topics are in elementary stages of development. From outcomes we move to processes and examine ways in which POS can inform research.

Studying outcomes in organizations with a POS lens

Thriving describes the psychological state whereby organizational members experience both vitality and learning simultaneously (Spreitzer et al., 2005). While failure to thrive has long been a serious interest of psychologists (Bergland and Kirkevold, 2001) organizational researchers have not given either failure to thrive or thriving much attention. Thriving as an optimal state is important because it captures individuals' sense of momentum and forward movement in organizations (and life more generally), either can be momentary or extended in time. Accordingly, thriving may be an important way that individuals gauge 'how are they doing' and whether they are on a forward path that can contribute to self-adaptation and growth at work (e.g., Tsui and Ashford, 1994). Thriving is also important in its own right; Spreitzer et al. (2005) propose that thriving (at work) may also be important in explaining health as a critical individual-level outcome.

Explaining positive states such as thriving at work necessitates consideration of how the context (e.g., job, unit, organizational) makes a difference. In their socially embedded model, Spreitzer et al. (2005) identify features of the work unit context as critical because of their pivotal role in shaping the everyday experience of people at work. In particular, they focus on how three contextual features (decision making discretion; information sharing; and trust and respect) foster agentic behaviors on the job; in turn, these produce resources (e.g. positive meaning, relational resources, knowledge and positive emotion) that fuel the behaviors that make thriving more likely. Their model opens up inquiries of eudemonic approaches, which focus on how individuals achieve potential at work (e.g., Ryan and Deci, 2001), as opposed to hedonic approaches which focus on pleasure, such as employee satisfaction (Spreitzer et al., 2005).

Flow captures the 'holistic sensation people feel when they act with total involvement in the activity' to the point of losing awareness of time and surroundings (Csikszentmihalyi, 1975: 36). Although interest in flow has been focused on the individual psychological state (e.g., Csikszentmihalyi, 1990), a POS perspective emphasizes the explanatory power of context (e.g., whole organization, profession, unit, team) in flow experiences. In an empirical study of the flow experience of knowledge workers at Sandia National Laboratories, Quinn (2005) revised the definition of flow as the experience of 'merging one's situational awareness with automatic application of activity-relevant knowledge and skills' (p. 615), which has distinctive antecedents and consequences. By focusing on this positively deviant state, new possibilities for understanding subjective performance, learning and motivation in organizations (Quinn, 2005) become evident.

Resilience captures a system's capacity to bounce back after setbacks. It is a form of positive adjustment to adversity of different kinds, and can be thought of as an important indicator and predictor of human flourishing. Studied most often in the case of children (Masten and Reed, 2002) who managed to adjust effectively to trauma and other challenging life circumstances (Wolin and Wolin, 1993), and recently with adults (Bononno, 2004), there is a growing practical (e.g., Coutu, 2002) and theoretical interest in how aspects of context can foster resilience at work (Caza, 2007) as well as in the organization as a whole (Sutcliffe and Vogus, 2003). Understanding how work contexts enable resilience on the job could provide valuable insights into processes that build adult resilience in all kinds of circumstances. Because people spend so much of their days at work, work contexts are potent social settings for developing and sustaining resilience. Organizational researchers have significant opportunities for making theoretical contributions into understanding the conditions that foster or diminish this vital human capacity.

Psychological capital. Rather than focus on one particular indicator of optimal functioning in organizations, Luthans and colleagues (Luthans et al., 2004; Luthans and Youssef, 2004) have advocated for an amalgam of four psychological states, i.e., 'psychological capital,' that can be developed in employees and are important for individual and organizational performance. Borrowing from psychological research, they identify these

four states as efficacy (Bandura, 1997), hope (Snyder, 2002), optimism (Seligman, 1998), and resilience (Masten, 2001), which other researchers have extended to the dyadic and group levels.

At the dyadic level, there is a rich vein of research on LMX (leader-member exchange) which focuses on well-functioning relationships between bosses and subordinates. LMX research has documented the consequences of such high-quality relationships for performance, satisfaction and career outcomes (e.g., Graen et al., 1982; Graen et al., 1982). In addition, research on developmental relationships at work (e.g., Kahn, 1998) like mentoring (Higgins, and Kram, 2001; Kram, 1985) has also shown the importance of positive relationships. Psychological research has demonstrated the importance of a range of positive relationships for human flourishing, but also notes the gap in understanding how these relationships have their effects (Berscheid and Reis, 1998; Reis and Gable, 2003).

POS redirects researchers to examine the nature of high quality relationships in work contexts, as well as their antecedents and consequences. A recent edited volume offers a set of papers that look across levels of analysis (individual, group, organizational and community) to identify core themes and insights around the dynamics of positive relationships at work, as well as their enabling contextual features and impact (Dutton and Ragins, 2007). The intentional look toward cross-level and multi-level theories of high quality connections at work stresses the importance of different levels of context, types of processes, and individual differences in creating and maintaining this form of vital human connection in organizations.

At the group level, there are several possible research programs that center on group flourishing. Wang and Thompson (2005) note three areas of group and teams research: group synergy and transactive memory (e.g., Lewis et al., 2005; Liang et al., 1995); positive group emotions (an area we discuss later in positive emoting); and group flow. Ancona and Isaacs (2007) note the lack of research on healthy functioning and outcomes in team and group research, characterizing current work as having a 'disease orientation' (p. 227). They propose a focus on team health, indicated by a team's capacity to do divergent thinking, repair poor dynamics and build new repertoires of action. Finally, Losada and Heaphy (2005) note that team flourishing can be detected in patterns of interaction among team members that have a high degree of connectivity with regard to patterns in positive to negative utterances (similar to Fredrickson and Losada's (2005) 'positivity ratio') as well as a balance of both inquiry to advocacy and self to other talk. All these studies encourage an examination of indicators of optimal team functioning that extend well beyond team or group performance.

At the organizational level, there has been an historical interest in studying organizational excellence, organizational performance or what some have called organizational effectiveness (Cameron, 2005). A POS perspective revitalizes and reaffirms this focus, offering new indicators of optimal organizational functioning or these as well as new notions of collective strengths such as compassion organizing competence (Dutton et al., 2006), mindful organizing (Weick et al., 1998), and collective courage (e.g., Quinn and Worline, 2008).

Organizational virtuousness, according to Cameron and colleagues (e.g., Cameron, 2003, Cameron et al., 2004), captures the pattern of organizational enablers or features associated with the virtuous actions of organizational members. Proposing that organizational virtuousness is positively associated with organizational performance, Cameron et al. (2004) found, in their sample of 52 organizations, that members' reports of higher levels of optimism, integrity and trust in their organizations were associated with a greater level of perceived organizational performance. These researchers suggest that there are sets of practices and cultural values and beliefs that are associated with overall organizational strength, which, in turn, contributes to higher performance. Relatedly, through telling the story of 'Rocky Flats,'

the cleanup of 'America's most dangerous nuclear weapons production facility' (p 3), Cameron and Lavine (2006) show how positively deviant performance, 'the achievement of extraordinary success well beyond the expectations of almost any outside observer' (p. 3), resulted from widespread organizational leadership that worked to fulfill the highest potential of individuals and the collective.

Organizational resilience describes a systems' capability of positively adjusting to setbacks, jolts and different forms of adversity (Sutcliffe and Vogus, 2003). In their review of the literature on organizational resilience, Sutcliffe and Vogus (2003) observe that this organizing competence does not always imply an organization is optimally functioning. Rather, it highlights the capacity of the organization to 'rebound from adversity strengthened and more resourceful' (p. 97). Thus, collective resilience captures a form of positive organizing that is a form of adaptive strength. Research points to the importance of everyday practices in cultivating the dynamics that undergird this capability (Worline et al., 2006), and implies that relational stocks and processes may be central in explaining resilience as a collective accomplishment (Gittell et al., 2006; Powley, 2005).

STUDYING PROCESSES AND MECHANISMS WITH A POS LENS

A POS lens offers a window on the mechanisms that explain flourishing and strength-building at different levels of analysis. Mechanisms are what Davis and Marquis (2005), borrowing from Elster (1989), refer to as the cogs and wheels in explanatory theories – for POS, this focuses on the motors of optimal functioning and the cultivation of strengths and capabilities for individuals, dyads, groups and organizations. We focus on the following three mechanisms because of their historical prominence in organizational studies, and because they are particularly relevant to the dynamics central of flourishing: positive meaning-making, positive emoting, and positive interrelating. We use verbs (rather than nouns) to emphasize the importance of *process* in accounting for flourishing at different levels of analysis. We define each of these process mechanisms next, and provide illustrations from current research.

Positive meaning-making

This refers to processes in which people imbue stimuli with significance, implications, and consequences that imply something is good, desirable or beneficial in some way. Researchers refer to positive meaning making using a variety of terms, including appraisals, sensemaking, interpretations, and belief formation. Positive meaning is often associated with beliefs such as heightened controllability, optimism and a greater sense of meaningfulness (e.g., Taylor et al., 2000), and states such as hopefulness (Feldman and Snyder, 2005). This type of meaning-making is also positive in that it is associated with resourcefulness (psychological and physiological) that fosters effective coping during traumatic events or diseases (Taylor et al., 2000), and in the case of work organizations, may contribute to individual or collective flourishing.

The potency of positive meaning-making as an important mechanism is revealed in multiple research domains in organizational research. For example, positive-meaning making is seemingly central to understanding the meaning and importance of work. Employees may come to understand the significance of what they are doing (e.g., their work, the project, the issue they are addressing) in ways that are positive (Pratt and Ashforth, 2003) which, in turn, activates emotions, motivations, and patterns of behaving that contribute to flourishing. Research on the meaning of work has increasingly focused on the variability in how people construe and craft jobs to derive different meanings (e.g., Pratt and Ashforth, 2003; Wrzesniewski, 2003; Wrzesniewski and Dutton, 2001). One study suggested that interpretations of work as a calling (e.g., defining work in ways that contribute to the common good or as an end in itself; Wrzesniewski, 2003)

were associated with more enjoyment, greater satisfaction and spending more time at work (Wrzesniewski et al., 1997). In a study of independent workers, people who framed their work positively (e.g., as having positive effects on others, as an opportunity for growth and personal development, or as a part of a larger enterprise) were more effective at sustaining productive action and were more resilient in the wake of setbacks (Blatt and Ashford, 2006). In both studies, making positive meaning of one's work produced outcomes that were associated with greater capacity to enjoy and take action at work.

In a very different research context, imposing positive meaning on ambiguous events and issues can affect flourishing or cultivate strengths. For example, managers' positive interpretation of strategic issues was associated with heightened capacities for action. Dutton (1993) argued that framing issues as opportunities (as an illustration of a positive categorization and interpretation of issues) is potent psychologically and organizationally because it (1) increases a sense of control; (2) increases positive affect; (3) suppresses threat, which increases search for, and use of, peripheral information; (4) focuses on the future; and (5) attracts involvement all of that contributes to a positive momentum for change. Barr and Glynn (2004) have shown that these perceptions tend to hold across different cultures. A variety of empirical studies lends further support. For example, Ginsberg and Venkatraman (1992) found that interpreting the issue of electronic filing as an opportunity by tax preparation firms was associated with a greater commitment to acquire new technology. In the context of strategic change implementation, Sonenshein (2007a) demonstrated empirically that employees who understand the change in terms of greater levels of hope and a greater sense of strategic significance evidence greater levels of effective change implementation behaviors. Sonenshein (2007b) posits a resource creation theory of change, where effective change implementation is due in part to the resourcefulness of individuals cultivated through positive meaning making about the change.

Research on individual and organizational identities lends further evidence on the impact of positive meaning on flourishing and strength-building. Most individuals desire to create positive identities or self-construals at work (Ashforth, 2001; Ibarra, 1999). When people are able to claim and be granted a more positive self-identity (e.g., by being affirmed as having desirable and valuable attributes; Bartel and Dutton, 2001), several psychological consequences result that may foster flourishing. Through a positive identity, people are able to construe possible selves in ways that foster the accomplishment of tasks (e.g., Ingelhart et al., 1988) and motivate and enable desirable career progressions (Ibarra, 1999). For example, the reflected best self intervention (e.g., Roberts et al., 2005) is designed to help individuals create a positive self identity based on assembling and integrating behavioral accounts from multiple people to show how the (target) individual has added value and had an impact. This purposeful use of 'real stories' to compose a positive identity is argued to foster well-being by better equipping people to socially construct jobs and situations so that they might fit their strengths. In this account, positive self meaning fosters an expanded capacity for action as a person feels more competent, efficacious and has a better sense of the strengths that they exhibit in the eyes of others (Roberts et al., 2005).

In the organizational identity literature, there has been interest in how the attractiveness of an organization's identity (as one indicator of positive meaning associated with an organization's identity) impacts on outcomes such as levels of employee commitment and cooperation (Dutton et al., 1994). Dukerich et al. (2002) found that attractiveness of physicians' construals of a health care system's identity was associated with greater levels of cooperative behaviors by physicians. Thus the positive meaning that organizational members impute to their collective (e.g., a positive organizational identity or image) can foster certain forms of flourishing through heightening levels of cooperation.

Organizations also impute positive meaning through a statement of 'corporate purpose' that integrates business and social needs so as to reframe work and position the organization in its environment. A statement of corporate purpose speaks to how a business meets social needs in the community in which it operates, provides goods or services that meet societal needs and aspires to something greater (Glynn and Smith, 2007). For instance, Chick-fil-A, a fast-food restaurant, cogently sums it up: 'We're here to serve. And not just sandwiches.' The organization implements policies and procedures consistent with its core purpose, including providing the cleanest dining rooms in the industry, kids' meals with a 'premium' that is designed to 'educate, build character, and foster interaction between parent and child,' responding to customer requests or thank-you's with 'My Pleasure,' and awarding over $19 million in college scholarships to Team Members (employees) since 1973. While individually these tactics seem like just good customer service and admirable employee relations, viewed within Chick-fil-A's purpose, there is a powerful message for employees and customers – this is who we are and what we stand for (Glynn and Smith, 2007).

Finally, individual efficacy and collective efficacy are positive beliefs about the ability of an individual or collective to produce desired outcomes (Bandura, 1995). Perceived efficacy enables positive meaning because the confidence in one's effectiveness often prompts actions (or yields outcomes) that are desirable; in turn, ongoing, efficacious action can increase the capabilities of a system through performance outcomes or psychological well-being. At the individual level, Bandura and colleagues (e.g., Bandura, 1997, 2002) have demonstrated how self-efficacy is related to a host of positive psychological states (including optimism, well-being and self-esteem), inversely related to negative outcomes (such as stress and performance outcomes). Moreover, general self-efficacy that extends beyond specific tasks has been shown to have similar effects across many different countries (Luszczynska et al., 2005).

Work in school settings has shown that the perceived collective efficacy of teachers is a major determinant of student learning at the school level (Goddard et al., 2004). Even when controlling for a wide range of rival explanations for student achievement (including school SES, size, demographic composition), perceived collective efficacy remained a key predictor of different forms of student achievement in a sample of 96 high schools. While this study did not test the mechanisms that account for these results, past research suggests that perceived collective efficacy is associated with resources such as greater commitment, collaboration, and more effective group processes (as cited in Goddard et al., 2004). Thus positive collective meaning, like greater perceived collective efficacy, is associated with a variety of resources that should contribute to manifestations of flourishing, such as higher levels of learning.

Positive emoting

The second major category of mechanisms is positive emoting, which refers to the felt experience of positive emotions for actors (individuals, dyads or groups). Positive emotions are short term states of felt activation by individuals or collectives that are associated with 'a pleasantly subjective feel' (Fredrickson, 1998: 300) and which trigger response tendencies that are manifest in subjective experiences and physiological changes (Fredrickson, 2003). Illustrations of positive emoting would include individual or group feelings of interest, joy, contentment, gratitude and excitement.

Fredrickson's 'broaden-and-build theory' of positive emotions proposes that when individuals feel positive emotions, their 'momentary thought action repertoires broaden' and the experience builds 'enduring personal resources' (2003: 166). This core claim, along with its empirical support, demonstrates that through the process of positive emoting, conditions for flourishing and strength-building are present. For example, Fredrickson and her colleagues

have argued that the emotion of joy prompts play which builds social bonds and physical strength which are resources that individuals carry forward beyond the event or circumstance that prompted the joy (Fredrickson, 1998). Fredrickson and her colleagues have empirically demonstrated that feeling positive emotions in the wake of trauma (in this case, students dealing with the aftermath of 9/11) is associated with resources (optimism, life satisfaction) that foster resilience (Tugade and Fredrickson, 2004).

Other research in organizational studies lends support for the idea that positive emoting creates resources that foster flourishing. At the individual level, researchers suggest that positive emotion is associated with creativity (Amabile et al., 2005). Fredrickson and Losada (2005) argue that this effect arises because positivity (a higher ratio of positive to negative emotions) prompts exploration in the moment leading to greater knowledge. At the group level, the induction of positive emotion in a group fosters distinctive ways of interacting (which Rhee identifies in three forms – building on ideas, morale-building communication, and active affirmation), which have been found to be associated with more creative solutions in a group problem solving task in the laboratory (Rhee, 2006). Thus, positive emotion increases resources through fostering creativity in individuals and groups.

As well, research indicates that positive emotions foster positive interrelating, which, as elaborated below, cultivates a variety of resources beyond the immediate connections. For example, the presence of positive emotions is associated with greater levels of cooperation and more integrative solutions in bargaining contexts. The most extensive work on this link has been conducted in the context of negotiations research. Carnevale and Isen (1986) showed that bargainers in the positive emotion conditions achieved greater joint gains by more accurately communicating their preferences and more accurately reading each other's interests. Anderson and Thompson (2004) demonstrated that negotiators who were higher in trait positive affect (and more likely to engage in positive emoting) induced greater mutual trust in the negotiation; this finding was used to help explain the higher integrative outcomes achieved when high power negotiators had more positive affect.

The patterns above are amplified through conditions of social contact and emotional contagion, as well as social influence through power and status differences. Simply put: Positive emotions are contagious. For example, Sy et al. (2005) found that leaders' positive moods spread to followers, resulting in greater levels of coordination and less effort expended. Further, positive emoting can be propagated by people in more powerful positions who express positive emotion. When groups are led by leaders who evoke positive emotion in others, people with less power likely feel more positive emotion (Anderson et al., 2003); as well, leaders expressing positive affect seem to foster better performance in group tasks such as negotiation (Anderson and Thompson, 2004).

Positive interrelating

The third mechanism focuses on what happens in the 'space between individuals' (Josselson, 1996), that is, in their patterns of interrelating. Positive interrelating captures modes of interacting where the parties engaged experience their connection as mutual, trusting, respectful of other high quality attributes and they experience some form of mutual benefit (Dutton and Ragins, 2007). A variety of studies suggest that positive interrelating contributes to flourishing or strength-building by fortifying people physiologically (e.g., Heaphy and Dutton, 2008), fostering greater collective mindfulness (Vogus, 2004), generating greater energy (Baeker et al., 2003; Quinn, 2007), allowing more efficient and effective coordination (Gittell, 2003), and in general, fostering trust which enables the favorable resource flows and exchanges that build economic, financial, reputational, human, and social capital (Aldrich and Fiol, 1994; Lounsbury and Glynn, 2001)

SOME FUTURE DIRECTIONS

Hopefully, future researchers will extend the reach of POS both theoretically and empirically. Theoretically, the manifestations and dynamics of flourishing merit far more elaboration; there is a need for more nuanced understandings of the moderators and conditions that contribute to flourishing. As well, the articulation of additional generative mechanisms, beyond the three we have discussed (positive meaning-making, positive emoting, positive interrelating), is much needed. Moreover, it is important to examine the relationships between these and other mechanisms. More finely-grained modeling is also need, relating these three mechanisms (either separately or interactively) to particular types of POS manifestations such as creativity, learning or thriving.

Empirically, the study of organizations using the POS lens is in its formative years. There are new opportunities to link research across the disparate and established domains in which researchers are studying POS-related outcomes and processes. In addition, emerging work in new POS-related topics attests to its vitality in organizations and offers explanations for the underlying dynamics of organizing. Further work is needed to distill some of the core processes and outcomes at multiple levels of analysis. And, although researchers to date have tended to use field studies and rich ethnographies in the service of model development, hypothesis testing awaits.

Finally, the POS perspective suggests important connections between theory and practice. Broadly speaking, POS is actionable. A POS lens focuses on creating organizational practices that enabling flourishing and strength-building. Aspects of the organizational culture, norms, structures, networks and other organizational features contribute to capabilities at the organizational level that might be considered collective organizational strengths. Organizations can get traction on flourishing by leveraging the mechanisms that underlie the processes, i.e., positive meaning-making, positive emoting, and positive interrelating. Cultivating these positive mechanisms can occur in a variety of ways. One important way is through leadership. The POS perspective alerts us to how leadership shifts from purely individual decision making and an exclusive focus on the instrumentality of results to the social, relational, and generative aspects of leadership that 'breathe life' (Snook, 2002) into organizations. In many ways, this view of leadership redounds to Selznick's view of leaders as involved in the work of institution-building, i.e., 'the reworking of human and technological materials to fashion an organism that embodies new and enduring values' (Selznick, 1957: 153). Like Podolny et al., (2005), POS takes an admittedly normative stance towards leadership that might be directed to the cultivation of positive states and process in organizational settings of benefit to the 'common good.' More generally, if leaders are to succeed in giving life to the organizations they lead, leadership must be generative, value-based, and social.

CONCLUSION

In this chapter, we have sought to capture the emerging perspective of Positive Organizational Scholarship (POS), which at its core focuses on flourishing, strength- or capacity-building, and generative dynamics, across levels of analysis in organizations. A POS perspective rests on several core assumptions, which include: *contextual potency*, such that organizational states and conditions affect individual and collective processes of strength and capacity-building; *negativity and positivity in relationships* that can be complementary and asymmetrical; *endogeneity and dynamism of resources* that enables creative bricolage for flourishing and the expansiveness of possibilities for action; and finally, a *normative basis* that favors what is 'good' or valued.

As promising as a POS perspective is we recognize its limitations. Within the field of organizational studies, there are debates as to its usefulness, generalizability and

moralistic overtones (e.g., Fineman, 2006; George, 2004; Roberts, 2006). In addition, there are challenges to seriously accounting for the culturally-embedded nature of what is good or what is 'optimal.' And yet, in spite of such concerns, the POS perspective seems to have found a footing in the field, as reflected in emerging publications, edited books, teaching content and cases, doctoral dissertations, professional conferences and workshops. All of these activities suggest interest and a vibrant research future.

NOTE

1 Thanks to Julian Barling, Scott Sonenshein and Gretchen Spreitzer for comments on earlier drafts of this chapter.

REFERENCES

Aldrich, H. and Fiol, M. (1994) 'Fools rush in? The institutional context of industry creation', *Academy of Management Review*, 19 (4): 645–670.

Amabile, T.M., Barsade, S.G., Mueller, J.S. and Staw, B.M. (2005) 'Affect and creativity at work', *Administrative Science Quarterly*, 50 (3): 367–403.

Ancona, D. and Isaacs, W. (2007) 'Structural balance in teams', in J. Dutton and B. Ragins (eds), *Exploring Positive Relationships at Work: Building a Theoretical and Research Foundation*. Mahwah, NJ: Lawrence Erlbaum Associates, Publishers, pp. 225–242.

Anderson, C., Keltner, D.K. and John, O.P. (2003) 'Emotional convergence between people over time', *Journal of Personality and Social Psychology*, 84 (5): 1054–1068.

Anderson, C. and Thompson, L.L. (2004) 'Affect from the top down: How powerful individuals' positive affect shapes negotiations', *Organizational Behavior and Human Decision Processes*, 95 (2): 125–139.

Ashforth, B.E. (2001) *Role Transitions in Organizational Life: An Identity-based Perspective*. Mahwah, NJ: Lawrence Erlbaum Associates.

Avilio, B.J. and Luthans, F. (2006) *The High Impact Leader: Moments Matter in Accelerating Authentic Leadership Development*. New York: McGraw-Hill.

Baker, W., Cross, R. and Wooten, M. (2003) 'Positive organizational network analysis', in K.E. Cameron, J.E. Dutton, and R.E. Quinn (eds), *Positive Organizational Scholarship: Foundations of a New Discipline*. San Francisco: Berrett-Koehler Publishers, pp. 328–342.

Bandura, A. (1997) *Self-Efficacy: The Exercise of Control*. New York: Freeman.

Bandura, A. (2002) 'Exercise of personal and collective efficacy in changing societies', in A. Bandura (ed.), *Self-Efficacy in Changing Societies*. Cambridge: Cambridge University Press, pp 1–46.

Barr, P.S. and Glynn, M.A. (2004) 'Cultural variations in strategic issue interpretation: Relating cultural uncertainty avoidance to controllability in discriminating threat and opportunity', *Strategic Management Journal*, 25 (1): 59–67.

Bartel, C. and Dutton, J. (2001) 'Ambiguous organizational memberships: Constructing organizational identities in interactions with others', in M. Hogg and D.J. Terry (eds), *Social Identity Processes in Organizational Contexts*. Philadelphia, PA: Psychology Press, pp. 115–130.

Bass, B.M. and Riggio, R.E. (2005) *Transformational Leadership*. Mahwah, NJ: Lawrence Erlbaum Publishers.

Baumeister, R.F., Bratslavsky, E., Finkenauer, C. and Vohs, K.D. (2001) 'Bad is stronger than good', *Review of General Psychology*, 5: 323–370.

Berscheid, E. and Reis, H.T. (1998) 'Attraction and close relationships', in D.T. Gilbert, S.T. Fiske, and G. Lindsey (eds), *The Handbook of Social Psychology* (4th edn). New York: McGraw Hill. Vol. 2, pp. 193–281.

Bergland, A. and Kirkevold, M. (2001) 'Thriving— A useful theoretical perspective to capture the experience of well-being among frail elderly in nursing homes?', *Journal of Advanced Nursing*, 36 (3): 426–32.

Blatt, R. and Ashford, S. (2006) 'Making meaning and taking action in knowledge and creative work: Insights from independent workers', Working paper, University of Michigan.

Blatt, R. and Camden, C. (2007) 'Positive relationships and cultivating community', in J. Dutton and B. Ragins (eds), *Exploring Positive Relationships at Work: Building a Theoretical and Research Foundation*. Mahwah, NJ: Lawrence Erlbaum Publishers, pp. 243–265.

Bononno, G.A. (2004) 'Loss, trauma, and human resilience: Have we underestimated the human capacity to thrive after extremely aversive events?', *American Psychologist*, 59 (1): 20–28.

Brief, A.P. and Motowidlo, S. (1986) 'Prosocial organizational behaviors', *Academy of Management Review*, 11 (4): 710–725.

Britt, T.W., Castro, C.A. and Adler, A.B. (2005) 'Self engagement, stressors and health', *Personality and Social Psychology Bulletin*, Nov, 1–12.

Bushe, G.R. and Kassam, A.F. (2005) 'When is AI transformational: A meta-case analysis', *Journal of Applied Behavioral Science*, 41 (2): 161–181.

Cameron, K. (2003) 'Organizational virtuousness and performance', in K. Cameron, J. Dutton, and R.E. Quinn (eds), *Positive Organizational Scholarship: Foundations of a New Discipline*. San Francisco: Berrett-Koehler Publishers, pp. 48–65.

Cameron, K. (2005) 'Organizational effectiveness: Its demise and re-emergence through Positive Organizational Scholarship', in K.G. Smith and M. Hitt (eds), *Great Minds in Management Theory: The Process of Theory development*. New York: Oxford University Press, pp. 304–330.

Cameron, K.S., Bright, D. and Caza, A. (2004) 'Exploring the relationship between virtuousness and organizational performance', *American Behavioral Scientist*, 47 (6): 766–790.

Cameron, K.S., Dutton, J. and Quinn, R. (2003) *Positive Organizational Scholarship: Foundations of a New Discipline*. San Francisco: Berrett-Koehler Publishers.

Cameron, K., Dutton, J., Quinn, R. and Wrzesniewski, A. (2003) 'Developing a discipline of positive organizational scholarship', in K. Cameron, J. Dutton, and R.E. Quinn (eds), *Positive Organizational Scholarship: Foundations of a New Discipline*. San Francisco: Berrett-Koehler Publishers, pp. 361–370.

Cameron, K.S. and Lavine, M. (2006) *Making the Impossible, Possible: Leadership Lessons on Creating Positive Deviance in Organizations*. San Francisco: Berrett-Koehler Publishers.

Carnevale, P. and Isen, A. (1986) 'The influence of positive affect and visual access on the discovery of integrative solutions in bilateral negotiation', *Organizational Behavior and Human Decision Processes*, 37 (1): 1–13.

Caza, B.B. (2007) *To Survive or Thrive: A Theory of Resilience in the Workplace*. Unpublished Ph.D. dissertation, University of Michigan.

Caza, B.B. and Caza, A. (2008) 'Positive organizational scholarship: A critical theory perspective', *Journal of Management Inquiry* 17 (1): 21–33.

Chun, R. (2005) 'Ethical character and virtue of organizations: An empirical assessment and strategic implications', *Journal of Business Ethics*, 57 (3): 269–284.

Cooperrider, D.L. (1990) 'Positive image, positive action: The affirmative basis of organizing', in S. Srivastva and D. Cooperrider (eds), *Appreciative Management and Leadership: The Power of Positive Thought and Action in Organizations*. San Francisco: Jossey-Bass, Inc, pp. 91–125.

Cooperrider, D.L. and Sekerka, L.E. (2003) 'Toward a theory of positive organizational change', in K. Cameron, J. Dutton, and R.E. Quinn (eds), *Positive Organizational Scholarship: Foundations of a New*

Discipline. San Francisco: Berrett-Koehler Publishers, pp. 225–241.

Cooperrider, D.L., Sorenson, P.F., Whitney, D. and Yeager, T.F. (eds) (2000) *Appreciative Inquiry*. Champaign, IL: Stipes.

Cooperrider, D.L. and Srivastva, S. (1987) 'Appreciative inquiry in organizational life', *Research in Organizational Change and Development*, 1: 128–169.

Coutu, D.L. (2002) 'How resilience works', *Harvard Business Review*, 80 (5): 46–51.

Csikszentmihalyi, M. (1975) *Beyond Boredom and Anxiety*. San Francisco: Jossey–Bass.

Csikszentmihalyi, M. (1990) *Flow: The Psychology of Optimal Experience*. New York: Harper Collins.

Dacin, T., Ventresca, M. and Beal, B.D. (1999) 'The embeddedness of organizations: Dialogue and Directions', *Journal of Management*, 25 (3): 317–356.

Dahsgaard, K., Peterson, C. and Seligman, M.E.P. (2005) 'Shared virtue: The convergence of valued human strengths across culture and history', *Review of General Psychology*, 9 (3): 203–213.

Davidson, M.N. and James, E.H. (2007) 'The engines of positive relationships across difference: Conflict and learning', in J. Dutton and B. Ragins (eds), *Exploring Positive Relationships at Work: Building a Theoretical and Research Foundation*. Mahwah, NJ: Lawrence Erlbaum Associates, Publishers, pp. 137–158.

Davis, G.F. and Marquis, C. (2005) 'Prospects for organizational theory in the early 21st century: institutional fields and mechanisms', *Organization Science*, 16 (4): 332–343.

DiMaggio, P.J. and Powell, W.W. (1991) 'Introduction to the new institutionalism', in W.W. Powell and P.J. DiMaggio (eds), *The New Institutionalism in Organizational Analysis*. Chicago: University of Chicago Press, pp. 1–38.

Drazin, R., Glynn, M.A. and Kazanjian, R.K. (1999) 'Multilevel theorizing about creativity in organizations: A sensemaking perspective', *Academy of Management Review*, 24 (2): 286–307.

Dukerich, J.M., Golden, B.R. and Shortell, S.M. (2002) 'Beauty is in the eye of the beholder: The impact of organizational identification, identity, and image on the cooperative behaviors of physicians', *Administrative Science Quarterly*, 47: 507–533.

Dutton, J. (1993) 'The making of organizational opportunities: An interpretive pathway to organizational change', in B.M. Staw and L.L. Cummings (eds), *Research in Organizational Behavior*. Greenwich, CT: JAI Press. Vol. 15, pp. 195–226.

Dutton, J.E. (2003) 'Breathing life into organizational studies', *Journal of Management Inquiry*, 12 (1): 5–19.

Dutton, J.E., Dukerich, J.M. and Harquail, C.V. (1994) 'Organizational images and member identification', *Administrative Science Quarterly*, 39 (2): 239–263.

Dutton, J.E. and Heaphy, E.D. (2003) 'The power of high quality connections at work', in K. Cameron, J. Dutton, and R. Quinn (eds), *Positive Organizational Scholarship: Foundations of a New Discipline*. San Francisco: Berrett-Koehler Publishers, pp. 263–278.

Dutton, J.E. and Ragins, B.R. (Eds.) (2007) *Exploring Positive Relationships at Work: Building a Theoretical and Research Foundation*. Mahwah, NJ: Lawrence Erlbaum Associates, Publishers.

Dutton, J., Worline, M., Frost, P. and Lilius, J. (2006) 'Explaining compassion organizing', *Administrative Science Quarterly*, 51 (1): 59–96.

Elster, J. (1989) *Nuts and Bolts for the Social Sciences*, New York: Cambridge University Press.

Feldman, M.S. (2004) 'Resources in emerging structures and processes of change', *Organization Science*, 15: 295–309.

Feldman, M.S. and Khademian, A.M. (2003) 'Empowerment and cascading vitality', in K. Cameron, J. Dutton and R. Quinn (eds), *Positive Organizational Scholarship: Foundations of a New Discipline*. San Francisco: Berrett-Koehler Publishers, pp. 343–358.

Feldman, D.B. and Snyder, C.R. (2005) 'Hope and the meaningful life: Theoretical and empirical associations between goal-directed thinking and life meaning', *Journal of Social and Clinical Psychology*, May, 24 (3): 401–421.

Fineman, S. (2006) 'On being positive: Concerns and counterpoints', *Academy of Management Review*, 31 (2): 270–291.

Fredrickson, B.L. (1998) 'What good are positive emotions?', *Review of General Psychology*, 2 (3): 300–319.

Fredrickson, B.L. (2003) 'Positive emotions and upward spirals in organizations', in K. Cameron, J. Dutton, and R. Quinn (eds), *Positive Organizational Scholarship: Foundations of a New Discipline*. San Francisco: Berrett-Koehler Publishers, Inc, pp. 163–175.

Fredrickson, B. and Losada, L. (2005) 'Positive affect and the complex dynamics of human flourishing', *American Psychologist*, 60 (7): 678–686.

Frost, P.J., Dutton, J.E., Maitlis, S., Kanov, J., Lilius, J. and Worline, M. (2006) 'Seeing organizations differently: Three lenses on compassion', in C. Hardy, S. Clegg, T. Lawrence, and W. Nord (eds), *Handbook of Organizational Studies*, Second edn. London: Sage Publications, pp. 843–866.

Gable, S.L. and Haidt, J. (2005) 'What (and why) is positive psychology?', *Review of General Psychology*, 9 (2): 103–110.

George, J.M. (2004) 'Positive organizational scholarship: Foundations of a new discipline', *Administrative Science Quarterly*, 49 (2): 325–330.

Ghoshal, S, (2005) 'Bad management theories are destroying good management practices', *Academy of Management Learning and Education*, 4 (1): 75–91.

Giacalone, R.A., Jurkiewicz, C. and Dunn, C. (2005) *Positive Psychology in Business Ethics and Corporate Responsibility*. Greenwich, CT: Information Age Publishing.

Ginsberg, A. and Venkatraman, N. (1992) 'Investing in new information technology: The role of competitive posture and issue diagnosis', *Strategic Management Journal*, 13 (Summer): 37–53.

Gittell, J.H. (2003) 'A theory of relational coordination', in K. Cameron, J. Dutton, and R. Quinn (eds), *Positive Organizational Scholarship: Foundations of a New Discipline*. San Francisco: Berrett-Koehler Publishers, pp. 279–295.

Gittell, J.H., Cameron, K.S., Lim, S. and Rivas, V. (2006) 'Relationships, layoffs and organizational resilience: Airline industry responses to September 11th', *Journal of Applied Behavioral Science*, 42 (3): 300–329.

Glynn, M.A, and Dutton, J. (2007) 'The generative dynamics of positive organizing', Working paper.

Glynn, M.A. and Smith, B.M. (2007) 'Competing on purpose', Working paper.

Glynn, M.A. and Wrobel, K. (2007) 'My family, my firm: How familial relationships function as endogenous organizational resources', in J.E. Dutton and B.R. Ragins (eds), *Exploring Positive Relationships at Work: Building a Theoretical and Research Foundation*. Mahwah, NJ: Lawrence Erlbaum, pp. 307–323.

Goddard, R.D., LoGerfo, L., and Hoy, W.K. (2004) 'High school accountability: The role of perceived collective efficacy', *Educational Policy*, 18 (3): 1–23.

Golden-Biddle, K., GermAnn, K., Reay, T. and Procyshen, G. (2007) 'Creating and sustaining positive orginational relationships: A cultural perspective', in J.E. Dutton and B.R. Ragins (eds), *Exploring Positive Relationships at Work: Building a Theoretical and Research Foundation*. Mahwah, NJ: Lawrence Erlbaum, pp. 289–330.

Graen, G., Liden, R.C. and Hoel, W. (1982) 'Role of leadership in the employee withdrawal process', *Journal of Applied Psychology*, 67: 868–872.

Graen, G., Novak, M.A. and Sommerkamp, P. (1982) 'The effects of leader-member exchange and job design on productivity and satisfaction: Testing a dual attachment model', *Organizational Behavior and Human Decision Processes*, 30 (1): 109–131.

Grant, A.M. and Ashford, S.J. (2008) 'The dynamics of proactivity at work', forthcoming in B.M. Staw and A. Brief (eds), *Research in Organizational Behavior*, Vol. 28.

Greenberg, J.J. and Colquitt, J.A. (2005) *Handbook of Organizational Justice*. Mahwah, NJ: Lawrence Erlbaum Associates.

Greenhaus, J.H. and Powell, G.N. (2006) 'When work and family are allies: A theory of work-family enrichment', *Academy of Management Review*, 31 (1): 72–92.

Hackman, J.R. and Oldham, G.R. (1980) *Work Redesign*. Reading, MA: Addison–Wesley.

Hargadon, A.B. and Bechky, B.A. (2006) 'When collections of creatives become creative collectives: A field study of problem solving at work', *Organization Science*, 17 (4): 484–500.

Harter, J.K., Schmidt, F.L. and Hayes, T.L. (2002) 'Business-unit-level relationship between employee satisfaction, employee engagement and business outcomes: A meta-analysis', *Journal of Applied Psychology*, 87 (2): 268–279.

Heaphy, E. (2007) 'Bodily insights: Three lenses on positive organizational relationships', in J.E. Dutton and B.R. Ragins (eds), *Exploring Positive Relationships at Work: Building a Theoretical and Research Foundation*. Mahwah, NJ: Lawrence Erlbaum, pp. 47–72.

Heaphy, E. and Dutton, J.E. (2008) 'Positive social interactions and the human body at work: Linking organizations and physiology', *Academy of Management Review*, 33 (1): 137–163.

Hess, E.D. and Cameron, K.S. (2006) *Leading with Values: Positivity, Virtue and High Performance*. Cambridge: Cambridge University Press.

Higgins, M.C. and Kram, K.E. (2001) 'Reconceptualizing mentoring at work: A developmental network perspective', *Academy of Management Review*, 26 (2): 264–288.

Hornstein, H. (1986) *Managerial Courage*. New York: Wiley.

Ibarra, H. (1999) 'Provisional selves: Experimenting with image and identity in professional adaptation', *Administrative Science Quarterly*, 44 (4): 764–791.

Inglehart, M.R., Markus, H. and Brown, D.R. (1988) 'The effects of possible selves on academic achievement: A panel study', Paper presented at the International Congress of Psychology, Sydney, Australia.

Jackson, S.E. and Schuler, R.S. (1985) 'A meta-analysis and conceptual critique of research on role ambiguity and role conflict in work settings', *Organizational Behavior and Human Decision Processes*, 36 (1): 16–78.

Josselson, R. (1996) *The Space Between Us: Exploring Human Dimensions of Human Relationships*. Thousand Oaks, CA: Sage.

Judge, T.Q., Thoresen, C.J., Bono, J.E. and Patton, G.K. (2001) 'The job satisfaction-job performance relationship: A qualitative and quantitative review', *Psychological Bulletin*, 127 (3): 376–407.

Kahn, W.A. (1990) 'Psychological conditions of personal engagement and disengagement at work', *Academy of Management Journal*, 33 (4): 692–724.

Kahn, W.A. (1998) 'Relational systems at work', in B.M. Staw and L.L. Cummings (eds), *Research in Organizational Behavior*. Greenwich, CT: JAI Press. Vol. 20, pp. 39–76.

Karasek, R.A. and Theorell, T. (1990) *Healthy Work: Stress, Productivity and the Reconstruction of Working Life*. New York: Basic Books.

Keyes, C. (2002) 'The mental health continuum: From languishing to flourishing in life', *Journal of Health and Social Behavior*, 43 (2): 207–222.

Kram, K. (1985) *Mentoring at Work: Developmental Relationships in Organizational Life*. Glenview, IL: Scott Foresman.

Lewis, K., Lange, D., and Gillis, L. (2005) 'Transactive memory systems, learning, and learning transfer', *Organization Science*, 16 (6): 581–598.

Liang, D.W., Moreland, R. and Argote, L. (1995) 'Group versus individual training and group performance: The mediating factor of transactive memory', *Personality and Social Psychology Bulletin*, 21 (4): 384–393.

Loehr, J. and Schwartz, T. (2003) *Power of Full Engagement: Managing Energy, Not Time, is the Key to High Performance and Personal Renewal*. New York: Free Press.

Losada, M. and Heaphy, E. (2004) 'The role of positivity and connectivity in the performance of business teams: A nonlinear dynamics model', *American Behavioral Scientist*, 47 (6): 740–765.

Lounsbury, M. and Glynn, M.A. (2001) 'Cultural entrepreneurship: Stories, legitimacy and the acquisition of resources', *Strategic Management Journal*, 22 (6/7): 545–564.

Luszczynska, A., Gutierez-Dona, B., and Schwarzer, R. (2005) 'General self-efficacy in various domains of human functioning: Evidence from five countries', *International Journal of Psychology*, 40 (2): 80–89.

Luthans, F. (2002) 'The need for and meaning of positive organizational behavior', *Journal of Organizational Behavior*, 23 (6): 695–706.

Luthans, F., Luthans, K.Q. and Luthans, B.C. (2004) 'Positive psychological capital: Beyond human and social capital', *Business Horizons*, 47 (1): 45–50.

Luthans, F. and Youssef, C.M. (2004) 'Human, social, and now positive psychological capital management: Investing in people for competitive advantage', *Organizational Dynamics*, 33 (2): 143–160.

Maslow, A. (1968) *Toward a Psychology of Being*. New York: Van Nostrand.

Masten, A.S. (2001) 'Ordinary magic: Resilience process in development', *American Psychologist*, 56 (3): 227–239.

Masten, A.S. and Reed, J.M. (2002) 'Resilience in development', in C.R. Snyder and S.L. Lopez, (eds), *Handbook of Positive Psychology*. New York: Oxford University Press, pp. 74–88.

Perry-Smith, J.E. (2006) 'Social yet creative: The role of social relationships in facilitating individual creativity', *Academy of Management Journal*, 49 (1): 85–101.

Perry-Smith, J.E. and Shalley, C. (2003) 'The social side of creativity: A static and dynamic social network perspective', *Academy of Management Review*, 28 (1): 89–106.

Podolny, J.M., Khurana, R. and Hill-Popper, M. (2005) 'Revisiting the meaning of leadership', in B.M. Staw and R.M. Kramer (eds), *Research in Organizational Behavior*. Greenwich, CT: JAI Press. Vol. 26, pp. 1–36.

Powley, E. (2005) *Connective Capacity and Resilience*. Unpublished dissertation, Case Western Reserve University.

Powley, E.H., and Cameron, K.S. (2006) 'Organizational healing: Lived virtuousness amidst organizational crisis', *Journal of Management, Spirituality, and Religion*, 3 (1): 13–33.

Pratt, M. and Ashforth, B. (2003)' Fostering meaningfulness in working and at work', in K. Cameron, J. Dutton, and R. Quinn (eds), *Positive Organizational Scholarship: Foundations of a New Discipline*. San Francisco: Berrett-Koehler Publishers, pp. 309–327.

Quinn, R.W. (2005) 'Flow in knowledge work: High performance experience in the design of national security technology', *Administrative Science Quarterly*, 50 (4): 610–642.

Quinn, R.W. (2007) 'Energizing others in work connections', in J.E. Dutton and B.R. Ragins (eds), *Exploring Positive Relationships at Work: Building a Theoretical and Research Foundation*. Mahwah, NJ: Lawrence Erlbaum, pp. 73–90.

Quinn, R.W. and Dutton, J.E. (2005) 'Coordination as Energy-in-Conversation: A process theory of organizing', *Academy of Management Review*, 30 (1): 36–57.

Quinn, R.W. and Worline, M.C (2008) 'Enabling courageous collective action: Conversations from United Airlines Flight 93', *Organizational Science*, published online before print Feb 20, 2008.

Ragins, B.R. and Verbos, A.K. (2007) 'Positive relationships in action: Relational mentoring and mentoring schemas in the workplace', in J.E. Dutton and

B.R. Ragins (eds), *Exploring Positive Relationships at Work: Building a Theoretical and Research Foundation*. Mahwah, NJ: Lawrence Erlbaum, pp. 91–116.

Reis, H.T. and Gable, S.T. (2003) 'Toward a positive psychology of relationships', in C.L.M. Keyes and J. Haidt (eds), *Flourishing: Positive Psychology and the Life Well-Lived*. Washington, DC: American Psychological Association, pp. 120–159.

Rhee, S.Y. (2006) 'Shared emotions and group effectiveness: The role of broadening-and-building interactions', in K. Mark Weaver (ed.), *Proceedings of the Sixty–fifth Annual Meeting of the Academy of Management* (CD), ISSN 1543–8643.

Roberts, L.M. (2006) 'Shifting the Lens on organizational life: The added value of positive scholarship', *Academy of Management Review*, 31 (2): 292–305.

Roberts, L.M. (2007) 'From proving to becoming: How positive relationships create a context for self-discovery and self-actualization', in J.E. Dutton and B.R. Ragins (eds), *Exploring Positive Relationships at Work: Building a Theoretical and Research Foundation*. Mahwah, NJ: Lawrence Erlbaum, pp. 29–46.

Roberts, L.M., Dutton, J., Spreitzer, G., Heaphy, E. and Quinn, R. E. (2005) 'Composing the reflected best self-portrait: Building pathways for becoming extraordinary in work organizations', *Academy of Management Review*, 30 (4): 712–736.

Rothbard, N.P. (2001) 'Enriching or depleting? The dynamics of engagement in work and family roles', *Administrative Science Quarterly*, 46 (4): 655–684.

Ryan, R.M. and Deci, E.L. (2001) 'On happiness and human potentials: A review of research on hedonic and eudaimonic well-being', *Annual Review of Psychology*, 52: 141–166.

Sandelands, L.E. (2003) *Thinking About Social Life*. Lanham, MD: University Press.

Sandelands, L.E. and Worline, M. (2007) 'Seeing life in organizations', Working paper, University of Michigan.

Seligman, M.E.P. (1998) *Learned Optimism: How to Change Your Mind and Your Life*. New York: Pocket Books.

Selznick, P. (1957) *Leadership in Administration*. New York: Harper and Row.

Snook, S. (2002) *Friendly Fire: The Accidental Shootdown of U.S. Black Hawks Over Northern Iraq*. Princeton: Princeton University Press.

Snyder, C.R. (2002) 'Hope theory: Rainbows of the mind', *Psychological Inquiry*, 13: 249–275.

Sonenshein, S. (2005) 'Positive organizational scholarship', in P.H. Werhane and R.E. Freeman (eds), *The Blackwell Encyclopedia of Management*,

Business Ethics. Oxford: Blackwell Publishing. Vol. II, pp. 410–414.

Sonenshein, S. (2007a) 'Communicating and constructing meaning during the implementation of strategic change', Unpublished Ph.D Dissertation, University of Michigan.

Sonenshein, S. (2007b) 'Resource creation theory: Antecedents, mechanisms and outcomes of a meaning-making approach', Working paper, University of Michigan.

Sonnentag, S. (1996) 'Work group factors and individual well-being', in M. A West (ed.), *The Handbook of Work Group Psychology*. Chichester: Wiley, pp. 346–367.

Sonnentag, S. (2003) 'Recovery, work engagement, and proactive behavior: A new look at the interface between nonwork and work', *Journal of Applied Psychology*, 88 (3): 518–528.

Spreitzer, G. (1995) 'Psychological empowerment in the workplace: Dimensions, Measurement, and Validation', *Academy of Management Journal*, 38: 1442–1465.

Spreitzer, G. (2007) 'Giving peace a chance: Organizational leadership, empowerment, and peace', *Journal of Organizational Behavior*, 28 (8): 1077–1095.

Spreitzer, G., Sutcliffe, K., Dutton, J.E., Sonenshein, S. and Grant, A. (2005) 'A socially embedded model of thriving at work', *Organization Science*, 16 (5): 537–549.

Srivastava, S. and Cooperrider, D. (1999) *Organizational Wisdom and Executive Courage*. Boston:Lexington Books.

Sutcliffe, K.M. and Vogus, T. (2003) 'Organizing for resilience', in K.S. Cameron, J.E. Dutton and R.E. Quinn (eds), *Positive Organizational Scholarship: Foundations of a New Discipline*. San Francisco: Berrett-Koehler Publishers, Inc, pp. 94–110.

Sy, T., Cote, S. and Saavadra, R. (2005) 'The contagious leader: The impact of leader's mood on the mood of group members, group affective tone and group processes', *Journal of Applied Psychology*, 90 (2): 295–305.

Taylor, S.E., Kemeny, M.E., Reed, G.M., Bower, G.E. and Gruenewald, T.L. (2000) 'Psychological resources, positive illusions and health', *American Psychologist*, 55 (1): 99–109.

Tsui, A.S. and Ashford, S.J. (1994) 'Adaptive self-regulation: A process view of managerial effectiveness', *Journal of Management*, 20 (1): 93–121.

Tugade, M.M. and Fredrickson, B.L. (2004) 'Resilient individuals use positive emotions to bounce back from negative emotional experiences', *Journal of Personality and Social Psychology*, 86 (2): 320–333.

Turner, N., Barling, J. and Zacharatos, A. (2002) 'Positive psychology at work', in C.R. Snyder and S.J. Lopez (eds), *Handbook of Positive Psychology*. New York: Oxford University Press, pp. 715–728.

Useem, M. (1998) *The Leadership Moment*. New York: Three Rivers Press.

Vogus, T. (2004) 'In search of mechanisms: How do HR practices affect organizational performance?', Unpublished Ph.D. Dissertation, University of Michigan.

Walsh, J.P., Margolis, J., and Weber, K. (2003) 'Social issues and management: Our lost cause found', *Journal of Management*, 29 (6): 859–881.

Wang, C.S. and Thompson, L.L. (2006) 'The negative and positive psychology of leadership and group research', in S.R. Thye and E.J. Lawler (eds), *The Social Psychology of the Workplace. Advances in Group Processes*. Amsterdam: JAI Press. Vol 23, pp. 31–61.

Weick, K. and Putnam, T. (2006) 'Organizing mindfulness: Eastern wisdom and western knowledge', *Journal of Management Inquiry*, 15 (3): 275–287.

Weick, K.E., Sutcliffe, K.M. and Obstfeld, D. (1999) 'Organizing for high reliability: Processes of collective mindfulness', in R.I. Sutton and B.M. Staw (eds), *Research in Organizational Behavior*. Stanford, CT: JAI Press, Vol. 21, pp. 81–123.

Weick, K., Sutcliffe, K. and Obstfeld, D. (2005) 'Organizing and the process of sensemaking', *Organization Science*, 16 (4): 409–421.

Wolin, S.J. and Wolin, S. (1993) *The Resilient Self*. New York: Villard.

Wooten, L. and Crane, P. (2004) 'Generating dynamic capabilities through a humanistic work ideology: The case of a certified–nurse midwife practice in a professional bureaucracy', *American Behavioral Scientist*, 47 (6): 848–866.

Worline, M., Dutton, J., Lilius, J., Kanov, J., Maitlis, S. and Frost, P. (2006) 'Organizing resilience by cultivating resources', Working paper, University of Michigan.

Wright, T. (2003) 'Positive organizational behavior: An idea whose time has truly come', *Journal of Organizational Behavior*, 24 (4): 437–442.

Wrzesniewski, A. (2003) 'Finding positive meaning in work', in K. Cameron, J.E. Dutton, and R.E. Quinn (eds), *Positive Organizational Scholarship: Foundations of a New Discipline*. San Francisco: Berrett-Koehler, pp. 296–308.

Wrzesniewski, A. and Dutton, J. (2001) 'Crafting a job: Employees as active crafters of their work', *Academy of Management Review*, 26 (2): 179–201.

Wrzesniewski, A., McCauley, C.R., Rozin, P. and Schwartz, B. (1997) 'Jobs, careers, and callings: People's relations to their work', *Journal of Research in Personality*, 31 (1): 21–33.

Youssef, C.M. and Luthans, F. (2005) 'A positive organizational behavior approach to ethical performance', in R.A. Giacalone, C.L. Jurkiewicz and C. Dunn (eds), *Positive Psychology in Business Ethics and Corporate Responsibility*. Greenwich, CT: IAP Publishing, pp. 1–22.

Index